BASIC TEXT

ON

INSURANCE LAW

By

ROBERT E. KEETON
Professor of Law, Harvard Law School

ST. PAUL, MINN.
WEST PUBLISHING CO.
1971

Keeton, Insurance Law BTB

5th Reprint—1978

PREFACE

The inventory of materials on insurance law is enormous—cases, statutes, administrative rulings, industry practices, and more if one chooses to extend his inquiry outward from this core. Also, the pace of weekly growth of the inventory is staggering. In such a context, several distinct functions of books on insurance law may be identified: first, to contribute to a reader's understanding of insurance law generally; second, to contribute to his working out solutions for particular problems by suggesting to him relevant general principles and avenues of inquiry, analogy, and comparison that he may usefully pursue; and, third, to provide references to the whole body of available materials. Perhaps every book and multi-volume set of books on the subject is intended to serve each of these objectives in some measure.

In this text I have chosen to emphasize the first and second of these objectives. Thus, though I have attempted in footnotes to cite a selection of cases and some useful secondary sources in which more materials and leads can be found, the emphasis is more on perspective than on comprehensive detail. The aim, then, is to serve principally those readers who are seeking a basic understanding of insurance law generally and those who are seeking assurance that they have recognized the varied currents of principle, policy, precedents, and practice that may be brought to bear upon some problem at hand.

The organization of this text is based primarily on principles of insurance law rather than types of insurance. This structure seems better suited to an emphasis on generalization—on principle and perspective. Nevertheless, the ultimate test of the validity of suggested generalizations is that they stand the rigors of application to the various particular problems about which they speak. In attempting complementary consideration of the general and the particular and testing one against the other, I have chosen in several instances to organize materials within a chapter along lines that happen also to be those separating different types of insurance. This is especially true within Chapter 4, Persons and Interests Protected, and within Chapter 7, Claims Processes. A large part of the latter chapter is devoted to problems distinctively associated with liability insurance claims—problems that have proved to be especially troublesome because of the conflicts of interest inherent in liability insurance relationships.

I gratefully acknowledge the excellent research assistance I received from Jack B. Birkinsha during early years of work on this manu-

PREFACE

script and from William Robinson during a later period. Also I gratefully acknowledge the essential and highly proficient secretarial services of Maria B. Hooks and Janet Johnson.

ROBERT E. KEETON

Cambridge, Massachusetts
December, 1970

SUMMARY OF CONTENTS

SUMMARY OF CONTENTS

TABLE OF CONTENTS

CHAPTER 1. CLASSIFICATION IN INSURANCE LAW

CHAPTER 2. MARKETING

TABLE OF CONTENTS

x

TABLE OF CONTENTS

TABLE OF CONTENTS

TABLE OF CONTENTS

TABLE OF CONTENTS

CHAPTER 5.   THE RISKS TRANSFERRED

TABLE OF CONTENTS

CHAPTER 6.   RIGHTS AT VARIANCE WITH POLICY PROVISIONS

TABLE OF CONTENTS

TABLE OF CONTENTS

CHAPTER 7. CLAIMS PROCESSES

TABLE OF CONTENTS

BASIC TEXT
ON
INSURANCE LAW

CHAPTER 1

CLASSIFICATION IN INSURANCE LAW

Sec.
1.1 The Role of Classification.
1.2 Meanings of "Insurance".
1.3 Classification by the Nature of the Risks.
1.4 Classification by the Nature of the Insuring Organization.
1.5 Classification of Representatives (Agents and Brokers).
1.6 Evaluative Standards of Classification; Flexibility.

SECTION 1.1 THE ROLE OF CLASSIFICATION

In the law of insurance, as elsewhere, categories are used and sometimes misused in developing and communicating ideas. There is always risk that a system of classification wisely designed for one purpose will be thoughtlessly extended to use in an unfitting context.

Classification is part of the process of seeking organizing principles. It is a useful—perhaps even inevitable—way of signifying similarities that warrant like treatment or differences that warrant contrasting treatment. Also, resort to classification in the analysis of a particular problem can serve the creative function of suggesting ideas that might be useful in dealing with it. But classification can also be constricting because of its influence toward limiting the perspectives from which the problem is examined.

The role of classification is closely related to the balance between generalization and particularization in a body of law. Some degree of generalization is essential to keeping the number of particularized rules of decision within administratively manageable bounds. Also, generalization helps one identify significant similarities that should cause like treatment of cases despite differences in less important particulars. Thus, wise generalization advances the quest for a system of predictable and evenhanded adjudication—for the "rule of law"—in contrast with a system that is wide open to whim and caprice, however well-intentioned its sponsorship may be.

The relative significance of similarities and differences is inevitably hard to determine in many instances. As a way of meeting this difficulty, the common law system accepts each judicial decision as a precedent, but with decreasing authoritative quality as grounds of factual distinction from a new situation increase. This system tends to develop distinctive rules for identifiable types of fact situations. In the absence of constant testing of these particularized rules by standards of generalization, inconsistencies of principle develop. Insurance law contains striking illustrations of this point.[1]

Since different purposes of inquiry call for classification by different criteria, the systems of classification used in insurance law are numerous. In this text a system of classification is presented, in some instances, only in relation to a particular body of law to which it is relevant.[2] However, some systems of classification that are used in numerous contexts are presented in the present chapter. The mere fact of presenting a particular set of ideas in this introductory material is a form of generalization—a suggestion that it is useful more widely than in some special area of insurance law. But this is not to assert universality for any of the systems of classification presented.

SECTION 1.2 MEANINGS OF "INSURANCE"

§ 1.2(a) PRINCIPAL CHARACTERISTICS OF INSURANCE

Determining whether a transaction falls within or outside the field of "insurance" is classification by a criterion so broad that its application is rarely in dispute. The likelihood that the characterization will generate dispute is further reduced by the fact that many of the principles underlying insurance law are principles of broader application as well—throughout the law of contracts, for example, or throughout the segment of law regarding contracts of adhesion or in wide areas of the law of torts or restitution. Thus, with respect to most of the problems encountered, it is unnecessary to define insurance—either because of a generally shared assumption that the transaction in question was insurance or because of an assumption that it would make no difference whether it was insurance or not. Occasionally, however, some legal consequence is made to turn on a disputable characterization of a transaction as insurance.

Because the purposes for which definitions of insurance are invoked differ, no single definition will serve always, even in a single jurisdiction. A way of approaching this problem of varied meanings of insurance is to state some characteristics always found in any transaction identified as insurance, without trying at the same time to make the catalog of characteristics complete.

Insurance is an arrangement for transferring and distributing risk. It is an arrangement under which one (called an insurer) con-

---

1. See, *e.g.*, § 4.6 *infra*.

2. See, *e.g.*, §§ 6.5(b), 6.6(b) (contrasts between coverage provisions and oth-

ers), 8.4 (classification for premium rating) *infra*.

tracts to do something that is of value to another (usually called an insured but sometimes called a beneficiary) upon the occurrence of a specified harmful contingency. Not all arrangements having these characteristics are treated as insurance, however. Some are never so treated; others are not uniformly so treated.

Whenever one is interested in knowing whether a transaction is insurance, a demonstration that it is part of an arrangement for transferring and distributing risk will not be sufficient to answer the question.[3] Thus, though these are the most obvious characteristics of insurance, cases on what constitutes insurance usually turn on other factors. One objective of this section is to expose and appraise other relevant factors in typical arrangements. This will be done through an examination of some common types of situations in which it may be important to ask whether a transaction is insurance, or to ask whether transactions in a series constitute doing an insurance business. First, however, the nature of risk and associated concepts will be examined.

§ 1.2(b) CONCEPTS UNDERLYING INSURANCE

(1) RISK

Risk is an abstract concept with no physical counterpart. Saying that one is subject to a risk of loss of a specified type during a specified period is a way of saying that we do not know whether he will suffer that type of loss or not. If one knew and fully understood all the facts about a given venture, including the influence of outside forces upon it, he could foresee that loss would or would not occur, just as, fully understanding all the forces coming to bear upon a tossed coin, he could foresee whether it would fall heads or tails. Knowing only part of the relevant facts, he must guess at the unknown; his prediction concerning potential loss, partly reasoned from things known and partly guesswork, is expressed as risk.[1]

A distinction may be drawn between two types of potential consequences of any venture. First, some potential consequences are recognized as harmful without reference to their legal significance; we often think of the risk of bodily harm in this sense, free of legal connotations. Second, other potential consequences of a venture are susceptible of description only in a context of legal relationships. The statement that an accident insurance company, having issued a policy of accident insurance, has assumed and is subject to a risk from bodily injury to the policyholder expresses a conclusion dependent upon the legal interpretation of the relation between the company and the policyholder.

---

3.   See § 1.2(c), *infra*.

1.   Risk "is a psychological phenomenon that is meaningful only in terms of human reactions and experiences."

Denenberg, Eilers, Hoffman, Kline, Melone & Snider, Risk and Insurance 4 (1964) [hereinafter cited as Denenberg *et al.*].

legal and nonlegal risks

Assume the issuance of a policy of accident insurance. Thereafter, the possibility of a single accident to the policyholder involves a nonlegal risk of bodily harm to him and a legal risk of harm to the insurer. It may also involve numerous other risks (or aspects of risk, if one thinks of the total risk as a unit). Suppose, for example, the possibility of accident arises from the fact that the policyholder is a pedestrian in the path of a speeding car. The pedestrian's fiancee is subject to a *nonlegal* risk of loss of his companionship, and if under the terms of her deceased grandfather's will she was to receive control of an estate on the day of her wedding, then she is subject to a *legal* risk of loss or postponement of that expectation. The driver is subject to a risk of legal liability to the pedestrian in tort. And if the driver carries liability insurance, his insurer is subject to a risk of legal liability both to the driver and to the pedestrian. Thus, a single incident, considered from different points of view and in the light of existing legal relations, involves a number of different risks, some nonlegal and some legal.

bundle of risks

In fact, the bundle of risks from any venture is much more complex than thus far indicated. Suppose, for example, with respect to the last illustration, that when the driver's liability insurance policy is obtained there is precedent against any liability of the driver to the fiancee of the pedestrian. The possibility that this precedent will be overturned and that the fiancee will be allowed to recover for loss of companionship is within the bundle of risks (or within the aspects of risk, if one thinks of the composite risk as a unit) transferred to the insurer by the driver's liability insurance policy.

Insurance literature sometimes draws distinctions among risks, hazards, and perils.[2] But there is no commonly accepted usage with separate and distinct meanings for these terms.[3] Rather, "hazard" and "risk" are often used interchangeably, and though "peril" more often connotes a potential physical cause of loss than a potential loss, even this term is occasionally used in a broader sense. In short, only by close study of the context, if then, can one ascertain the precise sense in which one of these terms is used.

(2) RISK MANAGEMENT

device for managing ignorance

Like other concepts based on probability, the concept of risk is a rational device for managing ignorance.[4] So too is insurance, since it is founded on the concept of risk.[5]

---

2. See Denenberg *et al.* 8. See also § 6.5(c) (2) *infra.*

3. *Cf.* Brainard, *Book Review*, 33 J. Risk & Ins. 344, 348 (1966) (review of Denenberg *et al.*).

4. Ignorance can be too profound for use of this device, however. In customary usage the concept of risk does not extend to a sequence of events, even though it is ineluctably leading

to loss, if human observers do not know enough to recognize the possibility that loss of that type will occur. Pressing this point further (and using what is perhaps an unusual sense of the term "created"), Denenberg *et al.* speak of risk as being "created" by a change in human knowledge. "For example, the recently discovered rela-

5. See Note 5 on page 5.

Though the insured normally collects much more or much less than the premium he pays for his insurance policy, it does not follow that he receives either more or less than a fair return. One benefit he receives is a measure of certainty about the cost of protection against specified types of losses. If loss of a specified type occurs, payment from the insurer offsets the loss. If no loss of the specified type occurs, that very fact offsets the lack of any payment. In either event, a risk of loss has existed because of uncertainty as to whether loss would occur. For a price adjusted to the risk, as best it could be estimated, the insured has traded off that possibility of heavy loss for a certain but more moderate cost.

As one understands a greater percentage of the relevant facts, the element of guessing in his description of risk is reduced, and his prediction is more reliable. That which in relative ignorance was regarded as part of the risk of the venture becomes, when fully understood, an item either certain to be among costs or else certain not to be. The best understanding that can be achieved with respect to a given venture, however, will leave some uncertainties. Not elimination but sound management of risk is the attainable goal.

(3) RISK CONTROL

One form of risk management is risk control, accomplished by so conducting a venture that risk is minimized.[6] Brakes, train whistles, fire escapes, and safety campaigns are common instruments of such risk management. Risk control may be effected either through risk avoidance (e. g., by effective enforcement of regulations against accumulations of flammable waste)[7] or through risk reduction (e. g., by removal of accumulated waste materials to reduce the risk of fire).

Insurance often results in overall risk reduction in another way, since the insurance company is more likely than the insured to be able to stand the specified loss without the necessity of an uneconomical forced sale of assets. That is, even though the main objective of the insurance contract is to transfer a specified loss, and the risk of that loss is not reduced, it may happen that there is an incidental re-

---

tion between smoking and lung cancer has created a risk where none previously existed. Losses may have occurred in the past as a result of excess smoking, but smoking involved no risk at that time because the relationship was not recognized; today we recognize the relationship, and risk does exist." Denenberg et al. 4.

5. See, e.g., Denenberg et al.; Mehr & Hedges, Risk Management in the Business Enterprise (1963) [hereinafter cited as Mehr & Hedges]; Williams & Heins, Risk Management and Insurance (1964) [hereinafter cited as Williams & Heins]; Bobbitt, Risk Management, 14 Annals Soc'y Chartered

Property & Cas. Underwriters 143 (1961).

6. See, e.g., Denenberg et al. 9, 87–120; Mehr & Hedges 41–59, 64–69; Williams & Heins 42; Bobbitt, n.5 supra, at 148–149.

7. Professors Williams and Heins offer another concept of risk avoidance as a tool of risk management: "Risk may be avoided by refusing to assume it even momentarily. For example, a firm that wishes to avoid the risks associated with a particular operation or business may refuse to engage in that activity." Williams & Heins 40.

duction of the risk that added loss will occur because of a forced sale of assets to meet the exigency arising from the specified loss. This reduction occurs because of the greater financial stability of the insurance company.

(4) RISK TRANSFERENCE

Another form of risk management is risk transference.[8] Though often accomplished through contracts, and especially insurance contracts, risk management may also be accomplished by measures that are more active and more concerned with nonlegal than legal risks. When the lighted squib of *Scott v. Shepherd*[9] was tossed into the crowd, each person who picked it up and tossed it again was changing the risk of bodily harm from one pattern to another, involving a new group of persons; even if some persons were in all groups, the degrees of risk to various persons changed as the squib moved.

All insurance contracts concern risk transference, but not all contracts concerning risk transference are insurance. The complex bundle of risks from a venture[10] gives rise to a variety of kinds of legal risk transference, some of which are not regarded as insurance for any purpose, and some of which are regarded as insurance for one purpose but not for another. Even in states having the broadest statutory or decisional definitions of insurance,[11] which if literally applied would include all or nearly all contracts transferring risk, many arrangements literally within such definitions are not treated as insurance transactions in legal contexts.

(5) RISK DISTRIBUTION; ADVERSE EXPERIENCE

Another form of risk management is risk distribution. Insurance, considered from the point of view of the insurer and from the point of view of society, is an instance of risk distribution. It approaches the objective of reducing uncertainty by treating as a unit the combined risk of multiple ventures of a given type.[12]

Risk distribution is a way of managing the risk of adverse experience—the risk that one's loss experience will be disproportionately great in comparison with the loss experience of similar ventures. As the number of ventures in the group under consideration is increased, protection is improved against the chance that the severity and number of harmful events will be spread over time or in other ways in

---

8. See, *e.g.*, Denenberg *et al.* 9; Mehr & Hedges 64–87; Williams & Heins 42; Bobbitt, n.5 *supra*, at 150.

9. 2 B.W. 892, 96 Eng.Rep. 525 (1775).

10. See § 1.2(b) (1) *supra*.

11. See § 8.2(a) *infra*.

12. See Williams & Heins 43, characterizing this tool of risk management

as "combination." "Insurers are the major users of this device for its own sake; they insure a large number of persons in order to improve their ability to predict their losses. In other words, the purchase of insurance, from the point of view of the insured, is a transfer; from the viewpoint of the insurer, it is a combination." *Ibid.* See also Denenberg *et al.* 9, 143–144; Bobbitt, n.5 *supra*, at 150.

groupings disproportionate to the overall risk. That is, with an increasing number of ventures in a combined pool, the unusually favorable and unusually harmful experiences tend to stay more nearly in balance, just as the percentages of heads and tails in the flipping of a coin tend to stay more nearly in balance as the number of tosses of the coin is increased. The prediction of harm to come from a single venture is still largely a guess. But, if the number of ventures is great and data about experience in like ventures in the past are very substantial, the prediction of total harm to come from the entire group of ventures can be close enough to accuracy for practical reliance. Thus the total cost of bearing the risk in such great number of like ventures can be reliably determined even though the cost of bearing the risk in any single venture in the group is quite uncertain. The policyholder pays as a premium an amount equal to a proportionate part of the total predicted cost of meeting specified types of losses in a great number of ventures like his, plus a sum for administrative and other costs. The insurer, collecting premiums from many policyholders, increases the number of ventures in the risk pool to the point that the principle of risk distribution operates satisfactorily. If a single insurer does not sell enough policies to reach this point of sufficient numbers of ventures at risk, it may likewise employ risk transference, turning to another insurer for reinsurance of part or all of the risk undertaken.

(6) SELF-INSURING; RISK RETENTION

Just as risk transference may be accomplished without insurance, so may risk distribution. If one engages in a sufficient volume of ventures of a given type, he can spread the risks of individual ventures among all the ventures in the group, paying losses from a fund created by charging a proportionate part of the total predicted cost against each venture without reference to which ones in fact produce harm. He is thus engaging in planned risk retention. Some large business enterprises handle tort claims in this manner. For example, a transit company against which hundreds of personal injury claims are made annually may prefer to have its own claims department and fund, rather than turning over to an insurer all or part of the management of its claims. An enterprise operating in this way is sometimes referred to as a self-insurer.[13] But this type of operation in-

---

13. Traditional thought is that "if a funded reserve is not used, one does not have self-insurance but instead has a system of non-insurance." Bobbitt, n.5 *supra*, at 150. "More recently, however, a different concept has been developed. Self-insurance is considered to be any plan of risk retention in which a program or procedure has been established to meet the adverse results of a financial loss. Although this does not exclude either the practice of pooling or the establishment of an inviolate reserve, it includes many other practices that the business world has considered self-insurance but insurance scholars have not. . . . This newer concept recognizes that the traditional requisites of self-insurance are seldom, if ever, achieved in practice but that a planned program of risk retention differs significantly from simple risk retention." Denenberg *et al.* 79–80.

volves no insurance as that term is ordinarily used in regulatory statutes, in tax statutes, and in other legal contexts.[14]

(7) ADVERSE SELECTION

Whenever a large group of potential insureds are treated alike irrespective of some factor that differentiates them as insurance risks, a disproportionately high percentage of applications for such insurance tends to come from the less desirable applicants because they get the better bargain. This is the principle of adverse selection.[15]

A good illustration of the process occurs in the case of "renewable term insurance." Such a policy grants the privilege of renewing the insurance for another term, irrespective of the insured's health at the time of the renewal. Thus, the renewal feature is a way of insuring one's insurability. Those who find themselves in bad health near the end of the earlier term of coverage will be likely to exercise the option to renew for another term. Those who are in good health at that time will be less likely to renew, especially since the premium rate for the new term is customarily higher than the rate for the earlier term, because fixed in accordance with attained age rather than age at the inception of the contract.[16] The death rate among those who renew their policies is therefore likely to be in excess of the normal death rate.

Other illustrations of adverse selection are referred to elsewhere.[17]

The probability of adverse selection is to be taken into account in devising any type of insurance, and any sound plan of insurance must have within it adequate protection against this phenomenon. In the case of renewable term insurance, for example, adverse selection accounts for only a small percentage of the overall risk transferred to

---

14. "Self-insurance as a technique for treating risk has long been surrounded with confusion and controversy. . . . For those who believe that transfer of risk is a requisite for insurance, the term self-insurance is a misnomer since it permits no transfer. For those who define insurance in terms of pooling, the term self-insurance is not a misnomer but an accurate description of a process by which uncertainty is reduced or eliminated." *Id.* at 79. See also Williams & Heins 41.

15. See, *e.g.*, Denenberg *et al.* 191–192.

16. *Cf.* Maclean, Life Insurance 33 (9th ed. 1962).

17. See §§ 2.3(c) (2) at n.19 (life insurance binding receipts), 2.8(a) at n.9 (group insurance), 8.6(c) at nn.10–11 (war risks in life insurance; flood insurance) *infra*.

Consider also the closely related concept of adverse financial selection, arising from the substantial investment element in many life insurance contracts. "A substantial proportion of the assets of life insurance companies [is] invested in long-term investments. As a result the average rate of investment return earned by life insurers at any given time seldom coincides with the going rate of interest on similar investments. Also, the rates of return earned by insurers often vary from the rate available on alternative investments. Thus, when the investment earnings rate of insurers is low relative to alternative investments, policyholders may be encouraged to withdraw their funds from the insurance company. The reverse is true when insurers are earning a higher return on investments than is available from other investment media." Denenberg *et al.* 192.

insurers, and adequate protection is provided by making the premiums charged during the earlier term, for the privilege of renewal at the end of that term, just a little higher than they would need to be if adverse selection were not operating—for example, just a little higher than if all policyholders could be expected to renew.

§ 1.2(c) CONTEXTS OF DISPUTE OVER WHAT IS INSURANCE

The most common source of controversy over what is insurance is dispute over the applicability of regulatory measures—statutory, administrative, and decisional.[1] Attempts have sometimes been made, in statutes and elsewhere, to formulate a general definition of insurance for use in determining the reach of these regulatory measures. The success of any such effort is bound to be limited because different regulatory measures are efforts to respond to needs of very different scope. Thus, as already noted,[2] no single concept of insurance is universally useful as a tool of thought and communication about such problems.

It is entirely appropriate that concepts of insurance be adaptable to widely differing circumstances of use rather than being so rigid that they become shackles to thought and expression. Though the principal characteristics of insurance are transferring and distributing risk,[3] demonstrating that a transaction has these characteristics falls short of proving that it is an insurance transaction. Whatever the context may be, something more is required.

Consider, for example, a warranty of quality of merchandise,[4] a contract to maintain a truck in good repair,[5] and a lawyer's retainer

1. Concerning the scope of regulatory measures generally, see § 8.2 *infra*.

2. See § 1.2(a) *supra*.

3. See § 1.2(a) *supra*.

4. See, *e.g.*, State *ex rel.* Herbert v. Standard Oil Co., 138 Ohio St. 376, 35 N.E.2d 437 (1941) (new tire guarantee applicable if used "under usual conditions" for a specified period of time; held not insurance although there was evidence that the company's agents orally represented that the guarantee protected "against such hazards as cuts, bruises, wheels out of alignment and blowouts" and that tires purposely mutilated had been replaced under the guarantee). See generally § 8.2(c) *infra*. *But see, e.g.*, State *ex rel.* Duffy v. Western Auto Supply Co., 134 Ohio St. 163, 16 N.E.2d 256 (1938), 119 A.L.R. 1236 (1939) (guarantee issued with new automobile tires found to be an illegal contract of insurance because the form

of agreement constituted "an undertaking to indemnify against failure from any cause except fire or theft and therefore covers loss or damage resulting from any and every hazard of travel, not excepting negligence of the automobile driver or another"). In later years Western Auto described its guarantee only a little more cautiously by including in its advertisements a footnote as follows: "In Ohio, complete tire service guaranteed under proper and normal operating conditions." Time, May, 1957, p. 23.

5. See, *e.g.*, Transportation Gee. Co. v. Jellins, 29 Cal.2d 242, 174 P.2d 625 (1946) ("guaranteed maintenance contract" to maintain truck in mechanical repair, to garage and fuel it, and to cause it to be insured; held not void as an insurance contract contrary to public policy since the "controlling object" of the contract was service, not insurance). See generally § 8.2(c) *infra*.

contract with the client, under which the fee is fixed in advance, at a time when neither can know precisely what legal services will be required during the period of the contract.[6] These transactions are generally not treated as insurance in legal contexts (*e. g.,* under a statute regulating those who are doing an insurance business). Yet they clearly involve risk transference and risk distribution.

Another set of disputes over what is insurance arises in relation to tax measures. For example, estate tax laws have commonly provided for special treatment of amounts receivable "as insurance under policies on the life of the decedent." [7] A tax loophole would exist if simultaneous and carefully dovetailed annuity and life insurance contracts (providing for payment of an annuity to the purchaser for life and payment of death proceeds to his designated beneficiaries at death) could be used to pass funds at death as proceeds of life insurance not includible within the estate of the decedent because at the time of his death he possessed none of the incidents of ownership. For this reason, a transaction in the form of traditional life insurance may yet be attacked as not "life insurance" within the meaning of the tax law.[8]

It may be suggested that the refund aspect of a refund annuity (one providing for a repayment of part of the premiums if death occurs early) is in essence hedging rather than insurance—that the refund annuity is partly insurance against the economic contingencies of long life and partly an investment providing for a minimum return even though death occurs early.[9] This analysis, however, is not conclusive of the question whether all or a portion of the payments before death should be treated as income for income tax purposes or those after death should be treated as "insurance proceeds" under estate or inheritance tax statutes (either for the purpose of bringing the proceeds within the estate of the decedent rather than excluding them altogether, or for the purpose of benefiting the taxpayer by application of statutory exclusions of insurance proceeds not exceeding a stated amount.) These issues of tax law must be resolved in the light of considerations relevant to the interpretation of the statutes involved rather than on the basis merely of some assumed general definition of insurance.

Similarly, disputes over the applicability to variable annuities [10] of measures for the regulation respectively of securities transactions

6. See Transportation Gee. Co. v. Jellins, 29 Cal.2d 242, 248, 174 P.2d 625, 629 (1946) (dictum that "the lawyer who contracts to prosecute a case to final judgment for a fixed or contingent fee assumes the risk of long litigation, of repeated trials and reversals . . . ." but is not engaged in the business of insurance).

7. See 26 U.S.C.A. § 2042 (1967); Annot., 14 L.Ed.2d 817 (1966).

8. See, *e.g.,* Fidelity-Philadelphia Trust Co. v. Smith, 356 U.S. 274, 78 Sup.Ct. 730, 2 L.Ed.2d 765 (1958), in which, however, the majority of the court treated the particular contracts in question as life insurance for purposes of the estate tax computation, the purchaser having divested herself, before death, of all interests in them.

9. Concerning the nature of annuities generally, see § 1.3(i) *infra.*

10. Concerning the nature of variable annuities generally, see § 1.3(i) *infra.*

and insurance transactions cannot be resolved satisfactorily by appeals to definitions of insurance and securities.[11]

SECTION 1.3 CLASSIFICATION BY THE NATURE OF THE RISKS

§ 1.3(a) GENERALLY

Under the combined influence of voluntary specialization and statutory classification for regulation, insurance contracts and organizations in the United States have developed into three main classes based on the nature of the risk covered. These classes are commonly referred to as life, fire and marine, and casualty insurance. Early regulatory statutes in the United States limited an insurer to writing within one of these three classes, although not every insurer had all the powers assigned to its class and some specialized in writing only one kind within a class. In England, this compartmentalization of authority for underwriting never existed. In the United States, during the first half of the twentieth century, "multiple-line" underwriting by one insurer of all types of insurance other than life came to be generally authorized by statute.[1] Multiple-line underwriting has been developed also by groups of affiliated companies, from whose common agents an insured may buy a single policy of multiple-line coverage, some of which is provided by each of the affiliated companies. This arrangement is sometimes made between a parent company and a subsidiary, and at other times among a group of otherwise independent insurers, sometimes referred to as a "fleet."

A still broader combination of underwriting includes life insurance as well as casualty and fire and marine, and is known as "all-line" underwriting. At present some fleets do such all-line underwriting.[2]

Despite multiple-line and all-line developments, the threefold classification of types of insurance is still important. Multiple-line legislation has not abolished the classes of insurance but has merely authorized one insurer to operate in the entire field of insurance other than life. Many companies still limit themselves for business and legal reasons to only a small part of the field that they might occupy. Also distinctive regulations, doctrines, and practices with respect to

---

11. See § 8.2(d) *infra.*

1. Michelbacher & Roos, Multiple-Line Insurers: Their Nature and Operation 4–9 (2d ed. 1970). See also Denenberg, Eilers, Hoffman, Kline, Melone & Snider, Risk and Insurance 335–346 (1964).

2. Woodson, *All-Lines Underwriting: New Fashion or New Era?*, 12 J.Am. Soc'y Chartered Life Underwriters 69, 75–76 (1957). With regard to authorization for all-line underwriting by a single company, but with special provision for life insurance reserves, see Wis.Stat. § 201.05(2) (1967). See also Connecticut Gen. Life Ins. Co. v. Superintendent of Ins., 10 N.Y.2d 42, 176 N.E.2d 63, 217 N.Y.S.2d 39 (1961) (licensed foreign life insurance company not barred, by N.Y.Ins.Law §§ 42(3) and 193(2) then in force, from purchasing 80 per cent or more of the common stock of a fire and casualty insurance company).

the different classes of insurance persist despite the growth of all-line underwriting.

Multiple-line insurers customarily use basically the same policy forms and offer the same types of coverages as other insurers. Thus the multiple-line development is not itself a trend toward "all-risk" insurance,[3] though in the long run it could facilitate such a trend.

§ 1.3(b) MARINE AND INLAND MARINE INSURANCE

Marine insurance developed into a standardized pattern at a relatively early time. In the 1600's, persons interested in arranging contracts of insurance against perils of the sea became accustomed to gathering at Lloyd's Coffee House in London to transact their business. A person interested in obtaining insurance on a vessel or cargo would pass around a slip containing relevant information, including an indication of the total amount of insurance desired, and each person interested in becoming an insurer would subscribe his initials and an amount for which he was willing to be responsible. Each of these "underwriters" became an insurer for the amount he had "underwritten." In 1769, the underwriters formed a society, and in 1779 this society adopted the "Lloyd's policy" as a standard form. Little change has been made in this policy form during intervening years, as you may infer from an examination of modern marine insurance forms.[1]

As insurance has developed in the 19th and 20th Centuries, the greater part of it is written by insurance companies rather than individual underwriters. Commonly the companies writing marine insurance have also extended their operations into other areas of property insurance. Some of these types of insurance, particularly those involving transportation of goods over inland waterways, have been referred to as "inland marine" insurance. As extensions have continued, however, inland marine insurance has come to include some risks that, if one were not familiar with the historical development, he would never expect to be classified as "marine" in even the most tenuous sense. "Inland marine" has spread to transportation risks generally, and further to insurance of any kind of goods that might be affected by movement.[2] The policies insuring moveable goods irrespective of location are known as "floater" policies.

Inland marine insurance now includes three main branches covering: domestic shipments; bridges, tunnels, and other instrumentali-

---

3. "All-risk" insurance is discussed in § 5.1(b) *infra*.

1. For illustrative modern marine insurance forms, see Appendix C *infra*. See also Russell Mining Co. v. Northwestern Fire & Marine Ins. Co., 207 F.Supp. 162 (1962), *reversed*, 322 F.2d 440 (6th Cir. 1963), for an example of the problems of applying antiquated terminology to current transactions.

The disputed insurance was coverage for a barge moored permanently on an inland waterway, and the case concerned application of the Inchmaree clause, devised in the late 1800's to apply to the insurance of ocean-going vessels.

2. See, *e.g.*, Denenberg, Eilers, Hoffman, Kline, Melone & Snider, Risk and Insurance 337–339 (1964).

ties of transportation and communication; and personal property floater risks.

§ 1.3(c) FIRE INSURANCE

Fire insurance, as the term is customarily understood, includes coverage of loss caused by hostile fire [3] or lightning. Fire insurance companies have customarily been authorized to write "allied lines" covering damage from wind, rain, collision, riot and civil commotion, explosion, water damage, and earthquake.

§ 1.3(d) CASUALTY INSURANCE

Casualty insurance includes liability, workmen's compensation, accident and health, glass, burglary and theft, boiler and machinery, property damage, collision, and credit insurance and fidelity and surety bonds.

§ 1.3(e) LIFE INSURANCE

Life insurance, as one of the three main classes, includes personal accident and health insurance and annuity contracts, in addition to life insurance in the narrower sense of contracts providing for payment of specified benefits upon the death of the person whose life is insured.

Life insurance in the narrower sense includes a variety of types. The term "ordinary life insurance" is sometimes used to signify a marketing arrangement; in this sense it refers to contracts, other than industrial insurance, marketed by individual solicitation as distinguished from group marketing.[1] In a more common usage this terminology concerns the structure of the policy—the terms and conditions that make up the "plan" of insurance. The following is a statement in outline form of terminology commonly used to distinguish different "plans" of insurance.[2]

Whole-life insurance (providing coverage for the entire lifetime and maturing for payment only at the death of the person insured):

(i) Ordinary life insurance (whole-life insurance in which premiums are payable either throughout the lifetime of the person insured or else until he has reached a specified advanced age—*e. g.,* 85). The term "straight life insurance" is sometimes used to refer to this same plan.

(ii) Limited-payment life insurance (whole-life insurance in which premiums are paid only during a specified number of years or until a specified event).

---

3. The distinction between "friendly" and "hostile" fires is discussed in § 5.3(d) *infra.*

(1935). *Cf.* Maclean, Life Insurance 406–412 (9th ed. 1962), using the phrase "ordinary life insurance" in this sense.

1. *E.g.,* see Fuller, Foreword to *The Wage-Earner's Life Insurance* [a symposium], 2 Law & Contemp.Prob. 2

2. *Cf.* Maclean, Life Insurance 21–34 (9th ed. 1962).

(iii) Single-premium life insurance.

(iv) Joint-life insurance.

Endowment life insurance (providing for payment of a specified amount either in the event of death within the endowment period, commonly twenty years, or upon survival to the "maturity" date at the end of that period).

Term life insurance (providing for payment of a specified amount only if death occurs within a limited period, the "term," specified in the policy). Term contracts may allow one, both, or neither of the options to convert and renew:

(i) Convertible term insurance (providing an option, without regard to health at the time of exercising the option, to change to a "permanent" plan of whole-life or endowment insurance).

(ii) Renewable term insurance (providing an option, without regard to health at the time of exercising the option, to renew for an additional term, and usually providing options for repeated renewals for a specified number of times or until the insured has reached a specified age).

Modified life insurance (combining term and ordinary life insurance).[3]

Most "plans" of life insurance involve, to a significant extent, features of savings and investment as well as purely insurance features.[4] Indeed, these features are so familiar that the particular form in which they exist in a contract may affect its classification as insurance or not.[5]

§ 1.3(f) INDUSTRIAL INSURANCE

The phrase "industrial life insurance" is used to refer to a type of life insurance that is written in small amounts (often barely adequate for burial expenses) and is paid for in frequent and modest premium installments, weekly collection being common. The shorter phrase "industrial insurance" usually refers to such life insurance, but also includes health and accident policies. In the frequency of premium installments, industrial life insurance is unlike "ordinary"[1] life insurance and is similar to the most common form of group insurance—that involving a group of employees whose contributions to the cost of the insurance are deducted from their pay.[2] But in con-

3. See Mowbray, Blanchard & Williams, Insurance 306 (6th ed. 1969).

4. See, *e.g.*, Denenberg, Eilers, Hoffman, Kline, Melone & Snider, Risk and Insurance 192, 243–249 (1964).

5. See, *e.g.*, Securities & Exchange Commission v. Variable Annuity Life Ins. Co., 359 U.S. 65, 79 Sup.Ct. 618, 3 L.Ed.2d 640 (1959), discussed in § 8.2 (d) *infra*.

1. The term "ordinary" is used here in the first of the senses explained in § 1.3(e) *supra*. Industrial life insurance is written on various plans (endowment, limited-payment life, *etc.*). Maclean, Life Insurance 408–409 (9th ed. 1962). An industrial policy on the ordinary (straight life) plan is sometimes referred to as an "ordinary" industrial policy.

2. The extent of the contrast between the methods of marketing "ordinary"

trast with the wholesale method of marketing used in group insurance, and in common with that of ordinary life insurance, the method of marketing industrial insurance is through direct solicitation by an agent.

The high cost of solicitation and collection (usually by the agent's calling on the policyholder), the minimal use of means of medical selection,[3] and the higher death rates of the low-income groups usually insured under such policies,[4] result in higher rates than for other forms of life insurance. Nevertheless, the convenience of small installment payments to persons in the low-income group, who find it difficult to budget for the less frequent but larger individual payments of ordinary life insurance, has combined with the effectiveness of solicitation to make industrial life insurance a very significant part of the total value of life insurance in force. In an article published in 1935, Patterson observed five methods of marketing wage-earner's insurance—industrial insurance, fraternal insurance, government insurance sold through post offices in England and Japan, savings-bank life insurance (originated in Massachusetts), and group insurance sold through employers.[5] He added that (in 1935) industrial insurance was the only one of these which had come near blanketing its field.[6] In 1955, approximately 112 million industrial life policies were in force, representing more than 39 billion dollars of insurance and more than ten per cent of the total amount of life insurance in force in the United States. The number of industrial life policies declined steadily from 1955 to 1969, and the total face amount of this coverage remained almost constant. In 1969, approximately 79 million industrial life policies were in force, representing somewhat less than 39 billion dollars of insurance, approximately three per cent of the total amount of life insurance in force in the United States.[7] The urban industrial class was the group among whom this type of insurance was first marketed, and is still the group accounting for most of such policies.[8] Hence the term "industrial" insurance.

Industrial insurance is distinctive not only because of the method by which it is marketed but also because of the combination of contract provisions commonly used. Some of the provisions referred to

and industrial insurance was reduced by rapid development during the late 1950's of monthly payment plans for "ordinary" life insurance under which the insured authorizes drafts on his bank account in the amount of the monthly premium signed by a representative of the insurer (called by various names, such as "check-o-matic" and "premiumatic"). See Eastern Underwriter, August 22, 1958, p. 10.

3. Maclean, Life Insurance 408 (9th ed. 1962).

4. *Ibid.*

5. Patterson, *The Distribution of Wage-Earner's Life Insurance*, 2 Law & Contemp.Prob. 3, 6 (1935).

6. *Ibid.*

7. Institute of Life Insurance, Life Insurance Fact Book, 1970, 32, 103. This compares to 118 million ordinary policies in 1969, representing over 678 billion dollars of insurance, a bit more than half of the total life insurance in force in the United States. *Id.* at 26, 103.

8. See Maclean, Life Insurance 406 (9th ed. 1962).

below can be found in one or more of the other types of life insurance, but in combination they set the distinctive pattern of industrial insurance.

One characteristic of industrial insurance is that the policyholder may return the policy in two or three weeks from the date of issue if he is not satisfied, receiving a refund of any premium payment.[9]

Unlike ordinary policies, industrial policies usually include, without additional premium, special benefits for loss of eyesight or limbs. For example, a typical industrial policy will pay the face amount of the insurance if the insured loses both hands or both feet or the entire sight of both eyes, and the company will also continue the policy in force with premiums waived.[10]   Also, industrial policies contain no suicide limitation.[11]   Due to the small amounts involved, however, they ordinarily have no loan provisions [12] or settlement options.[13]

As the company only rarely requires a physical examination, industrial policies contain a provision under which, subject to the incontestable clause, the policy is voidable on specific conditions—*e.g.*, if "the insured has received institutional, hospital, medical, or surgical treatment or attention, and the insured or any claimant under the policy fails to show that the condition occasioning such treatment or attention was not of a serious nature or was not material to the risk," unless the company was informed of the treatment, or attention.[14]   Another commonly used clause provides for invalidation of the policy if the insured was not in "good health" (or "sound health") on the inception date.[15]   The good-health clause is also sometimes used in ordinary life insurance, and especially in policies that are issued without a physical examination (usually $1,000 up to $5,000). [16]

Before the depression of the 1930's, most industrial policies allowed no cash return to the policyholder if he discontinued his premium payments before the eleventh year.[17]   In contrast, the holder of an ordinary policy would be entitled to "cash surrender" value after a much shorter period—under many policies, after the first year.   During the depression, some companies adopted a practice, in cases of hardship, of making cash payments upon discontinuance of industrial policies before they were eligible for cash surrender values.[18]   Also there was a movement, beginning in 1935, toward the use of provi-

9.   Davis, Industrial Life Insurance 36, 46 (1944); Maclean, Life Insurance 413 (9th ed. 1962).

10.   *Id.* at 416.

11.   Davis, Industrial Life Insurance 46 (1944).

12.   *Id.* at 44.

13.   *Id.* at 45.

14.   *Id.* at 34–35.

15.   *Id.* at 262.

16.   Concerning the effect of the good-health clause generally, see § 6.5(e) (4) *infra*.

17.   Davis, Industrial Life Insurance 198–199 (1944).

18.   Fuller, *The Special Nature of the Wage-Earner's Life Insurance Problem*, 2 Law & Contemp.Prob. 10, 25–26 (1935).

sions reducing the length of the period before eligibility for cash surrender values.[19]   Today, under most industrial policies, non-forfeiture benefits in the form of cash payments are not available for three to five years after date of issue, but non-forfeiture benefits in the form of insurance are commonly available as early as 26 weeks after date of issue.[20]   These non-forfeiture benefits, except for cash surrender value, are even more favorable than those of ordinary policies. One justification urged for treating industrial policies less favorably as to surrender terms is that more favorable treatment would be a disservice to the industrial policyholders, on the ground that as a class they need protection against the improvident surrender of their life insurance coverage.[21]

Two provisions within the pattern of industrial insurance prohibit any assignment of the policy or benefits thereunder and give the insurer some discretion over disposition of the death benefit.   The latter provision is known as the "facility of payment clause."   It authorizes payment to a person appearing to the insurer to be equitably entitled to the insurance proceeds by reason of having incurred expense on behalf of the insured for medical treatment, burial, or any other purpose.   This clause may avoid the necessity for appointment of an administrator, executor, or guardian to collect and use the insurance proceeds, and may serve to facilitate settlement of disputes among rival claimants without the delay and expense of litigation. The possibility of abuse of the discretion given to the insurer by the facility of payment clause is apparent.   The clause has nevertheless been defended as a wise provision.[22]   Group insurance often includes a similar "facility of payment clause." [23]

§ 1.3(g)   TRIP INSURANCE

Trip insurance is commonly available at airports both over the counter and through vending machines, and motoring trip insurance of similar characteristics has also been offered, though it is less readily available and less widely used.[1]

§ 1.3(h)   TITLE INSURANCE

Title insurance has been regarded as a separate type of contract not falling within any of the three basic classes of insurance.   The

---

19.   *Id.* at 26.

20.   See Maclean, Life Insurance 415 (9th ed. 1962), indicating also that in one company such non-forfeiture benefits are available after an even shorter period.

21.   See Fuller, *The Special Nature of the Wage-Earner's Life Insurance Problem*, 2 Law & Contemp.Prob. 10, 25–26 (1935).

22.   *Id.* at 28–29, expressing the opinion that "the companies have been guided by a sound instinct in preferring the dangers of paternalism to those of legalism."

23.   Gregg, Group Life Insurance 99 (3d ed. 1962).

1.   See § 2.9 *infra.*

risks insured against are more in the nature of incomplete information about legal rights already existing at the time the contract is written [1] and less in the nature of fortuitous subsequent events such as are the subject of other kinds of insurance. One can, however, view the subsequent assertion of a claim as a fortuitous loss-producing event against which insurance is being provided. The formulation of limitations on the scope of coverage under title insurance has produced distinctive problems of interpretation and application.[2]

§ 1.3 (i) ANNUITIES

An ordinary annuity contract provides for the payment of a fixed-dollar annual benefit commencing at a specified date and continuing as long as the annuitant lives. Such a contract is in many contexts treated as a form of insurance, closely associated in general with life insurance. The traditional annuity contract is in essence and principal purpose a risk-transferring-and-distributing contract. The risk in this instance is the risk of long life—the risk that in later years one's income-producing capacity will fall below his economic needs.

Many annuity contracts provide that if death comes early the company shall, in addition to paying annuities to the time of death, pay a specified sum as a refund of a part of the premium or premiums paid to purchase the contract. Perhaps this refund aspect of a refund annuity contract is properly regarded as not an incident of the insurance aspect of the contract but instead an incident of the refusal to make an annuity contract that is purely insurance against the risk of long life. That is, the refund aspect is more analogous to hedging; the refund annuity is partly insurance (against the economic contin-

---

1. In the nineteenth century, legal opinions of title validity were insured. But this gave way to title insurance. Brown, *Insured Legal Opinions*, 36 J.S.B.Calif. 411 (1961), reprinted in 1961 Ins.L.J. 712. Brown suggests the possibility of devising insurance to cover the risk of depending on the legal advice of counsel (*ibid.*); such insurance would probably be subsumed under the "casualty" classification.

2. See, *e.g.*, Hansen v. Western Title Ins. Co., 220 Cal.App.2d 531, 33 Cal. Rptr. 668 (1st Dist.1963), 98 A.L.R.2d 520 (1964) (a claim arising out of a poorly drafted option agreement between the insured and the claimant was settled by the insured, who then sought recovery from his title insurer; held, the defect was not "created by" the insured within the meaning of a coverage restriction); Demopoulos v. Title Ins. Co., 61 N.M. 254, 298 P.2d 938 (1956), 60 A.L.R.2d 969 (1958)

(mortgagee insured to the limit of $8,-500 its interest in a mortgage for that amount procured by a mortgagor who misrepresented the value and identification of the property involved, recorded a fraudulent deed to show his title to the property, and forged his wife's name to the mortgage contract; held, the mortgagee could recover only $1,200, the actual value of the land, since that was all the mortgagee could have recovered had the mortgage been valid and foreclosed); Shaver v. National Title & Abstract Co., 361 S.W. 2d 867 (Tex.1962), 98 A.L.R.2d 531 (1964) (unknown to the insured, a large gas main was buried under his land pursuant to a recorded easement that was not discovered when the insured bought the land; held, the defect in the title created by the easement was not within the coverage restriction concerning rights of persons in possession of the land).

gencies of long life) and partly investment (providing for a minimum return even though death occurs early).

The variable annuity is a relatively recent invention. Pioneered by the College Retirement Equities Fund (CREF) and its parent, Teachers Insurance and Annuity Association (TIAA), the variable annuity was first introduced in 1952. The CREF annuity was designed to provide retirement income based on common stock investments and to complement other provisions for fixed-dollar retirement income, such as one might obtain through an ordinary annuity.[3]

Variable annuity contracts differ in detail.[4] In general, however, during the pay-in period, the purchaser of a variable annuity buys units of ownership in a portfolio of common stocks. The cost of units purchased at different times and the value of the purchaser's accumulated holdings vary because of the changing value of the common stocks in the portfolio. During the pay-out period, the annuity holder receives payment of a number of units each year (or receives payments in smaller and more frequent installments, if so agreed). The number of units is actuarially calculated and depends on factors affecting life expectancy at the date of commencement of the pay-out period. Though the number of units received each year remains constant over the pay-out period (subject to agreed exceptions such as providing for more units while both the annuitant and his spouse are living than when only one is surviving), the money income varies because the value of the unit continues to change with the value of the common stocks in the portfolio.

Variable annuities have presented distinctive problems of regulation.[5]

SECTION 1.4   CLASSIFICATION BY THE NATURE OF THE INSURING ORGANIZATION

There is no single system of classification, from the point of view of the nature of the insuring organization, that has achieved general usage comparable to that of the three-fold classification as to the nature of the insured risks. For convenience, however, insurers (other than governmental units)[1] may be grouped in the following rough classification, though some organizations today are of mixed types that do not fit perfectly in any of these groups:[2] natural persons, as individuals; Lloyd's associations; stock companies; mutual companies; fraternal societies; and reciprocal associations or inter-insurance exchanges.

natural persons
Lloyds Assns
Stock Companies
Mutual Companies
Fraternal Societies
Reciprocal Assns
or
Inter-Insurance
exchanges

3. Greenough & King, Benefit Plans in American Colleges 43–99 (1969).

4. See generally Johnson & Grubbs, The Variable Annuity (2d ed. 1970).

5. See § 8.2(d) *infra*.

1. Greenough & King, Benefit Plans in tions as insurers, see § 8.6 *infra*.

2. See generally Patterson, Essentials of Insurance Law § 9 (2d ed. 1957); Vance, Law of Insurance 17–18, 122–125 (3d ed. Anderson 1951).

Though some insurance arrangements were developed earlier, modern Anglo-American insurance traditions are rooted in the practices of those who gathered at Lloyd's Coffee House in London in the latter part of the 17th century.[3] It became customary for persons desiring insurance to be represented by a Lloyd's broker and for persons willing to be insurers to operate in syndicates of several persons, with a single representative to do their underwriting. This practice continues today.[4] The arrangement is that members of such a syndicate are not to be jointly liable; rather it is agreed that each is to be separately liable for his specified fraction of the coverage underwritten by the representative of the syndicate. A high percentage of the world's insurance has been written by these Lloyd's syndicates, which are sometimes referred to as Lloyd's Associations. A small but substantial percentage of the insurance in the United States today, especially with respect to risks that do not fit one of the well-established patterns,[5] is written by English Lloyd's syndicates through brokers in the United States.

Though there is a Corporation of Lloyd's, organized in 1871, it does no underwriting. Rather, it is an organization that regulates the operations of the underwriters and provides various services, including the gathering and publication of data useful to the underwriters and others concerned with insurance.

Some organizations called Lloyd's Associations, patterned after the Coffee House syndicates, have been formed in the United States, but in general American legislation has either prohibited or else at least discouraged such associations.[6] Relatively, only a small amount of insurance is written by American Lloyd's Associations.

A stock company is a corporation, similar in organization to business corporations operating in other fields. Stockholders are the owners of the business but are not personally liable for losses if the company's reserves are depleted. Policies are sold on a fixed premium basis, but in some instances participating policies are issued, providing for the return to the policyholders of a share of profits.

Insurers of the three types considered above customarily operate for the profit of their owners. The remaining three types of insurers are mutual organizations—*i.e.*, nonprofit associations or corporations in which each member or shareholder is both an insurer and an insured. Some mutuals have operated by levying an assessment after losses have been determined.[7] Under the other plan of operation,

[margin note: Mutual Organizations]

3. See § 1.3(b) *supra.*

4. Denenberg, Eilers, Hoffman, Kline, Melone & Snider, Risk and Insurance 170–172 (1964) [hereinafter cited as Denenberg *et al.*].

5. For examples of the types of services provided by such associations, see *e.g.*, *id.* at 171; DeWolf, *The Proposed*

Surplus Line Law: Constructive or Destructive, 1961 Ins.L.J. 259.

6. See § 8.5 at n.3 *infra.*

7. Compare the system of assessments used in the early history of the arrangement that was involved in Commissioner v. Treganowan, 183 F.2d 288 (2d Cir.), *cert. denied*, 340 U.S. 853 (1950).

now generally required by statute, each member pays a premium in advance. If adequate reserves have been built up, mutuals may be permitted to issue non-assessable policies.[8] In some of the mutuals, however, the members are subject to assessment, usually limited to an amount equal to the advance premium.[9]

Most mutual insurers are incorporated under statutes providing specially for such organizations, and are referred to as mutual companies. There was a trend toward mutualization of stock companies in the early part of this century, especially in the life insurance field. At present the greater percentage of life insurance is written by mutual companies [10] though stock companies write more insurance than mutuals in the fields of fire and casualty insurance.[11]

A fraternal society (also called a mutual benefit society) is an organization providing insurance benefits to members of a fraternity or lodge. This is probably the most ancient form of insurance organization. Such organizations usually receive favored treatment under regulatory and tax laws; nevertheless, a disturbing number of financial failures has led to a tightening of regulations, especially with respect to the maintenance of reserves.

A reciprocal association or inter-insurance exchange is an association of individuals or juristic entities, providing insurance among themselves and operating through a person or corporation that serves as attorney-in-fact. Most of these organizations are either fire or automobile insurers.

SECTION 1.5   CLASSIFICATION OF REPRESEN-TATIVES (AGENTS AND BROKERS)

§ 1.5(a) GENERALLY

Courts and writers struggling with problems of insurance law have often yielded to the temptation to present fictional explanations of their decisions in distorted agency concepts. This tendency has produced confusion frequently and undesirable results occasionally. Illustrations of the misuse of agency concepts are presented in this

---

8. "The bulk of insurance coverage currently written by mutual insurance companies is nonassessable. . . . The nonassessable arrangement is made possible by the fact that before nonassessable insurers are licensed to operate in a particular state, they must meet, in general, the same financial requirements stipulated for stock insurers. Instead of having capital, however, the minimum surplus of nonassessable mutuals must equal the combined capital and surplus requirements of stock companies." Denenberg et al. 173.

9. Ibid.

10. "Of the 1812 companies in business at mid-year 1969, 1,656 or more than nine-tenths, were owned by stockholders. The remaining 156 were mutual companies. Mutual life companies, which are generally older and larger than the stockholder-owned companies, had about seven-tenths of the assets of all U. S. life companies and accounted for slightly over half of life insurance in force." Institute of Life Insurance, Life Insurance Fact Book, 1970, 108.

11. See, e.g., Denenberg et al. 179.

[margin note: Confusion in opinions re agency doctrine]

text in discussion of the various substantive problems in connection with which they have arisen.[1] Because of the high incidence of such distortion in references to agency concepts in judicial opinions and elsewhere, one should approach with skepticism any assertion that a particular decision on an insurance law problem is governed by agency doctrine. Frequently it is the case, instead, that some overriding principle of liability at variance with policy provisions [2] is the better explanation of the legal result. Nevertheless, insurers and insureds ordinarily conduct their business with each other through intermediaries, and the determination of rights arising under a particular transaction may depend upon the extent to which one or more intermediaries had and exercised power to represent one or the other of the parties to the transaction.

No attempt is made here, however, to align statutory or case authorities for various meanings of common agency concepts. As already suggested, the reason goes beyond that of almost insuperable difficulty because of the lack of a generally accepted set of fixed meanings. The more basic difficulty is that legal powers of representatives to bind insurers have been established in patterns too numerous to be reflected in a few categories identified by terms such as those presented in this section. These terms lack precision, and no others have been invented to serve the purpose of precise shorthand communication. Thus it is fundamentally erroneous to attempt to draw upon a particular usage of one of these terms as if it were an authoritative general definition. Moreover, close examination of the context is often essential to ascertaining the sense in which one of these terms is used.

§ 1.5(b) IN FIRE, MARINE, AND CASUALTY TERMINOLOGY

[margin note: Soliciting Agent — authority only to seek applications to transmit to insurer]

In relation to fire, marine, and casualty insurance, a distinction is customarily drawn between a *soliciting* or *special agent* and a *general agent*. In the strictest usage of the term, a *soliciting agent* is one who has authority only to seek applications and receive them for transmission to an office of the insurer. Such a person is also sometimes called a *special agent,* but more often the latter term, if referring to a member of the sales organization, means one having limited authority to make insurance contracts. The *general agent*, on the other hand, has wide authority to make insurance contracts for the insurer; ordinarily he reports transactions to the home office promptly, but his failure to do so does not affect the validity of the contracts of insurance.

[margin note: General Agent — wide authority to make it for insurer]

The terminology used in an agency contract is inconclusive and is often inconsistent with the distinctions just stated. It may happen that the agency contract refers to one as a soliciting agent but grants to him, expressly or by implication, limited authority to make con-

---

1. See §§ 2.5(c), 2.8(b), 7.10(b) *infra*.   2. See Chapter 6 *infra*.

tracts for the insurer in particular circumstances. Even if the term "special agent" were reserved to designate such persons, it would be indefinite because of the multitude of possible variations in the authority granted. In fact, the term "special agent" is even more indefinite because of its use in other senses as well. For example, it is sometimes used to designate a fieldman who is an intermediary between the field force and the home office,[1] and who also may have adjustment responsibilities.

The term "insurance broker" is used often in a narrow sense to indicate one who acts in the transaction primarily as a purchasing agent for the insured, though he receives his compensation in the form of a commission from the insurer and normally is an agent of the insurer for limited purposes such as collecting premiums on policies transmitted to him for delivery.[2] Less often, the term "insurance broker" is used in a broad sense to include also the various types of agents for the insurer, ranging from those who are soliciting agents in the strictest sense to those who have the broad authority customarily associated with the term "general agent."

§ 1.5(c) IN LIFE INSURANCE TERMINOLOGY

In the life insurance industry all final underwriting authority is customarily retained in the home office. The field organization is ordinarily patterned either on a general agency or branch office system and is headed by *general agents* or *branch managers*.[3] These general agents or branch managers do not have the wide authority to make contracts that is characteristic of general agents in the fire, marine, and casualty lines. Ordinarily their only authority to make insurance contracts concerns temporary, conditional, written contracts in the form of binding receipts, and this authority is usually delegated to *soliciting agents* whom they appoint.[4] Most soliciting agents of life insurers have this limited authority to make temporary contracts of insurance. The term "broker" in relation to life insurance usually refers to one who is a soliciting agent for more than one insurer.[5]

1. See, *e.g.*, Mowbray, Blanchard & Williams, Insurance 401–402 (6th ed. 1969).

2. See, *e.g.*, Patterson, Essentials of Insurance Law 45 (2d ed. 1957); Vance, Law of Insurance 443–445 (3d ed. Anderson 1951); Mowbray, Blanchard & Williams, Insurance 403–405 (6th ed. 1969).

3. See, *e.g.*, Maclean, Life Insurance 360–361 (9th ed. 1962).

4. See, *e.g.*, United Ins. Co. v. Headrick, 275 Ala. 594, 157 So.2d 19 (1963) ("soliciting agent" of life insurance company not authorized to bind company to oral contract of insurance).

5. See, *e.g.*, Maclean, Life Insurance 362 n.3 (9th ed. 1962).

SECTION 1.6 EVALUATIVE STANDARDS OF CLASSIFICATION; FLEXIBILITY

In some instances standards of classifications used in insurance law, as elsewhere in the legal system, require that the person applying the standard to a particular case make an interpretive judgment rather than merely a factfinding. That is, the criterion of classification is evaluative and not merely factual.[1]

The treatment of highly expectable losses is an example in point. Ordinarily insurance contracts do not cover instances of economic detriment of a type occurring so regularly that they are regarded as part of the cost of an activity or enterprise rather than the materialization of risks associated with it. Such a preclusion of coverage for highly expectable losses is sometimes incident to implied exceptions based on the general nature of insurance and at other times is expressed in policy clauses.[2] In either event, the criterion for classifying particular incidents as within or outside the preclusion is evaluative rather than merely factual in character.

It often happens, also, that the evaluative criterion cannot be applied to an individual case without resolving disputed issues of underlying fact. For example, applying the criterion of "permission" under the omnibus clause of an automobile insurance policy typically involves disputed issues of both fact (e. g., what was said or otherwise communicated by the named insured to the driver about the use of the car, and what was the use that was going on when the accident occurred?) and evaluation (e. g., was the use within the scope of the permission express or implied in the communication between the named insured and the driver?). This interrelation between fact issues and evaluative issues commonly leads courts to submit the entire mix to a jury rather than treating the evaluative issue as one for the court. As is well illustrated by the issue of permission under the omnibus clause of automobile policies, the interrelation between fact issues and evaluative issues also tends to breed litigation.[3] Though less notable as a source of litigation, the meaning of "use" in automobile policies also illustrates the case-by-case difficulties of applying standards that involve an element of evaluation as well as fact finding.[4]

One who applies an evaluative criterion to individual cases exercises a considerable measure of discretion, and as a practical matter this assures flexibility by giving a rather free hand to weigh factors that may be thought to affect equities in the individual case. However, such flexibility has its costs as well as its benefits. There is less assurance of consistency and evenhandedness than when less elastic criteria are used. And administrative costs tend to rise with the

1. Concerning evaluative standards generally, see Keeton, Venturing to Do Justice 65–74 (1969).

2. See § 5.4(c) *infra*.

3. See §§ 2.11(b) (2), 4.7(a), (b) (1) and (2), and (c) *infra*.

4. See § 5.2(b) *infra*.

degree of discretion committed to those responsible for applying the criterion to individual cases.[5] It is necessary, therefore, to strike an accommodation at some point between the competing demands for flexibility and certainty in any system of classification.[6] A number of rules of insurance law reflect decisions that favor in particular contexts the relatively high degree of flexibility inherent in evaluative criteria of classification.[7]

5. John Frank, American Law—The Case for Radical Reform 85–110 (1969), calls attention to the costs, in a broad sense, of multiplication of decision points in a legal system. The lawmaker's choice of an evaluative criterion confronts the law administrator with a type of decision point that is especially costly both because such a criterion has a capacity for generating numerous sub-points as factors to be taken into account and because its generality and imprecision reduce predictability and thereby impede the settlement process by which the necessity for formal decisions can often be avoided.

6. See, *e.g.*, Patterson's observations about the competing demands for flexibility and certainty in relation to the requirement of "delivery" of a life insurance policy, § 2.7 *infra*.

7. See, *e.g.*, §§ 4.7(a), (b) (1) and (2), and (c) ("permission" under omnibus clause); 4.11(d) (assignment of life policy by means not complying with formalities); 4.11(e) ("substantial compliance" with requisites for changing beneficiary of life policy); 5.2(b) ("arising" out of "use" of automobile); 7.2(a) ("reasonable time" for notice or proof of loss); 8.2 (definition of regulated "insurance" transactions); 8.4 (rates shall be "adequate" and neither "excessive" nor "unfairly discriminatory").

CHAPTER 2

MARKETING

SECTION 2.1 CONTROL OVER UNDERWRITING

§ 2.1(a) CENTRALIZATION OF THE POWER TO CONTRACT

The degree of centralization of the power to contract on behalf of the insurer is an important aspect of any system of insurance. Extreme centralization occurs when only a few persons, all situated in the home office, are empowered to make contracts for the insurer. Extreme decentralization occurs when this power is granted to numerous and widely scattered representatives.[1]

Many of the factors that affect a reasoned choice concerning the degree of centralization are related to the type of risk insured against. Thus, the tendency is for the various insurers of a particular combination of risks to adopt approximately the same degree of centralization. This tendency is further promoted by the pressure toward uniformity that is exerted by public regulation.

Life insurance is marketed by organizations with a high degree of centralization; the power to make formal contracts by issuance of policies, as distinguished from informal or temporary contracts, is customarily vested in the home office only. On the other hand, it is customary for fire and marine insurers and casualty insurers to grant to general agents the authority to countersign, issue and deliver policies; these general agents make reports to the home office, and an element of centralization of control over the insurer's underwriting is retained by a provision in the policy form giving the insurer a right of cancellation by notice to the insured.

---

1. Concerning the terminology commonly used to describe representatives empowered to contract for the insurer, see § 1.5 *supra*.

Though the power to make temporary or informal contracts is often widely dispersed in the marketing of life insurance, as well as other lines of coverage, there is nevertheless a marked difference of degree between life and other insurance organizations with respect to centralization of the power to make temporary or informal contracts, whether oral or written.

§ 2.1(b) FACTORS BEARING ON CENTRALIZATION

What degree of centralization of the power to contract do different types of insurers build into their marketing systems?

One factor bearing on this question is the extent to which there is or should be an element of discretion in accepting or rejecting an individual application for insurance. If much discretion is to be exercised, the success of the insurance operation depends heavily on the wisdom and experience of the group of persons entrusted with the power to make the discretionary choices. Thus, if there is a relatively large element of discretion in choosing insureds in a system for marketing a particular type of policy, the tendency is for the insurer to grant this power to contract to only a few persons situated in the home office; an extreme degree of centralization occurs. Decisions concerning medical and moral factors affecting the risk incident to a contract of insurance upon the life of a specific person involve such an exercise of discretion. On the other hand, if, for example, the insurer's governing board has decided that the insurer will make a given kind of insurance contract with anyone who is willing to pay the premium in cash, but with no one in the absence of cash payment, no element of discretion is left and the power to complete the contract on behalf of the insurer can be entrusted to a vending machine, as in the case of air travel trip insurance.[1] Between these extremes are many variations in the degree of centralization; such variations occur not only among types of insurance but also, though to less extent, from one insurer to another writing a single type and from one to another of the packages of insurance, covering a combination of risks, offered by a single insurer.

1) Degree of Discretion Involved

A second factor bearing on centralization of the power to contract is the extent to which it is possible and desirable to dispense with discretionary review of individual application by the wise exercise of discretion in accepting or declining substantial groups or classes of prospective insureds. Group life insurance contracts, for example, customarily involve less home office control over accepting or rejecting individual insureds (as distinguished from accepting or rejecting groups) than is exercised in other life insurance marketing.[2]

2) Group or Class involved rather than individual selection

The time period for which a policy is ordinarily written is a third factor relevant to centralization. Compare, for example, an in-

3) Time Period of policy

---

1. See § 2.9 *infra*.

2. See Denenberg, Eilers, Hoffman, Kline, Melone & Snider, Risk and In-surance 299, 305 (1964) [hereinafter cited as Denenberg *et al.*].

surance plan in which the policy is expected to continue for a very long period (*e. g.,* ordinary life insurance) with a plan in which the policy is expected to continue for one year (*e. g.,* automobile insurance) or for a few days (*e. g.,* trip insurance). Risks of very long-term character are more likely to be passed upon by the home office before a commitment is made. It is no coincidence that the types of insurance as to which the greater degree of centralization occurs are the longer-term types. Other things being equal, the longer the term is, the greater is the company's exposure and its need for caution in underwriting. Moreover, centralization is generally not practical for contracts of very short term, such as air travel trip insurance. The length of the term bears also upon the choice among techniques of control. Centralized control over underwriting is most fully achieved by denying to field representatives the power to bind the insurer even temporarily without home office approval. Granting field representatives power to bind on temporary contracts is a departure from centralization, and granting them power to issue formal long-term contracts is an even more substantial departure. But an insurer can authorize field representatives to make long-term contracts and still maintain substantially centralized control by requiring inclusion in those contracts of a right of cancellation at the discretion of the home office. This is commonly done, subject to provisions for a period of notice, in relation to fire insurance and allied lines.[3]

A fourth factor bearing on centralization is the likelihood that prospective insureds will want immediate coverage when they apply. This factor is an influence toward decentralization to avoid delay in effecting coverage.

A fifth factor is the risk of liability upon insurance transactions intended to be forbidden by company rules. It is an influence toward centralization, because proximity facilities control over performance. Agents in the field are less easily controlled than those in the home office, and more mistakes and misfeasance in underwriting are likely under a decentralized system.

SECTION 2.2 ORAL CONTRACTS OF INSURANCE

§ 2.2(a) LEGAL RESTRICTIONS AGAINST ORAL CONTRACTS

(1) DISTINCTIVE RESTRICTIONS AGAINST INSURANCE CONTRACTS

Despite early dicta [1] and occasional modern assumptions to the contrary,[2] it is well established that there is no prohibition of de-

---

3. See § 5.10(e) *infra.*

1. *E.g.,* Cockerill v. Cincinnati Mut. Ins. Co., 16 Ohio 148 (1847), discredited by later Ohio decisions, *e.g.,* Newark Mach. Co. v. Kenton Ins. Co., 50 Ohio St. 549, 555, 35 N.E. 1060, 1062 (1893).

2. See, *e.g.,* Gulbrandson v. Empire Mut. Ins. Co., 251 Minn. 387, 87 N.W. 2d 850 (1958), treating the question of validity of a partly oral contract of hail insurance as a debatable issue and resolving the issue in favor of validity after observing that previous cases in the same jurisdiction had up-

[margin note: Oral K's not forbidden by case law]

cisional origin against oral contracts of insurance.[3]   Even in the fields of life insurance and accident and health insurance, where the custom is that insurers insist upon written contracts, there have been occasional instances in which oral contracts have been made and enforced.[4]

It is generally conceded that a state legislature has the power to require insurance contracts to be in writing, and in some cases legislatures have done so.   Before the development of statutes of general application to the formation of insurance companies, a prohibition against oral contracts of insurance was sometimes included in a charter granted by special act of a legislature.[5]

[margin note: statutes sometimes forbid]

In Georgia, statutes require all contracts of insurance to be in writing in order to "be binding." [6]   In a minority of jurisdictions, other statutory provisions, such as those requiring standard provisions,[7] or regulating the manner in which a policy is to be executed,[8] have been interpreted as impliedly forbidding oral contracts of insurance.   Some jurisdictions have by statute limited the duration of oral contracts.[9]

In general, prohibitions against oral contracts have been imposed only rarely in relation to property insurance, though somewhat more frequently in relation to life, health, and accident insurance.[10]

held oral contracts of fire, collision, and workmen's compensation insurance.

3. See, *e.g.*, Rabb v. Public Nat'l Ins. Co., 243 F.2d 940 (6th Cir. 1957) (Kentucky law); Milwaukee Bedding Co. v. Graebner, 182 Wis. 171, 196 N.W. 533 (1923).   See generally 12 Appleman, Insurance Law § 7191 (1943).

4. *E.g.*, Whitehall v. Commonwealth Cas. Co., 125 Neb. 16, 248 N.W. 692 (1933) (accident and health); Bleam v. Sterling Ins. Co., 360 Mich. 208, 103 N.W.2d 466 (1960) (health and accident insurance policy reformed to conform with oral representations of agent that coverage for accidents was provided from date of application); Overton v. Washington Nat'l Ins. Co., 260 A.2d 444 (R.I.1970) (life insurance).

5. See, *e.g.*, Head & Amory v. Providence Ins. Co., 6 U.S. (2 Cranch) 127, 167, 2 L.Ed. 229, 242 (1804).   Concerning the effect of charter provisions on oral contracts, see, *e.g.*, Franklin Fire Ins. Co. v. Colt, 87 U.S. (20 Wall.) 560, 22 L.Ed. 423 (1873); Sanborn v. Fireman's Ins. Co., 82 Mass. (16 Gray) 448, 77 Am.Dec. 419 (1860).   See also Annot., 15 A.L.R. 995, 1001–1004 (1921).

6. Ga.Code Ann. §§ 56–2402, 56–2413 (1960).   *Cf.* Miss.Code Ann. § 5719 (Supp.1968).

7. *E.g.*, Pralle v. Metropolitan Life Ins. Co., 346 Ill. 58, 178 N.E. 371 (1931). *Contra, e.g.*, National Liberty Ins. Co. v. Milligan, 10 F.2d 483 (9th Cir. 1926); Lea v. Atlantic Ins. Co., 168 N.C. 478, 84 S.E. 813 (1915); Milwaukee Bedding Co. v. Graebner, 182 Wis. 171, 196 N.W. 533 (1923).   See 12 Appleman, Insurance Law § 7195 (1943); Annot., 92 A.L.R. 232, 235 (1934).

8. *E.g.*, Munhall v. Travelers Ins. Co., 300 Pa. 327, 150 A. 645 (1930) (life). *Contra, e.g.*, Sanford v. Orient Ins. Co., 174 Mass. 416, 54 N.E. 883 (1899).   See also Rossi v. Firemen's Ins. Co., 310 Pa. 242, 165 A. 16 (1932) (reaching a result contrary to *Munhall* in a case involving a temporary and preliminary contract of fire insurance).

9. Such a statute was considered in National Liberty Ins. Co. v. Jones, 165 Va. 606, 183 S.E. 443 (1936).   Similar statutes include N.J. Rev.Stat. § 17:36–5.16 (Supp.1954).

10. For an illustration of the contrasting treatment of the issue in these different contexts, see Milwaukee Bedding Co. v. Graebner, 182 Wis. 171,

(2) STATUTES OF FRAUDS

Statutes of frauds commonly contain a provision that contracts not to be performed within one year are unenforceable. There is a split of authority as to whether such a provision applies to an oral agreement by which an insurance agent or broker promises to keep certain insurance in force by periodic renewals. As a way of resolving in part the seeming conflict, it has been suggested that a distinction be drawn between two types of agreements—first, agreements to issue policies from year to year for three years [11] or to renew at the end of three years [12] (which are held to be unenforceable) and, second, agreements, terminable by the insured upon notice, for the issuance of yearly policies (which are held to be enforceable).[13] The distinction seems dubious, at best. Ordinarily, it would seem, the inference that the insured had an option to terminate would be a reasonable one in cases of the first group as well as those of the second group. Moreover, an option to terminate should not be decisive. The possibility of premature termination within a year, as distinguished from complete performance within that period, is not generally regarded as placing an agreement outside a statute of frauds.[14]

Another issue rarely discussed but surely presented by an attempt to enforce an alleged agreement for periodic renewal of an insurance policy concerns a conflict between the underlying principle of a statute of frauds and the underlying principle of granting redress for detrimental reliance. It may be argued that even if a statute of frauds would defeat a claim based merely on breach of an oral contract for periodic renewals, still a claim grounded on estoppel and supported by proof of detrimental reliance should be sustained. And this contention is strengthened by proof of a practice of renewals for several years before the occasion when renewal was overlooked.[15]

196 N.W. 533 (1923), holding that a fire insurance statute prescribing a standard form of coverage did not prohibit oral contracts, even though a previous decision had construed similar language in another statute as prohibiting oral contracts of health and accident insurance.

11. *E.g.*, Harrower v. Insurance Co. of N. Am., 144 Ark. 279, 222 S.W. 39 (1920).

12. Green v. Hartford Fire Ins. Co., 157 Miss. 316, 128 So. 107, 69 A.L.R. 554 (1930).

13. *E.g.*, First Baptist Church v. Brooklyn Fire Ins. Co., 19 N.Y. 305 (1859). *Contra, e.g.*, Klein v. Liverpool & London & Globe Ins. Co., 22 Ky.L.Rep. 301, 57 S.W. 250 (Ct.App.

1900). Patterson and Vance, in criticism of the *Klein* decision, argue that the latter agreement is outside the statute of frauds because it might be wholly performed within one year. Patterson, Essentials of Insurance Law 83 (2d ed. 1957) and Vance, Law of Insurance 222 n.42 (3d ed. Anderson 1951).

14. See Fuller & Braucher, Basic Contract Law 806 (1964); 3 Williston, Contracts § 498 (3d ed. 1960).

15. See, *e.g.*, Sanborn v. Maryland Cas. Co., 255 Iowa 1319, 125 N.W.2d 758 (1964), summarized in § 6.7(a) n.3 *infra*. Concerning detrimental reliance generally see § 6.3 *infra*; concerning this and other theories of rights at variance with policy provisions in marketing contexts, see § 6.7 *infra*.

Another type of provision appearing in many statutes of frauds requires that a promise to answer for the debt of another be in writing. Most decisions in point declare that guaranty insurance is not affected by such a statute,[16] and this seems sound. It is realistic to view guaranty insurance as insurance against the risk that the debtor will default. It is a more difficult question whether distinguishing between such an oral insurance contract and an oral "promise to answer for the debt of another" does not undercut the public policy underlying the statute of frauds. Probably it does not, however, at least in the case of the contract of insurance made by a professional insurer, whose business is in any event regulated extensively under other and more specialized statutes, and whose contracts of this type are made pursuant to a system of risk distribution.

It seems clear that contracts of reinsurance should not be affected by a statutory provision requiring that a promise to answer for the debt of another be in writing,[17] though a contrary result was reached in one state.[18] The reinsurance contract is an independent contract between the original insurer and a reinsurer, providing that the latter shall pay the former, rather than a contract by which the reinsurer promises to pay the original insurer's obligation to the original insured. It is the debtor who is being insured, not the creditor. This is not an agreement with the creditor to answer for a default of the debtor.

§ 2.2(b) USEFULNESS OF ORAL CONTRACTS

Difficulty of Proof problems

The principal disadvantages of oral contracts of insurance arise from difficulties of proving both the fact of an agreement and its terms. Though it is the common practice to use oral contracts for various types of fire, marine, and casualty insurance as temporary commitments, insurers and insureds alike ordinarily find it desirable to reduce their oral agreements to writing as soon as possible (using a temporary binder if issuing a policy will take any appreciable time). The juridical risk incident to uncertainty about evidence of the existence and the terms of the contract is thus reduced.

Associated with uncertainties of proof are risks of errors and malfeasance among the relatively large number of persons having power to bind the insurer when a typical system of oral contracting is used. For example, an agent in the field may be tempted after a loss to help a friend by false testimony that an oral contract had been made before the loss. Requirements of prompt reporting cannot eliminate this risk entirely but may reduce it. Another risk is that

risks of error & malfeasance

---

16. *E.g.*, Quinn-Shepherdson v. United States Fid. & Gy. Co., 142 Minn. 428, 172 N.W. 693 (1919). *Contra, e.g.*, Commonwealth v. Hinson, 143 Ky. 428, 136 S.W. 912 (1911). See 3 Williston, Contracts § 482 (3d ed. 1960).

17. *E.g.*, Commercial Mut. Marine Ins. Co. v. Union Mut. Ins. Co., 60 U.S. (19 How.) 318, 15 L.Ed. 636 (1857). See 3 Williston, Contracts § 482 n.19 (3d ed. 1960).

18. Egan v. Firemen's Ins. Co., 27 La. Ann. 368 (1875).

an agent may fail to raise with the applicant some question that should be faced in setting the terms of a contract, with the consequence that the applicant has no coverage when loss occurs or that the insurer affords coverage under conditions it would not have approved. Because of risks such as these, when an insurer operates under a marketing arrangement that allows oral contracts to be made in the field it must exercise closer supervision over its field personnel than if contracts are made only in the home office. Even this supervision has its price, since the relationship of a supervisor to a representative in the field is a fertile ground for evidence supporting a claim of rights at variance with policy provisions.[1]

That oral contracts are disadvantageous in some ways cannot be denied. The prevalent view that they are generally permissible and their prevalent use as temporary arrangements for some types of insurance reflect a consensus, however, that disadvantages are outweighed by a number of significant advantages.

Oral contracts can be effected more expeditiously than formal policies. Clearly it is in the public interest that needs for immediate coverage be met, if that can be done without undue sacrifice of other interests.

Situations in which immediate insurance coverage is desired may arise with respect to property insurance because of transfers of the property. This need lends support to the established practice of using temporary oral contracts of fire and collision coverage. It has less force in some other contexts. For example, occasions of compelling need for immediate inception of workmen's compensation coverage because of a business transfer are rare, since such a transfer is ordinarily negotiated and planned. Similarly, insofar as there are demands for prompt inception of hail insurance, they are rarely incident to a property transfer. But other reasons for allowing oral contracts can be found. For example, the desirability of making it as easy as possible to provide insurance protection for employees weighs heavily in favor of permitting oral contracts of workmen's compensation insurance. And, in relation to hail insurance, if one thinks of the social need as affected by the human tendency to postpone the buying of insurance until exposure to the risk reaches some high point in the curve of fluctuations (specifically, the tendency to wait until the hail season to buy hail insurance) and also considers it desirable to encourage large numbers of people to carry the insurance so as to spread the risk widely, he may conclude that there is even more reason for upholding an arrangement for immediate insurance in the case of the hail risk than in the case of fire and collision.[2]

Perhaps a better understanding of the differences among types of insurance with respect to the practice of using oral contracts can be reached by starting with the assumption that legal restrictions should

---

1. *E.g.*, Gulbrandson v. Empire Mut. Ins. Co., 251 Minn. 387, 87 N.W.2d 850 (1958). See Chapter 6 *infra*.

2. See Gulbrandson v. Empire Mut. Ins. Co., 251 Minn. 387, 87 N.W.2d 850 (1958).

not be imposed without good reason, and asking: Why not let parties make oral contracts of insurance if they want to do so? A system that allows oral contracts will also in practice be a system that decentralizes control over underwriting. Probably the most influential factor accounting for the difference in treatment of life and property insurance with respect to oral contracts [3] is this matter of centralization. The marketing systems with respect to written contracts are different,[4] and the inferences one may reasonably draw as to authority to make oral contracts are also different. The decentralization of underwriting control incident to oral contracts is a distinct disadvantage to the life insurer, but to the property insurer it is either consistent or nearly consistent with the marketing arrangement used even for written policies.

§ 2.2(c) REQUISITES OF ORAL CONTRACTS

(1) GENERALLY

If there is no applicable restriction impairing the effectiveness of an alleged oral contract of insurance, the requisites of an effective contract are in essence corollaries of basic contract law. There must be evidence of a manifestation of agreement on all essential terms, including the subject matter of the insurance (*e. g.,* an identified automobile), the risk insured against (*e. g.,* collision), the rate of premium, the duration and amount of the coverage, and identification of the parties.[1]

This is not to say, however, that the communications between the parties must refer to all these matters. Rather, many of the terms may be proved by evidence of an understanding, express or implied, that customary terms are to apply.[2] And in fact a contract is hardly ever entirely oral. Rather, evidence of customary terms will ordinarily be documentary. But the phrase "oral contract" is commonly used to refer to any contract of which a major aspect is oral, even though by far the greater portion is in a printed form that the oral understanding adopts by express or implied reference.

Beyond the problems of formulating the requisites of enforceable oral agreements, a court or legislature, if attempting to give full at-

---

3. See § 2.2(a) (1) *supra.*

4. See § 2.1 *supra.*

1. See, *e.g.,* Rabb v. Public Nat'l Ins. Co., 243 F.2d 940, 942, 944 (6th Cir. 1957) (Kentucky law; sustaining a lower court finding against the claim of an oral contract of automobile insurance for a soldier applicant who experienced difficulty in finding a company interested in writing insurance for his class of risk). See Annots., 14 A.L.R.3d 568 (1967) (fire, wind, or hail insurance), 12 A.L.R.3d 1304 (1967) (automobile insurance).

2. *E.g.,* Humenik v. Siwek, 266 Minn. 491, 124 N.W.2d 191 (1963) (oral contract of automobile liability insurance based only on uncontradicted testimony that agent had assured defendant that driver of car would be "covered"; terms of coverage apparently assumed by court to be those of earlier written policy issued by company or of written policy on car that did not provide coverage for driver); Milwaukee Bedding Co. v. Graebner, 182 Wis. 171, 196 N.W. 533 (1923) (statutory prescription).

tention to the set of problems associated with oral contracts, must consider what sanctions will be used to enforce the substantive requirements it chooses to impose. Arguably the policing of either outright restrictions against oral contracts or the less rigorous restrictions implicit in particular requisites of oral contracts would be most effective if in case of violation the loss were invariably caused to fall on the applicant. That is, it might be argued that consistently imposing the loss on the applicant whenever the requisites of valid oral contract are not met would lead, especially in the business community, to general knowledge of the restrictive rules and of the consequences of violating them. In turn, the argument goes, this would result in fewer of the pathological situations in which one thinks he is insured and finds otherwise after suffering loss. But it seems doubtful that even a uniform denial of recovery would accomplish this objective. Moreover, in a number of situations the surprised applicant for coverage has been allowed legal relief, either against the company on some theory of rights apart from contract,[3] or else against the agent—for example, on a theory of breach of his agreement to procure insurance.[4] Such results are supported by the argument that the applicant is an unskilled person dealing with a specialist and relying on the specialist to know his business. If the specialist purports to make a contract that he has no authority to make, or one that turns out to be defective in some other way, the applicant should have a cause of action against someone. If no cause of action can be made out against a company because of lack of proof that the agent was acting for the company within the scope of his power to bind it, personal liability of the agent is supportable.[5]

(2) DESIGNATION OF THE INSURER

It sometimes happens that, through the combination of oral communications and inferential adoption of form provisions, all terms are readily ascertainable except for identification of the company intended to be the insurer. If the agent with whom the applicant is dealing represents only one company that issues the kind of insurance applied for, the inference that this company was to be the insurer is strong, and this remains true even if the applicant does not know the identity of the company. Also, this is the most favorable context for proof that the agent was acting within his power to bind the company. But if the agent represents many companies, some evidence of selection of a particular company is required.[6] Moreover, it is commonly held that mere mental selection of the company by the agent is not

---

3. See Chapter 6 *infra.*

4. See § 2.5 *infra.*

5. *Ibid.*

6. *E.g.,* Employers Fire Ins. Co. v. Speed, 242 Miss. 341, 133 So.2d 627 (1961) (agent agreed to procure fire and extended coverage insurance on building to be constructed but failed to do so or to designate in any way which one or ones among the eight companies he represented were to be selected; held, no contract, even with the six of the eight companies with which the applicant was already insured for other fire insurance coverage).

[Handwritten margin note: Agent must manifest ID of Company in some way]

enough; the agent must have manifested the selection in some way. The designation is sufficient if he prepares a memorandum to guide later preparation of a written binder or longer-term contract. The memorandum, however, need not be completely explicit; it is necessary only that it show in some way a selection made by the agent before loss. For example, in *Milwaukee Bedding Co. v. Graebner*,[7] a case absolving an agent of personal liability, it was sufficient for purposes of identification that the agent, before leaving the office of the applicant, had noted on a card concerning renewal of fire insurance with another company "$2,000 add'l in L. & A. Co," and that the card had been so filed that in the ordinary course of the agency's business a contract would have been issued with the company thus identified.[8] Even if the agent's memorandum fails to designate a company, it may happen that the designation is effected, before loss, in some other way.[9]

[Handwritten margin note: Risk: Agent's selecting Co. after loss to protect himself against personal liability. Thus mental selection by agent not recognized]

The most serious shortcoming of any rule that would allow an insurance company to be bound even though it was not identified *before* loss, either in the conversation between the agent and the intended purchaser of insurance or in a memorandum prepared by the agent, would be the risk of the agent's dishonestly selecting a company *after* the fire, in order to protect himself against personal liability. Because of this risk, it seems appropriate to adopt a rule denying the agent the opportunity to escape responsibility by testifying that he had made a mental though unrecorded selection of the insurer. Such limited authority as can be found supports also the nonliability of the insurer whom the agent declares to have been mentally selected.[10]

It does not necessarily follow, however, that the intended purchaser of insurance should have no cause of action on any theory against any of the insurers whom the agent could have bound by a proper selection before loss. The agent's liability is little comfort to the applicant if the agent is financially irresponsible and does not have applicable errors and omissions coverage. In this situation it may be argued that the applicant ought not to have to bear the risk of combined inefficiency and financial irresponsibility of the agent. If this view were taken, one would be concerned also with allocation of the risk among several companies represented by one agent. Sure-

---

7. 182 Wis. 171, 196 N.W. 533 (1923).

8. 182 Wis. at 173, 196 N.W. at 534.

9. See, *e.g.*, Julien v. Spring Lake Park Agency, Inc., 283 Minn. 101, 166 N.W. 2d 355 (1969) (oral agreement for builder's risk policies on two houses; agent wrote such coverage with four or five companies, and his memorandum did not name company; another person in agent's office wrote policy with defendant on one of the houses but for "inexplicable reason" not on the other; agent had previously written eight such policies for applicant, all

in defendant company; agent testified that when making memorandum he did not remember which company, but he consciously intended it be the same company as before; held, though "the question is close," the designation was sufficient; company's claim against agent for indemnity denied because agent's failure to advise company caused no damage). Concerning builder's risk coverage generally, see Annot., 94 A.L.R.2d 221 (1964).

10. See, *e.g.*, Employers Fire Ins. Co. v. Speed, 242 Miss. 341, 133 So.2d 627 (1961).

ly their rights among themselves should not be governed by the agent's selection, which may have occurred after the fire. It is rather difficult, however, without the aid of legislation, to find some other basis for allocating this risk. Perhaps the best solution would be proportionate liability of the several insurers. An analogy is the joint and several liability of tortfeasors whose separate actions contribute to one indivisible injury. The acts of the several insurers in authorizing one agent to represent them, though independent acts in a sense, have contributed to creating a problem that would not have existed had the agent represented only one company, since identification of the company would then have been clear. Perhaps, like joint tortfeasors, the insurers should be jointly and severally liable to the applicant.

SECTION 2.3 WRITTEN BINDERS; BINDING RECEIPTS

§ 2.3(a) NEEDS FOR TEMPORARY WRITTEN CONTRACTS

Interval between application & issuance of policy

It often happens that there is a substantial interval between the time a policy of insurance is applied for and the time it is issued. Sometimes the applicant is dealing with an agent who has no power to issue a policy himself. In other instances, the agent, though having adequate power, does not issue a policy immediately; some delays result from clerical steps alone, but it may happen also that by a company rule or common practice the agent is expected to initiate some independent investigation and to await a report before issuing a policy. A lack of coverage during this interval before issuance of the policy, which may extend for days or weeks, is disadvantageous to the applicant. He is subject to the risk that a loss will occur during that interval, and secondly to the risk that a change of circumstances will make his risk of a future loss "uninsurable"—*e.g.*, illness arising in that period may cause the insurer to decline his application for life insurance. The insurer also suffers disadvantages from delay. It runs the risk that the applicant may change his mind and buy from a competitor or may decline insurance altogether, in either of which events it incurs a net loss from expenses of investigating and processing the application.[1]

Temporary K's by written memo of terms (vital terms) other terms inferred from std. forms, rates, etc.

memo issued after 1st installment of premium by cash or check

To meet some of the needs for insurance during this interval pending action of the insurer on an application, a practice has arisen of making a temporary contract of insurance by a written memorandum of vital terms, other terms of the agreement being ascertainable by reference to sources such as policy forms, rate schedules, and customary practices. Such memoranda with respect to life insurance are usually issued only after payment of the first installment of premium in cash or by check, and they are usually called "binding re-

Called "binding receipts"

---

1. *Cf.* Comment, *Operation of Binding Receipts in Life Insurance*, 44 Yale L.J. 1223 (1935).

"binders" issued w/o advance premium payment

ceipts" or "conditional binding receipts." With respect to the other two major classes of insurance (fire and marine, and casualty), these memoranda are often issued in advance of payment of any premium and are usually called "binders." The latter term is sometimes used more broadly to include the documents ordinarily called "binding receipts," and occasionally an oral agreement for temporary insurance is called an "oral binder" or simply a "binder."

§ 2.3(b) VALIDITY GENERALLY

It is obvious that some of the disadvantages of oral contracts are inherent also in these temporary contracts of insurance through abbreviated memoranda. There is enough difference, however, to account for a kindlier judicial and legislative response toward the latter. Almost universally their validity is assumed or expressly conceded and at most an attempt is made to regulate rather than to prohibit them.[2] Charter or statutory requirements concerning the manner of executing policies are usually held inapplicable to such memoranda.[3]

Reg's re binding receipts Statute Administration judicial rulings

There are three main types of regulations of memorandum contracts of insurance—statutory restrictions, administrative supervision, and judicial rulings, sometimes in the guise of interpretation of the agreements. Each of these is illustrated in the way binding receipts for life insurance are treated in insurance law.[4]

§ 2.3(c) BINDING RECEIPTS FOR LIFE INSURANCE

(1) FORMS USED

Binding receipts for life insurance have undergone a notable metamorphosis. At the beginning of the twentieth century, centralized control was the watchword of life insurance underwriting. Intrusion upon such centralization commenced with forms of binding receipts so rigorously qualified that they offered the applicant little more than an elusive hope for generosity in the company's exercise of unfettered discretion to back-date insurance coverage when approving it. Naturally such discretion would be exercised often when it provided no advantage for the applicant or his intended beneficiaries, but seldom when it profited them. The misleading quality of rigorously qualified binding receipts early led to judicial strictures against overreaching and to judicial interpretations that draftsmen of the interpreted receipts would never acknowledge as progeny of their pens. Thus began one of the many battles of wits between draftsmen and judges with which the history of insurance law is mottled.[1]

2. See, *e.g.*, Leube v. Prudential Ins. Co., 147 Ohio St. 450, 72 N.E.2d 76 (1947), 2 A.L.R.2d 936 (1948); 12 Appleman, Insurance Law § 7222 (1943).

3. *E.g.*, DeCesare v. Metropolitan Life Ins. Co., 278 Mass. 401, 180 N.E. 154, 81 A.L.R. 327 (1932).

4. See § 2.3(c) *infra*.

1. See generally § 6.3 *infra*.

[margin notes: metamorphosis of Forms ↓]

The critical passages in several binding receipt forms will serve to illustrate the various types used as the metamorphosis of forms has proceeded. In general the more rigorously restrictive forms are those of more ancient vintage; less restrictive forms have been increasingly used in more recent time. Illustrations follow, identified by letter designations to facilitate reference in further discussion.

[margin note: Least Desirable for applicant]

Form A: The insurance hereby applied for shall not take effect unless the first premium is paid and the policy is delivered to and received by me during my lifetime and good health, and unless otherwise agreed in writing the policy shall then relate back to and take effect as of the date of this application.[2]

Form B: If the application is approved at the home office of the company, in New York, the policy will be delivered if the insured is alive on its date of issue; and subject to the same conditions, should the death of the person upon whose life the policy is applied for occur prior to the date of issue of the policy and within eight weeks from the date of such application, the company will, upon surrender of this receipt, pay such amount as would have been due under the terms of the policy had it been issued on the date of such deposit.[3]

[margin note: Not clear. Encourages Litigation]

Form C: If the amount of such premium is paid to the said company's agent at the time of making this application the insurance (subject to the provisions of the said company's regular form of policy for the plan applied for) shall be effective from the date of my medical examination therefor and such a policy shall be issued and delivered to me or my legal representatives, provided the said company in its judgment shall be satisfied as to my insurability, on the plan applied for, on the date of such medical examination; and if said company shall not be so satisfied the amount of the premium paid shall be returned.[4]

---

2. *Cf.* Long v. New York Life Ins. Co., 106 Wash. 458, 180 P. 479 (1919) (recovery denied because policy issued by company, but not delivered to applicant before his death, substituted a date for taking effect different from the date stated in the application and was, therefore, a rejection of the applicant's offer by way of counter offer).

3. *Cf.* Gaunt v. John Hancock Mut. Life Ins. Co., 160 F.2d 599 (2d Cir.), *cert. denied*, 331 U.S. 849 (1947) (Form B type provision found ambiguous when combined with a "satisfaction of insurability" type provision like Form C; receipt construed to provide coverage though application not approved before applicant's death by homicide); DeCesare v. Metropolitan Life Ins. Co., 278 Mass. 401, 180 N.E. 154, 81 A.L.R. 327 (1932) (receipt dated March 7, policy delivered March 25 dated to take effect April 1, and applicant died March

31; held, coverage under the receipt); Allen v. Metropolitan Life Ins. Co., 44 N.J. 294, 208 A.2d 638 (1965) (coverage without regard to insurability subject only to termination on company's approval or rejection of permanent coverage applied for); Leube v. Prudential Ins. Co., 147 Ohio St. 450, 72 N. E.2d 76 (1947), 2 A.L.R.2d 936 (1948) (application was rejected before injury resulting in death occurred; coverage denied though actual notice of rejection was not given till after injury); Morgan v. State Farm Life Ins. Co., 240 Ore. 113, 400 P.2d 223 (1965) (combined Form B—"approval"—and Form C—"satisfaction of insurability" —provisions; held, coverage subject to insurability of applicant on date of application under objective test similar to that of Form D, *infra*).

4. *Cf.* Taylor v. New York Life Ins. Co., 324 F.2d 768 (10th Cir. 1963) (Colorado law; denial of coverage under

[Form D] If the first full premium is paid at the time of making this application, and if at that time the applicant is insurable under the company's rules and practices, for the amount and upon the plan applied for without modification, then the insurance (subject to the provisions of the company's regular form of policy for the plan applied for) shall be effective from the time of making application. If the underwriting rules of the company prevent issuance of a policy exactly as applied for but permit issuance on another basis, and the insured dies within sixty days and the issuable policy has neither become effective nor been refused, the insurance shall be in force for such lesser amount as the premium would have purchased when applied as the first premium on the issuable policy.

[Form E] If the first premium is paid at the time of application, the company will be liable from and after said payment to the same extent as if the policy, as applied for, had been issued and delivered at that time; provided, however, that (1) the company reserves the absolute right to reject said application and if said application is rejected (and without notice thereof) all liability on the part of the company shall thereupon terminate except as to claims maturing before such rejection; and (2) if said application is neither approved nor rejected by the company at its home office within 45 days from the date thereof it shall be deemed to have been rejected as of the last day of such 45 day period, without notice to that effect.[5]

[Form F] If the first premium is paid at the time of making application, the company will make payment in accordance with the

binder valid though application was rejected after applicant's death, since he failed to meet the insurer's requirements in not satisfactorily explaining weight loss before application; insurability in fact irrelevant); New England Mut. Life Ins. Co. v. Hinkle, 248 F.2d 879 (8th Cir. 1957), *cert. dismissed*, 358 U.S. 65 (1958) (Iowa law; the applicant customarily engaged in aviation activities, and the company did not customarily insure such persons at the rate the applicant applied for; coverage denied); Johnson v. Equitable Life Assur. Soc'y, 275 F.2d 315 (7th Cir. 1960) (Illinois law; provision inapplicable to contemporaneous temporary term life insurance for which a separate premium was stated and paid); Brunt v. Occidental Life Ins. Co., 223 Cal.App.2d 179, 35 Cal.Rptr. 492 (2d Dist.1963) (health and accident insurance; "satisfaction of insurability" held to be a condition subsequent to coverage); Reynolds v. Northwestern Mut. Life Ins. Co., 189 Iowa 76, 176 N.W. 207 (1920) (unclear whether subjective test of insurability or Form D type, objective test applied); Simpson v. Prudential Ins. Co., 227 Md. 393, 177 A.2d 417 (1962)

(construed to require an objective test of insurability "according to the general standards of the industry"); Morgan v. State Farm Life Ins. Co., 240 Ore. 113, 400 P.2d 223 (1965) (combined Form B and Form C provisions; held, coverage subject to Form D type objective test of insurability); Fanning v. Guardian Life Ins. Co., 59 Wash.2d 101, 366 P.2d 207 (1961) (accident occurred between dates of application for permanent policy of health and accident insurance and rejection and cancellation of the receipt by the company; coverage based on the agent's oral representation of immediate effectiveness, the agent having apparent authority to bind the company); United Founders Life Ins. Co. v. Carey, 363 S.W.2d 236 (Tex.1962) (plaintiff required to prove that a prudent, authorized officer acting in good faith would have found applicant insurable).

5. *Cf.* Western & So. Life Ins. Co. v. Lottes, 116 Ind.App. 559, 64 N.E.2d 405 (1946) (only question at issue whether or not applicant had paid first premium in full).

terms of the policy applied for, in the event applicant dies on the day of application or within 21 days thereafter.[6]

From the perspective of the applicant, forms D, E, and F are better than the others. The choice among these three depends on whether the applicant is more interested in long-term coverage or short-term coverage. If the former, D is the best, since it may more readily be construed as a commitment for the long term. If one is more interested in immediate short-term coverage, probably F is the best form since it plainly offers that commitment. Forms C, B, and A are increasingly less desirable in that order.

From an insurer's point of view, discretion in the acceptance of risks (of which the most is allowed under form A) is an advantage, but it may involve a competitive disadvantage in marketing since insureds will prefer other forms. Form C has the disadvantage of not being clear enough in its meaning that judicial interpretation can be predicted with assurance; litigation is encouraged.[7]

From the perspective of a public official (a commissioner of insurance, or a legislator, or a judge) with some kind of responsibility for approval or disapproval of proposed policy terms, a form like A should be disapproved as inequitable since the benefits received for the premium applicable to the period of "relation back" are minimal. It might be suggested, in reply, that a standard charge for less than standard coverage during the first year is justified by the higher administrative costs to the insurer during this year. But this argument does not justify the distribution of this cost among insureds in the way it occurs if the terms of such a receipt are rigorously enforced —a way that causes various insureds to pay in proportion to the length of delay between date of application and date of completion of all other requisites of a binding agreement. Thus, a higher cost is paid by those whose applications are acted upon with less dispatch. This seems an arbitrary way of allocating cost, wholly lacking foundation in any principle that appeals to one's sense of fairness.

Arguably form B is also inequitable.[8] And perhaps forms like C should be disapproved as misleading.[9]

---

6. *Cf.* Ranellucci v. John Hancock Mut. Life Ins. Co., 200 Misc. 1111, 112 N.Y. S.2d 94 (City Ct. of Albany 1951) (receipt constitutes a binding contract between applicant and company; materiality of misrepresentation in application a question of fact, not law, under N.Y. Laws 1939, ch. 882).

7. See the cases cited in n.4 *supra.* See also Duesenberg, *Recent Developments in Insurance Law*, 1965 Ins.L.J. 465, 468–469.

8. *Cf.* Allen v. Metropolitan Life Ins. Co., 44 N.J. 294, 208 A.2d 638 (1965) ("approval" provision construed as providing temporary coverage until the application had been rejected by the insurer, without regard to insurability).

9. *Cf.* Clark, J. concurring in Gaunt v. John Hancock Mut. Life Ins. Co., 160 F.2d 599, 603 (2d Cir.), *cert. denied,* 331 U.S. 849 (1947); O'Connell, J., dissenting in Morgan v. State Farm Life Ins. Co., 240 Ore. 113, 118, 400 P.2d 223, 225 (1965).

(2) JUDICIAL INTERPRETATION OF COMMON FORMS

Attempted generalizations about the effect of binding receipts suffer from the difficulty that the raw materials to which they apply —binding receipts—are not all of a kind. Such generalizations must be understood as subject to exceptions for binding receipt forms regarded as atypical by the person offering the generalization.

At one period in the history of life insurance binding receipts, it was quite common for companies to use forms that stated both a condition of "approval" like that of Form B and a condition of "satisfaction" as to insurability like that of Form C. Describing such a form of binding receipt, Patterson stated: "When issued by an agent having authority, this receipt makes a temporary contract of insurance, subject to a condition—rejection by the insurance company—which terminates the coverage." [10] He continued: "Apparently, the company must prove an honest rejection of the risk as it stood at the time of the application. Probably it need not prove that the rejection was reasonable or justifiable, but it could not reject, for instance, merely because a healthy applicant was accidentally killed before the policy was issued." [11]

"Patterson's Rule"

Even apart from the question whether a binding receipt imposes an obligation to issue a permanent policy [12] as well as an obligation of temporary coverage, Patterson's assertion seems grossly inconsistent with the language of Forms A and B and in lesser degree inconsistent with the language of Forms C and D. Such inconsistency seems clear whether Patterson's statement is interpreted as supporting temporary coverage regardless of insurability or instead as meaning that an honest rejection on grounds of uninsurability retroactively defeats all coverage. On balance it would seem likely that Patterson did not intend this latter interpretation. Probably he would have stated the point explicitly if he had intended that insurability be disregarded. But he used the phrase "terminates the coverage," which might be thought to imply the existence of coverage for some period of time and not merely the existence of a temporarily unresolved possibility of coverage.

Though different interpretations of Patterson's comment vary the degree of inconsistency of his rule with the language of the binding receipt, under any reasonable interpretation significant inconsistencies exist. Thus, candor compels recognition that there is judicial

10. Patterson, Essentials of Insurance Law 100 (2d ed. 1957), citing Gaunt v. John Hancock Mut. Life Ins. Co., 160 F.2d 599 (2d Cir.), *cert. denied*, 331 U. S. 849 (1947), and Reck v. Prudential Ins. Co., 116 N.J.L. 444, 184 A. 777 (Ct.Err. & App.1936).

11. Patterson, Essentials of Insurance Law 100–101 (2d ed. 1957), citing, in connection with the first sentence,

Reynolds v. Northwestern Mut. Life Ins. Co., 189 Iowa 76, 176 N.W. 207 (1920) (involving a binding receipt like Form C), and in connection with the second sentence, Gaunt v. John Hancock Mut. Life Ins. Co., n.10 *supra* (involving a combination of Form B and Form C type provisions).

12. See *infra* this section.

regulation of policy forms to whatever extent there is case support for applying Patterson's rule or for applying a rule, which Patterson probably did not intend, that if the company's rejection occurs after the applicant's death, the company is liable for death benefits despite its honest rejection of the application on evidence that at the time of application the applicant was uninsurable by the company's customary standards.[13] It would seem that the strongest justification for such judicial regulation lies in the principle of honoring reasonable expectations even when painstaking study of the policy provisions would have negated them.[14]

In contrast with Patterson's view is the following, advanced by an annotator in 1948: "The general rule adhered to by most of the courts, at least in their earlier decisions, is to the effect that where a binding receipt is issued to the applicant making the obligation of the insurance company conditional upon acceptance and approval by the company, the company is not bound until it approves and accepts the application, on the ground that the expressed condition of acceptance has not occurred."[15] However defensible this statement may have been as a reflection of "earlier decisions," surely it does not represent the prevailing trend of recent cases. Decisions that boldly rewrite conditions of "approval" or "acceptance" are numerous; often the opinions purport to interpret or to resolve ambiguities,[16] and some-

[margin handwritten note: Contrary view not prevalent today]

13. See, *e.g.*, Metropolitan Life Ins. Co. v. Wood, 302 F.2d 802 (9th Cir. 1962) (construing *Ransom, infra*, as establishing that under California law rejection of application only terminates temporary coverage and does not affect applicant's insured status before that action; the fact that applicant may not have been insurable does not negate insurer's liability); Prudential Ins. Co. v. Lamme, 83 Nev. 146, 425 P.2d 346 (1967) (Form C type receipt held to provide temporary coverage subject to rejection, even though applicant never took medical examination to establish insurability and died of heart attack about seven weeks after application; candid imposition of liability inconsistent with terms of the receipt). Though less candid and clear about adopting measures of judicial regulation, each of the following opinions is subject to being interpreted as disallowing a defense of honest rejection after death based on evidence of uninsurability at the time of application: Slobojan v. Western Travelers Life Ins. Co., 70 Cal.2d 432, 450 P.2d 271, 74 Cal.Rptr. 895 (1969) (Form C type receipt held to provide temporary life insurance subject to termination only by rejection of the application for permanent coverage; tendering a policy at a slightly higher rate was not a rejection; no showing

of uninsurability); Ransom v. Penn Mut. Life Ins. Co., 43 Cal.2d 420, 274 P.2d 633 (1954) (Form C type receipt held to provide temporary life insurance subject to termination; defense argument that applicant was uninsurable under company rules rejected, the court stating that a request for further medical examination indicated company had not yet decided whether applicant was an acceptable risk and that court need not decide whether temporary contract can be terminated only by actual rejection and return of premium); Allen v. Metropolitan Life Ins. Co., 44 N.J. 294, 208 A.2d 638 (1965) (Form B type receipt construed to provide temporary coverage without regard to insurability subject only to termination by the company's rejecting permanent coverage for which application was made).

14. See § 6.3(b) *infra*.

15. Annot., 2 A.L.R.2d 943, 964, 966 (1948).

16. See, *e.g.*, Gaunt v. John Hancock Mut. Life Ins. Co., 160 F.2d 599 (2d Cir.), *cert. denied*, 331 U.S. 849 (1947). See generally Note, *Life Insurance Policies and "Binding" Receipts: Is the Insurer Bound?* 1968 Utah L.Rev. 448; O'Neill, *Interim Coverage: Conditional Receipts*, 1964 U.Ill.L.Forum

times they disapprove onerous conditions more candidly on grounds of public policy.[17]

A difficulty that has received little direct attention is the question whether a binding receipt shall be interpreted and enforced as imposing on the insurer at most only a temporary obligation, or instead an obligation also to issue a permanent policy if the conditions of the binding receipt are met. In some instances this question is plainly answered in the negative by the terms of the binding receipt; there is little reason for imposing an obligation upon an insurer to issue a permanent policy when its binding receipt plainly negates that obligation. The area of difficulty concerns instead those cases in which the language of the binding receipt, standing alone, might be read as imposing an obligation to issue a permanent policy. May the company, in that situation, nevertheless terminate its potential liability by delivering to the applicant a notice of rejection of his application? The rule advanced by Patterson, quoted above, would seem to permit an effective rejection. But Patterson's comments were not focused on this question and it seems probable he would not have urged application of his suggested rule to a binding receipt whose terms unambiguously commit the insurer to issue a long-term policy on stated conditions. Even resolving ambiguity against the insurer on this point would be going beyond what it is clear that Patterson was urging. Certainly a decision against the insurer on a theory of resolving ambiguity in a clause that does not deal explicitly with the question seems less likely in relation to permanent coverage than in relation to temporary coverage. Such a decision on permanent coverage would make deeper inroads on underwriting control, and the result would be inconsistent with the general pattern of centralized control over underwriting in the marketing of life insurance.[18] Also, it is less likely that the insured can establish that he has been misled on the issue of his right to a permanent policy. For example, it might be said that a clause such as Form D is not likely to cause an applicant to believe that the company would be required to issue a long-term policy, as distinguished from being bound for temporary coverage, even though the form declares that "the insurance" is to be "effective from the time of making application" rather than more explicitly declaring, for

571; Comment, *"Binding Receipts" in California*, 7 Stan.L.Rev. 292 (1955); Comment, *Life Insurance Receipts: The Mystery of the Non-Binding Binder*, 63 Yale L.J. 523 (1954); Comment, *Operation of Binding Receipts in Life Insurance*, 44 Yale L.J. 1223 (1935).

17. *E.g.*, Prudential Ins. Co. v. Lamme, 83 Nev. 146, 425 P.2d 345 (1967) (Form C type receipt held to provide temporary coverage subject to rejection, regardless of insurability). See also Morgan v. State Farm Life Ins. Co., 240 Ore. 113, 400 P.2d 223 (1965) (re-

jecting the "fiction" of "constructive ambiguity" as inapplicable, yet finding temporary coverage under Form B and C type provisions subject to an objective, Form D type, test of insurability; O'Connell, J., dissenting, would have allowed temporary coverage without regard to insurability subject only to termination by the company's rejection of the permanent coverage for which application was made). See also § 6.3(b) *infra*, concerning application of the principle of honoring reasonable expectations.

18. See § 2.1(a) *supra*.

example, that "temporary insurance" is to be "effective from the time of making application until the company accepts or rejects the application."

The dearth of direct authority on this question is not surprising. When the company notifies the applicant of its refusal to issue a policy and encloses a draft refunding the premium, usually the applicant cashes the draft and thus, by accord and satisfaction, virtually precludes a successful contention at a later time that the company was obliged to issue a permanent policy.

It has been argued that the general tendency of courts to construe binding receipts so as to extend coverage beyond that apparently intended by the draftsmen of the receipt forms is objectionable because it provides free temporary insurance since the receipt typically provides for repayment of the full premium upon rejection of the application. To call the benefit of temporary coverage "free" is to overstate the point, however. There is consideration, but less per unit of insurance coverage than that paid by the applicant whose policy is accepted, since the consideration is merely a commitment of the premium subject to an obligation of the insurer to refund it if the application is rejected. Of course the "insurable" applicants make up for the relative underpayment, since the premiums will be set at a figure high enough to pay the claims under the temporary insurance coverage as well as those under permanent policies.

Thus, though there is no free insurance, there is an inequity in some degree among the different applicants. Before any justification for this inequity is offered, it may be well to note another argument against the tendency of courts to construe binding receipts in favor of coverage.

Construing binding receipts so as to extend coverage beyond that probably intended by draftsmen allows the process of adverse selection to operate.[19] For example, consider the effect of holding that, absent material misrepresentation by the applicant, there is a binding temporary contract of insurance despite the fact that the applicant's aviation activities prevent his qualifying for the plan and rate applied for and despite a stated condition in the binding receipt that the applicant must be "now insurable for the amount, plan and rating applied for."[20] Of course this kind of rule would be no advantage to the applicant who was so plainly uninsurable that his application could not be submitted except by material misrepresentation. And it would mean little more to the plainly insurable group than would the literal enforcement of the binding receipt. For the substantial group whose insurability was in doubt, however, the difference resulting from disregarding insurability would be quite significant. The fund for providing such temporary coverage, valid irrespective of

---

19. Concerning adverse selection generally, see § 1.2(b) (7) *supra*.

20. This is the position urged in the dissent of Woodrough, J., in New Eng-

land Mut. Life Ins. Co. v. Hinkle, 248 F.2d 879 (8th Cir. 1957), *cert. dismissed*, 358 U.S. 65 (1958). See also cases cited in n.13 *supra*.

the ultimate determination as to insurability under the plan and rate applied for, would come from premiums, and the only premiums collected and retained would be those from the insurables and the small percentage of uninsurables who died during the temporary period. The uninsurables who lived through that period would receive their premiums back, and not having made material misrepresentations in their applications, would have received temporary protection without contributing any premiums to the fund. This bargain for the border-line applicant who may prove to be uninsurable upon examination and investigation would provide a special inducement to border-line applicants to pay premiums in advance—a much stronger inducement than that operating upon the mind of the clearly insurable applicant. Thus, adverse selection would occur—that is, a disproportionately high percentage of advance premium payments would come from the border-line risks. Moreover, the premium rates paid by those contributing to the fund as well as receiving such temporary coverage would be at the same level as for an equivalent period of permanent coverage, since the method of handling premiums would be to treat the retained payments as if made on a permanent policy commencing at the date of the application. Thus, the losses paid would tend to be higher in proportion to the premiums collected for the temporary coverage than for permanent coverage, because of the lack of any adjustment of the premiums to take account of the adverse selection.

The inequity incident to providing some persons with almost free insurance and the disadvantages of adverse selection seem insufficient, however, to stem the tide of judicial extension of temporary coverage beyond the terms of binding receipts. Rates are never adjusted to the infinite variations in risks.[21] Rather, a range of variations is included within each rate category. The variations because of the "free" insurance and "adverse selection" in this situation are probably quite small, and the advantages of avoiding a marketing system likely to mislead a substantial percentage of applicants must be weighed against the inequity from the fact that those variations are not reflected in rates.

SECTION 2.4 DELAY IN ACTING ON THE APPLICATION

§ 2.4(a) DUTY TO ACT PROMPTLY

A substantial minority of the opinions in point have denied that an insurer has any duty to act promptly on an application for insurance.[1] On one theory or another, however, a majority have supported the proposition that the insurer is subject to liability in the

---

21. See § 8.4(b) *infra*.

1. *E.g.*, United Ins. Co. v. Headrick, 275 Ala. 594, 157 So.2d 19 (1963); Patten v. Continental Cas. Co., 162 Ohio St. 18, 120 N.E.2d 441 (1954); Zayc v. John Hancock Mut. Life Ins. Co., 338 Pa. 426, 13 A.2d 34 (1940); Levasseur v. Knights of Columbus, 96 R.I. 34, 188 A.2d 469 (1963).

Majority Rule:
Insurer liable
in event of negligent
delay in acting
on application

Theories:
1) Estoppel

2) Implied agreement
to act promptly

3) K of insurance
(offer accepted
by silence &
+ retention
of advance
payments)

4) Tort duty to act
(most common
ground)

event of negligent delay in acting on an application. Within that majority are substantial variations as to the scope and grounds of liability. Four principal theories of liability have been advanced: *estoppel* (by reason of the combination of actions and failure to act by representatives of the insurer, it is estopped to deny acceptance of the application);[2] *implied agreement to act promptly* (the course of conduct of the insurer's agents, including solicitation of the application and acceptance of an advance premium, amounts to an implied agreement that the insurer will act upon the application without unreasonable delay);[3] *contract of insurance* (the application is an offer, which was accepted by silence, or by silence combined with retention of advance payments);[4] *tort* (a duty to act on the application without unreasonable delay arises from the relation between the applicant and the insurer;[5] judicial recognition of such duty is supported by ordinary tort principles regarding duties of affirmative action,[6] and is further supported by the special nature of the insurance business,[7] which is affected with a public interest[8] and is carried on by companies operating under state franchise or charter.)[9] The tort theory is the ground of liability most often accepted.[10]

2. *E.g.*, Wille v. Farmers Equitable Ins. Co., 89 Ill.App.2d 377, 232 N.E.2d 468 (3d Dist.1967); Combined Am. Ins. Co. v. Parker, 377 S.W.2d 213 (Tex.Civ.App.1964, writ refused, no reversible error).

3. *E.g.*, Travelers Ins. Co. v. Anderson, 210 F.Supp. 735 (W.D.S.C.1962) (automobile trip insurance; applying South Carolina law, court recognizes both implied agreement from nature of coverage and tort theories); Gorham v. Peerless Life Ins. Co., 368 Mich. 335, 118 N.W.2d 306 (1962) (health and accident insurance; agreement to act without delay implied from advertising and application form).

4. Snyder v. Redding Motors, 131 Cal. App.2d 416, 280 P.2d 811 (3d Dist. 1955).

5. *E.g.*, Travelers Ins. Co. v. Anderson, 210 F.Supp. 735 (W.D.S.C.1962) (automobile trip insurance; applying South Carolina law, court recognizes both implied agreement from nature of coverage and tort theories); Duffie v. Bankers' Life Ass'n, 160 Iowa 19, 27, 139 N.W. 1087, 1090 (1913); Republic Nat'l Life Ins. Co. v. Chilcoat, 368 P. 2d 821 (Okla.1961); Hinds v. United

Ins. Co., 248 S.C. 285, 149 S.E.2d 771 (1966).

6. See § 2.4(b) *infra*.

7. See, *e.g.*, Duffie v. Bankers' Life Ass'n, 160 Iowa 19, 27, 139 N.W. 1087, 1090 (1913); Republic Nat'l Life Ins. Co. v. Chilcoat, 368 P.2d 821, 824 (Okla.1961); Hinds v. United Ins. Co., 248 S.C. 285, 149 S.E.2d 771 (1966).

8. *E.g.*, Duffie v. Bankers' Life Ass'n, 160 Iowa 19, 27, 139 N.W. 1087, 1090 (1913); Republic Nat'l Life Ins. Co. v. Chilcoat, 368 P.2d 821, 824 (Okla.1961).

9. *E.g.*, Duffie v. Bankers' Life Ass'n, 160 Iowa 19, 27, 139 N.W. 1087, 1090 (1913); Republic Nat'l Life Ins. Co. v. Chilcoat, 368 P.2d 821, 824 (Okla.1961). *But see e.g.*, Zayc v. John Hancock Mut. Life Ins. Co., 338 Pa. 426, 434, 13 A.2d 34, 38 (1940) (legal relevancy of operation under a state franchise rejected).

10. *Cf.* Funk, *The Duty of an Insurer to Act Promptly on Application*, 75 U. Pa.L.Rev. 207 (1927); Prosser, *Delay in Acting on an Application for Insurance*, 3 U.Chi.L.Rev. 39 (1935); 12 Appleman, Insurance Law § 7226 (1943); Annot., 32 A.L.R.2d 487 (1953).

§ 2.4(b) COMPARISON OF ASSERTED GROUNDS
FOR DUTY

True "estoppel" theory requires proof of detriment, and ordinarily if detriment can be proved, a case can also be made for tort liability. Note, moreover, that estoppel theory might be less advantageous to a plaintiff than tort theory since the duty in tort, by one view, arises upon commencement of performance, irrespective of detriment.[1] On the other hand, estoppel theory is better for plaintiff in that the tort theory requires proof of *negligence,* not merely delay, and is subject to the defense of contributory negligence.[2] Moreover, estoppel is sometimes invoked in insurance cases in which proof of genuine detriment is doubtful. Here, as elsewhere,[3] it would seem that the amorphous doctrine resulting from such an unexplained extension of estoppel theory is less desirable than a clear statement of grounds for imposed liability. Probably there is less risk of confusion if courts imposing liability for delay in acting on an application do so on a theory of liability in tort, rather than using a corrupted version of estoppel to bring the case under contract theory.

Can a theory of implied agreement to act promptly be sustained? In the face of a provision, common in application forms, that (except as modified by binding receipts) the company shall incur no liability until it acts on the application, it seems unreasonable to make either of two essential findings—first, that an agreement to act promptly is implied in fact and, second, that it is a bargained-for promise. Thus, the rationale of implied agreement seems fictional. Also, any theory of unjust enrichment is weak indeed as a basis for imposing liability in the amount that would have been payable had a policy been issued promptly, since the "enrichment" of the defendant insurer is insubstantial in comparison with that sum.

What of the theory that silence is a manifestation of consent to contract? Can it be sustained in the face of the common stipulation in application forms against the company's incurring liability before it acts on the application? Again, only by resort to fiction does this seem possible.

The argument for a tort action in these circumstances poses the "duty to act" problem and raises the question, much disputed in the "Good Samaritan" cases, whether a duty arises from mere commencement of performance [4] or only if the actor has proceeded far enough that if he stops the plaintiff's situation will have been made worse by the actor's total course of conduct.[5] Some of the decisions imposing liability are unclear as to which of these two theories of

---

1. See further discussion of this point in this subsection *infra.*

2. See, *e.g.,* Duffie v. Bankers' Life Ass'n, 160 Iowa 19, 139 N.W. 1087 (1913).

3. See generally § 6.4 *infra.*

4. See, *e.g.,* Prosser, Torts 339–343 (3d ed. 1965).

5. See, *e.g.,* Seavey, *Reliance on Gratuitous Promises or Other Conduct,* 64 Harv.L.Rev. 913 (1951).

[handwritten margin note: Estoppel theory requires proof of detriment & detriment, then tort liability can usually be proved but tort requires proof also of negligence & subject to defense of contrib. negligence]

liability, or some other, is being adopted.[6] Other decisions imposing liability, though perhaps consistent with the former theory, are plainly inconsistent with the latter. For example, it has been said that liability is supported by a jury finding that but for the negligence of the company a certificate of insurance would have been issued before the applicant's death.[7] In order to prove that the insurer's total course of conduct has worsened the situation of the applicant or his intended beneficiary, however, it would be necessary to show that if no application had been taken by the insurer's representative the applicant would have obtained effective insurance elsewhere before his death. It may be argued, also, that courts should adopt an intermediate position under which recovery would be allowed upon proof that, even though the applicant might not have taken the initiative to obtain insurance elsewhere had the agent never taken his application, once those negotiations had sparked his interest he relied upon the insurer to respond in reasonable time, and did so to the detriment of himself or his intended beneficiaries since he would then have sought and obtained insurance elsewhere had he not expected a response within reasonable time from the insurer.[8]

Two distinctive aspects of these insurance cases support a somewhat broader liability than that imposed in tort cases concerned with physical harm caused by negligent failure to act. The first is the capacity of insurers to bear and spread the risks of harm from delay in acting on applications. Insurers bear the risk only in a temporary sense, of course, since they pass it along to premium-payers. Does the burden fall fairly? (Perhaps it is not important to trace the shifting of the burden any further than to premium-payers, though in some instances that can be done—as when the insurance premium is a business cost that affects the pricing of products or services of the business.) Premium-payers whose applications are processed promptly pay a share of this burden, though they get none of the benefit except in the sense of the security of its availability in case of need. The burden is quite small, however, in relation to the total burden of the insurance program that must be paid for out of premium income, and one might think of a small fraction of the premium as a payment for insurance that there will be coverage if undue delay

[handwritten margin note: Insurance cases support a somewhat broader liability than usually imposed in Tort theory.]

[handwritten margin note: 1) capacity of insurance carriers to carry insured risk]

---

6. See, *e.g.*, Hinds v. United Ins. Co., 248 S.C. 285, 149 S.E.2d 771 (1966) (complaint alleged delay of about two months in issuing health and accident policy, containing an exclusion clause affecting liability for conditions arising within first six months; heart attack occurred five days before the policy had been in effect six months; held, complaint stated cause of action for the loss as one for which the applicant would have been covered "but for the negligence of the agent"). Does this mean it would be enough to show that the policy that was in fact issued would have been issued more than five days sooner but for the agent's negligence? Or would it be necessary to show a worsening in some sense—*e.g.*, that the agent's negligence made the applicant's position worse than it was before he took the application because otherwise the applicant would have effected coverage elsewhere?

7. *E.g.*, Duffie v. Bankers' Life Ass'n, 160 Iowa 19, 139 N.W. 1087 (1913).

8. Concerning standards of detrimental reliance in insurance law, see generally § 6.4(f) *infra*.

happens to occur.   The differences among policyholders as to need for this coverage, and consequently as to its value, may be regarded as a permissible degree of variation within a single rate category.[9]

A second factor weighing in favor of an extension of liability somewhat beyond ordinary tort theory is that insurance is affected with a public interest.   In this connection, compare the following three points of view:

First, a statute requiring insurance companies to act upon applications within a reasonable time would be constitutional, but the courts cannot impose a duty upon insurers merely because the legislature might do so.[10]   Though banking and employment are matters of great public interest, there is no duty to act without delay on an application for a bank loan or a job, and the business of insurance does not call for any different rule.[11]   Moreover, the harm complained of in cases of delay in acting on applications for insurance is nonphysical economic loss growing out of negotiations.   Comparable liability in other situations of negotiation is very limited—much narrower in scope than for physical harms.

Second, the standardized mass contract, developed by a large business firm (such as an insurance company) and used in substantially every bargain for its product or service, places the individual at a distinct disadvantage in bargaining with the firm.   The law of contracts, based upon the dogma of freedom of contract and developed primarily in relation to bargains between individuals, is unsuitable in relation to negotiations looking toward a "contract of adhesion," such as an insurance contract.   The courts should develop a different set of doctrines for such cases, rather than allowing technical doctrines of contract law to defeat liability when public interest would be served by imposing it.[12]

Third, railroad companies have been required to furnish transportation to all qualified passengers and shippers, and an insurance company might similarly be regarded as a public service company, under a legal duty to insure upon reasonable terms all properly qualified applicants.   It would then be unnecessary to consider vexing problems regarding unreasonable delay in acting on applications, since every person who applied would be insured from the date of application if it could be proved that he had the qualities of an acceptable risk.[13]

---

9.   See § 8.4(b) *infra.*

10.   *Cf.* Patten v. Continental Cas. Co., 162 Ohio St. 18, 120 N.E.2d 441 (1954); Levasseur v. Knights of Columbus, 96 R.I. 34, 188 A.2d 469 (1963).

11.   See Prosser, *Delay in Acting on an Application for Insurance,* 3 U.Chi.L. Rev. 39, 52–53 (1935).   *Cf.* Zayc v. John Hancock Mut. Life Ins. Co., 338 Pa. 426, 13 A.2d 34 (1940).

12.   See Kessler, *Contracts of Adhesion —Some Thoughts About Freedom of Contract,* 43 Colum.L.Rev. 629 (1943).

13.   See Patterson, *The Delivery of a Life Insurance Policy,* 33 Harv.L.Rev. 198, 216–217 (1919).   *Cf.* Denenberg, *Meeting the Insurance Crisis of our Cities: An Industry in Revolution,* 1970 Ins.L.J. 205, 210–212.

The case law in this area has not moved far enough to accept the third of these views, but it seems at least to have broken away from the first view, embracing results consistent with the second, though seldom expressed in this way.[14]

§ 2.4(c) WHOSE CAUSE OF ACTION

If the remedy for delay in acting on an application is in tort, the cause of action should belong to the person or persons who suffer a loss as a result of the insurer's breach of duty. Under this view, a person designated in the application as beneficiary is entitled to recover.[15] There is also authority, however, that the cause of action belongs to the estate of the insured.[16]

If the cause of action is contractual in nature, it would seem still that the intended beneficiary should be entitled to recover, since he is the one who would have been entitled to recover under the policy had the insurer performed its supposed contractual promise to act upon the application promptly.

Often, it would matter little who is entitled to the cause of action for delay in acting on an application, since the intended beneficiary of the policy applied for is so often also the beneficiary who would take through the estate of the deceased, if the cause of action is held to rest in the estate. But the decision concerning whose cause of action this is could be one of great consequence because of claims of creditors against the estate of the deceased, because of differences in identity of the two groups of claimants, or, if the amounts involved were sufficient, because of tax consequences.

SECTION 2.5   LIABILITY OF INTERMEDIARIES IN INSURANCE TRANSACTIONS

§ 2.5(a) GENERALLY

A transaction concerning insurance that gives rise to a claim of liability of a person other than an insurer ordinarily involves three parties—first, one desiring insurance coverage (who, for convenience, will be referred to as an applicant), second, an entity doing business as an insurer (referred to, for convenience, as an insurance company), and third, an intermediary between the applicant and the company (usually an insurance agent or broker, but in some cases a third party involved only in some other way).[1]

---

14. Concerning principles that may account for these decisions without resort to the "public utility" argument, see chapter 6 *infra*.

15. See, *e.g.*, Travelers Ins. Co. v. Anderson, 210 F.Supp. 735 (W.D.S.C.1962) (counter-claim in declaratory judgment action instituted by insurer against beneficiary).

16. *E.g.*, Rosin v. Peninsular Life Ins. Co., 116 So.2d 798 (Fla.App.1960); Duffie v. Bankers' Life Ass'n, 160 Iowa 19, 139 N.W. 1087 (1913).

1. A transaction may involve more than one intermediary. For example, the procurement of credit life insurance often involves two intermediaries —a lending institution and its em-

(handwritten margin notes: "usually no cause of action against it intermediary if transaction supports cause against Ins. Co. But, may have to indemnity.")

If the transaction in question supports an action by the applicant against the insurance company, whether in contract [2] or on some other theory,[3] it is commonly held that the applicant has no cause of action against the intermediary.[4] However, the intermediary may be bound to indemnify the company against the cost of discharging any liability to the applicant sustained by the company because of his deviation from authorized procedure.[5]

ployee who acts as an insurance agent or broker; in such transactions, questions sometimes arise as to the liability of one intermediary (the employee) to the other (the lending institution) for error in procuring insurance. See, *e.g.*, First Fed. Sav. & Loan Ass'n v. Continental Equity Life Ins. Co., 124 So.2d 802 (La.App.1960), discussed in § 2.5(c) n.4 *infra*. See also § 2.8(b) n.8 *infra*. Usually, however, litigation arising from such transactions is between the lending institution and the estate of the debtor-applicant or a joint debtor, and problems associated with the presence of a second intermediary do not arise. *E.g.*, Consumers Financing Corp. v. Lamb, 218 Ga. 343, 127 S.E.2d 914 (1962); In re Estate of Carter, 254 Iowa 138, 116 N.W.2d 419 (1962); Keene Inv. Corp. v. Martin, 104 N.H. 518, 191 A.2d 521 (1963); Mid-America Corp. v. Roach, 412 P.2d 188 (Okla.1966).

2. See §§ 2.2, 2.3 *supra* and §§ 2.6–2.10 *infra*.

3. See § 2.4 *supra* and Chapter 6 *infra*.

4. *E.g.*, Pennsylvania Millers Mut. Ins. Co. v. Walton, 236 Ark. 336, 365 S.W. 2d 859 (1963); Milwaukee Bedding Co. v. Graebner, 182 Wis. 171, 196 N.W. 533 (1923). In *Graebner* the agent called at the applicant's office on February 24 to see about renewal of a fire insurance policy in one company, due to expire on March 1. A renewal was agreed upon, and there was conversation asserted by the applicant to be an agreement for an additional $2,000 coverage, though no specific company was identified in the conversation. Before leaving plaintiff's office (it was assumed), the agent made a memorandum on a card that was construed as identifying a second company as the one with which the additional coverage was to be placed. This card was deposited in a customary place in the agent's office, where it remained until a time after a fire occurred shortly after noon the following day. A jury verdict in the ap-

plicant's action against the agent included a finding that by local custom fire insurance was dated to take effect from the noon preceding the order in the absence of agreement otherwise. The agent was held not liable, on the theory that a contract binding the second insurance company became effective before the fire. With respect to this basis for liability of the company, see § 2.2(c) *supra*.

But see Franklin v. Western Pac. Ins. Co., 243 Ore. 448, 414 P.2d 343 (1966) (allegation that insurance agent intermediary promised to procure $10,000 of unconditional fire insurance coverage but delivered a policy conditioned on the maintenance of a pre-existing policy, which resulted in applicant's recovering only $2,000 on the policy issued, states a cause of action against both the intermediary and the insurance company; the opinion does not explicitly consider whether liability of the company would relieve the intermediary of personal liability to the applicant).

The rule stated in the text above ordinarily does not apply in actions against the intermediary based on deceit; see § 2.5(c) n.8 *infra*.

(handwritten margin note: "doesn't apply in cases of deceit by intermediary")

5. *E.g.*, Manufacturers Cas. Ins. Co. v. Martin-Lebreton Ins. Agency, 242 F.2d 951 (5th Cir.), *cert. denied*, 355 U.S. 870 (1957). This proposition appears to be an assumption underlying the opinion in the *Walton* case, n.4 *supra*, although the company was denied recovery on its cross-claim against the agent for indemnification of its liability on a contract of insurance reformed to provide coverage because of mutual mistake of the applicant and the agent. The court held that there was no detriment to the company resulting from the agent's mistake because first, he was authorized to issue the coverage provided by the contract as reformed and, second, the applicants' recovery was reduced by the difference between the premium actually paid and that which would have been paid had the contract as reformed been issued originally.

But, it no cause against Ins. Co.; intermediary may be liable to beneficiary

Breach of K to procure insurance.

(If) on the other hand, the transaction in question fails to support a claim by the applicant against the insurance company, it may be that an intermediary is subject to liability to the applicant. Several supporting theories have been advanced.

Sometimes liability has been founded on breach of a contract to procure insurance for the applicant [6] or to perform some contractual function related to insurance coverage.[7] The requisites of a contract *to procure insurance* are not as stringent as those of an oral contract *of insurance.*[8] For example, a promise to procure complete insurance protection for a business is sufficiently definite, and failure to procure fire insurance is a breach of the contract created by that promise.[9] Similarly, it is sufficient that the intermediary agree to study an appraisal of the insured's property to determine its "insurable value" and to insure a certain percentage of that value. It is not necessary that a specific dollar amount of insurance be agreed upon, nor is it necessary that the rate of premium to be paid be agreed upon. The agreement can be to procure the desired coverage at the lowest obtainable premium rate.[10] Clearly identification of the insurance company, a requisite of an oral contract binding the company,[11] is not a requisite of an oral contract to procure insurance.

Breach of K to insure usually doesn't work as cause of action

It is occasionally suggested that liability be founded on breach of a contract *to insure.*[12] But this theory encounters the difficulties

6. *E.g.*, Consumers Financing Corp. v. Lamb, 218 Ga. 343, 127 S.E.2d 914 (1962) (assignee finance company failed to procure credit life insurance that assignor of debt, vendor of automobile, orally promised would be obtained); Sroga v. Lund, 259 Minn. 269, 106 N.W.2d 913 (1961) (contract to procure complete insurance coverage on business; failure to procure fire insurance); White v. Calley, 67 N.M. 343, 355 P.2d 280 (1960) (contract to procure increased fire insurance coverage, failure to get coverage effective immediately); Mid-America Corp. v. Roach, 412 P.2d 188 (Okla.1966) (lender failed to procure credit life insurance, $75 having been deducted from loan proceeds to pay first annual premium on insurance); Franklin v. Western Pac. Ins. Co., 243 Ore. 448, 414 P.2d 343 (1966) (failure to procure unconditional fire insurance coverage); Hamacher v. Tumy, 222 Ore. 341, 352 P.2d 493 (1960) (failure to procure additional fire insurance coverage as promised); Hause v. Schesel, 42 Wis.2d 628, 167 N.W.2d 421 (1969) (policy obtained stated effective date as April 3, rather than April 2 as orally promised; agent held liable; reasoned partly on inconsistency between applicant's proving agent's breach of contract to procure and applicant's attacking, on appeal, a di-

rected verdict for defendant company; court seems not to recognize agent's standing to attack the directed verdict on the ground that establishing the company's liability would have been a defense for the agent). See also 16 Appleman, Insurance Law §§ 8831, 8840, 8841 (1968); Annot., 29 A.L.R.2d 171 (1953).

7. *E.g.*, Spiegel v. Metropolitan Life Ins. Co., 6 N.Y.2d 91, 160 N.E.2d 40, 188 N.Y.S.2d 486 (1959) (insurance agent failed to pay premiums on life insurance policy as promised to prevent lapse); Walker Bank & Trust Co. v. First Security Corp., 9 Utah 2d 215, 341 P.2d 944 (1959) (bank failed to honor monthly drafts drawn by insurance company on insured's account as it had agreed to do).

8. Concerning oral contracts *of insurance*, see § 2.2(c) *supra.*

9. Sroga v. Lund, 259 Minn. 269, 106 N.W.2d 913 (1961).

10. Hamacher v. Tumy, 222 Ore. 341, 352 P.2d 493 (1960).

11. See § 2.2(c) (2) *supra.*

12. In Mid-America Corp. v. Roach, 412 P.2d 188 (Okla.1966), the court speaks

that, first, ordinarily the transaction cannot fairly be construed as an undertaking by the intermediary himself *to insure,* rather than *to procure insurance,* and second, rarely is the intermediary qualified to insure under regulatory statutes.

In other cases, liability of an intermediary has been founded in tort, usually on a theory of negligence.[13] Occasionally, the facts support a tort theory of deceit,[14] or a blend of tort-contract theory in the nature of breach of an express or implied warranty of authority to insure.[15]

Often the liability of an intermediary to an applicant is based upon his superior knowledge, or upon his holding himself out as an expert advisor on insurance matters, or both.[16] This supporting ar-

[Handwritten margin notes: Tort liability in negligence / deceit / or breach of warranty of authority to insure / superior knowledge — holding out as having]

of the intermediary's "liability as an insurer," but it is clear that the theory of the action was breach of a contract to procure insurance. See also Annot., 29 A.L.R.2d 171, 179–180 (1953). *But see, e.g.,* Bentley v. Fayas, 260 Wis. 177, 50 N.W.2d 404 (1951), 29 A.L.R.2d 205 (1953), specifically rejecting, in an alternative holding, the view that the intermediary can be held liable as an insurer.

13. *E.g.,* Hardt v. Brink, 192 F.Supp. 879 (W.D.Wash.1961) (insurance agent through whom insurance had been purchased for years negligent in failing to advise fire insurance coverage on leasehold of which he had been informed); Walker v. Pacific Indem. Co., 183 Cal.App.2d 513, 6 Cal.Rptr. 924 (1st Dist.1960) (insurance broker negligent in obtaining policy with smaller limits of coverage than had been agreed upon); Minor v. Universal C. I. T. Credit Corp., 27 Ill.App.2d 330, 170 N.E.2d 5 (1st Dist.1960) (credit company by exercising its option to purchase collision insurance on financed automobile assumed duty to provide insurance during term of loan contract or to notify debtor to procure own insurance and was negligent in failing to renew coverage without notice to debtor); Rider v. Lynch, 42 N. J. 465, 201 A.2d 561 (1964) (insurance broker negligent in obtaining non-owner motor vehicle liability policy knowing or charged with the duty of knowing that it would not provide the coverage desired); Riddle-Duckworth, Inc. v. Sullivan, 253 S.C. 411, 171 S.E. 2d 486 (1969) (agent undertook to procure complete business premises liability coverage for home and auto appliance business and represented that a policy he had procured afforded the desired protection; liable for negligent

failure to procure coverage for freight elevator occasionally used to transport people). See also McCall v. Marshall, 398 S.W.2d 106 (Tex.1965) (insurance agent not negligent in failing to procure fire insurance on additional location of customer's business though he had knowledge of that addition, because there is no duty to act unless there is evidence of previous dealings in which the agent customarily procured insurance for customer without consulting him); 16 Appleman, Insurance Law §§ 8831, 8840, 8841 (rev. ed. 1968); Annot., 29 A.L.R.2d 171 (1953).

14. *E.g.,* Anderson v. Knox, 297 F.2d 702 (9th Cir.), *cert. denied,* 370 U.S. 915 (1961) (insurance agent represented that $150,000 of bank-financed life insurance was a suitable plan for one earning less than $10,000 annually, knowing that it was not suitable or with wilful disregard as to the suitability of the plan); Clark v. Kelly, 217 Ga. 449, 122 S.E.2d 731 (1961) (insurance agent represented that he had issued binder of fire insurance, knowing that he had not and did not intend to do so; company identified but not liable on oral contract because of Georgia statutes forbidding oral contracts of insurance).

15. See, *e.g.,* Skyways Aircraft Ferrying Serv., Inc. v. Stanton, 242 Cal. App.2d 272, 51 Cal.Rptr. 352 (2d Dist. 1966), in which case, however, the intermediary was found to have had "ostensible authority."

16. See, *e.g.,* Hardt v. Brink, 192 F. Supp. 879 (W.D.Wash.1961); Riddle-Duckworth, Inc. v. Sullivan, 253 S.C. 411, 171 S.E.2d 486 (1969).

gument for liability more often applies when the intermediary is an insurance agent or broker than when not, since the liability of an intermediary who is not an agent or broker is generally founded on an explicit contractual undertaking.[17] This argument is also available, however, in many credit life insurance transactions involving a lending institution as intermediary.[18] If the conduct of the intermediary (of whatever type) induces the applicant to rely upon his obtaining insurance for the applicant, a legal duty of reasonable care should be and commonly is imposed upon the intermediary.[19] The recognition of such a duty is consistent with tort rules of general application, enforcing obligations of affirmative action when one has worsened another's position by leading him reasonably to expect action and then failing to fulfill the expectation.[20] The standard of reasonable care by which such an intermediary is judged is that of an ordinarily prudent person possessing the expert knowledge that the intermediary has or represents himself as having, whichever is greater.[21] Representations by which the intermediary holds himself out as an expert

17. See, *e.g.*, Mid-America Corp. v. Roach, 412 P.2d 188 (Okla.1966); Walker Bank & Trust Co. v. First Security Corp., 9 Utah 2d 215, 341 P.2d 944 (1959). See also Annot., 18 A.L.R.2d 1051 (1951). But one who is not an agent or broker may also be held to a noncontractual duty. See, *e.g.*, Wellens v. Perpetual Bldg. Ass'n, 184 A.2d 36 (D.C.Munic.Ct.App.1962) (mortgagee subject to liability for failure to act with reasonable care in obtaining fire insurance that did not cover garage detached from main building on mortgaged property).

18. *E.g.*: "[T]he plaintiff [lending institution] undertook to act . . . in a matter . . . where its knowledge and experience far exceeded [that of the defendant debtor] . . . ." Keene Inv. Co. v. Martin, 104 N.H. 518, 520, 191 A.2d 521, 522 (1963). See also, *e.g.*, Mid-America Corp. v. Roach, 412 P.2d 188 (Okla.1966).

19. *E.g.*, Hamacher v. Tumy, 222 Ore. 341, 352 P.2d 493 (1960); Hardt v. Brink, 192 F.Supp. 879 (W.D.Wash. 1961). *Cf.* McCall v. Marshall, 398 S. W.2d 106 (Tex.1965) (agent not liable because no evidence of previous conduct of agent acting to procure insurance coverage without specific instructions of applicant for him to do so).

20. See § 2.4 *supra* discussing this theory of liability in relation to delay in acting on an application for insurance.

21. *Cf.* 2 Restatement (Second) of Torts § 290 comment *f* (1965). In discussing *Hardt v. Brink*, n.16 *supra*, one writer has warned that "if the *Hardt* . . . approach is accepted, . . . [the agent] must review leases, contracts, etc., with a view to determining potential liability. This is a large undertaking. How many agents are aware, for example, of the risks in being a director or an officer of a corporation? . . . These and many other liability and loss exposures indicate that the agent either had better tell his client to see his lawyer and then request specific coverages or take the job of advisor and make sure his own errors and omissions coverage is in order." Hoeveler, *Architects, Engineers & Insurance Agents Professional Liability*, 1966 A.B.A. Section Ins., Neg. & Comp.L. Proceedings 222, 227–228. It seems unlikely, however, that courts would impose on the agent a duty that would amount to the unauthorized practice of law in the absence of a representation that, in effect, this was what the agent purported to undertake.

Concerning the coverage of agents' and brokers' errors and omissions insurance, see, *e.g.*, Otteman v. Interstate Fire & Cas. Co., 172 Neb. 574, 111 N. W.2d 97 (1961), 89 A.L.R.2d 1182 (1963).

may be made either to the applicant individually [22] or to the public generally.[23]

§ 2.5(b) CONTRIBUTORY FAULT

The question whether contributory fault of the applicant is a defense to his action against an intermediary is most obvious when the action is one in tort and is founded on negligence. It can arise also in a setting only slightly different, in substance, though the theory of the action is contract. This is true because, if the requisites of a contract to use reasonable care to obtain the desired coverage are present, conduct of the intermediary violating the standard of care by which he is judged ordinarily supports not only a tort action based on negligence [1] but also an action for breach of contract.[2] It may be argued that contributory fault should bar the action in contract as well as that in tort.

Consider a case in which the intermediary agrees to effect increased fire insurance coverage on the applicant's business premises immediately, but the policy issued provides that the increased coverage is to take effect one month after the agreement, at the expiration of pre-existing coverage. In such a situation, the intermediary has been held liable on a contract theory for damage from a fire occurring before the policy took effect,[3] and it has been said that contributory negligence in not ascertaining that the policy failed to take effect immediately does not bar liability when the action is for breach of contract.[4] But this line of reasoning is questionable and perhaps misleading as well. In the first place, if the theory of action is some failure of the intermediary that amounts to breach of a contract to use due care to procure insurance, it might be argued that contributory negligence should be a bar in the contract action as well as the tort action. Secondly, even if contributory negligence in a narrow technical sense is not recognized as a defense to an action for breach of contract, contributory fault in a broader sense may be quite relevant—for example, under theories that recovery is disallowed for consequences that were avoidable by the applicant's exercise of reasonable care and for consequences not within the contemplation of

22. *E.g.*, Sroga v. Lund, 259 Minn. 269, 106 N.W.2d 913 (1961); Spiegel v. Metropolitan Life Ins. Co., 6 N.Y.2d 91, 160 N.E.2d 40, 188 N.Y.S.2d 486 (1959).

23. *E.g.*, Rider v. Lynch, 42 N.J. 465, 201 A.2d 561 (1964).

I. See the cases cited in § 2.5(a) n.13 *supra*.

2. "For the breach of its agreement or for its negligent performance of it the plaintiff would be liable in damages to the defendant." Keene Inv. Corp. v. Martin, 104 N.H. 518, 520, 191 A.2d

521, 522 (1963). See also the cases cited in § 2.5(a) nn.6, 7 *supra*.

3. White v. Calley, 67 N.M. 343, 355 P. 2d 280 (1960).

4. 67 N.M. at 345, 355 P.2d at 281. *Accord*, Sroga v. Lund, 259 Minn. 269, 271–272, 106 N.W.2d 913, 915 (1961). See also Franklin v. Western Pac. Ins. Co., 243 Ore. 448, 453, 414 P.2d 343, 346 (1966), reasoning, however, that the intermediary was the agent of the applicant and that a principal is entitled to assume that his agent performed the duty as undertaken.

the contracting parties. Of course, in some instances the result of rejection of the contributory fault defense may be defended on the ground that the applicant's reliance upon an expert's assurances was reasonable. This has sometimes been an explicit ground of decision.[5]

The intermediary's holding himself out as an expert bears heavily not only upon the prima facie basis of liability but also upon the contributory fault question in whatever guise it may be presented.[6] This point is sound even when the applicant's theory of action is deceit; the applicant's reliance may be found reasonable even though the representations in other contexts might arguably be considered non-actionable misrepresentations of opinion [7] or law.[8]

§ 2.5(c) MISLEADING USE OF AGENCY CLASSIFICATIONS

By deliberate choice, the foregoing analysis of the liability of intermediaries has been expressed usually in terms of principles and rules that do not turn on whether the intermediary is an agent for the applicant in procuring insurance (commonly referred to as a broker).[1] Ordinarily the critical question is not whether such an agency relationship existed, but rather whether the relationship and dealings between the applicant and the intermediary support a duty of reasonable care to procure the promised insurance. Unfortunately, the focus upon this question has often been distorted by dicta about the existence or nonexistence of an agency relationship, liability of an intermediary being reasoned on the ground that he was an agent of the applicant to procure insurance or occupied a non-agency fiduciary relationship with the applicant. But even in cases in which either of these characterizations of the relationship is dubious, a finding of a

---

5. *E.g.*, Rider v. Lynch, 42 N.J. 465, 201 A.2d 561 (1964). The applicant desired liability insurance coverage for herself and her father while driving her fiancee's car, which had been left in her care, and the intermediary—an insurance broker—promised that such coverage would be obtained and stated that a policy subsequently issued provided the coverage desired. The applicant's father having been held liable for injuries to another arising from an accident involving the vehicle, liability was imposed on the intermediary on a theory of negligence, since the policy he procured (a non-owner contract) specifically excluded the coverage desired. The court held as a matter of law that the applicant was not contributorily negligent in failing to read the policy since she (and her father) were reasonable in relying on the broker's assurance that the policy provided the coverage desired. See also Riddle-Duckworth, Inc. v. Sullivan, 253 S.C. 411, 171 S.E. 2d 486 (1969) (treating the contributory

negligence issue as one of fact, taking into account the knowledge and means of knowledge of the agent and applicant respectively).

6. This is illustrated in *Rider* and in *Riddle-Duckworth*, n.5 *supra*.

7. *E.g.*, Anderson v. Knox, 297 F.2d 702 (9th Cir.), *cert. denied*, 370 U.S. 915 (1961) (representation that plan of life insurance was "suitable" held actionable).

8. *E.g.*, Clark v. Kelly, 217 Ga. 449, 122 S.E.2d 731, *opinion on remand sub nom.* Kelly v. Georgia Cas. & Sur. Co., 105 Ga.App. 104, 106–107, 123 S. E.2d 711, 713 (1961) (representation that binder providing immediate fire insurance coverage had been effected held actionable although state law required all contracts of insurance to be in writing). See also Annot., 29 A.L. R.2d 213 (1953).

1. See § 1.5(b) *supra*.

duty of reasonable care to procure insurance may nevertheless be well supported on straight contract grounds or because the conduct of the intermediary has created reasonable expectations in the applicant, who has relied to his detriment.

Perhaps there is minimal risk that the distortions caused by dicta about an agency relationship will lead to erroneous results when the intermediary is an insurance broker without authority to bind the company [2] or when the intermediary is one engaged in the insurance transaction only incidentally.[3] In either case, the intermediary is not bound by a pre-existing agency relationship with the insurance company that could complicate both the question of his liability to the applicant and the question of authority to bind the company. But some risk of erroneous results remains.[4]

2. *E.g.,* Walker v. Pacific Indem. Co., 183 Cal.App.2d 513, 6 Cal.Rptr. 924 (1st Dist.1960); Rider v. Lynch, 42 N.J. 465, 201 A.2d 561 (1964); Hamacher v. Tumy, 222 Ore. 341, 352 P.2d 493 (1960).

3. *E.g.,* Mid-America Corp. v. Roach, 412 P.2d 188 (Okla.1966); Walker Bank & Trust Co. v. First Security Corp., 9 Utah 2d 215, 341 P.2d 944 (1959).

4. See, *e.g.,* First Fed. Sav. & Loan Ass'n v. Continental Equity Life Ins. Co., 124 So.2d 802 (La.App.1960). An intermediary was held *not* to be liable to a lending institution because of an agency relationship held to have existed between the intermediary and the debtor-applicant. The debtor of the plaintiff lending institution applied for credit life insurance in the amount of his loan, placing the application through the assistant secretary of the lending institution. The application and assumed coverage was for $4,800 although the policy expressly limited coverage to $2,000; the mistake was not discovered until after the debtor's death, which occurred less than two weeks after the application was made. Plaintiff brought suit against the insurance company under the policy, against its own employee as an independent insurance broker, and against the employee's errors and omissions liability insurer, recovering in the trial court $2,056, $250, and $2,494, respectively, from the defendants. The employee's liability insurer appealed, and the judgment was reversed as to it. The court characterized the employee intermediary as an independent insurance broker and, as such, the agent of the applicant in the insurance transaction; basing its decision on this characterization, the court held that "plaintiff occupied the status of a stranger or a third party without interest or rights against the agent for acts of negligence or errors which were detrimental to the principal." 124 So.2d at 804. In credit life insurance transactions, the lending institution's employee through whom applications for insurance are made is, in fact, generally functioning on behalf of and under the control of the lending institution, regardless of his legal status as a licensed insurance agent or broker. See, *e.g.,* Mid-America Corp. v. Roach, n.3 *supra.* Moreover, the insurance coverage procured is often under a group contract (see *First Fed. Sav. & Loan Ass'n supra,* and § 2.8(b) n.8 *infra*) and the master policy or contract is usually issued to the lending institution. Characterizing the employee-intermediary as the agent of the applicant-debtor ignores these practical aspects of the transaction and implies a set of relationships between the parties that produces unacceptable legal consequences. The applicant-debtor's estate may thus be foreclosed from asserting liability of the lending institution as an intermediary and be left with recourse only against an individual who may be judgment proof. Under these circumstances, an analysis more consistent with the facts is to recognize the actual control of the lending institution and to allow the applicant-debtor recourse against the institution. In the *First Fed. Sav. & Loan Ass'n* case, this analysis would have called for resolving the question of the employee's liability to the lending institution on the basis of the employment relationship between them, also allowing the debtor's estate the possibility of holding the institution liable for the negli-

If there is a pre-existing agency relationship between the intermediary and the insurance company, introducing a theory that the intermediary owes a duty to the applicant *as his agent* spawns difficulties. First, an agency relationship is based fundamentally upon the principal's right of control of the agent, and it is difficult to sustain a finding that the applicant had such a right in the face of evidence of an inconsistent right of control in the company. Another problem is the general principle of agency law that an individual cannot act as the agent for both parties to a transaction without the informed consent of both [5]—a circumstance rarely if ever present in the insurance transaction upon which the liability of the intermediary is sought to be based. Yet some courts have characterized the intermediary as agent of the applicant in this kind of case.[6]

The most common mistake leading to erroneous characterization of a relationship as one of agency is overlooking the requirement of right of control over performance that is an essential characteristic of agency.[7] All too often the mere right to demand of the intermediary the accomplishment of a specified result has been treated as if it created an agency relationship; if that were so, the intermediary would be an agent for the applicant in every case of agreement to procure insurance—an obviously fallacious analysis. In such a situation, the contract to procure insurance sustains an action by the applicant against the intermediary without the fortification of an added duty incident to an agency or other fiduciary relationship. Similarly, in an applicant's action against an intermediary for deceit, the existence of an agency relationship between the intermediary and the applicant is not essential to liability of the intermediary; also, in such an action of deceit, unless based on misrepresentation of authority, existence of an agency relationship between the intermediary and the company does not defeat the intermediary's liability.[8]

Erroneously characterizing the relationship as one in which the intermediary is an agent of the applicant poses an improper obstacle

gence of its employee in the insurance transaction.

Concerning incorrect characterization of the relationship in an insurance transaction as one of agency, see generally § 1.5 *supra*.

5. See Restatement (Second) of Agency §§ 313, 391, 392 (1958).

6. *E.g.*, Franklin v. Western Pac. Ins. Co., 243 Ore. 448, 414 P.2d 343 (1966) (applicant not charged with duty of reading insurance policy to determine that coverage desired had not been obtained since intermediary held to have been acting as agent of the applicant in procuring the policy; yet, cause of action stated against insurance company because negligent intermediary was acting as its agent). When pur-

porting to found liability of the intermediary on his duty as an agent of the applicant, courts have generally ignored these special problems. See, *e.g.*, Hardt v. Brink, 192 F.Supp. 879 (W.D.Wash.1961); Sroga v. Lund, 259 Minn. 269, 106 N.W.2d 913 (1961); White v. Calley, 67 N.M. 343, 355 P.2d 280 (1960); Spiegel v. Metropolitan Life Ins. Co., 6 N.Y.2d 91, 160 N.E.2d 40, 188 N.Y.S.2d 486 (1959).

7. See Restatement (Second) of Agency § 14 (1958).

8. See, *e.g.*, Anderson v. Knox, 297 F.2d 702, 706 (9th Cir.), *cert. denied*, 370 U.S. 915 (1961). *Cf.* Clark v. Kelly, 217 Ga. 449, 122 S.E.2d 731, *opinion on remand sub nom.* Kelly v. Georgia Cas. & Sur. Co., 105 Ga.App. 104, 106, 123 S.E.2d 711, 713 (1961).

to relief in favor of the applicant against the insurance company. Ordinarily the company is bound only if the intermediary had actual or apparent authority as its agent, a position usually inconsistent with his being agent for the applicant in procuring insurance.

The question whether an agency relationship existed *between the company and the intermediary* with regard to the transaction in question is, of course, quite important since such a relationship may support liability of the company to the applicant, and, except as noted above in relation to an action against the intermediary based on deceit, ordinarily liability of the company is decisive against alleged liability of the intermediary to the applicant.[9]

SECTION 2.6 INSTRUMENTS OF OFFER AND ACCEPTANCE

[handwritten margin notes: Traditional Theory — applicant makes offer — Ins Co. makes acceptance]

The offer-and-acceptance theory traditionally applied to formal contracts of insurance is that the person desiring to be an insured (referred to for convenience as the applicant) makes an offer and the contract is made upon acceptance by the entity engaged in the insurance business (referred to for convenience as the company).[1] It often happens that an agent of the company has initiated negotiations and provided a form for the applicant to use in making known his interest in contracting. This preliminary initiative, however, is ordinarily referred to not as an offer but as an invitation for an offer.[2] This is an appropriate way of making the point, when it is so, that under the terms of the negotiations the company is not to be bound upon execution of the application but only after some representative of the company has considered and acted upon it favorably. Issuance of the policy is thus customarily essential to consummation of a formal contract of insurance, and in some instances the customary pattern of marketing requires, as an essential aspect of the company's manifesting its acceptance of the applicant's offer, not only that the policy be issued but also that it be delivered.[3]

[handwritten margin notes: agent is making "invitation to offer"]

[handwritten margin notes: Issuance of policy thus usually essential to consumation of it. Also, delivery often essential element]

Under the traditional theory, if the company responds to the applicant's offer by tendering an executed policy of different terms than those described in the application, this is a counter offer, and the contract is complete only if the applicant accepts the tendered policy.[4] Also, consummation of a contract is sometimes delayed beyond the response of the company to an application when the premium is not tendered with the application; this occurs when the company re-

[handwritten margin note: counter offer by Co.]

9. See § 2.5(a) *supra.*

1. See, *e.g.*, United Ins. Co. v. Headrick, 275 Ala. 594, 157 So.2d 19 (1963); 12 Appleman, Insurance Law §§ 7121, 7151 (1943). 1 Couch, Insurance Law § 7:8 (2d ed. 1959).

2. *Ibid.*

3. *E.g.*, Hartford Acc. & Indem. Co. v. McCullough, 235 Cal.App.2d 195, 44 Cal.Rptr. 915 (5th Dist. 1965). See § 2.7 *infra.*

4. *E.g.*, Long v. New York Life Ins. Co., 106 Wash. 458, 180 P. 479 (1919). See also 1 Couch, Insurance §§ 7:17, 7:20 (2d ed. 1959).

sponds with a tender of delivery of the policy upon payment of the premium to its agent.[5]

Insurance marketing practices, however, are not always in the pattern upon which the traditional theory is founded. For example, trip insurance marketed through vending machines at air terminals is in a different pattern.[6] The clear understanding is that the company cannot decline a completed application deposited in its machine before the applicant departs on his trip. In these circumstances it would appear that the communications from the company on the forms and in the notices posted on or near the vending machines constitute an offer to contract with virtually anyone on specified terms, and the execution and depositing of the "application" constitutes an acceptance.

The aptness of a theory of offer and acceptance depends in final analysis upon the communications between the parties. Only after a close examination of the communications can it be determined whether the traditional theory applies in a given context.[7]

SECTION 2.7 DELIVERY OF THE POLICY

Delivery of an insurance policy is a concept the principal use of which has occurred in life insurance. Delivery may be significant in the following ways:[1] First, it may have evidential value. Although possession of the policy by the applicant or another holding through him is not a conclusive demonstration that a contract is in effect, it requires that inference in the absence of explanation. Second, it may be the means of communication of the insurer's offer or acceptance. It may serve as an acceptance of an offer submitted by means of an application, such offer having been invited by the solicitation of an agent.[2] Also, it may serve as a counter-offer, if the policy delivered is different from that applied for.[3] Third, it may be a condition precedent to commencement of the insurer's responsibility for the risk that is the subject of insurance. Fourth, it may affect not only the time of commencement of a term of coverage but also the time of expiration.[4]

It is clear that there may be a contract before delivery if the parties so agree. Another form of communication of the insurer's acceptance or counter-offer may be used instead of delivery, and other

5. See *id.* §§ 7:16, 7:18.

6. Concerning trip insurance generally, see § 2.9 *infra.*

7. See, *e.g.*, Klos v. Mobil Oil Co., 55 N.J. 117, 259 A.2d 889 (1969) (under special arrangement for marketing to credit card holders, the company's communications constituted an offer and the completed "application" was an acceptance).

1. See generally Patterson, *Delivery of a Life Insurance Policy*, 33 Harv.L. Rev. 198 (1919); 1 Appleman, Insurance Law §§ 131–133 (rev. ed. 1965), 12 *id.* § 7156 (1943).

2. See § 2.6 *supra.*

3. *Ibid.*

4. See § 5.10(b) *infra.*

evidence of the consummation of an agreement may be available. Insurance is highly standardized and systematized, and it is usually possible to determine from written records what action has been taken on any particular application without reference to the evidential value of delivery.

Life insurers, however, have often inserted a clause in application and policy forms providing that the policy shall not take effect until delivered.[5] Though such clauses are valid, courts have sometimes rendered the requirement of delivery ineffectual by finding "constructive" delivery or by discovering some barrier to enforcement of the stipulation for delivery in circumstances involving want of compliance with the letter of the delivery clause.[6] Patterson aptly described these developments as a battle between the demand for certainty, with resulting formalism, and the demand for flexibility, with resulting judicial "flanking movements" to prevent apparent injustices that would result from strict adherence to form.[7]

Since binding receipts typically provide interim coverage before delivery if a premium has been paid in advance, their increased use has greatly reduced the significance of delivery. But even when a binding receipt is used, delivery may still be decisive of coverage. For example, this is true as to long-term coverage if by the terms of the receipt the insurer is free to decline to deliver a permanent policy even though bound by a contract of interim coverage; delivery of the policy is a decisive act that ordinarily marks the end of the insurer's opportunity to decline long-term coverage.[8]

5. A variation on this theme is a clause in an application form declaring that if the premium is not paid at the time of applying the insurance applied for "shall become effective on the date of issue stated in the policy PROVIDED the Company has approved this application at its Home Office, the premium has been paid, and the policy delivered to me while I am in good health." See Appendix E *infra.* Concerning the requirement of delivery during "good health" of the applicant, see generally § 6.5(e) (4) *infra.*

6. *E.g.*, New York Life Ins. Co. v. Ollich, 42 F.2d 399 (6th Cir. 1930) (constructive delivery); Prudence Mut. Cas. Co. v. Switzer, 253 Miss. 143, 175 So.2d 476 (1965), 19 A.L.R.3d 946 (1968) (under entire contract statute, requirement of delivery to applicant during lifetime ineffective when not incorporated into policy); Pierce v. New York Life Ins. Co., 174 Mo.App.

383, 160 S.W. 40 (1913) (finding a waiver of the requirement of delivery). *But cf.* Pruitt v. Great So. Life Ins. Co., 202 La. 527, 12 So.2d 261 (1942), 145 A.L.R. 1427 (1943) (held, when the policy clause specified *actual* delivery to and acceptance by the applicant of the policy while he was in good health, there was no coverage in effect when the applicant died after the policy had been issued and sent to the insurance agent but before the agent acted to deliver the policy). See generally Annot., 19 A.L.R.3d 953 (1968).

7. Patterson, *Delivery of a Life Insurance Policy*, 33 Harv.L.Rev. 198, 222 (1919). Concerning accommodation between demands for flexibility and certainty, and related problems of use of evaluative standards of judgment, see § 1.6 *supra.*

8. See § 2.3(c) *supra.*

SECTION 2.8 | GROUP CONTRACTS |

§ 2.8(a) GENERALLY

In the marketing of any product or service, economy can be achieved through high-volume dealings. The principal way of doing this in the insurance field is by group insurance.[1] In its original and most common form, group insurance covers the employees of one employer, but it has been extended to cover creditor-debtor groups, labor union groups,[2] industry groups (including the employees of two or more employers in the same industry),[3] and other groups such as professional associations.[4]

The terms on which the insurer agrees to make contracts available to individual members of the group are stated in a master agreement or policy between the insurer and the group representative (e. g., an employer). Ordinarily a separate instrument is issued to each participating individual, usually in the form of a certificate that sets out at least the principal conditions of the coverage, though it may refer to the master agreement for details, especially with reference to such matters as the conditions under which the coverage may be modified in the future.[5] If the group coverage is provided solely at the expense of the party to the master agreement (usually an employer), it is a non-contributory group plan; if the individual certificate holders pay part of the premiums, either directly or by payroll deductions, it is a contributory plan.

Early development of group insurance occurred almost exclusively in the areas of life, health, and accident coverage, and with emphasis on term policies.[6] Differences in the nature of life, health, and ac-

---

1. See, *e.g.*, Denenberg, Eilers, Hoffman, Kline, Melone & Snider, Risk and Insurance, 293–316 (1964).

2. See, *e.g.*, Dyer v. Occidental Life Ins. Co., 182 F.2d 127 (9th Cir. 1950), 17 A.L.R.2d 923 (1951) (members of the Teamsters Union).

3. See, *e.g.*, Vandenberg v. John Hancock Mut. Life Ins. Co., 48 N.J.Super. 1, 136 A.2d 661 (App.Div.1957) (merchant seamen).

4. See, *e.g.*, Washington Nat'l Ins. Co. v. Burch, 293 F.2d 365 (5th Cir. 1961) (members of the American Turpentine Farmers' Association Cooperative).

5. This secondary level of contract and the relationship of the master policy-holder to the certificate holder and the insurer create unique problems (see subsections (b) and (c) *infra*) and unique variations on problems that exist in other insurance contexts. See, *e.g.*, Larson v. Union Cent. Life

Ins. Co., 272 Minn. 177, 137 N.W.2d 327 (1965) (provision causing forfeiture for nonpayment of premiums by master policyholder held not to apply to non-contribution to premium by individual insured, and, in the absence of a specific forfeiture provision, contributing to premium by individual insured held to be a contractual obligation only, and not a condition precedent to coverage); Layman v. Continental Assur. Co., 416 Pa. 155, 205 A.2d 93 (1964) (statute precluding defenses based on statements in an insurance application unless a copy of the application is attached to the policy held not to apply to defense based on statements in the application of an individual certificate holder under a group policy). See also Annots., 5 A.L.R.3d 902 (1966); 68 A.L.R.2d 215 (1959); 68 A.L.R.2d 150 (1959); 68 A.L.R.2d 8 (1959); 35 A.L.R.2d 798 (1954); § 2.5 *supra*.

6. See Webb, *Group and Quasi-Group Property-Liability Insurance*, 24 C. L.U.J., No. 3, 31 (1970).

(margin note: mostly used in life, health, accident areas)

cident insurance, on the one hand, and casualty, fire, and marine insurance on the other, undoubtedly contributed to this circumstance of earlier and more rapid development of group insurance in the former area than in the latter. The principal variations of life, health, and accident risks among different individuals are associated with health, age, and occupation. If the percentage of participants in a group is high enough, undue effect of adverse selection on account of health can be avoided. Premiums can easily be adjusted according to age, even in group coverage. The nature of the group usually provides some degree of homogeneity as to occupation. In contrast, many of the principal variations of risk in relation to casualty, fire, and marine insurance are less readily dealt with on a group basis. For example, fire insurance on the scattered homes of a group of employees of one enterprise would involve coverage of quite different types of property risks. Probably a more important factor accounting for the growth of group insurance in the life, health, and accident area, however, is the opportunity for reducing administrative expense by eliminating the cost of home office review of individual applications —a cost not incurred under the decentralized system of marketing casualty, fire, and marine insurance even on an individual basis. But many of the economies through mass marketing can be achieved in the fields of casualty, fire, and marine insurance also.[7] In the late 1960's, interest in "group" or "mass" merchandising of automobile insurance intensified rapidly,[8] and it is reasonable to expect that a considerable percentage of these coverages will be written on this basis in the future.

(margin note: adverse selection problem)

The design of a sound group insurance system must take account of the process of adverse selection.[9] In a system of individual marketing, review of each application before acceptance is the principal protection against undue adverse selection. In contrast, a group insurer has less opportunity for exercising judgment on individual applications. It necessarily accepts somewhat more adverse selection and adjusts premiums accordingly. It protects against an undue degree of adverse selection by requiring that a high percentage of the presons within a group (*e.g.,* the employees of one employer) be participants in the insurance plan. By adjusting premiums to the average level of risk among the large number of participants, the insurer can maintain a financially sound plan. It happens, of course, that the better risks among the members of the participating group pay more in relation to the value received than do the poorer risks, but such a variation within a rate category may be justifiable.[10] Moreover, though the benefit to the poorer risks is greater, even the better risks

---

7. See, *e.g.*, Denenberg *et al.* 315.

8. See Kimball & Denenberg, Mass Marketing of Property and Liability Insurance (U.S. Dep't Transp. Auto. Ins. & Comp. Study 1970); Webb, *Group and Quasi-Group Property-Lia-*

bility Insurance, 24 C.L.U.J., No. 3, 31 (1970).

9. See § 1.2(b) (7) *supra.*

10. See § 8.4(b) *infra.*

among the participants may derive a net benefit from the group arrangement, because of economies in marketing.

§ 2.8(b) MISTAKES BY THE GROUP ADMINISTRATOR

It is bound to happen that from time to time mistakes will be made by the administrator of a group insurance program. The employer, for example, when the policy is for a group of its employees, will fall short of perfection in administering the plan. Who bears the risk of loss or hardship because of such a mistake? This question is not necessarily faced by a court that considers an action by an alleged group member against the insurer carrying the group policy. For example, a court may hold that the group insurer is not accountable for a mistake of the employer in omitting to remit premiums for an employee,[1] without considering whether the employee may have a remedy against the employer. Similarly, a decision against the insurer would not necessarily preclude a later action by the insurer against the employer. The question whether the group administrator (such as the employer in the foregoing example) should be liable for mistakes is part of a congeries of problems including those concerning claims of alleged members against the group insurer. Consideration of still other related questions may throw useful light on these problems.

If, in the example given, the employer had made an error in reporting to the insurer that a particular worker's employment had terminated, and had erroneously failed to remit a premium for his coverage, and if the errors had been discovered during the worker's lifetime, would the insurer have been entitled to recover the premium from the employer? If the risk of mistake is to be placed on the employee, then it is sound to deny the claim against the insurer and the insurer should not be able to recover the premiums from the employer; if a payroll deduction had been made, the worker should be entitled to reimbursement for the amount deducted, on the principle of unjust enrichment, though this would be small comfort. If the risk of mistake is to be placed on the insurer, then it is unsound to deny the worker's claim against the insurer, and the insurer should be able to recover the premiums mistakenly omitted from the employer's remittances to the insurer.

When a court denies the worker's claim against the insurer but does not discuss the possibility of an action by the employee against the employer, no doubt it is often assumed that the employee bears the risk of mistakes of the employer concerning payment of premi-

1. E.g., Magee v. Equitable Life Assur. Soc'y, 62 N.D. 614, 244 N.W. 518 (1932), 85 A.L.R. 1457 (1933). Accord, Gilford v. Emergency Aid Ins. Co., 252 Ala. 311, 40 So.2d 868 (1949) (company defense of alleged failure of employer to add employee's name to contract precludes liability of company); New-man v. Home Life Ins. Co., 255 N.C. 722, 122 S.E.2d 701 (1961) (termination of master contract for nonpayment of premium ended employee's rights against insurer though employer continued to deduct premium contributions from employee's pay).

ums. It might be argued, however, that an action should be allowed against the employer for the loss caused by his mistake. But neither of these solutions is a good way of dealing with this risk of administrative error.

Another method of dealing with this risk is illustrated by contractual provisions of the following type: "Unintentional neglect on the part of the employer to furnish the name of any employee eligible hereunder shall not invalidate the insurance on the life of such employee."[2] In the case of employee-group life insurance policies, at least, such a provision appears to be the common way of dealing with this problem.[3] But this arrangement results in the insurer's assuming some risk of employer dishonesty as well as the risk of mistakes. Compare the risk of dishonesty of an agent, considered in relation to liability for oral contracts of insurance.[4]

The desirability of a rule placing on the insurer the risk of mistakes of the employer in administration of the plan, irrespective of the terms of the group contract, is debatable, as is also the question whether it is appropriate for a court to adopt such a restriction on freedom of contract in the absence of statutory or administrative restriction.[5]

The decision concerning where the risk of mistake lies as between the insurer and the employee is independent of the question whether the plan is contributory or noncontributory. The argument for an action in favor of the employee against the employer might seem stronger under a contributory plan, but realistically viewed, either plan involves a contribution by the employee since the employer's contribution, whether the total premium or only part of it, is made not as a gratuity but as part of the consideration for the services of the employee.

Occasionally, confusion has arisen from an effort to describe the relationship among the parties to a group plan—for example, the employer, the employees, and the insurer—by referring to the group administrator as an agent for one or the other of the remaining two parties to a particular certificate.[6] The relationship is not ordinarily one of agency, however, since neither the insurer nor the individual insured has the power of direction and control that is characteristic of agency. The relationship of employer to employee with respect to the typical employee group plan is better described as that of a non-agent fiduciary.[7] If the agreement is that the insurer bears the risk of mis-

"fiduciary" is best view of relationship, not agency

2. See, *e.g.*, All States Life Ins. Co. v. Tillman, 226 Ala. 245, 248, 146 So. 393, 394 (1933) (coverage allowed although the insurer had not been notified of the re-employment of the worker, and, apparently, had not received premiums covering him under a contributory plan).

3. See Gregg, Group Life Insurance 39 (3d ed. 1962).

4. See § 2.2(c) (2) *supra*.

5. *Cf.* § 2.3(c) *supra* and Chapter 6 *infra*.

6. See, *e.g.*, Washington Nat'l Ins. Co. v. Burch, 293 F.2d 365 (5th Cir. 1961) (Georgia law).

7. See Restatement (Second) of Agency § 314F (1958). See also § 1.5 *supra*

takes in administration of the group plan, it is not necessary to enforcement of that agreement that the employer be characterized as agent of the insurer in receiving the premium contribution from the employee. Such an obligation can be merely contractual.

The argument for regarding the group administrator as an agent of the insurer generally lacks merit also in relation to a group credit life insurance plan.[8] It should be noted, however, that the parties can, if they wish to do so, establish an agency relationship, and in some instances a person employed by a credit life group administrator (such as a bank) has been designated by the insurer as its agent for the writing of individual certificates of insurance under the group policy.[9]

§ 2.8(c) MODIFICATION OF GROUP CONTRACTS

Is either consent of or notice to certificate holders required for modifications of a group contract affecting their interests? Either by reference to particular phrases in the master agreement and certificates, or by resort to arguments about the sense of the agreement as a whole, courts have been willing usually to infer a requirement of notice,[1] but unwilling (except when loss has already occurred or has commenced, as in the case of continuing disability) to infer a requirement of consent of the certificate holder to a change in the master policy.[2]

[margin note: notice, but usually not consent, of certificate holders required for modification of master plan]

Because of the practical obstacles to obtaining consent of all the certificate holders, a requirement of consent would prevent changes that might be improvements from various points of view. The requirement of notice is less burdensome, and has the great advantage of giving the certificate holder an opportunity to adjust his insurance program to the changes. Doubtless it is more reasonable to infer a requirement of notice than a requirement of consent.

Though it is customary to speak of a "requirement of notice" of a change in coverage, this is a way of saying that coverage is contin-

---

concerning misuse of agency terminology generally.

8. See, *e.g.*, South Branch Valley Nat'l Bank v. Williams, 151 W.Va. 775, 155 S.E.2d 845 (1967) (bank signed group contract with insurer, containing clause denying coverage on life of any debtor over 65 years of age when executing agreement for loan; held, no coverage; insurer not responsible for actions of bank cashier in transaction with two debtors one of whom was over 65). See also § 2.5(c) n.4 *supra*.

9. See, *e.g.*, Atlantic Nat'l Life Ins. Co. v. Bank of Sulligent, 271 Ala. 543, 125 So.2d 702 (1961) (vice-president of bank

said to have been designated by the insurer as its agent, though the opinion does not disclose details of the arrangement and designation; court declined to permit insurer to defend on grounds of agent's misrepresenting certificate holder's health; having established dual relation, insurer cannot assert it as limitation of authority).

1. *E.g.*, Vandenberg v. John Hancock Mut. Life Ins. Co., 48 N.J.Super. 1, 136 A.2d 661 (App.Div.1957).

2. *E.g.* Metropolitan Life Ins. Co. v. Korneghy, 37 Ala.App. 497, 71 So.2d 292 (1954), 68 A.L.R.2d 239 (1959).

ued unchanged in the absence of notice.[3] Similarly, notice to the insured of cancellation of coverage under a group policy has been required under the contractual provisions involved in many cases[4] and
notice that termination of employment ends coverage (either immediately or after a waiting period, as the case may be) is required for effective cancellation of group insurance coverage when that coverage
is coterminous with employment, particularly if the employee-in-
sured is allowed a conversion privilege on termination of the group
coverage.[5]

SECTION 2.9 OPEN INVITATIONS TO CONTRACT; VENDING MACHINE MARKETING

Air travel trip insurance is commonly available at airports not
only through over-the-counter sales but also through vending machines. The purchaser inserts a coin, takes a form that the machine
releases, completes and deposits part of the form and mails the remainder to an appropriate place such as his home or office. Motoring trip insurance of similar characteristics has been developed,[1] but
is neither widely used nor readily available.

Most of the few reported cases that have arisen from trip insurance have concerned alleged misunderstandings by an air-travel passenger with regard to limitations of the amount of coverage or the

---

3. See, *e.g.*, Vandenberg v. John Hancock Mut. Life Ins. Co., 48 N.J.Super.
1, 136 A.2d 661 (App.Div.1957) (employee died five and one-half months
after employment terminated; held,
covered by group contract of life insurance originally providing coverage
for approximately six months after
employment terminated, though master policy had been amended without
notice to provide coverage for only approximately three months after employment terminated).

4. *E.g.*, Parks v. Prudential Ins. Co.,
103 F.Supp. 493 (D.Tenn.1951), *aff'd
per curiam*, 195 F.2d 302 (6th Cir.
1952); Poch v. Equitable Life Assur.
Soc'y, 343 Pa. 119, 22 A.2d 590 (1941),
142 A.L.R. 1279 (1943). See Annot., 68
A.L.R.2d 249, 254 (1959).

5. *E.g.*, Neider v. Continental Assur.
Co., 213 La. 621, 35 So.2d 237, 2 A.L.
R.2d 846 (1948). See also Annot., 68
A.L.R.2d 8, 132 (1959). *But see, e.g.*,
Rivers v. State Capital Life Ins. Co.,
245 N.C. 461, 96 S.E.2d 431 (1957), 68
A.L.R.2d 205 (1959). *Cf.* Newman v.
Home Life Ins. Co., 255 N.C. 722, 122
S.E.2d 701 (1961) (employee's rights
against insurer ended on termination
of master contract for nonpayment of
premium though employee was not no-

tified of termination). In Magee v.
Equitable Life Assur. Soc'y, 62 N.D.
614, 244 N.W. 518 (1932), 85 A.L.R.
1457 (1933), the court held that the insurer was under no duty to notify the
employee of cancellation of coverage
because actual discharge of the employee would have been notice of cancellation without more, and from the
insurer's point of view, the employee
had been discharged and, therefore,
had been given notice of cancellation.
In effect this decision applies a rule
that the employee was "conclusively
presumed to know" that, under its
terms, the group insurance policy
ceased to cover him upon termination
of his employment and, therefore, that
the insurer was under no duty to notify him of its cancellation. In reality,
of course, this is a fictional way of
saying that the employee need not be
notified that termination of his employment also terminates his coverage
under the group insurance. This view
cannot be reconciled with the rule,
noted in the text above, that coverage
is not effectively terminated when the
employee has not had actual notice of
termination of his employment.

1. *Time*, April 13, 1959, p. 108. See, *e.
g.*, Travelers Ins. Co. v. Anderson, 210
F.Supp. 735 (W.D.S.C.1962).

trips covered.[2]   For example, one decision denied recovery on three
of eight $5,000 policies because of a limitation to $25,000 total insurance, plainly indicated on the vending machines and on the policies.[3]
Another allowed recovery for a trip on a non-scheduled flight since,
although a limitation to scheduled flights was stated on the vending
machine and on the policy, the policy provision was in fine print and
the vending machine was placed in front of an airport counter used
by all non-scheduled airlines as a processing point for their
passengers.[4]

SECTION 2.10   STANDARDIZATION OF INSURANCE CONTRACTS GENERALLY

§ 2.10(a)   THE ROLE OF STANDARDIZATION

The typical purchaser of insurance takes a packaged product.
Like the purchaser of an automobile, he knows the general purpose of
the product and the needs he wants it to serve.   He has chosen what he
regards as a suitable model, and has given moderate attention to the
choice of accessories or endorsements.   But he is content to leave to
specialists all concern about the detailed structure of his purchase.   If
a defect in an electrical contact for the starter makes it impossible for
him to use the car, he turns to a mechanic for help.   If a deficiency in
his insurance coverage results in rejection of his claim for reimbursement of some loss, he turns to an insurance consultant or to a lawyer
for help.   One's capacity to help is gravely restricted, however, when
he is first consulted at this late point.   Experience with a problem of
insurance law at this stage frequently demonstrates that the client as
an insurance purchaser had a deplorably inadequate understanding of
what he was buying.   If in the wisdom born of such an experience
the client, with the benefit of professional advice, sets about to get
precisely the insurance coverage he desires for the future, to what
extent can his wishes be made effective?   To what extent is he free

---

2. See, *e.g.*, Fidelity & Cas. Co., v.
Smith, 189 F.2d 315 (10th Cir. 1951),
25 A.L.R.2d 1025 (1952); Steven v. Fidelity & Cas. Co., 58 Cal.2d 862, 377
P.2d 284, 27 Cal.Rptr. 172 (1962).   See
also Mutual of Omaha Ins. Co. v.
Russell, 402 F.2d 339 (10th Cir. 1968),
29 A.L.R.3d 753 (1970), *cert. denied*,
394 U.S. 973 (1969) (general accident
policy enforced according to its terms
despite alleged misunderstanding as to
duration of coverage growing out of
insured's unsuccessful efforts to purchase airplane passengers' trip insurance of narrower coverage for longer
period).

3. Slater v. Fidelity & Cas. Co., 277
App.Div. 79, 98 N.Y.S.2d 28 (1st Dep't
1950).

4. Lachs v. Fidelity & Cas. Co., 306 N.
Y. 357, 118 N.E.2d 555 (1954).   See
also Steven v. Fidelity & Cas. Co., 58
Cal.2d 862, 377 P.2d 284, 27 Cal.Rptr.
172 (1962) (fatal accident in crash of
"air taxi" substituted by decedent for
cancelled scheduled flight; held covered, in spite of limitation of policy to
scheduled flights, because of ambiguity
in policy terms; clear notice test of
Lachs, supra, cited and used).   *But
see* Mutual Benefit Health & Acc.
Ass'n v. Brunke, 276 F.2d 53 (5th Cir.
1960) (Illinois law; ignorance of coverage of accidental injury while riding
in land conveyance arranged for by air
carrier insufficient answer to defense
based on untimeliness of notice two
years after date of accident).

to choose in the formulation of an insurance contract, and to what extent is he presented with a set of standard provisions and given only the option to take it or leave it?

It is clear that the use of standard provisions cuts down the scope of choice of the individual buying insurance, just as the automobile purchaser's scope of choice is far less than if cars were custom made. It is also clear that there are positive gains to the individual from such standardization in marketing. Perhaps the major gain is economy. With insurance, standardization serves another purpose as well. It makes risk distribution feasible. Consider the problem from the point of view of a group of persons contemplating mutual insurance. If the risks they want to transfer from individuals to the pool are varied, great difficulty will be encountered in negotiating the basis of contributions. Standardization of the definition of relevant risks thus serves individual policyholder interests and the public interest in having efficient and economical insurance operations, as well as the interests of insurance company management.[1]

There remains, however, the problem of maintaining an appropriate balance between standardization, on the one hand, and adaptability to individual needs, on the other. Among the factors relevant to such balance is the extent to which the policyholder is capable of intelligent definition of his insurance needs. The less he understands about insurance, the more standardization is useful; the standardized policy, if well constructed, is an approximation of his insurance needs developed from experience with the needs of others similarly situated. Another relevant factor bearing on the balance between standardization and adaptability is the degree to which the insured venture is a standardized venture. The greater the tendency of the venture toward the unique, the more useful is the characteristic of adaptability in the insurance available for the venture. To some extent, differences as to factors such as these will be reflected in different degrees of standardization of various types of insurance.

§ 2.10(b) TECHNIQUES OF STANDARDIZATION; REGULATION

Several techniques have evolved for formulating the terms of insurance contracts. They range from the extreme of a statutory prescription to the opposite extreme of free negotiation between insurer

---

1. For discussions of other advantages of standardization of insurance policies see, *e.g.*, Wenck, *The Historical Development of Standard Policies*, 35 J.Risk & Ins. 537 (1968); Grissom, *The Scope of Windstorm Coverage*, N.Y.L.J., Oct. 3, 1960, p. 4; Ward, *Policy Simplification*, 1959 Ins.L.J. 535.

For comments on standardization and contracts of adhesion generally, and for leads to other writings on this subject, see Restatement (Second) of Contracts § 237, comment *a* (Tent. Draft No. 5 1970); Llewellyn, The Common Law Tradition: Deciding Appeals 362–371 (1960); Leff, *Contract as Thing*, 19 Am.U.L.Rev. 131 (1970); Kessler, *Contracts of Adhesion—Some Thoughts About Freedom of Contract*, 43 Colum.L.Rev. 629 (1943).

and insured. To a great extent statutes determine whether standard-ization is to be required, and if so to what degree and by what method.[1]

Each of the techniques of standardization described below is typical of some kind of insurance today. In view of the multiplicity of kinds of insurance, and the fact that legal control over standardization is largely accomplished by state rather than federal regulation, the systems of policy formulation are numerous and they involve degrees of reliance upon the following techniques in various combinations.

(1) LEGISLATIVE PRESCRIPTION OF POLICY FORMS

Use of a form prescribed by statute is the most rigidly standardized method of formulating the insurance contract. This method is widely used for fire insurance. The 1943 New York Standard Fire Insurance Policy, with insubstantial modifications, is now used in nearly all of the United States. It is prescribed by statute in New York[2] and many other states, and elsewhere is prescribed by administrative regulation. A single form will not serve for all fire insurance contracts, however. Endorsements are needed. These have not generally been prescribed by statute. In New York, for example, there is provision for administrative prescription of endorsement forms.[3]

The greater degree of standardization in fire insurance than in other types of insurance may be accounted for, in part at least, by distinctive characteristics of this type of insurance. The insured venture (the maintenance of physical property) is common, and the variations in methods of maintenance that affect the risk from fire fit well into patterns to which rates and standardized endorsements can be readily adjusted.

Even though entire policy forms are not prescribed for other types of insurance, there are many statutes prescribing some clauses verbatim[4] or prescribing the content though not in the form intended for use in the policy.[5]

1. New York is among the states whose insurance regulatory statutes have been most carefully considered. In the appendix is a selection of New York statutes. For their bearing on standardization of policies, see N.Y. Ins.Law §§ 21, 141, 154, 164, 167–169, 183 (McKinney 1966) and N.Y. Vehicle & Traffic Law § 311(4) (McKinney 1960).

2. N.Y.Ins.Law § 168 (McKinney 1966).

3. N.Y.Ins.Law § 169 (McKinney 1966).

4. *E.g.*, N.Y.Ins.Law § 164 (McKinney 1966), prescribing "standard provisions" for accident and health insurance policies.

5. *E.g.*, Mass.Gen.Laws Ann. ch. 175, § 113A (1958 and Supp.1970), concerning compulsory motor vehicle liability insurance. Concerning legislative prescription generally, see Kimball & Pfennigstorf, *Legislative and Judicial Control of the Terms of Insurance Contracts: A Comparative Study of American and European Practice*, 39 Ind.L.J. 675 (1964).

(2) ADMINISTRATIVE PRESCRIPTION OF POLICY FORMS UNDER STATUTORY AUTHORIZATION

In one sense this method of standardization is as rigid as the statutory method; variations from the prescribed form are prohibited in either case. But in its practical operation administrative prescription involves less standardization than statutory prescription. It is normally more difficult to have a statute amended to meet a newly recognized need. Also, policy forms prescribed by administrative regulations are likely to provide for more variations by approved forms of endorsement. Not only is the administrator free of the concern that approval of a proposed form of endorsement will be inconsistent with a statute prescribing the basic form, but also he is more likely than a legislature to experiment with new forms, realizing that he can withdraw them if experience proves them undesirable.

To say that a policy form is prescribed by statute or by administrative regulation is not to say that the initiative for modification is, or should be, with the legislature or administrator. In fact, the initiative is more often elsewhere.

Perhaps changes in statutory forms are too infrequent to justify conclusions as to the usual source of initiative, but with respect to forms prescribed by administrative regulation, it appears that proposals for change more often come from insurers than from any other source, including the office of the administrator. The insurers are likely to become aware of needs for different forms to meet changing business circumstances, even without special attention to the problem. On the other hand, the administrative offices have no such daily contact with prospective insurance purchasers, and they rarely have anyone assigned to consider whether changes in policy forms should be initiated by the administrator. The administrator hears from insurance purchasers only in cases of acute dissatisfaction. Thus the administrator gets most of his information about new needs through insurers, and in most instances his action on proposed forms is based to a large extent on information presented by them in support of proposed changes.

(3) REQUIREMENT OF ADMINISTRATIVE APPROVAL OF POLICY FORMS

It has been observed in the preceding paragraph that a system of administrative prescription of policy forms approaches in practice a system of administrative action on proposals initiated by insurers. Some statutes specifically provide for such a practice by giving the administrator no power to prescribe, but rather power to disapprove forms proposed by the insurers who operate within the jurisdiction.[6] Under some statutes of this type approval must be obtained before

---

6. See, generally, Kimball & Pfennigstorf, *Administrative Control of the Terms of Insurance Contracts: A* *Comparative Study*, 40 Ind.L.J. 143, 144–177 (1965).

the form is used;[7] under others, the form may be used if filed with the administrator and not disapproved.[8] There is wide variation as to the standards governing the administrator's action, and under some statutes there is considerable doubt as to the range within which the administrator has discretion rather than being under the compulsion merely to examine proposals to determine that they do not violate some statute or common law doctrine.

(4) PROSCRIPTION OF POLICY PROVISIONS

In many instances policy forms are not prescribed, but certain provisions are proscribed. Proscriptions may occur by statute, or by administrative regulation under statutory authorization. The most extensive use of proscription has occurred in the field of life insurance, but to some extent it is used in other fields also. In all jurisdictions there are a few statutes of general application to all types of insurance, prohibiting certain provisions. For example, statutes regulating provisions regarding notice and proof of loss are common.[9]

(5) COOPERATION AMONG INSURERS IN DEVELOPING POLICY FORMS

The development of the standard forms of automobile insurance and other liability insurance policies is the outstanding example of this method of standardization. It will be considered more fully hereafter.[10]

(6) COMPETITION AMONG INSURERS

A policy form that proves attractive to purchasers and gives a competitive advantage to the insurer using it is likely to be imitated by other insurers. In this respect, competition works as an influence toward standardization. Competition works against standardization in another respect, however, since it encourages ingenuity in the development of new variations in the hope that they will be more attractive than others available on the insurance market.

(7) STANDARDIZATION OF A SINGLE COMPANY'S POLICY FORMS

Even in areas as to which there is no standard form developed among insurers generally, a single insurer usually develops its own forms and requires that they be used by its agents in making contracts.[11] Only in unusual circumstances are insurance contracts

---

7. *E.g.*, N.Y.Ins.Law § 154 (McKinney 1966) (life, accident, health, annuity); Pa.Stat.Ann. tit. 40, § 751 (1954) (accident and health); Pa.Stat.Ann. tit. 40, § 813 (1954) (workmen's compensation); Pa.Stat.Ann. tit. 40, § 477b (Supp.1970) (general section).

8. *E.g.*, Cal.Ins.Code § 10290 (West 1955) (disability) (if not disapproved in 30 days); N.J.Rev.Stat. § 17:35B–4 (Supp.1968) (life); N.J.Rev.Stat. §

17:38–1 (Supp.1953) (accident and health); Ohio Rev.Code Ann. § 3915.14 (Page 1953) (life); Wis.Stat. § 204.-31(3) (g) (2) (1967) (accident and sickness).

9. See §§ 6.8, 7.2 *infra*.

10. See § 2.11 *infra*.

11. For an example of a rather drastic and consciously undertaken standardi-

negotiated without primary reliance upon an assumption that the insurer offers only a limited range of forms of insurance, and the purchaser must accept one of these if he desires insurance with the company. It is for this reason that insurance is referred to as a contract of adhesion.[12]

§ 2.10(c) EFFECTIVENESS OF DIFFERENT TECHNIQUES COMPARED

To what extent do the various techniques for standardization of policy forms and endorsements afford representation to the interests of insurance companies, individual policyholders, and the public?

Under each of the techniques that involves legislative or administrative participation to any extent, there is opportunity for representation of the interests of all parties—insurers, policyholders, and the public. Only the insurers have an effectively organized lobby, however; policyholder interests and the public interest in a sound insurance system are independently represented to very little extent except insofar as individual legislators and administrators take the initiative in such representation. Thus, standardization by cooperation among insurers is effective in advancing the interests of policyholders and the public only insofar as these latter interests are consistent with those of the insurers. Perhaps in most respects there is consistency of interests, both as to the degree of standardization of insurance contracts and as to the choice of particular provisions over others that might be considered for use in a standard form. Examination of the development of automobile insurance forms bears out this point. But it also discloses some instances of competition between, on the one hand, the interests of the insurers as they have been appraised by the insurers' representatives, and on the other hand, public and policyholder interests as an objective observer might appraise them.[1]

SECTION 2.11　A STUDY IN STANDARDIZATION: AUTOMOBILE AND OTHER LIABILITY INSURANCE FORMS

§ 2.11(a) DEVELOPMENT OF THE STANDARD FORMS

Much of the standardization of policy forms occurs through voluntary cooperation among insurance companies. The automobile policy is the product of such cooperation, controlled only to a very limited extent by statutes and administrative rulings. The automobile

---

zation of policy forms by one company, John Hancock Mutual Life Insurance Company, see Ward, *Policy Simplification*, 1959 Ins.L.J. 535.

12. Concerning rights at variance with policy provisions, many of which can

be traced to recognition that insurance contracts are contracts of adhesion, see Chapter 6 *infra*.

1. See § 2.11(b), (c), and (d) *infra*.

policy is also the most prevalent form of policy involving both property and liability insurance, and is ideal as a specimen for study of the process of development of policy forms.

The standard provisions for automobile policies are prepared by cooperation among insurers through industry committees and national rating organizations. Publications issued to the companies by the rating organizations contain the standard provisions and instructions for preparation of policies by the companies. Allowance is made for the use of different policy forms by various combinations and modifications of standard provisions.

The adoption by cooperating stock and mutual casualty insurers of a nationally standardized form for automobile liability insurance policies first occurred in 1935.[1] Medical payments coverage was added in 1939.[2] The national rating organization for automobile physical damage insurance—the National Automobile Underwriters Association—joined the collaborating group at the time of the 1941 revision, and the standardized provisions were extended to automobile fire, theft, collision, and other physical damage coverages.[3] The next major revision occurred in 1955. It was preceded by a full review of the policy forms by representatives of the cooperating groups, and changes made at that time are of interest both for their effect on automobile insurance coverage and as an example of the process of voluntary standardization. Very soon thereafter a family automobile policy form was developed, including revisions definitely advantageous to policyholders. Also, package policies including coverage unrelated to the automobile risk were developed at about this time, but they have not been as widely used as the family automobile policies. Another major revision occurred in the automobile liability coverage, effective in 1966, and forms for liability coverages unrelated to automobiles were likewise revised at that time.

§ 2.11(b) THE 1955 AND 1958 REVISIONS OF AUTOMOBILE INSURANCE FORMS

(1) GENERALLY

Substantial changes in the coverages of the standard automobile form occurred at the time of the 1955 revision. Examples will be presented first, and then some generalizations about the process will

1. Faude, *The 1955 Revision of the Standard Automobile Policy—Coverage: Insuring Agreements and Exclusions*, 1955 ABA Section Ins. L. Proceedings 48, reprinted 1955 Ins.L.J. 647 [hereinafter cited as follows: Faude 48, 1955 Ins.L.J. at 647]; Thomas, *Other Provisions—Declarations and Conditions*, 1955 ABA Section Ins. L. Proceedings 56, reprinted 1955 Ins.L.J. 652. The Committee on Automobile Insurance Law of the American Bar Association also partic-

ipated in developing the first standard automobile insurance form. *Ibid.* See also Rust, *Automobile Liability Insurance Trends*, 1935–1936 ABA Section Ins. L. Proceedings 25, 26–27; *Report of the Committee on Automobile Insurance Law*, 1935 ABA Section Ins. L. Program & Committee Reports 8–9.

2. Faude 48, 1955 Ins.L.J. at 647.

3. *Ibid.*

be advanced. The 1958 revision did not supersede the 1955 form; rather, it merely created an additional form for a new package of coverage, called family automobile insurance.[1] Its provisions, somewhat expanding previous coverage to the benefit of policyholders generally, will be referred to by way of comparison with the 1955 provisions as they are discussed.

(2) MEDICAL PAYMENTS COVERAGE

The early form of medical payments coverage, introduced into the standard form in 1939, provided reimbursement for medical and funeral expenses of occupants of the insured automobile.[2] The 1955 revision offered extended benefits to the named insured and relatives residing in the same household when injured or killed as pedestrians or as occupants of the insured automobile or of any automobile not owned by any person in the eligible group.[3] The omission of coverage for injuries to one as an occupant of another automobile owned by a person in the eligible group can be justified on the ground that including such coverage without special upward rate adjustments for insuring one car in a two-car family would in effect allow medical payments coverage for two cars to be purchased for the price of such coverage for one.

The 1955 extension of coverage met a policyholder need by reducing the gap between the scope of a common risk and the scope of readily available coverage. From the point of view of public and policyholder interests it is to be criticized, if at all, only on the ground that further extension would have been even better.

Specific wording was added to the coverage to make it clear that the coverage extended to expenses of preparing and furnishing artificial teeth, limbs, and other prosthetic devices. This clarification seems desirable.

Consideration was given to modifying the clause declaring that, to be covered, medical and other expenses must be "incurred within one year from the date of accident." But no change was made. One of the draftsmen, in discussing the 1955 version, called attention to a decision [4] allowing an insured to recover reimbursement under this coverage when he made an advance contract and payment for medical services after the accident and before the expiration of one year, even though the treatment in question (such as surgery) could not be

1. For the complete text of the "1958 Standard Family Automobile Liability Policy," which includes the non-liability coverage forms, see Risjord & Austin, Automobile Liability Insurance Cases—Standard Provisions and Appendix 54–81 (1964) [hereinafter cited Risjord & Austin]. For excerpts from that form, see nn.15, 25, 26 *infra.*

2. Faude, *The 1955 Revision of the Standard Automobile Policy—Cov-* *erage; Insuring Agreements and Exclusions,* 1955 ABA Section Ins. L. Proceedings 48, reprinted 1955 Ins. L.J. 647 [hereinafter cited as follows: Faude 48, 1955 Ins.L.J. at 647].

3. *Id.* at 48–49, 1955 Ins.L.J. at 647.

4. Drobne v. Aetna Cas. & Surety Co., 66 Ohio L.Abs. 1, 115 N.E.2d 589 (Ct. Apps.1950). See also § 5.10(d) *infra.*

commenced during the year.[5] He added that such decisions might in time create a need for "revising this one-year requirement, lest the premium on foresight should become distorted to a temptation for the claims-conscious." [6] The failure to revise the policy form can be defended on the ground that the suggested interpretation of the clause is a distortion not likely to be followed by other courts generally,[7] and that it is not feasible to extend the language of policy forms to the lengths required to forestall or counteract all strained judicial interpretations. If this interpretation were generally followed, however, the result would be to make coverage depend upon the shrewdness of the injured person in making an advance contract for services, rather than upon the character of the fortuitous loss suffered—a plainly undesirable situation from the point of view of public interest and the interest of policyholders generally, as contrasted with the interest of the particular injured person, viewed after it appears that he has suffered the kind of injury that will require treatment beyond one year after the injury. But on another ground the retention of this clause, unchanged, is subject to criticism. Why have this one-year limitation in the policy? The pecuniary limit of coverage protects the insurer against any risk so extraordinary that it cannot be appraised well in calculating appropriate premiums. If, in establishing the terms of standard forms, policyholders (or some informed representative of their interests) were making a choice between one-year coverage at a specified premium and the longer-range coverage at the very slight increase in charge necessary to cover the added cost, it seems doubtful indeed that the one-year limitation would be chosen.

(3) THE DEFINITION OF "INSURED"

In general, an omnibus clause of an automobile insurance policy extends the definition of "insured" to persons using the automobile with permission.[8] The earlier forms of omnibus clauses required that the permission be that of the named insured, express or implied.[9] Much litigation resulted over situations in which permission was extended by another member of the family (for example, the insured's

---

5. Faude 49, 1955 Ins.L.J. at 648.

6. *Ibid.*

7. See, *e.g.,* Reliance Mut. Life Ins. Co. v. Booher, 166 So.2d 222 (Fla.App. 1964), 10 A.L.R.3d 458 (1966) (insurer not liable for payment for plastic surgery performed after the end of the 52-week coverage period although surgeon had been "engaged" prior to end of the period without payment or predetermination of fee, because the expense had not been incurred within that period; *Drobne* seemingly distinguished, however, because there the services had been engaged under a binding contract and payment had been made in advance).

8. See § 4.7 *infra.*

9. "III. Definition of Insured. With respect to the insurance for bodily injury liability and for property damage liability the unqualified word 'insured' includes the named insured and also includes any person while using the automobile and any person or organization legally responsible for the use thereof, provided the actual use of the automobile is by the named insured or with his permission. . . ." *1947 Standard Basic Automobile Liability Policy,* Risjord & Austin 4.

spouse) to a third member of the family (for example, a nephew) [10] or to one outside the family.[11]   The 1955 revision broadened the definition of "insured" to include the spouse of the insured even without proof of permission and any other person using the vehicle with the spouse's permission.[12]   One reason for the expansion was to make the policy coverage the same as if both husband and wife were named as insureds, thus sparing companies the nuisance arising from requests to name both spouses as insureds even though the car was owned by one alone.   Such requests were to be expected from knowledgeable applicants, since the same premium was charged whether one or both spouses were named as insureds.[13]

The 1955 broadening of the definition of "insured" was good as far as it went, but it did not go far enough.   Omnibus clauses have consistently bred controversy and litigation.   They were developed in response to a need and public demand, sometimes expressed in legislation.[14]   The need is broader than the scope of the clauses offered, however, and one charged with representing public and policyholder interests in developing policy forms probably would have been pressing constantly for more expansion than has occurred in the definition of "insured."   Of course each expansion produces somewhat higher insurance costs per automobile, but added benefits are more than commensurate with added costs to the extent that wasteful controversies over applicability of more restrictive omnibus clauses are avoided.   Even those current omnibus clauses that have been expanded somewhat beyond the 1955 version [15] are a spawning ground for

10. See, e.g., Hunter v. Western & So. Indem. Co., 19 Tenn.App. 589, 92 S.W. 2d 878 (1935) (husband of named insured lent car to fifteen-year-old nephew who, in turn, allowed a friend to drive the car; held, no coverage for the liability of either the nephew or his friend arising out of an accident that occurred while the friend was driving, because coverage of the nephew's liability was excluded by a policy provision requiring the driver to conform to minimum age requirements and the friend was not driving with the permission of either the named insured or an *adult* member of the named insured's household, as required by the omnibus clause).   See also Annot., 4 A.L.R.3d 10 (1965), especially at 33–34.

11. See, e.g., State Farm Mut. Auto. Ins. Co. v. Porter, 186 F.2d 834 (9th Cir. 1950), 52 A.L.R.2d 499 (1957) (wife of named insured lent car to third person with whom she was visiting; held, coverage under omnibus clause of accident occurring while third person was driving car although wife's use and loan of car were without the express consent of the named insured). See also Annot., 4 A.L.R.3d 10, *passim* (1965).

12. "III.   Definition   of   Insured. (a) With respect to the insurance for bodily injury liability and for property damage liability the unqualified word 'insured' includes the named insured and, if the named insured is an individual, his spouse if a resident of the same household, and also includes any person or organization legally responsible for the use thereof, provided the actual use of the automobile is by the named insured or such spouse or with the permission of either. . . ."   Risjord & Austin 18–19.

13. See Faude 49–50, 1955 Ins.L.J. at 648.

14. Cal.Ins.Code § 11580.1(d) (West Supp.1970).   See § 4.7(a) *infra*.

15. *E.g.*, "Persons Insured.   The following are insureds under Part I [Bodily Injury and Property Damage Liability]:

"(a) With respect to the owned automobile,

   "(1) the named insured and any resident of the same household,   .

   "(2) any other person using such automobile, provided the actual use

heavily fact-oriented controversies—the kind that depend on debatable inferences of fact from disputed testimony and thus lead to costly litigation. This is the inevitable result of causing coverage to depend on whether express or implied permission was given for use of the car by or on behalf of someone whose permission is required.[16] Moreover, in addition to the public interest against such waste there is a strong public interest in measures that increase the probability that motorists who are held liable for injuries will also be financially responsible.[17] Thus, it would seem to be plainly in the public interest —and probably in the long range interest of the companies as well— to expand the omnibus clause so that coverage would extend at least to every driver of the insured car other than a converter.[18]

(4) "DRIVE OTHER CARS" COVERAGE

Changes in the "Use of Other Automobiles" clause, also commonly referred to as the "Drive Other Cars" or "DOC" coverage, were contemporaneously declared to be among the most significant of the 1955 revisions.[19] This clause, previously applying only to liability and medical payments coverage, was made to apply also to collision coverage for operation of another private passenger automobile by the named insured or his spouse.[20] Previously, when the borrower of

thereof is with the permission of the named insured;

"(b) With respect to a non-owned automobile,

"(1) the named insured,

"(2) any relative, but only with respect to a private passenger automobile or trailer,

provided the actual use thereof is with the permission of the owner;

"(c) Any other person or organization legally responsible for the use of

"(1) an owned automobile, or

"(2) a non-owned automobile, if such automobile is not owned or hired by such person or organization, provided the actual use thereof is by a person who is an insured under (a) or (b) above with respect to such owned automobile or non-owned automobile.

"The insurance afforded under Part I applies separately to each insured against whom claim is made or suit is brought, but the inclusion herein of more than one insured shall not operate to increase the limits of the company's liability.

"Definitions. Under Part I:

"'named insured' means the individual named in Item 1 of the declarations and also includes his spouse, if a resident of the same household;

"'insured' means a person or organization described under 'Persons Insured' . . .."

1958 Standard Family Automobile Liability Policy, Risjord & Austin 57–58.

16. See § 1.6 *supra* and § 4.7(b) (1) and (c) *infra*.

17. See §§ 4.7(a), 4.8(d) *infra*.

18. See § 4.7(c) *infra*.

19. Faude 51–52, 1955 Ins.L.J. at 649.

20. "V. Use of Other Automobiles. If the named insured is an individual or husband and wife and if during the policy period such named insured, or the spouse of such individual if a resident of the same household, owns a private passenger automobile covered by this policy, such insurance as is afforded by this policy under coverages A [Bodily Injury Liability], B [Property Damage Liability], C–1, [Basic Medical Payments], E–1 [Collision or Upset], E–2 [Convertible Collision or Upset] and E–3 [Collision or Upset] with respect to said automobile applies with respect to any other automobile, subject to the following provisions:

"(c) Under coverages E–1, E–2 or E–3, this insurance applies only with

an insured car was in a collision while driving the borrowed car, the insurer paying the owner under his collision coverage was entitled to be subrogated to the owner's tort claim against the borrower. At first, insurers rarely asserted this subrogation claim, unless the borrower had insurance that would cover the loss. Shortly before the 1955 revision, however, some insurers became more active in doing so. For an additional charge an endorsement could have been purchased to protect the borrower in this situation, but it was not widely purchased.[21] The industry draftsmen, heeding the anguished complaints that arose from this gap in coverage, undertook to improve the situation in the 1955 revision. It was for this reason that they made the DOC coverage applicable to collision insurance. But because of their anxiety to avoid stimulating subrogation actions they inserted a condition that the DOC collision insurance of the borrower's policy would apply only if there was no other insurance applicable to the loss, whether in favor of the borrower, the owner, or any other interest.[22] Thus, if the owner had collision coverage, the borrower's DOC collision coverage was inapplicable, and he still was subject to a claim by the owner's insurer as subrogee to the owner's tort claim against the borrower.[23] The problem was further aggravated by the fact that the liability coverage (both under the omnibus clause of the owner's policy and under the DOC clause of the borrower's policy) was inapplicable because of an exclusion of injury to or destruction of property "in the charge of" the person claimed to be liable.[24] It is difficult to believe that this situation would have been tolerated had there been a participant in the process of revision charged with representing policyholder interests. To the credit of industry draftsmen, however, it should be noted that their 1958 revision of the family automobile form dealt with the problem very well indeed from the

respect to a private passenger automobile while being operated or used by such named insured or spouse. . . .

"(d) This insuring agreement does not apply:

.   .   .

"(4) under coverages E–1, E–2 or E–3, to any loss when there is any other insurance which would apply thereto in the absence of this insuring agreement, whether such other insurance covers the interest of the named insured or spouse, the owner of the automobile or any other person or organization."

National Bureau of Casualty Underwriters, Standard Provisions for Automobile Combination Policies, Basic Automobile Liability and Physical Damage Form (1955).

21. Faude 51, 1955 Ins.L.J. at 649.

22. See the quoted provision, subparagraph (d) (4), n.20 *supra*. See also Faude 52, 1955 Ins.L.J. at 649.

23. See, *e.g.*, Reserve Ins. Co. v. Fabre, 243 La. 982, 149 So.2d 413, *cert. denied*, 375 U.S. 816 (1963) (litigation arising out of a 1956 collision, though not involving the question of liability of a borrower's collision insurer).

24. **"Exclusions.** This policy does not apply:

.   .   .

"(f) under coverage B [Property Damage Liability], to injury to or destruction of property owned or transported by the insured, or property rented to or in charge of the insured other than a residence or private garage injured or destroyed by a private passenger automobile covered by this policy .   .   .." Risjord & Austin 25.

policyholders' point of view. Under that form the owner's collision coverage is double-interest (that is, the interest of the borrower as well as the owner is protected, and no longer can the owner's collision insurer proceed against the borrower as subrogee to the owner's tort claim against him).[25] Also, under that form the borrower's DOC collision coverage is excess insurance, applying only to whatever extent the loss is not covered by the owner's collision insurance and is not excluded from coverage by the borrower's deductible.[26]

The 1955 revision expanded DOC coverage in other ways, also. Previously this coverage had applied only so long as the policyholder continued to own the automobile described in the policy. The 1955 revision omitted this qualification, thereby continuing DOC coverage after disposition of the described car, even before amendment of the policy to describe the car obtained as a replacement, and even when an interval occurs between disposition of the described car and acqui-

---

25. "PART III—PHYSICAL DAMAGE

"Definitions. The definitions of 'named insured' . . . in Part I [see n.15 *supra*] apply to Part III, and under Part III:

" 'Insured' means (a) with respect to the owned automobile (1) the named insured and (2) any person or organization, other than a person or organization engaged in the automobile business or as a carrier or other bailee for hire, maintaining, using or having custody of said automobile with the permission of the named insured; (b) with respect to a non-owned automobile, the named insured and any relative provided the actual use thereof is with the permission of the owner . . .."

Risjord & Austin 66–67.

26. "PART III—PHYSICAL DAMAGE
. . .

"Coverage E—Collision. To pay for loss caused by collision to the owned automobile or to a non-owned automobile but only for the amount of each such loss in excess of the deductible amount stated in the declarations as applicable hereto.

. . .

"Other Insurance. If the insured has other insurance against a loss covered by Part III of this policy, the company shall not be liable under this policy for a greater proportion of such loss than the applicable limit of liability of this policy bears to the total applicable limit of liability of all valid and collectible insurance against such loss; provided, however, the in-

surance with respect to a temporary substitute automobile or non-owned automobile shall be excess insurance over any other valid and collectible insurance." Risjord & Austin 65, 68.

In Mancuso v. Rothenberg, 67 N.J.Super. 248, 170 A.2d 482 (App.Div.1961), the "other insurance" clause quoted above was held to be ambiguous, and the court allowed recovery against the borrower's collision insurer by the owner and the owner's subrogated collision insurer for the full amount of collision damage to the borrowed car, less a $50 deductible in the borrower's policy. The court rejected the contention that the coverage provided by the borrower's policy was excess insurance because the owner had collision coverage and that, since the owner's policy limits were not exhausted, there was no liability under the borrower's policy. Stressing the phrase "if the *insured* has other insurance," the court construed the clause to mean that coverage under the borrower's policy was excess insurance only when the "other insurance" on the borrowed car was taken out specifically by or for the benefit of the borrower. The court also rejected the contention that the borrower was an additional insured under the owner's collision coverage, since it was first raised on appeal. It seems doubtful that this litigation would have produced the same result if the interrelationship of the definition of "insured" under the owner's policy (see n.25 *supra*) and the "other insurance" clause in the borrower's policy had been properly raised.

sition of a replacement,[27] as might happen when the described car is totally destroyed in a collision. Another expansion of the DOC coverage concerned the use of hired automobiles. Before the 1955 revision, coverage did not extend to "the frequent use of hired automobiles"; the 1955 form allowed coverage except as to cars "furnished for regular use" by the policyholder or members of his household.[28]

The two expansions of coverage referred to in the next preceding paragraph probably benefit relatively few policyholders. It might be argued, therefore, that they are unnecessary additions to a package that the ordinary policyholder will be virtually forced to take, if he wants coverage at all. But they are desirable additions in avoiding pitfalls likely to be overlooked by the few policyholders who need such coverage.[29] Moreover, the added cost is slight and, as explained elsewhere, the spreading among policyholders of the costs for a package of insurance that includes numerous fringe coverages tends to produce equity among policyholders since no policyholder needs all the fringes, each needs some, and their needs tend to balance out.[30]

(5) THE CLAUSE CONCERNING FINANCIAL RESPONSIBILITY LAWS

The 1955 revision adds an introductory phrase to the clause concerning financial responsibility laws. With the new phrase quoted and the substance of the remainder briefly summarized, the clause provides: "when this policy is certified as proof of financial responsibility for the future under the provisions of the motor vehicle financial responsibility law of any state or province, . . ." the insurance afforded by the policy shall comply with requirements of financial responsibility laws up to the limits of coverage, and the insured agrees to reimburse the company for any payments the company is obligated to make under this clause but not obligated to make under other provisions of the policy.[31]

One effect of a certification is to prevent the company from prevailing against an injured person upon certain defenses it has against the policyholder, such as misrepresentation in the application for insurance.[32] The provision concerning consistency of the policy with financial responsibility laws was never intended by the industry draftsmen to deprive an insurer of these defenses on policies not certified. Also, this was quite manifest since in all states having financial responsibility laws, a contrary interpretation would have rendered completely nugatory those provisions in the policy establishing

27. Faude 52, 1955 Ins.L.J. at 649.

28. *Ibid.*

29. Compare the proposition that insurers should not be allowed to enforce qualifications of coverage that defeat reasonable lay expectations; § 6.3 *infra.*

30. See §§ 2.11 (d) and 8.4(b) *infra.*

31. Thomas, *The 1955 Revision of the Standard Automobile Policy: Other Provisions—Declarations and Conditions,* 1955 ABA Section Ins. L. Proceedings 56, 60, reprinted 1955 Ins.L.J. 652, 654–655 [hereinafter cited as follows: Thomas 60, 1955 Ins.L.J. at 654–655] See also Risjord & Austin 27–28.

32. See § 4.8(c) *infra.*

all the various defenses referred to in the financial responsibility laws as defeated by certification. Even so, the courts of a small minority of jurisdictions construed the clause on financial responsibility laws as a voluntary assumption by the insurer, even as to uncertified policies, of the specific burdens imposed by financial responsibility laws with respect to certified policies.[33] The 1955 amendment of this clause was designed to counter this minority doctrine,[34] and it appears to have been a fully justifiable change.

It might be suggested that the 1955 amendment is antagonistic to the public interest in assurance of financial responsibility of drivers so that tortiously injured victims may be compensated. This public interest lends support to a candid restriction on the freedom of contract, such as the statutory provision in New Hampshire that conduct of the insured that would violate the terms of various provisions customarily included in liability policies will not defeat liability.[35] But it is debatable whether this interest outweighs the disadvantages of imposing on all insured drivers the added cost of maintaining for the benefit of victims the coverage of those insureds who commit breaches of their policy obligations (*e.g.*, by failing to render assistance and cooperation to the insurer). Debatable also is the further question whether it is appropriate for a court to impose such a restriction on freedom of contract, when the legislature has not done so.[36] Moreover, in view of the unresolved debate over desirability of the result reached by the minority cases, industry draftsmen are not fairly subject to criticism for clarifying their policy forms to avoid that result.

Retention of the reimbursement clause seems wise and fair. The same is true of the use of the surcharge for certified policies, though it would seem the surcharge should have been higher, to achieve equity among policyholders, since the added costs of providing the insurance under certified policies appears to have been far greater than the income from the surcharge.

---

33. See Thomas 62, 1955 Ins.L.J. at 656.

34. For an example of its effectiveness in doing so, see Lynch-Davidson Motors v. Griffin, 182 So.2d 7 (Fla.1966), enforcing a clause declaring the financial responsibility law applicable only after the policy is certified, and distinguishing Howard v. American Serv. Mut. Ins. Co., 151 So.2d 682 (Fla. App. 3d Dist.1963), 8 A.L.R.3d 382 (1966), as not involving such a contractual requirement of certification.

35. "[N]o statement made by the insured or on his behalf, and no violation of exclusions, conditions, other terms, or language contained in the policy, and no unauthorized or unlawful use of the vehicle except as provided in paragraph VI of this section, whether or not a premium charge has been made and paid, shall operate to defeat or avoid the policy so as to bar recovery for such accidents within said limits of liability." N.H.Rev. Stat.Ann. § 268:16(III) (1966). See Annot., 1 A.L.R.2d 822 (1948), the subject of which is the New Hampshire provision.

36. If a court is to impose such a restriction, it would seem that the legal doctrine should be placed frankly on the ground of a judicially imposed regulation of the contract rather than on the spurious ground of interpretation. See Chapter 6 *infra*.

(6) SEVERABILITY OF INTERESTS

In earlier policy forms there was a provision, under the title "Limits of Liability," declaring that the inclusion of more than one insured under policy coverage would not operate to increase the limits. Under the 1955 revision the clause was changed to read as follows:

"Severability of Interests. The term 'the insured' is used severally and not collectively, but the inclusion herein of more than one insured shall not operate to increase the limits of the company's liability."[37]

Suppose that one lends his car to another and that the borrower damages the lender's garage when returning the car. Under the old policy form, it was debatable whether coverage was excluded because the damage was to "property owned or transported by the insured," the lender. With the new severability of interest clause, it is clear that the "insured" for the purpose of this claim is the borrower, not the lender, and the exclusion does not apply.[38] This is another illustration of a desirable broadening of coverage by amendments.[39]

§ 2.11(c) THE 1966 REVISION OF AUTOMOBILE AND LIABILITY INSURANCE FORMS

The first nationally standardized liability policy form was that developed for automobile liability insurance in 1935. Its provisions were easily adaptable for use in other liability policies, and in time standardization was extended to all the common types of liability insurance. The 1966 revision made significant changes in all these liability forms. It also changed the comprehensive automobile policy forms for the various other coverages as well as automobile liability insurance.

One change concerns the pattern of the policy. Earlier forms presented the coverage provisions in a group at the outset, just following the declarations, and the various qualifications of coverage (including "exclusions" and "conditions") in a separate group much later in the policy form.[1] Under the 1966 pattern the special qualifications of each particular coverage, usually called "exclusions," appear immediately after that coverage.[2]

Under the coverage provisions of earlier policy forms the company agreed to pay on behalf of the insured sums the insured becomes "legally obligated to pay as damages because of bodily injury, sick-

---

37. Risjord & Austin 27.

38. See Thomas 65, 1955 Ins.L.J. at 657–658.

39. See § 2.11(d) *infra*.

1. See, *e.g.*, Risjord & Austin, Automobile Liability Insurance Cases—Standard Provisions and Appendix 16–32, 56–81 (1964) [hereinafter cited Risjord & Austin].

2. See Wendorff, *The New Standard Comprehensive General Liability Insurance Policy*, 1966 ABA Section Ins., Neg. & Comp. L. Proceedings 250, 251–252. See also Appendix G *infra*.

ness or disease, including death at any time resulting therefrom, sustained by any person, caused by accident" and arising out of a specified activity. For example, under the automobile liability coverage, the specified activity was "the ownership, maintenance or use" of the insured automobile, or of other automobiles in limited circumstances.[3]

The 1966 form, among definitions, provides that " 'bodily injury' means bodily injury, sickness or disease sustained by any person" and that " 'damages' includes damages for death and for care and loss of services resulting from bodily injury." The new coverage clause provides that the company will pay on behalf of the insured sums the insured becomes "legally obligated to pay as damages because of bodily injury" to which the coverage applies, "caused by an occurrence" and arising out of a specified activity.[4] This change in the form of the provisions about "bodily injury," "death" and "damages" clarifies the point that one cannot double the amount within policy limits by claiming that death is a separate injury; it is treated as part of the original injury even when it occurs at a substantially later time.[5]

The 1966 form declares that " 'occurrence' means an accident, including injurious exposure to conditions, which results, during the policy period, in bodily injury . . . neither expected nor intended from the standpoint of the insured." One purpose of these changes in provisions about "accident" and "occurrence" was similar to that just noted in relation to "bodily injury"—"to clarify the intent with respect to the time of coverage and the application of policy limits . . .," [6] particularly in situations involving a related series of events attributable to the same factor, making it clear that such a series is to be treated as only one accident or occurrence in the application of policy limits.[7] Also, the phrase "including injurious exposure to conditions" was used to forestall any requirement that the injury result from a sudden event. This phrase in the definition of "caused by occurrence" makes the latter term suitable for use when the intent is to cover liabilities imposed by law for injuries caused by ingestion or inhalation of foreign substances, such as noxious fumes, over an extended period of time.[8] This expression favoring coverage is matched, however, by another aspect of the change that may prove disadvantageous to policyholders. Apparently the phrase "including injurious exposure to conditions, which *results,*

---

3. The quotations are from the 1955 form. See Risjord & Austin 16.

4. See Appendix G *infra.* The phrase "ownership, maintenance or use" is retained.

5. See Obrist, New Comprehensive General Liability Policy—A Coverage Analysis 13 (Defense Research Institute Monograph Series, 1966) [hereinafter cited as Obrist].

6. Obrist 6.

7. See *ibid.*

8. *Ibid. Cf.* Beryllium Corp. v. American Mut. Liab. Ins. Co., 223 F.2d 71 (3d Cir. 1955), 49 A.L.R.2d 1256 (1956), finding coverage under a comprehensive general liability insurance policy, without the aid of such a clarifying clause, for accidental death from repeated absorption of a poisonous substance over a long period of time.

during the policy period, in bodily injury . . .," was intended
to make coverage depend on whether bodily injury results during the
policy period,[9] with the consequence that, if this intent is enforceable
in the courts, an insurer might escape liability for known exposures
by cancelling or declining to renew coverage before bodily injury
resulted.[10]   Another purpose of the new definition of "occurrence"
was to forestall application of the concept of fortuity from the point
of view of the injured party [11]—certainly a justifiable objective.[12]
But the language chosen—"neither *expected* nor intended from the
standpoint of the insured"—is broader than it should be to serve this
purpose, and may prove to be a source of trouble for policyholders
and a source of litigation over coverage.[13]

These are examples of a host of changed phrases in the policy
form.   They serve to illustrate that the principal objective of the
draftsmen seems to have been "to clarify intent" that coverage be
less extensive than it has sometimes proved to be under court interpretations of the earlier forms.   Another example pointing this way
is a narrowing phrase in the omnibus clause—"provided his actual
operation or (if he is not operating) his actual use thereof is *within
the scope of such permission,* . . . ." [14] This change seems highly objectionable from the point of view of policyholder and public
interests.[15]

Another change that seems objectionable from the policyholder
and public interest points of view was an attempted narrowing of the
scope of the duty to defend.[16]

§ 2.11(d) SOME GENERALIZATIONS ABOUT EVOLUTION OF AUTOMOBILE AND OTHER LIABILITY FORMS

It has been noted earlier that standardization of policy forms by
cooperation among insurers is effective in advancing the interests of
policyholders and the public only insofar as they are consistent with
those of the insurers.[1]   The history of standard automobile insurance
forms suggests that public and policyholder interests have sometimes
been fairly well served.   It is within the enlightened self-interest of
the industry, after all, to develop forms of coverage that serve public
needs and desires and minimize dissatisfactions that might lead to reduced business or to outcries for more restrictive public regulation or
even more substantial governmental intrusion into the insurance busi-

---

9. See Obrist 6; Tarpey, *The New
Comprehensive Policy: Some of the
Changes,* 33 Ins.Counsel J. 223, 224
(1966).

10. Concerning ways of defining time
limits of coverage generally, see § 5.-
10(d) *infra.*

11. Obrist 6.

12. See § 5.4(a) *infra.*

13. See § 5.4(c) *infra.*

14. See Appendix G *infra.*

15. See § 2.11(b) (3) *supra* and § 4.7(c)
infra.

16. See § 7.6(c) *infra.*

1. Section 2.10(c) *supra.*

ness. But it also seems plain that the evolution of the standard forms has sometimes been less quickly and surely responsive to public and policyholder interests than would have been the case had there been participants in the consultations charged specifically with representing these interests, even when in conflict with the interests of the industry as appraised by its representatives. For example, separate representatives of public and policyholder interests (or one representative trying to serve well both these interests, which may themselves come into conflict) probably would have urged discontinuance of the one-year limitation in the medical payments coverage,[2] urged earlier expansions of this coverage to injuries other than those occurring to occupants of the insured vehicle,[3] urged earlier and further expansions of the group of drivers covered under the omnibus clauses,[4] balked at the very unsatisfactory revision of DOC coverage in 1955,[5] though applauding the improvements in this coverage incorporated into the 1958 family automobile form,[6] and urged earlier attention to the problem the industry draftsmen heeded in the 1955 clause on severability of interests.[7] Far more disturbing, however, is the tenor of the 1966 revisions. They seem to reflect an overriding aim to narrow the coverage [8] and fortify the policy defenses available to the company. The most favorable thing that can be said for the 1966 revisions is that in the process of fortifying defenses the draftsmen also produced a policy structure that contributes to greater clarity.[9] Even though the primary motivation for the new policy structure may have been the protection of company interests (for example, placing exclusionary clauses immediately after the coverage provision to

2. See § 2.11(b) (2) *supra.*

3. *Ibid.*

4. See § 2.11(b) (3) *supra.*

5. See § 2.11(b) (4) *supra.*

6. *Ibid.*

7. See § 2.11(b) (6) *supra.*

8. See § 2.11(c) *supra.*

9. The 1966 policy structure does not always favor clarity, however. Physical separation of the definitions of terms from the contexts in which they are used may lead to confusion, especially when terms are defined inconsistently with ordinary usage. Consider two examples. First, several coverage provisions declare that the company will pay damages because of bodily injury "caused by an occurrence." One who has read such a provision without turning back to the definition of "occurrence" in the "jacket" might be surprised to learn that this definition purports to re-

quire that the bodily injury be "neither expected nor intended from the standpoint of the insured." The second example concerns one who, being uninformed about the meshing of the comprehensive general liability coverage and the automobile liability coverage, reads in clause II(e) of the 1966 comprehensive general liability form that insureds are protected "with respect to the operation, for the purpose of locomotion upon a public highway, of mobile equipment registered under any motor vehicle registration law." He might be surprised to learn that "mobile equipment" is defined in a very special way that apparently is intended to exclude every "automobile." He might also wonder that this proposition is left to implication whereas the proposition that "automobile" does not include "mobile equipment" is explicitly stated in the definition of "automobile." Avoiding an overlap between the comprehensive general liability coverage and the automobile liability coverage is surely defensible, but the 1966 policy structure makes the meshing of the two coverages less clear than it could be.

which they relate in order to reduce the risk of their being disregarded in court tests) the result is to be applauded. But other aspects of the 1966 revisions are less praiseworthy and are destined to produce trouble for policyholders, and perhaps for courts and the industry too, as litigation develops over the meaning of some of the new and more restrictive phrases.[10]

Appraisal of the evolution of automobile and other liability insurance forms should take account also of a trend to which all the major revisions until that of 1966 had notably contributed—the trend toward expanded units of coverage. Has the expansion been desirable? It might be suggested that as the units of coverage available to policyholders grow larger and necessarily more expensive, it becomes increasingly difficult for one who desires a minimum of coverage to obtain it without paying for other coverage that he does not desire or need. Certainly it is true that many of the expansions have dealt with aspects of coverage that probably are not needed by most policyholders. This might be said, for example, of some of the expansions of DOC coverage in 1955,[11] or of the expansive application of the idea of severability of interest assured by a 1955 amendment.[12] It is true that most policyholders have needs for some of the fringes of coverage not needed by policyholders generally. But does the inclusion of all such fringes in one standard package tend to place potential policyholders in the position of being required to buy a case of dozens of exotic spices in order to get a little pepper and cinnamon?

In part at least, the answer to contentions that the automobile and liability insurance packages are growing too large lies in the fact that the differing values of the fringes of coverage to different policyholders tend to average out, each having a need for a few of them but not all. If some inequity among policyholders remains, perhaps it can be justified as a permissible variation within a rating category broad enough to be administratively feasible.[13]

Another factor favoring these expansions is that the likelihood of costly litigation over fringe questions of coverage is reduced as the number of exceptions and qualifications of coverage is reduced. Also, most of the expansions that have been occurring can be defended as dealing with gaps of the kind that can be covered at little cost but cause intense policyholder dissatisfaction on those rare occasions when they become operative and catch a policyholder by surprise. Few ideas about insurance have, over the years, caught public attention so much as the motion that the bold print giveth and the fine print taketh away. Expansions of the units of coverage in the evolution of automobile and other liability insurance forms are consistent with the aim of reducing the number of shocking surprises suffered by policyholders.[14]

10. See § 2.11(c) *supra*.

11. See § 2.11(b) (4) *supra*.

12. See § 2.11(b) (6) *supra*.

13. See § 8.4(b) *infra*.

14. Concerning other manifestations of this aim, consider the principle of honoring reasonable expectations, § 6.3 *infra*.

CHAPTER 3

THE PRINCIPLE OF INDEMNITY

SECTION 3.1   INTRODUCTION TO THE PRINCIPLE OF INDEMNITY

§ 3.1(a) THE MEANING OF THE PRINCIPLE

Insurance is a system for wide distribution of accidental losses.[1] One aspect of this system is the transfer of loss from an insured to an insurer by means of an obligation upon the insurer to confer an offsetting benefit (the insurance proceeds). To speak of "transferring loss" or providing an "offsetting benefit" is to imply that the value of the benefit shall not exceed the loss. That is, insurance is aimed at reimbursement, but not more. The principle that insurance contracts shall be interpreted and enforced consistently with this objective of conferring a benefit no greater in value than the loss suffered will be referred to in this book as the principle of indemnity. This principle does not imply, in converse, that the benefit must be no less than the loss. That is, partial reimbursement of a loss is not offensive to the principle of indemnity.

§ 3.1(b) POTENTIAL EVILS OF NET GAINS FROM INSURANCE

Any opportunity for net gain to an insured through the receipt of insurance proceeds is inconsistent with the principle of indemnity. Legal doctrine recognizes two principal evils from such opportunities —inducements to wagering and inducements to destruction of insured lives or property. A third evil, less often brought to the surface in legal discourse, is social waste incident to the fact that the benefits paid under an insurance plan are necessarily only a percentage of premiums paid; the remaining percentage, representing various ele-

---

1. See § 1.2(a) *supra.*

88

ments of overhead, is not well spent when it purchases only a wager for fortuitous profits rather than a socially useful protection against fortuitous losses.

It may be suggested that a distinction should be drawn between vocational wagering, in which the person who is to receive insurance proceeds enters into the transaction as a regular business, and non-vocational wagering, involving isolated transactions.[1] The purpose of making the distinction is, of course, to impose more severe legal restrictions against the former on the ground that it involves more substantial evils than the latter. But cases have arisen in which it might be argued that vocational wagering involving insurance policies has performed a socially useful function. For example, there was a time when industrial life insurance policies commonly contained no provisions for cash surrender value. In some communities a business developed of purchasing assignments of these policies.[2] It may well be that this was a form of vocational wagering, but enforcement of such assignments might also have served a socially useful purpose in enabling poverty-stricken holders of industrial life insurance policies to realize something on the potential value of contracts they might otherwise have allowed to lapse. Provision for cash surrender value is an alternative way of making it possible for the insured to realize the value of the contract in this situation. But if the person whose life is insured has become uninsurable, the value of the contract is much greater than cash surrender value, and the insured would have no enforceable way of realizing that higher value during his lifetime if assignments were void. Perhaps it is also true that the likelihood that a transaction will operate as an inducement to murder is greater in non-vocational wagering in one respect, since the vocational wagerer ordinarily would be in the business of making money by wagering only rather than by murdering as well. On the other hand, most non-vocational life-insurance wagerers would be related by consanguinity or affinity to the person whose life was insured, and love and affection would tend to counter the influence of the economic inducement to murder. Thus, in summary, there is not a clear-cut preponderance of policy arguments supporting the suggested distinction between vocational and non-vocational wagering, and little support can be found for the distinction in insurance law as it has developed.

An adverse judgment of wagering has been a major influence in development of the principle of indemnity and associated doctrines. A number of harmful social consequences have been thought to be caused by wagering. Patterson observed that they include the encouragement of idleness, vice, and a socially parasitic way of life, with a resulting increase of impoverishment, misery, and crime, and the discouragement of useful business and industry.[3] English judges

1. See Patterson, Essentials of Insurance Law 170–172 (2d ed. 1957).

2. See, *e.g.*, Hack v. Metz, 173 S.C. 413, 176 S.E. 314 (1934), 95 A.L.R. 196 (1935) (holding the assignments invalid).

3. Patterson, *Insurable Interest in Life*, 18 Colum.L.Rev. 381, 386 (1918).

were openly hostile to wagers, but wagering contracts, including those cast in the form of insurance, were nevertheless valid at common law.[4] In the United States, led by decisions in New England,[5] a majority of courts ruling on the point, in the absence of any controlling statute, have declared wagers illegal.[6]

§ 3.1(c) WAYS OF PREVENTING NET GAIN

The first four subdivisions below present in outline form the whole range of legal techniques that might reasonably be used to prevent net gain from receipt of those benefits that are stated by the insurance contract to be due. The techniques are described and classified here according to the nature of the results they produce. Terms of art that have become associated with various techniques are also sometimes indicated. The fifth subdivision concerns an associated problem regarding disposition of "unearned" premiums.

(i) *The Nonliability Rule.*[1] Under this rule, if enforcing the terms of the insurance contract would produce a net gain for the person designated to receive insurance proceeds, then the insurer will have a full defense and will not be liable for any part of the stated benefits. The situation presenting the strongest case for this result is that in which the person designated to receive insurance benefits has suffered no economic loss from the event insured against. It might also be argued that this result should be reached if the designee has suffered loss but less in amount than the stated benefits; the penalty thus imposed for seeking fortuitous gain is a stronger deterrent to wagering than mere denial of benefits in excess of loss would be. But such a penalty also has the disadvantage of denying socially useful reimbursement of fortuitous loss. Thus a reasoned judgment concerning the desirability of this rule depends on appraisal of the relative weight of these opposing interests.

(ii) *Liability-for-Net-Loss Rules.*[2] This set of rules declares that the insurer will be liable up to the amount of the net economic loss suffered by the person designated to receive insurance benefits, but in no case for more. "Net economic loss," as used here, means the remainder found by subtracting the real value of other rights of

---

4. See *id.* at 392, and Dalby v. India & London Life Assur. Co., 15 C.B. 365, 139 Eng.Rep. 465 (Ex.Ch.1854).

5. *E.g.*, Amory v. Gilman, 2 Mass. 1, 10–11 (1806).

6. *E.g.*, J. B. Lyon & Co. v. Culbertson, Blair & Co., 83 Ill. 33, 39, 25 Am.Rep. 349, 353 (1876). *Contra*, Dunman v. Strother, 1 Tex. 39, 46 Am.Dec. 97 (1846) (wager on horse race); Trenton Mut. Life & Fire Ins. Co. v. Johnson, 24 N.J.L. 576 (Sup.Ct.1854) (since wagering contracts were not illegal at common law, and no statute is applicable in New Jersey, there is no requirement of insurable interest for life insurance). See generally 1 Richards, Law of Insurance 329–330, § 65 (5th ed. Freedman 1952), and concerning New Jersey developments after *Johnson*, see *id.* at 371–372; Fulda Insurable Interest in Life, *New Jersey View*, 1 Rutgers L.Rev. 29 (1947).

1. Concerning applications of this rule, see § 3.1(d) *infra*.

2. Concerning applications of this type of rule, see § 3.1(d) *infra*.

indemnification (which might include rights against other insurers) from the designee's gross loss caused by the event insured against. This result can be reached by either of two different types of rules:

First, *an Insurance-as-Excess-Coverage Rule.* This kind of rule treats the right against the insurer as "excess" coverage, available only to the extent that other rights are not effective for indemnification.

Second, *a Proration Rule.*[3] This kind of rule treats the right against the insurer and one or more other rights as proratable, each being proportionately reduced just enough that their total value does not exceed the loss sustained.

(iii) *Modified-Gross-Liability-to-Designee Rules.*[4] These types of rules impose liability on the insurer up to the amount of the gross economic loss, but with the provision that to the extent necessary to prevent net gain incident to multiple rights of indemnification, the other indemnification rights of the person designated to receive insurance benefits are dealt with in one or the other of the following ways:

First, *a Subrogation Rule.*[5] Under this type of rule the designee's other rights of indemnification pass to the insurer (who may get indemnity or proratable contribution).

Second, *an Other-Rights-as-Excess-Coverage Rule.* Under this type of rule the designee's other rights of indemnification are reduced or terminated (thus being treated as "excess coverage").

(iv) *Distributed-Gross-Liability Rules.*[6] These rules impose liability on the insurer for the full amount of the benefits stated in the insurance contract, but with the provision that the insurer is liable to pay part of the amount to another rather than to the person designated in the contract to receive the insurance benefits. There are two types of such rules, and two sub-types of the second type, as follows:

First, *an All-Excess-to-Another Rule.* Under this type of rule the insurer pays to the designee an amount not exceeding his net loss, and it pays all of any excess to another person or persons sustaining loss.

Second, *Excess-over-Gross-Loss Rules.* These rules require the insurer to pay to another only the excess above gross loss, but with the further provision that, to the extent necessary to prevent net gain, the designee's other rights of indemnification are affected in one of the following two ways: First, *a Subrogation Rule.* Under this type of rule the designee's other rights of indemnification pass to the insurer (who may get either indemnity or proratable contribution). Second, *an Other-Rights-as-Excess-Coverage Rule.* Under this

---

3. Concerning application of this type of rule, see § 3.11(b) *infra.*

4. Concerning applications of this type of rule, see § 3.1(d) *infra.*

5. Concerning application of this type of rule, see § 3.10 *infra.*

6. Concerning applications of this type of rule, see § 3.1(d) *infra.*

type of rule the designee's other rights of indemnification are reduced or terminated (thus being treated as "excess coverage").

(v) *The "Unearned" Premium Problem.* Any one of the first three of the above four methods of preventing net gain from insurance presents an additional problem as to whether there is an unfair profit to the insurer on the theory that it does not pay as much in benefits as was contemplated in setting premiums. It might be concluded either that there is no obligation to return any part of the premiums or that the insurer must return "unearned premiums." An allocation between unearned and earned premiums might be made on the basis of the ratio between the insurer's enforceable risk of liability and the risk contemplated in setting the premium rates. Often there may be debate with respect to the scope of the risk contemplated in setting premium rates. But occasionally it seems clear that there is a disparity between the risk contemplated in rating and the risk actually insured. For example, if the designees of the policy benefits were never subject to a risk of economic loss from any event purportedly insured against by the policy, there would be no enforceable risk of liability and the entire premium would be "unearned." The desirability of denying insurers the benefit of unearned premiums is, however, only one among the factors influencing development of rules of law concerning disposition of unearned premiums in those situations in which the principle of indemnity is invoked to defeat claims for insurance benefits.[7]

§ 3.1(d) IMPAIRMENT OF THE PRINCIPLE OF INDEMNITY TO SERVE OTHER PRINCIPLES

Rules of law commonly develop from an accommodation among differing principles that are in some degree conflicting.[1] Consistently with this generalization, rules of insurance law fall short of compelling strict adherence to the principle of indemnity. Among the other principles that come into conflict with the principle of indemnity, three are discussed later in this chapter—the principle of freedom of contract,[2] the principles of equity underlying the doctrine of estoppel,[3] and the principle of repose underlying the doctrine of incontestability.[4]

As already noted,[5] the principle of indemnity is aimed chiefly at guarding against inducements to wagering and to destruction of lives or property. Any system of safeguards incurs costs. Perhaps the most significant costs of safeguards against violations of the principle of indemnity in insurance transactions are increases in the expense of administration and reductions in the flexibility of insurance arrange-

7.   See § 3.3(d) *infra.*

1.   See Keeton, Venturing to Do Justice 164–166 (1969).

2.   See § 3.3(a) *infra.*

3.   Section 3.3(b) (2) *infra.*

4.   See § 3.3(b) (3) *infra.*

5.   See § 3.1(b) *supra.*

ments. From another point of view, impairments of the support that might otherwise be given to principles of efficiency and flexibility are part of the price paid for the advantages realized from adhering generally to the principle of indemnity.

Another principle sometimes coming into conflict with the principle of indemnity deserves note. It is often said that insurance is a personal contract. Usually such a statement refers to the fact that the insurer has an interest in the identity of any person who is to receive benefits under the policy, primarily because of "moral hazards." The insurer is generally supposed to have a free choice of the persons and of the risks it will insure. And it is also supposed that by prudent exercise of this choice the insurer will be able to exclude undesirable persons and risks and thereby reduce the cost of insurance to those it accepts.

If this principle that insurance is personal were given full and rigorous enforcement, it would preclude the use of any among the ways of preventing net gain from insurance that involve payments by the insurer to someone other than a person it has agreed to pay. This would leave available the nonliability rule and the liability-for-net-loss rules as ways of preventing net gain,[6] but would preclude some modified-gross-liability-to-designee rules[7] and all distributed-gross-liability rules.[8] In fact, the principle that insurance is personal often yields to the principle of indemnity and to practical considerations bearing upon its implementation. But undoubtedly the converse is also true—that is, reasoning based upon the personal character of insurance has made inroads upon the principle of indemnity, steering courts away from resort to ways of preventing net gain from insurance that they otherwise might have chosen to use. For example, most courts have declined to order an insurer to pay directly to someone other than the person it had agreed to pay. Thus, they have confronted the hard choice of allowing the insured a net gain or else allowing the insurer to escape with liability for less than it agreed to pay. The pressures for avoiding this dilemma by deviating from the idea that insurance is personal have been growing.[9]

---

6. See § 3.1(c).

7. *Ibid.* It happens that some but not all instances of the third way of preventing net gain presented in § 3.1(c), referred to as modified-gross-liability-to-designee rules, involve impairments of the principle that insurance is personal. For example, subrogation rules remain consistent with the personal character of insurance insofar as they merely allow an insurer to assert in its insured's stead some other claim of its insured against another, but if the other claim of the insured is against an insurer too, then allowing the first insurer to benefit from it is an impairment of the personal character of the insurance provided by the second insurer.

8. See § 3.1(c). This last way of avoiding net gain involves provisions that the insurer make part of its payments to someone other than the person it agreed to pay, thus violating the principle that insurance is personal in character.

9. See, *e.g.*, §§ 3.3(b)(1), 4.3 *infra*.

§ 3.1(e) CHARACTERIZATION OF AN INSURANCE CONTRACT AS A CONTRACT OF INDEMNITY

Property insurance is quite generally referred to as a contract of indemnity. Some writers have called life insurance a contract of indemnity also.[1] Others have insisted that for various reasons it is not a contract of indemnity. For example, it has been observed that no attempt is made to value the insurable interest accurately and that rules concerning duration of the interest,[2] subrogation,[3] and overvaluation are inconsistent with indemnity.[4] It seems a better description of existing circumstances to say, first, that neither life insurance nor any other form of insurance is a pure indemnity contract, second, that all forms of insurance bear the marks of strong influence of the principle of indemnity, and third, that its influence is less extensive in life insurance than in property insurance. Though the generalization that a kind of insurance is or is not an indemnity contract may be useful as a statement of tendency, it is not a reliable guide for answers to specific problems of insurance law. Other illustrations of deviation of insurance law from the principle of indemnity, in relation to property insurance as well as life insurance, have been cited above.[5]

SECTION 3.2 THE HISTORY OF INSURABLE INTEREST DOCTRINE

§ 3.2(a) THE DOCTRINE AS AN AMALGAM

The modern doctrine of insurable interest is an amalgam. The substantive rules constituting the doctrine not only reflect the inroads of other principles upon the principle of indemnity [6] that underlies insurable interest doctrine but also reflect several somewhat inconsistent objectives of the doctrine itself (avoiding inducements to wagering and avoiding inducements to destruction of life or property, and perhaps avoiding waste as well).[7] And the doctrine is the handiwork mainly of two sets of institutions—courts and legislatures—each contributing so much that an assertion that the other is primarily responsible for the doctrine is not likely to go unchallenged. This sec-

---

1. *E.g.*, Richards, Law of Insurance 27–28, § 24 (3d ed. 1925). *But cf.* 1 Richards, Law of Insurance 370, § 89 (5th ed. Freedman 1952): "To call the contract of life insurance a contract of strict indemnity, on the one hand, or, on the other, to isolate it from the general law of insurance and classify it as an investment, as many have done, is unwise. It partakes of the nature of both arrangements."

2. See § 3.3(c) *infra*.

3. See § 3.10 *infra*.

4. Patterson, Essentials of Insurance Law 155 (2d ed. 1957); Patterson, *Insurable Interest in Life*, 18 Colum.L. Rev. 381, 388 (1918). *Cf.* Keckley v. Coshocton Glass Co., 86 Ohio St. 213, 225, 99 N.E. 299, 300 (1912).

5. See § 3.1(d) *supra*.

6. See § 3.1(d) *supra*.

7. See § 3.1(b) *supra*.

tion traces briefly the high points in development of this amalgam in Anglo-American law.

§ 3.2(b) THE STATUTE OF GEORGE II

Later English references to the history of insurable interest doctrine commonly trace its origin to an Act of Parliament in the year 1746, in the nineteenth year of the reign of George II.[1] Just before that time, it had become a prevalent practice to write marine insurance policies by which the underwriters agreed not to demand proof of the interest of the insured in the ship or cargo that was the subject of insurance.[2] The preamble of the Statute of George II declared that these types of contracts had "been productive of many pernicious practices, whereby great numbers of ships, with their cargoes, have either been fraudulently lost and destroyed, or taken by the enemy in time of war   .   .   ." and whereby there was introduced "a mischievious kind of gaming or wagering, under the pretence of assuring the risque on shipping." [3] The statute applied only to marine insurance. It declared that "no assurance or assurances shall be made   .   .   .   interest or no interest, or without further proof of interest than the policy, or by way of gaming or wagering, or without benefit of salvage to the assurer; and that every such assurance shall be null and void to all intents and purposes." [4]

§ 3.2(c) THE STATUTE OF GEORGE III

The second major statutory contribution to English insurable interest doctrine was enacted in 1774.[5] The preamble again made reference to "a mischievous kind of gaming," in this instance in relation to "the making of insurances on lives, or other events, wherein the assured shall have no interest." [6] Nothing was said of the other evil adverted to in the preamble of the marine insurance act of 1746 [7]— the destruction of the subject matter of insurance. Parliament was not prepared, apparently, to charge that no-interest insurance had produced a pernicious practice of murder.

The 1774 act declared that "no insurance shall be made   .   .   . on the life or lives of any person or persons, or on any other event or events whatsoever, wherein the person or persons for whose use, benefit, or on whose account such policy or policies shall be made, shall have no interest   .   .   .." [8]

1. 19 Geo. 2, c.37 (1746).

2. 1 Arnould, Marine Insurance [9 British Shipping Laws] § 364 (15th ed. 1961).

3. 19 Geo. 2, c.37, § 1 (1746).

4. *Ibid.*

5. 14 Geo. 3, c.48 (1774).

6. *Ibid.*

7. See § 3.2(b) *supra.*

8. 14 Geo. 3, c.48 (1774).

§ 3.2(d) BRITISH MARINE INSURANCE ACTS OF 1906 AND 1909

Early in the twentieth century a movement developed for codification and reform of the British law of marine insurance. The Marine Insurance Acts of 1906 and 1909 resulted.[9] A subdivision of the 1906 act concerned insurable interest, and reenacted the earlier statutory declaration that contracts of marine insurance "by way of gaming or wagering" are void.[10] It also defined more explicitly than the Acts of 1746 and 1774 what was meant by "gaming or wagering" contracts.[11] Further development of these explicit provisions occurred in the Marine Insurance (Gambling Policies) Act of 1909.[12]

§ 3.2(e) THE POLICY PROOF OF INTEREST (P.P.I.) CLAUSE AND HONOR POLICIES

As previously noted,[1] it had become a prevalent practice, just before enactment of the Statute of George II in 1746, to write marine insurance policies by which the underwriters agreed not to demand proof of the interest of the insured in the property that was the subject of insurance. When such policies became unenforceable in the courts by reason of legislation, their enforcement was dependent on the "honour" of the underwriter, and they came to be called "honour policies."[2] A form of words commonly used in the early agreements of this type was "policy proof of interest"; hence the terms "policy proof of interest" clause and "P.P.I." clause. Other forms of words that have been used are "interest or no interest," "all interest admitted," "without further proof of interest than the policy itself," and "without benefit of salvage to the insurer."[3] It is supposed that honor policies have been used primarily as a commercial convenience to persons having true interests in the property covered by insurance, but interests that might be very difficult to prove under legal standards. Nevertheless, the opportunity for wagering use is obvious, and the term "wager policy" has been used broadly to include not only pure wagers by those without interest but also honor policies used as a commercial convenience by those having an interest.[4] A policy containing a P.P.I. clause is unenforceable under the English decisions even if the insured has an insurable interest,[5] and the making of

---

9. Marine Insurance Act, 1906, 6 Edw. 7, c.41; Marine Insurance (Gambling Policies), Act, 1909, 9 Edw. 7, c.12.

10. Marine Insurance Act, 1906, 6 Edw. 7, c.41, § 4(1).

11. *Id.* § 4(2).

12. 9 Edw. 7, c.12, § 1(1).

1. See § 3.2(b) *supra.*

2. 1 Arnould, Marine Insurance [9 British Shipping Laws] § 11 (15th ed. 1961).

3. *Id.* § 363.

4. Arnould refers to the latter type as the "genuine *honour policy* as opposed to the mere wager." *Id.* § 11.

5. Cheshire v. Vaughn Bros. Co. [1920] 3 K.B. 240. See Gedge v. Royal Assur. Corp., [1900] 2 Q.B. 214.

such a policy is in some circumstances a criminal offense under the Act of 1909.[6] It may be argued that such a clause is not legally enforceable in the United States, but the P.P.I. clause, or the F.I.A. (full interest admitted) clause of similar import, is commonly used with respect to marine coverage.[7] Of course the parties to such policies act on the assumption that the presence of the P.P.I. or the F.I. A. clause in the policy does not affect the legal enforceability of other coverages in the policy. And this assumption appears to be legally sound.[8]

Skip to p. 101

§ 3.2(f) SOURCES OF THE AMERICAN DOCTRINE

In the United States, insurable interest doctrine appears to have been first recognized in most courts as a matter of decisional doctrine and in the absence of insurable interest legislation in the state. Usually, American courts have turned to English precedents on insurable interest without explicit reference to the fact that the English cases were interpretations and applications of statutes—usually either the Statute of George II or the Statute of George III.[1] In time, however, statutes on insurable interest have been adopted in a number of states. In California, for example, the Insurance Code contains numerous sections on insurable interest (the language of which, however, leaves considerable leeway for judicial interpretation).[2] The New York Insurance Law contains three sections, first enacted in 1939 and drafted with extreme care.[3] A third example of insurable interest legislation is a section of the Texas Insurance Code on insurable interest for life insurance,[4] first enacted in 1953 under the prodding of proponents for change in the decidedly distinctive rule that had prevailed in Texas before the statute.[5] It remains true, however,

---

6. Marine Insurance (Gambling Policies) Act, 1909, 9 Edw. 7, c.12, § 1(2). See 1 Arnould, Marine Insurance [9 British Shipping Laws] § 366 (15th ed. 1961).

7. "Disbursements insurance" is a common example. Originally such coverage applied to money that the master of the vessel spent during the voyage to pay charges incurred in various ways. Though the term is still used in this sense, it is also customary to speak of disbursements insurance as P.P.I. or F.I.A. insurance placed by the hull owner on the vessel in an amount over and above the hull valuation. See Winter, Marine Insurance 278–279, 385–386 (3d ed. 1952). Insurance of "anticipated freight" under an expected contract, not yet made at the time of insuring, is another example of P.P.I. or F.I.A. insurance. See *id.* at 320–321.

8. See Cabaud v. Federal Ins. Co., 37 F.2d 23 (2d Cir. 1930); Hall & Co. v.

Jefferson Ins. Co., 279 F. 982 (S.D. N.Y.1921).

1. See § 3.2(b) and (c) *supra.*

2. *E.g.,* Cal.Ins.Code §§ 280–287, 300–305 (West 1955).

3. N.Y.Ins.Law §§ 146–148 (McKinney 1966). These sections were part of an extensive recodification and revision of the insurance laws of New York enacted as N.Y. Acts 1939, ch. 882. This legislation was the product of a special committee chaired by Professor Patterson. Note, *New York Insurance Code of 1939,* 40 Colum.L.Rev. 880 n.3 (1940). Sections 146 and 147 have been amended since the 1939 recodification. *Ibid.* For a discussion of § 148, see § 3.4(a) (4) *infra.*

4. Tex.Ins.Code Ann. art. 3.49–1 (1963).

5. See § 3.5(d) *infra.*

despite their origin in English statutes, that insurable interest requirements have usually been treated in the United States as aspects of a decisional doctrine.

§ 3.2(g) LEGAL VERSUS FACTUAL INTEREST—THE EMERGENCE OF COMPETING THEORIES

Le Cras v. Hughes [1] was an action on a policy of insurance obtained by naval officers who had captured the Spanish ship "St. Domingo" in the harbor of St. Fernando de Omoa. The interest intended to be covered by the policy was that of the officers and crew of the naval squadron that participated, along with land forces, in the capture. The ship and part of its cargo were thereafter lost by perils of the sea during the voyage intended to be covered. Lord Mansfield observed that the Prize Act and proclamation granting rights to naval personnel participating in capture of an enemy vessel provided the "strongest ground" for upholding the contract against an attack for want of insurable interest. But he added that the expectation of benefit to the captors, growing out of the universal practice of grants by the Crown, was a sufficient interest to meet the requirements of the Statute of George II. Thus in *Le Cras* there was both a legal interest in the ship and cargo and a factual expectation of economic advantage from the continued existence of the ship and cargo (and, conversely, a factual expectation of loss in the event of damage to or destruction of the ship and cargo by the perils insured against).

Lucena v. Craufurd [2] was another case growing out of capture of a foreign vessel. This was an action on a policy of insurance obtained by Royal Commissioners on several vessels and their cargoes. The first count alleged interest in the commissioners who, under Act of Parliament, were authorized in wartime to take possession of ships and cargoes of inhabitants of the United Provinces, then neutral, "detained in or brought in to ports of this Kingdom." [3] The second count alleged interest in the Crown, and that the insurance was obtained for the benefit of the Crown. The third count alleged interest in foreigners. At various times in September, 1795, several of the vessels that were the subject of insurance were lost by perils of the sea during the voyage from the foreign port of seizure and before having reached a port of the Kingdom. There was a declaration of hostilities against the United Provinces on September 15, before the loss at sea of one of the vessels, the "Zeelelye", and after the loss of the others. After a verdict for the commissioners on the first count, and for the defendant below on the second and third counts, the House of Lords ordered a new trial because of misdirection of the jury on the first count. In the opinions on first appeal [4] were sugges-

---

1. 3 Doug. 81, 99 Eng.Rep. 549 (K.B. 1782).

2. 2 Bos. & P.N.R. 269, 127 Eng.Rep. 630 (House of Lords 1805); on appeal from second trial, 1 Taunt. 325, 127 Eng.Rep. 858 (House of Lords 1808).

3. 35 Geo. 3, c. 80, § 21 (1795).

4. 2 Bos. & P.N.R. 269, 127 Eng.Rep. 630 (House of Lords 1805).

tions that no recovery could be allowed under the first count for loss of the "Zeelelye" but that an opportunity ought to be allowed for the development of evidence that would sustain a recovery under the second count averring interest to be in the King. At the second trial there was a verdict for plaintiffs on the second count as to all the vessels, and it was sustained on appeal.[5] Thus, the conflicting views expressed in opinions in the House of Lords on first appeal were not critical to the disposition of the case, but they are of particular interest because of their influence on development of the doctrine of insurable interest. Support can be found in these opinions for at least three distinct and inconsistent theories of insurable interest.

The opinion of Lawrence, J., after noting various definitions of insurance, concludes that the contract of insurance "is applicable to protect men against uncertain events which may in anywise be of disadvantage to them . . .."[6] He observed that cases had arisen in which recovery on an insurance contract had been disallowed because the interest was too uncertain to be the subject of insurance, but for the reason of "impossibility of valuing, and not the want of property . . .."[7] To confine insurance "to the protection of the interest which arises out of property . . ." would be to add "a restriction to the contract which does not arise out of its nature."[8] Thus Lawrence formulated a view of insurable interest based on a broadly conceived factual expectancy of advantage from nonoccurrence of a peril insured against, or, conversely, factual expectancy of loss from its occurrence.

Lord Eldon, in contrast, declared that the "interest" required under the Statute of George II is an "intermediate thing between a strict right, or a right derived under a contract, and a mere expectation or hope," and that he could find no way of identifying that intermediate thing "unless it be a right in the property, or a right derivable out of some contract about the property, which in either case may be lost upon some contingency affecting the possession or enjoyment of the party."[9] He added: "If the Omoa case [*Le Cras v. Hughes*] was decided upon the expectation of a grant from the crown, I never can give my assent to such a doctrine. That expectation, though founded upon the highest probability, was not interest, and it was equally not interest, whatever might have been the chances in favour of the expectation."[10] The conclusion seems inescapable that Lord Eldon's conception of insurable interest included a requirement of some kind of legally enforceable right. It also appears that, when finding such a legally enforceable right, he would have found an insurable interest even if the factual expectation was that the right

---

5. 1 Taunt. 325, 127 Eng.Rep. 858 (House of Lords 1808).

6. 2 Bos. & P.N.R. 269, 301, 127 Eng. Rep. 630, 642 (House of Lords 1805).

7. 2 Bos. & P.N.R. at 301–302, 127 Eng.Rep. at 643.

8. 2 Bos. & P.N.R. at 302, 127 Eng.Rep. at 643.

9. 2 Bos. & P.N.R. at 321, 127 Eng.Rep. at 650.

10. 2 Bos. & P.N.R. at 323, 127 Eng. Rep. at 651.

would be economically worthless. "Suppose A. to be possessed of a ship limited to B. in case A. dies without issue; that A. has 20 children, the eldest of whom is 20 years of age; and B. 90 years of age; it is a moral certainty that B. will never come into possession, yet this is a clear interest." [11]

Professor Vance took the position that an expectation is not an insurable interest unless it "has a basis of legal right" and that the facts in *Lucena v. Craufurd* well illustrate what is meant by an expectation supported by a legal basis since "this expectation was based on an Act of Parliament, which must operate if the vessels come to port." [12]   This view seems inconsistent with the Lawrence opinion, because Lawrence did not require a basis of legal right. It seems inconsistent with the Eldon opinion both because Eldon did not require an expectation of advantage and because Eldon appeared not to regard the Act of Parliament as a sufficient legal basis for insurable interest.   Indeed Lord Eldon said, "If I were bound now to state my opinion judicially upon this first count [alleging interest in the commissioners authorized by the Act of Parliament to take possession of the ships and cargoes], I should be obliged very strongly to say, that the claims of the Plaintiffs could not be supported   .   .   ." [13]   A passage in a third opinion in *Lucena v. Craufurd*, attributed to seven members of the tribunal (Graham, B., Le Blanc, Rooke, Grose, and Heath, JJ., MacDonald, Ch.B., and Sir James Mansfield, Ch.J.), may be read as consistent with Professor Vance's position. It declares: "Where there is an expectancy coupled with a present existing title, there is an insurable interest .   .   .," [14] and it appears to proceed on the theory that the commissioners had such an expectancy.   But another passage in the same opinion seems inconsistent with requiring more than a mere expectation: "The case of *Le Cras v. Hughes* was a case of mere expectation, and the circumstances were not near so strong in favour of the assured as the circumstances of this case.   The doctrine there laid down by that great expositor of marine law Lord Mansfield, twenty-four years ago, has been recognized as law in subsequent cases; and if it were now to be decided that the interest of these commissioners was not insurable, it would render unintelligible that doctrine upon which merchants and underwriters have acted for years, and paid and received many thousand pounds." [15]   This passage seems to support the Lawrence view that a broadly conceived factual expectancy of advantage from nonoccurrence of a peril insured against is sufficient for insurable interest under the Statute of George II.

11. 2 Bos. & P.N.R. at 324, 127 Eng. Rep. at 652.

12. Vance, Law of Insurance, 157–158 (3d ed. Anderson 1951).

13. 2 Bos. & P.N.R. at 326, 127 Eng. Rep. at 652.

14. 2 Bos. & P.N.R. at 293, 127 Eng. Rep. at 639.

15. 2 Bos. & P.N.R. at 294, 127 Eng. Rep. at 640.

SECTION 3.3 THE NATURE OF INSURABLE INTEREST DOCTRINE

§ 3.3(a) IMPAIRING FREEDOM OF CONTRACT

Because of the distinctive risks associated with opportunities for net gain from receiving insurance proceeds,[1] insurers ordinarily wish to make contracts only with or for the benefit of persons who have an interest in the subject matter of the insurance, whether life or property. Ordinarily, also, they wish to make contracts only to pay benefits not in excess of the interest of the person or persons with whom or for whose benefit they are agreeing to make payments if a described fortuitous event occurs. Thus, they desire ordinarily either to include provisions in their contracts that require, as a contractual matter, a factual expectancy (that is, a factual interest in the preservation of the life or property that is the subject of insurance) or else to ascertain before entering into the contract that such an interest does in fact exist. The former procedure is customarily used for property insurance contracts; they ordinarily contain provisions limiting benefits to an amount not exceeding the interest of the insured. The latter procedure is customarily used for life insurance contracts; commonly they contain no limitations based on interest of the insured or designated beneficiaries, but the usual procedure is to obtain information in the application that gives the insurer a basis for estimating whether an appropriate interest exists before making the underwriting decision to accept the application.

As a result of the business judgments of insurers, therefore, the objectives underlying insurable interest doctrine are served by contractual procedures dictated by the self-interest of insurers. All this is accomplished without resort to a special doctrine of insurable interest.

In view of what has been noted in the preceding paragraph, insurable interest doctrine has no impact in most cases, because ordinarily insurers would not make contracts inconsistent with the doctrine even if it did not exist. The area of its practical impact is the area in which, for one reason or another, insurers would be willing to make and fulfill contracts that are unenforceable under this doctrine. Its impact is as an impairment of the freedom of contract. The doctrine must be justified, if at all, on the ground that the public interests at stake outweigh the interest in freedom of contract. And justification is the more difficult because whenever the doctrine is invoked to produce a result that would not have been accomplished anyway (either by enforcement of the policy provisions, or by enforcement of rights at variance with policy provisions that would have been available apart from the insurable interest doctrine), the result is to allow an insurer to deny coverage for which it has received consideration (if the benefits claimed were within policy provi-

---

1. See § 3.1(b) *supra*.

sions) or to which it would otherwise be bound because of the nature of its dealing (if the benefits were claimed on a basis of rights at variance with policy provisions). Thus, whenever insurable interest doctrine makes a difference, it produces a perfect defense for an undeserving insurer. To justify such a result, one must find that the public interest designed to be served by the doctrine has overpowering weight. That interest is, of course, the prevention of evils associated with opportunities for net gain from insurance.[2]

Why is it that the public interest would not be adequately served by procedures voluntarily developed by insurers to serve their own self-interest in avoiding the greater risks they would assume in making contracts that create opportunities for net gain through insurance proceeds? In part the answer to this question concerns not legitimate insurers but others who might wish to cloak strictly gambling transactions in an insurance form. The pernicious practices referred to in preambles to the Statutes of George II and George III suggest a realistic need for an insurable interest doctrine as part of any overall system of legal restraints on gambling.

Are there circumstances also in which legitimate insurers, as distinguished from gambling syndicates seeking to use the form of insurance as a cloak, would choose to make and fulfill contracts opening up opportunities for net gain were it not for insurable interest doctrine? If one examines the question as of the time a claim is presented, certainly it is true that insurers would sometimes choose to pay claims for business reasons, such as maintenance of good public relations and avoidance of expensive litigation, even though it appeared the claimant was making a profit. This situation might come about because of lack of foresight and skill in drafting policy provisions to protect adequately against opportunities for net gain. But it might also come about because of a considered decision to use standard policy provisions lacking fully effective restrictions against net gain. That is, if one examines the question whether legitimate insurers may choose at the underwriting stage, as distinguished from the claim stage, to leave open opportunities for net gain, he finds reasons for an affirmative answer. An example is the honor policy of marine insurance, on which an insurer pays claims voluntarily despite the fact that it could successfully assert a defense of want of insurable interest. These policies may be defended as designed to serve the commercial convenience of persons having legitimate interests in the property covered by the insurance, but interests difficult to prove under legal standards.[3] Even so, it is clear that they can be used for wagering. Insurers would be reluctant to decline to underwrite or to deny liability after underwriting even in cases in which they suspected wagering, however, since an insurer's reputation for doing so might cause it to lose a lucrative business in honor policies. Other il-

2. See § 3.1(b) *supra.*   3. See § 3.2(e) *supra.*

lustrations of underwriting decisions to allow opportunities for net gain can be found.[4]

Once a decision to underwrite has left open an opportunity for net gain under the contract terms, it is quite likely that the insurer, for business reasons such as those just referred to, will decline to raise a defense of want of insurable interest unless there are also other reasons for denying the claim. This fact casts doubt on the effectiveness of insurable interest doctrine to serve the public interest. In general there is no public representative available to invoke the doctrine. Indeed, there is even wide support for a doctrine, ill-considered though it be, that only the insurer can raise the question of insurable interest.[5] If that doctrine is accepted, then the public interest is poorly served because the insurer may choose not to invoke the doctrine, or when invoking it may do so for reasons extraneous to and perhaps inconsistent with those underlying the doctrine. Indeed, an examination of cases in which the doctrine is invoked leads one to suspect that the motivations for its being invoked are seldom concerned with the objectives the doctrine is designed to achieve. Rather, it appears that the defense is usually invoked to defeat a claim when the insurer has evidence or at least strong suspicions of another basis for denying the claim that might be more difficult to establish —usually fraud.[6]

In summary, the doctrine of insurable interest has its acknowledged impact only as an impairment of the freedom of contract. But curiously its enforcement depends primarily on the initiative of the insurer in contesting the claim and thereby causing it to come to the attention of the court, and enforcement is even further dependent on the insurer's initiative under the ill-considered rule that only an insurer may invoke the doctrine. Thus enforcement of the doctrine is left largely to the initiative of one of the parties whose freedom of contract it is impairing. In fact, then, its principal impact is as a defensive tool for insurers who wish to deny claims for other reasons, such as suspected fraud, and find it easier to establish this ground of defense.

§ 3.3(b) THE RIGHT TO QUESTION INSURABLE INTEREST

(1) GENERALLY

Though most of the judicial statements as to who may raise the question of insurable interest are either dicta or alternative grounds of decision at best, a clear majority of them state that only the insurer can raise the lack of insurable interest; the theory apparently is

usually held only insurer can raise question of lack of insurable interest

---

4. *E.g.*, insurers often decline to include any subrogation clause in health and accident insurance policies. See § 3.10 (a) *infra*.

5. See § 3.3(b) (1) *infra*.

6. *Cf.* Stebane Nash Co. v. Campbellsport Mut. Ins. Co., 27 Wis.2d 112, 133 N.W.2d 737 (1965), 16 A.L.R.3d 760 (1967). See also the discussion of *Macaura v. Northern Assur. Co.*, § 3.4 (b) (2) *infra*.

that the insurer, being a party to the contract, has a legitimate interest in raising want of insurable interest whereas nonparties have no such standing.

The assertion that only the insurer can raise lack of insurable interest has been made in relation to both property insurance [1] and life insurance.[2] Many decisions, however, are inconsistent with this assertion,[3] and it seems doubtful indeed that it represents a prevailing view.

Plainly there is an inconsistency between the idea that insurable interest doctrine is an impairment of freedom of contract imposed to serve overriding public interests and the idea that only the insurer can invoke the doctrine. The objectives of the doctrine of insurable interest would be better served if others who have suffered from the risk insured against, though not named as insureds or beneficiaries of the insurance contract, were permitted to use the doctrine as a means of recovering the insurance proceeds from one without insurable interest. This, of course, involves an intrusion on the principle that the contract is personal.[5] But it seems a more defensible accommodation among competing principles than that implicit in the rule that only an insurer is entitled to invoke the insurable interest doctrine.

(2) ESTOPPEL

As previously noted,[6] standard forms of property insurance commonly include provisions that in no event is the insurer to be liable for an amount in excess of the interest of the insured in the covered property. Thus an insurer desiring to defend on the ground that the insured has no interest or has only an interest of less value than the amount claimed can ordinarily do so under the terms of the contract rather than finding it necessary to invoke an insurable interest doc-

---

1. *E.g.*, Wheeler v. Insurance Co., 101 U.S. 439, 25 L.Ed. 1055 (1879).

2. *E.g.*, Poland v. Fisher's Estate, 329 S.W.2d 768 (Mo.1959). See Annot., 175 A.L.R. 1276 (1948); Vance, Law of Insurance 199 (3d ed. Anderson 1951). *But see* 1 Richards, Law of Insurance 372 (5th ed. Freedman 1952).

3. See, *e.g.*, Butterworth v. Mississippi Valley Trust Co., 362 Mo. 133, 240 S.W.2d 676 (1951), 30 A.L.R.2d 1298 (1953) (action for an accounting brought by insured's legal representatives against a trust to which the policy had been assigned by the insured's creditor, to whom the policy had been assigned by the insured, alleging lack of insurable interest and wagering); Allgood v. Wilmington Sav. & Trust Co., 242 N.C. 506, 88 S.E.2d 825 (1955) (permitting an action for money had and received against the trustee of a

pension trust, to get at proceeds of an insurance policy on a theory that involved challenging as a wagering arrangement the rules of the pension trust, purporting to make the proceeds payable to the trust). See also authorities allowing attacks upon the validity of assignments of life insurance policies, § 3.5(c) *infra*. And compare the former Texas rule on insurable interest for life insurance, under which the insurer could not invoke the doctrine as a defense but one to whom proceeds would go upon disqualification of the designated beneficiary was permitted to invoke it, § 3.5(d) *infra*.

4. See § 3.3(a) *supra*.

5. See § 3.1(d) *supra*.

6. See § 3.3(a) *supra*. See also Appendix A *infra*.

trine that overrides contract provisions. Even in this situation, however, the insurable interest doctrine may become relevant because the claimant asserts that the conduct of various representatives of the insurer estops it to stand on the restrictive provisions of the contract.[7] The insurer responds with a contention that the alleged claim, whether under policy provisions or at variance with them, is unenforceable because of want of insurable interest in the claimant. Thus the insurer prevails unless it is estopped also to assert lack of insurable interest.

It is arguable that the public interests underlying insurable interest doctrine (particularly interests in avoiding the evils of gambling and of inducements to destruction of life or property for profit),[8] outweigh the interests of fairness between contracting parties that underlie the doctrine of estoppel. If this be so, then the insurable interest defense should not be defeated by estoppel. This position has considerable support in judicial opinions.[9] Rather than taking either this or the opposite view that estoppel is fully applicable in this context, many courts have taken the intermediate position that an insurer cannot be estopped from asserting a complete want of insurable interest but that estoppel may be invoked to prevent a challenge that the interest is worth less than the amount otherwise due under the policy provisions, once some interest is established.[10] Most pronouncements on the subject do not make a clear choice among these competing views. The intermediate position is perhaps the more persuasively supported, however, at least in the sense that it is more readily reconcilable with results reached in a larger percentage of the cases.

(3) INCONTESTABILITY

Life insurance contracts generally contain, and in many states are by statute required to contain, a clause providing that the policy shall be "incontestable" after a specified period, usually either one year or two years. Such clauses are directed against stale defenses, and in general their objectives are like those of statutes of limitation. The need for protection against stale defenses is especially apparent as to cases in which the person whose life was insured was one party to the contract and the defense is raised after his death. Moreover, there is reason for special concern that the economic arrangements made for the benefit of survivors shall be reliable.

In contrast, it may be argued that the doctrine of insurable interest is based on public policies, concerned with wagering and inducements to destruction of life or property, and should be enforced despite unfairness to individual insureds who have been misled and

---

7. Concerning estoppel generally, see § 6.4 *infra*.

8. See § 3.1(b) *supra*.

9. *E.g.*, Colver v. Central States Fire Ins. Co., 130 Kan. 556, 287 P. 266 (1930); Rube v. Pacific Ins. Co., 131 So.2d 240 (La.App.1961).

10. See, *e.g.*, Liverpool & London & Globe Ins. Co. v. Bolling, 176 Va. 182, 10 S.E.2d 518 (1940). See also 4 Appleman, Insurance Law 112, § 2247 (rev. ed. 1969).

despite the desirability in general of requiring contests of life insurance policies to be instituted within a short period after the policy is written.

The public policy arguments underlying incontestability are thus in conflict with those underlying the requirement of insurable interest, and it is not surprising that there is conflict as to which shall prevail. It has been suggested that decisions upholding the defense of want of insurable interest despite an incontestable clause can be distinguished from those denying such defense; the former, it has been said, involve clauses voluntarily included in the policy whereas the latter are based upon a statutory requirement of inclusion of such a clause.[11] Usually, however, the rule is stated broadly (without qualification as to inclusion of the clause in the policy under statutory compulsion) that an incontestability clause does not bar the defense of want of insurable interest.[12]

§ 3.3(c) THE TIME WHEN INSURABLE INTEREST MUST EXIST

It is commonly said that insurable interest at the time of effecting a life insurance contract supports the contract despite want of insurable interest at the time of death.[1] As to property insurance, on the other hand, there was an early statement by Lord Chancellor

---

11. See, *e.g.*, Bogacki v. Great-West Life Assur. Co., 253 Mich. 253, 234 N.W. 865 (1931), denying the defense of want of insurable interest. An interesting sequel involving some of the same persons appears in Sun Life Assur. Co. v. Allen, 270 Mich. 272, 259 N.W. 281 (1935).

12. See *e.g.*, Bromley's Adm'r v. Washington Life Ins. Co., 122 Ky. 402, 92 S.W. 17 (1960); Wharton v. Home Security Life Ins. Co., 206 N.C. 254, 173 S.E. 338 (1934). See also 2 Appleman, Insurance Law § 764 n.46 (rev. ed. 1966). Concerning other aspects of the enforcement of incontestability clauses, see generally § 6.5(d) *infra*.

1. *E.g.*, Dalby v. India & London Life Assur. Co., 15 C.B. 365, 139 Eng.Rep. 465 (Ex.Ch.1854); Connecticut Mut. Life Ins. Co. v. Shaefer, 94 U.S. 457, 24 L.Ed. 251 (1876); Speroni v. Speroni, 406 Ill. 28, 92 N.E.2d 63 (1950). See 2 Appleman, Insurance Law 123, § 763 n.32 (rev. ed. 1966). *Contra*, McBride v. Clayton, 140 Tex. 71, 166 S.W.2d 125 (1935); but consider the effect of the 1953 Texas statute on this decision, § 3.5(d) *infra*. The rule that insurable interest at the time of effecting life insurance supports the contract despite want of insurable in-

terest at the time of death has been applied to validate a ten-year extension of term insurance on the basis of insurable interest at the inception of the original ten-year term. Marquet v. Aetna Life Ins. Co., 128 Tenn. 213, 159 S.W. 733 (1913). See also Butterworth v. Mississippi Valley Trust Co., 362 Mo. 133, 240 S.W.2d 676 (1951), 30 A. L.R.2d 1298 (1953) (insurable interest of beneficiary at time of "conversion" of term to ordinary life policy sufficient to validate later assignment of policy to beneficiary and reassignment of it by him to trust not having an insurable interest at insured's death).

Dalby applied this distinctive life insurance rule to a reinsurance agreement, even though reinsurance of a primary insurer's obligation on a life policy is more like property insurance than life insurance in that it is plainly intended as a contract of indemnity. Even if insurable interest at the time of loss were required in cases of reinsurance of a primary insurer's obligation on a life contract, however, the requirement would be met despite the primary insurer's lack of insurable interest at that time, so long as the primary insurer's obligation was enforceable. But in the peculiar circumstances of *Dalby*, the primary insurer's obligation had been discharged by settlement.

Hardwicke, in *Sadlers Co. v. Badcock*,[2] that it is necessary for the insured to have an interest at the time of insuring and at the time of the loss by fire. The person who obtained the insurance in that case was a lessee for years, whose lease expired before the fire occurred. Thus, the assertion of a necessity for insurable interest at the time of insuring was dictum and doubtlessly ill considered. It has been repeated often, however, in judicial opinions[3] and elsewhere, and many writers have been led to suppose that it is the majority rule.[4] But surely this is not so. Vance observed that, by well settled rules, an open marine policy may properly cover a return cargo to be purchased in the future; a floating policy on a fluctuating stock of goods is enforceable as to after-acquired property; alienation of insured property does not defeat recovery if the insured reacquires it before loss; the risk attaches under a builder's risk policy in proportion as the construction progresses and the builder's interest increases; and reinsurance against risks to be insured by the primary insurer in the future is valid.[5] Vance endorsed the validity of these various types of contracts, since they are not wagers and since valuable business interests would otherwise go unprotected because it often is impracticable to obtain insurance at the moment an interest is acquired. He concluded that the rule requiring insurable interest at the inception of the policy has no further meaning than that a policy intended as a wager will not be enforceable even if the policyholder subsequently acquires an interest in the property.[6] Patterson took the sterner view that there is no need for saving even as much of the rule as escaped Vance's assault. "For the purpose of setting a pious example, the courts might well deny . . . [a recovery to one who has taken out a policy while having no interest or expectation of in-

---

2. 2 Ark. 554, 555, 26 Eng.Rep. 733, 1 Wils.K.B. 10, 95 Eng.Rep. 463 (1743).

3. *E.g.,* Rube v. Pacific Ins. Co., 131 So. 2d 240 (La.App.1961) (alternate holding); Armbrust v. Travelers Ins. Co., 232 Ore. 617, 376 P.2d 669 (1963).

4. *E.g.,* 4 Appleman, Insurance Law 31, § 2122 (rev.ed.1969): "Probably the majority of cases hold that such insurable interest must exist both at the time of making the contract and at the time of loss." Appleman also observes, however: "If the insured had such interest during the duration of the risk and at the time of loss, a few well reasoned opinions . . . hold that sufficient." *Id.* at 32.

5. Vance, Law of Insurance 179–183 (3d ed. Anderson 1951). An interesting example of one of the situations cited by Vance is found in Osborne v. Pacific Ins. Co., 91 R.I. 469, 165 A.2d 725 (1960). Osborne purchased the insured property subject to an outstanding mortgage and took an assignment of a fire insurance policy with the consent of the insurer; the policy contained a standard mortgage clause (see § 4.2(b) *infra.*). Subsequently the mortgage was foreclosed, and the property was sold to a third party with an assignment of the mortgagee's rights under the policy (again with the insurer's consent). The mortgagee's vendee then reconveyed to Osborne and cancelled the insurance, receiving in return some twenty dollars in unearned premiums. Osborne then incurred loss from fire damage and claimed under the policy; held, Osborne could recover since, first, the intervening lack of insurable interest did not terminate Osborne's rights under the policy and, second, the mortgagee's vendee could effectively cancel only the rights the mortgagee had under the policy as mortgagee (see § 4.2 *infra*).

6. Vance, Law of Insurance 182–183 (3d ed. Anderson 1951).

terest and has subsequently acquired an interest], because he started out to wager; but the decision of such a bizarre case would have no effect on wagering generally, and such fanciful dangers ought not to be allowed to interfere with the protection of legitimate interests in a workaday world."[7] Counting opinions to determine a majority view on this point is fallacious not only because most of the pronouncements in accord with Lord Chancellor Hardwicke are dicta, but also because, as Patterson has observed,[8] insurers choose not to invoke a defense which, if successful, would destroy many lucrative kinds of insurance business.

Despite trenchant criticism of the view that an insurable interest is required for property insurance not only at the time of loss but also at the time of effecting the contract, one can find examples of application of the rule to produce undesirable results.[9]

It has been argued, in relation to life insurance, that it would be inequitable to enforce a requirement of insurable interest at the time of the death because this would result in payment of premiums calculated on an original fixed value of an interest in life, represented by the face amount of the policy, in return for a promise to pay a varying sum dependent upon alteration of the value of the interest at the time of death, and that this arrangement would be contrary to fair dealing and common honesty.[10] But the argument is unpersuasive. The quantity of interest and risk in property is as surely variable in amount as the quantity of risk and interest in life. Not only may the value of property change during the period of coverage, but also the loss may be either total or partial. Thus, a property insurance premium purchases coverage for a stated period during which the patterns of risk are changing. Still, fair rating can be achieved by taking these changes into account in setting the overall premium. Similarly, even when premiums for life insurance are paid in periodic installments of equal amount, fair rating can be achieved by taking the changing patterns of risk into account in fixing this amount. The alleged unfairness could also be avoided by allowing

---

7. Patterson, Essentials of Insurance Law 133 (2d ed. 1957).

8. *Id.* at 131.

9. *E.g.*, McCluskey v. Providence Wash. Ins. Co., 126 Mass. 306 (1879). *But cf.* Womble v. Dubuque Fire & Marine Ins. Co., 310 Mass. 142, 144, 146–147, 37 N.E.2d 263, 265–266 (1941): "If the person insured has no insurable interest in the property covered when the policy by its terms would become operative as to that property, the policy never takes effect as valid insurance on the property. McCluskey v. Providence Washington Ins. Co., 126 Mass. 306, 308 [(1879)]. . . .. [T]he insureds [trustees of a church group that had long used the insured church building, but did not have title to it] had an insurable interest in the building when the policy was issued, within the broad definitions of such an interest illustrated by the cases cited above. See also Liverpool & London & Globe Ins. Co., Ltd. v. Bolling, 176 Va. 182 [10 S.E.2d 518 (1940)]. The requirement of an insurable interest when the risk is assumed arose merely to prevent the use of insurance for illegitimate purposes. It should not be extended beyond the reasons for it by excessively technical construction."

10. See, *e.g.*, Dalby v. India & London Life Assur. Co., 15 C.B. 365, 139 Eng. Rep. 465 (Ex. Ch. 1854).

others with an economic interest in the life insured to have the benefit of the insurance.[11]

The contrast between *life* insurance and *property* insurance with respect to the time when insurable interest must exist (at inception of contract for life insurance and at time of loss for property insurance) may seem curious, but it is nevertheless rational. As previously noted,[12] property insurance adheres more closely than life insurance to the principle of indemnity. Strict adherence to the principle of indemnity requires insurable interest at the time of loss, but not at the time of making the contract. Under the principle of indemnity, the insurance benefit must offset loss. One can suffer loss from property damage arising out of an event insured against even though he had no interest at the time the contract was made, but not unless he has an interest in the insured property at the time it is damaged, destroyed or lost. But for life insurance the requirement of insurable interest at inception rather than at the time of loss may be rationally chosen as serving the objectives of the principle of indemnity in most instances, and without some difficulties of administration and sacrifice of other interests (such as that in making life insurance freely transferable) incident to requiring insurable interest at the time of loss.

§ 3.3(d) RETURN OF PREMIUMS WHEN INSURABLE INTEREST WAS LACKING

Vance summarized the law concerning return of premiums in two propositions. First: "When the risk has once attached the whole premium is deemed to be earned, and no portion thereof is returnable, in the absence of a stipulation to the contrary, even though the risk may terminate before the expiration of the term contracted for, unless—(a) Such termination is due to the wrong of the insurer, or (b) Such return is required by statute."[1] Second: "When the risk has never attached, the premium paid is always returnable unless—(a) The contract was rendered void ab initio by the fraud of the insured, or (b) The contract is illegal, and the parties in pari delicto."[2] These two statements might seem to leave little opportunity for the recovery of premiums when policy benefits have been denied because of want of insurable interest. In fact, however, premiums in such cases are very often returned. In the first place, the insurer is likely to tender the return of premiums in the hope of improving its chances of successful defense.[3] Moreover, even if one accepts Vance's statements as authoritative, he may argue that the purchaser of insurance that is invalid for want of insurable interest is ordinarily not

---

11. *Cf.* the Texas rule, § 3.5(d) infra.

12. See § 3.1(e) *supra*.

1. Vance, Law of Insurance 347, § 58 (3d ed. Anderson 1951).

2. *Ibid.*

3. See, *e.g.*, Commonwealth Life Ins. Co. v. Wood's Adm'x, 263 Ky. 361, 92 S.W. 2d 351 (1936); Colver v. Central States Fire Ins. Co., 130 Kan. 556, 287 P. 266 (1930).

in "pari delicto" with the insurer. Even without proof of fraud of the insurer's agent, a majority of the decisions in point have held that one may recover premiums paid with a bona fide belief that the insurance was valid.[4] Probably in most cases the person seeking the return of premiums could prove that his bona fide belief was induced by some type of representation (innocent, negligent, or fraudulent) of the insurer's agent,[5] but it seems doubtful that the majority would require such proof. A few decisions, however, have gone to the opposite extreme of denying the recovery of premiums even upon a showing of purchase with a bona fide belief of validity, induced by fraud of the insurer's agent.[6]

Concern about the inequity of allowing an insurer to collect premiums and then defend against a claim seeking the *promised benefits* has frequently been expressed in reasoning toward a denial of the defense of lack of insurable interest. For example, in one of the early cases involving insurable interest doctrine in English law, the court appeared to proceed on the theory that the choice to be faced was to allow recovery of the face amount of a thousand-pound life insurance contract or else deny relief altogether.[7] Another possibility would have been to hold the contract unenforceable and order a refund of premiums collected, with interest, as a means of redress for the unjust enrichment incident to collection of the premiums and nonpayment of the promised benefits. Such relief falls short of correcting the inequity when the fortuitous event on which the right to benefits turned has in fact occurred, but at least it represents a degree of amelioration of the inequity that makes it easier to accept the idea that on balance the advantages of non-enforcement of the promise to pay benefits outweigh the disadvantages.

SECTION 3.4   INSURABLE INTEREST IN PROPERTY

§ 3.4(a) TYPES OF INSURABLE INTEREST IN PROPERTY

(1) GENERALLY

It has been suggested that there are four broad types of insurable interest in property: property right, contract right, legal liability, and factual expectancy.[1] A contract right may also be a property

---

4. *E.g.*, Commonwealth Life Ins. Co. v. George, 248 Ala. 649, 28 So.2d 910, 170 A.L.R. 1032 (1947); Washington v. Atlanta Life Ins. Co., 175 Tenn. 529, 136 S.W.2d 493, 129 A.L.R. 54 (1940).

5. *E.g.*, Magers v. Western & So. Life Ins. Co., 344 S.W.2d 312 (Mo.App.1961).

6. *E.g.*, American Mut. Life Ins. Co. v. Mead, 39 Ind.App. 215, 79 N.E. 526 (1906) (on demurrer to complaint; the court was influenced by the notion that

a representation concerning validity of the contract was a representation of law).

7. Dalby v. India & London Life Assur. Co., 15 C.B. 365, 139 Eng.Rep. 465 (Ex. Ch. 1854).

1. Harnett & Thornton, *Insurable Interest in Property: A Socio-Economic Reevaluation of a Legal Concept*, 48 Colum.L.Rev. 1162 (1948). See also Stockton, *Analysis of Insurable Inter-*

interest such as a lien, but the concept of contract rights includes other cases in which one who has no property interest nevertheless is by contract so situated in relation to the property insured that he has an economic interest in its preservation.   Legal liability and factual expectancy are considered below.   Representative insurable interest, also discussed below, might be regarded as a fifth division of the concept of insurable interest in property, though most of the cases of representative insurable interest involve also one or more other types of interest.   Since the overlapping among these five types of insurable interest is extensive, and the courts have not given equal recognition to them as meeting the requirements of insurable interest doctrine, one who is seeking to prove insurable interest may profit from analysis of his case in terms of more than one of these types.

(2) LEGAL LIABILITY AS INSURABLE INTEREST

There is insurable interest to support any amount of liability insurance that is in other respects valid, since the legal liability insured against is itself a loss.[2]   Legal liability may also serve as an insurable interest for insurance against damage to property.   For example, a building contractor, being legally liable to the owner for completion of the building, has an insurable interest in the building under construction.[3]   And one who makes a legally enforceable agreement to obtain insurance on property for the benefit of another has an insurable interest supporting a contract of insurance of the property even in his own name.[4]

(3) REPRESENTATIVE INSURABLE INTEREST

It is often useful to have insurance on property taken out by one person for the interest of another.   In such situations it may happen that the person arranging the insurance has an insurable interest in his own right—e.g., because of a property interest, such as a lien, or because of a risk that he will be legally liable in the event of damage or destruction of the property.   But the desirability of allowing him to insure extends to situations and interests as to which he has no insurable interest in his own right, and in fact insurance arrangements

est Under Article Two of the Uniform Commercial Code, 17 Vand.L.Rev. 815 (1964).

2.   See, e.g., Western Cas. & Sur. Co. v. Herman, 318 F.2d 50 (8th Cir. 1963), 1 A.L.R.3d 1184 (1965).   But cf. Bendall v. Home Indem. Co., 238 So.2d 177 (Ala.1970) (named insured's automobile liability policy void because she was not the owner and had no insurable interest to support liability insurance coverage; it would seem the court errs in reasoning that the named insured would have to be "primarily liable for injury to persons or property that might arise out of the operation" of the described car in order to have an insurable interest to support automobile liability coverage; insured's liability for her own negligence in operating the described car, or another car under DOC coverage, is plainly an expectancy of loss arising from legal obligations).

3.   E.g., National Fire Ins. Co. v. Kinney, 224 Ala. 586, 141 So. 350 (1932).

4.   E.g., Liverpool & London & Globe Ins. Co. v. Crosby, 83 F.2d 647 (6th Cir.), cert. denied, 299 U.S. 587 (1936); Shaw v. Aetna Ins. Co., 49 Mo. 578, 8 Am.Rep. 150 (1872).

involving such broad coverage have been quite generally approved. The concept of representative insurable interest[5] includes situations in which the representative is not himself subject to a risk of economic loss from each of the events insured against; it is a more satisfactory rationale than is one dependent upon a showing of personal interest. Though the terminology of "representative" insurable interest is not often used, this kind of interest has long been recognized, particularly for insurance by bailees, trustees, receivers, administrators, and executors. Of course, an assumption underlying representative insurable interest is that the insurance is obtained for the benefit of another. Thus, the question whether this theory can fairly be applied to given circumstances will be resolved in conjunction with a construction of the insurance contract as to persons and interests protected.

(4) FACTUAL EXPECTANCY AS INSURABLE INTEREST

The theory that a factual expectancy of economic disadvantage from damage to property is an insurable interest in that property seems more consistent with the principle of indemnity than does a theory limiting insurable interest to property right, contract right and legal liability.[6] Despite this fact, and despite early roots in *Le-Cras v. Hughes* and the opinion of Lawrence, J., in *Lucena v. Craufurd*,[7] this theory has gained only limited acceptance.[8]

Perhaps the most notable American support for the factual expectancy theory of insurable interest is that developed in New York. Long before any legislation on insurable interest appeared in the New York statutes, the Court of Appeals had carefully considered and approved the factual expectancy theory of insurable interest in *National Filtering Oil Co. v. Citizens' Ins. Co.*[9] National Filtering had licensed Ellis & Co. to use a patent owned by it in Ellis' oil reduction and filtering works. The license was to be exclusive provided Ellis continued normal operations of its works, and was to remain exclusive even if royalties under the licensing contract were diminished because of damage to or destruction of Ellis' plant by fire; in the latter situation National Filtering would be entitled only to guaranteed minimum royalties. National Filtering procured insurance on Ellis' plant as protection against diminution of royalties because of fire damage to the plant; when a fire occurred, the insurer challenged National Filtering's claim on the basis of a lack of insurable interest in Ellis' property. The court held that the risk of loss of royalties above the guaranteed minimum because of damage by fire to the plant was placed by the contract on National Filtering and that this risk "had a direct and necessary connection with the safety of the structures burned. A fire

---

5. *Cf.* Patterson, Essentials of Insurance Law 123–130 (2d ed. 1957).

6. See § 3.4(b) (1) *infra*.

7. See § 3.2(g) *supra*.

8. Harnett & Thornton, *Insurable Interest in Property: A Socio-Economic Reevaluation of a Legal Concept*, 48 Colum.L.Rev. 1162, 1171–1175 (1948).

9. 106 N.Y. 535, 13 N.E. 337 (1887).

destroying them destroyed the royalties *pro tanto,* became the efficient cause of . . . [National Filtering's] loss, and so was established the needed connection between the premises insured and the royalties dependent upon their safety. . . . [A]n interest in property connected with its safety and situation as will cause the insured to sustain a direct loss from its destruction is an insurable interest . . . ."[10] The relationship thus noted by the court might have supported a theory of insurable interest in the property based on a contract right. But the court did not take that course. Instead, after citing three precedents,[11] the opinion declares: "They decide that an interest, legal or equitable, in the property burned, is not necessary to support an insurance upon it; that it is enough if the assured is so situated as to be liable to loss if it be destroyed by the peril insured against . . ." [12]

A section of the New York Insurance Law, first enacted in 1939 [13] and drafted by a committee of which Professor Patterson was chairman,[14] declares that no contract of insurance or property "shall be enforceable except for the benefit of some person having an insurable interest in the property insured . . ." and further declares that insurable interest "shall be deemed to include any lawful and substantial economic interest in the safety or preservation of property from loss, destruction or pecuniary damage."[15] It might be argued that the phrase *"lawful and substantial economic interest"* implies that the expectancy must be coupled with a legal interest. But it seems more reasonable to read "lawful . . . interest" as meaning merely a legitimate interest in the sense that it is not, for example, an interest that exists only because of an expectancy of profit from illegal activity, such as an interest in contraband liquor. This interpretation is supported by the history of the insurable interest doctrine in New York, since it is consistent with the opinion in *National Filtering,* and it should have been expected that the statutory draftsmen would be more explicit in rejecting the doctrine of that opinion if they meant to do so. Moreover, this statute was first enacted as part of a comprehensive set of statutes on insurance, and it seems likely that it was intended to declare the *National Filtering* doctrine rather than to modify it.[16] Certainly there were statutory models of a different ilk to which the draftsmen might have turned if they had intended to require a legally enforceable interest rather than merely a factual expectancy.[17]

---

10. 106 N.Y. at 541, 13 N.E. at 339.

11. *Ibid.,* citing Rohrbach v. Germania Fire Ins. Co., 62 N.Y. 47 (1875); Springfield Fire & Marine Ins. Co. v. Allen, 43 N.Y. 389 (1871); and Herkimer v. Rice, 27 N.Y. 163 (1863).

12. 106 N.Y. at 541, 13 N.E. at 339.

13. N.Y. Acts 1939, ch. 882.

14. Note, *New York Insurance Code of 1939,* 40 Colum.L.Rev. 880 n.3 (1940).

15. N.Y.Ins. Law § 148 (McKinney 1966).

16. See Note, *New York Insurance Code of 1939,* 40 Colum.L.Rev. 880, 893 (1940).

17. See, *e.g.,* Cal.Ins.Code § 283 (West 1955): "Contingent or expectant interests. A mere contingent or expectant

There is an instructive contrast between *National Filtering* and a Pennsylvania case of like vintage,[18] involving accidental destruction of a bridge on a county road that was an essential means of access to the privately owned New Holland Turnpike. The turnpike company had obtained a policy of insurance on the bridge and, as the court saw the issue, the critical question was "whether the turnpike company had any insurable interest in the bridge." The turnpike company had contributed $5,500 to the cost of erecting the bridge (one-third of the total cost), but the contribution was voluntary and the turnpike company had no obligation to contribute to reconstruction. The court denied recovery under the policy on the ground that the turnpike company had no insurable interest in the bridge. The opinion asserted that "all the definitions of an 'insurable interest' import an interest in the property insured which can be enforced at law or in equity."[19]

The *National Filtering* and *New Holland Turnpike* cases can be reconciled on the facts since there was a contract right to receive royalties in *National Filtering* and an explicit insuring against loss of royalties from specified perils, whereas there was no contract relation of any kind supporting the expectancy in *New Holland* and the policy apparently purported to insure against damage to the bridge itself rather than against loss of turnpike tolls because of damage to the bridge. But the rationale of the opinions is plainly inconsistent, *New Holland* supporting the Eldon view of insurable interest, requiring some legally enforceable right,[20] and *National Filtering* supporting the view that factual expectancy is sufficient for insurable interest.

The comparison between these cases is instructive in another way that has bearing on the relative merits of these competing views of insurable interest. Alert counsel, if consulted at the time the contract of insurance was being made, could have avoided the adverse impact of the insurable interest doctrine in *New Holland*. If part or all of the insurance was desired to reimburse the turnpike company for lost tolls rather than for the cost of contributing to reconstruction of the bridge, the intention could have been made explicit in the insurance contract, as was done in *National Filtering*. It may be that a strict legal-interest requirement would have imposed the need for also creating some arrangement under which the turnpike company would

interest in anything, not founded on an actual right to the thing, nor upon any valid contract for it, is not insurable."

18. Farmers Mut. Ins. Co. v. New Holland Turnpike Co., 122 Pa. 37, 15 A. 563 (1888).

19. 122 Pa. at 46, 15 A. at 565. *But cf.* Van Cure v. Hartford Fire Ins. Co., 435 Pa. 163, 253 A.2d 663 (1969) (majority opinion seems to favor "factual expectation" over "legally enforceable interest" theory, but finds that condemnee, though still in possession, had no insurable interest after condemning authority's bond had been filed and approved and title had passed; concurring opinion disapproves "factual expectation" theory; dissent finds insurable interest under "factual expectation" theory because the taking was conditional and the condemnor had absolute discretion to return the property to the condemnee). Concerning valuation of a condemnee's interest, see § 3.9(c) *infra*.

20. See § 3.2(g) *supra*.

[handwritten marginalia: How to avoid New Holland Bridge problem]

have had a legal interest in the continued existence of the bridge itself. That could have been done, for example, by entering into an enforceable legal obligation to contribute toward reconstruction of the bridge and designating part of the insurance coverage to fulfill that obligation.

This analysis of *New Holland* illustrates a proposition of broader application. Whenever there is a factual expectancy that leads one to desire insurance protection, fully informed counsel can devise legal relationships to attach to the factual expectancy some kind of legally enforceable obligations that would meet a legal-interest requirement. Thus the requirement of a legal interest rather than merely a factual expectancy serves not to enforce the underlying objectives of insurable interest doctrine but only to trap the unwary who may enter into insurance arrangements with basically legitimate objectives but badly designed details.

§ 3.4(b) RELATIONSHIPS BETWEEN OBJECTIVES AND THEORIES OF INSURABLE INTEREST

(1) GENERALLY

The objectives of avoiding inducements to wagering and avoiding inducements to destruction of insured property are keyed to avoiding net gain to an insured through receipt of insurance proceeds in excess of loss suffered.[1] These inducements depend upon factual expectancy as seen by the insured or one acting for him. The factual-expectancy theory of insurable interest[2] is therefore the theory truest to these objectives and to the principle of indemnity. As insurable interest doctrine has actually developed, however, many deviations have occurred from the factual-expectancy theory, and thus from the underlying objectives of avoiding inducements to wagering and destruction.

(2) DEVIATIONS TOWARD MORE RIGOROUS REQUIREMENTS THAN THE PRINCIPLE OF INDEMNITY

Some deviations of insurance law from the principle of indemnity are in the form of more rigorous requirements for insurable interest than mere adherence to that principle would require. For example, one who enters into a contract to purchase realty with improvements upon it, expecting to use it in establishing and maintaining a business, ordinarily would have a factual expectancy of occupying a less advantageous economic position if fire destroyed the improvements before the conveyance, even though the contract was oral and therefore legally unenforceable under a statute of frauds. Yet it has been held that such a person has no insurable interest in the property.[3] Of course a denial of liability under an insurance policy obtained by

---

1. See § 3.1 *supra*.

2. See § 3.4(a) (4) *supra*.

3. *E.g.*, Cherokee Foundries, Inc. v. Imperial Assur. Co., 188 Tenn. 349, 219 S.W.2d 203 (1949), 9 A.L.R.2d 177 (1951). See 4 Appleman, Insurance Law § 2185 (rev. ed. 1969).

the intending purchaser would be justified if the insurance policy purported to cover only a kind of interest different from the expectancy of the intending purchaser under the unenforceable contract.[4] But the denial of liability on grounds of want of insurable interest seems unwarranted. In answer it might be argued that the special economic value of the property to the intending purchaser would be so difficult to assess that a risk of overvaluation would be unavoidable, thus leaving open a prospect of gain from destruction of the property by fire and collection of the insurance proceeds. Also, it might be argued that at best insurance of interests so difficult to evaluate would be both expensive to administer and subject to abuse. But if regulation is needed to meet difficulties and abuses rather than to deny contracts of this nature on principle, the doctrine of insurable interest seems an unduly crude instrument for the purpose, rejecting contracts of net usefulness as well as others whose value would be outweighed by costs of administration and risks of abuse. The very development of business interruption insurance, and even more clearly the development of contingent business interruption insurance,[5] represents a departure from the rigorous view of insurable interest implicit in holding that the prospective purchaser of realty under an unenforceable oral contract has absolutely no insurable interest.

One may find other deviations from the principle of indemnity toward more rigorous requirements of insurable interest—that is, cases in which a claim for insurance benefits has been rejected for want of an interest qualifying as insurable interest, despite the existence of a factual risk of loss from the perils insured against. One example is the denial of insurable interest in the mortgagee under a title that was in litigation at the time a fire loss occurred, final judgment against that title having been entered before the action on the insurance policy was decided.[6] Again, the result might be defended on grounds concerned with the speculative character of the interest.

---

4. The terms of the policy are not quoted in Cherokee Foundries, Inc. v. Imperial Assur. Co., n.3 *supra*. If it was in the most common form, insuring against "direct loss by fire," it would provide no coverage except in so far as the worsening of Cherokee's economic position was due to damage to the physical property itself as distinguished from collateral consequences of such damage. Even as to the physical damage loss, it might be argued that the standard policy does not purport to cover the kind of expectancy the prospective purchaser has under an enforceable oral contract of purchase. It might be argued that this construction is supported by a customary policy clause, "nor in any event for more than the interest of the insured." *Cf.* Higgins v. Insurance Co. of N. Am., 469 P.2d 766 (Ore.1970) purchaser of building has insurable interest above actual cash value because of practical problem created by deprecia-

tion; under contractual provisions of "Replacement Cost" coverage, however, he cannot recover repair costs when he does not repair).

5. "Contingent Business Interruption Insurance is the coverage applicable where the Insured desires to be indemnified for the loss he sustains if business premises not owned or operated by him, but upon which his business is dependent in whole or in part, are prevented by property damage from operating." Klein, Business Interruption Insurance 140 (3d ed. 1957). This type of insurance serves a legitimate need, and insurable interest doctrine should not be a barrier to its development. But it might well be a barrier in jurisdictions not recognizing factual expectancy as insurable interest.

6. Colver v. Central States Fire Ins. Co., 130 Kan. 556, 287 P. 266 (1930).

Another, less defensible, example of denial of insurable interest in the face of a real economic interest occurred in a leading English case.[7] Macaura, owner of the Killymoon estate, obtain five policies of fire insurance on timber situated on the estate. Title to the timber was in the Irish Canadian Saw Mills, Ltd., of which Macaura was the sole stockholder. He was also the sole creditor of the corporation except for debts "trifling in amount." Yet it was held that he had no insurable interest in the timber. Plainly it would have been simple for counsel, if consulted at the time of insuring, to devise insurance arrangements that would not have run afoul of the doctrine of insurable interest applied in the case. For example, he could have arranged for insurance naming the corporation as an additional insured, or he could have arranged the transaction between Macaura and the corporation so as to give Macaura an insurable interest. The latter could have been done by giving Macaura a lien on the timber to secure payment of the debt, or by having Macaura agree to obtain insurance. The choice among these possibilities would depend on considerations other than the doctrine of insurable interest. Perhaps the arrangement involving least change from that in *Macaura* would have been to name the corporation as an insured; an added measure of protection to the creditor could have been provided by a loss payable clause in his favor. Thus, the doctrine as formulated in *Macaura* serves to trap the unwary person whose interest truly satisfies the principle of indemnity rather than to advance that principle. The case involved charges of fraud, and it is difficult to reject the inference that, though not proved, they influenced the court to reach a theory of insurable interest that is nothing short of pernicious. All too often, it would seem the doctrine of insurable interest has been invoked as the stated theory for denial of recovery when fraud was alleged and probably served both to induce the insurer to contest liability and to persuade the court that the insurer should prevail.[8] The risk of undesirable distortion of the doctrine under such influences is great.

The *Macaura* case is not representative of the law generally on the questions of insurable interest of stockholders and creditors.[9]

(3) DEVIATIONS TOWARD LESS RIGOROUS REQUIREMENTS THAN THE PRINCIPLE OF INDEMNITY

Some deviations in insurable interest doctrine from the principle of indemnity are in the form of less rigorous requirements than strict adherence to this principle would produce.

Such a deviation is inherent in the Eldon view of insurable interest, under which one with a legally enforceable right in property has an insurable interest in it, even though the right has no economic value.[10] And the Eldon view has prevailed in some cases. For exam-

7. Macaura v. Northern Assur. Co., [1925] A.C. 619.

8. See § 3.3(a) n.3 *supra*.

9. See § 3.4(c) *infra*.

10. See § 3.2(g) *supra*.

ple, the holder of a lien that was almost worthless has been allowed to recover in full on a policy in an amount not exceeding the debt secured by the lien.[11] Similarly, the owner of an equity of redemption has been said to have an insurable interest equal to the value of the insurable property, whether he is personally liable for the mortgage debt or not.[12] Also, the prospective purchaser in possession under a contract for sale of realty has been found to have an insurable interest, apparently to the extent of the full value of the insurable property, even though it had become apparent that the seller could never perfect title and under these circumstances the prospective purchaser had an option to cancel without ever having paid more than monthly installments, which then were to be treated as rent.[13] And tenants at will have sometimes been allowed to recover as if holding a far more valuable interest,[14] perhaps even as if holding a fee simple title.[15]

Arguably, such decisions as these can be justified despite the fact that they plainly deviate from the principle of indemnity, leaving open risks of gain from collecting insurance proceeds larger than losses. One argument is that in cases of these types ordinarily an insurable interest of some value exists and it is not worth the cost of administration to enforce a requirement that the insurance proceeds never exceed to any extent the value of the insured interest at the time of loss. Also, it might be thought desirable to allow the insured to be protected not only against the risk of economic loss caused by a hazard such as fire but also against the risk of his inability to establish the amount of that loss when interests less than full ownership are involved. Thus it might be thought desirable to estop insurers from contesting the value of economic rights of a type difficult to evaluate. This might be done with the purpose of causing insurers to investigate carefully before underwriting, as a safeguard against abuse by an insured of the opportunity to seek protection against the risk of inability to prove value. The notion that insurers would actually investigate more carefully under such a rule than under one disallowing recovery in excess of loss must be discounted, however, in light of the experience under valued policy laws.[16]

§ 3.4(c) COMMON FACTUAL PATTERNS

This subsection presents illustrative types of fact situations that arise frequently, and with respect to which some generalizations can be drawn about the ordinary existence or nonexistence of insurable interest.

11. Insurance Co. v. Stinson, 103 U.S. 25, 26 L.Ed. 473 (1880).

12. 103 U.S. at 29, 26 L.Ed. at 477 (dictum). *Accord*, First Westchester Nat'l Bank v. New England Ins. Co., 11 App. Div.2d 192, 204 N.Y.S.2d 754 (2d Dep't 1960) (alternative holding).

13. Hartford Fire Ins. Co. v. Cagle, 249 F.2d 241 (10th Cir. 1957).

14. *E.g.*, Liverpool & London & Globe Ins. Co. v. Bolling, 176 Va. 182, 10 S.E. 2d 518 (1940).

15. 176 Va. at 197–198, 10 S.E.2d at 524–525 (dissenting opinion so interpreting the majority opinion).

16. See § 3.8 *infra*. *Cf*. Thomas v. Penn Mut. Fire Ins. Co., 244 S.C. 581, 137 S.E.2d 856 (1964).

Each spouse ordinarily has an insurable interest in at least some of the property of the other spouse.[17] The factual-expectancy theory of insurable interest would almost invariably support a finding that each spouse has an insurable interest in virtually all property of the other spouse. Even under a doctrine requiring a legally enforceable interest, insurable interest would often be supportable—for example, by homestead rights, by rights of curtesy or dower, or by community property rights.

[margin note: Spouses in each others property]

With rare exceptions, American decisions support the view that a stockholder, although having neither legal nor equitable title to the property of a corporation, nevertheless has an insurable interest in such property.[18]

[margin note: stockholders in corp's property]

Although it is quite generally acknowledged both in legal doctrine and in practice that a creditor may have insurance on his debtor's life, it is usually said by American courts and writers that an unsecured creditor has no insurable interest in his living debtor's property.[19] The distinction between the creditor's interest in the debtor's life and his interest in the debtor's property can be defended on the ground that ordinarily a creditor depends less on the debtor's assets, aside from those in which a security interest is taken, than upon the debtor's personal reliability and earning power, both of which are dependent upon his life. There is less often a factual expectancy of loss to the creditor from destruction of a piece of the debtor's property in which the creditor has no security interest than from death of the obligor of an unsecured debt. Curiously, the argument for insurable interest of the unsecured creditor in the debtor's property is stronger after the debtor's death than while he is living, because of the special claim of the creditor against the property in the estate of the deceased debtor.

[margin note: creditor in debtor's life (but not property if unsecured)]

SECTION 3.5 INSURABLE INTEREST IN LIFE

§ 3.5(a) OBTAINING OR CONSENTING TO INSURANCE ON ONE'S OWN LIFE

It is often said that "every person has an insurable interest in his own life."[1] The quoted assertion implies a meaning of insurable

---

17. See, *e.g.*, North British & Mercantile Ins. Co. v. Sciandra, 256 Ala. 409, 54 So.2d 764 (1951), 27 A.L.R.2d 1047 (1953). See 4 Appleman, Insurance Law § 2149 (rev. ed. 1969).

18. *E.g.*, American Indem. Co. v. Southern Missionary College, 195 Tenn. 513, 260 S.W.2d 269 (1953), 39 A.L.R.2d 714 (1955); see 4 Appleman, Insurance Law § 2145 (rev. ed. 1969). Concerning English authority, see Macaura v. Northern Assur. Co., [1925] A.C. 619, discussed in § 3.4(b)(2) *supra.*

19. *E.g.*, Chapman v. England, 231 F.2d 606, 610–611 (9th Cir. 1956); 4 Appleman, Insurance Law § 2138 (rev. ed. 1969); Patterson & McIntyre, *Unsecured Creditor's Insurance*, 31 Colum. L.Rev. 212, 218–219 (1931). Concerning English authority, see Macaura v. Northern Assur. Co., n.2 *supra.*

1. *E.g.*, Langford v. National Life & Acc. Ins. Co., 116 Ark. 527, 173 S.W. 414 (1915), citing Cooley, Law of Insurance (1st ed. 1905): "That one has an insurable interest in his own life is an ele-

interest not easily reconcilable with the principle of indemnity. It would seem to be a corollary of the principle of indemnity that the test for interest adequate to support life insurance should be pecuniary interest in the continued life of the person whose death is the event insured against. No person can have a pecuniary interest in the continuance of his own life, in a strict factual sense. This is most clearly seen, perhaps, if pecuniary interest in continued life is examined in its converse form of expectancy of suffering pecuniary loss in the event of death. One has no such expectancy since, once his death occurs, he will no longer be in this vale of joy and tears where losses are suffered. Similarly, or perhaps one should say conversely, it is something of an anomaly to think of one's estate, the legal entity that succeeds him upon his death, as having a pecuniary interest in his life. One's estate, rather than suffering loss through his death, is thereby and only thereby enabled to come into possession of interests. Thus the assertion that "every person has an insurable interest in his own life" is a fictional way of saying that, despite the applicability of an insurable interest doctrine to life insurance contracts, every person sui juris—that is, everyone not under some type of legal disability—may validly contract for insurance on his own life, designating whomever he will as beneficiary. Despite debate over the form in which this rule is expressed, there is little dispute about it in substance.[2]

The power to contract for insurance on one's own life is not without qualification, however. It is a well accepted rule that courts will decline to enforce a policy of insurance one obtains on his own life as a cloak for what is in essence a genuine wager.[3] A later assignment of a valid contract is to be distinguished,[4] but the rule of nonenforceability would no doubt be extended to a case in which the policy was both obtained and assigned as part of an arrangement cloaking a genuine wager.

Relatively few cases have dealt with the question whether consent of the person whose life is insured is essential to the validity of an insurance contract obtained by another. Of course, if the other has no insurable interest, it is plain that it would be necessary to have at least the consent and perhaps even more active participation of the person whose life is insured, as by himself making the application.[5] Even when the other person obtaining insurance is one

---

mentary principle as to the existence of which the cases are unanimous."

2. E.g., American Cas. Co. v. Rose, 340 F.2d 469 (10th Cir. 1964); Ducros v. Commissioner, 272 F.2d 49 (6th Cir. 1959); Aetna Life Ins. Co. v. Patton, 176 F.Supp. 368 (S.D.Ill.1959); Corder v. Prudential Ins. Co., 42 Misc.2d 423, 248 N.Y.S.2d 265 (Sup.Ct.1964). See 2 Appleman, Insurance Law 109–113, § 761 n.12 (rev. ed. 1966).

3. E.g., Bromley's Admr. v. Washington Life Ins. Co., 122 Ky. 402, 92 S.W. 17 (1906).

4. See § 3.5(c) infra.

5. Consent of the person whose life was insured has been held not to be an adequate answer to the defense of lack of an insurable interest. E.g., National Life & Acc. Ins. Co. v. Middlebrooks, 27 Ala.App. 247, 170 So. 84 (1936); Na-

with an insurable interest, there is reason for requiring consent of the person whose life is insured. It may be that the insurable interest is quite adequate as a safeguard against evils of wagering, but there remains a concern about incentives to murder inherent in allowing one's life to be insured without his consent, even by another who has an insurable interest. This would be true even if a strict factual-expectancy theory of insurable interest were enforced in life insurance law. But in fact that theory does not prevail, and thus the risk of inducements to murder is even greater since the determination of insurable interest is often based on defined relationships of consanguinity or affinity, which in some situations involve little or no factual expectancy of pecuniary disadvantage from death of the person whose life is insured.

concern about incentives to murder

A modest body of law has been developed in the courts requiring consent of the person whose life is insured, even when the person obtaining the policy has an insurable interest,[6] and in a significant minority of jurisdictions statutes impose a similar requirement.[7]

§ 3.5(b) RELATIONSHIPS SUPPORTING INSURABLE INTEREST IN ANOTHER'S LIFE

Each person generally may obtain insurance on his own life without regard to insurable interest,[1] but to obtain valid insurance on the life of another[2] he must have an insurable interest in the other's life.[3]

Rule

It is generally recognized that one has an insurable interest in the life of his spouse[4] and his minor child,[5] and, while himself a mi-

---

tional Life & Acc. Ins. Co. v. Ball, 157 Miss. 163, 127 So. 268 (1930).

6. *E.g.*, Watson v. Massachusetts Mut. Life Ins. Co., 140 F.2d 673 (D.C. Cir.), *cert. denied*, 322 U.S. 746 (1944); Metropolitan Life Ins. Co. v. Monahan, 102 Ky. 13, 42 S.W. 924 (1897); Ramey v. Carolina Life Ins. Co., 244 S.C. 16, 135 S.E.2d 362 (1964), 9 A.L.R.3d 1164 (1966). *Cf.* Life & Cas. Ins. Co. v. Womack, 60 Ga.App. 284, 3 S.E.2d 791 (1940).

7. *E.g.*, Hawaii Rev.Laws § 431–416 (1968); Md.Ann.Code art. 48A, § 371 (1957); Mass.Gen.Laws Ann. ch. 175, § 123 (Supp.1970); N.Y.Ins.Law § 146 (3) (McKinney 1966); Va.Code Ann. § 38.1–330 (1953). Such statutes generally except from the consent requirement group insurance contracts and insurance procured on the life of a minor who is a dependent of the procurer or in whom the procurer otherwise has an insurable interest; many except insurance procured by one spouse on the life of the other though Massachusetts, for example, makes no such exception; and Maryland and Massachusetts, for example, except family policies procured by one or more adult members of the family, including a step-parent.

1. See § 3.5(a) *supra*.

2. It is useful to have a phrase other than "the insured" to designate the one whose life is insured (*i.e.*, whose death is the event insured against), when someone else procures the insurance contract or holds incidents of ownership. "*Cestui que vie*" ("CQV") is a phrase sometimes used to designate the one whose life is insured, whether or not he procures the insurance.

3. See generally Salzman, *Insurable Interest in Life Insurance*, 1965 Ins.L.J. 517.

4. *E.g.*, Bowers v. Missouri Mut. Ass'n, 333 Mo. 492, 62 S.W.2d 1058 (1933). See also the statutes cited in § 3.5(a)

5. See Note 5 on page 122.

nor, in the life of his parent.[6] Although such limited authority as can be found is inconclusive,[7] it would seem that an adult child and his parent do not have an insurable interest in the lives of each other without proof of a particular pecuniary interest. It has also been stated generally that one has an insurable interest in the life of his brother and sister,[8] but there are some decisions to the contrary.[9]

Concepts of insurable interest in the foregoing relationships of close family ties rest upon appraisal of the interests normally incident to the type of relationship, rather than appraisal of the particulars of each case. Moreover, these rules are often rationalized on the basis that in close family relationships love and affection supply insurable interest. Thus, in some instances, these rules appear consistent with the principle of indemnity only if one accepts as conclusive an assumption that pecuniary interests in all particular cases are consistent with those normally incident to the type of relationship—in short only by a fiction. Rigorous adherence to the principle of indemnity would require, on the contrary, a showing of factual expectancy of economic gain from the continued life and, conversely, economic loss from the death.

Beyond the group of close family ties discussed above, more attention is focused upon the interest between the two individuals con-

n.7 *supra*, which implicitly recognize the insurable interest of one spouse in the life of the other by excepting from the consent requirement policies procured on the spouse's life.

5. *E.g.*, Volunteer State Life Ins. Co. v. Pioneer Bank, 46 Tenn.App. 244, 327 S.W.2d 59 (1959). See also, *e.g.*, National Life & Acc. Ins. Co. v. Alexander, 226 Ala. 325, 147 So. 173 (1933) (dictum). *Cf.* Life & Cas. Ins. Co. v. Womack, 60 Ga.App. 284, 3 S.E.2d 791 (1940).

6. Judicial statements concerning the insurable interest of a minor child in his parent's life are generally dicta— *e.g.*, Rosenberg v. Robbins, 289 Mass. 402, 194 N.E. 291 (1935)—or are found in cases concerned with the interest of the child as beneficiary under rather than as procurer of insurance on the parent's life—*e.g.*, Drane v. Jefferson Standard Life Ins. Co., 139 Tex. 101, 161 S.W.2d 1057 (1942) (policy on life of godmother who was *in loco parentis*). This scarcity of direct authority is most likely the result of the improbability that a minor child would procure insurance on the life of his mother or father. Moreover, the minor's insurable interest is hardly open to doubt. In addition to the love-and-affection interest normally to be assumed, the minor child is owed a legal obligation of support by his parent and

ordinarily has a factual expectancy of pecuniary loss even greater than the minimum support required by law should his parent die.

7. *E.g.*, Life Ins. Clearing Co. v. O'Neill, 106 F. 800 (3d Cir. 1901) (applying Pennsylvania law; adult child has no insurable interest in father's life merely because of the relationship); Mitchell v. Union Life Ins. Co., 45 Me. 104 (1856) (dictum that parent has no insurable interest in life of adult child merely because of the relationship); Golden State Mut. Life Ins. Co. v. White, 374 S.W.2d 901 (Tex.Civ.App. 1964, writ refused, no reversible error) (absent fraud, no public policy against adult daughter procuring life insurance policy on her mother's life, naming daughter as beneficiary, on which daughter paid all premiums). See generally 1 Richards, Law of Insurance 389–391 (5th ed. Freedman 1952).

8. *E.g.*, Century Life Ins. Co. v. Custer, 178 Ark. 304, 10 S.W.2d 882 (1928), 61 A.L.R. 914 (1929); Rettenmaier v. Rettenmaier, 255 Iowa 952, 124 N.W.2d 453 (1963) (alternative holding).

9. *E.g.*, Gulf Life Ins. Co. v. Davis, 52 Ga.App. 464, 183 S.E. 640 (1936); Abernathy v. Springfield Mut. Ass'n, 284 S.W. 198 (Mo.App.1926). *Cf.* Magers v. Western & So. Life Ins. Co., 344 S.W.2d 312 (Mo.App.1961).

cerned. Still, something less than a clear demonstration of pecuniary interest has been held sufficient in particular cases in which the relationship of one to another was that of uncle, aunt, nephew, niece, step-brother, step-sister, step-child, step-mother, or step-father.[10]   For example, one who had supported her niece from infancy was held to have an insurable interest in the niece's life, on the basis of an expectation of pecuniary benefit incident to the moral obligation of the niece.[11]

The test for insurable interest beyond the foregoing relationships of consanquinity or affinity is concerned more directly with pecuniary interest in the particular case,[12] though in most cases such an interest is found to exist on behalf of a creditor in the life of his debtor,[13] a partner in the life of another partner,[14] and a business entity in the life of a key employee.[15]

In relation to property insurance it has been suggested that the factual-expectancy theory of insurable interest is most faithful to the principle of indemnity and generally is a more defensible theory than others.[16]   The arguments offered there are perhaps less compelling in relation to life insurance.   It might be said, for example, that the different treatment of close relationships of consanguinity or affinity is supported by the fact that love and affection normally existing in these relationships provide an extra safeguard against destruction of life and wagering on life.   Also it might be suggested that, since influences other than the doctrine of insurable interest are more likely to be effective in preventing destruction of life than destruction of

---

10. See generally Salzman, *Insurable Interest in Life Insurance*, 1965 Ins. L.J. 517, 523. *But cf.* Commonwealth Life Ins. Co. v. George, 248 Ala. 649, 28 So.2d 910, 170 A.L.R. 1032 (1947) (aunt has no insurable interest without showing of pecuniary interest); National Life & Acc. Ins. Co. v. Alexander, 226 Ala. 325, 147 So. 173 (1933) (cousin has no insurable interest without showing of pecuniary interest); National Life & Acc. Ins. Co. v. Ball, 157 Miss. 163, 127 So. 268 (1930) (son-in-law has no insurable interest without showing of pecuniary interest). Concerning the the interest of an aunt, see also § 3.5(e) n.3 *infra*.

11. Cronin v. Vermont Life Ins. Co., 20 R.I. 570, 40 A. 497 (1898). *Cf.* Young v. Hipple, 273 Pa. 439, 117 A. 185 (1922), 25 A.L.R. 1541 (1923) (assuming that a step-daughter had no insurable interest in the step-father's life merely by reason of that relationship; holding that an insurable interest based on moral obligation was proved).

12. *E.g.*, Poland v. Fisher's Estate, 329 S.W.2d 768 (Mo.1959).

13. *E.g.*, Metcalf v. Montgomery, 229 Ala. 156, 155 So. 582 (1934). See 2 Appleman, Insurance Law § 851 (rev. ed. 1966); 1 Richards, Law of Insurance 393–398 (5th ed. Freedman 1952).

14. *E.g.*, Gerstel v. Arens, 143 Fla. 20, 196 So. 616 (1940); Rahders, Merritt & Hagler v. People's Bank, 113 Minn. 496, 130 N.W. 16 (1911). See 2 Appleman, Insurance Law § 871 (rev. ed. 1966); 1 Richards, Law of Insurance 398–399 (5th ed. Freedman 1952). *But cf.* Lakin v. Postal Life & Cas. Ins. Co., 316 S.W.2d 542 (Mo.1958), 70 A.L.R.2d 564 (1960) (holding that the legal relation of partnership does not in itself create an insurable interest of one partner in the life of the other, and that evidence in the case at hand was insufficient as proof of such interest).

15. *E.g.*, Murray v. G. F. Higgins Co., 300 Pa. 341, 150 A. 629 (1930), 75 A.L.R. 1360 (1931) (corporation officer). See 2 Appleman, Insurance Law § 872 (rev. ed. 1966); Annot., 143 A.L.R. 293 (1943).

16. See § 3.4(a) (4) *supra*.

property, a more rigorous doctrine of insurable interest is needed in property insurance law than in life insurance law. Perhaps the same comparison is applicable to wagering on the likelihood of death and the likelihood of injury to or destruction of property. On the other hand, one might argue that a more rigorous doctrine is nevertheless justified in life insurance law because life is more precious than property and wagering on life is a greater evil than wagering on property. In fact, it appears that courts have been reluctant to recognize speculative interests incident to business relationships as sufficient insurable interest for life insurance—perhaps more reluctant than to recognize speculative interests as sufficient for property insurance.

§ 3.5(c) BENEFICIARIES AND ASSIGNEES WITHOUT INSURABLE INTEREST

It has been noted that there is general recognition of the rule that one may obtain insurance on his own life, designating whomever he wishes as beneficiary.[1] In contrast, there is considerable conflict regarding the question whether one may validly assign a policy on his own life to another who has no insurable interest. Cases involving use of the assignment as part of a cloak for a transaction in which the policy was originally obtained for wagering are to be distinguished; in such a case the entire policy is unenforceable.[2] A split of authority has developed, however, over the treatment of cases in which a valid policy was obtained by a person on his own life, and thereafter he attempted to assign it to another having no insurable interest in his life. The majority of decisions in point have upheld such assignments.[3] And this result is supported by the fact that often the objectives of assignment could easily be served, if the parties obtained skilled legal advice, by changing the beneficiary of the policy to the estate of the person whose life is insured, with provisions in his will for the insurance proceeds to go to the intended assignee, or even more simply by changing the beneficiary of the policy itself so as to designate the intended assignee.[4] Thus the rule of invalidity of an assignment serves usually to trap the unwary rather than to fulfill the objectives of insurable interest doctrine. But a substantial minority of the courts hold that an assignment of a life policy to one having no insurable interest is void as a matter of law without regard

---

1. See § 3.5(a) *supra*.

2. See *ibid.*

3. *E.g.*, Grigsby v. Russell, 222 U.S. 149, 32 Sup.Ct. 58, 56 L.Ed. 133 (1911). See also, *e.g.*, Butterworth v. Mississippi Valley Trust Co., 362 Mo. 133, 240 S. W.2d 676 (1951), 30 A.L.R.2d 1298 (1953) (upholding validity of assignment to trust not having an insurable interest in the insured life). *But cf.* Warnock v. Davis, 104 U.S. 775, 26 L. Ed. 924 (1881) (holding the assignment of a life policy to a trust association invalid for lack of insurable interest except as to sums advanced by the association upon the security provided by the policy); Bromley's Admr. v. Washington Life Ins. Co., 122 Ky. 402, 92 S.W. 17 (1906) (both initial procurement and assignment were part of a wagering arrangement). See 2 Appleman, Insurance Law §§ 854, 855 (rev. ed. 1966).

4. See § 4.11(e) *infra*.

to whether an intention to assign existed at the time of issuance of the contract.[5] Reasons urged in support of the minority rule are, first, that there is no material distinction between assignment of a policy to one without insurable interest and procurement of a policy by such person; second, that such assignment constitutes a wagering contract; and third, that the effect of such an assignment is to afford a temptation to murder.[6]

Can this minority rule of invalidity of assignments be reconciled with the virtually undisputed rule that one may validly obtain insurance on his own life and designate any beneficiary he wishes? If it appears that a beneficiary who pays the premium is the instigator of the insurance contract, the arguments against validity of an assignment to one without insurable interest seem equally applicable to validity of the basic contract. That case is analogous to one in which the person whose life is insured obtains the policy as a cloak for what is in essence a genuine wager.[7] On the other hand, if the person whose life is insured is the instigator of the contract, and the beneficiary is designated before any arrangement for his payment of subsequent premiums, the case can be distinguished from one of assignment on the ground that the original designation of the beneficiary is more likely to have been a choice free of the vices of the assignment to one without insurable interest.[8]

Some aspects of the arguments concerning encouragement of wagering and inducement to murder (which arguments account for the minority rule that an assignment to one without insurable interest is invalid) are applicable even to policies obtained and paid for by the person whose life is insured, but they are insufficient, in the face of countervailing considerations, to cause the courts to hold such contracts invalid. With regard to assignments, there is an added countervailing consideration in the desirability that the insured be free to use a policy to obtain cash. But in other respects it might be argued that there is more reason for holding assignments invalid. For example, the original arrangement for the policy is less likely than an assignment to be the product of pressure on the insured by the person who receives an interest in the policy. On balance, however, it seems doubtful that the minority rule on assignments should be maintained in view of the thoroughly established rule allowing one to obtain a policy on his own life and designate whomever he will as beneficiary.

Invalidation of an assignment leaves open the question whether the insurance company escapes liability or instead must pay the policy proceeds to the beneficiary. If the arguments supporting the majority rule, presented in *Grigsby v. Russell*,[9] do not make an adequate

---

5. *E.g.*, Griffin v. McCoach, 123 F.2d 550 (5th Cir.), *cert. denied*, 316 U.S. 683 (1941) (Texas law); Milliken v. Haner, 184 Ky. 694, 212 S.W. 605 (1919).

6. See, *e.g.*, 184 Ky. at 698–699, 212 S. W. at 606–607. See also Annot., 30 A.L.R.2d 1310, 1315–1316 (1953).

7. See § 3.5(a) *supra*.

8. *E.g.*, Langford v. National Life & Acc. Ins. Co., 116 Ark. 527, 173 S.W. 414 (1915).

9. 222 U.S. 149, 32 Sup.Ct. 58, 56 L.Ed. 133 (1911).

case against application of the indemnity principle, that principle could be adhered to under the fourth technique for honoring it (distributed-gross-liability rules),[10] with provision for any excess above the loss of the assignee to be paid to the designated beneficiary or to the estate of the deceased.

If an assignment is said to be "void", perhaps this implies that the beneficiary would be permitted to raise the point—an inconsistency with the idea that only the insurer can raise want of insurable interest. The results in *Grigsby* and in *Langford v. National Life & Acc. Ins. Co.*[11] are consistent with the view that only the insurer can raise the want of insurable interest, but the reason given in *Grigsby* is a more satisfactory one than this proposition would be, since the idea that only the insurer can raise the defense is inconsistent with the notion that it is a defense based on public interest.[12]

§ 3.5(d) THE DISTINCTIVE TEXAS RULE

Before the enactment of a statute in 1953, Texas decisions had allowed a rival claimant to defeat the designated beneficiary's right to life insurance proceeds by showing that the beneficiary had no insurable interest in the life of the insured at the time of death; the insurer, on the other hand, could not escape liability altogether by raising want of insurable interest since the estate of the deceased would be entitled to the proceeds in the absence of another qualified claimant.[1] This rule adhered more rigorously to the principle of indemnity than did the rules of other states, since it limited a beneficiary's recovery to his insurable interest. Also, it was more consistent with the public policy basis of insurable interest doctrine in allowing one other than an insurer to invoke the doctrine of insurable interest.[2] But the desirability of allowing rights in insurance policies to be assignable as property interests worked against the adoption of that rule elsewhere, and influenced the legislative development in Texas. The 1953 statute specifically declared that any person may obtain insurance on his own life and validly designate any beneficiary he wishes,[3] and similarly authorized assignments to persons without an interest in the sense of factual expectancy, though by the fictional technique of declaring that any beneficiary or assignee properly designated "shall at all times thereafter have an insurable interest" with specific statutory exceptions primarily concerned with legal entities engaged in the business of burying the dead.[4]

10. See § 3.1(c) *supra*.

11. 116 Ark. 527, 173 S.W. 414 (1915).

12. See § 3.3(b) *supra*.

1. See Swift, *Insurable Interest Changes*, 16 Texas B.J. 583 (1953), reprinted in 1953 Ins. L.J. 666. See also Note, 32 Texas L.Rev. 346 (1954).

2. On this matter, see § 3.3(b) *supra*.

3. Tex.Ins.Code Ann. art. 3.49–1, § 1 (1963).

4. *Id.* §§ 2–3. In McCain v. Yost, 155 Tex. 174, 284 S.W.2d 898 (1955), it was held that the statute applied when the insured died after its enactment, although the beneficiary—the insured's

§ 3.5(e) THE RISK OF INDUCEMENTS TO MURDER

Decisions that designations of beneficiaries without insurable interest and assignments to persons without insurable interest are valid when made by the person whose life is insured [1] have sometimes been reasoned on a theory that gives little, if any recognition to avoidance of inducements to murder as an objective of insurable interest doctrine; rather, it is said, the central objective is avoidance of wagering, and participation in the transaction by the person whose life is insured adequately protects against wagering.[2] But in other instances avoidance of inducements to murder has been recognized as an important objective too. Perhaps the most striking illustration is the recognition of a tort cause of action in favor of the father of a minor child against insurers issuing policies to an aunt without insurable interest, on the theory that their violation of the insurable interest doctrine contributed to the minor's death at the hands of the aunt.[3] Perhaps it is instructive to think of the basis of liability here in terms of negligence per se.[4] If insurable interest doctrine is expressed in a statute (as is true in some states), and if it be considered that an objective of the statute is to avoid inducements to murder, the murder that occurs in circumstances like those described above is a type of harm the statute is designed to prevent, and liability of the insurer can be based on the theory of negligence per se. On the other hand, if the statute is not aimed at prevention of murders that are in no way related to the freedom of "the whole world of the unscrupulous" [5] to wager then violation of the statute is not negligence per se. The doctrine of negligence per se relates to violations of statutes, and in some states to violations of ordinances or administrative regulations as well. Thus in a state in which insurable interest requirements are of decisional rather than statutory origin, negligence per se does not apply. But the analogy is close, and it seems reasonable to adopt a similar rule for a doctrine of decisional origin, to recognize avoidance of inducements to murder as one among the objectives of insurable interest doctrine, and thus to sustain a tort cause of action against the insurer if its issuance of a policy in violation of insurable interest doctrine is a cause in fact of murder of the person whose life was purportedly insured.

ex-wife at the time of his death—had been designated before the effective date of the statute, and that the beneficiary "had an insurable interest and was entitled under the law to have the proceeds of the policy paid to her." 155 Tex. at 178, 284 S.W.2d at 900. The contesting claimant was the insured's estate.

1. See § 3.5(a) and (c) *supra.*

2. See, *e.g.*, Grigsby v. Russell, 222 U.S. 149, 32 Sup.Ct. 58, 56 L.Ed. 133 (1911).

3. Liberty Nat'l Life Ins. Co. v. Weldon, 267 Ala. 171, 100 So.2d 696, 61 A.L.R. 2d 1346 (1958).

4. See 2 Restatement (Second) of Torts § 288B(1) (1965).

5. The quoted phrase is that of Holmes, J., in Grigsby v. Russell, 222 U.S. 149, 155, 32 Sup.Ct. 58, 56 L.Ed. 133, 136 (1911).

The foregoing discussion concerns insurable interest doctrine. A similar problem may arise in relation to requiring consent of the person whose life is insured at the instance of another. It has been held that a cause of action against the insurer for negligence was stated by a complaint alleging that the issuance of a policy on the life of the plaintiff to his wife without his knowledge or consent provided the motive for her attempt to murder him by arsenic poisoning.[6] This case did not involve insurable interest doctrine, strictly speaking; instead it was the closely related requirement of consent of the person whose life was insured.[7] But the foregoing comments about applicability of negligence per se theory to insurable interest requirements might also be extended to consent requirements.

§ 3.5(f) INSURABLE INTEREST IN INDUSTRIAL LIFE INSURANCE

It has often been asserted that insurable interest doctrine has no application to industrial life insurance.[1] The principal justification advanced in support of this immunity from insurable interest doctrine is that invoking the doctrine would interfere with free use of the "facility-of-payment" clause commonly appearing in industrial insurance—a clause authorizing prompt payment of funeral and burial expenses without resort to proceedings for administration of a deceased's estate, which would be very expensive in relation to the small amounts involved.[2] It might also be argued that the small amounts are not likely to operate as inducements to murder or to a substantial evil of wagering. Perhaps the absence of an applicable insurable interest doctrine also contributes to prompt and informal settlements that avoid wasting the modest proceeds in disputes that would be very costly in relation to the amounts involved. On the other hand, with the safeguard of insurable interest doctrine withdrawn, vocational wagering will arise.[3] But it may incidentally serve the useful purpose of enabling policyholders to realize the cash value of policies they would otherwise forfeit for nonpayment of premiums.[4] On balance the rule of nonapplication of insurable interest doctrine to industrial life insurance seems justified.

6. Ramey v. Carolina Life Ins. Co., 244 S.C. 16, 135 S.E.2d 362 (1964), 9 A.L.R. 3d 1164 (1966).

7. See § 3.5(a) supra.

1. E.g., Liberty Nat'l Life Ins. Co. v. Weldon, 267 Ala. 171, 100 So.2d 696, 61 A.L.R.2d 1346 (1958).

2. Ibid. As to "facility-of-payment" clauses generally, see § 1.3(f) supra.

3. See, e.g., Hack v. Metz, 173 S.C. 413, 176 S.E. 314 (1934), 95 A.L.R. 196 (1935); § 3.1(b) supra. Cf. Magers v. National Life & Acc. Ins. Co., 329 S.W. 2d 752 (Mo.1959).

4. See § 3.1(b) supra.

skip to p. 137

SECTION 3.6 THE MEASURE OF RECOVERY IN MARINE INSURANCE

§ 3.6(a) TYPES OF MARINE LOSSES

Marine losses are to some extent distinctive in nature, and the terminology traditionally used to describe them is even more distinctive. An introduction to this terminology is presented here.[1] Some of these terms are used also in relation to other types of insurance, but it is never safe to assume that the meaning is entirely consistent in the different contexts.

In marine insurance, "total" loss may be "actual" or "constructive." If a casualty from insured perils has made it impossible for the insured property to reach its destination in specie, an actual total loss has been suffered.[2] If it is still possible for the property to reach its destination in specie, but the cost of bringing this about would exceed the value of the property, then under both American and English law the insured may treat the loss as total by notifying the underwriter of his election to abandon to the underwriter all his rights in the property.[3] Under American law, but not English law, this election may also be made if such cost would be less than the value, but more than half the value.[4] The American rule is not often applicable to hull losses, however, since hull policies commonly include a clause providing that there shall be no recovery for a constructive total loss "unless the expense of recovering and repairing the vessel shall exceed the insured value." [5]

"Average," as used in admiralty and marine insurance law, means partial loss, in contrast with total loss. A "general average" is a partial loss that, under admiralty law, falls generally on all the interests at risk in a maritime venture and is incurred when some of the property at risk is sacrificed to save the remainder.[6] The typical

---

1. See generally Winter, Marine Insurance 369–371, 392–400, 405–412 (3d ed. 1952); Gilmore & Black, Admiralty 72–80 (1957).

2. *E.g.*, Roux v. Salvador, 3 Bing.N.C. 266–267, 286, 132 Eng.Rep. 413, 420–421 (Ex. Ch. 1836). See 2 Arnould, Marine Insurance [10 British Shipping Laws] 1023–1026, §§ 1046–1049 (15th ed. 1961). An actual total loss is also sometimes referred to as an absolute total loss. *Id.* at 1023.

3. See *id.* at 1085–1086, 1097–1099. See also Lord, *The Hull Policy: Actual and Constructive Total Loss and Abandonment*, 41 Tulane L.Rev. 347 (1967).

4. *E.g.*, Bradlie v. Maryland Ins. Co., 37 U.S. (12 Pet.) 378, 398–399, 9 L.Ed. 1123, 1132 (1838). See 2 Arnould,

Marine Insurance [10 British Shipping Laws] 1099 (15th ed. 1961).

5. See Winter, Marine Insurance 394–395 (3d ed. 1952). This stipulation for comparing the expense to *insured* value also effects a change from the rule, applied in the absence of such stipulation, that expense is to be compared with *actual repaired* value. See Gilmore & Black, Admiralty 78 (1957).

6. This proposition states the stricter English rule of general average. The American rule extends "the consequences of the general average act to include certain expenses incurred after safety has been attained. For example, expenses incurred for the mutual benefit of ship and cargo to enable the voyage to be completed, such as temporary repairs at a port of refuge, are made good [under the

case for which the legal rule of general average was developed was that presented when part of the cargo was cast overboard in a storm to save the ship and other cargo. Each of the owners of the property at risk in the venture was required to bear a proportionate share of the loss. Thus, each of the owners of the ship and cargo that was saved suffered a loss of the general average type because of the necessity of making a contribution to the owner of the cargo that was sacrificed, and the owner of the sacrificed cargo suffered a loss of the general average type because the reimbursement he received was less than full reimbursement, the deficiency being in the ratio of the value of his goods at risk to the total value of all goods at risk in the venture.

"Particular average" is a partial loss that falls on one interest because it is not due to the type of sacrifice to which the law of general average applies. A distinction is made between particular average and total loss of a part (as when one bale of cotton is totally destroyed by fire).

Marine underwriters developed a provision (known traditionally as the "Memorandum") excluding coverage of all particular average for some kinds of goods and excluding coverage of small percentages of particular average for others. The manner of expression may seem quaint. "It is also agreed, that . . . [1] tobacco . . . and all other articles that are perishable in their own nature, are warranted by the assured free from average, unless general; [2] . . . tobacco stems . . . free from average under *twenty per cent* unless general; [3] and sugar . . . and bread, are warranted by the assured free from average under *seven per cent* unless general; [4] and coffee in bags or bulk . . . free from average under *ten per cent* unless general." [7] The omitted phrases include a hodgepodge of other articles. The meaning of the part of the quoted passage that, for convenience, has been designated "[1]" is that particular average involving tobacco (*i. e.*, partial losses otherwise than by liability for general average contribution, or by sacrifice of the tobacco to save other property in a general average situation) is not covered, though general average and total losses of tobacco are covered. Clause "[2]" means that particular average involving tobacco stems, if under 20 per cent of the value, is not covered. That is, the insured bears any particular average involving tobacco stems if the loss is less than 20 per cent of the value, but if the loss is 20 per cent or more, the insurer bears the *whole* loss (not just the amount above 20 per cent). Again, of course, general average and total losses are covered. Clauses "[3]" and "[4]" provide different percentage exclusions for particular average involving other

American rule] as general average." Buglass, General Average and the York/Antwerp Rules, 1950, at 12 (1959). See *id.* at 11–17 for a comparison of the general principles of the American and English rules and their relation to the "York/Antwerp Rules, 1950," a set

of model provisions developed for inclusion in marine cargo contracts to facilitate uniformity of application of the law of general average.

7. See Winter, Marine Insurance 212 (3d ed. 1952).

products. The object of these provisions is primarily to exclude those partial losses that are normal and expectable in view of the "inherent susceptibility" of the goods to deterioration and secondarily to relieve the underwriter of the burden of adjusting for losses that, though accidental, are trifling in amount.

The "Memorandum" with its long list of products, most of which are irrelevant to any individual contract of insurance, is not as commonly used today as formerly, but a similar result is obtained by use of a "free of particular average" ("F.P.A.") clause, providing either for exclusion of all particular average or for exclusion of low-percentage particular average, depending upon the kind or kinds of goods at risk. The fixing of the percentage (called the "franchise")[8] is in the hands of specialists. Also, the F.P.A. clauses, by the addition of an "unless" phrase, allow coverage of most particular average that is plainly due to casualty rather than "inherent susceptibility" to deterioration. The F.P.A., E.C. clause (English conditions) provides: "Free of particular average unless the vessel be stranded, sunk, or burnt, or in collision." The F.P.A., A.C. clause (American conditions) provides: "Free of particular average unless caused by stranding, sinking, burning, or collision with another vessel." Note that under the English conditions the underwriter is liable for particular average if the vessel is "stranded, sunk, or burnt, or in collision," even though casualty to the vessel had no causal connection with the particular average.[9] Both the American and English F.P.A. clauses, as quoted above, have the same effect as the Memorandum with respect to coverage of total losses and general average. If the phrase "under x per cent" is added, they similarly have the effect of excluding a small percentage loss but covering the whole loss if it is as great as the specified percentage. Sometimes, however, there is added to the clause the phrase "under x per cent, which is deductible." In such case, the insured always bears that part of the loss up to the deductible percentage, and the underwriter pays only the excess.

§ 3.6(b) THE MEASURE OF RECOVERY FOR CARGO LOSSES

The obscurity of the traditional statement of rules concerning the measure of recovery in marine insurance tempts those who master it to preserve its labyrinths as an ordeal of initiation for others who dare to intrude. Once the obscurity is penetrated, however, an orderly and relatively uncomplicated set of rules is discovered.[1]

---

8. *Id.* at 201.

9. Burnett v. Kensington, 7 T.R. 210, 101 Eng.Rep. 937 (K.B. 1797). See London Assur. v. Companhia de Moagens do Barreiro, 167 U.S. 149, 162–168, 17 Sup.Ct. 785, 790–792, 42 L.Ed. 113, 121–123 (1897). See 2 Arnould, Marine Insurance [10 British Shipping Laws] § 882 (15th ed. 1961).

1. See generally 2 Arnould, Marine Insurance [10 British Shipping Laws] §§ 979–983, 991, 1004–1028. A lucid and less detailed treatment of the subject appears in Gilmore & Black, Admiralty 72–85 (1957). Many of the American cases are discussed in Gulf Refining Co. v. Atlantic Mut. Ins. Co., 279 U.S. 708, 49 Sup.Ct. 439, 73 L.Ed. 914 (1929).

According to the rules commonly applied by American and British courts, though there has been a lack of uniformity among them concerning details, the measure of recovery under a marine policy on cargo can be found by determining the fraction of loss and multiplying by the smaller of the underwritten amount and the value (using prime value if the policy is unvalued and stipulated value if the policy is valued).

Different and more complex statements of a rule for determining the measure of recovery are often used. In most instances, however, they are merely corollaries of this basic principle. Some of the variations in expression of the principle will be considered below. But at the outset, in order to understand the principle fully, one must take account of three characteristics of marine insurance.

First, marine insurance, unless in an amount as great as the "value" of the property insured, is customarily coinsurance. If the underwritten amount (i. e., the stated amount of insurance) is less than the "value" (to be explained presently) of the cargo that is the subject of insurance, the owner is a coinsurer in the sense that he bears a percentage of the risk.[2] For example, if he takes insurance in an amount that is 75% of the value, he bears 25% of the risk and recovers from the underwriter only 75% of the "loss" (to be explained presently). Thus, if the loss is $16,000, he recovers $12,000. In contrast, other forms of property insurance are customarily not coinsurance in the absence of a special endorsement. For example, if a householder has insurance of $15,000 on personal property worth $20,000, he recovers against the insurer the full amount of any loss, except that in no case does he recover more than $15,000. Thus, if the loss is $16,000, he recovers $15,000. A coinsurance endorsement is often added to fire insurance policies on commercial buildings and goods, and will be considered below.[3]

Second, the term "value" as used in the statement of principle above, if not referring to a stipulated value (to be explained presently), refers to the market value of the insured property at the port and time of departure (called "prime value"). A deviation from the principle of indemnity is implicit in this meaning of value.[4] The value of the cargo at the time and place of loss at sea may be either more or less than the prime value. If more, the insured who has insurance in the full amount of the stipulated or prime value nevertheless receives less than indemnity. If the value at time and place of loss is less than the stipulated or prime value, such an insured receives more than indemnity. Thus, in theory the marine contract on cargo,[5] even when enough insurance is obtained to avoid operation of

---

2. Section 81 of the British Marine Insurance Act of 1906, stating this rule, is declaratory of the distinctive rule that had been developed for marine insurance in the absence of legislation on the point.

3. Section 3.7 *infra.*

4. See 1 Arnould, Marine Insurance [9 British Shipping Laws] 360–363, §§ 391–393 (15th ed. 1961).

5. Note, however, that this statement does not apply to insurance against particular average to hull, at least under the British rule, and perhaps under

the coinsurance principle, is aimed at restoring the insured to the financial position he occupied at the commencement of the voyage, rather than either the position he occupied just before the casualty loss or the position he would have occupied if the voyage had been completed without casualty.

The simplest way of calculating this measure of recovery, aimed at restoring the position existing at commencement of the voyage, is to find the fraction of "loss" and multiply the underwritten amount by this fraction; this is the form in which the principle is stated above at the beginning of this discussion. Of course value at time of loss is not entirely ignored in this process. Rather, it is used in the determination of the fraction of loss. The value that the insured property would have had at the port of adjustment (usually the port of destination) in undamaged condition (called "sound value") is compared to the value at the port of adjustment in damaged condition to determine the fraction of loss.

Third, "value" of the cargo at commencement of the voyage may be stipulated by the terms of the policy, rather than being left to determination after loss. The policy in which value is so stipulated is referred to as a "valued" policy. If value is not so stipulated, the policy is referred to as an "open" or "unvalued" policy.[6] Most marine policies are valued. The use of valued policies is a further deviation from the principle of indemnity, since the prime value (for which the stipulated value is substituted) may be either more or less than the stipulated value.

This completes the statement of the three characteristics necessary to an understanding of the principle stated at the outset. The formulae discussed below can be derived from this principle, and need not be remembered if one finds it easier to work from the principle itself. The following symbols are used in the formulae:

X—amount of a single underwriter's liability

U—amount underwritten in the policy

P—prime value

V—value stipulated in the policy

S—sound value at port of adjustment

D—damaged value at port of adjustment

L—loss suffered by the insured as measured in monetary units of value at the port of adjustment

% L—fraction of loss (or percentage of loss, expressed in decimal form—*i.e.*, 60% being expressed .60)

---

the American rule as well. See § 3.6 (c) *infra*.

6. The term "open" has been more often used, but "unvalued" is adopted in the British Marine Insurance Act of 1906, since the term "open" is also used in a completely different sense to denote a "floating" policy (or "floater") that does not specify the property insured, but rather covers, for example, a number of cargoes to be shipped in the future during the definite or indefinite term of the policy. See 1 Arnould, Marine Insurance [9 British Shipping Laws] §§ 7, 8, 242 (15th ed. 1961). *Cf.* Winter, Marine Insurance 140, 149–150 (3d ed. 1952).

The following two propositions can be derived from the foregoing definitions of symbols:

$$L = S - D$$
$$\%L = \frac{S - D}{S} = \frac{L}{S}$$

Also, in terms of these symbols, the principle stated above can be expressed as below for all cases except the unusual cases (probably occurring, if at all, through mistake) of valued policies with U exceeding V and unvalued policies with U exceeding P. For these exceptional cases, the same formula may be used except that V or P, as the case may be, must be substituted for U.

$$X = (\% L)(U)$$

$$\text{or } X = \left(\frac{L}{S}\right) U$$

$$\text{or } X = \left(\frac{S - D}{S}\right) U$$

Traditionally the method of determining the amount due for partial damage under a valued policy is expressed in a way that is represented by the following algebraic formula:[7]

$$X = \frac{V(S - D)}{S}$$

But the formula is correct only if the valuation (V) is equal to or less than the underwritten amount (U). Commonly the sum of the amounts underwritten by separate underwriters is equal to the valuation, and this formula can be used to determine the total liability of all underwriters combined. To find the liability of a single underwriter, it is then necessary to multiply by the fraction of the total underwritten amount for which the single underwriter is responsible. In terms of the formula, this means multiplying by $\frac{U}{V}$. Put the two calculations together in one formula, and this is the result:

$$X = \frac{V(S - D)}{S} \left(\frac{U}{V}\right) = \left(\frac{S - D}{S}\right) U = \left(\frac{L}{S}\right) U = (\%L) U$$

The same answer can be derived in a less roundabout way by using the principle stated at the outset.

---

7. This formula is supported by the opinion of Lord Mansfield in Lewis v. Rucker, 2 Burr. 1167, 97 Eng.Rep. 769 (K.B. 1761). Also this is the formula for the "measure of indemnity" as defined in the British Marine Insurance Act of 1906. See § 3.6(c) n.7 *infra*.

Note from the next to the last simplification of the formula (and from the explanation above) that the principle stated at the outset can be expressed as follows:

$$X = \left(\frac{L}{S}\right) U$$

Algebraic rules tell us that this proposition may also be expressed as follows:

$$X = L\left(\frac{U}{S}\right)$$

Observe that this means that the underwriter's liability can be determined by finding the "loss" (in monetary units of value at port of adjustment) and multiplying by the "fraction of coverage" at the time of loss (determined by comparing the underwritten amount and the *sound value* at port of adjustment).[8] The reason for preferring the other form of stating the principle, used at the outset of this discussion, is that "fraction of coverage" is likely to be misunderstood as the comparison between underwritten amount and *stipulated value*. The risk of such confusion is increased by the fact that this latter meaning of "fraction of coverage" is sometimes applicable in hull insurance adjustments.[9]

§ 3.6(c) THE MEASURE OF RECOVERY FOR HULL LOSSES

Under the British rule with respect to hull losses, the underwriter's liability for *general* average under hull insurance can be determined by the formula used for cargo losses as well.[1] A different formula applies, however, to *particular* average. Liability for the latter can be computed by multiplying the loss by the "fraction of coverage" at commencement of the voyage, determined through a comparison between the underwritten amount and stipulated value (if the policy is valued) or prime value (if the policy is unvalued);[2] the loss

---

8. Compare the formulation in a clause of the American Institute Time (Hulls) form, under which American vessels are usually insured: "When the contributory value of the Vessel [that is, S] is greater than the valuation herein [that is, V], the liability of these Underwriters for General Average contribution . . . shall not exceed that proportion of the total contribution due from the Vessel that the amount insured hereunder bears to the contributory value . . . .." Buglass, General Average and the New York/Antwerp Rules, 1950, at 81 (1959).

9. See § 3.6(c) *infra*.

1. See 2 Arnould, Marine Insurance [10 British Shipping Laws] 923–927, 976–1008, §§ 1005–1008 (15th ed. 1961).

2. *Id.* at 997–998, § 1024; Winter, Marine Insurance 385 (3d ed. 1952). This difference between methods of computing liability for particular average to hull and cargo is customarily explained on the ground that a ship is not intended for sale, and it is presumed that repairs will be made by the owner, whereas cargo is intended for sale and is usually salable even in damaged condition. Perhaps an additional justification exists in the fact that this method of computing liability for hull loss avoids the difficult

is commonly the cost of making repairs minus the improvement resulting. Thus for partucular average to hull under a valued policy, by the British rule,

$$X = L \left(\frac{U}{V} \right)$$

And under an unvalued policy

$$X = L \left(\frac{U}{P} \right)$$

In case of total loss of the hull, the stipulated or prime value would also control the valuation of "L." Thus, the underwriter's liability would be U, the amount underwritten. Of course the underwriter's liability for total loss of cargo is also the underwritten amount; in the third from the last formula above, L and S would be identical, leaving X equal to U. Thus the simplified formula

$$X = U$$

is valid for total loss of either hull or cargo (except that in no event can the recovery under an unvalued policy exceed the prime value).

The American rule with respect to hull losses is in doubt. The opinion of the Supreme Court of the United States in *Gulf Refining Co. v. Atlantic Mut. Ins. Co.*[3] contains a statement of the petitioner's contention that in a case concerning loss to cargo by general average contribution, the rule applied "should be the same as that applied to insurance on hulls, where the insured is allowed to recover in full for a partial loss up to the amount of the insurance,"[4] and a dictum that "the insured may recover in full for partial losses under hull insurance."[5] Though rejecting the contention as to cargo loss, the court appears to have acquiesced in petitioner's statement of the rule as to hull loss. The cases cited in support of the dictum, however, are all cases of valued policies with a total underwritten amount equal to the stipulated value. Of course the British rule stated by Arnould would also produce full recovery, up to the amount of the insurance, in those circumstances. But the dictum has been repeated uncritically.[6]

---

problem of determining a sound value of the hull at port of adjustment. Sound value of cargo (which is used in the computation of liability for cargo losses, whether particular or general average) is usually less difficult to determine than sound value of a hull. In case of general average to hull, sound value must be determined for another purpose in any event, since it is used in the computation of the general average contribution for which the hull is liable.

3. 279 U.S. 708, 49 Sup.Ct. 439, 73 L.Ed. 914 (1929).

4. 279 U.S. at 711, 49 Sup.Ct. at 440, 73 L.Ed. at 916.

5. 279 U.S. at 713, 49 Sup.Ct. at 440, 73 L.Ed. at 917.

6. *E.g.*, Aetna Ins. Co. v. United Fruit Co., 304 U.S. 430, 435, 58 Sup.Ct. 959, 961, 82 L.Ed. 1443, 1446 (1938).

Some misunderstanding of the British rule may have arisen from the special sense in which "measure of indemnity" is used in the British Marine Insurance Act of 1906. The "measure of indemnity" and measure of recovery are not the same amount unless the underwritten amount is equal to the stipulated value (in case of a valued policy) or prime value (in case of an unvalued policy).[7]

SECTION 3.7   COINSURANCE IN NONMARINE COVERAGE

§ 3.7(a) GENERALLY

It has been noted that marine insurance, unless in an amount as great as the value of the property insured, is customarily coinsurance.[1] In contrast, other property insurance is not coinsurance unless the policy so provides. Instead the insurer is liable for the full amount of any insured loss up to the underwritten amount.

§ 3.7(b) THE NEW YORK STANDARD COINSURANCE CLAUSE

Rates for nonmarine property insurance have commonly been fixed as a percentage of the amount of insurance, regardless of the total amount insured under the policy. Thus, one pays the same number of dollars for the first thousand and for the fifteenth thousand under a $15,000 policy. Since the insurer will more often be required to pay the first thousand than the last, some losses being small, the cost to the insurer of providing the first thousand of coverage is considerably higher than the cost of providing the fifteenth thousand. These factors tend to cause insurance purchasers to take a

---

7. The following are relevant provisions of the British Marine Insurance Act of 1906:

"67.—(1) The sum which the assured can recover in respect of a loss on a policy by which he is insured, in the case of an unvalued policy to the full extent of the insurable value, or, in the case of a valued policy to the full extent of the value fixed by the policy, is called the measure of indemnity.

"(2) Where there is a loss recoverable under the policy, the insurer, or each insurer if there be more than one, is liable for such proportion of the measure of indemnity as the amount of his subscription bears to the value fixed by the policy in the case of a valued policy, or to the insurable value in the case of an unvalued policy.

"69. Where a ship is damaged, but is not totally lost, the measure of indemnity, subject to any express provision in the policy, is as follows:—

"(1) Where the ship has been repaired, the assured is entitled to the reason-

able cost of the repairs, less the customary deductions, but not exceeding the sum insured in respect of any one casualty:

"(2) Where the ship has been only partially repaired, the assured is entitled to the reasonable cost of such repairs, computed as above, and also to be indemnified for the reasonable depreciation, if any, arising from the unrepaired damage, provided that the aggregate amount shall not exceed the cost of repairing the whole damage, computed as above:

"(3) Where the ship has not been repaired, and has not been sold in her damaged state during the risk, the assured is entitled to be indemnified for the reasonable depreciation arising from the unrepaired damage, but not exceeding the reasonable cost of repairing such damage, computed as above."

1. Section 3.6(b) *supra.*

chance by purchasing an amount of insurance lower than the value of the property. To encourage the purchase of higher amounts, insurers have developed a type of provision that has eventually become the New York Standard Coinsurance Clause. An insurance policy with this clause attached is offered at a more favorable rate per thousand dollars of insurance than one without this clause. The clause reads, in part as follows:

> "This Company shall not be liable for a greater proportion of any loss or damage to the property described herein than the sum hereby insured bears to the percentage specified on the first page of this policy of the actual cash value of said property at the time such loss shall happen, nor for more than the proportion which this policy bears to the total insurance thereon."

It may facilitate understanding to translate the coinsurance clause into a formula, using symbols like those used in formulae for marine insurance,[1] except for having S here represent sound value in the sense of (quoting the policy) "actual cash value of said property at the time such loss shall happen"—a sense closely analogous to that of S in the marine formulae. To take an example, suppose the "percentage specified on the first page" of the policy is 80 per cent, which is a commonly used figure.[2] The measure of recovery can then be expressed in the following way (with the qualification that X cannot exceed L or U or L multiplied by the fraction derived by placing U over the total of all insurance on the property):

$$X = \left(\frac{U}{80\% \ S} \right) L$$

The measure of recovery under a New York standard coinsurance clause involves an element of coinsurance, but only if the total underwritten amount is not as high as the percentage of value designated in the coinsurance clause, and only in the proportion fixed by the relation between underwritten amount and the designated percentage of value rather than the relation between the underwritten amount and sound value. For example, if the value of the property, at both inception date and time of loss, is $100,000 and the total underwritten amount is $50,000, a loss of $8,000 resulting from damage to the property would be indemnified to the extent of

$$X = \left(\frac{\$50,000}{.80 \ \times \ \$100,000} \right) \$8,000 = \$5,000$$

If, however, the total underwritten amount is $80,000 (80 per cent of S) in a situation otherwise the same, then

$$X = \left(\frac{\$80,000}{.80 \ \times \ \$100,000} \right) \$8,000 = \$8,000.$$

---

1. See § 3.6(b) *supra.*

2. An earlier version of the clause was known as the New York 80% Average Clause.

Marine insurance, on the other hand, is customarily 100 per cent coinsurance. That is, the marine insurance rule produces the same result as would occur under a New York Standard Coinsurance clause in which the percentage specified was 100 per cent. Applied to the figures used above with the underwritten amount equal to $50,000, the marine result would be

$$X = \left(\frac{\$8,000}{\$100,000} \right) \ \$50,000 = \$4,000 \text{ [3]}$$

and the New York clause result would be

$$X = \left(\frac{\$50,000}{1.00 \ \times \ \$100,000} \right) \ \$8,000 = \$4,000.$$

Algebraically, the formulas are in this case equivalents since the marine formula

$$X = \left(\frac{L}{S} \right) U$$

can also be written

$$X = \left(\frac{U}{S} \right) L$$

which is the same as saying

$$X = \left(\frac{U}{1.00S} \right) L.$$

This last formula is the same as the New York formula with a specified percentage of 100 per cent.

The industry's customary use of the New York Standard Coinsurance Clause for insurance on commercial properties poses some practical problems for industrial and commercial insureds in a period of gradually rising price levels. The amount of insurance, though at least 80 per cent of the value of the property at the time of inception, might be less than 80 per cent at the time of loss, because of a rise in the dollar value of the property in the interval. Suppose, for example, the value of the property at inception was $100,000 and the total underwritten amount was $80,000 with a specified percentage of 80 per cent. And suppose that the value of the property rises so that at the time of a loss of $8,000 the value is $200,000. The resulting recovery would be

$$X = \left(\frac{\$80,000}{.80 \ \times \ \$200,000} \right) \ \$8,000 = \$4,000.$$

---

3. See § 3.6(b) *supra*.

This is only one-half of the recovery that would have been obtained if the property value had remained the same. Thus, once an increase of value is great enough to cause the face amount of coverage to be no more than the percentage stated in the coinsurance clause, the coverage of a particular loss decreases with any further rise in value of the property, in inverse proportion. Similarly, if the face amount of coverage is less than the percentage of value stated in the coinsurance clause, but only in that event, a decrease in value causes the coverage for a particular loss to increase (but in no case, of course, can the recovery exceed 100 per cent of loss).

Ordinarily the best way to avoid the risk that the coinsurance clause will come into operation is to set the original sum of insurance somewhat in excess of the stated percentage (usually 80 per cent) and to arrange for a periodic review of the valuation and an increase in the amount of insurance if the value has risen enough to make that desirable. Theoretically, another possibility would be to get a commitment from the insurer, preferably by endorsement on the policy, to a stipulated value for the purpose of the coinsurance clause, or an agreement that application of the principle of coinsurance will depend upon value at the time of inception of the contract rather than at the time of loss.[4] If the value thus agreed upon were such that the amount of the insurance equaled or exceeded the percentage stated in the coinsurance clause, the effect would be the same as if the clause were not in the policy. It is thus unlikely that an insurer would make such an agreement; rather, probably it would either strike the coinsurance clause by endorsement or else stand on the requirements implicit in the clause.

SECTION 3.8 | VALUED POLICIES

In marine insurance, a valued policy is one stipulating a value for the insured cargo or hull at commencement of the voyage (rather than leaving the value at that time, called prime value, to be determined after loss whenever relevant to calculating the measure of recovery). If no such stipulation appears in the policy, it is referred to as an "open" or "unvalued" policy.[1] As previously noted, most marine policies are valued, and this represents a potential deviation from the principle of indemnity since both the prime value (for which the stipulated value is substituted) and the sound value at time of loss may in fact be less than the stipulated value.[2]

In the absence of relevant statutes, nonmarine property insurance policies are seldom valued. Many states have adopted valued policy laws, however. They commonly apply to fire insurance and in some instances to other forms of nonmarine property insurance.[3]

---

4. Compare the effort of counsel, albeit quite properly unsuccessful, to have policies interpreted in this way in American Ins. Co. v. Iaconi, 47 Del. 167, 89 A.2d 141 (1952), 36 A.L.R.2d 604 (1954).

1. See § 3.6(b) n.6 *supra*.

2. See § 3.6(b) *supra*.

3. *E.g.*, Kans.Stat.Ann. § 40–905 (1964) (fire, tornado and lightning); Ky.

The most common form of valued policy law provides that in case of total loss the measure of recovery under the policy shall be the face amount of the policy, regardless of actual value of the insured property just before destruction.[4] In some instances valued policy laws apply also to partial losses. The most common provision, however, is for recovery of the "full" or "actual" amount of loss for partial damage,[5] thereby apparently establishing the same measure of recovery as would be used for partial loss if the valued policy law did not apply.[6] But both in the language of some statutes [7] and even independently of a statutory direction,[8] there is some support for allowing recovery of a percentage of the valuation equal to the percentage of damage suffered.

Rev.Stat. § 304.907 (1962) (livestock only).

As may be inferred from the foregoing the statutes generally are applicable to a type of risk or risks. The New Hampshire statute, however, is an example of one the application of which has been limited to a type of risk on a specific type of object—fire insurance on buildings owned by the insured. See, *e.g.*, Daeris, Inc. v. Hartford Fire Ins. Co., 105 N.H. 117, 193 A.2d 886 (1963), 97 A.L.R.2d 1238 (1964) (statute held not to apply to improvements and betterments fire insurance obtained by lessee of premises).

4.   *E.g.* Ark.Stat.Ann. § 66–3901 (1966); Minn.Stat. § 65A.08 (1969); Tex.Ins. Code Ann. art. 6.13 (1963). It has been held that a compromise or settlement between insured and insurer for an amount less than that stated in the policy is contrary to public policy and void. *E.g.*, Coddington v. Safeguard Ins. Co., 237 Ark. 457, 373 S.W. 2d 413 (1963). Also, it has been held that a clause in the policy giving the insurer an option to repair is void since the statutes state that the insured shall recover the face amount of the policy in the event of a total loss. *E.g.*, Tedder v. Hartford Fire Ins. Co., 246 S.C. 163, 143 S.E.2d 122 (1965). And the fact that the insured, as vendor under a contract to sell, has been paid the full purchase price out of proceeds of insurance separately obtained by the vendee does not defeat or reduce his claim. Hensley v. Farm Bureau Mut. Ins. Co., 243 Ark. 408, 420 S.W.2d 76 (1967).

5.   *E.g.* Fla.Stat.Ann. § 627.0801 (1960); Minn.Stat. § 65A.08 (1969); S.C.Code Ann. § 37–154 (1962). See also Hunt v. General Ins. Co., 227 S.C. 125, 87

S.E.2d 34 (1955), holding, partly because of the Valued Policy Statute, that life tenants could recover for the full amount of a partial fire loss although their interest in the property (as life tenants) had been grossly overvalued. This would seem to be a misapplication of the idea of awarding "full" or "actual" loss, since the court awarded an amount equal to the full loss on the entire property rather than the full loss to the life tenants' interest.

6.   See *e.g.*, American Ins. Co. v. Iaconi, 47 Del. 167, 89 A.2d 141 (1952), 36 A. L.R.2d 604 (1954). See also, Note, *Valuation and Measure of Recovery Under Fire Insurance Policies*, 49 Colum.L.Rev. 818, 827 (1949).

7.   *E.g.*, N.D.Cent.Code § 26–18–07 (1970).

8.   *Cf.* Billmayer v. Farmers Union Property & Cas. Co., 146 Mont. 38, 404 P.2d 322 (1965), 20 A.L.R.3d 916 (1968) (hail-crop policies held to be valued; measure of recovery based on percentage of damage and not limited to actual loss). The policies in *Billmayer* were not subject to the Montana Valued Policy Law, Mont.Rev.Codes Ann. § 40–4302 (1961), which applies only to total losses to improvements upon realty. The court found support for its application of a valued-policy rule in Mont.Rev.Codes Ann. § 40–4301 (1961), prescribing the measure of indemnity that applies when "there is no valuation in the policy."

See also Williams, *The Valued Policy and Value Determination*, 1961 Ins.L. J. 71, 78, suggesting that under laws providing a special measure of recovery for partial losses, the "criteria are either so broad or so ambiguous that any of the recognized standards of measurement may be applied."

The theory of the valued policy statutes is that the denial of any opportunity to contest the valuation when a claim is filed will cause insurers to investigate more carefully before underwriting and that policies in excessive amounts will not be written.[9] In fact, however, insurers find it more expensive to investigate fully before underwriting than to take the risks associated with increased moral hazards because some applicants will seek excessive insurance. Thus, in effect the insurer pays off on this added risk by paying the full sum of the insurance in all total loss cases in which it cannot prove another defense, including a few cases in which applicants obtained excessive coverage and destroyed the insured property to collect the insurance, but the insurer was unable to prove these facts. On balance, the principle of indemnity would be better served by repeal of valued policy statutes.

SECTION 3.9 THE MEASURE OF RECOVERY IN NONMARINE PROPERTY INSURANCE

§ 3.9(a) GENERALLY

Nonmarine property insurance policies commonly provide that, with qualifications, the company insures the designated property to the extent of the "actual cash value" at the time of loss, or, less often, the "actual value" at that time.[1]

With respect to property of such nature that market value can be determined readily, market value has usually been regarded as the measure of "actual cash value."[2] In some types of cases, however, it

---

9. *Cf.* Wisconsin Screw Co. v. Detroit Fire & Marine Ins. Co., 183 F.Supp. 183, 189 (E.D.Wis.1960), holding, however, that the valued policy provision was modified by another statute that limited recovery to actual loss when two or more policies were in effect covering the same property. Although recognizing that, if one policy had been issued in the same amount as the sum of the two policies before the court, the insured would have been entitled to the full amount stated in the policy, the court reasoned that to allow full recovery on several valued policies would encourage the procurement of excessive coverage by the insured. In a different phase of the same case, this resolution of the interaction between the statutes is adopted by the Court of Appeals for the Seventh Circuit as its own. Ludwig v. Detroit Fire & Marine Ins. Co., 342 F.2d 608 (7th Cir. 1965). If the multiple policies insure different interests, however, the face amount of each is collectible in the event of total loss. *E.g.,* Springfield Fire & Marine Ins. Co. v. Boswell, 167 So.2d 780 (Fla.

App.1964) (vendor and vendee of property subject to contract of sale).

1. By the customary phrasing of fire insurance policies on buildings and personal property generally, the insurer "does insure [*named insured*] and legal representatives, to the extent of the actual cash value of the property at the time of loss, but not exceeding the amount which it would cost to repair. . . . " See Appendix A *infra.* The comprehensive coverage clause of an automobile policy, on the other hand, customarily provides that the insurer agrees to pay for "direct and accidental loss of or damage to" the automobile; the phrase "actual cash value" is used only as the statement of the "limit of liability." See Appendix H *infra.*

2. The measure of recovery commonly applied is the difference between market value before and after damage. *E.g.,* Cassel v. Newark Ins. Co., 274 Wis. 25, 79 N.W.2d 101 (1956) (stock of merchandise); Engh v. Calvert Fire Ins. Co., 266 Wis. 419, 63 N.W.2d

is generally recognized that market value would not be a fair measure of indemnity of the insured's loss and that "actual cash value" is not synonymous with market value. Cases involving insurance on used household furniture illustrate the point.[3] With respect to buildings, although market value has sometimes been approved as the measure of "actual cash value," the two most common interpretations [4] of that phrase (and of the phrase "actual value," appearing in some policy forms) are, first, the view expressed in *McAnarney v. Newark Fire Ins. Co.*[5] that neither "market value" nor "reproduction cost less depreciation" is conclusive, these being merely factors relevant for consideration by a judge or jury,[6] and, second, the view that "actual cash value" or "actual value" means reproduction cost less depreciation.[7]

used household furniture example except...

§ 3.9(b) DEPRECIATION

The practical enforcement of a requirement that depreciation be considered may be more difficult under either the *McAnarney* or a market-value rule than under the reproduction-cost-less-depreciation rule, but it is clear in theory that the depreciated condition of property affects both its market value and its "actual cash value" as that phrase is interpreted in *McAnarney*. Some policies provide, however, that in case of partial loss the full repair cost will be paid without deduction on account of depreciation before the casualty loss. This type of coverage is sometimes referred to as "replacement insurance" (requiring the insured to repair in order to collect) or "depreciation insurance" (allowing the insured to collect in cash, whether he chooses to rebuild or not).[8] Though such coverage was first developed for large property holders, some of the comprehensive homeowner's policies, first developed in the 1950's, include coverage of this type under the title "replacement cost coverage." The following is an example of such a clause: "If at the time of loss the limit of liability for the dwelling [stated on the face of the policy] is 80 per cent or more of the full replacement cost of the dwelling covered, [the coverage under this policy is] extended to include the full cost of repair or replacement without deduction for depreciation." [9] However, further contractual

"replacement insurance" vs "depreciation insurance"

831 (1954) (motor vehicle). See Annot., 61 A.L.R.2d 711, 733–736 (1958).

3. *E.g.*, Fedas v. Insurance Co. of Pa., 300 Pa. 555, 151 A. 285 (1930); Crisp v. Security Nat'l Ins. Co., 369 S.W.2d 326 (Tex.1963).

4. Note, *Valuation and Measure of Recovery Under Fire Insurance Policies* 49 Colum.L.Rev. 818, 824 (1949).

5. 247 N.Y. 176, 159 N.E. 902, 56 A.L.R. 1149 (1928).

6. See, *e.g.*, Agoos Leather Cos. v. American & Foreign Ins. Co., 342

Mass. 603, 174 N.E.2d 652 (1961); Pinet v. New Hampshire Fire Ins. Co., 100 N.H. 346, 126 A.2d 262 (1956), 61 A.L.R.2d 706 (1958).

7. See, *e.g.*, Patriotic Order Sons of America Hall Ass'n v. Hartford Fire Ins. Co., 305 Pa. 107, 157 A. 259 (1931), 78 A.L.R. 899 (1932).

8. Note, *Valuation and Measure of Recovery Under Fire Insurance Policies,* 49 Colum.L.Rev. 818, 832 (1949).

9. It should be noted that a rise in value of the property insured carries the same potential for problems—and surprises—for the insured under this

stipulations may preclude recovery of repair costs when the policyholder does not in fact effect repairs.[10]

There is doubt about the extent to which depreciation is being taken into account in the settlement of losses covered by automobile physical damage insurance, and perhaps doubt as well about the desirability of its being deducted in calculating "actual cash value." [11] In favor of the deduction of depreciation, it might be argued that neither "loss" nor "actual cash value" is equal to the cost of repairs since the newly repaired property is somewhat more valuable than was the property just before it was damaged. On the other hand, a once-wrecked repaired vehicle ordinarily is not more valuable in the market place. But if the reduction in value of the automobile is caused by theft of a spare tire, rather than by collision, it might reasonably be argued that the new tire is clearly worth more than the used tire it replaces. If one thinks of the value of the car as a unit, however, rather than the value of the spare tire only, it is doubtful that it would make a difference that the spare is new rather than used. But perhaps a spare tire is different in this respect from a new door, since the extra value of the new door can never be realized because the rest of the car will wear out sooner than the door, whereas the same may not be true of a tire.

§ 3.9(c) OBSOLESCENCE AND CONDEMNATION PROCEEDINGS

McAnarney v. Newark Fire Ins. Co.,[1] apparently the first reported opinion explicitly considering the question whether obsolescence should be a factor in determining "actual cash value," [2] answers that question affirmatively. This view is supported in later cases as well.[3]

The reproduction-cost-less-depreciation rule of valuation appears to imply that a distinction will be drawn between obsolescence and depreciation with respect to whether a deduction should be made in arriving at "actual cash value." Such a distinction seems untenable. Both are relevant to value in virtually any sense in which that term is used except that sense implicit in equating value or "actual cash

---

homeowner's replacement provision as it does under the New York Standard Coinsurance Clause (see § 3.7(b) *supra*). A rise in value that causes 80 per cent of "the full replacement cost of the dwelling covered" to exceed the limit of liability would, in fact, cause the replacement provision to become completely inoperative.

10. See, *e.g.,* Higgins v. Insurance Co. of N. Am., 469 P.2d 766 (Ore.1970) (summarized in § 3.4(b) n.4 *supra*).

11. *Cf., e.g.,* Potomac Ins. Co. v. Wilkinson, 213 Miss. 520, 57 So.2d 158 (1952), 43 A.L.R.2d 321 (1955).

1. 247 N.Y. 176, 185, 159 N.E. 902, 905, 56 A.L.R. 1149 (1928). Another aspect of this case is discussed in § 3.9(a) *supra*.

2. Note, *Valuation and Measure of Recovery Under Fire Insurance Policies,* 49 Colum.L.Rev. 818, 824 (1949).

3. *E.g.,* American States Ins. Co. v. Mo-Lex, Inc., 427 S.W.2d 236 (Ky. 1968); Doelger & Kirsten, Inc. v. National Union Fire Ins. Co., 42 Wis.2d 518, 167 N.W.2d 198 (1969).

value" with reproduction cost less depreciation. For example, both are surely relevant to market value, though ordinarily no separate calculation of either is made when market value is determined by evidence as to what a willing buyer would pay a willing seller for the property.

A distinction may be observed between obsolescence and depreciation, however, with respect to the method of calculation. By custom, depreciation is computed on a mathematical basis, and often by a method that is known to allow more or less reduction for particular years than the actual decrease in market value because of depreciation. There is no such custom with reference to obsolescence, and often the only defensible way to determine a figure for obsolescence is in terms of the market. This is not always so, however. For example, if a theatre is obsolescent only in the sense that it has excessive space backstage, designed for vaudeville, one might rationally defend a computation under which obsolescence is accounted for by deducting the unuseable space and estimating the current reproduction cost of a building equal in size to the useable space.[4]

Closely related to the problem of valuing obsolescent property is the problem of valuing property subject to pending condemnation proceedings. It has been held that so long as the condemnation order is not final, a risk of loss from destruction of the property remains with the condemnee (assuming him to be the owner but for the effect of the condemnation proceeding) and he may recover in full under his property insurance.[5] Perhaps such a rule can be reconciled with *McAnarney* on the theory that as long as the condemnation proceeding may be abandoned there is only a prospective obsolescence, and not obsolescence in fact. But this is a dubious distinction at best since the allowance of compensation to the full extent of damage to the property (as distinguished from reduction in value of the insured's interest in the property) produces substantial overcompensation. Even more dubious, it would seem, is a decision directing the trial court to disregard, in valuing an aged fraternity house, a city resolution declaring the building a nuisance and ordering it to be demolished.[6]

A distinguishable problem is presented when a leasehold is prematurely terminated because of fire damage and a court must determine the measure of recovery under improvements and betterments coverage.[7]

---

4. *Cf.* B. F. Keith Columbus Co. v. Board of Revision, 148 Ohio St. 253, 74 N.E.2d 359 (1947).

5. *E.g.*, Edlin v. Security Ins. Co., 269 F.2d 159 (7th Cir. 1959); American Nat'l Bank & Trust Co. v. Reserve Ins. Co., 38 Ill.App.2d 315, 187 N.E.2d 343 (1st Dist. 1962); Heidisch v. Globe & Republic Ins. Co., 368 Pa. 602, 84 A.2d 566 (1951), 29 A.L.R.2d 884 (1953). *Cf.* Redevelopment Agency of City & County of San Francisco v.

Maxwell, 193 Cal.App.2d 414, 14 Cal. Rptr. 170 (1st Dist. 1961), 89 A.L.R. 2d 1070 (1963). *But cf.* Van Cure v. Hartford Fire Ins. Co., 435 Pa. 163, 253 A.2d 663 (1969), summarized in § 3.4(a) (4) n.19 *supra*.

6. Bailey v. Gulf Ins. Co., 406 F.2d 47 (10th Cir. 1969) (Oklahoma law).

7. In Daeris, Inc. v. Hartford Fire Ins. Co., 105 N.H. 117, 193 A.2d 886 (1963), 97 A.L.R.2d 1238 (1964), a fire policy

§ 3.9(d) USE AND OCCUPANCY LOSSES

The measure of recovery under property insurance policies, as customarily written and interpreted, does not include economic loss apart from damage to an interest in the property itself, unless there is a special provision in the policy for this purpose. Thus, the 1943 New York Standard Fire Insurance Policy provides that the insurer "does insure [named insured] and legal representatives, to the extent of the actual cash value of the property at the time of loss, but not exceeding the amount which it would cost to repair . . . ., nor in any event for more than the interest of the insured, against all direct loss by fire . . . to the property described hereinafter . . . ." [8] Of course the economic risk is often much greater, because of the risk of loss of use of the property pending repairs. Types of insurance that have been developed to cover the latter risk are variously referred to as "use and occupancy," "loss of rents or profits," and "business interruption" insurance.[9] Modern package policies commonly include some insurance of this kind; for example, a homeowner's comprehensive policy usually includes coverage for additional living expense, within specified limits, if the insured dwelling becomes "untenantable" because of one of the casualties insured against. Also, "business interruption" or "loss of rents and profits" endorsements are commonly added to fire insurance policies on commercial buildings.

§ 3.9(e) RELATION TO THE PRINCIPLE OF INDEMNITY

How well does the measure of recovery in nonmarine property insurance serve the principle of indemnity? "Actual cash value" and "reproduction cost less depreciation" may each be different from value to the insured. Probably even by its theory, as well as in practice, neither of these measures is aimed at accomplishing exact indemnity of the insured's loss. Either of them might produce more than indemnity to an insured who was about to sell at a lower price when the fire occurred. Also, either might produce less than indemnity. In the first place, if the insured had an old building, for the de-

provided that the measure of damages was the proportion of the original cost of the improvements that the unexpired term of the lease bore to the period from the date of making the improvements to the date of expiration; the insurer resisted a claim under the policy because the lessor had exercised its option to terminate after the fire. The court's decision allowing the lessee to recover is defensible since the lessee probably would not have been deprived of the use of the improvements by premature termination of the lease but for the fire damage; that is, the loss to the lessee was the result of the risk insured against since the premature termination of the lease was a result of the fire damage.

8. See Appendix A *infra*.

9. The development of such coverages has, as might be expected, created further variations of measure of recovery problems. In Washington Restaurant Corp. v. General Ins. Co., 64 Wash.2d 150, 390 P.2d 970 (1964), for example, the insured was allowed to recover under its business interruption policy even though its continuing expenses after fire damage were less than its operating loss before the fire.

preciated value of which he is compensated, and he must replace it with a new building, there is a problem of financing the difference between new value and depreciated value, and this affects the economic loss he suffers. Second, any special relationship that he bears to the property is not taken into account in a valuation at reproduction cost less depreciation, and perhaps not in the *McAnarney* concept of actual cash value. On grounds of administrability, however, the *McAnarney* concept is nevertheless defensible; getting into the area of special value to the insured would substantially increase problems of proof.

In some policies today there is an element of insurance at reproduction cost, without deduction for depreciation.[10] This seems a reasonable arrangement to protect the homeowner against the cost of making a cash outlay beyond what the amount of the insurance proceeds would be if a deduction were made for depreciation. On the other hand, in a strictly commercial context, this arrangement would probably not be desirable. In either case, the proceeds are likely to exceed indemnity of the insured's loss.[11]

Less defensible, it would seem, are rules allowing overcompensation for a building destroyed by fire or other casualty after its real value to the insured had been reduced by condemnation proceedings or a demolition order.[12]

SECTION 3.10 | SUBROGATION |

§ 3.10(a) SUBROGATION RIGHTS BY TYPE OF INSURANCE

In relation to property insurance, it is generally recognized, first, that the insurer is subrogated to claims of its insured against others (in contract as well as in tort) if neither the insurance contract nor the agreement made in settling the claim under the insurance policy contains any reference to subrogation or assignment of the insured's claims against others [1] and, second, that the insurer may waive all or part of its subrogation rights by stipulation in the policy [2] or by other means.[3] In practice, however, property insurance policies commonly include a subrogation clause, and the question whether such rights exist in particular circumstances in the absence of express stipulation

Property Ins

---

10. See § 3.9(b) *supra*.

11. See generally Williams, *The Principle of Indemnity: A Critical Analysis*, 1960 Ins.L.J. 471.

12. See § 3.9(c) *supra*.

1. See, *e.g.*, Pelzer Mfg. Co. v. Sun Fire Office, 36 S.C. 213, 267, 15 S.E. 562, 582 (1892); 6 Appleman, Insurance Law § 4052 n.46 (1942). Concerning subrogation to contract claims, see § 4.2(d) n.4 *infra*.

2. See, *e.g.*, Aetna Ins. Co. v. United Fruit Co., 92 F.2d 576 (2d Cir. 1937), *aff'd*, 304 U.S. 430 (1938); Fire Ass'n of Philadelphia v. Schellenger, 84 N. J.Eq. 464, 94 A. 615 (1915).

3. *E.g.*, Powers v. Calvert Fire Ins. Co., 216 S.C. 309, 57 S.E.2d 638 (1950), 16 A.L.R.2d 1261 (1951); Leonard v. Bottomley, 210 Wis. 411, 245 N.W. 849 (1933).

usually arises only when it is asserted that the express stipulation is too narrow to include the right in issue.[4]

Liability insurance policies also commonly include a subrogation clause, and validity of such a clause is not questioned.[5] Moreover, there is support for recognizing subrogation in circumstances beyond the terms of the policy clause.[6]

Though recognition of subrogation rights is the general rule for property and liability insurance, it is not a universal rule for all forms of casualty insurance. The right of an insurer to be subrogated to its insured's claims against a third party for losses due to check forgeries, for example, is limited. In this context subrogation depends upon the nature of the third party (whether the original wrongdoer, i.e., the forgerer, or an "innocent" intermediary, e.g. the bank upon which the forged check was drawn) and the specific type of insurance under which the loss is covered, and it is further complicated by the allocation-of-loss rules of negotiable instruments law.[7] If the insured is a drawee-bank (i.e., the bank upon which the forged check was drawn) with coverage under a forgery bond, the insurer is generally allowed to be subrogated to the bank's claim against the "innocent" party who had cashed the check for the forger.[8] But if the insured is an employer with coverage against forgery by an employee under a general fidelity bond, the insurer is generally not allowed to be subrogated to the employer's claim against an "innocent" intermediary, usually the drawee-bank.[9] In either case, the insurer is

4. See, e.g., Home Ins. Co. v. Bishop, 140 Me. 72, 34 A.2d 22 (1943).

5. See, e.g., Aetna Cas. & Sur. Co. v. Porter, 181 F.Supp. 81 (D.D.C.1960) (liability insurer subrogated to indemnity claim of insured against joint tortfeasor who was primarily liable for the tort); Zeglen v. Minkiewicz, 12 N.Y.2d 497, 191 N.E.2d 450, 240 N.Y.S. 2d 965 (1963) (subrogated insurer of tortfeasor on behalf of whom high limits—$50,000—of liability policy were paid out allowed contribution from another tortfeasor, also an insured of the same company under a policy with lower limits—$10,000— with the result that the second tortfeasor-insured was personally liable to the insurer for $20,000); Aetna Cas. & Sur. Co. v. Buckeye Union Cas. Co., 157 Ohio St. 385, 105 N.E.2d 568 (1952), 31 A.L.R.2d 1317 (1953) (driver's own liability insurer, which had provided coverage under a temporary substitute vehicle clause, subrogated to driver's claim as an additional insured for primary coverage under car owner's liability policy).

6. See, e. g., Hartford Acc. & Indem. Co. v. Pacific Indem. Co., 249 Cal.App.2d

432, 57 Cal.Rptr. 492 (2d Dist. 1967) (subrogation to effect sharing of malpractice insurers in costs of defense). See also § 3.11(b) n.2 infra.

7. See generally, Farnsworth, Insurance Against Check Forgery, 60 Colum.L.Rev. 284 (1960).

8. E.g., Borserine v. Maryland Cas. Co., 112 F.2d 409 (8th Cir. 1940) (applying Missouri law); First & Tri State Nat'l Bank & Trust Co. v. Massachusetts Bonding & Ins. Co., 102 Ind.App. 361, 200 N.E. 449 (1936); Metropolitan Cas. Ins. Co. v. First Nat'l Bank, 261 Mich. 450, 246 N.W. 178 (1933). See Farnsworth, n.7 supra, at 319–320.

9. American Sur. Co. v. Bank of Cal., 133 F.2d 160 (9th Cir. 1943) (applying Oregon law); Meyers v. Bank of Am. Nat'l Trust & Sav. Ass'n, 11 Cal.2d 92, 77 P.2d 1084 (1938); Baker v. American Sur. Co., 181 Iowa 634, 159 N.W. 1044 (1916); Oxford Prod. Credit Ass'n v. Bank of Oxford, 196 Miss. 50, 16 So.2d 384 (1944). See Farnsworth, n.7, supra, at 316–319. This rule is subject to considerable criticism, however, and Professor Farnsworth concludes that "as oppor-

subrogated to the claim against the forger, which is generally of little value.[10]

In relation to life and accident insurance, it is generally recognized that the insurer is not subrogated to claims of its insured, or claims for wrongful death, in the absence of contract stipulations so providing.[11] Issues regarding the validity and interpretation of any such clause seldom arise since life and accident insurance policies commonly do not contain any subrogation clause.

Life & accident Ins

In relation to medical, surgical, and hospitalization insurance, practices as to inclusion or omission of a subrogation clause have varied. The subrogation clauses of standard automobile insurance forms from the beginning through the 1958 family form were by their terms not applicable to medical payments coverages. But nonstandard forms containing subrogation clauses applicable to medical payments coverages were occasionally used,[12] and some of the standard forms devised more recently, and particularly some of the so-called package policies built around automobile insurance, allow subrogation under medical payments coverages. Many courts have sustained subrogation clauses in automobile medical payments coverages,[13] and a

tunities to spread the risk of forgery increase, and as more states adopt the *Uniform Commercial Code* [which changes much of the former negotiable instruments law underlying the denial-of-subrogation rule], the popularity of the rule . . . can be expected to wane." *Id.* at 325.

10. See *id.* at 299 n.71 for "salvage" figures on forgery bonds and fidelity insurance.

11. See, *e.g.*, Connecticut Mut. Life Ins. Co. v. New York & N. H. R. R., 25 Conn. 265 (1856).

12. See, *e.g.*, Smith v. Motor Club of Am. Ins. Co., 54 N.J.Super. 37, 148 A. 2d 37 (1959).

13. *E.g.*, Sentry Ins. Co. v. Stuart, 246 Ark. 663, 439 S.W.2d 797 (1969) (insurer, having paid $1,000 under medical payments coverage, sued insured and third parties with whom insured settled tort claim; trial court's action in sustaining demurrer reversed); DeCespedes v. Prudence Mut. Cas. Co., 193 So.2d 224 (Fla.App.1967), *aff'd*, 202 So.2d 561 (Fla.1967) (suit by insured under medical payments coverage after insured had settled with tortfeasor; held, violation of subrogation rights is a defense); Damhesel v. Hardware Dealers Mut. Fire Ins. Co., 60 Ill.App.2d 279, 209 N.E.2d 876 (1965) (denying insured recovery under medical payments coverage because of in-

sured's release to tortfeasor, which violated insurer's subrogation provision, and distinguishing subrogation right from assignment of cause of action for personal injury, which is prohibited by Illinois law); National Union Fire Ins. Co. v. Grimes, 278 Minn. 45, 153 N.W.2d 152 (1967) (insurer paid insured $970.20 under medical payments coverage; thereafter insured settled with tortfeasor, Stanek; insurer sued insured only for $970.20; declining to pass on issues of assignability since this action was against insured for a share of proceeds of settlement, held, insurer entitled to recover, subject to an offset to the extent of "the reasonable worth and value of the efforts expended and expenses incurred by defendant properly chargeable to that portion of the recovery from Stanek attributable to these medical expenses"); Motto v. State Farm Mut. Auto. Ins. Co., 81 N. M. 35, 462 P.2d 620 (1969) (suit by insured under medical payments coverage after insured had settled with tortfeasor; held, violation of subrogation rights is a defense); Geertz v. State Farm Fire & Cas., 451 P.2d 860 (Ore.1969) (suit by insured under medical payments coverage after insured had settled with tortfeasor; held, violation of subrogation rights is a defense; see n.16 *infra* for a sequel in Oregon); State Farm Mut. Ins. Co. v. Farmers Ins. Exch., 22 Utah 2d 183, 450 P.2d 458 (1969) (summary judgment holding subrogation clause val-

few have struck them down, usually on the theory that they violate rules against the assignability of causes of action for injury to person.[14]   A third position, untenable it would seem,[15] is that traditionally phrased subrogation clauses are enforceable against both the insured and the third party tortfeasor, but a clause phrased to grant rights in the proceeds of any settlement or judgment (a phrasing adopted to meet the rule against assignments) is enforceable only as a claim in the proceeds and not as a claim against the tortfeasor for violation of the subrogee's rights by settling with the insured after notice of those rights.[16]

Similarly, from an early practice of almost uniformly omitting any provisions for subrogation under medical, surgical, and hospitalization insurance, there has been a movement toward inclusion of rights of subrogation in some instances.[17]

id; affirmed); Travelers Indem. Co. v. Rader, 166 S.E.2d 157 (W.Va.1969) (declaratory judgment of validity of subrogation clause).

See Kimball & Davis, *The Extension of Insurance Subrogation*, 60 Mich.L.Rev. 841, 858, 866–868 (1962) [hereinafter cited as Kimball & Davis], persuasively distinguising between subrogation, whether legal or conventional, and assignment.

14.   *E.g.*, Peller v. Liberty Mut. Fire Ins. Co., 220 Cal.App.2d 610, 34 Cal. Rptr. 41 (4th Dist. 1963) (medical payments subrogation clause was void because contrary to common law and legislative prohibition against assignment of causes of action for personal injury); Travelers Indem. Co. v. Chumbley, 394 S.W.2d 418 (Mo.App. 1965), 19 A.L.R.3d 1043 (1968) (denying subrogation right of medical payments insurer because of prohibition against assignment of cause of action for personal injury).   Even in a jurisdiction denying subrogation for medical loss because of prohibitions against the assignment of a cause of action for personal injury, however, a "trust receipt" or "loan receipt" giving the insurer a share in any *recovery* obtained by the insured may be found valid.   *E.g.*, Block v. California Physicians' Serv., 244 Cal.App.2d 266, 53 Cal.Rptr. 51 (2d Dist. 1966) (medical services coverage).   For other examples of using such agreements to avoid problems related to subrogation practices, see § 3.10(b) (2) and (c) (1) *infra*.

15.   See § 3.10(c) (2) *infra*.

16.   State Farm Mut. Auto. Ins. Co. v. Pohl, 464 P.2d 321 (Ore.1970).   It may be suggested that the distinction drawn in this case is also supported by decisions that, in a context that might be regarded as a converse of the problem considered here, recognize the validity of a "loan receipt" type of transaction even in a jurisdiction that strikes down a traditionally phrased subrogation clause as an invalid attempt to assign a claim for personal injury; concerning that context see n.14 *supra*.   Just as the "loan receipt" sometimes proves to be an effective way around the rule against assignability, might the insurer get around the rule of *Pohl* by suing the third party tortfeasor, or his liability insurer, on the theory that they knowingly participated in an arrangement under which the insured intended to break his contract with the insurer by declining to pay to the insurer its share of the proceeds of the settlement?

17.   See, *e.g.*, Michigan Medical Serv. v. Sharpe, 339 Mich. 574, 64 N.W.2d 713 (1954) (action allowed against subscribers but not against tortfeasor); Associated Hosp. Serv., Inc. v. Milwaukee Auto. Mut. Ins. Co., 33 Wis. 2d 170, 147 N.W.2d 225 (1967) (action by Blue Cross against tortfeasor's liability insurer; judgment for Blue Cross affirmed).   Compare cases sustaining a clause excluding coverage of injuries for which a third person is legally liable unless insured is unable to recover from that person: Smith v. Idaho Hosp. Serv., Inc., 89 Idaho 499, 406 P.2d 696 (1965); Barmeier v. Oregon Physicians' Serv.,

Vance observed a split of authority as to whether a workmen's compensation insurer, in the absence of an explicit statutory provision one way or the other, is subrogated to the employee's rights against a third party tortfeasor, and he argued that the jurisdictions denying subrogation were misled by a false analogy to cases involving life and accident insurance.[18] "[T]he primary reason for refusing subrogation to the life or accident insurer is that the insurer's liability is fixed by his contract, and not by the principle of indemnity to the insured. But the [workmen's compensation] insurance carrier recovers from the tort-feasor, not on the basis of subrogation strictly speaking, but directly on the ground that it has been injured by the negligence of the tort-feasor. The loss suffered by the insurance carrier, being fixed by the terms of a public statute, was clearly foreseeable by the tort-feasor, and therefore may properly be regarded as a proximate consequence of such negligence."[19] Vance's observation of a contrast between life insurance and workmen's compensation insurance with respect to judicial recognition of insurer's rights of recoupment from tortfeasors is well supported. That is, a right of recoupment is hardly ever recognized for life insurance but is often recognized under particular workmen's compensation statutes and policies.[20] But his explanation of a workmen's compensation insurer's direct right in tort against the third party whose negligence injured the worker is unpersuasive. The argument for such a direct action, as distinguished from "subrogation strictly speaking," seems as easily applicable to life insurers as to workmen's compensation insurers. Yet it has been rejected when urged by an insurer having a life policy on one who allegedly was killed by the negligence of a railroad; the railroad had paid the insured's administratrix damages for causing his death, and the insurer then sued the railroad for the amount it had been required to pay under the terms of its policy. Judgment was rendered for the defendant railroad.[21] As to the theory of a right by direct action, the court placed its decision on the ground that the injury to the insurer by the tortfeasor was too remote.[22] Remoteness or proximity seems identical in relation to life insurers and workmen's compensation insurers, unless one considers that customs and policy provisions in relation to subrogation make the difference. Thus the contrasting treatment of life insurers and workmen's compensation insurers in relation to a direct tort action is nothing

194 Ore. 659, 243 P.2d 1053 (1952). See also Kimball & Davis 842–844.

18. Vance, Law of Insurance 798 (3d ed. Anderson 1951).

19. *Id.* at 798 n.59.

20. See, *e.g.*, Travelers' Ins. Co. v. Brass Goods Mfg. Co., 239 N.Y. 273, 146 N.E. 377, 37 A.L.R. 826 (1925); Fort Worth Lloyds v. Haygood, 151

Tex. 149, 246 S.W.2d 865 (1952); N.Y. Workmen's Comp.Law § 29 (McKinney 1965) (enacted subsequent to the *Brass Goods* decision, *supra*, and specifying a different result though retaining subrogation).

21. Connecticut Mut. Life Ins. Co. v. New York & N. H. R. R., 25 Conn. 265 (1856).

22. 25 Conn. at 276–277.

more than a reflection of the contrasting treatment in relation to subrogation.[23]

Some basic differences between property insurance, on the one hand, and life and accident insurance on the other, may be cited to support the contrasting rules with respect to subrogation rights. They do not make an overwhelming case for the distinctions that have developed, but at least they help to explain them. Three differences, in particular, are notable. First, life and accident insurance policies are rarely in amounts sufficient to provide full indemnity; property insurance often does so. Second, the amount of loss is not as readily evaluated in life and accident cases as in property cases. Third, life insurance is said to be an "investment" rather than an "indemnity" contract. Of course whole life insurance has an investment feature.[24] But the existence of that feature is consistent with the conclusion that the contract is one of indemnity as well as investment. The statement that life insurance is not an indemnity contract seems merely a legal conclusion (of which denial of subrogation is a corollary) rather than a reason for reaching the conclusion of denying subrogation or otherwise treating the contract as not one of indemnity.

In relation to subrogation, medical and hospitalization coverages occupy a middle ground between property insurance and life and accident insurance. Medical and hospitalization policies often provide full indemnity for small losses, though large losses may exceed the limits of coverage. The amount of recovery is usually dependent on amount of loss (in contrast with the designation of a fixed sum for death or scheduled sums for injuries and disabilities of specified types, in life and accident insurance). The losses are liquidated. In all these respects medical and hospitalization insurance contracts are more closely analogous to property and liability insurance than to life and accident. Even so, medical and hospitalization insurers have generally been denied subrogation rights in the absence of an express provision,[25] and the more recently developed express subrogation clauses have sometimes been held to be invalid because of statutory

---

23. Kimball and Davis note that there is a two-level subrogation problem in relation to workmen's compensation, expressed by two questions: First, is the employer subrogated to its employee's claims against third persons, and second, is the employer's insurer subrogated to the employer's rights against the third person tortfeasor. They argue that the answer to the second question should clearly be yes by analogy to the liability insurer's generally accepted right to be subrogated to its insured's claims for indemnity and contribution and that the primary question is, therefore, whether the employer is subrogated to its employee's claims. Kimball & Davis 846–847. In contrast to Vance's anal-

ysis, they conclude that the divergent answers given to this question are dependent upon the applicable workmen's compensation statutes, that "it would seem that on the authorities there is no subrogation of the employer to the rights of the employee absent a statutory provision to that effect." *Id.* at 848.

24. See § 1.3(e) *supra.*

25. *E.g.*, Hack v. Great Am. Ins. Co., 175 So.2d 594 (Fla.App.1965) (medical payments); Michigan Hosp. Serv. v. Sharpe, 339 Mich. 357, 63 N.W.2d 638 (1954), 43 A.L.R.2d 1167 (1955) (hospitalization).

or common law prohibitions against the assignment of causes of action for personal injuries.[26] Only rarely have judicial decisions denied liability under medical payments coverage to avoid double recovery, and generally only on a theory of policy construction.[27]

In general, the attitude of the courts toward subrogation is perhaps best described as one of allowing complete freedom of contract, and trying to determine and enforce the expressed intention of the contracting parties. A competing theory is that, though acknowledging a large measure of freedom of contract, some courts have favored certain resolutions in relation to asserted subrogation rights, varying with the type of insurance involved, and have held the favored resolution applicable in the absence of a clear statement in the contract of a different resolution. Whichever of these two ways of describing judicial attitudes toward subrogation rules is deemed more accurate, it stands in contrast with the judicial attitude expressed in relation to insurable interest doctrine, since there the courts have in general enforced, irrespective of the intention of the contracting parties, a doctrine founded on a recognized public policy. This contrast is all the more intriguing when one takes account of the fact that rules fashioned under both doctrines (insurable interest and subrogation) are techniques for preventing an insured from realizing a net gain from insurance proceeds.[28] Both doctrines are corollaries of the principle of indemnity.[29]

---

26. See n.14 *supra*.

27. In Gunter v. Lord, 242 La. 943, 140 So.2d 11 (1962), for example, it was held that a passenger in the insured's car could not recover twice for the same loss, once under the medical payments coverage of the insured's policy and once under the liability coverage of the same policy, because it was not the intention of the insured and insurer that double recovery under the two provisions be allowed. *Accord*, Yarrington v. Thornburg, 205 A.2d 1 (Del.1964), 11 A.L.R.3d 1110 (1967). *But cf.* Blocker v. Sterling, 251 Md. 55, 246 A.2d 226 (1968) ("we find nothing in the policy implicitly suggesting an intent that medical expense payments were not to be in addition to liability payments"). When two or more policies are involved, however, double recovery, even from the same insurer, has been allowed, the rationale being that a different result would allow the third-party tortfeasor to benefit from the contri-

butions of another and that the identity of the insurer is irrelevant. *E.g.*, Sonnier v. State Farm Mut. Auto. Ins. Co., 179 So.2d 467 (La.App.1965). This, of course, is a restatement of the collateral source rule of tort law, a rule not applicable when only one policy is involved (since the insured tortfeasor is the "contributor" of the benefit, whether it be through medical payments or liability coverage). Yarrington v. Thornburg, *supra*. If a valid right of subrogation had been recognized, whether express or not, double recovery could have been avoided in all of these cases in spite of the collateral source rule. Of course this is not to say that recognizing subrogation rights is the best means of denying double recovery.

28. See § 3.1(c) concerning techniques of preventing net gain.

29. See § 3.1 concerning that principle generally.

§ 3.10(b) IMPEDIMENTS TO SUBROGATION

(1) GENERALLY

It has sometimes been argued that either because of the basic nature of the type of insurance or because of the terms of a particular policy clause, an insurer in paying policy benefits is discharging a primary and not a secondary obligation and for that reason has no rights by way of subrogation.[1] This argument is patently fallacious, however, since all the insurer's payments in question are made in satisfaction, wholly or partially, of the insurer's contractual obligation. The characterization of that obligation as primary or secondary is merely a legal conclusion, expressing in another way, and without any statement of supporting reasons, the proposition that subrogation is sometimes disallowed but at other times allowed.

A second type of impediment to subrogation claims is a "volunteer" theory sometimes asserted. That is, it is said that an insurer paying a claim for which it is not liable is a volunteer and is not entitled to subrogation. Most decisions in point do not bear out this broad statement.[2] Even the minority decisions denying subrogation on the ground that the insurer was a volunteer have seldom, if ever, done so when liability was genuinely in dispute. Instead, they have invoked the volunteer rule when the circumstances clearly indicated that the insurer had a valid defense but nevertheless paid the policy claim.[3] Patterson suggested that the insurer is entitled to subroga-

---

1. *E.g.*, Michigan Hosp. Serv. v. Sharpe, 339 Mich. 357, 63 N.W.2d 638 (1954), 43 A.L.R.2d 1167 (1955); United States Fid. & Gy. Co. v. Valdez, 390 S.W.2d 485 (Tex.Civ.App.1965, writ refused, no reversible error) (alternate holding; voluntary workmen's compensation insurance). In a companion case to *Michigan Hosp. Serv.*, however, it was held that an express subrogation provision in a contract for medical and surgical services supported a suit for breach of contract by the Sharpes in settling with the tortfeasor. Michigan Medical Serv. v. Sharpe, 339 Mich. 574, 64 N.W.2d 713 (1954). The court thus impliedly recognized that the "primary" obligation argument for denying rights of subrogation, at most, applies only in the absence of an express subrogation provision.

2. See, *e.g.*, North-West Ins. Co. v. Western Pac. Ins. Co., 249 Ore. 662, 439 P.2d 1006 (1968) (action by liability insurer of one car against liability insurer of second car, owned by same insured, to recover money paid on property damage claims under mistaken belief plaintiff's coverage was involved).

3. *E.g.*, Old Colony Ins. Co. v. Kansas Public Serv. Co., 154 Kan. 643, 121 P. 2d 193, 138 A.L.R. 1166 (1942) (husband's homestead interest in residence owned by wife was not "unconditional and sole ownership" required by policy naming him as the insured; insurer was a "mere volunteer" in paying husband's claim). See also, *e.g.*, Grain Dealers Mut. Ins. Co. v. White, 103 Ga.App. 260, 119 S.E.2d 38 (1961) (insurer's statutory cause of action for indemnity against insured defeated by lack of proof that insurer was not a volunteer in paying liability claims against insured); Motorists Mut. Ins. Co. v. Buckeye Union Cas. Co., 81 Ohio L.Abs. 236, 161 N.E.2d 422 (Ct.App. 1959) (liability insurer not entitled to contribution from other insurer whose policy was applicable to liability of insured because payment of total claim against insured by it made it a volunteer since its liability was limited by an "other insurance" clause to only a proportionate share of the claim); American Reliable Ins. Co. v. St. Paul Fire & Marine Ins. Co., 79 S. D. 226, 110 N.W.2d 344 (1961) (fire insurer could not recover contribution from second fire insurer, both having issued policies on the same property

tion although it pays a claim despite a good defense "based upon a breach of condition which an honest insurer would ordinarily be willing to overlook . . .," but not if the loss "is not covered by the policy or falls within an exception." [4] The effect of the minority doctrine can be avoided by the insurer's taking an assignment of the claim of the "insured" at the time of its payment to him, in the absence of applicable restrictions on assignability,[5] or perhaps by resorting to a "loan receipt" type of transaction even in the face of a rule against assignability.[6]

A rule denying subrogation to a "volunteer" insurer tends to discourage an insurer from settling with the insured in a case of doubtful coverage, especially unless the insurer is able to obtain, as part of the settlement agreement, an effectual assignment of the insured's claims against third parties. Such a rule seems undesirable.

(2) CLAIMS AGAINST COMMON CARRIERS

Insurers and carriers for many years engaged in an extended struggle, sometimes referred to as the "battle of the forms," [7] with regard to the insurers' assertion of claims against carriers for damage to goods covered by insurance obtained by shippers. A statement of some main events in this struggle, though not reflecting the detailed manipulation of forms that occurred, will indicate the nature of the controversy and its relation to subrogation.[8] An early event in the struggle was the adoption by carriers of a bill-of-lading clause giving the carrier the benefit of insurance effected by the shipper.[9]

containing "other insurance" clauses, because payment to insured of amount in excess of insurer's pro rata share of loss was voluntary).

4. Patterson, Essentials of Insurance Law 149 (2d ed. 1957), citing the *Old Colony* case, n.3 *supra*, for the latter proposition.

5. See, *e.g.*, Atlantic Mut. Ins. Co. v. Cooney, 303 F.2d 253, 262–263 (9th Cir. 1962) (fire insurer reimbursed insured for loss in excess of $300,000 although applicable policy limit was $100,000; held, insurer could recover under California law as subrogee to insured's contract claim against bailee of property, rejecting the volunteer argument on the alternate grounds, first, that the insured had given express assignments of its rights to the insurer and, second, that the *moral* obligation of the insurer to reimburse its insured was sufficient to support equitable subrogation); Freeport Motor Cas. Co. v. McKenzie Pontiac, Inc., 171 Neb. 681, 107 N.W.2d 542 (1961) (volunteer argument irrelevant when insured's release of automobile comprehensive insurer expressly states

that insurer is subrogated to claims of insured).

6. For instances of use of "loan receipts" in other contexts, see § 3.10(a) *supra* and § 3.10(b) (2) and (c) (1) *infra*. See also the reference to "loan receipts" in the majority opinion and the discussion of the "volunteer" argument in both the majority and dissenting opinions in Employers Cas. Co. v. Transport Ins. Co., 444 S.W.2d 606 (Tex.1969), which concerns conflicting "other insurance" clauses discussed in § 3.11(b) *infra*.

7. Entitlement to recognition as *the* battle of the forms has also been claimed for other controversies. See, *e.g.*, Apsey, *The Battle of the Forms*, 34 Notre Dame Law. 556 (1959).

8. See generally Vance, Law of Insurance 794–796 (3d ed. Anderson 1951); Campbell, *Non-Consensual Suretyship*, 47 Yale L.J. 69, 81–85 (1935).

9. See, *e.g.*, Phoenix Ins. Co. v. Erie & W. Transp. Co., 117 U.S. 312, 6 Sup. Ct. 750, 29 L.Ed. 873 (1886).

Insurers responded with a policy clause providing for nonliability of the insurer upon shipment under a bill of lading that gave the carrier the benefit of the shipper's insurance.[10]   Since the carriers then had nothing to gain and the shippers had much to lose by retention of the clause previously used in bills of lading, the carriers modified the clause to give the carrier the benefit of any insurance effected on the goods so far as this did not defeat the insurer's liability.[11]   This strategic retreat by the carriers still left the insurers with a problem.   If an insurer paid a shipper, would it be a "volunteer"[12] and not entitled to subrogation to the shipper's claim against the carrier?   If it did not pay the shipper, how could it maintain good business relations with an insured who wanted prompt payment from somebody and did not like waiting for the carrier and insurer to resolve a dispute as to ultimate responsibility for the loss?   To meet this problem, insurers resorted to the loan receipt; the insurer paid the shipper an amount equal to the promised insurance benefits, but the transaction was cast as a loan repayable out of the prospective recovery from the carrier. The effectiveness of this technique of preserving rights against the carrier has been recognized in a number of judicial decisions.[13]   Thus the insurers emerged as the victors in the struggle with carriers over form provisions concerning responsibility for losses of insured property during shipment.   And this result is fortified by decisions that a "benefit of insurance" clause in a bill of lading is invalid under statutory prohibitions against rate discrimination, since the carrier would be receiving greater compensation from a shipper who had insurance than from one who did not.[14]

§ 3.10(c) ENFORCEMENT OF SUBROGATION RIGHTS

(1) Parties to Actions

In a case against a third party involving an insurer's subrogation rights, the insurer usually prefers to present the controversy to the jury as one between the insured and the third party, in order to avoid the effect of jury prejudice against insurers.   In some cases it has been held that the insurer is entitled to have the case presented in this way, even if it is clear in fact that the insurer's subrogation rights will entitle it to the full amount recoverable in the event of a

10. See, *e.g.*, Fayerweather v. Phenix Ins. Co., 118 N.Y. 324, 23 N.E. 192 (1890); Hartford Fire Ins. Co. v. Payne, 199 Iowa 1008, 203 N.W. 4, 39 A.L.R. 1109 (1925).

11. See, *e.g.*, Adams v. Hartford Fire Ins. Co., 193 Iowa 1027, 188 N.W. 823 (1922), 24 A.L.R. 182 (1923); Richard D. Brew & Co. v. Auclair Transp., Inc., 106 N.H. 370, 211 A.2d 897 (1965), 27 A.L.R.3d 978 (1969).

12. See § 3.10(b) (1) *supra*.

13. *E.g.*, Luckenbach v. McCahan Sugar Refining Co., 248 U.S. 139, 39 Sup.Ct. 53, 63 L.Ed. 170 (1918), 1 A.L.R. 1522 (1919).   Concerning loan receipts and their validity, see also § 3.10(a) and (b) (1) *supra* and § 3.10(c) (1) *infra*.

14. *E.g.*, Salon Serv., Inc. v. Pacific & Atl. Shippers, 24 N.Y.2d 15, 246 N. E.2d 509, 298 N.Y.S.2d 700 (1969). *Contra*, *e.g.*, Home Ins. Co. v. Northern Pac. Ry., 18 Wash.2d 798, 140 P.2d 507, 147 A.L.R. 849 (1943).

favorable result from trial.[1] The argument for permitting the action to be brought solely in the name of the insured is perhaps even stronger when the insurer has paid only part of the loss and the insured thus retains a beneficial interest in the claim.[2] But other courts have treated the insurer as a real party in interest and, indeed, as *the* real party in interest when it has paid the loss in full.[3] In an effort to improve the chances that the claim, if carried to trial, can be presented as one between the insured and the third party, often an insurer "advances" to the insured the amount due on the insurance contract, using a "loan receipt," by which the insured agrees to repay the insurer out of the recovery from the third party.[4] The question whether a transaction of this type should be given effect to avoid the insurer's being a party to the action against the third person has been sharply controverted.[5]

1. *E.g.*, Catalfano v. Higgins, 55 Del. 470, 188 A.2d 357 (1962) (held, "real party in interest" provision of Civil Procedure Act did not change common law rule that an insurer's subrogation suit must be brought in insured's name); Butera v. Donner, 177 Misc. 966, 32 N.Y.S.2d 633 (Sup.Ct.1942) (insured had released all his interest in claim against tortfeasor to his collision insurer; note that proceedings in the name of the insured are now specifically allowed by N.Y.Civ.Prac.L.R. § 1004 (McKinney 1963), quoted in n.5 *infra*); Morales v. Roddy, 250 S.W.2d 225 (Tex.Civ.App.1952, no writ history) (subrogation claim of automobile collision insurer; held that the insurer, subrogated to part of plaintiff's claim, is a necessary party to the action and that its interest must be revealed to the court although not to the jury). See Myers v. Thomas, 143 Tex. 502, 186 S.W.2d 811 (1945) (pro tanto subrogation claim of workmen's compensation insurer).

2. *E.g.*, Ellsaesser v. Mid-Continent Cas. Co., 195 Kan. 117, 403 P.2d 185 (1965), 13 A.L.R.3d 133 (1967) (car owner, paid by his insurer for all but a small part of damages to his car, sued alleged tortfeasor and others; trial court ruled that insurer, as a real party in interest, be made a party plaintiff or suit would be dismissed; held, order reversed; in a case of partial coverage and partial payment for loss, insurer is not a necessary party, and insured is proper party plaintiff, holding in trust such part of recovery as belongs in equity to insurer).

3. *E.g.*, Ellis Canning Co. v. International Harvester Co., 174 Kan. 357,

255 P.2d 658 (1953) (overruling earlier decision to the contrary); Shambley v. Jobe-Blackley Plumbing & Heating Co., 264 N.C. 456, 142 S.E.2d 18 (1965), 13 A.L.R.3d 224 (1967) (insurer having paid in full for damages to home resulting from explosion of defective heaters, it was real party in interest in tort action; action in name of insured dismissed).

4. With regard to other uses of the "loan receipt," see § 3.10(a) and (b) (1) and (2) *supra*.

5. See, *e.g.*, Crocker v. New England Power Co., 348 Mass. 159, 202 N.E.2d 793 (1964) (held, receipt was not shown to be other than the loan arrangement it purported to be, and the insurer's payment to plaintiff under the terms of the receipt did not extinguish plaintiff's rights against defendant); Waterway Term. Co. v. P. S. Lord Mech. Contractors, 242 Ore. 1, 406 P.2d 556 (1965), 13 A.L.R.3d 1 (1967) (action by property owner against contractor and subcontractors for damage from fire caused by defendants' negligence; trial court dismissed pleas in abatement founded on theory property owner was not real party in interest since it had been paid for the loss under fire insurance coverage; jury verdict for defendants; held, reversed for new trial because of errors in rulings on evidence and instructions to jury; pleas in abatement were properly dismissed since payments were made under loan receipts). *Contra, e.g.*, Kopperud v. Chick, 27 Wis.2d 591, 135 N. W.2d 335 (1965) (held, insured's suit against tortfeasor for indemnity properly dismissed since insurer was real party in interest, the execution of a

Arguments for the special treatment of insurance subrogation claims, for the purpose of avoiding disclosure to the jury that an insurer has an interest, are much like those against disclosure of liability insurance. They are directed at minimizing the effect of unavoidable bias of jurors against insurers. In addition to the opposing arguments for full disclosure, whether of liability or of subrogation interests, it might be urged that subrogation of insurers is of doubtful value from an overall point of view and that a rigid real-party-in-interest rule would be one practical step toward a goal of eliminating wasteful subrogation practices. Against this last argument stands the proposition that such a piecemeal attack on a practice is not warranted unless there is justification for it independently of reasons of broader application; the disadvantages of the duplicity it introduces into the legal system outweigh advantages of such a technique of law reform.[6]

(2) REMEDIES; INTERESTS IN CLAIMS

Legal protection against interference with an insurer's subrogation interest is in some instances granted in proceedings between the insurer and the third party against whom the insured had a claim subject to subrogation, in other instances in proceedings between the insurer and insured, and occasionally in proceedings involving all three parties.

By the majority rule the subrogated insurer may proceed against the tortfeasor who settled with the insured in violation of its subrogation rights; thus, payment to the insured or another by a third party who knew of the insurer's interest is disallowed as a discharge of the third party's liability to the extent of the insurer's subrogation interest.[7]

loan receipt between insurer and insured not having preserved the insured's status as the real party in interest on the claim; dicta, however, that loan receipts are valid and effective in some contexts). See also N.Y. Civ.Prac.L.R. § 1004 (McKinney 1963): "Except where otherwise prescribed by order of the court, an . . . insured person who has executed to his insurer either a loan or subrogation receipt, trust agreement, or other similar agreement . . . may sue or be sued without joining with him the person for or against whose interest the action is brought."

6. *Cf.* Keeton, Venturing to Do Justice 74–77 (1969).

7. *E.g.*, Sentry Ins. Co. v. Stuart, 246 Ark. 663, 439 S.W.2d 797 (1969) (medical payments coverage; trial court's action in sustaining demurrer reversed); Cleaveland v. Chesapeake &

Potomac Tel. Co., 225 Md. 47, 169 A.2d 446 (1961); Nationwide Mut. Ins. Co. v. Spivey, 259 N.C. 732, 131 S.E.2d 338 (1963) (held, fact that consent judgment had been entered was irrelevant since consent judgment is a contract and is to be interpreted as such); Great Am. Ins. Co. v. Watts, 393 P.2d 236 (Okla.1964) (settlement was expressly limited to excess of loss over insurance proceeds); Calvert Fire Ins. Co. v. James, 236 S.C. 431, 114 S.E.2d 832 (1960) 92 A.L.R.2d 97 (1963). See also Farm Bureau Mut. Ins. Co. v. Anderson, 360 S.W.2d 314 (Mo.App. 1962) (holding that since a release obtained by the tortfeasor with knowledge of the insurer's subrogation interest did not extinguish that interest or the insurer's rights against the tortfeasor, the insurer could not maintain an action against the insured for giving a release without the insurer's knowledge or consent).

The subrogated insurer may also be entitled to enforce one or another among a wide variety of remedies against the insured. If the insurer has not yet paid policy benefits to the insured, the insured's violation of the insurer's subrogation rights serves as a partial or complete defense to liability for such benefits.[8] If, on the other hand, policy benefits have been paid to the insured, the insurer may be allowed to prosecute a separate action against the insured. Causes of action, subject to some qualifications,[9] have been recognized on each of the following theories: *breach of contract* (conduct of the insured, such as settling with a third party tortfeasor responsible for the insured loss, is a breach of subrogation stipulations in the original insurance contract between the insurer and the insured, or in a collateral agreement such as an assignment, "loan receipt," or subrogation agreement executed at the time of payment of the policy claim, and damages may be recovered for the breach)[10]; *quasi-contract* (the insured has received from a third person money for which in equity and good conscience he ought to account to the insurer, in view of the subrogation interest of the latter)[11]; *constructive trust* (since in equity and good conscience the insurer is entitled to money received by the insured from the third person, the insured is regarded as a constructive trustee, receiving and holding the money for the

8.   *E.g.*, Continental Mfg. Corp. v. Underwriters at Lloyds London, 185 Cal. App.2d 545, 8 Cal.Rptr. 276 (2d Dist. 1960) (lease provision relieving lessee of liability for negligence, executed without consent of lessor's insurer, held to interfere with insurer's subrogation rights and to provide an adequate defense to lessor's claim under the policy); DeCespedes v. Prudence Mut. Cas. Co., 193 So.2d 224 (Fla.App. 1967), *aff'd*, 202 So.2d 561 (Fla.1967) (medical payments coverage); Damhesel v. Hardware Dealers Mut. Fire Ins. Co., 60 Ill.App.2d 279, 209 N.E.2d 876 (1st Dist. 1965) (medical payments coverage); Flanary v. Reserve Ins. Co., 364 Mich. 73, 110 N.W.2d 670 (1961) (automobile collision insurance); Motto v. State Farm Mut. Auto. Ins. Co., 81 N.M. 35, 462 P.2d 620 (1969) (medical payments coverage); Armijo v. Foundation Reserve Ins. Co., 75 N.M. 592, 408 P.2d 750 (1966) (automobile collision insurance); Hilley v. Blue Ridge Ins. Co., 235 N.C. 544, 70 S.E.2d 570 (1952), 38 A.L.R.2d 1090 (1954) (automobile collision insurance); Geertz v. State Farm Fire & Cas., 451 P.2d 860 (Ore.1969).

9.   Under some decisions an insurer has no right of direct action against an insured who has allegedly interfered with the insurer's subrogation rights if the insured's settlement with the tortfeasor does not preclude action by the insurer against the tortfeasor—*e. g.*, Farm Bureau Mut. Ins. Co. v. Anderson, 360 S.W.2d 314 (Mo.App.1962) (tortfeasor having knowledge of insurer's subrogation interest)—or if the insured has, without the insurer's knowledge or consent, prosecuted to an unsuccessful conclusion a tort action against the third party—*e.g.*, Providence Wash. Ins. Co. v. Hogges, 67 N.J.Super. 475, 171 A.2d 120 (App. Div.1961) (adverse result in the insured's tort action treated as a determination that the third party was not liable and therefore that the insurer's rights were valueless).

10.   *E.g.*, Sentry Ins. Co. v. Stuart, 246 Ark. 663, 439 S.W.2d 797 (1969) (subrogation clause in medical payments coverage; trial court's action in sustaining demurrer reversed); National Union Fire Ins. Co. v. Grimes, 278 Minn. 45, 153 N.W.2d 152 (1967) (medical payments coverage; breach of agreement to repay insurer out of settlement proceeds; offset allowed for expenses); United States Fid. & Gy. Co. v. Covert, 242 Miss. 1, 133 So.2d 403 (1961) (action based on "subrogation receipt" rather than insurance policy).

11.   *E.g.*, General Exch. Ins. Corp. v. Driscoll, 315 Mass. 360, 52 N.E.2d 970 (1944).

benefit of the insurer)[12]; _injunction_ (because remedies at law are inadequate, though the subrogation interest of the insurer is clear, an insured may be restrained from settling or receiving proceeds of a settlement with a third person in derogation of such interest).[13]

The pecuniary value of the remedy to the insurer may be affected by the choice among these different grounds of relief, whether the choice is made by an insurer or instead by a court despite an insurer's effort to elect a different remedy. For example, under the quasi-contract theory of money had and received by the insured from a third person, the insurer would recover from the insured the sum that the insured had recovered from the alleged tortfeasor on account of the claim (or that proportion of the claim) to which the insurer was subrogated. In contrast, under the theory that violation of subrogation rights is a complete defense to the insurer's liability, the insurer would pay nothing to the insured. Also, the insurer might get back the entire sum paid if it had paid before violation or without notice of violation.[14] If the theory is one of damages for breach of contract by the insured, troublesome questions may arise concerning the measure of damages. The answers depend to a large extent on views regarding the respective interests of the insured and the subrogated insurer in the third party claim.

It may be useful to consider the range of possible methods of allocating rights in an insured's claim against a third party. The present discussion is limited by two assumptions. The validity of these assumptions for particular transactions will be examined in the next chapter;[15] as will appear there, courts sometimes reject these assumptions, bypassing the problems they present and encountering another set of problems instead. The first assumption is that a contract of insurance is personal in nature in the sense that it runs to the insured and its existence does not affect the third party's liability to the insured. The second assumption is that the existence of a claim of the insured against the third party does not affect the liability of the insurer to the insured.

After an insurer has paid to an insured the benefits specified in the insurance contract, what are the interests of the insurer and the insured in the insured's claim against a third party allegedly responsible for the loss? Each of the following five rules has been urged as the answer to this question.

First Rule: The insurer is the sole beneficial owner of the claim against the third party and is entitled to the full amount recovered,

---

12. _E.g._, Norwich Union Fire Ins. Soc'y v. Stang, 9 Ohio C.C.Dec. 576 (Cir.Ct. 1897). See also, _e.g._, Providence Wash. Ins. Co. v. Hogges, 67 N.J.Super. 475, 171 A.2d 120 (1961) (dictum). _Cf._ North River Ins. Co. v. McKenzie, 261 Ala. 353, 74 So.2d 599 (1954), 51 A.L.R.2d 687 (1957).

13. _E.g._, Hartford Ins. Co. v. Pennell, 2 Ill.App. 609 (3d Dist. 1878).

14. _E.g._, Illinois Auto. Ins. Exch. v. Braun, 280 Pa. 550, 124 A. 691 (1924), 36 A.L.R. 1262 (1925).

15. See especially §§ 4.1–4.6 _infra_.

whether or not it exceeds the amount paid by the insurer to the insured.[16]

Second Rule: The insurer is to be reimbursed first out of the recovery from the third party, and the insured is entitled to any remaining balance.[17]

Third Rule: The recovery from the third person is to be prorated between the insurer and the insured in accordance with the percentage of the original loss for which the insurer paid the insured under the policy.[18]

Fourth Rule: Out of the recovery from the third party the insured is to be reimbursed first, for the loss not covered by insurance, and the insurer is entitled to any remaining balance, up to a sum sufficient to reimburse the insurer fully, the insured being entitled to anything beyond that.[19] Thus, if there is any windfall, it goes to the insured.[20]

16. *E.g.* Travelers' Ins. Co. v. Brass Goods Mfg. Co., 239 N.Y. 273, 146 N.E. 377, 37 A.L.R. 826 (1925) (applying this rule under the then-existing workmen's compensation law that required an injured employee to make an exclusive election either to receive compensation benefits or to sue in tort). See Kimball & Davis 865–866.

17. *E.g.*, Fort Worth Lloyds v. Haygood, 151 Tex. 149, 246 S.W.2d 865 (1952) (so interpreting the state workmen's compensation law).

18. *E.g.*, Pontiac Mut. County Fire & Lightning Ins. Co. v. Sheibley, 279 Ill. 118, 116 N.E. 644 (1917); General Exch. Ins. Corp. v. Driscoll, 315 Mass. 360, 52 N.E.2d 970 (1944).

19. *E.g.*, Union Ins. Soc'y v. Consolidated Ice Co., 261 Mich. 35, 245 N.W. 563 (1932); Yorkshire Ins. Co. v. Nisbet Shipping Co., [1962] 2 Q.B. 330. Kimball and Davis seem to rely implicitly on what is here called the Fourth Rule as a means of allocation that would protect the rights of the insured yet allow a rational extension of subrogation to life insurance and related coverages. See Kimball & Davis, *The Extension of Insurance Subrogation*, 60 Mich.L.Rev. 841, 850–860 (1962).

20. In the *Nisbet* case, n.19 *supra*, the insured had several valued hull policies on one of its ships in a total amount of £72,000, each policy stating a value for the ship of that amount. The ship was wrecked and sunk in 1945, the result of a collision with a ship owned by the Canadian

government. Nisbet was paid £72,000 by the insurers in 1945 and, with the insurers' permission and subject to their subrogation rights, commenced suit against the Canadian government in 1946. After a long history of litigation (including one appeal to the Privy Council), Nisbet won. The ship was valued at £74,514 as of the date of the collision, and payment was made in Canadian dollars at the 1945 exchange rate. However, the English pound sterling had been devalued in 1949, so Nisbet's recovery in Canadian dollars was worth somewhat over £126,971 in 1955. Nisbet admitted its obligation to reimburse the insurers and paid £72,000 to them. But one of the insurers claimed and brought suit to recover its pro tanto share of the excess retained by Nisbet, on the theory that the *entire* recovery belonged to the insurers. The court held that the insurers were entitled only to what they had paid Nisbet and gave judgment denying recovery beyond the £72,000 that Nisbet had voluntarily paid them. The adoption of what is here called the Fourth Rule seems sound, but the judgment does not. Because of the devaluation in 1949, the £72,000 paid Nisbet in 1945 was not equivalent to the £72,000 paid the insurers in 1955. If the rule had been correctly applied, both the recovery equal to the full 1945 loss and the £72,000 paid by the insurers in that year would have been converted to 1955 pounds sterling; Nisbet would have been allowed to retain the difference between the two as unreimbursed loss, and the insurers would have been allowed the 1955 equivalent of

Fifth Rule: The insured is the sole owner of the claim against the third party and is entitled to the full amount recovered, whether or not the total thus received from the third party and the insurer exceeds his loss. This rule is a rejection of subrogation. It is in effect the rule applied to types of insurance under which subrogation is customarily disallowed—for example, life insurance.[21]

A court rejecting the first and fifth rules may find it necessary not only to choose among rules two, three, and four but also to decide whether splitting of a tort cause of action will be allowed—that is, whether the insured and the subrogated insurer will each be allowed to proceed independently with respect to his or its share of the cause of action or instead will be required to proceed jointly if at all. Decisions are in conflict, a majority holding that splitting is not allowed.[22] Perhaps some of the apparent conflict can be resolved. Cases involving two separate claims by a single person, holding all the legal and equitable interests in both claims, might be distinguished from cases in which one of the claims in reality involves an insurer's subrogation interests and the other involves the insured's residual interests. Also, cases involving a *settlement* of one claim (or even an agreed judgment as distinguished from a judgment reached in a trial on the merits) followed by the filing of an action in court might be distinguished from cases applying the rule against splitting when a second action is filed after a trial on the merits in a first action. Thus a court that had disallowed splitting in the latter type of case might nevertheless permit splitting by settlement when, for example, settlement of the property damage claim asserted by the subrogated insurer has been consummated before the plea in bar, based on the rule against splitting, is brought to decision in an action on the personal injury claim by the insured. And, similarly a court might allow the insured to settle with the alleged tortfeasor as to his share of the

their 1945 payment. The rule of allocation chosen by the court would have had practical significance, therefore, even if the court had properly revalued the amount paid by the insurers; it had special meaning under the court's method of disposition because Nisbet was allowed to retain the "excess" over the sum of his unreimbursed loss and the amount paid by the insurers. The court speaks of the "windfall" produced by the devaluation of the pound sterling in relation to the last part of the allocation, but Nisbet's windfall was produced by the court's decision concerning the effect of the devaluation, not by the devaluation itself.

21. See § 3.10(a) *supra*.

22. See, *e.g.*, Rush v. City of Maple Heights, 167 Ohio St. 221, 147 N.E.2d 599 (1958), and Spinelli v. Maxwell, 430 Pa. 478, 243 A.2d 425 (1968), both denying recovery for personal injuries sustained in automobile accidents because of previous adjudications of property damage claims. See also Warner v. Hedrick, 147 W.Va. 262, 126 S.E.2d 371 (1962) (judgment for plaintiff on $300 property damage claim precluded subsequent assertion of his cause of action for medical expense and loss of consortium because of injury to his wife). *Contra, e.g.*, Carter v. Hinkle, 189 Va. 1, 52 S.E.2d 135 (1949). Compare Holbert v. Safe Ins. Co., 114 W.Va. 221, 171 S.E. 422 (1933) (allowing insured to recover from insurer after settling with tortfeasor for amount of loss in excess of part covered by insurance, the release involved preserving for the insured and his insurer the right to proceed against the tortfeasor for the amount of loss equal to the part insured). See also Annot., 62 A.L.R.2d 977 (1958).

cause of action without affecting the subrogated insurer's share of the cause of action, even if disallowing splitting in other contexts. Perhaps, then, in some of the jurisdictions having precedents against splitting exceptions will be recognized; in this context of genuinely disparate interests it may be found that the desirability of preventing a burden of litigation is outweighed by the desirability of avoiding the difficulties arising from conflicting interests between insurer and insured if splitting is disallowed—a conflict that is especially troublesome when personal injury as well as property damage is involved. If the rule against splitting is applied in this context despite the conflict of interests between insurer and insured, then it would seem appropriate to hold the subrogated insurer to a requirement that it give reasonable consideration to the interest of the insured in the claim rather than being free to assert its subrogation claim without accountability for the collateral effect on the insured's interests.[23] Such an obligation, imposed by the courts because of the nature of the relationship of the parties, would be a counterpart of the insured's obligation, imposed under equitable doctrine even in the absence of contractual stipulations, to respect the insurer's subrogation interest.

In a number of respects, precedents concerning subrogation rights are insufficient to support the formulation of answers that could fairly be called a majority or prevailing set of rules. For example, there is no clear answer in precedents as to whether the choice a court makes among rules two, three, and four as a method of allocating rights in the proceeds of a *settlement* with the tortfeasor is to be applied also to a recovery *in full* upon a judgment against the tortfeasor. One reason for the lack of a clear answer to this question is that full recoveries by collection of a judgment occur in an extremely small percentage of cases. A second reason is that usually such a full recovery by judgment is just enough to reimburse fully both the insurer and the insured as long as litigation expenses are disregarded, and in these circumstances rules two, three, and four all produce the same result.

In contrast, almost invariably a settlement involves a reduced recovery—one insufficient to reimburse fully both the insurer and the insured—and poses the necessity of choosing among rules two, three, and four. There is precedent supporting each rule, at least in some limited context. The second rule—reimbursing the insurer first—has been applied to interests in the claim of an injured worker against a third party, after workmen's compensation benefits have been paid.[24] The third rule—reimbursing under a proration formula—has been applied occasionally in contested cases,[25] and is no doubt very often the result achieved by compromise settlement between the insured and

---

23. Compare the argument for accountability of the liability insurer for affecting adversely the interests of its insured in his reciprocal claim, § 7.-10(a) *infra*.

24. See n.17 *supra*.

25. See n.18 *supra*.

insurer, whether or not it is consistent with the legally enforceable rule of allocation. The fourth rule—reimbursing the insured first—has the greatest support of the three in precedents.[26] Perhaps the argument for this rule is fortified by the fact that ordinarily there has been no barrier to the insurers' drafting policy forms containing a stipulation for proration—the third rule—or an even more pro-insurer disposition of recoveries against third persons, and yet they have not so drafted policies generally.

It might be argued, on the other hand, that neither an insurer nor an insured is entitled to insist that the claim against the third party be compromised and that ordinarily a tort claim against the third person, if collected in full, would make both the insurer and the insured whole. Thus, each is entitled to be made whole (if the tort claim is valid) or to get nothing (if the tort claim is invalid). It might be suggested, too, that if it is held that the insured is entitled to be reimbursed first out of any compromise settlement, insurers will tend to reject settlement proposals and insist on trials, unless this rule is supplemented by another establishing that the insurer has a duty not to oppose a settlement it would have found acceptable, had it held the entire interest in the claim against the third party.[27]

In view of the fact that all but a very low percentage of the tort claims against third persons are settled, the frequency of agreement between the insurer and the insured for proration of settlement proceeds produces a substantial deviation from the principle that the insured should be fully indemnified first, even in jurisdictions where that might be the theoretical rule of allocation.

Often issues concerning the allocation of rights of the insurer and the insured in the latter's claim against a third person are presented for determination after the insured has violated the insurer's rights by taking some independent action that affects the insurer's subrogation interest. One line of precedents holds that the insured's violation of the insurer's subrogation rights totally relieves the insurer of liability under the policy if it has not yet paid the insured [28] and entitles the insurer to recover from the insured any payment made by it to the insured before the violation occurred.[29]

A conflicting line of precedents, with numerous variations, undertakes to limit the insurer's relief to an amount consistent with the harm done by the breach. It has been said in a leading case that in order to prove the harm done by violation of its subrogation rights an insurer "must show that in fact it might have recovered against . . . ." the third party, in that case a railroad company, "as a wrongdoer." [30] The insurer had issued collision coverage for a car and had a

Re Insured's violation of Insurer's Subrogation right

26. See n.19 *supra*.

27. Compare the rules developed in relation to the duty of a liability insurer with a low policy limit not to decline a claimant's settlement offer within that limit if it would have accepted the offer had no policy limit applied. See § 7.8 *infra*.

28. See n.8 *supra*.

29. See n.14 *supra*.

30. Hamilton Fire Ins. Co. v. Greger, 246 N.Y. 162, 169, 158 N.E. 60, 62 (1927), 55 A.L.R. 921, 926 (1928). See also, *e.g.*, Twin States Ins. Co. v. Bush, 183 So.2d 891 (Miss.1966), hold-

subrogation interest in the claim for damage to the car but not in the very substantial claim for personal injury. The word "might" in the opinion is ambiguous. Was it intended to mean that, in order to recover, the insurer must show that it would have litigated the tort claim and would have recovered judgment against the alleged tortfeasor if the settlement had not been made? Or only that the prospect of its doing so was such that it would have effected some recovery by way of compromise of disputed liability in tort? Or only that there was a prospect of effecting some recovery by compromise? The last interpretation seems implausible, since any value placed on such a prospect would be more speculative than damages findings are ordinarily allowed to be. The second interpretation seems the fairest, since it is best calculated to put the insurer in the position it would have occupied had the insured not violated its subrogation rights. But it is not at all clear that this is the choice intended by the court.

If the quoted passage means that the insurer must prove that it would have recovered if the claim had been litigated rather than being settled, then the compromise settlement figure is not treated as the true value of the third party claim. If the passage means that the insurer must show only that there is such a possibility of recovery that the claim had settlement value, then it would be open to the insurer to show that it was damaged in an amount equal to the compromise settlement figure allocable to that part of the claim to which it was subrogated (the property damage claim, but not the personal injury claim); though the insurer would be free to urge that the reasonable compromise settlement value exceeded the amount that the insured accepted in settlement, it would seem that the insured would have no cause for complaint if the insurer were satisfied to treat the actual settlement figure as the true value.

If the insurer recovers against the insured on the quasi-contract theory of money had and received by the insured by virtue of his compromise settlement, that part of the compromise settlement allocable to the claim to which the insurer was subrogated is the measure of recovery, not on the theory that it represents true value of the claim but rather upon the theory that it represents the amount had and received.

Costs of investigation and litigation of the tort claim pose an additional problem. For example, suppose the payment by the insurer to the insured is $2,000, the total loss suffered by the insured is $4,000, the judgment collected from the third party on account of the loss is $4,000, and the cost of investigation and litigation to effect the collection is $1,000. Is the allocation to be computed on the basis of the net recovery of $3,000 or on the basis of the gross recovery of $4,000? That is, if the fourth rule of allocation is applied—reim-

ing that the insurer must prove that it "could have recovered from the person to whom the release was given . . . ," *i.e.* that it must allege and prove, in its claim against the insured, "that the other driver caused or contributed to the accident . . . ." 183 So.2d at 893.

bursing the insured first—is the recovery a net of $2,000 to the insured and $1,000 to the insurer or is it a gross of $2,000 to each, leaving responsibility for litigation costs to be determined independently? This is a debatable question, and very little authority in point can be found.

Independent treatment of the costs of effecting collection would be consistent with the usual treatment of attorneys' fees in American law; ordinarily a measure of damages is established on the assumption that it will be paid without litigation, and attorneys' fees are not an element of damages. The argument for this result is strengthened when each of the parties having an interest in the claim against the third party is represented by a separate attorney and the tort claim is tried to judgment rather than being compromised. The law on the measure of recovery is fashioned on the theory that obligations will be paid in full, and to the extent that one must incur expenses because this is not so, they are his to bear. The theoretical recovery, then, is the full amount of the judgment when the case is not settled. Thus, if in pursuing the tort claim against the third person the insurer and insured had separate attorneys and separate expenses, each should receive his full share of the judgment and bear his own expenses, each thus realizing a net recovery somewhat less than full reimbursement. If the insurer and insured were represented by one attorney and incurred other expenses jointly in pressing the tort claim, proration would achieve virtually this same result. Similarly, one might argue for proration when the insured and his attorney press the claim to conclusion without participation of any separate attorney employed by the insurer. There is some support in precedents for such proration of the expenses of collection.[31]

On the other hand, independent treatment of the costs of effecting collection produces a net result inconsistent with the theory purportedly being applied as to division of interests in the claim that is the subject of subrogation. And there is support for the proposition that in applying the fourth rule—reimbursing the insured first—one should not regard the insured as reimbursed fully unless the net recovery above all expenses of effecting it is at least as much as the amount by which the insured's loss exceeded the benefits paid to him by the insurer.[32]

---

31. *E.g.*, National Union Fire Ins. Co. v. Grimes, 278 Minn. 45, 153 N.W.2d 152 (1967) (subrogated insurer recovered part of proceeds of insured's settlement with tortfeasor, but subject to an offset to the extent of "the reasonable worth and value of the efforts expended and expenses incurred" by the insured properly chargeable to that portion of the claim attributable to medical expenses, for which the insurer had paid under medical payments coverage). *Cf.* United Services Auto. Assoc. v. Hills, 172 Neb. 128, 109 N.W.2d 174 (1961), 2 A.L.R.3d 1422 (1965) (when collision insurer abandoned its hostility to inclusion of its subrogation claim in insured's attorney's negotiations with tortfeasor, by seeking to collect a share of the settlement fund secured solely by the efforts of the insured and his attorney, attorney had claim against insurer's share of settlement fund for expenses, including value of his services).

32. *E.g.*, Union Ins. Soc'y v. Consolidated Ice Co., 261 Mich. 35, 245 N.W. 563 (1932).

It might be argued that the choice among the rules for allocating rights in the tort recovery from a third person should depend on why a share of the loss was to be borne by the insured in the absence of third party claims. That is, was the insured's share solely an excess of the loss over the amount of the insurance coverage (as when the coverage under a fire insurance policy is $10,000 and the loss is $12,000, leaving the insured a $2,000 share of the loss to bear personally in the absence of a tort cause of action against a third person for negligently starting the fire), or did it arise entirely or in part from a policy provision for a deductible (as when $1,450 of a $1,500 collision loss is paid by an automobile collision insurer under a policy with a $50 deductible) or from a coinsurance clause (as when a fire insurance policy on commercial property, with a New York Standard Coinsurance Clause, provides for payment of only a stated percentage of the loss, leaving the insured to bear the remaining percentage)? The reasons that, absent a tort recovery against a third person, part of the loss would be borne by the insured are arguably relevant to interpretation of the contract between the parties as it bears upon any express subrogation clause and upon the question whether the rights of subrogation, as they would have existed in the absence of contractual stipulation, have been impliedly modified by the terms of the contract. For example, if the contract provides for coinsurance of the loss, with the insured bearing part of the risk, it may be argued that this implies an agreement that the rule for allocation of recovery from a third party should be the third rule—proration. But it might be answered that the coinsurance principle is aimed at creating an inducement to the maintenance of full insurance and not at division of recoupment from other sources. Similarly, it might appear that a clause providing that there shall be a "deductible" of $50 is fairly construed as an agreement that the insured shall bear the first $50 of loss and that the subrogation interest should be computed on the basis that, if the total recovery against the third party is just $50 less than the total loss of the insured, the insurer shall have full reimbursement of its insurance payment and the $50 loss remaining shall be borne by the insured. On the other hand, it might be argued that the deductible provision is not an agreement about bearing net loss after recoupment from other sources but only a clause designed for administrative convenience and for the elimination of concern with losses so small that they are better borne as costs of the activity than as casualty losses. Thus the arguments for preferring one over another of the rules of allocation are rather inconclusive in principle, and they are unsettled in the precedents. There is a tendency in the few decisions facing such an issue to reach some kind of compromise (for example, applying a proration principle to the $50 of a collision loss within the deductible, rather than giving preference either to the insurer or to the insured).[33]   And no doubt there is a similar tenden-

33. See, *e.g.*, General Exch. Ins. Corp. v. Driscoll, 315 Mass. 360, 52 N.E.2d 970 (1944).

cy for insurers and their insureds to settle these issues on a compromise basis rather than pressing for an adjudication.

SECTION 3.11 OTHER INSURANCE CLAUSES

§ 3.11(a) PURPOSES AND TYPES OF OTHER INSURANCE CLAUSES

Other insurance provisions in a policy are designed to reduce or eliminate the liability of the insurer in whose policy they appear because of the insured's obtaining or having available to him other coverage of a type specified. In general, their purpose is to protect the insurer against the moral risks incident to over-insurance. Obviously, if by going to two or more insurers for policies a person has obtained insurance on property in an amount exceeding its value, he has an inducement to destroy it for the purpose of collecting the insurance.[1] Also, on a plane of less wilful action, inducements to take care to preserve the property against hazards operate less forcefully upon him than upon one who has an interest in the property beyond the amount of his insurance.[2]

Some clauses, more commonly used in the past than currently, declare that the company shall have no liability if the policyholder has other insurance applicable to the loss.[3] In some instances this result was declared to apply whether the other insurance was valid and collectible or not;[4] thus, if the policyholder had obtained two policies containing such clauses, literal enforcement of their provisions precluded him from recovering under either. As might be expected, courts have tended to seek assiduously a way around literal enforcement, at least whenever it appeared that an unwitting violation of the other insurance clause had occurred.[5]

The 1943 New York Standard Fire Insurance Policy[6] omits all of the many moral hazard clauses previously in use, including the other

---

1. Compare § 3.1(b).

2. Concerning moral hazard clauses generally, see § 6.5(e)(3) *infra.*

3. See, *e.g.*, General Acc. Fire & Life Assur. Corp. v. Continental Cas. Co., 287 F.2d 464 (9th Cir. 1961); Continental Cas. Co. v. Weekes, 74 So.2d 367 (Fla.1954), 46 A.L.R.2d 1159 (1956); St. Paul Fire & Marine Ins. Co. v. Crutchfield, 162 Tex. 586, 350 S.W.2d 534 (1961); American Ins. Co. v. Kelley, 160 Tex. 71, 325 S.W.2d 370 (1959).

4. See, *e.g.*, Wilson & Co. v. Hartford Fire Ins. Co., 300 Mo. 1, 254 S.W. 266 (1923). See also § 2.11(b)(4) *supra* concerning provisions of this type under the 1955 Standard Automobile Policy, DOC coverage.

5. *E.g.*, St. Paul Fire & Marine Ins. Co. v. Crutchfield, 162 Tex. 586, 350 S.W. 2d 534 (1961) (interests of mortgagor and first mortgagee under policy obtained by mortgagor not avoided by policy procured by agent of second mortgagee without their knowledge); American Ins. Co. v. Kelley, 160 Tex. 71, 325 S.W.2d 370 (1959) (recovery allowed under policy first obtained; policy obtained subsequently was unenforceable from inception and insured had acted in good faith in obtaining second policy). Decisions of this type may be regarded as illustrations of the principle of honoring reasonable expectations; see § 6.3 *infra.*

6. N.Y.Ins.Law § 168 (McKinney 1966), reproduced in Appendix A *infra.*

insurance provisions, except that it provides for attachment of an endorsement imposing restrictions concerning other insurance,[7] and includes a provision that the insurer "shall not be liable for a greater proportion of any loss than the amount hereby insured shall bear to the whole insurance covering the property against the peril involved, whether collectible or not."[8]

In the foregoing paragraphs two types of sanctions against other insurance have been referred to—first, declaring that the insurer shall have no liability if there is other insurance and, second, declaring that the insurer's liability shall be limited to a proportion of the loss not exceeding its proportion of the insurance coverage. A third type of sanction often used is to declare that "this policy" shall apply only as excess insurance over any other insurance.[9] Clauses of this nature often produce litigation because of the conflict occurring if each of two policies declares that it is excess insurance and the other is primary.[10]

As might be inferred from the illustrations given above, other insurance clauses of one type or another are commonly used in all

7. "Other insurance may be prohibited or the amount of insurance may be limited by endorsement attached hereto." *Id.*, lines 25–27.

8. *Id.*, lines 86–89. In contrast to the general reluctance of courts to honor the total exclusion of coverage when each of the policies involved purportedly denies all coverage because of the presence of other insurance, in some instances proration resulting in recovery less than the face amount of coverage under one policy containing the clause quoted in the text has been allowed although another policy covering the same "peril," *i.e.* fire, was not applicable to the specific loss for other reasons. *E.g.*, Ekelchik v. American Cas. Co., 56 N.J.Super. 171, 152 A.2d 156 (1959). Such a result may be criticized as defeating reasonable expectations of the policyholder for coverage up to his policy limit from one source or the other. It seems rather likely, in a situation not involving total coverage exceeding his interest, that the untutored layman would be surprised to learn that his buying a second policy had reduced his total coverage in some circumstances. Concerning reasonable expectations generally, see § 6.3 *infra*.

9. *E.g.*, the following clause appears in a form of Mercantile Open Stock Policy: "If there is any other valid and collectible insurance which would apply in the absence of this policy, the insurance under this policy shall apply only as excess insurance over such other insurance; provided, the insurance shall not apply to property otherwise insured unless such property is owned by the insured." Compare the following clause, appearing in a form of American marine policy on cargo: "If an interest insured hereunder is covered by other insurance which attached prior to the coverage provided by this Policy, then this Company shall be liable only for the amount in excess of such prior insurance; the Company to return to the Assured premium equivalent to the cost of the prior insurance at this Company's rates. If an interest insured hereunder is covered by other insurance which attached subsequent to the coverage provided by this Policy, then this Company shall nevertheless be liable for the full amount of the insurance without right to claim contribution from the subsequent Insurers. Other insurance upon the property of same attaching date as the coverage provided by this Policy shall be deemed simultaneous, and this Company will be liable for a ratable contribution to the loss or damage in proportion to the amount for which this Company would otherwise be liable under this Policy, and will return to the Assured an amount of premium proportionate to such reduction of liability." See also the clauses discussed in § 3.11(b) *infra*.

10. See § 3.11(b) *infra*.

forms of property insurance. In contrast, policies of insurance on life ordinarily do not contain a clause concerning other insurance.[11] But it is common to include questions on this subject in application forms.

There is less need for "other insurance" provisions in life insurance than in other types, not only on the theory that the indemnity principle is less rigorously followed, but also because of the fact that the total life insurance on a single life is rarely as great as the total risk of economic loss to interested persons from early death, whereas the total insurance on property is often as great as the total interest in the property.

Some policies providing health, accident, medical, or hospitalization coverage do not contain any clause concerning either subrogation [12] or other insurance. Others contain clauses on both subjects. The forms of such clauses in these coverages vary widely.[13]

"Other insurance" clauses of uninsured motorist coverage, like other restrictive provisions of such coverage,[14] in some instances have been held invalid because in conflict with legislation requiring that uninsured motorist coverage be included in liability insurance policies.[15]

§ 3.11(b) CONFLICTS AMONG OTHER INSURANCE CLAUSES

It sometimes happens that other insurance provisions of two or more policies are in conflict. A clear case of conflict occurs when the applicable other insurance provision in each of the policies declares that the policy in which it appears shall be excess insurance. The great weight of authority supports proration in such a case,[1] and

11. Note, however, that this statement applies to "life insurance" in a narrow sense that excludes health and accident coverage. "Life insurance" as one of the three main classes of insurance is a broader concept that includes health and accident coverage. See § 1.3(e) *supra*. Also, though uncommon, other insurance provisions are occasionally used in some forms of life insurance in the narrow sense. For an example of such a policy, containing a clause concerning "other insurance" and limiting coverage to a scheduled amount, according to age, less the face amount of the other insurance, see Prudential Ins. Co. v. Fuqua's Adm'r, 314 Ky. 166, 234 S.W.2d 666 (1950), 22 A.L.R.2d 803 (1952) (holding, however, that the insurer was precluded by the incontestability clause of the policy from defending on the basis of the other insurance clause).

12. See § 3.10(a) *supra*.

13. See, *e.g.*, Laurie v. Holland Am. Ins. Co., 31 Ill.App.2d 437, 176 N.E.2d

678 (1st Dist. 1961) (involving two accident insurance policies with "other insurance" clauses of the "excess" coverage type); Slater v. Fidelity & Cas. Co., 277 App.Div. 79, 98 N.Y. S.2d 28 (1st Dep't 1950) (recovery denied on three of eight $5,000 air travel trip insurance policies because of express limitation in policies to $25,000 total insurance).

14. See § 4.9(e) *infra*.

15. *E.g.*, Harleysville Mut. Cas. Co. v. Blumling, 429 Pa. 389, 241 A.2d 112 (1968). See Annot., 28 A.L.R.3d 551 (1969).

1. *E.g.*, State Farm Mut. Auto. Ins. Co. v. Union Ins. Co., 181 Neb. 253, 147 N.W.2d 760 (1967); Cosmopolitan Mut. Ins. Co. v. Continental Cas. Co., 28 N. J. 554, 147 A.2d 529 (1959), 69 A.L.R. 2d 1115 (1960); Pacific Indem. Co. v. Federated Am. Ins. Co., 456 P.2d 331 (Wash.1969); Farmers Ins. Exch. v. Fidelity & Cas. Co., 374 P.2d 754 (Wyo.1962). See 8 Appleman, Insurance Law § 4913 (rev. ed. 1962).

most decisions in point allow a liability insurer that defends and settles a claim against the insured of two such policies to recover proportionately from the other insurer.[2] If the coverage limits of the applicable policies are not identical, a choice must be made among different methods of proration. In some instances, the rule of proration has been that all of the insurers with applicable policies are to pay equal shares of the loss up to the limits of their respective coverages.[3] Occasionally proration has been based on a comparison of premiums paid.[4] The method of proration most frequently used, however, is that the insurers pay shares of the loss proportional to their limits of coverage.[5]

The rule of proration applied when each of the policies contains a clause declaring it to be "excess" of other insurance has sometimes been extended to cases of less than clear and explicit conflict. That

---

2. *E.g.*, Truck Ins. Exch. v. Maryland Cas. Co., 167 N.W.2d 163 (Iowa 1969) (recovery allowed on theory of contribution, explicitly not on theory of subrogation to insured's rights). *But cf.* Employers Cas. Co. v. Transport Ins. Co., 444 S.W.2d 606 (Tex.1969) (action by truck lessee's insurer against truck lessor's insurer to recover pro rata contribution of sum paid in settlement and as costs of defense of tort claim against insured; held, since insurers' obligations were independent, payment by plaintiff insurer of more than its pro rata part of loss gave it no right of contribution; its remedy lies in a suit based on "contractual or conventional" subrogation to the right of the insured, which was not within the pleadings; intermediate court's remand for new trial affirmed). See also, however, the persuasive dissenting opinion, 444 S.W.2d at 611, taking the position that the insurer's remedy should not be limited to contractual subrogation and that an independent right of contribution should be recognized in this context, with the consequence that the trial court's summary judgment for five-eighths contribution (based on policy limits of $500,000 and $300,000) should be reinstated. See also § 3.-10(a) at n.6 *supra*. Multiple liability insurance coverage also gives rise to special problems concerning the duty to defend; see § 7.6(d) *infra*.

3. *E.g.*, Cosmopolitan Mut. Ins. Co. v. Continental Cas. Co., 28 N.J. 554, 147 A.2d 529 (1959), 69 A.L.R.2d 1115 (1960).

The "other insurance" clause of the 1966 Standard General Liability-Automobile Policy provides for equal-share proration when the other insurance also so provides. See Appendix G *infra*.

4. *E.g.*, Insurance Co. of Tex. v. Employers Liab. Assur. Corp., 163 F. Supp. 143 (S.D.Cal.1958).

5. *E.g.*, Liberty Mut. Ins. Co. v. Truck Ins. Exch., 245 Ore. 30, 420 P.2d 66 (1966); Lamb-Weston, Inc. v. Oregon Auto. Ins. Co., 219 Ore. 110, 341 P.2d 110, 346 P.2d 643 (1959), 76 A.L.R.2d 485 (1961); United Services Auto. Assoc. v. Hartford Acc. & Indem. Co., 433 S.W.2d 850 (1968), 220 Tenn. 120, 414 S.W.2d 836 (1967); Pacific Indem. Co. v. Federated Am. Ins. Co., 456 P. 2d 331 (Wash.1969); Farmers Ins. Exch. v. Fidelity & Cas. Co., 374 P. 2d 754 (Wyo.1962). When proration is provided for by the terms of a policy, rather than being ordered by the court because of inconsistency between the provisions of two policies, this rule that the insurers shall pay shares proportional to their limits of coverage is often expressed in both policies. See the 1943 N.Y. Standard Fire Insurance Police provision quoted in § 3.11(a) *supra* and the 1966 Standard General Liability-Automobile Policy, Appendix G *infra*, which provides in part:
"6. *Other Insurance* . . . .
"(b) Contribution by Limits. If any of such other insurance does not provide for contribution by equal shares, the company shall not be liable for a greater proportion of such loss than the applicable limit of liability under this policy for such loss bears to the total applicable limit of liability of all valid and collectible insurance against such loss."

is, the field of application of the judicially imposed rule of proration has been expanded by declaring that clauses are in conflict despite a reasonable theory of reconciliation. One justification offered is that the interests of the insured are better served in this way since, for example, he may otherwise be prejudiced by delay in the disposition of claims against him. Perhaps it may also be said that because of the public interests at stake courts should decline to legitimate the development of labyrinthian policy provisions the reconciliation of which requires inordinately complex analysis and occasions wasteful litigation. Examples of extension of the rule of proration include cases involving one policy with an "excess" clause and another with a "nonliability" or "escape" clause,[6] and occasionally a case involving one policy with an "excess" clause and another with a proration clause.[7] In this last context, however, the insurer whose clause declares its policy to be excess insurance only may contend that, either because of the specific language of the clause of the other policy or because of its general sense, it applies only to other "applicable" coverage and when one coverage is declared to be excess and the other is not, the excess coverage is applicable only to loss in an amount exceeding the limit of the other coverage and not to the loss up to that limit. The other insurance provisions of the 1955 and 1958 automobile liability forms (invoked, for example, when an owner's policy and a borrower's policy both apply) have been construed in this way by most courts, with the result that the owner's policy is primary coverage, and the borrower's is excess.[8] This result is perhaps more clear-

---

6. *E.g.*, Union Ins. Co. (Mut.) v. Iowa Hardware Mut. Ins. Co., 175 N.W.2d 413 (Iowa 1970); Hardware Dealers Mut. Fire Ins. Co. v. Farmers Ins. Exch., 444 S.W.2d 583 (Tex.1969). *Contra, e.g.*, Federal Ins. Co. v. Prestemon, 278 Minn. 218, 153 N.W.2d 429 (1967).

7. *E.g.*, Liberty Mut. Ins. Co. v. Truck Ins. Exch., 245 Ore. 30, 420 P.2d 66 (1966); Lamb-Weston, Inc. v. Oregon Auto. Ins. Co., 219 Ore. 110, 341 P.2d 110, 346 P.2d 643 (1959), 76 A.L.R.2d 485 (1961). See also Note, *"Other Insurance" Clauses: The Lamb-Weston Doctrine*, 47 Ore.L.Rev. 430 (1968).

8. See, *e.g.*, Continental Cas. Co. v. American Fid. & Cas. Co., 275 F.2d 381 (7th Cir. 1960) (applying Illinois law; result characterized as subrogation of excess insurer to rights of insured against primary insurer); Citizens Mut. Auto. Ins. Co. v. Liberty Mut. Ins. Co., 273 F.2d 189 (6th Cir. 1959) (applying Michigan law); Continental Cas. Co. v. Zurich Ins. Co., 57 Cal.2d 27, 366 P.2d 455, 17 Cal.Rptr. 12 (1961) (involving three liability policies, one with a pro rata clause and

two with excess coverage provisions; the pro rata clause policy insurer was held to be primarily liable to the extent of the policy limits, and the other two were held liable for the excess of the judgment over the primary limits to be shared proportionately, in some unspecified manner); Annot., 76 A.L.R. 2d 502 (1961). See also Harkavy v. Phoenix Ins. Co., 220 Tenn. 327, 417 S.W.2d 542 (1967), treating medical payments coverage on the car in which the claimant was a passenger as "other valid and collectible" medical payments insurance, which precluded recovery under the excess clause of the medical payments coverage of her own automobile policy, even though she was compelled in effect to return what she had received from the insurer of the car in which she was a passenger because that policy contained a subrogation clause.

The 1958 form clause reads as follows: "If the insured has other insurance against a loss covered by Part I of this policy the company shall not be liable under this policy for a greater proportion of such loss than the applicable limit of liability stated in the declarations bears to the total applica-

ly directed by the 1966 revision of the automobile liability forms.[9] If careful reading of the language used in two policies serves to reconcile them, then unless enforcement produces adverse and unexpected consequences for the insured or the interlocking provisions are so complex that they are likely to breed inordinate litigation, it seems appropriate to enforce the clauses as written. In these circumstances, the rights of the insured are protected, and the controversy is merely one concerning allocation among insurers of responsibility for the loss.

ble limit of liability of all valid and collectible insurance against such loss; provided, however, the insurance with respect to a temporary substitute automobile or non-owned automobile shall be excess insurance over any other valid and collectible insurance." Risjord & Austin, Automobile Liability Insurance Cases—Standard Provisions and Appendix 62 (1964).

9. "With respect to a hired automobile or a non-owned automobile, this insurance shall be excess insurance over any other valid and collectible insurance available to the insured." Appendix G *infra*. Primary coverage is provided for the owner's vehicle when other coverages are excess, and proration is called for when two or more policies are either all primary or all excess. *Ibid.*

CHAPTER 4

PERSONS AND INTERESTS PROTECTED

SECTION 4.1   METHODS OF DEFINING PERSONS AND INTERESTS PROTECTED

§ 4.1(a)   GENERALLY

Even though the notorious tendency of early policy draftsmen to grant in large print and take away in fine print is no longer so prevalent, still it is a standard and perhaps inevitable part of the method of defining coverage to use primary definitions broader than the intended scope of the coverage, qualified by restrictive provisions that take away something.

Policy coverages are commonly identified by the broad grants and are classified by types on that basis. The distinctions among major classifications of insurance relate mainly to portions of the definitions of coverage according to the nature of the risk transferred—a subject treated in the next chapter.

Restrictive provisions, though less central to classification of types of coverage, are more likely than the language of broad grants to be sources of dispute and litigation. Since no coverage is truly unlimited, a so-called "all risk" [1] pattern of defining the scope of protection afforded by an insurance policy makes use of restrictive provisions, and they are used also to deny protection for some losses that would otherwise fall within the primary definition of specified-risk coverages—for example, coverages that make up the package of protection commonly offered in an automobile insurance policy.

Restrictive provisions vary greatly both in substantive content and in form. Some concern the identity of persons entitled to benefits under the policy, as insureds or as beneficiaries in some other sense. Others concern the identification of interests protected. Vari-

---

1. See § 5.1(b) *infra*.

ous provisions of these two types are discussed in this chapter. Still other restrictive provisions concern the nature of the risks against which the policy protects. Most provisions of that type are considered in the next chapter, but some are also included in this chapter.[2]

In form, restrictive provisions are sometimes incorporated into the basic definition of coverage, through qualifying phrases. At other times, they are set apart. Some, for example, are introduced by a statement such as "This policy does not apply . . . ," and in some cases appear in sections of the policy designated by headings such as "Exclusions" or "Conditions."

Terminology applied to restrictive provisions varies also. For example, Patterson constructed a system of terminology carefully distinguishing between a provision defining "excluded events" (which he called an "exclusion," though he also used the term "exclusion" for a provision restrictive with respect to persons or interests rather than events) and a provision defining "excepted causes" (which he called an "exception").[3] But Patterson's terminology is not adhered to generally, and it is quite common to find the term "exclusion" used to designate a restrictive provision of any type, whether dealing with "events" or "causes" or with persons or interests.

Among the whole array of varied interests of persons who happen to be among the insureds and beneficiaries of an insurance policy, which particular interests does the policy cover? In the context of property insurance, most of the problems in this area are embraced within the question: What property is the subject matter of the contract?[4] This is true because ordinarily whatever interest the insured has in the property that is the subject of the insurance contract is covered.[5] Similarly, a recurring question concerning what interest of the insured is covered by an automobile insurance contract is expressed in the question: What automobiles are the subject of the contract? That is, was the automobile that was involved in the fortuitous loss for which claim is made one to which the contract applied? This question has given rise to substantial difficulty.[6]

In contrast, in relation to life insurance it does not appear useful to press such a question concerning the interest covered. This seems

---

2. See, *e.g.*, § 4.9(c) *infra*.

3. See Patterson, Essentials of Insurance Law 248–257 (2d ed. 1957). See also § 5.5(a) *infra*.

4. For example, a dispute may arise concerning whether a particular item of the insured's personal property is included within coverage under a fire insurance policy that does not identify the property except by reference to the location where it is kept. With respect to the effectiveness of such a provision concerning location as a "coverage" provision rather than a "warranty," see § 6.6(b) *infra*.

5. This is not always the case, however. For example, it may happen that a fire insurance contract is unclear as to whether it is intended to protect the insured's interest in the property itself, or instead in the insured's expectations of profit from uses of the property, or both. See § 3.4(a) (4) *supra*. In this context, identifying the interest covered involves more than merely identifying property to which the contract relates.

6. See § 4.9(b) *infra*.

clear when, as is usually the case, the person referred to as the insured is also the person whose death is the occasion for the insurer's
liability; obviously it is his life that is the subject of the contract. If
someone else obtains the contract and is referred to as the insured,
perhaps it seems more sensible to inquire: What is the subject of the
contract? That is, whose life is the subject? Even in this context,
however, it seems neither necessary nor helpful to separate this question of identifying the interest that is the subject of the contract
from the question of identifying the risk transferred by the contract.
It seems artificial to describe the risk transferred as merely death,
rather than describing it in a way that includes this question of interest as well by saying it is the death of a specified person—or, to put
it another way, the death of the person whose life is the subject of
the contract. There are, however, other problems concerning interests protected that are distinctive to life insurance.[7]

§ 4.1(b) "INSUREDS" DISTINGUISHED FROM OTHERS BENEFITTING FROM INSURANCE

In the context of property and casualty insurance the term "insured" ordinarily signifies a person whose risk of economic loss of a
designated type is part of the subject matter of the contract—a person whose loss is an occasion for liability of the insurer to pay benefits. Ordinarily the benefits are payable to the insured whose loss
has occasioned them, but it also may happen that benefits are payable to someone else, usually because of the insured's assignment of
his chose in action against the insurer.[1] It is common that the other
person to whom such an assignment is made also has an interest that
was adversely affected by the incident insured against; that is, ordinarily he too has suffered a loss. But this happens by coincidence rather than as a corollary of his being the assignee of the chose in action.
And even though this happens, he is not an "insured" if his loss is not
one insured against; his loss is neither the occasion for nor the measure of the insurer's liability. Thus, if the insurance transaction is such
that a mortgagee is an assignee of the mortgagor's chose in action
against the insurer but it is solely loss to the mortgagor's interest that
is the occasion for and the measure of the insurer's liability, the mortgagee is not an "insured" as that term is ordinarily used and as it is
being defined here. This remains true even though it may have been
agreed that the insurance benefits would be paid to the mortgagee or
to the mortgagor and mortgagee jointly. Also, the mortgagee's
rights against the insurer in these circumstances are derivative from
the mortgagor's and are defeated by defenses good against the mortgagor. If this is not implicit in what has already been said, it is at
least by customary usage an additional facet of the distinction between being an "insured" and being merely an assignee of an insured's
chose in action against an insurer. Thus if the terms of the transaction entitle the mortgagee to receive benefits even when the insurer

7. See § 4.11 infra.

1. See § 4.1(d) (1) infra.

has a good defense against the mortgagor, the mortgagee is referred to as an "insured," though of course the mortgagee may in addition be an assignee of the mortgagor's chose in action.

"Insured" is sometimes used in a narrower sense than that described above. For example, policy forms that in fact confer on a mortgagee independent rights essential to being an insured in the sense described above often make no reference to the mortgagee as either a named or an additional "insured," though the mortgagor is so designated, with the implication that only the mortgagor is an "insured" in the sense in which that term is used in that insurance policy.

Both the broad and narrow usages of the term "insured" in property and casualty insurance, described above, stand in contrast with the usage of that term in life insurance. There, the insured is the person whose life is the subject of the insurance contract, but it is the economic detriment of others from his death that the insurance is intended to repair.[2] "Beneficiary" is a term commonly used to signify one other than an "insured" who is to receive the proceeds of a life insurance contract. This term is not commonly used in relation to property and casualty insurance, however, despite the fact that there are contexts, particularly under liability insurance, in which rights of a third person under the coverage are well described as making him in some respects a third party beneficiary of the contract.[3]

§ 4.1(c) WAYS OF DESIGNATING INSUREDS IN PROPERTY AND CASUALTY INSURANCE

The primary way of designating a person as an insured is to place his name in a blank on the policy form following the words "does insure" or some phrase of similar import. A policy may designate more than one person in this way, and it may or may not indicate the nature of their respective interests. For example, several persons holding various interests in a building that is the subject of a fire insurance policy are often listed as insureds without specification of their respective interests. Sometimes the phrase "as their interests may appear" is added, generally signifying that they are entitled to share in the insurance proceeds in proportion to the damage to their respective interests in the insured property.[1] On the other hand, it may happen also that the relationship of the insureds to the property is indicated; for example, one insured may be described as "owner" and another as "mortgagee," or one as "life tenant" and another as "remainderman." It is particularly likely that an insured whose interest in the property is that of a fiduciary will be described by his fiduciary title to avoid any question about the capacity in which he obtains the insurance.

---

2. See § 3.5 *supra* and § 4.11 *infra*.

3. See § 4.8 *infra*.

Keeton, Insurance Law BTB—12

1. See § 4.1(d) (1) *infra* with respect to the different meaning of this phrase in another context.

It often happens that other persons, commonly referred to as "additional insureds," are named or described elsewhere in the policy as persons whose interests are insured. This may be done in other clauses of the primary policy form, as when a separate clause on the face of a fire insurance policy names a mortgagee as such and, when read together with a standard mortgage clause appearing elsewhere in the policy, expresses the understanding that the mortgagee is an additional "insured" rather than being merely an assignee of the mortgagor's chose in action against the insurer.[2] Also the designation of additional insureds may occur by endorsement, as is commonly done when a person having a contract to purchase a building is designated as an additional insured of the vendor's insurance policy pending consummation of the sale.

An "omnibus" clause is another method of designating additional insureds, used primarily in liability insurance (both automobile and general) and recently in other forms of automobile insurance as well. The forms of omnibus clauses have been many and varied.[3] Rather than designating persons by name, they do so by described relationships. For example, omnibus clauses of automobile liability insurance policies ordinarily declare that persons driving the insured automobile with permission of the "named insured" are additional insureds.[4]

Medical payments coverages often contain provisions that, though not referred to as omnibus clauses, similarly designate additional insureds by description of a class of persons bearing some relationship to the named insured. The group most often included are members of the named insured's household, but in some instances the group definition is expanded to include, for example, guests in the insured's household.[5]

§ 4.1(d) ASSIGNMENTS

(1) Types of Assignments

Two types of multi-party property insurance arrangements should be distinguished. First, there is an arrangement under which several different persons having varied interests in "the insured property"[1] are designated (either by name or by a descriptive term

---

2. See §§ 4.1(d) (1), 4.2 *infra*.

3. See § 4.7 *infra*.

4. See § 4.7(b) (1) *infra*.

5. *E.g.*, this is commonly done in the medical payments coverage of homeowners policy forms, as well as in automobile medical payments forms. But it often happens that the insurance policy itself does not refer to these persons as "insureds." See Appendix H *infra*.

1. The phrase "the insured property" is misleading, since it might be thought to suggest that insurance is automatically transferred whenever there is a transfer of the property. In fact, this phrase is a shorthand expression for "the property that is the subject of the insurance." In a strict sense, there is no "insured property" but rather only insurance of the interests of various persons in the property that is the subject of the insurance.

adequate for their identification) as persons whose interests are insured; each is entitled to receive part of the insurance proceeds if his interest is damaged by the casualty insured against. Their different interests in the property are insured under one joint policy.

The second type of arrangement is one under which some person, though not designated as one whose interest in the property is insured, is nevertheless designated to receive all or part of the proceeds, without regard to whether he has any interest in the property.

As has been indicated,[2] the first of these two types of arrangements is commonly referred to as a designation of "insureds" or "additional insureds," and under this arrangement when the phrase "as their interests may appear" is added, it ordinarily means "in proportion to the damage to their respective interests in the insured property."

The second type of arrangement is what is normally intended when one person's name appears in the blank following the words "does insure," or elsewhere as a designation of the "insured," and another person is named as payee of the policy proceeds—e.g., in a clause stating, "loss, if any, payable to _____." The phrase "as his interest may appear" is often added to this designation of the payee. In this context, it has a different meaning from that stated in the preceding paragraph. For example, this type of arrangement is often used when a policy of property insurance is being pledged as collateral for an otherwise unsecured debt, the creditor having no lien on the property; in such a situation, "as his interest may appear" means that the insurance proceeds are payable to the creditor up to the amount of his debt, even though he has no interest in the property other than that remote interest of any unsecured creditor in the property of his debtor.

Because of the phraseology commonly used in setting up the second of these types of arrangements, it is often referred to as a "loss payable clause." Occasionally, however, that term is used more broadly to include also transactions in which additional "insureds" are designated not in the blank on the face of the policy after the words "does insure" but rather by a separate clause using "loss payable" phraseology; of course this broader meaning includes many transactions of the first type of arrangement here described.

Often a distinction is made between an "assignment of the policy" and an "assignment of the chose in action." This distinction is closely related to the one described above.

An "assignment of the chose in action" is an arrangement that involves a transfer of the right to receive insurance proceeds but need not involve any transfer of interests in the insured property and does not affect the designation of insureds. This kind of assignment is often referred to as a "loss payable clause," even if written on a separate document from the insurance policy and not consented to by the

2. See § 4.1(b) *supra*.

insurer. Such an assignment may occur either before or after loss. If it occurs before loss, it is sometimes referred to as an anticipatory assignment of the chose in action.

"Assignment of the policy," in relation to property insurance, is ordinarily (but not uniformly) used to mean an arrangement under which the insured transfers all his interest in the policy to another who is substituted as a new insured. This type of assignment is used when the original insured is also transferring all his interest in the insured property to the new insured. When such a transfer is made, if the policy is not assigned it no longer provides coverage, since the original insured no longer has any insurable interest. "Assignment of the policy" is one way of designating an insured; in the case of assignment, however, it is a *substitute* and not an *additional* insured that is designated. It is this difference that prevents the distinction between "assignment of the policy" and "assignment of the chose in action" from being identical with the distinction, described above, between designation of insureds and designation of payees of the policy proceeds. Property insurance policies usually contain a clause prohibiting an assignment of the policy such as is described in this paragraph, except with the consent of the insurer; the insurer wants the privilege of deciding whether the new owner of the property is a desirable insured.

In relation to life insurance, an "assignment of the policy," as that phrase is commonly used, does not involve any change in the designation of the person whose life is insured or in the designation of the "beneficiaries." It is a transfer of incidents of ownership of the policy such as the right to change the designation of beneficiaries, the right to obtain policy loans, the right to convert the policy to another form of insurance, and the right to surrender for cash. It may also have an effect similar to a change of beneficiaries, since the assignee may have rights in policy proceeds upon maturity that are superior to those of the beneficiaries.[3] Often the assignment of a life insurance policy is part of a transaction in which the policy is being pledged as security for a loan from some person other than the insurer.

Since questions concerning rights of various persons under insurance policies are primarily questions of contract law, it follows that even if the parties have used a phraseology commonly associated with one of these forms of transaction, clear indications in the terms of their agreement that they intended the other form will be given effect, absent conflict with some regulatory statute or decisional restriction such as that incident to insurable interest doctrine. For example, the fact that the phrase "loss payable" appears somewhere in the agreement will not prevent a finding, based on other indications of the parties' intention, that the arrangement is a designation of either substitute or additional insureds, rather than a "loss payable clause" in the narrower and more common usage.

3. See § 4.11(d) *infra*.

Either of these two types of arrangements can be used when each of the persons who is to receive any part of the proceeds has an interest in the insured property. Also, it happens that in most situations each payee has an interest in the property consistent with his interest in the insurance proceeds. For example, when a secured creditor is included in the arrangement, the parties ordinarily would choose to give him an interest in the insurance proceeds consistent with his lien on the insured property. For this reason, in relation to most insurance claims the practical effect of the two different arrangements is the same. In some situations, however, the effects are quite different. For example, this is true if a mortgagor of realty has obtained a policy of insurance with a clause declaring that loss, if any, is payable to the mortgagee. If the transfer of interest in the insurance by the loss-payable clause is held to be one of the second type (an assignment of the chose in action), then the realty interest purportedly insured continues to be that of the mortgagor-assignor, even though the mortgagee is designated to receive the insurance proceeds. Thus, if the insurer has a defense against a claim for loss to the mortgagor's interest, it is a good defense also against the claim of the mortgagee designated to receive the insurance proceeds.[4] In contrast, if the transfer of interest by the loss-payable clause is held to be a transaction of the first type (an assignment of the policy) then the interest of the mortgagee is insured and the mortgagee's claim is not necessarily defeated by a defense to a claim for insurance of the mortgagor's interest; it would be necessary to determine whether the grounds of defense to a claim of insurance of the mortgagor's interest would also be good grounds for defense to a claim of insurance of the mortgagee's interest.

---

4. *E.g.*, Grosvenor v. Atlantic Fire Ins. Co., 17 N.Y. 391 (1858), in which the insurer's defense was upheld, the mortgagor having committed policy violations, presumably in transferring to another his interest in the realty that was the subject of insurance. Note, however, that there is an inconsistency between terminology used in *Grosvenor* and that described in the text above. The court refers to "an assignment of the policy to a mortgagee to be held by him as collateral security for his debt, with the consent of the insurer," though they are speaking of a transaction in which "the insurance is upon the interest of the mortgagor" and "the money shall be paid, not to the party who has sustained the loss, but to his appointee or assignee for his benefit." 17 N.Y. at 395. See also, *e.g.*, Armbrust v. Travelers Ins. Co., 232 Ore. 617, 376 P.2d 669 (1963) (recovery denied assignee of loss payee because of failure to prove insurable interest of insured although loss payee had clear interest in her own right because of an outstanding debt from her conditional sale of the insured vehicle to another person).

It has also been held that construction of a loss payable clause as an assignment of the chose in action permits subrogation of the insurer to tort claims of the mortgagor-assignor against the mortgagee-assignee. *E.g.*, Insurance Co. of N. Am. v. Gulf Oil Corp., 106 Ga.App. 382, 127 S.E.2d 43 (1962). Gulf had sold products to North America's insured, holding a mortgage on them; the insured also leased from Gulf part of a warehouse where the products were stored. After loss from a fire caused by the negligence of one of Gulf's employees, North America paid the policy proceeds to its insured and Gulf, the payment to the latter being made under an "open" loss payable clause (as opposed to a "union" or "standard" clause—see § 4.2(b) *infra*). The insurer was then allowed to recover from Gulf as subrogee to its insured's claim in tort.

It is often difficult to determine which type of transaction was intended by the parties and sometimes difficult even to determine which way a court treated the transaction. An early New York case illustrates these difficulties.[5] The policy in suit provided that it would no longer be effective if other insurance on the property was obtained without notice to this insurer within a reasonable time. The insured (mortgagor of the insured property) transferred an interest in the insurance to a mortgagee with the consent of the insurers. Thereafter he (the mortgagor) effected other insurance without notice. In an action against the first insurer, brought by the mortgagee but in the name of his assignor, the mortgagor, the Supreme Court held that the conduct of the mortgagor in obtaining other insurance did not bar the mortgagee's rights. No appeal was taken, and this decision in the name of the mortgagor against the insurer became the law of the case. The mortgagee then received payment of the mortgage debt, apparently from the mortgagor, and the mortgagor sought to collect upon the judgment in his name against the insurer. The Supreme Court stayed proceedings for collection, but its order was reversed by the Court for the Correction of Errors.[6] The rationale of the first opinion included the statement that "after the assignment of the policy [to Bolton, the mortgagee], Robert [the mortgagor], in whose name it was originally taken, had no interest in it, and . . . the rights of the parties are the same as if the policy . . . had been given to . . . Bolton. . . ."[7] This would be accurate only as to a substitution of insureds (a transaction of the first type, but to be distinguished from addition of an insured, another transaction of the first type). But if there had been a substitution, then the insurer should have been subrogated to the contract claim of its substituted insured (the mortgagee) against the mortgagor Robert, who by reason of the substitution would no longer be an insured. Allowing Robert to collect on Bolton's judgment against the insurer, as assignee of that judgment, would be ignoring this right of subrogation, which should be offset so as to produce the result that the casualty loss would fall ultimately on the uninsured (as to this policy) mortgagor, the insurance having served its purpose as a guarantee to the mortgagee alone that he would not suffer the casualty loss. Thus the protection actually afforded under the second opinion to the mortgagor Robert against the casualty loss was in effect either treating him as continuing to be an insured or else declining (perhaps on procedural grounds) to give effect to the subrogation right. A holding that Robert continued to be an insured is a result that is possible under a transaction of the first type, if it be addition rather than substitution of an insured. Such a holding is also possible under a transaction of the second type. In either case, this holding would be dependent on rejection of the policy

5. Traders' Ins. Co. v. Robert, 9 Wend. 404 (N.Y.Sup.Ct.1832).

6. Robert v. Traders' Ins. Co., 17 Wend. 631 (1836).

7. 9 Wend. 404, 409–410 (N.Y.Sup.Ct. 1832).

defense of alleged violation of the no-other-insurance clause. Since such rejection is not suggested in the opinions, it seems more likely that the explanation of the case is that the transaction was treated as the first type and the subrogation right was overlooked or denied on procedural grounds—for example, that the right of subrogation was lost by nonassertion, or that it was inappropriate as an offset in the suit on the mortgagee's judgment, in which case it might still be available for independent assertion against the mortgagor.

The illustrations given suggest the need for interpreting with caution not only statements in which the terminology of assignment is used, because of lack of uniformity of usage, but also the substantive precedents themselves, because it may happen that a result superficially appearing to be dependent on treating the transaction as one of these two basic types can in fact be explained consistently too with its being treated as a transaction of the other type.

(2) INSURER'S CONSENT TO ASSIGNMENT

It is not necessary generally to have the insurer's consent to an "assignment of the chose in action." In the absence of a policy provision to the contrary, such an assignment without the insurer's consent is valid whether made after loss [8] or before.[9] Insurance policies commonly do not contain any provision against assignment of the chose in action. Moreover, there have been indications that attempted restrictions against such an assignment after loss would be invalid.[10]

On the other hand the insurer's consent is normally necessary to the validity of an attempted "assignment of the policy," if it is not a marine policy.[11]

[handwritten margin notes: "Consent not generally necessary for assignment of chose in action valid before or after loss" and "consent normally necessary for assignment of policy"]

8.   E.g., Ocean Acc. & Gee. Corp. v. Southwestern Bell Tel. Co., 100 F.2d 441, 122 A.L.R. 133 (8th Cir. 1939) (employer's liability insurance); Windey v. North Star Farmers Mut. Ins. Co., 231 Minn. 279, 43 N.W.2d 99 (1950) (tornado insurance). See 5A Appleman, Insurance Law § 3459 (rev.ed.1970).

9.   E.g., Hartford Fire Ins. Co. v. Mutual Sav. & Loan Co., 193 Va. 269, 68 S.E.2d 541 (1952), 31 A.L.R.2d 1191 (1953). See Vance, Law of Insurance 760–761 (3d ed. Anderson 1951).

10.   E.g., Max L. Bloom Co. v. United States Cas. Co., 191 Wis. 524, 210 N. W. 689 (1926) (burglary insurance). See Vance, Law of Insurance 761 (3d ed. Anderson 1951). Contra, e.g., Dallas County Hosp. Dist. v. Pioneer Cas. Co., 402 S.W.2d 287 (Tex.Civ.App.1966, writ refused, no reversible error) (insured assigned her rights under her $1,000 limit medical payments coverage to hospital that had already provided services worth $400; after insured had incurred expenses in excess of $1,000, the hospital gave the insurer notice of the assignment, after which the insurer, not having consented to the assignment, paid its $1,000 limit to the insured, who subsequently disappeared without paying the hospital; held, the hospital could not recover anything from the insurer since the policy prohibited the assignment of "any interest" without the insurer's consent).

11.   E.g., McHugh v. Manhattan Fire & Marine Ins. Co., 363 Mich. 324, 109 N. W.2d 842 (1961). Transfers by operation of law, however, are distinguishable. See, e.g., Gulf Ins. Co. v. Thieman, 356 P.2d 360 (Okla.1960) (trustee in bankruptcy claimed for fire loss under policy issued to insured prior to his filing in bankruptcy; held, transfer of policy to trustee by operation of bankruptcy laws not an assignment

Life insurance policies ordinarily contain a clause establishing formalities to be complied with for valid assignment, and consent of the insurer is a customary requirement.[12]

It has been suggested that an attempted assignment of a fire insurance policy would be ineffective without the insurer's consent even in the absence of a policy clause so providing; support for this proposition has been found in the theory that the fire insurance contract is by its nature "personal" in the sense that it is intended to insure interests of the insured rather than to insure and run with the property itself.[13] Although some early policies did not contain any provision against assignment, it came to be the practice to include a clause stating that the entire policy would be void in the event of assignment without the insurer's consent. More recently, under the widespread influence of the 1943 New York fire insurance form, it has become customary to include in fire policies a provision that "assignment of this policy shall not be valid except with the written consent of this Company" [14] and to include a similar provision in other nonmarine property and liability policies.

In the absence of policy stipulations to the contrary, marine insurance policies have been considered generally to be assignable without the consent of the insurer.[15] This rule of the common law was incorporated into the British Marine Insurance Act of 1906.[16] In American policies today, however, and to less extent in English policies, there are commonly provisions against assignment of the policy without the insurer's consent.

Even though an assignment of a policy of property insurance is permissible, transfer of the insured property otherwise than by operation of law [17] does not automatically effect such assignment.[18] In one

within meaning of policy clause prohibiting assignment of policy without consent of insurer); Loomis v. Vernon Mut. Fire Ins. Co., 14 Wis.2d 470, 111 N.W.2d 443 (1961) (insured under three year fire policy obtained in 1954 died intestate later that year, and property passed to insured's heirs, the final probate decree being filed in 1955; held, heirs could recover under policy for fire loss in 1956 on alternative grounds that assignment-without-consent provision was inapplicable to transfer by operation of law and that heirs were within meaning of clause naming insured as intestate "and his legal representatives").

12.   For further treatment of assignment of life insurance policies, see § 4.11 *infra.*

13.   See, *e.g.,* Wilson v. Hill, 44 Mass. (3 Metc.) 66 (1841); Vance, Law of Insurance 757–758 n.1 (3d ed. Anderson 1951). See also § 3.1(d) *supra.* Non-

assignability of these insurance claims might also have been supported originally on the broader ground that choses in action generally were not assignable at common law.

14.   See the face of the 1943 New York Standard Fire Insurance Policy, Appendix A *infra.*

15.   See, *e.g.,* Spring v. South Carolina Ins. Co., 21 U.S. (8 Wheat.) 268, 5 L. Ed. 614 (1823); 1 Arnould, Marine Insurance [9 British Shipping Laws] §§ 231, 236 (15th ed. 1961); Vance, Law of Insurance 756 (3d ed. Anderson 1951).

16.   6 Edw. 7, c. 41, § 50.

17.   See n.11 *supra* and n.18 *infra.*

18.   *E.g.,* Davis v. Oregon Mut. Ins. Co., 71 Wash.2d 579, 429 P.2d 886 (1967) (fire insurance on house; conveyance of house does not transfer insurance;

type of situation, however, the result under another rationale may be the same as if such automatic assignment were recognized. This situation involves policies, usually of marine insurance, "for the account of whom it may concern" (the phrase used in American policies) or for all persons to whom an interest in the property "doth, may, or shall appertain" (the phrase used in English policies). As an original proposition, it might reasonably be argued that these phrases imply an expression of the insurer's agreement that a future transfer of the insured property will carry with it the right to protection under the insurance policy. American decisions appear to accept this result in cases in which it can be said that the transferee is among those whom, by name or by present or future status in relation to the property, the person named intended to insure.[19] But English courts have indicated that one claiming as a beneficiary of a marine policy of this type, if he does not prove a valid assignment of the policy, must offer extrinsic proof that the named insured had the claimant in contemplation at the time of making the insurance contract.[20] Perhaps the explanation for such favor toward assignees and disfavor toward unnamed beneficiaries of the original agreement is primarily historical. In the middle of the eighteenth century the practice arose in England of effecting policies in blank, without inserting the name either of the party for whom the insurance was obtained or of the party by whom it was obtained. Legislation aimed at prevention of such blank policies culminated in a provision in the British Marine Insurance Act of 1906 that "a marine policy must specify the name of the assured or of some person who effects the insurance on his behalf." [21] Although neither this act nor the earlier legislation specifies that the named insured must have the claimant in contemplation at the time of making the contract, the legislation and the circumstances out of which it arose probably contributed to the development of this rule.[22]

assignment to third person of vendor's interest under policy obtained in part for his benefit by purchaser distinguished). The following provision appears in the British Marine Insurance Act of 1906, 6 Edw. 7, c. 41, § 15: "Where the assured assigns or otherwise parts with his interest in the subject-matter insured, he does not thereby transfer to the assignee his rights under the contract of insurance, unless there be an express or implied agreement with the assignee to that effect.

"But the provisions of this section do not affect a transmission of interest by operation of law."

If the vendor retains an interest in the property, *e.g.* as a purchase-money mortgagee, his interest will continue to be protected under the policy in the absence of a provision voiding the pol-

icy on alienation of the property. *E. g.*, American Equitable Assur. Co. v. Pioneer Coop. Fire Ins. Co., 100 R.I. 375, 216 A.2d 139 (1966).

19.   *E.g.*, Hagan v. Scottish Union & Nat'l Ins. Co., 186 U.S. 423, 22 Sup.Ct. 862, 46 L.Ed. 1229 (1902). See generally 5A Appleman, Insurance Law § 3336 (rev.ed.1970).

20.   *E.g.*, Boston Fruit Co. v. British & Foreign Marine Ins. Co., [1906] A.C. 336. See 1 Arnould, Marine Insurance [9 British Shipping Laws] §§ 227–229 (15th ed. 1961).

21.   6 Edw. 7, c. 41, § 23(1).

22.   See generally 1 Arnould, Marine Insurance [9 British Shipping Laws] §§ 225, 226 (15th ed. 1961).

SECTION 4.2 MORTGAGES AND CONDITIONAL SALES

§ 4.2(a) QUESTIONS UNDERLYING CONFLICTING CLAIMS (INCLUDING SUBROGATION)

The following four questions concerning persons and interests protected by an insurance policy on mortgaged property (or property under conditional sale) are intimately related: First, is the insurer subrogated to rights of the mortgagee (or conditional vendor)? Second, does the insurer's payment of insurance benefits due under the policy discharge the mortgage debt pro tanto? Third, if all parties are solvent and all rights are enforced, will the loss ultimately fall on the mortgagor, the mortgagee, or the insurer? Fourth, may the mortgagee collect and retain the proceeds of both the insurance contract and the mortgage debt?

On the theory that fire insurance is "personal," Chief Justice Shaw of the Massachusetts Supreme Judicial Court wrote an opinion giving an affirmative answer to the fourth question above in a case involving a policy with no subrogation clause.[1] But this opinion has not been accepted generally,[2] and in any event it is not applicable to current fire policies, either in Massachusetts or elsewhere, since they commonly include a subrogation clause.

If one takes the view that the principle of indemnity should prevail and that the mortgagee should not be allowed to profit by double recovery, then in answering the remaining three of the four questions above he faces but one more choice. Either he answers that, first, the insurer is subrogated to the mortgagee's rights, second, the mortgage debt is not discharged by the insurance payments, and third, the ultimate loss if all parties are solvent and all rights are enforced will fall on the mortgagor, or else he answers that, first, the insurer is not subrogated to the mortgagee's rights, second, the mortgage debt is discharged pro tanto, and third, the ultimate loss will fall on the insurer. This group of questions brings into issue the validity of the assumptions, referred to in an earlier section,[3] that, first, the existence of insurance coverage does not affect the liability of "third persons" to the "insured" and, second, the existence of claims of the "insured" against "third persons" does not affect the liability of the insurer. Indeed, as will appear in the next subsection, one important step toward an answer to the four questions stated above is implied if one classifies the mortgagor as a "third person" rather than an "insured."

1. King v. State Mut. Fire Ins. Co., 61 Mass. (7 Cush.) 1, 54 Am.Dec. 683 (1851).

2. See § 3.10(a) *supra* for expressions of the prevailing view that the prop-

erty insurer is entitled to be subrogated to claims of the insured against third persons even if the insurance contract is silent on the subject.

3. Section 3.10(c) (2) *supra*.

§ 4.2(b) SUBROGATION UNDER THE STANDARD MORTGAGE CLAUSE

Allowing an insurer to be subrogated to rights against an "insured" on account of a payment of benefits under the coverage with respect to which the person is an "insured" would have the effect of withdrawing the insurance benefits. Accordingly, it is generally stated that an insurer cannot have subrogation against its own insured.[1] But the meaning of this statement depends on the interpretation given to the word "insured." Insurance on mortgaged property presents a good example of this problem of meaning. In most insurance policies on mortgaged realty, the mortgagor's name is typed in a space within a printed statement that the insurer "does insure _____ and legal representatives . . ."; the mortgagee's name is typed in another space within a printed statement that, subject to provisions of the printed mortgage clause, loss "shall be payable to: _____." Nearly all such policies on realty contain a "standard" mortgage clause (also called "union" mortgage clause)[2] providing that loss shall be payable to the mortgagee "as interest may appear," that insurance as to the interest of the mortgagee "shall not be invalidated by any act or neglect of the mortgagor . . .," and that whenever the insurer pays the mortgagee and establishes that it has no liability to the mortgagor because of his act or neglect the insurer shall be subrogated to the rights of the mortgagee on the mortgage debt but without impairment of the mortgagee's right to recover the full amount of his claim. Similar clauses often appear in automobile

---

1. See, *e.g.*, Federal Ins. Co. v. Tamiami Trail Tours, Inc., 117 F.2d 794 (5th Cir. 1941). *Cf.* Mutual Fire Ins. Co. v. Dilworth, 167 Md. 232, 173 A. 22 (1934), 83 U.Pa.L.Rev. 273 (1934) (policy having a standard mortgage clause with loss payable to first mortgagee and second mortgagee as interest may appear; insurer claimed nonliability as to mortgagor, paid to the first mortgagee a sum equal to the full amount of his mortgage, receiving an assignment, and asserted a lien superior to that of the second mortgagee; insurer's claim of priority over second mortgagee disallowed).

2. In contrast, a "loss payable clause" in the narrower sense, described in § 4.1(d)(1) *supra*, is sometimes called an "open" mortgage clause. See Insurance Co. of N. Am. v. Gulf Oil Corp., 106 Ga.App. 382, 127 S.E.2d 43 (1962); Conard v. Moreland, 230 Iowa 520, 523, 298 N.W. 628, 629 (1941).

As previously suggested, § 4.1(d)(1) *supra*, the manifested intentions of the parties and not a technical interpretation of the language used should de-

termine whether the "loss payable" clause is given the narrower effect of an assignment of the chose in action or instead the broader effect of the standard-mortgage clause. In *Gulf Oil, supra*, however, the clause involved was characterized as the "open" type, apparently without regard to the parties' intentions, and the insurer was allowed to recover as subrogee to its insured's (the mortgagor's) tort claim against the mortgagee. In contrast, it was held in Commercial Credit Corp. v. Premier Ins. Co., 12 Utah 2d 321, 366 P.2d 476 (1961), that cancellation of a policy of collision insurance by the named insured without notice to the mortgagee did not defeat the latter's claim under the policy, although the clause involved was practically identical to that in *Gulf Oil*. The broader construction was not based explicitly on the parties' manifested intentions, however, but on the principle of construing against the insurer an ambiguity with respect to whether cancellation without notice to the mortgagee affected his interests. See § 6.3 *infra*.

insurance policies.[3] Under such a policy, the mortgagor is an "insured" in the absence of act or neglect in violation of policy terms, and the group of four questions stated above should be answered so as to place the ultimate loss on the insurer.[4] On the other hand, if some act or neglect of the mortgagor prevents his direct recovery against the insurer on the policy, the mortgagor is not an "insured" with respect to the enforceable insurance coverage, and allowing the subrogation rights as stated in the mortgage clause is not allowing an

3. See, *e.g.*, Bennett Motor Co. v. Lyon, 14 Utah 2d 161, 380 P.2d 69 (1963), holding that the insured's intentional burning of the insured vehicle did not preclude recovery by the insured's conditional sale vendor and that as to the latter the loss was accidental. See also, *e.g.*, Southwestern Funding Corp. v. Motors Ins. Corp., 5 Cal.2d 91, 378 P.2d 361, 28 Cal.Rptr. 161 (1963) (clause provided coverage for mortgagee in spite of insured's violation of "terms or *conditions*" of policy; held, mortgagee can recover for loss from accident that occurred in Mexico although policy provided, under heading "Conditions," that coverage was applicable only while automobile was within the United States). *But cf.* Savings Soc'y Commercial Bank v. Michigan Mut. Liab. Co., 118 Ohio App. 297, 25 Ohio Ops.2d 143, 194 N.E. 2d 435 (1963), 98 A.L.R.2d 1312 (1964) (insurer not required to give notice to mortgagee under standard mortgage clause of its exercising option to repair damaged automobile, since policy did not so require).

4. *E.g.*, Palisano v. Bankers & Shippers Ins. Co., 276 App.Div. 523, 95 N.Y.S.2d 543 (4th Dep't 1950).

If the mortgage debt is wholly satisfied, even subsequent to fire damage to the mortgaged property, the mortgagor becomes the only "insured" still entitled to a share of the insurance proceeds and is thus entitled to the full amount. But inequitable results may be produced if a court regards the debt as wholly satisfied when the mortgagee has in fact received less than full payment. Rosenbaum v. Funcannon, 308 F.2d 680 (9th Cir. 1962), and Northwestern Nat'l Ins. Co. v. Mildenberger, 359 S.W.2d 380 (Mo. App.1962), are interesting illustrations of this point. In both cases the debt was "extinguished" by foreclosure sale at which the mortgagee bid in and bought the property for the amount of the outstanding debt, and the mortgagor was held to be entitled to the full insurance proceeds. In an extreme case such as *Rosenbaum*, this injudicious action of the mortgagee, together with the court's treating the debt as extinguished, produces a massive windfall for the mortgagor, who retains the insurance proceeds and is relieved of the debt as well as the damaged property. In that case, the original debt of $25,000 had been reduced only to $24,898 when an insured fire loss of $22,500 occurred. The mortgagee subsequently foreclosed, exercising his power to have the property sold, and bid the amount of the outstanding debt for the damaged property. Subsequently the mortgagee-purchaser sued to recover the insurance proceeds from the mortgagor and lost. As a result, the mortgagor, though having lost the property, had a large net gain (perhaps over $22,000, depending on whether the property was worth more than the debt, before the fire) and the mortgagee suffered a loss of approximately the same amount.

In a similar (though arguably distinguishable) case, Kolehouse v. Connecticut Fire Ins. Co., 267 Wis. 120, 65 N. W.2d 28 (1954), 46 A.L.R.2d 983 (1956), a more equitable result was reached by allowing a conditional vendor to recover collision insurance proceeds equal to the mortgage debt at the time of the accident, although shortly thereafter the vendor had improperly repossessed and resold the vehicle for its salvage value, with the result that the vendee was released from all obligation under the conditional sale contract. In so deciding, however, the court held that rights in the insurance proceeds were fixed as of the date of loss and subsequent cancellation of the debt was of no effect. Surely such a broad holding would have to be qualified to apply only to a somewhat technical "cancellation" of the debt as distinguished from a discharge by actual payment. Perhaps an analogous qualification is implicit in the court's requiring an allowance to the vendee for the amount realized in sale of the damaged truck at salvage.

insurer to "have subrogation against its own insured." Enforcement of the express stipulation for subrogation to the mortgagee's rights against the mortgagor on the mortgage debt is therefore compatible with the rule forbidding subrogation against an insured.

If the mortgagor conveys to a purchaser who agrees to pay the mortgage debt and no change is made in the insurance policy obtained by the mortgagor, which contains a standard mortgage clause, the insurer, who has paid the mortgagee in full following a fire and has taken an assignment of the mortgagee's claims, should not be allowed to recover on the mortgage debt against the mortgagor, unless the conveyance violates a policy clause. The mortgagor remains an insured and continues to have an insurable interest. The insurer should not be allowed subrogation against its own insured. But the principle that a fire insurance contract is personal supports a rule allowing the insurer to assert its subrogation claim against a purchaser who is not an insured. To argue against subrogation in this latter situation is to argue that the insurance should run with the property —that the purchaser should be treated as an insured even without the insurer's consent. Precedents on this issue are inconclusive.[5]

If a policy containing a standard mortgage clause has become unenforceable by the mortgagor because of his act or neglect, the case is analogous to one arising under mortgagee-only insurance, which is discussed in the next subsection.

§ 4.2(c) SUBROGATION AND RATING UNDER MORTGAGEE-ONLY INSURANCE

Another form of insurance, less commonly used than the standard mortgage clause, is written with only the mortgagee's name in the blank space after the printed phrase "does insure." Unless the mortgagor is to be treated as an additional insured,[1] such insurance

---

5. For an expression of different points of view concerning this problem, see Palisano v. Bankers & Shippers Ins. Co., 193 Misc. 647, 84 N.Y.S.2d 637 (Sup.Ct. Special Term 1948), aff'd, 276 App.Div. 523, 95 N.Y.S.2d 543 (4th Dep't 1950), and Note, *Subrogation of Insurer to Mortgagee's Rights Against Substituted Mortgage Debtor*, 49 Colum.L.Rev. 866 (1949).

1. See generally King, *Subrogation Under Contracts Insuring Property*, 30 Texas L.Rev. 62, 72–76 (1951), arguing that the mortgagor should be given the benefit of the insurance in a number of situations in which most courts have concluded that the mortgagor has no beneficial interest in the policy and that the insurer is subrogated to the mortgagee's claims against him. In re Future Mfg. Coop., 165 F.Supp. 111 (N.D.Cal.1958), 72 Harv.L.Rev. 1380 (1959), is a decision consistent

with the result urged by King. The conditional sales contract in that case provided that the vendee was to assume the risk of casualty loss and was to insure in the vendor's favor. The vendee failed to obtain insurance, and the vendor arranged for a policy naming only the vendor as insured. The court held that insurance proceeds received by the vendor, less an amount equal to the insurance premiums paid by the vendor, were to be credited on the contract price. *But cf.* Flint Frozen Foods, Inc. v. Firemen's Ins. Co., 8 N.J. 606, 86 A.2d 673 (1952), denying a claim against the creditor's insurer presented by the debtor, who also held an assignment of the creditor's rights under a policy obtained by the creditor after the debtor failed to comply with the contractual obligation to obtain insurance for the creditor's benefit.

imposes a less onerous burden on the insurer than the more common form of policy, and one might expect that it would be available at lower rates. But the rates for these two different forms of insurance are not customarily different.[2] Also, it has been suggested that subrogation in general plays no part, or only a minor part, in rate schedules and that subrogation is a windfall to the insurer.[3] There is no windfall to the insurer, however, if the overall rate for both types of insurance is adjusted to take account of the subrogation recoveries that are realized. But there is an apparent inequity among insureds. Perhaps the inequity is so small that it is a permissible variation within a single rate category.[4] Also, the suggestion may be made that a request for insurance of the mortgagee's interest alone is a sign of trouble with the mortgagor, indicating both a higher than normal moral risk and a higher than normal likelihood that a subrogation interest would be of no value because of financial irresponsibility of the mortgagor. Thus the advantage of insuring only the mortgagee's interest may be more than offset by increase of risk in other respects. That is, it may be that if the loss data for these two different types of policies were separated rather than being combined it would appear that actual net losses of insurers under coverage for mortgagees only are no less than under coverage for mortgagees and mortgagors as well.

If subrogation of the insurer to the mortgagee's rights against the mortgagor is denied even though the mortgagor is not designated as an "insured," the mortgagor receives a windfall if the debt is held to be discharged, and the mortgagee receives a windfall if the debt is held to be still enforceable. These points make a compelling argument for allowing subrogation in the absence of evidence of an understanding, express or implied, that the mortgagor was to be an additional insured. Most opinions in point have reached this result.[5]

§ 4.2(d) SUBROGATION UNDER OTHER POLICY PROVISIONS

Ordinarily the basic standard automobile collision insurance forms do not contain a clause with provisions like those of the standard mortgage clause. But when collision insurance is written as part of a transaction involving a loan secured by a mortgage (or conditional sale) of an automobile, commonly an endorsement is attached with provisions substantially the same as those of the standard (union) mortgage clause. This endorsement is ordinarily attached upon request and without an extra premium charge. It includes an express provision for subrogation of the insurer to the rights of the mortgagee against the mortgagor who could not recover directly against the insurer on the policy (that is, against the mortgagor

2. Note, 72 Harv.L.Rev. 1380, 1382 (1959).

3. Patterson, Essentials of Insurance Law 151–152 (2d ed. 1957).

4. See § 8.4(b) infra.

5. E.g., Drewicki v. Fidelity & Gy. Fire Corp., 162 Kan. 10, 174 P.2d 75 (1946).

whose own recovery directly against the insurer is barred by his wrongful act or neglect). In the absence of such an express provision, precedents are divided as to whether the insurer, having paid the mortgagee in these circumstances, is subrogated to the mortgagee's contractual claim (on the debt) against a mortgagor whose default bars his direct claim against the insurer. A leading New York decision, *Fields v. Western Millers Mut. Fire Ins. Co.,*[1] rendered by a divided court, denied subrogation. The default of the conditional vendee (referred to hereafter as the mortgagor) in that case was failure to pay premiums, because of which the insurer had cancelled the policy by notice to the mortgagor (failing, however, apparently by inadvertence to give notice to the mortgagee). The insurer acknowledged its liability to the mortgagee but sought to be subrogated to the mortgagee's claim against the mortgagor. The position taken by the dissent, which would have allowed subrogation, seems sound since, as to this loss, the mortgagor was not an insured. The only basis for liability of the insurer for the loss was a promise made for the benefit of the mortgagee to whom it had not given notice of the cancellation for nonpayment of premium. The majority opinion, asserting that the mortgagor "was, and remained, the insured under the policy, so long as the policy remained in existence . . .,"[2] does not meet the point that it is quite possible to treat the total arrangement as one of a coverage for the mortgagee distinct from that for the mortgagor, the former being free of some defenses available against the latter. It is hard to find any argument, from the point of view of contractual expectations or otherwise, in favor of insisting that a notice of cancellation for nonpayment of premiums delivered to the mortgagor is no defense even as against him. If the notion of distinct coverages is accepted, then the situation in *Fields* is analogous to one in which the mortgagee obtains a separate policy explicitly covering his interest alone and not that of the mortgagor.

This analysis, appropriate in the absence of any subrogation clause, is strengthened by the existence of such a clause applying to "all right of recovery against any party." The majority opinion in *Fields* responds that this means "a claim against some third party for damaging the vehicle."[3] But why does it not also refer to a contract claim, in view of the phrase "all right of recovery"?[4] And is not the

1. 290 N.Y. 209, 48 N.E.2d 489, 146 A. L.R. 434 (1943).

2. 290 N.Y. at 212, 48 N.E.2d at 490, 146 A.L.R. at 437.

3. 290 N.Y. at 216, 48 N.E.2d at 492, 146 A.L.R. at 439.

4. For precedent allowing subrogation to contract claims of the insured in other contexts, see, *e.g.*, Atlantic Mut. Ins. Co. v. Cooney, 303 F.2d 253 (9th Cir. 1962) (applying California law; bailor's insurer subrogated to contract claim against bailee). *Cf.* Employers Mut. Cas. Co. v. Shepherd-Vineyard Motors, Inc., 189 Kan. 525, 370 P.2d 388 (1962) (insurer subrogated to contract right of insured under "warranty" of new car destroyed by fire caused by defect in construction). *But cf.* Patent Scaffolding Co. v. William Simpson Construction Co., 256 Cal.App.2d 506, 64 Cal.Rptr. 187 (2d Dist.1967); Levit, *Court Denies Subrogation to Contractual Rights*, 1968 Ins.L.J. 105 (commenting on *Patent Scaffolding*).

mortgagor a "third party" as to the special coverage available to the mortgagee despite cancellation as to the mortgagor?

With regard to the problem of scope of the rights created, can something be made of the practice of not charging extra for an endorsement extending coverage to a mortgagee even after a mortgagor's default, as distinguished from the fact of its omission from a particular policy?

By the inclusion of a provision giving special protection to the mortgagee, the company incurs greater risk. This is true regardless of the answer given to the question presented in *Fields*. Under the doctrine of the dissenting opinion, the company would be required to pay off the mortgagee and might not be able to collect on its subrogation claim against the mortgagor because of the risk of the mortgagor's financial irresponsibility. The increase of risk is even greater under the doctrine of the majority opinion. For the insurer it might be argued that the practice of not charging an added premium points to an expectation that the added risk undertaken would be minimal —only that incident to the doctrine of the dissent in *Fields*. For the mortgagor it might be argued that the practice of not charging an added premium points to the conclusion that rates are set in contemplation of double-interest coverage—that is, coverage for both mortgagee and mortgagor. The latter argument, however, still does not clear the hurdle that the scope of the coverage of the two separate interests might be different, and particularly so when the ground of defense urged is a neglect of one party only.

§ 4.2(e) ASSIGNABILITY OF THE MORTGAGEE'S INTEREST

When coverage has become unenforceable by the mortgagor, a debatable problem arises if the mortgagee, before loss, has purportedly assigned its interest without the consent of the insurer to a person to whom the mortgagee was transferring the mortgage debt and all security for its payment. Such an assignment has been held valid,[1]

---

1. Central Union Bank v. New York Underwriters Ins. Co., 52 F.2d 823 (4th Cir. 1931), 78 A.L.R. 494 (1932). In this case, the mortgagee named in the fire policy was a life insurance company that had taken an assignment of the mortgage under an agreement that it would be repurchased by one to whose interests plaintiff succeeded, in the event of default of the mortgagor. Pursuant to this agreement to repurchase, plaintiff took an assignment from the life insurance company shortly before the fire loss occurred. On first appeal, the Court of Appeals reversed a judgment on directed verdict for the insurer and remanded for a new trial. On new trial, the insurer contended that the plaintiff was barred from recovering because of failure to give notice of change of ownership in accordance with the requirement of the standard mortgage clause that the mortgagee should notify the insurer of any change of ownership coming to its knowledge. Directed verdict for the plaintiff against the insurer was affirmed on the theory that a reasonable length of time for notification of the insurer had not expired, since, though plaintiff had knowledge of the change of ownership at an earlier time, it was not until the policy was received in the mail, on the day before the fire, that the plaintiff could have had knowledge that the policy as written was not consistent with the

and this seems a sound ruling. That is, it seems appropriate to hold that the interest of the mortgagee under the standard mortgage clause is assignable without the consent of the insurer to a transferee of the mortgagee's interests in the debt and security. Against this result stands the suggestion that, since the mortgagee is himself an insured under this clause, there is a need for consent of the insurer because the assignee of all the mortgagee's interests must then claim any special rights under the standard mortgage clause as himself an insured, rather than merely as assignee of interests derivative from the mortgagor. But this argument is outweighed by the desirability of making the debt and security freely assignable and by the probability that insurers do not have as great an interest in identity of the mortgagee as in identity of the mortgagor.

If knowledge of a breach by the mortgagor came to the mortgagee before assignment, the mortgagee's assignee should be barred by the mortgagee's failure to notify the insurer. Otherwise the change of insureds would have the effect of curing a policy defense, all without the consent of the insurer. The issue is more debatable if knowledge of the breach is acquired by the mortgagee after he is no longer directly interested. It might be said that the insurer still has the benefit of an obligation of reporting by the party most interested and most likely to have knowledge of the mortgagor's breach, and that this should be adequate protection. But it may be that the assignee is often a distant financial institution, less likely than the mortgagee to be well informed about the physical property and the mortgagor. Thus it would be imposing a greater risk on the insurer, and without its consent, to deprive it of the protection of the mortgagee's obligation to report defaults of the mortgagor. In the absence of a contractual provision that is explicit on this point, however, perhaps this factor is outweighed by the desirability of free assignability of mortgagee interests.

§ 4.2(f) SUBROGATION TO A MORTGAGEE'S TORT CLAIM AGAINST A THIRD PERSON

It often happens that a bank or finance company holding a mortgage interest in an automobile (or a similar interest under a transaction in the form of a conditional sale) also has an interest in insurance against damage to the automobile. In such circumstances, if the insurance is written to apply to the interests of both the mortgagor and the mortgagee and both have good claims against a third person for tortiously damaging the insured car, the insurer, having paid insurance benefits due for the joint interests of the mortgagor and mortgagee, is subrogated to their tort claims against the negligent third person.

ownership after the change. It did not appear that the mortgagee named in the insurance policy (*i.e.*, the life insurance company) had notice of the breach. New York Underwriters Ins. Co. v. Central Union Bank, 65 F.2d 738 (4th Cir. 1933).

A more difficult question arises if a collision damaging the insured automobile results from the negligence of both the mortgagor and a third person. In these circumstances ordinarily the mortgagor's tort claim against the third person is barred in jurisdictions applying the contributory negligence doctrine. But under the prevailing rule the mortgagee is still entitled to recover in tort against the third person; that is, the mortgagor's negligence is not imputed to the mortgagee.[1] Is the collision insurer of the mortgaged automobile subrogated to the mortgagee's claim in tort against the third person? *Harvard Trust Co. v. Racheotes*[2] answers this question affirmatively. The tort action was being pressed in the Trust Company's name but for the interest of the collision insurer. The balance outstanding on the mortgage debt was $318; the cost of repairing the car was $506.11; the insurer issued a check in the amount of $456.11 payable to the Trust Company and the mortgagor, and it was endorsed over to the repairman. The Court reasoned that the insurer should recover $318 as subrogee to the mortgagee's claim. But what was the nature of the mortgagee's claim? That is, what would have been the rights of the various parties, incident to the mortgagee's claim, in the absence of insurance?

Before *Racheotes* it had been decided that the mortgagee or conditional vendor can recover against the negligent third party despite contributory negligence of the mortgagor or conditional vendee.[3] After such a recovery, what is the status of the debt? Only three possibilities can be suggested: First, the mortgagee still retains the debt, thus enabling him to obtain double payment if the debtor is solvent. Second, the negligent third party's payment to the mortgagee has discharged the debt pro tanto, thus enabling the debtor to obtain indirectly a benefit he could not obtain directly because of his contributory negligence. Third, the negligent third party is entitled to receive any sum that can be collected on the debt. The first choice unjustly enriches the mortgagee, by giving him double payment. The second unjustly enriches the mortgagor.[4] The third is the best choice. As between the two negligent drivers, it places the ultimate

---

1. *E.g.*, Commercial Credit Corp. v. Satterthwaite, 107 N.J.L. 17, 150 A. 235 (Sup.Ct.1930), *aff'd per curiam*, 108 N.J.L. 188, 154 A. 769 (Ct.Err. & App. 1931); Lacey v. Great N. Ry., 70 Mont. 346, 225 P. 808 (1924), 38 A.L.R. 1331 (1925). See also n. 3 *infra*.

2. 337 Mass. 73, 147 N.E.2d 817 (1958), 67 A.L.R.2d 596 (1959). The discussion of this case in the text is adapted from my discussion in 1958 Annual Survey of Mass. Law 33–37 (Huber ed. 1959). A contrary appraisal of the case is presented by Professor Hogan, *id.* at 78–80.

3. See, *e.g.*, Bell Finance Co. v. Gefter, 337 Mass. 69, 147 N.E.2d 815 (1958), 67 A.L.R.2d 578 (1959) (involving a conditional sale and indicating that mortgages and conditional sales are similarly treated in this context); Morris Plan Co. v. Hillcrest Farms Dairy, Inc., 323 Mass. 452, 82 N.E.2d 889 (1948) (involving a conditional sale). See also Annots., 67 A.L.R.2d 582 (1959), 67 A.L.R.2d 599 (1959).

4. Note that a reason given by the Court in *Racheotes* for disallowing any recovery in excess of the debt was that the mortgagor would then obtain indirectly a recovery he could not obtain directly. 337 Mass. 73, 76, 147 N.E.2d 817, 819, 67 A.L.R.2d 596, 598.

legal responsibility in the same place, irrespective of mortgages and conditional sales; yet it gives the non-negligent mortgagee or conditional vendor a claim against the negligent third party to protect itself against the risk of non-payment by the debtor. Thus the mortgagee's claim against the third party is good only for shifting to the latter the risk of financial irresponsibility of the mortgagor and is not good for an added benefit to either the mortgagee or the mortgagor.

Whatever it may be called—a security interest in property, or a chose in action—the mortgagee's interest that is harmed by the third party's negligence is an interest intended only as security for payment of a debt. Ordinarily the amount remaining due on the debt is a fair measure of the maximum possible harm done to the mortgagee's interest. The actual harm will be less if subsequently the debtor makes some payment or if something is realized from the remaining value of the damaged chattel. Nevertheless, if there is uncertainty about the debtor's payment or about the value of the damaged chattel, it would be unfair to the mortgagee to make his award against the negligent third party less than the sum remaining due on the debt, since it may finally turn out that he loses the entire amount still owed him. To make certain that the mortgagee is not undercompensated for the loss caused by the negligent third party, it is sound to measure the amount of the mortgagee's recovery by the sum outstanding on the debt. But, to make certain that the negligent third party is not required to pay more than compensation, it is a necessary corollary that when he pays the full sum to the mortgagee he becomes the beneficial owner of whatever value remains in the mortgagee's security interest. This legal relation may be described as an instance of subrogation, in which the third party's payment to the mortgagee entitles him to sue on the mortgagee's claim in debt against the mortgagor. Or it may be said that any further recovery by the mortgagee against the mortgagor is held in trust for the third party, who has fully compensated the mortgagee. Also the legal relation may be thought of as one of forced purchase, analogous to that imposed by the action of trover upon one whose tortious damage to a chattel is so severe as to amount to conversion; the tortfeasor must pay a sum equal to the full value of the interest in an undamaged condition, but in return the judgment vests in him the title to the interest in its damaged condition. Thus, if the mortgagor is financially responsible, the third party will recover on the debt and the mortgagor will be left with his damaged chattel; the ultimate loss will fall on the mortgagor as would have been true if there had been no mortgage.

Before *Racheotes* the court had not been required to choose among these three possibilities as to what effect the mortgagee's recovery against the third party has upon the debt. It is easy to imagine why the point had not been presented for decision. A mortgagee would ordinarily sue on the claim more easily established—the debt —except when the debtor is not financially responsible, and in that case the negligent third party would not ordinarily bother to preserve and press a potential claim against the mortgagor.

It is conceded in *Racheotes* that the insurer can recover only as subrogee of the mortgagee, and if the foregoing analysis is correct, the mortgagee's claim is not one by which the result of placing the ultimate loss on the negligent third party can be reached. Yet that is the result reached in *Racheotes*, unless after the judgment for the insurer against Racheotes the latter still has a subrogation claim on the debt against the mortgagor. This possibility surely would not be conceded, since it would result in loss by the mortgagor, who would then have received no net benefit from his own collision insurance, unless in turn he were allowed to complete the circle by recovering again from the insurance company.[5]

There is a second ground for criticism of *Racheotes*, entirely independent of the foregoing analysis. The mortgage included an assignment by the mortgagor of the insurance proceeds not exceeding the unpaid balance of the debt, and an agreement that the insurance proceeds would be paid to the mortgagee to be "applied" to the unpaid balance of the debt.[6] Neither the opinion nor the record contains a copy of the insurance policy; stipulations make it apparent, however, that the insurer was aware of the mortgagee's interest and perhaps also inserted in the policy a loss payable clause providing for payment to the mortgagee "as its interest may appear." Thus it would be inconsistent with the policy obligations as well as the mortgage to make payment otherwise than to the mortgagee to be "ap-

---

5. A similar problem may have been created by the decision in Broadview Seafoods, Inc. v. Pierre, 248 La. 533, 180 So.2d 694 (1965). A truck owned by Broadview was damaged in a collision while being used by one of its employees on a personal errand. Both the employee and Pierre, the driver of the other vehicle, were negligent. In the absence of insurance, Broadview could have recovered from Pierre as a joint tortfeasor (since the employee's relation to Broadview in this situation was that of a bailee whose negligence was not imputed to his employer-bailor), and Pierre would then have had a right of contribution against the employee. Broadview was partially reimbursed, however, by its collision insurer and the suit was brought for the benefit of both Broadview and the insurer. A lower court judgment allowed Broadview to recover its unreimbursed loss but denied recovery to the insurer on the ground that the employee was an omnibus insured under the collision coverage and, therefore, that the insurer's recovery was barred by his contributory negligence. This decision against the insurer was reversed. Although speaking in terms of the employee as an omnibus insured, the Louisiana Supreme Court held that the insurer was subrogated to the rights of the *named* insured against both the employee and Pierre. The dictum about the insurer being subrogated to Broadview's claim against its employee is clearly wrong if the employee was indeed an omnibus insured under the collision coverage. Not only would this go against the rule that an insurer may not be subrogated to claims against its insured (see § 4.2(b) *supra*), but it would also contravene the intention behind extending the omnibus clause to collision coverage (see § 2.11(b) (3) *supra*). Therefore, if the employee was an omnibus insured, either the court's decision would indirectly deprive him of his rights as an insured, or after the insurer recovered against Pierre and Pierre recovered contribution from the employee, the employee would have the right to recover again from the collision insurer.

6. 337 Mass. 73, 74 n.1, 147 N.E.2d 817, 818 n.1, 67 A.L.R.2d 596, 597 n.1.

plied" to the unpaid balance of the debt. Of course the insurer, mortgagor, and mortgagee are free to, and often do, agree on another form of payment, as they did in this case by using a check payable jointly to mortgagee and mortgagor, which was then applied toward the repair bill. But such an arrangement as to manner of payment, agreed upon after loss, should not give rise to a claim against the negligent third party that would not have been available if the manner of payment had been that provided in the combined terms of the mortgage and the insurance policy. If the proceeds had been paid as those documents provided, then the debt would have been fully discharged; the insurance proceeds exceeded the unpaid balance, and "applied" surely means "applied toward discharge" since any other meaning would leave the mortgagor owing further payment even if the proceeds were "applied" to the debt rather than being used to pay the repair bill. Thus, because of the discharge of the debt, the mortgagee would be fully compensated and would have no further claim for harm to his security, and there would then be no basis for the insurer's subrogation claim.

It is not an adequate answer to argue that the insurer-subrogee should be allowed to assert the claim that existed just before it made payment. That would be giving the payment the effect of purchasing an assignment of the claim rather than the declared effect of being applied to the unpaid balance of the debt. It would leave the debt outstanding; the mortgagor would still owe the full balance to the mortgagee (or its subrogee) and would be holding a damaged car with no fund to repair it, since we are now assuming that payment has been made to the mortgagee as provided in the documents and not to the repairman. The effect of allowing the insurer its alleged subrogation claim would thus be to cause the mortgagor to receive no net benefit from the insurance. It would be treating him as if he were not an insured—as if the policy had been insurance of the mortgagee's interest only. If the negligent third party had been named as an additional insured, it would never have been argued that the insurer should have a subrogation claim against him. In a sense, that is the effect of the agreement that proceeds will be applied to the unpaid balance of the debt; the agreement is one for the discharge pro tanto of the debt and all other claims dependent upon the debt.

The foregoing criticisms of *Racheotes* may be regarded as essentially doctrinal in character. If that be a detraction, however, they are fully supported on grounds of public policy as well, even without resort to the view sometimes urged [7] that subrogation is generally undesirable. If subrogation is to be justified, it is upon the bases that it reduces insurance costs by reducing insurance losses and that it carries out the theme that insurance should effect indemnity only by allowing the insurer to capitalize on other rights for indemnification of the insured loss rather than leaving an insured to profit by recover-

---

7. See, *e.g.*, James, *Indemnity, Subrogation and Contribution and the Effi-* *cient Distribution of Accident Losses*, 21 NACCA L.J. 360 (1958).

ing twice. In this instance, it is plain both that denial of subrogation will not cause anyone to recover more than he lost and that any saving on collision insurance rates that results from allowing subrogation will be exceeded by an increase of liability insurance rates because of administrative costs incurred and losses paid by the liability insurers of persons occupying the position of the negligent third party.

In the next legislative session after *Racheotes* was decided a statute was enacted, providing as follows: "In any action to recover for damage to a motor vehicle brought in the name of a person or persons holding a security interest in said motor vehicle, any defense which would be available as against any registered owner thereof shall be available as against the person or persons holding said security interest." [8]   Literal enforcement will change not merely the insurance-subrogation rule of *Racheotes* but, more basically, the tort rule that the mortgagor's negligence is not imputed to the mortgagee. It might be questioned whether the legislative objective was this broad, however. A narrower objective is suggested by the title of the act, "An Act Relative to Subrogated Automobile Property Damage Claims." [9]

SECTION 4.3   VENDOR AND PURCHASER OF REALTY

§ 4.3(a) GENERALLY

Liability of an insurer and rights in proceeds of a policy insuring against casualty loss to a building that is under contract of sale are dependent in part on determinations concerning, first, insurable interest of each of the parties to the contract of sale, second, placement of the risk of casualty loss as between vendor and purchaser, third, defenses of the insurer based on alleged violations of policy clauses, and fourth, an interrelated combination of questions concerning measure of insurance recovery, subrogation, assignment, proration, and single-interest or multiple-interest construction of the policy or policies of insurance obtained by the vendor and purchaser. The first of these factors (insurable interest) has been considered in the preceding chapter. The second and third factors will be considered briefly before attention is directed to the sharp controversy concerning the fourth combination of factors.

§ 4.3(b) RISK OF CASUALTY LOSS AS BETWEEN VENDOR AND PURCHASER

A substantial number of American courts, following a doctrine of English origin,[1] hold that the purchaser under an enforceable con-

---

8. Mass.Acts 1959, ch. 300; Mass.Gen. Laws Ann. ch. 231, § 85E (Supp.1969).

9. Mass.Acts 1959, ch. 300.

1. Paine v. Meller, 6 Ves.Jr. 349, 31 Eng.Rep. 1088 (1801). See Williston, *The Risk of Loss After an Executory Contract of Sale in the Common Law*, 9 Harv.L.Rev. 106 (1895).

Equitable Conversion

purchaser as equitable owner of property thus bears risk of loss before legal title has legal title (Majority Rule)

tract for sale of realty, in the absence of contract stipulations to the contrary, is the equitable owner of the property and bears the risk of casualty loss even before receipt of either possession or title.[2] The term "equitable conversion" is commonly used to describe this result.[3] Somewhat fewer courts, following a doctrine more nearly like that applicable to contracts for sale of personalty, hold that, in the absence of contract stipulations to the contrary, the risk of casualty loss is on the vendor until conveyance.[4] Some of the apparently conflicting decisions could be reconciled on the facts by adoption of the theory that the person in possession pending conveyance, whether vendor or purchaser, bears the risk of loss in the absence of contract stipulations in point.[5] Possession is a crucial factor under the Uniform Vendor and Purchaser Risk Act § 1, which provides as follows: [6]

exception when in possession. One in possession bears risk of loss

Uniform Vendor-Purchaser Risk Act

"Any contract hereafter made in this State for the purchase and sale of realty shall be interpreted as including an agreement that the parties shall have the following rights and duties, unless the contract expressly provides otherwise:

"(a) If, when neither the legal title nor the possession of the subject matter of the contract has been transferred, all or a material part thereof is destroyed without fault of the purchaser or is taken by eminent domain, the vendor cannot enforce the contract, and the purchaser is entitled to recover any portion of the price that he has paid;

"(b) If, when either the legal title or the possession of the subject matter of the contract has been transferred, all or any part thereof is destroyed without fault of the vendor or is taken by eminent domain, the purchaser is not thereby relieved from a duty to pay the price, nor is he entitled to recover any portion thereof that he has paid."

§ 4.3(c) VIOLATIONS OF POLICY CLAUSES

In many of the older cases and a smaller percentage of recent cases concerning insurance rights as affected by a contract of sale

---

2. *E.g.*, McGinley v. Forrest, 107 Neb. 309, 186 N.W. 74 (1921), 22 A.L.R. 567 (1923).

3. See, *e.g.*, Coolidge & Sickler, Inc. v. Regn, 7 N.J. 93, 80 A.2d 554 (1951), 27 A.L.R.2d 437 (1953).

4. *E.g.*, Libman v. Levenson, 236 Mass. 221, 128 N.E. 13 (1920), 22 A.L.R. 560 (1923); Thompson v. Gould, 37 Mass. (20 Pick.) 134 (1838). See also Annot., 27 A.L.R.2d 444, 454–459 (1953).

5. See Anderson v. Yaworski, 120 Conn. 390, 398, 181 A. 205, 208, 101 A.L.R. 1232, 1237–1238 (1935): "Now that we are directly confronted with the question whether, under [a contract for

sale of land] . . . the risk of loss is upon the vendee, we are not able to accept as authoritative the statement in [Hough v. City Fire Ins. Co., 29 Conn. 10, 76 Am.Dec. 581 (1860)] . . . that it is, at least where possession has not passed, but hold that risk of loss is upon the vendor."

6. 9C Uniform Laws Annotated 314 (1957). The remaining sections of the Act concern uniformity of interpretation, short title, repeal, and time of taking effect. The Act has been adopted in a substantial number of states, though a minority, and in some instances with modifications. *Id.* at 194 (Supp.1967).

of the insured property, the insurer contended that there was a violation of one or more of the moral hazard clauses—*e.g.,* a provision against other insurance, or a provision against change of interest or ownership, or a provision requiring that the interest of the named insured be unconditional and sole ownership. The 1943 New York Standard Fire Insurance Policy omits all moral hazard clauses except that concerning other insurance and provides for a limitation against other insurance only if such limitation is added by special endorsement. Thus, in view of the widespread adoption of the 1943 form, the danger that all insurance protection will be lost by inapt arrangement of the transaction of sale has been greatly reduced. Some danger remains, however. For example, there is at least a small danger from operation of other insurance clauses and from possible violation of one or more of the clauses concerning vacancy, unoccupancy, and increase of hazard.

§ 4.3(d) EXPLICIT CONTRACTUAL PROVISIONS CONCERNING INSURANCE

The careful draftsman of a contract for sale of realty rarely leaves the rights of the parties concerning insurance and the risk of casualty loss to be determined by rules of law applicable in the absence of contract stipulations in point; rather, unless deliberately preferring not to focus attention upon the problem for a reason such as concern that negotiations would then resolve it against the interests he is representing, he covers these matters in the contract stipulations and makes certain that the policy or policies of insurance obtained by the vendor, the purchaser, or both are consistent with those stipulations. Ordinarily the simplest and best way of arranging the insurance is to have each policy endorsed by the insurer to specify that it covers both the vendor and the purchaser, "as their interests may appear"; usually this endorsement will be added upon request and without additional premium charge. It does not resolve all problems, however. For example, it does not resolve questions about the rights of the vendor and purchaser if the damage causes the property to be unsuitable for the intended use during an extended period of repairs.

§ 4.3(e) LEGISLATIVE AND JUDICIAL SOLUTIONS WHEN CONTRACTUAL PROVISIONS ARE INCONCLUSIVE

The first four subdivisions below present, in outline form, a set of possible ways of dealing with those pathological cases in which contract stipulations are silent on the entire insurance problem or on some major aspects of it. Though not all-inclusive, this list is intended to cover the most plausible solutions that a court or legislator might consider. A brief comparison of the merits of the different rules is presented thereafter.

(i) *Liability-for-Insurable-Interest Rules.* Each insurer is liable only to the extent of its insured's insurable interest at the time of the loss, and rights in the policy proceeds are allocated in one of the following three ways: First, a *no-subrogation rule*. Each insured is entitled to retain the proceeds of his policy and is required to comply with his obligations to the other party under the contract of sale, and no insurer is subrogated to the rights of its insured against the other party under the contract of sale. Second, a *subrogation rule*. Each insurer is subrogated to its insured's claim against the other party to the contract of sale, subject to defenses which would be available against the insured. (*E.g.*, if the risk of loss under the contract of sale is on the purchaser, the vendor's insurer is able to recover against the purchaser on his agreement to pay the purchase price; the purchaser, if himself fully insured, is made whole by his recovery against his own insurer. Likewise, if the risk of loss under the sale contract is on the vendor, the purchaser's insurer is able to recover on the purchaser's claims against the vendor for repair of the damage, or for a reduction of the purchase price, or for rescission and return of the down payment.) Third, a *trust-for-the-purchaser rule*. Any recovery by the vendor is to be retained by him to the extent needed to give him total receipts (from the purchaser and the insurer) equal to the agreed purchase price, and any excess is held by him for the benefit of the purchaser.

(ii) *Liability-for-Full-Loss Rules.* Subject to its policy limit, each insurer is liable for the full loss to the property, and one of the three choices stated in paragraph (i) is made as to rights in the policy proceeds.

(iii) *A Primary-and-Excess-Coverage Rule.* The insurance in the name of the party having the risk of loss under the contract of sale will be treated as primary coverage and the insurance in the name of the other party to the contract as excess coverage of the loss to the property, and the total insurance recovery will not exceed that loss.

(iv) *A Prorated-Coverage Rule.* The vendor's insurance and the purchaser's insurance will be treated as complementary coverage, with the total recovery not exceeding the loss to the property and the part paid by each insurer being determined by a principle of proration.[1]

It may happen that the first of the several rules presented here (a *liability-for-insurable-interest rule* with *no subrogation* allowed) works out inconsistently with the principle of indemnity since insurable interests may overlap, their sum exceeding the value of the property, when each insurable interest is valued at the highest amount of loss it might cover under the various contingencies involved. For example, if as between vendor and purchaser the risk of loss is on the purchaser and both parties have fire insurance to the full extent of their insurable interests (valued according to contingent rather than

---

1. Concerning the choice among principles of proration, compare § 3.10(c) (2) *supra*.

actual loss), then each will recover from his insurer, and the vendor will also get either specific performance or damages from the purchaser. Thus the vendor profits from the fire. This first rule, when insurable interests are valued according to contingent rather than actual loss, therefore has the disadvantage of working against the objectives underlying the doctrine of insurable interest.[2] The simplicity of the rule in operation and the avoidance of a second round of loss shifting through operation of subrogation rights (an uneconomic process from an overall point of view) are arguable advantages of this solution, but seem clearly outweighed by this disadvantage.

The second variation among rules of the first type suggested (a *liability-for-insurable-interest rule* with *subrogation* allowed) adheres to the principle of indemnity. If it seems objectionable in some circumstances, probably that is due either to the objectionable character of the rules allocating the risk of loss as between vendor and purchaser or to inconsistency between the total complex of rules and the common expectation of laymen that insurance will run with the property. This rule is supported by English authorities, particularly *Castellain v. Preston*[3] and *Rayner v. Preston*.[4] Under those decisions,

2. If one rejects contingent valuation however, and adopts the rationale that the vendor incurs no legal loss if it later turns out that the executory contract is completed subsequent to the fire loss—*e.g.*, see Paramount Fire Ins. Co. v. Aetna Cas. & Sur. Co., 163 Tex. 250, 353 S.W.2d 841 (1962) (refusing to allow the vendee's insurer pro rata recovery from the vendor's insurer)—the objectives of the insurable interest doctrine are indirectly affirmed. The dissent in this case, however, makes a good case for valuing loss as of the time of the fire without regard to subsequent events (*i. e.*, the completion of the sale transaction), a result more consistent with the express terms of most policies. In that event, the vendor's loss might be termed "contingent." Even so, one of various possible arrangements might be adopted to take the contingency into account and yet not allow a profit to the vendor; for example, in this case, the vendee's insurer sought a proration between the insurers to prevent net profit to the vendor. See the text *infra*, this section.

3. 11 Q.B.D. 380 (1883). Before contracting to sell a house, the owner had procured fire insurance on it; the contract of sale mentioned neither the insurance nor the risk of casualty loss pending completion of the sale. The house was damaged by fire after the date of the contract of sale and before completion of the transaction;

the vendor recovered under the insurance without the insurer's knowing of the contract of sale, but the purchase price was not reduced because of the damage to the house. In *Rayner*, n.4 *infra*, the vendee was denied recovery of the insurance proceeds from the vendor, but in *Castellain* the insurer was allowed to recover out of the purchase money received by the vendor an amount equal to the benefits paid because of its right to be subrogated to the vendor's contract claim against the vendee. *Compare* these cases *with* Paramount Fire Ins. Co. v. Aetna Cas. & Sur. Co., 163 Tex. 250, 353 S.W.2d 841 (1962) (holding that, when the vendor and the vendee are insured by different insurers, the entire loss must be borne by the vendee's insurer; reserving the question of rights in the proceeds when only the vendor is insured).

4. 18 Ch.D. 1 (1881). The decision in *Rayner* (and, therefore, that in *Castellain* in regard to vendor-vendee interests) was changed in 1922 by statute. Law of Real Property Act, 1922, 12 & 13 Geo. 5, c. 16, § 105. See also Law of Property Act, 1925, 15 Geo. 5, c. 20, § 47; Ivamy, General Principles of Insurance Law 373 (1966). Compare Hepburn v. A. Tomlinson (Hauliers) Ltd., [1966] 1 All E.R. 418 (H.L.), reaching in a bailment situation, without benefit of statute, a result directly contrary to *Rayner* in the sense that the bailee was allowed to recover

the vendor's insurer was subrogated to the vendor's rights incident to the fact that the rules of law applicable to the contract of purchase and sale placed the risk of loss on the purchaser.   The leading New York decision in *Brownell v. Board of Education*[5] might be thought inconsistent with this rule.   But the purchaser's inability in that case to recover the vendor's insurance proceeds is consistent with this rule because the contract of purchase and sale, as construed, gave the purchaser no cause of action against the vendor for more than $3,000 (apparently merely in effect the return of $3,000 deposited by the purchaser and not $3,000 in addition to return of the deposit).   The profit to the vendor produced by the decision and the resulting inconsistency with the underlying objectives of the doctrine of insurable interest arise from the fact that the value placed on the vendor's insurable interest was unrealistically high in view of the obsolete character of the building.

The third variation among rules of the first type suggested (a *liability-for-insurable-interest rule* with a *trust for the purchaser*) incorporates to a degree the idea that insurance runs with the land.[6]   It also allows a deviation from the principle of indemnity since the combination of the purchaser's own insurance and that of the vendor, accruing to the purchaser's benefit in trust, may exceed his loss.   The idea that insurance may run with the land is also expressed in the third type of rule (a *primary-and-excess-coverage rule*) but without the potential deviation from the principle of indemnity.   The result in a leading New York decision, *Raplee v. Piper*,[7] is consistent with both of these solutions.   On the facts of that case it was not necessary to make the choice between them.   Moreover, the opinions in *Raplee* make it appear that the result of allowing the purchaser to benefit from the vendor's insurance was dependent on the fact that the premiums on the vendor's policy were paid by the purchaser, pursuant to terms of the contract of purchase and sale; perhaps also the terms of the contract and the fact that premiums were paid by the purchaser were known to the insurer, though this is not made clear.

in full with the understanding that he would hold in trust for the bailor any surplus above the sum necessary to indemnify himself.   See Ivamy, *op. cit. supra* at 374–375, 460, 462, indicating that this result would be reached only if the parties to the insurance contract so intended at the time of effecting it.

5.   239 N.Y. 369, 146 N.E. 630, 37 A.L.R. 1319 (1925).

6.   See, *e.g.*, Skelly Oil Co. v. Ashmore, 365 S.W.2d 582 (Mo.1963) (vendee allowed specific performance of contract to purchase property with the purchase price reduced by the amount of insurance proceeds paid vendor because of fire damage that occurred before sale was completed); Dubin Pa-

per Co. v. Insurance Co. of N. Am., 361 Pa. 68, 63 A.2d 85, 8 A.L.R.2d 1393 (1949) (contract to sell property entered into before loss and consummated after loss but before payment of insurance proceeds held not to affect insurer's liability, although vendor would hold proceeds in trust for the benefit of the vendee).

7.   3 N.Y.2d 179, 143 N.E.2d 919, 164 N.Y.S.2d 732 (1957), 64 A.L.R.2d 1397 (1959).   See also Gard v. Razanskas, 248 Iowa 1333, 85 N.W.2d 612 (1957), 65 A.L.R.2d 982 (1959) (lessee-optionee entitled to credit on purchase price in the amount of insurance proceeds paid to lessor-optionor on loss occurring after option to purchase was created and before it was exercised).

The second type of rule (*liability-for-full-loss*) is not supported by decisions.[8] It would be inconsistent with that provision of the fire insurance policy forms stating that the amount of the insurance shall not be "in any event for more than the interest of the insured."

The fourth type of rule (a *prorated-coverage rule*) is consistent with the principle of indemnity but offensive to the principle that the fire insurance contract is personal. This result has been achieved in many cases by agreement among the insurers after dispute has arisen. *Insurance Co. of N. Am. v. Alberstadt*[9] is an example. Rose Alberstadt, while the owner of the property in question, obtained a $3,500 fire insurance policy. Thereafter, the property was sold to Patterson at sheriff's sale for delinquent taxes. The sale price was $2,600. Patterson then obtained a $2,500 fire insurance policy. A few weeks later a fire occurred, damaging the property (the court assumed) to the extent of $3,175. After the fire Patterson paid the sheriff the amount of his bid and obtained the sheriff's deed. Though the policies reserved to the insurers the right to discharge their obligations by repairing the property, they lost that right by failing to assert it within the time stipulated in the policies.[10] Rose Alberstadt demanded $3,175 (the full loss) from her insurer, and Patterson demanded $2,500 (the policy limit) from his insurer. The lower court entered judgments for both Alberstadt and Patterson.

8. Perhaps one reason for lack of precedents supporting this rule is that, as stated in the text, policy forms ordinarily declare that in no event shall the insurer's liability be for an amount in excess of the interest of the insured in the property. Thus, the question whether a larger recovery can be obtained is not likely to arise except when a valued policy statute applies (although even then it is subject to the qualification that the statutes proscribe any challenge of the dollar amount of the insured's interest so that, in form at least, an *insurable-interest* and not a *full-loss* rule is applicable). In Springfield Fire & Marine Ins. Co. v. Boswell, 167 So.2d 780 (Fla.App.1964), for example, the insured property was to be sold for $12,500, and the vendor and vendee independently obtained valued policies in the amounts of $6,000 and $15,000 respectively. After a fire that totally destroyed the improvements on the property, vendee collected the face amount of his policy and paid $12,000 of the proceeds (an amount equal to the then unpaid part of the purchase price) to his vendor in return for the conveyance of the property to him. The vendor then claimed and recovered the face amount of his policy, the court not questioning the amount of the vendor's loss but, rather, speaking of the total loss as having been $21,000 since that was the sum of the two policies on the property.

9. 383 Pa. 556, 119 A.2d 83 (1956).

10. If the vendor's insurer were to elect to repair the property in a situation like that in *Alberstadt*, however, it might lose its opportunity to cause the loss to be borne either primarily by the purchaser's insurer, with its own coverage being treated as excess, or else proportionately by the two insurers. The disputed rule denying subrogation to a volunteer could be invoked by the purchaser's insurer. See § 3.10(b) (1) *supra*. Moreover, if —mindful of the fact that when the option to repair is exercised, the insured cannot compel appraisal of the damage, see, *e.g.*, Michigan Fire Repair Contractors' Ass'n v. Pacific Nat'l Fire Ins. Co., 362 Mich. 552, 107 N.W.2d 811 (1961)—the company was considering the repair option because of a belief that the insured's claim might be padded and that the total cost to the insurer could be reduced by contracting directly for the repairs, it would be unlikely that the insurer could get an assignment from its insured for the purpose of avoiding the rule against volunteers.

The companies offered to pay $3,175, by proration agreed upon between them, and the Supreme Court of Pennsylvania modified the judgments so as to limit the total recovery to $3,175 [11] and to distribute the loss between the insurers consistently with their proration agreement.   The court also concluded that as between Rose Alberstadt and Patterson, she was entitled to retain none of the insurance proceeds because she sustained no loss.   This conclusion seems dubious.   It was based on a presumption that the price the property brought at sheriff's sale was the value of the property, in the absence of averment to the contrary.   This is surely contrary to fact with respect to sheriffs' sales generally and this one in particular since the admitted amount of loss exceeded the price at sheriff's sale.   It would seem that she should have been allowed to retain proceeds of her own policy equal to the value of her right of redemption.   One way, but not necessarily the only way, of arriving at that value would be to determine the excess of the market value of the property over the amount she would have had to pay to redeem it.   The fact that the right was not exercised and that it expired before trial, but after the fire, does not establish that it was worthless.   The uncertainties arising from the fire and the disputed insurance claims may have made it impractical to exercise the right even though it had value just before the fire.

Alberstadt and *Brownell* may seem to be in conflict since *Alberstadt* permits the purchaser to benefit from the vendor's insurance and *Brownell* declines to allow that result.   But the cases can be reconciled.

Despite the fact that the contract of purchase and sale in *Brownell* placed the risk of loss on the vendor, the contract was held to place a limitation on the purchaser's remedy for breach that was inconsistent with the purchaser's argument that he was entitled to insurance proceeds;   the return of the $3,000 deposit discharged the vendor's obligations to the purchaser.   Also, the cases might be distinguished on the ground that in *Alberstadt* the insurers were resisting payment in excess of loss to the property whereas in *Brownell* the payment had been made by the insurer and the dispute was one between vendor and purchaser over the insurance proceeds.

11.   In reaching this result, the Pennsylvania court acted differently from a federal court's prediction of its action made in Vogel v. Northern Assur. Co., 219 F.2d 409 (3d Cir. 1955).   Subsequent to agreeing on the terms of a sale of improved property for $15,000, Vogel and his vendor independently obtained fire insurance on the property in amounts of $9,000 and $6,000 respectively.   Before conveyance of the property to Vogel, a fire caused $12,000 damage.   Vogel completed his part of the transaction and received from the vendor, in addition to the deed to the property, an assignment of the vendor's rights against his insurer. Vogel brought suit against both his insurer and the vendor's and obtained a verdict for the full amount of each policy, a total recovery $3,000 in excess of the loss.   The Court of Appeals affirmed, holding that, although there were good arguments against the result, it was supported by Pennsylvania law, which governed the case.

Shup
206-221

SECTION 4.4 LEASES, LIFE ESTATES, AND OTHER LIMITED INTERESTS IN REALTY

§ 4.4(a) RULES APPLICABLE WHEN CONTRACTUAL PROVISIONS ARE INCONCLUSIVE

A division of authority exists with respect to the rights of parties to a lease of the insured property to recover under insurance policies. One line of decisions, adhering to the principle of indemnity, protects insurers of the lessor and lessee against liabilities that exceed loss because of other rights of indemnity. *Ramsdell v. Insurance Co. of N. Am.* [1] is an example. The lessee under a five-year lease was permitted, by terms of the lease, to repair or remodel at his own expense and had an option to purchase at the expiration of the lease. The lessee remodeled at an expense of $7,800 and obtained fire insurance of $7,500 on the leased building. Independently, the lessors had obtained insurance in the amount of $3,000 (policies of $1,000 each in three different companies). Neither the lessee nor the lessors were required to restore the building after damage by fire, but after such damage in the amount of $4,264 the lessee restored the building and sued its insurer. The lessors, too, sued on their policies. All these suits were consolidated. In the trial court, the lessors recovered their limit of coverage ($3,000) and the lessee an amount equal to the total damage ($4,264). The latter judgment was paid in full. On appeal by the lessors' insurers, the judgment against them was reversed on the ground that, the damage having been repaired by the lessee, the lessors could not show any loss. The court suggested the possibility of proration: "[T]he insurance companies might lawfully pool their losses and restore the building at the cost of the damage to the building.. . . . In equity and good conscience the insurance companies may yet prorate the loss, but we cannot see how it can be held that plaintiffs below had any actual loss."[2]

The possible solutions of the contest, if the lessee's insurer, as well as the lessor's insurers, had chosen to appeal from the trial court judgment in this case, would have been similar to those outlined elswhere with respect to contracts of purchase and sale.[3] It might be argued that this lease was analogous to a contract of purchase and sale placing the risk of casualty loss on the purchaser. Here neither party was required to restore the building, and apparently the lessee was not excused from his rental obligation because it had been damaged through casualty. But there is only an analogy, not a perfect parallel, since the lessor would still bear the risk of loss incident to the fact that the lessee might elect not to repair, in which event the lessor would receive back a damaged building at the end of the lease term. Arguably the division of loss between insurers ought

---

1.   197 Wis. 136, 221 N.W. 654 (1928). See also 6 Appleman, Insurance Law § 3861 (1942); Annot., 97 A.L.R.2d 1243, 1249–1250 (1964).

2.   197 Wis. at 139, 221 N.W. at 655.

3.   See § 4.3(e) *supra*.

to be on a basis consistent with this division of the risk of loss between lessor and lessee, each insurer being subrogated to its insured's rights. But the complexity of the problem of determining the allocation on this basis is a cogent argument for proration among insurers, as if all policies were written for the joint interests of lessor and lessee. If the conclusion is reached that a rule of proration is the best solution here, that result ought not to be defeated either by the argument that the insurer who pays in full to its insured is a volunteer to the extent of payment above its prorated share or by the argument that the insured who repairs and then sues its insurer is a volunteer in making the repairs, so as to bar his insurer from seeking contribution after being held liable for the full cost of repairs. Unfortunately, however, the closing sentence in the quotation from *Ramsdell*, above, offers only a little hope for recognition that the lessee's insurer has an enforceable right of contribution from the lessor's insurer. The argument for proration would have been strengthened, however, if the actions in the *Ramsdell* fact situation had all been prosecuted to final judgment before any repairs were effected. The "volunteer" arguments against this result would not then have been available.

Some lessee's "improvements and betterments" policies declare the measure of recovery to be a fraction of the original cost, related to the proportion of the term of the lease yet to run at the time of loss. Decisions applying this measure of recovery [4] can easily be reconciled with the *Ramsdell* rule when, as is ordinarily the case, no recovery in excess of loss results.

In contrast with *Ramsdell*, another line of authority departs from the principle of indemnity, permitting a net profit from an insured loss. *Citizens Ins. Co. v. Foxbilt, Inc.*[5] is an illustration. An insurance policy on improvements to a leased building, obtained by Foxbilt, the lessee, provided that the insurer agreed "to accept and consider the insured in the event of loss in the position of sole and unconditional owner of such Improvements and Betterments, any contract or lease the insured may have made to the contrary notwithstanding." [6] The lease provided for termination in the event of casualty damage not repairable in ninety days and for suspension of rent in the event of casualty damage rendering the premises unfit for occupancy but repairable within ninety days, and it provided further in the latter event that the lessor should make repairs with reasonable speed. The District Court held the insurer liable for damage to the improvements, despite the fact that the lessor had restored them without expense to the insured,[7] and the Court of Appeals affirmed.[8]

---

4. See, *e.g.*, Daeris, Inc. v. Hartford Fire Ins. Co., 105 N.H. 117, 193 A.2d 886 (1963), 97 A.L.R.2d 1238 (1964).

5. 226 F.2d 641 (8th Cir. 1955), 53 A.L.R.2d 1376 (1957).

6. 226 F.2d at 642, 53 A.L.R.2d at 1379.

7. See also Alwood v. Commercial Union Assur. Co., 107 Ga.App. 797, 131 S.E.2d 594 (1963) (lessee's "gratuitous" repair of fire damage does not defeat lessor's claim, which arose when dam-

8. See Note 8 on page 208.

The possibility of profiting from fire damage to the leased building was inherent in the *Foxbilt* policy clause declaring that the lessee should be regarded as sole and unconditional owner of the improvements irrespective of the terms of the lease. Thus the insurer had little basis for complaint as a matter of contract, but the opposite result might have been reached on the basis of a judicially imposed rule aimed at serving the principle of indemnity (*i.e.*, as an aspect of insurable interest doctrine). The argument that the insurer cannot benefit from the insured's recoupment of his loss from another source opposes the principle of indemnity. If this argument is made in a case in which the insured has a legal right to recoupment from the other source, it opposes also the right of subrogation (a particular application of the principle of indemnity).

Even in a jurisdiction not following *Ramsdell*, perhaps insurers could effectively cooperate to prevent total liabilities in excess of the damage to the insured property. Perhaps they could limit the total payments to the cost of repair by cooperating in the exercise of the option to repair. It may be, however, that they would not in this way get the benefit of any reduction for depreciation, and to this extent their total outlay would exceed damage to the insured property. Significantly, some policies are now providing for cash recovery to this same extent—that is, without deduction for depreciation.[9]

§ 4.4(b) SUBROGATION OF THE LESSOR'S INSURER TO THE LESSOR'S CLAIMS FOR INDEMNITY BY THE LESSEE

It may happen that a lessor's insurer, under a line of authority adhering to the principle of indemnity,[1] will be subrogated to the lessor's claims against the lessee for indemnity.[2] The potential liability

age occurred); Alexandra Restaurant, Inc. v. New Hampshire Ins. Co., 272 App.Div. 346, 71 N.Y.S.2d 515 (1st Dep't 1947), *aff'd*, 297 N.Y. 858, 79 N. E.2d 268 (1948) (structural improvements to leased property were made and insured by lessee; subsequent to fire damage, repairs were made by lessor, which was his obligation under the lease; held, lessee could recover under his insurance).

8. 226 F.2d 641, 644, 53 A.L.R.2d 1376, 1381: "Since the liability of the insurer is for indemnity against loss to property and attaches on the happening of the loss and since the amount of the liability is determinable as of that time, it reasonably can be argued that the subsequent repair or restoration of the insured property by a third party without cost to the insured cannot relieve the insurer of its accrued liability. That is the law in

some of the states." The Court of Appeals, though allowing this result, seems not to adopt the rule as its own but merely to hold that the District Court's adoption of this rule is permissible. It seems a strange notion that under *Erie* the District Court's choice of a rule of law should be sustained if a "permissible" one among conflicting views, none of which has been authoritatively adopted by the state courts. In this aspect, *Foxbilt* treats the issue as if it were a question of fact rather than a question of law.

9. See § 3.9(b) *supra*.

1. See § 4.4(a) *supra*.

2. *E.g.*, Wichita City Lines, Inc. v. Puckett, 156 Tex. 456, 295 S.W.2d 894 (1956).

of lessees in these circumstances was given scant attention before a trial court decision in the late 1940's, which imposed a heavy liability ($142,500) upon the lessee of a commercial building.[3] Fire insurers had rarely made claims against lessees on the basis of subrogation to the lessor's rights either in tort or in contract.[4] In the 1950's it became possible to obtain an endorsement on a lessor's fire policy by which the insurer waives any right of recovery against a tenant for loss to insured property. Ordinarily, also, no additional premium is charged for such an endorsement.[5]

A lessee alert to this risk may seek protection by insisting upon such an endorsement of the lessor's insurance or in other ways. For example he might seek to obtain lease provisions that place all the insurable risks on the lessor as between lessor and tenant, or to obtain joint insurance so the insurer would be precluded from asserting a subrogation claim against the tenant as one of its insureds (a result achieved also by the endorsement referred to), or to obtain separate insurance that would protect the tenant against the insurable risks it assumes under the lease. The first of these protective methods has the advantage that, if it can be negotiated with the lessor, it is more likely to involve a lease provision that relieves the tenant of any concern about responsibility for fortuitous losses to the property—even those caused by the tenant's negligence. But this has the disadvantage of possible resistance of the lessor in negotiations for the lease; the likelihood of such resistance is increased by the possibility that the provision, if not consented to by the insurer, will be held to be an interference with the insurer's rights of subrogation and, as such, a defense to a claim by the lessor under his policy.[6] Moreover, the lessee may need insurance to protect him against loss from business interruption or, in some situations, loss incident to destruction of improvements made at the expense of the lessee; ordinarily it would be preferable to obtain these coverages as part of a policy that also pro-

3. See General Mills, Inc. v. Goldman, 184 F.2d 359 (8th Cir. 1950), *cert. denied*, 340 U.S. 947 (1951), reversing the trial court decision on the basis of the higher court's interpretation of the lease and without rejecting the possibility of subrogation of a lessor's insurer to the lessor's claims against the lessee in the absence of inconsistent provisions in the lease.

4. See Friedman, *Landlords, Tenants and Fires—Insurer's Right of Subrogation*, 43 Cornell L.Q. 225 (1957); Brewer, *An Inductive Approach to the Liability of the Tenant for Negligence*, 31 B.U.L.Rev. 47, 50 (1951).

5. Compare the rating practices in relation to insurance protecting both the mortgagor and mortgagee, or both the vendor and purchaser. See §§ 4.2(c), 4.3(d) *supra*.

6. See, *e.g.*, Continental Mfg. Corp. v. Underwriters at Lloyds London, 185 Cal.App.2d 545, 8 Cal.Rptr. 276 (2d Dist.1960). See also § 3.10(c) (2) *supra*.

Moreover, inexplicit attempts at contractual exculpation from responsibility for negligence may be ineffectual. *Cf.*, *e.g.*, Poslosky v. Firestone Tire & Rubber Co., 349 S.W.2d 847 (Mo.1961) (lessee held liable for its negligence even in the face of lease provisions obligating the lessor to carry fire insurance, declaring that the insurance proceeds should on demand by the lessee be used to repair, and allowing the lessee to terminate if the premises were untenantable or if the lessor failed to repair on demand; thus, the court concluded the lessor and its subrogated insurer could recover against the lessee).

tects the lessee's interest in the property incident to his obligations to the lessor for repair of damage caused, for example, by a fire arising from the lessee's negligence.

Probably it is undesirable, from the point of view of public interest, that the risk of loss from a fire negligently caused by a lessee be upon the lessee rather than the lessor's insurer. Allowing the lessor's insurer to proceed against the lessee is surely contrary to expectations of persons other than those who have been exposed to this bit of law either during negotiations for a lease or else after a loss. The question whether the desired result (that the lessee be given the benefit of the lessor's insurance) should be reached by judicial imposition of such a rule in the absence of statutory or administrative sanctions is debatable. Probably the courts should not so rule if the lease and insurance provisions together clearly express an agreement that the lessor's insurer shall have the right of subrogation. But perhaps they should at least adopt a rule against allowing the lessor's insurer to proceed against the lessee when lease provisions are ambiguous in this regard and the insurance policy is silent or ambiguous.[7]

§ 4.4(c) LIFE TENANT AND REMAINDERMAN

One context in which a dispute may exist with respect to rights of a life tenant and a remainderman in insurance proceeds arises when an owner of insured property dies and persons in these two groups are his successors in interest. It is commonly held that if a building has been insured before and is destroyed after the creation of a life tenancy, the destruction converts the interests in the property to personalty and the life tenant is entitled only to a life estate in the proceeds of the insurance contract.[1] Thus the policy is given effect as insurance for the separate interests of both the life tenant and the remainderman; it is neither insurance for the benefit of one to the exclusion of the other nor insurance providing proceeds that either party could use to repair the loss without the agreement of the other. Neither the life tenant nor the remainderman is well protected in these circumstances. Similarly, a life tenant obtaining separate coverage in an amount that does not exceed the present cash value of his life estate, computed on the basis of his life expectancy and a reasonable rate of return on investment, has inadequate protection. The insurance proceeds would be inadequate to repair the fortuitous damage to the property, and the life tenant might be in a much less advantageous economic position than before the damage occurred if he were unable to arrange for repairs. He would face both the problem of obtaining additional funds from sources other than insurance proceeds and the problem of possible disagreement with the remainderman over the arrangements for repairs. It would be better that these problems be worked out in advance of loss by an arrangement for joint insurance with a further understanding for application of the in-

7. See generally § 6.3 *infra.*   1. *E.g.,* Millard v. Beaumont, 194 Mo. App. 69, 185 S.W. 547 (1916).

surance proceeds toward repairs and for financing additional costs, if any, of full repairs.

If a life tenant obtains an insurance policy not designating the remainderman as an additional insured, a question may be raised with respect to the existence of any insurable interest in excess of the present cash value of his life estate. If the full expectation of economic loss to the life tenant from fortuitous destruction of the property is recognized as the measure, his insurable interest exceeds present cash value of his life estate. This is true because it may be that no investment he could acquire with an amount of insurance proceeds equal to the present cash value of his interest would be as valuable to him as his life estate in the fully repaired property. But it is debatable whether this risk of economic loss beyond the present cash value of his life estate is within the coverage of the fire policy, which ordinarily is an agreement that the company does insure the named person "and legal representatives, to the extent of the actual cash value of the property at the time of loss, but not exceeding the amount which it would cost to repair .   . ., nor in any event for more than the interest of the insured, against all DIRECT LOSS BY FIRE .   . ." [2] Even if the policy does not cover this phase of the risk, however, an insurer might choose as a matter of business judgment not to seek to limit its liability. In the first place, by contending for the limitation it would be asserting a position inconsistent with its being entitled to the full amount of premiums if the stated limit of liability was higher than the maximum value of the interest actually covered under its contention. Second, the amount saved by contending successfully for the limitation might not be worth the cost of the fight, even in terms of litigation costs and aside from considerations of goodwill.

It might also be argued that, even without explicit provisions so stating, a contract of insurance in an amount equal to full value of a building, obtained by a life tenant, ought to be upheld on the theory of representative insurable interest [3]—an interest in the life tenant to obtain insurance for the benefit of the remainderman. If this theory is accepted, it follows that the proceeds, if recovered by the life tenant, should be held in part for the benefit of the remainderman. In these circumstances it might be argued, however, that the form of the transaction supports the further conclusion that the life tenant acts properly in using the proceeds to repair the damage—a step that protects the interests of the remainderman as well as the life tenant and is therefore consistent with his obligations as trustee of the proceeds in excess of the amount of his own interest. Some decisions have gone still further, allowing the life tenant to collect the insurance proceeds in full for his own interest, even over the opposition of the remainderman. [4] Usually such results have been reasoned in part

2. See the standard fire insurance policy form in Appendix A *infra*.

3. See § 3.4(a) (3) *supra*.

4. *E.g.*, Farmers' Mut. Fire & Lightning Ins. Co. v. Crowley, 354 Mo. 649, 190 S.W.2d 250 (1945) (life tenant had endorsement added to policy originally

on the ground that a property insurance contract is personal in character.[5] Standing alone, however, this is not an adequate justification for allowing the life tenant to recover an amount in excess of his interest and hold it for himself; consistency with both the principle of indemnity and the principle that fire insurance is personal could be achieved by limiting recovery to the amount of the life tenant's interest.

If the insurance proceeds collected by a life tenant do not exceed the present value of the life tenant's interest, the arguments for allowing him the full beneficial interest in the proceeds are compelling. In general, in the absence of stipulations to the contrary in the insurance contracts and documents creating the life tenancy, the life tenant is not bound to keep the premises insured for the remainderman's benefit[6] or to repair fortuitous damage to the property occurring without his fault.[7]

§ 4.4(d) PERSONAL REPRESENTATIVES; SURVIVORSHIP

It has been said that the executor or administrator of a deceased insured is the proper person to collect under a fire policy for a loss, whether occurring before the insured's death[1] or after.[2] It is also recognized, however, that the personal representative collecting may be obligated to apply proceeds in a special way rather than as part of the personal assets of the estate. For example, in a case involving fire loss shortly before the insured's death, it was held that the proceeds of the policy received for destruction of a barn should be treated as real estate in place of the barn, not as personalty.[3]

obtained by his grantor that recognized the demise of the grantor and named life tenant as the owner of the property; after a fire causing damage to the property the insurer interpleaded the adverse claimants, *i.e.* the life tenant and the remainderman; held, life tenant was entitled to receive and use as his own the entire proceeds of the policy). *Cf.* Hunt v. General Ins. Co., 227 S.C. 125, 87 S.E.2d 34 (1955) (life tenants procured an $8,000 valued fire policy on their interest and remainderman procured a $3,000 fire policy on his interest, by coincidence with the same insurer; after a fire causing $1,290.45 damage, insurer offered to repair the damage, but remainderman would not consent to repair; held, though their interest was grossly overvalued, life tenants could recover full amount of loss because of Valued Policy Statute and insurer's retention of full premiums; majority opinion noted that the court was not here concerned with any judgment rendered in favor of the remainderman; the dissenting opinion disclosed

that the remainderman had been awarded a judgment by the trial court on the basis of a percentage of total loss in proportion to the remainderman's interest in the total value of the property, 71.5 per cent, as determined on the basis of a mortality table used by the court).

5. *E.g.*, Farmers' Mut. Fire & Lightning Ins. Co. v. Crowley, n.4 *supra*.

6. *Ibid.*

7. 1 Restatement of Property § 146 (1936).

1. *E.g.*, *In re* Mullin's Estate, 121 Misc. 867, 202 N.Y.Supp. 758 (Surr.Ct.1921).

2. *E.g.*, Oldham's Trustee v. Boston Ins. Co., 189 Ky. 844, 226 S.W. 106 (1920), 16 A.L.R. 305 (1922).

3. *In re* Mullin's Estate, 121 Misc. 867, 202 N.Y.Supp. 758 (Surr.Ct.1921). *Accord*, Rock County Sav. & Trust Co. v. London Assur. Co., 17 Wis.2d 618, 117

SECTION 4.5 "IN TRUST OR ON COMMISSION" AND ANALOGOUS COVERAGES

§ 4.5(a) GENERALLY

Warehousemen's insurance policies have commonly included a type of provision, referred to as an "in trust or on commission" clause, extending coverage to damage to property held but not owned by the insured. A great number of different forms of such clauses have been used, many of which do not contain exactly this phrase. Even among those containing this phrase there have been great variations in the remainder of the clause.

Other types of coverage, as well as "in trust or on commission" clauses, may also extend to property of persons other than the named insured. For example, mercantile forms covering furniture, fixtures, equipment, and supplies have sometimes included coverage of property of others for which the insured is "liable" while located in the described building.[1]

In general, courts have tended to construe these clauses to afford greater coverage than literal enforcement would have provided. Often this has been done by resort to the rule of resolving ambiguities against the insurer.[2] In some instances when this theory has been used, the conclusion of ambiguity has been strained and a more candid explanation is that for some other reason of policy—such as honoring reasonable expectations [3]—a court has declined to enforce the limitations of coverage as written. *United States v. Globe & Rutgers Fire Ins. Co.*[4] is an example. The Commodity Credit Corporation had contracted with the McCoy Gin Company for the latter to purchase for the corporation cotton seed from eligible producers under the Federal price support program. A fire at the McCoy premises destroyed 114,130 pounds of seed purchased under that contract and in McCoy's custody at the time. Without claiming that the fire was due to the negligence of McCoy, the government brought suit to recover under six Texas-standard-form fire insurance policies obtained by

---

N.W.2d 676 (1962), 4 A.L.R.3d 422 (1965) (joint tenant died one day after fire loss; held, in denying claim of deceased's estate, insurance proceeds to be treated in equity as if they were the insured building, thereby passing entirely to surviving tenant). *But cf. In re* Estate of Barry, 208 Okla. 8, 252 P.2d 437 (1952), 35 A.L.R.2d 1052 (1954) (collision insured died shortly after accident that severely damaged insured vehicle; held, legatee of vehicle was entitled only to salvage value of vehicle after the accident and not to the collision insurance proceeds).

1. *E.g.*, Penn v. Commercial Union Fire Ins. Co., 233 Miss. 178, 101 So.2d 535 (1958), 67 A.L.R.2d 1238 (1959) ("liability" referred to general liability of bailee and did not condition coverage on proof of "particular fixed legal liability as a consequence of a fire").

2. See § 6.3 *infra.*

3. *Ibid.*

4. 104 F.Supp. 632 (N.D.Tex.1952), *aff'd*, 202 F.2d 696 (5th Cir.1953). See also 4 Appleman, Insurance Law §§ 2345–2346 (rev. ed. 1969); Annot., 67 A.L. R.2d 1241 (1959).

McCoy and in force at the time of the fire, each of which contained the following coverage clause:

"On cotton, ginned and unginned, baled and unbaled, seed cotton, cotton seed, supplies of sacks and other packaging material containing or to contain cotton seed, and bagging and ties, their own, and provided the insured is legally liable therefor, this policy shall also cover such property sold but not delivered, held in trust or on consignment or for storage." [5]

It was argued by the insurer in this case that the court's interpretation of the clause in favor of broad coverage rendered sterile the limiting phrase "provided the insured is legally liable therefor." The trial court answered that this argument overlooks "the frequent tendency of bailees to attempt contractual stipulations against their common law liability." [6] Presumably the suggestion is that to give effect to the stated limitation that this clause grants coverage only if "the insured is legally liable" for the damaged property would be to render the clause virtually worthless because bailees are so seldom liable. But the court's answer is unconvincing since the bailee's attempt to contract away its potential liabilities can seldom, if ever, be so fully effective as to render virtually worthless an "in trust or on commission" clause covering only the property for which the insured is legally liable. Rather, warehousemen continue to need protection against the risk of legal liability for property damaged by hazards such as fire while in their custody. Even though this protection could be obtained in other ways—for example, through liability insurance—still the "in trust or on commission" clause of a property insurance policy is a suitable way of arranging for such protection. To deny effect to the limiting phrase "provided the insured is legally liable therefor" is to hold that the warehouseman who wants this protection through property insurance cannot obtain it without also buying further coverage against losses for which he is not legally liable. Plainly this demand that he buy protection applicable to all loss from designated hazards to property he holds in order to get protection to the extent of his legal liability cannot be justified if he is to receive the proceeds for his own benefit, thereby making a profit. Thus, it must be contemplated that the bailors or others having interest in the property will be entitled to part or all of the proceeds.[7] In effect then, the court's refusal to enforce the limiting language forces the warehouseman to confer added benefits on others if he wishes to buy the protection he needs for himself. And, if rates are appropriately adjusted to loss experience, this means also that warehousemen must pay

5. 104 F.Supp. at 633.

6. 104 F.Supp. at 634.

7. Cf. Hepburn v. A. Tomlinson (Hauliers) Ltd., [1966] 1 All E.R. 418 (H.L.) (a carrier procured an inland marine policy on goods in transit, which was in force when goods were stolen from the carrier's truck without its negligence; held, carrier could recover under the policy the full value of the goods although it was not legally liable to the owner for the loss, but the carrier would then be under a duty to turn over to the owner of the goods any proceeds in excess of its own loss).

higher rates for this coverage than if they were allowed to buy the more limited form of coverage the clause was plainly designed to give. The requirement thus imposed on the contracting parties to afford coverage beyond the terms of their agreement does not appear to be justified by any considerations of policy advanced in cases of this type. In short, judicial insistence on granting coverage inconsistent with the limiting phrase seems an unwarranted intrusion on freedom of contract between warehousemen and insurers. Moreover, even if a concept of representative interest is invoked to avoid inconsistency with insurable interest doctrine, with the consequence that some other person is entitled to the proceeds from this coverage, still it may reasonably be asserted that the interest of such other persons is not within the terms of the policy. This is true because the provisions of the basic policy declare that the coverage is not "in any event for more than the interest of the insured." It is debatable whether an "in trust or on commission" clause modifies this provision of the basic policy form or instead merely expands the description of property beyond that owned by the insured.

Another argument advanced in favor of judicial expansion of liability under "in trust or on commission" clauses is that in basic nature the policies in which these clauses appear are policies of insurance on *property* and not on *liability*. This argument, pressed to its logical conclusion, would preclude any definition of coverage under an "in trust or on commission" clause by standards concerned with the bailee's legal liability for the property in his possession. Yet, with curious logical inconsistency, the argument that the coverage is basically *property* insurance has been invoked only in aid of construing a particular clause in favor of broader coverage while conceding that judicial precedents giving effect to legal-liability limitations in forms of "in trust or on commission" clauses with only slightly different phrasing remain authoritative.[8]

In summary, reasons advanced for such expansive construction of "in trust or on commission" clauses are unconvincing and a more faithful adherence to the policy language seems appropriate.[9]

§ 4.5(b) RELATION TO COINSURANCE PROVISIONS

The coinsurance provisions customarily included in commercial property insurance contracts invoke the coinsurance principle if the amount of the insurance is less than a stated percentage (80 per cent, for example) "of the actual cash value of the property described

8. See, *e.g.*, United States v. Globe & Rutgers Fire Ins. Co., 104 F.Supp. 632 (N.D.Tex.1952), *aff'd*, 202 F.2d 696 (5th Cir. 1953).

9. *Cf.* Aaro Packaging Corp. v. Fire Ins. Exch., 280 Minn. 159, 158 N.W.2d 586 (1968) (denying a bailor's claim to policy proceeds, by giving effect to the limitation, "provided the insured is legally liable therefor"; distinguishable, however, because the contest was one for priority among creditors of the insured warehouseman after the insurer had made a payment, by settlement, to the receiver). See also § 4.5(b) *infra* (relation to coinsurance provisions) for another context in which enforcement of the limiting language seems especially likely.

herein" immediately before loss.[1] If a policy contains both a coinsurance clause and an "in trust or on commission" clause, is the property of other persons held in trust or on commission includible in calculating the "actual cash value of the property described herein"?

One finds little in precedents that is directly relevant to this difficult question.[2] Sometimes it has been avoided by a narrow construction of the "in trust or on commission" clause, in sharp contrast with the expansive construction accorded those clauses to increase the insurer's liability.[3] Here, of course, the expansive construction of

1. See § 3.7 *supra*.

2. See Conklin, *Insurance of Warehousing and Other Risks*, 1957 U.Ill.L.Forum 560, 579, reprinted 1959 Ins.Counsel J. 76, 88–89: "There has been little or no litigation which has reached the higher courts with respect to this controversial question. It is obvious that this is of great importance because the value of property of others in the possession of bailees may fluctuate from time to time from a very small quantity to values running into millions, as in . . . [Texas City Terminal Ry. v. American Equitable Assur. Co., 130 F.Supp. 843 (S.D.Tex. 1955)]." See n.3 *infra*.

3. *E.g.*, Texas City Terminal Ry. v. American Equitable Assur. Co., 130 F.Supp. 843, 853–856 (S.D.Tex.1955). Property of the plaintiff railway with an actual cash value of $4,437,864 was destroyed in the Texas City disaster of April 16, 1947. This property was covered by an explosion insurance policy in the amount of $2,300,000 that contained both coinsurance and "in trust or on commission" clauses which read:

"Coinsurance, Reduced rate contribution or average clause—In consideration of the reduced rates and/or form under which this policy is written, it is expressly stipulated and made a condition of this contract that in the event of loss this Company shall be liable for no greater proportion thereof than the amount hereby assured bears to Ninety Per Cent of the actual cash value of the property described herein at the time when such loss shall happen, nor for more than the proportion which this policy bears to the total insurance thereon.

. . .

"It is understood and agreed that this insurance also covers the interest of the assured in and/or liability for similar property belonging in whole or in part to others, and held by the assured either sold but not removed on storage or for repairs, or otherwise held." *Id.* at 853.

American Equitable, the insurer, contended that the policy covered all of the goods of others on plaintiff's property at the time of the explosion (having an actual cash value of $19,-632,143) or, in the alternative, that plaintiff was liable for the loss of that property and that the property was thereby covered; that, in either case, the value of the property of others was includible in applying the coinsurance clause; and, therefore, that it was liable for only 10.617% of plaintiff's own loss. (The owners of the other property had all been impleaded in the case but had either defaulted or disclaimed any interest in the policy proceeds.) Citing the approval in United States v. Globe & Rutgers Fire Ins. Co., 104 F. Supp. 632 (N.D.Tex.1952), *aff'd*, 202 F.2d 696 (5th Cir. 1953), of cases in which "in trust or on commission" clauses were held to cover liability only (see § 4.-5(a) *supra*), the court in *Texas City* so construed the above clause and held that plaintiff was not legally liable for the loss to the property of others, thereby avoiding the question whether the value of the other's property was includible in the coinsurance computation.

Against the interpretation of the "in trust or on commission" clause in *Texas City* it might be argued that "the interest of the assured in . . . similar property" of others held by the assured includes the assured's representative interest —that the coverage is as broad as the doctrine of insurable interest permits when the phrase "interest of the assured" is used. Also, the phrases "interest of the insured in" and "liability for" appear as alternatives, being connected by "and/or," and to be given any meaning the former phrase must be construed as providing some cover-

the "in trust or on commission" clause would reduce the insurer's liability because of the coinsurance provisions.

It might be said that the phrase "the property described herein," as used in the coinsurance clause, refers only to the insured's property and not to the added property that is "described," if at all, only in the separate "in trust or on commission" clause. Or, it might be said that the amount included, in calculating actual cash value, because of property covered by the "in trust or on commission" clause would be the valuation of the insured's interest in such property, rather than its total value. The latter contention is perhaps less readily squared with the policy language than the former, which happens also to be the position more favorable to insureds generally. The probability that the former contention will prevail is fortified by the availability of the argument that the policy is unclear on this point and that the ambiguity should be resolved against insurers.[4]

Since the answer to questions about the relationship between these two types of clauses is in doubt, a bailee with a property insurance policy including both should either be certain that he carries coverage in an amount adequate to avoid application of the coinsurance clause even if the property held in trust or on commission is included in the calculation or get an explicit agreement from the insurer that property of others will not be taken into account in determining applicability of the coinsurance clause.

SECTION 4.6   GENERALIZATION CONCERNING LIMITED INTEREST PROBLEMS IN PROPERTY INSURANCE

The relationships of mortgagor-mortgagee, vendor-purchaser, lessor-lessee, life tenant-remainderman, and bailor-bailee, which have been considered thus far in this chapter, have in common the fact that they involve multiple interests in one property. An insurance policy obtained by one of the persons in such a relationship presents what is commonly referred to either as a "multiple-interest" or as a "limited-interest" problem. There are, of course, other relationships involving multiple interests in one property.[1] Can some generaliza-

---

age in situations in which the insured was not liable for damage to the other property. It has been argued, however, that other differences in phraseology between the clauses in *Texas City* and *Globe & Rutgers* (see § 4.5(a) supra) justify the different interpretations given by the two courts, despite the points made here. Also, in view of the different purposes for which the broad interpretation of the clause was invoked—being invoked in *Globe & Rutgers* by the owner of the property held by the insured to expand the insurer's liability and being invoked

in *Texas City* by the insurer to limit its liability through application of the coinsurance clause—one might argue that the cases are reconcilable on the theory of resolving ambiguity against the insurer in both instances. See § 6.3 *infra*. The most vulnerable aspect of this last argument is the assumption that the clauses were ambiguous in relation to the point at issue.

4. See § 6.3 *infra*.

1. See, *e.g.*, Newsome v. St. Paul Mercury Ins. Co., 331 S.W.2d 497 (Tex.

tions be drawn concerning rules of insurance law applicable to all these problems, or instead, has a separate body of rules developed for each type of relationship?

The difficulty of generalization is affected by the fact that these problems are a battle ground for several competing principles—the principle of indemnity, the principle that nonmarine property insurance is "personal", the principle that an insurer should not be allowed the "unjust enrichment" incident to collection of premiums computed on the assumption of a higher limit of coverage than is in fact provided, and the principle that reasonable expectations should be honored. The courts are faced with a hard choice among three major solutions[2] or a mixture with elements of at least two of the three.[3] First, let the insurer escape responsibility for the loss above its named insured's interest despite computation of premiums on a higher stated maximum of insurance coverage, thus serving the principle of indemnity and the personal-contract principle but disappointing reasonable expectations and allowing what might be regarded as unjust enrichment of the insurer, not wholly avoidable by provision for refunding of "unearned" premiums. Second, let the named insured recover the entire amount of damage to the property, up to the amount of the insurance, for his own benefit, thus violating the principle of indemnity while remaining faithful to the principles concerned with the personal nature of nonmarine insurance and with

Civ.App.1960, no writ history) (a husband and wife were divorced without a division of their community property, and the ex-husband continued to reside in and obtained insurance on their residence, which under Texas law became a tenancy in common; after fire loss, the ex-wife sought a share in the insurance proceeds; held —without discussing whether that amount exceeded the value of the insured's interest or, if it did, what effect that would have—the contract was personal, and the insured could retain the full amount of proceeds received); Rock County Sav. & Trust Co. v. London Assur. Co., 17 Wis.2d 618, 117 N.W.2d 676 (1962), 4 A.L.R.3d 422 (1965) (joint tenant who had insured property in names of both tenants died one day after fire loss and her estate sought a share in the insurance proceeds; held, insurance proceeds to be treated in equity as if they were the property, passing thereby to the surviving tenant).

2. *Cf.* Godfrey, *Some Limited-Interest Problems,* 15 Law & Contemp.Prob. 415, 419–420 (1950). See also Young, *Some "Windfall Coverages" in Property and Liability Insurance,* 60 Colum. L.Rev. 1063 (1960).

3. *Cf.* J. McCoid, *Allocation of Loss and Property Insurance,* 39 Ind.L.J. 647 (1964), adding to the solutions identified in the text above two more: though limiting the insured to indemnity, let the source of recovery be left to his choosing; let the loss be apportioned between the insurer and the third party. The first of these additional solutions permits the insured to choose between allowing the insurer to escape responsibility (the first of the three solutions in the text above) and imposing the loss entirely on the insurer (the third solution in the text) or perhaps partly on the insurer (a further mixture). The second of these additional solutions (apportionment) involves a mixture, or perhaps one would wish to say a compromise, between the first and third of the text rules. The apportionment might also involve a compromise in still another dimension by allocating part of the loss to the insured himself, as happens when rights in a tort claim against a third person are apportioned between the insurer and the insured, leaving part of the insured's loss uncompensated from either of the two sources (the insurer and the third party) against whom he has claimed. Concerning subrogation claims generally, see § 3.10 *supra.*

avoidance of unjust enrichment of the insurer and arguably remaining faithful to the principle of honoring reasonable expectations. Third, let the persons other than the named insured recover against the insurer, either directly or by holding that the named insured must effect the recovery but holds insurance proceeds in excess of his own interest for the benefit of others having interests in the property, thus violating the personal-contract principle though remaining faithful to the principle of indemnity and the principle concerned with unjust enrichment of the insurer and arguably remaining faithful to the principle of honoring reasonable expectations.

The range of available solutions has been described above without mention of subrogation. But issues concerning subrogation arise often in relation to limited-interest problems. Allowing the insurer to be subrogated to a claim of the insured against another serves the principle of indemnity by giving the insurer the benefit of the insured's other claim for indemnity; the loss then falls on the other indemnitor rather than the insurer. Allowing other persons to be subrogated to the insured's claim against the insurer in excess of the insured's own interest (or holding that the insured must effect the recovery but holds the proceeds in excess of his own interest for the benefit of such other persons) also serves the principle of indemnity, but the loss then falls on the insurer. Thus, while subrogation is a useful device for effectuating the principle of indemnity, the choice of a particular subrogation doctrine is dependent also on the influence of the other principles referred to above.

If several persons with limited interests in one property obtain separate insurance policies, another dimension is added to the difficulty. The third solution above might violate the principle of indemnity in that situation, since total recovery might exceed damage to the property. In such a situation the court faces a further choice of, first, allowing such total recovery to exceed damage to the property, or second, classifying the policies as primary and excess coverage, or third, allowing proration or contribution.

Of course a court may be moved toward one or another of the three major solutions by particular provisions in the insurance contract or in a separate contract concerning the limited-interest relationship. If both contracts specify that the insurance coverage is for the benefit of all owners of limited interests "as their interests may appear," the court readily adopts a solution that allows these persons to recover (whether referring to them as additional "named insureds" or instead as persons other than the "named insured"). Also, it has sometimes been considered a factor favoring this solution that, even though the stipulations of the insurance policy designate only one insured, a separate contract between the owners of various interests in the property contains a stipulation that one party is to obtain insurance for the benefit of another; this factor is greatly weakened, however, if the insurer has not contracted in contemplation of such separate agreement.

In resolving these conflicts among different principles, should courts aim for a uniform set of rules for all types of limited-interest cases though allowing for variations dependent upon stipulations in the relevant documents?

As has been noted elsewhere,[4] some degree of generalization is essential to keeping the number of particularized rules of decision within administratively manageable bounds, and wise generalization advances the quest for the "rule of law," in contrast with arbitrary adjudication. It does so by identifying significant similarities that should cause like treatment of cases despite differences in immaterial particulars. But whether similarities are significant and whether differences are immaterial are hard questions. The common law system, accepting each judicial decision as a precedent but with decreasing authoritative quality as grounds of factual distinction from a new situation increase, tends to develop distinctive rules for identifiable types of fact situations. But, in the absence of constant testing of these particularized rules by standards of generalization, inconsistencies of principle will develop.

Such inconsistencies have developed in limited-interest cases. Consider an example. Application of the principle that nonmarine property insurance is "personal" has the consequences that such insurance will not be treated as coverage of the property for the benefit of whoever may happen to have interests in it and that it will not "run with the property." Judicial decisions have produced a considerable departure from this principle in the vendor-purchaser situations, allowing the purchaser to benefit from the vendor's insurance. Another departure has occurred in life tenancy cases, in which many decisions allow the remainderman to benefit from the life tenant's insurance. And perhaps bailment cases disclose a tendency favoring construction of the coverage as multiple interest. On the other hand, the principle of the "personal" character of the insurance appears to have greater vitality in lease cases.

It seems unlikely that these differences can all be accounted for on the basis either of differences in types of relationships to the insured property or of differences in insurance policy terms. To some extent the different decisions probably represent conflicts among jurisdictions rather than different treatment of multiple-interest cases within a single jurisdiction.

Perhaps such differences as now exist in the treatment of different types of multiple-interest cases are explainable as different degrees of movement in a general trend away from rigid adherence to the principle that insurance is personal and toward the principle that it will be treated as insurance of the property for the benefit of whatever persons happen to be its owners. If so, attempts at generalization should advance that trend, which on the whole seems a desirable one.[5] The principle that insurance is personal, it may be argued, is

---

4. See § 1.1 *supra.*

5. *But cf.* J. McCoid, *Allocation of Loss and Property Insurance,* 39 Ind.L.J.

justified on the theory that the insurer has an interest in selecting its insureds because of moral hazards. In fact, however, it is only a very low percentage of the multiple-interest cases in which the insurer would have hesitated to revise its contract to multiple-interest coverage if requested to do so. Moreover, insurers do not in practice treat multiple-interest situations as involving greater moral hazard, and indeed they commit very little effort and expense to considering moral hazard at all. Thus, their practical assessment of the significance of moral hazards raises serious doubts about the desirability of adhering to the principle that fire insurance is personal in character.

Perhaps, too, whatever justifications may have existed for this principle at the time it evolved are weakened in the modern context, since single ownership of all interests in a physical unit of property is less common today than the fractioning of ownership into multiple interests. Probably most properties are rarely held for significant periods of time in single ownership. Typically, for example, when an individual purchases a residence there is first a temporary period of the vendor-vendee relationship, followed by consummation of the transaction and simultaneous creation of a mortgagor-mortgagee relationship. In turn, the mortgagor is apt to become a vendor himself before the mortgage debt is paid, or he may become a lessor (as to commercial property, particularly, this is likely); and there is the possibility that some kind of joint ownership (joint tenancy, tenancy in common, or tenancy by the entirety) will exist in relation to a given residence at any given time—between husband and wife or among heirs or devisees. Perhaps this continuum of limited interests, shifting from one pattern to another, militates against treating nonmarine property insurance as personal. Certainly it increases the probability that applying that principle faithfully will produce results in many cases that are both harsh and contrary to the expectations of laymen unfamiliar with the details of insurance law and theory.[6]

SECTION 4.7   OMNIBUS CLAUSES AND STATUTES

§ 4.7(a)   GENERALLY

The term "omnibus clause" is ordinarily used to signify a provision of a liability insurance policy designating additional insureds by an expansive class description in terms of some relationship to the insured. Although this usage is prevalent in discourse about policy forms, the forms themselves ordinarily do not refer to such a provision as an omnibus clause. Rather, the clause usually appears under a caption such as "persons insured" or "definition of insured."

The most familiar use of omnibus clauses occurs in automobile liability insurance. The clauses used have been many and varied;

647, 664–674 (1964), generally favoring allocation of loss to the "third party" rather than the insurer, by means of subrogation.

6. Concerning the principle of honoring reasonable expectations generally, see § 6.3 *infra*.

virtually all, however, have had as a central theme that other persons driving the insured car with permission of the named insured are additional insureds.

A second theme that has appeared in omnibus clauses of automobile liability insurance forms beginning with the 1955 revision [1] is that other members of the named insured's household are additional insureds. This theme is readily transferable to other types of insurance. Such a provision commonly appears in comprehensive personal liability insurance forms (both in independent policies and in such package policies as those developed for homeowners). The provision is seldom referred to as an "omnibus clause," however, in this context of non-automobile liability insurance. And in still other contexts it is even rarer that such a provision is referred to in this way. For example, clauses in health and accident policies extending coverage to members of the policyholder's family are virtually never referred to as omnibus clauses.

The omnibus clauses initially used in automobile insurance forms applied only to the liability insurance coverages. Clauses of this type are currently used also for collision coverages and medical payments coverages.[2] Indeed, the most common medical payments provision extends coverage, with qualifications, to each person who sustains injury while "occupying"—that is, while "in or upon or entering into or alighting from"—a designated automobile.[3] Though this is written into the primary definition of coverage rather than in a separate omnibus clause, these persons are "insureds" in the usual sense of that term, since they are entitled to collect benefits in their own right and in reimbursement of their own losses.[4] The other phase of earlier omnibus clauses—that extending coverage to members of the named insured's household—is also written into the primary definition of medical payments coverages in some current forms.[5]

Perhaps the major objective underlying the development of omnibus clauses has been to serve the interests of the insurance purchaser (usually the named insured) in having the benefits of the coverage extend to certain other persons as well as himself—persons who are natural objects of his concern. For example, the purchaser of an automobile insurance policy ordinarily has both economic and non-economic reasons for desiring the extension of the various coverages of the policy to other members of his household. Also, he has an interest in the extension of the liability and collision coverages to others who drive his car with his permission, both because he may feel that he has a moral obligation to them and because, as a practical matter, he may face a troublesome situation if his insurer is obligated to protect him but free to press a claim for reimbursement against the person driving his car with his permission. This is a

---

1. See § 2.11(b) (3) *supra*.

2. See § 2.11(c) *supra*.

3. See *ibid.*; Appendix H *infra*.

4. Compare § 4.1(c) *supra*.

5. See Appendix H *infra*.

course the insurer could take as subrogee to the named insured's interests if the driver were not an additional insured.[6]

A second objective—to serve the interests of potential victims of incidents to which the insurance coverage applies—has been at most a subsidiary influence in the voluntary expansion of coverage through omnibus clauses, but it has been a primary influence upon legislation requiring or encouraging the inclusion of omnibus clauses in liability insurance coverages. Some state statutes, designed to serve this objective of reducing the probability that an automobile accident victim will be unable to collect against a legally responsible driver only because of his financial irresponsibility, have required that automobile liability insurance policies include an omnibus clause of a specified scope.[7]

Even though the motivations for the development of omnibus clauses may have been primarily concerned with benefits to others, it is nevertheless clear that a person who comes within the terms of such a clause is himself an insured. In the absence of some special relationship beyond that of permission to use the vehicle, he is ordinarily in the position of a donee beneficiary.[8]

§ 4.7(b)   PROBLEMS OF INTERPRETATION AND APPLICATION

(1) GENERALLY

The omnibus clause, in its various forms, has been a prolific source of litigation. Many of the cases have involved disputes about "permission, express or implied"—usually questions as to whether a person who was using[1] the car at the time of the accident had been allowed by the named insured to use it only for a limited time or limited purpose. Some distinctive lines of authority have developed, and the jurisdictions have commonly been classified into three groups, as follows: First, those giving a "strict" construction to the omnibus clause and requiring proof that the use was rather clearly within the scope of the permission;[2] second, those giving a "liberal" construc-

---

6. This could occur under the liability coverage if, for example, the named insured were vicariously liable for negligent operation of the vehicle by the driver. It could occur under the collision coverage if the driver negligently caused the damage to the insured car; see §§ 2.11(b) (4), 3.10 supra.

7. E.g., S.C.Code Ann. § 46–750.31–.32 (Supp.1969). See also § 4.7(b) nn.11, 25 infra.

8. See, e.g., Johnson v. Doughty, 236 Ore. 78, 385 P.2d 760 (1963) (as a donee beneficiary, driver had a right to be notified that the contract existed

and that he had certain duties under it before his rights could be terminated for failure to communicate with insurer).

1. As to the meaning of "use," see this section n.11 infra and § 5.2(b) infra.

2. E.g., Eagle Fire Co. v. Mullins, 238 S.C. 272, 120 S.E.2d 1 (1961) (implied consent of dealer for employee to use car in transportation to and from work and for employee's son to use it in transportation to and from college did not extend to son's use for pleasure trip to beach; consent limited "to the purpose for which it was given").

tion to the clause and finding almost any use to be within the coverage so long as the vehicle was being operated by one to whom the named insured entrusted it for some purpose;[3] and third, those, probably a majority, following the "minor deviation rule," under which coverage is defeated by a material violation of the scope of permission contemplated by the named insured but not by minor deviation.[4] Of course the classification is inexact. And significant variations can occur on associated issues within any one of these lines of authority.[5] Also, the particular language of the omnibus clause is relevant. A change at the time of the 1966 revision appears to have been designed to weigh against the "liberal" construction; "within the scope of such permission," was substituted for the phrase "with the permission," used in earlier forms.[6] Moreover, considerable variation

---

3. *E.g.*, Matits v. Nationwide Mut. Ins. Co., 33 N.J. 488, 166 A.2d 345 (1960) (initial permission of husband of named insured made driver an omnibus insured although she used the car for "bar hopping" after completing the trip for which initial permission was given).

4. See, *e.g.*, Mid-Continent Cas. Co. v. Everett, 340 F.2d 65 (10th Cir. 1965) (applying Kansas law; intoxicated driver of empty bus who was off route and two and one-half hours behind schedule when accident occurred was no longer permissive user of bus under omnibus clause); Employers Mut. Cas. Co. v. Mosqueda, 317 F.2d 609 (5th Cir. 1963) (applying Texas law; use of indirect and unauthorized route by employee was within scope of permission under omnibus clause even though employer was relieved of liability because that use was a deviation from the employee's scope of employment); Fisher v. Firemen's Fund Indem. Co., 244 F.2d 194 (10th Cir. 1957) (applying Kansas law; personal trip of employee in employer's truck to a town fifteen miles away on Christmas day authorized; use for a trip out of state, during which an accident occurred at a point one hundred miles from the place of residence and garaging was a flagrant violation); Allied Mut. Cas. Co. v. Nelson, 274 Minn. 297, 143 N.W.2d 635 (1966) (date of named insured's daughter was given permission to drive to movie and directly back to insured's home; accident occurred while the couple were "driving around," after they decided not to go to the movie; held, permittee was an omnibus insured); Ryan v. Western Pac. Ins. Co., 242 Ore. 84, 408 P.2d 84 (1965) (employee of the named insured truck had permission to use insured's truck to move furni-

ture but was using it for entertainment when accident occurred; held, employee was an omnibus insured since the general use—*i.e.*, personal use as opposed to business use—was that for which permission had been granted and the deviation from the specific use was not "gross"); Foote v. Grant, 56 Wash.2d 630, 354 P.2d 893 (1960) (driver was furnished car for drive from Chicago to West Coast in return for driving it to specified destination by specified route—accident occurred while driver was on an unauthorized side trip from a route to the specified destination, which was itself a deviation from the specified route; held, the original deviation would have been permissible since it was on route to the specified destination, but the off-route deviation was not permissible and avoided omnibus clause coverage). See Annot., 5 A.L.R.2d 600, 621–660 (1949).

5. One such issue is the question whether the individual through whom it is claimed permission was given was in a position to give effective permission. One phase of this issue is the problem of the permittee's permittee, discussed in § 4.7(b) (2) *infra*. See also, *e.g.*, Underwood v. National Grange Mut. Liab. Co., 258 N.C. 211, 128 S.E.2d 577 (1962) (insurer not liable on policy after car title had been transferred without endorsement of policy; transferee's driver was not permittee of named insured because he no longer had the legal right to give or withhold consent to the use of the car); Young, *Some "Windfall Coverages" in Property and Liability Insurance*, 60 Colum.L.Rev. 1063, 1078–1082 (1960); Annot., 36 A.L.R.2d 673 (1954).

6. See § 2.11(c) and (d) *supra*.

can be concealed within identically-phrased rules of law, since these problems of permission are primarily fact-oriented rather than law-oriented. That is, determining in a particular case whether the driving of the vehicle at the time of collision was within the scope of the permission of the insured does not depend merely upon the legal standard laid down in choosing among the three major lines of authority just described and variations on each. Rather it depends quite heavily on resolving controversies over, first, the raw facts with respect to what was said and done that bears on permission and, second, the evaluation of those raw facts in terms relevant to the chosen legal standard (for example, is a particular violation of conditions stated by the insured severe enough to defeat coverage under the chosen legal standard regarding severity of deviations).[7]

The relationship between the named insured and the driver is an important factor affecting the determination whether his use was within or outside the scope of the named insured's permission. It has been suggested, for example, that a comprehensive permission is much more readily to be inferred when "the use of the car is for social or non-business purposes" than when "the relationship of master and servant exists and the usage of the car is for business purposes."[8] Also, the nature of the violation of instructions is significant. For example, an employee's use of his employer's automobile for personal purposes in violation of express instructions or use of the vehicle by a third person to whom the employee gave permission despite an express prohibition is generally considered not to have been with the permission of the employer within the meaning of the omnibus clause,[9] but a majority of jurisdictions find permission despite an employee's violation of an express prohibition against permitting riders.[10]

Ordinarily a claim of coverage under an omnibus clause is made by or on behalf of a person operating the vehicle. Occasionally, however, claims have been asserted successfully on a theory of permitted "use" by a passenger or even by a person not occupying the vehicle either as operator or passenger.[11]

---

7.   Concerning raw-fact and evaluative findings generally, see § 1.6 *supra*.

8.   Jordan v. Shelby Mut. Plate Glass & Cas. Co., 51 F.Supp. 240, 242 (W.D. Va.1943). This idea was approved and further developed by the Court of Appeals in the same case, 142 F.2d 52, 56 (4th Cir. 1944). See also, *e.g.*, Foote v. Grant, 56 Wash.2d 630, 354 P.2d 893 (1960); Young, *Some "Windfall Coverages" in Property and Liability Insurance*, 60 Colum.L.Rev. 1063, 1077 (1960).

9.   *E.g.*, Boyd v. Liberty Mut. Ins. Co., 232 F.2d 364 (D.C.Cir. 1956) (use for personal purposes); Hopson v. Shelby Mut. Cas. Co., 203 F.2d 434 (4th Cir. 1953) (use by third person); Smith v.

Insurance Co. of Pa., 161 So.2d 903 (La.App.), *writ refused*, 245 La. 344, 164 So.2d 350 (1964) (use by third person). See also Annot., 5 A.L.R.2d 600, 651–654, 657–660 (1949).

10.   *E.g.*, Hardware Mut. Cas. Co. v. Milwaukee Auto. Ins. Co., 229 Wis. 215, 282 N.W. 27 (1938). See also Annot., 5 A.L.R.2d 600, 654–657 (1949).

11.   See § 5.2(b) *infra*. See also Lukaszewicz v. Concrete Research, Inc., 43 Wis.2d 335, 168 N.W.2d 581 (1969) (exclusion as to accidents during loading, attached to trucker's policy, held void as in violation of statutory requirement of omnibus clause; liability coverage of trucker's policy extended to concrete company and its employee

(2) THE PERMITTEE'S PERMITTEE

It often happens that the person driving the insured car at the time of the accident was one with whom no named insured of the policy on that automobile had communicated directly; rather, a named insured had given permission to a second person for use of the car, and that person in turn had given permission to a third. This type of fact situation has bred much litigation.[12]

Issues arising from use of the insured vehicle by a third person with whom the named insured has not directly communicated, usually called the permittee's permittee (or the "second" permittee, as opposed to the "original" permittee with whom the insured communicated directly) are complicated by the major shortcoming of omnibus clauses in general; that is, all too often there is room for doubt and debate about one or more decisive fact-oriented questions. This serious shortcoming of omnibus clauses has been a factor in the development of a minority rule that initial permission to one person will be held effective as to that person's permittee, regardless of the fact that the named insured attempted to limit the scope of his consent to the first person only.[13] Most courts, not adopting this stern measure of judicial regulation of the terms of the omnibus clause, have had to face a number of fact-oriented questions. Had the original permittee received permission from a named insured to use the car?[14] Had

who, while moving concrete slabs with a travel-lift vehicle to load truck, injured truck driver; "operating" construed broadly to include participation in loading).

12. Perhaps it has also helped to stimulate redrafting of policy forms in an effort to preclude the extension of coverage to the permittee's permittee. This may have been one of the objectives of the 1966 adoption of the phrasing "provided his actual operation or (if he is not operating) his actual use thereof is *within the scope of such permission.*" See Appendix H *infra.* The corresponding provision in the 1955 form was "provided the actual use of the automobile is by the named insured or such spouse or *with the permission* of either." Risjord & Austin, Automobile Liability Insurance Cases—Standard Provisions and Appendix 19 (1964) [hereinafter cited as Risjord & Austin]. The corresponding provision in an earlier form was "provided the actual use of the automobile is by the named insured or with his permission." 1947 Standard Basic Automobile Liability Policy, *id.* at 4. It seems doubtful, however, that this modest change of phrasing will lead many, if any, courts to adopt a more restrictive interpretation of

the omnibus clause in relation to the problem of the permittee's permittee. Perhaps it will have greater impact in another respect; see § 4.7(b) (1) at n.6 *supra.*

13. *E.g.,* Odolecki v. Hartford Acc. & Indem. Co., 55 N.J. 542, 264 A.2d 38 (1970) (overruling an earlier case directly in point; son permitted friend to drive in direct violation of parent's attempted limitation of scope of consent; friend held to be covered under omnibus clause). Note that even this rule does not avoid the first of the fact-oriented questions referred to immediately after the statement in the text above.

14. See, *e.g.,* Travelers Indem. Co. v. State Farm Mut. Auto. Ins. Co., 330 F.2d 250 (9th Cir. 1964) (named insured's minor, unlicensed son took the car against the express orders of his parents and allowed another minor to drive it; held, no coverage under owner's policy); Rondina v. Employers' Liab. Assur. Corp., 286 Mass. 209, 190 N.E. 35 (1934) (driver against whom judgment was rendered had borrowed the car from its true owner, who had fraudulently registered and insured the car in the name of a third person without that person's knowl-

the original permittee consented to the third person's use of the car?[15] Was the nature of the use of the car (apart from *who* was using it) within the scope of the permission granted?[16] Did the named insured authorize the original permittee to allow a second permittee to operate or use the vehicle? Did the named insured himself authorize the second permittee's operation or use? These last two questions, peculiar to the permittee's-permittee situation, have proved to be especially troublesome issues, as an examination of illustrative cases will show.

If the named insured's original permission is broad in scope, and the original permittee is expressly authorized to allow others to use the car, it is generally recognized that the permittee's permittee is covered as an additional insured under the omnibus clause, even when using the car for personal purposes.[17] If, however, use of the vehicle by third persons is expressly prohibited by the named insured, it has been generally agreed that the permittee's permittee is not covered when using the car for his own purposes,[18] unless an implied permission by the named insured can be shown in spite of the express general prohibition;[19] when the permittee's permittee is using the car contrary to the named insured's prohibition but for the benefit of the original permittee, the courts are divided as to whether the permittee's permittee is an additional insured.[20]

In the more typical case, however, the original permittee is neither expressly authorized to allow others to drive the car nor expressly prohibited from doing so. In these situations, more often than not the second permittee is allowed coverage. Often courts have relied on a theory that the second permittee's use of the car was for the benefit of the original permittee.[21] When it has been found that

edge or consent; held, no coverage under the policy naming the third person as insured).

15. See, *e.g.*, Rosenbloom v. St. Paul Fire & Marine Ins. Co., 214 F.Supp. 301 (S.D.N.Y.1963) (applying Virginia law); Nationwide Mut. Ins. Co. v. Chandler, 151 F.Supp. 365 (D.N.C. 1957).

16. See § 4.7(b) (1) *supra*.

17. *E.g.*, Davis v. St. Paul-Mercury Indem. Co., 294 F.2d 641 (4th Cir. 1961) (applying Texas law).

18. *E.g.*, Baesler v. Globe Indem. Co., 33 N.J. 148, 162 A.2d 854 (1960), overruled in Odolecki v. Hartford Acc. & Indem. Co., 55 N.J. 542, 264 A.2d 38 (1970). *Cf.* American Home Assur. Co. v. Czarniecki, 255 La. 251, 230 So. 2d 253 (1970).

19. See, *e.g.*, Schevling v. Johnson, 122 F.Supp. 87 (D.Conn.1953), *aff'd per*

curiam, 213 F.2d 959 (2d Cir. 1954); Haspel v. Treece, 150 So.2d 120 (La. App.), *writs refused*, 244 La. 218, 219, 151 So.2d 692 (1963).

20. Allowing coverage, see, *e.g.*, Metcalf v. Hartford Acc. & Indem. Co., 176 Neb. 468, 126 N.W.2d 471 (1964). Denying coverage, see, *e.g.*, Coco v. State Farm Mut. Auto. Ins. Co., 136 So.2d 288 (La.App.1961); State Farm Mut. Auto. Ins. Co. v. American Cas. Co., 150 W.Va. 435, 146 S.E.2d 842 (1966); Prisuda v. General Cas. Co., 272 Wis. 41, 74 N.W.2d 777 (1956). See also Annot., 5 A.L.R.2d 600, 657 (1949).

21. *E.g.*, State Farm Mut. Auto. Ins. Co. v. Automobile Underwriters, Inc., 255 F.Supp. 404 (S.D.Ind.1966); Small v. Schuncke, 42 N.J. 407, 201 A.2d 56 (1964) (applying the "initial permission" rule—see § 4.7(b) (1) *supra*—to find the use of the car within the scope of the permission given by the named insured); Teague v. Tate, 213 Tenn. 269, 375 S.W.2d 840 (1964). See

use of the car was for personal purposes of the second permittee, however, the courts generally have denied coverage if the original permission was found to be limited in some way [22] and have divided in result if the original permission was broad. Classification of cases on this basis is somewhat unreliable because so much depends on evaluation of the facts as to whether an unrestricted grant for general use carries with it authority to allow other persons to use the car. Some cases have allowed coverage on a theory of such an implied authority.[23] Others have concluded that the original permittee was without power to authorize use by a second permittee.[24]

In a number of cases courts have by-passed the question whether the insured's permission extended to the permittee's permittee, holding that the permittee was still using the car, that his use was still within the scope of the named insured's permission even though another was driving, and that the permittee was vicariously liable to a victim because the driver was his servant, acting within the scope of employment.[25]

also Annot., 5 A.L.R.2d 600, 643, 648 (1949).

22. *E.g.*, Horn v. Allied Mut. Cas. Co., 272 F.2d 76 (10th Cir. 1959) (applying Kansas law; named insured's step-daughter who was only allowed to drive the car to and from school lent it to a friend who had an accident while driving by herself on business of her own; held, no coverage); Hays v. Country Mut. Ins. Co., 28 Ill. 2d 601, 192 N.E.2d 855 (1963) (named insured's son and stepdaughter, who were permitted to take car into town on a pleasure drive on the condition that they not use it for "driving around" while in town, lent the car to a friend who wrecked it while returning from a trip out of town; held, no coverage).

23. See, *e.g.*, Utica Mut. Ins. Co. v. Rollason, 246 F.2d 105 (4th Cir. 1957) (applying Virginia law); Hardware Mut. Cas. Co. v. Shelby Mut. Ins. Co., 213 F.Supp. 669 (N.D.Ohio 1962); Krebsbach v. Miller, 22 Wis.2d 171, 125 N.W.2d 408 (1963), 4 A.L.R.3d 1 (1965).

24. See, *e.g.*, Duff v. Alliance Mut. Cas. Co., 296 F.2d 506 (10th Cir. 1961) (applying Oklahoma law); Ewing v. Colorado Farm Mut. Cas. Co., 133 Colo. 447, 296 P.2d 1040 (1956).

25. *E.g.*, Melvin v. American Auto. Ins. Co., 232 Md. 476, 194 A.2d 269 (1963). This is one of the grounds on which Souza v. Corti, 22 Cal.2d 454, 139 P.2d 645, 147 A.L.R. 861 (1943) is explained

in the majority opinion in Norris v. Pacific Indem. Co., 39 Cal.2d 420, 247 P.2d 1 (1952). In *Norris*, the permittee's permittee sued the owner's insurer, seeking a declaration of coverage with respect to a pending tort claim against him. It appears that the controversy was primarily one among insurers, since the insurer of the father of the permittee's permittee presumably covered the statutory vicarious liability imposed on the father as signer of his son's application for an operator's license. The majority held that the owner's policy did not apply. *Souza v. Corti*, in which it was held that the owner's policy did apply, was dstinguished apparently on two grounds—one, that the original permittee was the user in that case and, two, that provisions concerning express or implied permission in two California statutes, though they appear not to be materially different in phrasing in the view of the dissenters (and this writer), carried different meanings. The statute involved in *Souza* imposed vicarious liability on the vehicle owner for the negligence of a person operating it with his permission. The statute involved in *Norris* required that an omnibus clause of specified terms be included in automobile liability insurance policies. The majority opinion in *Norris* thus construes the omnibus clause statute as using a narrower concept of permission than the vicarious liability statute. Curiously, a later decision takes just the reverse view—that the latter statute is narrower in scope than the former. A victim who had lost his

(3) INJURY TO A NAMED INSURED BY AN ADDITIONAL INSURED

It sometimes happens that one who is a named insured of a liability insurance policy has a claim in tort, based on negligence, against another who is an additional insured under his policy. For example, the owner of an insured automobile lends it to another whose operation of the vehicle injures the owner (the named insured). *MacBey v. Hartford Acc. & Indem. Co.*,[26] one of the earliest cases dealing with a question of this type, arose under the Massachusetts compulsory automobile insurance coverage. The statute pur-

action against the owner under the vicarious liability statute was then permitted to proceed against the driver (a car-wash employee driving the car away from the end of the line and near to a polishing enclosure), claiming against the insurer under the omnibus clause; the contention that a verdict of non-permission under the vicarious liability statute barred a claim of permission under the omnibus-clause statute was rejected on the ground that the former statute should be construed more narrowly because it imposes a harsh liability on an otherwise innocent owner. Exchange Cas. & Sur. Co. v. Scott, 56 Cal.2d 613, 364 P.2d 833, 15 Cal.Rptr. 897 (1961). In one respect, however, there is consistency throughout this line of decisions; in each case some insurer was held liable somehow. Perhaps both *Norris* and *Scott* are unwarranted decisions. Surely the first action in *Scott* presented the issue of permission in a context less favorable to a jury verdict of permission than did the later action, but a tactical error of counsel in pursuing the less promising action is hardly a justification for allowing retrial of what is in fact an identical issue of permission. With respect to *Norris*, if the policy clause had been unaffected by statute, one could reasonably argue that it was intended only to serve the interests of the named insured, the purchaser of the policy—that is, to afford coverage to other persons whom he would want to be covered while using his automobile —whereas plainly the purpose of the vicarious liability statute was to benefit victims by assuring financial responsibility of drivers. As noted in the *Norris* dissent, however, the omnibus-clause statute requires that clause in the policy. This fact weakens any argument based on the theory that the omnibus clause is not intended for the benefit of victims. The argument was further weakened by a line of California cases invalidating, as con-

trary to the public policy expressed by the statute, specific exclusions from the omnibus coverage, the leading case being Wildman v. Government Employees' Ins. Co., 48 Cal.2d 31, 307 P.2d 359 (1957) (invalidating clause purporting to limit coverage to named insured and specified relatives only, and holding that the omnibus clause required by the financial responsibility law must be included in all automobile liability policies written in California). Note, however, that the California legislature has since curtailed in a number of ways the broad requirements of the statute construed in *Wildman*. Cal.Laws of 1970, ch. 300, amending Cal.Ins.Code 11580.1 (West 1955). For other decisions striking down provisions less expansive than the then required omnibus clause, see, *e.g.*, Atlantic Nat'l Ins. Co. v. Armstrong, 65 Cal.2d 100, 416 P.2d 801, 52 Cal.Rptr. 569 (1966) (exclusion from coverage of all drivers of leased vehicle except lessee and exclusion of coverage of liability to occupants of vehicle); Interinsurance Exch. v. Ohio Cas. Ins. Co., 58 Cal.2d 142, 373 P.2d 640, 23 Cal.Rptr. 592 (1962) (exclusion of prospective buyer of vehicle); Exchange Cas. & Sur. Co. v. Scott, *supra* (exclusion of service station employees). Note also that it is the user who is seeking the benefit of the coverage in *Norris*—to discharge his liability—rather than a victim who otherwise would have a tort claim on which he could not collect because of financial irresponsibility. But this difference between *Norris* and the earlier case of *Souza* hardly justifies a different construction of virtually identical language. Surely the language will not bear the construction that it means coverage for the benefit of the victim but not for the benefit of the driver.

26. 292 Mass. 105, 197 N.E. 516 (1935), 106 A.L.R. 1248 (1937).

suant to which the compulsory coverage was issued required that the policy provide "indemnity for or protection to the insured and any person responsible for the operation of the insured's motor vehicle with his express or implied consent against loss by reason of the liability to pay damages to others for bodily injuries." [27]   The court concluded that "others" could not be construed to include the named insured.[28]   This point of view was subsequently criticized, and validly so it would seem, in an opinion of Chief Justice Maltbie of Connecticut.   The Connecticut court followed the Massachusetts precedent in construing the extraterritorial provision of a Massachusetts policy.[29] Chief Justice Maltbie concurred in the result but indicated that he would have reached a different result if not bound by the Massachusetts precedent.   He remarked: "The word 'others' in the clause under which the company agrees to indemnify the named insured or any person operating the car with his consent 'against loss by reason of the liability to pay damages to others' means persons other than the one invoking the protection of the policy, whether it be the named insured or one who is operating the car with his consent." [30] The weight of decisions in other jurisdictions supports this latter position.[31]   The addition of the severability clause in the 1955 revision of policy forms fortifies this conclusion since it supports the proposition that "the insured" is used severally in relation to each claim,[32] and in that light the named insured is not an insured at all in relation to his claim in tort against the additional insured.

How would the claim of a spouse of a person named as insured in a policy fare in a jurisdiction following *MacBey*?   The reasoning of that court was based on the theory that the word "others" in the Massachusetts statute indicates that "inclusion of the named assured within the class of beneficiaries was not within the legislative intent." [33]   It proceeds on the theory that the owner of a motor vehicle is placed in a different position from other members of the public in relation to assurance of financial responsibility for injuries from operation of the vehicle.   Since the point is expressed in relation to the "owner" or "named assured" rather than in relation to omnibus insureds, it may be argued that the spouse of the owner is not preclud-

27.   Mass.Gen.Laws Ann. ch. 90, § 34A (1969).

28.   292 Mass. 105, 107, 197 N.E. 516, 517, 106 A.L.R. 1248, 1250.

29.   Cain v. American Policy Holders Ins. Co., 120 Conn. 645, 183 A. 403 (1936).

30.   120 Conn. at 655, 183 A. at 407.

31.   *E.g.*, Bachman v. Independence Indem. Co., 214 Cal. 529, 6 P.2d 943 (1931); Iowa Mut. Ins. Co. v. Meckna, 180 Neb. 516, 144 N.W.2d 73 (1966), 15 A.L.R.3d 698 (1967); Commercial Ins. Co. v. Papandrea, 121 Vt. 386, 159 A.

2d 333 (1960) (dictum). *Cf.* Ottinger v. Falkenberg, 11 Wis.2d 506, 105 N.W.2d 560 (1960) (reformation allowed to strike name of wife as named insured, because it was included without her knowledge or consent, after injury to her while her brother was driving the insured car with permission; the court reserved the question whether, had she been a named insured, liability for injury to her could have been excluded).

32.   See § 2.11(b) (6) *supra*.

33.   292 Mass. 105, 107, 197 N.E. 516, 517, 106 A.L.R. 1248, 1250.

ed from recovery if either the owner or someone else with his permission drives the automobile and negligently injures the spouse.   This distinction is a debatable one, but the likelihood of its being drawn is perhaps increased by the fact that the *MacBey* interpretation of the Massachusetts statute is itself dubious.   The problem is further complicated by the fact that the 1958 family automobile form defines "named insured" to include the spouse.   Apparently the drafting objective was to do away with differences based on whether a policy was issued to one spouse alone or to the two spouses jointly.[34]   One might nevertheless distinguish the non-owning spouse from the owner, with respect to potential application of the *MacBey* rule, on the theory that *MacBey* was an interpretation of the statutory requirement rather than the omnibus clause and that "others" in the statute includes all persons other than the owner, irrespective of relationship to the owner.

Distinguishable from the cases discussed above are those involving policies containing a clause, not commonly included in automobile insurance coverage, declaring explicitly that the bodily injury liability coverage does not apply to bodily injury to an insured; in those cases, absent statutory provisions precluding such a limitation of the omnibus clause, coverage may be denied not on the ground discussed here but on the ground that the exclusion clause applies.[35]

§ 4.7(c)   AN APPRAISAL OF OMNIBUS CLAUSES

Over the span of years since an omnibus clause was first used, there has been a general trend toward expanding the scope of such clauses.   This trend probably reflects, first, an increased preference on the part of insurance purchasers, incident to changing social attitudes, to have the benefits of their policies extend quite broadly to others and, second, a diminished apprehension on the part of insurers concerning the costs of supplying more expanded coverage, in light of their experience under omnibus clauses previously used.   The trend has not been advanced by every revision of standard forms, however. After notable expansions in 1955[1] and 1958,[2] company draftsmen attempted a retreat to less expansive coverage in the 1966 revision.[3]

The revisions that have occurred, however, have failed to come to grips with a central deficiency of the omnibus clauses in automobile policies.   Because they have used "permission" in one sense or another as a standard for determining the scope of coverage, they have bred litigation.[4]   Moreover, it has been litigation of a most wasteful and expensive type—litigation concerning controversies that

---

34.   See § 2.11(b) (3) *supra.*

35.   See § 4.9(c) *infra.*

1.   See § 2.11(b) (3) and (d) *supra.*

2.   *Ibid.*

3.   See § 2.11(c) and (d) *supra.*

4.   See, *e.g.,* Annots., 4 A.L.R.3d 10 (1965);   36 A.L.R.2d 673 (1954);   5 A.L.R.2d 600 (1948).   See also § 4.7(b) (1) and (2) *supra.*

are essentially fact-oriented.[5]   One way of avoiding this waste would be to limit omnibus insureds to a group definable in terms less likely to give rise to fact disputes (for example, limiting the group to members of the household of the named insured).[6]   This would be an undesirable revision from another point of view, however, since it would work against the public interest in favor of maximizing the probability that drivers will be financially responsible.   Another way of avoiding the waste and expense incident to using a concept of permission in omnibus clauses would be to expand the group of covered drivers at least to a point that only very exceptional cases would spawn any controversy over whether the driver was an insured.   For example, a clause might be written to cover all persons using the designated automobile unless under circumstances amounting to conversion.[7]   It may be suggested that the question whether a conversion had occurred is also a fact-oriented question likely to produce litigation. But the number of cases in which there would be an issue for the jury would be fewer because the requirements for conversion are far more rigorous than the requirements for non-permission.   Thus the resulting saving in litigation costs would go far toward meeting the added cost of extending coverage to additional drivers not covered by clauses that make coverage depend on permission.   Moreover, other means are used in every state to provide to some extent for availability of compensation to victims of financially irresponsible motorists. The costs of these measures would be reduced if omnibus clauses were expanded in the way suggested.   When all costs are considered, then, it seems highly probable that the suggested expansion of omnibus clauses would result in net savings to the motoring public as well as reduced friction among automobile liability insurers, their insureds, and accident victims.

SECTION 4.8   INTERESTS IN LIABILITY INSURANCE

§ 4.8(a) GENERALLY

Liability insurance was initially designed to protect an insured against loss caused by his tort liability to a third person.   From a very early time in its development, however, liability insurance has included elements of protection for the benefit of third parties. First, the omnibus clause provides protection for certain other persons against loss resulting from their liability to victims.[1]   Second, victims too are often third party beneficiaries of liability insurance

---

5.   See §§ 1.6, 4.7(b) (1) and (2) *supra*.

6.   *Cf.* Jones v. Mid-South Ins. Co., 358 F.2d 887 (5th Cir. 1966) (applying Louisiana law; held, omnibus clause limiting coverage to named insured, spouse, and an additional named insured valid in absence of statutory re-

quirement of broader omnibus clause coverage).   *But see* § 4.7(b) n.25 *supra*.

7.   *Cf.* Keeton & O'Connell, Basic Protection for the Traffic Victim 391 (1965).

1.   See § 4.7 *supra*.

coverage. If coverage were restricted to pure liability insurance, victims would benefit only incidentally if at all. But liability insurance has come to be used openly and extensively as a device for insuring compensation to victims. The principal areas of explicit protection for victims will be considered in this section. Further protection has occurred through the impact of financial responsibility legislation.[2]

The impact of varied liability insurance interests on claims processes and the distinctive conflicts of interest problems that result are considered elsewhere.[3]

§ 4.8(b) INSOLVENCY CLAUSES AND STATUTES

In its original form liability insurance was an agreement by the insurer to indemnify the insured against loss arising from his tort liability to a third person. In the earliest policies, the insured was an employer, obtaining protection against tort liability to employees based on work injuries. If an injured victim attempted to proceed against the insurer, even after obtaining a tort judgment against the insured, the insurer could defend successfully since its obligation was only to the insured. Indeed, on the theory that the contract was one of "indemnity" in the narrowest possible sense, it was held in numerous cases that even the insured could not recover against the insurer without having previously sustained loss by discharging the liability to the victim as distinguished from merely being adjudged to be liable.[4] Thus, insolvency of the insured not only prevented the victim from realizing anything on his tort judgment against the insured but also prevented the insured from realizing anything under the insurance policy.

The obvious inequity of this situation led to legislation in some states requiring a policy provision that insolvency or bankruptcy of the insured shall not release the insurer from liability.[5] No doubt such legislation would have been adopted in every state in time had not insurers revised their policy forms to include such a provision in all policies.

The insolvency provision of current forms appears in a clause commonly entitled "Action Against Company." In addition to declaring that bankruptcy or insolvency "shall not relieve the company of any of its obligations hereunder," that clause declares: "No action shall lie against the company . . . until the amount of the insured's obligation to pay shall have been finally determined either by judgment against the insured after actual trial or by written agreement of the insured, the claimant and the company."[6] Thus the right of the insured to proceed against an insurer under the payment

---

2. See, *e.g.*, § 4.7(a) n.7 *supra* and § 4.8 (c) *infra*.

3. See §§ 7.5–7.11 *infra*.

4. *E.g.*, Hebojoff v. Globe Indem. Co., 35 Cal.App. 390, 169 P. 1048 (2d Dist.

1918); Shea v. United States Fid. Co., 98 Conn. 447, 120 A. 286 (1923).

5. *E.g.*, N.Y.Ins.Law § 167 (McKinney 1966).

6. Appendix H *infra*.

provisions, as distinguished from the provisions for defense, ripens when a victim obtains a tort judgment. It is commonly recognized that at that time the victim may proceed against the insurer by garnishment or otherwise, even without the insured's cooperation.[7] At least in this limited sense, then, the victim may be referred to as a third party beneficiary of the liability insurance contract.[8] As will appear in the later subdivisions of this section, other developments in some jurisdictions have given the victim further rights as a third party beneficiary of the liability insurance contract.

§ 4.8(c) NON-DERIVATIVE LIABILITY (LIMITATION OF DEFENSES)

Insolvency statutes [1] were supported by a rather limited objective of curing the inequity arising when a liability insurer escaped all liability because of the insolvency of its insured. Other legislation of more recent vintage, referred to here as non-derivative liability statutes, is more broadly aimed at protecting tort victims against financial irresponsibility of tortfeasors [2] by depriving liability insurers of policy defenses that would be good against the insureds—for example, such defenses as late notice or noncooperation.[3] This type of statute has been enacted in every state, though with very limited application in many. The most common form of such a statute is the provision in financial responsibility laws applying to those policies certified to a public official in order for a motorist to comply with insurance requirements imposed upon him because of his having been convicted of a serious driving offense or having failed to provide compensation for the victim of an accident in which he was involved.[4] The financial

---

7. See, *e.g.*, Lachenmyer v. Central Mut. Ins. Co., 384 Ill.App. 391, 2 N.E. 2d 177 (3d Dist. 1936); Hall v. Harleysville Mut. Cas. Co., 233 N.C. 339, 64 S.E.2d 160 (1951).

8. Other advantages of third party beneficiary status are also sometimes judicially conferred. In State Farm Mut. Auto. Ins. Co. v. Kendall, 104 Ga.App. 481, 122 S.E.2d 139 (1961), for example, the court held that an attempted rescission of an automobile liability policy by the named insured and his insurer, after an accident involving an employee of the named insured who was driving with permission, did not defeat the rights of an injured person under the policy. See also § 4.8(d) *infra* concerning agreements, after an accident, between the insured and the insurer to assert an immunity that the policy declared would not be asserted.

1. See § 4.8(b) *supra*.

2. Concerning the implementation of this objective through omnibus clauses and statutes requiring them, see § 4.-7(a) *supra*.

3. See, *e.g.*, Sobina v. Busby, 61 Ill. App.2d 1, 210 N.E.2d 769 (1st Dist. 1965) (after notice of a suit in Illinois against its insured, insurer obtained a judgment in Alabama that its policy was void ab initio because of misrepresentation by the insured; held, the victims of the insured's negligence were unaffected by the Alabama judgment since they were neither parties to nor given notice of that action); Aetna Cas. & Sur. Co. v. O'Connor, 8 N.Y.2d 359, 170 N.E.2d 681, 207 N.Y.S. 2d 679 (1960), 83 A.L.R.2d 1099 (1962) (held, policy issued under pre-compulsory insurance law assigned-risk plan can be cancelled for fraud but cannot be rescinded to the prejudice of innocent third parties). See also Annots., 34 A.L.R.2d 1297 (1954); 1 A.L.R.2d 822 (1948).

4. See, *e.g.*, Nimeth v. Felling, 282 Minn. 460, 165 N.W.2d 237 (1969).

responsibility statutes of a minority of the states have been construed to apply more broadly to all motor vehicle liability insurance policies issued in the state.[5] Similarly, some compulsory liability insurance statutes include such a provision.[6]

Standard automobile insurance forms provide that the insurance afforded by the policy shall comply with statutes of this type when the policy is certified, and the negative implication that this obligation attaches only when the policy has been so certified is ordinarily honored in the courts.[7] The standard clause also provides that the insured shall reimburse the company for any payment the company must make under this clause but would not otherwise have been obligated to make.[8]

§ 4.8(d) IMMUNITY OF INSUREDS

When an institution with a partial immunity from tort liability has obtained a liability insurance policy, the question may arise whether the liability insurer is obligated to make payments equivalent to those that would have been due in the absence of the immunity.

An endorsement is sometimes added to the policy declaring that the company will not assert the insured's immunity and will not deny liability because of it.[1] It would seem that such an agreement should be enforced, even against the contention that the added premium an insured must pay to obtain such an endorsement is an improper use of its trust funds. That contention is based on an unduly narrow conception of what is the proper fiduciary concern of the persons responsible for managing the institution. Surely, for example, the charity that a charitable hospital dispenses ought to include provisions for compensating, at least as well as non-immune institutions are obligated to do, the victims of carelessness in its operations. In relation to liability insurance purchased by the governing body of a municipality the problem may be more difficult because of the terms

5. See, *e.g.*, Farmers Ins. Exch. v. Rose, 411 F.2d 270 (9th Cir. 1969) (forecasting Arizona law; defense of fraud in application for insurance unavailable); Farm Bureau Auto. Ins. Co. v. Martin, 97 N.H. 196, 84 A.2d 823 (1951), 29 A.L.R.2d 811 (1953) (defense of failure to give notice of replacement of insured vehicle unavailable).

6. See, *e.g.*, Lane v. Iowa Mut. Ins. Co., 258 N.C. 318, 128 S.E.2d 398 (1962) (failure of insured to give insurer notice of suit did not relieve insurer of liability to insured's victims). See Annots., 31 A.L.R.2d 645 (1953); 29 A.L.R.2d 817 (1953). *But see, e.g.*, National Grange Mut. Liab. Co. v. Fino, 13 App.Div.2d 10, 212 N.Y.S.2d 684 (3d Dep't 1961) (noncooperation of insured

allowed as a defense to claims of third parties against company).

7. See, *e.g.*, Fidelity & Cas. Co. v. McConnaughy, 228 Md. 1, 179 A.2d 117 (1962) (filing of form acknowledging coverage of one for whom proof of financial responsibility was · not required does not preclude assertion of noncooperation); Annot., 8 A.L.R.3d 388 (1966).

8. See § 2.11(b) (5) *supra* and § 5.4(b) n.2 *infra*. See also Annot., 29 A.L.R. 3d 291 (1970).

1. See, *e.g.*, Taylor v. Knox County Board of Education, 292 Ky. 767, 167 S.W.2d 700 (1942), 145 A.L.R. 1333 (1943).

of legislative authorizations for expenditure of funds. But it would seem that here also, in the absence of a clearly manifested legislative prohibition, it should be held that municipal officials who are authorized to purchase liability insurance are not misusing funds in paying the added premium necessary to obtain an endorsement of the type under discussion.[2]

Another type of immunity endorsement sometimes used provides that the insurer will not assert the insured's immunity except with the consent in writing of the insured. An insurer's premium rate for such an endorsement must be set in contemplation of the possibility that consent of the insured will never be given. Thus, such a clause is likely to be virtually as expensive as one in which the insurer unqualifiedly agrees not to assert the immunity. But an insured institution might nevertheless desire the consent clause in order to make certain that the immunity defense is preserved for use whenever a claim is being asserted that appears unjustified but perhaps difficult or expensive to defeat on grounds other than immunity.

An immunity endorsement containing a consent clause clearly implies that the right of the insured and insurer to agree to assert the immunity is preserved. If the endorsement does not contain such a clause, the question arises whether a victim is a third party beneficiary of the immunity endorsement in his own right—that is, whether he can enforce the contractual stipulation that the immunity not be asserted even though the insured, after the victim's injury was suffered, has agreed to the insurer's asserting it. Authorities on the issue are inconclusive,[3] but it seems likely and proper that the rights of the victim will be regarded as fixed when the injury occurs. The resulting liability is no greater than the insurer should have anticipated in setting premiums. And to give the insured a chance to exercise unpoliced choice between favoring the insurer and favoring the victim after accident would invite fraud and chicane.[4] It may be answered, and cogently, that such an invitation results, also, from enforcing an express-consent clause. But in that instance the interest in freedom of contract supports enforcement of the agreement; perhaps that interest may be assessed as having sufficient weight to justify distinguishing the case of the express-consent clause from that involving no explicit provision on this point.

Most courts confronting the question have held that if a liability insurance policy contains no immunity endorsement the insured's im-

2. A contrary result was reached in Pohland v. City of Sheboygan, 251 Wis. 20, 27 N.W.2d 736 (1947), later overruled by Marshall v. City of Green Bay, 18 Wis.2d 421, 118 N.W.2d 715 (1963).

3. See, e.g., Walton v. Glens Falls Indem. Co., 192 F.2d 189 (5th Cir. 1951), decided for the insurer, following what were conceived to be the implications of a decision of the Supreme

Court of Georgia in the related tort suit. The Georgia law is now clearly different, however. See n.6 infra.

4. This is a specific illustration of a principle of general application that it is undesirable to give one person an unpoliced discretion to make a choice decisive of the allocation of interests between two others. For other illustrations of the principle see §§ 4.11(e) at n.10, 7.9(c) infra.

munity continues to be available to both the insured and the insurer.[5] But the courts of several jurisdictions have reached the contrary result.[6] These decisions cannot be justified as reasonable interpretations of the contract provisions. The agreement of the insurer is to pay on behalf of the insured the liability imposed by law, and no liability is imposed when the immunity is invoked. Moreover, it is apparent that the premiums, if reasonably related to the risks involved, will be much higher if the immunity is not available than if either it definitely is available or there is uncertainty as to whether it is available (as has been the situation in states in which the immunity was being eroded and ripened for outright abandonment). Thus the minority rule must be justified, if at all, as a doctrine overriding intent of the parties. If applied consistently, this would mean that the same result of liability of the insurer would be reached even in the face of an explicit statement in the policy that the insurer was not obligated to make any payment if the insured would not have been liable in tort in the absence of liability insurance. Thus, the doctrine would be a judicial restriction of freedom of contract, making it impossible for an institution with a partial immunity to take liability insurance against its limited liability without losing its immunity altogether up to the limits of the liability coverage. Certainly the trend toward abandonment of tort immunities is soundly supported in public policy, but using that argument in this context proves too much, since it supports denial of the tort immunity irrespective of the existence of an applicable liability insurance policy. Nevertheless, it may be that a court adopting the minority position would take the doctrine to this extreme, as a way of chipping away another segment of immunity, rather than limiting its expansive doctrine to cases in which the policy does not explicitly state that immunity is to be preserved.[7] Arkansas legislation adopts this restraint-on-free-contract position, declaring that, "notwithstanding the terms of the policy itself . . . .," an injured person shall have a cause of action against the liability insurer of "any cooperative nonprofit corporation, association or organization or . . . any other organization or association . . . not subject to suit for tort . . . ."[8]

5. *E.g.*, McGrath Bldg. Co. v. City of Bettendorf, 248 Iowa 1386, 85 N.W.2d 616 (1957), 68 A.L.R.2d 1429 (1959); Kesman v. Fallowfield Township School Dist., 345 Pa. 457, 29 A.2d 17 (1942); Mann v. County Board of Arlington County, 199 Va. 169, 98 S.E.2d 515 (1957).

6. *E.g.*, O'Connor v. Boulder Colo. Sanitarium Ass'n, 105 Colo. 259, 96 P.2d 835 (1939), 133 A.L.R. 819 (1941); Morehouse College v. Russell, 219 Ga. 717, 135 S.E.2d 432 (1964); Geislinger v. Village of Watkins, 269 Minn. 116, 130 N.W.2d 62 (1964); Vendrell v. School Dist. No. 26C Malheur County,

226 Ore. 263, 360 P.2d 282 (1961). See Annot., 25 A.L.R.2d 29, 89, 139–142 (1952).

7. *Cf.* Vendrell v. School Dist. No. 26C Malheur County, 226 Ore. 263, 360 P. 2d 282 (1961).

8. Ark.Stat.Ann. §§ 66–3240, 66–3242(2) (1966). See Michael v. St. Paul Mercury Indem. Co., 92 F.Supp. 140 (D. Ark.1950). Perhaps the statute was intended to protect victims, being enacted in the hope that if hospitals were deprived of the opportunity to buy coverage against only the limited liability existing under the immunity

SECTION 4.9 INTERESTS IN AUTOMOBILE INSURANCE

§ 4.9(a) GENERALLY

Under many types of insurance coverage, including some in the typical automobile insurance policy, even when it is possible to determine readily both the identity of the principal insured and the nature of the risks transferred from the insured to the insurer by the contract,[9] it may be difficult to determine exactly what other persons receive protection as additional insureds or beneficiaries and which interests are covered among the whole array of varied interests of insureds and beneficiaries.

This section treats a set of recurring instances in which such problems have arisen under automobile insurance coverages. Additional problems concerning the scope of protection under automobile insurance are considered elsewhere.[10]

§ 4.9(b) IDENTIFYING COVERED VEHICLES

Automobile insurance is often referred to as a system of insuring vehicles rather than insuring drivers. There is a germ of truth here. The package of coverage in the basic standard automobile policy is centered around a designated vehicle, and the omnibus clause[1] extends coverage to the operation of that vehicle not only by the named insured but by others in specified circumstances that include nearly all the expected uses. If an insured has more than one vehicle to insure, either a separate policy is issued or else each of the automobiles to be covered is described on the face of the policy or in a schedule that is a part of the policy. When such a policy covers a large number of vehicles, it is commonly referred to as a "fleet" policy.

It happens, however, that standard automobile insurance contracts not only insure vehicles in the sense indicated but also insure people in the sense that the named insured and relatives of his household have coverage while driving other automobiles under specified circumstances. Thus, in order to determine whether a vehicle involved in an accident producing loss for an insured was covered at the time, one must sometimes look beyond the clause designating a particular vehicle to other clauses of the policy that describe vehicles in terms of the insured's relationship to them.

---

rule, they would then choose the more expensive coverage that waives the immunity within policy limits rather than choosing not to insure at all.

9. Concerning the nature of the risks transferred see Chapter 5 *infra*.

10. See §§ 4.7 (omnibus clauses), 4.8 (liability insurance generally) *supra* and §§ 4.10 (nonfault insurance), 5.2(b) ("ownership, maintenance and use"), 7.5–7.11 (claims processes under liability insurance) *infra*.

1. See § 4.7 *supra*.

The basic statement of liability coverages in pre-1966 forms ordinarily declared that the company agreed "to pay on behalf of the insured . . . damages . . . . arising out of the ownership, maintenance or use of *the* automobile." [2] A separate clause defined "automobile" to include not only the automobile described in the declarations on the face of the policy but also, under restricted circumstances, a "trailer," a "temporary substitute automobile," and a "newly acquired automobile," thereby expanding coverage to cases involving use of vehicles in these other groups in addition to the described automobile.[3]

Coverage was further expanded, in the pre-1966 forms, by inclusion of a clause under the caption "Use of Other Automobiles," often referred to as the "Drive Other Cars" or "DOC" coverage.[4] Both the definition of "automobile" and the DOC clause were applicable to some extent to medical payments and collision coverages as well as liability coverages.[5] The principle of the DOC clause was to extend coverage to the use [6] by an insured of other automobiles, with excep-

---

2. Emphasis added. See, *e.g.*, the "1955 Standard Basic Automobile Liability Policy," Risjord & Austin, Automobile Liability Insurance Cases—Standard Provisions and Appendix 16 (1964) [hereinafter cited Risjord & Austin].

3. See *id.* at 20–22.

4. In the 1958 revision, the DOC coverage was provided along with coverage of the insured's own vehicle in a single coverage clause (see Risjord & Austin 56), and the omnibus clause was revised to include the enumeration of persons insured under the DOC coverage:
"**Persons Insured**
"The following are insureds under Part I:
        . . .
"(b) With respect to a non-owned automobile,
    "(1) the named insured,
    "(2) any relative, but only with respect to a private passenger automobile or trailer,
    provided the actual use thereof is with the permission of the owner . . . ."
Risjord & Austin 57.

The "permission of the owner" provision did not appear in the 1955 form (see *id.* at 22–24); there have been holdings that in these circumstances permission is irrelevant to the question whether DOC coverage was applicable. *E.g.*, Sperling v. Great Am. Indem. Co., 7 N.Y.2d 442, 166 N.E.2d 482, 199 N.Y.S.2d 465 (1960) (insurer liable under "family" policy not containing

requirement of permission for judgment against sixteen-year-old family member who at the time of the accident was driving a stolen car and fleeing from the police). *Cf.* Home Indem. Co. v. Ware, 285 F.2d 852 (3d Cir. 1960) (insured's liability policy provided coverage for liability resulting from collision caused by insured's step-son while driving a stolen car). The "permission of the owner" provision was added in spite of the volume of litigation produced by the permission requirements of omnibus clauses generally. See § 4.7(b) *supra*. It has been successfully contended, however, that the "permission of the owner" requirement qualifies only sub-part (b) of the quoted clause and not the named insured's coverage under sub-part (a), the failing contention of the insurer being that the structure of the clause clearly evidences an intent that the requirement qualify both sub-parts (a) and (b). *E.g.*, McMichael v. American Ins. Co., 351 F.2d 665 (8th Cir. 1965) (applying Missouri law); Harleysville Mut. Cas. Co. v. Nationwide Mut. Ins. Co., 248 S.C. 398, 150 S.E.2d 233 (1966).

5. See, *e.g.*, the 1955 form, Risjord & Austin 20–24, and see § 2.11(b) (4) *supra* discussing shortcomings of the DOC collision coverage in the 1955 form.

6. An issue sometimes arises with respect to whether the individual claiming coverage under a DOC clause was

tions concerning other effective insurance or concerning the insured's opportunity to arrange for other insurance separately.[7] A theme underlying the exceptions is to preclude a person from insuring several cars for the price of one but to effect this preclusion without undue impairment of the general objective of the DOC clause to protect the insured during his occasional use of some vehicle other than his own.[8]

actually "using" the vehicle involved in the accident. See, e.g., Potomac Ins. Co. v. Ohio Cas. Ins. Co., 188 F. Supp. 218 (N.D.Cal.1960) (male passenger was negligent in distracting female driver, thereby causing an accident; held, he was not using the vehicle so as to qualify for DOC coverage under the policy of which he was the named insured). But cf. decisions concerning the meaning of "use" of an automobile in other contexts, § 4.7 (b) (1) n.11 supra and § 5.2(b) infra.

7. As to the exceptions, clause V(d) of the 1955 form read:
"This insuring agreement does not apply:
"(1) to any automobile owned by or furnished for regular use to either the named insured or a member of the same household other than a private chauffeur or domestic servant of such named insured or spouse;
"(2) to any accident arising out of the operation of an automobile sales agency, repair shop, service station, storage garage or public parking place;
"(3) under coverages A, B or C–1, to any automobile while used in a business or occupation of such named insured or spouse except a private passenger automobile operated or occupied by such named insured, spouse, private chauffeur or domestic servant;
"(4) under coverages E–1, E–2 or E–3, to any loss when there is any other insurance which would apply thereto in the absence of this insuring agreement, whether such other insurance covers the interest of the named insured or spouse, the owner of the automobile or any other person or organization."

8. See, e.g., Carr v. Home Indem. Co., 404 Pa. 27, 170 A.2d 588 (1961), 83 A. L.R.2d 922 (1962) (insured is not covered while driving a car owned by brother residing at same address since it is not a car "not owned by . . . any relative"); Schoenknecht v. Prairie States Farmers Ins. Ass'n, 27 Ill. App.2d 83, 169 N.E.2d 148 (2d Dist. 1960) (car regularly used by insured during his employment was not ex-

cluded as a car provided for his regular use when accident occurred while he was using it for personal pleasure outside the scope of his employment); Palmer v. Glens Falls Ins. Co., 58 Wash.2d 88, 360 P.2d 742 (1961) (insured regularly used son-in-law's car for business purposes for over two months, but accident occurred when he was using it with owner's consent for trip to a repair shop; held, special use interrupted regular use and DOC coverage applied); Texas Cas. Ins. Co. v. Wyble, 333 S.W.2d 668 (Tex.Civ.App.1960, no writ history) (insured claimed medical payments coverage for injury to son incurred in an accident with an automobile while the son was riding on a motor scooter owned by him; held, scooter was not an "automobile" owned by or furnished for the use of a member of the family). See also Annots., 86 A.L.R. 2d 937 (1962); 85 A.L.R.2d 502 (1962); 83 A.L.R.2d 926 (1962).

Coverage otherwise excluded under the DOC coverage is under some circumstances afforded by other policy provisions, e.g., the temporary-substitute-automobile provision or the after-acquired-automobile provision. See, e.g., Imperial Cas. & Indem. Co. v. Relder, 308 F.2d 761 (8th Cir. 1962) (applying Missouri law; insured purchased a second car and insured it with another company but, after an accident involving the second car, reported the purchase to the insurer of his original car and claimed coverage under the after-acquired-automobile clause of that policy; held, for the insured since the policy required notice of the purchase of another automobile only during the policy period, which notice the insured had given, and nothing in the policy indicated that the coverage applied only to after-acquired replacements of the described vehicle); Densmore v. Hartford Acc. & Indem. Co., 221 F.Supp. 652 (W.D.Va.1963) (after demolishing his own car, insured stole another car with which he had an accident; held, coverage under substitute automobile clause of policy on demolished car); McKee v. Exchange Ins. Ass'n, 270 Ala. 518, 120 So.2d 690 (1960) (insured's car was de-

The 1966 changes in liability insurance policy forms thoroughly revised the definitions, including that for "automobile," and eliminated the clause formerly appearing under the caption "Use of Other Automobiles." Nevertheless, in effect it continued what had formerly been referred to as temporary-substitute-automobile, newly-acquired-automobile, and DOC coverages by incorporating them into a more inclusive basic statement of liability coverages. The 1966 form substitutes the phrase "*any* automobile" for "*the* automobile" (emphases added) in the basic statement of the liability coverages.[9] It states exceptions at the end of Section II of the form, entitled "Persons Insured," in the following language: "This insurance does not apply to bodily injury or property damage arising out of (1) a non-owned automobile used in the conduct of any partnership or joint venture of which the insured is a partner or member and which is not designated in this policy as a named insured, or (2) if the named insured is a partnership, an automobile owned by or registered in the name of a partner thereof."[10] It will be noted that this exclusion says nothing about a non-designated automobile that an insured might own in addition to the one designated. But the schedule on the face of the new policy form provides for a listing of more than one owned automobile under a single policy, and presumably it is intended that this form not be used to write coverage for only one of two automobiles owned by the named insured;[11] thus it is unneces-

molished in an accident, after which he was in another accident while driving an automobile owned by his mother, who was a resident of the same household; held, coverage under the substitute automobile provision of the insured's policy); Mid-Continent Cas. Co. v. West, 351 P.2d 398 (Okla.1959) (insured had an accident while on a business trip in his father's car, which was being used because the tires on his car were too dangerous for use on a long trip; held, coverage under the substitute automobile provision of his policy, the fact that new tires had been ordered for his car evidencing that the use of the father's car was more than merely for convenience); Baxley v. State Farm Mut. Auto. Liab. Ins. Co., 241 S.C. 332, 128 S.E.2d 165 (1962) (insured was driving wife's car when involved in an accident; although "insured" was defined to include spouse, held, coverage under substitute automobile provision since the involved vehicle was not owned by the named insured either solely or jointly with his wife). *But see, e.g.,* Gabrelcik v. National Indem. Co., 269 Minn. 445, 131 N.W.2d 534 (1964) (while her regular taxi was disabled, insured used for her taxi business a car lent by her husband, which was registered in the name of his sole

proprietorship; held, no coverage); Fullilove v. United States Cas. Co., 240 La. 859, 125 So.2d 389 (1961) (insured used his son's car on a business trip since the tires on his own car were in poor condition; held, no coverage since on the day of the accident in the son's car the insured's car was being used by his wife for in-town driving, which had become the "normal use" of the car).

9. See Appendix G *infra*.

10. *Ibid.* For illustrations of situations that produced litigation under earlier forms that appear to be governed by this exclusion, see Mission Ins. Co. v. Feldt, 62 Cal.2d 97, 396 P.2d 709 (1964) (insured, under a policy covering him only while driving cars he did not own, covered in an accident that occurred while driving a car owned by a joint venture in which he was a partner); Farley v. American Auto. Ins. Co., 137 W.Va. 455, 72 S.E.2d 520 (1952), 34 A.L.R.2d 933 (1954) (partnership covered by policy on car owned by it for accident involving car owned by one partner, which had been temporarily substituted for partnership car).

11. Or, presumably, for only one of two cars owned separately by the named

sary to include in the form an exclusion of coverage as to a non-designated owned automobile.

§ 4.9(c) EXCLUSIONS OF INJURY TO DESCRIBED PERSONS AND CLASSES

"employee" excluded

Automobile liability policies generally contain clauses excluding coverage of liability for bodily injury to an "employee of the insured."[1] Less frequently, a policy contains a clause declaring that coverage does not apply to injury to insureds. In some instances the exclusion has referred to *named insureds*; that is, the clause has declared that coverage does not apply to "bodily injury to or death of any person who is a named insured."[2] In the absence of statutory provisions (such as those requiring omnibus clauses)[3] construed as precluding their use, such restrictive provisions have usually been effective to protect insurers against liability on claims of named insureds against additional insureds.[4] The same result has often been reached under clauses precluding coverage for bodily injury "to the insured or any member of the family of the insured residing in the same household as the insured," or words of similar import.[5] But this is a more debatable position because of doubt about whether "insured" means the "named insured" rather than the person who is the insured of liability coverage with respect to the tort claim at issue. A closely analogous problem arises under employee exclusions.

A kind of factual situation that has given rise often to litigation involving the "employee of the insured" exclusion is that of injury to an employee of the *named* insured caused by one otherwise an *additional* insured. In many instances an employee of the named insured has been injured while the insured vehicle was being loaded or unloaded by employees of the additional insured.

It has been noted that the weight of authority supports coverage of an additional insured's liability for injury to a named insured[6]

insured and his spouse. The 1955 definition of "temporary substitute automobile" included the phrase "an automobile not owned by the named insured or his spouse if a resident of the same household . . . ." See Risjord & Austin 21.

1. See, *e.g.*, Appendix H *infra*.

2. See, *e.g.*, Frye v. Theige, 253 Wis. 596, 34 N.W.2d 793 (1948), 50 A.L.R.2d 124 (1956).

3. See § 4.7(a) *supra*.

4. *E.g.*, Hepburn v. Pennsylvania Indem. Corp., 109 F.2d 833 (D.C.Cir. 1939); Jenkins v. Morano, 74 F.Supp. 234 (E.D.Va.1947); Shaw v. State Farm Mut. Ins. Co., 107 Ga.App. 8, 129 S.E.2d 85 (1962); Frye v. Theige,

253 Wis. 596, 34 N.W.2d 793 (1948), 50 A.L.R.2d 124 (1956). *Cf.* Employers' Liab. Assur. Corp. v. Aresty, 11 App. Div.2d 331, 205 N.Y.S.2d 711 (1st Dep't 1960), *aff'd per curiam*, 11 N.Y.2d 696, 180 N.E.2d 916, 225 N.Y.S.2d 764 (1962) (held, insured's move to Connecticut and endorsement of policy to change the address of the insured did not expand coverage to include injury to spouse, which was excluded under New York statute applicable to policy as originally issued).

5. *E.g.*, Fuchs v. Cheeley, 285 Minn. 356, 173 N.W.2d 358 (1969); Tomlyanovich v. Tomlyanovich, 239 Minn. 250, 58 N.W.2d 855 (1953), 50 A.L.R.2d 108 (1956).

6. See § 4.7(b) (3) *supra*.

when the policy contains no exclusion clause regarding such claims. Those precedents have little weight, however, for cases involving an exclusion clause; the issue becomes primarily one of construction of that clause. It would seem that when injury to an employee of the named insured is caused by one otherwise an additional insured, "employee of the insured," as it appears in the exclusion, should be read as "employee of the insured *invoking the protection of the policy*," *i. e.*, the "additional insured." This interpretation is arguably negated by the general definition of "insured"—for example the 1966 form provision that "insured" means any person or organization qualifying as an insured in the 'Persons Insured' provision . . . ." [7]— which may be said to imply that the use of the unqualified phrase "insured" includes the named insured at all times, regardless of who is invoking the protection of the policy. That definition, however, is immediately followed in the 1966 form by the statement that "the insurance afforded applies separately to each insured against whom claim is made or suit is brought . . . .." [8] If not completely reversing the implications of the primary definition, this severability clause at least makes the meaning of "employee of the insured" ambiguous and, therefore, subject to construction against the insurer.[9]

There is a close division of authority on this question,[10] with a substantial number of precedents for [11] and against [12] coverage.

7. See Appendix G *infra*.

8. *Ibid*. The "severability of interest" clause first appeared in the 1955 form. See § 2.11(b) (6) *supra*.

9. See § 6.3 *infra*.

10. The rule allowing coverage was characterized as the "majority" rule in Travelers Ins. Co. v. Auto-Owners (Mut.) Ins. Co., 1 Ohio App.2d 65, 203 N.E.2d 846 (1964), but coverage was denied in Michigan Mut. Liab. Co. v. Continental Cas. Co., 297 F.2d 208 (7th Cir. 1961), on the basis of the "majority rule," the court having found no decision of the question by the courts of Delaware, the law of which controlled the case. Although a three-year period of time separates these cases, an examination of cases in point decided during that period revealed no perceptible shift in the weight of authority. After another five years, the Minnesota Supreme Court decided against coverage because of an exclusion of "bodily injury to . . . the insured or any member of the family of the insured residing in the same household as the insured," making no special point of the fact that this was a family exclusion rather than an "employee of the insured" exclusion. The court re-

ferred to one of its own 1964 opinions containing a dictum that it might have decided an earlier case differently if there had been a severability clause in the contract, and added: "The decisions handed down since 1964 clearly indicate the view that where an exclusionary clause refers to the word 'insured' it includes the named insured, regardless of a severability clause." Fuchs v. Cheeley, 285 Minn. 356, 365, 173 N.W.2d 358, 364 (1969). But the inference that the tide may have turned toward non-coverage is countered by the actions of the Florida Supreme Court in 1967, resolving a conflict between lower court decisions by approving the decision favoring coverage, and of the Texas Supreme Court in 1970, overruling its own 1960 decision for non-coverage and commenting that the earlier decision had not given adequate emphasis to the severability clause; see the Florida and Texas cases cited in n.11 *infra*. See generally Annots., 34 A.L.R.3d 1397 (1970); 50 A.L.R.2d 78 (1956).

11. *E.g.*, Shelby Mut. Ins. Co. v. Schuitema, 183 So.2d 571 (Fla.App. 4th Dist. 1966), *aff'd*, 193 So.2d 435

12. See note 12 on page 244.

It might be questioned why one should be precluded from being an additional insured under a policy containing the "employee of the insured" exclusion simply because the injury he causes is to an employee of the named insured. For example, why should the employer of an individual unloading the insured vehicle be an additional insured when that employee causes injury to an uninvolved bystander but not when that employee causes injury to the driver of the vehicle, an employee of the named insured? The widespread applicability of workmen's compensation laws has little bearing on the significance of this distinction, since ordinarily in this situation the "additional insured's" workmen's compensation coverage would not provide benefits for the named insured's employee and the applicability of the named insured's workmen's compensation coverage would not preclude a tort claim against the "additional insured" by the injured employee (or by his employer or the employer's workmen's compensation insurer as subrogee to his claim).[13] The significance of the problem is reduced, however, by the applicability of the general liability coverage of the tortfeasor, if he has such coverage; thus many of the litigated cases have arisen from the general liability carrier's attempt to invoke the "other insurance" of the automobile liability carrier rather than the tortfeasor's search for insurance protection.

Changes in the 1966 automobile liability form apparently were intended to deny coverage in some typical circumstances of injury to an employee of the named insured caused while the insured vehicle is being loaded or unloaded by one otherwise qualifying as an additional insured. In addition to the "employee of the insured" exclusion, the 1966 form contains a provision that excludes as additional insureds any person "with respect to bodily injury or property damage arising out of the loading or unloading   .   .   ." of the insured vehicle except "(1) a lessee or borrower of the automobile, or (2) an employee of the named insured or of such lessee or borrower .   .   .   ." [14] Apparently this eliminates, too, the possibility of

---

(1967); Greaves v. Public Serv. Mut. Ins. Co., 5 N.Y.2d 120, 155 N.E.2d 390, 181 N.Y.S.2d 489 (1959); Cimarron Ins. Co. v. Travelers Ins. Co., 224 Ore. 57, 355 P.2d 742 (1960); American Gen. Ins. Co. v. Commercial Std. Ins. Co., 455 S.W.2d 714 (Tex.1970), *overruling* Transport Ins. Co. v. Standard Oil Co., 161 Tex. 93, 337 S.W.2d 284 (1960). *Cf.* Lackey v. Virginia Surety Co., 209 Va. 713, 167 S.E.2d 131 (1969) (action for damage to named insured's automobile sustained in collision with another of named insured's automobiles while driven by employee; coverage). See also Western Cas. & Sur. Co. v. Teel, 391 F.2d 764 (10th Cir. 1968), 34 A.L.R.3d 1387 (1970) (child helping employed mother at laundry was not an employee within meaning

of employee-of-insured exclusion of non-automobile liability policy).

12. *E.g.*, Michigan Mut. Liab. Co. v. Continental Cas. Co., 297 F.2d 208 (7th Cir. 1961); Kelly v. State Auto. Ins. Ass'n, 288 F.2d 734 (6th Cir. 1961); G. C. Kohlmier, Inc. v. Mollenhauer, 273 Minn. 126, 140 N.W.2d 47 (1966); Benton v. Canal Ins. Co., 241 Miss. 493, 130 So.2d 840 (1961); Pennsylvania Mfrs. Ass'n Ins. Co. v. Aetna Cas. & Sur. Ins. Co., 426 Pa. 453, 233 A.2d 548 (1967).

13. See § 3.10 *supra* concerning subrogation generally.

14. See Appendix G *infra* for the complete phrasing of the exclusion.

coverage for injuries to uninvolved bystanders caused by negligence of a person not within the two excepted groups; the questionable distinction between injury to employees of the named insured and injury to uninvolved bystanders is thus bypassed.

§ 4.9(d) UNINSURED MOTORIST COVERAGE

The uninsured motorist coverage of the automobile insurance policy is a hybrid coverage. It is fault-based like liability insurance, but first-party like accident insurance.

This coverage, aimed at meeting one of the problems of uninsured losses,[1] was evolved in response to pressures for reform of the automobile accident reparations system.[2] Most states have enacted legislation either requiring that it be included in every automobile liability insurance policy or requiring at least that it be offered to the policyholder.[3]

Uninsured motorist coverage protects named insureds and certain others, primarily members of a named insured's household, against loss from inability to collect valid claims in tort against uninsured motorists. The definition of uninsured motorist ordinarily includes hit-and-run drivers as well.[4]

Despite the inclusion of an arbitration clause in policy forms [5] the uninsured motorist coverage has spawned an extraordinary amount of litigation, in trial and appellate courts as well.[6] Both for this reason and because of its relation to automobile insurance reform, it seems destined for major modification.

1. See § 8.6(e) *infra.*

2. As pressure was increasing in 1955 for the adoption of compulsory insurance in New York, insurance industry representatives were actively opposing such legislation. Keeton & O'Connell, Basic Protection for the Traffic Victim 91–102, 111 (1965). In this setting, "a group of stock companies offered a liability insurance policy endorsement providing benefits for guests in the policyholder's car, and for the policyholder and members of his family in the car or elsewhere, in the event of injuries for which the driver or owner of an uninsured car is legally liable. [New York Times, Oct. 5, 1955, pp. 1, 25.] A number of mutual companies forthwith offered an endorsement providing benefits for the policyholder and members of his family injured in an accident with an uninsured car, regardless of legal liability of the uninsured driver or owner. [New York Times Oct. 6, 1955, pp. 20, 31.] Out of this activity came a new coverage, now generally called uninsured motorist coverage." Keeton, Compensation Systems—The Search for a Viable Alternative to Negligence Law 7 (1969), reprinted in Seavey, Keeton & Keeton, Cases and Materials on the Law of Torts 225–226 (Supp.1970) (footnotes accompanying the quoted passage inserted in brackets here). See also Widiss, A Guide to Uninsured Motorist Coverage §§ 1.7–1.10 (1969).

3. *Id.* § 3.1. See also Notman, *A Decennial Study of Uninsured Motorist Endorsements*, 1968 Ins.L.J. 22.

4. See Generally Widiss, A Guide to Uninsured Motorist Coverage §§ 2.40–2.44 (1969). Concerning the physical-contact requirement, see § 5.2(b) n.13 *infra.*

5. See § 7.3(c) *infra.*

6. See Laufer, *Embattled Victims of the Uninsured: In Court with New York's MVAIC, 1959–1969,* 19 Buffalo L.Rev. 471 (1970); Laufer, *Insurance Against Lack of Insurance? A Dissent from the Uninsured Motorist Endorsement,* 1969 Duke L.J. 227.

SECTION 4.10 NONFAULT INSURANCE

*Skip
246-248*

Most forms of insurance provide for payment of benefits upon the occurrence of described events and without regard to whether those events were caused by the fault of some person, either the insured or another. Thus, most insurance is, in a broad sense, nonfault insurance. But the term "nonfault" (or "no-fault") insurance is often used in a narrower sense to signify a type of insurance designed to replace, to some extent at least, the system of negligence law and liability insurance that came to maturity in the nineteenth and twentieth centuries. The development of nonfault insurance in this narrower sense was an outgrowth of public dissatisfaction with the performance of the system for compensation of losses suffered in traffic accidents, which in turn led to a succession of legislative measures over the span of several decades.

Among the varied coverages in the automobile insurance package, the liability insurance coverages (Bodily Injury and Property Damage) were the principal targets of legislative attention. They were the chief coverages involved in financial responsibility legislation generated in the first half of the twentieth century and as well in more far-reaching proposals for reform advanced soon after mid-century. But more of the coverages of the automobile policy are nonfault insurance in the broad sense of that term. The principal coverages of this type in use in the late 1960's were collision coverage (for damage to the insured vehicle, with occasional extension to damage to other vehicles),[1] medical payments coverage,[2] and comprehensive coverage (including fire, theft, and a variety of other risks).[3] Loss of income and disability coverages for motoring victims were marketed only to a very limited extent.[4] In general, interests protected by these coverages have been confined to named insureds and others closely associated with them, such as members of their households, authorized drivers, and guest passengers.

It was in the latter part of the 1960's that proposals for dramatic expansion of the use of nonfault automobile insurance coverages became the center of an active controversy over reform of the automobile accident reparations system.[5]

Puerto Rico adopted a state-insurance plan of nonfault coverage, effective January 1, 1970, providing extensive medical benefits and

1. See § 2.11(b) (4) *supra*.

2. See § 2.11(b) (1) and (c) *supra*.

3. For common policy provisions concerning all these nonfault automobile insurance coverages, see Appendix H *infra*.

4. See generally Keeton & O'Connell, Basic Protection for the Traffic Victim 121–123 (1965).

5. See, *e.g.*, N.Y.Ins.Dep't, Report, Automobile Insurance . . . For Whose Benefit? (1970); Keeton & O'Connell, Basic Protection for the Traffic Victim (1965). Numerous proposals are summarized in Keeton, Compensation Systems—The Search for a Viable Alternative to Negligence Law 11–23 (1969), reprinted with additions in Seavey, Keeton & Keeton, Cases and Materials on the Law of Torts 229–250 (Supp.1970).

limited nonfault benefits of other types while preserving tort actions for larger claims.[6]   Though the level of nonfault coverage is relatively low and tort actions are preserved for larger claims, the Puerto Rican legislation marked the adoption of one of the most radical of the various proposals in another sense; it resorts to state rather than private enterprise to provide the nonfault insurance.

In August of 1970 Massachusetts became the first state of the United States to enact a nonfault automobile insurance law.[7]   Retaining the long-standing requirement that Massachusetts motorists carry automobile bodily injury liability insurance with limits not lower than $5,000 per person and $10,000 per accident, the nonfault statute adds $2,000 of nonfault insurance to the compulsory coverage. Under the terms of the new coverage, nonfault benefits extend to the following: reasonable expenses incurred within two years from the date of the accident for necessary medical and hospital services, without deduction for benefits from other sources; costs of substitute services—that is, payments to persons outside the family for services that would have been performed for the family by the injured person had he not been injured; net loss of wages or equivalent for employed persons, including those self-employed, and net loss of earning power for unemployed persons, subject to a limit such that the sum of these nonfault benefits and payments under a wage (or wage-equivalent) continuation program shall not exceed 75 per cent of the injured person's average weekly wage (or equivalent) for the year immediately preceding the accident.

The Massachusetts statute declares that the nonfault benefits are granted in lieu of damages otherwise recoverable in tort, and it permits an injured person to recover tort damages for pain and suffering only if one of the following conditions is satisfied: the reasonable and necessary expenses for medical and hospital services exceed $500; the injury causes death; the injury consists in whole or in part of loss of a body member, or permanent and serious disfigurement, or loss of sight or hearing as defined in specified sections of the workmen's compensation law, or a fracture.

The act also requires that the insurer offer the policyholder a deductible under which he would give up all nonfault benefits for himself, or for himself and members of his household, to the extent of the deductible he selects among the figures $250, $500, $1,000, and $2,000. Thus a policyholder may elect to give up all nonfault benefits by electing the $2,000 deductible. The stated purpose of the provision was to allow persons with extraordinarily good coverages under other policies or wage continuation plans to avoid double coverage

---

6. See Aponte & Denenberg, *The Automobile Problem in Puerto Rico: Dimensions and Proposed Solution*, 35 J.Risk & Ins. 227 (1968), reprinted with updating amendments in 1968 Ins.L.J. 884; An Addendum, 35 J.Risk & Ins. 637 (1968).

7. Mass.Laws 1970 ch. 670 as amended by Mass.Laws 1970 ch. 744; Mass. Genl.Laws ch. 90, §§ 34A, 34D, 34M, 34N, ch. 175, §§ 22E–22H, 113B, 113C, ch. 231, § 6D (Supp.1970).

and reduce their automobile insurance costs accordingly. The election of a deductible does not affect tort actions, however. That is, any person electing the deductible is subject to the same reductions of his tort rights as would apply if he had not elected the deductible.

The act does not extend either the nonfault benefits or the partial tort exemption to property damage. As this book goes to press, however, proposals for amendment of the Massachusetts act abound, and extension of the nonfault system to the area of damage to vehicles is perhaps the most widely supported of all the proposals advanced.[8]

SECTION 4.11 | INTERESTS IN LIFE INSURANCE

§ 4.11(a) GENERALLY

The principal rights created by life insurance policies are the rights to borrow from the insurer on the security of the policy, to surrender the policy for cash, to receive matured endowment benefits, to receive dividends (under mutual policies commonly, and occasionally under others), to change the beneficiary, to elect among settlement options, and to receive proceeds upon death of the person whose life is insured. Usually the ownership of these various rights is divided. Typically a person obtains the policy on his own life, designating another to receive proceeds upon his death and reserving all other rights to himself. Sometimes, however, ownership of the rights under a life insurance policy is fractionated further. This may occur by operation of law under a community property system.[1] It may also result from an assignment, whether to serve tax and estate planning purposes or merely to secure a loan.[2]

§ 4.11(b) COMMUNITY PROPERTY AND LIFE INSURANCE

Ordinarily community property law does not affect the power of the person designated by the policy as holder of a certain right to enforce that right in a proceeding against the insurer and does not affect the protection that the insurer receives upon taking a release from that person.[3] But in many situations the holder of the right in a policy that is classified as community property is, with respect to its exercise, responsible to the other spouse and persons claiming

---

8. See generally Keeton & O'Connell, *Alternative Paths Toward Nonfault Automobile Insurance*, 71 Colum.L. Rev. 241 (1971).

1. See § 4.11(b) *infra.*

2. See § 4.11(d) *infra.*

3. There may be exceptions to this generalization. See, *e.g.,* Swift, *House Bill 900 and Your Life Insurance Pol-* *icy*, 20 Texas B.J. 691, 722 (1957), suggesting that in Texas, at the time Swift was writing, if the insurance contract vested in the wife the legal title to rights under a policy that was classified as community, it might be that only the husband could dispose of those rights since Tex.Rev.Civ.Stat. Ann. art. 4619, then in effect, provided that during marriage community property "may be disposed of by the husband only . . . ."

~~through such spo~~use. For example, "all of the decided cases in community property jurisdictions agree that if the husband takes out during the marriage a policy on his own life payable at his death to his estate, or to his executors, administrators, or assigns, and pays the premiums with community funds, when the marriage is dissolved by the death of the husband, the proceeds received by the husband's legal representatives belong to the community." [4] Also, "when the wife is named the beneficiary in a policy taken out by the husband upon his own life and paid for with community funds, the proceeds received by the wife at the husband's death are her separate property. . . . By making the policy payable to the wife, the cases usually reason, the husband has manifested an intent to make a gift to her of the proceeds." [5]

Community property laws vary considerably among the states recognizing the concept and so do decisions concerning the impact of the laws on rights in insurance policies. The varied rules are not developed in this text.[6]

§ 4.11(c) BENEFICIARY CLAUSES OF LIFE INSURANCE POLICIES

Before twentieth century developments in policy forms, the beneficiary clauses of life insurance policies often simply designated a named person or persons to receive the policy proceeds in cash and included no alternative disposition of the policy proceeds payable upon death of the person whose life was insured. At present, however, policy forms commonly reserve to the policyholder the right to change the beneficiary and provide in some detail for contingent beneficiaries, designated by relationship to the person whose life is insured; usually the ultimate designee is the estate of the person whose life is insured. Moreover, rather than merely providing for cash payment of the policy proceeds, current forms ordinarily offer the applicant for life insurance a wide choice concerning modes of settlement; the beneficiary clause of his policy may be tailor-made to his estate plan. Most of the considerations that bear on this choice are not peculiarly insurance considerations; rather, they are much like the questions one faces in drafting a will. Insurance serves a unique function in the estate plan, however, because it may provide a significant part of the assets of the estate, especially in the case of death at

4. Huie, *Community Property Laws as Applied to Life Insurance*, 17 Texas L.Rev. 121 (1939).

5. *Id.* at 123–124.

6. See Huie, *Community Property Laws as Applied to Life Insurance*, 17 Texas L.Rev. 121 (1939), 18 Texas L.Rev. 121 (1940); Ray, *Life Insurance, Community Property and Death Taxes in Texas*, 26 Texas B.J. 835 (1963);

Thurman, *Federal Estate and Gift Taxation of Community Property Life Insurance*, 9 Stan.L.Rev. 239 (1957); Annot., 168 A.L.R. 342 (1947). See also Abel, Barry, Halsted & Marsh, *Rights of Surviving Spouse in Property Acquired by a Decedent While Domiciled Outside California*, 47 Calif.L.Rev. 211 (1959); Fritz, *Survivorship Agreements Between Spouses*, 24 Texas B.J. 395 (1961).

an early age. Even in cases involving substantial properties of other types, insurance may provide an important fund of ready cash.[7]

A plan for use of life insurance proceeds is sometimes expressed completely in a policy endorsement composed of a combination of printed provisions and clauses especially drafted for the particular case. At other times, the beneficiary clause or endorsement of the policy provides for payment to a specified person, and a separate document (*e.g.*, a contract, a will, or an inter vivos trust instrument) or group of documents completes the plan. The latter arrangement, though having disadvantages in other respects, allows greater flexibility in the disposition of the insurance proceeds, since the settlor may act to establish or amend the arrangement without the concurrence of the insurer in all the details. The insurer may require that the beneficiary clause of the policy include a provision protecting it from further liability upon payment to the specified person [8] but usually does not insist on having the separate documents submitted for its approval. It has become common to use an arrangement of this type in buy-and-sell agreements among business associates, funded by life insurance; the survivors acquire the interests of a deceased associate, and insurance on the life of the deceased provides ready cash that makes it possible for the deceased's beneficiaries to be compensated without withdrawal of needed cash from the business. Tax considerations have greatly influenced the shaping of such agreements.

§ 4.11(d) ASSIGNMENTS; PRIORITY AMONG BENE-FICIARIES AND ASSIGNEES

In the absence of assignment of a life insurance policy one who is designated as beneficiary of the policy is ordinarily entitled to the proceeds payable upon death of the person whose life is insured. But if the policy has been assigned the question arises whether the assignee is entitled to all or part of the proceeds with priority over the beneficiary.

As to policies not reserving to the policyholder a right to change the beneficiary—a situation more common in the past than currently —it has been held generally that no assignment of the policy could impair the beneficiary's rights without his consent.[1] The development and recognition of this rule led to a demand for policies reserving greater rights to the policyholder to change beneficiaries or to make assignments that would be effective to give the assignees priority over beneficiaries. From the point of view of an outside observer, the reponse to this demand may appear curious, almost as if designed for ambiguity rather than clarity. The companies developed forms of

---

7. See generally Wojta, *Life Insurance Funding of Stock Purchase Agreements*, 48 Neb.L.Rev. 961 (1969).

8. Compare the "facility of payment" clause of industrial policies, § 1.3(f) *supra*.

1. See, *e.g.*, Davis v. Modern Indus. Bank, 279 N.Y. 405, 409, 18 N.E.2d 639, 640 (1939), 135 A.L.R. 1035, 1037 (1941), characterizing this rule as "the law in every jurisdiction in this country except Wisconsin."

change-of-beneficiary clauses and assignment clauses that not only established different formalities for assigning the policy and changing the beneficiary—surely a defensible arrangement—but also did not say whose claim to death proceeds is superior—that of the beneficiary or that of the assignee—in commonly recurring factual situations.[2] In these circumstances, by the great weight of precedent, the assignee of the policy takes ahead of the beneficiary.[3] Thus he recovers the entire death proceeds unless his assignment is for a lesser share, as is often the case when the assignment is made to secure a debt.[4] There is a difference of opinion, however, with respect to whether a purported assignment that does not comply with the formalities described in the assignment clause of the policy may nevertheless be effective to give the assignee a claim superior to that of the beneficiary when the interests of the company are not thereby prejudiced. The dispute may be characterized as one over whether the formalities described in the assignment clause are intended only for the protection of the company, and may be waived by it, or instead are intended to protect interests of the beneficiary as well, with the consequence that he may successfully challenge a purported assignment not complying with those formalities. The forms in use have been little help in resolving this dispute. There is precedent for the view that the assignee should prevail.[5] This rule is fortified by anal-

2. Compare the more explicit clauses of Appendix E, *infra*, with the following clauses, taken from a form still widely used as late as 1960 and reproduced in Keeton, Basic Insurance Law, Appendix E (1960):

"*Assignment.* No assignment of this policy shall be binding on the Company unless a duplicate thereof be filed with the Company at its Home Office. The Company assumes no responsibility as to the validity of any assignment. Any assignment shall be subject to any indebtedness to the Company on account of or secured by this policy."

"*Change of Beneficiary.* The beneficiary designation may be changed at any time, and from time to time, by written request filed at the Home Office of the Company and accompanied by this policy for endorsement. The new designation shall be subject to any existing assignment and shall take effect only upon endorsement hereon by the Company at its Home Office. If there is no beneficiary surviving at the death of the Insured, then, unless otherwise provided herein, the proceeds of this policy shall be paid to the person or persons who, upon proof by affidavit or other written evidence satisfactory to the Company, appear to be the then living lawful bodily and legally-adopted child or children of the Insured, equally if more than one, or, if none, to the executors or administrators of the estate of the Insured. The words 'child' and 'children' are used herein to refer to only the first generation. The right to revoke and change any beneficiary designation is reserved to the Insured unless otherwise specified herein."

3. *E.g.*, Davis v. Modern Indus. Bank, 279 N.Y. 405, 18 N.E.2d 639 (1939), 135 A.L.R. 1035 (1941); McAllen State Bank v. Texas Bank & Trust Co., 433 S.W.2d 167 (Tex.1968). The beneficiary, however, may have a claim against the estate of the decedent for an amount equal to the part of the policy proceeds applied in discharge of a debt of the decedent. See, *e.g.*, Rountree v. Frazee, 282 Ala. 142, 209 So.2d 424 (1968). *But cf. In re* Estate of Green, 415 Pa. 161, 202 A.2d 17 (1964). See Annot., 91 A.L.R.2d 496 (1963).

4. See § 4.11(f) *infra*.

5. Farmers' State Bank v. Kelley, 155 Ga. 733, 118 S.E. 197 (1923). *Cf.* Abruzise v. Sposata, 306 Mass. 151, 27 N.E.2d 722 (1940). See generally 2A Appleman, Insurance Law §§ 1193, 1196, 1219–1221, 1246–1250 (rev. ed. 1966).

ogy to a rule of assignability of the rights of "third-party owners" of interests in life insurance policies,[6] and, at least when it can be said that there has been substantial though not strict compliance with formalities, this result is supported also by a large body of precedent regarding formalities for change of beneficiary.[7] Moreover, this rule results in fulfilling a clearly manifested intention of the policyholder, even when expressed in a way not complying with formalities described in the policy. Also, it results in free assignability, thereby permitting the policyholder to use a life insurance policy as an asset available to serve his needs.

Weighing against the public interest in free assignability of life insurance policies by informal means are dangers of the type that have given rise to statutes of frauds. In response to this problem a statute was enacted in New York, rendering unenforceable any "contract to assign or an assignment .   .   . of a life .   .   . insurance policy, or a promise .   .   . to name a beneficiary of any such policy .   .   ." unless the agreement or a memorandum of it is in writing.[8] A leading New York case arising under the statute [9] poses the familiar questions, first, whether apparent injustice in particular cases from rigid enforcement of a statute of frauds is too great a price to pay for the prevention of other injustices at which such a statute is aimed and, second, whether the statute can be properly construed as allowing exceptions for oral agreements the genuineness of which is attested by some independent evidence. In this instance, the independent evidence, which might be regarded as analogous to part performance, included payment of the premiums by the plaintiff, delivery of the policy to the plaintiff, and continued possession by her until surreptitious removal by the deceased's sister and the deceased. The issue reached the Court of Appeals in a procedural context most favorable to the plaintiff, since her complaint had been dismissed in the trial court. Taking her allegations as true for the purpose of decision of the issue presented, the Court of Appeals sustained her contention that her claim was not barred by the Statute of Frauds. Three of the seven judges dissented, contending that the arrangement alleged by the plaintiff was precisely the kind the statute rendered void.[10]

6. Concerning assignments by "third-party owners" generally, see Dibrell, *Life Insurance Policies—Transfers by Third Party Owners*, 4 Forum 25 (ABA Section Ins., Neg. & Comp.L. 1968). Concerning rights of creditor-assignees generally, see § 4.11(f) *infra*.

7. Concerning the rule of substantial compliance with respect to change of beneficiary, see § 4.11(e) *infra*.

8. N.Y.Laws 1943, ch. 104, carried forward as N.Y.Gen.Obligations Law § 5–701(9) (McKinney 1964).

9. Katzman v. Aetna Life Ins. Co., 309 N.Y. 197, 128 N.E.2d 307 (1955).

10. 309 N.Y. at 205, 128 N.E.2d at 311.

§ 4.11(e) CHANGING BENEFICIARIES

The designation of the beneficiary of a life insurance contract may be made irrevocable except with the consent of the beneficiary, and forms not reserving the right to change the beneficiary have been construed generally as having this effect.[1] But most policies now in effect and most new contracts being made reserve to the policyholder (usually the person whose life is insured) the right to change the beneficiary by formalities specified in the change-of-beneficiary clause. Ordinarily the formalities include, first, the policyholder's written request to the company at its home office for a change of beneficiary, in a form approved by the company, second, delivery to the company of the original policy or proof that it has been lost, and, third, the company's endorsement of the change upon the original policy, or upon the substitute issued in lieu of a lost policy. When the formalities prescribed for a change of beneficiary are fully observed, the change is effective against a person claiming under an earlier designation, even though the change was made without his consent or even without his knowledge.[2]

The rights of rival claimants are less clearly defined, however, if the policyholder attempts to change beneficiaries by a procedure not complying with the formalities specified in the policy.[3] Cases involving irregular attempts to change beneficiaries present sharply a conflict between the interests served by insistence upon formalism with its attendant certainty, on the one hand, and the interests served by enforcement of intention, however manifested, on the other.[4] If one could always be confident of the fairness of inferences drawn from

---

1. *E.g.*, Garner v. Germania Life Ins. Co., 110 N.Y. 266, 18 N.E. 130 (1888).

2. Contractual agreements, however, between the policyholder and the original beneficiary (or another for his benefit) have been held to create a vested equitable interest in the insurance proceeds superior to the claim of the subsequently designated beneficiary. See, *e.g.*, Kelly v. Layton, 309 F.2d 611 (8th Cir. 1962) (applying Missouri law; insured, to induce divorced wife not to levy on arrears in support payments, agreed not to change designation of daughter as beneficiary but subsequently filed a "lost policy" form with the company and named his second wife as beneficiary; held, daughter entitled to proceeds); Yates v. Yates, 272 F.2d 52 (5th Cir. 1959) (applying Florida law; insured was obligated by property settlement in divorce from first wife to pay off mortgage on home retained by wife and to have his estate assume the obligation if he died before the debt was retired, and he promised to have insurance made payable to his estate for that purpose; held, second wife named as beneficiary in policies and named as executrix in will omitting any reference to mortgage obligation took subject to first wife's equitable interest, measured by outstanding debt on home at time of insured's death plus interest); Lee v. Preiss, 18 Wis.2d 109, 118 N.W.2d 104 (1962) (insured, to prevent action for nonsupport, orally agreed with former wife not to change designation of her and children as beneficiaries; held, agreement gave wife and children a cause of action for equitable relief against subsequently designated beneficiary).

3. Compare the issue of validity of an assignment not complying with specified formalities, § 4.11(d) *supra*.

4. Concerning the conflict between formalism and flexibility generally, see § 1.6 *supra*.

informal evidence of intention, including the inference that the policyholder made a deliberate choice without undue influence, he would surely prefer the rule giving effect to intention over that giving effect only to a formal expression of intention. But the former rule involves great uncertainty and the prospect of wasteful litigation, as well as the risk of mistakes of the fact finders in determining what the intention was. Formalism protects against these risks. That degree of formalism implicit in a rule requiring at least substantial compliance with a policy provision concerning change of beneficiary seems well justified. The majority of the decisions in point adopt this position.[5] The predictability of results under this line of authority is complicated by the fact that "substantial compliance" is a fact-oriented, evaluative concept. That is, various courts using this same concept as a guide line may reach quite inconsistent conclusions about the meaning given to the concept in its practical application to cases presented for decision.[6] Thus, sharp conflict may arise as to what courses of conduct are sufficient to amount to substantial compliance. To predict reliably, then, one must not only consider whether the precedents for his jurisdiction support the "substantial compliance" rule but also, if so, what is the meaning of "substantial compliance" implicit in those precedents and how that meaning comes to bear upon the facts of the case at hand.

It has been argued that change-of-beneficiary clauses are inserted in policies solely for the company's protection against rival claims and that the original beneficiary has no standing to contest the effectiveness of an attempted change of beneficiary when the company waives its right to insist upon the formalities specified.[7] Without

---

5. *E.g.*, Continental Assur. Co. v. Platke, 295 F.2d 571 (7th Cir. 1961) (Illinois law); Equitable Life Assur. Soc'y v. Hitchcock, 270 Mich. 72, 258 N.W. 214 (1935), 106 A.L.R. 591 (1937); Boehne v. Guardian Life Ins. Co., 224 Minn. 57, 28 N.W.2d 54 (1947); Fidelity Union Life Ins. Co. v. Methven, 162 Tex. 323, 346 S.W.2d 797 (1961); Kotch v. Kotch, 151 Tex. 471, 251 S.W.2d 520 (1952). See 2 Appleman, Insurance Law § 943 (rev. ed. 1966), 2A *id.* §§ 1021, 1022, 1063; Annot., 19 A.L.R.2d 5 (1951).

6. Concerning fact-oriented, evaluative issues generally, see § 1.6 *supra*.

7. See, *e.g.*, Davis v. Modern Indus. Bank, 279 N.Y. 405, 18 N.E.2d 639 (1939), 135 A.L.R. 1035 (1941). In *Davis*, the insured had effected a valid assignment to a creditor "as his interest may appear." After the insured's death a dispute arose between the named beneficiary (the insured's widow) and the creditor-assignee as to the creditor's rights to the proceeds. The beneficiary contended that the as-

signment did not entitle the creditor to any of the proceeds because there was no formal designation of the creditor as a beneficiary and because the assignment itself did not carry the effect of entitlement to proceeds. The court held for the creditor-assignee on the grounds that the named beneficiary had no right to question the deficiency in meeting the formal requirements of a change of beneficiary when the insurance company had not done so.

In the context of conflicting claims of prior and subsequently designated beneficiaries, it has often been stated that the policy provisions were primarily (or even solely) for the protection of the company. See, *e.g.*, Continental Assur. Co. v. Platke, 295 F.2d 571 (7th Cir. 1961) (Illinois law; interpleader action); Sears v. Austin, 292 F.2d 690 (9th Cir.), *cert. denied*, 368 U.S. 929 (1961) (federal law; interpleader action); Fidelity Union Life Ins. Co. v. Methven, 162 Tex. 323, 346 S.W.2d 797 (1961).

doubt, protection of the company's interests, was a significant and perhaps even exclusive objective of company draftsmen.   But to declare it the sole objective of the specification of formalities in the change-of-beneficiary clause, as part of a contract, would be to disregard the fact that, viewed by the usual standards for determining the manifested intent of contractual documents, the clause is subject to another reasonable interpretation.   That is, it may be read as being aimed also at serving the interests of the policyholder (protecting his considered choice of a beneficiary against frustration through enforcement of a supposed choice inferred from informal evidence) and the interests of the third party beneficiary (protecting against his being superseded by unreliable evidence of change in the policyholder's intention).[8]   This interpretation is fortified by a public interest in requiring a set of formalities for changing beneficiaries, analogous to but not identical with the public interest in requiring a set of formalities, though a different set, for designating beneficiaries of one's estate.[9]   Also this refusal to read the change-of-beneficiary provision as one solely for the company's protection is supported by the availability of interpleader, which seems an adequate, though less than perfect, protection for the company.

In light of support in precedents for the proposition that the original beneficiary has standing to contest the effectiveness of an attempted informal change of beneficiary, insurers are subject to a risk of double liability.   An insurer might be held liable to an original beneficiary after having previously paid policy proceeds to the person

8.   *Cf.* Kotch v. Kotch, 151 Tex. 471, 477, 251 S.W.2d 520, 523 (1952): "But there is also merit in our existing view, which, while disclaiming to recognize a 'vested' right in the named beneficiary and while not denying that the policy provisions may be waived by the insurer, yet regards the matter as one of contract between insurer and insured for the benefit of a third party—the named beneficiary— and apparently represents a policy to forestall belated, informal treatment of these serious economic affairs, which is generally suspicious in appearance and nearly always confusing and litigious in result."

In Fidelity Union Life Ins. Co. v. Methven, 162 Tex. 323, 346 S.W.2d 797 (1961), the court decided against the original beneficiary, holding that the change of beneficiary requirements were for the benefit of the insurer and had been waived by the insurer *during the lifetime* of the insured.

9.   *Cf.* Stone v. Stephens, 155 Ohio St. 595, 99 N.E.2d 766 (1951), 25 A.L.R.2d 992 (1952), involving an attempt to

change the beneficiary by will—a procedure that might seem formal enough in one sense because it complied with the requirements for wills.   But it failed to comply with the terms of the change-of-beneficiary clause.   The court noted the public interest in having insurers pay the beneficiary of a life insurance policy as soon as possible after death of the person whose life was insured, and remarked: "There is sound reason both in law and in public policy for holding that a change of an insurance policy beneficiary by last will and testament of the insured is ineffective unless authorized by the terms of the policy." 155 Ohio St. at 600, 99 N.E.2d at 769, 25 A.L.R.2d at 996.   *But cf.*, Sears v. Austin, 292 F.2d 690 (9th Cir.), *cert. denied*, 368 U.S. 929 (1961) (designation of beneficiary of Federal Employees' Group Life Insurance policy by holographic will held valid under Federal law).   Of course a policy designating the insured's estate as the beneficiary enables him to provide in his will for the disposition of the proceeds of the policy.

designated in an attempted change of beneficiary that not only failed to comply with the formalities specified in the policy but also failed even to measure up to those lesser formalities implicit in a judicially created standard such as "substantial compliance." The magnitude of this risk could be affected by a court's position with respect to whether the insurer's action in endorsing or declining to endorse a policy as requested by a policyholder is relevant to the issue of substantial compliance with the policy requirements. It is the nature of the policyholder's request, rather than the insurer's response, that bears upon the reliability of evidence of the policyholder's intention. And it would seem, therefore, that the nature of the policyholder's request should be decisive of the issue of substantial compliance. Moreover, as a general principle it is undesirable to have rules of law that permit one party to have a power to allocate burdens or benefits between two other parties without responsibility for its exercise; such an unpoliced power is an open invitation not only to arbitrary action but also to corruption.[10] Thus, if it is held that the company's response to the policyholder's informal request is decisive of rival claims, it should also be held that the company is subject to liability at least for bad faith in exercising this power and perhaps also for negligence. Such a combination of rules seems less desirable than a criterion for substantial compliance based on the nature of the policyholder's steps toward change of beneficiary rather than the company's response. This would not mean that the company's response was totally irrelevant, however; in those situations in which a sequence of communications occurred, it might be necessary to take into account company responses to assess properly the significance of later communications of the policyholder.

Recognition of the standing of the original beneficiary to contest the effectiveness of an irregular attempt to change the beneficiary also implies that the duly designated beneficiary has something more than a mere expectancy during the life of the insured, since he benefits from some qualifications as to the kinds of attempted changes of beneficiary that will be effective. This conclusion is not necessarily inconsistent with the theory that it is the interest of the insured, and not that of the duly designated beneficiary, that the court is seeking to protect by introducing the requirement of such formalities; it might be said that the beneficiary is aided incidentally by a requirement that is established for the purpose of protecting the insured's considered choice against frustration by evidence of belated and informal indications of an intent contrary to the considered choice. But, as has been indicated, there is support too for the theory that the rule allowing the beneficiary to contest the change is aimed in part at protecting his interests rather than merely accomplishing this result coincidentally.

In a line of cases concerning National Service Life Insurance it has been said that noncompliance with specified formalities for

10. See § 4.8(d) n.4 *supra*.

change of beneficiary is of less significance under that type of coverage than under private contracts, because the courts should "brush aside all legal technicalities in order to effectuate the manifest intention of the insured."[11] This is a proposition of doubtful validity. The choice courts make for some degree of formalism in preference to a rule for enforcing even the most informally expressed intention is based on consideration of the interests of the policyholder and the potential claimants and not merely the interests of the insurer. Thus one may be disserving the interests of the serviceman by brushing aside all formalities—which one views as "technicalities" only after deciding that they are not useful requirements. Perhaps a different rule for National Service Life Insurance cases can be justified, however, because of a greater likelihood of an ill-considered designation by the serviceman in the first instance, in view of the varied circumstances under which the insurance forms are completed and because of the greater likelihood of changes of circumstances and the greater difficulties of communicating both rapidly and formally the serviceman's desire that the beneficiary be changed.[12]

§ 4.11(f) CREDITORS AS BENEFICIARIES OR ASSIGNEES

It often happens that a creditor of a life insurance policyholder is designated as a beneficiary or as an assignee of the policy. Questions may arise with respect to his rights under the policy, including rights in proceeds of the policy at the death of the person whose life is insured.

In relation to death proceeds, ordinarily no special problem is presented by designation of a creditor as beneficiary or assignee if the proceeds do not exceed the amount of the debt, including any accumulation of interest and charges. If the debt is less than the policy proceeds, however, it often happens that another person claims to be entitled to all policy proceeds in excess of the debt.

---

11. United States v. Pahmer, 238 F.2d 431, 433 (2d Cir. 1956), quoting from Roberts v. United States, 157 F.2d 906, 909 (4th Cir.), cert. denied, 330 U.S. 829 (1946). See Annot., 2 A.L.R. 2d 489 (1948).

12. Without regard to the relevance of such special considerations, the National Service Life Insurance cases—and, specifically, the quotation from Pahmer in the text, supra—were relied on in Sears v. Austin, 292 F.2d 690 (9th Cir.), cert. denied, 368 U.S. 929 (1961), to validate a beneficiary designation by holographic will made by a former Internal Revenue Service employee under his Federal Employees Group Life Insurance. Before making that will, the insured had not designated any beneficiary; his group certificate stated that, if no specific beneficiary was designated according to the prescribed procedure, the proceeds would pass, in his case, to his children in equal shares. After the insured's death, the children as well as the beneficiary designated in the will (an unrelated woman who had apparently provided the insured with nursing services) claimed the proceeds. In validating the designation by will, the court held that the policy formalities were for the benefit of the insurer only, which in this case had interpleaded the rival claimants rather than rely on the protection of the provisions. See also Annot., 2 A.L.R.3d 1141 (1965).

One argument commonly advanced by the non-creditor claimant is that the designation of the creditor as beneficiary or assignee was intended as security for payment of the debt and no more. If such an intention is manifested, it will surely be enforced. Thus, validity of this type of contention turns on construction of such evidence as is available regarding manifested intention. Ordinarily the document designating the creditor as beneficiary or assignee is the principal evidence of the policyholder's intention. If it explicitly limits the designation as one securing payment of the debt, that limitation will be enforced. Often, however, the document lacks any such explicit provision. In these circumstances, the creditor's claim that his rights in death proceeds are not limited to the amount of the debt is ordinarily stronger if he was designated as beneficiary of the policy than if designated as assignee, provided no one else was designated as assignee.[1] This conclusion is supported by the fact that it is common to make an assignment as security for a debt but uncommon to change the beneficiary for this limited purpose. Thus, if no better indication of intent appears, a court is likely to infer that the policyholder who designated the creditor as beneficiary of the policy (even by a change-of-beneficiary endorsement, and a fortiori by an original designation) intended that his right to proceeds at death not be limited to the amount of the debt. But circumstances of the designation are surely relevant. For example, if it appears that the designation of the creditor was made by a change-of beneficiary endorsement at the time the policyholder obtained a loan from the creditor and that he had no other relationship with the creditor, it is perhaps a more compelling inference that the designation was made in this way because the creditor insisted upon it to avoid any doubt about the priority of his rights over those of the beneficiary, though not with the understanding that he would receive more than full payment of his debt, including interest and charges.[2]

It might be argued that, even if the intention is manifested that the creditor's interest in proceeds at death not be limited to the amount of the debt, as a matter of public policy he should not be allowed to recover more than that amount. Such an argument is based on the principle of indemnity. The weight of precedents appears to be against this position, however. In the first place, it is generally recognized that the person whose life is insured may designate anyone he wishes as beneficiary, without regard to insurable interest.[3] And even as to assignments, the majority rule favors free assignability of life insurance contracts to persons without insurable interest.[4] It may be, however, that despite the weight of precedents against en-

---

1. The reason for the proviso is that ordinarily an assignee's claim is prior in right to that of a beneficiary. See § 4.11(d) *supra*.

2. Perhaps a better way of accomplishing this assurance, from the point of view of the policyholder and the beneficiary at least, would be to have the beneficiary join in an assignment, acknowledging the priority of the assignee's rights, and to have the assignment specify that it is for security only.

3. See § 3.5(c) *supra*.

4. *Ibid*.

forcement of the principle of indemnity as a firm barrier against the creditor's being allowed an interest in excess of his debt, this principle has its influence as a factor bearing on construction of inexplicit documents.

Looking to results rather than theory, one finds that most of the decisions involving a creditor as beneficiary or assignee of a life insurance policy have, on the facts, allowed the creditor to retain for his own benefit only a sum equal to the debt, including interest and charges, among which are often included premiums paid to keep the policy in force.[5] But this preponderance of results might be attributed to the probability that most assignments to creditors are in fact so intended and are surrounded by indicia of this intent that influence decisions.   Thus this preponderance does not establish even that courts apply a rebuttable presumption of such an intention, much less that they apply an irrebuttable presumption.   Opinions that might be said to bear more directly on the question add up to a close split of authority as to whether a creditor who has taken out a policy on the life of his debtor (or is the beneficiary or assignee of a policy taken out by the debtor on his own life) may recover for his own benefit the full amount of the policy, even though it exceeds the debt, if that is found to be the intention manifested by the parties to the transaction.[6]

In an attempt to reconcile most of the apparently conflicting authorities on a basis that he thought acceptable in principle, Vance suggested that the creditor should have the entire recovery when it is he who obtains the policy; his theory was that the debtor then has no interest in the contract.[7]   But it would seem that the debtor and his successors should be accorded an interest, perhaps equitable in nature, at least whenever the understanding is that the insurance is obtained to secure the debt.   Whenever the policy is obtained as a part of the arrangements contemplated in the consummation of the original transaction (rather than being obtained by the creditor at a later time, at his own instance), the debtor in a sense bears the burden of the cost of the insurance, since the creditor's agreement to terms of the loan is influenced by the amount of the insurance premium he ex-

5. *E.g.*, Dunn v. Second Nat'l Bank, 131 Tex. 198, 113 S.W.2d 165, 115 A.L.R. 730 (1938).

6.   See, *e.g.*, Urquhart v. Alexander & Alexander, Inc., 218 Md. 405, 147 A.2d 213 (1958) and Forster v. Franklin Life Ins. Co., 135 Colo. 383, 311 P.2d 700 (1957), supporting the creditor's right to the entire policy proceeds, though they exceeded the indebtedness. See generally, Annot., 115 A.L. R. 741 (1938). Compare the two opinions in Albrent v. Spencer, 275 Wis. 127, 81 N.W.2d 555 (1957), and 3 Wis. 2d 273, 88 N.W.2d 333 (1958), adding up to the proposition that "any pur-

ported absolute assignment by a debtor to a creditor of a policy, which had previously been pledged as security to the creditor is only valid between the immediate parties to the extent of enabling the creditor to realize . . . ." an amount not exceeding the debt. 275 Wis. at 139, 81 N.W.2d at 561. This is, of course, inconsistent with the generally applicable rule of free assignability of a life insurance policy by the person whose life is insured when he is also the owner of the policy interests relevant to assignment.

7.   Vance, Law of Insurance § 123 (3d ed. Anderson 1951).

pects to pay for the life insurance. Moreover, the fact that the creditor obtains the policy does not demonstrate that the debtor and his estate have no legal interest in it. It would be important to determine whether there is a beneficiary clause designating the estate of the debtor (the person whose life is insured) as the contingent beneficiary. If so, the debtor is not a stranger to the contract, though it may still be necessary to rely on equitable principles to give the debtor's estate a right to that part of the proceeds in excess of the debt, the creditor having been designated as primary beneficiary.

Neither should the fact that the creditor pays the insurance premiums entitle him to the entire proceeds of the policy. It is true that this payment of premiums may affect the amount of his interest, as when he is entitled to be reimbursed by the debtor and this is a charge added to the basic amount of the debt. Also, the source of payment of premiums has some bearing on construction of the agreement of the creditor, debtor, and insurer. Unless the policy is obtained by the creditor subsequently, however, and not as a part of the arrangements for the loan, the channel through which the premiums are paid may be less significant than the fact that the debtor probably bears the burden of the premiums. The latter fact is quite clear both when the debtor is obligated to reimburse the creditor and when he pays the premiums himself; it may also be demonstrated to be the case even when he does not reimburse the premiums as such but pays a higher interest rate or service charge than would have been required had he been providing the insurance separately.

§ 4.11 (g) DISQUALIFICATION OF BENEFICIARIES

(1) GENERALLY

A person otherwise entitled to receive the proceeds of a life insurance policy may be disqualified from doing so because of his participation in bringing about the death of the person whose life was insured.

The principle underlying this disqualification is often stated to be that "no one shall be allowed to benefit from his own wrong."[1] This proposition is too broad, however, to reflect precisely the rules that have evolved for disqualification of the beneficiary of a life insurance policy.[2] The disqualification applies at most to cases of intentional, unlawful killing, and not to cases of negligently or recklessly causing death.[3] And even the scope of its applicability to killings treated in law as intentional may be questioned. The meaning of "intentional" for the purpose of classifying an offense under the criminal law as in-

---

1. Carter v. Carter, 88 So.2d 153, 157 (Fla.1956), quoting 29 Am.Jur., Ins. § 1310, p. 979 (1940) [now 29A Am.Jur., Ins. § 1643, p. 725 (rev. ed. 1960)].

2. See, *e.g.*, Minasian v. Aetna Life Ins. Co., 295 Mass. 1, 3 N.E.2d 17 (1936).

3. *E.g.*, Commercial Travelers Mut. Acc. Ass'n v. Witte, 406 S.W.2d 145 (Ky. 1966), 27 A.L.R.3d 784 (1969) (applying New York law; wife convicted of involuntary manslaughter in death of husband from stabbing during domestic quarrel not disqualified).

battery

intention to cause death usually required to disqualify

tentional homicide (or instead as a lesser crime) or for the purpose of classifying an offense under tort law as battery (or instead as a reckless or negligent invasion of interests in bodily security) need not necessarily be the same as the meaning of the term when used in stating a criterion for determining whether one is disqualified as a life insurance beneficiary.[4]   Some offenses classified as intentional crimes or torts involving death of the victim do not involve an intent to bring about death (whether that of the victim or another) or even to bring about an intrusion on bodily security likely to produce serious bodily injury or death.   Such offenses probably would not disqualify a life insurance beneficiary.   For example, "if one brother, in a boyish quarrel, should give another a slight blow or push, and death should unexpectedly result, a forfeiture of insurance or of inheritance would be a consequence undesired by the deceased and shocking to the community."[5]   Thus probably the rule of disqualification is confined in most jurisdictions to cases involving intent either to cause death or to cause the type of intrusion on another's physical security that is likely to cause death.[6]

Clearly, then, the asserted principle that "no one shall be allowed to benefit from his own wrong" is not useful as a premise for logical deduction of the answer to particular questions about the scope of disqualification of slaying beneficiaries.   But a broad statement of principle such as this may nevertheless be useful as an expression of an underlying public interest with which courts must be concerned in working out the legal rules for particular cases.   It is common that two or more broad principles, based on different public interests, come into competition with each other so that neither alone can be taken as an accurate expression of the foundation for the resulting legal rules.[7]   Often the task of formulating a strictly accurate and complete expression of the underlying aims of a rule would be virtually as complex as stating the precise rule itself.   Still, understanding may be aided by a generalization that identifies a broad objective without specifying the extent to which it is carried out in particular applications.

(2) EFFECT OF STATUTES

The disqualification of a person to receive life insurance proceeds as beneficiary of a life insurance policy because he intentionally caused the death of the person whose life was insured is in many jurisdictions entirely decisional rather than statutory in ori-

---

4.   See, *e.g.*, Davis v. Aetna Life Ins. Co., 279 F.2d 304 (9th Cir. 1960) (applying California law; guilty plea of beneficiary to charge of voluntary manslaughter was admissible as an admission against interest in dispute over insurance proceeds but was not conclusive on issue); Rose v. Rose, 79 N.M. 435, 444 P.2d 762 (1968) (statute disqualifying convicted murderers held to express a legislative intent not to disqualify wife convicted of voluntary manslaughter).

5.   Minasian v. Aetna Life Ins. Co., 295 Mass. 1, 6, 3 N.E.2d 17, 19 (1936).

6.   *Cf. ibid.*

7.   See Keeton, Venturing to Do Justice 164–166 (1969).

gin. In most such states there is no statute governing the rights of life insurance beneficiaries generally and no statute referring specifically to the problem of the slaying beneficiary. A difference may be observed between the question whether life insurance beneficiaries are to be disqualified and the question whether beneficiaries of an estate are to be disqualified. Though many states have no statute speaking directly to this question in either context, there are statutes governing descent and distribution generally. It appears to have been assumed in most judicial references to this problem that, because of the statutes of descent and distribution, courts are less free to work out details of disqualification in relation to rights of estate beneficiaries than in relation to rights of life insurance beneficiaries. Thus, though there is a split of authority, some courts disqualifying the slayer to recover as a claimant on the insurance policy have nevertheless allowed him to recover the insurance proceeds indirectly as a beneficiary of the estate of the decedent.[8]

With respect to situations in which statutes contained no explicit provisions concerning a slaying beneficiary, Dean Wade commented, in an article published in 1936:

"With the exception of the insurance cases, the courts have taken three different views: (1) that complete ownership of the property will pass to the slayer in spite of his wrongs; (2) that no title will pass to the slayer; and (3) that title will pass to the slayer, but that equity will hold him a constructive trustee for the heir or next of kin of the decedent.

"The first view was adopted in the first case in which the problem arose, and since that time it has been the majority ruling, especially in cases of intestacy." [9]

Dean Wade also noted a trend toward the second view [10] and observed that in most of the jurisdictions in which the courts refused to engraft on a statute an exception to exclude an acquisition by the willful killer, a rectifying statute was passed shortly thereafter.[11] But it may be doubted that the rectifying statutory solutions are consistent with the decisional doctrines developed in insurance cases; statutes never deal explicitly with all the possible cases that may arise, and courts have been most reluctant to extend the statutory policy of disqualification beyond the cases to which the statute is expressly applicable.[12]

It would seem that different rules of disqualification for estate beneficiaries and life insurance beneficiaries are not justified. Thus, unless required to do so because of its duty of fidelity to a legisla-

---

8.   *E.g.*, Moore v. Prudential Ins. Co., 342 Pa. 570, 21 A.2d 42 (1941). See Annot., 39 A.L.R.2d 477, 500–505 (1955).

9.   Wade, *Acquisition of Property by Willfully Killing Another—A Statutory Solution*, 49 Harv.L.Rev. 715, 717 (1936).

10.   *Id.* at 717–718.

11.   *Id.* at 716.

12.   See, *e.g.*, Rose v. Rose, 79 N.M. 435, 444 P.2d 762 (1968).

ture's mandate, a court should not allow one who is disqualified by judicial doctrine from receiving life insurance proceeds directly to receive them indirectly as beneficiary of the estate of the decedent. Courts have been unduly timorous in failing to apply to descent and distribution the same doctrines of disqualification they have applied to life insurance beneficiaries. When the statute of descent and distribution is silent on this question, the court should give its own best answer rather than adhering to a fiction that the legislature's silence on the issue amounts to a mandate against disqualification.[13] If courts are as reluctant in the future as in the past to deal with this issue on the merits, legislation will be needed. But the problem is one more appropriately resolved through case-by-case development of judicial doctrine.

The disadvantages of the statutory method of meeting this problem are well illustrated in statutes thus far enacted. Some statutes adopted specifically to govern disqualification have referred to estate beneficiaries and not to life insurance beneficiaries and have been too narrow in their definition of the cases of disqualification. For example, one statute disqualifies "any person convicted of the murder of a decedent . . ." from inheriting or taking by will.[14] Perhaps there is danger that such a statute, narrower in scope than the judicial doctrine applicable to life insurance beneficiaries, may be urged successfully as a basis for narrowing the judicial doctrine to the same limits.[15] But more courts have treated such a statute as applying only to estate beneficiaries and not to life insurance beneficiaries.[16]

---

13. Concerning the role of courts in the interpretation of statutes, and the harmful consequences of contrary-to-fact presumptions from legislative silence on an issue, see Keeton, Venturing to Do Justice 78–82, 92–95 (1969).

14. Fla.Stat.Ann. § 731.31 (1964).

15. Rosenberger v. Northwestern Mut. Life Ins. Co., 182 F.Supp. 633 (D.Kan. 1960) (question of beneficiary's intent in killing insured could not be relitigated when beneficiary had been convicted of involuntary manslaughter, and she could therefore receive insurance proceeds because Kansas statute required conviction of "felonious killing," interpreted to mean intentional killing, for forfeiture; in so holding, court construed the phrase "inherit or take by will *or otherwise* from such other person" as applying to a claim as beneficiary of a life insurance policy, and it found support for applying statute to insurance in another statutory provision stating that insurance proceeds inure to the benefit of beneficiaries free of all claims).

16. *E.g.*, Continental Bank & Trust Co. v. Maag, 285 F.2d 558 (10th Cir. 1960)

(circumstantial evidence that beneficiary had killed his insured wife, then taken his own life; in interpleader action between beneficiary's estate and contingent beneficiaries, held that public policy prevented beneficiary's estate from taking and that Utah statute providing for forfeiture of "any property or benefit by succession, will, or otherwise" in case of conviction—thus arguably implying no forfeiture in the absence of conviction—was inapplicable); Davis v. Aetna Life Ins. Co., 279 F.2d 304 (9th Cir. 1960) (primary beneficiary pleaded guilty to voluntary manslaughter of his wife, insured under two policies with Aetna; held, in interpleader action involving primary beneficiary and the contingent beneficiaries under the policies, that a California probate statute barring one convicted of murder or voluntary manslaughter from benefitting from the victim's estate was inapplicable to insurance and that the confession was admissible as an admission against interest but was not conclusive on the issue of the beneficiary's rights to the proceeds of the policies); Carter v. Carter, 88 So.2d 153 (Fla.1956) (held, summary judg-

Certainly a court is justified in inferring that the legislature did not mean to overturn the body of decisional doctrine on disqualification of life insurance beneficiaries when it enacted a statute that speaks only of inheriting or taking by will. The court nevertheless faces a difficult issue—a choice between evils—if, as is suggested here, it considers, first, that the rules for disqualification of estate beneficiaries and life insurance beneficiaries should be alike and, second, that the statutory rules for disqualification of estate beneficiaries are less suitable and just than the decisional rules for disqualification of life insurance beneficiaries.

Dean Wade has proposed a comprehensive statutory solution, which at least one state has adopted,[17] including the following section on insurance: [18]

"(a) Insurance proceeds payable to the slayer as the beneficiary or assignee of any policy or certificate of insurance on the life of the decedent or as the survivor of a joint life policy shall be paid to the estate of the decedent, unless the policy or certificate designates some person not claiming through the slayer as alternative beneficiary to him.

"(b) If the decedent is beneficiary or assignee of any policy or certificate of insurance on the life of the slayer, the proceeds shall be paid to the estate of the decedent upon the death of the slayer, unless the policy names some person other than the slayer or his estate as alternative beneficiary, or unless the slayer, by naming a new beneficiary or assigning the policy, performs an act which would have deprived the decedent of his interest in the policy if he had been living.

"(c) No insurance company shall be subject to liability on any policy on the life of the decedent procured and maintained by the slayer or on which all the premiums were paid by him."

On most of the insurance issues dealt with, it would seem that Dean Wade's proposed statute is admirable. One might question, however, the broad rule of non-liability for insurers, under paragraph (c), when the slayer has procured and maintained the policy or paid all the premiums. For example, it seems doubtful that the insurer should escape liability if the policy was procured by the slayer twenty years before the slaying and was maintained by the slayer for all that period, and particularly so in the absence of some evidence of connection between the insurance and the slaying. Perhaps it could be objected, too, that a statutory declaration that the insurer shall not be "subject to liability *on* any policy" might be construed as negating

ment was properly denied because the issue whether the wife-beneficiary had feloniously killed her husband-insured was one of fact, despite her previous acquittal in a criminal proceeding; the statute disqualifying "any person convicted of the murder of the decedent . . ." and by implication declining to disqualify one acquitted—was construed as applying to estate beneficiaries only and not life insurance beneficiaries).

17. S.D. Compiled Laws Ann. § 29-9-13 through 29-9-16 (1967).

18. Wade, *Acquisition of Property by Willfully Killing Another—A Statutory Solution*, 49 Harv.L.Rev. 715, 741 (1936).

tort liability, which has been imposed, for example, because of the insurer's issuing life insurance to one without insurable interest.[19]   It seems likely, however, that such liability would be held not affected because in its nature it is tort liability rather than liability "on" the policy.

(3) WHO IS ENTITLED TO PROCEEDS AFTER THE BENEFICIARY'S DISQUALIFICATION?

When the primary beneficiary of a life insurance policy is disqualified because of his killing the person whose life was insured and the insurer nevertheless acknowledges or is held to liability, a contest for the proceeds may arise between the contingent beneficiary and the estate of the insured.

One position taken is that the slaying beneficiary is legally entitled to recover the proceeds but holds them in "constructive trust for the estate of the insured."[20]   This result would often frustrate the probable intention of the deceased insured.   The preferable rule, well supported by precedents,[21] is that the proceeds will be distributed as if the slaying beneficiary had predeceased the insured. This comes as near as possible to carrying out the intention expressed by the insurance policy with respect to disposition of insurance proceeds.   Ordinarily the policy does not expressly cover this situation, since it says only that the contingent beneficiary will take if the primary beneficiary predeceases the insured.   But the result desired by the insured in a situation closely analogous to the case of disqualification is expressed, and that result is the one that the insured probably would have chosen had he faced this question.

(4) THE INSURER'S ARGUMENTS FOR NON-LIABILITY

Professor Vance asserted that the insurer is not liable to anyone on a life insurance policy taken out by one who is also the named beneficiary and the murderer of the person whose life is insured.

---

19. See § 3.5(e) *supra*.

20. *Cf.* Restatement of Restitution § 189 (1937).   Perhaps the implication of the quoted passage from the black-letter section is that the estate takes as against a contingent beneficiary. But that reading may not be sound in view of Comment *a*, stating: "In such a case ordinarily the executor or administrator of the insured is entitled to receive the proceeds of the policy from the insurer and to apply them in the same way in which they would have been applicable if the beneficiary had predeceased the insured or was otherwise incapable of taking or disqualified from taking the proceeds." Perhaps the drafters of this section of the Restatement of Restitution were thinking of a type of policy that designated no contingent beneficiary at all or one that designated the estate of the insured as the only contingent beneficiary.

The "constructive trust" rule is more appropriately applied in non-insurance situations, in which there is no conflict with secondary designees. *E.g.*, *In re* Cox' Estate, 141 Mont. 583, 380 P.2d 584 (1963) (husband murdered wife, then committed suicide; held, husband held wife's share of jointly owned property in trust for wife's heirs, and his estate had no rights in the half of the property so held).

21. *E.g.*, Carter v. Carter, 88 So.2d 153 (Fla.1956); Metropolitan Life Ins. Co. v. Wenckus, 244 A.2d 424 (Me.1968). See Annot., 26 A.L.R.2d 987 (1952).

His rationale was based on the theory that the interest of a beneficiary who did not procure the insurance contract is equitable. If he murders the insured, Professor Vance reasoned, this equitable interest fails and there is a resulting trust for the benefit of either the murdered person's estate or another beneficiary.[22] "We have a different case, however, where the murderer has taken out the policy upon the life of the slain man, and has himself paid the premiums. Here the murderous beneficiary is party to the contract. He has the legal as well as the equitable title to the policy. The insured was absolutely without interest in it. There is no basis for a resulting trust. The entire right in the policy having been forfeited by the crime of its sole owner, the duty of the insurer to pay is wholly extinguished."[23]

Vance's argument is based on the assumption that the beneficiary of a contract procured by another has only an equitable interest, the failure of which makes possible a resulting trust in favor of another rather than a denial of the insurer's liability. This distinction fails once it is recognized that the third party beneficiary of a contract has a legal interest.

It is less difficult, perhaps, to support Vance's proposition that the entire right in a policy obtained by the beneficiary is forfeited by his crime of murdering the insured because the beneficiary was "sole owner." This argument may be persuasive if no other person than the murderer is named as owner of any of the rights of the policy or even as contingent beneficiary. Under current practices, this would be a very unusual policy, but such policies were common in the early American history of life insurance. In relation to policies in which "no one but the beneficiary or one claiming through him has any interest in the policy," Vance's position that the insurer is relieved of liability is supported also by Professor Scott,[24] and the result is also supported by a section of the statute proposed by Dean Wade.[25]

Most modern policy forms have printed clauses, rarely stricken out even in policies purchased by the primary beneficiary, making contingent provisions for payment to relatives or to the estate of the person whose life is insured.[26] Under such a policy, it cannot be said that "no one but the beneficiary or one claiming through him has any interest in the policy."

The cases cited by Vance in support of his position, as well as those cited by Scott for non-liability of the insurer when no one but the beneficiary or one claiming through him has any interest in the policy, all involve either fact situations on which liability was imposed, non-liability in other situations being discussed in dicta, or fact situations that are suggestive of the plainly cogent defense of fraud

22. Vance, Law of Insurance 721 (3d ed. Anderson 1951).

23. *Id.* at 722.

24. 5 Scott, Trusts 3531, § 494.2 (3d ed. 1967).

25. See § 4.11(g) (2) *supra*, quoting Dean Wade's proposal and questioning this particular aspect of it though applauding his draft statute in general.

26. See § 4.11(d) n.2 *supra*; Appendix E *infra*.

(*i. e.*, obtaining a policy as part of a plan to murder for profit),[27] although some of the opinions do not appear to limit the rule of nonliability to cases in which fraud is proved. In *New York Mut. Life Ins. Co. v. Armstrong*,[28] relied upon by Professor Vance and generally recognized as a leading case, it appeared that the insurer had on December 8, 1877, issued an endowment policy on the life of Armstrong, payable to him or his assigns on the eighth of December, 1897, or if he should die before that time to his legal representatives. The policy was assigned to Hunter. Armstrong died on January 25, 1878; Hunter was convicted of the murder of Armstrong and was hanged for the offense. Armstrong's widow, as administratrix of Armstrong's estate, sued the insurer. The defendant contended, inter alia, that the policy had been obtained by Hunter with intent to defraud the insurer by bringing about the death of Armstrong. The Supreme Court of the United States reversed a judgment for plaintiff and remanded for a new trial. After holding that it was error to exclude evidence that Hunter obtained insurance policies in other companies on the life of Armstrong at or near the time the policy was obtained from defendant, the opinion of the court by Field, J., continues: "But, independently of any proof of the motives of Hunter in obtaining the policy, and even assuming that they were just and proper, he forfeited all rights under it when, to secure its immediate payment, he murdered the assured. It would be a reproach to the jurisprudence of the country, if one could recover insurance money payable on the death of a party whose life he had feloniously taken. As well might he recover insurance money upon a building that he had willfully fired." [29]

It will be noted that the concluding sentence in this quoted passage suggests the theory that murder by the person who procured the policy was an excepted risk.[30] Of course, most policies do not contain any provision on this point, and as applied to such policies the theory must be one of implied exception. Ordinarily that theory applies to losses that are either so regular as to be regarded as a cost rather than a risk of an activity or enterprise or else are not fortuitous from the point of view of the person who would be entitled to the proceeds of the insurance contract were it enforceable.[31] That the death was fortuitous from the point of view of the murder victim, in a case in which he obtained the policy, is not conclusive against the analogy to the friendly-fire and inherent-vice exceptions of property insurance. In life insurance cases, it happens that the person who obtains the contract is ordinarily the one whose life is insured, but the interests of others against the risk of economic loss from his death are the in-

27. A more recent decision that can be explained on the same basis is Travelers Ins. Co. v. Thompson, 281 Minn. 547, 163 N.W.2d 289 (1969), *app. dism'd* and *cert. denied*, 395 U.S. 161 (1969).

28. 117 U.S. 591, 6 Sup.Ct. 877, 29 L. Ed. 997 (1886).

29. 117 U.S. at 600, 6 Sup.Ct. at 881, 29 L.Ed. at 1000.

30. *Cf.* 5 Scott, Trusts 3531, § 494.2 (3d ed. 1967).

31. See § 5.3 *infra*.

terests protected by the policy. Applying the excepted-risk theory to these cases would allow the insurer to escape liability in all cases in which the person whose life was insured was murdered by a beneficiary. The contrary result has been consistently reached when the policy was obtained by the insured, and these decisions appear to be a rejection of the theory of implied exception. It is difficult to see why this theory should be invoked in cases of policies obtained by the beneficiary but not in cases of policies obtained by the insured. Undoubtedly the practice is to charge the same premium in both cases; yet the insurer's risks would be different if the narrower theory of implied exception were adopted.

If the result of non-liability on the ground of an implied exception is reached, no problem of unjust enrichment is presented, and no occasion is presented for return of premiums to avoid a supposed unjust enrichment. An apt analogy would be the fire insurance policy for a period during which no insured loss occurred. But if the ground of non-liability is merely that no one but the beneficiary had an interest in the policy and his interest was forfeited by murder, the argument that non-liability of the insurer produces an unjust enrichment is stronger. In no event, however, should the insurer be required to return any premium collected for that period of time (before the murder) during which it was subject to the risk of death under circumstances that would have given rise to liability.

CHAPTER 5

THE RISKS TRANSFERRED

SECTION 5.1   METHODS OF DEFINING THE RISKS TRANSFERRED

§ 5.1(a) GENERALLY

The determination of "the risks transferred" is the subject of the entire body of insurance law if that phrase is understood in the broadest possible sense. As the title of the present chapter, however, it is used in a narrower sense as a common denominator for insurance problems concerning the scope of the insurer's liability as affected by the nature of the loss-producing circumstances, in contrast with problems concerning persons and interests protected, which were considered in Chapter 4.

The purpose of this chapter is to consider, first, some typical limitations of the scope of liability in kinds of insurance that are common today and, second, the processes and principles by which these limitations have been developed—processes and principles that, in many respects, will continue to be applicable despite changes in insurance forms and practices.

Basically the determination of the risks transferred is dependent upon contract. But the materials presented in this chapter and the next reflect considerable regulation of the freedom of contract by the actions of legislatures, administrators, and courts.

§ 5.1(b) ALL–RISK AND SPECIFIED–RISK POLICIES

(1) GENERALLY

The draftsman of an insurance policy form might adopt the approach of stating that the policy covers all risks with exceptions specified, or the opposite approach of stating that the policy covers only the risks specified. A policy drafted in the former manner is called an all-risk policy. Invariably, however, there are qualifications of

all-risk policy
vs
specified-risk

269

the scope of coverage. In form they may appear, first, as a designation of the subject matter and of the persons and interests protected, or, second, as a qualifying phrase after the words "all risks," or, third, as qualifications separately stated under a heading such as "conditions," "exclusions," or "exceptions." The first two types of qualifications are illustrated by a policy insuring the policyholder's interests in designated property against "all risks by land and water by any conveyance." [1] The first and last are illustrated by a currently used personal property floater (inland marine insurance) that describes the property covered as "personal property owned, used or worn by the person in whose name this policy is issued and members of the Insured's family of the same household, while in all situations, except as hereinafter provided." In the same form, under the heading "exclusions," appear provisions of such different nature as a limitation of the scope of coverage by physical location ("property on exhibition at fairgrounds") and a limitation by cause ("against loss or damage caused by . . . insurrection, rebellion, revolution, civil war . . .").[2]

Since the scope of coverage of an all-risk policy is limited in various ways, the contrast between all-risk and specified-risk policies is merely one of tendency and method of defining the scope of coverage. Yet it may have practical significance. Certainly it has influenced decisions on the burden of proof, the insured receiving the benefit of a more favorable rule under all-risk coverage than under specified-risk coverage.[3] Perhaps also all-risk coverage is more favorable to insureds in relation to avoiding gaps of coverage.[4] It may be argued, too, that it is more difficult for an insurer to establish a defense of implied exception under all-risk coverage, because exceptions are less likely to be implicit when the coverage is relatively broad than when relatively narrow in scope. It is nevertheless true that even all-risk coverages are subject to implied exceptions.[5]

As indicated by the illustrations thus far given, marine insurance policies are to a considerable degree all-risk in character. Life insurance, too, though not commonly referred to as such, is all-risk in character. Life policies do not purport to specify all the risks of death that are covered. Rather, the approach to defining the coverage is to start with the proposition that death from whatever cause is covered and to depend on exceptions, express or implied, to limit that broad proposition.[6]

---

1. See Schloss v. Stevens, [1906] 2 K.B. 665.

2. See Appendix I *infra*.

3. See § 5.1(b) (3) *infra*.

4. See § 5.1(b) (2) *infra*.

5. See § 5.3(b) and (c) *infra*, concerning implied exceptions in life and marine insurance respectively.

6. Formerly it was common that the insurer would have *no liability at all* if death resulted from an excepted cause. At present, under the combined influence of insurer practices and regulatory compulsion, the policy commonly provides that if death results from an excepted cause the insurer shall pay *a sum less than the face amount of insurance (e.g.,* the cash surrender value or a sum equal to premiums paid). See § 6.5(b) (2) nn.23–25 *infra*.

(2) GAPS OF COVERAGE

One reason for significance of the contrast between the all-risk and the specified-risk methods of defining risks transferred appears in a comparison of "package" and all-risk policies. Much of the trend toward more comprehensive policies has been manifested by merely combining in one package various specified-risk coverages previously available in separate policies. Gaps that exist in the coverage provided by all the separate policies remain when they are brought together in one "package" policy.[7] For example, the Homeowners Policy forms are for the most part merely combinations of specified-risk coverages previously available in separate policies. Thus, under prevailing doctrine the policyholder still has no coverage for loss of a diamond ring accidentally tossed into a furnace.[8] On the other hand, the holder of a personal property floater, an all-risk form, would recover for such a loss to the extent that specified exceptions (including special limitations on the amount of liability for precious stones) were not applicable.

In view of the all-risk characteristics of marine insurance incident to use of the phrase "perils of the sea"—a group designation of perils—gaps in coverage are less likely than they would be under a specification of the individual perils; it is also likely that in some instances the insured will be able to prove that the loss resulted from some cause among "perils of the sea" without proving exactly what caused the loss.[9]

Similarly, comprehensive coverage "against all risks of physical loss" to specified property, except as otherwise provided in the policy, is a group designation of perils that reduces the likelihood of gaps. Here, too, it is likely that in some instances the insured will be able to prove a fortuitous loss within the comprehensive coverage though not proving exactly what caused it.[10]

---

7. *Cf.* Hedges, *Improving Property and Casualty Insurance Coverage*, 15 Law & Contemp.Prob. 353, 374–375 (1950). There may be limitations on the scope of protection under an all-risk policy, however, that are inapplicable to specified-risk coverage. For example, it has been held that certain conditions of a jewelers' block policy are valid, though they would be invalid under the statute prescribing the fire insurance form if that statute were applicable to the fire coverage that is included in this all-risk policy. Woods Patchogue Corp. v. Franklin Nat'l Ins. Co., 5 N.Y.2d 479, 158 N.E.2d 710, 186 N.Y.S.2d 42 (1959).

8. See § 5.3(d) *infra*, discussing the friendly-fire defense.

9. *Cf.* Boston Ins. Co. v. Dehydrating Process Co., 204 F.2d 441 (1st Cir. 1953) (insured's barge sank during calm weather after being loaded at a sheltered berth; subsequent inspection of the barge did not reveal any structural defects that could have caused the sinking, and the trial court found that the insured had rebutted the presumption of unseaworthiness due to overloading or improper loading of the barge; held, affirmed). The likelihood that the insured can recover without proving exactly what happened is affected also by the burden of proof; see § 5.1(b) (3) *infra*.

10. See § 5.1(b) (3) *infra*.

(3) BURDEN OF PROOF

The contrast between all-risk and specified-risk policies has significant bearing on the burden of proof. The policies in *British & Foreign Marine Ins. Co. v. Gaunt*,[11] a leading English case, provided coverage for wool, "including all risk of craft, fire, coasters, hulks, transhipment and inland carriage by land and/or water and/or risks from the sheep's back and/or stations while awaiting shipment and/or forwarding and until safely delivered . . . ."[12] The wool arrived in damaged condition, and the evidence did not establish exactly when or how the damage was done but made it clear that it occurred at some time during the period covered by the policies. After recognizing that the words "all risk" cannot be held to cover "such damage as is inevitable from ordinary wear and tear and inevitable depreciation . . ." and that damage "must be due to some fortuitous circumstance or casualty . . . ,"[13] Lord Birkenhead further remarked, "[W]here all risks are covered by the policy and not merely risks of a specified class or classes, the plaintiff discharges his special onus when he has proved that the loss was caused by some event covered by the general expression, and he is not bound to go further and prove the exact nature of the accident or casualty which, in fact, occasioned his loss."[14] Although there has been relatively little development of the point in the courts, probably the rule of the *Gaunt* case will be followed generally.[15]

11. [1921] 2 A.C. 41.

12. [1921] 2 A.C. at 42.

13. [1921] 2 A.C. at 46–47. This implied exception is commonly referred to as the "exception of loss from inherent vice." See § 5.3(c) *infra*.

14. [1921] 2 A.C. at 47. *Cf.* Lord Sumner's statement: "When he avers loss by some risk coming within 'all risks,' as used in this policy, he need only give evidence reasonably showing that the loss was due to a casualty, not to a certainty or to inherent vice or to wear and tear." [1921] 2 A.C. at 58. See 2 Arnould, Marine Insurance [10 British Shipping Laws] 817–818, § 856 (15th ed. 1961).

15. *E.g.*, Jewelers Mut. Ins. Co. v. Balogh, 272 F.2d 889 (5th Cir. 1959) (jewelry placed in safe on Saturday was missing on Monday with no visible evidence of theft; held, coverage under all-risk policy that stated there would be no liability for "unexplained loss," "mysterious disappearance," etc., since insurer had failed to prove the applicability of the restriction); Advance Piece Dye Works, Inc. v. Travelers Indem. Co., 64 N.J.Super. 405, 166 A.2d 173 (App.Div.1960), 88 A. L.R.2d 1114 (1963) (claiming under an all-risk policy that stated there would be no liability for "mysterious disappearance" and theft by employees and, alternatively, under a policy covering loss from employee dishonesty, the insured proved only that the property had disappeared from its place of storage in an unnatural manner; held, reversing the trial court, a dismissal with prejudice could not be directed for the all-risk insurer because it had the burden of proving the applicability of the restrictions on coverage, nor should a dismissal with prejudice be granted the employee-dishonesty insurer since the success of the all-risk insurer's defense based on employee dishonesty would cure the deficiency of the insured's case against the employee-dishonesty insurer); Glassner v. Detroit Fire & Marine Ins. Co., 23 Wis.2d 532, 127 N.W.2d 761 (1964) (action for damage to submersible pump under comprehensive coverage of dwelling "against all risks of physical loss" except as otherwise provided; held for policyholder since, after stipulating loss was fortuitous, insurer has burden of showing an ap-

Along with the reduced chance of a gap in coverage as to one or more of the speculative causes of a loss,[16] the fact that the burden of proof is on the insurer materially improves the insured's prospects for proving his case without proving exactly what happened.[17]

SECTION 5.2   EXPRESS RESTRICTIONS OF RISK
§ 5.2(a) GENERALLY

Despite pervasive regulation of insurance transactions, the coverage afforded by an insurance policy is in most respects subject to restriction by the terms of the contract. Some restrictive stipulations concern the persons and interests protected.[1] Others concern the nature of the risks transferred by the contract. Illustrative provisions of the latter type are considered in this section. Further illustrations, together with discussion of basic issues they raise, are considered in a later section treating distinctions concerning the nature of causal contributions to a loss.[2]

Some restrictions of the risks transferred by a policy are expressed in the primary definition of coverage. Even in policies that are all-risk in character[3] the primary definition of coverage serves

plicable exclusion; dictum that under all-risk coverage insured has burden of proving loss was fortuitous and not the result of "an ordinary and almost certain consequence of the inherent qualities and intended use of the property"; question reserved as to where burden would be, absent stipulation, concerning whether loss was caused by "wear and tear, deterioration, and mechanical breakdown," since arguably the policy form treated these causes "as if they were excluded risks"); *cf.* 21 Appleman, Insurance Law § 12238 (rev. ed. 1962). *Contra, e.g.,* Hardware Dealers Mut. Fire Ins. Co. v. Berglund, 393 S.W.2d 309 (Tex.1965) (the insured claimed under all-risk policies containing various water-damage "exclusions" for loss to several properties caused by hurricane; held, reinstating the trial court verdict that awarded only the portion of loss due to wind damage, that the burden of proof was on the insured to show the inapplicability of the "exclusions").

16. See § 5.1(b) (2) *supra.*

17. *Compare* cases cited in n.15 *supra with* Austin v. American Cas. Co., 193 A.2d 741 (D.C.Cir. 1963), 12 A.L.R.3d 860 (1967) ("extended theft coverage" under endorsement of homeowners policy, defining theft to include "mys-

terious disappearance"; insured proved she had bracelet on at luncheon and when entering a store to try on clothes, and did not realize it was gone until 48 hours later; held, not an "all loss" policy, and insured's proof was insufficient since circumstances suggested bracelet was lost or mislaid rather than stolen); Brier v. Mutual Ins. Co. of Hartford, 3 Conn. Cir. 326, 213 A.2d 736 (1965) ("extended theft coverage" defining theft to include "mysterious disappearance"; insured proved only that the insured property, a watch, had been last seen at a given time, then later could not be found; held, not an all-risk form and insured's proof was insufficient since it indicated that theft, even including "mysterious disappearance," was improbable). *But see, e.g.,* Alexandre of London v. Indemnity Ins. Co. of N. Am., 183 F.Supp. 715 (D.D.C. 1960) (claiming under a policy requiring "conclusive" proof of loss from a covered risk, insured offered proof that loss resulted from either burglary or employee dishonesty, both covered risks under the policy; held, coverage allowed).

1. See generally Chapter 4 *supra.*

2. See § 5.5(a) and (b) *infra.*

3. See § 5.1(b) *supra.*

not only as the affirmative basis for support of a claim of coverage but also, on occasion, as the language to which the insurer appeals in urging a restriction that defeats the claim. The more strongly oriented toward all-risk character a coverage is, however, the less often it serves effectively such a restrictive function. Conversely, specified-risk definitions of coverage are more frequently useful to insurers in such a restrictive way. For example, the phrase "arising out of the ownership, maintenance or use" in a motor vehicle liability insurance policy expresses not only an affirmative identification of the subject matter of the coverage but also a significant limitation of its scope.[4]

Other restrictions are expressed in clauses separated from the primary definition of coverage. Policies of insurance, whether all-risk or specified-risk in character, commonly include separately stated provisions limiting the primary definition of the risks transferred by the contract. For example, coverage against "all risks of loss" of the insured property is commonly subject to a special provision against liability for loss caused by nuclear accident,[5] and a similar clause commonly appears in specified-risk policies such as liability insurance contracts.[6]

A pecuniary limit of liability is another common type of separately stated restrictive provision.[7]

The draftsman's choice between incorporating restrictive phrases in the primary definition of coverage and stating them separately may be influenced by his concern about the judicial tendency toward less rigorous adherence to those restrictions that are widely separated, in the policy form, from the primary definitions of risk they modify. This judicial tendency is usually reasoned on grounds of resolving ambiguities but extends beyond cases of literal ambiguity and is perhaps better explained as a corollary of the principle of honoring reasonable expectations even when inconsistent with painstaking reading of the policy provisions.[8] The 1966 revision of liability insurance forms moved substantially in the direction of placing restrictive clauses within or close by the primary definition of coverage they modify, for the declared purpose of clarifying the draftsmen's intent and reducing the likelihood of judicial constructions contrary to that intent.[9]

§ 5.2(b) ILLUSTRATIONS IN AUTOMOBILE INSURANCE

The phrase "arising out of the ownership, maintenance or use" of the insured vehicle,[1] appearing in automobile liability policies, illustrates the way in which a primary definition of coverage serves not only affirmatively to support coverage but also on occasion re-

---

4. See § 5.2(b) *infra.*

5. See Appendix I *infra.*

6. See Appendix G *infra.*

7. See § 5.9 *infra.*

8. See § 6.3 *infra.*

9. See § 2.11(c) *supra.*

1. See Appendix H *infra.*

strictively to defeat it. It would seem a fair construction that "use" refers to use *as a vehicle*. This interpretation conforms with the basic idea that the automobile policy is designed to cover motoring risks. There is support for this interpretation in some cases,[2] but other cases support a broader interpretation of use.[3]

Is a passenger, as well as the driver, engaged in "use" of a vehicle within the meaning of the liability insurance coverage? This is a significant question when a claim is made against a passenger on the ground that he negligently distracted the driver and caused injury to the driver or another (whether a passenger, a pedestrian, or an occupant of another car). There is no other common insurance coverage applying to the potential liability of a passenger in such circumstances, and a potentially serious gap of coverage would exist if the term "use" (in various coverages, including the primary coverage, the omnibus clause, and drive-other-cars coverage) were not construed to extend coverage to the defendant passenger with respect to such claims against him. There is case law favoring coverage for claims against the passenger in this context,[4] and other case law opposed to coverage.[5]

---

2. *Cf.* Mason v. Celina Mut. Ins. Co., 161 Colo. 442, 423 P.2d 24 (1967) (death of one person in parked car caused by accidental discharge of a pistol in hands of another person in the car does not arise out of the "use" of the insured vehicle; to be covered, "the injury would have to be one originating from the use of the vehicle as such"). See 7 Appleman, Insurance Law § 4317 (rev.ed. 1962). In *Mason*, the defendant and the victim were not using the car as a vehicle—neither for transportation nor even for entering or leaving incident to transportation. But the result should be the same even if the car was moving at the time but its movement did not contribute to the accidental discharge of the pistol; the injury would not have been one "arising out of the . . . use" as a vehicle. A more difficult case would be presented if movement of the vehicle contributed to the accidental discharge of the pistol. It might then be said both that the car was being used as a vehicle and that such use was a factor in bringing about the injury. But the mere fact that the vehicle was moving at the time the gun was accidentally discharged is insufficient to establish the causal connection required for coverage; see National Union Fire Ins. Co. v. Bruecks, 179 Neb. 642, 139 N.W. 2d 821 (1966). For other decisions on the meaning of "use," see §§ 4.7(b) n.11, 4.9(b) n.6 *supra*.

3. See, *e.g.*, Fidelity & Cas. Co. v. Lott, 273 F.2d 500 (5th Cir. 1960) (forecasting Texas law; bullet from deer rifle resting on top of the insured car failed to clear the curved top and was deflected downward, killing the hunter's companion sitting in the right front seat; held, the death arose out of use of the insured vehicle). *Cf.* Carter v. Bergeron, 102 N.H. 464, 160 A.2d 348 (1960), 89 A.L.R.2d 142 (1963) (insured, driving the insured pick-up truck, was allegedly driving ahead of a two-ton truck loaded with horses and signalling its driver, his employee, to drive faster; the larger truck struck a car at an intersection, killing the driver of the car; held, death arose out of use of the insured pick-up truck). Arguably *Carter* may be explained as a case in which operation of the insured pick-up truck— its use as a vehicle—was one of the contributing causes of the accident.

4. *E.g.*, Gronquist v. Transit Cas. Co., 105 N.J.Super. 363, 252 A.2d 232 (1969). *Cf.* National Union Fire Ins. Co. v. Bruecks, 179 Neb. 642, 139 N.W.2d 821 (1966) (accidental discharge of gun in hands of minor passenger; held, passenger was "using" automobile but the injury did not arise out of that use); Coletrain v. Coletrain, 238 S.C. 555, 121

5. See note 5 on page 276.

Some automobile insurance policies have contained clauses restricting coverage to circumstances in which the vehicle in question was being "operated" by one of a described group of persons (e. g., members of the insured's family), or denying coverage when the vehicle was being "operated" by one of a described group (e. g., members of the armed services). In the first of these contexts, coverage is expanded by an expansive interpretation of "operate" and its derivatives; in the second, by a narrow interpretation. Not surprisingly, decisions can be found that interpret "operate" differently in these separate contexts so as to favor coverage in both instances. That is, some decisions have sustained coverage by construing "operate" expansively,[6] and others, in a different context, by construing it narrowly.[7] There is also support, however, for construing "operate"

S.E.2d 89 (1961) (woman's hand injured when caught in taxi door slammed shut by her husband, a fellow passenger; held, he was "using" the vehicle and was an insured under omnibus clause of coverage on the taxi). See 7 Appleman, Insurance Law § 4316 (rev.ed. 1962). See also n.6 *infra*.

5. *E.g.*, Potomac Ins. Co. v. Ohio Cas. Ins. Co., 188 F.Supp. 218 (N.D.Cal. 1960) (male passenger was negligent in distracting female driver, thereby causing accident; held, he was not using the vehicle so as to qualify for drive-other-cars coverage under a policy of which he was the named insured). *Cf.* Dunlap v. Maryland Cas. Co., 242 Ark. 533, 414 S.W.2d 397 (1967) (Dan, teen-age son of named insured was passenger in car driven by his friend, Glenn, and owned by Glenn's father; Glenn collided with another car, injuring a child in that car; held, no coverage under Dan's father's insurance for the claim against Glenn since Dan, as passenger, was not "using" Glenn's father's car). Although the narrow interpretation these opinions place on "use" is subject to criticism, the result in *Dunlap* probably was justified on other grounds; though the clause there involved is not quoted, references to it support the inference that it was like the "drive-other-cars" or "non-owned automobile" provisions of automobile liability insurance forms in common use. Such a clause extends coverage principally to the named insured and his relatives. To the extent that it extends coverage to others it does so only for their liability because of acts or omissions of the named insured or one of his relatives —that is, for their vicarious liability. In *Dunlap*, the claim was that the driver was liable because of his own neg-

ligence, not that he was vicariously liable for negligence of his passenger. Concerning drive-other-cars coverage see § 4.9(b) *supra* generally, and see n.6 thereto with respect to the meaning of "use" under the drive-other-cars coverage.

6. See, *e.g.*, Trans-Continental Mut. Ins. Co. v. Harrison, 262 Ala. 373, 78 So.2d 917 (1955), 51 A.L.R.2d 917 (1957) (coverage only when operated by named insured or member of his immediate family; car driven by third person in company of named insured; insured guilty of separate negligence in exhorting driver to speed; held, vehicle was being "operated" by named insured); Mayflower Ins. Exch. v. Kosteriva, 84 Ida. 42, 367 P.2d 572 (1961) (accident occurred while car was being driven by member of armed services, who had been requested to drive by the named insured, also a member of the armed services, because the named insured was intoxicated; held, car was being "operated" by wife of named insured, who was also in the car, and, therefore, clause denying coverage for operation by members of the armed services other than the named insured was not applicable). *Cf.* Hay v. Ham, 364 S.W.2d 118 (Mo.1962) (while shifting her position to allow another passenger to enter the car, the defendant accidentally touched the accelerator of a car parked in gear by her husband; held, she was "operating" the car within the meaning of a statute requiring the "highest" degree of care of persons operating motor vehicles).

7. See, *e.g.*, Ayres v. Harleysville Mut. Cas. Co., 172 Va. 383, 2 S.E.2d 303 (1939) (clause denying coverage for injury to an employee of the insured while "operating" the vehicle; injury

in a narrower sense even when this defeats coverage.[8]   Although the meaning of a term may be affected substantially by the context, a factor weighing strongly in favor of construing "operate" in a narrower sense is that the ordinary usage of "operate" suggests a narrower meaning, more like that associated with "drive" than like the broader meaning commonly associated with "use."

Since motor vehicle policies often extend coverage to "loading and unloading," an issue may arise as to whether the vehicle in question was being "used" or "operated" by the individual claiming coverage for events occurring at a time when he was not in the vehicle at all—neither as driver nor as passenger.[9]

A phrase such as "arising out of the   . . .   use" predictably produces also a body of decisions that are concerned with the nature of the causal relation between use and result [10]—decisions turning on questions that are heavily fact-oriented in character.[11]

to plaintiff, sitting beside driver, held covered even though he was to assist the driver in loading and unloading, and at times in driving).

8. See, *e.g.*, Schaffer v. Mill Owners Mut. Ins. Co., 242 Ore. 150, 407 P.2d 614 (1965) (clause denying coverage while automobile "is being operated by any male operator under 25 years of age"; named insured was ill and asleep while 17-year-old son drove; held, no coverage; when used in this context "operator" is synonomous with "driver").

9. The precedents are not entirely in harmony. See, *e.g.*, Commercial Standard Ins. Co. v. New Amsterdam Cas. Co., 272 Ala. 357, 131 So.2d 182 (1961) (after having loaded shrubbery in car and talking with driver for a few minutes, nursery employee slammed car door on hand of passenger; held, loading had been completed before the accident and employee was not, therefore, an omnibus insured under the policy on the car); Travelers Ins. Co. v. Buckeye Union Cas. Co., 172 Ohio St. 507, 178 N.E.2d 792 (1961), 95 A.L.R. 2d 1114 (1964) (named insured's tank-truck driver was knocked off the back of the truck and injured as a spout was being swung into place for the purpose of filling the truck with a cargo of fuel; in a contest between insurance companies, held, third person responsible for operation of the spout was not "using" the truck, since the loading of it had not yet begun, and he therefore was not an omnibus insured under the truck owner's policy); Coletrain v. Coletrain, 238 S.C. 555, 121 S.E.2d 89 (1961), n.4 *supra*;

Amery Motor Co. v. Corey, 46 Wis.2d 291, 174 N.W.2d 540 (1970) (owner-lessees of bulk plant brought third party action against insurers of gasoline transporter, alleging they were additional insureds under liability policies; held, for insurers; furnishing key to unlock pipes to tanks when no employee of plant was present and furnishing defective tanks and storage equipment that led to explosion did not constitute "use of truck during unloading operation"); Lukaszewicz v. Concrete Research, Inc., 43 Wis.2d 335, 168 N.W.2d 581 (1969) (exclusion as to accidents during loading, attached to trucker's policy, held void as in violation of statutory requirement of omnibus clause; liability coverage of trucker's policy extended to concrete company and its employee who, while moving concrete slabs with a travel-lift vehicle to load truck, injured truck driver; "operating," as used in statute requiring omnibus, clause, construed broadly to include participation in loading; though statute did not require coverage for loading and unloading, it required that any such coverage for named insured be extended also to omnibus insureds).

10. See, *e.g.*, Red Ball Motor Freight, Inc. v. Employers Mut. Liab. Ins. Co., 189 F. 2d 374 (5th Cir. 1951) (Texas law; explosion caused by truck driver's negligently failing to close a valve between underground and overground tanks upon completing fueling of the truck; loading and unloading clause not re-

11. See note 11 on page 278.

Uninsured motorist coverage provides an array of illustrations of restrictive policy clauses.[12]   An example is the physical-contact requirement for coverage of hit-and-run accidents.[13]

SECTION 5.3 IMPLIED EXCEPTIONS

§ 5.3(a) PRINCIPLES UNDERLYING IMPLIED EXCEPTIONS

The phrase "implied exception" as used in insurance law ordinarily refers to a basis for an insurer's non-liability that is not expressed anywhere in the contract but is said to be implicit in the nature of the agreement and the circumstances to which it applies. Common examples of implied exceptions are the rules denying recovery under fire insurance for losses caused by "friendly fires," [1] under marine insurance for losses caused by ordinary deterioration of goods or by inherent vice,[2] and under liability insurance for losses caused intentionally by the insured.[3]

An examination of the whole array of implied exceptions recognized in insurance law reveals that most of the losses to which implied exceptions apply can be explained as illustrations of one or the other of two principles. First, insurance contracts do not ordinarily cover economic detriment of a type occurring so regularly in relation to an insured enterprise or activity that it is commonly regarded as a cost rather than a risk of that activity or enterprise.[4] Second, insurance contracts do not cover economic detriment that is not fortuitous from the point of view of the person (usually the insured) whose detriment is asserted as the basis of the insurer's liability. For example,

lied upon by the two-to-one majority; accident resulted from fueling and "fueling the truck for the journey was just as much a 'use' of it . . . [as] making the journey would be"); Carter v. Bergeron, 102 N.H. 464, 160 A.2d 348 (1960), 89 A.L.R.2d 142 (1963) (discussed in n.3 *supra*); Green Bus Lines, Inc. v. Ocean Acc. & Gy. Corp., 287 N.Y. 309, 39 N.E.2d 251 (1942), 162 A.L.R. 241 (1946) (passenger of common carrier attacked by fellow passenger; coverage under a policy issued to meet the requirements of a special statute applicable to vehicles for hire). Concerning fact-oriented disputes over causal relation between loading or unloading and loss, see, *e.g.*, Ocean Acc. & Gee. Corp. v. J. B. Pound Hotel Co., 69 Ga.App. 447, 26 S.E.2d 116 (1943) (pedestrian slipped on oil leaked from the load of an oil tank truck; no coverage under policy on the truck); Caron v. American Motorists' Ins. Co., 277 Mass. 156, 178 N.E. 286 (1931) (pedestrian slipped on ice dropped in unloading ice truck; no

coverage under a policy issued under the compulsory automobile insurance statute); Schmidt v. Utilities Ins. Co., 353 Mo. 213, 182 S.W.2d 181 (1944), 154 A.L.R. 1088 (1946) (pedestrian tripped over wooden blocks negligently left on sidewalk by coal deliveryman; held, injury arose from "use" of delivery truck).

11.   Concerning evaluative, fact-oriented issues generally, see § 1.6 *supra*.

12.   See §§ 4.9(d) *supra*, 7.3(c) *infra*. See generally Widiss, A Guide to Uninsured Motorist Coverage (1969).

13.   See § 8.6(e) n.7 *infra*.

1.   See § 5.3(d) *infra*.

2.   See § 5.3(c) *infra*.

3.   See § 5.3(f) *infra*.

4.   See, *e.g.*, § 5.3(c) and (d) *infra*. See also § 5.4(c) *infra*.

a loss is not fortuitous in this sense if caused intentionally by that person.[5]

These two criteria for implied exceptions may contribute to an understanding of the rules developed and may serve as useful aids in examining the merits of rules drawn into question. But they lack precision for marginal cases. Also, they are not altogether consistent with each other. For example, the first is concerned with a common understanding of what kinds of detriment constitute part of the routine costs as distinguished from the risks of an activity and thus has little if any force in the face of an explicit agreement contrary to the alleged common understanding. The second, on the other hand, is concerned with whether an economic detriment is fortuitous—a matter that may be regarded as so central to the concept of insurance that it is contrary to public policy to permit the enforcement of an agreement, purportedly an insurance contract, that violates it. Thus one of these basic principles supports the notion that an implied exception is a rule of interpretation designed only to apply in the absence of explicit agreement; the other, that it is a rule of public policy applicable regardless of explicit agreements to the contrary.

Implied exceptions have in some instances been shaped in part under the influence of other public policies as well as the two principles already stated. For example, objectives assertedly served by implied exceptions in life insurance cases have included, first, avoiding profit from wrongdoing, second, deterring crime, third, avoiding frauds against insurers, and fourth, maintaining coverage of a scope probably consistent with the reasonable expectations of the contracting parties on matters as to which no intention or expectation was expressed.[6]

The last of these objectives, like the first principle stated above, supports a rule of interpretation of contracts that can be rendered inapplicable by explicit agreement.[7] The other three, however, lend support to a rule of overriding public policy. In most instances, the state of precedents does not resolve this question about the nature of the implied exception in a given area of insurance law. More often than not, the point need not be decided in the particular case and the reasons advanced for decision tend to include variations on both these somewhat competitive ideas.[8]

§ 5.3(b) IMPLIED EXCEPTIONS IN LIFE INSURANCE

It has sometimes been argued that courts should decline to recognize any implied exceptions in life insurance cases because the occurrence of the insured event, death, is a certainty and the

---

5. See §§ 5.3(f), 5.4(b) *infra*.

6. See § 5.3(b) *infra*.

7. This objective is thus distinguished from the principle of honoring reasonable expectations even though inconsistent with a painstaking reading of the policy provisions, which is considered in § 6.3 *infra*.

8. See, *e.g.*, Burt v. Union Cent. Life Ins. Co., 187 U.S. 362, 23 Sup.Ct. 139, 47 L Ed. 216 (1902).

risk is concerned with time only. This argument is plainly fallacious as to term insurance, however, since under all such contracts it is uncertain whether death will occur during the term and under many it is highly improbable. Thus life insurance is not by nature preclusive of implied exceptions. Perhaps it is nevertheless true that courts have evidenced greater reluctance to find implied exceptions in life insurance cases. Partly this may be due to the all-risk character of life insurance contracts.[1] Perhaps even more it represents enforcement of a common understanding among laymen that life insurance covers death from any cause.[2] Another factor lending added weight to a reluctance to recognize implied exceptions is paternalistic concern for the third party beneficiaries of life insurance.

Barely more than half of the cases in point have denied recovery on a life insurance policy for death by execution for crime, even in the absence of an express exception in the policy.[3] But some of these decisions involved situations in which the criminal's estate was designated as the beneficiary of the policy, and it may be that a majority of jurisdictions would allow recovery when there is provision either in the policy or in the law (statutory or decisional) for the proceeds to go elsewhere than to the criminal's estate.[4]

If a life insurance policy contains no clause excepting death or injury resulting from a criminal act of the insured, and death results from such an act but not by legal execution, only a minority of the decisions deny recovery to a designated beneficiary other than the insured or his estate.[5]

---

1. See § 5.1(b) (1) *supra*.

2. *Cf.* § 6.3 *infra*.

3. *E.g.*, Smith v. Metropolitan Life Ins. Co., 125 Misc. 670, 211 N.Y.S. 755 (App.Div.1925); Collins v. Metropolitan Life Ins. Co., 27 Pa.Super. 353 (1905). See Annot., 36 A.L.R. 1255 (1925). The rationale of some cases following the minority view has been based in part on the untenable argument that the denial of recovery is inconsistent with statutory and constitutional provisions against corruption of blood and forfeiture for crime. *E.g.*, American Nat'l Ins. Co. v. Coates, 112 Tex. 267, 246 S.W. 356 (1923). See also 6 Williston, Contracts § 1750 (rev. ed. 1938).

4. See, *e.g.*, John Hancock Mut. Life Ins. Co. v. Tarrence, 244 F.2d 86 (6th Cir. 1957) (2–1 decision that recovery by a beneficiary other than the estate of the criminal is allowed under the law of New York, one of the jurisdictions classified with the "majority" in n.3 *supra*); Prudential Ins. Co. v. Petril, 43 F.Supp. 768 (E.D.Pa.1942) (applying the law of Pennsylvania, another jurisdiction classified with the

"majority" in n.3 *supra*; recovery allowed; rationale based on grounds that the decisional public policy disallowing recovery is applicable only to cases in which the criminal's estate profits and that a similar public policy is expressed in a Pennsylvania statute, one section of which applies directly to this case; under this statute, the proceeds of a policy *on the life of a slayer* designating the slain as beneficiary are to be paid to the estate of the slain, unless the contingent beneficiary is one other than the slayer or his estate).

5. Home State Life Ins. Co. v. Russell, 175 Okla. 492, 53 P.2d 562 (1936), is an example of the majority rule. Molloy v. John Hancock Mut. Life Ins. Co., 327 Mass. 181, 97 N.E.2d 422 (1951), 23 A.L.R.2d 1103 (1952), is an example of the minority view: "Decisions of this court have established the proposition that public policy forbids even an innocent beneficiary of a policy of life insurance to recover on the policy where the death of the insured is the result of his own criminal conduct." 327 Mass. at 182, 97 N.E.2d at 423, 23 A.L.R.2d at 1104.

suicide

Under the English [6] and minority American [7] view, it is against public policy to allow a life insurance recovery for death by suicide while sane, regardless of whether the terms of the contract are silent on this matter or instead purport to allow coverage under some circumstances. But contracts allowing recovery for death by suicide are enforceable by the great weight of American authority, and at least when the policy names a beneficiary other than the estate of the insured, the weight of authority among American cases allows recovery upon a policy that contains no express provisions concerning suicide.[8] Policies now commonly contain a provision disallowing coverage for death by suicide only under specified conditions (*e. g.*, while sane and within two years from the date of the policy),[9] and in many states there are regulatory statutes forbidding suicide clauses more favorable to the insurer.[10]

A similar question occasionally arises in connection with other kinds of insurance—for example, whether loss caused by a fortuitous collision is covered by collision insurance when the collision occurs because of criminal conduct of the insured. See, *e.g.*, Acme Fin. Co. v. National Ins. Co., 118 Colo. 445, 195 P.2d 728 (1948), 4 A.L.R.2d 131 (1949) (mortgagee of car totally demolished in collision occurring during "getaway" from robbery and murder denied coverage on grounds of public policy).

6. *E.g.*, Beresford v. Royal Ins. Co., [1938] A.C. 586 (no recovery though there was a clause saying the company would not be liable if the insured committed suicide "whether sane or insane, within one year" and the policy had been in force nearly ten years; it appeared that the insured was financially embarrassed and committed suicide for the purpose of making insurance proceeds of 50,000 pounds available to his creditors).

7. *E.g.*, Ritter v. Mutual Life Ins. Co., 169 U.S. 139, 18 Sup.Ct. 300, 42 L.Ed. 693 (1898).

8. *E.g.*, Patterson v. Natural Premium Mut. Life Ins. Co., 100 Wis. 118, 75 N.W. 980 (1898). See 2 Richards, Law of Insurance 827 (5th ed. Freedman 1952). *Cf.* 43 Am.Jur.2d 1111, Insurance §§ 1191, 1192 (1969), which is in accord as to a policy payable to a third person, but asserts that "[i]n the case of a policy payable to the estate of the insured, it is without doubt the rule that intentional self-destruction by the insured when of sound mind is itself a defense to an action on the policy, even if the policy does not ex-

pressly declare that it shall be void in such a case." *Id.* § 1191.

9. See Appendix E *infra*. The suicide clause of life and accident insurance policies often includes the phrase "sane or insane," thereby disallowing coverage, for the period stated in the clause even for a suicide induced by insanity. In the absence of a statute to the contrary, such clauses are generally held valid. Insanity may, however, be found to have negated suicide. Thus, though it is generally held that the insured need not have comprehended the moral or legal nature and consequences of his act for the clause to apply, the decisions are in conflict as to whether the insured must have comprehended the *physical* nature and consequences of his act for application of the clause. See, *e.g.*, Aetna Life Ins. Co. v. McLaughlin, 380 S.W.2d 101 (Tex.1964), 9 A.L.R.3d 1005 (1966) (insured under an accident policy providing a death benefit but excluding loss or death caused by "suicide, sane or insane," died after falling or lunging in front of a bus while intoxicated; held, reversing judgment for the insured's widow because of an error in instructions, no coverage if insured died as the result of an act that would be considered suicide if committed by a sane person, regardless of whether he was conscious of the physical nature and consequences of his act or had an intent to kill himself). See also 1 Appleman, Insurance Law § 363 (rev. ed. 1965).

10. *E.g.*, N.Y. Ins. Law § 155 (McKinney 1966) allows a provision against liability for suicide within two years from the date of the policy but forbids clauses more favorable to

Another theory of implied exception for which there is support, at least in limited circumstances, concerns cases in which the life insurance beneficiary kills the person whose life is insured.[11]

Reasons given for the denial of recovery in these various types of cases—suicide, legal execution, death caused by criminal act of the insured, and death at the hands of the beneficiary—have included, first, avoiding profit from wrongdoing,[12] second, deterring crime,[13] third, avoiding frauds against insurers,[14] and fourth, maintaining coverage of a scope probably consistent with the reasonable expectations of the contracting parties on matters as to which no intention or expectation was expressed.[15]

The last two of these considerations are clearly relevant to the insurer's liability and not merely to disqualifying the wrongdoer from receiving proceeds. But the first two objectives—avoiding profit from wrongdoing and deterring crime—would be served by rules merely disqualifying the wrongdoers from receiving insurance proceeds. They afford only weak support, at best, for granting the insurer a defense against liability. It is not surprising then that many decisions in this area have denied benefits of the insurance to the wrongdoer but allowed others to recover the insurance proceeds[16] rather than recognizing an implied exception to coverage of the life insurance policy.

§ 5.3(c) INHERENT VICE

Though all-risk in character,[1] marine insurance is subject to a well established implied exception of inherent vice.[2] That is, deterioration of a vessel or goods due to ordinary wear and tear and inevitable depreciation does not come within coverage for loss from "perils of the sea."[3] However, when the natural decay of goods results from delay caused by a peril insured against, recovery for the loss is permitted.[4]

---

the insurer. It has been construed as supporting recovery for suicide while insane, even though within two years of the date of the policy. See Franklin v. John Hancock Mut. Life Ins. Co., 298 N.Y. 81, 80 N.E.2d 746 (1948).

11. See § 4.11(g) (4) *supra.*

12. *Cf.* New York Mut. Life Ins. Co. v. Armstrong, 117 U.S. 591, 6 Sup.Ct. 877, 29 L.Ed. 997 (1886).

13. *Cf.* Burt v. Union Cent. Life Ins. Co., 187 U.S. 362, 365–366, 23 Sup.Ct. 139, 140, 47 L.Ed. 216, 219 (1902).

14. *Cf.* New York Mut. Life Ins. Co. v. Armstrong, 117 U.S. 591, 6 Sup.Ct. 877, 29 L.Ed. 997 (1886).

15. *Cf.* Burt v. Union Cent. Life Ins. Co., 187 U.S. 362, 363–364, 23 Sup.Ct. 139–140, 47 L.Ed. 216, 218 (1902).

16. *E.g.,* Continental Bank & Trust Co. v. Maag, 285 F.2d 558 (10th Cir. 1960); Carter v. Carter, 88 So.2d 153 (Fla.1956). See § 4.11(g) *supra.*

1. See § 5.1(b) (1) *supra.*

2. See generally British Marine Insurance Act, 1906, § 55(2) (c); 2 Arnould, Marine Insurance [10 British Shipping Laws] 717–719, § 762 (15th ed. 1961); 5A Appleman, Insurance Law § 3272 (rev. ed. 1970).

3. See, *e.g.,* Reisman v. New Hampshire Fire Ins. Co., 312 F.2d 17 (5th Cir. 1963). As to the burden of proof relating to inherent vice, see § 5.1(b) (3) *supra.* It would appear that the plaintiff has the burden of showing that deterioration of the goods was

---

4. See note 4 on page 283.

[handwritten margin notes: confined in; eg. in stove or furnace; ie, in its intended place]

§ 5.3(d) THE FRIENDLY FIRE RULE

Despite want of any specific language in policies to support the result, courts have commonly recognized an implied exception under which loss caused by a "friendly" as distinguished from a "hostile" fire is not covered by a fire insurance policy. In general, a friendly fire is one contained in an ordinary place for a fire in use, such as a stove or furnace.[1] Hostile fires include not only those accidentally occurring in a place where fire is ordinarily not maintained but also those that are in origin friendly but escape their usual confines. There is limited but perhaps increasing support for classifying as hostile, also, a fire that gets out of control and becomes excessive even though remaining within the intended place.[2]

The precise line between friendly and hostile fires has been a subject of considerable conflict in decisions.[3] Patterson has suggested that, in the friendly-fire exception, the courts are aiming at a functional distinction "between mere irregularities in the process of manufacture or other use of fire as an instrument [as in the case of the baker who inadvertently overbakes his bread], which would be charged off to the cost of doing business, and those ex-

---

not due "to a certainty or to inherent vice or to wear and tear." This is implied in British & Foreign Marine Ins. Co. v. Gaunt, [1921] 2 A.C. 41, both in Lord Birkenhead's comment that "the plaintiff discharges his special onus when he has proved that the loss was caused by some event covered by the general expression . . . ." and in Lord Sumner's comment that "he need only give evidence reasonably showing that the loss was due to a casualty . . . ." [1921] 2 A.C. at 46, 58. See also Goldman v. Rhode Island Ins. Co., 100 F.Supp. 196 (E.D.Pa.1951).

4. See Lanasa Fruit Steamship & Importing Co. v. Universal Ins. Co., 302 U.S. 556, 58 Sup.Ct. 371, 82 L.Ed. 422 (1938); 5A Appleman, Insurance Law § 3269 (rev. ed. 1970).

1. See, *e.g.*, Youse v. Employer's Fire Ins. Co., 172 Kan. 111, 238 P.2d 472 (1951). See also, *e.g.*, Levert-St. John, Inc. v. Birmingham Fire & Cas. Co., 137 So.2d 494 (La.App.1961), in which the court recognized that the "friendly fire" distinction is not usually made in Louisiana but held that the distinction was relevant to the applicability of a fire insurance clause excluding coverage of loss caused by explosion (holding that an explosion set off by a welder's ignition spark was caused by

a friendly fire and, therefore, that the exclusionary clause was applicable). *But see, e.g.*, Harris v. Poland, [1941] 1 K.B. 462 (apprehensive of theft, the insured hid her jewelry under wood and coal on a grate, which she lighted later, having forgotten about the jewelry; held, coverage under a Lloyds Householders Comprehensive Policy insuring "against loss or damage caused by Fire . . . ."). See 5 Appleman, Insurance Law § 3082 (rev. ed. 1970).

2. *E.g.*, L. L. Freeberg Pie Co. v. St. Paul Mut. Ins. Co., 257 Minn. 244, 100 N.W.2d 753 (1960) (excessive heating of commercial baking oven caused by a malfunctioning thermostat resulted in structural damage to the oven and heat damage to hardwood floor underneath and in front of the oven; held, "hostile" fire covered by standard fire policy). See Mooney, *Is the "Friendly" Fire Doctrine Becoming Obsolete?*, 1968 Ins.L.J. 945; Annot., 17 A.L.R.3d 1155 (1968). *But cf.* 5 Appleman, Insurance Law § 3082 n.27.25 (rev. ed. 1970).

3. *Compare, e.g.*, Harris v. Poland, [1941] 1 K.B. 462, *with, e.g.*, Youse v. Employer's Fire Ins. Co., 172 Kan. 111, 238 P.2d 472 (1951). See Reis, *The Friendly Versus Hostile Fire Dichotomy*, 12 Vill.L.Rev. 109 (1966).

traordinary, accidental fires against which a prudent business man insures. . . . However, . . . the functional distinction is rather vague, and it is not surprising to find that the test commonly applied by the courts is a mechanical one, namely, was the 'fire' (in the chemical sense) confined to the receptacle or other *place where* it was intended to be."[4] Perhaps, however, cases cited since the date of Patterson's article have tended to expand the meaning of "hostile" somewhat more than this mechanical test would support.[5]

Some friendly fire losses are not fortuitous. This is true, for example, of the destruction of a ring deliberately tossed into a furnace for the purpose of destroying it, whatever the motivation for such destruction might be. Non-coverage for some other friendly fire losses can be justified under one of the principles underlying implied exceptions generally—namely, that insurance is designed to cover risks, not costs of an activity.[6] That is, some losses are of such nature that they are part of the regular costs of maintaining fires rather than being extraordinary losses. This latter explanation may be offered for denying liability for damage from soot and smoke that escape when one builds in a fireplace a fire larger than it was designed for but not large enough to cause the escape of flame.[7] But it is clear that the friendly-fire exception has sometimes been extended even further. For example, almost uniformly courts have held that damage to or loss of jewelry thrown inadvertently into a stove, furnace, or fireplace is not covered by fire insurance.[8] The explanation cannot be that there is a public policy against such coverage, since it is undisputed that this type of loss is insurable under floater policies.[9] The explanation must lie elsewhere.

Many opinions have advanced the explanation that in common parlance one has not "had a fire" if the fire has burned only in the place where it was intended to burn.[10] But to ask whether one has "had a fire" is to ask a question not posed by policy language itself, since the policy requires not that one "have a fire" but that he suffer a "direct loss by fire."[11] The question whether, in common parlance, the person who accidentally tossed his diamond ring into a stove has suffered a direct loss by fire might well be answered in the affirmative.

---

4. Patterson, *The Apportionment of Business Risks Through Legal Devices*, 24 Colum.L.Rev. 335, 338 (1924) (emphasis is Patterson's).

5. See n.2 *supra*.

6. See § 5.3(a) *supra*.

7. It might be argued also that "direct loss by fire" (the phrase customarily appearing in fire insurance policies) refers to flame damage rather than damage from soot, smoke, or heat. But that rationale would involve one in an inconsistency since it is well established that these kinds of damage from a *hostile* fire are included within the losses for which an insurer is liable, even though the requirement that they be regarded as within the phrase "direct loss by fire" applies here too.

8. *E.g.*, Youse v. Employer's Fire Ins. Co., 172 Kan. 111, 238 P.2d 472 (1951).

9. See *ibid*.

10. *Ibid*.

11. See Appendix A *infra*.

Another explanation of the friendly fire rule often advanced and perhaps less vulnerable is that, whatever the merits or demerits of the exception initially, its existence is now common knowledge, and it is in fact understood by most policyholders. The counter-argument that this interpretation of the fire policy is contrary to reasonable expectations of policyholders[12] gains force, however, in the context of residential as distinguished from commercial insureds, since householders generally are less likely than business men to know of the understanding common in insurance circles.[13]

As extended to a case involving damage to a ring accidentally tossed into a stove, the friendly fire rule, it would seem, is less cogently supported by the language of the fire insurance policy or by the probable expectations of the policyholder without experience in insurance matters than would be a rule recognizing coverage. It may thus be regarded as one of a limited number of instances in which courts have resolved ambiguities of policy language or have filled in lacunae in favor of insurers.[14]

§ 5.3(e) NEGLIGENCE, GROSS NEGLIGENCE, AND RECKLESSNESS

The questions, first, whether it is against public policy for insurance to apply to losses caused by the insured's negligence and, second, if not, whether particular contract provisions provide such coverage have produced a surprisingly large number of strikingly misleading judicial opinions. One such group of opinions, discussed in a later section, concerns coverage under liability insurance policies for highly expectable losses.[1] Another group of misleading judicial opinions concerns fire insurance coverage.

It has been said to be the general rule that gross negligence or recklessness on the part of the insured "may preclude a recovery" under a fire policy.[2] In most and perhaps all instances, however, the statements to this effect in judicial opinions have been at least arguably dicta, if not plainly so. Moreover, in many instances, the statement is in such form that it is subject to the interpretation that it refers to conduct of a type supporting the inference that the actor probably intended to cause the destruction of the insured property.[3]

---

12. See § 6.3 *infra*.

13. See, *e.g.*, Harris v. Poland, [1941] 1 K.B. 462.

14. See § 6.9(a) *infra*.

1. See § 5.4(c) *infra*.

2. See, *e.g.*, Fidelity-Phenix Fire Ins. Co. v. Lawler, 38 Ala.App. 245, 81 So. 2d 908 (1955), quoting Annot., 10 A.L. R. 728 (1921). *Cf.* 5 Appleman, Insurance Law § 3114 (rev.ed.1970).

3. See, *e.g.*, Todd v. Traders & Mechanics' Ins. Co., 230 Mass. 595, 120 N.E. 142 (1918). One of the plaintiffs started a fire in tall grass overhanging a raspberry bed to see if a grass path could be burned over without scorching the berries. Being satisfied with the experiment, he stamped out the flames. Shortly thereafter, a flame flared up 15 or 20 feet on the other side of the raspberry bed and burned a barn before it could be controlled. Plaintiff had violated a statute prohibiting the lighting of a fire

Thus, despite the consistent repetition of the proposition, it seems doubtful that gross negligence or recklessness will be recognized as a defense in the absence of a statute[4] or policy clause[5] so providing. Perhaps even a statutory adoption of the dictum will be narrowly construed so as to amount to little enlargement of the defense of deliberate destruction of the insured property.[6]

§ 5.3(f) INTENTIONAL TORTS AND PUNITIVE DAMAGES UNDER LIABILITY INSURANCE

The proposition that losses intentionally caused by the insured are not covered by liability insurance often appears in policy clauses.[1] Even when not expressed in the contract, this proposition is supported by an implied exception[2] based on the fact that the loss is not for-

in the open air without permission of a town official. The insurers denied liability on fire insurance policies, and this action was brought. In holding for the plaintiffs the court declared: "Mere negligence on the part of the insured does not prevent recovery on a policy of insurance. One of the objects of insurance is to protect the insured from loss due to carelessness. In *Johnson v. Berkshire Mutual Fire Ins. Co.*, 4 Allen [86 Mass.], 388 [(1862)], it was held that the insured could recover for the loss by fire of his barn and contents, where he had lighted some straw under the barn in order to smoke out bees, and the fire rapidly spread and destroyed the property. On the other hand the insurer is not liable for a fraudulent loss, due to the intentional destruction of property by the insured, or to such reckless and inexcusable negligence as tends to show a fraudulent purpose or design." 230 Mass. at 598–599, 120 N. E. at 144.

4. See Ga.Code Ann. § 56–819 (1953) (repealed, Ga.Laws 1960, p. 289): "The insured shall be bound to ordinary diligence in protecting the property from fire, and gross negligence on his part shall relieve the insurer. Simple negligence by a servant or the insured, unaffected by fraud or design in the latter, shall not relieve the insurer." This is not a common type of statute.

5. Concerning policy clauses restricting coverage because of negligence, gross negligence, or recklessness of the insured in failing to protect property after an accident, see § 5.4(d) *infra*.

6. Compare the scope-limiting interpretations of statutes prohibiting liability insurance against intentional wrongdoing or relieving liability insurers of liability for "wilful" acts of the insured; see § 5.3(f) *infra*. But *cf*. Pennsylvania Threshermans & Farmers Mut. Ins. Cos. v. McCall, 102 Ga.App. 137, 115 S.E.2d 740 (1960) (insured extinguished tractor fire by throwing sand and dirt on it, then failed to clean the tractor thoroughly before using it; a complete breakdown occurred after the tractor was operated for a short time; held, Ga. Code Ann. § 56–819 (1953) [subsequently repealed] would preclude recovery if the jury should find that insured's use of sand and dirt to extinguish the fire and his subsequent failure to clean the tractor thoroughly were gross negligence, which was equated with failure to exercise even *slight* diligence).

1. See § 5.4(b) *infra*.

2. *Cf.* Haser v. Maryland Cas. Co., 78 N.D. 893, 53 N.W.2d 508 (1952), 33 A.L.R.2d 1018 (1954) (liability coverage for rapist would be contrary to public policy; coverage denied even though "caused by accident" defined coverage of broader scope than merely for negligence). There is a dearth of direct authority for an implied exception of this nature, perhaps in part because of the fact that policies rarely fail to include express requirements and in part because the proposition is so clearly sound in principle that it would ordinarily go unchallenged even if there were no policy clause in point. *But cf.* Wolff v. General Cas. Co., 68 N.M. 292, 361 P.2d 330 (1961) (reversing summary judgment for insurer, obtained on theory that insurer was not bound to defend and pay

tuitous from the point of view of the person whose interest the liability insurance contract is designed to protect.[3]

The concept of intentionally-caused loss underlying this implied exception does not include all losses for which recovery is awarded under the theory of intentional tort. In many instances damages awarded against a defendant under a theory of intentional tort are nevertheless fortuitously caused from his point of view.[4] Even when the prohibition against coverage for intentional wrongdoing is expressed in a statute rather than a judicially-created implied exception, a court may recognize this distinction and correspondingly limit the scope of the statutory prohibition.[5]

If the facts underlying a claim support denial of coverage under an implied exception as to intentionally-caused loss, both punitive and compensatory damages are beyond coverage. If, on the other hand, the loss is not intentionally caused within the meaning of the implied exception, even though tort law classifies the cause of action as intentional tort, there remains a question whether coverage should be limited to compensatory damages because of a separate implied exception denying coverage for punitive damages. The principal argument for such an exception is that the purpose of assessing punitive damages is not to recognize any special merit of the victim's claim but to punish the wrongdoer; allowing the wrongdoer to shift the responsibility for punitive damages to an insurer would thwart this public policy favoring punishment.[6]

It may be noted that even compensatory tort judgments serve punitive and deterrent objectives, and it has been argued that liability insurance thwarts these objectives. Such arguments have been found insufficient to justify outlawing liability insurance generally,[7] but

judgment on claim for assault and battery by its insured; "Blanket Liability Policy" did not expressly exclude intentional injury from the coverage and referred to "accident" only in a "per-accident" limit on the amount of coverage; note, however, that insured claimed he discharged a tear-gas pencil at victim because he believed himself in danger; see § 5.-4(b) and n.18 thereto *infra*).

3. Concerning the proper point of view for considering whether loss is fortuitous, see § 5.4(a) *infra*. Note that if a financial responsibility statute is construed as intended to protect victims even in cases of intentional tort, allowing the victim to recover does not offend this principle of implied exception; see § 5.4(b) and n.2 thereto *infra*.

4. See § 5.4(b) *infra*.

5. See, *e.g.*, Capachi v. Glens Falls Ins. Co., 215 Cal.App.2d 843, 30 Cal.Rptr.

323 (App.Dep't Super.Ct.1963) (restaurant owner covered for liability arising out of false arrest although Cal. Ins.Code § 533 (West 1955) provided that "wilful" acts of an insured did not subject the insurer to liability; "[i]t is significant that the liability . . . in the false arrest action . . . need not have been founded on an implied finding of ill will or desire to injure, for although intent is necessary as an element of the tort of false arrest, malice, in the sense of ill will or desire to injure, is not . . ."). See also § 5.4(b) *infra.*

6. See, *e.g.*, American Sur. Co. v. Gold, 375 F.2d 523 (10th Cir. 1967), 20 A.L. R.3d 335 (1968) (forecasting Kansas law).

7. *E.g.*, Breeden v. Frankford Marine Acc. & Plate Glass Ins. Co., 220 Mo. 327, 423–435, 119 S.W. 576, 606–610 (1909). Concerning the validity of liability insurance generally, see 7 Ap-

they have greater force as to awards of punitive damages not only because punishment of the wrongdoer is the prime objective but also because countervailing interests favoring compensation of victims are in this context limited if not totally absent. Thus, there is precedent for denial of coverage for punitive damages on public policy grounds.[8] A court may take this view, however, and still permit coverage for the compensatory damages awarded for precisely the same conduct.[9] Some courts, however, have disagreed with the basic principle of an implied exception for punitive damages, holding that liability insurance covers punitive as well as compensatory damages in the absence of policy provisions to the contrary.[10]

SECTION 5.4 REQUIREMENTS CONCERNING THE ACCIDENTAL NATURE OF LOSS

§ 5.4(a) GENERALLY

A requirement that loss be accidental in some sense in order to qualify as the occasion for liability of an insurer is implicit, when not express, because of the very nature of insurance. Such a requirement is one of the principles underlying implied exceptions recognized in insurance law.[1]

Also, insurance contracts often contain explicit provisions requiring that loss be accidental in some sense to sustain coverage. Sometimes such provisions are in the form of a basic definition of covered risks in terms of accidental loss [2] or some variation on this idea.[3] In other instances the requirement that loss be accidental in some sense is a separately stated restriction of the basic definition of coverage.[4]

Such policy clauses may restrict coverage to an extent well beyond the effect of the public policy underlying the implied exception

---

pleman, Insurance Law § 4252 (rev. ed. 1962); Gardner, *Insurance Against Tort Liability—An Approach to the Cosmology of the Law*, 15 Law & Contemp.Prob. 455, 462–463 (1950).

8. See cases cited in n.6 *supra* and n.9 *infra*.

9. *E.g.*, Crull v. Gleb, 382 S.W.2d 17 (Mo.App.1964) (reckless operation of automobile). *Cf.* Northwestern Nat'l Cas. Co. v. McNulty, 307 F.2d 432 (5th Cir. 1962) (forecasting Virginia and Florida law; disallowing coverage for punitive damages and distinguishing cases holding insurers bound for compensatory damages awarded on the basis of recklessness or wilful and wanton misconduct).

10. *E.g.*, Southern Farm Bureau Cas. Ins. Co. v. Daniel, 246 Ark. 813, 440 S.W.2d 582 (1969) (automobile colli-

sion); Carroway v. Johnson, 245 S.C. 200, 139 S.E.2d 908 (1965) (automobile collision); Lazenby v. Universal Underwriters Ins. Co., 214 Tenn. 639, 383 S.W.2d 1 (1964) (automobile collision). See 7 Appleman, Insurance Law § 4312 (rev. ed. 1962); 8 *id.* § 4900; Note, *Insurance Coverage and the Punitive Award in the Automobile Accident Suit*, 19 U.Pitt.L.Rev. 144 (1957).

1. See § 5.3(a) *supra*.

2. See, *e.g.*, New York Life Ins. Co. v. Harrington, 299 F.2d 803 (9th Cir. 1962) ("accidental bodily injury" clause).

3. See § 5.4(b) *infra*.

4. See, *e.g.*, the "Assault and Battery" clause of some liability insurance forms, described in § 5.4(b) *infra*.

from coverage of non-fortuitous losses. For example, even apart from more restrictive phrases sometimes incorporated in life and personal accident policies, the terms "accidental death" and "accidental bodily injury" themselves express an intention to narrow coverage to something far short of all fortuitous harms to the insured. Disease and bodily deterioration, for example, are not within the risks covered by such contract provisions, even though they produce losses that are fortuitous and as to which there is no public policy against insurance coverage.

It is also possible, though perhaps less likely, that an implied exception of broader scope, enforced as a rule of interpretation and not as an overriding rule of public policy,[5] will be narrowed by language of a policy clause expressing or implying an understanding of coverage for a type of risk that would have been treated as impliedly excepted in the absence of the policy clause.

In view of the impact of both public policy and contract provisions, the grounds of decision in precedents concerning the requirement that loss be fortuitous, or that it be accidental in some more restrictive sense, are a medley of interpretation of expressed qualifications of coverage and application of implied exceptions, some based on a theory of interpretation and some on overriding public policy. As might be expected, these lines of thought are not always carefully distinguished, and it is sometimes difficult to ascertain whether the court has been influenced by one, or the other, or both.

Confusion has arisen with respect to the point of view from which a court should examine the question whether loss is accidental. Some opinions and other legal writings have declared that the question is to be examined from the point of view of the insured;[6] others, from the point of view of the person injured.[7] But, with perhaps a

---

5. See § 5.3(a) *supra.*

6. *E.g.,* New York Life Ins. Co. v. Harrington, 299 F.2d 803 (9th Cir. 1962) (applying California law; insured under a life policy providing double indemnity in the event of death caused by "accidental bodily injury" shot himself by placing a loaded gun to his temple and pulling the trigger, thinking, however, that the safety catch was engaged; held, the insured's widow could collect the accidental death benefits—"[o]nce it is established that . . . [the insured's] belief in the safety was not unreasonable as a matter of law, the death was as to him unexpected . . ." and, therefore, accidental).

7. *E.g.,* Jernigan v. Allstate Ins. Co., 269 F.2d 353, *opinion on denial of rehearing,* 272 F.2d 857 (5th Cir. 1959) (applying Louisiana law; coverage for injury deliberately inflicted by

omnibus insured; dissent on ground the driver was later determined to be insane and that neither the driver nor the insurer should be liable; perhaps the result reached by the majority could have been rested solely on the impact of the Louisiana Direct Action Statute, but the opinion is reasoned also on the broader ground that the injury was accidental from the point of view of the victim); Haser v. Maryland Cas. Co., 78 N.D. 893, 53 N.W.2d 508 (1952), 33 A.L.R.2d 1018 (1954) (liability insurance coverage for rapist denied on grounds of public policy; dictum approving coverage for vicarious liability of his employer and saying that "accident" in contract provisions is to be interpreted from the point of view of the victim); Fox Wis. Corp. v. Century Indem. Co., 219 Wis. 549, 263 N.W. 567 (1935) (liability insurer held liable for judgment recovered against insured and for cost of defense of suit resulting from an

few exceptions [8] cases in these opposite groups may in fact be quite consistent by a more appropriate standard of classification. The meaning of "fortuitous," "accidental," or like terms should be determined from the point of view of the person whose interest is protected by the policy.[9]

In the case of property insurance and accident insurance, ordinarily the insured and the victim of the accident are the same person; his is the interest protected by the policy.[10]

In the case of liability insurance, absent some statutory requirement that it be available in order to protect potential victims,[11] the person whose interest is protected is the insured rather than the victim of physical harm, and the economic loss against which he is protected is legal liability.

In the case of life insurance, it is not the economic interest of the person whose life is insured but rather the interest of his beneficiaries that is being protected under the customary policy. The designated beneficiaries are third party beneficiaries in their own right and not merely as a practical incident of the protection of some other person, as in the case of the victim who ultimately receives the benefit of liability insurance coverage by being able to collect against a tortfeasor who might otherwise have been judgment proof. This suggests that not only homicide but also suicide may be accidental from the point of view of those whose interests are protected; therefore recovery of life insurance proceeds by a named beneficiary following homicide or suicide is not contrary to the public policy opposing insurance against non-fortuitous losses.[12] Subject to statutory restrictions, however, the terms of life insurance contracts may exclude coverage for suicides and homicides in some circumstances. Also, provi-

---

assault by an employee of the insured on a patron of the insured's theatre). See also § 5.4(b) and n.2 thereto *infra*.

8. *Jernigan*, n.7 *supra*, might be such an exception.

9. This is not to say, however, that a contract expressly providing otherwise would be invalid for reasons of public policy. See, *e.g.*, the accident insurance clause quoted in Butler v. Peninsular Life Ins., 115 So.2d 608 (Fla. App.1959) ("agreement as to benefits under this policy . . . shall be null and void if the insured's . . . loss . . . results directly or indirectly from . . . intentional act or acts of any person or persons"), and the life insurance clause quoted in Colonial Life & Acc. Ins. Co. v. Wagner, 380 S.W.2d 224 (Ky.1964) ("insurance under this [group life] certificate shall not cover death or other loss caused . . . by in-

juries intentionally inflicted upon the Insured Employee by any other person").

10. See, *e.g.*, Nuffer v. Insurance Co. of N. Am., 236 Cal.App.2d 349, 45 Cal. Rptr. 918 (4th Dist. 1965) (hotel manager intentionally set fire to the structure; held, recovery by insured-owner, since the manager acted without authority from or knowledge of the insured). *But see*, *e.g.*, Klemens v. Badger Mut. Ins. Co., 8 Wis.2d 565, 99 N.W.2d 865 (1959) (husband set fire to property owned jointly with his wife, who did not have knowledge of his wrongdoing; held, no recovery under policy issued to husband and wife jointly).

11. See § 5.4(b) and n.2 thereto *infra*.

12. But note the English view supporting an implied exception for suicide; see § 5.3(b) *supra*.

sions for double indemnity in case of "accidental" death [13] may define "accidental" in a way that excludes suicides and homicides.

§ 5.4(b) INTENTIONAL LOSSES UNDER LIABILITY INSURANCE

One corollary of the central idea that insurance concerns fortuitous losses only is that there is no coverage for intentional loss. The question whether loss is intentional, like the more comprehensive question whether loss is fortuitous, should be examined from the point of view of the person whose loss is the asserted basis of the insurer's liability.[1] Thus, in liability insurance cases, ordinarily this question should be examined from the point of view of the person who is the insured as to the particular claim. There is some support, however, for an exception with respect to cases affected by a statutory requirement of liability insurance coverage, imposed for the protection of victims rather than insureds. Certainly fidelity to the principle that loss must be fortuitous may be preserved without precluding liability of the insurer to the victim. The victim, as to whom loss is fortuitous, can be allowed protection without giving coverage to a tortfeasor who intentionally injured him. For example, the insurer may be required to pay the victim but granted a right of reimbursement from the tortfeasor.

Several state courts of last resort have construed their "compulsory" automobile insurance or "noncompulsory" financial responsibility acts as so providing.[2] A decision construing a statute for the

---

13. See § 5.4(e) *infra*.

1. See § 5.4(a) *supra*.

2. *E.g.*, Wheeler v. O'Connell, 297 Mass. 549, 9 N.E.2d 544, 111 A.L.R. 1038 (1937) (wilfull, wanton and reckless operation of truck, causing injury to officer who was on running board attempting to halt it; declaration of public policy in compulsory automobile insurance law for protection of victims supersedes any rule of public policy in ordinary insurance law); Hartford Acc. & Indem. Co. v. Wolbarst, 95 N.H. 40, 57 A.2d 151 (1948) (deliberate bumping of another car, unintentionally causing injury to occupants; in declaratory proceedings, held coverage under liability insurance policy containing customary provision that the insurance afforded "shall comply" with any applicable financial responsibility law; opinion notes statutory and policy provisions for insurer's right of reimbursement from tortfeasor); Nationwide Mut. Ins. Co. v. Roberts, 261 N.C. 285, 134 S.E.2d 654 (1964) (deliberate driving of car against pedestrian; in declaratory

proceedings, held coverage under compulsory liability insurance policy; opinion notes statutory and policy provisions for insurer's right of reimbursement from tortfeasor, as to which see §§ 2.11(b) (5), 4.8(c) n.8 *supra*). *But cf.* Peerless Cas. Co. v. Cole, 121 Vt. 258, 155 A.2d 866 (1959) (insurer's settlement with victims constitutes election; cannot rely on insurance contract for right to settle and at the same time claim it is ineffectual; the facts were, however, that settlements were made before notice to the insured that the insurer denied coverage). See also Jernigan v. Allstate Ins. Co., 269 F.2d 353, *opinion on denial of rehearing*, 272 F.2d 857 (5th Cir. 1959) (applying Louisiana law; coverage for deliberate injury inflicted by omnibus insured; majority note the Louisiana Direct Action Statute, designed to protect victims, but reason also on broader ground that this was an accident from the point of view of the victim; dissent on the ground that the driver had later been determined to be insane and that neither the driver nor the insurer should be liable); New Amsterdam Cas. Co. v.

protection of motoring victims as applying even to a case of deliberate use of a car to commit a battery may be criticized as an unwarranted interpretation of the statute aimed at assuring compensation for victims of motoring risks, as distinguished from deliberate use of a vehicle as a weapon,[3] but this construction is not offensive to the principles underlying implied exceptions in insurance law so long as the insurance protection is not extended also to the tortfeasor—the person from whose point of view the injury was intended.

Under liability insurance, except to the extent that special rights are granted to victims even though coverage for the alleged insured (the tortfeasor) is denied, it is not enough to escape the preclusion against coverage of nonfortuitous losses that the loss is fortuitous from the point of view of the victim. And, conversely, it is not enough to preclude coverage for a named or additional insured of a policy that the harm was intentionally caused from the point of view of another named or additional insured of the same policy. This latter proposition is consistent with the principles of public policy underlying implied exceptions, and it also is the most common interpretation of policy provisions precluding coverage for intentionally-caused injuries.[4]

As previously noted, the proposition that intentional losses are not covered is supported by an implied exception even when not explicitly stated.[5] It appears also in many policy clauses.[6] But the

---

Jones, 135 F.2d 191 (6th Cir. 1943) (purportedly applying Michigan law; allowing victim of battery to recover under tortfeasor's liability insurance policy; interpretation of Michigan statutes regulating liability insurance seems unpersuasive).

3. Among the cases cited in the preceding note, only *Roberts* plainly goes this far, but the opinions in the other cases are susceptible of being read in this way.

4. *E.g.*, Employers Mut. Liab. Ins. Co. v. Hendrix, 199 F.2d 53 (4th Cir. 1952), 41 A.L.R.2d 424 (1955) (applying South Carolina law; named insured allowed coverage as to claim he was vicariously liable for assault committed by employee); Arenson v. National Auto. & Cas. Ins. Co., 45 Cal.2d 81, 286 P.2d 816 (1955) (minor son started fire that damaged school property; school district obtained judgment against parent under vicarious liability statute; parent's liability covered by liability policy of which parent was named insured); Morgan v. Greater N. Y. Taxpayers Mut. Ins. Ass'n, 305 N.Y. 243, 112 N.E.2d 273 (1953) (victim of assault by one member of partnership obtained judgment against that partner individually and against the partnership; proceeding to recover the amount of the judgment from the partnership's public liability insurer; held, for victim on the theory that a second partner, who was individually liable for judgment against partnership, was a named insured and that the assault and battery clause did not preclude coverage for his liability since the assault was not by him or at his direction); Employers Surplus Lines v. Stone, 388 P. 2d 295 (Okla. 1963) (partner of claimant's assailant settled assault claim and then sued liability insurer for reimbursement; held, recovery, citing and following *Morgan, supra*). See also 7A Appleman, Insurance Law § 4492 (rev. ed. 1962).

5. See § 5.3(f) *supra*.

6. See, *e.g.*, the 1966 liability insurance form, Appendix G *infra*, declaring that the company is obligated to pay on the insured's behalf damages imposed by law because of bodily injury or property damage "caused by an occurrence," and defining "occurrence" to mean "an accident, including injurious exposure to conditions, which results, during the policy period, in

concept of intentionally-caused loss applied in determining the scope of either an implied exception or an express stipulation against coverage of such losses does not extend to all damages awarded under the theory of intentional tort. For example, even though the theory of judgment is intentional tort, the harm for which damages are awarded may nevertheless be fortuitous, from the point of view of the defendant as well as the victim, when one is held vicariously liable for the intentional tort of another.[7] From the defendant's point of view, harm is likewise fortuitous when a parent is held liable for his own negligence in failing to prevent his child from committing a battery upon another person.[8] Also, as will be developed presently, it would seem that the principal reasons—and especially those of public policy —for disallowing insurance against intentionally-caused loss are inapplicable to some cases in which the defendant himself is the "intentional" tortfeasor.

Consistently with the foregoing analysis, coverage for intentionally-caused harm has been denied under liability insurance policy provisions including the phrase "caused by accident" in the basic definition of coverage,[9] and a fortiori when the policy provisions explicitly preclude coverage for "injury . . . caused intentionally."[10] Some opinions suggest that contract provisions such as these are merely declaratory of a public policy that would have precluded coverage in any event.[11]

Many liability insurance policies have included a provision, separate from the primary definition of coverage, declaring that "assault and battery shall be deemed an accident unless committed by or at the direction of the insured."[12] By negative implication, this clause

bodily injury or property damage neither expected nor intended from the standpoint of the insured . . . ." The significance of the requirement that the bodily injury or property damage not be "expected" is discussed in § 5.4(c) infra.

7. See n.4 supra.

8. E.g., Pawtucket Mut. Ins. Co. v. Lebrecht, 104 N.H. 465, 190 A.2d 420 (1963), 2 A.L.R.3d 1229 (1965) (suit against parents of seventeen-year-old delinquent boy who attacked plaintiff, a girl).

9. E.g., Sontag v. Galer, 279 Mass. 309, 181 N.E. 182 (1932) (cooking utensil, thrown by landlady at boys who had come on her premises without leave, struck plaintiff).

10. E.g., Rankin v. Farmers Elevator Mut. Ins. Co., 393 F.2d 718 (10th Cir. 1968) (applying Kansas law; farmer chasing motorcyclists who had trespassed on his land, deliberately

swerved his pick-up against a cyclist and ran him into ditch; declaratory summary judgment against coverage affirmed; reasoning, however, included the hoary fiction that one is "presumed to intend the natural and probable consequences" of his acts).

11. E.g., Haser v. Maryland Cas. Co., 78 N.D. 893, 53 N.W.2d 508 (1952), 33 A.L.R.2d 1018 (1954) (passenger in taxi who had been raped by driver and another passenger sought coverage of default judgment against driver under policy making driver an additional insured; held, for the insurer, since coverage would be contrary to public policy even though the phrase "caused by accident" defined coverage of broader scope than merely for negligent acts of insured; note that such a case might also be decided for the insurer on the ground that the liability did not arise "out of the . . . use" of the vehicle as a vehicle; see § 5.2(b) supra).

12. See the 1955 Standard Basic Automobile Liability Policy, "Conditions"

would seem to preclude liability of the insurer for all damages imposed on the insured under the theory that he committed or directed the commission of an assault and battery.[13] Thus, it would be of no use to the insured to show that the purpose of his intended impact upon the victim was self-defense and that, though he acted in good faith, his defense failed because his belief that he was being attacked arose from his negligent mistake. Also, it would not avail the insured to show that he intended an impact of relatively little significance and that, though the theory of liability for the severe injury resulting was battery, in fact the severe injury was unintended.

Coverage for cases such as the two illustrations just given seems consistent, however, with the requirement that loss be fortuitous in the sense of the implied exception that would apply in the absence of a policy clause more broadly preclusive. This position is supported also by cases arising under a clause precluding coverage for "injury caused intentionally," or other phrases of similar import. It seems reasonable to expect an assault-and-battery clause to be interpreted as precluding coverage of every claim made on the theory of assault or battery, even though the injury may have been fortuitously caused from the point of view of the defendant (for example, because he negligently believed there was a need for acting in self-defense). There is a somewhat lower probability, it would seem, that the phrase "injury caused intentionally" will be construed as precluding coverage for every claim asserted under the rubric of intentional tort; it is less likely that the phrase "injury caused intentionally" will be construed as words of art than that "assault" and "battery" will be so construed. There are precedents to sustain an interpretation of "injury caused intentionally" that allows coverage for some claims asserted under the rubric of intentional tort. For example, it has been held that when a six-year-old insured pushed a four-year-old girl, knowing the contact to be offensive, thereby committing a battery and being held liable for a broken arm, the injury "was not caused intentionally" but was an unintended result of the boy's conduct.[14] Such a case of "battery" by a young child may properly

clause 6, Risjord & Austin, Automobile Liability Insurance Cases—Standard Provisions and Appendix 28 (1964).

13. See, *e.g.*, Huie v. Phoenix Ins. Co., 413 F.2d 613 (8th Cir. 1969) (Arkansas law; defense of insanity unavailable in action against insurer on tort judgment, since that defense could have been raised in tort action; in view of "assault and battery" exclusion, not necessary to consider whether same result would be reached under an "intentional injury" exclusion). Distinguish, *e.g.*, Maryland Cas. Co. v. Mitchell, 322 F.2d 37 (5th Cir. 1963) (applying Texas law; liability insurer declined to defend suit against insured

in which the claimant's pleadings stated both negligence and assault and battery theories; held, insurer liable for judgment against insured and costs of insured's defense; see §§ 7.-6(a), 7.7 *infra* concerning the duty to defend when a negligence claim is joined with a claim of intentional tort).

14. Baldinger v. Consolidated Mut. Ins. Co., 15 App.Div.2d 526, 222 N.Y.S.2d 736 (2d Dep't 1961), *aff'd mem. decision*, 11 N.Y.2d 1026, 183 N.E.2d 908, 230 N.Y.S.2d 25 (1962) (comprehensive personal liability coverage within a homeowners policy, including a provision against coverage for "injury . . . caused intentionally by

be distinguished from an attack on another person by an adult; thus, it has been held that it is not enough to escape the exclusion of "injury . . . caused intentionally" that one who approached the victim from behind, spun him around, and struck him on the cheek, knocking him down, "did not intend to inflict . . . the specific injuries sustained." [15]

A clause excluding "injury . . . caused intentionally" may also be construed as not precluding coverage when the insured is found to have been incapable of forming an "intent," as that term is used in the insurance policy, even though the theory of recovery against the insured is one of intentional tort.[16]   Even more clearly,

or at the direction of the insured"). *Cf.* Capachi v. Glens Falls Ins. Co., 215 Cal.App.2d 843, 30 Cal.Rptr. 323 (App.Div.Super.Ct.1963) (coverage for claim of false arrest, which "need not have been founded on an implied finding of ill will or desire to injure, for although intent is necessary as an element of the tort of false arrest, malice, in the sense of ill will or desire to injure is not . . ."); Haynes v. American Cas. Co., 228 Md. 394, 179 A.2d 900 (1962) (insured's employees, being mistaken about location of boundary line, cut trees on land adjoining that on which they were supposed to be working; loss held to be "caused by accident" within meaning of liability policy); J. D'Amico, Inc. v. City of Boston, 345 Mass. 218, 186 N.E.2d 716 (1962) (insurer required to defend action against insured in which the claimant's declaration was broad enough to state a claim for trespass by mistake; concerning the scope of the duty to defend, particularly in light of ambiguity about whether a claim within the definition of policy coverage will be asserted, see § 7.6(a) *infra*); York Industrial Center, Inc. v. Michigan Mut. Liab. Co., 271 N.C. 158, 155 S.E.2d 501 (1967) (surveying mistake and damage to trees on 20-foot strip mistakenly believed to be insured's own land; coverage); City of Burns v. Northwestern Mut. Ins. Co., 248 Ore. 364, 434 P.2d 465 (1967) (judgment sustaining insurer's demurrer and dismissing complaint reversed; intent to disinter and move body does not establish intent to cause resulting harm; tort complaint on which judgment was entered stated claim within coverage, even though there was no duty to defend against original complaint alleging the insured's act was done with malice; concerning duty of defense, however, see § 7.6(a) *infra*); Eisenman v. Hornberger, 438 Pa. 46, 264 A.

2d 673 (1970) (teenagers, including son of named insured of homeowners policy, broke into another person's house to steal liquor; one of the matches they used to find their way lodged in overstuffed chair and started fire; held, loss not intentionally caused within the meaning of exclusion clause; coverage for the teenage son).

15.   Pendergraft v. Commercial Standard Fire & Marine Co., 342 F.2d 427 (10th Cir. 1965). *But cf.* Smith v. Moran, 61 Ill.App.2d 157, 209 N.E.2d 18 (2d Dist. 1965) (insured accidentally shot one waitress in a tavern when shooting at another waitress; held, insurer was bound to defend the suit against the insured; decision seems unsound, since the mere fact that the harm fortuitously fell on one other than the person the insured intended to injure seems a poor reason for allowing the insured to escape the preclusion of coverage). See also General Ins. Co. v. Whitmore, 235 Cal.App. 2d 670, 45 Cal.Rptr. 556 (2d Dist. 1965) (trial court's sustaining of demurrer to complaint in declaratory proceedings reversed; intimations of noncoverage for claims that juveniles deliberately tampered with switches and derailed train, injuring numerous passengers; coverage for claim based on negligence not disputed).   This case, too, might be distinguished from *Baldinger*, n.14 *supra*, on the basis of the nature of the actors' intent, the expectability of the consequences, and the capacity of the actors to foresee and understand those consequences.

16.   See, *e.g.*, Rosa v. Liberty Mut. Ins. Co., 243 F.Supp. 407 (D.Conn.1965) (sixteen-year-old schizophrenic beat and shot a young girl; held, recovery under personal liability coverage of homeowners policy of which the assailant was an additional insured); Ruvolo v. American Cas. Co, 39 N.J.

cases involving bodily injury resulting from conduct intended to accomplish some other unlawful result but not to cause bodily harm to anyone do not involve injury caused intentionally, even though courts may for other purposes refer to the injuries as wilfully, wantonly, recklessly, or even intentionally caused.[17]

The type of self-defense case in which the insured acted mistakenly is another instance in which it might be argued that injury was not "caused intentionally." [18]   A difficulty with this position is that

490, 189 A.2d 204 (1963) (insured shot and killed third person; held, if he did so while derangement deprived him of capacity to govern his conduct, acting on an irrational impulse, his act could not be treated as "intentional" as that term is used in policy exclusion); 1A Appleman, Insurance Law § 482 (rev. ed. 1965). *But cf.* Wagner v. Colonial Life & Acc. Ins. Co., 380 S.W.2d 224 (Ky.1964), *opinion on second appeal*, 408 S.W.2d 612 (Ky. 1966) (held, whether or not the killer of the insured had the mental capacity to form an intent to kill, the homicide was intentional within the meaning of a group life insurance policy exclusion of death caused by "injuries intentionally inflicted upon the Insured Employee by any other person"); State Farm Mut. Auto. Ins. Co. v. Treas, 254 Md. 615, 255 A.2d 296 (1969) (insured denied intent to strike woman who stood in front of vehicle to stop it, with her hands on it, backing up, as insured drove it out driveway; insured accelerated and she fell under car and was dragged and killed; insured testified he blacked out and went berserk; held, trial court finding death was "caused by accident" was clearly erroneous; injuries could not be said to be "unforeseen, unusual, or unexpected"); Aetna Life Ins. Co. v. McLaughlin, 380 S.W.2d 101 (Tex.1964), 9 A.L.R.3d 1005 (1966) (held, if insured of accident policy committed the act of throwing himself in front of bus on highway, his beneficiary could not recover, in face of clause precluding liability for "suicide, sane or insane," even on proof that he did not appreciate the physical consequences of his act). *Wagner* and *McLaughlin* can be distinguished from cases of liability insurance since they involved life or accident insurance and policy language different from that of the clauses under discussion here.

17. *Cf.* Travelers Indem. Co. v. Hood, 110 Ga.App. 855, 140 S.E.2d 68 (1964), 20 A.L.R.3d 314 (1968) (racing cars on public highway; coverage allowed, the court observing that the fact that an injury is treated for other purposes as "constructively intentional does not remove it from the category of injury 'caused by accident' in the terms of an insurance contract").

18. *Cf.* Putman v. Zeluff, 372 Mich. 553, 127 N.W.2d 374 (1964) (coverage, despite exclusion clause, for claim against young boy who shot pedigreed coon hound, thinking it was a wild dog and shooting for his own safety; reasoned, however, on the ground that in the confused circumstances it was not clear that he had the intent to destroy the animal). The comment in the text concerns a type of case in which the plea of self-defense *fails* because the person asserting it was unreasonable in believing it necessary to act in self-defense. A somewhat stronger case for coverage as to the duty to defend is presented when the circumstances *support* the plea of self-defense.

In Walters v. American Ins. Co., 185 Cal.App.2d 776, 8 Cal.Rptr. 665 (1st Dist. 1960), the insured claimed against his liability insurer for both the costs of defense and the amount of settlement of an assault and battery claim against him that the insurer had refused to defend. There being no "assault and battery" exclusion clause in the policy, the court held, assuming an implied trial court finding that the insured "acted reasonably and in self-defense," that self-defense took the matter out of the intentional injury exclusion and, therefore, that the insurer had wrongfully refused to defend and was liable for the amount of the settlement, which the court found reasonable.

In Maxon v. Security Ins. Co., 214 Cal. App.2d 603, 29 Cal.Rptr. 586 (1st Dist. 1963), the court held that a liability insurer was not liable for the cost of the insured's successful defense of a malicious prosecution action, distinguishing *Walters* on the tenuous, if

the actor intended the physical impact he caused and his mistake concerned the right of self-defense rather than the impact and its results suffered by the victim. If no policy clause is held to preclude coverage of intentional injury, however, and one is thus faced with determining the scope of the implied exception against coverage of non-fortuitous loss, it seems a cogent argument that regardless of whether the insured intended the impact on the victim, the illegality of the insured's behavior, as well as his loss from liability for damages, was fortuitous since it resulted from a mistake that was no worse in nature than ordinary negligence.

The question whether loss is fortuitous even though the victim is entitled to recover against the insured under a theory of intentional tort may arise under medical malpractice coverage. For example, a psychiatrist recommending commitment of a patient as dangerously psychotic may be held liable on a theory of false imprisonment, if liable at all. Yet if he was acting in good faith, and his defense of privilege failed only because he made a negligent mistake, the loss is surely fortuitous in the sense of the implied exception that would apply in the absence of a more preclusive policy provision.[19]

Liability insurance policies carried by business enterprises often include coverages for claims that may be classified as intentional torts but nevertheless involve losses that are fortuitous from the point of view of the insured.[20]

§ 5.4(c) HIGHLY EXPECTABLE LOSSES

Non-coverage of intentional losses is, as already observed,[1] a corollary of the central idea that insurance concerns fortuitous losses only. A second corollary, perhaps less obvious and certainly more difficult to formulate precisely, is that insurance contracts do not cover certain highly expectable losses. Ordinarily they do not cover economic detriment of a type occurring so regularly that it is com-

---

not untenable, ground that a pleading was available by which the insurer's duty to defend could be measured (whereas in *Walters* the insurer had refused to defend and the insured had settled before suit was filed by the claimant). Concerning the ambiguity arising from lack of a pleading, see § 7.6(a) *infra*. The successful plea of probable cause in *Maxon* was not a negation of intent but rather an assertion of privilege, as was the plea of self-defense in *Walters*; it would seem that the cases cannot be satisfactorily distinguished. See § 7.6(a) *infra* for further criticism of the *Maxon* decision.

19. *Cf.* Sommer v. New Amsterdam Cas. Co., 171 F.Supp. 84 (E.D.Mo. 1959), denying summary judgment for either plaintiff-insured or defendant-

insurer. The insured, a psychiatrist, settled a suit for assault brought by a patient wrongfully committed to a mental institution, then sought recovery against his malpractice insurer for the cost of his defense and the amount of the settlement. The insurer defended on the basis of a clause excluding from coverage "injury arising out of the performance of a criminal act . . . ."

20. See generally Allen, *Coverage Problems in Libel, Slander and Assault and Battery Cases*, 1968 ABA Section Ins., Neg. & Comp.L.Proceedings 531; Dane, *Insurance of Liability for Business Torts*, 2 Forum 85 (ABA Section Ins., Neg. & Comp.L.1967).

1. See § 5.4(b) *supra*.

monly regarded as a cost rather than a risk of the insured enterprise or activity. This proposition is supported in a measure by implied exceptions, recognized in the absence of policy provisions in point.[2] An even broader preclusion of liability is sometimes expressed or implied in policy clauses.

Tort actions based on nuisance often present issues regarding coverage for highly expectable losses. In some cases it has been held that the effects of a nuisance maintained by the insured were not "caused by accident" within the meaning of liability coverage [3] and, similarly, that results of an insured's act were not accidents when, though not intended, they were a calculated risk.[4] Often, however, the rationale for such decisions has been that the loss was the "normal" or "foreseeable" result of the insured's intentional or negligent conduct [5] and, therefore, not an accident. Denying coverage on this rationale is difficult to reconcile with allowing coverage, for example, in automobile negligence cases in which the relevant policy language

---

2. See § 5.3(a) *supra. Cf.* Patterson's explanation of the friendly fire exception, § 5.3(d) *supra.*

3. *E.g.,* Farmers Elevator Mut. Ins. Co. v. Burch, 38 Ill.App.2d 249, 187 N.E.2d 12 (4th Dist. 1962) (loss caused by dust, noise, and vibrations from insured's operation of a grain elevator); Clark v. London & Lancashire Indem. Co., 21 Wis.2d 268, 124 N.W.2d 29 (1963), 98 A.L.R.2d 1037 (1964) (loss caused by rats, flies, hydrogen sulfide gas, and odors from refuse dumped into gravel pit operated by insured). *Cf.* Harleysville Mut. Cas. Co. v. Harris & Brooks, Inc., 248 Md. 148, 235 A.2d 556 (1967) (smoke and soot damage to nearby owners from intentionally set fires was not "caused by accident"). *But see* n. 12 *infra.*

4. *E. g.,* City of Aurora v. Trinity Universal Ins. Co., 326 F.2d 905 (10th Cir. 1964), 7 A.L.R.3d 1257 (1966) (insured maintained sewer system known to be inadequate during periods of heavy rainfall, which were not infrequent; held, liability policy did not cover loss to property caused by backed up sewage); Albuquerque Gravel Prods. Co. v. American Employers Ins. Co., 282 F.2d 218 (10th Cir. 1960) (insured built a ramp in an arroyo—a normally dry watercourse—in such a way that it diverted water onto adjoining land during heavy rainfall; held, no coverage under liability policy for loss thus caused by flooding; Casper v. American Guar. & Liab. Ins. Co., 408 Pa. 426, 184 A.2d 247 (1962) (insured contractor failed adequately to seal off area being remodeled from other areas in

same building; held, no coverage under liability policy for loss due to the settling of dust and debris on merchandise of a shopowner in the building); Gassaway v. Travelers Ins. Co,, 439 S.W.2d 605 (Tenn.1969) (storm sewer leaked so house foundation settled; developer-insured, knowing of the risk, failed to disclose it to buyer, who made claim for damage to house; no coverage); Town of Tieton v. General Ins. Co., 61 Wash.2d 716, 380 P.2d 127 (1963) (town had been warned that proposed sewer installation might contaminate nearby wells but proceeded with plan anyway; held, no coverage for loss due to contamination).

5. See especially the line of cases in the Tenth Circuit represented by *City of Aurora v. Trinity Universal Ins. Co.* and *Albuquerque Gravel Prods. Co. v. American Employers Ins. Co.,* n.4 *supra*; these later cases have virtually dissipated hopes, based on the opinion in Hutchinson Water Co. v. United States Fid. & Gy. Co., 250 F.2d 892 (10th Cir. 1957), that this court had come to appreciate the unacceptable implications of its extraordinary construction of "caused by accident" and like phrases. *Cf.* Calvert Fire Ins. Co. v. Little, 421 S.W.2d 584 (Ky. 1967) (no recovery under collision coverage for damage allegedly sustained when truck passed over drainage ditch; impact was not "unforeseen, accidental, sudden or violent" and not such "as normally could be calculated to cause damage," and was not a "collision" in either the ordinary sense or the policy sense).

is the same. Indeed, it is generally recognized that automobile liability insurance coverage extends even to cases of gross negligence and recklessness.[6]

To explain insurance law decisions in this area, distinctions must be drawn among different kinds of expectable losses, and perhaps the most useful distinction for this purpose is one between highly expectable losses and those less expectable.[7] This is, of course, a distinction of degree, involving evaluative findings case by case, with standards of judgment difficult to formulate and results difficult to predict.[8] It seems likely, too, that courts applying such a distinction will tend to resolve doubts in favor of coverage.[9]

The distinction between highly expectable and less expectable losses affects the scope of products liability coverage. Here, expectability of loss may be gauged in terms of recurrence, and highly expectable loss may be characterized generally as a "cost" rather than a "risk" of the insured business. To a very considerable extent con-

---

6. *E.g.*, Peterson v. Western Cas. & Sur. Co., 5 Wis.2d 535, 93 N.W.2d 433 (1958) (insured, chased and stopped by police, rapidly backed his car in an attempt to escape, striking the plaintiff officer, who had opened the insured's car door; jury finding that insured did not intentionally injure plaintiff sustained by court, stating that although insured was probably guilty of gross negligence, and although such conduct may be treated as the equivalent of intentional wrongdoing for some purposes, it is not so treated for the purpose of an intentional-injury exclusion in a liability policy). *But cf.* American Surety Co. v. Gold, 375 F.2d 523 (10th Cir. 1966), 20 A.L.R.3d 335 (1968) (forecasting Kansas law; disallowing coverage for punitive damages as a matter of public policy and observing that this would require juries to distinguish between ordinary negligence and gross and wanton negligence). See § 5.3(f) *supra* concerning the argument for an implied exception as to punitive damages.

7. *Cf., e.g.*, Harleysville Mut. Cas. Co. v. Harris & Brooks, Inc., 248 Md. 148, 235 A.2d 556 (1967) (smoke and soot damage from fires intentionally set in ten to twelve foot high brush piles, topped with tires and fuel oil, during clearing of wooded tract; held, not "caused by accident"; "not 'an event that takes place without one's foresight or expectation,'" quoting the definition of accident in Webster's Twentieth Century Dictionary, 1950). Concerning ordinary negligence that aggravates damages from a covered loss, see § 5.4(d) *infra*.

8. Concerning evaluative findings generally, see § 1.6 *supra*.

9. *Cf.* Baker v. American Ins. Co. of Newark, 324 F.2d 748 (4th Cir. 1963) (South Carolina law; extraordinary rainfall and grading of site for shopping center combined to cause flooding of neighboring lands; held, an accident, even though the court expressed in dictum the untenable view that "[o]rdinarily, 'accident' would exclude an event caused by negligence or nuisance alone and followed by a foreseeable or natural consequence, for then neither the cause nor the effect is unexpectable"); Taylor v. Imperial Cas. & Indem. Co., 82 S.D. 298, 144 N.W.2d 856 (1966) (damage to adjoining property from underground leakage of gasoline from storage tanks was caused by accident); Bosko v. Pitts & Still, Inc., 75 Wash.2d 856, 454 P.2d 229 (1969) (damage done by slide of waste material was accidental; damages included cost of stabilizing against future slides, materials requiring stabilization being on the claimant's land so a trespass had already occurred); Ramco, Inc. v. Pacific Ins. Co., 249 Ore. 666, 439 P.2d 1002 (1968) (coverage for claim against manufacturer of electric baseboard heaters based on "actual loss" sustained when defective heating coils "failed to produce the heat they were designed to produce"; precise nature of the loss not disclosed, but demurrer sustained to count for "consequential loss of good will and credit").

cern about products liability coverage was the impetus for the 1966 revision of policy forms, and this may have been a major factor leading the draftsmen to include the requirement that the bodily injury or property damage not be "expected" from the point of view of the insured. This requirement appears in the definition of "occurrence" as "an accident, including injurious exposure to conditions, which results, during the policy period, in bodily injury or property damage *neither expected* nor intended from the standpoint of the insured." [10] It would seem that "expected" should be and probably will be construed by courts in the sense of a high degree of expectability; otherwise the appearance of this term in the automobile liability coverage would be at odds, as noted above, with coverage in the great bulk of negligence cases that are the daily grist of automobile liability insurance.[11]

It may be noted also that using the term "occurrence" instead of "accident" in the coverage language and defining it to include "injurious exposure to conditions," as the 1966 policy forms do, appear to have been intended to broaden coverage in another sense—not in relation to degree of expectability of loss but by avoiding an implication that there was no coverage for a continuing condition as distinguished from a sudden event.[12] Because of the broadening of coverage in this other respect, the limitation of coverage in terms of de-

---

10. See Appendix G *infra.*

11. See n.6 *supra.* See also Even, *The Corporate Insurance Administrator—Problems with the 1966 Revised Liability Policy,* 3 Forum 95 (ABA Section Ins., Neg. & Comp.L.1968).

12. *E.g.,* Address by H. G. Mildrum [a member of the industry committee responsible for drafting the 1966 forms], Chartered Property and Casualty Underwriters Seminar (Oct. 12, 1966). See generally Hall, *Contractors' Liability Insurance for Property Damage Incidental to Normal Operations—The Standard Coverage Problem,* 16 U. Kan.L.Rev. 181, 203–207 (1968). *Cf.* Massachusetts Turnpike Authority v. Perini Corp., 349 Mass. 448, 208 N.E. 2d 807 (1965). The Massachusetts Supreme Judicial Court, considering a liability policy using the term "occurrence" and rejecting coverage of loss that was "inevitable" in a public construction project and for which the contractor-insured was not liable to the government, stated: "One purpose of the substitution of the word 'occurrence' for 'accident' may have been to include in the coverage a suitable provision for indemnity against injuries . . . gradually occurring . . . . The use of the term 'occurrence' also may be designed to expand the coverage so that it will be more nearly as extensive as negligence and possibly also other forms of tort liability." 349 Mass. at 456–457, 208 N.E.2d at 813. And, assuming the insurance contract to have been designed to cover the liability assumed by Perini under the construction contract, the court stated as dictum: "[The insured] will be liable [under the construction contract] only if its acts or omissions were tortious by reason of negligence or strict liability, *maintaining a nuisance,* . . . or otherwise." 349 Mass. at 454, 208 N.E.2d at 811 (emphasis added). See also Aerial Agricultural Serv., Inc. v. Till, 207 F. Supp. 50 (N.D.Miss.1962) (policy defining "occurrence" as an "accident" or a "condition created by the insured which during the policy period accidentally causes injury or destruction provided that such condition, injury or destruction is not caused by accident"; held, coverage of insured's liability to farmer for damage resulting when a seeding device that was intentionally created as designed nevertheless improperly distributed seed); Bean, *The Accident Versus the Occurrence Concept,* 1959 Ins.L.J. 550.

gree of expectability of loss may become even more significant under the 1966 forms than before.[13]

§ 5.4(d) FAILURE TO PREVENT THREATENED INJURY

Property insurance policies ordinarily contain a provision concerning the insured's failure to protect against further damage to property damaged but not destroyed by an event of the type against which the policy offers protection. Thus, a standard fire insurance policy, under a clause headed "perils not included," lists "neglect of the insured to use all reasonable means to save and preserve the property at and after a loss, or when the property is endangered by fire in neighboring premises." [1]

Homeowners policies have commonly included not only the foregoing clause from fire insurance forms but also a clause precluding coverage for loss "resulting from freezing while the building covered is vacant or unoccupied, unless the insured shall have exercised due diligence with respect to maintaining heat in the building, ..." [2] It has been held, however, that one may exercise due diligence "with respect to" maintaining heat by leaving the heat off and employing a qualified person to place anti-freeze in the system and test its adequacy, even though it later turns out to have been inadequate.[3]

Automobile policies covering *physical damage to the insured automobile* customarily provide that if a loss occurs the insured shall "protect the automobile, whether or not the loss is covered by this policy, and any further loss due to the insured's failure to protect shall not be recoverable under this policy; reasonable expenses incurred in affording such protection shall be deemed incurred at the company's request; . . . ." [4] Provisions of this type have been construed as limiting coverage only in situations in which the insured's failure to act for protection of the automobile is negligence; usually this result is reasoned on the ground that the failure to act is not a legal cause of the additional loss unless such failure is negligence.[5] It may even be argued, with support in analogies from

---

13. *Cf.* Hall, *Contractors' Liability Insurance for Property Damage Incidental to Normal Operations—The Standard Coverage Problem,* 16 U.Kan.L. Rev. 181, 203–207 (1968); Even, *The Corporate Insurance Administrator—Problems with the 1966 Revised Liability Policy,* 3 Forum 95 (ABA Section Ins., Neg. & Comp.L.1968).

1. See Appendix A *infra.*

2. See, *e.g.,* the Homeowners Policy in Insurance Information Institute, Sample Insurance Policies, Property-Lia-

bility Coverages, Advanced Book 89, 94 (1969).

3. Palmer v. Pawtucket Mut. Ins. Co., 352 Mass. 304, 225 N.E.2d 331 (1967).

4. See Appendix H *infra.*

5. See, *e.g.,* Centennial Cas. Co. v. Snyder, 142 Colo. 198, 350 P.2d 337 (1960) (after a collision with a telephone pole, the insured drove the car home, thinking that only its fender and bumper were damaged; in fact, the brake fluid line was broken and a

other areas of insurance law, that gross negligence or worse will be required to defeat the claim for the added loss.[6]

Surely the insured is entitled to recover from the insurer reasonable costs he incurs in protecting his property in such circumstances. As appears from the foregoing quotation, automobile policies customarily contain a clause explicitly so providing, and consistently with the general doctrine of avoidable consequences [7] such a right should be recognized even when not stated in the policy.

Another aspect of automobile policies presents an issue that is more debatable, however. The 1966 revision of *liability* insurance forms introduced a new provision, under paragraph four of the "conditions," requiring that the named insured "promptly take at his expense all reasonable steps to prevent other bodily injury or property damage from arising out of the same or similar conditions, but such expense shall not be recoverable under this policy." [8] The scope of the duty imposed by this clause and the remedy for its breach are yet to be determined. When the insurer asserts that the insured's failure to take specified protective measures bars or limits the insurer's liability, surely the amount of expense that would have been involved is relevant to the issue whether the suggested measures come within "all *reasonable* steps."

It may be that the scope of this duty of the insured will be even more basically restricted. In their fundamental nature, protection-of-property clauses are designed to preclude recovery for a certain type of accidental harm because of the policyholder's negligence. Thus, in a sense, they are contrary to the more general tendency of insurance policies to cover accidental loss even when due to the policyholder's own carelessness. Arguably they are nonetheless defensible because of their modest scope and the special problem of limiting loss to which they are directed. But it seems likely that they will be rather narrowly construed by courts, and this attitude toward them can be justified on the principle of honoring reasonable expectations.[9]

§ 5.4(e) ACCIDENTAL MEANS

Draftsmen of many accident insurance policy forms have sought to narrow the scope of coverage, much more than does the requirement that loss be fortuitous, by providing coverage only against loss

---

wheel was flat, and the continued operation of the car caused the fluid to ignite, burning a wheel, a tire, and the car; held, recovery); Runner v. Calvert Fire Ins. Co., 138 W.Va. 369, 76 S.E.2d 244 (1953), 44 A.L.R.2d 1075 (1955) (insured ran over large rock on highway in construction area and, unaware that the collision had caused an oil leak, continued driving, which caused additional damage to the car; held, judgment for the insured affirmed, since the question of violation

of the protection clause had been properly submitted to the jury).

6. Compare the precedents concerning negligence or gross negligence leading to the initial loss, § 5.3(e) *supra*.

7. See Restatement of Torts § 918 (1939).

8. See Appendix G *infra*.

9. See § 6.3 *infra*.

by "accidental means." Such provisions have appeared also in double
indemnity clauses of some life insurance policies. It seems clear that,
if literally enforced, provisions of this type, particularly when rein-
forced by such a commonly used phrase as "directly and independently of all other causes," [1] would afford much less coverage than provisions for coverage of accidental injury or accidental loss. Before
1946, a clear majority of the states that had passed on the question
recognized a distinction in scope of coverage between policies using
the language of accidental means and those using the language of accidental results.[2] In that year, however, the New York Court of Appeals declared, in the leading case of *Burr v. Commercial Travelers
Mut. Acc. Ass'n* [3]: "In this State there is no longer any distinction
made between accidental death and death by accidental means, nor
between accidental means and accidental results." [4] An annotator of

1. See, *e.g.*, the clauses involved in
Commercial Travelers Ins. Co. v.
Walsh, 228 F.2d 200 (9th Cir. 1955), 56
A.L.R.2d 796 (1957) (applying Washington law; insured who had a short
history of mild heart trouble died of a
heart attack following accidental over-
exertion; held, coverage, without express consideration of the "sole cause"
problem); Silverstein v. Metropolitan
Life Ins. Co., 254 N.Y. 81, 171 N.E.
914 (1930) (insured who accidentally
dropped a large milk can, which hit
him in the stomach, died of peritonitis
caused by perforation of the stomach
at a point where it was found there
had been a pea-sized ulcer; held, recovery, since the ulcer was at most a
"predisposing tendency" and not a disease or infirmity contributing to the
death within the meaning of the policy clause); Hammer v. Mutual Benefit Health & Acc. Ass'n, 158 Ohio St.
394, 109 N.E.2d 649 (1952), 36 A.L.R.2d
1084 (1954) (insured who apparently
had no history of heart trouble died
of a heart attack brought on by heat
exhaustion; held, recovery, the court
treating the death as resulting from
accidental means that were the sole
cause of death); Britton v. Prudential
Ins. Co., 205 Tenn. 726, 330 S.W.2d
326 (1959), 82 A.L.R.2d 605 (1962) (insured who had a history of arterio-
sclerosis died of an acute coronary
thrombosis after surgery for a fracture caused by an accident; held, action to recover accidental death benefits dismissed); Pan American Life
Ins. Co. v. Andrews, 161 Tex. 391, 340
S.W.2d 787 (1960), 93 A.L.R.2d 560
(1964) (psychic trauma incurred when
insured witnessed fire that burned his
office; death, 34 days later and after
intervening brain operation, held not
covered under double indemnity provision).

"Sole cause" provisions are also used in
conjunction with "accidental injury"
clauses. See, *e.g.*, Adkins v. American
Cas. Co., 145 W.Va. 281, 114 S.E.2d
556 (1960), 84 A.L.R.2d 169 (1962),
opinion on second appeal, 146 W.Va.
1045, 124 S.E.2d 457 (1962) (insured received an accidental blow to his head
after which he was continually af-
flicted with severe shoulder and back
pains, which, it was determined, were
due to aggravation of a degenerative
condition of intervertebral discs not
uncommon for one of the insured's
age; held, no coverage under a policy
insuring against "accidental bodily injury which is the sole cause . . ."
of loss).

2. *E.g.*, John Hancock Mut. Life Ins.
Co. v. Plummer, 181 Md. 140, 28 A.2d
856 (1942). See Annot., 166 A.L.R. 469
(1947). See also, *e.g.*, Prudential Ins.
Co. v. Gutowski, 49 Del. 233, 113 A.2d
579 (1955), 52 A.L.R.2d 1073 (1957).
Cf., *e.g.*, Haynes v. American Cas. Co.,
228 Md. 394, 179 A.2d 900 (1962).

3. 295 N.Y. 294, 67 N.E.2d 248 (1946)
166 A.L.R. 462 (1947) (insured died
after trying to dig his automobile out
of a snow-filled ditch where it had
come to rest after a minor collision
with another car; he had told his
wife after walking some distance to
get a shovel that he had been
"knocked out" by the strong winds accompanying the snow storm, and his
wife had seen him "hit himself or slip
and fall against the shovel and then
against the rear wheel or rear fender
of the car . . ." shortly before
his death; held, coverage under a policy providing "against loss by accidental means").

4. 295 N.Y. at 302, 67 N.E.2d at 252,
166 A.L.R. at 466. See 1A Appleman,

Burr observed that an increasing number of jurisdictions were rejecting the distinction between accidental means and accidental results,[5] and that trend has continued.[6]

The affirmance of the judgment on the jury verdict for the plaintiff in *Burr* cannot be supported as faithfully applying the meaning expressed in the policy clause extending coverage for death only if caused solely and exclusively by external, violent, and accidental means.[7] In this case and in others reaching similar results, despite their theoretical basis of interpreting the manifested intention of the contracting parties, the courts have, to serve a public interest, imposed a very considerable judicial restriction upon the freedom of contract. This restriction can be justified on the grounds that literal enforcement of the provisions on accidental means would afford such minimal coverage as to be patently disproportionate to the premiums paid and that there would be little occasion for buying insurance of such narrow scope, thus providing only against a risk defined in a bizarre way that would never be conceived by one stating his insurance needs. These considerations support the conclusion that literal enforcement would be inconsistent with reasonable expectations of insureds.[8]

Insurers had little reason to hope that they would be permitted to enforce accidental means clauses as restrictively as written. It seems more likely that they designed such restrictive language with the purpose of invoking it to defeat with ease claims that they regarded as fraudulent or exaggerated, thus establishing better control of claims. But the courts have wisely determined here, as elsewhere,[9] to deal harshly with the efforts of insurers to achieve less fettered discretion over claims by placing in their policy forms a

---

Insurance Law §§ 391–393 (rev. ed. 1965).

5. Annot., 166 A.L.R. 469, 473 (1947).

6. *E.g.*, Schonberg v. New York Life Ins. Co., 235 La. 461, 104 So.2d 171 (1958) (repudiating the distinction though it had been recognized by an earlier Louisiana Supreme Court decision); Scott v. New Empire Ins. Co., 75 N.M. 81, 400 P.2d 953 (1965); Beckham v. Travelers Ins. Co., 424 Pa. 107, 225 A.2d 532 (1967) (death from overdose of narcotics without suicidal intent; distinction between accidental means and accidental results expressly abandoned). *But cf.* Perrine v. Prudential Ins. Co., 56 N.J. 120, 265 A.2d 521 (1970). See also, *e.g.*, Commercial Travelers Ins. Co. v. Walsh, 228 F.2d 200 (9th Cir. 1955), 56 A.L.R. 2d 796 (1957) (applying Washington law; insured died of a heart attack caused by over-exertion in straining to prevent a mishap in unloading

heavy grain sacks from a truck; held, coverage; decision involved distinguishing between "deliberate" and "unintentional" acts of the insured that caused the fatal heart attack rather than distinguishing between "accidental means" and "accidental death").

7. It seems clear, first, that exertions of the deceased in shoveling snow, after being stalled on a highway in a snowstorm, were not within the phrase "external, violent and accidental means," second, that it was a permissible fact inference from the evidence that these exertions contributed to the death, and third, that the trial court's charge permitted the jury to find for the plaintiff even though taking this view of the evidence.

8. Perrine v. Prudential Ins. Co., 56 N. J. 120, 265 A.2d 521 (1970).

9. See generally § 6.3 *infra*.

standard of coverage far more restrictive than that actually enforced in practice.

§ 5.4(f) RESULTS OF AN INSURED'S CRIMINAL ACTS

Many accident insurance policies have included provisions explicitly precluding coverage for losses resulting from specified criminal acts of the insured.[1]

Even in the absence of a policy provision precluding coverage for injuries one suffers unintentionally but as the result of his own seriously criminal conduct, he is often denied the benefit of accident insurance.

The proposition that the insured did not die "accidentally" or by "accidental means" if his injury or death was a "natural" and "reasonably foreseeable" consequence of his wrongful act in assaulting another appears to be supported by nearly all of the opinions commenting on the question.[2] Most of the judicial expressions have been dicta in opinions sustaining jury verdicts for the insured or the beneficiary. Also, most of the opinions containing such dicta have involved policy clauses using the phrase "accidental means." But it appears probable, in view of the frequent repetition of the proposition, that it will be adopted as the rule of decision whenever the issue is clearly presented, at least as to policies phrased in terms of "accidental means."[3] The fact that the proposition is often stated in terms of "accident" makes it appear not unlikely that it will be applied also to policies using the phrase "accidental injury or death," rather than injury or death from "accidental means."

Probably the most influential factors leading to these holdings have been moral aversion to the conduct that produced the loss and recognition that such conduct substantially increased the risk. Perhaps such factors outweigh the fact that these are plainly unintended consequences. To say that they are not fortuitous, however, is to apply a meaning of that term perhaps even more restrictive than that involved in policy clauses denying coverage for "expected" loss.[4] Thus, these holdings are among the relatively few instances in which insurers are allowed defenses at variance with policy provisions.[5]

---

1. See, *e.g.*, the limitation on the double indemnity, accidental death provision of the life insurance policy involved in Powell v. New York Life Ins. Co., 120 So.2d 33 (Fla.App.1960), 86 A.L.R. 2d 437 (1962), excluding payment of the accidental death benefit if the death resulted from the commission by the insured of "an assault or felony." The court affirmed summary judgment for the insurer in an action to recover the benefit (the face value of the policy having been paid), since the insured was shot and killed by his son while beating his wife.

2. *E.g.*, Bernhard v. Prudential Ins. Co., 134 Neb. 402, 278 N.W. 846 (1938); Shields v. Prudential Ins. Co., 6 N.J. 517, 79 A.2d 297 (1951), 26 A.L.R.2d 392 (1952).

3. *E.g.*, Jaudon v. Prudential Ins. Co., 279 F.2d 730 (6th Cir. 1960) (applying Tennessee law); Powell v. New York Life Ins. Co., 120 So.2d 33 (Fla.App. 1960), 86 A.L.R.2d 437 (1962).

4. See § 5.4(c) *supra*.

5. See § 6.9(a) *infra*.

SECTION 5.5 CAUSATION PROBLEMS

§ 5.5(a) CONCLUSIVE AND INCONCLUSIVE CAUSATION CLAUSES

(1) THE CAUSE-EVENT-RESULT TRICHOTOMY

Frequently provisions affecting determination of the risks transferred by insurance have been classified on the basis of distinctions concerned with cause, event, and result. The problem of understanding a statement about insurance law that employs terminology used in such distinctions is greatly complicated by the extraordinary ambiguities arising from lack of any clearly prevailing usage.

The most carefully constructed system of terminology in this area of insurance law is that adopted by Professor Patterson.[1] "Coverage" provisions are those that serve to "identify the risk."[2] They are to be distinguished from provisions relating to potential causes of loss, which he calls warranties.[3] "Coverage" provisions include statements of the insured event, "exceptions," the subject matter of insurance and "exclusions" from the subject matter, interests insured, "consequences of the insured event" declared either to be covered or to be not covered, duration of the insurance, and the amount of insurance.[4]

According to Professor Patterson's system, a provision limiting liability in terms of consequences of the insured event is to be distinguished from an "exception" and from an "exclusion."[5] An "exception" concerns a cause of the insured event and is thus an antecedent link in the chain of causation; an "exclusion" concerns the central link, the event; the consequence of the insured event is a subsequent link.[6]

Among those not committed to Patterson's system of terminology, one common way of speaking has been to use the term "exceptions" for all provisions in the pre-1966 standard automobile policies preceded by the word "except," wherever appearing in the clauses under the heading "Insuring Agreements," and to use the term "exclusions" for all those provisions under the heading "Exclusions." In Patterson's terminology, however, an "exclusion" is distinguished from an "exception" not on the basis of the place where it appears or the heading under which it appears in the policy form but rather on grounds concerned with the kind of condition of liability it imposes.

1. This system of terminology appears in Patterson, Essentials of Insurance Law (2nd ed. 1957), as well as in other writings by Professor Patterson. The explanation here was presented in slightly different form in my review of Patterson's book, 36 Texas L. Rev. 545 (1958).

2. Patterson, Essentials of Insurance Law 230 (2d ed. 1957).

3. *Id.* at 230–231, 273. More detailed treatment of Patterson's concept of warranty appears *infra*, § 6.5.

4. Patterson, Essentials of Insurance Law 230–235 (2d ed. 1957).

5. *Id.* at 249.

6. *Id.* at 267.

An "exception" is a provision limiting the insurer's liability in terms of a cause of the insured event; the cause to which it refers is an "excepted cause." [7] An "exclusion" (aside from exclusions of certain persons or of certain kinds of property) [8] is a provision limiting the insurer's liability in terms of an event; the event to which it refers is an "excluded event." [9]

An illustration of an exclusion is the marine insurance clause "warranted free from any claim for loss . . . caused by capture . . ."; capture is an event excluded from the broader clause "perils of the sea." [10] An illustration of an exception is the clause in the automobile comprehensive coverage provision indicating that there shall be no liability for "loss caused by collision . . . or upset." [11] Observe the phrase "loss caused by" in both the capture and the collision clauses. If capture is to be viewed as an event, rather than as a cause of the event of harm to the vessel, then why is not collision to be viewed as an event, rather than as a cause of the event of harm to the automobile?

Patterson, it seems, was not suggesting that collision could not be an excluded event or that capture could not be an excepted cause; he was not suggesting a distinction in the nature of the physical incidents, which would overlook the truth that every incident is alike cause, event, and consequence and appears to us in one or another of these ways only because of the perspective from which we view it. Rather, he was expressing a difference between the clauses as to their legal effects, or perhaps as to the legal effects they would have if enforced according to their expressed meaning.

One kind of clause says (or is given the legal effect of saying) that there shall be no liability in case of capture; it makes no difference that some peril of the sea contributed by making possible a capture that otherwise would not have occurred; capture is an excluded event and the clause is an "exclusion."

A second kind of clause says (or is given the legal effect of saying) that collision does not supply the basis for liability of the insurer under the comprehensive coverage of the automobile policy, but if a covered incident (such as fire) occurs and the collision follows as a consequence (as when fire causes the driver to lose control and crash), the collision damage is within the scope of the insurer's liability.

Another form of the second kind of clause says that if a fire occurs after a collision there is liability for only the harm of which the fire was a contributing cause.

7. *Id.* at 249.

8. *E.g.*, in the automobile comprehensive coverage in effect when Patterson was writing, "This policy does not apply . . . to robes, wearing apparel or personal effects . . . ." *Id.* at 232.

9. *Id.* at 249.

10. *Id.* at 249, 255, 272.

11. *Id.* at 232.

Under both forms of the second type of clause, collision is not an "excluded event" or a non-covered "consequence" of an insured event, but is only an "excepted cause." If some insured event (fire) is produced by the collision, or if collision is a consequence of an insured event (fire), or if some covered cause (fire) combines with collision to produce a loss, liability follows.

In other terminology than Patterson's, the first kind of clause excepts, or excludes, or negates liability for (the choice among these forms of expression being left to one's taste) all damages caused by capture, regardless of whether there is a cooperating cause that is among those designated in the policy coverage provisions; that is, the clause negates liability for damage caused by capture, even if there is another cause that, but for this negation, would have provided the affirmative basis for liability.

This first kind of clause states a criterion *conclusive* against liability—a purging criterion. If its requirements are satisfied in relation to a claim, there is no coverage under the policy for that claim, regardless of what the other circumstances may have been.

In other terminology than Patterson's, one form of the second kind of clause does not defeat coverage for damages caused by the specified incident (collision) if that incident is caused by a covered incident (fire), but if the order of causation is the reverse, and the first incident produces the covered incident, there is no coverage beyond the damages of which the covered incident was a contributing cause.

In other terminology than Patterson's, another form of the second type of clause excepts or excludes a specified incident (collision) from the causes that can supply an affirmative basis of liability under the policy, but does not except, or exclude, or negate liability for damage resulting from the combined influence of that incident (collision) and another incident (fire) that is among those designated in policy coverage provisions.

Each form of the second type of clause states a criterion that is itself *inconclusive* of liability. It merely states that the facts specified in the clause are themselves insufficient to support liability—that they do not supply an affirmative basis for liability. This kind of clause does not foreclose the possibility of coverage under some other clause of the policy that supplies the affirmative basis for liability.

In cases of multiple causation (cases in which two or more causes are arguably relevant to the liability of the insurer), the distinction identified by Patterson—and characterized by him as a distinction between "exceptions" and "exclusions"—is quite useful in expressing a decision, as distinguished from reaching it. In this respect it is superior to a usage in accordance with whether the clause appears after the word "except" or instead under a heading "Exclusions" in the policy form. Also, it is useful in marshaling precedents for whatever bearing they should have on the decision of a new case, provided great care is taken to classify the precedents according to the expression of one or the other meaning in the policy clause rather than, for example, treating all collision clauses alike without regard to which of these meanings is expressed. But on the other hand, and without minimizing the importance of those uses, it should be noted that this terminology is not very helpful in deciding what result should be reached in a given case, since it involves definition in terms of legal consequences. Except as an appeal to similarly characterized precedents (*e. g.,* by arguing that a clause not materially different was previously held in effect to be an "exception" and this one should be so treated because of the precedent), use of one or the other characterization of a clause as a reason for applying one of these sets of legal consequences is question-begging. The principal problems for one who is deciding a question of first impression or criticizing precedents are those of interpreting the clause (does it express the meaning that it have one legal effect rather than the other) and applying any statutory or judicial restrictions on the insurer's freedom to use the clause it prefers.

Thus, observing the distinction between these two types of insurance clauses is useful to a significant, even if limited, degree. But it is doubtful that there is merit in expressing that distinction as one between "exceptions" and "exclusions." The terminology chosen by Patterson has the disadvantage of giving to terms commonly used in other senses the new significance of special terms of art. Perhaps it would be less confusing to speak of Patterson's "exceptions" as inconclusive clauses and his "exclusions" as conclusive clauses.

Patterson also used "consequences" as a term of art in his further distinction between "exceptions" and "exclusions," on the one hand, and clauses declaring "consequences" to be covered or not covered. This kind of provision, like the provision Patterson called an "exception," is an inconclusive clause—one that does not dispose of the issue of liability entirely but merely describes or limits one possible basis for affirmatively supporting liability. This usage, also, gives to a commonly used word a new and special significance. Moreover, there is less scope for fruitfully using this distinction, even as a mode of communication, than for using the distinction between "exceptions" and "exclusions."

Many courts and writers have not accepted Patterson's terminology at all; [12] others have accepted it only to a very limited extent and even then, it seems, without faithful and accurate use.[13]

12. See, *e.g.*, 4 Appleman, Insurance Law § 2303 (rev. ed. 1969), omitting any reference to Patterson's terminology, speaking in a way inconsistent with it, and citing opinions that do likewise.

13. See, *e.g.*, 2 Richards, Law of Insurance § 208 (5th ed. Freedman 1952): "An Excepted Cause or Exception Clause generally provides that an insurer is not liable for loss or damage if the Insured Event actually resulted from or was caused by the subject matter of the Excepted Cause or Exception Clause. . . . The Exclusion Clause simply excludes from coverage certain events which otherwise would fall within the scope of the Insured Event. Technically

(2) Precedents on Conclusive and Inconclusive Causation Clauses

Clauses concerning automobile collisions have been a fertile field for precedents bearing on the question whether a policy clause is to be treated as stating a criterion conclusive against coverage or instead making the inconclusive statement that a specified set of facts is in itself insufficient to afford an affirmative basis for coverage.

A widely used combination automobile insurance policy form states that the insurer agrees to pay the insured for physical damage to his own car *under collision coverage* for loss "caused by collision" and *under comprehensive coverage* for loss "from any cause except collision; but, for the purpose of this coverage, breakage of glass and loss caused by missiles, falling objects, fire, theft, or larceny, windstorm, hail, earthquake, explosion, riot or civil commotion, malicious mischief or vandalism, flood, or (as to a covered automobile of the private passenger type) colliding with a bird or animal, shall not be deemed loss caused by collision; . . . ." [14] Family automobile policy forms have included provisions of generally similar import.[15]

The quoted passages plainly assign to "collision" when used as a qualification of comprehensive coverage a narrower meaning than when used to define the separate "collision" coverage.[16] This sug-

---

such a clause does not pertain to causative connections with the Insured Event, but few courts have appreciated this distinction in definition."

The first sentence of this passage is ambiguous on the question whether the "exception" clause precludes liability, regardless of other circumstances, when its criterion is met. In contrast, Patterson makes it clear that an exception clause does not have this effect but an exclusion clause does. Also, the assertion in the third sentence, in light of the use of "event" in the first and second sentences, may seem to deny the proposition that a collision, for example, is not inherently a "cause," or an "event," or a "result" but appears to us in one or another of these ways according to the perspective from which we view it.

See also Mooney, *Functional Analysis of Exceptions in Accident Insurance,* 1964 U.Ill.L.Forum 495, which appears to place a different interpretation on Patterson's distinction between "exceptions" and "exclusions" from that expressed in the text above.

14. See, *e.g.,* Automobile Physical Damage Part of the Combination Automobile-General Liability Policy in the American Mutual Insurance Alliance Study Kit distributed in 1969.

15. See Appendix H *infra.*

16. The special-purpose definition of "collision" used to limit the extent to which the phrase "except collision" confines the scope of the *comprehensive* coverage is plainly narrower than "collision" in the ordinary sense. In that context, the narrower definition produces broader coverage for the policyholder. In contrast, when the policyholder has *collision* coverage, he is favored by giving "collision" a broader meaning. In this latter context, some courts have construed "collision" in varying senses that go beyond what might be considered the "ordinary sense" of "collision." See, *e.g.,* Trinity Universal Ins. Co. v. Evans, 93 Ariz. 9, 377 P.2d 1020 (1963) (driver of truck carrying insured tractor lost control, and truck went off the road and down into a ravine, striking the bottom of it; held, coverage under policy insuring against loss to the tractor caused "by . . . collision . . . of any conveyance upon which the Caterpillar [tractor] is being transported"); Tuten v. First of Ga. Ins. Co., 117 Ga.App. 409, 160 S.E.2d 903 (1968), 34 A.L.R.3d 988 (1970) (insured's car totally destroyed by submersion in salt water when it slipped down boat ramp into river while car was chocked and motor was

gests the possibility of double coverage for a loss, but that result is precluded by a provision stating a limit of the company's liability for loss to any one covered automobile.[17] This narrower meaning of "collision" as used in defining the qualification of comprehensive coverage plainly expresses a meaning that any occurrence within certain types—e. g., loss caused by windstorm [18] or loss caused by the impact between a "falling object" and the car [19]—shall not defeat coverage under the comprehensive clause, even though being a "collision" in the broader sense of that term as used in the collision coverage. It is not entirely clear, however, whether the occurrence of a "collision" in the narrower sense in which that term is used in the comprehensive coverage clause is conclusive against coverage under the comprehensive clause—that is, whether it denies comprehensive coverage even when there was also some other cause within the meaning of "any cause except collision." In other words, it is not clear whether "except collision" is a conclusive clause, intended to defeat coverage if a collision occurred, or instead is an inconclusive clause, merely saying that a collision is not itself an affirmative basis for liability under the comprehensive coverage, thus leaving the issue of liability to be decided by answering the question whether there was some other circumstance of the loss that would be a sufficient basis for liability. In Patterson's terminology, the question is whether the language "except collision" is an "exclusion" or instead only an "exception." [20] Patterson took the view that the corresponding language in earlier

not running; held, collision coverage applied because there was a collision between car and water); Payne v. Western Cas. & Sur. Co., 379 S.W.2d 209 (Mo.App.1964) (the wheels of the insured tractor-trailer rig slipped off the paved highway onto the shoulder, the softness of which caused an abrupt stop that wrenched the heavily loaded trailer; held, a collision); Morton v. Blue Ridge Ins. Co., 255 N. C. 360, 121 S.E.2d 716 (1961) (the insured car accidentally rolled down a boat ramp into a canal; held, a collision). *But see, e.g.*, Mercury Ins. Co. v. McClellan, 216 Ark. 410, 225 S.W.2d 931, 14 A.L.R.2d 806 (1950) (insured cars were damaged as the result of a tornado, one by having a brick wall and timber blown upon it, another by being rolled over several times and being blown into a tree; held, no coverage under "collision and upset" provisions, since the policies contained an express provision for windstorm damage, which the insureds had not purchased, and a provision that limited the insurance to coverages for which a premium had been paid).

An expansive view of collision coverage has been encouraged, perhaps, by the inclusion of the word "upset" in the definition of collision coverage in policy forms. See Appendix H *infra*.

17. See Appendix H *infra*.

18. *Cf.* Friedman v. Insurance Co. of N. Am., 4 Wis.2d 641, 91 N.W.2d 328, (1958), 68 A.L.R.2d 1417 (1959) (tractor-trailer overturned in executing a left turn in strong winds; that the windstorm could not have produced the result without the aid of centrifugal force does not defeat recovery under windstorm coverage since it is not necessary that wind be the sole cause).

19. For opinions observing this distinction and sustaining claims of collision coverage against arguments that the narrower meaning of "collision" in the comprehensive clause should be applied, see, *e.g.*, Barnard v. Houston Fire & Cas. Ins. Co., 81 So.2d 132 (La.App.1955), 54 A.L.R.2d 374 (1957); Jones v. Virginia Sur. Co., 145 Mont. 440, 401 P.2d 570 (1965).

20. See § 5.5(a) (1) *supra*.

versions of this clause was an "exception." [21]   His interpretation of the provision as inconclusive is supported by the results reached in most decisions.[22]

21. Patterson, Essentials of Insurance Law 232 (2d ed. 1957).

22. See, *e.g.*, Friedman v. Insurance Co. of N. Am., 4 Wis.2d 641, 91 N.W.2d 328 (1958), 68 A.L.R.2d 1417 (1959). It might be argued that Bruener v. Twin City Fire Ins. Co., 37 Wash.2d 181, 222 P.2d 833 (1950), 23 A.L.R.2d 385 (1952), treats the collision clause in the comprehensive coverage provision as conclusive against coverage—as an "exclusion" in Patterson's terminology. But the decision can be explained on other grounds. The plaintiff's car skidded on icy pavement, went out of control, straddled a ditch, and jammed into an embankment. In the suit to recover under a comprehensive coverage clause for damage to the car, the court denied liability. The court reasoned that insurance law is concerned "with the nature of the injury and how it happened . . ." (37 Wash.2d at 184, 222 P.2d at 835, 23 A.L.R.2d at 388) and does not "reach back of both the injury and the physical cause to fix the blame . . ." as do "the tort rules of proximate cause . . .." 37 Wash.2d at 183, 222 P.2d at 835, 23 A.L.R.2d at 388. Thus, the court concluded, "the loss resulting from this collision is within the exception of the policy." One might interpret this passage as treating the phrase about collision as a conclusive provision. A different analysis supporting the same judgment in the case is to treat collision as only an "excepted cause" in Patterson's sense rather than an "excluded event" but yet to hold for the insurer because of the absence of evidence to support a finding of any covered cause. A difficulty with this argument is that the comprehensive coverage of *Bruener* was defined as applying to "any direct and accidental loss of or damage to the automobile except loss caused by collision . . .." 37 Wash.2d at 182, 222 P.2d at 834, 23 A. L.R.2d at 387. It might be said that the loss of control because of skidding on ice comes within the range of causes included in this broad definition of comprehensive coverage. But it seems doubtful that the comprehensive coverage was designed to cover or should be construed to cover risks of this nature, which are in essence traffic or operational risks. More-

over, many collisions involve loss of control of one or both vehicles, and such a construction of the comprehensive coverage would lead to the conclusion that there is a very substantial overlap between it and collision coverage. Though the point is debatable, it would seem more appropriate to hold that "loss of control" and "skidding" are not among the causes within the comprehensive coverage. Also, it might be argued that a loss of which skidding is an antecedent, but which occurs only after collision following the skidding, is not a "direct" loss caused otherwise than by collision. Thus the result that ought to be reached if one treats the collision clause as an "exception" and not an "exclusion" in Patterson's sense is still unclear because of uncertainty whether there was any other cause that was a covered cause. *Cf.* 5 Appleman, Insurance Law § 3222 (rev. ed. 1970).

In the earlier case of Ploe v. International Indem. Co., 128 Wash. 480, 223 P. 327 (1924), the court held that there was no liability under collision coverage for a loss resulting when the insured car skidded from the road, struck a stump, and rolled down an embankment. The court in *Bruener* felt impelled to overrule *Ploe* because of a line of reasoning in *Ploe* that the proximate cause of the accident was the skidding or its passing from the roadway from whatever cause, and the instant it left the roadway its doom was sealed. Fallacious as this latter line of reasoning in *Ploe* may have been, the views on proximate cause advanced in *Bruener* seem equally unsatisfactory. See § 5.5(c) *infra*. It seems a different and closer question, however, whether *Bruener* is sound in overruling the holding in *Ploe* that skidding, passing from the roadway, and striking an object such as a stump or an embankment do not constitute a collision. Arguably the result reached in *Ploe* is defensible on the ground that there was no collision in the ordinary sense of that term (and, in contrast with current collision forms, the collision clause in *Ploe* did not state that "upset" was included within its coverage). This view would serve to reconcile the results of non-liability in both *Ploe* and *Bruener*, avoiding any need for overruling

The insured ordinarily recovers when he proves that he obtained comprehensive but not collision coverage and then suffered a loss caused by the combination of collision and some other cause plainly among those that, at least when not combined with collision, would be within the comprehensive coverage. For example, courts have so ruled when a fire [23] or a theft [24] was a cause of an ensuing collision.

In contrast, if a collision produces a fire and the owner of the vehicle had obtained fire but not collision coverage, the insurer is liable for only that part of the damage caused by fire.[25]

A more difficult question was raised in a case in which a car insured under comprehensive coverage but not under collision coverage after being driven into a puddle of water 50 feet long and eight inches deep, mounted an embankment and turned over. Evidence was offered that a tie rod was bent by the contact with the water, causing loss of control. It was conceded that the comprehensive coverage applied to "loss caused by water," but the court concluded that this was not a case of "loss caused by water" within either the ordinary sense or the sense of the policy.[26]

It often happens that policy language is far from clear with respect to whether a clause is intended to be conclusive against coverage (an exclusion in Patterson's terminology) or merely a declaration that a certain kind of cause of loss is not an affirmative basis of recovery (an exception in Patterson's terminology). This is well illustrated in the provisions of a policy invoked when a claim was

Ploe. But it would lead to non-liability under both collision and comprehensive coverages for some accidental losses—for example, skidding off the road into mud, without upset, the sudden stopping causing damage to the vehicle. Some courts have construed "collision" so broadly as to include this type of case. See n.16 *supra*.

23. Tonkin v. California Ins. Co., 294 N.Y. 326, 62 N.E.2d 215 (1945), 160 A. L.R. 944 (1946). Similar results have been reached in relation to other types of restrictions on comprehensive coverage. See, *e.g.*, Standard Acc. Ins. Co. v. Christy, 235 Ark. 415, 360 S.W. 2d 195 (1962) (a fire of unexplained origin burned the radiator and air conditioner hoses of the insured car while it was being operated; water from the radiator extinguished the fire, but the loss of water in the cooling system caused severe damage to the motor before the insured became aware of the fire and was able to stop the car; held, coverage for the entire loss under comprehensive coverage excluding loss due to mechanical failure, which the insurer argued included the damage to the motor caused by overheating). See also

Smith v. M. F. A. Mut. Ins. Co., 337 S.W.2d 537 (Mo.App.1960) (gas leaking from the load of a propane tank-truck was ignited by some unknown source, and the resulting fire caused heavy damage to the truck; held, recovery under coverage excluding loss "caused by bottled or compressed gas"; reasoned, however, on the ground that the loss was not "caused by" though it may have arisen from compressed gas).

24. Bolling v. Northern Ins. Co., 280 N. Y. 510, 19 N.E.2d 920 (1939) (thief abandoned insured car; collision occurred while policeman was driving it to police station).

25. *E.g.*, Mammina v. Homeland Ins. Co., 371 Ill. 555, 21 N.E.2d 726 (1939).

26. Harris v. Allstate Ins. Co., 309 N.Y. 72, 127 N.E.2d 816 (1955). See also nn.16, 22 *supra*, discussing the question whether there is a collision in the ordinary sense and in the sense of a policy clause when a car skids and jams into an embankment, and whether there is in such a fact situation some other cause within the coverage of "any cause except collision."

presented for destruction of a residence at the top of a bluff overlooking a lake.[27]   Landslides occurred after heavy rainfall, and severe faults appeared in the ground immediately under the house, resulting in the loss in question. The owners sued their insurer under coverage for "All Physical Loss"—with certain qualifications, of course, among which were the following:

"Exclusions: This Policy Does Not Insure Against: . . .

"B. Loss by . . . normal settling . . . ; this Exclusion, however, shall not apply to loss by . . . Landslide, Total or Partial Collapse, Water Damage, and Glass Breakage, caused by perils excluded in this paragraph;

"C. Loss by surface waters, flood waters, waves, tide or tidal waves, high water, or overflow of streams or bodies of water, all whether driven by wind or not . . . ."[28]

Evidence indicated that waves and high water on the lake, driven against the bluff by storms, combined with heavy rains that soaked the ground above to create extensive erosion over a period of years. The trial court instructed the jury, in effect, that if the loss was caused by a combination of covered and non-covered causes, they should find for the plaintiffs. Judgment on the verdict for the plaintiffs was affirmed, apparently because "the jury presumably found [first] that the erosion and action of high water, surface water and waves were not predominant and efficient causes of the landslide . . . ."[29] and, second, that "the factors causing the landslide at or near the time of the loss were the constant rainfall, the increase of weight from water percolating into the clay and the presence of a huge weight of ground water in clay-sand strata lying 20 to 30 feet below the top of the bluff . . . ."[30] With these findings assumed, the court resolved ambiguities in the policy clauses against the insurer. Certainly the provisions concerning landslide in this policy are unclear. Perhaps "normal settling" in clause "B" under the heading "Exclusions" is an "excepted cause" in Patterson's terminology, and "Landslide" in this clause would therefore be either an exception from this "excepted cause" of "normal settling" or perhaps merely a thing distinguished from "normal settling."[31] The clause appears to imply that landslide is not an "excepted cause," and certainly not an "excluded event." Arguably it implies that landslide is a covered cause, particularly in view of the provision that the policy covers "All Physical Loss" except that referred to in the "Exclusions."

27. Fireman's Fund Ins. Co. v. Hanley, 252 F.2d 780 (6th Cir. 1958).

28. 252 F.2d at 781–782.

29. 252 F.2d at 784.

30. 252 F.2d at 786.

31. A *"normal* settling" restriction such as that in the *Hanley* case has been construed to permit coverage for sudden and extraordinary settling. See, *e.g.*, Prickett v. Royal Ins. Co., 56 Cal.2d 234, 363 P.2d 907, 14 Cal.Rptr. 675 (1961), 86 A.L.R.2d 711 (1962) (one wall of insured house settled five to twelve inches very suddenly due to improper earth fill underneath it; held, sudden settling to the extent involved in the present case was not "normal" settling within meaning of restriction).

The provision concerning surface water, in clause C under the heading "Exclusions," appears to be, in Patterson's terminology, an "excepted cause" provision. Perhaps it could be interpreted as an "exclusion," but one not applicable unless surface water is the predominating cause. That question was not reached because the court held that surface water was not a substantial cause, the water being regarded as no longer surface water once it had gone into the ground one inch. The trial court instruction, it may be noted, treated all the qualifying provisions as "excepted cause" provisions in Patterson's sense.[32]

There have been other decisions dealing with similar policy language that have also treated provisions under the heading "Exclusions" as inconclusive—as "excepted cause" provisions in Patterson's terminology.[33]

The discussion here has referred to several contexts, scattered through various branches of insurance law, in which the need arises for determining whether a policy clause restricting coverage should be given effect as conclusive against coverage or instead as negating one ground of coverage and remaining inconclusive as to other possible grounds. This problem has been presented in other contexts as well, including, among others,[34] those in which the following holdings

32. The trial court charged, "if you find as a fact that the damage to the plaintiffs' property resulted from a combination . . . of causes within the coverage of the policy and causes excluded from the coverage of the policy, . . . the plaintiffs are entitled to recover in this action." 252 F.2d at 783.

33. See, *e.g.*, Sabella v. Wisler, 59 Cal. 2d 21, 377 P.2d 889, 27 Cal.Rptr. 689 (1963) (loss caused by settling covered since settling was caused by flooding from sewer pipe that resulted from negligence of building contractor); Sauer v. General Ins. Co., 225 Cal. App.2d 275, 37 Cal.Rptr. 303 (2d Dist. 1964) (perils covered included accidental discharge of water from plumbing; break in water pipe beneath house; clauses under the heading "Exclusions" pertaining to water damage, earth movement, settlement, and cracking; held, efficient cause was peril insured against and "Exclusions" were inapplicable).

34. See, *e.g.*, Mann v. Service Life Ins. Co., 284 F.Supp. 139 (E.D.Va.1968) (Marine officer, acting as co-pilot of helicopter in Vietnam, killed by rifle fire from ground; policy provision that coverage did not apply if death resulted from "operating or riding in, or descending from any kind of air-craft if the Insured is a pilot . . ."; held, coverage on the theory that the limitation was not intended to be effective if death resulted from an intervening cause totally unrelated to operation of the aircraft); Dickson v. United States Fid. & Gy. Co., 466 P.2d 515 (Wash.1970) (all-risk contractor's equipment floater policy with "exclusion" for "latent defect"; insured crane damaged when its boom with a defective weld collapsed, while pulling "H" beams out of ground on highway job, when earth collapsed onto "H" beam; held, coverage on alternate grounds, first, that "latent defect" exclusion applied only to cost of repairing the defect, not to resulting damage and, second, that not the latent defect but an external cause, collapsing earth, was the "direct, violent and efficient cause," and thus the "responsible cause of the loss"). *Cf.* Harris v. Carolina Life Ins. Co., 233 So.2d 833 (Fla.1970) (insured died in collision, as passenger in car, while under influence of alcohol; policy "exception" saying "death . . . resulting . . . from any of the following causes are risks not assumed under this policy . . . bodily injury which under the influence of alcohol . . ."; held, ambiguous, and insurer has burden of proving causal relationship).

have been reached. Damage from an explosion incident to a fire has been held to be covered under a fire insurance policy not covering explosion.[35] Damage to a house from freezing after vandals cut off heat has been held to be within vandalism coverage despite a provision disallowing coverage for loss from change in temperature.[36]

As one among possible explanations of this last illustration will show, the problem is more complicated than choosing merely between conclusive and inconclusive effect. It is possible also, for example, to treat a clause as having conclusive effect against coverage when the conditions it states are met, but construing the statement of those conditions restrictively. Thus, it may be held that a clause declaring that there shall be no coverage for "loss resulting from change in temperature" is conclusive against coverage when the required condition is met, but that the required condition is that the loss be "directly caused" by change of temperature as distinguished from being directly caused by vandalism and "incidentally aggravated" by a change of temperature that would not have occurred but for the vandalism.[37] Pushed far enough, however, this kind of construction ordinarily produces the same result as classifying the clause as inconclusive—as merely saying that a "change of temperature" is not itself a basis for coverage but that there may be coverage for a loss to which a change of temperature contributes as long as there was a cooperating cause that was covered by the policy. Of course, there is only coverage for such loss as the covered cause does cause. If a change of temperature causes loss by freezing, and then vandalism occurs, the vandalism would not be a cause of the loss from freezing before the vandalism occurred.

In general the relevant precedents display a strong judicial tendency to favor construing a clause as, in Patterson's terminology, an exception rather than an exclusion. Yet there are decisions construing clauses as conclusive against coverage despite the existence of additional causes that would otherwise support coverage—as "exclusions" in Patterson's terminology.[38] Of course the particular lan-

35. Cook v. Continental Ins. Co., 220 Ala. 162, 124 So. 239 (1928), 65 A.L.R. 921 (1930) (concussion damage from explosion set off by firemen); Wheeler v. Phenix Ins. Co., 203 N.Y. 283, 96 N.E. 452 (1911) (evidence sustained finding that fire preceded explosion in grain elevator); Merrimack Mut. Fire Ins. Co. v. Lanasa, 202 Va. 562, 118 S.E.2d 450 (1961), 82 A.L.R.2d 1118 (1962) (evidence sustained finding that fire preceded explosion in fruit storage building). *But see, e.g.,* Levert-St. John, Inc. v. Birmingham Fire & Cas. Co., 137 So.2d 494 (La.App.1961) (applying the exclusion because the explosion was set off by a "friendly" fire—a welder's arc; see § 5.3(d) *supra*, concerning the general distinction between "friendly" and "hostile" fires).

36. Fawcett House, Inc. v. Great Cent. Ins. Co., 280 Minn. 325, 159 N.W.2d 268 (1968).

37. *Cf. Fawcett House*, n.36 *supra.*

38. *E.g.,* Insurance Co. v. Boon, 95 U.S. 117, 24 L.Ed. 395 (1877) (insurance on stock of goods in Glasgow, Mo., in 1864; stipulation that "the company shall not be liable to make good any loss or damage by fire which may happen or take place by means of any invasion, insurrection, riot, or civil commotion, or of any military or usurped power"; commander of Union forces set fire to city hall to prevent stores from falling into hands of opposing troops, and fire spread through two intermediate buildings to the building containing the insured goods;

guage of the policy may clearly express an intent that the clause be conclusive against coverage despite the fact that because of a cooperating cause there would otherwise be coverage. If there is doubt, however, a construction that the clause is only an "exception," in Patterson's terminology, is likely. This result is often justified on the theory of resolving ambiguities against the insurer. In some instances it may be justified on the theory of disallowing unconscionable advantage [39] or on the theory of honoring expectations of policyholders who cannot reasonably be expected to read complex policy provisions closely enough to discover an intent to preclude coverage in some described circumstance, even if that intent is unambiguously manifested to one who takes the time and trouble to puzzle his way through all the details of the policy.[40]

§ 5.5(b) PROBLEMS OF LEGAL CAUSE

Multiple-cause cases sometimes involve not only the questions of interpretation referrred to as the choice between conclusive and inconclusive clauses (between exclusions and exceptions in Patterson's terminology), but also problems perhaps appropriately characterized as legal cause questions.

Many judges and writers have suggested that there are basic differences between principles of legal cause applying to tort cases and those applying to contract cases generally or to insurance cases particularly. For example, Cardozo remarked that "there is a tendency [in tort law] to go farther back in the search for causes than there is in the law of contracts . . . . Especially in the law of insurance, the rule is that, 'You are not to trouble yourself with distant causes.'" [1] Others, pushing to what is perhaps a more extreme position than Cardozo's, have said that in tort law proximate cause "is not limited to one link back in the chain of causation . . ." and that "it excludes the immediate physical cause of injury, with which insurance is concerned, from its purview and includes any number of

---

held, not covered); United States Fid. & Gy. Co. v. Morgan, 399 S.W.2d 537 (Tex.1966), Paulson v. Fire Ins. Exch., 393 S.W.2d 316 (Tex.1965), and Hardware Dealers Mut. Ins. Co. v. Berglund, 393 S.W.2d 309 (Tex.1965) (these three Texas decisions give conclusive—"excluded event"—effect to provisions in windstorm policies against liability for loss caused by such things as rain, tidal wave, high water, or overflow, "whether driven by wind or not"; the insured is allowed to recover, however, for so much of his loss as he can prove to have been caused solely by a covered cause, such as windstorm, before a non-covered cause, such as flooding, could have had any effect on the property).

39. See § 6.2 infra.

40. See § 6.3 infra.

1. Bird v. St. Paul Fire & Marine Ins. Co., 224 N.Y. 47, 53, 120 N.E. 86, 88 (1918), 13 A.L.R. 875, 878 (1921) (denying liability, under a policy including fire insurance on a canal boat, for concussion damage from an explosion about 1,000 feet distant from the boat, the explosion being part of a chain of events started by a fire in a freight yard).

unbroken links of causation with which insurance is not concerned." [2] Also, judicial opinions in insurance cases, especially those of earlier vintage, often express the idea that the proximate cause is the efficient or predominant cause. Perhaps the idea that proximate cause is a more limited concept in insurance law than in tort law has been encouraged by the presence of the phrase "direct loss by" in many insurance policies.[3] But it has often been held that a loss caused jointly by an insured cause and a cause operating later in time was a "direct loss by" the insured cause.[4] And the language of efficient or predominant cause appears not only in insurance cases but also in tort cases, and especially those of earlier vintage. In some insurance cases this language appears to have been adopted not as a distinctive theory for insurance law but on the assumption that problems of proximate cause in tort and insurance cases are essentially alike.[5]

More significant, perhaps, than the varied theories expressed on this issue is the fact that the results reached in a host of insurance cases contradict the view that insurance law is concerned with only the immediate and not the more distant causes, or only the efficient or predominant and not other causes.[6]

On the whole, an inventory of results supports the conclusion that the analogy between insurance and tort cases on issues of proximate cause is quite close.[7] Where differences appear, they are more

---

2. Bruener v. Twin City Fire Ins. Co., 37 Wash.2d 181, 184, 222 P.2d 833, 835 (1950), 23 A.L.R.2d 385, 388 (1952).

3. See, *e.g.*, the fire insurance form in Appendix A *infra*.

4. See, *e.g.*, Fred Meyer, Inc. v. Central Mut. Ins. Co., 235 F.Supp. 540 (D.Ore. 1964) (food spoilage caused by failure of refrigeration when windstorm destroyed electric power lines held a "direct loss by windstorm"); Providence Wash. Ins. Co. v. Weaver, 242 Miss. 141, 133 So.2d 635 (1961) (both death of cattle resulting immediately from injuries received in collision and upset of the truck in which they were being carried and presumed death of cattle the last traces of which were tracks into quicksand along river's edge, where they proceeded when freed by the accident, held "direct loss by overturning" of the vehicle on which they were being transported). *Cf.* 5 Appleman, Insurance Law § 3083 (rev. ed. 1970).

5. See, *e.g.*, Russell v. German Fire Ins. Co., 100 Minn. 528, 111 N.W. 400, 10 L.R.A.(n.s.) 326 (1907) (building gutted by fire but walls left standing; several days later a strong wind, expectable in that area, blew one of the walls down onto plaintiff's building;

plaintiff recovered under his fire insurance policy; citing tort and insurance cases without suggesting that they involve different principles, the court observed, "what is meant by proximate cause is not that which is last in time or place, not merely that which was in activity at the consummation of the injury, but that which is the procuring, efficient, and predominant cause").

6. See, *e.g.*, *Russell*, n.5 *supra*, and cases cited in n. 4 *supra*, allowing recovery because an earlier link in the chain was a covered cause, even though the most immediate physical cause was not. See also, *e.g.*, Levert-St. John, Inc. v. Birmingham Fire & Cas. Co., 137 So.2d 494 (La.App.1961) (holding that an explosion exclusion applied because the explosion was set off by a "friendly" fire, although explosion caused by hostile fire would be covered; as to the general distinction between "friendly" and "hostile" fires, see § 5.3(d) *supra*).

7. *Cf.* Levit, *Proximate Cause—First Party Coverage*, 1965 ABA Section Ins., Neg. & Comp.L.Proceedings 157, reprinted 1966 Ins. L.J. 340; Gorman, *A Reply to "Proximate Cause—First Party Coverage,"* 34 Ins. Counsel J. 98 (1967). [continued on page 319]

accurately explained, it would seem, not as manifestations of a general tendency of insurance cases in contrast with tort cases but rather as consequences of enforcing one kind of contractual provision in contrast with another. Subject to overriding regulatory measures,[8] explicit policy provisions regarding multiple-cause cases are ordinarily enforceable as written and may provide either for broader or for narrower coverage than would result in the absence of contractual specification. Thus, for example, the rules of insurance law applicable to what Patterson calls excluded events [9] are quite unlike the rules of proximate cause applied in torts cases and in other insurance cases, since these rules of insurance law deny recovery for losses arising from multiple causes some of which could have been affirmative bases for coverage but for the exclusionary provision.

§ 5.5(c) INEQUITIES FROM OVERLAPPING COVERAGES

The arrangement of various coverages in a policy form so they overlap in multiple-cause situations produces problems of equity.

One form of inequity is that of overpayment for loss under overlapping coverages. This occurs, for example, in those jurisdictions that allow a guest passenger in an automobile to recover for his medical expenses under the medical payments coverage of his host driver's policy and again under the bodily injury liability coverage of the same policy. Such overpayment is inconsistent with the principle that insurance is intended as indemnity against loss, and some courts have achieved the better result of denying such fortuitous profit by holding that the amount paid under the medical payments coverage is also credited against any claim under the liability coverage.[1] The case for using this technique of crediting is arguably less persuasive when the medical payments coverage is part of a policy other than that containing the applicable liability coverage. In that context, the technique of subrogation may be used to avoid overpayment, but more often medical payments coverages have not been construed as providing for subrogation.[2]

Another form of inequity from overlapping coverages concerns premium rates. For example, suppose a loss caused by what is construed to be a "collision" of the insured car with a stream of water across a highway [3] or with debris that falls upon the car as a wind-

See also Brewer, *Concurrent Causation in Insurance Contracts*, 59 Mich.L. Rev. 1141 (1961), which draws a contrast between tort and insurance cases with respect to the treatment of causation issues but perhaps is less at odds with the view expressed in the text above than might appear on the surface, since much of the contrast is concerned with the impact of contractual provisions in modifying rules of causation otherwise applicable.

8. See generally Chapter 6 *infra*.

9. See § 5.5(a) *supra*.

1. See § 5.9 and n.8 thereto *infra*.

2. See § 3.10(a) *supra*.

3. See, *e.g.*, Providence Wash. Ins. Co. v. Proffitt, 150 Tex. 207, 239 S.W.2d 379 (1951). *Cf. e.g.*, cases cited in § 5.5(a) n. 16 *supra*.

storm demolishes a building,[4] or suppose the car is "upset" by a windstorm.[5] In each situation it is likely that courts will find the loss covered if the insured has either collision or comprehensive coverage alone. Also, it is clear that, if he has both, he is allowed to recover for his loss only once because of policy clauses so providing. If the total premium for a policy including both coverages is the sum of the premiums for the two separate coverages, the insured is in a sense paying twice for coverage of loss of this type. This is an inequity in the rate structure, favoring the person who buys only one of the two coverages over the person who buys both. Of course that is not a conclusive indication that the rate structure is unsound. If the inequity is slight, it may be outweighed by the desirability of having each coverage include a loss that is difficult to classify.[6]

This inequity occurs to some extent even if courts adhere to a relatively narrow construction of the separate coverages. It is increased by expansive construction of each of the coverages to apply when the other coverage has not been obtained. The net effect is also to increase the premium that must be charged for each of the coverages alone, since the funds for the insurance payouts must be provided from premiums.

The problem of inequity among policyholders may be avoided, of course, by establishing a lower charge for the two overlapping coverages than the sum of the charges for the two separately. This has been done in the marketing of some special package policies.

SECTION 5.6 WARRANTY

Primary responsibility for development of the concept of warranty in insurance law has been attributed to Lord Mansfield.[1] Summarizing the early development of the concept, Professor Vance observed that apparently the term "warranted" was in general use in the seventeenth century, but in a more limited sense than it later came to have; "in the few insurance cases reported as being tried in the common law courts prior to Lord Mansfield's accession as Chief Justice of the Court of King's Bench, in 1756, there is nothing to indicate that the term had any other significance than to introduce a

4. See, e.g., United States Ins. Co. v. Boyer, 153 Tex. 415, 269 S.W.2d 340 (1954). Cf., e.g., Barnard v. Houston Fire & Cas. Ins. Co., 81 So.2d 132 (La.App.1955), 54 A.L.R.2d 374 (1957) (a tree cut by workmen hit insured vehicle; held, within collision coverage); Jones v. Virginia Sur. Co., 145 Mont. 440, 401 P.2d 570 (1965) (log felled in logging operation struck insured vehicle; held, within collision coverage). But see, e.g., Mercury Ins. Co. v. McClellan, 216 Ark. 410, 225 S.W.2d 931, 14 A.L.R.2d 806 (1950) (tornado rolled over one insured car and caused brick

wall and timber to strike another insured car; held, not within collision and upset coverage).

5. See, e.g., Farmers Ins. Exch. v. Wallace, 275 S.W.2d 864 (Tex.Civ.App. 1955, writ refused, no reversible error).

6. See generally § 8.4(b) infra.

1. Vance, The History of the Development of the Warranty in Insurance Law, 20 Yale L.J. 523, 525–532 (1911).

condition that had to be strictly performed." [2] This meaning appears to encompass what have later been called "promissory" or "continuing" warranties (which are merely "executory terms of the contract agreed to be material"),[3] but not "affirmative" warranties stipulating that specified facts exist.

In contrast, concluded Vance: "The practical result reached by the courts before Mansfield retired from the bench may be stated thus: The description of the risk upon which the underwriter relied in determining whether he would assume the risk or not, or at what premium he would assume it, might be found within the policy or without it. So far as the descriptive terms chanced to be within the policy [warranties], they must be literally true, irrespective of their materiality, but if they chanced to be without the policy [representations] the insurance remained valid unless the misdescription was of such character as really to injure the underwriter; that is, unless the misdescription was substantial and material." [4]

Vance was not critical of the rule requiring promissory warranties to be strictly performed.[5] But his criticism of the strict enforcement of affirmative warranties was severe. He asserted that it makes no difference to the insurer whether statements descriptive of the risk appear within the policy or instead appear (orally or in writing) outside it; he considered that in both instances the insurer should not be expected to pay if the risk differed materially from that described. On the other hand he saw no reason why the insurer should not pay if the risk did not differ in any material respect, "even though the shibboleth 'warranty' be found in the policy." [6]

The harsh rule of warranty developed by Mansfield in marine insurance cases was extended to life and fire insurance, although the reasons advanced for it in the marine cases were not applicable to the other forms of insurance.[7] Policy forms became "overgrown with a wilderness of warranties, many of the most trivial character, in which the rights of the policyholder, however honest and careful, were in grave danger of being lost. It was necessary for the courts to go to the rescue of the public. It was too late to do what Lord Mansfield should have done; that is, declare that an immaterial warranty should have no more effect upon the rights of the insured than an immaterial representation; but they did hold that no stipulation, though written in the policy, should be construed as a warranty, unless it was clearly and unmistakably so intended by the parties, as indicated by the unequivocal language of the policy.[8] The unseemly

---

2. *Id.* at 526–527.

3. *Id.* at 532.

4. *Id.* at 531.

5. *Id.* at 532. See the statement quoted in the first paragraph of this section, from which one may infer that Vance considered it quite appropriate that a

warranty be used to impose a "condition that had to be strictly performed."

6. *Id.* at 533.

7. *Id.* at 533–534.

8. Vance's footnote 33 renumbered: "For examples of such liberal con-

struggle that ensued between the unwise insurers who sought so to frame their policies as to compel the courts to allow them the dishonest benefit of forfeitures unsuspected by the insured, and the courts who sought by liberal construction, and sometimes distortion of the language of the policies, to do justice in spite of the warranties, resulted in a mass of litigation and confused precedent, the like of which cannot be found in any other field of our law." [9]

The rigors of the common law rule requiring strict compliance with warranties in insurance law have been greatly relieved by the combination of decisional developments, reducing its range of application, and statutory developments either making further inroads on its effective range or else directly changing the effect of warranties. [10]

With respect to life insurance, little range for the operation of the rule of strict compliance remains. Statutes commonly either provide, or else require that the policy provide, that the policy shall be incontestable after a short period (one year or two). [11] Also, there is now commonly either a statutory provision or a statutory requirement of a policy provision that statements made in an application for life insurance shall be considered representations and not warranties. [12]

With respect to types of insurance other than life insurance, statutory relief against the rigors of the common law rule [13] has been less pervasive. Quite generally with respect to marine insurance [14]

struction see *Moulor v. Insurance Co.*, 111 U.S., 335 [4 Sup.Ct. 466, 28 L.Ed. 447 (1884)]; *Phoenix Mut. Life Ins. Co. v. Raddin*, 120 U.S., 183 [7 Sup.Ct. 500, 30 L.Ed. 644 (1887)]; *Alabama Gold Life Ins. Co. v. Johnston*, 80 Ala., 467 [2 So. 125 (1887)]; *Globe Mut. Life Ins. Ass'n v. Wagner*, 188 Ill., 133 [58 N.E. 970 (1900)]."

9. Vance, *The History of the Development of the Warranty in Insurance Law*, 20 Yale L.J. 523, 534 (1911).

10. See § 6.5 *infra*.

11. See § 6.5(d) *infra*.

12. See, *e.g.*, N.Y.Ins.Law § 142(3) (McKinney 1966).

13. See § 6.5 *infra*.

14. But marine insurance has not completely escaped the impact of statutory modification of the law of warranty. See, *e.g.*, Wilburn Boat Co. v. Fireman's Fund Ins. Co., 348 U.S. 310, 75 Sup.Ct. 368, 99 L.Ed. 337 (1955). An action was brought in 1949 on a policy insuring a house boat that burned on Lake Texoma, an artificial lake on the Texas-Oklahoma border. The insurer denied liability because of alleged breach of "warranties" providing that the boat would not be sold, transferred, assigned, pledged, hired, or chartered without the insurer's consent. The Wilburns contended that Texas law was applicable to the contract and that under Texas statutes, now carried forward as Texas Ins. Code Ann. arts. 6.14 and 21.16 (1963), the defense was unavailing. The District Court held that the policy was a maritime contract governed by federal admiralty law and that literal fulfillment of warranties is required under such law. The Court of Appeals affirmed. The Supreme Court (Justice Frankfurter concurring in result and Justices Reed and Burton dissenting) reversed and remanded for a trial "under appropriate state law," the court's opinion by Justice Black declaring: "We, like Congress, leave the regulation of marine insurance where it has been—with the States." 348 U.S. at 321, 75 Sup.Ct. at 374, 99 L.Ed. at 346. The subsequent District Court decision on remand in favor of the insured was reversed by the Court of Appeals for insufficiency of evidence to support the District Court's application of Texas law. 259 F.2d 662 (5th Cir. 1958), *cert. denied*, 359 U.S. 925 (1959). Finally, after a new trial that also re-

and in a substantial number of states with respect to most other types of insurance, the rule requiring strict compliance with warranties is still recognized.

SECTION 5.7   REPRESENTATIONS

§ 5.7(a) GENERALLY

Under the rule that prevails in the absence of statutory modification of the decisional law, a material misrepresentation in reliance upon which a policy is issued is ground for avoidance of the policy, whether the misrepresentation is made with knowledge of its falsity or instead is made through a good faith mistake.[1] In some circumstances, however, intent to deceive has been required. Most of the cases so requiring have concerned representations of intention [2] or representations in life and accident insurance applications concerning health of the applicant (often treated as a matter of opinion).[3] But a minority of the courts have stated the requirement of intent to deceive as one applicable to misrepresentation generally,[4] and in a few

sulted in judgment for the insured— 199 F.Supp. 784 (E.D.Tex.1960)—the Court of Appeals reversed and remanded for entry of judgment in favor of the insurer, holding that the insured's misrepresentation of facts concerning use of the vessel was material to the risk insured against and that, under the applicable Texas law, therefore, the insured could not recover. 300 F.2d 631 (5th Cir.), *cert. denied*, 370 U.S. 925 (1962).

See generally Healy, *The Hull Policy: Warranties, Representations, Disclosures and Conditions*, 41 Tulane L. Rev. 245 (1967).

1. *E.g.*, Metropolitan Life Ins. Co. v. Becraft, 213 Ind. 378, 12 N.E.2d 952, 115 A.L.R. 93 (1938); Bankers' Life Ins. Co. v. Miller, 100 Md. 1, 59 A. 116 (1904). See 12 Appleman, Insurance Law §§ 7293, 7294 (1943).

2. *E.g.*, Bryant v. Ocean Ins. Co., 39 Mass. 200 (1839) (representation, in applying for marine insurance, that the vessel was taking in paving stones and would fill up with hay; instead a cargo of paving stones without hay was taken and was allegedly heavier and more perilous).

3. *E.g.*, Franklin Life Ins. Co. v. William J. Champion & Co., 350 F.2d 115, 353 F.2d 919 (6th Cir. 1965), 26 A.L.R. 3d 1034 (1969), *cert. denied*, 384 U.S. 928 (1966) (Michigan law); Metropolitan Life Ins. Co. v. Johnson, 105 Ark.

101, 150 S.W. 393 (1912); Clark v. National Life & Acc. Ins. Co., 145 Tex. 575, 200 S.W.2d 820 (1947). But a court so holding may nevertheless enforce a stipulation that the insurance shall not be effective until the policy is delivered to the insured while he is in good health. See § 6.-5(e) (4) *infra*.

4. See Vance, Law of Insurance 390–392 (3d ed. Anderson 1951), deploring the fact that such misleading dicta "are becoming unfortunately frequent in recent judicial opinions." Vance suggests that these dicta have resulted from confusion over the grounds of decision in several special types of cases wherein proof of fraud has properly been required. These special types include (a) cases in which the insured or beneficiary claims that the answer given to the examining physician or agent of the insurer was correct, but was incorrectly recorded, and good faith of the applicant has been required to support equitable estoppel against the insurer's assertion of the false answer; (b) cases involving statements of opinion, expectation, or intention; (c) cases in jurisdictions where an applicable statute has been construed to mean that misrepresentations are not ground for avoidance of a policy unless fraudulent as well as material; and (d) cases involving concealment rather than misrepresentation.

instances have applied the rule in such way as to support the conclusion that it will not be limited to misrepresentations of intention and opinion.[5]

The decisions requiring intent to deceive with respect to representations of intention and representations of health can be distinguished from cases holding that in general an innocent but material misrepresentation is ground for avoidance of an insurance policy. Intent is a state of mind. If the representor did not have the state of mind represented he must have known his statement was false and, if he intended it to be relied upon, he intended to deceive. Likewise, since a representation of health by a layman is reasonably interpretable as no more than a representation of his own opinion about his health, in the light of his limited knowledge,[6] it may be regarded as a representation of his state of mind. If he intended his representation to be relied upon, it is proved false only by evidence that proves intent to deceive as well. Thus the purported requirement of intent to deceive in these cases is not in real conflict with the general rule that innocent, material misrepresentation is ground for avoidance of an insurance policy, since in these types of cases both rules produce the same results.

There are now many statutory modifications of these common law rules concerning representations in insurance transactions.[7]

§ 5.7(b) PARTIAL INVESTIGATION AND RELIANCE

To defend successfully on the ground of misrepresentation, or on the ground of breach of warranty if materiality is required by statute, ordinarily an insurer must establish that it relied upon the false representation or warranty. A counterargument frequently advanced is that the insurer did not rely or was not entitled to rely either because it had an initial and unfulfilled duty to investigate or because, having undertaken an investigation, it can no longer defend on the ground of continued reliance even though its partial investigation was not pressed far enough to uncover the falsity of the representation or warranty.

It might be suggested that some of the seeming conflict on this question can be explained on the ground that most cases in which the insurer's defense was denied were cases of good faith misrepresenta-

---

5. *E.g.*, Grand Lodge v. Massachusetts Bonding & Ins. Co., 324 Mo. 938, 25 S. W.2d 783 (1930) (rule stated broadly as applying to all representations; "promissory representations" held not a ground for avoidance, since they could not be found to be fraudulent).

6. See, *e.g.*, Fuchs v. Old Line Life Ins. Co., 46 Wis.2d 67, 174 N.W.2d 273 (1970) (statement by applicant he was "free of any sickness or physical im-

pairment" was not misrepresentation though he later died of acute myocardial infarction and had suffered a similar attack two years before applying; healed myocardial infarct did not interfere with his normal activities and occupation and from his point of view was not "sickness or physical impairment").

7. See § 6.5(c) *infra*.

tion (either innocently or negligently) by an applicant.[8] Perhaps the insurer should have a "duty to investigate" if, either from the information furnished by the applicant or from that obtained in a partial investigation, it appears that there is a likelihood of innocent misunderstanding by the applicant. That is, the insurer should bear the risk of misunderstanding. But this view seems the equivalent of saying that good faith misrepresentation by the applicant is not a defense for the insurer—a proposition in conflict with a basic principle that is the best organizing principle of this body of law—namely, that material misrepresentation is a defense, irrespective of intent to deceive, provided the insurer relies.

Perhaps the apparent conflict can be explained on the ground that in most cases in which the insurer's defense is denied it can reasonably be inferred that the insurer learned the relevant facts from its partial investigation and considered that they did not warrant rejecting the application.

If decisions precluding the insurer's defense of misrepresentation because of its failure to investigate cannot be explained on such a ground as this, they are subject to valid criticism. If an applicant is intentionally deceitful and the insurer is only careless, the deception should be a good defense for the insurer. And the insurer's defense should not be barred merely because it relied in part on its own investigation as well as relying in part on the applicant's

---

8. *Compare, e.g.*, the following two cases: New York Life Ins. Co. v. Strudel, 243 F.2d 90 (5th Cir. 1957) (Florida law; insurer denied liability on life insurance policies because of false answers to questions the correct answers to which might have revealed the fact that he had suffered a heart attack about five years previously and had since been under treatment by various doctors; the insurer made limited independent investigation after receiving the application, but with negative results; the applicant died about seven months later; the insurer again investigated with negative results; thereafter an agent of the insurer received an anonymous telephone call directing him to a doctor and to a Heart Institute, from which in due course the history of the applicant's heart trouble was obtained; held, for the insurer; the partial investigation did not bar the insurer's reliance on the undisputed misrepresentations); Columbian Nat'l Life Ins. Co. v. Lanigan, 154 Fla. 760, 19 So.2d 67 (1944) (suit by insurer for "rescission and cancellation" of two life insurance policies because of alleged misrepresentations in disclosing appendectomy in 1934 and perforated ulcer in 1925 but not an operation for perforated duodenal ulcer in 1933 and again in 1935, hospitalization for a chronic peptic ulcer of the stomach in 1934 and 1936, hospitalization for lobar pneumonia in 1936, and receipt of indemnity for accidents and illnesses in 1936 and twice in 1939; Lanigan contended that the insurer's medical examiner came to Lanigan's farm and examined him while he was at work, and that he answered questions according to his best memory and suggested that further information could be obtained at Rhode Island Hospital; the chancellor found that Lanigan acted in good faith and that the insurer made an independent investigation rather than placing entire reliance on Lanigan's answers; held, decree dismissing the bill affirmed). Arguably the different results in these cases can be explained on the basis of a finding in *Lanigan* that the applicant acted in good faith and the absence of such a finding in *Strudel*. Another potential ground of distinction is that a lead to a source of full information was provided by the applicant in *Lanigan* but not in *Strudel*. The nature of the investigation undertaken by the company in *Lanigan* is not disclosed in the opinion.

misrepresentation.[9] The equities in such cases are in sharp contrast with those in a case in which the applicant is honestly mistaken in making material representations and the insurer is careless. In the latter instance, the problem is one between an innocent or at most careless applicant and a careless insurer, and a defensible argument can be made that the insurer should bear the risk of misunderstandings of that type.

SECTION 5.8 CONCEALMENT

Intentional concealment of a material fact by an applicant for insurance is generally a good defense for an insurer unaware of that fact, regardless of the type of insurance involved.[1]

An applicant's good faith failure to disclose a material fact, however, is ordinarily not a good defense for the insurer under nonmarine policies.[2] A distinctive rule for marine insurance allows the insurer a defense of concealment even in these circumstances. It has been argued that the marine rule should be extended also to inland marine coverage, such as a floater on jewelry, but the prevailing precedents are to the contrary.[3]

It may be questioned whether the circumstances of modern marine insurance are more closely analogous to the circumstances of marine insurance in the days when the distinctive marine rule arose than to the circumstances of modern fire and life insurance. It has been said that the marine rule is explained by the fact that, in the early days of marine insurance, the underwriter had to rely heavily upon the insured for disclosure of facts bearing upon the degree of risk. With improvements in communication and the availability of data on ships and shipping, any differentiation on this ground between marine and other types of insurance is much less significant today. Perhaps there are other factors, however, that still justify a more stringent rule of disclosure for marine insurance. For example, perhaps marine contracts are more likely than others to involve parties of relatively equal bargaining power and business acumen. In any event, the distinctive rule is firmly entrenched, and it does not seem likely that it will be modified soon.

9. Cf. Praetorian Mut. Life Ins. Co. v. Sherman, 455 S.W.2d 201 (Tex.1970) summarized in § 6.5(c) n.32 infra.

1. See, e.g., Sebring v. Fidelity-Phenix Fire Ins. Co., 255 N.Y. 382, 174 N.E. 761 (1931) (nondisclosure of the fact that new insured added to policy had been convicted of conspiracy to defraud insurance companies and that original insured, an attorney, had defended him in his trial for that crime; trial court judgment of coverage reversed). For a dissenting view on the doctrine of concealment, urging that it be excised from the law of insurance, see Harnett, The Doctrine of Concealment: A Remnant in the Law of Insurance, 15 Law & Contemp.Prob. 391 (1950).

2. Ibid.

3. E.g., Blair v. National Security Ins. Co., 126 F.2d 955 (3d Cir. 1942); Stecker v. American Home Fire Assur. Co., 299 N.Y. 1, 84 N.E.2d 797 (1949).

Under the nonmarine rule, disclosures by the applicant about his own character ordinarily are not required in the absence of specific inquiry.[4] But if an applicant intentionally conceals material facts, even of such an intimate nature, the policy is subject to being avoided.[5] Thus, the applicant is not free to withhold facts he believes would affect the insurer's action on his application. One who has expert knowledge of insurance practices because of his professional experience is thus required to disclose facts that he knows to be material, even though a layman might not know of their materiality. Moreover, if he submits an application to a company he represents as agent, the agency relationship supports a duty of disclosure under an objective standard based on what one with such experience in insurance matters should know about materiality of the fact in question, rather than under a subjective standard concerned with his own belief.[6]

In fire insurance, the rule that innocent concealment by the applicant is no defense for the insurer is fortified by a passage in the standard fire insurance form, declaring, "This entire policy shall be void if, whether before or after a loss, the insured has wilfully concealed or misrepresented any material fact or circumstance . . . ."[7] It seems unlikely that a court would recognize innocent concealment or misrepresentation as a ground of avoidance in view of the negative implication of the quoted passage.[8]

A special problem is presented with respect to failure to report material facts coming to the attention of an applicant between the time he applies and the time the insurer acts on his application. In principle, the duty of disclosure during this interim period is the same as at the time of applying.[9] That is, intentional concealment of a material fact coming to the attention of the applicant during this period is generally a good defense for the insurer unaware of that fact, and good faith nondisclosure is no defense. But the practical

---

4. See, *e.g.*, Penn Mut. Life Ins. Co. v. Mechanics' Savings Bank & Trust Co., 72 F. 413, 73 F. 653 (6th Cir. 1896) (opinion by Taft, J.).

5. *Ibid.*

6. *Cf.* Pederson v. Life of Mid-Am. Ins. Co., 164 N.W.2d 337 (Iowa 1969) (failure of insurance-agent-applicant to disclose shortages and discrepancies in bank accounts under his control; he signed application as applicant and agent, stating as agent that he knew nothing unfavorable regarding the applicant's character, habits, etc.; held for the insurer).

7. See Appendix A *infra*.

8. *Cf.* Di Leo v. United States Fid. & Gy. Co., 50 Ill.App.2d 183, 200 N.E.2d

405 (1st Dist. 1964), 9 A.L.R.3d 1399 (1966) (failure to inform insurer of pending condemnation proceedings on building in which insured leased space for their business was not such concealment as would void fire insurance policies on contents of insured's store and for business interruption).

9. See, *e.g.*, Stipcich v. Metropolitan Life Ins. Co., 277 U.S. 311, 48 Sup.Ct. 512, 72 L.Ed. 895 (1928) (recurrence of duodenal ulcer that later caused death; applicant made disclosure to the agent who had taken the application, but neither disclosed to the home office; held, in reversing a directed verdict for defendant and ordering new trial, that the agent was authorized by statute to receive information on behalf of the company).

impact of the rule may be quite different because the insurer does not customarily submit any questions to the insured at the close of this period. Thus, the argument that the applicant may infer that a given fact is not material since the insurer did not include it among the inquiries on the application form—often a persuasive argument in response to a contention of concealment at the time of applying—has little force in relation to concealment of facts coming to the attention of the applicant during the period between application and delivery of the policy.

The problem of nondisclosure of facts coming to the attention of the applicant after the time of applying is sometimes dealt with under the rubric of misrepresentation,[10] though in many instances this method of analysis involves a fiction of "continuing" representation since there is no act or communication of the applicant after the time of applying that can fairly be interpreted as in fact (rather than by contrary-to-fact presumption of law) making a representation on the matter in question.

To be distinguished are cases in which the terms of a binding receipt make changes of health after the date of receipt irrelevant to the insurer's obligation to issue the permanent policy; in that event, the argument for a duty of disclosure of such changes would fail.

It might be argued, on similar grounds, that the protection afforded to the company by a delivery-in-good-health clause or a continued-insurability clause would make disclosure unnecessary.[11] But the duty of disclosure should remain, since the company's action might still be influenced by a change in conditions affecting insurability. Moreover, the delivery-in-good-health clause is a clear indication that the contract is intended to be made with reference to the conditions at the time of delivery if they are different from those at the time of application. If a duty is recognized, however, it is likely to be limited to a duty of disclosure of what the applicant believes to be a change in his health between the time of application and delivery, and his nondisclosure of a change of which he had no knowledge would not violate this duty.[12]

---

10. See, *e.g.*, MacKenzie v. Prudential Ins. Co., 411 F.2d 781 (6th Cir. 1969) (forecasting Kentucky law; undivulged, increased blood pressure reading exceeding normal limits after application for life policy and before issuance was "material misrepresentation" voiding policy).

11. *Cf.* paragraphs 4 and 5, Cal.Ins. Code § 333 (West 1955), saying there is no duty to disclose information, which is not otherwise material, on matters "which prove or tend to prove the existence of a risk excluded by a warranty" and those that relate "to a risk excepted."

12. See, *e.g.*, Harte v. United Benefit Life Ins. Co., 66 Cal.2d 148, 424 P.2d 329, 56 Cal.Rptr. 889 (1967) (application clause declaring no liability until policy delivered "in good health and free from injury"; "good health" interpreted from point of view of applicant's understanding and not from point of view of then unknown facts or from point of view of what treating physician or member of the family knew; recovery allowed if applicant believed in good faith that his health had not materially changed between the time of application and delivery). This decision seems to treat a stipulation for a condition of coverage (good

SECTION 5.9   LIMITS OF LIABILITY

Pecuniary limits of liability are common in various types of insurance. Automobile liability insurance is usually written with both a per-person and a per-accident (or "per occurrence") limit.[1] Fire insurance and allied coverages are commonly written with a pecuniary limit as well as form provisions limiting coverage to the value of the insured's interest in the property.[2] Health, accident, and medical payments coverages are commonly written with overall limits of liability[3] and may also contain special limits for certain losses—e.g., a provision placing a $500 limit on benefits for prior illness recurring within three months after the application for the policy.[4]

Application of pecuniary limits of liability has led to dispute and litigation in a number of situations involving multiple claims, multiple policies, or multiple units of coverage under a single policy.

A problem of multiple units of coverage under a single policy may arise, for example, under automobile medical payments coverage of a policy covering two automobiles. There is a split of authority as to whether such a policy, having a per-person limit and containing no stipulation against accumulation, provides coverage up to twice the stated limit for medical expenses incurred because of injury to a named insured in a single accident.[5]

It may happen that a claimant alleging that he was injured by an insured tortfeasor asserts that he is entitled to recover for medical expenses both under the medical payments coverage and under the bodily injury liability coverage of the tortfeasor's insurance policy. Such a claim gives rise to a problem of multiple coverage under a single policy, affecting the right to recover separately under each coverage even when it is plain that no limit is exceeded,[6] as well as a prob-

---

health at delivery) as if it were only a stipulation for a duty to disclose material changes in health between the times of medical examination and delivery. Though the proper resolution of the issue may be debated, surely the question whether a stipulation that good health or continued insurability at time of delivery (or absence of treatment or consultation between the times of medical examination and delivery) is enforceable is distinct from the question whether there is a duty to disclose changes in health (or the occurrence of treatment or consultation) after the medical examination and before delivery of the policy. Concerning enforceability of such a stipulation, see § 6.5(e) (4) *infra*.

1. See Appendices G, H *infra*.

2. See Appendix A *infra*.

3. See Appendices F, H *infra*.

4. See, *e.g., In re* Estate of Clement, 220 Tenn. 114, 414 S.W.2d 644 (1967) (limit held enforceable and insurer allowed to recover amounts paid in excess of the limit before learning of the previous illness).

5. Government Employees Ins. Co. v. Sweet, 186 So.2d 95 (Fla.App.1966), 21 A.L.R.3d 895 (1968) (held, coverage up to twice the limit; the coverage associated with each automobile applied regardless of whether the insured was in that automobile or elsewhere when injured). *Contra*, Sullivan v. Royal Exch. Assur., 181 Cal.App.2d 644, 5 Cal.Rptr. 878 (2d Dist. 1960).

6. Concerning other problems of overlapping coverages, see §§ 3.10, 3.11, 5.5(c) *supra*.

lem of chargeability against limits. Double recovery for loss has been allowed in some cases [7] and denied in others.[8] Allowing such double recovery is inconsistent with the principle that insurance is intended as indemnity for loss.[9] Denial of such fortuitous profits seems the preferable rule.

Consortium claims have led to litigation because of disputes, for example, as to whether the damages paid to a husband for loss of consortium resulting from injury to his wife are chargeable against the per-person limit of liability for injury to his wife. Most contractual provisions have been cast in terms of "bodily injury to one person" or a like phrase, and most decisions in point have answered that consortium damages are chargeable against the limit applying to the person suffering the physical injury, thus defeating, for example, the effort of a husband to recover an additional sum from the insurer after its payment of the per-person limit on his wife's claim.[10]

SECTION 5.10 DURATION OF COVERAGE

§ 5.10(a) GENERALLY

Duration of the coverage, like other terms of an insurance arrangement, is ordinarily governed by the provisions of the insurance policy. However, overriding interests have sometimes resulted in the recognition of claims or defenses at variance with the policy stipulations. Some illustrations are presented in this section. Also, this section presents other illustrations of provisions within the policy itself that modify the period of coverage initially stated.

§ 5.10(b) VARIANCE FROM THE POLICY DATE

It sometimes happens that the date of commencement of coverage is not that stated on the face of the policy as its anniversary date. Ordinarily the reason for this discrepancy is that some condi-

---

7. *E.g.*, Long v. Landy, 35 N.J. 44, 171 A.2d 1 (1961) (collateral source rule applied even as between a wife and the estate of her deceased husband, who was the tortfeasor).

8. *E.g.*, Yarrington v. Thornburg, 205 A.2d 1 (Del.1964), 11 A.L.R.3d 1110 (1967) (held, tortfeasor entitled to credit, in reduction of damages, for medical payments to guest passenger under tortfeasor's insurance policy, even though the policy did not so stipulate; since the tort judgment exceeded the liability insurance limit, this is not merely a question of the insurer's contractual liability). See also Yarrington v. Thornburg, 208 A.2d 60 (Del.Super.1965) (Thornburg was judgment proof and his carrier paid $10,-000 under liability coverage and $5,-

000 under medical payments coverage; tort judgment of $40,000 had been entered against Thornburg and two others as joint tortfeasors; having received $25,000 from the other two, plaintiff sought to recover an additional $5,000 on the theory they should not be credited with the $5,000 paid under Thornburg's medical payments coverage; held for defendants, the credit being allowed).

9. See generally § 3.1 *supra*.

10. *E.g.*, Sheffield v. American Indem. Co., 245 S.C. 389, 140 S.E.2d 787 (1965), 13 A.L.R.3d 1220 (1967) (uninsured motorist coverage). See 8 Appleman, Insurance Law § 4891 (rev. ed. 1962).

tion concerned with prepayment of a premium or delivery of the policy has not been satisfied.[1] In such instances, does an "annual" premium buy coverage only for the period up to the end of a year from the date stated as the anniversary of the policy or instead for a full year after the date on which coverage commenced (plus, in either instance, a grace period if the policy so provides)?

Consider, first, the type of situation in which a later annual premium was not paid within the grace period following the anniversary date stated in the policy, and the insured dies (or tenders the premium) thereafter, but before expiration of the grace period following the anniversary of the date on which coverage actually commenced.

Most decisions in point have held that the date stipulated in the policy as that from which premiums are to be calculated must be given effect in determining when the grace period commences and ends, notwithstanding the fact that the coverage was not actually in force until a later date.[2] In a minority of the cases, coverage has been upheld on the theory that a full year's coverage is to be provided for the annual premium, and the grace period therefore commences running a year after coverage becomes effective, rather than on the earlier anniversary date stated in the policy.[3]

The foregoing majority and minority rules concern cases in which coverage is alleged to have terminated before the event insured against occurred. In appraising these rules, one may appropriately take into account the converse factual situation in which the event insured against occurs before some alleged prerequisite to coverage has been satisfied, though after the date stated on the face of the policy. For example, an application for insurance providing benefits in case of disability caused by accident is signed and delivered to an agent on the tenth of the month; an accident causing disability occurs on the fifteenth; and a policy issued and delivered thereafter states that the tenth is the anniversary date but also declares that coverage does not take effect until delivery of the policy and payment of the first full premium, which, we will assume, occurs on the twentieth. According to the traditional theory, the application was an of-

1. See § 2.7 *supra* concerning delivery.

2. *E.g.*, Kampf v. Franklin Life Ins. Co., 33 N.J. 36, 161 A.2d 717 (1960). See 14 Appleman, Insurance Law § 7953 (1944).

3. *E.g.*, Lentin v. Continental Assur. Co., 412 Ill. 158, 105 N.E.2d 735 (1952), 44 A.L.R.2d 463 (1955); Duerksen v. Brookings Int'l Life & Cas. Co., 166 N.W.2d 567 (S.D.1969). See also State Security Life Ins. Co. v. Kintner, 243 Ind. 331, 185 N.E.2d 527 (1962). Though reasoned as an exception consistent with the majority rule, perhaps this decision is more easily aligned with the minority. The policy in question specified that the annual premium payments (or the first of semi-annual or quarterly premium payments) were due on the anniversary of the date of issuance. Monthly payments were made by the insured and accepted by the company; since there was no specific reference in the policy to monthly payment of premiums, it was held that the payments were due on the monthly anniversary of the date the policy went into effect (the date of delivery), allowing recovery for the death of the insured within the grace period based upon the date the coverage took effect even though the grace period based upon the date of issuance had passed.

fer; the acceptance occurred when the executed policy was delivered;[4] and, in the absence of adequate grounds for liability at variance with policy provisions,[5] the applicant's claim for benefits on account of the disabling accident of the fifteenth would be denied.

If the rule stated in the preceding paragraph is combined with the majority rule stated earlier in this subsection, the result is that the insured receives less than a year's coverage for his first annual premium.[6] And, on the other hand, if a court applies the minority rule described earlier in this subsection (imposing liability for death or disabling injury occurring after expiration of the grace period based on the stated anniversary date) and then, in the converse situation now under discussion, imposes liability also for the disabling accident occurring on the fifteenth of the first month, the result is that the insured receives more than a year's coverage for his first annual premium.

The decision on one of these two types of situations lends support to an argument for resolving the converse problem in a way that produces exactly a year's coverage, plus the grace-period privileges, for the first annual premium. That argument has limited force, however, since there are many ways in which disparities in a rate structure are accepted as a reasonable price to pay for other advantages. Such a disparity is a normal consequence of invoking any theory of resolving ambiguities against the insurer or any theory of recognizing rights at variance with contract terms, such as waiver or estoppel. In these situations, the disparity of more than a year's coverage for an annual premium is deemed an acceptable result. The converse disparity of less than a year's coverage for an annual premium may be deemed an acceptable result also. The conclusion that the first premium, if not paid at the time of applying, buys less than a full year's coverage might be justified, for example, on grounds favoring certainty of the anniversary date. Moreover, an inequity among different policy holders, who get different amounts of coverage for the same premium, might be regarded as a permissible range of variation within a rate category, since premiums can never be adjusted precisely to the infinite variations in value of coverage.[7]

Another type of situation involving a potential variance of the period of effective coverage from that indicated by the date of the policy concerns the time of commencement of coverage, and whether the date of termination of coverage is correspondingly extended, when the purchase of the property intended to be covered is consummated at a time subsequent to the policy date. It has been held, on the basis of enforcing the understanding of the parties, that coverage on an automobile commenced when the purchase was consummated, not when the application for credit to purchase the automobile was

---

4. See §§ 2.6, 2.7 *supra*.

5. See Chapter 6 *infra*.

6. See, *e.g.*, Lentin v. Continental Assur. Co., 412 Ill. 158, 105 N.E.2d 735 (1952), 44 A.L.R.2d 463 (1955).

7. See § 8.4(b) *infra*.

made, and that coverage thus was still in effect when an accident occurred on the second day beyond a year after the policy date but less than a year after the purchase.[8]

§ 5.10(c) PRE-CONTRACT LOSSES

Occasionally it happens that a policy is so written that if literally enforced it provides coverage for a loss occurring before the contract is made. The question whether such a provision is enforceable may be answered differently depending on the circumstances.

In the early days of marine insurance, it was a common occurrence that an agreement for insurance would be made at a time when the insured vessel was already at sea or in a foreign port. Quite frequently agreements were made to cover the vessel "lost or not lost" —with an explicit understanding that if, unknown to both parties to the transaction, the vessel had already been lost or damaged from covered perils, the underwriter would be liable for the loss within the terms and limits of his underwriting.[1] Such agreements are entirely consistent with the fundamental principle that insurance is a contract for coverage of fortuitous loss.[2] Although other persons somewhere in the world knew the facts as to whether the vessel had already been lost, from the point of view of the contracting parties there was a risk that it had been lost rather than a certainty one way or the other.[3] From their point of view, with the limited knowledge available to them at the time of contracting, the loss that the insurer agreed to pay was fortuitous in nature even though it might later become known to them that in fact loss had already occurred before they had made their contract.

Rarely circumstances arise in which the underlying principle of "lost or not lost" coverage in marine insurance applies in a nonmarine context.[4]

Another type of case stands in sharp contrast with a marine contract covering a ship "lost or not lost." It sometimes happens that a

8. Marathon Ins. Co. v. Arnold, 433 P. 2d 927 (Okla.1967).

1. See, *e.g.*, Bond v. Nutt, 2 Cowp. 601, 98 Eng.Rep. 1262 (K.B.1777) (opinion by Mansfield, J.) (contract made on August 20, 1776, on a vessel warranted to have sailed on or before August 1 from Jamaica to London; in July the vessel sailed from one port in Jamaica to another in Jamaica for the sole purpose of joining a convoy and proceeding to England; an embargo delayed the departure of the convoy from the second port until August 6; thereafter, the vessel was separated in passage and "was taken by an American privateer"; held, coverage).

2. Concerning this principle generally, see § 5.3(a) *supra*.

3. See § 1.2(b) (1) *supra* regarding the meaning of "risk."

4. See, *e.g.*, Burch v. Commonwealth County Mut. Ins. Co., 450 S.W.2d 838 (Tex.1970) (damage to automobile occurring on July 18 held to be covered by policy issued by agent on July 19 for period of one year commencing at 12:01 on July 18; insured applied on July 18 before accident occurred, and agent told him he was covered, though not specifying the company; insured was unable to notify agent of accident for several days after it occurred; neither insurer nor agent knew of accident when policy was issued on July 19 with defendant company).

person is moved to arrange for coverage because he has just had an accident. It may also happen that the dating of the contract, together with printed provisions about the time of day coverage commences, results in a policy stipulation for coverage commencing a few hours before the contract was made. If, for example, he applies for coverage at 3:00 p. m., knowing, that the agent with whom he deals will write the contract so that coverage purportedly commences at 12:00 noon and fails to disclose that he had an accident within the terms of the coverage between 12:00 and 3:00, a claim of coverage should be denied. Knowing that the insurer would not make the contract if he disclosed the accident, he should be held to a duty to disclose even under the rather limited stringency of the doctrine of concealment applied in nonmarine cases.[5] Moreover, to permit coverage in such a case would be inconsistent with the fundamental premise that insurance is concerned with risk of loss, whereas loss in this instance is already known by the applicant to be certain. Thus it is generally held that in such circumstances a contract does not cover a loss occurring before it was made.[6]

§ 5.10(d) WAYS OF DEFINING TIME LIMITS

Do time limits stated in various types of insurance coverage define the period within which loss must be suffered or instead the period within which a defined event must occur, the covered loss from which may be suffered, wholly or in part, at a time beyond the stated time limit?

In relation to most problems arising under automobile insurance coverages, policy forms commonly state the period within which an accident must have occurred if there is to be any coverage under the policy based on that accident. Thus, under automobile liability coverage, an insured has coverage for a judgment entered against him years after the policy has terminated, if it is based on an accident occurring within the stated time limits and other conditions of coverage have been met. The requirement that an "accident" occur within the period of the policy coverage may be more troublesome under other forms of liability coverage than under automobile liability coverage. For example, under products liability coverage, it may happen that a loss is not covered because the "accident" occurred after the policy period had elapsed, even though the negligence or other actions of the insured on which liability is predicated occurred during the policy period.[1]

---

5. See § 5.8 *supra.*

6. See, *e.g.,* General Ins. Co. v. Lapidus, 325 F.2d 287 (9th Cir. 1963) (California law; coverage for gradual landslide that, unknown to applicant, had already started; dictum that if loss had already occurred or if quick process of destruction was already under way, there would be no coverage).

See generally 4 Appleman, Insurance Law § 2291 (rev. ed. 1969).

1. *E.g.,* National Aviation Underwriters, Inc. v. Idaho Aviation Center, Inc., 471 P.2d 55 (Ida.1970) (aircraft policy applying "only to occurrences, and losses to the insured aircraft which are sustained, during the policy period . . .", included "Airport

There are exceptions to the general pattern of basing the timing of the coverage on the occurrence of an "accident" within the period of policy coverage. One occurs in the medical payments coverages, which, in addition to stating the customary time limits within which an accident must have occurred to furnish the basis for coverage, commonly provide that the only expenses for medical services covered by the policy are those incurred within one year after the injury.[2] There is a close division of authority as to whether expenses are incurred within the period of coverage under such a policy provision when an agreement for the medical services in question is made within the year but the services are to be performed at a later time.[3]

A second and potentially more significant exception to the general pattern of stating that the coverage applies for accidents occurring in the policy period, regardless of when the loss is suffered, arises from a modification of the liability insurance forms in 1966. The 1966 forms provide coverage for an "occurrence," defining "occurrence" to mean "an accident, including injurious exposure to conditions, which results, during the policy period, in bodily injury or property damage neither expected nor intended from the standpoint of the insured."[4] The apparent intent was to give the insurer a defense on the ground, for example, that although an accidental exposure to impurities negligently discharged into the air by the liability insured occurred during the policy period, coverage does not apply because the claimed bodily injury did not result before the policy period had expired.[5] Whether that intent will be enforced by the courts remains to be seen.

Similar problems concerning the duration of coverage are presented even more sharply under certain specialized types of lia-

---

Liability Endorsement" with coverage for losses to property "caused by accident . . ."; held, no coverage for propeller failure after cancellation of the policy, even though the failure allegedly resulted from negligent repair occurring before cancellation); Silver Eagle Co. v. National Union Fire Ins. Co., 246 Ore. 398, 423 P.2d 944 (1967) (defective "fifth wheel"—a truck coupling device—sold by insured distributor during period of policy coverage; held, products liability insurer not liable for accident occurring after cancellation under 10-days-notice provision exercised after insurer was notified of several damage claims). See Annots., 57 A.L.R.2d 1385 (1958), 45 A.L.R.2d 994, 999 (1956).

2. See Appendix H *infra*. See also § 2.11(b) (2) *supra*.

3. See, *e.g.*, Reliance Mut. Life Ins. Co. v. Booher, 166 So.2d 222 (Fla.App. 1964), 10 A.L.R.3d 458 (1966) (recovery

denied for cost of plastic surgery for which a general agreement had been made within the stated period; however, rather than explicitly declining to follow certain cases allowing recovery for services performed after the stated period this court distinguished such cases as involving prepayments or fixed obligations to pay rather than mere agreements for such services to be performed without the obligation of payment having been fixed); Czarnecki v. American Indem. Co., 259 N.C. 718, 131 S.E.2d 347 (1963) (denying recovery for services performed after the stated period but distinguishing rather than declining to follow a case in which recovery had been allowed because an obligation to pay for dental work had been entered into within the stipulated period). See also § 2.11(b) (2) *supra*.

4. See § 2.11 (c) *supra*.

5. *Ibid*.

bility insurance.[6]   A prime example is coverage for the liabilities of corporate directors.[7]   The policies commonly used require that loss occur within the primary time limits of the coverage or within a stated extension period in case of cancellation.   Yet, it may happen that a claim is first made after even the extension period has passed, though based on conduct occurring within the primary time limits.   Such a problem may arise also in relation to claims based on physical injury under other liability coverages—e.g., a claim against a builder for an injury, allegedly caused by his negligent performance of a building contract, sustained years after the performance was completed.   In general, there are few statutes or judicial decisions concerning these problems, and they are largely governed by contractual provisions developed by insurers.   In dealing with such a problem, however, one should consider analogies that might be brought to bear from the precedents on rights at variance with policy provisions.[8]

Special problems of duration of coverage may arise under other forms of insurance also.[9]

§ 5.10(e) TERMINATION OF COVERAGE

(1) GENERALLY

Methods of termination of coverage, apart from expiration of the agreed period, are to some extent specially provided for in insurance contracts.   Among the subjects treated under common policy provisions are termination for nonpayment of premiums,[1] cancellation (either for nonpayment or on other grounds), and surrender.[2]   Under group policies issues have often arisen concerning termination of individual coverage because of cancellation or modification of the master policy,[3] because of mistake or misconduct of the group administrator in remission of premiums,[4] or because of termination of the association of an individual certificate holder with the group,[5] and con-

---

6. In addition to the example that follows in the text above, see Long v. Sakleson, 328 Pa. 261, 195 A. 416 (1937).

7. See generally Note, *Liability Insurance for Corporate Executives*, 80 Harv.L.Rev. 648, 651 (1967).

8. See Chapter 6 *infra*.

9. See, *e.g.*, Bartulis v. Metropolitan Life Ins. Co., 72 Ill.App.2d 267, 218 N.E.2d 225 (4th Dist. 1966) (group hospitalization insurer not liable for surgery after policy period, though injury occurred during period of coverage; coverage not for injuries during the period but for expenses incurred during the period; policy provided some post-termination coverage, but none applicable to this case).

1. See § 5.10(e) (2) *infra*.

2. See § 5.10(e) (3) *infra*.

3. See, *e.g.*, Metropolitan Life Ins. Co. v. Korneghy, 37 Ala.App. 497, 71 So.2d 292, *cert. petition stricken*, 260 Ala. 521, 71 So.2d 301 (1954), 68 A.L.R.2d 239 (1959) (coverage effectively discontinued by agreement between employer and insurer with notice to but without consent of employee).

4. See § 2.8(b) *supra*.

5. See, *e.g.*, Lineberger v. Security Life & Trust Co., 245 N.C. 166, 95 S.E.2d 501 (1956), 68 A.L.R.2d 1 (1959) (coverage terminated with termination of employment, none of the special provisions for extension of coverage being applicable).

cerning applicability of provisions for extensions of coverage in special cases.[6] Other methods of termination, including rescission, are considered elsewhere.[7]

(2) NONPAYMENT OF PREMIUMS

If the insurance policy is silent on the question, ordinarily failure to pay a premium when due merely produces a debt in favor of the insurer rather than a termination of coverage. Most policies, however, contain explicit provisions for termination.

Life insurance contracts commonly have a provision extending coverage during a "grace period" immediately following the due date of a second or later premium. Such a grace period is sometimes provided for also in health and accident coverage but is uncommon in other types of policies.

Individual life insurance policies usually provide for automatic termination after the grace period, subject to temporary continuance by the application of dividends or surrender value.[8] Types of coverage that routinely go into effect on a credit basis, however, usually contain provisions for a cancellation notice rather than automatic termination.[9]

Group life insurance contracts have given rise to a number of special problems related to termination of individual coverage. Under typical policies covering employee groups, an issue has often arisen concerning allocation of the risk of mistake or misconduct of the employer in remission of premiums to the insurer.[10]

An insurance policy that is intended not only for the protection of the policyholder but to some extent for protection of the interests of certain other persons may contain provisions extending protection to such other persons even after the termination of protection for the policyholder for nonpayment of premiums.[11]

6. See, *e.g.*, Johnson v. Equitable Life Assur. Soc., 239 N.C. 296, 79 S.E.2d 776 (1954), 68 A.L.R.2d 147 (1959) (evidence insufficient for jury issue on claim of former employee that she was disabled at time of discharge so as to qualify under provisions extending coverage).

7. See §§ 6.9 *infra* (rescission by company), 6.1 *infra* (rescission by policyholder).

8. See, *e.g.*, Simmons v. Cambridge Sav. Bank, 346 Mass. 327, 191 N.E.2d 681 (1963), 8 A.L.R.3d 856 (1966) (insured elected to pay premiums annually and to have dividends applied to payment of premiums; an annual premium was still unpaid when the insured died six days after the end of the grace period; dividend was insufficient to cover an annual premium though sufficient for a quarterly premium; held, no coverage).

9. See § 5.10(e) (3) *infra*.

10. See § 2.8(b) *supra*. *Cf.* Rivers v. State Capital Life Ins. Co., 245 N.C. 461, 96 S.E.2d 431 (1957), 68 A.L.R.2d 205 (1959) (nonpayment of premiums to insurers terminated coverage, despite efforts of employee to continue paying them through the employer after termination of his employment).

11. *E.g.*, the provisions of the standard mortgage clause protect the mortgagee beyond the time the mortgagor's protection is terminated for nonpayment of premiums. See § 4.2(b) and (d) *supra*.

(3) Cancellation and Surrender

Some insurance policies say nothing about cancellation *by the insured*. But ordinarily the insured nevertheless has power to terminate the contract at the end of any premium period by simply declining to pay a further premium. That is, insurance contracts do not customarily bind the insured to continue the relationship beyond a specified premium period, if that long. The length of the premium period in this sense, however, may be different from the period between payments. This commonly occurs, for example, when provisions are made for payment of an annual premium in semi-annual, quarterly, or monthly installments.

Life insurance policies other than term policies ordinarily include provisions *for surrender* of the policy and refund of a sum specified, representing return of the portion of the premiums not applied to the purchase of coverage up to the time of surrender, together with some allowance for interest.[12]

Modern fire and casualty policies ordinarily include a clause permitting *the insured* to cancel by written notice to the company stating when thereafter the cancellation is to be effective.[13] Usually the refund due the insured in such cases is somewhat reduced by provisions for applying a short-rate table under which the refund is something less than proportionate to the period of coverage cancelled.[14]

Life insurance policies ordinarily do not provide for cancellation *by the company* and do not even permit a contest on grounds such as fraud beyond a limited period, usually one or two years, after the date of the contract.[15]

Policy contracts for health and accident insurance vary widely with respect to provisions for cancellation *by the company*.

Fire and casualty contracts customarily authorize cancellation *by the company* effective within a relatively short period after the delivery of written notice.[16]

The differences among types of cancellation clauses in different types of insurance contracts are related to marketing practices. In general, rights of cancellation are retained by insurers whose marketing systems contemplate that agents in the field will consummate not merely temporary binders but principal contracts as well. In contrast, to meet the public need for long-term non-cancellable life insurance, the contracts offering such coverage sharply limit the insurer's rights of cancellation or contest, and insurers tend far more to maintain centralized control over underwriting rather than allowing

---

12. See, *e.g.*, Appendix E *infra*.

13. See, *e.g.*, Appendices A, H *infra*.

14. *Ibid.*

15. See, *e.g.*, Appendix E *infra*. See also § 6.5(d) *infra*.

16. See, *e.g.*, Appendices A, H *infra*.

agents in the field to commit them except on temporary binding receipts.[17]

During the period of intensified public criticism of automobile insurance and insurers in the 1960's, company practices with respect to cancellation of automobile insurance policies came under heavy fire. One consequence of this public pressure was the adoption in some states of regulatory legislation limiting rights of cancellation.[18] Also, regulatory officials have, by conducting investigations and in other ways, encouraged insurers voluntarily to limit the grounds of cancellation used.[19]

Efforts of insurers to cancel have also been restricted occasionally by statutes or case decisions of relatively narrow scope. For example, the provisions for cancellation notice in a compulsory automobile insurance law may be interpreted as allowing only prospective cancellation, thus impliedly precluding a rescission for fraud that would defeat the rights of the victim of an accident occurring before the attempted rescission,[20] though such a fully retroactive annulment of coverage would ordinarily be effective, in the absence of overriding legislation.[21] And under ordinary automobile insurance coverage, some courts have held that a cancellation notice was ineffectual unless received by the policyholder even though the policy clause provided that it would be effective if timely mailed to the proper address, without proof of receipt.[22] Also, it has been held that the acceptance of a refund is not conclusive when it was tendered under circumstances of overreaching that amounted to "an attempt to perpetrate a constructive fraud. . . ."[23] And, it has been held, alle-

17. Concerning degrees of centralization over underwriting generally, see § 2.1 *supra.*

18. See, *e.g.,* N.Y. Ins. Dep't, Report, The Public Interest Now in Property and Liability Insurance Regulation 43 (1969); Ghiardi & Wienke, *Recent Developments in the Cancellation, Renewal and Rescission of Automobile Insurance Policies,* 51 Marquette L.Rev. 219 (1968).

19. The National Association of Insurance Commissioners, at its 1969 meeting in Philadelphia, after receiving the report of a staff study of automobile insurance, declared that each state should be free to choose its own legal liability system and that, regardless of the legal framework, a set of minimum criteria should be met, among them being the ready availability of insurance to all licensed drivers at reasonable rates and protection against arbitrary and unfair cancellations and nonrenewals. See, *e.g.,* The Standard (New England's Insurance Weekly), June 27, 1969, pp. 1, 20–21.

20. See Aetna Cas. & Sur. Co. v. Garrett, 31 A.D.2d 710, 296 N.Y.S.2d 12 (3d Dep't 1968), *aff'd,* 26 N.Y.2d 729, 257 N.E.2d 284, 309 N.Y.S.2d 34 (1970).

21. See, *e.g.,* Fierro v. Foundation Reserve Ins. Co., 81 N.Mex. 225, 465 P.2d 282 (1970) (fully retroactive cancellation of automobile insurance after accident because of misrepresentations, in application, of no cancellation within previous 36 months; held for insurer; applicant bound by application he signed, regardless of who filled it out).

22. *E.g.,* Koehn v. Central. Nat'l Ins. Co., 187 Kan. 192, 354 P.2d 352 (1960); Donarski v. Lardy, 251 Minn. 358, 88 N.W.2d 7 (1958). *Contra,* Westmoreland v. General Acc. Fire & Life Assur. Corp., 144 Conn. 265, 129 A.2d 623 (1957), 64 A.L.R.2d 976 (1959).

23. Lewis v. Snake River Mut. Fire Ins. Co., 82 Ida. 329, 353 P.2d 648 (1960). See also Annot., 34 A.L.R.3d 385 (1970).

gations of cancellation of a dentist's malpractice coverage because he had testified in malpractice cases would, if proved, establish a breach of contract.[24]

24. L'Orange v. Medical Protective Co., 394 F.2d 57 (6th Cir. 1968) (Ohio law).

CHAPTER 6

RIGHTS AT VARIANCE WITH POLICY PROVISIONS *

SECTION 6.1 PRINCIPLES, PATTERNS, AND DOCTRINES OF VARIANCE

In any area of law it is instructive to study simultaneously the doctrinal currents, the decisional patterns by fact types, and the underlying justifications for each. In few areas is it so difficult to reconcile what one sees from these different perspectives as in that area of insurance law concerning rights of policyholders and other claimants at variance with policy provisions. Perhaps as a corollary, judicial opinions in this area are less than ordinarily enlightening about principled bases for decision. Often, too, the favorite generalization advanced by outside observers to explain a judgment against an insurance company at variance with policy provisions is the ambivalent, suggestive, and wholly unsatisfactory aphorism: "It's an insurance case."

Yet one can find in the patterns of decision some compelling currents of principle. Particularly, two broad principles, it is submitted, account for such a high percentage of what might otherwise appear to be deviant decisions that the remainder can be accepted as within the margin of error one should expect in the administration of any set of guidelines. Under these two principles, an insurer will be denied any unconscionable advantage in an insurance transaction, and the reasonable expectations of applicants and intended beneficiaries will be honored. The first of these principles is candidly recognized in some contexts, though less often than it accounts for results. Open acknowledgment of the second began to emerge only in the 1960's. Although the same or closely analogous ideas may be expressed elsewhere in the law, the conditions for their application arise

---

* Parts of this chapter were published in advance of this book, as a two-part article, *Insurance Law Rights at Variance with Policy Provisions*, 83 Harv.L.Rev. 961, 1281 (1970).

in insurance transactions with distinctive frequency. It is hardly surprising, then, that insurance law decisions, viewed apart from these two principles, have so often seemed arbitrary.

Among other principles particularly relevant to rights at variance with policy provisions, the most significant is the principle of granting redress for detrimental reliance. Doctrines related to the application of this principle have often been distorted by the undeclared influence of the two distinctive principles alluded to above. Once these two principles are openly declared, it becomes possible to trace more precisely the influence of this third principle.

The next three sections of this chapter develop these three major principles, along with some of their corollaries and implications. This pattern of organization cuts across a number of doctrinal theories frequently invoked in recognizing rights at variance with policy provisions. These doctrines include waiver, estoppel in its various forms, election, reformation, rescission, the defense of breach by the other party of a contractual or non-contractual duty, modification of rights under the policy by subsequent agreement (either before or after a claim arises), and a considerable range of agency law, as well as less supportable theories.[1] Defensive responses to affirmative theories for variance include an alleged immunity of "coverage" provisions from variance, the parol evidence rule, entire-contract statutes, reservation-of-rights notices, nonwaiver agreements, and infrequently a statute of frauds of general application or one tailored especially to insurance transactions. Of the defensive doctrines, two will be separately examined in the latter part of this chapter: the theory of immunity from variance [2] and the effect of reservation-of-rights notices and nonwaiver agreements.[3] Less obviously than doctrines such as waiver and estoppel, but no less surely, statutory and decisional controls over defenses based on warranty, representation, or concealment create rights at variance with policy provisions. These regulatory controls will also be discussed separately.[4]

With the three exceptions noted, the various doctrines are considered only as they relate to implications of the major principles under examination. Also, despite the recognized usefulness of examining cases by fact types,[5] the present chapter adopts this focus only to a limited extent,[6] and not in a fully systematic way.

---

1. A rarely invoked and, it would seem, aberrational theory is that the payment of a claim is a practical construction of latent ambiguity in a policy, binding the insurer to coverage of a later claim that is of the same type, though much larger. See § 6.8(a) *infra*.

2. See § 6.6(b) *infra*.

3. See § 6.6(a) *infra*.

4. See § 6.5 *infra*.

5. *Cf.* Morris, *Waiver and Estoppel in Insurance Policy Litigation*, 105 U. Pa.L.Rev. 925 (1957). Professor Morris, recognizing that there are some "main intellectual currents that cut across the law of waiver and estoppel," *id.* at 951, nonetheless emphasizes classification of the cases by fact type:

"The cases are a buzzing confusion when different kinds of insurances

6. See Note 6 on page 343.

The different legal theories commonly invoked to sustain rights at variance with policy provisions reflect somewhat different sets of substantive reasons for variance.

Reformation is customarily grounded on mutual mistake of the parties in reducing their oral agreement to writing or upon mistake of the aggrieved party induced by the other. The basic theory is that the formal contract is being corrected to reflect accurately the enforceable agreement (that mutually intended if there was mutual mistake, or that intended by the innocent party if his mistake was induced by the other).[7]

Rescission is likewise commonly grounded on mutual mistake or mistake of the aggrieved party induced by the other, but here the mistake is one negating agreement rather than incorrectly recording it. Rescission is more often sought by an insurer than by an insured or third party beneficiary, since its effect is to restore the parties to their pre-contract positions; thus the insurer is required only to return premiums rather than to pay the larger benefits that would be due under specified contingencies.

Subsequent contractual agreements modifying rights of the parties under policy provisions are in most instances incorporated into riders and attached to the policy. Such agreements may be regarded as in essence modifying the policy provisions themselves rather than creating rights at variance. In other instances, however, the new agreement does not purport to modify policy provisions but does in fact alter their impact. A so-called nonwaiver agreement may have this effect because a party to it may give up a right to invoke some provision of the policy to his advantage.[8]

Waiver is typically defined as the voluntary relinquishment of a known right. This is a rare phenomenon. Yet opinions declaring a waiver as the explanation of rights at variance with policy provisions are numerous. In fact, things well short of voluntary relinquishment of a known right have often been referred to as waivers.[9]

To invoke estoppel, according to customary doctrine, one must show detrimental reliance upon some representation, express or implied in words or in conduct. But deviations from strict adherence to the underlying theory are frequent.[10] The most common pattern of deviation is dilution of the standard for proof of detrimental reliance. This seems a departure from sound principle.[11]

---

are talked about at the same time. Many, though of course not all, of the inconsistencies disappear or become understandable when the cases are classified in terms of business functions."

Id. at 950.

6. See particularly §§ 6.5(e), 6.7, 6.8 *infra.*

7. See generally Covington, *Reformation of Contracts of Personal Insurance,* 1964 U.Ill.L.Forum 548.

8. See § 6.6(a) *infra.*

9. See, *e.g.,* §§ 6.2, 6.7(b), (c), and (d), 6.-8(a), (b), and (d) *infra.*

10. See, *e.g.,* §§ 6.2, 6.7(b), (c), and (d), 6.8(a), (b), and (d) *infra.*

11. See § 6.4(f) *infra.*

Genuine waiver is by nature based on consent and thus is closely analogous to contract. Liability because of estoppel, on the other hand, is by nature an imposed liability, more like tort than contract. This basic difference between waiver and estoppel reflects different underlying justifications for rights at variance with policy provisions. The difference is relevant to the concepts of agency invoked when a policyholder or other claimant, asserting rights at variance with policy provisions, bases his claim on the conduct of persons alleged to have acted on behalf of the insurer. Estoppel is more compatible than waiver with applying a relatively broad agency concept, imposing liability based on representations incidental to the employment of the agent—a concept analogous to "scope of employment" in master-servant cases concerned with physical harm.[12] Waiver is more compatible with a somewhat narrower agency concept, comparable to "scope of authority" in contract cases. To a plaintiff estoppel is in this respect more useful than waiver. Estoppel theory also escapes the requirement of proof of voluntary relinquishment of a known right, which is the basis of strictly defined waiver. On the other hand, estoppel theory is less favorable to the plaintiff in that detrimental reliance is supposedly required.

Since estoppel and waiver, rigorously defined, reflect different theories of variance with separate grounds of justification, a claimant is entitled to have the benefit of whichever theory sustains his claim, if either does.

Election is a cross between waiver and estoppel. It is a theory under which a rule of law imposes upon the actor the restriction that he has only a limited number of sets of legal consequences among which he may choose.[13] Election is somewhat like estoppel because its essence is an imposed rule of law—one which in this instance limits the range of choice of the person against whom it is imposed. Election is also somewhat like waiver because the particular legal result it imposes depends in part upon a choice made by the actor. This hybrid theory is often more useful to the plaintiff than either waiver or estoppel because it softens their respective requirements of voluntary relinquishment and detrimental reliance. It is also a more troublesome and often a more dubious theory for courts to employ because of the common deficiencies in statement of both the terms of the choice left open to the insurer and the reasons for the regulatory restrictions implicit in the court's prescription of those terms.

Courts often adopt a doctrine of the type referred to here as election under the name of waiver or estoppel. For example, this sometimes happens when a court holds that because one agent of an insurance company collected an insurance premium at a time when a

---

12. See § 6.4(d) *infra*. Compare § 6.4(b) *infra*.

13. Concerning election generally, see J. Ewart, Waiver Distributed 66–123 (1917); Ewart, "*Waiver*" *in Insurance*

Law, 13 Iowa L.Rev. 129 (1928); Ewart, *Waiver or Election*, 29 Harv. L.Rev. 724 (1916). For illustrations in insurance law, see §§ 6.2, 6.7(b), (c), and (d), 6.8(a), (b), and (d) *infra*.

second agent knew of a policy violation that would defeat coverage if enforced, the company is precluded from asserting the violation.   A court may, in so holding, say its theory is waiver, even though it is not in fact based on the insurer's voluntary relinquishment of a known right.   Or it may say the theory is estoppel, even though not in fact based on detrimental reliance by the insured.   To use either waiver or estoppel in such a context is to confuse by diluting the requirements of those doctrines, and usually without candid definition of the scope of dilution.[14]

What the court has actually done in such a case is to construct a doctrine that confronts the insurer with a limited range of choice under which the insurer cannot collect a new premium without losing full defenses, and perhaps partial defenses as well, then known to any of its agents even though not known to the agent collecting the premium.   There is an advantage in recognizing the nature of this doctrine as one of election—one limiting the range of choice of the insurer in specified ways—because doing so tends to focus attention on the terms of those imposed limitations and on the question whether such limitations are justified.

Election remains a difficult concept to cope with, even when dealt with candidly.   No single standard has been employed to explain it—nothing comparable to the voluntary relinquishment of known right that is the essence of waiver or the detrimental reliance that is the essence of estoppel.   Rather, the election doctrine has depended for its content upon the terms of choice imposed by statutes or decisions and has not been generalized as waiver and estoppel have been.   Thus, merely classifying a judicial deviation from rigorously defined waiver and estoppel as in essence election is only one small step toward understanding it and clarifying its impact.   In appraising such a case it is helpful, and often virtually essential, to describe the result it achieves in terms of a rather particularized rule for a common type of fact situation and then to subject that rule to arguments of justification and opposition that may reasonably be advanced.   If this is done, the principle of disallowing unconscionable advantage [15] emerges, it would seem, as the justification for most cases of election.

The point along the time sequence when given events occur has a bearing on what theories of variance are available to a claimant because of those events;   it affects also the applicability of defensive responses that might be advanced by an insurer.

If a claim for variance is based on events occurring before the insurance contract was consummated, the theories to be considered include reformation, rescission, waiver, estoppel, and election.   This is true also if the events occurred after consummation of an original insurance agreement but the claim is for variance from the terms of a rider that was later attached to the original agreement.   For example, a rider may be reformed or rescinded, or its terms may be affect-

14. See, *e.g.*, §§ 6.2, 6.7(d), 6.8(a) *infra*.   15. See § 6.2 *infra*.

ed by waiver, estoppel, or election, on the basis of events occurring after the original contract was consummated but before the rider was attached. This same group of theories as well as another—subsequent agreement—should be considered, also, when the agreement could have been attached as a rider but was not.

One defensive theory sometimes available against a claim based on pre-contract (including pre-rider) events is that the claimed right at variance is precluded by a nonwaiver agreement or a reservation-of-rights notice.[16] Other defensive theories one should examine include the parol evidence rule, entire-contract statutes, and statutes of frauds.

Reformation and rescission are clear-cut qualifications of the parol evidence rule. Whether waiver is to be recognized on the basis of pre-contract events is more debatable, however. It is at least a reasonable contention that a claim of waiver of policy provisions is so fundamentally inconsistent with the parol evidence rule that it should only be recognized when the claimed variance is based on post-contract events. On this point, in cases involving events occurring after consummation of the original contract, it makes a difference whether the claim is one for modification of a rider attached after the alleged events or instead is a claim of oral agreement for a rider never attached. In the former case, the parol evidence rule applies, since there is an integrated, written agreement—the rider—that the parol evidence of events preceding its execution purports to modify. But when no rider was issued, the only integrated agreement the parol evidence seeks to modify is one entered into before the events to which the parol evidence refers. Thus, the parol evidence rule is inapplicable.

Entire-contract statutes commonly apply only to life or to life, health, and accident insurance. Such a statute ordinarily declares that the application must be attached to the policy and that the policy constitutes the entire contract between the parties. It is often invoked against an insured's claim that the false answers appearing in his application (relied upon by the insurer to defeat the contract) came about because a representative of the insurer incorrectly recorded his truthful oral responses.[17]

The application of statutes of frauds to insurance transactions is uncommon, but a few illustrations can be found.[18] When there is a writing that satisfies the statute of frauds and an effort is being made to vary its terms, it is the parol evidence rule rather than the statute of frauds that must be overcome. It is possible, however, for a statute of frauds to apply to a claim of oral modification agreed upon after the original contract was reduced to writing and never incorporated into a rider.[19]

---

16. See § 6.6(a) *infra.*

17. See § 6.7(b) *infra.*

18. See §§ 2.2(a) (2), 4.11(d) *supra.*

19. See § 4.11(d) *supra.*

Another respect in which claims for variance based on post-contract events face a distinctive hurdle concerns agency powers. Powers incidental to consummation of the contract may not exist after consummation. In this respect, it is vital to determine whether the agent is clothed with power to issue riders modifying the original contract, as is ordinarily the case with respect to automobile insurance but not, for example, with respect to life insurance. The proof of power to modify a contract in this way greatly strengthens a claim for variance based on post-contract events.

In relation to post-casualty events, as in other contexts, genuine waiver can only rarely be proved. Estoppel, too, is ordinarily most difficult to sustain in this context because it is rare that the claimant can show detrimental reliance on post-casualty representations express or implied in the conduct of representatives of the insurer. Yet there are cases in which genuine estoppel applies, and more still in which courts have used the terminology of estoppel in constructing a doctrine that is better described as election and in many instances is open to challenge on the merits even as a form of election.[20]

A common context for invoking the theory that the insurer's breach precludes its assertion of a defense concerns subrogation rights. When, for example, an automobile collision insurer defends on the ground that the claimant has interfered with its subrogation rights by pursuing the tort claim against a third person for negligently damaging the insured vehicle, the claimant may respond that the insurer's breach of its obligation of prompt payment for the collision loss precludes this defense.[21]

This classification of theories according to the time of occurrence of events on which a claim for variance is based makes no reference to incontestability. The reason is that this theory, rather than being based upon events outside those integrated into the contract, is a response to an insurer's effort to defeat the contract either on the basis of pre-contract events such as misrepresentations or, less often, post-contract or even post-casualty events. Whenever the insurer invokes a defense of misrepresentation, the question whether there is an applicable incontestability statute or clause should be considered. Indeed, it may be said that the theory of incontestability should be considered as a potential response to other types of defenses as well, but in light of the terms and construction of incontestability statutes and clauses, its applicability in other contexts is less often a realistic possibility.[22]

---

20. See, *e.g.*, § 6.7(d) *infra*.

21. See, *e.g.*, § 6.8(b) *infra*.

22. See § 6.5(d) *infra*.

SECTION 6.2 DISALLOWING UNCONSCIONABLE ADVANTAGE

Some rights against insurers at variance with policy provisions can be accounted for as instances of the following principle:

An insurer will not be permitted an unconscionable advantage in an insurance transaction even though the policyholder or other person whose interests are affected has manifested fully informed consent.

This principle explains much that is called waiver or estoppel in insurance law, in circumstances involving neither voluntary relinquishment nor detrimental reliance—the essence of waiver and estoppel respectively. It also accounts for most of the distinctive controls over defenses based on warranty, representation, or concealment.

Typically there is disparity between the bargaining positions of the insurer and the insured. The insurer's opportunity to draft the proposed terms of agreement is an opportunity as well for over-reaching. Quite naturally, there have been enough abuses of that opportunity to generate remedial action. In part, the controls developed have been statutory or administrative regulation of policy forms —occasionally by prescription of forms but more often by less rigid regulation.[1] But such explicit regulation of policy forms is only one segment of a more comprehensive pattern of statutory and decisional controls against overreaching.

Opportunities for overreaching in the drafting of policy provisions were confirmed and enhanced by the strict and unyielding law of warranty initially fashioned by Lord Mansfield for marine insurance and extended with perhaps less justification to life and fire insurance.[2] Warranty law opened an expansive and fertile field for insurers to conceive imaginative and sharply restrictive limitations— unconscionable even in bold face and the more so if concealed in the fine print of an obscure passage in a lengthy, bewildering form. In this setting controls were inevitable. They have been developed not only in statutes and in administrative regulation of the potential effect of warranties, but also in doctrines fashioned by courts.[3] And, as we shall see elsewhere in this chapter,[4] controls fashioned in these various ways have been extended to closely similar though perhaps less severe abuses of defenses based on representation or concealment. Many of the legal consequences of these controls are, from another

---

1. See § 2.10(b) *supra.*

2. See § 5.6 *supra.*

3. Closely akin to the discredited myth that courts only find and apply law and do not make it is the myth that courts only enforce measures of insurance regulation and never create

them. The history of insurance cases in the courts is in fact replete with instances of judicially created regulatory doctrines. Court-made doctrines are particularly pervasive in the area of rights at variance.

4. See § 6.5 *infra.*

perspective, rights against insurers at variance with policy provisions. Perhaps these two areas—regulation of policy forms and controls over defenses based on warranty, representation, or concealment—have accounted for most applications of the principle of disallowing unconscionable advantage.

In addition, the principle underlies the formulation of the precise terms of choice imposed upon insurers in the most common applications of the doctrine of election, and in still more cases that are better explained under a theory of election than under the theories of waiver or estoppel expressed in the opinions. Among the examples are cases in which insurers, accepting late premiums, are precluded from asserting a lapse of coverage even though the policyholder is unable to prove either genuine waiver (that is, that the insurer voluntarily relinquished a known right) or genuine estoppel (that is, that the policyholder detrimentally relied on some representation for which the insurer is accountable).[5] These cases, as is always true under a doctrine of election, impose some limit on the insurer's range of choice. That is, they disallow adherence to one way of treating premiums if no casualty has occurred (collecting and applying premiums to a period already past) and another in other cases (declaring a lapse), the insurer thereby attempting a course advantageous to itself in each instance. If sustainable, the decisions imposing liability in this context despite the fact that the tender of a renewal premium occurred after loss are best explained as responses to an insurer's effort to gain unconscionable advantage—revealed in this instance in the insurer's treatment of the whole body of cases rather than in the way it treated the single case of late tender after a casualty had already occurred. Treating cases of this type as cases of waiver or estoppel, as courts have more often done, has tended to make them seem less defensible than they are; theories of waiver or estoppel are obviously strained in such an application, and the better explanation is obscured.

"Unconscionability" is by nature an elusive standard.[6] As might be expected, courts of different jurisdictions are not in full accord concerning applications of the principle of disallowing unconscionable advantage. The Supreme Court of New Jersey has been notably more active in invoking this principle and has pressed its application to a greater extreme than courts generally. It has, for example, invoked the principle in imposing on an insurer a duty to disclose its knowledge of the reach of a policy provision that had received a surprisingly broad judicial construction.[7]

5. See § 6.7(d) *infra*.

6. See, *e.g.*, Restatement (Second) of Contracts §§ 234, 237 (Tent. Draft No. 5 1970). See also the materials on judicial treatment of standardized contracts cited in § 2.10(a) n.1 *supra*.

7. Bowler v. Fidelity & Cas. Co., 53 N. J. 313, 327–328, 250 A.2d 580, 588 (1969):

"In situations where a layman might give the controlling language of the policy a more restrictive interpretation than the insurer knows the

SECTION 6.3 HONORING REASONABLE EXPECTATIONS

§ 6.3(a) EMERGENCE OF THE PRINCIPLE

At Lloyd's Coffee House in the early days of its history, perhaps insurance contracts were negotiated among persons of relatively equal bargaining power. At the least, it was common for the proposal for insurance to be written by the person desiring insurance, the insurers merely underwriting for designated amounts. It may well be, however, that the nature of the provisions contained in the proposal were very early dictated by the demands of the underwriters. In any event, as the marketing of various kinds of insurance outside the Coffee House developed in magnitude, standardization of terms for contracting, almost invariably drafted by insurers, became progressively more common.

Insurance contracts continue to be contracts of adhesion, under which the insured is left little choice beyond electing among standardized provisions offered to him, even when the standard forms are prescribed by public officials rather than insurers. Moreover, although statutory and administrative regulations have made increasing inroads on the insurer's autonomy by prescribing some kinds of provisions and proscribing others,[1] most insurance policy provisions are still drafted by insurers. Regulation is relatively weak in most instances, and even the provisions prescribed or approved by legislative or administrative action ordinarily are in essence adoptions, outright or slightly modified, of proposals made by insurers' draftsmen.

courts have given it and as a result the uninformed insured might be inclined to be quiescent about the disregard or non-payment of his claim and not to press it in timely fashion, the company cannot ignore its obligation. It cannot hide behind the insured's ignorance of the law; it cannot conceal its liability. In these circumstances it has the duty to speak and disclose, and to act in accordance with its contractual undertaking. The slightest evidence of deception or overreaching will bar reliance upon time limitations for prosecution of the claim."

In *Bowler* the court also invoked several theories of estoppel. One of these was founded on the insurer's failure to make the last of 200 weekly-benefits payments when due, which payment might have indicated that the insurer was also liable for a lump-sum payment in an amount equal to 600 additional weekly benefits. The insurer's conduct, said the court, "constitutes conduct incompatible with the insurer's obligation to exercise good faith in dealing with its insured, and *of itself* creates an equitable estoppel against the plea of the statute of limitations." 53 N.J. at 329, 250 A.2d at 589 (emphasis in original). It is not difficult to find detrimental reliance by the insured on his assumption, not contradicted by the insurer, that he did not have a valid claim. But in *Bowler* the New Jersey court went well beyond other courts generally in holding that the insured is entitled to rely upon *nondisclosure* by the insurer. In effect the court held that the insurer has a duty to volunteer information about the insured's rights, which duty it violates by a "mere naked rejection" of the claim when "it has a reasonable doubt as to whether the evidence is sufficient to require payment   .   .   ." 53 N.J. at 328, 250 A.2d at 588. Concerning detrimental reliance generally, see § 6.3 *infra.*

1. See § 2.10(b) *supra.*

Under such circumstances as these, judicial regulation of contracts of adhesion, whether concerning insurance or some other kind of transaction, remains appropriate. Several of the doctrines serving this regulatory purpose—notably the contract law doctrine that ambiguities in contract documents are resolved against the party responsible for its drafting—will be discussed below. Underlying this congeries of doctrines, however, one can discern a principle broader than the separate bodies of doctrine it has sustained. With a focus limited to insurance cases (though surely it applies in other contexts as well), this principle may be stated in the following way:

Principle

> The objectively reasonable expectations of applicants and intended beneficiaries regarding the terms of insurance contracts will be honored even though painstaking study of the policy provisions would have negated those expectations.

Although too general to serve as a guide from which particularized decisions can be derived through an exercise of logic, and too broad to be universally true, this principle points in the direction insurance law appears to be moving. It is also, I submit, a principle that insurance law ought to embrace. This section explores some characteristics and implications of the principle as an ideal—and as it appears to be emerging—and then examines particular instances of its operation in the case law.

First, as an ideal this principle incorporates the proposition that policy language will be construed as laymen would understand it and not according to the interpretation of sophisticated underwriters. Arguably that proposition should be regarded as a corollary of the principle of resolving ambiguities against the insurer. The principle of honoring reasonable expectations should be extended further, protecting the policyholder's expectations as long as they are objectively reasonable from the layman's point of view, in spite of the fact that had he made a painstaking study of the contract, he would have understood the limitation that defeats the expectations at issue. The question whether the policyholder has sufficiently examined the policy is only one part of the overall calculation of the objective reasonableness of his expectations. An objective standard produces an essential degree of certainty and predictability about legal rights, as well as a method of achieving equity not only between insurer and insured but also among different insureds whose contributions through premiums create the funds that are tapped to pay judgments against insurers.

An important corollary of the expectations principle is that insurers ought not to be allowed to use qualifications and exceptions from coverage that are inconsistent with the reasonable expectations of a policyholder having an ordinary degree of familiarity with the type of coverage involved. This ought not to be allowed even though the insurer's form is very explicit and unambiguous, because insurers know that ordinarily policyholders will not in fact read their policies. Policy forms are long and complicated and cannot be fully understood without detailed study; few policyholders ever read their policies as carefully as would be required for moderately detailed understanding. Moreover, the normal processes for marketing most kinds of insurance do not ordinarily place the detailed policy terms in the hands of the policyholder until the contract has already been made. In life insurance marketing, for example, the policyholder does not ordinarily see the policy terms until he has signed the application (his offer to contract with the company) and has paid a premium, and the company has approved the application and has executed and issued the policy. This often means a delay of weeks, and occasionally even longer, between making an application and having possession of the policy— a factor enhancing the policyholder's disinclination to read his policy carefully or even to read it at all. Thus, not only should a policyholder's reasonable expectations be honored in the face of difficult and technical language, but those expectations should prevail as well when the language of an unsual provision is clearly understandable, unless the insurer can show that the policyholder's failure to read such language was unreasonable.

It is important to note, however, that the principle of honoring reasonable expectations does not deny the insurer the opportunity to make an explicit qualification effective by calling it to the attention of a policyholder at the time of contracting, thereby negating surprise to him. The doctrines developed in relation to notice of limitations of liability of an innkeeper [2] provide an analogy to which courts might turn in formulating more precise guidelines on this matter. There are limits, however, on the extent to which full notice to a particular policyholder can be effective; probably it cannot defeat a claim at variance with a clause that is fundamentally unconscionable because it misleads the great majority of policyholders. [3]

As was suggested earlier, though the principle has broader application, among the decisions that can be explained in this way are most, at least, of the decisions resolving genuine ambiguities against the policy draftsman. To this proposition it might be objected that resolving ambiguities against the insurer would sometimes be more favorable to the insured than would honoring reasonable expectations. For example, even though the contractual language was ambiguous, there might be no expectation at all, or the expectation might be unreasonable, thus defeating a claimed expansion of coverage beyond the letter of the contract. It seems likely, however, that, even though not often expressed, there has always been an implicit understanding that ambiguities, which in most cases might be resolved in more than just one or the other of two ways, would be resolved favorably to the insured's claim only if a reasonable person in his position would have expected coverage. [4]

---

2. See generally 9 Williston, Contracts § 1069 (3d ed. 1967).

3. See § 6.3(b) *infra*.

4. See, *e.g.*, Steven v. Fidelity & Cas. Co., 58 Cal.2d 862, 869–870, 377 P.2d 284, 288–289, 27 Cal.Rptr. 172, 176–177 (1962); Allen v. Metropolitan Life Ins.

Opinions proceeding generally on the theory of resolving ambiguities against the insurer have often included passages stretching toward but not reaching the broader principle of honoring reasonable expectations. A leading example is an opinion by Judge Learned Hand.[5] After referring to the insurer's contention that the language of a binding receipt for a life insurance premium unambiguously postponed commencement of coverage until the insurer's approval of the application and provided a half dozen assorted advantages to the applicant as well, the opinion continued: [6]

"An underwriter might so understand the phrase, when read in its context, but the application was not to be submitted to underwriters; it was to go to persons utterly unacquainted with the niceties of life insurance, who would read it colloquially. It is the understanding of such persons that counts; and not one in a hundred would suppose that he would be covered, not 'as of the date of completion of Part B,' as the defendant promised, but only as of the date of approval."

He added that in Connecticut (the state whose law the court was applying) as elsewhere "the canon contra proferentem is more rigorously applied in insurance than in other contracts, in recognition of the difference between the parties in their acquaintance with the subject matter." [7]

Other examples of opinions that strain the outer limits of the theory of resolving ambiguity, but do not explicitly go beyond it, have involved such varied matters as restrictive clauses in air travel trip insurance purchased through vending machines [8] and a liability insurer's duty of defense against a claim of assault and battery.[9]

Co., 44 N.J. 294, 305, 208 A.2d 638, 644 (1965).

5. Gaunt v. John Hancock Mut. Life Ins. Co., 160 F.2d 599 (2d Cir.), *cert. denied*, 331 U.S. 849 (1947).

6. 160 F.2d at 601 (footnote omitted).

7. 160 F.2d at 602 (footnote omitted).

8. The decisions allowing coverage in this context contrary to the insurer's intentions are generally grounded on lack of notice to the insured, before his purchase of the insurance, of specific exclusions from coverage. See, *e.g.*, Lachs v. Fidelity & Cas. Co., 306 N.Y. 357, 118 N.E.2d 555 (1954). It has been reasoned that this lack of notice creates an ambiguity, to be resolved against the insurer. But some decisions emphasize also that the marketing arrangement—vending machine sales in airports—creates reasonable expectations of the insured contrary to the terms of the policy as the in-

surer urges it be construed. For example, it has been said:
"In this type of standardized contract, sold by a vending machine, the insured may reasonably expect coverage for the whole trip which he inserted in the policy, including reasonable substituted transportation necessitated by emergency."

Steven v. Fidelity & Cas. Co., 58 Cal.2d 862, 868, 377 P.2d 284, 288, 27 Cal. Rptr. 172, 176 (1962). Moreover, the court added, the question of ambiguity of the policy language is to be determined in view of the insured's "knowledge and understanding as a reasonable layman, his normal expectation of the extent of coverage of the policy .   .   .   ." 58 Cal.2d at 869, 377 P.2d at 288, 27 Cal.Rptr. at 176 (footnote omitted).

9. Gray v. Zurich Ins. Co., 65 Cal.2d 263, 419 P.2d 168, 54 Cal.Rptr. 104 (1966); Lowell v. Maryland Cas. Co., 65 Cal.2d 298, 419 P.2d 180, 54 Cal. Rptr. 116 (1966). In *Gray*, insured defended a tort claim unsuccessfully and

Some more recent decisions, in particular, have seemed rather clearly to press beyond the rationale of ambiguity—even beyond the outer limits of the idea of ambiguity to laymen as distinguished from underwriters. Opinions of this kind have been handed down in cases involving such different areas of insurance law as restrictively defined coverage for loss from accidental bodily injuries,[10] other accident insurance issues,[11] life insurance binding receipts,[12] and various cover-

---

was allowed recovery against the insurer for the amount of the tort judgment as well as costs of defense; the court held that standard provisions concerning the duty of defense, in a Comprehensive Personal Liability Endorsement, "are uncertain and undefined," and that they should be construed to fulfill the insured's reasonable expectations. In *Lowell*, on the same holding as to ambiguity, the insured who had defended a tort claim successfully was allowed recovery against the insurer for costs of defense but not for the attorneys' fees incurred in the separate action against the insurer.

Even though one supports not merely the resolution of ambiguities in favor of the insured but also the still broader principle of honoring reasonable expectations, he may differ with the California court's conclusions that the insureds' beliefs were reasonable. It was at least arguably unreasonable even for a layman to have expected that the policy provided for defense against claims of assault and battery generally—as distinguished from claims based on circumstances that in fact involved mistake, as when the insured acted in self-defense but without a privilege to do so because his belief that he was under attack was unreasonable. For a thoughtful criticism of the California court's decision in *Gray*, see Note, *The Insurer's Duty to Defend Made Absolute: Gray v. Zurich*, 14 U.C.L.A. L.Rev. 1328 (1967). See also §§ 7.6(a) n.32 and 7.6(e) n.11 *infra*.

10. Perrine v. Prudential Ins. Co., 56 N.J. 120, 265 A.2d 521 (1970) (see § 6.-3(b) n.3 *infra*); Kievit v. Loyal Protective Life Ins. Co., 34 N.J. 475, 170 A.2d 22 (1961). In *Kievit*, after being hit on the head by a piece of lumber, the insured suffered from continuing body tremors, which, according to testimony of a defense physician, resulted from pre-existing but latent Parkinson's disease activated by the blow. Held, insured could recover under a policy insuring against loss "resulting

directly and independently of all other causes from accidental bodily injuries" and excluding "disability . . . resulting from or contributed to by any disease or ailment," since the pre-existing disease was dormant and unknown to the insured and was activated by the accident into a disabling condition. The court remarked:
"When members of the public purchase policies of insurance they are entitled to the broad measure of protection necessary to fulfill their reasonable expectations. . . . Where particular provisions, if read literally, would largely nullify the insurance, they will be severely restricted so as to enable fair fulfillment of the stated policy objective."
34 N.J. at 482–483, 170 A.2d at 26.

11. Klos v. Mobil Oil Co., 55 N.J. 117, 259 A.2d 889 (1969) (complicated conflict among brochure sent to credit card holders, application, and policy, regarding effective date of accident insurance coverage; resolved for coverage on the basis of honoring reasonable expectation; opinion notes that the principle applies to contracts *for* as well as contracts *of* insurance).

12. In Prudential Ins. Co. v. Lamme, 83 Nev. 146, 425 P.2d 346 (1967), holding that a conditional receipt creates a temporary contract of life insurance subject to rejection and that during the period before rejection it covers the applicant regardless of whether he is insurable by the company's standards referred to in the receipt, the court remarked:
"A conditional receipt tends to encourage deception. We do not mean to imply affirmative misconduct by the soliciting insurance agent. We suggest only that if nothing is said about the complicated and legalistic phrasing of the receipt, and the agent accepts an application for insurance together with the first premium payment, the applicant has reason to believe that he is insured."
83 Nev. at 149, 425 P.2d at 347–348. After declaring its holding that the

ages under fire and casualty insurance policies.[13]   Moreover, the principle of resolving ambiguities against the draftsman is simply an in-

receipt created a temporary contract subject to rejection, the court concluded: "The life insurance companies may still write 'COD' [cash on delivery] insurance, or, in the light of experience, choose to assume the risk sometimes involved in the use of the conditional receipt."   83 Nev. at 149–150, 425 P.2d 348 (footnote omitted).

In Allen v. Metropolitan Life Ins. Co., 44 N.J. 294, 302, 208 A.2d 638, 642 (1965), the court stated:
"Much of the difficulty may be laid at the doorstep of the life insurance industry itself for .   .   . it has persisted in using language which is obscure to the layman and in tolerating agency practices which are calculated to lead the layman to believe that he has coverage beyond that which may be called for by a literal reading."

Though recognizing that "[w]hen read literally, the receipt gave no interim protection at all in the absence of an approval by the company at its home office," 44 N.J. at 304, 208 A.2d at 643, the court held that the applicant's
"reasonable expectations in the transaction may not justly be frustrated and courts have properly molded their governing interpretative principles with that uppermost in mind.   Thus we have consistently construed policy terms strictly against the insurer and where several interpretations were permissible, we have chosen the one most favorable to the assured."
44 N.J. at 305, 208 A.2d at 644.

In Morgan v. State Farm Life Ins. Co., 240 Ore. 113, 118–122, 400 P.2d 223, 225–227 (1965), the dissenting opinion (joined in by three of seven judges) also seems clearly to support the principle of honoring reasonable expectations.   240 Ore. at 120–121, 400 P.2d at 226–227.

13.   National Indem. Co. v. Flesher, 469 P.2d 360 (Alaska 1970) (resolving, on the basis of reasonable expectations, a dispute in favor of coverage with respect to duty to defend under liability insurance; citing the advance publication of this section in 83 Harv.L.Rev. 961; other details are stated in § 7.-6(a) n.14 infra); Gerhardt v. Continental Ins. Cos., 48 N.J. 291, 225 A.2d 328 (1966).

In Gerhardt, sustaining coverage under a homeowners policy for a workmen's compensation claim of a domestic employee, the court observed that in deciding an earlier case it had "stressed that insureds are entitled to the measure of protection necessary to fulfill their 'reasonable expectations' and that they should not be subjected to 'technical encumbrances or to hidden pitfalls.' "
"While the insured is always supposed to read the policy, only a very hardy soul would have plowed through all of the fine print here in an effort to understand the many terms and conditions."

.   .   .

"The insurer explains .   .   . references favoring residence employees by pointing to the fact that its policy form was used in various states including those where residence employees are not within workmen's compensation laws. .   .   . But so far as the New Jersey insured here was concerned, she was entitled to treat the policy as solely a New Jersey one.   She was not at all interested in any extra-state matters and her reasonable expectations are to be determined and fulfilled entirely from the point of view of a local policy purchased in a local relationship."
48 N.J. at 297, 299–300, 225 A.2d at 332–334.

Cf.   Cooper v. Government Employees Ins. Co., 51 N.J. 86, 237 A.2d 870 (1968) (placing burden on insurer to prove breach of late-notice provision and "a likelihood of appreciable prejudice" therefrom in order to fulfill reasonable expectations of the purchaser "so far as its language will permit"; trial court's fact-finding of no breach by insured of notice provision sustained).

See also Harr v. Allstate Ins. Co., 54 N. J. 287, 255 A.2d 208 (1969) (insurer estopped to deny coverage under fire policy because of contrary representations of agent; the court resorted to a theory of reasonable expectations in rejecting the contention that policy provisions negated the alleged representations); Barth v. State Farm Fire & Cas. Co., 214 Pa.Super. 434, 257 A.2d 671 (1969) (policy, received several weeks after insured had applied for coverage, afforded robbery protection only when the premises

adequate explanation of the results of some cases. The conclusion is inescapable that courts have sometimes invented ambiguity where none existed, then resolving the invented ambiguity contrary to the plainly expressed terms of the contract document.[14] To extend the principle of resolving ambiguities against the draftsman in this fictional way not only causes confusion and uncertainty about the effective scope of judicial regulation of contract terms but also creates an impression of unprincipled judicial prejudice against insurers. If results in such cases are supportable at all, generally it is because the principle of honoring policyholders' reasonable expectations applies.

In addition to cases that have been reasoned on a theory of resolving ambiguities against the insurer there are decisions, invoking a variety of other doctrines, for which the principle of honoring reasonable expectations is an alternative and arguably better justification. Examples include cases involving such things as delivery of a policy that deviates in some marked fashion from the coverage applied for,[15] and delivery of a renewal policy of lesser scope than the previous policy without calling the insured's attention to the reduction of coverage.[16]

were open for business; brochure relied upon as the basis for coverage until the policy was received referred to all-risk comprehensive crime insurance and had an artist's representation of a burglary occurring during non-business hours; judgment for insurer reversed and remanded for trial on fact question whether policyholder had in fact been informed before loss that policy did not cover loss of cash during non-business hours; reasoned on ground of rights based on reasonable reliance, not available if he had been correctly informed before loss).

14. See, *e.g.*, Mosby v. Mutual Life Ins. Co., 405 Ill. 599, 92 N.E.2d 103 (1950), 18 A.L.R.2d 1054 (1951), discussed in § 6.8(c) *infra*.

15. Under customary theory, the transmission of such a policy is a counter offer by the insurer. Acceptance by the insured concludes the transaction and makes the substituted policy the binding contract. *E.g.*, Long v. New York Life Ins. Co., 106 Wash. 458, 180 P. 479 (1919). See generally § 2.6 *supra*.

But in some cases involving deviations not specifically brought to the insured's attention, the policy has been construed to provide the coverage applied for, regardless of express language to the contrary. See, *e.g.*, Providential Life Ins. Co. v. Clem, 240 Ark. 922, 403 S.W.2d 68 (1966); Lawrence v. Providential Life Ins. Co., 238

Ark. 981, 385 S.W.2d 936 (1965). Although this result has been based upon a duty of the insurer to issue the insurance applied for in the absence of adequate notice of variations, it may be suggested that the reasonable expectations of the insured created by the description of coverage contained in the application form constitute the best reason for recognizing such a duty.

See also Stamps v. Consolidated Underwriters, 205 Kan. 187, 468 P.2d 84 (1970) (automobile liability insurance coverage less than applied for was issued without notice to applicant; reformation allowed).

16. *E.g.*, Bauman v. Royal Indem. Co., 36 N.J. 12, 174 A.2d 585 (1961), 91 A. L.R.2d 535 (1963) (renewal policy declared no coverage for workmen's compensation claims of resident employees as well as other employees; held, claim of part-time domestic employee covered). A later New Jersey case sustained coverage for a workmen's compensation claim of a domestic employee on a ground more broadly supporting the principle of honoring reasonable expectations. In this later instance there was no history of an earlier, broader policy on which the insured might base his claim of reasonable expectations. Gerhardt v. Continental Ins. Cos., 48 N.J. 291, 225 A.2d 328 (1966), discussed in n.13 *supra*.

Thus, the principle of honoring reasonable expectations, though only occasionally recognized explicitly, is a better explanation of results in many cases than a strained rationale such as that of resolving ambiguities against the insurer. Also, as stated above, insurance law appears to be moving in the direction the principle indicates. It must be recognized, however, that precedents provide illustrations of deviations from this principle in result as well as in reasoning. For example, authority can still be found among modern cases for the proposition that even if it be assumed that a conditional receipt was intentionally drafted to be confusing, still if there is no ambiguity in it, there is nothing for the court to construe and no basis for finding coverage contrary to the terms of the receipt.[17]

The expectations principle considered here and the reliance principle considered in the next section overlap, but they are distinct theories of liability. Neither wholly embraces the other. The expectations principle goes beyond the reliance principle in sustaining relief for a claimant without regard to whether he has suffered detriment from his own or another's change of position in reliance on expectations created by the insurer. But the reliance principle has the broader range of application in another respect. When detrimental reliance is proved, it will sometimes be appropriate to grant relief even on the basis of unauthorized and deviational representations by an agent in the field. By way of contrast, the illustrations we have examined here involve expectations created by policy language and structure and by marketing patterns and general practices. These are expectations shared by many and based on matters emanating from a source relatively near the command center of the insurer's operational structure. It seems both appropriate and likely that the expectations principle identified here will be extended only to expectations of a somewhat common rather than exceptional character and that agency doctrines associated with this principle will be less expansive than those associated with the reliance principle.

§ 6.3(b) INDIVIDUAL KNOWLEDGE OF LIMITING PROVISIONS

Are rights at variance that would otherwise be recognized under the expectations principle defeated by a policyholder's specific knowledge of the policy provisions that limit protection in a surprising way? It would seem that knowledge of the limiting provisions should defeat any claim based alone on the principle of honoring reasonable expectations, since such knowledge negates the surprise that would be the basis for departing from ordinary contract principles. But this principle combines with the principle of disallowing uncon-

---

17.   Morgan v. State Farm Life Ins. Co., 240 Ore. 113, 400 P.2d 223 (1965) (4–3 decision enforcing an insurability requirement; the dissenting opinion supports the principle of honoring reasonable expectations, favoring temporary coverage subject to rejection even though the receipt was unambiguous to the careful reader).

scionable advantage to support recovery in some cases even in the face of the claimant's unusual knowledge of the surprising provisions. The following generalization is a corollary of the combined principles of honoring reasonable expectations and disallowing unconscionable advantage:

Corollary principle

If the enforcement of a policy provision would defeat the reasonable expectations of the great majority of policyholders to whose claims it is relevant, it will not be enforced even against those who know of its restrictive terms.

Judicial decisions supportable on this ground have imposed controls over not merely form and method but the substantive content of insurance contracts as well—controls that apply even to provisions so central to the contract that they are referred to as coverage clauses. These legal controls are based upon factual assumptions concerning the extent to which substantively complex or otherwise unexpectable policy terms can be effectively brought to the attention of policyholders in a mass marketing process. In such circumstances, no amount of care in drafting and in marketing will avoid the creation of reasonable expectations contrary to the literal terms of policy provisions. It is a sound rule to strike down a surprising policy provision uniformly, sustaining even the claim of that occasional policyholder who can be shown to have known of its restrictive terms. To apply a different rule among various policyholders would produce the result that those who remained ignorant of the terms would receive substantially more protection for their premium dollars than those aware of them. At least when such a knowledgeable policyholder would receive coverage disproportionately small in comparison with his premiums (which ordinarily would be the case if the total premiums received from all policyholders combined were adequate for the coverage afforded), it would be unduly harsh to deprive him of the protection the great majority of policyholders receive at the same price.

In addition to illustrations that may go beyond settled practice,[1] there are a number of areas in which rather well established decisions are supportable on this ground—areas in which courts have disallowed literal enforcement of policy provisions without regard to whether the individual policyholder read or had ample opportunity to read the restrictive provision in question. For example, courts have quite commonly refused to enforce intolerably restrictive definitions of total disability,[2] accidental means,[3] or accidental bodily injury.[4]

---

1. Perhaps Prudential Ins. Co. v. Lamme, 83 Nev. 146, 425 P.2d 346 (1967), is properly read as pressing beyond settled practice in declaring temporary coverage under a life insurance binding receipt form, as a matter of public policy, even though the applicant is uninsurable and the form unambiguously indicates that insurability is a prerequisite of coverage.

2. *E.g.*, Mason v. Loyal Protective Life Ins. Co., 249 Iowa 1167, 91 N.W.2d 389 (1958); Rudder v. Ohio State Life Ins. Co., 389 S.W.2d 448 (Ky.1965), 26 A.L.R.3d 707 (1969); Struble v. Occi-

3. See Note 3 on page 359.

4. See Note 4 on page 360.

Ordinarily they have justified these results as exercises in construction of the language of the clauses. But it often happens that the

dental Life Ins. Co., 265 Minn. 26, 120 N.W.2d 609 (1963); Bowler v. Fidelity & Cas. Co., 53 N.J. 313, 250 A.2d 580 (1969), discussed in § 6.2 n.7 *supra.*

In *Mason* a doctor of medicine, compelled to give up practice because of nerve deafness, undertook a residency for training as a radiologist, receiving compensation about one-tenth as much as he had earned during his last year in practice. The policy defined "total disability" as "complete loss of business time due to inability of the Insured to engage in his regular occupation or any gainful occupation for which he is reasonably fitted." Held, for the insured:

" 'Total disability' as used in this connection does not mean, as its literal construction would require, a state of absolute helplessness.

. . . .

"[S]uch words as 'any gainful occupation' in this policy mean any occupation, reasonably approximating the same livelihood of the insured's regular occupation as he might fairly be expected to follow, in view of his station, circumstances, and capabilities."

249 Iowa at 1171, 1177, 91 N.W.2d at 392, 395.

In *Rudder*, the policy provided for benefits if plaintiff-insured's disability prevented him "from engaging in any and every occupation or employment." There was evidence he engaged in supervision of others and himself performed minor physical tasks incident to operation of his farm. Held, it was nevertheless error to enter judgment on verdict for defendant and to deny plaintiff's motion for judgment n.o.v.

In *Struble*, a policy clause conditioned coverage on insured's being "necessarily and continuously confined within the house and therein regularly visited and attended by a legally qualified physician or surgeon other than himself." The verdict for plaintiff was upheld despite the fact that he had worked at ordinary laborer's tasks for pay as part of the prescribed therapy while under treatment for mental illness, the court commenting that the policy must be construed so as "to give a realistic meaning to the words and provide some measure of the protection" bargained for.

See generally 1A Appleman, Insurance Law §§ 632, 671–674 (rev. ed. 1965); Annot., 24 A.L.R.3d 8 (1969). *But see, e.g.,* Walsh v. United Ins. Co., 265 N. C. 634, 144 S.E.2d 817 (1965) (insured was totally disabled from engaging in farming, his pre-accident occupation, but he engaged in activities advised by his doctor—short walks, driving, etc.; held, engaging in these activities excluded coverage under policy containing a "continuous confinement" clause).

"Liberal" judicial construction of disability clauses was a factor contributing to the general withdrawal of life insurance companies from this field of insurance during the 1930's. Claim costs proved to be far greater, especially during the depression years, than had been anticipated at the time premium rates were fixed. See, *e.g.,* Rhine v. New York Life Ins. Co., 273 N.Y. 1, 11, 6 N.E.2d 74, 77 (1936), 108 A.L.R. 1197, 1202 (1937): "[T]he 'extra premium' . . . paid to obtain a policy with additional *'disability benefits'* has, in every year since 1931, been less than the cost of furnishing those benefits."

3. See, *e.g.,* Schonberg v. New York Life Ins. Co., 235 La. 461, 104 So.2d 171 (1958); Perrine v. Prudential Ins. Co., 56 N.J. 120, 265 A.2d 521 (1970) (double indemnity "accidental means" clause; deceased leaned cabinet-type 600–700 pound equipment against body while moving it on Friday; complained of feeling unwell that evening; felt worse on Sunday and was hospitalized then; surgery disclosed perforation of his large bowel; died within days from inflammation of abdominal cavity; held, fact question whether he suffered injury from "accidental means" as construed according to reasonable expectations of average policyholder, the test being "whether the average policyholder would consider that there was something about the preceding acts and events, in the light of the unexpected injurious result and at the same time having in mind the limiting language of the insuring clause, which would lead him, reasonably to call the means 'accidental,' even though, strictly speaking, nothing unexpected or unforeseen occurred in the course of the preceding acts"; quotes with approval

construction is one the language itself will not bear.   A better explanation of these precedents is that the language of the policy provision unambiguously provides so little coverage that it would be unconscionable to permit the insurer to enforce it—perhaps even without regard to the premiums it has charged but the more clearly when those premiums are compared with the cost of affording such restricted coverage.

Another example concerns the construction of the increase-of-hazard clause of fire insurance policies.   Such a clause commonly contains the following declaration: [5]

"Unless otherwise provided in writing added hereto this Company shall not be liable for loss occurring (a) while the hazard is increased by any means within the control or knowledge of the insured . . . . ."

Is it enough for a defense that an "increase of hazard," however that phrase is construed,[6] is within the potential control of the insured, even though he does not know about it?   Likewise, is it enough that the increase is known to him, though beyond his control?   Literal reading of the phrase "control or knowledge" would support an affirmative answer to both these questions.   Results, however, are generally contrary to this position.[7]   The degree of judicial regulation in-

from the advance publication of this section in 83 Harv.L.Rev. 961; distinguishes earlier case of heart attack, held as a matter of law not to involve accidental means); Scott v. New Empire Ins. Co., 75 N.M. 81, 400 P.2d 953 (1965); Burr v. Commercial Travelers Mut. Acc. Ass'n, 295 N.Y. 294, 67 N.E. 2d 248 (1946), 166 A.L.R. 462 (1947); Beckham v. Travelers Ins. Co., 424 Pa. 107, 225 A.2d 532 (1967).   *But cf.* Gordon v. Metropolitan Life Ins. Co., 256 Md. 320, 260 A.2d 338 (1970) (affirming directed verdict for insurer on claim under clause for double indemnity; court refuses to declare there is no distinction between accidental means and accidental results; decedent illegally used heroin, which combined with pain killer to produce death; use of heroin caused substantial risk and was prime cause of death).

4.   See, *e.g.*, Kievit v. Loyal Protective Life Ins. Co., 34 N.J. 475, 170 A.2d 22 (1961), discussed in § 6.3(a) n.10 *supra*.

5.   See, *e.g.*, lines 28–32 of the policy form prescribed in N.Y. Ins. Law § 168 (McKinney 1966), Appendix A *infra*.   Since this provision appears in a statutorily prescribed form, the argument for a measure of judicial regulation to prevent an unconscionable advantage is arguably less strong than

when the policy form is drafted by the insurer.   But there remains the point of great disparity between the level of premiums charged and the scope of coverage that would be provided under a literal enforcement of the clause.

6.   See § 6.5(c) (2) *infra*.

7.   See, *e.g.*, Goldman v. Piedmont Fire Ins. Co., 198 F.2d 712 (3d Cir. 1952), 34 A.L.R.2d 706 (1954) (New Jersey law); Di Leo v. United States Fid. & Gy. Co., 50 Ill.App.2d 183, 200 N.E.2d 405 (1st Dist. 1964), 9 A.L.R.3d 1399 (1966).   The majority opinion in *Goldman* asserts that the court is enforcing the increase-of-hazard clause as written, but also speaks of the condition as one applicable upon proof that the increase of hazard was within the insured's knowledge *and* control rather than knowledge *or* control.   The opinion indicates on procedural grounds, however, that the plaintiff cannot complain of the trial court's failure to charge that the increase of hazard must be within the insured's "knowledge *and* control."   198 F.2d at 715, 34 A.L.R.2d at 714.   In *Di Leo*, the insurer defended against recovery under policies on the contents of the insured's store and for business interruption, citing changes in use and occupancy incident to a pending condem-

volved in giving the clause the same effect as if it read knowledge "and" control is arguably justified because of the unduly severe and, from the layman's point of view, surprising effect the clause would have if it were literally enforceable. Literal enforcement would result in such minimal coverage that few policyholders would find the coverage acceptable, and the premiums customarily charged could not possibly be justified.

Among still other insurance law developments that may be regarded as examples of the combined force of the principles of honoring reasonable expectations and disallowing unconscionable advantage are decisions concerning receipt-of-due-proof clauses in disability insurance policies [8] and "other insurance" clauses in various kinds of coverage.[9]

Because it is based on the combined ideas of disallowing unconscionable advantage and honoring reasonable expectations, the corollary generalization suggested here would not preclude an agreement with a fully informed policyholder for exceptional limitations of his coverage at a premium rate fairly adjusted to the narrow scope of the coverage. Since most insurance contracts are standardized, however, either under regulatory compulsion or as a matter of practice, it is not likely that such agreements will be negotiated often.

SECTION 6.4 DETRIMENTAL RELIANCE

§ 6.4(a) GENERALLY

Many aspects of the law applying to insurance transactions, as to other transactions generally, are founded on a pervasive principle of granting redress for loss resulting from detrimental reliance. To state the principle more precisely one must take a position on issues that are controversial. The following formulation is submitted not as a universally recognized principle but as a principle that is supportable on policy grounds and is fully consistent with the results attained by most relevant modern decisions:

A policyholder or other person intended to receive benefits under an insurance policy is entitled to redress against the insurer to the extent of detriment he suffers because he or another person justifiably relied upon an agent's representation incidental to his employment for the insurer.

Principle

This formulation focuses on rights of policyholders and intended beneficiaries against insurers. The principle applies more broadly, of course. It may apply among insurers, for example, and it may apply

---

nation of the building in which insureds leased space for their business. Held, "knowledge AND control of the increase of hazard must be shown before the clause can be used to avoid liability." 50 Ill.App.2d at 191, 200 N.E.2d at 409, 9 A.L.R.3d at 1407 (emphasis in original). See 5 Appleman, Insurance Law § 2941 (rev. ed. 1970).

8. See § 6.8(c) *infra.*

9. See §§ 3.11(a) n.5 and 3.11(b) nn.6, 7 *supra.*

to other than insurance transactions. The more particular formulation expresses the sense of the principle in its most common application to insurance transactions.

Most applications of this principle have been referred to as applications of the doctrine of estoppel. But this principle also accounts for much that has loosely been called waiver, and it applies in other contexts as well. An example is the set of decisions imposing liability for negligent delay in processing an application for insurance. The majority of such decisions are reasoned, quite appropriately, as imposing tort liability for negligence,[1] but these cases also illustrate an aspect of the principle of granting redress for detrimental reliance.

§ 6.4(b) PERSONS PROTECTED

The principle of granting redress for detrimental reliance supports legal relief apart from contract. By nature it may apply even when no contract has been consummated, and it may apply in favor of persons other than the policyholder or intended policyholder.

This is true, for example, when an intended policyholder applies for life insurance, designating intended beneficiaries, and dies before a policy is issued, the insurer having unreasonably delayed in acting on the application. Some courts allowing legal relief in these circumstances have declared that the cause of action belongs to the deceased's estate rather than to the intended beneficiary.[2] Such a decision grants the estate a benefit it would never have received if the contract had been issued. It is also a benefit the estate would not have received if the intended policyholder, not relying upon the insurer to act with reasonable diligence, had instead obtained an identical policy elsewhere. Other courts, consistently with the principle of granting redress for detrimental reliance, have adopted the better rule that the cause of action belongs to the intended beneficiary.[3]

As this last example also illustrates, the cause of action for relief may exist in favor of a person who has not himself relied. In this context, reliance of the intended policyholder, with resulting loss to the intended beneficiary, is the essence of the cause of action. Similarly, reliance of an intended policyholder may cause loss to persons beyond the group commonly called "beneficiaries." Thus a pedestrian struck down by a negligent "omnibus insured" of an automobile liability policy (that is, a person driving with the permission of a

1. *E.g.* Duffie v. Bankers' Life Ass'n, 160 Iowa 19, 27, 139 N.W. 1087, 1090 (1913); Republic Nat'l Life Ins. Co. v. Chilcoat, 368 P.2d 821 (Okla.1961). See generally § 2.4 *supra*.

2. *E.g.*, Rosin v. Peninsular Life Ins. Co., 116 So.2d 798 (Fla.App.1960); Duffie v. Bankers' Life Ass'n, 160 Iowa 19, 29, 139 N.W. 1087, 1090 (1913).

3. See, *e.g.*, Travelers Ins. Co. v. Anderson, 210 F.Supp. 735 (W.D.S.C.1962) (counterclaim in declaratory judgment action instituted by insurer against beneficiary; but court did not discuss whether right of action runs to beneficiary or estate). See also § 2.4(c) *supra*.

named insured) may have a right of action upon proof that the intended policyholder relied on a representation of an agent of the insurer that he would forthwith endorse a change in the place of principal garaging of the vehicle. Even in jurisdictions where the pedestrian would not be among those allowed to recover as third party beneficiaries, he should be protected under the principle of granting redress for detrimental reliance if he can prove that, had the contract been consummated, its benefits would have been available to him directly or indirectly. The principle of granting redress for detrimental reliance is in essence more like tort than contract; it imposes liability on the basis of conduct rather than sustaining it on the basis of manifested consent. It is appropriate, then, that the persons protected be identified on grounds more like those of tort than those of contract.

§ 6.4(c) REPRESENTATIONS TO WHICH THE PRINCIPLE APPLIES

In applying the principle of granting redress for detrimental reliance under the rubric of estoppel, courts and writers have sometimes distinguished among representations of existing fact (*e.g.*, a statement by an agent that he *has issued* a binder or an endorsement changing the specified location at which personal property of the insured is protected under a fire policy), promissory representations (*e.g.*, a statement by an agent that he *will issue* a binder or endorsement before the date of the intended move), and representations of law or opinion (*e.g.*, a statement that without endorsement the policy provisions extend coverage to the new location, either because of the oral notice given to the agent or independently). Such distinctions have been founded on the theory that an estoppel must be based on representations of existing fact, not representations of law, opinion, or promise.[1] Generally, it would seem, courts should not decline to recognize an estoppel merely because the representation on which it is based is promissory [2] or is a representation of law or opinion rather than existing fact. Moreover, it is seldom indeed that one can find a modern case in which denial of a claimed right at variance with policy provisions is stated to have been founded on this kind of distinction and rarer still that it appears in fact that but for this distinction the case would have been decided differently.[3]

Though it seems inappropriate to deny all claims of estoppel based on promissory representations or on representations of opinion

---

1. *Cf.* 28 Am. Jur. Estoppel & Waiver §§ 46–47 (2d ed. 1966).

2. *Cf.* Restatement of Contracts § 90 (1932); 28 Am.Jur. Estoppel & Waiver §§ 48–49 (2d ed. 1966).

3. As an example of opinions stating the requirement of a representation of fact but resting decision on other grounds, see Breen v. Aetna Cas. & Sur. Co., 153 Conn. 633, 220 A.2d 254 (1966) (claim of estoppel to deny coverage rejected because of lack of proof of change of position in reliance on alleged acknowledgement of coverage). See generally 16A Appleman, Insurance Law §§ 9081, 9088 (rev. ed. 1968).

or law, it may nevertheless be reasonable to establish by other standards some limits regarding the kinds of representations that may serve as the basis for estoppel. For example, it seems sound to deny a claim of estoppel based on evidence that an agent of the insurer stated that he would take whatever action should become necessary in the future to keep the policy in force even should changed circumstances result in increased risk.[4] To give effect to such a broad undertaking by the agent would be to cut deeply into the authorized plan of marketing the insurance. Even when agents in the field are authorized to make binding commitments for coverage, they are not generally authorized to extend coverage without advance commitment for the appropriate increase in premium charges. The juridical risk in resolving disputes over evidence of such a broad undertaking would be considerably greater than the juridical risk, substantial though it is, of undertaking to decide the trustworthiness of evidence that the agent made a representation of some type (whether of fact, opinion, or promise) after having notice of the changed circumstances.

Similarly, precedent in most jurisdictions does not permit recovery for an insured's detrimental reliance because of an insurer's nondisclosure. Yet one court has granted redress for presumed detrimental reliance because of an insurer's failure to disclose to its policyholder that courts have generally interpreted certain policy language more favorably than a layman might read it.[5]

§ 6.4(d) THE AGENCY PROBLEM

Since liability founded on the principle of granting redress for detrimental reliance is by nature an imposed, nonconsensual liability, more like tort than contract, it is not surprising that the agency concept associated with this principle is broader than that associated with liability based on contract. Ordinarily an agent must have "authority" or "apparent authority" to bind his principal to a contract.[6] Normally (and appropriately) representations "incidental" to the employment of the agent expose the principal to liability for detrimental reliance.[7] This broader standard is more nearly analogous to the

---

4. *Compare* Home Fire Ins. Co. v. Wilson, 109 Ark. 324, 159 S.W. 1113 (1913), rejecting a claim based on evidence that the agent agreed to take whatever action was necessary to continue in force a fire insurance policy that denied coverage for a vacant building, *with* Home Fire Ins. Co. v. Wilson, 118 Ark. 442, 176 S.W. 688 (1915), sustaining a claim on retrial of the same case, based on evidence of assurances given by the agent after a vacancy arose and he was notified.

5. See § 6.2 n.7 *supra*, discussing Bowler v. Fidelity & Cas. Co., 53 N.J. 313, 250 A.2d 580 (1969).

6. Restatement (Second) of Agency § 140 (1958). However, a "general agent" is held to have additional "inherent agency powers" to bind his principal. The law attributes these additional powers to the relationship even when the "general agent" and his principal did not so intend. The basis of these powers is thus analogous to the basis of the master's liability for the torts of his servant. See *id.* § 161, Comment *a*.

7. This position is supported by a growing body of precedent denying to an insurer a defense based on false answers in the application when it ap-

concept of scope of employment in master-servant cases concerned with physical harm.[8]

§ 6.4(e) JUSTIFIABLE RELIANCE

If the claimant asserts detrimental reliance on an honest but carelessly inaccurate representation, recovery is in general not permitted if the claimant too was careless.[1] This is consistent with the usual common law rule that contributory negligence is a complete bar to a claim based on negligence. Modern trends toward apportioning the loss in cases of contributory fault rather than barring relief entirely [2] seem not to have had noticeable impact, as yet, upon the doctrine of estoppel.

If the agent's representations are fraudulent, however, contributory negligence ought not to bar relief. This view is consistent with the disputed but nevertheless prevailing common law rule that contributory negligence is no defense against an intentional tort.[3] Thus, an insured's negligent failure to read his policy ought not to bar him from relief for his detrimental reliance on the intentional misrepresentations of an insurer's agent.[4] However, when the agent's wrongdoing is unauthorized, the equities favoring the insured have less force against the insurer than against the agent.[5] In such a case, the insurer as well as the insured is a victim of the agent's

---

pears that the applicant answered truthfully and the agent incorrectly recorded his answers. See § 6.7(b) *infra*.

8. *Cf.* Restatement (Second) of Agency § 258 (1958), concerning tort liability of a principal for "incidental misrepresentations" of his agent. The Restatement points out that the liability is broader than that for contracts within the agent's authority or apparent authority.

"Under the rule stated in this Section, the principal is subject to liability for statements concerning such matters as the other party to the transaction may reasonably believe have been confided to the agent to deal with."

Id. Comment *a*.

1. *But cf.* General Electric Credit Corp. v. Aetna Cas. & Sur. Co., 437 Pa. 463, 263 A.2d 448 (1970) (two of seven fire policies failed to include allegedly agreed-upon special lender's loss payee clause; allegations support reformation; negligence "in failing to discover the mistake will not bar reformation in the absence of prejudice or a violation of a positive legal duty"; held, same rule applies when suit, though it could have been brought on

theory of reformation, is founded instead on waiver or estoppel).

2. See generally James, Kalven, Keeton, Leflar, Malone & Wade, *Comments on Maki v. Frelk—Comparative v. Contributory Negligence: Should the Court or Legislature Decide?*, 21 Vand.L.Rev. 889–948 (1968).

3. See Restatement (Second) of Torts § 481 (1966) (intentional injury); *cf.* Restatement of Torts § 918 (1939) (avoidable consequences).

4. See, *e.g.*, both supporting and opposing precedents in cases concerning an agent's falsely recording an applicant's correct answers to inquiries, § 6.7(b) *infra*.

5. *Cf.* Restatement (Second) of Agency § 259A (1958), stating not a distinctive rule for insurance cases but a rule of general application. The stated rule approves reformation based on an agent's misrepresentation as to the contents of an agreement executed in writing with the representee, and comment *a* indicates that the rule "applies whether or not the third person was negligent, unless the principal would be adversely affected by a delay in discovering the facts."

wrong. Thus, it might be suggested that the insured's rights against the insurer should be more limited than his rights against the agent. For example, it might be urged that the insured not be entitled to recover for detrimental reliance on the agent's fraudulent representation if the insured himself was careless and nothing worse than carelessness could be attributed to the insurer, apart from the conduct of the agent who was dishonest with the insurer as well as the insured. Such a distinction would have great practical significance in those cases in which the agent was not financially responsible to the full extent of his liability. But, whatever rule might be desirable outside the context of insurance, perhaps a distinctive rule for insurance cases is justified. A rule that would include protection against the fraud of insurance agents within the scope of the insurance arrangement—thus causing such losses to be distributed widely—seems wiser and fairer than a rule placing the loss entirely on a single victim of the fraud.

§ 6.4(f) PROOF OF DETRIMENT AND SCOPE OF RELIEF

The principle of granting redress for detrimental reliance justifies compensation only to the extent of the resulting detriment, and no more.[1] Nevertheless, courts sometimes impose liability beyond redress for detrimental reliance—either finding liability when there was no detriment or permitting recovery in excess of the detriment sustained. This has sometimes occurred in cases involving acceptance of premiums tendered late.[2] And it has occurred in other contexts as well.[3] For example, detriment is properly measured by the terms of an intended insurance contract whenever the policyholder would have had a valid contract with the defendant insurer or another but for his reliance on the agent's representations. Sometimes, however, liability has been imposed in accordance with the terms of a proposed contract despite the absence of proof that the insured would have concluded a comparable contract but for his detrimental

1. Probably Restatement of Contracts § 90 (1932) was at odds with this position. *But cf.* Restatement (Second) of Contracts § 90 (Tent. Draft No. 2 1965): "A promise which the promisor should reasonably expect to induce action or forbearance on the part of the promisee or a third person and which does induce such action or forbearance is binding if injustice can be avoided only by enforcement of the promise. *The remedy granted for breach may be limited as justice requires.*" (Emphasis added.) See also *id.*, comment e.

2. See, *e.g.*, § 6.7(d) n.2 *infra.*

3. In addition to illustrations discussed in the text above, see, *e.g.*, Bayer v. Lutheran Mut. Life Ins. Co., 184 Neb. 826, 172 N.W.2d 400 (1969) (summary judgment for defendant insurer reversed and remanded with directions to enter judgment for insured on 30-year endowment policies issued at age 17; in answer to a letter from insured's mother a month after issuance of policy, agent quoted, as sum to which insured would be entitled, an amount larger than that provided for in policy and rate book; held statement was "promissory rather than illustrative" and insured and her mother had a right to rely; dissent on ground there was no evidence of fraud or change of position).

reliance.[4] Any justification for such decisions must be found either in some entirely different principle or else in a principle of granting redress for detrimental reliance more generous to policyholders than that advanced here.

A more generous principle of detrimental reliance might be thought justified as a punitive measure, to encourage insurers to police the activities of their agents more effectively. But it is relevant to ask who is likely to suffer the impact of the punishment. Experience with another effort to achieve a desired marketing practice by imposing higher liability on insurers in individual cases of deviation from the desired practice is instructive. The underlying theory advanced for the enactment of valued policy laws, fixing an insurer's liability at the value stated in the policy even though true value of the insured property is lower, was that they would encourage insurers to inspect the property and decline to insure for more than its true value. In practice, however, insurers have generally preferred to forego the expense of inspections and pay the penalty when necessary.[5] It seems likely indeed that the consequence of imposing a penalty of liability in excess of resulting detriment, under a modified principle of granting redress for detrimental reliance, would merely be to pay an occasional and rather fortuitous bonus, and in the long run probably not at the expense of insurers but rather at the expense of policyholders generally, whose premiums would be calculated on the basis of loss experience including these occasional bonuses. Moreover, efforts to sort out this element of the loss experience and deny insurers credit for it in rating procedures would probably not be worth the cost.

Another argument for permitting recovery absent proof of any detriment invokes in combination this principle of granting redress for detrimental reliance and the principle of disallowing unconscionable advantage. We have seen that the latter principle serves to buttress a principle of honoring expectations of policyholders that in some contexts favors an individual policyholder who fully understood the restrictive terms of the policy with which his claim is at variance.[6] It might be suggested, by analogy, that a claimant should be permitted to recover against an insurer upon proving a course of conduct likely to cause detriment generally to persons in the claimant's class, without proving detriment in the particular instance.[7] But the argument is less persuasive in this context. Here, the claimant seeks benefits beyond those other policyholders in general will re-

---

4. *E.g.*, Duffie v. Bankers' Life Ass'n, 160 Iowa 19, 139 N.W. 1087 (1913). See § 2.4 *supra*.

5. See § 3.8 *supra*.

6. See § 6.3(b) *supra*.

7. *Cf.* Bogle v. Conway, 199 Kan. 707, 433 P.2d 407 (1967) (insurer precluded from asserting exclusion of racing accidents; nonwaiver agreement ineffectual because of presumed prejudice from want of full notice to the insured concerning the claimed defense). For further comments on *Bogle* and on nonwaiver agreements generally, see § 6.6(a) and n.3 thereto *infra*.

ceive for comparable premiums. In the other instance, a purpose of allowing the claim of the knowledgeable policyholder is to award him benefits comparable to those other policyholders receive for the same premium. Also, in the present context the choice of a measure of recovery would seem arbitrary and unrelated to the theory of claim if not tied to detriment in fact rather than presumed detriment, whereas in the context of the asserted analogy the court is enforcing for all policyholders a given type of clause that the court in effect rewrites because it was unconscionably restrictive. The lack of availability of a comparable standard distinguishes the cases.

Yet another theory supporting recovery absent proof of any detriment might be premised on the unavailability in some cases of clear evidence as to whether detriment resulted. Such a problem may arise, for example, when a liability insurer takes over the defense and the insured, relying on an express or implied representation that the insurer acknowledges coverage, takes no steps to obtain independent counsel. If the insurer thereafter denies liability and the insured then employs an attorney, the latter may argue that the insured's reliance has caused him to lose the opportunity of early, independent investigation that would have been essential not only to the most effective defense but also to the discovery of evidence that the insurer's defense did not measure up to the standard required. There is some authority for invoking estoppel in such a context with no evidence of detriment beyond the fact of the insurer's exercise of exclusive control over the defense for a substantial period of time.[8] It would seem, however, that more should be required. In the absence of evidence that the insurer's conduct of the defense was in some respect substandard, there is a compelling inference that a defense conducted at the insured's instance would have been no better. To "presume" detriment in such circumstances is essentially a departure from the principle of redressing detrimental reliance without the saving grace of candor and, in the absence of some other explanation, without a satisfactory guideline for determining when and how far the alternative principle, whatever it may be, supports relief.

A distinguishable case is presented, however, if the insured proves not only that in reliance on the insurer's assumption of the defense he failed to take defensive measures himself but also that the insurer's conduct of the defense was negligent. In these circumstances it would seem reasonable to shift to the insurer the burden of

---

8. *E.g.*, Tomerlin v. Canadian Indem. Co., 61 Cal.2d 638, 394 P.2d 571, 39 Cal.Rptr. 731 (1964) (insured's attorney withdrew after insurer's attorney represented there was coverage for assault and battery claim under comprehensive personal liability policy; held, insurer estopped to deny coverage); National Union Fire Ins. Co. v. Bruecks, 179 Neb. 642, 654, 139 N.W. 2d 821, 829 (1966) ("the assumption of complete control . . . for a period of 17 months, with the consequent need of cooperation [between insurer and insured] under the terms of the policy, in itself constitutes a sufficient showing of prejudice [as a basis for urging estoppel]"; but the court held that the defense of noncoverage lacked merit in any event). See also § 6.8(a) *infra*.

proof on the issue of detriment resulting from its negligence, since the careless conduct of the defense would be likely to deprive the insured of not only the fruits of a well-conducted defense but also evidence of what those fruits would have been. Somewhat analogous theories of shifting or relaxation of the burden of proof have developed in various tort law contexts,[9] and such a theory can be justified here without resort to a distinctive rule for insurance cases. It remains, however, a theory more procedural than substantive in nature —a theory of administration aimed at reaching results that, in the face of uncertainties of proof, seem likely to be consistent in most cases with a substantive standard of detriment in fact.

SECTION 6.5 REGULATION OF DEFENSES BASED ON WARRANTY, REPRESENTATION, OR CONCEALMENT

§ 6.5(a) DECISIONAL LIMITATION OF WARRANTY

The common law of warranty in insurance cases was extraordinarily rigorous.[1] Though the term itself and many of the phrases commonly used in policies to provide for "warranties" suggest affirmation, or promise, or both, a warranty was, and is, significant in insurance law primarily as a condition of the insurer's promise to pay, not as an assertion of fact or as a promise of performance by the insured. At common law, noncompliance with a provision construed as a "warranty" was a complete defense for the insurer regardless of materiality of the "breach."

This drastic consequence of characterizing a provision as a warranty was clearly settled. It was less clear what would be so characterized, and the lack of precision about what is treated as a warranty continues today under most regulatory statutes as well as applicable decisions.

More often than not, "warranty" has been defined in writings on insurance law in terms of consequences rather than identifying characteristics. Thus Vance, expressing the traditional view, defined a warranty as

"a statement or promise set forth in the policy, or by reference incorporated therein, the untruth or nonfulfillment of which in any respect, and without reference to whether the insurer was in fact preju-

---

9. *Cf.* Summers v. Tice, 33 Cal.2d 80, 199 P.2d 1 (1948), 5 A.L.R.2d 91 (1949) (plaintiff, a member of a hunting party, was hit when two other hunters shot at quail in a negligent manner; held, neither hunter is relieved from liability unless he proves it was not his shot); Loui v. Oakley, 50 Haw. 260, 438 P.2d 393, *rehearing denied*, 50 Haw. 272 (1968) (in absence of sufficient evidence to apportion damages among consecutive tortfeasors more precisely, damages to be allocated equally among all); Maddux v. Donaldson, 362 Mich. 425, 108 N.W.2d 33 (1961), 100 A.L.R.2d 1 (1965) (successive impacts in chain collision; joint and several liability for total damage in absence of evidence supporting an apportionment).

1. See § 5.6 *supra.*

diced by such untruth or nonfulfillment, renders the policy voidable by the insurer, wholly irrespective of the materiality of such statement or promise." [2]

The common law established a key distinction between warranties and "representations." Misrepresentation was ground for avoidance only if material to the risk assumed. Vance, observing that representations are statements made to give information to the insurer, distinguished them from warranties as follows:

"(a) Warranties are parts of the contract, agreed to be essential; representations are but collateral inducements to it.

"(b) Warranties are always written on the face of the policy, actually or by reference. Representations may be written in the policy or in a totally disconnected paper, or may be oral.

"(c) Warranties are conclusively presumed to be material. The burden is on the insurer to prove representations material.

"(d) Warranties must be strictly complied with, while substantial truth only is required of representations." [3]

Inevitably, pressure developed for amelioration of the law of warranty because its results were often unconscionable, or inconsistent with most policyholders' reasonable expectations, or both. Even before modern statutory developments, judicial decisions had moved far in a remedial direction, and they continue to be the only regulation of warranties in some contexts since in many jurisdictions there still are no warranty statutes generally applicable to all types of insurance.

In addition to developing doctrines of waiver and estoppel rather expansively,[4] courts commonly apply several methods of policy construction to reduce the impact of the harsh law of warranty. First, courts often construe in some other way policy provisions that might arguably have been intended as warranties. For example, words describing insured property may be treated as merely identifying property rather than stipulating that it must continue to meet the description in every detail to remain within the coverage.[5] Similarly, phrases specifying such circumstances as the insured's age may be treated as mere representations of present fact,[6] rather than warran-

---

2. Vance, The Law of Insurance 408 (3d ed. Anderson 1951). "Warranty" is often used in another sense to mean a policy provision expressing an intention that it be given the effect stated in the Vance definition, regardless of whether the courts will so enforce it. *Id.* at 408–409, following the definition quoted in the text.

3. *Id.* at 412.

4. See §§ 6.1–6.4 *supra.*

5. *E.g.,* Joyce v. Maine Ins. Co., 45 Me. 168, 172, 71 Am.Dec. 536, 537–538 (1858) (description of house as occupied by insured). *But cf.* Wood v. Hartford Fire Ins. Co., 13 Conn. 533, 544–545, 35 Am.Dec. 92, 93–94 (1840) (dictum) (description of insured premises as a "paper-mill" relates to risk and thus is a warranty; change of use is complete defense, even if change diminishes risk); however, see n.8 and accompanying text *infra.*

6. See, *e.g.,* Spence v. Central Acc. Ins. Co., 236 Ill. 444, 448–450, 86 N.E. 104, 106 (1908) (statement of insured's age not a warranty because contained in application and thus not part of in-

ties.   Also, written provisions may be treated as negating printed warranty clauses.[7]

Second, when treating a policy provision as a warranty, courts tend to construe it so as to minimize its impact. For example, in a leading case the court held that the descriptive warranty "paper-mill" did not mean that the building must be used as a paper mill but only that it must be ready for use as a paper mill—a state of fact that existed even while the building was being used as a grist mill.[8]

Third, courts favor construing a clause as an "affirmative warranty" rather than a "continuing" or "promissory warranty." Thus, compliance at the commencement of the contract term is enough to satisfy the warranty, and noncompliance at a later date during the policy term is no defense.[9] Similarly, courts often construe a warranty clause as severable or distributable, so that noncompliance with a clause bearing on one type of risk does not defeat coverage for other types of risks within the policy.[10] Finally, courts tend to construe a warranty clause as suspending liability during the period of noncompliance rather than construing it as terminating all potential liability for loss thereafter [11] and, a fortiori, rather than construing it to

surance contract); Morris v. Sovereign Camp, W.O.W., 9 So.2d 835, 837 (La.App.1942) (construing provision that delinquent payment implied warranty of good health).

7. See, *e.g.*, McClure v. Mutual Fire Ins. Co., 242 Pa. 59, 65–67, 88 A. 921, 923–924 (1913) (alternative holding) (printed clause prohibited the keeping of specified articles among which were some items that were normal, if not essential, stock of a country store, for which the insured building was used; the court applied the rule that written provisions—apparently those designating the use of the building as a country store—prevail over printed provisions as being more immediately expressive of the intention of the parties and allowed recovery despite the keeping of the specified articles as part of the stock of the store).

8. Wood v. Hartford Fire Ins. Co., 13 Conn. 533, 35 Am.Dec. 92 (1840). *Cf.* § 5.5(a) (2) *supra*, referring to an analogous tendency to construe coverage provisions less restrictively than their language might bear.

9. *E.g.*, Blood v. Howard Fire Ins. Co., 66 Mass. (12 Cush.) 472 (1853).

10. *E.g.*, Diesinger v. American & Foreign Ins. Co., 138 F.2d 91 (3d Cir. 1943) (breach of the warranty in a jeweler's block policy limiting the amount of jewelry to be displayed in

the window was material to the risk of burglary by window-smashing but did not bar a claim for loss by armed robbery by persons who did not smash or cut the window). *But cf.* Pollock v. Connecticut Fire Ins. Co., 362 Ill. 313, 199 N.E. 816 (1936), in which the court upheld the insurer's refusal of liability for a loss by lightning because Pollock was not the "unconditional and sole owner" within the meaning of a clause in a fire and lightning policy declaring that "[t]his entire policy . . . shall be void . . . if the interest of the insured be other than unconditional and sole ownership . . . ." 362 Ill. at 314, 199 N.E. at 817. It would seem that the risks this clause was intended to avoid have no relevance to the risk of loss by lightning; yet the court denied recovery.

11. See, *e.g.*, McClure v. Mutual Fire Ins. Co., 242 Pa. 59, 63, 88 A. 921, 922 (1913) (alternative holding). Courts have sometimes stated the rule favoring suspension of liability over termination of all potential liability in terms broad enough to suggest that they would apply it even in the face of a clearly stated contractual provision for termination. *E.g.*, Dale v. Mutual Fire Ins. Co., 376 Pa. 470, 472, 103 A.2d 414, 415 (1954), 44 A.L.R.2d 1044, 1046 (1955) (breach of a promissory warranty that "[w]hen a portable internal combustion engine is used as a motive power for threshing grain

mean, as suggested in a dictum by Lord Mansfield,[12] that there is no liability even as to a loss occurring before the breach.[13]

Though such techniques of construction as these can markedly relieve the rigors of the rule requiring strict compliance with warranties, they nevertheless leave a considerable range for the operation of that rule whenever the clause is so carefully drafted that the court cannot plausibly decline to apply it as a matter of construction. Thus, in the absence of legislation, courts have had to determine whether public policy demands that a warranty clause not be enforced, regardless of its clear meaning. In general they have decided to enforce (subject only to the kinds of doctrinal limitations they apply against even those clauses so central as to be treated as "coverage" provisions).[14] That is, courts have not developed any general doctrine aimed specifically at limiting the enforcement of warranties on grounds of public policy. Further amelioration has been left to state legislatures. However, more candid recognition of the principles of disallowing unconscionable advantage and honoring reasonable expectations may work a practical change in this area of the law, whether or not it is reasoned as a regulation of warranties. Since the kinds of clauses commonly referred to as warranties are more likely than coverage provisions to be surprising to laymen or unconscionably restrictive if rigorously enforced, they are more likely, regardless of terminology, to call for application of one of these general grounds for recognizing rights at variance with policy provisions.

. . . it shall not be located nearer than 25 feet from any building"; recovery allowed despite use of such an engine in the insured barn for a period terminating a few hours before the fire). *Contra, e.g.*, German Ins. Co. v. Russell, 65 Kan. 373, 69 P. 345 (1902) (the court enforced a clause declaring the policy forfeited if the property should become vacant or unoccupied without the insurer's consent; reoccupancy after twelve day vacancy did not revive the forfeited policy).

12. DeHahn v. Hartley, 1 T.R. 343, 99 Eng.Rep. 1130 (K.B. 1786). An underwriter brought an action to recover from the insured the amount of a payment under a policy of insurance upon the ship "Juno," "warranted copper-sheathed, and sailed from Liverpool with 14 six-pounders, (exclusive of swivels, &c.) 50 hands or upwards." The ship sailed from Liverpool with only forty-six hands on board. At Beaumaris, which she reached six hours thereafter, with the pilot from Liverpool on board, she took on six hands more, and she continued to have fifty-two hands or more from that time until she was captured on the high seas. Judgment was awarded to the underwriter. The following passage appears in Lord Mansfield's opinion: "A warranty in a policy of insurance is a condition or a contingency, and unless that be performed, there is no contract. It is perfectly immaterial for what purpose a warranty is introduced; but, being inserted, the contract does not exist unless it be literally complied with." 1 T.R. at 345–346, 99 Eng.Rep. at 1131. Concurring opinions were delivered by Ashhurst, J., and Buller, J., and the decision was thereafter unanimously affirmed, 2 T.R. 186, 100 Eng.Rep. 101 (Ex. 1787).

13. See, *e.g.*, Tyrie v. Fletcher, 2 Cowp. 666, 670, 98 Eng.Rep. 1297, 1299 (K.B. 1777) (Mansfield, J.) (dictum). See generally Annot., 59 A.L.R. 611, 614–615 (1929).

14. *But cf.* Dale v. Mutual Fire Ins. Co., 376 Pa. 470, 103 A.2d 414 (1954), 44 A.L.R.2d 1044 (1955).

§ 6.5(b) CONCEPTS OF WARRANTY, REPRESENTATION, AND COVERAGE

(1) GENERALLY

The distinction between warranties and representations has had significance since Lord Mansfield's time. A second important distinction—between warranties and coverage provisions—is principally significant in relation to modern statutory regulation of insurance contracts. Restrictions on the enforceability of warranties, imposed by statutes enacted during the late nineteenth century or thereafter, are generally inapplicable to coverage provisions.

The primary import of this latter distinction is the same as that formerly accorded, before statutory controls, to the distinction between misrepresentation and warranty. Under most modern statutes, either a misrepresentation *or* a breach of warranty is ground for avoidance only if material in some sense, but noncompliance with a coverage provision is a defense regardless of materiality.

Before the modern statutory development got under way, there was relatively little need to distinguish between a warranty and any other policy provision stating a condition of liability—whether called a coverage clause, an exception, an exclusion, or something else. Whatever the terminology, if the policy provision clearly stated that the existence of specified facts was a condition of liability, so it was. But as the art of drafting exculpatory fine print reached maturity and the political climate grew warmer toward public control of insurance, a need was recognized for restrictions against "technical" defenses. Such legislation was primarily directed against an evil of overreaching by insurers—their gaining an unconscionable advantage by the use of complex policy provisions concerning facts that the untutored purchaser would be surprised to find relevant to his insurance coverage. The objective was to preclude defenses not materially related to the maintenance of a sound, nondiscriminatory insurance plan (that is, one under which total premiums collected are adequate but not excessive and premium charges to individual policyholders are properly adjusted to the risks). Historically, the awkward but rhetorically impressive language of warranty, though also used for what Patterson called coverage provisions (*e.g.*, "warranted free of . . . capture"),[1] was commonly used in the policy provisions on which "technical" defenses were based. For this reason, and perhaps also because the word suggested that the insured was assuming some new responsibility rather than merely contracting not to pass part of his risks along to the insurer, warranty was a natural target for re-

---

1. See Patterson, Essentials of Insurance Law 272 (2d ed. 1957). See also *id.* at 249, 255. Compare another use of a derivative of the term "warranty" in a clause that is commonly regarded as a coverage provision—"warranted free of particular average." This is a way of saying that the insurer will not pay a particular average loss. See *id.* at 272; Gilmore & Black, The Law of Admiralty 61 (1957).

strictive legislation. The term warranty commonly appeared in such legislation, but usually without statutory definition.

Some statutes declared that certain types of provisions, formerly treated as warranties, would thereafter be treated as representations.[2] Other statutes, as we shall see presently, declared a new set of legal consequences for warranties, without undertaking a change of terminology. Regardless of the type of legislation, draftsmen of policy forms predictably attempted to avoid the statutory sanctions by rewriting policy clauses in the language of coverage rather than warranty. The efforts of courts and legislatures to deal with this problem have produced a maze of variant rules about warranties in insurance law.

(2) THE NEW YORK STATUTORY DEFINITION OF WARRANTY

As the draftsmen of insurance policy forms made increasing use of the idiom of coverage in an effort to circumvent judicial and statutory regulation of warranties, a need developed for a concept of warranty substantively distinguishable from other conditions of liability. Thus arose the occasion for Patterson's careful distinction between warranties and other policy conditions,[3] and for its enactment in a New York statute.[4]

Patterson's concept of warranty relies on a distinction between an actual or efficient cause of a loss and a potential cause—a distinction he noted as early as 1924.[5] Six years later Chief Judge Cardozo, in *Metropolitan Life Insurance Co. v. Conway,*[6] wrote an opinion for the court that can reasonably be read as distinguishing between a provision (held valid) declaring death from specified causes not to be covered and a provision (held invalid) declaring death under specified circumstances not to be covered, regardless of the cause. Patterson so interpreted Cardozo and, writing in 1934, cited the *Conway* opinion in support of a more elaborate development of the distinction between efficient and potential causes.[7] In 1939 this concept was incorporated

---

2. This type of statute has been used especially in relation to life insurance. See, *e.g.,* N.Y. Ins. Law § 142(3) (McKinney 1966).

3. See generally Patterson, Essentials of Insurance Law 272–309 (2d ed. 1957). Comments in the text here are adapted from my review of Patterson's book, 36 Texas L.Rev. 545 (1958).

4. N.Y. Ins. Law § 150 (McKinney 1966).

5. Patterson, *The Apportionment of Business Risks Through Legal Devices,* 24 Colum.L.Rev. 335, 340–341 (1924):

"Here [by the conditions or warranties in fire insurance policies] the risk is defined in terms, not of *efficient* but of

potential causes. For instance, the fire insurer does not attempt to exclude the risk of fire caused by ten gallons of gasoline by inserting a provision that no liability is assumed by him for fire *actually* so caused; he stipulates that if such a quantity of gasoline is on the insured premises—that is, is a *potential* cause—no liability is assumed. Thus he avoids the juridical risk of interpretation of a risk defined in terms of efficient cause, as well as the juridical risk of not being able to prove that the gasoline was the actual cause of the fire."

6. 252 N.Y. 449, 169 N.E. 642 (1930).

7. Patterson, *Warranties in Insurance Law,* 34 Colum.L.Rev. 595, 600 & n.27 (1934).

into the New York statute governing warranties, drafted by Patterson.[8]

A warranty, in a succinct statement of Patterson's concept, is a "clause in an insurance contract that prescribes, as a condition of the insurer's liability, the existence of a fact affecting the risk." [9] It is to be contrasted with a "coverage" clause, one example of which is an exception.[10] "The warranty . . . seeks to exclude *potential* causes of an insured event; the exception . . . excludes certain *actual* causes of an insured event."[11]

A statement of this contrast in several forms may help to clarify it. The condition of liability imposed by warranty can be seen as one concerning:

One: Potential cause of loss.

Two: The existence of a fact affecting risk that an insured event will occur.

Three: Amelioration of the risk.[12]

Four: Suspension of coverage irrespective of the cause of loss.[13] (A suspensive condition is usually a "while" clause, *e.g.,* a clause saying the life insurer is not liable for death occurring while the insured is engaged in specified aviation.)

In contrast a coverage provision can be seen as one concerning:

One: Actual cause of loss.

Two: The existence of a fact determining whether an insured event has occurred.

Three: Identification of the risk.[14]

Four: Scope of coverage as determined by cause of loss.[15] (*E.g.,* a clause saying the life insurer is not liable for death caused by specified aviation.)

The New York statute states that any provision that purports to relieve the company of liability upon the occurrence of a specified state of facts tending to increase the risk of loss within the contract coverage *is a warranty and that breach of warranty* is no defense unless the breach of such provision materially increased the risk of loss within the coverage.[16]

One fairly minor objection to the New York statute lies in the decision to use, and define in a new way, the term "warranty." The use of "warranty" is not essential to the statutory rule. The concept

8.   Ch. 882, § 150, [1939] Laws of New York 2636. See also Patterson, Essentials of Insurance Law 275 n.9 (2d ed. 1957).

9.   Patterson, Essentials of Insurance Law 308 (2d ed. 1957).

10.   *Id.* at 230, 273.

11.   *Id.* at 273 (emphasis by Patterson).

12.   *Id.* at 282–283.

13.   *Id.* at 254.

14.   *Id.* at 230–231.

15.   *Id.* at 249.

16.   N.Y. Ins. Law § 150 (McKinney 1966).

identified in the statute as a warranty might just as well have been called "X," or the label might have been omitted altogether. The preceding paragraph might be read without the phrases in italics; the meaning is the same. Why then give such a new definition to the old term "warranty," long used in different senses and bound to be so used still by those not converted to the new faith? May not the incomplete acceptance of this terminology heap new confusions on the old? This result seems especially likely if the new terminology is urged upon courts, writers, lawyers, and insurance men by persuasion rather than by statute, for substantial inconsistency of usage even within a single jurisdiction is thus almost certain to follow.

Such difficulties are compounded because the concept of warranty has been invoked in relation to other problems of insurance law in addition to the major one considered here. Three problems deserve particular mention. First, can a defense raised by an insurer be enforced despite incontestability statutes?[17] Second, how is the defense affected by waiver, estoppel, and election?[18] Third, will the insurer's payment in spite of the availability of a defense restrict its subrogation rights by relegating it to the status of a volunteer?[19] Can Patterson's definition of warranty be appropriately carried over into these contexts? Probably not (as indicated below in relation to the first two questions),[20] and therefore, at the least, additional definitions must be used. Better, the common references to warranty in these contexts might be declared inappropriate. Moreover, any variety of definitional approach is probably inapt in these contexts; the answers to the questions posed should in most instances depend on factors that do not correlate well with the nature of the provision upon which the insurer rests his defense.

More important than the terminology is the substance of the distinction at which the New York statute and Patterson's definition of warranty are aimed. In this respect, Patterson's contribution deserves high praise as clearly the most careful and orderly statement that can be found in any of the statutes having comparable aims or in writings concerning such statutes. Even with this contribution, however, there remain substantial difficulties in applying the New York statute.

One of these difficulties is that though all provisions concerning *actual cause* of loss are coverage provisions, not all provisions concerning *potential cause* of loss are warranties; as Patterson himself recognized, some of the latter are coverage provisions. That is, although the coverage of the policy can be partly defined in terms of actual causes of loss, provisions defining coverage can also refer to

17. See Patterson, Essentials of Insurance Law 280–281 (2d ed. 1957). See also § 6.5(d) *infra*.

18. See Patterson, Essentials of Insurance Law 506, 530–533 (2d ed. 1957). See also § 6.6(b) *infra*.

19. See Patterson, Essentials of Insurance Law 149 (2d ed. 1957). See also § 3.10(b) (1) *supra*.

20. See §§ 6.5(d), 6.6(b) *infra*.

potential causes. For example, the typical fire insurance policy on personalty designates certain premises as the location of the property. This clause is properly considered a coverage provision, as courts generally hold, because it serves to identify the subject matter of the policy. In the language of the New York statute, it is one of the elements of "the coverage of the contract,"[21] even though the location of the goods does affect the risk of occurrence of a loss within the coverage. Of course, provisions describing location are not always intended to serve the function of identification. To take Patterson's own example, "where *specified* personal property is insured at a given location, the correct interpretation of the contract seems to be that the location is not an essential term of identification, that at most it is a warranty of a fact relating to the risk as a potential cause . . . . ."[22] Thus the potential-cause versus actual-cause distinction expressed in the New York statute must be supplemented— again, as Patterson apparently advocated—by a functional analysis of whether a provision that in fact relates to potential cause of loss was intended to serve the purpose of identification.

It is no easy task to devise a test for distinguishing warranties, in Patterson's sense, from potential-cause provisions that are coverage clauses because of the functions they serve. Any test that operates with a high degree of precision will in some instances operate inconsistently with the underlying purpose of guarding against overreaching by insurers. On the other hand, a test stated simply in terms of this general purpose will be vague and difficult to apply in a considerable body of marginal cases. No solution entirely escapes both these difficulties. Arguably Patterson's approach is the best so far developed. Yet in the troublesome cases in which it is necessary to distinguish warranties from clauses that, though concerning potential cause of loss, appear to serve the function of coverage clauses, perhaps it will be best, despite objections of vagueness and generality, to resort to a test that is purposive in a broader sense than that necessarily implied in Patterson's urging a "functional" analysis. One might ask whether the clause under study is likely to serve as an instrument of overreaching, or whether instead it concerns a fact that the ordinary insured would realize was significant for insurance purposes. This standard appears to be consistent with both Patterson's objective and his functional test for achieving it, as far as he developed that approach.

Stepping back momentarily from the New York statute, one may say that its basic technique—distinguishing coverage from other clauses and protecting insured's only with respect to the latter—suggests by negative implication that overreaching is not a significant danger with respect to coverage clauses. Although it is probably true that coverage clauses, on account of their prominence and cen-

21. N.Y. Ins. Law § 150(1) (McKinney 1966); See Patterson, Essentials of Insurance Law 296–297 (2d ed. 1957).

22. See Patterson, Essentials of Insurance Law 297 (2d ed. 1957) (emphasis in original).

trality to a policy, are less susceptible to abuse than other clauses (the distinction is in this respect far more valid than that between "warranties" and "representations"), nonetheless statutes in several states reflect a legislative judgment that the evils of misleading policy clauses extend in some degree to coverage provisions as well as warranties. Thus, it has been thought desirable to restrict the use of some kinds of coverage clauses in life insurance. In New York[23] and elsewhere[24] statutes have restricted the use of provisions against liability for death caused in a specified manner or while the insured occupies a specified status.[25]

Such a legislative judgment appears also to be one of the factors supporting provisions for compulsory standardization of insurance contracts,[26] insofar as they extend to coverage provisions as well as warranties. Moreover, some judicial applications of the principles of honoring reasonable expectations and disallowing unconscionable advantage are responsive to the need for controlling coverage clauses.[27]

(3) WARRANTY STATUTES OF OTHER STATES

A number of states have statutes providing generally, though with variations in detail, that no false representation or warranty shall defeat a claim of coverage unless, for example, the representation or warranty was made with intent to deceive or increased the risk of loss. More often than not such statutes contain no definition of the operative terms.

What is the meaning of "representation" and "warranty" as used in these statutes? It is unnecessary, of course, to distinguish between representations and warranties in this context. Together they occupy a middle ground between what are commonly called coverage provisions and statements or promises the falsity of which would in no circumstances affect the enforceability of the insurance contract. In comparison with the problem of distinguishing warranties from coverage clauses, relatively few problems have arisen with respect to drawing the dividing line between representations and these latter kinds of statements or promises.

To illustrate the confusion that arises under these statutes, consider a policy stipulation that insured property shall not be mortgaged. Some courts have sustained the insurer's defense upon proof of a violation of a chattel mortgage clause suspending liability "during

---

23. See N.Y. Ins. Law § 155(2) (McKinney 1966).

24. *E.g.*, Tex.Ins.Code Ann. art. 3.45 (1963).

25. Such a statute may, however, permit a clause allowing a recovery in the nature of a return of the reserve value (or the somewhat larger sum of the premiums paid), rather than the face amount in specified circumstances—for example, in case of suicide or

in case of death resulting from military service.

26. As in the statutory prescription of the fire insurance form, N.Y. Ins. Law § 168 (McKinney 1966). See generally § 2.10 *supra*.

27. Consider, for example, the treatment of policy provisions regarding "accidental means," discussed in § 6.-3(b) *supra*.

the time" of an impermissible encumbrance, holding the chattel mortgage clause to be a coverage provision, not a warranty.[28] Such an interpretation is clearly contrary to the New York statute's explicit definition of warranty (Patterson's concept), with the consequence that, in New York, breach would provide a good defense only if materiality were proved. The meaning of warranty assumed in such opinions is contrary also to the prevailing idea that the primary significance of warranty in insurance law is as a condition of the insurer's promise; that is, rejection of this prevailing idea is commonly implicit in opinions holding that a statute regulating warranties does not apply to a chattel mortgage clause.[29]

As this example also illustrates, the confusing variations among courts are increased by the distinction sometimes drawn—under statutes that do not define their operative terms—between a warranty and a condition precedent, the latter being held enforceable without regard to materiality or deceit.[30] Of course compliance with a warranty is by definition a condition precedent, if that phrase is used to include all prerequisites of liability. And if the phrase were construed to mean only those prerequisites the absence of which would determine that no coverage under the policy ever became effective,[31] it still would include some provisions commonly treated as warranties within the scope of these statutes. Thus it must be that the phrase is being used as one of art, with a meaning different from both of these. The distinction intended is rarely if ever systematically expounded by the courts that draw it.[32]

Other instances of uncertainty concern the questions whether these regulatory statutes apply to misrepresentation in presenting a claim as distinguished from misrepresentation in the negotiation of the contract,[33] and to violations of moral hazard clauses.[34]

28. *E.g.*, Moe v. Allemannia Fire Ins. Co., 209 Wis. 526, 244 N.W. 593 (1932). For disputed interpretations of *Moe* see the majority and dissenting opinions in Emmco Ins. Co. v. Palatine Ins. Co., 263 Wis. 558, 58 N.W.2d 525 (1953).

29. See, *e.g.*, Moe v. Allemannia Fire Ins. Co., 209 Wis. 526, 244 N.W. 593 (1932), in which the court reasons that no warranty or representation was made, the insured not having represented that the property was free from encumbrance and not having warranted that it would remain so. This reasoning suggests that "warranty" connotes an assertion, affirmation, or promise by the insured rather than merely a qualification or condition of the insurer's promise.

30. See, *e.g.*, Krause v. Equitable Life Ins. Co., 333 Mass. 200, 129 N.E.2d 617 (1955).

31. *Cf.* Healy, *The Hull Policy: Warranties, Representations, Disclosures and Conditions*, 41 Tulane L.Rev. 245, 251 (1967): "In the law of insurance, a condition precedent is one which must be met before the attachment of the risk; a condition subsequent is one which must be maintained or met after the risk has attached, in order that the insurance contract may remain in force."

32. *Compare Krause*, n.30 *supra, with* Mutual Life Ins. Co. v. Mandelbaum, 207 Ala. 234, 92 So. 440 (1922), 29 A.L.R. 649 (1924).

33. See § 7.2(b) *infra*.

34. See § 6.5(e) (3) *infra*.

The absence of coherent exposition is characteristic of decisions applying statutes of the type we have been considering. As a consequence, analysis of the results reached in relation to common kinds of policy clauses usually will guide the practitioner better than analysis of what courts say generally about the meaning of warranties, either in this context or in others.[35]

§ 6.5(c) REGULATORY STANDARDS

(1) DECEIT PROVISIONS

Several state statutes permit a defense of misrepresentation or false warranty only on proof of intent to deceive or a resultant "increase in risk."[1] The difficult problem of giving content to the concept of increase in the risk will be considered in the next subsection. At this point we turn to separate problems concerning intent to deceive.

Is fraudulent, immaterial misrepresentation a ground for avoidance of an insurance contract? Are these regulatory statutes to be construed as so declaring, regardless of what the answer may have been under common law decisions?

Although many judicial opinions contain dicta that fraud is a defense without regard to materiality,[2] and literal interpretation of some statutes would seem to support this result, Patterson found no case in which, on the facts, under either statutory or decisional rules, "a clearly immaterial misrepresentation was held to be fatal merely because fraudulent."[3] In exceptional instances there is statutory phrasing, such as "in the absence of fraud," supporting the construction that the statute makes no prescription for cases of fraud (whether material or not) rather than a prescription by negative implication.[4] But even in the absence of such a phrase, consideration

---

35. For such an analysis in relation to some common policy clauses, see § 6.-5(e) infra.

1. E.g., Ala.Code tit. 28, § 6 (1958); Mass.Gen.Laws Ann. ch. 175, § 186 (1958); Wis.Stat. § 209.06(1) (1967).

2. See, e.g., Campbell v. Prudential Ins. Co., 15 Ill.2d 308, 155 N.E.2d 9 (1959).

3. Patterson Essentials of Insurance Law 433 (2d ed. 1957). Cf. Johnson v. National Life Ins. Co., 123 Minn. 453, 457, 144 N.W. 218, 220 (1913):

"Some of the cases cited [construing statutes providing that no oral or written misrepresentation shall avoid a policy unless made with intent to deceive or unless the matter misrepresented increases the risk of loss] seem to hold that a misrepresentation made with intent to deceive and defraud, though the matter misrepresented is immaterial in character, avoids the policy. We do not stop to inquire how many, if any, directly and necessarily so hold. We cannot adopt such a doctrine. Long prior to the statute this court held that a fraudulent misrepresentation of an immaterial matter did not avoid the policy; and the 1895 law was not intended to make the insurer's liability less."

4. See, e.g., Tex.Ins.Code Ann. art. 3.-44(4) (1963), declaring that life insurance policies shall contain a provision "[t]hat all statements made by the insured shall, in the absence of fraud, be deemed representations and not warranties." This interpretation is fortified by id. art. 21.18, declaring that recovery under a life, accident, or health insurance policy shall not be defeated because of a misrepresenta-

of statutory purpose points to the conclusion that the statute should not be read as creating a new defense for the insurer. It seems likely that, as Patterson found at the time of his search, there will continue to be a dearth of holdings that immaterial misrepresentation is a defense.

The converse problem has been presented often—that is, whether under such a statute a material misrepresentation is a good defense for the insurer even though it was made in good faith. An affirmative answer is supported not only by literal construction of the statute but also, it would seem, by a fair analysis of the statutory purpose.[5] That is, policyholders can properly be expected to anticipate that coverage would be suspended for a violation if it materially increased the risk (or, a fortiori, if it caused the loss), regardless of the absence of intent to deceive. Nonetheless, some decisions seem in result to have converted the statutory word "or" to "and," requiring both materiality and intent to deceive.[6]

(2) CONTRIBUTE-TO-LOSS AND INCREASE-OF-RISK PROVISIONS

Apart from the intent-to-deceive criterion, statutory standards fall into two major classes with respect to what an insurer must show, if anything more than violation of a policy provision, to sus-

---

tion "which is of an immaterial fact and which does not affect the risks assumed."

5. *Cf.* Campbell v. Prudential Ins. Co., 15 Ill.2d 308, 155 N.E.2d 9 (1959).

6. Arguably Metropolitan Life Ins. Co. v. Burno, 309 Mass. 7, 33 N.E.2d 519 (1941), is such a case. The company filed a bill to "rescind and cancel" a policy of life insurance issued by plaintiff on the life of Burno. One ground of relief was that Burno made a false answer "no" to a question, purportedly addressed to him by the medical examiner for plaintiff, asking whether he had ever had any disease of the stomach. The trial judge found that Burno had cancer of the stomach but did not know that fact at the time of the answer or before the policy was issued. A second ground of relief was that Burno made a false answer "none" to a question concerning what clinics and physicians he had consulted within five years. The trial judge found this answer false because Burno had consulted a physician shortly before making application, complaining of belching gas, stomachache, heartburn, and constipation. He also found, however, that plaintiff insurer had not proved an actual intent to deceive or an increase

in the risk of loss. From a decree dismissing the bill, the plaintiff insurer appealed; thereafter Burno died and the executrix of his will was made a defendant. Held, decree affirmed.

Arguably, the question whether the insured had suffered from any disease of the stomach, when addressed to a layman, called for no more than the layman's state of mind — his knowledge and belief on a matter as to which he might not know the objective facts. But the answer concerning clinics and physicians consulted cannot be explained in this way. However, the authority of *Burno* appears to have been undermined by Pahigian v. Manufacturers' Life Ins. Co., 349 Mass. 78, 206 N.E.2d 660 (1965), 18 A. L.R.3d 749 (1968). In *Pahigian*, the policyholder had been hospitalized several times within two years before the policy application and treated for Hodgkins disease, of which he subsequently died. Without discussing whether misrepresentations concerning his medical history were intentional, and expressly declining to follow *Burno*, the court held that the misrepresentations increased the risk of loss as a matter of law and entitled the insurance company to avoid the policy.

tain a defense. One is that the violation must increase the risk.[7] The other is that the violation must contribute to the loss. A few statutes invoke both these standards in the alternative. The dominance of these two standards invites comparative analysis and raises common questions of interpretation. This discussion will proceed first to the comparison.

Referring again to the general purpose of these statutes—to bar technical, immaterial defenses—one may note that the strongest showing of materiality is proof that the breach contributed to the loss. Although statutes requiring this showing thus go farthest toward protecting insureds,[8] they sacrifice other interests in doing so.

First, a contribute-to-loss standard of materiality tends to produce an inequity in rate structure. Insurers will sometimes lack proof that a violation contributed to a loss, even when it in fact did so. From the insurer's point of view, because of this juridical risk it is more expensive to service the contracts of those policyholders who engage in policy violations than to service the contracts of those who conform; the risk that the company undertakes for those who commit policy violations is somewhat higher than the risk it undertakes for others. Despite this, the same premiums are paid by the two groups. Of course one might argue that this discrimination is justified on the same basis as any other rate classification that is broad enough to include some persons whose risks are greater than others within the same classification.[9] Also, similar inequities probably arise from juridical risks under any standard of liability. For example, if the decisive question is merely whether a violation of policy terms has occurred, the nonviolators help to pay for the losses of those violators whose violations cannot be proved. The effect of the juridical risks on equity of the rate structure is undoubtedly greater, however, under a contribute-to-loss statute than under an increase-of-risk statute. In cases of fire loss, for example, the evidence needed to prove that a violation contributed to the loss will often be destroyed by the fire. In any event it is so much more difficult to prove contribution to loss than increase of risk that a much higher percentage of cases will be decided by lack of adequate evidence if the former is the decisive issue.

---

7. The phrase "materially affected" the risk or a variant, e.g., Ill.Rev.Stat. ch. 73, § 766 (1969), sometimes used instead of a phrase "increased" the risk, is apparently intended to convey the same meaning, since an insurer is in no position to complain about a statement that has a material bearing on risk, but in a way that pictures the risk as more substantial than if a true statement had been made.

8. It may be theoretically possible for a breach to contribute to loss (thus sustaining the insurer's defense) though not having increased the risk. See n.20 infra. In such an instance, a contribute-to-loss standard would be less favorable to the policyholder than an increase-of-risk standard. But even if the standards as interpreted create this theoretical possibility, the occasions of its occurrence in fact would be very rare.

9. See § 8.4(b) infra.

Rate pattern inequity caused by a contribute-to-loss standard may also hinder the structuring of insurance so as to enable a purchaser to buy just what he needs. For example, under a contribute-to-loss standard, it is less likely that an insurer can afford to sell to the owner of a building with an especially fire-resistant roof a policy covering his relatively lower risk at a charge reduced in full proportion to the reduction of risk. If it did so while not incurring the cost of inspections before underwriting, it would be collecting only this lower rate from other policyholders who misrepresented the construction of their roofs, some of whom would nevertheless be able to collect for loss to which the flammability of the roof contributed, since the insurer might be unable to prove contribution to loss.

Others factors also favor the choice of an increase-of-risk over a contribute-to-loss standard. The latter standard can be expected to generate more wasteful litigation of disputed facts than the former. Also, an insured may be more likely to avoid violating a warranty if he knows that the insurer need only show increased risk in order to defeat liability. If insureds were thus to take fewer chances, the result should be not only a reduction in insured losses but also a reduction in losses generally.

A more sophisticated comparison of these regulatory standards depends on the meaning assigned to the concepts "increase of risk" and "contribution to loss." For example, does "contribute" suggest merely that a violation must be one among connected antecedents of the loss, or is the term used in some narrower sense? Consider a case involving collision coverage on a truck under a policy including a clause stating that the truck is not to be driven beyond a radius 500 miles from a designated point of principal garaging. If the truck is in a collision while on the last 100 miles of the return leg of a 1050 mile round trip, should the travel slightly beyond the permitted radius be said to have "contributed" to the loss? Or must something more be proved, such as that the added hour of driving the extra fifty miles had put an extra strain on the driver by reason of which he made a mistake he would not otherwise have made? Would it make a difference that the accident occurred 150 miles from final destination, at which point the driver would ordinarily be less tired than during the last fifty miles of the return from a trip to the edge of the radius and back? Would proof that the trip would not have been made but for the violation be decisive? What would be the effect of an insurer's showing that in the aggregate truckers who permitted trips beyond the radius made more trips, or more tiring trips, than otherwise? Would such proof of increase of risk, in one of the possible senses of that phrase, be evidence also that the particular violation contributed to the particular loss? Alternatively, a court might construe the radius clause as requiring that the vehicle be beyond the stipulated radius at the time of a collision. But suppose the truck is properly parked, although outside the 500-mile radius, when struck by a car out of control. Might it be held that since the radius clause concerns movement of the vehicle, implicitly it applies only when the vehicle is in operation and not when it is parked? Or might it be said that even though the violation continued as long as the vehicle was beyond the radius, it did not "contribute" because the presence of the vehicle in a legitimate parking place was a purely passive rather than contributory factor?

As a general answer to these difficulties, it seems likely that courts will attribute a rather broad meaning to terms like "contribute." A narrower meaning would push to an even greater extreme the effect of statutes that are already among the most extreme of regulatory measures in the extent to which they protect policyholders from the consequences of violating policy stipulations.

Similar disputes may arise over the meaning of "risk" in statutes using the increase-of-risk formula. Closely analogous definitional difficulties have arisen under the standard "increase-of-hazard" clause in fire insurance policies. It is difficult, if not impossible, to discover any significance in the difference between "hazard" and "risk." One might nonetheless expect to find differences in interpretation, reflecting the different contexts and purposes giving rise to the two formulations. With due awareness of such possible variations, it is instructive to consider together the problems of construing these parallel phrases.

In many cases there can be no doubt about increase of risk or hazard. For example, if a building that is the subject of a fire insurance policy is declared to be in use as a residence and during the policy term the policyholder establishes a dry cleaning business on the premises, using highly inflammable cleaning fluids, probably no court would hesitate to find an increase of risk.[10] And, when automobile insurers are customarily charging higher premiums to a policyholder if there is a driver under 25 years of age in his household, plainly the fact that among those who drive the car there is such a person, contrary to the policyholder's representation, increases the risk on the basis of which the policy is written.[11] Conversely, it is not

10. *Cf.* Fleet v. National Fire Ins. Co., 167 La. 74, 118 So. 697 (1928) (building and outbuilding, insured under a dwelling policy, burned while in use for dance hall and gambling purposes; premiums for insuring buildings so used would have been four and a half times those for insuring a dwelling); Progress Spinning & Knitting Mills Co. v. Southern Nat'l Ins. Co., 42 Utah 263, 130 P. 63 (1913) (building insured as water power woolen mill used to manufacture "cotton bats," an operation that, according to evidence introduced, could be conducted safely only in a fireproof building). See generally 4A Appleman, Insurance Law § 2579 (rev. ed. 1969); Annot., 19 A.L.R.3d 1336 (1968).

11. *E.g.*, Stockinger v. Central Nat'l Ins. Co., 24 Wis.2d 245, 128 N.W.2d 433 (1964) (insurer not liable under collision coverage for value of car destroyed when driven into a tree by the insured's nineteen-year-old son). See generally Annot., 29 A.L.R.3d 1139 (1970). *Cf.* Fierro v. Foundation Reserve Ins. Co., 81 N.M. 225, 465 P.2d 282 (1970) (fully retroactive cancellation of automobile insurance after accident because of misrepresentations, in application, of no cancellation within previous 36 months; held for insurer; applicant bound by application he signed, regardless of who filled it out) [concerning the binding effect of false answers written into the application by an agent, however, see § 6.7(b) *infra*]; Odom v. Insurance Co. of the State of Pa., 455 S.W.2d 195 (Tex.1970) (questions, in application attached to and made part of automobile policy, whether within 36

likely that a court would hesitate about declaring that there is no increase of risk, even if there is a violation of the principal-place-of-garaging clause, when the policyholder changes the place of garaging his car to a territory with the same or a lower rate as to each of the coverages under the policy. One need not be precise about the meaning of risk he applies in answering such questions as these.

There are instances, however, in which the choice among debatable meanings of risk can be decisive. Precedents provide relatively little guidance. In part, perhaps, this comes about because the question of materiality calls for an evaluative finding [12] and there is a tendency to treat it as a fact question,[13] often without explicit consideration of the criterion of materiality that the factfinder should employ.

One important question of interpretation common to both the increase-of-risk type of regulatory statute and the increase-of-hazard provision in fire insurance policies concerns the degree and duration of the increased risk sufficient to trigger the two tests. Although the problems are analytically similar, the question arises under the two standards in somewhat different ways.

The fire insurance clause provides that the insurer "shall not be liable for loss occurring (a) while the hazard is increased by any means within the control or knowledge of the insured   .   .   .   ."[14] Plainly this stipulation should not be and is not literally construed. Risk and hazard are concepts concerned with estimation of the probability of harm on the basis of incomplete data.[15] Since the data are constantly changing, sometimes to make the situation appear safer and at other times more dangerous, it is virtually

---

preceding months insured had been convicted of any moving traffic violations or had been involved in any accidents; false negative answers written into an application by agent; declaratory judgment for insurer affirmed; applicant knew or had means of knowing that such statements were in application and were false; case distinguished from precedents not involving attachment of application to policy; delivery of copy of application though not as part of policy, also gives policyholder means of knowing of answers and binds him, and a precedent to the contrary is overruled); Utica Mut. Ins. Co. v. National Indem. Co., 210 Va. 769, 173 S.E.2d 855 (1970) (application for automobile insurance; negative answer to question asking for a list of "impairments"; applicant had epilepsy by reason of which his license to drive had been disallowed for a period ending shortly before application; renewal policy issued a little more than a year later; accident during epileptic sei-

zure; held, for insurer, declaring policy void ab initio).

12. Concerning evaluative findings generally, see § 1.6 *supra*.

13. See, *e.g.*, Mayflower Ins. Exch. v. Gilmont, 280 F.2d 13 (9th Cir. 1960), 89 A.L.R.2d 1019 (1963) (Oregon Law; issue of materiality of representations concerning license revocations or suspensions, driving charges and fines, and previous insurance in application for automobile insurance; held, a question of fact for the jury). *But cf.* Mutual of Omaha Ins. Co. v. Echols, 207 Va. 949, 154 S.E.2d 169 (1967) (erroneous statement in application with resulting nondisclosure of fainting spells; held, material, the issue being one for the court, not the jury).

14. N.Y. Ins. Law § 168(6) (McKinney 1966).

15. See generally § 1.2(b)(1) *supra*.

certain that during a major portion of the policy period there would be some increase of hazard above the minimum existing at another time during the period. It is clear that the increase-of-hazard clause of the fire insurance policy will not be construed to mean that such fluctuations would necessarily violate it. One obvious way of avoiding such an untenable rule is to require that in some sense the policyholder must be responsible for any increased hazard, or to require that the increase result from actual changes in the condition of the insured premises, rather than merely from new data about previously existing conditions. These readings would not, however, avoid the further difficulty of suspending coverage for any slight increase of hazard caused by the policyholder. Thus, a court might require that to qualify as an increase of hazard within the meaning of a policy clause the increase must be substantial. Such a rule is supported by precedent.[16] The need to avoid suspension of coverage upon any violation that trivially increases risk exists also in relation to increase-of-risk statutes. Probably the rule requiring that an increase of risk be "substantial" should apply here as well.[17] An alternative way of meeting the same problem, under both provisions, is to hold that the fluctuation must result from a use of the property not within the "contemplation of the contracting parties."[18]

A corollary of these requirements concerning the substantiality of increased risk is that the increase should in most instances persist for some substantial period of time. In fact there is much case support for the proposition that to invoke successfully the increase-of-hazard clause an insurer must show that the increase was not "temporary."[19] Probably the intended meaning of these decisions is

---

16. *E.g.*, Smith v. Peninsular Ins. Co., 181 So.2d 212 (Fla.App.1965), 19 A.L. R.3d 1326 (1968) (judgment on jury verdict for insured under charge that, to be a defense, a change in occupancy must result in "material and substantial increase in hazard"); *cf.* Nathan v. St. Paul Mut. Ins. Co., 243 Minn. 430, 441, 68 N.W.2d 385, 393 (1955) (statement, in applying for $12,000 fire insurance, that building was unencumbered; a mechanic's lien for $200 had been filed; "[i]t can hardly be said, under those circumstances, that this factor would increase the risk by reducing [the insured's] pecuniary interest in the property, thereby increasing the moral hazard").

17. See, *e.g.*, Mutual Benefit Health & Acc. Ass'n v. McCranie, 178 F.2d 745, 747 (5th Cir. 1949) (judgment for insurer, applying Georgia statute concerning materiality of misrepresentations in life insurance application; dictum that "*substantial* increase in risk" is required (emphasis in origi-

nal), *quoting from* Preston v. National Life & Acc. Ins. Co., 196 Ga. 217, 237, 26 S.E.2d 439, 450 (1943)).

18. *Cf.* Hartford Fire Ins. Co. v. Chenault, 137 Ky. 753, 756, 126 S.W. 1098, 1099 (1910) (building insured as barn; storage of tobacco did not constitute a violation, since this was one of the purposes for which barns in the area were commonly used); Aurora Fire Ins. Co. v. Eddy, 55 Ill. 213, 221 (1870) (building insured as flax factory; installing and operating machinery for manufacturing rope held to be a "usual part of the business" of a flax factory).

19. *E.g.*, Orient Ins. Co. v. Cox, 218 Ark. 804, 812, 238 S.W.2d 757, 761 (1951), 26 A.L.R.2d 799, 806 (1952) (judgment on verdict for insured reversed because of error in instructions; rejected insurer's contention that eighteen or twenty scattered containers of gasoline, altogether over fifteen gallons, violated increase-of-hazard clause as a matter of law;

better conveyed by the term "transitory." Rather than brevity of duration, "temporary" suggests only lack of permanence—which surely should not be required in most instances when the increased risk is substantial.

Unlike a finding of insubstantiality, a finding that the increase was transitory should probably not in itself defeat an insurer's defense. For example, it may be that a very severe increase would qualify as an increase of hazard or risk, though quite transitory, especially if the risk resulted from a use of the insured premises inconsistent with customary use of similar property or, a fortiori, if loss occurred because of that use.[20] Of course, by the explicit terms of the policy clause, the defense would be available only as to losses occurring during the continuance of the violation. Against such a loss, the defense should be recognized without proof that the violation contributed to the loss. Not requiring proof of causality is, after all, a primary characteristic of the increase-of-risk formulation.

Another question of interpretation common to the two provisions is this: does "risk" or "hazard" refer to a net risk (in which case, for example, an increase from the specified circumstances constituting a violation, such as storage of prohibited combustibles, may be offset by decreases from, say, addition of automatic sprinklers). Or does it instead refer only to the effect of a prohibited use, without regard to offsetting changes of circumstance? It would seem that a narrower meaning than the total of all risks under the policy is intended. A policyholder should not be permitted to defeat the defense by showing that his risk-increasing violation was outweighed by risk-ameliorating steps he was not required to take. The kinds of changes in circumstances that an insured might raise in mitigation of a violation are countless, and case-by-case comparative evaluation of total risk would be extremely expensive and wasteful. Moreover to forgive violations on such an ad hoc basis would often make decisions turn on the resolution of closely balanced issues of fact and highly debatable evaluations of risk. The unpredictability of results would work against one of the primary goals of insurance regulation stated earlier: to maximize equity among insureds as well as between insureds and insurers.

"casual or temporary change in the use or condition of the insured property will not ordinarily be sufficient to avoid the policy").

20. If it were held that there was no increase of risk in such a case because of the transitory nature of the increase, the contribute-to-loss standard would be potentially broader in relation to cases of transitory increase, though much narrower generally, than the increase-of-risk standard. This would supply a justification for the clause, which appears in some regulatory statutes, that viola-tion of a policy provision shall not be a defense unless it is either "material to the risk or actually contributed to the [loss]." See, e.g., Tex.Ins.Code Ann. art. 21.16 (1963); Wis.Stat. § 209.06(1) (1967). On the other hand, if "risk" were considered to refer to the risk, whether transitory or not, from specified circumstances (for example, the risk from storing prohibited combustibles), then one could not prove contribution without also proving increase in risk: the violation must have increased the risk of just such a loss.

The core question, of course, remains: what is meant by "increase of risk" and "hazard," assuming we are concerned with only substantial increases in risk that arise from specific violations or aberrant uses, regardless of changes in net risk from all circumstances. The formula "increase of risk" is undefined, and there is no better general guide to its meaning than the broad statutory purpose— to protect against unconscionable advantage while honoring reasonable expectations. Posing a few of the many difficulties that may arise in interpreting these words should suffice to illustrate this central point. For example, is an increase of risk to be determined from the point of view of a standard or typical effect of a specific violation upon the risk assumed under policies of a given type or from the point of view of the effect of the violation upon the risk assumed under the individual policy, taking into account all the particulars of the situation of that policyholder? Or, should it be determined from some point of view different from both of these?

Perhaps considerations of predictability and economy of litigation would suggest that a standard or typical meaning is to be preferred over one that would involve detailed factual inquiries in each case. But the standard or typical meaning cannot treat alike all cases involving one "type" of provision, when the type is defined according to the specific act or use proscribed by the provision.

For example, consider the claim of a policyholder of fire insurance on an automobile that is destroyed by fire after he has mortgaged it without notice to the insurer. The size of a mortgage in relation to the value of the property would surely be relevant. In fact, sound precedents disallow a defense based on a mortgage trivial in amount.[21]

Consider also the meaning of "increase of risk" as applied to the collision radius clause discussed earlier, stating that the insured truck is not to be operated more than 500 miles from the designated place of garaging. Suppose the truck is driven for several weeks within a territory that lies partly within and partly without the prescribed area. Consider two different cases that may arise.

Suppose, first, that an accident occurs outside the permitted 500-mile radius. The insurer might argue that the violation increased risk—because, for example, the truck was driven more often than it otherwise would have been, or driven in an area unfamiliar to the driver. But if the territory of operation, outside the radius, is a lower-rate territory than the place of principal garaging, the insured might respond that because of this the violation reduced total risk. Permitting insureds to balance such effects would give rise to the same kinds of dislocations from sound insurance principles as would result if insureds were entitled to offset the risk-effects of violations against effects of other changes in circumstance.

21. *E.g.*, Nathan v. St. Paul Mut. Ins. Co., 243 Minn. 430, 68 N.W.2d 385 (1955) (mechanic's lien of $200 when applicant for $12,000 fire policy stated building was unencumbered).

Suppose, now, that the collision occurs within the prescribed area, but during a trip that began outside the 500-mile radius, after several weeks of local use there. Would the increase-of-risk statute permit an insurer to raise its defense, on the theory that the violation materially increased the risk of a collision occurring on the trip in which it occurred in fact? The insured might argue that the concept of a "single trip" cannot serve to distinguish the last few miles of the collision trip from later travel entirely within the 500-mile radius. Again, however, the insurer might respond that the violation increased the danger of collision by increasing the number of trips taken, or by tiring the driver.

One coherent approach to interpreting the increase-of-risk language could be fashioned with reference to statutory purpose. These statutes, it would seem, are aimed primarily at regulating policy clauses to disallow unconscionable advantages to insurers (and consistently with honoring policyholders' reasonable expectations). Therefore they are not intended to interfere with clauses defining the scope of the risk in a reasonable way, understandable to policyholders generally and having a substantial relation to what premiums are fairly to be charged for the coverage. Pursuing this approach, one might conclude that the underlying reason for the 500-mile radius clause is to avoid certain identifiable risks such as the greater exposure to accidents that generally occurs when a truck is used in long-distance trips or when a truck garaged in a thinly populated area is driven in a generally more congested area beyond the 500-mile radius. It might then be found that the violation did not increase the risk within the objectives of the 500-mile radius clause except for the long trips between the place of garaging and the point that was outside the 500-mile radius but within a lower-rate territory. In contrast, if the territory in which the truck was being driven was a highly congested high-rate area and the place of principal garaging was a thinly populated, low-rate area, it might be found that the violation had increased the risk within the objectives of the 500-mile radius clause throughout the period of use beyond the 500-mile radius as well as during the journey to and from.

One way to make clearer the approach to interpreting increase-of-risk statutes here recommended is to restate the basic question from yet another perspective. In fixing a standard for determining increase of risk, courts must choose a point of view from which the increase is to be determined. Is the standard subjective, based on the practices of the particular insurer, or is it objective? If objective, is the standard based on the customary practices of insurers (either in the particular community or more generally), or is it set by legislation and judicial decisions rather than by custom? Is the standard the same under different statutes and policy clauses?

This is a form of statement to which courts have long been accustomed. However, precedents on the issue are inconclusive generally, and there is conflict among the authorities. As one might expect, the choice with respect to increase-of-hazard clauses may be different than that under increase-of-risk statutes. Reasoning that the policy clause should be construed as the lay policyholder would read it, a court may apply a prudent-man standard.[22] In contrast, most precedents concerned with the application of regulatory statutes have adopted either a this-insurer or a prudent-insurer standard.[23]

In this latter context, particularly, the choice of standard emerged as a choice among rules of evidence. Under the common law doctrine making defenses of misrepresentation or concealment depend on materiality, Wigmore supported a this-insurer standard of materiality to risk.[24] A leading opinion by Judge (later Chief Justice) Taft appears to support in effect a prudent-insurer standard.[25] An-

---

22. See Note, *The Increase-of-Hazard Clause in the Standard Fire Insurance Policy*, 76 Harv.L.Rev. 1472, 1478–1480 (1963). But note that the insurer's point of view, expressed through the rate structure, may be treated as relevant. *Id.* at 1475–1478. Probably this would result in deviation from a prudent-layman standard in some cases.

23. See nn.24–31 *infra.*

24. Wigmore advanced the position that the question is, "in truth, Is the circumstance in question one which *would have influenced the insurer* (or promiser) to fix a higher rate of premium" or to refuse the insurance altogether. 7 Wigmore, Evidence § 1946, at 60 (3d ed. 1940) (emphasis is Wigmore's). The inquiry, therefore, is primarily one concerning the insurer's system of classification and "secondarily, the *usage of insurers* in the same community, because their custom will tend to show what the individual insurer's practice is, as conforming presumably to the local methods." *Ibid.* Wigmore disapproves of asking the question, though addressed to an expert witness, whether there was, in his opinion, an increase of risk. *Id.* at 59–60. He distinguishes "*actual* [or objectively real] *increase* of danger" from increase of danger "as determined by the insurer's classification of the various circumstances affecting the rate of premium," and declares that it is the latter, not the former, that is ordinarily the true issue. *Id.* at 60. But, he observes, "it may clearly appear in a given case that the phrase was *not* used with reference to the insurer's sense or classification, and that it is to be interpreted according to the sense used *by the insured, i.e.* the ordinary sense

of 'increase of risk,' which therefore is to be applied by the jury acting on the standards and knowledge of the average layman." *Id.* at 62. A dispute involving the increase-of-hazard clause may be such a case, since the standard clause requires that the increase be within the knowledge *of the insured,* suggesting that the standard may be the ordinary sense rather than the insurer's sense. *See ibid.*

See also Columbia Ins. Co. v. Lawrence, 35 U.S. (10 Pet.) 507, 516 (1836). Mr. Justice Story appears to choose a this-insurer standard by stating the question to be whether concealed facts about the title of property to be covered by a fire insurance policy "would have, or might have a real influence upon the underwriter, either not to underwrite at all, or not to underwrite except at a higher premium." *But cf.* Hare & Chase, Inc. v. National Sur. Co., 60 F.2d 909, 912 (2d Cir.), *cert. denied,* 287 U.S. 662 (1932), which appears to adopt a prudent-insured standard regarding facts concealed. One might reasonably distinguish concealment cases on the ground that the obligation to disclose facts not inquired about should be tested by a standard concerned with the insured's point of view, even if a different standard is used with respect to materiality under common law or statutory regulation of defenses based on misrepresentation.

25. Penn Mut. Life Ins. Co. v. Mechanics' Sav. Bank & Trust Co., 72 F. 413, 428–430 (6th Cir. 1896). Judge Taft's approval of questions concerning insurers' practices appears to be founded on acceptance of a prudent-insurer standard (in contrast with Wigmore's acceptance of a this-insurer standard and allowance of evidence of insurer's

other leading opinion, by Judge Richman of the Supreme Court of Indiana, says the test is whether "the facts if truly stated *might* reasonably have influenced the company in deciding whether it should reject or accept the risk,"[26] and again, "the final inquiry is what that company *might* reasonably have done."[27] If Judge Richman was deliberately drawing a distinction by using "might" rather than "would" as the modifier of "reasonably," his standard is in this respect more favorable to the insurer than a this-insurer standard, which would have required a showing of consistency with the company's practice rather than merely with what it might reasonably have chosen to do.[28] In another respect, however, Richman's standard is less favorable to the insurer since it requires a showing of reasonableness — requiring the court to invoke an objective test rather than employing only a this-insurer standard.

It has not been common for statutory draftsmen to express a clear choice among the various possible standards concerning the point of view from which materiality is determined. Such a choice was expressed, however — in favor of this-insurer standard — in the New York statute regarding misrepresentation.[29] It is puzzling that the statutory draftsman (Professor Patterson) phrased the materiality standard differently for the warranty statute. The latter statute[30] is silent on this question, unless the phrase "materially increased the risk of loss" is interpreted as implying either a prudent-insurer standard[31] or else a wholly different point of view (perhaps that of the court rather than an insurer, and perhaps with hindsight on judgment day rather than with hypothetical foresight before loss).

It may be that the difference between the misrepresentation and warranty statutes in this respect arose from the notion that representations are assertions of fact made to influence the insurer's action on the application, whereas warranties are continuing nonassertive conditions of liability, the prospective deviation from which would influence the underwriting decision in only a very indirect way, if at all.

practices as secondary evidence). Apparently Judge Taft would disapprove of some questions, directed to the conclusion of materiality as distinguished from the usage of insurers generally, that Wigmore would approve.

26. New York Life Ins. Co. v. Kuhlenschmidt, 218 Ind. 404, 420, 33 N.E.2d 340, 347 (1941), 135 A.L.R. 397, 405 (1941) (emphasis added).

27. 218 Ind. at 424–425, 33 N.E.2d at 348, 135 A.L.R. at 407 (emphasis added).

28. Perhaps this interpretation is rendered less plausible by the fact that the court was responding to a contention of the insurer that the issue was "what action appellant would have taken" as opposed to "what action other companies would have taken." 218 Ind. at 422, 33 N.E.2d at 347, 135 A.L.R. at 406. Thus it seems more likely that Judge Richman was stating "might reasonably have taken" as an added requirement beyond what the company conceded, rather than using "might" instead of "would" to soften the requirement.

29. N.Y. Ins. Law § 149 (McKinney 1966).

30. *Id.* § 150.

31. See Equitable Life Assur. Soc'y v. Milman, 291 N.Y. 90, 97, 50 N.E.2d 553, 554 (1943) (stating the test to be whether the facts in question "might reasonably affect the choice of the insurance company").

The contrast between applying an objective standard from the insurer's viewpoint in interpreting increase-of-risk provisions and applying an objective standard from the insured's viewpoint in interpreting increase-of-hazard clauses seems consistent with a purposive approach.

The increase-of-hazard clause is placed before policyholders in the policy itself, with the consequence that at least occasionally expectations will be based on the policyholder's reading it. Moreover, it seems consistent with honoring reasonable expectations (or even the narrower principle of resolving ambiguities against the draftsman) to construe increase of hazard from the policyholder's point of view; the clause requires that the increase be within his "control or knowledge." The increase-of-risk statutes, on the other hand, were enacted primarily to protect against unconscionable advantage, at a time when the broad principle of honoring reasonable expectations (as distinguished from a narrower principle of resolving ambiguities) was not openly recognized. It seems reasonable in this context of securing evenhanded treatment of policyholders to apply a prudent-insurer viewpoint in determining materiality to risk.

This kind of purposive approach seems appropriate not only to construction of the increase-of-risk provision but also to interpretation of the alternative wording discussed earlier, suspending coverage only as to violations that "contribute to the loss." This interpretation thus may suggest a way of meeting some of the difficulties raised earlier with respect to the "contribution" standard. Nonetheless, it remains unclear whether this approach will be generally adopted.

Closely related but distinguishable from the issue whether a this-insurer or a prudent-insurer standard applies is the question whether the insurer must, to establish a defense based on misrepresentation, prove reliance as well as materiality to risk. There is some precedent for an affirmative answer,[32] though the issue has rarely come into sharp focus. Perhaps proof of reliance is generally assumed to be a part of the proof of materiality to the risk under a particular contract. It seems especially likely that under a this-insurer standard it will be considered implicit that proof of reliance is part of the showing of materiality to this insurer. In any event, it would seem that reliance should be required not only under a this-insurer standard but also under a prudent-insurer standard. In the latter instance, the effect is that the insurer cannot defend successfully

32. See, *e.g.*, Praetorian Mut. Life Ins. Co. v. Sherman, 455 S.W.2d 201 (Tex. 1970) (false answer that applicant had not within the past five years consulted or been attended by any doctor; had done so at least 43 times, on some occasions for lung ailment; report of physical examination for insurance showed good health; died from lung cancer fifteen months later; jury found false answer was material to the risk and was made for purpose of "wrongfully inducing" issuance of policy; judgment for insurer reversed and remanded because of failure to obtain jury finding that insurer relied on the truth of the answer; opinion recognizes that insurer may rely partly on examination and partly on answers in application).

by proving that it relied — that applying its own rigorous standards and practices it would have declined the application if a truthful answer had been given — even though a "prudent insurer" would have treated the answer as immaterial.

§ 6.5(d) INCONTESTABILITY

Life insurance policies customarily contain a clause declaring that, subject to stated exceptions, the policy is incontestable after a specified period of time, ordinarily one or two years.[1] Such clauses are now commonly required by statute.[2] In some instances statutes extend the requirement to related types of coverage such as disability or health and accident insurance, and such clauses are sometimes included in these other types of policies even though not required by statute. Also, provisions similar to the incontestability clauses commonly used in life insurance policies but less favorable to policyholders sometimes appear in these other types of policies, either under statutory compulsion or by voluntary action of insurers.[3]

Apart from these statutory and voluntary provisions affecting life, disability, and accident coverages, there is no generally recognized principle of incontestability. There is limited support, however, for applying a somewhat similar principle to sustain recovery by a third-party victim under automobile insurance in exceptional circumstances.[4]

1. Incontestability clauses also commonly apply to applications for reinstatement of lapsed coverage, and it is usually held that the period of contestability commences to run anew for any defense based on the application for reinstatement. See, e.g., McCary v. John Hancock Mut. Life Ins. Co., 236 Cal.App.2d 501, 46 Cal.Rptr. 121 (1st Dist. 1965), 23 A.L.R.3d 733 (1969). See generally McCarthy, *Reinstatement: Misrepresentation and Incontestability: A Polysyllabic Puzzle,* 4 Forum 40 (ABA Section Ins., Neg. & Comp.L.1968).

2. See, e.g., N.Y. Ins. Law § 155(1) (b) (McKinney 1966). See also Salzman, *The Incontestable Clause in Life Insurance Policies,* 1969 Ins.L.J. 142.

3. See e.g., Bronson v. Washington Nat'l Ins. Co., 59 Ill.App.2d 253, 207 N.E.2d 172 (2d Dist. 1965), 13 A.L.R.3d 1375 (1967) (statute regulating disability insurance construed as less restrictive than corresponding statute regulating life insurance; disability insurer permitted to contest an action filed more than two years after date of policy for disability commencing within two years; clause provided that

after two years no misstatements in application could be used to void policy or to deny claim for disability commencing after two years); Taylor v. Metropolitan Life Ins. Co., 106 N.H. 455, 461–462, 214 A.2d 109, 114–115 (1965) ("time limit on certain defenses" clause in accident and sickness policy declaring that, as to disability commencing after two years from the date of issue, "no misstatements, except fraudulent misstatements, made by the applicant in the application for such policy shall be used to void the policy or to deny a claim;" held inapplicable to a claim of disability commencing within the two years, thus allowing a defense of nonfraudulent misstatement as to such claim though not raised in a judicial contest within two years from the date of issue).

4. See, e.g., Barrera v. State Farm Mut. Auto. Ins. Co., 71 Cal.2d 659, 456 P.2d 674, 79 Cal.Rptr. 106 (1969). In *Barrera,* the victim obtained judgment against the tortfeasor and sought payment from the insurer, which cross-complained for a declaration that the policy was void because issued in reliance on a material misrepresentation, in an application ten-

The potential defenses that incontestability statutes and clauses affect are almost entirely those based on warranty, representation, or concealment, even though the language of the statutes and clauses commonly includes no specific reference to these concepts.

Incontestability statutes are in one respect a more rigorous type of regulation than the usual statutes of the type that refer explicitly to warranties and representations. An incontestability statute unconditionally bars the potential defenses to which it refers unless the insurer has taken action that constitutes the institution of a contest [5] before the period of contestability has passed. The warranty-representation type of statute, on the other hand, continues to permit defenses based on breach of warranty or misrepresentation, subject to a condition of materiality in some sense.[6] But an incontestability statute is ordinarily far less comprehensive in scope than a warranty-representation type of statute because it applies only to life insurance or to life and closely related types of insurance, whereas many of the warranty-representation statutes apply to all kinds of insurance.

In those instances in which both types of statutes apply to a policy, a potential defense must clear the requirements of both statutes to be effective. One corollary of this proposition is that in such cases the materiality standard of the warranty-representation statute has practical significance only during the short period of contestability.

Under both types of statutes, it is either express or implicit that certain policy defenses — commonly called "coverage" defenses — are beyond the scope of the statutory regulation. The distinction between what is and what is not affected by the statutory scheme of regulation is extraordinarily difficult to formulate in relation to warranty-representation statutes, and perhaps only slightly less so in relation to incontestability statutes. The considerations bearing on the appropriate standards of distinction are quite similar, and precedents in one area have often influenced the development of the standard in the other.[7]

---

dered one and a half years before the accident, that the insured's driver's license had never been suspended. The trial court found that the insurer relied on the material misrepresentation and acted promptly to rescind upon discovery of it. The supreme court reversed, holding that because of the quasi-public nature of insurance and the public policy underlying the financial responsibility law, an automobile liability insurer has a duty reasonably to investigate an insured's insurability within a reasonable time after issuance of a policy. The insurer cannot "take advantage of a breach of its duty" for the purpose of avoiding liability to an innocent victim, though it may recover against the insured for misrepresentation or may defend against the insured if the insured sues after paying the tort judgment.

5. As to what constitutes the institution of a contest, see, *e.g.*, Franklin Life Ins. Co. v. Bieniek, 312 F.2d 365 (3d Cir. 1962), 95 A.L.R.2d 407 (1964) (Pennsylvania law; letter denying liability insufficient; court proceedings required).

6. See, *e.g.*, N.Y. Ins. Law § 150 (McKinney 1966); § 6.5(b) (2) and (3), (c) (2) *supra*.

7. Perhaps the most striking example is the influence of Cardozo's opinion in Metropolitan Life Ins. Co. v. Conway, 252 N.Y. 449, 169 N.E. 642 (1930), an incontestability case, on the devel-

Two leading New York cases well illustrate the difficulty of determining what defenses are and what defenses are not precluded by an incontestability statute.

In the first of these cases, *Metropolitan Life Insurance Co. v. Conway,* [8] the insurer attacked the refusal of the superintendent of insurance to approve a rider, to be attached to its policies, in the following form: "Death as a result of service, travel or flight in any species of air craft, except as a fare-paying passenger, is a risk not assumed under this policy; but, if the insured shall die as a result, directly or indirectly, of such service, travel or flight, the company will pay to the beneficiary the reserve on this policy."[9] The court, in an opinion by Chief Judge Cardozo, held this clause to be a permissible rider under the New York statute, despite the fact that by its terms it might preclude a claim arising after the close of the period of contestability. One passage in the opinion draws a distinction between a provision setting the "limits of coverage" (a permissible rider, enforceable though it defeats claims arising after the period of contestability) and a provision establishing a "condition" (not permissible if it would defeat claims arising after the period of contestability has passed).[10] Other parts of the opinion seem to distinguish between a provision that is a "limitation of coverage" and a provision "for a forfeiture" in the sense that it denies all recovery, not even providing for return of premiums or surrender value.[11] On the whole, it would seem that the opinion is reasonably read as distinguishing between a provision declaring death from specified causes not to be covered (a permissible rider) and a provision declaring death under specified circumstances not to be covered, regardless of the cause (not a permissible rider). So interpreting Cardozo's opinion, Patterson cited it in support of his distinction between efficient and potential causes of loss — a key idea in his concept of warranty, which as draftsman he later incorporated into the New York warranty statute.[12] If this interpretation were taken to be authoritative, the distinction between a coverage clause and a warranty under the New York warranty statute would be identical with the distinction, under the New York incontestability statute, between clauses that continue to be enforceable and those no longer enforceable after the period of contestability has passed. But it is debatable whether this standard for determining what kinds of clauses are permissible under the incontestability statute remains authoritative today, if it ever was.

In *Simpson v. Phoenix Mutual Life Insurance Co.,*[13] the suit of a beneficiary of a group life policy for death proceeds was challenged

opment of the New York warranty statute. See § 6.5(b) (2) *supra.*

8.   252 N.Y. 449, 169 N.E. 642 (1930).

9.   252 N.Y. at 451, 169 N.E. at 642.

10.   252 N.Y. at 452, 169 N.E. at 642.

11.   252 N.Y. at 453, 169 N.E. at 643.

12.   N.Y. Ins. Law § 150 (McKinney 1966). See § 6.5(b) (2) *supra.*

13.   24 N.Y.2d 262, 247 N.E.2d 655, 299 N.Y.S.2d 835 (1969).

on the ground that her decedent was not eligible for membership in the employee group because he had not been employed for as much as thirty hours a week as required by the master policy. The decedent, a practicing attorney, was the assistant secretary of the group employer, a cemetery association, and devoted only a few days a month to the association's business. The opinion of the court, by Judge Keating, stated the question at issue to be "whether employment, as defined in this group life insurance policy, is a condition of insurance or a limitation of the risk which the insurer contracted to underwrite. If employment is a condition, the defense is now barred by the policy's incontestable clause."[14] The court, recognizing a conflict among precedents from other jurisdictions,[15] classified the provision at issue as a condition, declaring:[16]

"In New York the incontestable clause is viewed normally with reference to the manner of death. Risks which are considered limitations are those which could not be ascertained by the insurer by investigation at the time the policy of insurance was issued. . . . . If the additional risk to the insurer of issuing a policy to a particular applicant could have been discovered at the time the contract was entered into, the insurer is precluded from raising this fact as a defense after the period provided for in the incontestable clause has elapsed. It is only those risks which could not be ascertained at the time of contracting which can properly be viewed as a limitation on the risk of insurance."

The reference, in the opening sentence of this latter passage, to "the manner of death" might suggest a distinction between efficient causes and potential causes — the same distinction that is suggested by part at least of the *Conway* opinion. But the next sentence speaks of a distinction turning on whether the risks could or "could not be ascertained by the insurer by investigation at the time the policy of insurance was issued," and the opening sentence of the next paragraph emphasizes this test: "The hallmark of the distinction between conditions and limitations is discoverability."[17]

These leading New York opinions leave much room for debate about what grounds of defense or avoidance of liability constitute a contest, and much uncertainty exists in other jurisdictions as well.[18]

---

14. 24 N.Y.2d at 266, 247 N.E.2d at 657, 299 N.Y.S.2d at 838.

15. See, *e.g.*, Fisher v. Prudential Ins. Co., 107 N.H. 101, 218 A.2d 62 (1966), 26 A.L.R.3d 625 (1969) (deceased was listed as a participant in group insurance plan and as an employee, and premiums were paid; in fact, she was never an employee; held, no coverage; incontestability clause does not apply to the insurer's defense that the risk is excluded from the definition of the hazards to be borne by the insurer).

16. 24 N.Y.2d at 267, 247 N.E.2d at 657–658, 299 N.Y.S.2d at 839–840.

17. 24 N.Y.2d at 267, 247 N.E.2d at 658, 299 N.Y.S.2d at 840.

18. See, *e.g.*, First Pa. Banking & Trust Co. v. United States Life Ins. Co., 421 F.2d 959 (3d Cir. 1969); *cf.* Rall & Sfikas, *Group Insurance — Is the Incontestable Clause a Bootstrap Which Enlarges Coverage?* 5 Forum 51 (ABA Section Ins., Neg. & Comp.L. 1969.) See also Young, *"Incontestable" — As to what?* 1964 U.Ill.L.Forum 323.

Compare the test of *Conway*, interpreted as suggested above (that is, as distinguishing between efficient-cause and potential-cause provisions), with the test of *Simpson* (distinguishing between discoverable and nondiscoverable matters) as applied to a provision stating that the insurer shall have no obligation, except for return of premiums, unless the applicant is in good health when the policy is delivered. Reliance on a defense that the applicant was not in good health would seem to be a prohibited contest under the suggested interpretation of *Conway,* since the clause invoked purports to afford a defense whether or not the pre-existing condition of health contributed to the death. That is, it purports to apply even if the applicant was killed in an accident wholly unrelated to his pre-existing bad health. Under the *Simpson* test of discoverability, on the other hand, it would seem that some conditions of health would be discoverable and others would not be, under any of the various meanings likely to be given to "good health." Thus, the *Simpson* test would seem to allow a defense based on the "good health" clause in some instances and to deny it in others.

It is usually held that an incontestability clause bars a defense that the policy never took effect because the insured was not in good health as required by an explicit policy provision.[19] This conclusion had been reached in New York [20] before *Simpson*. Whether *Simpson* has effected a change in this respect is open to debate.

A distinction might be drawn between a good-health clause, which purports to deny liability altogether except for return of premiums, and does so regardless of the cause of death, and a clause (more often found in disability or accident and health than in life policies) declaring that there is no coverage for disability or death resulting from a disease existing at the time the policy was issued. Most jurisdictions, including New York, have permitted this defense after, as well as during, the period of contestability,[21] though some have held that it is precluded after the period of contestability has passed.[22] In line with precedents enforcing resulting-from-existing-

19. *E.g.*, McDaniel v. Insurance Co., 243 Ore. 1, 410 P.2d 814 (1966). See generally 1 Appleman, Insurance Law § 333 (rev. ed. 1965).

20. Allick v. Columbian Protective Ass'n, 269 App.Div. 281, 55 N.Y.S.2d 438 (1st Dep't 1945). It might be argued that by holding the applicant to be in "good health" as that term is used in the policy unless he has a "discoverable" ailment the *Simpson* test can be reconciled with treating a defense based on the "good health" clause as a contest. Thus, even if he has cancer, but in such an early state of development that it is undetectable, he is in "good health." But since *Simpson* speaks of conditions "discoverable" from the point of view of

the insurer, this reconciliation depends on attributing a rather bizarre meaning to "good health."

21. *E.g.*, Apter v. Home Life Ins. Co., 266 N.Y. 333, 194 N.E. 846 (1935), 98 A.L.R. 1281 (1935) (policy coverage was defined as extending to disability from "disease originating after the date on which" the policy became effective; held, incontestability clause bars the defense of fraud but not the defense that disease of tuberculosis originated before delivery of the policy). See 1 Appleman, Insurance Law § 333 (rev. ed. 1965).

22. *E.g.*, Blackwell v. United Ins. Co., 231 S.C. 535, 99 S.E.2d 414 (1957) (incontestability statute read into policy

disease clauses, it may be argued that a good-health clause, rather than being totally inoperative after the period of contestability, should be given the more limited effect of a resulting-from-existing-disease clause. That is, it may be argued that an incontestability statute, like a contribute-to-loss statute, should be construed to have the effect of converting a potential-cause-of-loss provision ("good health") into an actual-cause provision. Combining this idea with the time limit clearly expressed in incontestability statutes, one might say that an incontestability statute has the effect of rewriting a good-health clause in two ways to bring it within permissible bounds: first, by placing a time limit (the period of contestability) on its effectiveness as a potential-cause provision and, second, by changing it to an actual-cause provision thereafter. A weakness in the analogy is that contribute-to-loss statutes plainly declare that a potential-cause provision, rather than being stricken entirely from the contract, shall be given the more limited effect of an actual-cause provision. Incontestability statutes, on the other hand, say nothing of limited enforcement of the condemned provision except insofar as they express or imply that the provision is enforceable during the limited period of contestability. Perhaps it is more consistent with the legislative expression contained in incontestability statutes to hold that when the insurer attempts to take unfair advantage of the policyholder by inserting a prohibited clause in its policy, it should lose the benefit of that clause entirely. Moreover, *Simpson* casts doubt on the authority of the earlier precedent for enforcing resulting-from-existing-disease clauses. The rationale of *Simpson* would seem to bar the defense, after expiration of the period of contestability, in those cases in which the pre-existing disease was discoverable by the insurer at the time the policy was issued, even if the death or disability did thereafter result from it. Here too there is a counterargument based on regulation of warranties. Patterson's concept of warranty, incorporated in the New York warranty statute, treats potential-cause provisions as coverage provisions rather than warranties when they are designed to serve a coverage function such as identifying the property that is insured.[23] Arguably provisions concerning "discoverable" conditions of health could likewise be treated as coverage provisions in exceptional cases. The *Simpson* opinion gives no hint of any such qualification, but perhaps the likelihood of its recognition is increased by the essentially fair nature of a resulting-from-existing-disease clause of which the policyholder has effective notice.

When a policy provides for the contingency of misstatement of age and stipulates what the rights of the parties shall be, ordinarily the enforcement of this stipulation is held not to be a contest prohib-

with no incontestability clause; policy contained both a clause declaring no liability unless insured was in sound health on date of delivery and a clause denying liability, other than for refund of premiums, for death resulting from pre-existing disease; held, coverage for death from "heart trouble" despite pre-existing heart disease).

23. See § 6.5(b) (2) *supra.*

ited by the incontestability clause.[24] Indeed, a clause stating that the amount payable shall be such as the premium paid would have purchased at the correct age may be enforced not on the theory of successful contest but on the theory of fulfillment of the contract itself. Although an action by an insurer for enforcement of such a clause has sometimes been referred to as an action for reformation [25] because it has the effect of substituting the correct age for the misstated age in the policy, it may be viewed instead merely as a proceeding seeking a declaration of rights under the contract as written.[26] That is, the contract itself makes plain an intention that the age adjustment clause override the stated age if the stated age is not correct.

For cases in which the result is merely a scaling down of benefits, as is common in life insurance contracts, this view produces a result difficult to challenge. But if the result is to deny benefits altogether, the counterargument that the attempted enforcement is in essence a contest is more disquieting. For example, suppose that a policy of disability insurance purchased by a sixty-year-old applicant incorrectly states his age as fifty-five and provides elsewhere that no benefits shall be due for a disability commencing before the inception of the policy or after the applicant has attained the age of sixty. To enforce the latter clause is to deny that any benefits could ever become due. Thus, the policy must have been obtained by fraud or mistake. Ordinarily an insurer's denial of liability because of the applicant's fraud is treated as a contest and must be brought within the short period allowed for contests under an incontestability clause. Surely the insurer is in no better position if the misstatement resulted instead from honest mistake. But may the insurer bypass this problem with the contention that its position is grounded not upon fraud or mistake in the statement of age but rather upon the overriding stipulation for correction of the stated age? It would seem reasonable to permit such a contention to prevail, subject to allowance of a suitable remedy for any reliance damage the insured may have suffered, absent fraud on his part. The rights the insured is seeking by opposing this contention are rights beyond any he would have been granted but for mistake, and he has no just ground for complaint if his reliance damages are provided for and he is merely denied the windfall of a mistake. One might advance a similar argument about contests of all types based on fraud or mistake, but a distinction can reasonably be made. The incontestability statutes and clauses are aimed at protecting insureds and third party beneficiaries against stale claims of fraud or mistake, difficult to disprove. The problem of stale proof is not one of great consequence in the case of erroneous statement of age. Thus, although a policy clause declaring the contract unenforceable in case of fraud of the applicant cannot be permitted generally to bypass the incontestability clause since it would defeat the central objective of the clause, a different view may be

24. *E.g.*, New York Life Ins. Co. v. Hollender, 38 Cal.2d 73, 237 P.2d 510 (1951).

25. 38 Cal.2d at 76, 237 P.2d at 512.

26. 38 Cal.2d at 84, 237 P.2d at 516.

taken of a policy clause providing specifically for correction of age in case of misstatement, whether by fraud or by honest error.

The reliance damages an insured not himself guilty of fraud should be permitted to recover in such cases would include, at the least, the return of his premiums with interest. They might be higher if, for example, he could prove that, had he known this contract to be worthless because of the clause denying benefits for disability commencing after age sixty, he would have obtained elsewhere a contract paying benefits for the disability he later suffered in fact.[27]

Although an action for enforcement of an age adjustment clause in life insurance is held not to be a contest, if a disability insurance case of the type last stated above were treated as a contest it would be necessary to face cases on a spectrum between these two. For example, what of cases in which a disability policy with the clause suggested above was taken at age fifty-five or at age fifty-nine, the age being understated five years (at fifty or fifty-four)? Enforcement of the age adjustment clause would afford coverage only for disability commencing after inception of the policy and before age sixty — in the latter illustration, a period of less than a year. Would coverage for a few days, or months, be enough to save the insurer's contention from classification as a contest? To answer this question one would find it necessary to draw a sharp line of distinction along a continuum of cases differing only in degree. Enforcing the stipulation for correction of age, but allowing an action for reliance damages as recommended above, has the advantage of avoiding this problem.

A similar solution may be appropriate in other cases to avoid arbitrarily drawing a bright line between cases different only in degree. Sometimes it happens that a policy incorrectly states the period of coverage or the amount of benefits due for the premium paid. For example, in one case the sum payable at age sixty-five under endowment provisions was stated to be $57,098.26, whereas the sum intended was $5,798.26. This was treated as a scrivener's error and the federal court confronted with the issue concluded that both generally and in California particularly the precedents allow reformation to correct such an error, as against a contention that the action for reformation is a contest prohibited by the incontestability clause.[28] This result seems irreproachable when the discrepancy is so great as to negate any detrimental reliance by the insured. Even if the discrepancy is small enough that a claim of detrimental reliance is reasonable, it would seem proper to allow reformation of a scrivener's error[29]

27. Concerning detrimental reliance and reliance damages generally, see § 6.4 *supra*.

28. Mutual Life Ins. Co. v. Simon, 151 F.Supp. 408 (S.D.N.Y.1957). Concerning scrivener's errors generally, see Merriman, *Scrivener's Errors and the Mischief They Cause*, 1969 ABA Section Ins., Neg. & Comp.L. Proceedings 166.

29. *But cf.* Richardson v. Travelers Ins. Co., 171 F.2d 699 (9th Cir. 1948), 7 A.L.R.2d 501 (1949) (forecasting California law; insurer by mistake issued a pension policy rather than the intended life insurance policy on a

while also awarding reliance damages if any can be proved. Otherwise the insured or third-party beneficiaries would be receiving a pure windfall, well beyond the objectives of an incontestability statute or clause.

§ 6.5(e) PATTERNS OF TREATMENT OF COMMON CLAUSES

(1) GENERALLY

Interpretation and use of the statutes and decisional precedents bearing on the area identified with the concepts of warranty and representation are hampered by the conflicting meanings given by different courts and legislatures to terms of art.

One way of cutting through the fog enshrouding this body of statutes and decisions is to separate and then analyze respectively the instances in which policy stipulations defeating protection were enforced without regard to materiality and the instances in which policy stipulations were declared unenforceable unless one or another among varied standards of materiality could be satisfied.

In the older law, stipulations designed to limit protection were usually referred to as either warranties or representations. The former were enforceable without regard to materiality; the latter, only upon a showing of materiality. Under modern statutes the terminology and the scope of the two categories have changed, but it continues to be true that a distinction is made between a kind of stipulation that is enforceable regardless of materiality (commonly called a coverage provision), and a kind of stipulation enforceable only upon a showing of materiality.[1] The latter category includes sub-types, one of which is often called warranty and another of which is often called representation. Thus one can classify by result to a considerable extent within the framework of terminology customarily used. It happens, however, that the meaning of common terms varies from state to state. For example, states having statutes regulating warranties commonly rely on a contrast between warranty and coverage, but their definitions of the contrast differ.

It may be useful, then, to attempt another way of classifying— not by whether a stipulation is called a coverage provision, or a warranty, or a representation, but by what the nature of the stipulation is in some respect more closely related to what it attempts to do. Two jurisdictions both of which hold that coverage clauses are enforceable without regard to materiality and that warranties are enforceable only upon a showing of materiality may be achieving sharply different results because, for example, one says a typical chattel mortgage clause is a coverage provision and the other says it is a

[handwritten margin note: Distinctions based on whether or not materiality need be shown to defeat protection]

"uniform premium plan;" action for reformation twenty years later was held to be a contest prohibited by the incontestability clause). For criticisms

of *Richardson*, see 62 Harv.L.Rev. 890 (1949); 97 U.Pa.L.Rev. 741 (1949).

1. See § 6.5(a) and (b) (1).

warranty.[2] Conversely, two jurisdictions whose theories and terminology stand in sharp contrast may be reaching essentially consistent results.

The purpose of this section is to make comparisons both on a theoretical plane and in terms of practical outcome in relation to some illustrative clauses and the results reached when their application is challenged.

(2) CLAUSES CONCERNING PHYSICAL LOCATION

Many insurance policies contain clauses purporting to limit protection according to the physical location of property or of an event.

Sometimes such a clause concerns the customary physical location of property that is the subject of the insurance. For example, fire insurance policies have commonly identified a building by street address, then designating the personal property to be included in the subject matter of the contract as "contents" of the described building.[3] Automobile insurance policies commonly include a clause specifying a place of principal garaging.[4]

Sometimes a limiting clause concerns the place where an event occurs. For example, family automobile policies usually include the following clause:

"This policy applies only to accidents, occurrences and loss during the policy period while the automobile is within the United States of America, its territories or possessions, or Canada, or is being transported between parts thereof."[5] Policies on commercial vehicles often contain also a "radius" clause purporting to defeat liability because of use of the vehicle beyond the area marked by a radius of specified length from the place of principal garaging. Forms of such clauses have varied considerably.[6]

Is insurance protection unavailable under such provisions as these when the automobile or personal property is outside the specified physical location?

If the clause in question is treated as a coverage clause, the insurer, by showing merely that the property was beyond the specified

---

2. See § 6.5(b) (3) and n.28 thereto, *supra*.

3. See Appendix A *infra*.

4. See Appendix H *infra*.

5. See Appendix H *infra*.

6. One example is a policy form containing two clauses as follows:

"In consideration of the premium at which the policy is written, it is agreed that the automobile or automobiles described in the policy will be used and operated entirely within a radius of 500 miles of the place where such automobile or automobiles as described in said policy are principally garaged."

"It is further agreed that the company shall not be liable for, nor will it pay any loss or claim whatsoever that results from any accident or loss occurring while the automobile or automobiles described in the policy are being operated outside of the radius of 500 miles of the place where such automobile or automobiles described in the policy are principally garaged."

See Wallace v. Virginia Sur. Co., 80 Ga.App. 50, 55 S.E.2d 259 (1949).

physical area, establishes a perfect defense against an insured responsible for the departure of the vehicle from the territory of coverage.[7] If the clause is treated as a warranty, the same result would have been reached under the common law,[8] but in a state having a statute that applies to the type of insurance in question and restricts the effectiveness of warranties[9] it is necessary that the insurer prove something more—usually that the "breach of warranty" (that is, the violation of the clause) increased the risk that the insurer agreed to cover by the terms of the policy.[10] If the clause is treated as a representation, also, such a showing is generally required to sustain an insurer's defense.[11]

The clause in a fire insurance policy stating that the personalty it covers consists of the "contents" of a building described by street address is commonly regarded as a coverage clause, noncompliance with which is a defense without proof of increased risk.[12] One might reasonably argue that such a clause concerns potential cause of loss in Patterson's terminology, but Patterson himself cites this as an example of a coverage clause, not a warranty.[13] This conclusion can be defended on the ground that it serves the special coverage function of identifying the goods that are the subject matter of the contract.

Each of the other physical location clauses among the illustrations above may also be said to be a "potential cause" as distinguished from an "actual cause" provision. As to each, the question arises whether it, too, will be treated as a coverage clause on the theory that it serves some special coverage function. The answers may vary not only among the different types of clauses but also among different jurisdictions.

Patterson appears to have regarded the clause concerning place of principal garaging as a warranty.[14] Certainly it concerns potential cause of loss rather than actual cause, and it seems unlikely that it will be treated as a coverage provision in states where its classification as a warranty would invoke a requirement that violation be material. If the actual place of principal garaging was a lower rated

---

7. See, *e.g.*, Herzog v. National Am. Ins. Co., 2 Cal.3d 192, 465 P.2d 841, 84 Cal.Rptr. 705 (1970) (homeowners policy provision excluding automobile accidents "while away from the premises or the ways adjoining" defeated coverage for insured son's operation of nonowned motor bike on freeway several miles from home; reasonable expectations of parties did not encompass such extended coverage; distinguishes an earlier case but nevertheless says "to the extent it is inconsistent herewith" it is overruled). However, the defense may not be valid against a lienholder who is independently an insured under a "loss payable" clause of the standard mortgage

type. See nn.23–25 and associated text *infra*.

8. See § 5.6 *supra*.

9. See § 6.5(b) *supra*.

10. See § 6.5(c) *supra*.

11. See §§ 5.7, 6.5(c) (1) and (2) *supra*.

12. See § 6.5(b) (2) and n.21 thereto, *supra*.

13. See Patterson, Essentials of Insurance Law 296–297 (2d ed. 1957).

14. *Id.* at 290, 297–299, 404.

territory than the stated place, it would be difficult at best for the insurer to show that the violation was material. It is arguable, however, that the provision is neither a coverage provision nor a warranty but merely a representation.[15] The typical provision appears under the heading "Declarations," a term more suggestive of representation than warranty.

It is clear that a clause stating the place of garaging can be a warranty—a continuing condition of liability—if that intention is expressed. It is also clear that it can be merely a representation as to the present place of garaging, if that intention is expressed. The current use of the term "declarations" and the omission of the term "warranty" point to the conclusion that this is a representation only. But in New York, where promissory representations are not recognized,[16] the use of the words "will be" in reference to the place of garaging suggests that the provision is a warranty.

If the provision is a representation of an existing fact or an affirmative warranty of that fact, the insurer cannot establish a defense by showing merely a change in the place of garaging during the policy period.

The place-of-garaging declaration might also be treated as a representation of an existing state of mind—intention that the automobile continue to be garaged at that location during the entire policy period.[17] A change in place of garaging incident to a change of intention thereafter would not be a defense, but proof that the insured did not have the intention stated at the time of the application would be a defense, if the requirement of materiality were met.

If the policyholder of a policy having a radius clause takes the automobile to a higher-rate territory beyond the specified radius and keeps it there,[18] he may be violating the principal-place-of-garaging clause as well as the radius clause.[19] In any event, in such a case there

15. *Cf.* Allstate Ins. Co. v. Stinger, 400 Pa. 533, 163 A.2d 74 (1960) (insured had license suspended because of mental illness within two-year period to which an answer on his application related; held, no defense, without proof of bad faith and materiality; dictum that declarations of automobile policy are representations, not warranties).

16. N.Y. Ins. Law § 149 (McKinney 1966) defines a representation as "a statement as to past or present fact." See also Patterson, Essentials of Insurance Law 297–299 (2d ed. 1957).

17. Compare the question as to the nature, under the New York statutes, of a statement concerning the future (*e. g.*, concerning expected travel in a foreign country or expected aviation activity) appearing in an application for life insurance. It is not a warranty since it is a statement made by the applicant for the insurance. N.Y. Ins. Law § 142(3) (McKinney 1966). It is not a representation, except insofar as it impliedly represents the existing intention of the applicant, since it is not otherwise a "statement as to past or present fact." N.Y. Ins. Law § 149 (McKinney 1966). The conclusion is that it is a nullity, except insofar as it is a representation of existing intention.

18. See, *e.g.*, Indiana Rolling Mill Baling Corp. v. National Auto. & Cas. Ins. Co., 240 F.2d 74 (7th Cir. 1957).

19. But compare the argument that the declaration of principal place of garaging is merely a representation of intention. See this section at n.17 *supra*.

is ordinarily no occasion for determining whether the radius clause is a warranty or a coverage provision since materiality of the violation is so clear.[20] If, on the other hand, he takes the vehicle to a lower-rate territory, difficult questions are presented. What are the risks the radius clause is directed against? Long trips, with added expense of the vehicle and fatigue of the driver, are surely within the relevant risks. But are short trips, starting and ending beyond the area of the radius, also within the risks sought to be precluded? Also, in determining whether the violation increased risk, could one take into account, as an offset against the increased risk from a long trip beyond the radius, that the area to which the policyholder drove was a low-rate territory and that he kept the vehicle there for a long time? These are questions on which there is little authority. [21] Another source of uncertainty is that even if a radius clause is carefully drafted to avoid the use of language suggestive of warranty, the question whether it will be treated as a warranty or instead as a coverage provision, when classification makes a difference, is debatable and unsettled. The probability of its being treated as a warranty is, no doubt, greatly increased if the language of the radius clause includes the term "warranty" or some derivative.[22]

The clause of the automobile policy purporting to deny coverage for accidents occurring while the automobile is outside the United States and Canada is a "potential cause" provision in Patterson's terminology, but it might be argued that it, like the "contents" location clause of the fire insurance policy, serves a coverage function,[23] and

---

20. With respect to possible qualification of this assertion because of uncertainties about the meaning of "materiality" or of such cognate concepts as "increase of risk," see § 6.5(c) (2) *supra*.

21. See § 6.5(c) (2) *supra*.

22. *E.g.*: "It is warranted by the insured that no regular or frequent trips . . . will be made . . . to any location beyond a 50-mile radius from the limits of the city or town of principal garaging of said vehicle." This phrase appeared in the policy before the court in Indiana Rolling Mill Baling Corp. v. National Auto. & Cas. Ins. Co., 240 F.2d 74 (7th Cir. 1957).

23. *Cf.* Herzog v. National Am. Ins. Co., 2 Cal.3d 192, 465 P.2d 841, 84 Cal.Rptr. 705 (1970) (homeowners policy provisions excluding automobile accidents "while away from the premises or the ways adjoining" defeated coverage for insured son's operation of nonowned motor bike on freeway several miles from home; reasonable

expectations of parties did not encompass such extended coverage; distinguishes an earlier case but nevertheless says "to the extent it is inconsistent herewith" it is overruled). In another case, cited below, an argument that the "United States and Canada" clause was a coverage clause in contrast with a "condition" failed. But the insurer was advancing the contention to defeat a lienholder, and the court's result can be justified on the ground that even coverage provisions may be modified by a "loss payable" clause that expressly or impliedly grants such independent protection to the loss payee. Southwestern Funding Corp. v. Motors Ins. Corp., 59 Cal.2d 91, 378 P.2d 361, 28 Cal.Rptr. 161 (1963) ("loss payable" clause extending coverage to lienholder despite policyholder's violation of "terms and *conditions*" of policy; insurer liable to lienholder for damage to vehicle sustained in Mexico, despite provision that coverage applied only to accidents in the U.S. and Canada; reasoned on grounds of resolving ambiguities against the company). See also § 4.2(b) *supra*.

especially so since the geographical area in which the car is operated may be of central importance because of the different legal, social, and economic circumstances encountered outside the permitted territory.

The territorial clause of the automobile physical damage coverage serves to illustrate another possible consequence of distinguishing between coverage and warranty. If the clause is a warranty, the mortgagee has a strong argument that the mortgagor's taking the car beyond the permitted territory falls within the concept of "an act or neglect of the mortgagor" that does not bar the mortgagee's claim.[24] The mortgagee's position is arguably weaker if the clause is classified as a coverage provision, but there is neverthless some support for the mortgagee's recovery.[25]

(3) MORAL HAZARD CLAUSES

Before 1943, fire insurance policies customarily contained "moral hazard" clauses declaring the policy to be void in specified circumstances unless otherwise provided in writing added to the policy. Among the specified circumstances were the following: if the insured was not unconditional and sole owner of the property that was the subject of insurance; if the subject of insurance was a building on ground not owned by the insured in fee simple; if, with the insured's knowledge, foreclosure proceedings were commenced; if any change in interest, title, or possession occurred except by death of an insured or by change of occupants without increase of hazard; if the policy was assigned before loss.[26] Also, there were additional clauses that, under the fairest of the forms then in use, suspended coverage for the duration of noncompliance with specified conditions rather than declaring the policy void. Among these were conditions concerned with other moral hazards in addition to those named above.[27] In the case of *Pollock v. Connecticut Fire Ins. Co.*,[28] involving a claim for loss from lightning, the insurer successfully defended on the ground that the insured was not the unconditional and sole owner of the dwelling that was purportedly insured, since it was owned by the insured and his wife as joint tenants. Professor Goble conducted a survey in Champaign and Urbana, Illinois, shortly after *Pollock* was decided, and found that approximately 28 per cent of the fire insurance policies examined were policies naming only one insured though he was not the sole owner.[29] Even more policies were potentially unenforceable, of course, in view of the effect of other moral hazard clauses.

The 1943 New York Standard Fire Insurance Policy form omits all "moral hazard" clauses previously in use, except that it provides

24. See § 4.2(b) *supra*.

25. See, *e.g.*, Southwestern Funding Corp. v. Motors Ins. Corp., n.23 *supra*.

26. Goble, *The Moral Hazard Clauses of the Standard Fire Insurance Policy*, 37 Colum.L.Rev. 410, 415 (1937).

27. *Id.* at 414.

28. 362 Ill. 313, 199 N.E. 816 (1936).

29. 37 Colum.L.Rev. 410, 418 (1937).

for attachment of an endorsement imposing restrictions concerning other insurances. Automobile policies, also, now contain fewer moral hazard provisions than were formerly in common use.[30]

In the absence of relevant statutory provisions, encumbrance clauses are generally enforced, and recovery is denied upon proof of violation of such a clause without regard to materiality and prejudice.[31] In Texas there is a statute, befittingly distinctive, directed specifically against an encumbrance clause.[32] And statutes of wider application to representations and warranties have sometimes been held applicable to encumbrance clauses,[33] though other courts have held such statutes inapplicable either on the questionable theory that the encumbrance clause is an enforceable "condition" or "coverage" provision [34] or on the still more dubious theory that these regulatory statutes do not apply to moral hazard clauses.[35]

It might be argued that the omission of the moral hazard clauses from the 1943 revision of the fire insurance policy form implies that they are not to be conditions of liability any longer. But since increase of risk in fact may be a good defense under the increase-of-hazard clause, the circumstances that formerly would have invoked a moral hazard clause may still be a defense on the independent basis of the increase-of-hazard clause.[36] This is entirely harmonious with the deletion of moral hazard clauses since the evil aimed at was that they operated to defeat liability in many situations in which there was in fact no increase of risk as a result of the violation.

(4) GOOD HEALTH; MEDICAL TREATMENT; PRE-EXISTING DISEASE

Life insurance policies (especially those of relatively low amount, including policies of industrial life insurance)[37] and health and accident policies often contain a clause declaring that the insurer shall have no obligation, other than to return premiums, unless the

---

30. See Appendix H *infra*.

31. *E.g.*, Globe & Rutgers Fire Ins. Co. v. Segler, 44 So.2d 658 (Fla.1950), 16 A.L.R.2d 731 (1951) (automobile insurance).

32. Tex.Ins.Code Ann. art. 5.37 (1963).

33. *E.g.*, Davidson v. American Cent. Ins. Co., 80 N.H. 552, 119 A. 707 (1923).

34. *E.g.*, Moe v. Allemannia Fire Ins. Co., 209 Wis. 526, 244 N.W. 593 (1932), discussed in § 6.5(b) (3) nn.28, 29 *supra*.

35. See Hawkins v. New York Life Ins. Co., 176 Kan. 24, 269 P.2d 389 (1954), overruling earlier decisions that had interpreted a contribute-to-loss statute on life insurance as being inapplicable to "moral risk."

36. *Cf.* Nemojeski v. Bubolz Mut. Town Fire Ins. Co., 271 Wis. 561, 74 N.W.2d 196 (1956), 56 A.L.R.2d 414 (1957). The increase-of-hazard clause would be classified as a warranty under the New York statutes. See § 6.5(b) (2) *supra*. Under statutes of the types enacted in other states, the classification would be debatable. See § 6.5(b) (3) *supra*. But the classification would be immaterial to the result in most instances, since proof of the violation would also meet the restrictive requirements of the statute, unless it was a contribute-to-the-loss statute. The classification might make a difference, however, if the suit was brought by a mortgagee, claiming that under the standard mortgagee clause he should not be barred by any act or neglect of the mortgagor. See § 4.2(b) *supra*.

37. See § 1.3(f) *supra*.

applicant is in good health on a specified date (ordinarily either the date of issue or the date of delivery of the policy).

A defense based on such a good-health clause is generally held to be a prohibited contest under incontestability clauses.[38] Within the period of permitted contestability, may a further challenge to the defense based on a statute regulating warranties be successful? Under the test of the New York warranty statute,[39] a good-health clause is surely a warranty rather than a coverage clause, since it concerns potential cause rather than actual cause of death or disability and is not likely to be treated as one of those exceptional potential-cause provisions that serve some coverage function. But it is nevertheless plainly effective as a defense since the statutory requirement of materiality is so clearly satisfied. It is unclear whether a good-health clause will be characterized as a warranty under warranty-representation statutes of other states or instead as a coverage provision free of the regulatory effect of such statutes. In most cases, however, this is not likely to be a significant question since good health is material to the risk. In any event there is less doubt about results than about applicable theories; noncompliance with the good-health clause is usually recognized as an effective ground of defense when not barred by an incontestability clause or statute.[40] If, however, a statute requires that a breach of warranty contribute to the loss in order to be an effective defense, then in those cases in which death or disability resulted from other causes and not from the pre-existing ill health the defense would prevail if the clause were classified as a coverage provision but would fail if it were classified as a warranty.

A good-health clause, though not adversely affected by a statute regulating warranties, may be subjected to regulation also by restrictive judicial interpretation. For example, there is some support for construing "good health" in a sense that classifies an applicant as being in good health as long as he in good faith believes he is, even though his physician and family may know he is incurably ill.[41] Also, when the company requires a physical examination even though there is a good-health clause in the policy, perhaps the principal significance of the clause, as commonly construed, is to defeat recovery

---

38.   See § 6.5(d) *supra*.

39.   See § 6.5(b)(2) *supra*.

40.   *E.g.*, Great Nat'l Life Ins. Co. v. Hulme, 134 Tex. 539, 136 S.W.2d 602 (1940). See 1 Appleman, Insurance Law § 151 (rev. ed. 1965).

41.   See, *e.g.*, Harte v. United Benefit Life Ins. Co., 66 Cal.2d 148, 424 P.2d 329, 56 Cal.Rptr. 889 (1967) (application clause declaring no liability until policy delivered while applicant "in good health and free from injury";

"good health" interpreted from point of view of applicant's understanding and not from point of view of then unknown facts or from point of view of what treating physician or members of the family knew; recovery allowed if applicant believed in good faith that his health had not materially changed between the time of application and delivery). See also §§ 5.-7(a), 5.8 *supra*, concerning defenses based on representation or concealment as distinguished from a good-health clause.

in case of an adverse change in the applicant's health between the date of the examination and the date of delivery of the policy.[42]

In some instances application forms contain a stipulation that the contract shall take effect only upon payment of the premium and delivery of the policy and only if the applicant has not consulted or been examined or treated by a physician after the completion of the medical examination in connection with the application. Under such a clause it has been held that the insurer may defend on the ground of intervening visits to a physician without regard to the seriousness or triviality of the applicant's ailment.[43] But it would seem that a somewhat different result should be reached under a warranty statute like that of New York, since this is plainly a potential-cause provision and is not likely to be treated as one of those exceptional potential-cause provisions that serve some coverage function.[44] As a warranty, it would be subject to the materiality requirement of the statute. Whether this clause would be classified as a warranty under the statutes of other states, or instead as a coverage clause free of the materiality requirement, is more doubtful.[45]

Often in health and accident policies and less often in life policies there is a provision declaring that the insurer shall not be liable for death or disability resulting from a disease existing on the date the policy becomes effective. Most courts have permitted defenses under this clause even after termination of the period when contests are permitted under an incontestability clause.[46] And such clauses fare well also under statutes regulating warranties and representations. Under the New York warranty statute this would seem to be a coverage clause since it concerns actual cause of the claimed loss. And it seems likely that it will be regarded as a coverage clause under the warranty-representation statutes of other states as well.[47] Moreover, even if the clause is treated as a warranty, it is an effective basis for a defense since by proving its applicability to a claim the insurer is also proving that the breach contributed to the claimed loss.

---

42. See, *e.g.*, Bronx Sav. Bank v. Weigandt, 1 N.Y.2d 545, 136 N.E.2d 848, 154 N.Y.S.2d 878 (1956), 60 A.L.R.2d 1422 (1958).

43. *E.g.*, Girouard v. John Hancock Mut. Life Ins. Co., 98 R.I. 1, 199 A.2d 307 (1964). The defense was raised early enough that incontestability was not an issue. It would seem that a defense based on this clause should be classified as a prohibited contest in states where a defense under the good-health clause is so treated, but this issue is debatable.

44. See generally § 6.5(b) (2) *supra*.

45. See generally § 6.5(b) (3) *supra*.

46. See § 6.5(d) *supra*. *But cf.* Young, *"Incontestable" — As to what?* 1964 U.Ill.L.Forum 323, 326–329.

47. See generally § 6.5(b) (3) *supra*.

SECTION 6.6 AVOIDING CLAIMS FOR VARIANCE

§ 6.6(a) RESERVATION-OF-RIGHTS NOTICES AND NONWAIVER AGREEMENTS

It often happens that an insurer attempts to defeat a claim of rights at variance with policy provisions by relying upon a reservation-of-rights notice or a nonwaiver agreement. The former is a unilateral declaration by the insurer, delivered to the insured or other potential claimant, or both, stating in effect that the insurer reserves its rights to contest liability and that its conduct in investigating the claim or taking other action in relation to it is not to be construed otherwise. A nonwaiver agreement is a similar declaration in the form of a contractual agreement between the insurer and the insured or other potential claimant.

Since a reservation-of-rights notice is unilateral, its potential effectiveness is significantly limited. Generally it serves the purpose of refuting inferences that might otherwise be drawn from the conduct of the insurer. For example, when a liability insurer engages in a thorough and extended investigation of the facts bearing on potential liability of its insured for an injury to another person resulting from the insured's operation of an automobile, its conduct, continuing after it has acquired information relevant to a potential defense against coverage, may be thought to imply an acknowledgement of coverage despite that defense. But a reservation-of-rights notice, delivered promptly after the insurer acquires information of the potential defense, negates such an inference. Thus the notice tends to disprove voluntary relinquishment of a known right to contest coverage.

The notice may have a bearing on other theories of rights at variance with policy provisions as well. For example, it may be that the insured is not justified in relying solely upon the insurer's investigation of the accident rather than employing his own attorney, even though such reliance would have been reasonable if the reservation-of-rights notice had not been delivered.[1] But it may happen, on the other hand, that the insured's decision not to employ his own attorney is reasonable on the ground that two simultaneous investigations on his behalf would interfere with each other or would create adverse reactions among witnesses whose cooperation may be needed at trial. The insurer's agent may have made clear his intent to preserve all rights to contest coverage, but there may be grounds for recognizing

---

1. *Cf.* Salonen v. Paanenen, 320 Mass. 568, 573–574, 71 N.E.2d 227, 231–232 (1947) (when insurer seasonably notifies insured that it is continuing to defend under reservation of rights, insured is not misled and the basis for estoppel is lacking; insured can take protective steps, such as assuming control of defense; dictum that insured is entitled to assume control of defense if he so demands after receiving reservation notice). For a different view concerning the insured's assertion of a right to assume control of the defense, at least in circumstances of conflict of interest between the insurer and the insured, see § 7.7 (c) and n.5 thereto *infra*.

rights at variance with both his intent and the policy provisions on which the insurer's defense is based.

A nonwaiver agreement has a broader range of effectiveness because it is consensual. The insured agrees to give up certain rights at variance with policy provisions in return for the insurer's incurring costs of investigation and defense with respect to which its obligation is in dispute. The agreement is, in short, a kind of partial settlement of disputed claims. In circumstances such as those of the last illustration, a court might appropriately hold an insured to his agreement that the insurer's continuing to investigate would not preclude its later assertion of the coverage defense.

As the last example in part illustrates, the term "nonwaiver agreement" is misleading in several ways. First, nonwaiver may seem to imply that the agreement is intended to defeat only claims of waiver in the strict sense, involving a state of mind of voluntary relinquishment of known right. If nonwaiver agreements were so intended, they would have little impact since such a waiver is seldom provable in any event. In fact the term "nonwaiver" is to be understood in a much broader sense, comparable to the loose way in which courts often use waiver in insurance cases. Thus, the purpose of the agreement is to preclude various other assertions of rights at variance with policy provisions, as well as assertions of waiver in the strict sense. Certainly claims of estoppel and election are ordinarily intended to be precluded by nonwaiver agreements.

The term "nonwaiver" also misleads to the extent it implies that the very making of the agreement may not itself constitute a "waiver," in the loose sense. Thus, there have been some cases in which a nonwaiver agreement has been held to constitute a "waiver" of a policy provision. For example, in one case the insurer's joinder in a nonwaiver agreement dated five days after the date of the insured's proof of loss defeated its assertion that the insured's demand for appraisal, made seventeen days after the proof of loss, was too late under a policy provision requiring notice of the demand within fifteen days; the court held that the demand was timely, reasoning that the nonwaiver agreement suspended the running of the fifteen-day period until there was a definite failure of the parties to agree on the amount of the loss.[2]

It may be noted that the insurer's relinquishment in this case of its right to insist on compliance with the fifteen-day limit probably was not a waiver in the strict sense of voluntary relinquishment of a known right. But this is not to say that the court's decision was improper. A state-of-mind standard is quite defensible, and even preferable, when the legal theory is one of unilateral relinquishment of a legal right. But a nonwaiver agreement is a contract and as such is subject to an objective standard of interpretation. Thus, in the illus-

---

2. Milwaukee Ins. Co. v. Kogen, 240 F. 2d 613 (8th Cir. 1957) (forecasting Minnesota law).

tration last given, proof that the agent representing the insurer in making the nonwaiver agreement intended that the fifteen-day limit for an appraisal demand should remain in effect would not save the insurer's defense of late demand; by the objective standard of interpretation, the nonwaiver agreement manifested an understanding that the right to demand an appraisal, among others, would be preserved. Thus, a full catalog of theories of rights at variance with policy provisions must include subsequent contractual agreements at variance with policy provisions, of which a so-called nonwaiver agreement is an example.

Neither a nonwaiver agreement nor a reservation-of-rights notice will serve to give an insurer the protection sought in some circumstances. For example, the principles of disallowing unconscionable advantage and honoring reasonable expectations may be applied not only to preclude enforcement of the insurance contract itself but also to preclude the effectiveness of a nonwaiver agreement or a reservation-of-rights notice.[3] It is possible, too, that later conduct of the insurer's agents will induce detrimental reliance that supports rights at variance with the the terms of a nonwaiver agreement or a reservation-of-rights notice. In short, just as there may be grounds for rights at variance with policy provisions, so too there may be grounds for rights at variance with nonwaiver agreements and reservation-of-rights notices.[4]

3. *Cf.* Bogle v. Conway, 199 Kan. 707, 433 P.2d 407 (1967) (insurer precluded from asserting exclusion of racing accidents; nonwaiver agreement ineffectual because of presumed prejudice — as to which see § 6.4(f) *supra* — from want of full notice to the insured concerning the claimed defense). See also Note, 18 Def.L.J. 612, 619 (1969), suggesting that because defense counsel represented conflicting interests growing out of the fact that the insurer had policies applying to both of the vehicles in the collision, *Bogle* is distinguishable from many decisions for insurers that are inconsistent with the broad language in *Bogle*. With respect to possible limitations of various defenses and of the effectiveness of nonwaiver agreements and reservation-of-rights notices because of conflict-of-interest relationships, see also § 7.7(b) and (c) *infra*. Concerning the effect of a demand by the insurer that the insured execute a nonwaiver agreement relieving the insurer of the effect of its previous misconduct, see § 6.8(d) n.5 *infra*.

4. *Cf.* Allstate Ins. Co. v. Gross, 27 N.Y.2d 263, 265 N.E.2d 736, 317 N.Y.S. 2d 309 (1970) (in declaratory action, liability insurer contended it was not required to decide to disclaim liability within any particular time, in absence of prejudice to an insured or an injured party, though N.Y.Ins.Law § 167, subd. 8, requires "notice as soon as is reasonably possible of such disclaimer of liability"; shortly after insurer first received notice, it sent letter to insured stating that it reserved right to disclaim because of late notice of accident; almost seven months after letter of reservation insurer filed this declaratory proceeding for determination of its right to disclaim; insurer argued in Court of Appeals, seven years later, that it had not yet disclaimed but was seeking determination of its right to do so; held, insurer has obligation of prompt decision as well as prompt notice thereafter and right of disclaimer is defeated by unreasonable delay; statutory requirement is part of scheme for protection of New York's MVAIC as well as insured and injured persons). See also § 6.8(a) *infra*.

§ 6.6(b) COVERAGE CLAUSES

Are certain stipulations in an insurance policy so important that they are beyond the reach of some or all theories of rights at variance with policy provisions?

As we have seen, the New York warranty statute explicitly exempts coverage provisions from its protection,[1] and the same distinction — between unregulated coverage clauses and regulated defenses based on warranties, representations, or concealments — is implicit in other warranty statutes. A similar distinction is made under incontestability statutes between coverage provisions and those the assertion of which constitutes a prohibited contest.[2] There is case support, too, for the theory that some contractual stipulations are beyond the reach of doctrines of waiver and estoppel because they are the heart or essence of the contract.[3] Ordinarily this theory is also

---

1. N.Y. Ins. Law § 150 (McKinney 1966). See § 6.5(b)(2) *supra*.

2. See, *e.g.*, N.Y. Ins. Law § 155 (McKinney 1966); Simpson v. Phoenix Mut. Life Ins. Co., 24 N.Y.2d 262, 247 N.E.2d 655, 299 N.Y.S.2d 835 (1969). See § 6.5(d) *supra*.

3. *E.g.*, Inland Mut. Ins. Co. v. Hightower, 274 Ala. 52, 145 So.2d 422 (1962) (per curiam) (adjuster, while uncertain whether covered or noncovered trailer was involved in accident, told injured party to get best medical care possible and insurer would care for everything; held, on rehearing, for the insurer; coverage cannot be enlarged by waiver or estoppel); Washington Nat'l Ins. Co. v. Craddock, 130 Tex. 251, 109 S.W.2d 165 (1937), 113 A.L.R. 854 (1938); Summers v. Oakfield Town Mut. Fire Ins. Co., 245 Wis. 40, 13 N.W.2d 518 (1944). *Contra, e.g.*, Harr v. Allstate Ins. Co., 54 N.J. 287, 255 A.2d 208 (1969) (claim of estoppel to deny coverage under fire policy because of contrary representations of agent; in granting a new trial the court held the parol evidence rule inapplicable and rejected the assertion that estoppel does not apply to coverage provisions); State Auto. Cas. Underwriters v. Ruotsalainen, 81 S.D. 472, 136 N.W.2d 884 (1965) (waiver and estoppel available to expand coverage to trailer in view of assurances by insurer's agents); Farmers Mut. Auto. Ins. Co. v. Bechard, 80 S.D. 237, 122 N.W.2d 86 (1963), 1 A.L.R.3d 1124 (1965) (provision in death and disability coverage of automobile policy declaring no liability for "death sustained in the course of his occupation" while operating a "commercial" vehicle; deceased was operating the insured truck in the course of his work; held, insurer barred from asserting the defense because of representations he would be covered regardless of what he might be driving). See also Note, 15 Vill.L.Rev. 505 (1970).

The phrase "the heart, the very essence, of the contract" appears in the course of the court's statement of an unsuccessful defense raised in State Farm Fire Ins. Co. v. Rakes, 188 Va. 239, 243, 49 S.E.2d 265, 267 (1948), 4 A.L.R.2d 862, 864 (1949).

In *Craddock*, the court stated: "The question presented . . . is whether a contractual liability may be created by a waiver. . . . [The waiver] doctrine can not be made to serve that purpose." 130 Tex. at 253, 109 S.W.2d at 166. But it is plain that the voluntary relinquishment of a known right that is the essence of genuine waiver could not be proved in *Craddock*. Nor could the claimant prove detrimental reliance. The plaintiff's accident insurance policy stipulated that gunshot wounds were not within the class of injuries for which protection was given. After plaintiff accidentally shot himself through the leg with a pistol, he presented a claim and for eleven weeks received payments. The insurer then declined to make further payments, and plaintiff claimed that by making payments for eleven weeks the insurer waived the policy provision on gunshot wounds.

In *Summers*, a town mutual company issued a fire insurance policy covering

expressed as a doctrine disallowing variance from coverage provisions.

Courts and writers have not generally attempted to correlate the definitions of coverage in these different contexts. For example, it has been said that in the great majority of cases provisions relating to the location of insured property are subject to waiver or estoppel.[4] Yet, in the context of statutes regulating defenses based on warranties, Patterson classifies such a provision as a coverage clause rather than a warranty.[5] Moreover, it has been stated that most cases distinguish an "estoppel to assert breach of warranty or condition" from an estoppel that would "prevent the insurance company from maintaining that certain risks are not covered by the policy."[6] Thus, both in these decisions and in some construing incontestability statutes,[7] a condition is classified with a warranty in contrast with a coverage clause, whereas other courts, construing statutes regulating warranties, would classify a condition with a coverage provision in contrast with a warranty.[8]

Of course, surface confusion does not conclusively establish undesirable substantive inconsistency. These discrepancies may only reflect variations among jurisdictions rather than variations according to what kind of regulatory measure is involved — whether a warranty statute, an incontestability statute, or some such judicial doctrine as waiver, estoppel, or election. Moreover though these regulations may be characterized as legal restrictions against technical defenses used to gain unconscionable advantage, the contexts differ materially. Thus, the controls over defenses based on warranty, representation, or concealment are primarily concerned with risks of overreaching by the use of shrewdly drafted policy provisions. The doctrines of waiver and estoppel, and the miscellaneous set of additional theories often associated with them, apply most often to conduct of agents of the in-

---

property while located in a described building in a specified town, but not elsewhere. By its charter the company's authorization to do business was limited to a specified territory. The insured moved his property to a town outside this territory and claimed coverage on the ground that with knowledge of his move the company continued to collect assessments. Perhaps the claimant did prove, or at least could have proved if required to do so, that the agent accepting the payments knew of the move and that the claimant detrimentally relied upon the representation of continued coverage implicit in accepting payments after the claimant had moved his property outside the company's authorized territory. In that case, however, *Summers* might still be explained on grounds other than immunity of coverage provisions from the doctrine of estoppel.

Arguably the case turned on the distinctive geographical limits of the company's power to insure. Perhaps the soundness of the result reached by the court is open to question, since there are better remedies than this for a company's ultra vires conduct.

4. Annot., 4 A.L.R.2d 868, 871 (1949). *But see* Annot., 1 A.L.R.3d 1139, 1170 (1965). See also § 6.7(c) *infra.*

5. Patterson, Essentials of Insurance Law 296–297 (2d ed. 1957). See § 6.-5(b) (2) *supra.*

6. Ivey v. United Nat'l Indem. Co., 259 F.2d 205, 207 (9th Cir. 1958) (dictum).

7. See § 6.5(d) *supra* [discussing *Simpson*].

8. See § 6.5(b) (3) *supra.*

surer in relation to marketing. These different contexts may well call for legal controls different in reach as well as in kind.

For example, application of theories of waiver and estoppel may produce exceptionally favored treatment for limited numbers of policyholders, giving some a far better bargain than others with the same class of coverage. Moreover, this inequity is not mitigated by broader considerations of fairness, as when a knowledgeable policyholder benefits by an objectively reasonable construction of an onerous provision.[9] Also, the cumulative effect of individual applications of these doctrines may be a severe interference with control over underwriting since the acts of agents in the field may frustrate underwriting decisions made at the home office. In contrast, regulation of warranty clauses in policy forms raises no similar problem of equity among policyholders, and it frustrates underwriting decisions only to the extent that they are part of an unconscionable pattern the regulation is designed to defeat. Thus, it may be argued that courts should recognize an even broader immunity from variance by waiver and estoppel than the immunity from another kind of variance implicit in holding that coverage clauses are unaffected by statutory regulation of warranties. But immunity is not the only way, and probably is not the best way, of protecting against excessive proliferation of cases of variance.

Granted, among the alternative ways of achieving this protection are some that, though using distinctions other than the coverage-warranty dichotomy, nevertheless depend on the notion that certain stipulations are immune from variance. One possibility, already noted, is to determine whether provisions are within reach of such doctrines as waiver and estoppel on the basis of whether the provisions are part of the heart, the very essence of the contract. One way to give content to such a standard would be to ask whether the condition serves a function basic to identification of the subject matter or to determination of the character of the insurance contract — a method similar to Patterson's functional analysis of clauses being tested under statutes regulating warranties.[10] Still another possible standard is whether adherence to the condition is essential to a reasonable degree of control over underwriting and rate fixing and to equity among policyholders in light of their respective contributions to the insurance arrangement through premiums.

It would seem wiser, however, to dispense with all these theories of immunity from variance. Some interference with centralized underwriting and with consistent treatment of different policyholders is inherent in most theories of variance. But courts can limit this interference reasonably (and without resort to the crutch of a theory of immunity) by simply adhering to sound requisites for entitlement

---

9. For discussion of the knowledgeable policyholder, see § 6.3(b) *supra*.

10. See Patterson, Essentials of Insurance Law 296–297 (2d ed. 1957) and § 6.5(b) (2) *supra*.

to variance case by case. Moreover, the risk that there will be successful nonmeritorious claims is easily exaggerated.

One factor that helps to control the risk of nonmeritorious claims is the liability of the agent to the insurer for representations beyond the scope of his authority. Even if the policyholder chooses to proceed against the insurer and not the agent, the insurer's rights against the agent and its bargaining position with him give it a degree of protection against his abuse of power, especially if deliberate. Also, the increasing use of errors and omissions coverage — a form of malpractice liability insurance — encourages policing of agents by their liability insurers.

A second and perhaps more important factor limiting the risk of nonmeritorious claims at variance with policy provisions operates when genuine estoppel is the theory of variance. Dubious claims are tested by the requirement that to establish estoppel the claimant must prove detrimental reliance on a misleading representation. This does not remove risks of injustice entirely, since there will be cases of undetected fraudulent testimony and even undetected collusion with an insurer's agent to establish a claim of estoppel. But at least the risks of nonmeritorious claims of such misrepresentations are minimized by the detrimental reliance requirement.

There are positive gains, too, from rejecting the theory that some kinds of stipulations should be immune from variance claims. Doctrines based on genuine waiver and estoppel are intended to protect against agents' misleading oral representations, just as statutes concerning warranties protect against draftsmen's misleading policy clauses. To accomplish this, their application should not depend merely on the nature of the policy provision that a representation contradicts. Misleading oral representations are no less possible in relation to provisions of central importance than in relation to less significant provisions.

Moreover, there is reason to think that the doctrine of immunity from waiver and estoppel has proved unnecessary to its apparent intended function and that the rule that coverage provisions are not subject to variance is a less reliable basis for prediction, even in jurisdictions whose courts persistently state the rule, than is a set of rigorously applied rules of waiver, estoppel, election, reformation, and breach.

Among the decisions denying claims of waiver or estoppel on the ground that coverage provisions were involved, it is difficult indeed to find cases in which it does not seem likely that the claims could have been properly denied on other grounds. In most instances, denial might have rested on the claimant's failure to prove the requisites of genuine waiver, estoppel, or reformation as they are commonly applied in other contexts, along with failure to prove an election soundly grounded on the principle of disallowing unconscionable advantage. Cases not explainable on this basis may be distinguished on more specialized grounds.[11]   The development of extensive regulation of policy forms demonstrates a recognition of needs for regulating provisions that are of the very essence of the contract.   Although such regulation is accomplished in a way that is consistent in theory with enforcement of policy provisions, in substance it is often founded on the same principles that give rise to rights at variance with policy provisions.   It is noteworthy, by way of analogy, that incontestability and warranty statutes exclude from their reach — thus treating as coverage provisions — a number of common clauses with respect to which some legislatures have enacted regulatory statutes.   Among these are life insurance policy provisions concerning death caused in a specified manner.[12]

It seems, then, that even coverage provisions should be subject to carefully limited application of waiver and estoppel, as well as other doctrines such as election, reformation, and rescission.   The need sensed by some courts to hold certain types of policy provisions beyond reach of waiver and estoppel may be avoided if courts adhere to the general formulations of waiver and estoppel rather than stretching them beyond their normal scope.   Rather than distorting waiver and estoppel, courts should candidly rely on the principles of honoring reasonable expectations and disallowing unconscionable advantage when there are compelling reasons for protecting the insured beyond the normal scope of waiver and estoppel.   As a practical matter, in light of agency and marketing practices in the industry, insurance cases would continue to be distinctive in calling for relatively frequent applications of waiver, estoppel, and election.

SECTION 6.7   REGULATION OF MARKETING

§ 6.7(a) GENERALLY

Perhaps the most common context in insurance law for invoking waiver, estoppel, and related theories has been the assertion of rights based on occurrences during the marketing process.   A wide range of theories presented at the beginning of this chapter[1] is relevant to the subject matter of the present section, in which their application is considered in types of cases falling within some of the most common fact patterns.

An error in a policy resulting from mutual mistake is ordinarily a ground for reformation.   Thus, for example, a policy may be reformed to identify correctly the persons or interests insured.[2]

---

11. See, *e.g.*, the discussion of *Summers*, n.3 *supra*.

12. See § 6.5(b)(2) nn.23–25 *supra*.

1. See § 6.1 *supra*.

2. *E.g.*, Gillis v. Sun Ins. Office, Ltd., 238 Cal.App.2d 408, 47 Cal.Rptr. 868 (1st Dist. 1965), 25 A.L.R.3d 564 (1969) (corporation named as insured had ceased to exist because of a merger before policy was written; reformation to substitute surviving corporation as insured and to cover certain other interests as intended).

More often, however, variance claims growing out of incidents during the marketing process are rationalized on grounds of waiver or estoppel,[3] and, as will appear in this section, frequently on untenable extensions of those theories when the facts warrant relief but on other grounds.

Ordinarily an insurer is not estopped, however, to assert fraud in which the party claiming coverage participated. In that circumstance, if the claimant cannot prove that the agent knew of the fraudulent scheme there is no basis for estopping the insurer, and if he does prove complicity of the agent, he proves the agent's collusion against his principal, which ordinarily precludes imputing the agent's knowledge to the insurer.[4]

In addition to the rights discussed in the present section, there are other instances of judicial recognition of rights at variance with policy provisions because of incidents occurring during the marketing process. These include rights against insurers based on unreasonable delay in processing an application for insurance,[5] rights inconsistent with cancellation provisions,[6] and rights against agents and other intermediaries based on occurrences during the marketing process.[7]

§ 6.7(b) ERRONEOUSLY RECORDED ANSWERS

When an application for insurance contains false answers, should the insured or third party beneficiaries be able to recover benefits upon proof that the applicant gave truthful answers that were incorrectly recorded by an intermediary (agent or broker) or medical examiner?

An initial line of defense for the insurer is that the applicant is responsible for whatever appears in the application. This defense is

3. *E.g.*, Sanborn v. Maryland Cas. Co., 255 Iowa 1319, 125 N.W.2d 758 (1964) (oral agreement in 1956 for annual renewal of liability insurance policy; without request or application, renewal policies issued in 1957, 1958, and 1959; application signed for 1960 policy, but applicant testified he signed it in November, 1961, believing it was an application for renewal of plate glass insurance in the same company; accident occurred in October, 1961, four months after expiration of the last policy; defendant's Des Moines office had customarily sent ticklers to agent concerning policies about to expire, but could not find any record of such a tickler on this policy in 1961; oral "agreement for coverage and automatic renewal" enforced; estoppel applied; see also § 2.2(a) (2) at n.15 *supra*); Dodge v. Aetna Cas. & Sur. Co., 127 Vt. 409, 250 A.2d 742 (1969) (agent, having agreed to obtain all the insurance plaintiff needed for new venture added to his business, issued liability policy that excluded products hazard, which agent negligently thought to be included; policyholder, unfamiliar with insurance, relied on the agent; held, insurer estopped from taking advantage of the exclusion).

4. *E.g.*, Southern Farm Bureau Cas. Ins. Co. v. Allen, 388 F.2d 126 (5th Cir. 1967) (Texas law; after application for automobile insurance was rejected, paper title to car was transferred to brother and new application was filed and approved in brother's name, although original applicant continued to hold and use car; claim of widow of victim of negligent driving by original applicant; held, for insurer).

5. See § 2.4 *supra*.

6. See § 5.10(e) *supra*.

7. See § 2.5 *supra*.

buttressed with arguments that the person recording the answers was, in doing so, acting as the applicant's agent and not as agent for the insurer; that the applicant's opportunity to read the recorded answers before signing makes him responsible for their content even if he failed to take advantage of that opportunity; and, if the application or a copy of it was attached to the policy or otherwise delivered to the policyholder, that his opportunity to read the recorded answers at that time and to call the insurer's attention to any discrepancy makes him responsible thereafter for their content. This last point is strengthened by invoking, when applicable, an entire-contract statute requiring that the application be made a part of the policy and declaring that no agreement outside the policy is binding.

Despite all these defensive theories, claimants often recover, at least in egregious cases, on grounds of rights at variance with policy provisions.

Perhaps most of the decisions considering this problem and allowing the insured or third party beneficiary to prove that the applicant answered correctly and his answers were falsely recorded are life or health and accident insurance cases.[1] But the rule has been applied in other types of cases as well. For example, a 17-year-old, newly-licensed applicant for automobile liability insurance was afforded protection under a policy even though the policy declared that the insurance did not apply when the car was operated by a person licensed less than a year or by a person under 25, except the applicant, stated to be age 23. Upon findings and conclusions that the applicant acted in good faith, that the false answers resulted from the agent's actions, that the policy form was complex and confusing, that the agent represented that liability coverage would be issued to the applicant, and that the insurer was responsible for the agent's unconscionable conduct, the court allowed reformation on the theory of honest mistake of the applicant induced by unconscionable conduct of the insurer's agent. The court further observed that in the face of fraud or other unconscionable conduct of its agent, an insurer cannot successfully defend on the ground that if the insured had exercised due care he would not have been defrauded.[2]

1.   *E.g.*, Pennsylvania Life Ins. Co. v. McReynolds, 440 S.W.2d 275 (Ky.1969), 57 Ky.L.J. 714 (1969) (nonmedical accident and health policy; agent considered facts too inconsequential to be included in application; insurer must show applicant's bad faith to establish defense; dissent on ground this in effect overrules recent decisions based on a statute); John Hancock Mut. Life Ins. Co. v. Schwarzer, 354 Mass. 327, 237 N.E.2d 50 (1968), 26 A.L.R.3d 1 (1969) (hospital expense policy; answers recorded by soliciting agent); Brasier v. Benefit Assoc. of Ry. Employees, 369 Mich. 166, 119 N.W.2d 639 (1963), 94 A.L.R.2d 1385 (1964) (health and accident insurance; answers recorded in report of medical examination); Hughes v. John Hancock Mut. Life Ins. Co., 351 Mich. 302, 88 N.W.2d 557 (1958) (life insurance; answers recorded in report of medical examination); Kelly v. Madison Nat'l Life Ins. Co., 37 Wis.2d 152, 154 N.W. 2d 334 (1967) (life insurance; answers recorded in report of medical examination; jury findings that doctor and applicant did not collude). See 17 Appleman, Insurance Law § 9401 (1945).

2.   Heake v. Atlantic Cas. Ins. Co., 15 N.J. 475, 105 A.2d 526 (1954).

In a case such as this, involving positive representations by the intermediary to the applicant as well as falsely recorded answers in the document forwarded to the insurer, the argument for reformation is compelling if the necessary relationship of the agent to the insurer can be proved. Such proof is commonly available in automobile insurance cases; indeed, customary marketing practices permit the agent to go even further and bind the insurer rather than merely to act for it in taking applications.

The argument for estoppel faces not only the requirement of detrimental reliance but also the difficulty that in some jurisdictions estoppel must be based on an agent's representations of fact, whereas in this context it often happens that some of the essential representations of the agent are promissory in character—assertions that the insurer will issue a policy with stated terms in the factual circumstances reported to the agent by the applicant. However, this is no obstacle in jurisdictions adhering to the preferable rule that an estoppel may be founded upon promissory representations. In such a jurisdiction, estoppel theory might be employed to afford protection if there were hesitation about allowing reformation because of the agency issue. Since estoppel is more analogous to tort than contract, the agency issue may be resolved favorably to the applicant on a theory that the agent's representations were incidental to his employment (a concept analogous to scope of employment in master-servant cases) even though beyond the scope of his authority or apparent authority to contract for the insurer.[3] The mere fact that the agent acted fraudulently to serve his own interests and in violation of instructions is insufficient to defeat either the claim of apparent authority on which reformation rests or the claim of representations incidental to his employment by the insurer on which estoppel rests.

Contributory negligence might be used as a defense to a claim of the type under consideration, but it should not bar relief against fraud, under either a theory of reformation or a theory of estoppel.[4] Indeed, it would seem that contributory negligence should not bar relief against a false record that the agent knew to be different from the applicant's answers, even if the agent's motives were not such as to warrant the characterization "fraud" in its ordinary sense. Even then the case is still not one of mere negligence and contributory negligence. Rather, an agent (or a medical examiner) and the applicant are not on a parity ordinarily with respect to their understanding of what is sought by the inquiries in the application and what is an appropriate way of expressing the response. This point has special force in relation to the rephrasing of an applicant's answers about medical history, whenever the answers are such as to require anything more than a report of physical facts or events within the applicant's knowledge at the time the inquiry is submitted to him.

In the absence of an applicable entire-contract statute, probably most courts would reach results consistent with the foregoing analy-

---

3. See § 6.4(d) *supra.*   4. See § 6.4(e) *supra.*

sis. But there are contrary decisions.[5] Also, a result unfavorable to the insured might be reached on the separate ground that, though not barred by his carelessness in reading, the insured is barred by the terms of an independent provision of the insurance contract, such as a clause declaring that the policy shall not become effective unless at the time it is delivered the intended insured is in good health; a court may hold that it is not the erroneous answers about his health, but the fact of his not being in good health in conformity with this clause that defeats his insurance coverage.[6]

Entire-contract statutes express an underlying policy somewhat at odds with the view expressed here that carelessness in failing to read a contract should not bar relief based on a claim that the agent or medical examiner knew the answers he recorded to be different from those given orally by the applicant. Perhaps the primary objective of these statutes is to avoid uncertainties for an insured about his rights by giving him access to a copy of the application rather than permitting the insurer to hold it and yet incorporate it by reference into the policy. But it is also within the purpose of these statutes, as most courts construe them, to achieve greater certainty in another way as well, by disallowing an insured's contention that he was not aware of the record, in the application attached to the policy, of what purports to be his answers. Thus most courts hold that, within the scope of their application, entire-contract statutes bind the insured by the record of his answers, even though it may be an inac-

---

5. *E.g.*, Gillan v. Equitable Life Assur. Soc., 143 Neb. 647, 10 N.W.2d 693 (1943), 148 A.L.R. 496 (1944):

"[W]e conclude that there is no sufficient reason in contracts of insurance why a party should be relieved from the duty of exercising the ordinary care and prudence that would be exacted in relation to other contracts." The validity of their assumption about the rule applying to other contracts may be challenged. Note, for example, that under the rule of Restatement (Second) of Agency § 295A, comment *a*, this would depend on whether the principal (the insurer) "would be adversely affected by a delay in discovering the facts." Certainly there would be cases of such adverse effect, but whether *Gillan* was one is not clear. Moreover, for reasons developed in § 6.4(e) *supra*, it seems preferable that the qualification set forth in the *Restatement* not be applied to insurance cases.

Gillan is interesting on another ground as well. It disapproved a contrary holding in German Ins. Co. v. Frederick, 57 Neb. 538, 77 N.W. 1106 (1899),

but applied the old rule to the case at hand because the defense attorney (very likely in reliance on the precedent) had not objected to the parol evidence of the plaintiff that she gave correct answers to defendant's medical examiner and he inserted incorrect answers in the application. This seems hardly fair to the defendant insurer, or to defense counsel, unless there was special reason for limiting the overruling decision to prospective application—for example, because the plaintiff in the particular case detrimentally relied on the old rule or because insureds generally would have detrimentally relied on that rule (both of which possibilities seem rather unlikely). Concerning the relevance of reliance interests to prospective overruling, see generally Keeton, Venturing to Do Justice 41–43 (1969).

6. See *e.g.*, Great Nat'l Life Ins. Co. v. Hulme, 134 Tex. 539, 136 S.W.2d 602 (1940), which, however, involved an "entire contract" statute as well as a good health clause. Regarding enforcement of good-health clauses generally, see § 6.5(e) (4) *supra*.

curate record.[7] Most statutes of this type, however, apply only to life or to life, health, and accident insurance.

A closely balanced issue arises in those exceptional circumstances in which, though not required to do so by statute, the insurer attaches the application to the policy or otherwise delivers a copy to the policyholder. On the one hand, under a rule barring the policyholder's claim because of his opportunity to read his copy of the application there is a risk that some policyholders will be the victims of a dishonest agent's fraud, and on the other hand under a rule barring the policyholder's claim only on proof of his knowledge of the false answers there is a risk of a substantial body of successful claims by dishonest policyholders. The former risk weighs less heavily and the latter more heavily in these circumstances than when no copy of the completed application is delivered to the policyholder. There is some support for extending the rule of preclusion under entire-contract statutes to these circumstances as well.[8]

§ 6.7(c) NOTICE CONCERNING LOCATION, USE, OR OCCUPANCY

Fire insurance contracts on personalty have customarily included a clause declaring that the policy covers personal property of the insured while located at a specified physical location, "but not elsewhere" unless otherwise provided (for example, with respect to limited coverage for property temporarily away from the specified location). Often it has happened that the insured has moved from the residence designated in the policy to another without having his insurance policy endorsed with the change of location. In Patterson's terminology, this location clause of the fire insurance policy is a coverage provision rather than a warranty.[1] But among courts purportedly adhering to the view that coverage provisions cannot be defeated by claimed rights at variance with them, this clause is usually not classified as a coverage provision for this purpose.[2] Thus, most jurisdictions recognize that a claim for continued coverage at the new location may be based on representations by an agent to the insured occurring after the consummation of the original contract.[3]

Fire insurance contracts on buildings have customarily included a clause declaring that, unless otherwise provided in writing by an endorsement attached to the policy, the insurer is not liable for loss occurring while the building is vacant or unoccupied beyond a speci-

---

7. *E.g.*, Minsker v. John Hancock Mut. Life Ins. Co., 254 N.Y. 333, 173 N.E. 4 (1930), 81 A.L.R. 829 (1932), which also calls attention to the fact that the New York decisional rule had been otherwise before the statute was enacted.

8. See, *e.g.*, Odom v. Insurance Co. of the State of Pa., 455 S.W.2d 195

(Tex.1970) (summarized in § 6.5(c) n.11 *supra*).

1. See § 6.5(b) (2) *supra*.

2. See § 6.6(b) and n.4 thereto *supra*.

3. *E.g.*, State Farm Fire Ins. Co. v. Rakes, 188 Va. 239, 49 S.E.2d 265 (1948), 4 A.L.R.2d 862 (1949).

fied length of time.   Often it has happened that the insured has claimed coverage for a loss occurring after a longer period of vacancy or unoccupancy, basing his claim on notice to the agent and conduct or representations of the agent thereafter.   Though decisions on the issue are not entirely in harmony, the insured has frequently prevailed on grounds of rights at variance with policy provisions.[4]

§ 6.7(d) ACCEPTING PREMIUMS TENDERED LATE OR OTHERWISE IMPROPERLY

Claims of rights at variance with policy provisions have sometimes been based on evidence that a person alleged to be an agent of the insurer received and exercised control over a premium in a way inconsistent with the insurer's theory of defense.

The most common context in which this problem arises involves a defense of nonpayment or late tender of the premium.   A claim that late payment revives the coverage under the terms of the policy itself is, of course, a claim within rather than at variance with policy provisions.   But claims based on acceptance of a late payment are often presented even though the policy does not provide for revival or reinstatement of coverage, or does not provide for retroactive effect to cover a loss occurring before late payment.   In such an instance, the claim is one for rights at variance with policy provisions.

If a casualty of the type insured against occurs after the policy has lapsed for nonpayment of a premium, an agent's receiving a premium with the understanding that he will tender it to the home office, but without any commitment that it will be accepted, is plainly insufficient, standing alone, to support a claim of coverage at variance with the policy provisions.   In considering what more is essential to a claim at variance, a wide range of theories is relevant.

Waiver is among the theories one should consider in this context.   Life, health, and accident policies commonly contain a clause establishing a grace period within which premiums may be paid without loss of coverage.   Under such a clause, it does not matter that a casualty has occurred before payment of the premium during the grace period.   The claim is valid under the contract itself.   Similarly, a right at variance with the contract—a claim of genuine waiver— might be established by evidence that the insurer had adopted a custom of conducting its operations on a grace-period basis, though without adding the grace-period clause to its policies.   The custom would be a voluntary extension of rights analogous to an insurer's sending out endorsements, without added premium charge, providing for such a grace period, or its publishing advertisements [1] announcing

---

4.   *E.g.*, McKinney v. Providence Washington Ins. Co., 144 W.Va. 559, 109 S. E.2d 480 (1959).   See 16A Appleman, Insurance Law § 9214 (rev. ed. 1968).

1.   See, *e.g.*, advertisement of John Hancock Mutual Life Insurnace Company announcing increased benefits for death or dismemberment under

that it was granting such an extension or had, for example, decided to increase benefits or to disregard a restrictive clause in its policies concerning military service in time of war.

Waiver is often relied upon when less appropriate to the circumstances. If a late premium is accepted at the home office, a question may be presented as to whether the home office agent accepting the premium did so with full knowledge of the circumstances—including both the late tender and the intervening casualty. In order to establish the voluntary relinquishment of known right that is the essence of waiver, such full knowledge should be required. To charge the insurer as if there were voluntary relinquishment because one agent knew of the casualty and the late tender when another agent accepted the premium is to dispense with a requirement of genuine voluntariness and substitute a fiction. Yet this is sometimes done.[2] The

certain paid-up weekly premium life insurance policies, Boston Globe, Jan. 2, 1968, p. 9.

2. See, *e.g.*, Seavey v. Erickson, 244 Minn. 232, 246, 69 N.W.2d 889, 898 (1955), 52 A.L.R.2d 1144, 1156 (1957):

"While the authorities are not in agreement, we believe that the rule to which we are committed is that acceptance and retention of a premium on a policy of insurance after knowledge of a loss is a waiver of a forfeiture, at least unless the insurance can have some application to the property which remains after the loss."

The court noted that the car allegedly covered by its policy of collision insurance had been completely demolished, and observed that the insurer's "contention that it accepted the premium to reinstate the policy as of the day and hour when the premium was paid, to operate prospectively on an automobile it then knew was no longer in existence as an automobile, is hardly tenable." *Ibid.* It seems highly improbable, however, that the person who accepted the premium in the home office knew what the court here says the insurer knew; rather, it appears likely that the court was attributing knowledge to the company from different agents and treating the company as if it were a single mind having the sum of this knowledge from different sources. The result reached by the court may be defended on other grounds, however. It may be that a genuine waiver could be established not on the basis of acceptance of this premium itself but on the basis of voluntarily adopting a general practice of issuing notices and accepting late

premiums as a routine, regardless of intervening casualty losses. Or estoppel, which was invoked by the court as an alternate ground of decision, might be supportable. For example, though this is not made clear it may be that the facts would have supported a claim that the insured detrimentally relied on company practices of sending notices inviting late payments and accepting them when tendered. Or, finally, one might argue that candid adoption of a doctrine of election for this type of case is justified. Concerning election generally, see J. Ewart, Waiver Distributed 66–123 (1917); Ewart, *"Waiver" in Insurance Law*, 13 Iowa L.Rev. 129 (1928); Ewart, *Waiver or Election*, 29 Harv. L.Rev. 724 (1916). Regarding the efforts of company draftsmen to forestall such decisions as that in *Seavey* by stipulations against waiver, and the frequent refusal of courts to enforce such clauses, see 3 Merrill, Notice §§ 1233, 1237, 1238 (1952).

See also American Nat'l Ins. Co. v. Cooper, —— Colo. ——, 458 P.2d 257 (1969) (delinquent premium accepted after injury; company precluded from defense that it did not reinstate coverage retroactively); Home Ins. Co. v. Caudill, 366 S.W.2d 167 (Ky.1963), 7 A.L.R.3d 406 (1966) (expressing reservations about a jury finding that premium payment was made before loss but affirming judgment for insured on grounds of that finding and waiver by the insurer in failing to cancel and then accepting an installment after the fire); German Ins. Co. v. Shader, 68 Neb. 1, 93 N.W. 972 (1903) (opinion by Roscoe Pound, Commissioner) (premium delivered to agent, and by him delivered to and accepted by the com-

result is, in reality, a doctrine of election, with a strong element of imposed liability rather than liability based on conduct reasonably interpretable as manifesting voluntary relinquishment.[3] To the extent that waiver is applied inconsistently with the theory that it is consensual, it has the effect of election, but without the saving grace of candor.

In this context, a candid doctrine of election would deny the insurer the option of retaining the premium and at the same time contesting coverage for an accident occurring during the period for which the premium was tendered. This would mean, among other things, that the insurer could not retain the premium and successfully claim that it did so in recognition only of coverage commencing with the date of tender or of acceptance. The argument for such a limitation on the insurer's range of choice in dealing with the tendered premium may be based on the proposition that insurers would otherwise be free to overreach policyholders, charging the premiums to the period for which late premiums were tendered as a routine, but thereafter treating differently those few late premiums that turned out on further inquiry to have been tendered after a casualty loss had occurred. If the limitation of such a rule of election is imposed, the insurer can protect itself by requiring the home office personnel to make inquiry before accepting late premiums, or it can take its chances by allowing them to accept late premiums without inquiry, the consequence being that occasionally it will become liable for an intervening casualty occurring after lapse and before tender. Against such a doctrine it may be argued that it converts what is supposed to be an insurance system into a system under which the premium is tendered to purchase coverage not for a risk of future loss but a loss certain—one that has already occurred. Nor is this argument adequately countered by the analogy to marine coverage for ships at sea, lost or not lost. In that context, neither the insurer nor the insured knows of the loss when the coverage is consummated. Here the insured knows of the loss, even if the person accepting the premium on behalf of the insurer does not. On balance it would seem better not to impose such a doctrine of election based merely on acceptance of a late premium in a case at bar. A legal consequence that is in nature a doctrine of election may result, however, from the enforcement of a statute regulating the disposition of tendered premiums.[4]

pany, after destruction of all the insured property; the money was sent back to the agent afterwards, but was not by him tendered to Shader; held, the agent had general authority to receive and collect premiums, and the course of conduct of the company and its agent "waives a provision that the insurer shall not be liable for a loss occurring before payment of the premium"; opinion observes that there has been a "contest between the courts on the one hand and counsel for insurance companies on the other, the latter devising skillfully framed clauses and provisions, and the former largely thwarting the purpose of those clauses by construing them strictly against the insurer").

3. For further development of this point, see §§ 6.1, 6.2 *supra*.

4. See, *e.g.*, Bousquet v. Transportation Ins. Co., 354 Mass. 152, 235 N.E.2d 807

The argument for election is strengthened if there is evidence of a custom of accepting premiums at the home office without inquiry and charging them in part to pay for the period of lapse except in those cases in which further inquiry discloses that a casualty has occurred during that period. It is reasonable to impose a limitation against such an unconscionable custom. Imposing on the insurer, by a doctrine of election, the choice of applying the premium in part to the period of lapse in all cases or none is one way of regulating such conduct.

It may be asserted that agents of the insurer—those in the home office, those in the field, or both—have made express or implied representations concerning acceptance of late premiums on which the insured has detrimentally relied. For example, the insured might offer evidence that over a course of years of dealing the insurer had always sent him a second notice before lapse for nonpayment of premium, that the second notice was not sent in this instance, and that the insured failed to pay on time because he relied on the opportunity of paying promptly after receipt of the second notice. Such proof would establish genuine estoppel.[5]

In some instances courts have permitted a claim of alleged estoppel upon proof of the custom of giving notice and failure to give it in the instance at hand, without requiring the further showing of detrimental reliance.[6] This is in substance a doctrine of election, on yet another set of terms. The limitation imposed here is that when an insurer establishes a general custom of sending notices that permit late payment within established periods of time, routinely applying the premiums as if collected on time and thus purchasing coverage that terminates sooner than if they were applied to coverage commencing when tendered, it will not be permitted to deviate from that custom in isolated cases in which it learns of the occurrence of a casualty before receiving the late premium. It must discontinue the custom altogether or adhere to it when disadvantageous as well as when advantageous. The unconscionable course of acting always to its own advantage is precluded.

Tender of a premium sometimes fails to measure up to policy provisions on a ground other than tardiness. For example, life insurance policies often provide that premiums are payable only at the home office of the company or, if elsewhere, only to a designated collector. If over a course of time the policyholder delivers premi-

---

(1968) (failure to issue conditional receipt for premium tendered with application for reinstatement caused statutory automatic reinstatement provisions to apply, with the result that coverage was in effect at the time of the insured's accidental death).

5. Perhaps Seavey v. Erickson, 244 Minn. 232, 69 N.W.2d 889 (1955), 52

A.L.R.2d 1144 (1957) is such a case. See n.2 *supra*.

6. *Seavey*, n.2 *supra*, may be considered such a case if not interpreted as resting on the assumption that the evidence sustained a finding of detrimental reliance in fact on company practices of sending notices inviting late payments and accepting them when tendered.

ums elsewhere—to a soliciting agent, for example—and they are consistently accepted, theories of rights at variance with the policy provisions may be invoked when the insurer later denies liability for nonpayment of a premium that was tendered at the accustomed place but not accepted.   If detrimental reliance can be proved—for example, because the policyholder made tender at the accustomed place on the last permissible day and made tender at the proper place reasonably soon thereafter but beyond the stated period—a compelling case of estoppel is established.   A materially different case is presented when it appears that a soliciting agent who had been receiving and transmitting premiums discontinued that practice and refused the tendered premium, and neither the policyholder nor anyone else on his behalf made any further effort to pay the premium.   Even though death of the person whose life was insured occurs within the period for which the tendered premium would have continued the policy in force, there is in such case no good ground for waiver [7] and, in the absence of proof of detrimental reliance, none for estoppel either.

SECTION 6.8   REGULATION OF CLAIMS PROCESSES

§ 6.8(a)   GENERALLY

Insurance policies commonly include clauses designed to govern claims processes.   Provisions concerning timeliness of notice, proof of loss, and suit [1] are examples.   So, too, are clauses concerning subrogation,[2] clauses concerning protection of property damaged under circumstances within the coverage of property insurance,[3] and liability insurance clauses concerning assistance and cooperation in defense.[4]

In general, the drafting of such provisions has been strongly influenced by the desire of claims officers of insurers to reduce delays

---

7.   Southland Life Ins. Co. v. Lawson, 137 Tex. 399, 153 S.W.2d 953 (1941), 136 A.L.R. 1212 (1942).   A further argument for the insured in such a case is that apparent authority of the agent to accept the premium is established by the insurer's practice of accepting previous premiums, and that a valid tender to the agent is thus consummated momentarily before the agent declines to accept the premium in issue.   If it has happened, however, that all of the agent's transmittals have reached the home office within the permitted time, it may be argued that the insurer's conduct has been equivocal because consistent with treating the payments as made at the home office through an agent for the insured.   To counter this argument the claimant might assert that the in-

surer should be aware of the policyholder's reasonable expectations that the agent was acting for the insurer and not the policyholder and should be required to honor those expectations in the absence of notifying the policyholder to the contrary.   The *Lawson* opinion does not disclose whether in fact each of the transmitted premiums was received in the home office before expiration of the applicable grace period.

1.   See § 7.2(a) *infra.*

2.   See §§ 3.10, 4.2–4.6 *supra* and § 6.8(b) *infra.*

3.   See § 5.4(d) *supra.*

4.   See § 7.5 *infra.*

and uncertainties about the disposition of claims. As a result, it has happened that in many instances the stated terms have been more restrictive than can be permitted under the principles of disallowing unconscionable advantage[5] and honoring reasonable expectations.[6] Thus, occasionally courts have dispensed entirely with the requirement of filing proof of loss,[7] and quite often provisions establishing rigid time limits for giving notice, presenting proof of loss, or filing suit have been tempered by the recognition of excuses that in combination virtually amount to and occasionally have even been expressed as a rule declaring the notice, proof, or filing adequate if it occurs within a reasonable time.[8] Another way in which such provisions have been tempered is by disallowing the insurer's defense based on a stated time limit if it appears that the incident at first seemed trivial to the insured[9] or if it does not appear that the insurer was prejudiced by the delay in presenting the claim.[10] In all these cases, judicial opinions have often been reasoned on grounds of construction of policy provisions or of resolving ambiguities in them. A more candid explanation is that rights at variance with policy provisions are being recognized. There is limited support for extending this principle even to the point of holding that an insurer will be estopped from relying on a statute of limitation because of its failure to inform the insured that coverage of a restrictively worded policy clause is held to be broader than literal construction would indicate.[11]

The theory has been advanced that payment of a claim that might have been contested is a practical construction of a latent ambiguity in a policy, binding the insurer to coverage of a later claim, even though the earlier claim was small and the later relatively large.[12] It would seem, however, that this theory should be rejected. It is not supported by any of the several principles underlying rights at variance with policy provisions.[13] If there is a true ambiguity in the policy, it may well be that a straightforward application of the principle of resolving ambiguities against the insurer justifies coverage.[14] Or, if detrimental reliance can be proved, coverage may be justified.[15] But an independent theory that practical construction by the insurer in paying a single claim should bind it to pay future claims of that type seems insupportable on grounds of principle.

---

5. See § 6.2 *supra*.

6. See § 6.3 *supra*.

7. *E.g.*, Maynard v. National Fire Ins. Co., 147 W.Va. 539, 129 S.E.2d 443 (1963) (insurer "waived" requirement of filing proof of loss by requiring examinations under oath).

8. See § 7.2(a) *infra*. Compare also the treatment of clauses concerning timeliness of a demand for appraisal, § 7.3(b) *infra*.

9. See § 7.2(a) *infra*.

10. See § 7.1(b) *infra*.

11. Bowler v. Fidelity & Cas. Co., 53 N.J. 313, 250 A.2d 580 (1969), discussed in § 6.2 *supra*.

12. Aetna Cas. & Sur. Co. v. Haas, 422 S.W.2d 316 (Mo.1968).

13. Concerning such principles generally, see § 6.1 *supra*.

14. See § 6.3(a) *supra*.

15. See § 6.4 *supra*.

Another set of cases in which courts have occasionally recognized rights at variance with policy provisions concerns appraisal and arbitration clauses.[16] Here, as in relation to rights at variance generally, the relevant theories are numerous. For example, cases recognizing rights at variance with policy provisions concerning the timeliness of a demand for appraisal have included instances of subsequent contractual agreement (a nonwaiver agreement) inconsistent with the policy clause,[17] genuine estoppel, and election.[18] As in other contexts, courts have tended to speak of waiver even when the real ground was not voluntary relinquishment of known right but one among other theories.

An additional context in which rights at variance with policy provisions are frequently recognized involves a liability insurer's actions in relation to a tort claim against the insured after knowledge of a policy defense. For example, a claim of rights at variance with policy provisions may be based on the insurer's receiving suit papers served upon the insured in the tort action and failing to notify the insured of the disclaimer of liability in time for the insured to take other protective action,[19] or on the insurer's undertaking the defense with knowledge of the insured's breach of the assistance and cooperation clause.[20] Reservation of rights notices and nonwaiver agree-

---

16. Concerning such clauses generally, see § 7.3 *infra*.

17. *E.g.*, Milwaukee Ins. Co. v. Kogen, 240 F.2d 613 (8th Cir. 1957) (Minnesota law). Concerning nonwaiver agreements generally, see § 6.6(a) *supra*.

18. In Chainless Cycle Mfg. Co. v. Security Ins. Co., 169 N.Y. 304, 62 N.E. 392 (1901), the court held that the insurer, having permitted its agent to engage in protracted negotiations over the amount of a fire loss while the damaged property was deteriorating rapidly, was precluded from requiring an appraisal by demand made a few days after the insured had sold the property, several weeks after the fire. Though the opinion characterized defendant's conduct as a waiver, the supporting rationale was that the court could not say the insurer's demand for appraisal was made within reasonable time since the evidence warranted an inference the insurer had no intention of requiring an appraisal until it thought it could take unfair advantage of the insured. Perhaps the evidence proved detrimental reliance on an implied representation the insurer did not wish an appraisal; if so, a genuine case of estoppel was presented. At another point the opinion refers to the fact that the demand

came after the insured, misled by the insurer's acts, had been placed in such a position that an appraisal was impossible. Concerning genuine estoppel, see § 6.4 *supra*; concerning election, see § 6.1 *supra*.

19. *E.g.*, Zak v. Fidelity-Phenix Ins. Co., 34 Ill.2d 438, 216 N.E.2d 113 (1966). See also § 6.6(a) n.4 *supra*.

20. See, *e.g.*, Allstate Ins. Co. v. Keller, 17 Ill.App.2d 44, 149 N.E.2d 482 (1st Dist. 1958), 70 A.L.R.2d 1190 (1960) (breach by insured's false representation that he was the driver of his car at the time of accident; after receiving knowledge of contrary facts, insurer's attorneys continued in defense and took insured's deposition to strengthen policy defense; insurer barred from relying on the breach, the court loosely employing waiver and estoppel theories); Rose v. Regan, 344 Mass. 223, 181 N.E.2d 796 (1962) (entering general appearance and having default removed without having reserved rights growing out of insured's failure to forward suit papers; waiver and election reasoning, but without using the terminology of election); Merchants Indem. Corp. v. Eggleston, 37 N.J. 114, 179 A.2d 505 (1962) (insurer precluded because it defended without reservation of rights or nonwaiver agreement; discussion of waiver and

ments are frequently used, sometimes effectively and sometimes not, for the purpose of avoiding variance claims incident to the insurer's undertaking the defense.[21]

Some of the decisions favoring insureds appear to do so on very ill-defined and unclear grounds—for example, allowing recovery on a theory of waiver when there are clear indications the insurer's representatives did not intend to relinquish a known right,[22] or on a theory of estoppel but without any showing of detrimental reliance.[23]

Liability insurers are sometimes confronted with the contention that denial of liability on one ground precludes later assertion of another policy defense. Although in particular circumstances it may happen that a communication denying liability on one ground impliedly represents that no other ground of defense will be asserted, more often this is not the case and theories of waiver, estoppel, or election grounded on a contrary assumption seem ill-founded.[24]

Improper conduct of a liability-insurer-appointed counsel in a tort action, serving the insurer's interests that conflict with those of the insured, may lead to granting rights to the insured at variance with the assistance and cooperation clause of the policy.[25]

estoppel, and some language of election); Van Dyke v. White, 55 Wash. 2d 601, 349 P.2d 430 (1960) (when the insured refused to attend trial and the insurer proceeded with defense despite offer of continuance because of absence of the insured, the insurer "waived" breach of cooperation clause, since it cannot use its right of defense to improve its own position against the interests of the policyholder). See also § 7.7(b) and n.13 thereto infra.

21. See § 6.6(a) supra.

22. See, e.g., Nationwide Mut. Ins. Co. v. Thomas, 306 F.2d 767 (D.C. Cir. 1962) (defense counsel's request to withdraw upon discovery of breach of assistance and cooperation clause denied by trial court; motion for new trial resulted in reduction of judgments; insurer then appealed on merits; held, voluntary appeal waived defense of noncooperation, though there was no waiver in attorneys' acting in trial court under court order; concerning withdrawal of defense attorney, see § 7.7(b) at nn.22–24 infra; Van Dyke in n.20 supra.

23. See, e.g., Meirthew v. Last, 376 Mich. 33, 135 N.W.2d 353 (1965) (after the insurer knew of facts bearing on applicability of an exclusion it answered for the insured, and only later gave notice that it reserved rights as to any

defense it might have under policy; held, notice was unreasonably and prejudicially tardy and insufficient to preserve a policy defense later asserted in garnishment proceeding); National Union Fire Ins. Co. v. Bruecks, 179 Neb. 642, 139 N.W.2d 821 (1966) (accidental discharge of gun when insured attempted to unload it in back seat of moving car; held, not within coverage of automobile policy—as to which point, see § 5.2(b) supra—but was within coverage of homeowners policy; also held that homeowners insurer, having taken over control of defense for seventeen months and having represented that the policy afforded coverage, was, without any further showing of prejudice, estopped to deny coverage). See also § 6.4(f) supra concerning what is required as a showing of prejudice or detriment generally. Concerning the necessity for an insurer to show prejudice to sustain a defense, see § 7.1(b) infra.

24. See, e.g., Clark v. London & Lancashire Indem. Co., 16 Wis.2d 30, 113 N. W.2d 555 (1962) (denial of liability as beyond policy coverage and simultaneous assertion of noncompliance with notice provisions; held, no waiver or election by the insurer), on later appeal involving other issues, 21 Wis.2d 268, 124 N.W.2d 29 (1963), 98 A.L.R.2d 1037 (1964).

25. See § 7.7(b) infra.

§ 6.8(b) PRECLUSION OF SUBROGATION RIGHTS

Fire and casualty insurance contracts ordinarily provide that the insurer, in some circumstances at least, shall upon payment of loss be subrogated to rights of the insured against third persons.[1]

Perhaps the most common context for a claim of rights at variance with such a policy provision is that of collision damage to an insured automobile caused by the negligent operation of another vehicle. The insured may wish to assert his tort claim against the third party—for example, because his own insurer is dilatory in paying his claim, or because he suffered personal injury as well as damage to the insured car, or because his collision coverage is subject to a substantial deductible and he hopes to recover in full against the tortfeasor or the latter's liability insurer. If he pursues the tort claim without his collision insurer's consent, however, he may endanger his collision coverage. If his insurer has not yet paid the collision claim, it may deny liability because of interference with its subrogation rights; if it has already paid, it may seek damages or restitution from the insured.[2]

In some circumstances, however, the insured may succeed in asserting rights at variance with the subrogation clause of his collision coverage. For example, the insurer's subrogation rights may be barred by laches.[3] Also, it has been held that if the collision insurer declines to act—failing either to make payment or to deny liability—it is precluded from asserting that the insured's subsequent pursuit of his tort claim against the third party defeats his coverage.[4] The theory of preclusion has sometimes been stated as waiver or estoppel.[5] But a claim of waiver faces the difficulty that the insurer, rather than voluntarily relinquishing its defense, was plainly trying to avoid the legal consequence of losing it. In most cases of this general type, a claim of estoppel faces the difficulty that the insured did not detrimentally rely upon any representation of the insurer. Even election, though a more plausible theory than waiver or estoppel since by nature it involves judicial imposition of limits on the insurer's range of choice, does not fit this situation well. Although there is a good argument for the result reached, it is awkward to express it as a doctrine of election precluding the insurer from simultaneous breach

1. See § 3.10 *supra*.

2. See § 3.10 *supra*.

3. *E.g.*, Sun Ins. Office v. Hohenstein, 128 Misc. 870, 875, 220 N.Y.S. 386, 389 (Munic. Ct., Manhattan 1927).

4. Powers v. Calvert Fire Ins. Co., 216 S.C. 309, 57 S.E.2d 638 (1950), 16 A.L. R.2d 1261 (1951).

5. *E.g.*, Weber v. United Hardware & Implement Mutuals Co., 75 N.D. 581,

31 N.W.2d 456 (1948) (waiver and estoppel). See also Powers v. Calvert Fire Ins. Co., 216 S.C. 309, 57 S.E.2d 638 (1950), 16 A.L.R.2d 1261 (1951), in which the court characterizes the ground of preclusion as waiver but also observes that the subrogation rights are not available to the insurer "because of its conduct which amounted to a breach of the contract of insurance . . . ." 216 S.C. at 316, 57 S.E.2d at 642, 16 A.L.R.2d at 1266.

of its own contract obligation and assertion of its subrogation rights. If election is to be applied to this breach, then why not to all others? In short, to expand the theory of election this far is to incorporate within its scope every breach of contract by the insurer, at least if as substantial in character as that here involved.

A more suitable rationale for the result is that the insurer is barred from asserting violation of its subrogation rights as a defense because it has committed a material breach of contract in failing to pay the collision claim when due. The insured is privileged to pursue the tort claim against the third party in order to mitigate his damages flowing from the insurer's breach, and perhaps is even bound to do so under pain of having his claim against the insurer limited by the doctrine of avoidable consequences. To the argument that the insured should sue the insurer first rather than proceeding against the tortfeasor, it may be answered that if this course is less attractive to the insured, the insurer has no cause to complain that the insured pursues diligently what will be his only remedy if it turns out that there is justification for the insurer's refusal to pay the collision claim. Moreover, when the tort claim for the property damage that is also the subject of collision insurance is related to a very substantial personal injury claim, it would be grossly unfair to the insured, the victim of the insurer's breach of contract, to require him to suffer delay or other disadvantage in the pursuit of his personal injury claim in order to serve the interests of the insurer. This theory of denial of the insurer's defense as a consequence of its own material breach of contract has support in precedent as well as principle.[6]

§ 6.8(c) RECEIPT-OF-DUE-PROOF AND RELATED CLAUSES

The clause stating the principal agreement of a life or health and accident insurer to pay benefits for disability has in many instances been conditioned "upon receipt of due proof" of the disability.[1] Often other conditions are added, either in the principal statement of the insurer's promise or elsewhere in the policy.[2]

6. This appears to be the theory counsel for the plaintiff and the court were expressing in speaking of the insured's action against his collision insurer in *Powers*, n.5 *supra*, as an action "not for enforcement of the contract of insurance but for damages for its breach." 216 S.C. at 315, 57 S.E.2d at 641, 16 A.L.R.2d at 1265.

1. Compare the provisions in the waiver-of-premiums clauses of the life insurance policy in Appendix E and the health and accident insurance policy in Appendix F *infra*.

2. For example, such a policy may require written notice to the insurer at its home office during the lifetime of the insured and during the continuance of the disability. And it may declare that due proof must be received at the home office before the expiration of one year after default in payment of premium and in any event, whether or not there be a default, not later than one year from the anniversary of the policy on which the insured's rated-up age at nearest birthday is 60 or one year after maturity of the policy, whichever is the earlier date, otherwise the claim shall be invalid. Compare the provisions in the waiver-of-premiums clauses of the life insurance policy in Appendix E *infra* and the health and accident insurance policy in Appendix F *infra*.

Strict enforcement of such conditions would give the insurer strong protection against late claims and would sharply reduce the amount needed at any given time in reserves for claims not yet presented. It would also limit protection in a way not well related, if at all, to policyholder needs, and often would reduce protection substantially below reasonable expectations. Not surprisingly, then, controls over such clauses have been developed both in statutes and in judicial decisions.

Statutory controls are ordinarily in the form of prescription or proscription of policy provisions.[3] Thus it usually happens that they operate to cause the policy provisions themselves to be more favorable to policyholders than they might otherwise be. The controls effected by judicial decision, on the other hand, often establish rights at variance with policy provisions, even when reasoned as if mere interpretations of policy language.

Sometimes the refusal to enforce restrictive provisions concerning receipt of due proof is based on an alleged conflict between provisions in different parts of the policy form, the principal promise of the insurer being treated as less restrictive than qualifying clauses appearing elsewhere in the policy.[4] On the theory of resolving ambiguity, enforcement of the more restrictive provisions is then disallowed. But it is seldom indeed that company draftsmen have been so thoughtless as not to include in the principal promise a reference to the part of the policy in which the more restrictive provisions appear. Thus, painstaking study of the policy would have revealed to the policyholder the restrictions of which he or his beneficiary complains. In these circumstances, it has been said that a majority of the decisions enforce the restrictive clauses.[5] But, as indicated, other courts have declined to enforce such clauses, often reasoning that there was conflict among different policy provisions and thus ambiguity in the policy as a whole. The result they have thus reached is in fact to recognize rights at variance with policy provisions. In some instances, at least, the principle of honoring reasonable expectations [6] supports this result.

If decisions for policyholders in this context are based on a theory of conflict and ambiguity, it should follow logically that company draftsmen could fashion a policy stating all the qualifications in the insuring clause in such way as to avoid any ambiguity. This would be awkward and perhaps undesirable from the point of view of marketing, however. Moreover, even if such a policy form were fashioned, the company would not be absolutely safe from liability at variance with the policy provisions. For example, if any less carefully

---

3. *E.g.*, N.Y. Ins. Law § 164 (McKinney 1966). See also § 2.10 *supra*.

4. *E.g.*, Johnson v. New York Life Ins. Co., 212 F.2d 256 (7th Cir. 1954), *cert. denied*, 348 U.S. 836 (1954); Mosby v. Mutual Life Ins. Co., 405 Ill. 599, 92

N.E.2d 103 (1950), 18 A.L.R.2d 1054 (1951).

5. See Annot., 18 A.L.R.2d 1061 (1951). See also 3 Appleman, Insurance Law § 1395 (rev. ed. 1967).

6. See § 6.3 *supra*.

qualified description of the coverage were used in the company's brochures describing the policy, or perhaps even in agents' oral statements about it, there would be a risk that a court would hold the company bound by the misleading advertising, particularly if it regarded the carefully qualified policy clause as too complex for the lay reader to understand. In this respect, the principle of honoring reasonable expectations combines with the principle of disallowing unconscionable advantage to support a regulation of substance and not merely form. That is, these principles support a rule prohibiting insurers from enforcing strictly those policy provisions that are so complex or otherwise unexpectable substantively that no amount of care in drafting can avoid the creation of reasonable expectations contrary to their terms.[7]

§ 6.8(d) INSURER'S BREACH AS EXCUSING INSURED'S NONCOMPLIANCE WITH CLAIM PROCEDURES

An insurer's unjustified denial of liability may serve as an excuse for failure of the insured to comply thereafter with policy provisions concerning claim processes. For example, when the insurer in subsequent litigation bases its denial of liability on lack of timely presentment of a claim, either alone or in conjunction with the defense previously asserted, the defense of lateness may be precluded because of the recognition of rights at variance with policy provisions. Such rights, if based on the insured's detrimental reliance, are an instance of genuine estoppel. The recognition of such right may also be justified on the ground that the insurer's material breach of contract excuses the insured's noncompliance with prescribed claims procedures. The stated theory of decision in such cases has often been waiver.[1] But ordinarily genuine waiver cannot be proved in this context. And if the insurer's denial of liability was justifiable, in view of the nature of the claims made up to the time it occurred, such denial does not preclude the insurer from asserting noncompliance with claims procedures (such as timely filing of proof of loss) when the insured subsequently presents a revised claim on grounds within coverage.[2]

As already noted, a property insurer may be precluded from asserting violation of its subrogation rights because of its own breach.[3]

A liability insurer's failure to defend on behalf of the insured, if it proves to be inconsistent with policy terms,[4] is a material breach that defeats the insurer's later claim of interference with its right of control (whether exclusive or joint) over defense.[5]

---

7. See § 6.3(b) *supra*.

1. See, *e.g.*, Covey v. National Benefit Life Ins. Co., 77 N.M. 512, 424 P.2d 793 (1967).

2. *Cf.* A. Perley Fitch Co. v. Continental Ins. Co., 99 N.H. 1, 104 A.2d 511 (1954) 49 A.L.R.2d 156 (1956).

3. See § 6.8(b) *supra*.

4. See generally § 7.6 *infra*.

5. *Cf.* Krutsinger v. Illinois Cas. Co., 10 Ill.2d 518, 141 N.E.2d 16 (1957), in which, however, the court refers to the theory of preclusion as waiver. In this case, judgment creditors

A liability insurer's denial of coverage, unless qualified by an indication of willingness to defend without requiring more of the insured than the assistance and cooperation he owes under the policy provisions, is at least by implication a declaration of unwillingness to fulfill its legal obligation to defend on behalf of the insured. Thus, if it occurs after the occasion for taking preparatory defensive steps has already arisen, it may constitute an immediate breach of a duty to make early preparations for defense at trial,[6] regardless of whether in other respects it constitutes an anticipatory breach. Such an immediate breach of a duty to take essential preparatory steps supports the preclusion of the insurer's later claim of interference with its right of control over the defense.

An errors-and-omissions liability insurer's unreasonable delay in the handling of a claim against its insured, an insurance agent, even though it did not deny coverage altogether, has been held to defeat the insurer's reliance on a clause prohibiting the insured from settling.[7]

SECTION 6.9 INSURER'S RIGHTS AT VARIANCE WITH POLICY PROVISIONS

§ 6.9(a) GENERALLY

An insurer, as well as a policyholder, may have rights at variance with policy provisions.

Insurer's rights to reformation, though based on principles of general application, arise most often in patterns of circumstances rather distinctive to insurance transactions. Perhaps the most common ground for reformation of policy provisions at the instance of

brought an action against a liability insurance company for failure to satisfy judgments on tort claims against the insureds and others based on the sales of alcoholic beverages to a known habitual drunkard in violation of a dram shop act, thus interfering with the claimants' means of support. The policy covered only part of the period during which the sales occurred. The defendant insurer had failed to participate in the defense or settlement negotiations and in this action against it contended that the insureds had violated the policy condition that the insurer should have the exclusive right to contest any suits against the insureds. Affirming a judgment against the insurer, the court held that since some asserted grounds of liability were within and others were outside the policy coverage, the insurer had a duty to participate in the defense, and none of the parties had a right to exclude the oth-

ers from participation in the absence of breach. The insurer was precluded from asserting a violation of its rights to participate in the defense because of its inaction for months followed by unjustified demands for execution of a nonwaiver agreement not only avoiding any waiver from the insurer's then undertaking the defense but also seeking to avoid waiver from previous events and stating conclusions of fact with implications of fraud by the insureds. Obviously the insurer did not voluntarily relinquish a known right. The result can be justified, however, on the ground of breach of contract by the insurer.

6. Concerning the obligation of taking preparatory defensive steps, see § 7.-6(a) *infra*.

7. Otteman v. Interstate Fire & Cas. Co., 172 Neb. 574, 111 N.W.2d 97 (1961), 89 A.L.R.2d 1182 (1963).

the insurer is mistake in the preparation of the policy—mistake of a type often referred to as a scrivener's error.[1]

One common fact pattern involves misstatement of the insured's age in an application for life, health, or accident insurance. An overstatement of age would ordinarily be a disadvantage to the insured, and although there has been little litigation on the point, reformation would surely be available to the insured if the overstatement came about through mutual mistake or because of an error of some representative of the insurer, as when an agent erroneously recorded a correct statement of age by the applicant.

A more frequently litigated problem arises when the insured's age is understated and the insurer contends that benefits should be reduced or denied altogether in accordance with what it asserts would have been the contract provisions with one of the insured's true age. In this situation, the insurer rather than the insured is asserting rights that are arguably at variance with policy provisions, and the insured may seek to invoke an incontestability statute or policy clause.[2]

An insurer's defenses based on misrepresentation or concealment are sometimes provided for in policy provisions. In other instances, they are rights at variance with policy provisions. In either event, they may be sharply limited by statutory and policy provisions for incontestability, or by more general statutory or judicial restriction of defenses based on warranty, misrepresentation, or concealment.[3]

There are also some instances in which insurers' rights at variance with policy provisions are recognized on grounds of rather narrow application. Among these are some deviations from the general rule of resolving ambiguities of policy language against the party responsible for its drafting. This is not to say that the rule of resolving ambiguities against the draftsman are cited and rejected in these contexts. More often there is no reference at all to this rule. Yet enough illustrations can be found to establish the point beyond dispute that courts occasionally grant to insurers the benefit of defenses not supported by policy language. Examples follow.

Fire insurance policies ordinarily declare that the insurer shall pay the insured for "direct loss by fire," without specifying that the loss be "accidental" or that the fire be "hostile." An inference that only "accidental" losses were intended to be covered is reasonable. One need not resort to any theory of ambiguity to support such a limitation; indeed, any other reading of the agreement would be contrary to ordinary principles of reading contractual instruments consistently with implications in fact of the language in the context of its use. But the rule that a fire insurer is not liable for loss from a "friendly" fire (as opposed to a "hostile" fire) goes well beyond any such factual implications that only accidental losses are intended to

---

1. See § 6.5(d) *supra* generally and nn. 28, 29 thereto in particular.

2. See § 6.5(d) *supra*.

3. See § 6.5 *supra*.

be covered.   For example, according to most courts considering the question, it precludes coverage under fire insurance for damage to a ring accidentally thrown into an incinerator.[4]   The rule denying recovery from loss caused by a "friendly" fire, such as one in an incinerator, is often explained as consistent with the probable understanding of the contracting parties.   This explanation seems supportable only to the extent that the friendly-fire rule is known to insureds, as perhaps is often the case in relation to fire insurance on commercial risks.   But to infer that the ordinary householder understands that his fire insurance will not cover the destruction by fire of a valuable ring tossed into an incinerator by mistake is to engage in fiction. Certainly the policy language does not clearly negate coverage.   Perhaps it may reasonably be regarded as ambiguous in this instance, rather than clearly supporting coverage.   If that be so, we have here an instance of resolving an ambiguity in favor of rather than against the insurer.

Another type of case in which ambiguities have been resolved in favor of the insurer concerns the applicability of accident insurance coverage to injuries suffered by an insured as a result of his engaging in seriously criminal behavior.   For example, courts have often reasoned that one who was killed by another's measures of self-defense against his unlawful attack did not suffer "accidental death" within the meaning of that phrase in an accident insurance policy, even though the policy contained no explicit provision against coverage in such a case.[5]   Yet it seems clear that the death in nearly all such cases was accidental from the point of view of the deceased; that is, he did not want to die and did not know that his death was virtually certain to occur as a result of his attack.   Thus, courts denying liability in these cases have either resolved an ambiguity against the insured or, perhaps more likely, have declined to enforce a provision unambiguously supporting coverage.

Perhaps there is no single explanation for these and other examples of resolving ambiguities in favor of insurers.   They are all deviations from the principle that ambiguities are resolved against the draftsman of the policy form, the insurer.   And each deviation is designed to serve some other principle having overriding significance in the context.   But the other principles served are different.   For example, the rule that the insured's death resulting from another's defense against his assault is not "accidental" can be explained as a sanction against seriously antisocial behavior.   And the friendly-fire rule—when extended to denying coverage for the ring mistakenly tossed into the incinerator—if not explained as an unwarranted and perhaps unwitting deviation from ordinary rules for construing insurance contracts, may be thought to be designed to reduce the opportunities for fraud that would be opened up by allowing recovery in this type of case.

---

4.   See § 5.3(d) *supra*.   5.   See § 5.4(f) *supra*.

Whatever one's explanations may be, it is clear that there are types of cases in which prevailing rules of insurance law in effect resolve ambiguities in favor of insurers. It remains true, however, that ordinarily ambiguities of insurance policy language are resolved against insurers.[6]

§ 6.9(b) RESCISSION AND CANCELLATION

In addition to the option to pursue the formally prescribed procedure for cancellation of fire and casualty insurance,[1] a company may have a right to terminate a contract by rescission because of mutual mistake, misrepresentation, or concealment.[2]

If at a time when a substantial part of the policy term has passed an insurer claims the right to terminate coverage because, for example, of misrepresentation at the time of application, there are varying advantages and disadvantages of the different ways it might proceed. Except insofar as statutes or decisions have regulated rights of cancellation,[3] if the insurer cancels pursuant to the procedure described in the policy, it avoids any dispute over its right to do so. Also, it is entitled to retain that portion of the premium allocable to the period before the effective date of the cancellation. But in so doing the insurer runs the risk that it will be held to have exercised an election [4] under which it will be liable for any losses within policy coverage occurring during that period. Rescission avoids this risk but requires the return of the full premium. Also, a notice of rescission may prove to be ineffective since the insured may contest the insurer's grounds for rescission. It might be suggested that an insurer wishing to discontinue coverage for the future and also to contest coverage for a loss that has already occurred should deliver notices of both rescission and cancellation. But this course would somewhat reduce the prospects of successful defense against liability for the previous loss, because of the risk that a doctrine of election would be invoked to declare that the cancellation notice, even if also accompanied with a full return of premium, could only be given effect for the future on the condition that it affirmed the validity of coverage up to its effective date.

An insurer desiring termination of the coverage is best served by reaching an understanding with the insured under which part or all of the returned premium is accepted on the conditions desired by the

---

6.   See § 6.3(a) *supra.*

1.   See § 5.10(e) (3) *supra.*

2.   See generally §§ 5.6–5.8, 6.1 *supra.* Standards of materiality applied and doctrines available to an insured to defeat such a claim, even when based on explicit policy provisions, are considered in §§ 6.5, 6.7 *supra.* Concerning imposition of a duty to the public, arising from the public policy under-

lying financial responsibility laws, to investigate an insured's insurability within a reasonable time after issuing a policy and not to "take advantage of a breach" of that duty to avoid liability to an innocent victim, see § 6.5(d) n.4 *supra.*

3.   See § 5.10(e) (3) *supra.*

4.   *Cf.* § 6.7(d) *supra.*

insurer. But negotiations for rescission or cancellation by mutual agreement may turn out badly for the company, even when the position it takes in the negotiations is consistent with its rights of cancellation.[5]

5. See, *e.g.*, Merchants & Farmers Mut. Cas. Co. v. St. Paul-Mercury Indem. Co., 214 Minn. 544, 8 N.W.2d 827 (1943). The insurer's agent informed the insured that the company would no longer continue her automobile liability policy without an endorsement eliminating coverage for a son convicted of a traffic offense. She insisted on return of the full premium, though coverage had been provided for some time. Though the agent finally agreed to the full refund, it had not been delivered when another son was involved in an accident. Even though another policy had already been obtained by the insured, a divided court reversed a judgment for the insurer, holding that a jury could have found that there was no rescission because her intent to rescind was dependent upon her getting back the full refund as well as getting other insurance.

CHAPTER 7

CLAIMS PROCESSES

SECTION 7.1   CLAIM–PROCESSING REQUIRE-MENTS AND THE EFFECTS OF NONCOMPLIANCE

§ 7.1(a) GENERALLY

Insurance contracts customarily contain provisions concerning the process by which claims are to be presented to the insurer by an insured or other claimant.

It is sometimes said that such policy provisions impose obligations. Perhaps this is the case occasionally, even in the strictest sense of the term obligation, under which a violation of the policy provision by the insured supports affirmative legal relief for the insurer. For example, when an insured violates the assistance and cooperation clause of a compulsory liability insurance policy, or one that is certified under a financial responsibility statute, and the insurer is held liable to the tort claimant, ordinarily the insurer is allowed an action over against the insured.[1] In such a case, it may be said that the policy provisions, either alone (if they fully express this obligation) or in conjunction with the applicable law (including compulsory insurance or financial responsibility legislation), impose an obligation of assistance and cooperation.

More often, however, policy provisions concerning the processing of claims impose merely a qualification (a condition in the broadest sense of that term)[2] of the insurer's obligation to pay benefits. That is, noncompliance with such a provision may be a defense for the in-

---

1. See generally § 7.5 *infra*.

2. Concerning other meanings sometimes ascribed to the term "condition"

see, *e.g.*, §§ 5.6, 6.5(b) at nn.29–32 *supra* and § 7.1(b) *infra*.

surer, but ordinarily it does not give the insurer a basis for affirmative relief against the insured.

The policy provisions of this kind that are most commonly involved in controversy are those, under any type of insurance, regarding prompt presentment of claims,[3] those, under liability insurance, regarding assistance and cooperation of the insured,[4] and, during the 1960's, those under uninsured motorist coverage regarding arbitration of disputes.[5]

Events occurring during claims processing may also affect the rights of the parties to an insurance contract because of statutory provisions rather than policy clauses; most claims against insurers for penalties and attorneys' fees because of delayed payment are founded on statutes.[6]

There are also contractual and regulatory measures of various types concerning other rights and obligations of the insurer in relation to the processing of claims. Examples include measures bearing on subrogation rights,[7] the insurer's option to repair property damaged by an event insured against under property insurance,[8] and a congeries of rights and duties associated with liability insurance claims.[9]

§ 7.1(b) PREJUDICE TO THE INSURER

A requirement of prejudice as a prerequisite to an insurer's taking advantage of rights based on violation or nonfulfillment of a policy provision concerning claims processing is ordinarily not expressed in the policy itself. Unless it can be said to be implied in fact, which seems a highly dubious theory in most instances,[1] its recognition, in some contexts at least, by a majority of courts [2] is a form of judicial

---

3. See § 7.2 *infra.*

4. See § 7.5 *infra.*

5. See § 7.3 *infra.*

6. See § 7.4 *infra.*

7. See § 3.10 *supra.*

8. For an option-to-repair clause, see the fire insurance form in Appendix A, lines 141–147, *infra.* See also § 4.-4(a) *supra.*

9. See §§ 7.6–7.11 *infra.*

1. *Cf.* comments of Cardozo, J., in Coleman v. New Amsterdam Cas. Co., 247 N.Y. 271, 276–277, 160 N.E. 367, 369 (1928), 72 A.L.R. 1443, 1446 (1931):

"The plaintiff makes the point that the default should be condoned, since there is no evidence that co-operation, however willing, would have defeated the claim for damages or diminished its extent. For all that appears, the insurer would be no better off if the assured had kept its covenant, and made disclosure full and free. The argument misconceives the effect of a refusal. Co-operation with the insurer is one of the conditions of the policy. When the condition was broken, the policy was at an end, if the insurer so elected. The case is not one of the breach of a mere covenant, where the consequences may vary with fluctuations of the damage. There has been a failure to fulfill a condition upon which obligation is dependent."

2. See Note, *Liability Insurance Policy Defenses and the Duty to Defend,* 68 Harv.L.Rev. 1436 (1955); 8 Appleman, Insurance Law § 4773 (rev. ed. 1962). *But cf.* State Farm Mut. Auto. Ins. Co. v. Cassinelli, 67 Nev. 227, 216 P.2d 606 (1950), 18 A.L.R.2d 431 (1951); *but cf.* Comment, *The Materiality of Preju-*

regulation giving rise to rights at variance with policy provisions.[3] This occurs, for example, when the decision on a liability insurer's defense of breach of the assistance and cooperation clause is conditioned on prejudice to the insurer.[4] When the burden is placed on the insurer to prove prejudice,[5] the practical impact of the regulatory doctrine is very substantial. When the burden is placed on the policyholder to prove that the insurer was not prejudiced,[6] the impact of the doctrine is less severe but still significant.

Another common example of such judicial regulation occurs when a court that purportedly enforces a rigid time limit for presenting a claim introduces a great degree of flexibility into the standard for enforcement by holding that a transgression of the limit defeats the claim only if prejudicial to the insurer.[7]

There are wide variations in the standards used in different cases to determine what constitutes prejudice to an insurer.

Arguably a court adhering faithfully to a rigorous standard of genuine prejudice would require the insurer, when it has the burden, to show that the result was different in the particular instance because of the event in question.[8] Relief would be limited to an extent

---

dice to the Insurer as a Result of the Insured's Failure to Give Timely Notice, 74 Dick.L.Rev. 260, 261–262 (1970), indicating that the majority hold prejudice to be immaterial except when "the terms of the policy are ambiguous or unemphatic."

3. See generally § 6.8(a) *supra.*

4. See § 7.5 *infra.*

5. See, *e.g.,* Billington v. Interinsurance Exch., 71 Cal.2d 728, 456 P.2d 982, 79 Cal.Rptr. 326 (1969) (summarized in n.10 *infra*); Campbell v. Allstate Ins. Co., 60 Cal.2d 303, 384 P.2d 155, 32 Cal.Rptr. 827 (1963); Cooper v. Government Employees Ins. Co., 51 N.J. 86, 237 A.2d 870 (1968) (summarized in n.10 *infra*).

6. See, *e.g.,* Western Mut. Ins. Co. v. Baldwin, 258 Iowa 460, 472–475, 137 N.W.2d 918, 925–927 (1965) (confirming the rule of *Henderson, infra*); Henderson v. Hawkeye-Security Ins. Co., 252 Iowa 97, 106 N.W.2d 86 (1960) (rebuttable presumption of prejudice from delay of more than a year in giving notice under automobile medical payments coverage; though declaring that allowing recovery "unless the company proves prejudice" would be truly to "rewrite the contract and [would] be most unreasonable," the court seems curiously unaware that it also rewrites the contract by holding

that a claimant's showing of lack of prejudice overcomes the defense of late notice); Mountainair Municipal Schools v. United States Fid. & Gy. Co., 80 N.M. 761, 461 P.2d 410 (1969) (injury to student when door-closing mechanism fell on her head in gymnasium; first report nineteen months later was not "as soon as practicable"; school superintendent's ignorance of existence of liability policy was no excuse; late notice is presumptively prejudicial to insurer; though presumption is rebuttable, it was not rebutted in this case).

7. See § 7.2(a) *infra.*

8. See State Farm Mut. Auto. Ins. Co. v. Walker, 382 F.2d 548 (7th Cir. 1967), *cert. denied,* 389 U.S. 1045 (1968) (Indiana law; insured told attorney engaged by insurer to defend him that insured's earlier version of accident was false and accident occurred because insured lost control in passing another car; held, fact issues whether breach of cooperation clause prejudiced the insurer and whether counsel's participation in defense after learning of the breach constituted a "waiver" by the insurer; "it has been said that an insurer is not prejudiced unless the breach will produce a judgment less favorable to it in the tort suit"). See generally Note, *Liability Insurance Policy Defenses and the Duty to Defend,* 68 Harv.L.Rev.

corresponding with the difference in result shown.[9]   Under such a test, it would be rare indeed that the insurer could escape liability completely because of the stipulated event.   Support in precedents for faithful application of so stringent a view, however, is slight at best.

One of many possible intermediate standards would require that a liability insurer, asserting a defense of noncooperation, show a "substantial likelihood" that but for the noncooperation the trier of fact would have found for the defense in the tort action.[10]   Another of the possible intermediate positions would preclude the insurer from asserting its defense in the absence of a showing of prejudice in the particular case, but would recognize the event as a complete defense upon a showing that the result would have been different in any substantial respect if the event had not occurred.[11]   Probably the majority of decisions requiring some showing of prejudice, however, accept something still less as adequate proof of prejudice.   It would appear to be enough, under most precedents, to show that the claim was substantially more dangerous, onerous, or troublesome to the insurer than it would have been in the absence of the event in question.[12]

1436 (1955).   Regarding preclusion of the defense by actions of counsel in a conflict-of-interest setting, see § 7.7(b) *infra*.

9.   *Cf.* Fidelity & Cas. Co. v. McConnaughy, 228 Md. 1, 179 A.2d 117 (1962) (without clearly resolving a conflict in precedents regarding what showing of prejudice is required, the court accepted insurer's assertion that insured's breach of cooperation clause by bringing in false witnesses caused insurer to decline to accept claimant's $3,500 settlement offer; relief limited, however, to excusing insurer from liability for excess above $3,500 for which insurer claims it would have settled but for insured's breach; insurer-appointed counsel acted improperly in taking insured's deposition to confirm its defense of noncooperation, but insurer did not thereby lose its rights).

10.   See, *e.g.*, Billington v. Interinsurance Exch., 71 Cal.2d 728, 456 P.2d 982, 79 Cal.Rptr. 326 (1969) (car owner insured under the assigned risk plan; held, lack of cooperation, if established, was a proper defense despite the Financial Responsibility Law; however, judgment for insurer was reversed because trial judge used erroneous standard on prejudice; insurer has burden of proving prejudice, and it is not enough that jury "could reasonably and properly have accepted a defense" of assumed risk because of plaintiff's knowledge of insured's in-

toxication; must at least show "substantial likelihood the trier of fact would have found in the insured's favor").   *Cf.* Cooper v. Government Employees Ins. Co., 51 N.J. 86, 237 A.2d 870 (1968) (placing burden on insurer to prove breach of late-notice provision and "a likelihood of appreciable prejudice" therefrom in order to fulfill reasonable expectations of the purchaser "so far as its language will permit"; trial court's fact-finding of no breach by insured of notice provision sustained).

11.   *Cf.* Western Mut. Ins. Co. v. Baldwin, 258 Iowa 460, 137 N.W.2d 918 (1965) ("existence of prejudice does not depend on the amount," and extent of prejudice from "ending up with an insured whose credibility was self-destroyed cannot be determined" but cannot "be brushed aside as inconsequential").

12.   See, *e.g.*, Renner v. State Farm Mut. Auto. Ins. Co., 392 F.2d 666 (5th Cir. 1968) (Florida law; late report of automobile accident due to misunderstanding between husband and wife; lack of opportunity to photograph cars and talk with witnesses while facts were fresh, including one witness who died of an unrelated cause nineteen days after the accident; trial court finding of prejudice sustained); Canadian Universal Ins. Co. v. Northwest Hosp., Inc., 389 F.2d 559 (7th Cir. 1968) (Illinois law; two-year delay in reporting accident to hospi-

Under such a standard, it is not necessary to show that the end result was different. The likelihood of applying such a standard, or even dispensing entirely with a requirement of proof of prejudice, is increased by a showing that the policyholder has acted in bad faith.[13] Also, rules of thumb may be developed for recurring factual patterns.[14]

Each of the foregoing standards is phrased in terms implying that the burden of proof of prejudice, within whatever sense the standard of prejudice requires, is upon the insurer. If the burden of showing lack of prejudice is placed on the claimant,[15] the insurer's position is stronger, whatever the standard may be.

There is good reason for declining to enforce a rigorous requirement that the insurer prove that a different result has occurred in the particular case because of the insured's breach. In relation to a defense of late claim, for example, the very delay of which the insurer complains has deprived it of the normal opportunity for early investigation that might have disclosed defenses, if they existed. Thus, it can never be known whether the case is in fact one in which the result would have been different. If the insurer is deprived of its defense unless it can prove that a different result would have come about in the particular case, it must pay a whole body of claims some of which it could have defeated but for the delayed presentment. Narrowing the insurer's defense in this way would produce injustice not only to the insurer but also to other policyholders whose premiums must pay for this risk if the insurer is required to bear it.

It may be noted that the standard for the insurer's showing of prejudice is generally less demanding than the standard for an insured's showing of detrimental reliance to support a right at variance with policy provisions.[16] But this seems entirely appropriate since the insurer here, as in cases involving regulatory measures regarding warranty and representation,[17] is seeking to enforce a policy provi-

tal's liability insurer gave rise to presumption of prejudice, which was not rebutted but strengthened by evidence that the condition of the area where patient fell had been changed between accident and notice).

13. See, *e.g.*, Elliott v. Metropolitan Cas. Ins. Co., 250 F.2d 680 (10th Cir. 1957), 66 A.L.R.2d 1231 (1959), *cert. denied*, 356 U.S. 932 (1958) (Kansas law; collusion with claimants to travel from Kansas to Missouri to accept service of process; in such cases, insurers need not show a resulting substantial and actual prejudice, as they must do in cases involving disappearance of an insured before trial).

14. See, *e.g.*, dictum in Henderson v. Rochester Am. Ins. Co., 254 N.C. 329, 333, 118 S.E.2d 885, 888 (1961): "Where there has been evidence tend-

ing to show collusion between the injured and the insured, courts have been careful to protect the insurer. Courts usually hold that misstatements persisted in until the trial or subsequent to the filing of pleadings by insured requiring a shifting of ground and a new and different defense suffice as a matter of law to establish a failure to cooperate. Except for these classes of cases, courts generally hold the question of materiality and prejudice is a question for the jury."

15. See Henderson v. Hawkeye-Security Ins. Co., 252 Iowa 97, 106 N.W.2d 86 (1960), discussed in n.6 *supra*.

16. Regarding the latter standard, see § 6.4(f) *supra*.

17. See § 6.5 *supra*.

sion and is being required to prove even more than breach of that provision in order to establish its defense. In both settings, then, the insured is being granted greater rights than strict enforcement of policy provisions would give him. To apply a standard of prejudice in this setting analogous to the standard of detriment applied in the other setting would be to make here a far greater extension of the insured's rights at variance with policy provisions than is made by recognizing an insured's rights based on detrimental reliance. Moreover, the argument that the wrongdoer's conduct has deprived the other party of the evidence of detriment (or prejudice) from that wrong—which favors claimants in the context of rights at variance based on detrimental reliance [18]—favors the insurer in the present context.

SECTION 7.2 PRESENTMENT OF CLAIMS

§ 7.2(a) TIMELINESS

Insurance policies commonly include provisions concerning the timeliness of claims. Among these are provisions requiring prompt notice of loss [1] and provisions either requiring submission of proof of loss within a stated time [2] or purportedly conditioning liability of the insurer on submission of due proof of loss.[3] In some policies there is also a stipulation concerning the time within which suit may be filed; [4] in many instances statutes restrict the potential effectiveness of such stipulations for a short limitation period.[5]

Reasonable policy stipulations conditioning liability of the insurer on prompt notice of loss are enforceable.[6]

It is often stated that the purpose of the requirement of notice is to give the insurer reasonable opportunity to protect its rights.[7] In so doing, however, the insurer is sometimes protecting the interests of the particular insured in the instant case as well and often is serving the best interests of its insureds as a group. Thus problems involving enforcement of such provisions cannot properly be regarded as raising merely issues of competing interests between the insurer and the insured in the particular case. When a claim under a fidelity

18. See § 6.4(f) *supra.*

1. See Appendices A, F, G, H *infra.*

2. See Appendices A, F *infra.*

3. See § 6.8(c) *supra.*

4. See Appendix A *infra.*

5. See, *e.g.,* N.Y.Ins.Law § 164(3) (McKinney 1966) (accident and sickness policy provisions).

6. See, *e.g.,* Henderson v. Hawkeye-Security Ins. Co., 252 Iowa 97, 106 N.W. 2d 86 (1960) (automobile medical payments coverage requiring notice "as soon as practicable"); American Fid. Co. v. Schemel, 103 N.H. 190, 168 A.2d 478 (1961) (liability coverage requiring notice "as soon as practicable"); Britz v. American Ins. Co., 2 Wis.2d 192, 86 N.W.2d 18 (1958), 66 A.L.R.2d 1271 (1959) (theft coverage requiring notice "as soon as practicable").

7. *E.g.,* Brown v. Maryland Cas. Co., 111 Vt. 30, 11 A.2d 222, 129 A.L.R. 1404 (1940); Jellico Grocery Co. v. Sun Indem. Co., 272 Ky. 276, 282, 114 S.W.2d 83, 86 (1938).

bond is based on misappropriations,[8] for example, prompt notice may help to prevent further losses, an objective consistent with the best interests of the insurer, the insured in the instant case, and insureds generally.

The interests of insureds generally and the public interest may also be served in some instances in which the requirement of prompt notice is a disadvantage to the insured in the instant case. Under any type of insurance, early investigation reduces the risk of successful fraudulent claims. This is a disadvantage to the specific claimant, who often is also the insured, but it is a disadvantage fully supportable in the public interest.

In liability insurance cases early notice has an added advantage to both the insurer and the insured in that it provides a better opportunity for controlling the claim and, by favorable settlement, avoiding both the expense of litigation and the risk of higher damages.

Provisions designed to require timely presentment of claims—including those concerning proof of loss and filing of suit as well as initial notice—are advantageous to insurers and insureds, under all types of insurance, in the control of claims in a very broad sense. First, they reduce the overall cost of the coverage below what it would be in the absence of such provisions, since they preclude some claims (including late claims in which fraud is more difficult to ferret out). Second, they reduce the burden of providing reserves for undetermined claims by reducing the period and degree of uncertainty concerning the number of claims (or claim frequency, as it is often called) and their amounts (or average claim cost). Provisions operating in these ways may, of course, be disadvantageous to particular insureds, and not alone to those who would present dishonest or exaggerated claims but as well to the scrupulously honest. They leave the insured to bear a risk of loss from inadvertent failure to perfect his rights under the coverage. Notice and time-of-suit provisions have sometimes been regarded as so harsh in this respect that they have been subjected to rather stringent regulation—judicial, administrative, and legislative. Among such regulations are judicial doctrines (including waiver, estoppel, and election) supporting claims at variance with policy provisions [9] and judicial construction of notice and time-of-suit provisions to establish a flexible requirement of notice within reasonable time and in the absence of reasonable excuse, rather than the more rigid requirement that literal interpretation of the policy provisions would produce.[10] Also, though there is a conflict of

---

8. *E.g.*, Brown v. Maryland Cas. Co., 111 Vt. 30, 11 A.2d 222, 129 A.L.R. 1404 (1940).

9. See § 6.8 supra.

10. *Cf. e.g.*, St. Paul Fire & Marine Ins. Co. v. Petzold, 418 F.2d 303 (1st Cir. 1969) (New Hampshire law; policyholder's counsel did not advise noti-fying the company because he thought policyholder could not be held liable for damage to a third person by blasting done on policyholder's premises by another; held, reasonable excuse for delayed notice; remarking that this alone did not dispose of the issue whether the insured notified the insurer in reasonable time, the court considered the issue of prejudice and

authorities on the point, many courts introduce an added regulatory measure by holding that late notice is not a good defense in the absence of prejudice.[11]

One who (whether as policy draftsman, legislator, administrator, or judge) is formulating provisions concerning timely presentment of claims must make a choice between a specific time limit and a more generalized limit—for example, a requirement that the notice or suit be presented within reasonable time. This is essentially a choice between certainty and flexibility—a choice faced in many other contexts in insurance law and law generally.[12] Insurers' draftsmen have tended to push further toward rules of rigid certainty than regulators (legislative, administrative, and judicial) have been willing to permit. One important reason for regulatory controls is that a rigid time limit has the consequence of imposing on the insured the risk of loss by failure to perfect his rights in time. That risk includes not only cases of negligent failure but also cases in which the failure occurs without fault of the insured. Most insurance coverages provide protection to some extent at least against losses to which a mistake of the insured contributes. For example, fire insurance covers losses caused by the insured's negligence; life insurance covers even a case of death to which negligence of both the insured and the beneficiary contributed; and liability insurance is chiefly intended to protect against the consequences of liability based on negligence. But there is ample precedent for taking a more stringent attitude toward negligence in the presentment of a claim than toward negligence in causing the loss. Similarly, negligence of an insured in protecting property already damaged under circumstances covered by property insurance is commonly treated less favorably than negligence contributing to the initial loss.[13]

At what point does a limited period for taking some act in presentment of a claim commence to run?

In some instances, relevant policy provisions state that the time commences with occurrence of the casualty that serves as the basis of claim—for example, an accident to which liability insurance ap-

---

then concluded that defendant policyholder was entitled to judgment in the declaratory action); Abington Mut. Fire Ins. Co. v. Drew, 109 N.H. 464, 254 A.2d 829 (1969) (accidental shooting by insured's son while hunting; notice was given three months after accident, when insured and son consulted an attorney upon son's being arrested and were informed that insured's homeowners policy provided coverage; held, insurer obliged to defend son in tort action; there was evidence to support trial court's finding of no "substantial breach"). See also nn.21–24 *infra.*

11. See, *e.g., Petzold* and *Drew* in n.10 *supra. But cf.* Sterling State Bank v. Virginia Sur. Co., 285 Minn. 348, 173 N.W.2d 342 (1969) (notice of theft of tractor-trailer more than one year after the incident; violation of notice and proof of loss clauses barred claim, since compliance was a "condition precedent of liability"; however, the opinion discloses a finding of no plausible reason for failure to notify and a finding of prejudice to the insurer). See also § 7.1(b) *supra.*

12. See § 1.6 *supra.*

13. See § 5.4(d) *supra.*

plies,[14] or a loss to which a health and accident policy [15] or a fidelity bond applies. In general, if there is no explicit reference to the insured's having either specific knowledge of the event or facts that in some sense put him on notice—for example, knowledge of facts on the basis of which a reasonable person in his position would have inferred that the event had occurred—he is excused from acting until he acquires such knowledge.[16] But it has been held that a homeowner who delayed five months after knowing of fully developed damage, before making repairs and discovering that the damage was due to a cause within the coverage of his homeowners policy, was barred for failure to bring his suit within a year after he knew of the fully developed damage, even though he brought suit within a year after discovering the cause.[17] Also, if it appears that the insured knew that the event on which the claim is based had occurred, his lack of knowledge of the amount of resulting loss is no excuse for his delay in notifying the insurer.[18]

An insured may be confronted with a contention that "discover" is used in an objective sense that is fulfilled if a reasonable person in his position would infer from facts he knows that a loss had occurred, even though he did not himself draw that inference. But even precedents relatively more favorable to insurers draw a distinction between knowing facts from which the inference of loss would be drawn by a reasonable person and knowing facts that would create in a reasonable person's mind no more than a suspicion of possible loss. The latter is insufficient to require the insured to give notice to the insurer.[19] Moreover, it may reasonably be argued, first, that "discover" itself implies a more subjective standard and, second, that if it does not there is at least ambiguity that should be resolved against the insurer by application of a subjective standard excusing delay unless the insured knows of the event itself rather than merely knowing facts on the basis of which a reasonable person would infer that the event had occurred, even though the insured did not so infer. Be-

---

14. See Appendices G, H *infra* (notice "as soon as practicable" after the accident, occurrence, or loss; notice of steps in the process of claim or suit "immediately" after the "demand, notice, summons or other process" is received).

15. See Appendix F *infra*.

16. *E.g.*, National Mut. Cas. Co. v. Cypret, 207 Ark. 11, 179 S.W.2d 161 (1944) (the mortgagee-bank, the insured of a theft policy, held to be excused when the insured car disappeared under ambiguous circumstances and the mortgagee-bank gave notice within 60 days after learning that it had been stolen); Johnson Ready-Mix Concrete Co. v. United Pac. Ins. Co., 11 Utah 2d 279, 358 P.2d 337 (1961) (corporate insured not barred by late notice to liability insurer since no employee of insured with authority to receive such information for the insured knew that the incident occurred and that it was not trivial).

17. Naghten v. Maryland Cas. Co., 47 Ill.App.2d 74, 197 N.E.2d 489 (1st Dist. 1964), 24 A.L.R.3d 1001 (1969) (policy requirement that suit be brought within "twelve months next after inception of the loss").

18. *E.g.*, Brown v. Maryland Cas. Co., 111 Vt. 30, 11 A.2d 222, 129 A.L.R. 1404 (1940).

19. *E.g.*, Gilmour v. Standard Sur. & Cas. Co., 292 Mass. 205, 197 N.E. 673 (1935).

yond these arguments, moreover, is the possibility that a court would refuse to enforce a provision if it purportedly barred the insured from protection because, for example, he negligently failed to realize that a loss had occurred.[20]

An insured may claim that his delay in taking steps essential to timely presentment of a claim was due to triviality of the occurrence. For example, the insured of a liability policy may assert that the incident on the basis of which a tort claim is presented against him by a third person was so trivial that he reasonably believed that no claim for damages would arise. There is substantial precedent supporting this excuse.[21]

Reasonable mistake, in a broader sense than failure to realize the occurrence of the event in question, is also sometimes recognized as an excuse for delay. For example, there is some support for the position that a liability insured may be excused for delay in giving notice of an accident if, "acting as a reasonably prudent person, he believed that he was not liable for the accident."[22] It seems proper that a reasonable belief by the policyholder that he was in no way involved in an accident should excuse his delay in reporting,[23] but an excuse as broad as the implications of the quoted phrase seems not justified either as an interpretation of the policy or on grounds of rights at variance with policy provisions. Certainly the insured should be required to give notice when he realizes that a claim might be made, even though as a layman he reasonably believes that any claim made would lack merit.

With varied results, policyholders have also urged as an excuse for delayed notice the failure to realize that the policy included coverage for the type of incident involved.[24]

---

20. See generally § 6.8(a) *supra*.

21. *E.g.*, Leytem v. Fireman's Fund Indem. Co., 249 Iowa 524, 85 N.W.2d 921 (1957); Bennett v. Swift & Co., 170 Ohio St. 168, 163 N.E.2d 362 (1959) (failure to give notice for 18 months; directed verdict for insurer reversed for new trial of fact issues on triviality). *But cf.* State Farm Mut. Auto. Ins. Co. v. Ranson, 121 So.2d 175 (Fla.App.2d Dist. 1960) (failure to give notice for more than a year was a good defense as a matter of law, though the policyholder claimed that the incident seemed trivial); however, *Ranson* is severely undermined in American Fire and Cas. Co. v. Collura, 163 So.2d 784, 789–794 (Fla.App. 2d Dist. 1964), *cert. denied without opinion*, 171 So.2d 389 (Fla.1964).

22. See *e.g.*, Frederick v. John Wood Co., 263 Minn. 101, 116 N.W.2d 88 (1962), quoting with approval from 29A Am.Jur.Ins. § 1393 [carried for-

ward as 44 Am.Jur.2d Ins. § 1474 (1969)].

23. *Cf.* Pawtucket Mut. Ins. Co. v. Lebrecht, 104 N.H. 465, 190 A.2d 420 (1963), 2 A.L.R.3d 1229 (1965) (claim against policyholder-parents growing out of assault by their son on another person; delay excused on the theory that the parents "were justifiably ignorant of any connection between that incident and the bringing up of their son on which a claim of liability against them might be based").

24. Denying recovery because of delayed notice: *E.g.*, Mutual Benefit Health & Acc. Ass'n v. Brunke, 276 F.2d 53 (5th Cir. 1960) (under Illinois law, plaintiff was barred from recovering under air trip insurance for injury sustained in taxicab; notice two years after injury was not notice within a reasonable time; plaintiff alleged he lost policy and failed to realize that injury en route to airport

§ 7.2(b) PROOF OF LOSS; FRAUD AND FALSE SWEARING

Fire insurance policies, as well as some others, commonly provide for the filing of a proof of loss.[1] Attacks on the timeliness of proofs of loss have led to decisions at variance with policy provisions,[2] and so too have defenses based on the total failure to present a proof of loss.[3]

Fire insurance policies commonly provide also that "the entire policy shall be void if, whether before or after a loss, the insured has wilfully concealed or misrepresented any material fact or circumstance concerning this insurance or the subject thereof, or the interest of the insured therein, or in case of any fraud or false swearing by the insured relating thereto . . . ."[4]

Although this provision is sometimes the basis of a successful defense by the insurer,[5] it is hardly surprising that such broad language as this is not literally enforced, even when appearing in policy forms prescribed by statute. As we have seen, defenses based on misrepresentation in the application for insurance are subject to regulatory statutes in some states.[6] In most instances such statutes explicitly apply only to representations made at the time of or before issuance of the policy.[7] In some instances, separate statutes regulate defenses based on misrepresentation in the proof of loss,[8] precluding such a defense unless the misrepresentation was fraudulent and concerned a matter material to the liability of the insurer. In other instances a statute regulating defenses based on misrepresentation during nego-

---

was covered); Mountainair Municipal Schools v. United States Fid. & Gy. Co., 80 N.M. 761, 461 P.2d 410 (1969) (injury to student when door-closing mechanism fell on her head in gymnasium; first report nineteen months later was not "as soon as practicable"; school superintendent's ignorance of existence of liability policy was no excuse; late notice is presumptively prejudicial to insurer; though presumption is rebuttable, it was not rebutted in this case).

Excusing delay: *E.g.*, Home Indem. Co. v. Ware, 285 F.2d 852 (3d Cir. 1960) (Delaware law; delay of almost three months not a breach of notice requirement since insured would have no reason to believe his automobile liability policy afforded coverage when his stepson, an unlicensed driver, stole the car and became involved in a collision).

See also Annot., 28 A.L.R.3d 292 (1969) (concerning ignorance of existence of life or accident policy).

1. See Appendix A *infra*.

2. See § 7.2(a) *supra*.

3. See § 6.8(a) and n.7 thereto *supra*.

4. See Appendix A *infra*.

5. See, *e.g.*, Lakes v. Buckeye State Mut. Ins. Ass'n, 110 Ohio App. 115, 168 N.E.2d 895 (1960) (jury found that plaintiff wilfully concealed that some of the personalty reported in proof of loss was not destroyed by fire). *Cf.* Teitelbaum Furs, Inc. v. Dominion Ins. Co., 58 Cal.2d 601, 375 P.2d 439, 25 Cal.Rptr. 559 (1962), *cert. denied*, 372 U.S. 966 (1963) (plaintiff company's claim, based on the assertion that a robbery occurred, barred by collateral estoppel since one of its officers was convicted of filing false insurance claim; the issue whether robbery occurred was the same in both cases).

6. See § 6.5(b) *supra*.

7. *E.g.*, Mass.Gen.Laws Ann. ch. 175, § 186 (1958), applying to "oral or written misrepresentation or warranty made in the negotiation of a policy of insurance . . . ."

8. *E.g.*, Tex.Ins.Code Ann. art. 21.19 (1963).

tiation of the contract explicitly extends also to defenses based on misrepresentation in the proof of loss.[9] In still other instances a statute that is aimed at least primarily at defenses based on misrepresentation during negotiation of the contract is inexplicit as to whether it applies as well to fraud and false swearing in the presentment of a claim. Debatable problems of meaning are thus presented. For example, consider a regulatory statute adopting the severe standard that denies a defense based on misrepresentation unless it concerns a matter that contributes to the loss. False swearing about the amount of loss never concerns a matter that contributes to the policyholder's loss, in the sense of being a causative factor in its occurrence, as distinguished from contributing to a loss by the insurer if the false swearing succeeds. What inference, then, should a court draw concerning the statutory meaning—that the statute precludes the insurer from establishing that this kind of false swearing renders the policy void, or instead that this kind of false swearing is beyond the intended scope of the statute so the court must fashion its own answer to the insurer's contention?[10]

Even in the absence of an applicable statute, courts have tended to impose some requirement of materiality as a prerequisite for application of a defense based on fraud or false swearing in presenting a claim.[11] Also, decisions have tended to limit the scope and effectiveness of the defense in other ways. For example, some courts hold that the fraud-or-false-swearing clause does not apply to testimony given at trial.[12] And in some instances it has been held that misconduct of one insured does not bar recovery by an innocent co-insured holding a separable interest.[13]

---

9. See *e.g.*, Ala.Code tit. 28, § 6 (1958).

10. See, *e.g.*, McPherson v. Camden Fire Ins. Co., 222 S.W. 211 (Tex. Comm'n App.1920) (breach of "iron safe clause" requiring plaintiff to take inventory and keep books in a fireproof safe was a good defense for insurer;   contribute-to-loss statute held inapplicable to "iron safe clause" and to "proof of loss clause" because the breach could in no event contribute to bring about the loss). See also Hawkins v. New York Life Ins. Co., 176 Kan. 24, 269 P.2d 389 (1954) (overruling earlier decisions that had interpreted a contribute-to-loss statute on life insurance as being inapplicable to "moral risk").

11. See, *e.g.*, Firemen's Ins. Co. v. Smith, 180 F.2d 371 (8th Cir.), *cert. denied*, 339 U.S. 980 (1950) (Missouri law; on other issues in the case the court cited a Missouri statute concerning warranties *incorporated in* a fire policy; without referring to any statute or decision, the court stated that

whether the policy was rendered void by false swearing "depends also upon whether the alleged false swearing by the insured related to any material fact or circumstance concerning the insurance or the subject thereof"). See generally 5A Appleman, Insurance Law § 3587 (rev. ed. 1970).

12. *E.g.*, American Paint Service v. Home Ins. Co., 246 F.2d 91 (3d Cir. 1957), 64 A.L.R.2d 957 (1959) (New Jersey law); Home Ins. Co. v. Cohen, 357 S.W.2d 674 (Ky.1962), *overruling* World Fire & Marine Ins. Co. v. Tapp, 279 Ky. 423, 130 S.W.2d 848 (1939) (false statements in deposition).

13. *E.g.*, Mercantile Trust Co. v. New York Underwriters Ins. Co., 376 F.2d 502 (7th Cir. 1967), 24 A.L.R.3d 443 (1969) (Illinois law; fraud of life tenant of dwelling in relation to contents coverage under homeowners policy did not bar trustee holding remainder interest in dwelling). By virtue of explicit policy provisions, a similar rule applies to protect the mortgagee under

SECTION 7.3   APPRAISAL AND ARBITRATION

§ 7.3(a) GENERALLY

Standard fire insurance forms provide that if the company and the insured fail to agree upon the value of the property or the amount of loss either may demand an appraisal by two appraisers, one appointed by each party, with an umpire resolving differences between them.[1]

Uninsured motorist coverage within automobile insurance policies commonly provides for arbitration with respect to some, though not all, of the disputed issues of fact and law that may arise under this coverage.[2]

The general hostility of courts to agreements for arbitration of future disputes has cast doubt on the enforceability and effect of appraisal and arbitration clauses in insurance policies. Since appraisal clauses are more limited in scope, ordinarily applying only to an issue of valuation of property or loss, they have fared somewhat better than arbitration clauses, and if the terms of an appraisal clause have been strictly adhered to by the party invoking it, he has usually been protected against a contest of the appraisal by the opposing party.[3]

Arbitration clauses, representing a far greater threat than appraisal clauses to availability of the full panoply of legal processes for resolving disputes, have been less favorably treated by the courts, and their enforcement, when allowed, has created many more problems because of their wider scope and the wider range of problems for which clear-cut answers are not provided in the policy provisions themselves.[4]

The general judicial hostility to arbitration clauses does not extend to an agreement for arbitration made after a dispute has arisen or to a general agreement for arbitration made before a particular dispute arises and affirmed with respect to that dispute by mutual acquiescence in its submission to arbitration under the earlier general agreement. Many subrogation claims of an automobile collision insurer against an automobile liability insurer are submitted to arbitration under such an arrangement.[5] Only rarely, however, are other third-party claims submitted to arbitration.[6]

the standard mortgage clause. See § 4.2(b) *supra*. But in the absence of policy provisions such as those of the standard mortgage clause, probably the mortgagee would be barred by the mortgagor's false swearing. *Cf.* Reserve Ins. Co. v. Aguilera, 181 Neb. 605, 150 N.W.2d 114 (1967), 24 A.L.R. 3d 431 (1969).

1. See § 7.3(b) *infra*.

2. See § 7.3(c) *infra*.

3. See § 7.3(b) *infra*.

4. See § 7.3(c) *infra*.

5. See Smith, *Arbitration of Automobile Subrogation Claims*, 1962 Ins.L.J. 279. *But cf.* Rosenbloom, *Arbitration of Automobile Subrogation Claims: A Dissent*, 1962 Ins.L.J. 413.

6. See generally Santoorgian, *Arbitration of Third-Party Liability Claims: One Company's Experiment*, 1969 Ins. L.J. 588.

§ 7.3(b) APPRAISAL CLAUSES

The New York statutory standard fire insurance policy,[1] which has been widely copied in other states,[2] contains a clause declaring that if the insured and insurer fail to agree on the amount of a loss, "then, on the written demand of either, each shall select a competent and disinterested appraiser   .   .   ." and the two are to appraise the loss, with the participation if necessary of a disinterested umpire selected by them, or by a judge, and their award "shall determine the amount of actual cash value and loss."[3]

In general such appraisal clauses, applying only to valuation questions and not to all manner of disputed issues, have been held valid and enforceable even in jurisdictions in which agreements to arbitrate all future disputes are unenforceable.[4] Nevertheless, appraisal clauses have given rise to legal controversy.[5]

One source of recurring controversy is a lack of specificity of such clauses regarding the time within which appraisal may be demanded. The general standard adopted by courts in the absence of an explicit policy provision on the point is that a demand for appraisal must be made within a reasonable time.[6]

However, even if the demand comes at a time later than an explicit policy provision permits,[7] or at a time that is beyond what would ordinarily be regarded as reasonable, a demand for appraisal is sometimes sustained. If the policy provision does not specify a time limit, this result is in some instances justified as a determination that the length of time that is reasonable in a particular case is affected by the conduct of the parties in their dealings concerning settlement of the loss. In some cases it can also be justified on grounds of rights at variance with policy provisions,[8] and this theory may be applied even if an explicitly stated time limit has been violated.

The procedure for appointment of an umpire is another source of potential dispute. It is commonly provided that if an umpire is needed he is to be selected by the two appraisers appointed by the parties, or by a judge of a court of record. It has been held that since no formal procedure is prescribed an appointment on ex parte application of the insured was a valid appointment.[9] But another court took a con-

---

1. See Appendix A *infra*.

2. See § 2.10(b) *supra*.

3. See Appendix A *infra*.

4. *E.g.*, School Dist. No. 1 of Silver Bow County v. Globe & Republic Ins. Co., 146 Mont. 208, 404 P.2d 889 (1965), 14 A.L.R.3d 666 (1967) (judgment for policyholder reversed and remanded for compliance with the insurers' demand for appraisal).

5. See generally Torshen, *Current Problems Relating to Demands for Appraisals*, 1961 Ins.L.J. 835.

6. *E.g.*, School Dist. No. 1 of Silver Bow County v. Globe & Republic Ins. Co., 146 Mont. 208, 404 P.2d 889 (1965), 14 A.L.R.3d 666 (1967).

7. *E.g.*, Milwaukee Ins. Co. v. Kogen, 240 F.2d 613 (8th Cir. 1957) (Minnesota law).

8. See §§ 6.1, 6.8(a) *supra*.

9. Agricultural Ins. Co. v. Holter, 201 Tenn. 345, 299 S.W.2d 15 (1957), 69 A. L.R.2d 1292 (1960).

trary view, pointing out that unless the clause is construed as requiring a judicial order as distinguished from a personal act of a judge on informal ex parte application, serious problems might arise from conflicting appointments by different judges at the instance of different parties, each without notice to the other.[10]

Appraisal proceedings are commonly even less formal than arbitration. For example, an appraisal may occur without any formal opportunity being extended to the parties to present or challenge evidence. Thus, in the absence of some special need for taking testimony and in the absence of statutory or policy requirements for notice and hearing, some courts have sustained an appraisal in the face of a challenge on the ground of failure on the part of the appraisers and umpire to give the insured notice of the time and place of the meeting of the appraisers with the umpire to whom they were submitting their differences.[11]

§ 7.3(c) ARBITRATION IN UNINSURED MOTORIST COVERAGE

Policy provisions for Uninsured Motorist Coverage—a coverage first developed in the mid-1950's in response to threats of more far-reaching reform of automobile insurance[1]—commonly include a stipulation for settling disputes by arbitration.[2] In some states the common law rule against enforcing agreements to arbitrate future disputes still prevails, and there are precedents for applying this rule to the arbitration clause in uninsured motorist coverage.[3] In other states, there are statutes that are sufficient to authorize enforcement of agreements to arbitrate future disputes under uninsured motorist coverage.[4] There is the possibility, too, though it seems remote, that exceptional cases will be reached by the Federal Arbitration Act.[5]

10. Caledonian Ins. Co. v. Superior Court, 140 Cal.App.2d 458, 295 P.2d 49 (1st Dist. 1956).

11. *E.g.*, Hendricks v. American Fire & Cas. Co., 247 S.C. 479, 148 S.E.2d 162 (1966), 25 A.L.R.3d 671 (1969).

1. See § 4.9(d) *supra*.

2. See Appendix H *infra*. See also Aksen, *Arbitration Under the Uninsured Motorist Endorsement*, 1965 Ins.L.J. 17.

3. See, *e.g.*, Heisner v. Jones, 184 Neb. 602, 169 N.W.2d 606 (1969) (insurer held entitled to intervene in tort action and forfeited its right to contest default judgment by failing to intervene); Boughton v. Farmers Ins. Exch., 354 P.2d 1085 (Okla.1960), 79 A.L.R.2d 1245 (1961); Barnhart v. Civil Service Employees Ins. Co., 16

Utah 2d 223, 398 P.2d 873 (1965). See Generally Widiss, A Guide to Uninsured Motorist Coverage §§ 6.2–6.16 (1969).

4. Clear examples are Cal.Ins.Code § 11580.2(f) (West Supp.1969) (also authorizing discovery) and Ore.Rev. Stat. § 743.792(1) (a) (1969), including arbitration provisions in the uninsured motorist statutes. It is debatable whether broad arbitration statutes of other states apply, since it may be argued that a policyholder's acquiescence in the inclusion of the arbitration clause in the policy is not such a voluntary, written agreement as is contemplated by the arbitration statutes. See Widiss, A Guide to Uninsured Motorist Coverage §§ 6.6–6.14 (1969). *But cf.* Aksen, *Arbitration*

5. See Note 5 on page 455.

Insofar as the clause purports to deny a right to jury trial to persons not parties to the insurance contract—and perhaps even as to a policyholder who is given no option but to accept the arbitration stipulation if he is to have any uninsured motorist coverage—it is arguably subject to attack on constitutional grounds.[6] There would appear to be no constitutional obstacle, however, to an insurer's including in its policy a clause under which the company would in effect make a standing offer to arbitrate any dispute arising under the coverage and the policyholder would have the option, after a dispute arises under the coverage, to submit it to arbitration.

The arbitration clause in the uninsured motorist coverage—though intended to simplify procedure and expedite disposition of claims—has itself been the source of an extraordinary amount of litigation.[7]

SECTION 7.4   NONPAYMENT AND LATE PAYMENT

§ 7.4(a) GENERALLY

Some states have statutes providing special remedies for an insurer's nonpayment or late payment of a valid claim under specified types of insurance contracts,[1] and a few states have statutes of this kind applying to many [2] or all types of insurance.[3]

Under the Uninsured Motorist Endorsement, 1965 Ins.L.J. 17, 20–21.

5. The Federal Arbitration Act, 9 U.S.C.A. §§ 1–14 (1970), applies only to an arbitration agreement in maritime transactions and transactions involving interstate or foreign commerce. Thus, before it could be applied to the arbitration clause in the uninsured motorist coverage, it would be necessary to classify the contract for this coverage as a transaction involving interstate or foreign commerce. Moreover, it is doubtful that the act will be applied, as a rule of national substantive law, in *state* as well as federal courts. See Prima Paint Corp. v. Flood & Conklin Mfg. Co., 388 U.S. 395, 87 Sup.Ct. 1801, 18 L.Ed.2d 1270 (1967), and Aksen, *Prima Paint v. Flood & Conklin—What Does It Mean?* 43 St.John's L.Rev. 1 (1968). If the act applies only to proceedings in federal courts, the jurisdictional requirement that the amount in controversy exceed $10,000 would be an obstacle to its application to most claims under uninsured motorist coverage as long as this coverage is rarely written with a limit higher than $10,000. If the act applies only to

proceedings in federal courts, it would also be necessary to clear another jurisdictional hurdle that there be a federal question or diversity of citizenship. 28 U.S.C.A. §§ 1331, 1332 (1966).

6. Note, 78 Harv.L.Rev. 1250 (1965).

7. See Laufer, *Insurance Against Lack of Insurance? A Dissent from the Uninsured Motorist Endorsement,* 1969 Duke L.J. 227, 240–242. See also Annot., 29 A.L.R.3d 328 (1970).

1. *E.g.,* Mass.Gen.Laws Ann. ch. 175B, § 4 (1958) (attorney's fee against unauthorized foreign insurer when insurer has failed for 30 days after demand prior to commencement of action to pay according to contract). See generally 22 Appleman, Insurance Law § 14532 (1947); Annot., 126 A.L.R. 1439 (1940).

2. See, *e.g.,* Neb.Rev.Stat. § 44–359 (1968), construed in Otteman v. Interstate Fire & Cas. Co., 172 Neb. 574, 111 N.W.2d 97 (1961), 89 A.L.R.2d 1182 (1963).

3. See, *e.g.,* Fla.Stat.Ann. § 626.0508–09 (1960), § 627.0127 (Supp.1970).

The sanctions customarily include liability for a claimant's attorney's fee and for a penalty in addition, often calculated as a percentage of the contract benefit due.[4]

As a general rule, in the absence of an applicable statute, there is no liability for either penalty or attorney's fee because of late payment of an insurance claim.[5] This is an application of the broader rule, applied throughout the United States, that ordinarily parties are to bear their own attorneys' fees regardless of the outcome of litigation.[6] Thus, for example, when a liability insurer denies coverage and is later held to have done so wrongfully, the insured may recover as damages for the breach whatever reasonable attorneys' fees he has paid to attorneys defending him against a tort claim that was covered.[7] In the absence of an applicable statute or rather exceptional circumstances,[8] however, the insured is not allowed to recover for the fees paid in compensation for representing him in the action against the insurer.[9]

4. See *e.g.*, Harmon v. Lumbermens Mut. Cas. Co., 247 La. 263, 283, 170 So. 2d 646, 653 (1965) (observing variations among Louisiana statutes and noting that the penalty for refusal to settle small claims is relatively high —100 per cent for refusal to pay claims such as are common under hospital and medical coverages for periodic benefits—but much lower on types of coverage commonly involving large lump-sum payments).

5. *E.g.*, Millers' Nat'l Ins. Co. v. Wichita Flour Mills Co., 257 F.2d 93, 102– 103 (10th Cir. 1958), 76 A.L.R.2d 385, 400 (1961).

6. See generally MacKinnon, Contingent Fees for Legal Services—A Study of Professional Economics and Responsibilities 141–146 (Report of the Am. Bar Foundation 1964). Concerning the law of England, under which attorneys' fees are commonly treated as part of the costs taxed against a losing party, see *id.* at 142– 143.

7. See generally § 7.6(e) *infra*.

8. See, *e.g.*, Siegel v. William E. Bookhultz & Sons, Inc., 419 F.2d 720 (D.C. Cir. 1969) (insurer of a bankrupt corporation quit corporation's defense of a products liability action; insurer held liable for fee of corporation's court-appointed attorney in a subsequent action against the insurer for its breach of duty to defend; "[o]nly by grace of the court's appointment of counsel was the corporation able to sue to regain the protection of the policy, and only because it was compelled to sue did the expense arise of which St. Paul [the insurer] now complains"; ". . . in the circumstances here, a fee for appointed counsel's successful effort to secure for Surrey Corporation the coverage of the policy and the protection it promised was within the sphere of damages awardable for St. Paul's breach of contract").

9. *E.g.*, Utica Mut. Ins. Co. v. Plante, 106 N.H. 525, 214 A.2d 742 (1965) (insured cannot recover fees paid to attorney representing him in declaratory judgment proceeding); Baker v. Northwestern Nat'l Cas. Co., 26 Wis. 2d 306, 132 N.W.2d 493 (1965) (insured cannot recover attorneys' fees beyond statutory costs incurred in prosecuting action against insurer, but if not otherwise barred may recover attorneys' fees incurred in litigation with third parties because of insurer's wrongdoings). *But cf.* Equity Mut. Ins. Co. v. Southern Ice Co., 232 Ark. 41, 334 S. W.2d 688 (1960) (insureds asked for additional fees for services of attorneys in appeal of declaratory judgment proceeding; without further discussion, the court declared, "[W]e find that they are entitled to such amounts and fix the same at a total of $250 for both The Borden Company and Gober").

§ 7.4(b) STANDARDS FOR IMPOSING PENALTY
AND ATTORNEYS' FEES

Statutes and judicial decisions interpreting them have differed with respect to whether assessments of penalties and attorneys' fees against insurers are limited to cases in which the insurer has contested a claim or otherwise delayed payment without having reasonable grounds for doing so.

Two principal lines of argument may be advanced in support of statutory imposition of added liability even though the insurer's decision to contest the claim was reasonable. First, it may be argued that the threat of higher liability without dependence on a finding of unreasonableness of the contest is a surer deterrent to unfounded contests. Second, it may be argued that higher liability should be imposed on an insurer when it unsuccessfully contests a claim, even though it acts reasonably in doing so, in order to compensate the insured for the costs of the contest to him.

The second argument does not support imposition of a penalty, but it is a better ground than the first for imposing added liability to the extent of attorneys' fees and other litigation costs. If the insured has to bear the expense of litigation to prove his claim, he is effectively denied a substantial share of the relief from an economic risk against which he was seeking protection when he obtained insurance. If this argument seems vulnerable on the ground that the risk of litigation over insurance benefits in borderline cases is distinct from the initial economic risk, it may be answered that the layman would be more likely to count the net than the gross as the benefit he received from his insurance, and the net recovery in contested cases would fall short of offsetting his initial economic loss even if he had obtained what he thought to be full insurance coverage. It is surely a defensible position that this risk of the expense of successful litigation by the insured should be borne by the insurer and that its cost should be distributed among insureds through premiums, as part of the cost of the coverage.

On the other hand, such an added liability will tend to cause insurers to pay claims of doubtful merit, with the result that the insurers' function of holding down the cost of coverage by vigorous policing of claims will not be as effectively performed. Thus, the balance that most statutes and interpreting decisions have struck in disallowing either penalty or attorneys' fees in cases of contest on reasonable grounds [10] is also a defensible position. It would seem clearly undesirable, moreover, to allow a penalty, as distinguished from a compensatory allowance of attorneys' fees and litigation costs, when the insur-

10. See, *e.g.*, Koch v. Prudential Ins. Co., 205 Kan. 561, 470 P.2d 756 (1970) (attorney's fee disallowed since there was reasonably disputable fact issue on whether insured was 66 and thus beyond age limit of group credit life policy, rather than 65 as he represented); Seguin v. Continental Serv. Life & Health Ins. Co., 230 La. 533, 89 So.2d 113 (1956), 55 A.L.R.2d 1014 (1957) (discussed in n.11 *infra*).

er has acted reasonably though unsuccessfully in contesting a claim. No penalty is deserved by the insurer, and the deterrent to contests would affect those cases in which the available grounds seemed fair and just as well as those in which contesting liability was unreasonable. Since policyholders in general have an interest, along with insurers, in defeating claims that are without merit, it seems unwise to introduce such a strong deterrent to the useful activity of insurers in contesting claims that they reasonably conclude they should contest.

It might be argued that recognizing the grounds of contest as reasonable when they have been proved by litigation to be unsound is contradictory. But the standard of reasonableness quite properly used here is concerned with the reasonableness of the judgment of the insurance claims representatives in deciding to contest a claim the merit of which will not be determined until the litigation is ended. For example, a statute may declare that a claim shall be paid within thirty days after proof of the claim is submitted "unless just and reasonable grounds, such as would put a reasonable and prudent business man on his guard, exist." [11]

SECTION 7.5 ASSISTANCE AND COOPERATION OF THE INSURED

Liability insurance policies customarily provide that the insured shall cooperate with and assist the company in the investigation and defense of tort claims against the insured.[1] Such provisions ordinarily refer explicitly to attendance at hearings and trials and assistance in effecting settlements, securing and giving evidence, obtaining the attendance of witnesses, and otherwise aiding in the conduct of suits. They also include negative stipulations—that, except at his own cost, the insured shall not voluntarily make any payment, assume any obligation or incur any expense other than for imperative medical and surgical relief to others immediately after the accident.

Despite early and highly respected authority to the contrary,[2] the weight of authority, consisting in part of cases reasoned to some

---

11. La.Rev.Stat.Ann. 22:1057 (West Supp.1970). In *Seguin,* n.1 *supra,* applying this statute, it was held that penalties should be assessed, the insurer having unsuccessfully contested a claim for diaphragmatic hernia on the ground it did not come within hernia either in the ordinary usage of that term or in the policy usage. If a court construes the concept of what would put a prudent business man on guard so narrowly that it does not encompass the problem whether "hernia" as used in the policy includes "diaphragmatic hernia," then surely there can be but few cases in which the company will be held liable for the policy benefits but not for the penalty. A holding that the insurer

could not escape the penalty even if acting on the advice of its medical and legal advisers in declining to pay a claim such as that in *Seguin* would seem to be a distortion of the statute. Arguably the result in *Seguin* might be justified, however, on the narrower ground that the company not only must have an adequate ground for being "on guard" but also must prove that it acted on that ground rather than arbitrarily, through the decision of a claims representative unqualified to appraise that ground.

1. See Appendices G, H *infra.*

2. *E.g.,* Coleman v. New Amsterdam Cas. Co., 247 N.Y. 271, 160 N.E. 367

extent on special recognition of the interests of third party victims,[3] requires that the insurer show prejudice to establish a defense based on breach of the assistance and cooperation clause.[4]

Collusion with a claimant to establish his claim is a violation of the assistance and cooperation clause, and in some jurisdictions there is support for the position that this is such a serious violation that the insurer need not meet the ordinary requirements of proof of prejudice.[5] But it would seem that an insured cannot be required to falsify or even to withhold facts from a victim claiming against him. And it has been held that the actions of a parent in arranging for an attorney for a minor child to bring suit against the parent do not

(1928), **72** A.L.R. 1443 (1931) (opinion by Cardozo, J.). Perhaps few, if any, would contend that the insurer's defense of breach of the assistance and cooperation clause should not have been recognized on the facts of the case, since, first, the secretary of the insured drug company, which was sued on the theory of a negligently filled prescription, said there had been a mistake and refused to say more unless the insurer would undertake to pay any recovery against him as well as any recovery against the insured and, second, the insured failed to respond to the insurer's letters requesting that some officer be sent to verify an answer for the defendant and requesting a conference as to the merits of the claim. But the opinion placed the holding on the ground that cooperation was one of the "conditions" of the policy, adding: "When the condition was broken, the policy was at an end, if the insurer so elected. The case is not one of the breach of a mere covenant, where the consequences may vary with fluctuations of the damage." Opinions citing *Coleman* with apparent approval include, *e.g.*, Pennsylvania Ins. Co. v. Horner, 198 Tenn. 445, 281 S.W.2d 44 (1955) (statement by the insured admitting fault and accepting responsibility for damages to the other vehicle, signed apparently because the insured was worried about hit-and-run charges; arguably this conduct was such clear proof of prejudice that the opinion does not have weight as a considered choice among the competing views on the necessity for proof of prejudice). See also Alabama Farm Bureau Mut. Cas. Ins. Co. v. Mills, 271 Ala. 192, 123 So.2d 138 (1960) (deliberate persistence in false statements; prejudice not required; in fact, however, risk of loss was increased when insur-

er was caused to defend rather than settle).

3. See, *e.g.*, Stippich v. Morrison, 12 Wis.2d 331, 107 N.W.2d 125 (1961) (breach by submitting to adverse examination without insurer's knowledge; overruling one of two earlier decisions reconcilable on facts but conflicting in rationale). *Cf.* Campbell v. Allstate Ins. Co., 60 Cal.2d 303, 384 P.2d 155, 32 Cal.Rptr. 827 (1963) (failure to respond to letters requesting assistance; default judgment); MFA Mutual Ins. Co. v. Sailors, 180 Neb. 201, 141 N.W.2d 846 (1966) (concealing identity of driver and failing to forward summons).

4. In addition to cases cited in the next preceding note, see, *e.g.*, American Fire & Cas. Co. v. Vliet, 148 Fla. 568, 4 So.2d 862 (1941), 139 A.L.R. 767 (1942); Automobile Club Ins. Co. v. Turner, 335 S.W.2d 889 (Ky.1960) (insured at first said he was driving but later corrected the misstatement; insurer, having failed to show prejudice, could not avoid liability); Henderson v. Rochester Am. Ins. Co., 254 N.C. 329, 118 S.E.2d 885 (1961) (conflicting versions as to who was driving). See generally 8 Appleman, Insurance Law § 4773 (rev. ed. 1962); 8 Blashfield, Automobile Law § 342.14 (3d ed. 1966). As to the standard for showing prejudice in this and other contexts, see § 7.1(b) *supra*.

5. See, *e.g.*, Elliott v. Metropolitan Cas. Ins. Co., 250 F.2d 680 (10th Cir. 1957), 66 A.L.R.2d 1231 (1959), *cert. denied*, 356 U.S. 932 (1958) (collusion to travel to Kansas to accept service of process). *But cf. Chapman*, n.15 *infra*. Concerning the prejudice requirement generally, see § 7.1(b) *supra*.

constitute collusion.[6] However, entering into an agreement to admit critical facts in return for a covenant by the claimant not to levy execution for any judgment in excess of the liability insurance coverage limit has been held to be a breach of the assistance and cooperation clause.[7]

Like collusion, the insured's wilful obstruction of the insurer's handling of a claim against the insured is a violation of the assistance and cooperation clause. But an insurer cannot successfully defend under this theory on evidence merely that the insured has been unavailable to cooperate in the defense; it must at least prove that it has exercised reasonable diligence to locate the insured.[8]

The unexcused refusal of an insured to attend the trial of an action against him is a violation of the assistance and cooperation clause.[9] But there are areas of uncertainty with respect to what constitutes an adequate excuse.

It has been said that the insured may be required to attend trial without pay for lost time.[10] But this proposition is open to challenge, at least in cases of severe impact on the insured's income or job status and perhaps more generally. As a matter of practice, moreover, liability insurers often reimburse lost wages, especially for an insured who works at an hourly or daily wage, and it would seem that this practice is both permissible and desirable. Some current policies provide for compensation, within a stated limit per day, for loss of wages because of attendance at trial.[11]

6. *E.g.*, Jordan v. Standard Mut. Ins. Co., 50 Ill.App.2d 12, 199 N.E.2d 423 (2d Dist. 1964), 8 A.L.R.3d 1338 (1966). However, the problem of collusive intra-family claims has led to enactment of a statute in New York declaring that no policy "shall be deemed to insure against any liability of an insured because of death of or injuries to his or her spouse or because of injury to or destruction of property of his or her spouse unless express provision relating specifically thereto is included in the policy." N.Y.Ins.Law § 167 (3) (McKinney 1966). Concerning conflicts of interest in litigation, in this and other contexts, see § 7.7 *infra.*

7. *E.g.*, Western Mut. Ins. Co. v. Baldwin, 258 Iowa 460, 137 N.W.2d 918 (1965) (farmer's comprehensive policy; insured first denied he started fire that destroyed railroad bridge and later covenanted with railroad, in return for railroad's agreement not to levy execution in excess of policy limit, to admit he started fire; declaratory judgment for insurer).

8. See, *e.g.*, Thrasher v. United States Liab. Ins. Co., 19 N.Y.2d 159, 225 N.E. 2d 503, 278 N.Y.S.2d 793 (1967) (insur-

er's attempts to locate insured were limited and ineffectual; evidence presented by insurer that insured knew insurer's investigator was looking for him was "equivocal, at best," and did not discharge insurer's burden of proving that insured's "attitude was one of 'willful and avowed obstruction' "); Johnson v. Doughty, 236 Ore. 78, 385 P.2d 760 (1963) (borrower of insured car involved in hit-and-run collision abandoned car after driving away from accident and left state without leaving forwarding address; sending a letter addressed to him at a known improper address did not constitute reasonable effort to give him an opportunity to demonstrate his willingness or lack of willingness to cooperate with insurer).

9. See *e.g.*, Morrison v. Lewis, 351 Mass. 386, 221 N.E.2d 401 (1966) (involving noncompulsory guest coverage).

10. See, *e.g.*, American Fire & Cas. Co. v. Vliet, 148 Fla. 568, 4 So.2d 862 (1941), 139 A.L.R. 767 (1942).

11. See Appendix G *infra*. Though this provision would serve to clarify the insurer's liability for lost time

It is generally recognized that the insured need not incur expense to attend trial and does not violate the assistance and cooperation clause by declining to make an expensive trip to attend at the request of the insurer when reimbursement of expenses is not offered.[12] This result is supported by a supplementary-payments clause, commonly included in policies, stating that the insurer shall reimburse expenses other than loss of earnings.[13]

Ordinarily the questions whether particular conduct on the part of the insured amounts to noncooperation and, if so, whether the insurer was prejudiced are fact questions.[14] Directly relevant to litigation over the assistance and cooperation clause is the general trend of increasing reluctance of courts to rule that reasonable jurors could not differ concerning a particular fact issue on the evidence before them.[15] This change has a very significant impact upon the practical meaning of the duty of cooperation.

and to fix a limit on the amount in the absence of an agreement otherwise, still in particular cases the argument might prevail that it would be unreasonable to demand that the insured attend trial without reimbursement of his loss of income if the loss would be much greater than the stated amount per day.

12. *E.g.*, American Fire & Cas. Co. v. Vliet, 148 Fla. 568, 4 So.2d 862 (1941), 139 A.L.R. 767 (1942). *Cf.* Beam v. State Farm Mut. Auto. Ins. Co., 269 F.2d 151 (6th Cir. 1959).

13. See Appendix G *infra*.

14. See, *e.g.*, Henderson v. Rochester Am. Ins. Co., 254 N.C. 329, 118 S.E.2d 885 (1961) (calling attention both to the usual treatment of these issues as fact questions and to the tendency of courts to decide the issues as a matter of law in certain recurring factual patterns). See also § 7.1(b) and nn.13, 14 thereto *supra*.

15. See, *e.g.*, Lumbermens Mut. Cas. Co. v. Chapman, 269 F.2d 478 (4th Cir. 1959). The act of noncooperation charged by the company was collusion between the insured, Foster, and the claimant, who was his sister-in-law. On the evening before the trial, Foster, at the request of the claimant's attorney extended through the claimant, went to the office of the claimant's attorney, for an interview. The attorney stated that his purpose was to get information to prepare his case properly, and he assured Foster that in the event of a verdict beyond the coverage the claimant would release

Foster of any responsibility for the excess. The company's attorney did not know of this meeting. Previous to this meeting, the settlement figure demanded by the claimant was $15,-000; at the start of trial, the claimant's attorney raised his settlement demand to $20,000 and gave notice to the company that he would also look to the company for any amount of the verdict beyond $20,000. The claimant's attorney called Foster as a witness during the presentation of claimant's case. In answering a question, Foster expressed the opinion that he was legally responsible for the accident. In his opening statement the claimant's attorney had described the occurrence just as Foster outlined it in his testimony, and the claimant's account closely paralleled Foster's. Trial resulted in a verdict for $7,500, which was within policy limits, and thereafter the claimant commenced this action against the company. The court of appeals sustained a jury verdict for the claimant on this evidence. The court noted that the conduct of the claimant's counsel in arranging an interview with the insured after he was represented by counsel appointed by the company was a violation of the canons of ethics but observed that the misconduct of the claimant's attorney was not chargeable to the insured. The court considered that ordinary candor demanded of the insured that he inform the company of the conference, but that this breach of obligation by the insured was not so substantial as to require a conclusion that the company was relieved of liability. Perhaps even in a day of great permissiveness toward jury ver-

SECTION 7.6 THE LIABILITY INSURER'S DUTY OF DEFENSE

§ 7.6(a) THE SOURCE AND NATURE OF THE DUTY

A liability insurance policy ordinarily contains provisions that require the company to defend any suit against an insured alleging bodily injury or property damage within the scope of the insuring agreements, "even if such suit is groundless, false or fraudulent." [1] This phrase makes clear that the duty to defend sometimes applies even when under the facts there will be no duty to pay on behalf of the insured.[2] But, as we shall see, there is dispute and uncertainty about the application of this standard in some contexts. There are also other areas of conflict with respect to the scope of the duty to defend. For example, it has been held that the duty to defend is not necessarily limited to actions for damages. That is, in some instances a suit for injunction may be within the insuring agreements.[3]

It is often stated that the obligation to defend is determined by the nature of the claim against the insured, regardless of whether it is meritorious.[4] There is support in a scattering of cases, though no precedent squarely in point in many jurisdictions, for qualification of this standard when, in addition to a formally alleged claim within coverage, there is a potential or actual claim of intentional tort that

dicts other courts would have found the defense of noncooperation established as a matter of law in these circumstances. Certainly a different result would have been probable in earlier times.

1. See Appendices G, H *infra*.

2. The duty to pay is established by showing that there was in fact an occurrence within the scope of the insuring agreements under which the insurer agreed "to pay on behalf of the insured all sums which the insured shall become legally obligated to pay as damages . . ." because of bodily injury or property damage arising out of defined incidents. See the policy forms, Appendices G, H *infra*. On the other hand, ordinarily the mere filing of a suit alleging that such an incident has occurred would invoke the duty to defend without regard to whether such an incident did in fact occur.

3. *E.g.*, Taylor v. Imperial Cas. & Indem. Co., 82 S.D. 298, 144 N.W.2d 856 (1966) (damage to adjoining property from underground leakage of gasoline from storage tanks was damage caused by accident within coverage of

liability policy; in suit for injunction and damages, no damages were awarded; insured held entitled to recover from insurer his costs of defense). *But cf.* Aetna Cas. & Sur. Co. v. Hanna, 224 F.2d 499 (5th Cir. 1955), 53 A.L.R.2d 1125 (1957) (duty to defend did not extend to suit for injunction or subsequent proceedings in which the plaintiff unsuccessfully sought damages for violating injunction decree).

4. *E.g.*, Wilson v. Maryland Cas. Co., 377 Pa. 588, 105 A.2d 304 (1954), 50 A. L.R.2d 449 (1956). See generally, Comment, *The Insurer's Duty to Defend Under a Liability Insurance Policy*, 114 U.Pa.L.Rev. 734 (1966); 7A Appleman, Insurance Law § 4683 (rev. ed. 1962). The majority opinion in *Wilson* seems not to distinguish clearly between the claimant's allegations in the tort action and the insured's allegations in his action against the company. In view of the majority decision against coverage, it was unnecessary for the court to face squarely a problem arising from the fact that the insured settled with the claimant after the company's alleged breach. This problem is considered in § 7.6(e) *infra*.

is beyond coverage; [5] other precedents, however, cast doubt at the least as to whether such a qualification of this standard will be recog-

5. *E.g.*, Stout v. Grain Dealers Mut. Ins. Co., 307 F.2d 521 (4th Cir. 1962) (after intentional shooting of "peeping Tom," insured was convicted of manslaughter on plea of guilty; insurer declined to defend wrongful death action; insured instituted this declaratory proceeding; held, plaintiff-insured placed himself outside the coverage by his plea of guilty to manslaughter, and insurer therefore has no duty to defend wrongful death action; to compel insurer to defend would create impossible situation because of conflict of interest); Weis v. State Farm Mut. Auto. Ins. Co., 242 Minn. 141, 64 N.W.2d 366 (1954), 49 A.L.R.2d 688 (1956) (claimant alleged insured "negligently, carelessly, and recklessly, deliberately" ran into rear of claimant's car; insured's statement to insurer declared it was no accident and that he ran into claimant's car deliberately several times; held, no duty to defend in view of insured's admission the incident was not an accident; under these circumstances insurer cannot be bound by any contrary implications of the judgment in the tort case it properly refused to defend); Burd v. Sussex Mut. Ins. Co., 56 N.J. 383, 267 A.2d 7 (1970) (tort action against insured of homeowners policy with one count alleging that, while intoxicated, he intentionally shot his friend and second count alleging he did so negligently; insurer refused to defend; general verdict and judgment against insured in tort action; trial court entered summary judgment for insured in action on policy; held, reversed; carrier should not be permitted to defend in such a conflict-of-interest situation, and should not be estopped by result in tort action; its covenant to defend is translated into an obligation "to reimburse the insured if it is later adjudged that the claim was one within the policy covenant to pay").

In *Stout* the court relied heavily on Farm Bureau Mut. Auto. Ins. Co. v. Hammer, 177 F.2d 793 (4th Cir. 1949), *cert. denied*, 339 U.S. 914 (1950), in which the court declined to hold the insurer collaterally estopped to challenge findings that its insured caused injuries negligently, the insurer having declined to defend the insured because it contended he caused the injuries intentionally. It would seem that conflict of interest is a sound reason for hold-

ing that the insurer is not collaterally estopped by findings in a civil action when it has declined to defend; see § 7.7 *infra*. And this has the practical consequence of translating the duty to defend, if it is still recognized, into an obligation to reimburse costs of defense. But whether the insurer should be freed even of an obligation to pay the costs of defense (by reimbursing the insured) is a distinguishable and more debatable question. On the one hand, such an obligation seems reasonably supportable in the policy language. On the other hand, one might argue, on grounds of public policy, that an insured guilty in fact of an especially heinous offense should be denied the benefit of the insurer's agreement to defend him against a claim of a less serious offense based on the same incident. And one might challenge the good faith of the claimant's allegations of only the less serious offense of negligence; perhaps the insurer should be permitted to make such a challenge in a proceeding to which both the claimant and the alleged insured are parties. But conflict of interest would itself seem to be an inadequate reason for allowing the insurer to escape its obligation to bear the costs of defense against any claim of a type within the scope of the insuring agreements; this and other conflicts of interest inhere in the nature of liability insurance, as is noted in § 7.7 *infra*. *Cf.*, however, Williams v. Farmers Mut. of Enumclaw, 245 Ore. 557, 423 P.2d 518 (1967) (plaintiff swore out a complaint against defendant's omnibus insured charging that he intentionally drove his car against plaintiff; conviction for assault with a dangerous weapon; plaintiff then sued for damages, alleging negligence only; insurer declined to defend, calling attention to the conflict of interest; plaintiff took a default judgment against the omnibus insured and then brought this action against the insurer to collect the amount of that judgment, asserting that the insurer was estopped to challenge the findings of negligence implicit in the default judgment; held, insurer is not estopped by default judgment and is entitled to judgment on its policy defense of assault committed by the insured). Note that in both *Hammer* and *Williams* the victim (or his representative) was proceeding against the insurer to collect the

nized, and may be interpreted as definitely opposing such a qualification.[6] There is also a scattering of cases supporting qualification of this standard on other special grounds.[7] Subject to these possible qualifications, this standard of determining the obligation to defend by the nature of the claim alleged in the tort action against the insured is consistent, it would seem, with most decisions involving cases in which the claimant has filed a suit against the insured alleging an injury under circumstances that happen to be within the scope of the insuring agreements of the policy. Thus, as an *inclusionary* test, this standard (the nature of the claim against the insured) is, with the possible qualifications noted, consistent with the weight of authority. Quite clearly, however, it is not reliable as an *exclusionary* standard. That is, it cannot be relied upon as the basis for answering a number of questions that may be raised by an insurer's contention that it has no duty to defend because the victim alleges only a claim against the insured that falls outside the scope of the insuring agreements.

First, is there a duty to defend when the accident victim, in his tort action against the insured, presents pleadings that take no position one way or the other on some point determinative of coverage? For example, the liability policy often contains a provision that it will not apply to claims for bodily injury sustained by an "employee of the insured."[8] Suppose there is doubt about whether the injured person was an "employee" as that term is used in the policy clause and, if so,

---

amount of his own judgment for tort damages. In neither case was cost of defense included in the claim. Thus neither of these cases is directly in point on the duty of defense, though both opinions are reasoned in part on denial of the duty to defend in these circumstances. In *Burd*, however, the costs of defense were included in the claim, and the opinion may be interpreted, it would seem, as saying, first, that full costs of defense of the entire action (including the count for intentional tort and that for negligence) are recoverable if in the action on the insurance policy it is found that the insured did not commit an intentional tort and, second, that no costs of defense (not even the costs of defending against the negligence count) are recoverable if in the action on the policy it is found that the insured did commit an intentional tort.

6. *E.g.*, Employers' Fire Ins. Co. v. Beals, 103 R.I. 623, 240 A.2d 397 (1968) (claimant alleged that insured child negligently struck claimant in eye with pencil; insurer's declaratory proceedings based on contention insured child intentionally struck claimant, dismissed; as to conflict of inter-

est problem noted in the opinion, see § 7.7 *infra*.)

7. See, *e.g.*, Commercial Ins. Co. v. Papandrea, 121 Vt. 386, 159 A.2d 333 (1960) (mutually repugnant claims for injury or death of each of two occupants of a vehicle, each claim being founded on the theory that the other occupant was driving; trial court's dismissal of declaratory judgment reversed and cause remanded; contention that insurer is bound to defend against both claims rejected; roots of the problem go deeper than the obligation to defend even false or fraudulent claims, since there was no obligation whatsoever to one of the tort defendants—the one who was not the named insured—unless he was in fact the driver and was thus an omnibus insured; also he makes inconsistent claims in demanding that the insurer defend the action against him, a defense to which he is entitled only if he was the driver, while claiming in his separate action as tort plaintiff that he was not the driver).

8. For an example of such a policy provision, see Appendix G *infra*. Concerning interpretation of this clause, see § 4.9(c) *supra*.

whether he was employed by one who was "the insured" in the sense in which those words are used. The disputed fact issues determinative of coverage may not have to be decided in reaching a disposition of the tort claim against the insured. Although there is impressive support for a more expansive duty to defend,[9] it would seem that in such circumstances the insured should be entitled to recover damages for breach of the duty to defend only upon a finding of the decisive facts in his favor in an action to which he and the company are parties.[10] To hold otherwise would often deprive the insurer of any

9. *E.g.*, Lee v. Aetna Cas. & Sur. Co., 178 F.2d 750 (2d Cir. 1949) (opinion by L.Hand, C.J.) (New York law; claimant alleged that through insured's negligence claimant was caused to fall into pit of elevator shaft; liability policy did not apply to "use of any elevator," and insurer declined to defend; insured defended unsuccessfully and sued insurer for reimbursement of payment on judgment and for defense costs; summary judgment for insurer against claim for reimbursement of payment on judgment, since the claim finally established was outside coverage, but summary judgment for recovery of $2500 cost of defense affirmed; "it was the duty of the defendant [insurer] to undertake the defence, until it could confine the claim to a recovery that the policy did not cover"); National Indem. Co. v. Flesher, 469 P.2d 360 (Alaska 1970) (discussed in n.14 *infra*); Hartford Acc. & Indem. Co. v. Pacific Indem. Co., 249 Cal.App.2d 432, 57 Cal.Rptr. 492 (2d Dist. 1967) (in malpractice action against dentist, plaintiff alleged a date of contracting for services falling near the end of period of coverage of one insurer and did not state when malpractice occurred; second insurer, whose coverage applied to later period, held liable for contribution but not indemnity of costs of defense, though it acknowledged liability for full amount of judgment against dentist for malpractice occurring during its coverage period); McFayden v. North River Ins. Co., 62 Ill.App.2d 164, 209 N.E.2d 833 (2d Dist. 1965) (homeowners coverage; insurer declined to defend dog-bite claim on the ground that a "business" was being conducted on the premises; policyholder defended unsuccessfully and sued insurer for reimbursement of the tort judgment and costs of defense; insurer held liable for full amount; estopped because of its refusal to defend; duty to defend because the claimant in the tort action alleged a claim "potentially within"

coverage, even though it was indefinite as to matters decisive of the policy defense); Sims v. Illinois Nat. Cas. Co., 43 Ill.App.2d 184, 193 N.E.2d 123 (3d Dist. 1963) (Ruark, riding with Sims, injured in collision with vehicle owned by Watson and driven by Kinsel, Watson's servant; insurer, having issued policies on both vehicles, denied coverage under Sims' policy on ground Ruark was Sims' employee in scope of employment and thus excluded; held, duty to defend Sims since allegations stated claim "potentially" within coverage, there being no allegations as to whether Ruark was or was not an employee of Sims as well as a passenger in his truck; because of unjustified refusal to defend, insurer held liable in this garnishment proceeding for the amount of tort judgment); Magoun v. Liberty Mut. Ins. Co., 346 Mass. 677, 195 N.E.2d 514 (1964) (tort allegations insufficiently explicit to show that a loading exclusion applied, since they failed to mention that the incident involved loading a truck; held, insurer bound to defend, or pay costs of defense, "even if the proof would ultimately relieve" the insurer from liability to indemnify); Burnett v. Western Pac. Ins. Co., 469 P.2d 602 (Ore.1970) (discussed in n.12 *infra*). See also United States Fid. & Gy. Co. v. National Paving & Contracting Co., 228 Md. 40, 178 A.2d 872 (1962) (allegations that did not state a case clearly within coverage for "operations performed by independent contractors" but indicated potentially a claim within that coverage were sufficient to invoke duty of defense, and insurer was bound by settlement made by insured after insurer refused to defend; in this case, however, since the court also held that the accident did in fact arise from "operations performed by an independent contractor," the result is consistent with the rule urged in the text above).

10. *E.g.*, Cook v. Ohio Cas. Ins. Co., 418 S.W.2d 712 (Tex.Civ.App.1967, no writ

opportunity ever to get an adjudication on the merits with respect to fact issues that the policy provisions declare to be decisive. If those policy provisions are themselves unconscionable, their enforcement should be denied for that reason. If they are not unconscionable, they should be enforced. In any event, there is no adequate justification for a doctrine that bases the duty to defend on the fortuity that a tort action can be alleged with ambiguity about a fact that would be decisive against coverage if the insurer were given an opportunity to prove it. Such a rule would also reward lack of candor, encourage undercover deals, and invite manipulation of the tort pleadings for reasons irrelevant to the merits of the tort actions. Moreover, the additional protection such a rule would give to a few policyholders is not related to reasonable expectations and would be distributed among policyholders quite fortuitously.

Is there a duty to defend when the accident victim, in his tort action, makes allegations that are surplusage with respect to a tort cause of action against the insured but, if credited, are decisive of coverage? In general, despite arguable support for a contrary view,[11] it would seem that such surplusage should be disregarded [12]

history) (insurer declined to defend because of exclusion applying when insured drove car belonging to relative in same household; summary judgment for insurer affirmed; facts shown by affidavit and stipulations in present action against insurer are decisive). See *dicta* supporting this view in Burd v. Sussex Mut. Ins. Co., 56 N.J. 383, 267 A.2d 7 (1970).

11. See nn.13, 16 *infra*. It might be argued also that there is support for the view that the surplus allegation should be credited and not disregarded in Brown v. Green, 204 Kan. 802, 466 P.2d 299 (1970) (action by plaintiff against his employer-insured, a licensed motor carrier, against the employer's public liability insurer, and against a fellow employee; allegations of petition disclosed that plaintiff was an employee of the defendant employer-insured; among insurer's pleas was a cross-claim for declaratory judgment of no coverage because of employee exclusion clause; held, no duty to pay or to defend). But there was no focus on this issue in that opinion, and indeed no occasion to focus on it, since there was apparently no objection from any party to the court's assumption that in fact as well as according to the plaintiff's allegation the plaintiff was an employee of the defendant employer-insured.

12. See nn.14, 15 *infra*. For a case that holds the surplusage not control-

ling but goes beyond the view stated in the text above by saying also that the duty to defend is established by the mere fact that it is "possible, under the complaint" against the insured, "to impose liability for conduct covered by the policy," see Burnett v. Western Pac. Ins. Co., 469 P.2d 602 (Ore.1970) (Hartford had liability coverage for Burnett; Western had coverage for two corporations of which Burnett was employee and Anderson was salaried officer and principal stockholder; Burnett was driving and Anderson was passenger when both were killed in single-car accident; Western's omnibus clause covered Burnett's driving, but was limited by cross-employee exception; Western declined to defend; tort judgment entered against Burnett's estate; held, Western had duty to defend because it was "possible, under the complaint" against Burnett's estate, "to impose liability for conduct covered by the policy" since, although all factual requirements of the cross-employee exception were alleged, it was not necessary to prove them to recover; costs of defense to be prorated between insurers as the rest of a loss would be prorated—in relation to policy limits; remanded to determine whether cross-employee exception defeated coverage for payment of judgment, however; Western not estopped by findings in the action against Burnett's estate that were not "actually or necessarily adjudicated" in that action).

and that the court should apply rules consistent with those it would apply if there were no allegation either way on facts decisive of coverage but not decisive of the tort action. In examining the problem more particularly, consider, first, the case in which such surplusage will, if credited, defeat coverage but the insured, if allowed to do so, can prove that the facts were contrary to the allegation. Allowing the insurer's promise to defend to be limited by such surplusage in the claimant's allegations [13] is not supported by the language of the defense clause of the policy and would defeat the reasonable expectations of policyholders.[14] Consider, next, the case in which a surplus allegation will, if credited, establish coverage but the insurer, if allowed to do so, can prove that the facts were contrary to the allega-

---

13. Language in some opinions might seem to support such a defense, but of course the issue is not squarely faced unless it appears that such surplus allegations are inconsistent with what actually happened. For an opinion containing such language but not squarely facing the issue, see Amundsen v. Great Cent. Ins. Co., 451 S.W. 2d 277 (Tex.Civ.App.1970, writ refused, no reversible error) (summary judgment for insurer affirmed; suit to recover damages for failure to defend bar and lounge owners in action by inebriated male customer alleging he was shot by inebriated female companion with whom he had been engaged in pleasantries; exclusion for selling, serving, or giving alcoholic beverages in violation of statute; since pleadings in tort action stated case within scope of exclusion, insurer had no duty to investigate whether facts did or did not fall within exclusion; court notes, however, absence of allegations in present suit that true facts were not within the exclusion).

14. *E.g.*, National Indem. Co. v. Flesher, 469 P.2d 360 (Alaska 1970) (declaratory action initiated by Flesher, insured of automobile liability policy; exclusion of use of vehicle "in a business or occupation"; Steineman disabled a Broadway cab; Flesher, a Broadway stockholder and employee, had Al's Service send wrecker and driver, Van Buren, to tow cab; Flesher rather than Van Buren was driving wrecker with cab in tow when it ran off highway, injuring Steineman; Steineman sued various defendants in tort, alleging Flesher was Al's "borrowed servant or employee" and also an "agent of Broadway in the course and scope of his employment" when he negligently drove off road; Flesher's attorney demanded that insurer defend Flesher, and insurer refused on grounds of no coverage for the accident; tort action was settled, Flesher stipulating entry of judgment for $23,575 plus attorney's fees, Steineman covenanting not to execute against Flesher and taking assignment of Flesher's rights against insurer; third amended complaint, filed after stipulation for judgment, eliminated allegations Flesher was acting in scope of employment for Broadway, thus stating a claim within coverage for the first time; held, because filed after stipulation for judgment, the third amended complaint is not relevant to duty to defend; tort action pleadings thus alleged only a claim "within an exception to coverage"; but applying the rule that duty to defend is determined by tort action pleadings, when they allege a claim beyond coverage arising from a factual setting within coverage, would frustrate reasonable expectations of the insured; insurer must defend if "true facts are within, or potentially within, the policy coverage and are known or reasonably ascertainable to the insurer"; case remanded for determination whether insurer "knew or through a reasonable investigation would have ascertained that the facts of the accident came within, or potentially within, the coverage . . ."). Though consistent with the position taken in this text that surplus allegations in the tort action should not control the duty of defense, *Flesher* goes beyond this text in stating that the insurer has a duty to defend if on reasonable investigation it "would have ascertained that the facts of the accident came within, *or potentially within,* the coverage." (Emphasis added). See text at nn.9–10 *supra* and at nn.28–31 *infra*.

tion. Again it would seem that the surplusage should not control. To hold otherwise is to invite undercover deals, lack of candor, and manipulation of the tort pleadings as a device for involving an insurer who could not otherwise be involved. The insurer should be permitted to prove a state of facts contrary to the surplusage and decisive against the duty to defend.[15] However, there is support for a contrary view.[16]

It often happens that the victim's allegations include claims beyond coverage as well as claims within coverage. Plainly the insurer is not relieved from a duty of defense merely because of the inclusion of allegations of a claim outside coverage.[17] Thus, the inclusion of al-

---

15. See *dicta* supporting this position in Burd v. Sussex Mut. Ins. Co., 56 N.J. 383, 267 A.2d 7 (1970) ("when coverage, *i.e.*, the duty to pay, depends upon a factual issue which will not be resolved by the trial of the third party's suit against the insured, the duty to defend may depend upon the actual facts and not upon the allegations of the complaint").

16. See, *e.g.*, Holland Am. Ins. Co. v. National Indem. Co., 75 Wash.2d 909, 454 P.2d 383 (1969) (claimant sued both owner and driver; owner's insurer accepted defense for owner but declined to defend for driver, contending he did not have owner's permission to drive; driver also had a policy and his insurer assumed control of defense for driver; owner's insurer negotiated settlement; then driver's insurer, as driver's subrogee, sued owner's insurer for attorneys' fees and recovered; claimant's allegation that driver was operating car with owner's permission appears, for all the report shows, to have been surplusage even as to liability of the owner; plainly it was surplusage as to liability of the driver; yet it was held to have established the duty to defend). Another decision that might seem to be in accord with *Holland* but can easily be distinguished is Travelers Ins. Co. v. Tymkow, 91 N.J.Super. 184, 219 A.2d 625 (1966) (Travelers issued policy to Kowalsky; Nationwide issued policy to Walter Tymkow; truck owned by Walter Tymkow and driven by Bryant Tymkow was in collision injuring Brooks; Brooks' complaint alleged that Bryant Tymkow was acting as servant for Kowalsky; although the allegation that Kowalsky was responsible for operation of the truck appeared to be almost certainly insupportable in fact, held nevertheless that the allegations of Brooks' complaint established Nationwide's duty

to defend Kowalsky as an additional insured). In *Tymkow* the insurer that admittedly has coverage for the *owner and driver* is seeking to escape the duty to defend another person alleged to be responsible for the driver's actions, and the only circumstances in which the other person will be liable are the very circumstances that also establish the duty to defend. Thus the case is within the general rule that an action invokes the duty of defense if the claim alleged would be within coverage if proved, even though it may turn out that it cannot be proved. In *Holland*, on the other hand, the allegation that the driver was acting with permission of the owner is urged as establishing that the *owner's* policy covers the *driver*, and the allegation of facts that would make this so is irrelevant to the tort liability of the *driver*. Thus, *Holland* is a case of surplus allegations, at least as to coverage for the driver, and *Tymkow* is a case of relevant allegations.

17. *Cf.* Krutsinger v. Illinois Cas. Co., 10 Ill.2d 518, 141 N.E.2d 16 (1957) (action by judgment creditors against insurer for failure to satisfy judgments on tort claims against the insured and others based on the sale of alcoholic beverages to a known habitual drunkard in violation of a dram shop act, thus interfering with claimants' means of support; defendant insurer's policy covered only part of the period on which the tort action was based; held, defendant insurer had a duty to participate in defense, but without right to exclude others from participation; for additional details on *Krutsinger*, see § 6.8(d) n.5 *supra*); Waite v. Aetna Cas. & Sur. Co., 467 P.2d 847 (Wash.1970) (comprehensive liability policy; tort action on multiple items of damages, some items claimed being outside policy coverage; insurer de-

legations of intentional tort does not alone relieve the insurer of liability, even if the claim of intentional tort is itself not within coverage.[18] It seems appropriate, however, to hold that because of the conflict of interest between the insurer and the insured regarding defense in such circumstances, the duty to defend should be translated into an obligation to reimburse the insured for costs of defense insofar as the claim is otherwise within the scope of the duty to defend.[19]

A different case is presented if the victim's allegations in his action against the insured cannot support liability of the insured on any theory that is consistent with a set of facts falling within the insuring agreements. It would seem clear that the victim's allegations do not in themselves invoke a duty of defense in these circumstances. Examples are cases in which the victim alleges only an intentional tort of a type not within the insuring agreements,[20] or alleges a claim arising under circumstances that happen to be outside policy coverage because of a provision excluding specified persons or events.[21]

clined to defend entire case but offered to defend against the claim as to admittedly covered item of damages or pay the cost of such defense; insured rejected the insurer's offers and demanded it defend entire case, which insurer declined to do; after insured settled, insurer paid insured a sum it regarded as portion of settlement allocable to admittedly covered item, plus expenses incurred by the insured for defense of that part of the claim; trial court imposed liability for additional item covered, and allocable portion of defense costs, but declined to hold the insurer for costs of settlement or costs of defense as to items not covered; held, affirmed; intimations in the opinion that because of conflict of interests regarding one item, insurer offered more than it was required to offer in leaving defense entirely in insured's hands and agreeing to pay an allocated part of defense costs). Concerning control over the defense when the pleadings allege both covered and non-covered claims, see §§ 7.6(d) and 7.7 infra.

18. E.g., Alm v. Hartford Fire Ins. Co., 369 P.2d 216 (Wyo.1962) (negligence and assault counts; insured defended successfully and then sued insurer for costs of defense; held, coverage, reasoning broadly for coverage if a claim "potentially" within coverage is alleged). Cf. Ferguson v. Birmingham Fire Ins. Co., 460 P.2d 342 (Ore.1969) (complaint alleging willful trespass to land and cutting of trees; held, since plaintiff could, without amending pleadings, recover damages for the lesser included offense of non-willful entry, the insurer had a duty to defend because the complaint embraced covered as well as noncovered grounds of liability; contrary holding in an earlier case explicitly modified; however, Isenhart, n.27 infra, adhered to, the "lesser included offense" notion being inapplicable to an allegation of assault and battery; insurer not estopped to raise its coverage defense in later action since there was a conflict of interest; neither does insured's improper demand that insurer defend without a nonwaiver agreement preclude insured from asserting coverage, since insured's breach did not prejudice insurer).

19. See, e.g., Burd v. Sussex Mut. Ins. Co., 56 N.J. 383, 267 A.2d 7 (1970), discussed in n.5 supra.

20. E.g., Harbin v. Assurance Co. of Am., 308 F.2d 748 (10th Cir. 1962) (New Mexico case; claim of assault; held, in declaratory proceedings, no duty to defend as matters stand, but this judgment is not determinative of insurer's liability if facts as later established bring injury within policy coverage); McKee v. Allstate Ins. Co., 246 Ore. 517, 426 P.2d 456 (1967) (nightclub owners sued to recover cost of defending action by patron for assault by them and unidentified third person; assault action was eventually dismissed for want of prosecution; held, for insurer).

21. See, e.g., Lewis v. Mid-Century Ins. Co., 152 Mont. 328, 449 P.2d 679 (1969)

But a duty to defend may nevertheless arise because of matters outside the allegations of the complaint, including matters contrary to these allegations. Consider cases in which the victim's allegations would place the claim outside coverage but the actual circumstances of the incident in question are within coverage. For example, the policy in question excludes employee claims and the victim alleges that he was an employee of the defendant, but the facts are that he was not. In such circumstances the insurer should be required to defend.[22] A similar problem arises when the victim alleges an intentional tort but the insured contends that he caused the injury to the victim accidentally. It would seem that a duty to defend should be recognized in these circumstances if the insured's contention about the facts is sound.[23] The insured has sought protection against economic loss from his negligent conduct (negligent driving, for exam-

(allegations of claims disclosing that plaintiff was a family member, thus being within a group precluded from coverage by a special policy clause).

22. See, e.g., Hardware Mut. Cas. Co. v. Hilderbrandt, 119 F.2d 291 (10th Cir. 1941) (Oklahoma case; insured settled after insurer refused to defend; upon findings that the injured persons were not employees, insurer held liable for the amount of the settlements plus attorneys' fees for defense); see also n. 31 infra. Cf. Milliken v. Fidelity & Cas. Co., 338 F.2d 35 (10th Cir. 1964) (Kansas case; liability policy on oil and gas operations, excluding coverage for injury to or destruction of "underground property" such as oil, gas, and water "not reduced to physical possession above the earth's surface"; claimants sued for injury to land, livestock, and poultry allegedly caused by pollution saturating the subsurface of the claimant's property; the insurer declined to defend on the grounds, among others, that the actions involved an occurrence and not an "accident" and were for damage to underground property; the insured engaged counsel who defended successfully; insured then brought this action for reimbursement of defense costs, proving that without dispute the alleged pollution consisted of the escape of salt water on two occasions involving accidents; held, for insured; facts extraneous to the pleadings, which were discoverable by the insurer and could be proved in the tort litigation in federal court, under liberal pleadings practice, showed a case within coverage); American Motorists Ins. Co. v. Southwestern Greyhound Lines, Inc., 283 F.2d 648 (10th Cir. 1960) (Oklahoma case; policy excluded coverage for injuries sustained

by passenger while alighting from buses; claimant alleged such an injury but insured contended injury was suffered on platform after alighting from bus; after insurer's refusal to defend, insured settled; held, upon findings that injury occurred on platform after alighting, insurer liable for amount of settlements and defense costs).

23. Cf. McGettrick v. Fidelity & Cas. Co., 264 F.2d 883 (2d Cir. 1959) (Vermont case; liability policy on restaurant operations, with provision that assault and battery shall be deemed an accident unless committed by or at the direction of the insured; claim and action against insured for assault and battery, and insured contended he acted properly in self-defense; insurer refused to defend; insured's personal attorney handled defense and obtained offer of settlement for $1,-000; adjuster for insurer then negotiated and settled for $400; insured sued for costs of defense and other damages; jury found that if insurer had investigated before declining to defend it would have found that the insured had not committed assault and battery; held, recovery for cost of defense; the insurer had a duty "to reasonably investigate" and since it did not, the only possible substitute for what its investigation would have shown is the jury's finding as to the merits of the injured person's claim). Note that although this opinion is founded on a duty to investigate, arguably at variance with the view stated in the text above, the actual facts as found in the action between insured and insurer were held to be controlling. Thus the result is entirely consistent with the text above on this point. Another ground on which both

ple) and would reasonably expect to be protected against the costs of defending against claims arising out of such conduct, even though unfounded claims of worse conduct are made.[24]   The policy provisions, even under painstaking analysis, do not clearly negate this expectation.   And it may be doubted that the expectation would in fact be negated among policyholders generally if a provision were included that would communicate this message to those who undertook the painstaking analysis.   Perhaps this is an instance in which, on the basis of honoring reasonable expectations, even if inconsistent with painstaking analysis of policy provisions,[25] the duty to defend should be recognized.   Results consistent with this proposition have been reached in some cases,[26] and it would seem that most, though not all,[27] of the authority that can be marshaled against it consists of broad statements of the rule that the claimant's allegations against the insured determine the scope of the duty of defense.   When that statement is made in some other context it is weak authority indeed against recognizing a qualification of the broad rule for cases in which the facts support the insured's contention that his striking the victim was accidental, even though the victim claims otherwise.

the result and the reasoning might be questioned is whether there is a duty to defend if the evidence shows that the injury was intentionally inflicted and the only dispute is over self-defense.   Whether this was such a case is not clear, and it might be argued that such a case is distinguishable from one in which the injury was negligently inflicted in fact even though an unfounded claim of battery was asserted by the injured person. See generally § 5.4(b) *supra.*

24. *Cf.* Comment, *The Insurer's Duty to Defend Under a Liability Insurance Policy,* 114 U.Pa.L.Rev. 734, 748 (1966).

25. See § 6.3 *supra.*

26. See n.22 *supra.*

27. *E.g.,* McKee v. Allstate Ins. Co., 246 Ore. 517, 426 P.2d 456 (1967) (nightclub owners sued to recover cost of defending action by patron for assault by them and unidentified third person; assault action was eventually dismissed for want of prosecution; held, for insurer); Isenhart v. General Cas. Co., 233 Ore. 49, 377 P.2d 26 (1962) (no duty to defend assault action even if allegations are groundless and actual facts bring case within coverage; even if allegations that contract provided for coverage be accepted as true, "a clause in a contract of insurance purporting to indemnify the insured for damages recovered against him as a consequence of his intentional conduct in inflicting injury upon another is unenforceable by the insured on the ground that to permit recovery would be against public policy," and, though recognizing shortcomings in so holding, court adheres to rule that duty to defend is determined by allegations of victim's complaint, believing such rule to be supported by sounder reasoning; the scope of potential application of *Isenhart* was narrowed in *Ferguson,* n.18 *supra*); Travelers Ins. Co. v. Newsom, 352 S.W. 2d 888 (Tex.Civ.App.1962, writ refused, no reversible error) (no duty to defend when claim is one of assault; dissent on ground actual facts known to insurer may support duty of defense though claim of victim is otherwise).   *Cf.* Harbin v. Assurance Co. of Am., 308 F.2d 748 (10th Cir. 1962) (New Mexico case; claim of assault; held, in declaratory proceedings, no duty to defend as matters stand, but this judgment is not determinative of insurer's liability if facts as later established bring injury within policy coverage).   Although the court held there was no duty to defend as matters stood in the declaratory proceeding, perhaps the opinion is properly interpreted as leaving open the possibility of liability not only under the "duty to pay" but also under the "duty to defend" if it should later be established that the facts bring the claim within coverage. See Note, 30 N.Y.U.L.Rev. 1019 (1955).

Under the view advanced here,[28] if the company declines to defend when the insured contends that the striking alleged by the victim to be intentional was in fact accidental, and a court later determines, in an action to which the insurer is a party,[29] that the insured's contention is consistent with the facts, that determination establishes a breach of the duty to defend and entitles the insured to recover his costs of defense and, as we shall see later,[30] perhaps the amount of a settlement as well. The view advanced here does not support a duty of defense merely because the *insured contends* that his striking the victim was accidental rather than intentional, or because the insured so contends and it appears on incomplete information that his contention may be correct—that is, that there is "potentially" a claim within coverage. It is true, however, that there is some support for that more expansive view of the duty to defend.[31] Nor does the view advanced here support a duty of defense against a meritorious claim of intentional tort. Some support for such an extreme position exists,[32] but it would seem that it is not well founded

---

28. A view of the duty to defend quite similar in substance to that proposed here is stated in the concluding paragraph of Comment, *The Insurer's Duty to Defend Under a Liability Insurance Policy*, 114 U.Pa.L.Rev. 734 (1966), though the point is there expressed in a fictional form that pays homage to a theory of duty of reasonable investigation. The Comment concludes that there is an obligation of the insurer to defend "if a 'reasonable' investigation does or would disclose facts within" the scope of the policy coverage, and explains in a footnote: "An investigation is reasonable only if it finds the facts as a court later does. . . ." *Id.* at 758 and n.102.

29. See § 7.7 *infra* regarding the division of authority concerning what adjudications bind the insurer.

30. See text at n.39 *infra* and *cf.* § 7.-6(e) *infra.*

31. See cases cited in nn.9, 12 *supra. Cf.* Crum v. Anchor Cas. Co., 264 Minn. 378, 119 N.W.2d 703 (1963) (victim's amended pleadings stated a claim under workmen's compensation act and insurer, previously defending, withdrew; insured's attorney then assumed the defense and settled for $600; trial court findings that the claimant was not acting within the scope of employment when injured; held, insured entitled to recover from the insurer the cost of settlement and defense attorney's fees; syllabus by the court states that when "insurer

learns from an independent investigation that the true facts, if established, present a potential liability on the part of the insured, the insurer is under an obligation to defend until it appears that the facts upon which liability is predicated exclude the insurance coverage"); Mavar Shrimp & Oyster Co. v. United States Fid. & Cas. Co., 187 So.2d 871 (Miss.1966) (obligation to defend despite claimant's allegation of employee status; *Crum* cited and quoted with approval). In both *Crum* and *Mavar* there were findings of fact in the action against the insurer establishing that the incident in question was of a type within the policy coverage. Thus, the results the courts reached are consistent with the view advanced in the text above, though the opinions support a more expansive duty to defend.

With respect to a possible duty to prepare for defense, less expansive in nature than a duty to defend whenever there is potentially a claim within coverage, see this subsection *infra.*

32. See, *e.g.*, Gray v. Zurich Ins. Co., 65 Cal.2d 263, 419 P.2d 168, 54 Cal. Rptr. 104 (1966) (holding that standard provisions concerning the duty of defense, in a Comprehensive Personal Liability Endorsement, "are uncertain and undefined," and that they should be construed to fulfill the insured's reasonable expectations; the measure of recovery allowed in this case for breach of the duty to defend included the amount of the tort judgment against the insured, and in this re-

in principle. With possibly an exception for cases in which tort liability is classified as intentional though based on mistake, the assertion that there are public expectations of a duty to defend in circumstances in which the insured committed an intentional tort seems ill-founded, even aside from the question whether courts should recognize such expectations as reasonable if they existed.

On a theory of ambiguity of the defense provisions of a liability insurance policy, a few courts have expanded the duty of defense well beyond the views expressed here.[33]

The discussion thus far has focused on disputes over whether there is a duty to defend a pending tort action. Has the liability insurer any duty to the insured regarding preparations for defense even before a tort action has been filed? Liability insurers insist upon prompt notice of accidents, commonly initiate prompt investigation, and in some instances take the initiative in approaching potential claimants rather than waiting for a claim to be made. Experience has demonstrated that these are prudent practices for controlling potential claims and minimizing the costs of defending against them. If the circumstances of an injury are such that a liability insurer with acknowledged coverage for the injury, or an ordinarily prudent person of ample means and without liability insurance, would take precautionary measures against the possibility of future claims, has the liability insurer any duty to its insured to take such precautionary measures?

Perhaps the support that can be found in precedents for an expansive view of a duty to defend whenever there is "potentially" a

spect also the decision represents, it would seem, an untenable extreme); Lowell v. Maryland Cas. Co., 65 Cal.2d 298, 419 P.2d 180, 54 Cal.Rptr. 116 (1966) (similar holding in a case in which, however, the insured successfully defended the tort action). See Note, *The Insurer's Duty to Defend Made Absolute: Gray v. Zurich,* 14 U.C.L.A.L.Rev. 1328 (1967). For other cogent criticism of *Gray,* see, *e.g.,* Burd v. Sussex Mut. Ins. Co., 56 N.J. 383, 267 A.2d 7 (1970). See also § 6.-3(a) n.9 *supra.*

33. See, *e. g.,* Gray v. Zurich Ins. Co., 65 Cal.2d 263, 419 P.2d 168, 54 Cal. Rptr. 104 (1966), n.32 *supra.* Cf. Zurich Ins. Co. v. Rombough, 384 Mich. 228, 180 N.W.2d 775 (1970) (tort action alleging insured defendant owned vehicle that was in collision with victim's car and was liable under owner-liability statute; insurer instituted this action seeking declaratory judgment that it had no duty to defend under its "bobtail coverage" containing clause stating it did not apply while vehicle was "used to carry property in business"; insured contended

he was not owner because title to vehicle had been transferred before accident and that vehicle was being used in another person's business with stolen plates; *held,* policy was ambiguous as to whether exclusion clause controlled over defense clause requiring defense of even groundless claims; ambiguity resolved in favor of duty to defend; this court cites *Gray* with approval and perhaps the court's opinion may fairly be read as supporting a broad rule that the agreement to defend groundless claims precludes enforcement of any clause denying a duty to defend a complaint alleging "bodily injuries caused by collision with a vehicle allegedly owned" by the insured; thus, even one who would support coverage on a finding that the facts were as the insured claimed—see n.10 *supra*—or would support coverage without that finding on the theory that reasonable investigation would have disclosed a claim potentially within coverage—see n.9 *supra*—may consider that the assertion of ambiguity in this instance is strained and that the court's rationale is untenable).

claim within coverage [34] can be largely accounted for on the basis of concern about this problem of preparation for defense. But a distinction may be drawn between concluding that there is a present duty *to defend a pending tort action* making no claim within coverage, just because reasonable investigation would disclose the possibility of a future claim within coverage, and, on the other hand, concluding merely that there is a duty to take reasonable precautions, such as investigation, so as to be prepared to defend a claim within coverage, if presented in the future, even though the pending claim is not within coverage. Thus, it may be useful to distinguish between a duty to defend and a duty to prepare for defense—that is, a duty to take reasonable steps in preparation for defense against claims that may be asserted in the future. With occasional exceptions, as noted at the beginning of this section, the duty to defend is recognized, first, whenever an injured person files an action alleging a claim within policy coverage. Second, though there is conflict in the precedents, the duty to defend is recognized in some instances when the injured person files an action alleging a claim outside policy coverage but in fact the incident on which the claim is based is within policy coverage. Third, although there is little precedent on the point, it would seem on principle that the duty to defend applies also when the injured person, although not yet having filed an action, in some way asserts a claim against the insured that would invoke the duty of defense under the foregoing rules if he made the same assertion of claim in a legal action. One may reasonably distinguish these three types of fact situations from those in which the injured person has given no indication whether or not he expects to make a claim. Here, there is no present duty to defend since there is as yet no claim to defend against; if there is a duty, it is a duty to prepare for defense against potential claims rather than a present duty to defend.

If a duty to prepare for defense is recognized, it might arise when no action has been filed and no claim has been made. It might also arise when an action has been filed (or a claim has been made) solely upon a basis that does not invoke a present duty to defend. The fact that the nature of the allegations (or claims) is not such as to invoke a duty to defend does not preclude the possibility that the nature of the underlying fact situation may give notice of a sufficient likelihood of later amendments, in which claims within coverage will be asserted, that the ordinarily prudent person would take immediate preparatory steps. It should be noted, however, that if this duty to prepare for defense is recognized, it does not arise because of the mere possibility that the injured person will later file a complaint, or an amended complaint, alleging a claim within policy coverage. That possibility could be said to exist in every case. The source of the duty is, instead, a probability of such degree that an ordinarily prudent person would act in advance to be prepared to meet it if it should arise. In judging whether some particular step of advance preparation should be undertaken, one would appropriately weigh costs against benefits, including in the assessment the degree of probability of a later claim within coverage and the benefits of preparing to meet it.

There is some precedent against recognizing any duty *to prepare for defense* against claims not yet made.[35] But on principle it would seem that such a duty should be recognized, and it is supported indirectly, at least, by analogy to decisions regarding the duty *to defend.*

In the first place, in most cases, at whatever time a duty to defend ripens because an injured person has made a claim, the liability insurer can discharge that duty properly only if it has previously taken preparatory steps including prompt investigation. Thus, at the least, the insurer will be accountable, under the rubric of the duty to defend, when it is disabled from complying with that duty by its earlier failure to take reasonable preparatory steps. It might be argued that, nevertheless, the insurer has only a duty to defend and cannot be held accountable unless a claim is made and the insurer thereafter fails to defend properly, whether because disabled by lack of earlier preparation or for other reasons. This view of the relationship between the insurer and the insured would leave the insurer free to make no immediate investigation as long as it stood ready to pay for the consequences if a claim within coverage was later asserted. When the insurer chose not to investigate, the insured would be confronted with the hard choice of investigating at his own expense or taking the converse risk from that elected by the insurer. That is, the insured would take the risk that claims outside coverage would be made (and perhaps only such claims) and late investigation would be ineffectual in protecting against them. Moreover, the insured might have difficulty proving that the insurer's failure to investigate had adversely affected the defense. A shifting of the burden of proof on this issue to the insurer would be one way of meeting this difficulty. On the whole, however, it would seem a less complicated and fairer rule to acknowledge that a duty to defend implies a duty to do whatever a reasonably prudent person would do in preparation for defense when circumstances involve such likelihood of future claims within policy coverage that the ordinarily prudent person would act promptly to prepare for defense against them rather than waiting to see whether they would be presented.

Among the factors to be taken into account in determining whether an ordinarily prudent person would act to prepare for defense are any assertions by the victim, formal or informal, indicating what he might claim. As in the case of allegations in a complaint filed by the victim, however, such assertions would not necessarily be conclusive. For example, if battery is outside the scope of the insuring agreements and the victim has indicated that he believes the in-

---

35. *E.g.,* Gibbs v. St. Paul Fire & Marine Ins. Co., 22 Utah 2d 263, 451 P.2d 776 (1969) (suit by owner of ski resort to recover attorney's fees paid for preparations against the possibility of a claim never made; held, for insurer; no duty to defend or investigate unless suit is filed or claim is made).

sured intentionally attacked him, this would not end the inquiry regarding a duty to prepare for defense against a future claim by the victim that the insured negligently rather than intentionally injured him. Since human experience includes many cases of later claims inconsistent with early assertions by the victim, prudence may require prompt investigation in preparation for the possibility that different assertions will be made by the victim in the future. If the circumstances are such that an ordinarily prudent person would take precautionary measures against the possibility, among others, of a later claim of negligence, the company should be obligated to take comparable steps on the insured's behalf.

The company's duty to prepare for defense against one or more potential claims arising from a given incident should not be treated as a duty to prepare for defense against every claim that might arise from that incident. The company should be required only to take steps appropriate for protecting against those potential claims that, if asserted, would invoke the duty to defend.

It must be acknowledged that to approve the views advanced here is to recognize a duty to prepare for defense somewhat at odds with customary policy language. The usual policy provision declares that the company *shall* defend and may "make such investigation, negotiation and settlement of any claim or suit as it deems expedient." [36] But, as we have noted above, ordinarily it will be impossible for the company to discharge its duty of defense at trial without having made advance preparations even before the existence of that duty had become determinable. It would seem then that the word "may" before "investigation" cannot properly be construed as so qualifying the duty to defend that the company is excused from liability for failure to take due steps in preparation before an action is filed.[37] This conclusion is fortified by the analogy to the company's duty regarding settlement. Virtually the same argument of contradiction of the policy language can be made in that context. Thus, the overwhelming support for a duty regarding settlement [38] reinforces the argument for recognizing the duty of early preparations for defense. It would seem likely, then, that a duty to take reasonable steps in preparation for defense, even before assertion of a claim of a type within policy coverage, will be recognized when the circumstances are such that preparations against the possibility of such a claim would be made by an ordinarily prudent person.[39]

One might question whether it will make any practical difference to recognize a duty to prepare for defense, as distinguished from merely recognizing that the duty to defend is violated at some later

---

36. See Appendices G, H *infra.*

37. With respect to application of this reasoning to negotiation and settlement as well as investigation, see § 7.-8 *infra.*

38. *Ibid.*

39. The phrasing used in the text above is premised on applying to the duty a standard of ordinary care, rather than a standard merely requiring good faith. With respect to this issue regarding the standard, see generally § 7.6(b) *infra.*

point, after a claim has been formally asserted, if the company's conduct of the defense is then deficient because of its earlier lack of preparation. It would seem that in rare cases, at least, the consequences of recognizing this duty might be quite significant. For example, if a policyholder demanded that his company take appropriate steps of early preparation, including an initiative in exploring possibilities of early and favorable settlement, and the company refused to do so, the policyholder might then assert the right to act on his own behalf, consummating a reasonable settlement and suing the company for reimbursement. It would seem that this right is more likely to be recognized [40] under a theory of breach of a duty to prepare for defense than if the policyholder must rely upon a theory of anticipatory breach of the duty to defend.

§ 7.6(b) THE STANDARD OF CONDUCT

In cases concerning a liability insurance company's duty to defend it is usually assumed or stated that the insurance company must exercise ordinary care.[1] On some occasions, however, it has been said that good faith is the standard of performance required of the insurer. Some of these statements have occurred in cases in which both breach of the duty to settle [2] and breach of the duty to defend were alleged. Nevertheless, the acts or omissions usually involved in cases holding or assuming that ordinary care is required could be distinguished from the act of deciding not to settle. That is, these cases of negligence in defense have concerned inadvertence or thoughtless omissions such as failure to discover important evidence, failure to advert to and develop a particular ground of defense that apparently was sound, failure to answer, or failure to perfect appeal in due time. In contrast, the conduct involved in the cases concerning liability for failure to settle is usually a considered exercise of judgment. If this distinction between inadvertence and mistake of judgment is given effect, marginal cases will arise in which it will be difficult to determine factually whether an omission (for example, failure to urge a particular ground of defense) was due to inadvertence or instead to an error of tactical judgment. Often the issue in marginal cases will be one of fact or evaluation. These difficulties of administration weigh against the desirability of making the suggested distinction,[3] but perhaps they are not alone enough to condemn it.

If inadvertence and mistake of judgment are distinguished, a considered decision not to appeal an adverse judgment in excess of

---

40. Concerning recognition of a comparable right after breach of the duty to defend, and possible extension to breach of the duty to prepare for defense, see § 7.6(e) *infra*.

1. See, *e.g.*, Anderson v. Southern Sur. Co., 107 Kan. 375, 191 P. 583 (1920), 21 A.L.R. 761 (1922); Abrams v. Factory Mut. Liab. Ins. Co., 298 Mass. 141, 10 N.E.2d 82 (1937).

2. Concerning the duty to settle, see § 7.8 *infra*.

3. Concerning the administrative disadvantages of evaluative issues generally, see § 1.6 *supra*.

policy limits is more nearly analogous to the decision not to settle than the failure to discover a witness or inadvertent failure to heed a deadline for answer or appeal. This suggestion has some support in precedent.[4] But, by the same line of reasoning, one would surely classify as a "mistake of judgment" rather than inadvertence a considered decision to plead a claim of indemnity on behalf of the insured defendant against another party but not to plead contribution since expecting to be allowed to assert contribution as a lesser claim and preferring an "all-out" strategy. Yet there is precedent for applying a negligence rather than a bad faith test in ruling upon the insured's claim for liability of the insurer in excess of policy limits in this setting.[5]

One might urge, in support of the suggested distinction between inadvertence and mistake of judgment, the analogy of the dual standard adopted by some courts in relation to the failure to settle, requiring only good faith as to the decision regarding settlement but ordinary care as well in the investigation leading to such decision.[6] But that body of precedent is itself of doubtful merit.[7] Moreover, there is another instructive analogy—the troublesome distinction between discretionary and ministerial acts in relation to governmental immunity from liability for negligence. Perhaps there are public policy justifications for retaining an area of immunity for discretionary acts in that context, even in the face of the difficulties of administration. It

4. *E.g.*, Hawkeye-Security Ins. Co. v. Indemnity Ins. Co., 260 F.2d 361 (10th Cir. 1958), 69 A.L.R.2d 684 (1960). A claimant recovered a tort judgment of more than $22,000 against the insured, Northern Utilities. The attorney for the primary liability insurer, Hawkeye, recommended appeal on the ground that no specific acts of negligence were proved and that the trial court erred in applying the doctrine of *res ipsa loquitur* to the case. Hawkeye declined to appeal except on condition that the costs of appeal be prorated between it and the insured—or an excess insurer, Indemnity, occupying the position of the insured in these negotiations. The excess insurer arranged for the appeal to be prosecuted in the name of the insured and after the appeal proved to be unsuccessful, brought suit as subrogee of the insured to recover the cost of appeal. The court denied recovery on the theory that mere proof that Hawkeye declined to follow the advice of its counsel failed to establish the bad faith necessary for liability. It might also have been considered that such proof was insufficient to establish negligence in failing to appeal. but the opinion plainly indicated that the standard of liability was bad faith rather than negligence.

5. Steedly v. London & Lancashire Ins. Co., 416 F.2d 259 (6th Cir. 1969) (Kentucky case; held, jury issue as to whether it was negligence not to seek contribution). In the tort action, the Kentucky Court of Appeals held that though perhaps the insured could have succeeded in a claim for contribution, the issue was not presented because the third-party complaint was confined to a claim for indemnity. Schuster v. Steedley, 406 S.W.2d 387 (Ky.1966).

6. *E.g.*, Ballard v. Citizens Cas. Co., 196 F.2d 96 (7th Cir. 1952); Olympia Fields Country Club v. Bankers Indem. Ins. Co., 325 Ill.App. 649, 60 N. E.2d 896 (1st Dist. 1945); Southern Fire & Cas. Co. v. Norris, 35 Tenn. App. 657, 250 S.W.2d 785 (1952). See Radio Taxi Serv., Inc. v. Lincoln Mut. Ins. Co., 31 N.J. 299, 157 A.2d 319 (1960). In Hilker v. Western Auto. Ins. Co., 204 Wis. 1, 231 N.W. 257 (1930), *affirmance upheld on rehearing*, 204 Wis. 12, 235 N.W. 413 (1931), the duty of care was extended also to negotiation, though only good faith was required with respect to the insurer's decision to settle or not.

7. See § 7.8 *infra*.

seems less likely that this is so in the present context. A consistent requirement of ordinary care in all matters pertaining to defense seems preferable. However, there is support for the contrary view.[8]

§ 7.6(c) EFFECT OF PAYMENT OR TENDER UP TO POLICY LIMITS

May a liability insurance company discharge its entire duty by paying out the policy limit in settlement, or else tendering the policy limit for application to settlements at the discretion of the policyholder? The few decisions in point are not in harmony, and the problem has been further complicated by changes in policy forms.

In some instances it has been held that the company's duty of defense was not discharged by payment of the policy limit on a judgment obtained against the insured.[1] Other cases have held that the company's duty was discharged after such payment,[2] and it has even been held that the company was not required to defend after tendering to the insured, for his free use in disposition of claims, an amount equal to the policy limit.[3]

8. See, *e.g.*, Detenber v. American Universal Ins. Co., 372 F.2d 50 (6th Cir. 1967), 34 A.L.R.3d 526 (1970), *cert. denied*, 389 U.S. 987 (1967) (applying Kentucky law, as to which, however, see also n.5 *supra*).

1. *E.g.*, American Cas. Co. v. Howard, 187 F.2d 322 (4th Cir. 1951) (the judgment against the insured was obtained under the South Carolina Death Act, and the insurer was held to be obligated to defend a second suit, the latter under the Survival Act, for conscious pain and suffering of the same decedent); St. Paul Fire & Marine Ins. Co. v. Thompson, 150 Mont. 182, 433 P.2d 795 (1967), 27 A. L.R.3d 1048 (1969) (employee's insurer paid out limits on judgment against employer and employee; insurer nevertheless obligated to defend employee in employer's action for indemnity). See also American Employers Ins. Co. v. Goble Aircraft Specialities, Inc., 205 Misc. 1066, 131 N.Y.S.2d 393 (Sup. Ct.1954). *Howard* might be explained on the ground that the property-damage claim remained outstanding and the duty to defend cannot be discharged by *promising to pay* the property-damage limit as distinguished from actually *paying*. But the result reached may be sustained also on the broader ground that the duty to defend is an independent duty.

2. *E.g.*, Liberty Mut. Ins. Co. v. Mead Corp., 219 Ga. 6, 131 S.E.2d 534

(1963) (limits paid out in settlement of two claims with insured's consent and contribution); Travelers Indem. Co. v. New England Box Co., 102 N.H. 380, 157 A.2d 765 (1960) ($25,000 limit paid in settlement of property damage claims arising from fire on insured's premises); Lumbermen's Mut. Cas. Co. v. McCarthy, 90 N.H. 320, 8 A.2d 750 (1939), 126 A.L.R. 894 (1940) (limit paid out in discharging some among multiple claims). See Faude, *The 1955 Revision of the Standard Automobile Policy, Coverage: Insuring Agreements and Exclusions*, 1955 ABA Section Ins. L. Proceedings 48, 53–54, reprinted 1955 Ins.L.J. 647, 650; Gavin, *The Insurance Carrier's Obligation to Defend When Claims Against the Insured Exceed the Policy Limits*, 35 Ins. Counsel J. 92 (1968), reprinted 1968 Personal Injury Annual 571 (Frumer & Friedman eds.); DesChamps, *The Obligation of the Insurer To Defend Under Casualty Insurance Policy Contracts*, 26 Ins. Counsel J. 580 (1959); Kemper, *Avoiding the Hazard of Excess Liability and the Expense of Defense by Settlements for Policy Limits*, 17 Ins. Counsel J. 145 (1950).

3. *E.g.*, Denham v. La Salle-Madison Hotel Co., 168 F.2d 576 (7th Cir. 1948), *cert. denied*, 335 U.S. 871 (the insured contended that regardless of whether the company was liable for payment of claims in excess of its limit, which it had tendered, the com-

It has been argued that placing the company in control of the litigation after it no longer has a stake is inconsistent with prohibitions against corporate practice of law.[4] But the point is debatable. Certainly an agreement of a company to reimburse the insured for whatever costs of defense are incurred, including fees to an attorney selected by himself, would not violate prohibitions against corporate practice of law. If the company's right of control over litigation under these circumstances is inconsistent with prohibitions against corporate practice of law, would not this reasoning apply irrespective of payment or nonpayment of the policy limit in damages? The only difference is that the company has a direct interest in the result of the litigation in one instance and not in the other. But surely prohibitions against corporate practice of law, if applicable at all to this problem, should not be subject to evasion by the corporation's contracting for an interest in the very litigation the handling of which is urged to amount to corporate practice of law. That would be exactly the effect of liability insurance. It seems preferable to acknowledge that recognizing the validity of the defense clause of liability insurance policies inherently implies that the kind of control of litigation that a liability insurance company exercises in selecting and instructing an attorney who appears as counsel for the insured is not corporate practice of law within the meaning of prohibitions against such practice, and that the potential evils and countervailing benefits are not so different in the case of defense after the company's payment of the policy limit in damages as to warrant a conclusion that an insurance contract expressly providing for such a benefit to the insured would be against public policy. It follows that the issue whether such benefit is available should be determined on the basis of a fair and reasonable construction of the policy clause.

pany had severable obligations to defend the insured against liability with respect to each of about 250 claims for damage to or loss of property of guests of the insured's hotel incident to a fire that compelled all guests to leave in haste; held that the company was obligated only "as respects insurance afforded by this policy," and was not required to defend after tendering the policy limit; the insured's theory "would produce the incongruous situation" that the insurance company would have a continuing obligation to defend, notwithstanding that it had "exhausted" its obligation to pay, 168 F.2d at 584). *Contra*, Sutton Mut. Ins. Co. v. Rolph, 109 N.H. 142, 244 A.2d 186 (1968) (bill of interpleader filed by insurer, depositing a sum equal to the total of property damage claims arising from a three-car collision and an additional $20,000—the per-accident limit on personal injury claims—less $250 paid out in settlement of one claim; other personal injury claims totaling $175,000 were still pending; held, insurer cannot in this way discharge its duty to defend); see also Lumbermen's Mut. Cas. Co. v. McCarthy, 90 N.H. 320, 8 A.2d 750 (1939), 126 A.L.R. 894 (1940) (duty discharged by payment in disposition of some among multiple claims; dictum, however, 90 N.H. at 323, 8 A. 2d at 752, 126 A.L.R. at 898, that the duty is not discharged by merely paying the limit to the insured and casting on him the burden of investigation, settlement, or defense). It has been reported that the position taken by most insurance companies in 1955 was consistent with the foregoing dictum in *McCarthy*. Faude, n.2 *supra*, at 53–54, 1955 Ins.L.J. at 650.

4. See 7A Appleman, Insurance Law § 4682 and n.18.5 (rev. ed. 1962); Appleman, *Conflicts in Injury Defenses*, 1957 Ins.L.J. 545, 560; Faude, n.2 *supra*, at 53, 1955 Ins.L.J. at 650; DesChamps, n.2 *supra*, 26 Ins. Counsel J. at 583.

Some policy forms in use in the early history of liability insurance clearly gave the company a three-way option of defending, settling, or paying to the insured the face amount (thus leaving the insured to defend at his own expense, or settle).[5] Under those circumstances, the insurer could avoid any liability for defense by tendering the face amount of the policy. The forms commonly used just before the 1955 revision included a provision as follows:

"As respects the insurance afforded by the other terms of this policy under coverages A [Bodily Injury Liability] and B [Property Damage Liability], the company shall [defend, etc.] . . . ." [6]

The corresponding provision in the 1955 revision of forms is as follows:

"With respect to such insurance as is afforded by this policy for bodily injury liability and for property damage liability, the company shall:

"(a) defend any suit against the insured alleging such injury, sickness, disease or destruction and seeking damages on account thereof, even if such suit is groundless, false or fraudulent. . . . ." [7]

It has been stated that the editorial amendments of the 1955 revision,

"while seemingly minor in nature, are designed to make the defense provision more clearly subordinate to the main introductory paragraph of the policy, which [after the 1955 revision as well as before] states the company's entire contractual undertaking as '*subject to the limits of liability, exclusions, conditions and other terms of this policy.*' " [8]

Apparently this statement refers to the change from the expression "the insurance afforded by the other terms of this policy under coverages A and B" to the expression "such insurance as is afforded by this policy for bodily injury liability and for property damage liability." Perhaps the idea is that the former expression could be construed as referring only to the other terms stated under the sections of the policy designated coverages A and B, and not also to the "main introductory paragraph of the policy" that included the phrase "subject to the limits of liability." But even if this main introductory phrase is accepted as a qualification of the duty to defend, it is far

5. See, *e.g.*, Brassil v. Maryland Cas. Co., 210 N.Y. 235, 104 N.E. 622 (1914).

6. This phrasing appears in a specimen stock-company form supplied in the early 1950's by the Association of Casualty and Surety Companies for use in college insurance courses. The same phrasing appears in the specimen mutual-company policy, printed in Patterson, Cases on Insurance Law 792–793 (3d ed. 1955). See also Des-

Champs, n.2 *supra*, 26 Ins. Counsel J. at 582.

7. *Standard Provisions for Automobile Combination Policies, Basic Automobile and Physical Damage Form, Insuring Agreements*, para. II (2d rev. 1955).

8. Faude, n.2 *supra*, at 54, 1955 Ins.L.J. at 650 (emphasis Faude's). *Cf.* DesChamps, n.2 *supra*, 26 Ins. Counsel J. at 582–584, 586–587.

from clear that it means that such duty is exhausted by payment of the policy limits. If that was the intention of the drafters of the amended form, it was not clearly expressed, and the vagueness is the more significant in view of the former use of a clause clearly specifying a three-way option. The better rule, it would seem, is that under provisions such as those in the 1955 revision the company's duty to defend continues even after payment of the policy limits in damages, and a fortiori after a mere tender of the policy limit to the insured. But, as we have seen, the precedents are divided.

It was reported immediately after the 1955 amendment that the associations were considering a further clarifying amendment on this subject,[9] but the next revision (the Family Automobile Form) did not contain any such clarification, though there were editorial changes incident to incorporation of the defense clause into the coverage clauses.[10]

In 1966, however, significant changes were made. Within the coverage clause itself the following phrase appears: "but the company shall not be obligated to pay any claim or judgment or to defend any suit after the applicable limit of the company's liability has been exhausted by payment of judgments or settlements." [11]

This provision, like many others in the 1966 revision,[12] seems objectionable from policyholder and public interest points of view. It is likely that it will receive unfriendly treatment at the hands of the courts. Certainly, for example, it seems unlikely that any court will allow mere tender, as distinguished from payment in disposition of claims, to exhaust the duty to defend. Also, it would seem that a policyholder might attack a particular settlement on the ground that the company was acting for the purpose of terminating its duty to defend and would not have made the settlement had it been giving due consideration to the policyholder's overall exposure to all the claims outstanding against him.

---

9. Faude, n.2 *supra*, at 54, 1955 Ins.L.J. at 650.

10. *Standard Provisions for Automobile Combination Policies, Family Automobile Form*, (1st rev. 1958), includes the following clause within *Part I—Liability:*

Coverage A—Bodily Injury Liability

Coverage B—Property Damage Liability
To pay on behalf of the insured all sums which the insured shall become legally obligated to pay as damages because of:

A. bodily injury, sickness or disease, including death resulting therefrom, hereinafter called "bodily injury," sustained by any person;

B. injury to or destruction of property loss of use thereof, hereinafter called "property damage";

arising out of the ownership, maintenance or use of the owned automobile or any non-owned automobile and the company shall defend any suit alleging such bodily injury or property damage and seeking damages which are payable under the terms of this policy, even if any of the allegations of the suit are groundless, false or fraudulent; but the company may make such investigation and settlement of any claim or suit as it deems expedient.

11. See Appendix G *infra*.

12. See § 2.11(c) *supra*.

§ 7.6(d) CONTROL OF THE DEFENSE; MULTIPLE OBLIGATIONS TO DEFEND

When the insured has no reciprocal claim [1] and the only tort claims against him are within the insuring agreements of his liability coverage, the customary defense clause imposes on the company exclusive responsibility to defend. In turn, it is ordinarily treated as granting the company exclusive control over the defense. This rule applies even when there are tort claims in excess of the policy limits, but in these circumstances companies customarily invite advisory participation of any independent counsel the insured may wish to employ. Perhaps the company is obliged to do this. At the least, its conduct in the discharge of its obligations of defense would be viewed with greater suspicion should it oppose such advisory participation.

The defense clause makes no provision for cases of varied interests in the defense arising from multiple claims, some within coverage and some outside. Such interests arise, for example, when a tort claim on grounds beyond coverage is made by one who is also claiming on another ground within coverage. Certainly the duty of defense continues in these circumstances.[2] Difficulties must be faced in accommodating the varied interests of the parties in relation to different claims, but they do not justify absolving the company from a duty. Nor do these difficulties justify granting the company exclusive control over the defense. Thus, both the duty of defense and the rights of control over the defense are non-exclusive in these circumstances.[3] This duty is violated by a refusal to participate in the defense,[4] and it would seem also that it is violated by insistence upon full control over the defense when the insured asserts his right to share in the conduct of the defense insofar as it affects the non-covered claims.[5]

In some situations, however, sharing control of the defense is impractical because the separate interests are so sharply in conflict that their protection requires inconsistent contentions. In these circumstances, courts should and perhaps will recognize other procedures than joint participation for according full protection to the conflicting interests of the company and the insured.[6]

Multiple obligations to defend against a single claim may arise from separate liability insurance policies with coverage applicable to the claim. In such circumstances, some courts have disallowed a claim for recovery of defense costs (or of a portion of such costs),

1. Concerning reciprocal claims generally, see § 7.10 *infra*.

2. See § 7.6(a) nn.17, 18 *supra*.

3. *E.g.*, Krutsinger v. Illinois Cas. Co., 10 Ill.2d 518, 141 N.E.2d 16 (1957), discussed in §§ 6.8(d) n.5, 7.6(a) n.17 *supra*.

4. *Ibid.*

5. *Cf.* Fidelity & Cas. Co. v. Stewart Dry Goods Co., 208 Ky. 429, 271 S.W. 444 (1925), 43 A.L.R. 318 (1926).

6. See § 7.7(c) *infra*.

brought by a defending insurer against another insurer that wrongfully refused to defend.[7] Others have held, with more justification it would seem, that when only one insurer has fulfilled the obligation of defense, it should be allowed to recover all[8] or part[9] of the costs from a defaulting insurer. If two or more insurers, rather than sharing the costs of a single defense effort, seek to have separate attorneys representing the insured, the risk of disservice to the insured is substantial and a court may appropriately hold that only one of the attorneys will be permitted to appear for the insured.[10]

§ 7.6(e) REMEDIES FOR WRONGFUL FAILURE TO DEFEND

If, after a company's wrongful refusal to defend, the insured employs an attorney who defends the tort action to a final judgment for the insured, full reimbursement of reasonable costs of defense is obviously due. Ordinarily, however, the insured is not entitled to recover attorney's fees or other costs incurred in the action on the policy against the insurer.[1]

If the final judgment in the tort action is against the insured, the company may contend that the doctrine of avoidable consequences

7. *E.g.*, United States Fid. & Gy. Co. v. Tri-State Ins. Co., 285 F.2d 579 (10th Cir. 1960) (Oklahoma case; action by excess insurer against primary insurer for a share of defense costs incurred by excess insurer in successfully defending after primary insurer refused to do so; held, for defendant; agreements to defend were several and personal to the insured); Farmers Elevator Mut. Ins. Co. v. American Mut. Liab. Ins. Co., 185 Neb. 4, 173 N.W.2d 378 (1969) (when two separate liability insurers have duty to defend, one defends, and the second declines, the first has no remedy against the second since the insured suffers no damage from the second's refusal to defend, the first having defended as it was obligated to do; if the insured suffers it is because the first company's defense is not such as to fulfill its duty, and the first company cannot impose liability on the second on that account).

8. National Farmers Union Property & Cas. Co. v. Farmers Ins. Group, 14 Utah 2d 89, 377 P.2d 786 (1963) (excess carrier subrogated to insured's rights against primary carrier; claim was well within primary carrier's coverage limit).

9. *E.g.*, Continental Cas. Co. v. Zurich Ins. Co., 57 Cal.2d 27, 366 P.2d 455, 17 Cal.Rptr. 12 (1961) (one insurer defended and two others refused to participate; first insurer then sued for contribution; after reviewing conflicting precedents, held, proration of defense costs among three insurers in the same ratio as their liability for payment of the judgment against the insured); Burnett v. Western Pac. Ins. Co., 469 P.2d 602 (Ore.1970) (summarized in § 7.6(a) n.12 *supra*). See also § 3.11(b) n.2 *supra*. *Cf.* American Fid. & Cas. Co. v. Pennsylvania Threshermen & Farmers' Mut. Cas. Ins. Co., 280 F.2d 453 (5th Cir. 1960) (Georgia law; all insurers with applicable liability coverage, whether primary or excess, agreed by their policy contracts to defend; held, none is excused because others are involved; tort action is still pending and disputes over how costs of defense will be borne are not now justiciable).

10. *E.g.*, Jackson v. Trapier, 42 Misc.2d 139, 247 N.Y.S.2d 315 (S.Ct. Special Term 1964) (two insurance carriers with separate coverage and conflicting interests appointed separate counsel for defendant, liability insured; court discharged second and ruled that first should represent insured only, not insurer, though insurer pays fee).

1. See § 7.4(b) *supra*. See also the discussion, in § 7.6(a) n.5 *supra*, of Burd v. Sussex Mut. Ins. Co., 56 N.J. 383, 267 A.2d 7 (1970).

applies and limits liability to something less than the sum of the defense costs and the judgment within policy limits. This doctrine has no impact if the conduct of the insured and his attorney were reasonable. If the insured acted reasonably but his attorney did not, it may be doubted that the insurer should be able to impose this risk of malpractice on the insured. The company was obligated to provide an attorney and would have been liable for his malpractice. It would seem they should not escape this risk by breach. Of course there would be a possibility of imposing the cost finally on the attorney guilty of malpractice, if financially responsible, or upon his malpractice insurer if he carried applicable coverage.

If the insured himself has been heedless in failing to protect his own interests—for example, if he has done nothing to prevent a judgment against him by default—he should be precluded from recovering reimbursement in excess of what his losses would have been had he acted responsibly. Some cases appear to have taken a contrary view,[2] but it is submitted that they do not take due account of the doctrine of avoidable consequences, which by the weight of authority applies even to cases of intentional wrongdoing.[3]

It is possible for the company's breach of its duty to defend to be a legal cause of loss in excess of policy limits, and such loss should be included within the measure of damages. This could happen, for example, if an opportunity for early and favorable settlement of the case was lost only because of delay incident to the company's breach.

The company might contend that if the insured could have settled the case himself, he should be precluded from claiming reimbursement for more than the amount for which settlement could have been made. This contention might be advanced not only in relation to amounts in excess of policy limits but also with respect to amounts above what the case could have been settled for and yet within policy limits. But the full implications of such a rule make it appear undesirable in principle, and it is supported only slightly, if at all, in precedents.[4]

Different issues are presented if the insured chooses to settle after the company's wrongful refusal to defend.

---

2. See, *e.g.*, Aetna Cas. & Sur. Co. v. Hase, 390 F.2d 151 (8th Cir. 1968) (purportedly applying Missouri law; insurer collaterally estopped to assert exclusion as to liability under workmen's compensation law and as to liability for injury to employee; preclusion applied even though lower court opinion, 266 F.Supp. 952, 957, discloses that insured's attorney withdrew by agreement with plaintiff and permitted a default judgment). See also Gray v. Zurich Ins. Co., 65 Cal.2d 263, 419 P.2d 168, 54 Cal.Rptr. 104 (1966) (summarized in §§ 6.3(a) n.9 and 7.6(a) n.32 *supra*), the rationale of which might be extended this far, although the case is easily distinguishable on the facts as involving an issue of the scope of harm caused by the insurer's breach rather than an issue of avoidable consequences.

3. See, *e.g.*, Restatement of Torts § 918 (1939), which recognizes, however, that the standard for judging the plaintiff's conduct may be less demanding in cases of injury intended by the defendant than in cases of negligence.

4. See § 7.8(e) *infra*.

Consider, first, a settlement by the insured for a sum within policy limits. Though some decisions have indicated that the insured cannot recover from the company the cost of such a settlement unless the insured was in fact liable to the claimant,[5] the usual statement of the requirements for full reimbursement is merely that the insured's settlement must be a reasonable one made in good faith.[6] Moreover, there is some support for the proposition that the company has the burden of challenging the reasonableness of the settlement.[7] Almost invariably it has been found that these requirements for reimbursement were satisfied, but comments in some opinions suggest that sanctions might be applied upon a finding of noncompliance. If the insured settles at an unreasonably high figure, the sanction might be to limit his recovery against the company to the maximum amount he might reasonably have paid in settlement.[8] Another possibility would be to disallow any recovery, but it seems unlikely that such a severe sanction would be applied.

The insured's right of reimbursement for a settlement within policy limits has been extended to cases in which the company's denial of policy coverage was accompanied with conduct short of an absolute refusal to defend. For example, the insured was allowed reimbursement against a company whose conduct in denying policy coverage, filing a declaratory judgment proceeding, pressing for a trial therein before trial of the claimant's suit (though offering to defend under a reservation of rights pending a decision in the declaratory judgment proceeding), and opposing a reasonable settlement consummated by the insured, did "not square with the standard of good faith and fair dealing which underlies the contract between the parties. . . . ."[9]

With respect to a settlement by the insured for a sum in excess of policy limits, the insured's claim for reimbursement up to policy limits should be determined upon the same rules as those applied to cases of settlement for a figure within policy limits. Reimbursement above policy limits, however, would be justifiable only if the cost of disposition of the claim would have been less had the company complied with its duties regarding defense and settlement. When this

---

5. See, *e.g.*, Butler Bros. v. American Fid. Co., 120 Minn. 157, 139 N.W. 355 (1913) (dictum).

6.   See, *e.g.*, Hardware Mut. Cas. Co. v. Hilderbrandt, 119 F.2d 291 (10th Cir. 1941); Continental Cas. Co. v. Shankel, 88 F.2d 819 (10th Cir. 1937); United States Fid. & Gy. Co. v. National Paving & Contracting Co., 228 Md. 40, 178 A.2d 872 (1962); Berke Moore Co. v. Lumbermens Mut. Cas. Co., 345 Mass. 66, 185 N.E.2d 637 (1962); Nixon v. Liberty Mut. Ins. Co., 255 N.C. 106, 120 S.E.2d 430 (1961),. *on later appeal*, 258 N.C. 41, 127 S.E.2d 892 (1962). See generally 7A Appleman, Insurance Law § 4690

(rev. ed. 1962); Annot., 49 L.R.2d 694, 744–751 (1956).

7. See, *e.g.*, Butler Bros. v. American Fid. Co., 120 Minn. 157, 139 N.W. 355 (1913).

8.   See Employers Mut. Liab. Ins. Co. v. Hendrix, 199 F.2d 53, 59 (4th Cir. 1952), 41 A.L.R.2d 424, 433 (1955) (South Carolina case).

9.   Traders & Gen. Ins. Co. v. Rudco Oil & Gas Co., 129 F.2d 621, 628 (10th Cir. 1942), 142 A.L.R. 799, 809 (1943). *Cf.* Evans v. Continental Cas. Co., 40 Wash.2d 614, 245 P.2d 470 (1952).

condition is met, it would be proper to treat the added cost of disposition in the same way as a settlement for a sum within policy limits, even though part or all of that added cost was in excess of policy limits. When this condition is not met, the company's breach would not be a cause of the insured's loss in excess of policy limits; that loss would have occurred even if the company had complied with its duties.

Thus far we have been considering the insured's remedies in the context of an assumption that the insurer had wrongfully refused to defend. Often, however, questions about potential remedies must be faced at a time when the duty of defense is somewhat in doubt because of uncertainty about the nature of claims that have been or may be made against the insured, with resulting uncertainty about whether the claims made or to be made fall within the scope of the insuring agreement. It may be noted, first, that even if a claim proceeds to a final judgment establishing a set of facts that fall outside the insuring agreements, it does not necessarily follow that there were not such probabilities of claims within the insuring agreements as to raise a duty to defend or a duty to take steps in preparation for defense.[10] It is unlikely under such circumstances, however, that the costs of these steps would amount to a very substantial percentage of the total costs expended by the insured in defense. And, though there is authority to the contrary,[11] it would seem that damages for breach of the duty to defend should not include the cost of discharging an adverse judgment on grounds outside policy coverage; in the assumed circumstances, that adverse result would have occurred even if the insurer had fulfilled its duty of defense. To assume otherwise is to assume that an improper result was reached by the court that decided the tort case against the insured. It would seem an unjustified judicial policy to permit such an assumption or finding when no evidence to support it has been presented by the insured. Perhaps injustice will be done in rare cases because of lack of proof, but it would seem far outweighed by the injustice of extending unwarranted coverage in more numerous cases, and under circumstances that may raise serious problems of conflict with policies of the law such as those regarding intentional torts.

If, conversely, a claim as to which coverage has been doubtful proceeds to a final judgment in which the facts are determined in a way that places the claim within the insuring agreements (regardless of whether this is favorable or unfavorable to the insured on the question of tort liability), ordinarily the insurer would be bound by this determination, but in exceptional circumstances of conflict of interest regarding the defense, the company should not be bound be-

---

10. See generally § 7.6(a) *supra*.

11. *E.g.*, Gray v. Zurich Ins. Co., 65 Cal.2d 263, 419 P.2d 168, 54 Cal.Rptr. 104 (1966) (summarized in §§ 6.3(a) n.9 and 7.6(a) n.32 *supra*). See also Sims v. Illinois Nat. Cas. Co., 43 Ill.App.2d 184, 193 N.E.2d 123 (3d Dist. 1963) (discussed in § 7.6(a) n.9 *supra*).

cause such a rule would deprive the insurer of any reasonable opportunity to contest the issues of fact that determine coverage.[12]

In other types of cases, also, the doubt over coverage may remain to be resolved independently, even after disposition of the tort claim. This occurs when the tort case proceeds to a final judgment in which the facts determining the duty to defend are not adjudicated. If the result reached is a judgment in tort against the insured, the dispute over coverage applies to both the company's duty to pay on the insured's behalf and its duty to defend (enforceable in this context by a judgment requiring the company to reimburse the insured for the costs of defense of the tort action reasonably incurred as a result of the company's alleged breach). If the result reached in the tort action is a judgment for the insured, the dispute over coverage concerns only the duty to defend.

Does the right of the insured to make a reasonable settlement with the claimant and obtain reimbursement from the insurer extend to the various types of cases in which facts decisive of the duty to defend are in doubt at the time the company denies liability? It would seem, by analogy to the rule stated earlier in this section and generally applied when the only claim is one within policy coverage, that the insured should be permitted to settle, rather than incurring the costs and risks of litigation, when an ordinarily prudent person without insurance coverage might reasonably have done so. Thus, he should recover whatever proportion of a reasonable settlement made after the company's breach can be allocated to any claim later determined to be within the insuring agreements.[13]

The proportion of the full amount expended by the insured that should be included in the measure of damages in these circumstances would depend on the facts of the particular case. The insured's cause of action against the company should not be rendered valueless, however, by an overly rigorous burden of proving this proportion. Indeed, it might be argued that the burden should fall on the insurer since the problem arises because of the combination of circumstances in which, first, there are covered and noncovered claims, second, there are under policy provisions non-exclusive obligations of defense with corresponding non-exclusive rights of control, and third, the company's breach (which the insured must prove before the problem under discussion here is reached) makes it necessary to prorate amounts expended by one party rather than leaving each party to discharge his own obligation of participation in defense. However, imposing an overly rigorous burden on the insurer would also work out unfairly, since it would so often happen that there were conflicts of interest in defense by reason of which the necessity of proration would arise not from the insurer's breach but from the impossibility of complying with its obligation to defend otherwise than by paying

12. See § 7.7(c) *infra*.

13. *Cf.* Employers Mut. Liab. Ins. Co. v. Hendrix, 199 F.2d 53, 59 (4th Cir. 1952), 41 A.L.R.2d 424, 433 (1955) (South Carolina case).

an appropriate share of the costs of employing an attorney responsible to the insured only.[14]   Thus, wherever the burden is placed, it should not be a rigorous requirement of evidence for proration that could hardly be met.   Settlements are achieved by a willingness on both sides to accept rough estimates of uncertain value.   Proration of amounts expended in achieving settlement should be approached in like spirit.   A court should strive to achieve as fair a proration as is possible under the evidence rather than causing the decision to turn one way or the other on a rule of burden of proof.

It might be suggested that this right of reimbursement for a proportionate share of a settlement should be limited by a rule that, just as the insurer may be held to have acted at its peril in refusing to defend, the insured should be held to act at his peril in settling.   That is, the question whether the insurer will be liable and whether the insured will be entitled to reimbursement will depend on a final adjudication (in an action the insured brings against the company) as to whether in fact there was or was not either a claim of an incident or an incident in fact of a type within the insuring agreements and, if so, what part of a reasonable settlement can properly be allocated to it.   If findings were favorable to the insured, the company's denial of liability would thereby be established as wrongful, and the company would be required both to reimburse (all or proportionally, as the case may be) the amount expended in settlement and to reimburse (all or proportionally) costs of defense.   If the findings were unfavorable, the insured would recover neither.   But it may be objected that this rule would be inadequate to remedy the breach of a duty to take precautionary defensive measures against potential future claims, if such a duty is recognized.[15]   At the least, the insured should be entitled to recover any added defense costs reasonably incurred in preparing for defense against potential future claims within coverage, and arguably he should be entitled to recover any part of the amount expended in settlement that he could show to be reasonably attributable to protecting against such potential future claims.

The insured, not the tort victim, is the person to whom the insurer owes the duty to defend.[16]   May the victim nevertheless bring an action against the insurer for breach of this duty, once the victim has obtained a tort judgment against the insured?   The problem is closely analogous to that arising with respect to the cause of action for breach of the insurer's duty to the insured regarding settlement. In this context, as in that,[17] there is support for permitting the victim to bring the action as successor, by assignment or otherwise, to the insured's cause of action.[18]

---

14.   See generally § 7.7 *infra*.

15.   Concerning possible recognition of such a duty, see § 7.6(a) *supra*.

16.   *Cf.* § 7.8(f) *infra*; Keeton, *Liability Insurance and Responsibility for Settlement*, 67 Harv.L.Rev. 1136, 1175–1176 (1954).

17.   See § 7.8(f) *infra*.

18.   See, *e.g.*, Damron v. Sledge, 105 Ariz. 151, 460 P.2d 997 (1969) (upheld, against claims of fraud and collusion, a prejudgment assignment by defendant driver to the plaintiff in an automobile accident case of whatever claims he might have against his in-

SECTION 7.7 CONFLICTS OF INTEREST UNDER LIABILITY INSURANCE

§ 7.7(a) SOURCES AND NATURE OF CONFLICTS

Liability insurance relationships create numerous and troublesome conflicts of interest. The present section is primarily concerned with conflicts affecting the presentment of claims or defenses. Other sections treat conflicts of interest associated with settlement.[1]

Ordinarily both the company and the insured wish to resist the tort claim of a third person against the insured. The insured is motivated to do so by self interest as well as duty to cooperate with the company; similarly the company is motivated by both duty and self interest to defend effectively. Yet there are many sources of potential conflict of interest with respect to duties of cooperation and defense.[2] A common example is the situation in which there is coverage for negligence but not for intentional tort and the available evidence raises jury issues as to whether the defendant committed an intentional tort, a negligent tort, or no tort at all.[3]

Though there are few precedents concerning the respective obligations of the insurer and the insured to each other in conflict-of-interest situations, on principle it would seem that the company and the insured should be held to mutual obligations to give to each other's interests such weight as would be given by an individual holding both interests. There have been indications of a contrary view, which would permit the company to protect its own interest even at the expense of the interest of the insured.[4] But the suggestion of

surer and car owner's insurer for alleged bad faith in failing to defend; defendant driver's personal attorney intended to allow the action to go by default and plaintiff announced dismissal with prejudice against defendant car owner; counsel for defendant car owner, designated by her insurer, was denied permission to continue to participate in trial to rebut evidence as to the extent of the plaintiff's injuries). Cf. Coblentz v. American Sur. Co., 416 F.2d 1059, 421 F.2d 187 (5th Cir. 1969) (summarized in § 7.7(c) n.8 infra).

1. Concerning conflicts of interest regarding settlement within policy limits, see §§ 7.8, 7.9 infra. Concerning conflicts of interest regarding settlement of reciprocal claims, see § 7.10 infra.

2. See generally A. E. Smith, The Miscegenetic Union of Liability Insurance and Tort Process in the Personal Injury Claims System, 54 Cornell L.Rev. 645, 656–666 (1969); Note, The Effect of Collateral Estoppel on the Assertion of Coverage Defenses, 69 Colum. L.Rev. 1459 (1969); Note, Conflicts of Interests: Insurance Cases, 55 A.B.A. J. 262 (1969); Note, Insurance Policy Defenses and Collateral Estoppel, 43 N.Y.U.L.Rev. 140 (1968), reprinted 1968 Personal Injury Annual 616 (Frumer & Friedman eds.); Comment, The Insurer's Duty to Defend Under a Liability Insurance Policy, 114 U. Pa.L.Rev. 734, 736–740, 745–746 (1966); Note, Use of the Declaratory Judgment to Determine a Liability Insurer's Duty to Defend: Conflict of Interests, 41 Ind.L.J. 87 (1965).

3. See § 7.7(c) infra.

4. E.g., Abrams v. Factory Mut. Liab. Ins. Co., 298 Mass. 141, 10 N.E.2d 82 (1937); Davison v. Maryland Cas. Co., 197 Mass. 167, 83 N.E. 407 (1908) (stating that the company had the privilege of appealing to protect its own interest, even though the insured's interest might be prejudiced by the additional legal proceedings).

mutual obligations in other conflict-of-interest settings is strongly supported by the analogy to the company's obligation with respect to liability in excess of policy limits for failure to settle.[5]

Reciprocal claims may also give rise to a conflict of interest in litigation, as well as in settlement. In a typical situation C, the claimant, is asserting a claim against D and D's liability insurance company, and D is also asserting a claim against C and C's liability insurance company. A conflict may arise either in litigation in which both claims are at issue, or in litigation deciding one of these claims and collaterally affecting the other. Both D and D's liability insurance company are interested in proving that C was negligent and that D was not. But their interests do not always coincide. For example, trial tactics will be affected by the fact that in some cases the company would be as well served by findings of negligence against both parties as by a finding of no negligence against D, whereas D would be well served by the latter result only.[6] Another potential conflict of interest is that concerning the advisability of an appeal that might result in a new trial as to both the claim against D and D's claim against C.[7]

Conflicts of interest in litigation may arise from the possibility of claiming against more than one defendant, as when a passenger in one vehicle is injured in a collision with another vehicle. In such circumstances, if an attorney interested in the defense of claims against the driver or owner of the first vehicle undertakes also to represent the injured passenger he is almost certain to be representing persons with conflicting interests since the interests of the passenger and his host driver are likely to be in irreconcilable conflict.[8]

Conflicts of interest in defense may arise from the policy limit per person. For example, interests may differ with respect to the allocation of damages among different claims within a suit, since the allocation might affect the total amount the company would be required to pay on the insured's behalf.[9]

---

5. See § 7.8 *infra.*

6. This idea is developed in more detail in Keeton, *Liability Insurance and Reciprocal Claims from a Single Accident,* 10 Sw.L.J. 1, 16–19 (1956), reprinted 1957 Ins.L.J. 29, 37–38.

7. *Ibid.*

8. See, *e.g., In re* Paders, 250 App.Div. 418, 294 N.Y.S. 252 (2d Dep't 1937). *Cf. In re* Conrad, 19 App.Div.2d 644, 241 N.Y.S.2d 291 (2d Dep't 1963), *aff'd,* 14 N.Y.2d 500, 197 N.E.2d 621, 248 N.Y.S.2d 224 (1964). Concerning what constitutes representation of conflicting interests generally, see Annot., 17 A.L.R.3d 835 (1968).

9. This is illustrated in Perkoski v. Wilson, 371 Pa. 553, 92 A.2d 189 (1952). In the tort suit, a judgment was entered in favor of the wife-plaintiff for $10,000 and in favor of the husband-plaintiff for $3940, after verdicts of $10,000 and $6,000 respectively and the filing of a remittitur to avoid new trial. The jury were permitted by the instructions to award to the husband damages for loss of consortium and loss of the wife's services. The company refused to pay more than the $10,000 on the wife's claim and $769.13 of the award to the husband, asserting that the remainder of the award to the husband was damages consequential to the wife's injury and therefore in excess of the $10,000 limit per person. The court

Another situation of conflict is that arising from collision between two automobiles insured in the same company. It has been held that the ordinary implications of the insured's obligation of assistance and cooperation are inapplicable in these circumstances and that the company is liable for any judgment, costs, and reasonable attorney's fees incurred by the insured in his own defense, such fees being recoverable in lieu of the defense required by the insurance contract.[10]

Some companies have attempted to meet this problem by assigning different claims personnel and different attorneys to the two sides of the controversy, and this arrangement has received limited encouragement in judicial pronouncements.[11] But obviously such an arrangement is less desirable from the insured's point of view than his employment of an attorney of his own choosing, and it would seem to be his right to insist upon the latter arrangement.[12] Moreover, communications that under ordinary circumstances would be the subject of work-product or attorney-client privileges may be subject to discovery by each insured because occurring at a time before a separate attorney was employed (either by him or by the insurer) to represent him.[13]

declined to allow the company's contention, one ground of decision being that the lower court, though requiring a remittitur, had left it to the plaintiffs to determine which of the verdicts should suffer the reduction, and counsel for the company, still representing the insured, stood by and permitted the husband-plaintiff to accept the reduction without disclosing to him or to the insured that the company would then invoke a policy-limit argument that would not have been available if the remittitur had been applied to the verdict for the wife-plaintiff.

10. *E.g.*, O'Morrow v. Borad, 27 Cal.2d 794, 167 P.2d 483, 163 A.L.R. 894 (1946); noted 59 Harv.L.Rev. 1316, 45 Mich.L.Rev. 515, 31 Minn.L.Rev. 380, 14 U.Chi.L.Rev. 102. After Borad sued O'Morrow, O'Morrow obtained counsel and through such counsel filed a cross-complaint, notifying the insuring group (affiliated companies) that his counsel would also present his defense to Borad's cause of action. O'Morrow then brought the suit in question for declaratory relief against Borad and the insuring group. The appellate court approved O'Morrow's conduct, noting that it would be contrary to public policy to allow a person to control both sides of litigation.

11. *Cf.* Employers' Fire Ins. Co. v. Beals, 103 R.I. 623, 240 A.2d 397

(1968) (child in third grade struck another child in eye with lead pencil; tort suit included allegations of negligence and recklessness; discretionary dismissal of insurer's declaratory proceeding affirmed; opinion includes suggestions, explicitly not all-inclusive, for ways of dealing with conflict-of-interest problems by having two attorneys for the defense, both paid by the insurers). See also Cloer v. Superior Court of Tulare County, 271 Cal.App.2d 143, 76 Cal.Rptr. 217 (5th Dist. 1969) (trial court acted beyond its jurisdiction in discharging the two attorneys appointed by an insurer that had coverage on both automobiles in collision; parties had been fully informed and had accepted representation by the attorneys).

12. Among the difficulties encountered if the company attempts to remain in control of the defense when it has coverage on both sides of the case is the problem of settlement. In Tully v. Travelers Ins. Co., 118 F.Supp. 568 (N.D.Fla.1954), the company was held liable in excess of policy limits for a failure to settle resulting from its refusal to discuss settlement with attorneys for either claimant, on the asserted theory that it could not place itself "in the position of showing partiality to one assured" over another.

13. See, *e.g.* Monier v. Chamberlain, 35 Ill.2d 351, 221 N.E.2d 410 (1966), 18

An additional type of competing interest is that incident to a close personal relationship between the insured and the claimant. This problem of potential collusion has led to the enactment in New York of a statute declaring that no policy "shall be deemed to insure against any liability of an insured because of death of or injuries to his or her spouse or because of injury to, or destruction of property of his or her spouse unless express provision relating specifically thereto is included in the policy." [14] This is an unusual statute, and it affects only a part of the field of relationships potentially giving rise to collusion. Thus, across the nation generally, numerous claims are presented in circumstances such that the company suspects collusion between the claimant and the insured.

Uninsured motorist coverage frequently produces a conflict of interest between the policyholder and the insurer because of the relationship between the claim of the insured against the uninsured motorist, on the one hand, and claims of the uninsured motorist and others against the policyholder on the other hand.[15]

§ 7.7(b) ATTORNEYS' ROLES AND RISKS

A company confronted with a tort claim against its insured in excess of policy limits usually advises the insured that he may obtain his own attorney and that the company and the attorney it employs to represent the insured in court will undertake to cooperate with any attorney appointed by the insured. The insured's employment of a separate attorney, however, does not relieve the company of its duty regarding settlement.[1] Nor can the company discharge its responsibility to the insured by employing a competent attorney and accepting his judgment on settlement proposals.[2]

The attorney employed by the insurer to represent the insured may be confronted with serious problems of conflict of interest between his two clients not only in relation to issues arising during the defense against a claim, including proposals for settlement [3] and choices regarding defenses to be advanced at trial, but also in relation

A.L.R.3d 471 (1968) (insurer having issued coverage for both parties to automobile accident required to produce various documents, reports, memoranda, and statements for inspection by one of the parties; work-product and attorney-client privileges held inapplicable to matter accumulated up to the time the insurer employed an attorney for the defendant).

14. N.Y.Ins.Law 167(3) (McKinney 1966).

15. See, *e.g.*, Allstate Ins. Co. v. Hunt, —— S.W.2d —— (Tex. 197—) [see 450 S.W.2d 668 for Civ.App. opinion, error granted]. See also § 7.7(c) n.10 *infra.*

1. *E.g.*, Ballard v. Citizens Cas. Co., 196 F.2d 96 (7th Cir. 1952) (Illinois law).

2. *E.g.*, Dumas v. Hartford Acc. & Indem. Co., 94 N.H. 484, 56 A.2d 57 (1947); see Highway Ins. Underwriters v. Lufkin-Beaumont Motor Coaches, Inc., 215 S.W.2d 904, 932 (Tex.Civ. App.1948, writ refused, no reversible error). *But cf.* Abrams v. Factory Mut. Liab. Ins. Co., 298 Mass. 141, 144, 10 N.E.2d 82, 84 (1937) (reserving the question whether "an attorney employed by the insurer to defend is an independent contractor for whose negligence the insurer is not liable").

3. See § 7.8 *infra.*

to the preliminary question whether a nonwaiver agreement should be executed.[4]

There are cases in which the conflict of interest is of such nature that it is impossible for one attorney to represent both the company and the insured, even with the fully informed consent of both.[5] When the conflict is less fundamental some particular courses of action may be precluded,[6] but it may nevertheless be possible for one attorney to represent both with their fully informed consent. Thus it would seem permissible, on principle, that an attorney represent both parties with respect to their mutual interest in effective defense against the tort claim, but represent neither with respect to settlement, or that he represent only the company with respect to settlement, the insured fully understanding the situation.[7] However, it would violate canons of ethics for an attorney to represent both the company and the insured unless both were fully aware of the nature and degree of the conflict and nevertheless consented to his representing them.[8] Moreover, it would seem that many companies and their attorneys tread on dangerous ground in relying upon a letter from the company to the insured to serve the function of notice to the insured, since many of the forms of letters used fall short of giving full information about the nature of the conflict.[9]

---

4. Concerning the risk an attorney selected by the insurer takes in advising the insured concerning his entering into a nonwaiver agreement, or even failing to make explicit to the insured the fact and nature of the conflict of interest regarding execution of a nonwaiver agreement, see, *e.g.*, Comment, *The Insurer's Duty to Defend Under a Liability Insurance Policy*, 114 U. Pa.L.Rev. 734, 745–746 (1966). Concerning nonwaiver agreements generally, see § 6.6(a) *supra*. See also § 7.-7(c) *infra*.

5. See § 7.7(c) *infra*.

6. *Ibid.*

7. For more detailed consideration of this question, see Appleman, *Conflicts in Injury Defenses*, 1957 Ins.L.J. 545; Keeton, *Liability Insurance and Responsibility for Settlement*, 67 Harv. L.Rev. 1136, 1167–1173 (1954).

8. See A.B.A. Code of Professional Responsibility, Canon 5, EC 5–16 (1969). Compare the problem of the duty of the company to disclose to the insured a conflict of interests, as exemplified in Perkoski v. Wilson, 371 Pa. 553, 92 A.2d 189 (1952).

9. See Committee on Interpretation of Canons of Ethics, State Bar of Texas,

Opinion No. 179 (June 1958), reprinted 21 Texas B.J. 593 (1958). The Committee rendered an advisory opinion in response to questions whether the attorney designated by the company to appear on behalf of the insured is required "to fully inform" the insured and whether, in particular, he must inform the insured of the holding in G. A. Stowers Furniture Co. v. American Indem. Co., 15 S.W.2d 544 (Tex. Comm'n App. 1929), which imposed liability in excess of policy limits for negligent failure to settle. The Committee answered both questions in the affirmative. The lack of more explicit disclosure may not be significant in those cases in which the insured employs independent counsel. But if the insured is not fully aware of this conflict and does not employ independent counsel, the failure of the attorney to make the more explicit disclosure suggested in the Texas opinion is not only a probable violation of canons of ethics but also a potential source of liability of the attorney and the company for loss resulting to the insured from a tort judgment against him in excess of policy limits.

On May 22, 1969, the ABA National Conference of Lawyers and Liability Insurers adopted a statement of Guiding Principles, widely published with an invitation for submission of suggestions or ideas regarding the Princi-

Is an attorney likely to be held liable for damages on a malpractice theory if he has acted with lack of due sensitivity to the conflict of interest inherent in some liability insurance relationship?

There is some direct authority for such liability [10] and some against it.[11] The view that the attorney is subject to liability for harm resulting from his misconduct in relation to a conflict of interest seems likely to prevail.

---

ples. 5 Forum 296 (ABA Section Ins., Neg. & Comp. L. 1970). Paragraph IV is as follows:

"IV. Conflicts of Interest Generally—Duties of Attorney

"In any claim or in any suit where the attorney selected by the company to defend the claim or action becomes aware of facts or information which indicate to him a question of coverage in the matter being defended or any other conflict of interest between the company and the insured with respect to the defense of the matter, the attorney should promptly inform both the company and the insured, preferably in writing, of the nature and extent of the conflicting interest. In any such suit, the company or its attorney should invite the insured to retain his own counsel at his own expense to represent his separate interest."

See also Statement of Principles Relative to Claims Adjusting, adopted January 8, 1939, by the Conference Committee on Adjusters [name later changed to National Conference of Lawyers, Insurance Companies, and Adjusters by resolution adopted by ABA House of Delegates, Feb. 1961], five of whom, including the Chairman, represented the American Bar Association. This statement was approved by the American Bar Association, American Mutual Alliance [name later changed to American Mutual Insurance Alliance], Association of Casualty and Surety Companies [name later changed to American Insurance Association], International Claim Association, National Board of Fire Underwriters, National Association of Independent Insurance Adjusters, and National Association of Independent Insurers. The statement is printed in full in the prefatory section of Vol. III, Martindale-Hubbell Law Directory, 218A–219A (1970). The following is an excerpt from the Committee statement, a footnote construing "representatives" being omitted here:

"4(b). The companies and their representatives, including attorneys, will inform the policyholder of the progress of any suit against the policyholder and its probable results. If any diversity of interest shall appear between the policyholder and the company, the policyholder shall be fully advised of the situation and invited to retain his own counsel. Without limiting the general application of the foregoing, it is contemplated that this will be done in any case in which it appears probable that an amount in excess of the limit of the policy is involved, or in any case in which the company is defending under a reservation of rights, or in any case in which the prosecution of a counterclaim appears advantageous to the policyholder."

See also Committee on Interpretation of Canons of Ethics, State Bar of Texas, Opinion No. 201 (June 1960).

But cf. Murach v. Massachusetts Bonding & Ins. Co., 339 Mass. 184, 158 N. E.2d 338 (1959). Though apparently reserving the question whether further disclosure might be required in some circumstances, the court found adequate, in the case at hand, a letter calling attention to the fact that the claim was in excess of policy limits and inviting the insureds to obtain their own counsel to protect their interests as to the excess. The evidence indicated that the insureds were experienced in business and legal matters and were unconcerned with the possibility of involvement of their own property because it appeared they had no equity of substance. Under these circumstances the court held that there was no obligation even to disclose to the insureds an offer of settlement, since it appeared that they were not concerned with knowing about it.

10.   *E.g.*, Lysick v. Walcom, 258 Cal. App.2d 136, 65 Cal.Rptr. 406 (1st Dist. 1968), 28 A.L.R.3d 368 (1969).

11.   *E.g.*, Waters v. American Cas. Co., 261 Ala. 252, 73 So.2d 524 (1954).

In the first place, on principle there are strong reasons for concluding that the attorney is subject to such potential liability both to the insured and to the insurance company. He occupies a fiduciary relation to both and implicitly, if not explicitly, holds himself out as exercising his professional competence and skill on behalf of each. This is not to say, however, that the attorney would be held responsible in each situation in which one of his clients, the insured, is able to recover against his other client, the company, because of its misconduct in relation to the conflict of interest. Probably in most instances the total conduct of the company on which liability is based involves not only the conduct of the attorney but also that of other representatives, including adjusters and home office claims examiners. Also, the attorney has some practical protection in the tactical undesirability, from the insured's point of view, of having an individual attorney as a defendant in the suit.[12] Despite the practical and doctrinal arguments against liability of the attorney, however, the potential exposure is enough to cause concern to any attorney, unless he has complete confidence that the company he is representing will not seek indemnity from him.

In addition to the limited direct authority for the attorney's liability to the insured, there is persuasive support for liability in opinions disapproving conduct of the attorney and penalizing the insurer in some way because of it. An example is an opinion indicating that the attorney's nondisclosure of the purpose of taking the deposition of the insured—that is, to use it in support of a policy defense—was improper conduct and that its occurrence precluded the insurer's reliance upon the policy defense.[13] If some special damage had been suffered by the insured, not reparable by allowing him to recover on the

---

12. See Peerless Ins. Co. v. Inland Mut. Ins. Co., 251 F.2d 696, 701 (4th Cir. 1958), explaining on a comparable basis the conduct of the primary insurer (who was seeking reimbursement from a reinsurer) in failing to assert a potential claim against its attorney.

13. See, e.g., Allstate Ins. Co. v. Keller, 17 Ill.App.2d 44, 149 N.E.2d 482 (1st Dist. 1958), 70 A.L.R.2d 1190 (1960) (the company asserted a coverage defense based on the insured's false statement to the company that he rather than another occupant of the car was driving at the time of the accident; the insured corrected the statement about nine months later; the court stated in dicta that "timely revelation of the truth might render an incipient breach immaterial . . ." but that an actual showing of prejudice is not required, 17 Ill.App.2d at 50, 149 N.E.2d at 485; concluding that the revelation in this case was not timely, the court found a breach of the assistance and cooperation clause but held that the company was precluded from asserting this defense because it failed to attempt a reservation of its rights for a period of almost a year and a half, during which interval its attorney took the insured's deposition in contemplation of the filing of a declaratory judgment action concerning the breach, but without notifying the insured of such purpose). But cf. Fidelity & Cas. Co. v. McConnaughy, 228 Md. 1, 179 A.2d 117 (1962) (insured's breach of cooperation clause by bringing in false witnesses caused insurer to decline to accept claimant's $3,500 settlement offer; insurer-appointed counsel acted improperly in taking insured's deposition to confirm its defense of noncooperation, but insurer is not thereby barred from asserting noncooperation; relief limited, however, to excusing insurer from liability for excess above $3,500 for which insurer claims it would have settled but for insured's breach).

insurance policy, would he not have been allowed a cause of action against the attorney?

Another example is an opinion indicating that it was improper to withhold disclosure of the fact that the company was hoping to fall back on a policy defense as a final resort and was therefore not considering settlement.[14]

It has been held that communications between the company and the attorney are not privileged as against the insured.[15] The insured can often use evidence of such communications to great advantage in proving his claim of negligence or bad faith of the company in relation to settlement. Such communications might also be used effectively in a suit by the insured against the attorney himself.

Is it permissible for an insurer to designate "house counsel" to appear for insureds in defense of tort claims covered by liability insurance? Obviously conflict-of-interest problems will arise from time to time. However, a court requested to adopt a proposed rule against representation of insureds by house counsel declined to do so on the ground that such a rule would be discriminatory against a class since conflict-of-interest problems are present also when non-house-counsel attorneys appear for insureds.[16]

Attorneys for claimants, as well as those representing defendants, are likely to be confronted with problems of professional conduct related to the conflicts of interest arising in the liability insurance context. Some examples follow.

Is it permissible for an attorney for a claimant, seeking to increase the likelihood of a favorable settlement, to communicate to the insured information about the company's potential liability in excess of policy limits for failure to settle? A bar association committee charged with interpreting canons of ethics has answered that this conduct would be improper.[17]

May one attorney represent several persons who are making claims arising out of the same accident and involving conflicts of interest? For example, suppose a father, his fifteen-year-old son, and a friend, all in a car driven by the father, are injured in a collision with a car driven by another person. May one attorney properly represent the father, the son, and the friend in their claims against the other driver and his liability insurance company? This arrange-

---

14. Home Indem. Co. v. Williamson, 183 F.2d 572 (5th Cir. 1950).

15. Henke v. Iowa Home Mut. Cas. Co., 249 Iowa 614, 87 N.W.2d 920 (1958). See also § 7.7(a) n.13 *supra*.

16. *In re* Rules Governing Conduct of Attorneys in Florida, 220 So.2d 6 (Fla.1969).

17. Committee on Interpretation of Canons of Ethics, State Bar of Texas, Opinion No. 97 (April 1954). The

opinion answers that it would not violate canons, however, merely "to write to the tort-feasor putting such party on notice of the attorney's employment, and offering to make compromise settlement of the claim without litigation for the amount of the tort-feasor's liability insurance policy limits, where, at the time the offer is made, no suit has been instituted and the tort-feasor is not represented by any counsel on account of the accident."

ment, sometimes followed in practice, raises serious problems because of the potential conflict of interest among the claimants. The father has a strong interest in contending both that he was careful and that the other driver was negligent. The claim for the son's medical expense and wage loss would also be affected by the father's negligence in many jurisdictions, and in some arguably even the claim for the son's pain and suffering would be affected. In contrast, the friend might have an economic interest in showing that both the father and the other driver were at fault since he might establish a valid claim against both and reach the liability insurance of both.

It would seem that in order to represent all three a single attorney must obtain their fully informed consent.[18] This is an especially troublesome requirement when one of the claimants is under legal disabilities, such as those of minority.[19] Moreover, here as in the case of some liability insurance relationships presenting conflicts of interest in defense, referred to above, it may happen that the facts and relevant legal doctrines present such sharp conflicts that it is not practicable for one attorney to represent the different claimants. An additional factor having greater force here than in the defense context, however, is the increase in cost of representation if separate representation is required.[20] This factor of cost does not weigh against a requirement of full disclosure and explanation of the conflict, however. At most it weighs in favor of freedom for the parties whose interests are affected, after being fully informed of the conflict, to agree upon a course of action in which one attorney can represent them, even at the sacrifice of potential claims that might have been made if each had been separately represented.

Sharp conflicts of interest among claimants may arise in relation to settlement as well as trial. A practice occasionally followed of proposals between a liability insurance company and an attorney for settlement of a number of claims as a group for a stated figure, the allocation to be made by the attorney, plainly places him in a position of conflict. He cannot properly make such an allocation without full disclosure to all the parties whose claims are affected,[21] and it would seem that an insurance company participating in a group settlement

---

18. See A.B.A. Code of Professional Responsibility, Canon 5, EC 5–16, DR 5–105, 5–106 (1969). *Cf.* Jedwabny v. Philadelphia Transp. Co., 390 Pa. 231, 135 A.2d 252 (1957), *cert. denied*, 355 U.S. 966 (1958).

19. *Cf.* Smith v. Price, 253 N.C. 285, 116 S.E.2d 733 (1960) (friendly suit to approve settlement with infant plaintiff; one attorney represented defendants—two insurers and their several insureds including an infant defendant; the infant defendant's injuries were not called to court's attention; held, judgment irregular because of conflict of interest among defendants;

infant defendant's motion to vacate judgment as to him allowed). Note, however, that the issue in this case was not the effect of the judgment as to the infant plaintiff but rather its effect on the reciprocal claim of the infant defendant; concerning reciprocal claims generally, see § 7.10 *infra.*

20. See the dissenting opinion of Bell, J., in Jedwabny v. Philadelphia Transp. Co., 390 Pa. 231, 135 A.2d 252 (1957), *cert. denied*, 355 U.S. 966 (1958).

21. *Cf.* ABA Code of Professional Responsibility DR 5–106 (1969).

with notice that the attorney was acting without such full disclosure would be a party to the improper action, with the consequence that the settlements might be subject to later attack by an aggrieved party.

Attorneys finding themselves in an untenable conflict-of-interest position may seek to withdraw from representation of a client in litigation. On occasion, trial courts have denied permission for withdrawal. Perhaps it is within the discretion of the trial court to deny permission for withdrawal if the circumstances are such that the attorney can function with clear directions from the court that he is to serve the interests of a designated client only, and with the understanding that no other person will be bound by the results of the trial. For example, trial courts have sometimes denied insurer-appointed defense counsel the right to withdraw,[22] and such an order has been said to have the effect that the attorney's actions under the order did not waive the insurer's defense of noncooperation.[23] But there is other precedent supporting the right of an insurer-appointed attorney to withdraw from the representation of the insured in a tort case whenever he is dissatisfied with the arrangements between him and the insured and the withdrawal can be accomplished without harm to any of the parties to the tort action.[24] For stronger reasons, it would seem that withdrawal should be permitted when there is a conflict of interest between the attorney's two clients—the insurer and the insured—that affects the manner in which the defense of the tort claim is to be conducted.

§ 7.7(c) COURSES OF ACTION WHEN INTERESTS IN DEFENSE CONFLICT

If a liability insurance company suspects collusion between its insured and a claimant, what courses of action may it take to protect its own interests?

One course attempted on occasion is to attack the character and motives of both the claimant and its insured in the trial of the tort claim, contending that the two are in collusion to present a false claim because the facts do not support a valid claim. Since the company is ordinarily not a party in the tort litigation, the attack is made by the attorney whom it has engaged to represent the insured.

22. *E.g.*, Cascella v. Jay James Camera Shop, Inc., 147 Conn. 337, 160 A.2d 899 (1960) (trial court did not err in denying motion of defense counsel to withdraw on theory insured had failed to cooperate; "[a]ny question concerning coverage . . . was foreign to the issues" of tort trial and could not be determined on motion of counsel to withdraw).

23. Nationwide Mut. Ins. Co. v. Thomas, 306 F.2d 767 (D.C.Cir. 1962) (however, a motion for new trial resulted in reduction of judgments and the insurer then appealed on the merits; held, voluntary appeal waived defense of noncooperation; concerning preclusion of defenses as a result of actions in defending a claim, see § 6.8(a) *supra*).

24. See, *e.g.*, Swedloff v. Philadelphia Transp. Co., 409 Pa. 382, 187 A.2d 152 (1963) (order denying permission to withdraw reversed).

Quite plainly, the attorney, in attacking his own client's motivations and honesty, is acting improperly, and it has been held that the claimant may obtain a reversal of a judgment on a verdict obtained in this way since it is prejudicial to his interests for the factfinder to be exposed to such an attack by counsel who purportedly represents one of the persons whose credibility is challenged.[1]

When counsel is instructed by the company or otherwise concludes that it is in the company's best interests that he assert such a contention of collusion, he can no longer properly represent both the company and the insured since their interests are in sharp conflict. If he continues to defend on behalf of the insured in these circumstances without presenting a contention in the tort litigation that there is collusion, will the company be precluded from asserting this contention later?

If the attorney and the company do not make full disclosure of the conflict and obtain the insured's fully informed consent to the attorney's continuing to represent him, the company should be precluded from asserting the defense later under a doctrine of election based on an attempt to obtain the unconscionable advantage of maintaining control of the litigation through an attorney selected by the company, while secretly preparing to contest liability thereafter on grounds of collusion; the risks of overreaching of the insured in such circumstances are sufficient to justify the imposition of a limited choice upon the company that precludes such secret qualifications of the attorney's representation of the insured.[2]

It may be doubted that it is even proper for the attorney selected by the insurer to continue to represent the insured when a contention of collusion is being considered by the company. Perhaps the conflict is of such nature that even fully informed consent should not be held adequate to permit such representation. But even if a fully informed consent of the insured is obtained for postponing decision of the dispute over collusion, and even if this is held sufficient to permit the attorney selected by the insurer to continue to represent the insured in the tort action, it may be asserted that the company will be precluded from raising the issue of collusion later because it will be bound by the factfindings in the tort action—findings that are at the least inconsistent with any theory that the company has been prejudiced by collusion, if not inconsistent with collusion itself. This is a problem ordinarily treated under the rubric of res judicata or estoppel by judgment. Before proceeding to a proposed answer, let us observe other conflict of interest situations that present similar problems.

One such problem arises when there is a conflict of interest with respect to what defense should be asserted as a tactical matter, even

---

1. *E.g.*, Pennix v. Winton, 61 Cal. App.2d 761, 143 P.2d 940 (1st Dist. 1943), *hearing denied*, 145 P.2d 561 (1944).

2. See generally §§ 6.2–6.4, 6.6(a) *supra.*

though there is no claim of collusion. For example, when a passenger sues his host driver because of injuries sustained during an outing in which drinking had occurred, there may be a conflict of interest with respect to whether the defense should be based on denial of the degree of fault in driving required to sustain the claim or instead should be based on conceding recklessness and asserting a defense of contributory fault or assumption of risk. Though counsel engaged by the insurer as defense attorney for the insured might in some circumstances reasonably conclude that the interests of the insured as well as the insurer are best served by presenting the latter type of defense,[3] it is easy to imagine circumstances in which the conflict of interest is so sharp that this course of conduct should not be permissible.

Another similar conflict-of-interest problem arises when the claimant sues the insured, alleging that his injuries were caused by the insured's negligence, and the available evidence suggests that the injuries may have been caused not by negligence but by intentional misconduct not covered by the insurance policy. Often the claimant prefers to proceed on the theory of negligence rather than intentional tort, because the insured is judgment proof and the claimant's only hope for monetary recovery is to bring the case within insurance coverage. When the insured is sued on the theory of negligence, his interests require that the attorney representing him contend, first, that his conduct was not even negligence and, in the alternative, that it was merely negligence and not an intentional tort. The insurance company's interests would be served by establishing the first contention, but when the evidence makes such a finding improbable, the company's interests are best served by making a third contention— that the insured committed an intentional tort, beyond the scope of policy coverage. If the attorney employed by the company to represent the insured undertakes to make the third contention, he is acting in violation of his duty to the insured, with whom he has an attorney-client relation.[4]

In circumstances of this last type, insurer-designated attorneys have sometimes continued to represent the insured, withholding the

---

3. Consider the questionable decision in Detenber v. American Universal Ins. Co., 372 F.2d 50 (6th Cir. 1967), 34 A.L. R.3d 526 (1970), *cert. denied*, 389 U.S. 987 (1967) (Black dissenting), denying the insured's claim for liability in excess of $10,000 policy limit, even though the insurer had offered $10,000 in settlement before trial and at the commencement of trial the attorney changed from a defense of no negligence to a sole defense of assumption of risk, emphasizing the insured's guilt, without either consultation with or notice to the insured and his private attorney, who did not participate in the trial. See also § 7.6(b) *supra*.

4. See, *e.g.*, Newcomb v. Meiss, 263 Minn. 315, 116 N.W.2d 593 (1962) (trial court did not err in submitting negligence theory over insurer-appointed defense attorney's contention that defendant wilfully rather than negligently struck plaintiff; trial court's instructions directed jury not to award damages for an intended impact on plaintiff but only for a separate impact on plaintiff of car driven by defendant, negligently according to plaintiff's claim though intentionally according to defense attorney's contention; dicta that the attorney acted improperly, though in good faith, in contending the latter impact was intentional).

contention for the insurer in the expectation it could be asserted in a later proceeding against the insurer in the event of a tort judgment against the insured. And this course of action has occasionally been approved in judicial opinions [5] and other writings.[6] But this method of dealing with the problem is unsatisfactory because of the irreconcilable conflict between the insurer's and insured's interests. It is undesirable to place the attorney designated by the insurer in the position of being charged with responsibility for making a contention contrary to the interests of the insurer. This does not mean, however, that the company's right to defend its own interests must be wholly sacrificed. Two possible solutions avoiding that result may be suggested.

The first is to allow separate adjudication of the tort and coverage disputes. Under this arrangement the insured is allowed to decline permission for the insurer-appointed attorney to represent him and is, upon proof of coverage, allowed to recover his expenses of defense by an attorney he engages.[7] Similarly, the insurer is allowed to refuse to defend for the insured and to raise its policy defense (the third contention) in the later suit on the policy, and it is not estopped by the judgment in the tort suit. This result is both supported [8] and

5. See, e.g., Great Am. Ins. Co. v. Ratliff, 242 F.Supp. 983 (D.Ark.1965) (state court's decision in tort case that collision was negligently caused was not res judicata against insurer even though its attorneys defended; held for insurer in declaratory proceedings); Crum v. Anchor Cas. Co., 264 Minn. 378, 119 N.W.2d 703 (1963) (held, insurer liable for expenses of defense and $600 settlement made by insured with claimant after insurer withdrew from defense, though knowing facts that brought incident within coverage despite victim's allegations of a claim excluded by policy terms; statement in opinion that when conflict arises, attorney must act as if retained by insured personally, and insurer may assert its defense in separate proceedings). Cf. Ferguson v. Birmingham Fire Ins. Co., 460 P.2d 342 (Ore.1969) (since there was a conflict of interest, insurer was not estopped to raise in later action its coverage defense that trespass to land was willful; neither did insured's improper demand that insurer defend without a nonwaiver agreement preclude insured from asserting coverage, since insured's breach did not prejudice insurer; other details of this case are stated in § 7.6(a) n.18 supra. For a different view concerning the insured's assertion of a right to assume control of the defense unless the insurer will defend without a nonwaiver agreement, see § 6.6(a) n.1 supra.

6. See, e.g., Note, Insurance Policy Defenses and Collateral Estoppel, 43 N. Y.U.L.Rev. 140 (1968), reprinted 1968 Personal Injury Annual 616 (Frumer & Friedman eds.), which appears to support this arrangement at least when there is full disclosure to the insured and a reservation of rights.

7. E.g., Magoun v. Liberty Mut. Ins. Co., 346 Mass. 677, 195 N.E.2d 514 (1964) (with insurer's acquiescence, insured employed his own counsel, refusing to permit insurer to proceed under an attempted reservation of rights; insurer held liable for fee of insured's counsel as part of expense of defending); Burd v. Sussex Mut. Ins. Co., 56 N.J. 383, 267 A.2d 7 (1970) (discussed in n.8 infra). Cf. Prashker v. United States Gee. Co., 1 N.Y.2d 584, 593, 136 N.E.2d 871, 876, 154 N.Y. S.2d 910, 917 (1956), observing that in another situation of conflicting interest, "the selection of the attorneys to represent the assureds should be made by them rather than by the insurance company, which should remain liable for the payment of the reasonable value of the services of whatever attorneys the assureds select."

8. See, e.g., American Sur. Co. v. Coblentz, 381 F.2d 185 (5th Cir. 1967) (insured shot person who had been loitering around motel and was fleeing from chase; after insurer withdrew from defense, judgment was entered

opposed [9] by precedents.   Often an insurer asserting this right to refuse to defend without being estopped to raise its policy defense

for plaintiff on a stipulation of evidence at non-jury trial; summary judgment for plaintiff in an ensuing garnishment proceeding reversed; insurer entitled to a chance to prove its policy defense based on assault and battery exclusion), which still remains authoritative, it would seem, after Coblentz v. American Sur. Co., 416 F. 2d 1059, 421 F.2d 187 (5th Cir. 1969) (liability insurer denied liability and withdrew; insured stipulated judgment for victim to be satisfied only out of liability insurance; in garnishment action, jury finding that motel owner's shooting of prowler was negligence, not assault; court holds insurer liable; one passage in opinion seems to say insurer was bound by judgment in tort case, but this is misleading since insurer had its opportunity for jury trial of assault-negligence issue in the garnishment proceeding); Farm Bureau Mut. Auto. Ins. Co. v. Hammer, 177 F.2d 793 (4th Cir. 1949) (2–to–1 decision), *cert. denied*, 339 U.S. 914 (1950) (insurer sought declaratory judgment that its policy did not cover damages awarded against its insured in five tort actions from the defense of which the insurer-appointed attorney withdrew after the insured had been convicted of murder in the second degree for intentionally causing the death of a passenger in another vehicle by driving his truck into it; thereafter the insured made no defense, and judgments grounded on allegations of negligence were entered against him; the district judge entered summary judgment against the company on the theory that it was estopped to assert that the injuries were intentionally caused in view of the determination in the tort judgments that they were negligently caused; held, reversed and remanded); Glens Falls Ins. Co. v. American Oil Co., 254 Md. 120, 254 A.2d 658 (1969) (tort action against decedent insured's estate alleging decedent negligently drove car into plaintiff's gasoline pumps, damaging them; a few days after the incident, decedent died from other causes under circumstances suggestive of suicide; insurer declined to defend, and default judgment was entered for plaintiff; in later action against insurer, held, remanding for trial, insurer not estopped by the judgment in tort case); Weis v. State Farm Mut. Auto. Ins. Co., 242 Minn.

141, 64 N.W.2d 366 (1954), 49 A.L.R.2d 688 (1956) (claimant alleged insured "negligently, carelessly, and recklessly, deliberately" ran into rear of claimant's car; insured's statement to insurer declared it was no accident and that he ran into claimant's car deliberately several times; held, no duty to defend in view of insured's admission the incident was not an accident; under these circumstances insurer cannot be bound by any contrary implications of the judgment in the tort case it properly refused to defend); Burd v. Sussex Mut. Ins. Co., 56 N.J. 383, 267 A.2d 7 (1970) (tort action against homeowners policy insured with one count alleging that, while intoxicated, he intentionally shot his friend and second count alleging he did so negligently, insurer refused to defend; general verdict and judgment against insured in tort action; trial court entered summary judgment for insured in action on policy; held, reversed; carrier should not be permitted to defend in such a conflict-of-interest situation, and should not be estopped by result in tort action; its covenant to defend is translated into an obligation "to reimburse the insured if it is later adjudged that the claim was one within the policy covenant to pay"); Sims v. Nationwide Mut. Ins. Co., 247 S.C. 82, 145 S.E.2d 523 (1965) (victim sued on negligence theory; insurer refused to defend, asserting that the injury was intentional; victim recovered and insured sued insurer; held, insurer not bound by negligence finding; entitled, because of conflict of interest, to refuse to defend and thereafter assert intentional injury exclusion). See also Stout v. Grain Dealers Mut. Ins. Co., 307 F.2d 521 (4th Cir. 1962) and Williams v. Farmers Mut. of Enumclaw, 245 Ore. 557, 423 P.2d 518 (1967), discussed in § 7.6(a) n.5 *supra*. See generally Note, *The Effect of Collateral Estoppel on the Assertion of Coverage Defenses*, 69 Colum.L.Rev. 1459 (1969); Note, *Insurance Policy Defenses and Collateral Estoppel*, 43 N.Y.U.L.Rev. 140 (1968), reprinted 1968 Personal Injury Annual 616 (Frumer & Friedman eds.).

9. *E.g.*, Miller v. United States Fid. & Cas. Co., 291 Mass. 445, 197 N.E. 75 (1935) (insurer contended that the insured, while driving on a highway,

also files declaratory judgment proceedings, especially when it is asserting not merely that conflict of interest prevents its fulfilling a duty of defense in the usual way but more broadly that it has no duty of defense. If it wins on the broader ground, it has no obligation to pay either a tort judgment against the insured or the insured's costs of defending against the tort claim. If, on the other hand, the insurer has a duty to defend but because of conflict of interest is excused from discharging that duty in the usual way, then the insurer is not estopped by the tort judgment against the insured from proving facts that are inconsistent with that judgment and defeat the insurer's alleged liability to pay the tort judgment on the insured's behalf. But the insurer is nevertheless obligated to discharge its duty to defend by reimbursing the insured's reasonable expenses incurred in defense.

The second possible solution that offers a fair opportunity for an insurer to have an adjudication of its coverage defense is to allow the company to refuse to defend for the insured (again with the expectation of holding the company liable for costs of defense if its policy defense finally fails), and further allow the company to be made a party to the suit in which the tort claim against the insured is adjudicated. This might be done by intervention at the instance of the company,[10] by third party proceedings at the instance of the

had an altercation with the driver of another car, sped past him and cut in sharply, causing the other driver to lose control of his car, which then overturned; the claimant sued the insured, alleging negligence only, and recovered a judgment, the company having refused to defend; in this later proceeding on the policy, held that the company was estopped to litigate its contention that the injury was not caused accidentally, since theories of negligence and wilful and wanton conduct were mutually exclusive and the company was bound by the determination in the previous suit that the insured was guilty of negligence). *Cf.* B. Roth Tool Co. v. New Amsterdam Cas. Co., 161 F. 709 (8th Cir. 1908) (insured suffered a judgment against itself in favor of its employee for injuries allegedly due to its negligence in allowing use of metals of explosive nature; held, that when suing its insurer on an employer's liability policy containing a warranty against use of explosives on the property, insured was estopped to claim that the injuries were not due to explosives); Gray v. Zurich Ins. Co., 65 Cal.2d 263, 419 P.2d 168, 54 Cal.Rptr. 104 (1966), discussed in § 7.6(a) n.5 *supra*, and explicitly disapproved by the New Jersey Supreme Court in *Burd*, n.8 *supra*.

See also Stefus v. London & Lancashire Indem. Co., 111 N.J.L. 6, 166 A. 339 (1933) (10–to–4 decision), *cert. denied*, 290 U.S. 658 (1933) (liability insurer bound by tort action record indicating judgment on a claim of negligence and recklessness in starting car while plaintiff was on running board; insurer precluded from contending injury was wilfully caused), which, however, can no longer be taken as authoritative on this point in view of the comments about it in *Burd*, n.8 *supra*.

10. *Cf.* State *ex rel.* State Farm Mut. Auto. Ins. Co. v. Craig, 364 S.W.2d 343 (Mo.App.1963), 95 A.L.R.2d 1321 (1964) (insurer under uninsured motorist coverage permitted to intervene in suit between its insured and an uninsured motorist who had defaulted); Doe v. Moss, 120 Ga.App. 762, 172 S. E.2d 321 (1969) (under Georgia statute, insurer permitted to intervene in action against uninsured motorist without conceding coverage or liability). *But cf.* Newcomb v. Meiss, 263 Minn. 315, 116 N.W.2d 593 (1962) (defense attorney unsuccessful in attempting to get court to submit intentional tort issue to jury; but observe that the insured was not separately represented in this proceeding).

insured,[11] by joinder at the instance of the claimant,[12] or by declaratory proceedings that adjudicate the tort claim as well as the coverage issue. The considerations accounting for the customary refusal of courts to allow an insurance company to be a party to the tort suit are less forcefully applicable here than to the ordinary case involving no such conflict of interest between the company and the insured. Especially is this so if the joinder is at the instance of the company or the insured, rather than the claimant, since the rule against joinder is designed for their protection rather than the claimant's protection. Probably the allowance of a three-party proceeding that will dispose of the entire set of controversies in one trial is the ideal solution of this problem. If this solution is denied on principle or is foreclosed by nonsatisfaction of procedural or jurisdictional requisites, however, it is plainly unjust to deny also the first solution suggested above. That would be to hold that the company shall never have any opportunity to urge its defense. Indeed, such a denial of hearing on its contention should be found to be offensive to principles of due process.

This type of case, involving irreconcilable conflict between the interests of the company and the insured concerning defense, is distinguishable from the more frequently occurring case in which there is a disputed policy defense of such nature that the insured and the company still have consistent interests in the defense of the tort claim (e. g., defenses of late notice, cancellation, or nonpermissive use by one other than named insureds). In a case of the latter type, the problem of estoppel by judgment usually does not arise in any event, since the issue determinative of the dispute over coverage is not one of the issues decided in the tort case. Moreover, a specious argument of estoppel founded on so-called findings that were in fact not actual adjudications on essential issues should not be accepted.[13] If the same issue does arise (as when the claimant alleges that the insured was driving, the insured denies this, and the policy contains an endorsement by reason of which it provides no coverage unless the insured was driving [14]) it might be argued that estoppel by judgment should not apply.[15] But the fact remains that here the company and

---

11. *Cf.* Jenkins v. General Acc. Fire & Life Assur. Corp., 349 Mass. 699, 212 N.E.2d 464 (1965) (insurer's argument it had no duty to settle a claim it refused to defend held to be without merit; suit by victim against insured; insured allowed to implead insurer).

12. See § 7.11 *infra*.

13. See, *e.g.*, Burnett v. Western Pac. Ins. Co., 469 P.2d 602 (Ore.1970) (discussed in § 7.6(a) n.9 *supra*).

14. Public Nat'l Ins. Co. v. Wheat, 100 Ga.App. 695, 112 S.E.2d 194 (1959) (company held estopped by the judgment in the tort suit that it refused to defend; it might have been inferred from the evidence that the insured was honest but mistaken in his statement that he was not driving, having been severely intoxicated at the time of the incident).

15. It might be thought that this argument is supported by State Farm Mut. Auto. Ins. Co. v. Coughran, 303 U.S. 485, 58 Sup.Ct. 670, 82 L.Ed. 970 (1938). The policy provided coverage only if the vehicle was "being operated by the Assured, his paid driver, members of his immediate family, or persons acting under the direction of

the insured have only consistent interests in the manner of defense. Thus, either the company or the insured can defend in a way that serves the interests of both, and the opportunity for hearing on defensive contentions can be preserved without imposing on the claimant the burden of trying one issue twice in order to recover on the liability insurance policy. In this situation, it would seem appropriate that the company be bound by the results of the tort trial.[16]

Because of uncertainty about judicial recognition of either or both of the two solutions suggested here, in some jurisdictions there is no clearly safe way for the company to preserve an opportunity for hearing on its policy defense in cases involving a conflict of interest between the company and the insured in relation to defense. Even in jurisdictions permitting declaratory proceedings,[17] they cannot serve this purpose unless they are extended to adjudicating the tort claim as well as coverage issues, which is one version of the second of the two solutions discussed here. If a court declines to extend declaratory proceedings this far and also declines to recognize the first solution, the judgment in the declaratory proceedings will simply advise the insurer that it has no way of obtaining an adjudication of its policy defense.

In view of the indisposition of the companies to attempt intervention in the tort suit, their more common course of action is to

the Assured" and not in violation of any law as to age or driving license. At the tort trial, defended by the company under a nonwaiver agreement, the claimant recovered a judgment against the assured and wife, on the theory of negligence of the wife as operator, imputed to the husband; the company successfully defended the later suit on the policy by showing that an unlicensed 13-year-old girl was operating the car under the wife's direction, in violation of law and contrary to the assured's express instructions, the wife being at most a joint operator. The case is not good support for the argument suggested in the text above, since the issue determinative of policy coverage was not exactly the same as any issue decided in the tort case. The court's opinion includes the following passage: "Defenses now presented by the Insurance Company against liability under the policy were not involved. Joint driving by Mrs. Anthony and the girl was not subject to inquiry." 303 U.S. at 492, 58 Sup. Ct. at 673, 82 L.Ed. at 975.

16.   See, *e.g.*, Burd v. Sussex Mut. Ins. Co., 56 N.J. 383, 267 A.2d 7 (1970) (discussed in n.8 *supra*). See also Public Nat'l Ins. Co. v. Wheat, 100 Ga.App. 695, 112 S.E.2d 194 (1959); Annot., 27 A.L.R.3d 350 (1969). Concerning a dis-

tinguishable situation in which a car was occupied by two persons, each being injured or killed, and two inconsistent actions are filed, the plaintiff in each claiming that the other person was the driver, see § 7.6(a) n.7 *supra*.

17.   See Tennessee Farmers Mut. Ins. Co. v. Hammond, 200 Tenn. 106, 290 S.W.2d 860 (1956) (suit in chancery by a liability insurance company for declaratory judgment to determine whether it was subject to liability in excess of policy limits; decree sustaining a plea in abatement affirmed on the theory that the plaintiff insurance company was anticipating a tort action against it for alleged lack of good faith, which involved a fact issue, and that it was appropriate for the lower court to refuse to entertain a suit when a disputed issue of fact was determinative of the rights of the parties; the tort action was subsequently filed in the circuit court of the same county and was tried before a jury). This opinion might arguably be read as precluding the use of declaratory proceedings with respect to any claim of liability in excess of policy limits, since an issue of bad faith or negligence is always involved. It need not be read so broadly, however, and on principle it would seem that should not be the rule.

deny coverage and to decline to defend the tort case. There are disadvantages in this course of action beyond the risk that a rule of estoppel by judgment will be invoked. First, it is likely to increase the cost of defense since the amount allowed to the insured's independent counsel as a reasonable fee, in the event the dispute on the policy defense is eventually resolved against the company, will ordinarily be higher than would have been the payment to the company's own counsel. Of as much or more concern to the company, however, is the fear that the case will not be as effectively and vigorously defended as if it were in the hands of the company's counsel. Also, there is danger that the insured will settle for an amount that the company would have considered too high, and that the company will be bound by the settlement if it loses the suit on the policy.[18] The combined force of all these disadvantages often leads a company to continue in control of the defense of the tort claim, even at the expense of giving up the potential policy defense, unless there is a very strong probability that the policy defense will eventually be sustained in court.

Some of the shortcomings of declaratory proceedings in this context have been noted above, and there are others.[19] Among them is the fact that such proceedings take time, and it is likely that the company will be required to make an election to act in defense or decline to do so before declaratory proceedings can be brought to issue, unless it can preserve some freedom of action by a nonwaiver agreement with the insured or by a declaration of reservation of rights. An attempted reservation of rights [20] seems unlikely to be effective. Even if a court adopts the view, urged here, that the company should have some reasonable opportunity to present its policy defense, it does not follow that it should be able to remain in control of the defense under a so-called reservation of rights.

Occasionally an insurance company has preferred to seek the advantage of two chances by trying to win in the defense of the tort claim against the insured and, if unsuccessful in that attempt, then trying to win on the policy defense in the garnishment proceeding or the independent suit on the policy. That is a risky course, however, because of the settlement problem. Proof that the company offered less in settlement than would have been the case if it had not been relying in part upon the opportunity for a second chance under the policy defense may lead to a finding that the company was represent-

---

18. See § 7.6(e) *supra*.

19. See, *e.g.*, Central Sur. & Ins. Corp. v. Anderson, 445 S.W.2d 514 (Tex. 1969) (trial court declared insurer obligated to defend and to pay any judgment that might be rendered against insureds; held that insofar as judgment declared insurer would be obligated to pay any judgment rendered against insured it was an advisory opinion prohibited by the state constitution).

20. Concerning nonwaiver agreements and reservations of rights generally, see § 6.6(a) *supra*. Concerning the defense attorney's conflict of interest in relation to advising his clients to enter into a nonwaiver agreement, see § 7.7(b) n.4 *supra*.

ing conflicting interests without disclosure of the conflict; misleading the insured in this way may even vitiate a nonwaiver agreement.[21]

When there is no conflict of interest in defense itself but a policy coverage defense is in dispute, ordinarily an insurance company would prefer to have an immediate determination of the issue of coverage. Declaratory judgment proceedings have been much used for this purpose.

Moreover, trial of issues of fact by a jury is generally permissible in declaratory proceedings.[22] It is a sound proposition, however, that no declaratory judgment act should be distorted for use as an instrument of procedural fencing—to secure delay, to affect the choice of a forum, or to affect the question whether the issue will be tried by a jury.[23]

SECTION 7.8 THE LIABILITY INSURER'S DUTY TO INSUREDS REGARDING SETTLEMENT

§ 7.8(a) SOURCE AND THEORY OF THE DUTY

Liability insurance policies customarily provide that the company *shall* defend but "may make such investigation, negotiation and settlement of any claim or suit as it deems expedient." [1] As an original question such a clause might have been thought to give the company a privilege but not a duty regarding settlement of the tort claim against the insured.[2] But it is now clear that under such a clause the company has a duty to the insured in this matter.

The company's duty regarding settlement, according to the most common rationale, arises not from any particular contractual provision but rather from the relationship created by the liability insur-

---

21. *E.g.*, Home Indem. Co. v Williamson, 183 F.2d 572 (5th Cir. 1950).

22. See Uniform Declaratory Judgments Act § 9; Declaratory Judgment Act, 28 U.S.C. §§ 2201–2202 (1958); Annot., 142 A.L.R. 8, 58 (1943). The original federal act provided for the submission of issues of fact to a jury on interrogatories. Declaratory Judgment Act ch. 512, 48 Stat. 955 (1934). This provision was omitted in the revision of the code as being covered by Rule 49 of the Federal Rules of Civil Procedure. Reviser's Note to 28 U.S. C. § 2202.

23. *Cf.* Annot., 142 A.L.R. 8, 58 (1943). Also see Annot., 28 A.L.R.2d 957 (1953), suggesting that even though there is nothing in the Uniform Declaratory Judgments Act to exclude declaratory proceedings involving fact issues, yet the discretion of the court to deny declaratory relief has general-

ly been thought to exclude such relief in "ordinary negligence cases."

1. See Appendices G, H *infra*.

2. See, *e.g.*, Rumford Falls Paper Co. v. Fidelity & Cas. Co., 92 Me. 574, 43 A. 503 (1899); Schmidt v. Travelers Ins. Co., 244 Pa. 286, 90 A. 653 (1914). But in such cases it does not appear that the insured was urging liability on a theory of negligence or bad faith in failing to give consideration to the insured's interests. The contention expressly rejected was that the policy limit no longer applied after the company had declined a settlement offer within the limit. *Cf.* Wilson v. Aetna Cas. & Sur. Co., 145 Me. 370, 76 A.2d 111 (1950), which appears to interpret the *Rumford* opinion as consistent with the imposition of excess liability for either bad faith or negligence of the company in failing to settle.

ance contract as a whole. The principal aspect of the relationship that supports the duty is the company's power of control over settlements that affect not only its own interests but also the interests of the insured. If, for example, the policy limit per person is $10,000 and the claimant, having sued for $100,000 or more, offers to settle for $10,000, accepting the offer would ordinarily best serve the insured's interests because the settlement would foreclose the risk of a judgment against the insured in excess of his policy limits. On the other hand, apart from potential liability for noncompliance with a legal duty to settle, refusal to settle would ordinarily best serve the company's interests because the defense might be successful at trial and, even if the defense loses, the company's only added loss from unsuccessful litigation would be the cost of defense.

The company's duty regarding settlement is usually referred to as a duty sounding in tort rather than contract,[3] and there is some support for allowing the offended party to proceed on either theory.[4] There are a few situations, though only a few, in which the classification is critical. For example, characterizing the cause of action as one sounding in contract may result in the application of a longer period of limitation [5] and tends to favor assignability of the chose in action.[6] On the other hand, characterizing the cause of action as one sounding in tort may broaden the measure of damages.[7]

Both on principle and under such few precedents as there are, it appears that the duty extends not only to cases involving only one claim, which is potentially in excess of the per-person limit of coverage, but also to cases of multiple claims adding up to potential liability in excess of the per-accident limit of coverage.[8]

3. See, *e.g.*, Norwood v. Travelers Ins. Co., 204 Minn. 595, 284 N.W. 785 (1939), 131 A.L.R. 1496 (1941); Zumwalt v. Utilities Ins. Co., 360 Mo. 362, 228 S.W.2d 750 (1950); Hart v. Republic Mut. Ins. Co., 152 Ohio St. 185, 87 N.E.2d 347 (1949); Tennessee Farmers Mut. Ins. Co. v. Hammond, 200 Tenn. 106, 290 S.W.2d 860 (1956); Evans v. Continental Cas. Co., 40 Wash.2d 614, 245 P.2d 470 (1952). *But cf.* Hilker v. Western Auto. Ins. Co., 204 Wis. 1, 231 N.W. 257 (1930), 204 Wis. 12, 16, 235 N.W. 413, 415 (1931), referring to the obligations of the company as arising "by reasonable implication from the express terms of the contract." And see nn.4, 5, *infra.*

4. *E.g.*, Crisci v. Security Ins. Co., 66 Cal.2d 425, 426 P.2d 173, 58 Cal.Rptr. 13 (1967).

5. *E.g.*, Comunale v. Traders & Gen. Ins. Co., 50 Cal.2d 654, 328 P.2d 198 (1958), 68 A.L.R.2d 883 (1959) (cause of action sounds in both contract and tort; plaintiff may take advantage of the longer limitation period under contract theory).

6. *E.g.*, Gray v. Nationwide Mut. Ins. Co., 422 Pa. 500, 223 A.2d 8 (1966).

7. *E.g.*, Crisci v. Security Ins. Co., 66 Cal.2d 425, 426 P.2d 173, 58 Cal.Rptr. 13 (1967) (cause of action sounds in both contract and tort; plaintiff may recover damages for mental distress under tort theory, whether or not she could do so under contract theory in this setting).

8. See § 7.9(a) *infra.*

§ 7.8(b) THE STANDARD OF CONDUCT

The standard used in judging whether a liability insurance company has complied with its duty regarding settlement involves two major issues.

The first issue is whether the basis of liability is bad faith, or negligence, or some variant on one of these standards.[1] Some cases have held that only good faith toward the insured is required,[2] and at the opposite extreme some have held that both good faith and ordinary care are required.[3] In the middle ground fall numerous cases that do not make a clear-cut choice; many of these recognize at least a duty of good faith and either expressly or silently leave unresolved the question whether there is also a requirement of ordinary care.[4]

It seems likely that in most cases the final result would not depend on the court's choice between bad faith and negligence standards. The standards themselves are less different than they might seem since virtually the same evidence will be relied upon to prove breach of duty, and the general reaction of the jury to a particular case is likely to be the same under either standard. But some difference of practical consequence remains. For example, circumstances may arise in which it is unlikely that a jury will make the nominally harsh finding of bad faith, yet likely that they will find negligence. This might be true when the conduct on which the case against the company must be made is exclusively the conduct of a lawyer who is known and respected in the community; in such a case, a jury will ordinarily be more hesitant to find bad faith than to find negligence.

The special meaning ascribed to bad faith in this context, however, sharply limits the practical significance of the choice between bad faith and negligence standards. The bad faith referred to may exist even though the representatives of the company have been scrupulously honest in their handling of the claim. For example, in many jurisdictions bad faith can be established by proof that the defendant engaged in a course of conduct manifesting a deliberate preference for the company's interests over the insured's, even though the com-

---

1. Concerning suggestions of a stricter standard, see Crisci v. Security Ins. Co., 66 Cal.2d 425, 426 P.2d 173, 58 Cal.Rptr. 13 (1967).

2. *E.g.*, Kohlstedt v. Farm Bureau Mut. Ins. Co., 258 Iowa 337, 139 N.W.2d 184 (1965); Georgia Cas. Co. v. Mann, 242 Ky. 447, 46 S.W.2d 777 (1932); City of Wakefield v. Globe Indem. Co., 246 Mich. 645, 225 N.W. 643 (1929); Radio Taxi Serv., Inc. v. Lincoln Mut. Ins. Co., 31 N.J. 229, 157 A.2d 319 (1960) (4–2 decision); Best Bldg. Co. v. Employers' Liab. Assur. Corp., 247 N.Y. 451, 160 N.E. 911 (1928), 71 A.L.R. 1464 (1931); Aetna Cas. & Sur. Co. v. Price, 206 Va. 749, 146 S.E.2d 220 (1966);

Berk v. Milwaukee Auto. Ins. Co., 245 Wis. 597, 15 N.W.2d 834 (1944).

3. *E.g.*, Douglas v. United States Fid. & Gy. Co., 81 N.H. 371, 127 A. 708 (1924), 37 A.L.R. 1477 (1925); Dumas v. Hartford Acc. & Indem. Co., 94 N.H. 484, 56 A.2d 57 (1947); G. A. Stowers Furniture Co. v. American Indem. Co., 15 S.W.2d 544 (Tex.Comm'n App.1929). See also Gedeon v. State Farm Mut. Auto. Ins. Co., 410 Pa. 55, 188 A.2d 320 (1963).

4. Concerning varied rules falling in the middle ground, see Keeton, *Liability Insurance and Responsibility for Settlement*, 67 Harv.L.Rev. 1136, 1139–1148 (1954).

pany's representatives honestly believed that such a course of conduct was within their legal rights.[5]

The second major issue involved in setting the standard by which the company's conduct regarding settlement is tested concerns the relative degree of consideration the company must give to the insured's interests in comparison with its own, when they come into conflict. The prevailing view among courts that have squarely faced this issue is that the company must give the insured's interests at least equal weight. This formulation is somewhat confusing, since in deciding to settle or to decline settlement one interest may seem to be sacrificed. The concept of equality referred to is like the concept of equality of men before the courts. It refers to impartiality—in this instance, impartiality in the weighing of the two competing interests. The easiest way to conceive of the exercise of such impartiality is to conceive of the two competing interests as being held by a single person, who thus would have no inducement to sacrifice one over the other except on the basis of their relative merit. The rule is better expressed in another form. The following proposition, which can appropriately be used as an instruction to the jury, expresses the combination of the requirements of good faith and equal consideration:

With respect to the decision whether to settle or try the case, the insurance company must in good faith view the situation as it would if there were no policy limit applicable to the claim.[6]

The following proposition, likewise appropriate as a jury instruction, expresses the combination of the requirements of ordinary care and equal consideration:

With respect to the decision whether to settle or try the case, the insurer, acting through its representatives, must use such care as would have been used by an ordinarily prudent insurer with no policy limit applicable to the claim. The insurer is negligent in failing to settle if, but only if, such ordinarily prudent insurer would consider that choosing to try the case (rather than to settle on the terms by which the claim could be settled) would be taking an unreasonable risk—that is, trial would involve chances of unfavorable results out of reasonable proportion to the chances of favorable results.[7]

---

5. This point is illustrated in Tennessee Farmers Mut. Ins. Co. v. Hammond, 43 Tenn.App. 62, 306 S.W.2d 13 (1957) (trial judge, in passing on the motion for a new trial, remarked that it was clear that the attorney employed by the company to represent the insured in the tort claim had not been guilty of dishonesty; appellate court nevertheless affirmed a judgment for the insured on the theory that the conduct of the company's representatives, including the attorney, amounted to "bad faith" such as to support liability in excess of policy limits).

6. This standard is applied in *e.g.*, Herges v. Western Cas. & Sur. Co., 408 F.2d 1157 (8th Cir. 1969) (Minnesota law). For a more detailed statement of the arguments supporting this formulation, see Keeton, *Liability Insurance and Responsibility for Settlement*, 67 Harv.L.Rev. 1136, 1142–1148 (1954).

7. *Cf.* Dumas v. Hartford Acc. & Indem. Co., 94 N.H. 484, 56 A.2d 57 (1947). See also Keeton, *Liability Insurance and Responsibility for Settlement*, 67 Harv.L.Rev. 1136, 1147 (1954).

§ 7.8(c) SETTLEMENT DEMANDS AND OFFERS

Neither a demand by the insured that the company settle nor an offer by the claimant is a prerequisite of liability in excess of policy limits.[1] But without the claimant's offer and the insured's demand, the insured might sometimes find himself unable to prove an opportunity to settle and bad faith or negligent refusal to act upon it; in any case, the insured's problems of proof are greatly reduced if the claimant has made an offer of settlement and the insured has advised the insurer of his contention that the offer should be accepted.

Even though a settlement demand exceeds the policy limit, the duty to settle can nevertheless be invoked if the insured is willing to contribute the difference between the policy limit and the total settlement demand.[2] A company invites trouble, however, if it suggests such a contribution without making it clear that the company stands ready to contribute its entire policy limit. Such a proposal clearly supports the inference that the company is preferring its own interests over those of the insured by declining to offer its policy limit

---

1. For its bearing on both points, see Fidelity & Cas. Co. v. Robb, 267 F.2d 473 (5th Cir. 1959) (jury found for the insurer in relation to a theory that it acted unreasonably in declining claimant's settlement offer before trial, but against the insurer on a second theory that it acted unreasonably, after the tort case had developed unfavorably at trial, in failing to accept the original offer if it remained open or to initiate new discussions and bring about settlement if it did not remain open; though reversing because of error in the charge, the appellate court were "of the view that the district judge did not err in instructing the jury that they could consider whether the insurer was negligent either or both in rejecting the firm offer and in not thereafter undertaking to make a settlement"). See also Young v. American Cas. Co., 416 F.2d 906 (2d Cir. 1969), *cert. dism'd*, 396 U.S. 997 (1970) (New York law; trustees in bankruptcy of insured sued liability insurer for the amount of a judgment against insured in excess of policy limit of $20,000; insureds, operators of laundromat, held liable for $90,330.-25 on tort claim of plaintiff who slipped and fell on wet floor; insurer paid $20,000 limit and insureds paid $7,278.61 to tort plaintiffs before insureds were discharged in bankruptcy; bankruptcy proceeding remained open pending disposition of this case; evidence was offered that insurer failed to investigate properly before trial, failed to enter into settlement negotiations, did not inform insureds of the possibility of settlement, never asked if insureds were willing to contribute to a possible settlement, and made no counteroffer to a $40,000 settlement demand from claimant's counsel; evidence also supported the view that had counsel responded with a counteroffer "a settlement within the $20,000 limit of the policy might have been reached, or, that had the insureds been fully advised a settlement could have been made with some small contribution from them," though neither possibility was established by "proof"; doubt in speculating on these possibilities should be resolved in favor of insureds; insurer held liable for the full $70,330.25, about $63,000 of which is expected to pass through the bankrupts' estates to the claimant); Brockstein v. Nationwide Mut. Ins. Co., 417 F.2d 703 (2d Cir. 1969) (applies rule of *Young* to a case in which the insured's contribution would have been to a settlement for a total sum within policy limits, whereas *Young* itself might be interpreted as concerning a potential settlement of which the insurer would have paid all of the settlement figure within the policy limit, even though the insureds might have been required to contribute also).

2. See, *e.g.*, Boling v. New Amsterdam Cas. Co., 173 Okla. 160, 46 P.2d 916 (1935). *Cf.* Peerless Ins. Co. v. Inland Mut. Ins. Co., 251 F.2d 696 (4th Cir. 1958).

though the settlement proposal in excess of the policy limit is a reasonable one.[3]

It may be a useful step toward self-protection for a company to offer to settle for the maximum sum within its policy limits. But this does not discharge the company's duties of defense [4] and perhaps does not fully discharge its duties regarding settlement. It may well be that it is required to use its expert capabilities for negotiation on behalf of the insured, as well as offering its policy limit when it would be acting in bad faith or unreasonably not to offer that much. Certainly an offer of the full policy limit would not alone serve to defeat a claim in excess of policy limits based on an earlier refusal to settle for the same or an even smaller sum.[5]

§ 7.8(d) MULTIPLE INSURERS AND CLAIMANTS

The duty regarding settlement applies, though its application is considerably more complex, in situations involving several insurance companies (because of reinsurance or other insurance), several claimants, or both.

A company cannot, by obtaining reinsurance, escape its duty to its insured.[1]

Has a reinsurer a duty, to either the primary insured or the primary insurer, regarding the decision whether to settle? It may be argued that a duty to the primary insurer arises from the relationship between it and the reinsurer. But the answer to the question whether that relationship is analogous to the one on which the primary insurer's duty to its insured is based depends on the terms of the reinsurance contract. If the primary insurer is in control of the *decision* concerning settlement, its remedy is to settle and compel reimbursement by the reinsurer under their contract, rather than yielding to a demand by the reinsurer not to settle. On the other hand, if the reinsurance contract places the reinsurer in control of the settlement decision, the analogy is close. Perhaps it is unlikely that such an issue will be presented to the courts often, however, since it can be avoided by contract stipulations, or may be dealt with by negotiation or arbitration even after it arises.

3. See, *e.g.*, American Mut. Liab. Ins. Co. v. Cooper, 61 F.2d 446 (5th Cir. 1932), *cert. denied*, 289 U.S. 736 (1933); Maryland Cas. Co. v. Cook-O'Brien Construction Co., 69 F.2d 462 (8th Cir.), *cert. denied*, 293 U.S. 569 (1934); Boling v. New Amsterdam Cas. Co., 173 Okla. 160, 46 P.2d 916 (1935); Johnson v. Hardware Mut. Cas. Co., 108 Vt. 269, 187 A. 788 (1936). See also Keeton, *Liability Insurance and Responsibility for Settlement*, 67 Harv. L.Rev. 1136, 1149 (1954).

4. See § 7.6 *supra*.

5. *E.g.*, Vanderbilt Univ. v. Hartford Acc. & Indem. Co., 109 F.Supp. 565 (M.D.Tenn.1952), *aff'd*, 218 F.2d 818 (6th Cir. 1954); *cf.* Southern Fire & Cas. Co. v. Norris, 35 Tenn.App. 657, 250 S.W.2d 785 (1952).

1. *E.g.*, Zumwalt v. Utilities Ins. Co., 360 Mo. 362, 228 S.W.2d 750 (1950). *Cf.* Royal Transit, Inc. v. Central Sur. & Ins. Corp., 168 F.2d 345 (7th Cir.), *cert. denied*, 335 U.S. 844 (1948) (Wisconsin law).

Whether the reinsurer has a duty to the primary insured also depends on whether in the total relationship it has control in some degree over the decision concerning settlement. If not, the basis for the duty is lacking; if so, it exists. This issue, too, is unlikely to be presented for decision often since the insured has a more clear-cut case against the primary insurer, which could not escape its duty to the insured even by surrendering control over the settlement decision to the reinsurer as between itself and the reinsurer. Thus, the insured would not be likely to press a claim against a reinsurer unless the primary insurer was insolvent. If the primary insurer, having paid a claim in excess of its limits, sought reimbursement from the reinsurer, it would be necessary to look to the terms of the reinsurance contract and relationship to determine whether such reimbursement is due.[2]

With respect to other insurance, whether proratable or excess coverage, it would seem that each insurer has a duty to each person who is its insured with respect to the claim in question.

In the case of proratable coverage, it would seem that each insurer should have a duty to the other insurer.[3] In the case of excess coverage, the primary insurer should be held responsible to the excess insurer for improper failure to settle, since the position of the latter is analogous to that of the insured when only one insurer is involved.[4] The right of the excess carrier might be supported either on the theory that it is subrogated to the right of the insured against the primary carrier[5] or on the theory that the relationship between primary and excess carriers gives rise to an independent duty of the former to the latter.[6]

The analogy to a case of involving a single insurer and single claimant holds also for a case involving multiple claimants as well as multiple insurers. For example, a case might involve one policy providing $10,000 of primary coverage, a second providing $10,000 of excess coverage, and total claims of three claimants that could be settled within the limits of the policies. These added factual complexities increase the difficulties of proof that misconduct of one or both insurers blocked a potential settlement within policy limits, but they do not negate the underlying basis for duties regarding settlement.

Situations involving multiple claimants and limited coverage present problems of preferential settlement also.[7]

2. See Peerless Ins. Co. v. Inland Mut. Ins. Co., 251 F.2d 696 (4th Cir. 1958).

3. See Keeton, *Liability Insurance and Responsibility for Settlement*, 67 Harv.L.Rev. 1136, 1152–1153 (1954).

4. See, *e.g.*, Hawkeye-Security Ins. Co. v. Indemnity Ins. Co., 260 F.2d 361 (10th Cir. 1958), 69 A.L.R.2d 684 (1960); American Fid. & Cas. Co. v. All American Bus Lines, Inc., 190 F.2d 234 (10th Cir.), *cert. denied*, 342 U.S. 851 (1951) (Oklahoma law). See also St. Paul-Mercury Indem. Co. v. Martin, 190 F.2d 455, 457 (10th Cir. 1951) (Oklahoma law).

5. American Fid. & Cas. Co. v. All American Bus Lines, Inc., 190 F.2d 234 (10th Cir.), *cert. denied*, 342 U.S. 851 (1951) (Oklahoma law).

6. See, *e.g.*, St. Paul-Mercury Indem. Co. v. Martin, 190 F.2d 455, 457 (10th Cir. 1951) (Oklahoma law).

7. See § 7.9 *infra*.

§ 7.8(e) AVOIDABLE CONSEQUENCES AND RENUNCIATION OF CONTROL OVER SETTLEMENT

It has sometimes been suggested that a company sued for liability in excess of its limit might urge in defense that the insured's excess liability claim is barred under the doctrine of avoidable consequences, often expressed as a duty to mitigate damages. That is, he is barred if he could have settled at a figure within policy limits but unreasonably failed to do so.[1] A grave doctrinal difficulty with this notion is that it rests on an assumption of transfer of control over the settlement decision from the company to the insured. It would be indefensible for a court to invoke such a doctrine against the insured unless it would also hold the company bound by a reasonable settlement made by him after the company's wrongful refusal to settle; that is, the insured would be able to recover from the company the amount he paid in settlement. It seems most improbable that this theory will be accepted upon mature consideration.[2] Cases involving breach of the duty to defend rather than merely the duty to settle are to be distinguished.[3]

Nor is it likely that the company can escape its duty regarding settlement by complete withdrawal from handling the case. After so doing, it is true, it may argue not only an avoidable consequences theory but also a theory that it renounced control over the settlement decision—the control that serves as the foundation for judicial recognition of the duty regarding settlement. And some precedents seem to support nonliability in excess of policy limits in this setting, even though the refusal to defend was wrongful.[4] But there is stronger support for the view that since the attempted renunciation of control is itself wrongful, it will not be permitted to insulate the company from excess liability.[5]

§ 7.8(f) REMEDIES FOR BREACH

What are the available remedies for breach of the company's duty to the insured regarding settlement, and to whom are they available?

One problem concerns the measure of damages. Do the damages recoverable in an action for improper failure to settle include com-

---

1. See, *e.g.*, Southern Fire & Cas. Co. v. Norris, 35 Tenn.App. 657, 250 S.W.2d 785 (1952).

2. See Keeton, *Liability Insurance and Responsibility for Settlement*, 67 Harv.L.Rev. 1136, 1153–1167 (1954).

3. See *id.* at 1155–1167. See also § 7.6 (e) *supra*.

4. *E.g.*, Fidelity & Cas. Co. v. Gault, 196 F.2d 329 (5th Cir. 1952) (Mississippi law). See generally Keeton, *Liability Insurance and Responsibility for Settlement*. 67 Harv.L.Rev. 1136, 1159–1161 (1954).

5. *E.g.*, Gedeon v. State Farm Mut. Auto. Ins. Co., 342 F.2d 15 (3d Cir. 1965) (Pennsylvania law); Comunale v. Traders & Gen. Ins. Co., 50 Cal.2d 654, 328 P.2d 198 (1958), 68 A.L.R.2d 883 (1959); Jenkins v. General Acc. Fire & Life Assur. Corp., 349 Mass. 699, 212 N.E.2d 464 (1965).

pensation for mental illness suffered by the insured as a result of the insurer's wrong? There is limited support for an affirmative answer.[1]

Controversy over remedies for breach of the company's duty regarding settlement have more often centered on various theories by which the proceeds of a cause of action against the insurer might become available to compensate the injured person. Courts have been sharply divided on this set of problems and issues subsidiary to it.[2]

One view is that the insured's cause of action against the insurer for liability in excess of policy limits (usually treated as a cause of action in tort) [3] does not accrue until the insured pays something on the judgment,[4] "or at least until his financial status is such that the excess judgment is sure to be collected." [5]

This view leads to the conclusion that, when the insured has no assets available for collection of the judgment by legal process and there is no evidence he has paid or will pay in some other way, the insurer is not liable in excess of policy limits because its failure to settle has not caused damage to the insured.[6] The case of the insolvent insured is the context most favorable to this view that the cause of action depends on payment or proof (measuring up to a standard of reasonable probability) that payment will occur in the future, even if nothing is recovered on the excess liability claim.[7] Arguments that the insured has been damaged by the increase in his debts [8] are rath-

---

1. *E.g.*, Crisci v. Security Ins. Co., 66 Cal.2d 425, 426 P.2d 173, 58 Cal.Rptr. 13 (1967) (insured, a 70-year-old widow, became indigent as a result of personal injury judgment of $101,000 against her in action brought by her tenant, which could have been settled within $10,000 liability insurance limit; $25,000 recovery for mental suffering allowed).

2. In addition to precedents discussed in this section, see those dealing with the closely analogous problem concerning remedies for breach of the duty to defend, § 7.6(e) *supra*.

3. See § 7.8(a) *supra*.

4. *E.g.*, Universal Auto. Ins. Co. v. Culberson, 126 Tex. 282, 86 S.W.2d 727, 87 S.W.2d 475 (1935); State Auto. Mut. Ins. Co. v. York, 104 F.2d 730 (4th Cir.), *cert. denied*, 308 U.S. 591 (1939) (North Carolina law; alternate ground for decision).

5. Dumas v. Hartford Acc. & Indem. Co., 92 N.H. 140, 141, 26 A.2d 361, 362 (1942). See also Norwood v. Travelers Ins. Co., 204 Minn. 595, 284 N.W. 785 (1939), 131 A.L.R. 1496 (1941) indicating that there is no "resulting injury" to the insured if he is judgment-proof;

the opinion is not concerned with whether payment—not merely certainty of payment in the future—would be required.

6. *E.g.*, Harris v. Standard Acc. & Ins. Co., 297 F.2d 627 (2d Cir. 1961), *cert. denied*, 369 U.S. 843 (1962) (insured insolvent before rendition of the excess judgment, paid no part of it, and was discharged in bankruptcy).

7. Dumas v. Hartford Acc. & Indem. Co., 92 N.H. 140, 26 A.2d 361 (1942), speaks of a showing that "the excess judgment is sure to be collected." But it would seem that the jury would be told to resolve this fact issue as they are told generally to resolve issues about future events—by a standard of proof that falls short of certainty and is often phrased as reasonable probability.

8. See Schwartz v. Norwich Union Indem. Co., 212 Wis. 593, 250 N.W. 446 (1933) (cause of action "in tort for fraudulent and negligent handling of the defense" rather than for failure to settle; analogy to expenses incurred, but unpaid, by reason of an injury); Southern Fire & Cas. Co. v. Norris, 35 Tenn.App. 657, 250 S.W.2d 785 (1952). The Tennessee court noted the New

er weak support for any cause of action at all, much less for a measure of damages equal to the amount of the increase in his debts, when it seems almost certain he will never pay anything at all on the excess judgment if his claim against the insurer is denied. The claimant, moreover, is in no position to assert that he was harmed. In the first place, the insurer's duty was to the insured, not the claimant,[9] and in the second place the claimant has benefited from the insurer's refusal to settle because he has obtained a judgment far in excess of the amount he had offered to accept in settlement. Also, it would seem that public interest would disfavor allowing the claimant a cause of action in his own right. He deserves further compensation, but no more so than the victims of insolvent and underinsured tortfeasors whose liability insurers had not refused a settlement offer within policy limits. The practical effect of allowing him a cause of action is to introduce a fortuitous and occasional protection beyond policy limits.[10] If a public policy in favor of higher insurance coverage is to be invoked for the protection of victims it ought to be formulated in a more regular and evenhanded way.[11]

A case involving a thoroughly solvent insured poses no substantial difficulty. If to support the cause of action for excess liability it is necessary to prove that payment has been made or will be made in the future (even if there is no recovery on the excess liability claim), the requirement can be met without the insured's suffering anything worse than temporary inconvenience. But the view requiring such proof runs into very substantial difficulties in relation to the case of the insured who falls in the great middle ground—one who is neither thoroughly insolvent nor thoroughly solvent.[12]

Surely when such a person has assets taken from him by legal process for part payment of the excess judgment against him, or when he makes part payment voluntarily to avoid such legal process,

Hampshire and Fourth Circuit decisions, nn.4, 5 *supra*, opposed to its conclusions, stated that the "courts of Wisconsin and Texas are aligned with the contrary view," and concluded that the "latter cases, it seems to us, are supported by the sounder reasoning." 35 Tenn.App. at 671–672, 250 S. W.2d at 791. It misconstrued the Texas rule, however. See Universal Auto. Ins. Co. v. Culberson, 126 Tex. 282, 289, 86 S.W.2d 727, 731 (1935): "As to his alleged cause of action [for excess liability] . . . Culberson cannot assert same until he has paid some sum on the judgment in excess of the $5,000.00 limit in the policy; and then only to the extent of his payment."

9. The duty involved in these cases is to be distinguished from the duty regarding preferential settlement. That duty, if recognized at all, is surely a duty to claimants, though it may ex-

tend to the insured also. See § 7.9 *infra*.

10. For example, compare the following two cases: Case 1—obvious liability; severe injury; settlement value, apart from financial responsibility, $50,000; policy limit, $10,000; insured's net non-exempt assets, $15,000; the company offers $10,000, which the claimant refuses; the claimant does not get the benefit of the excess-liability rule. Case 2—doubtful liability; other factors the same as case 1; the claimant's offer to settle for $10,000 is refused by the insurer; the claimant gets the benefit of the excess-liability rule.

11. See generally Keeton, *Liability Insurance and Responsibility for Settlement*, 67 Harv.L.Rev. 1136, 1175–1177 (1954).

12. See *id.* at 1179–1182.

he should be allowed to recover that much from the insurer. But what is to keep the claimant (the judgment creditor) from attaching whatever the insured recovers from the insurer? If the answer is nothing, then the ratchet process may continue until the insurer has finally paid the full excess, the claimant has collected all of it, and the insured has served as a conduit for payment of far more in so-called damages than any realistic measure of the harm he suffered. This result is basically inconsistent with the idea that the remedy should be limited to the damage suffered by the person wronged—the insured. It imposes a penalty on the insurer and grants a windfall to the claimant in fortuitously added insurance protection. Neverthe-less, if one must choose between this result and inadequate protection for the insured, he is likely to choose this result as the lesser of two evils.[13] Perhaps this factor has been the principal force toward al-lowing recovery to the full extent of the excess judgment without proof of payment or future payment (probable or certain, as may be required) by the insured. In any event, it appears that a majority of the decisions in point have reached this result.[14] And probably other opinions, upholding the insured's assignment of his cause of action to the tort claimant, are reasonably interpreted as implying that there may be recovery to the full extent of the excess judgment without proof of payment, past or future.[15]

The possibility remains, however, of an intermediate solution that avoids the dilemma of choice between two rules neither of which seems desirable. Perhaps one reason no such solution has been devel-oped is that opposing advocates have generally chosen to advance the more extreme positions rather than an intermediate measure of dam-ages. On the one hand, counsel for the claimant have willingly as-sumed the burden of pressing the insured's cause of action, either in his name or in the name of the claimant as assignee or successor to the insured's right,[16] and naturally have sought to establish liability to the full extent of the excess judgment, regardless of the insured's financial status. On the other hand, counsel for insurers have gener-ally attempted to establish that proof of the amount paid or of the

13. See Note, 72 Harv.L.Rev. 568, 569–573 (1959).

14. *E.g.*, Comunale v. Traders & Gen. Ins. Co., 50 Cal.2d 654, 328 P.2d 198 (1958), 68 A.L.R.2d 883 (1959); Swee-ten v. National Mut. Ins. Co., 233 Md. 52, 194 A.2d 817 (1963); Ammerman v. Farmers Ins. Exch., 22 Utah 2d 187, 450 P.2d 460 (1969) (payment on judgment not essential to cause of ac-tion; new trial granted).

15. See, *e.g.*, Nationwide Mut. Ins. Co. v. McNulty, 229 So.2d 585 (Fla.1970), citing with approval Gray v. Nation-wide Mut. Ins. Co., 422 Pa. 500, 223 A.2d 8 (1966), in which the court ex-plicitly allowed recovery of the full

amount of the excess judgment in an action on an assigned claim.

16. Most decisions in point have sup-ported assignability of the insured's cause of action against the company for breach of its duty regarding set-tlement: Liberty Mut. Ins. Co. v. Davis, 412 F.2d 475 (5th Cir. 1969) (Florida law); Critz v. Farmers Ins. Group, 230 Cal.App.2d 788, 41 Cal. Rptr. 401 (3d Dist. 1964), 12 A.L.R.3d 1142 (1967) (holding valid an assign-ment executed even before trial of the tort claim against the insured); Gray v. Nationwide Mut. Ins. Co., 422 Pa. 500, 223 A.2d 8 (1966). *Contra, e.g.*, Dillingham v. Tri-State Ins. Co., 214 Tenn. 592, 381 S.W.2d 914 (1964).

certainty, or at least reasonable probability, of an amount of future payment is essential to the cause of action.

Is it possible to formulate a workable doctrine that fully protects the insured from loss and yet does not in fact result in either a penalty to the insurer or a windfall to the claimant? Perhaps so. The aim should be to make the insured whole (placing him in the same position he would have been in had there been no breach by failure to settle) at minimum cost and without reducing the amount the claimant could have realized upon his rights against the insured if there had been no cause of action for liability in excess of policy limits.

This might be done by permitting a single recovery against the insurer on the excess liability claim, at the instance of either the insured or the claimant, in an amount equal to the insured's net assets not exempt from legal process,[17] and holding that the claimant's tort judgment against the insured is fully discharged by payment of this sum to the claimant either by the insured or by the insurer on the insured's behalf. Probably this is a bit more than the net amount the claimant would have realized, apart from the excess liability claim, whether or not the insured went through bankruptcy proceedings. Also, it fully protects the insured's financial position from the consequences of the insurer's wrong to him in failing to settle. The financial interests of both the insured and the claimant are better served by this solution than by leaving them to other legal processes, including bankruptcy, the costs of which would have an adverse impact on the interests of each. Perhaps this proposal is not within the scope of avoidable consequences rules as thus far developed, since they have been concerned with mitigating damages in a different sense. But the underlying principle of an avoidable consequences rule is that even though a person can show that in fact his losses have been greater, his legal relief is limited to what he would have been entitled to receive if he had acted reasonably to minimize harm. Even though the claimant's tort claim has already been reduced to judgment, the underlying spirit of exemption and bankruptcy laws expresses a public policy of reasonable limitation of the hardship he is permitted to impose by strict enforcement of his judgment. In the present context, it happens that the availability of a cause of action against the insurer in excess of its policy limits offers a distinctive opportunity, not generally existing in other settings, for accomplishing at least as much as could be accomplished for the claimant through enforcement of his judgment as far as the exemption and bankruptcy laws would permit, but without incurring the costs of bankruptcy to himself and to the insured. It seems consistent with the principles underlying both the avoidable consequences doctrine and the exemption and bankruptcy laws to adopt this intermediate measure of damages in excess liability claims. No doubt the application of this measure of

---

17. The present discussion refers only to the damages for economic loss. Concerning possible recovery for mental distress as well, see § 7.8(a) n.7 *supra*.

damages will present problems of proof not heretofore faced, but they would seem to be manageable. At the least, the insurer should have the right to offer satisfactory evidence on these issues if it can, shouldering the burden as one customarily does in advancing an avoidable consequences defense.

It may be objected that the insured suffers a loss of privacy because of the necessity of disclosing his financial situation fully. This is, however, a consequence to which he has contributed by committing a tort against the claimant that has caused damages of such severity that the limited liability insurance coverage he had chosen to carry was inadequate. The only realistic alternative to an intermediate solution such as this is to set the measure of damages in these cases at the full amount of the judgment—a solution that would disadvantage the insured and others like him by increasing the costs of low-limit liability insurance. A bit of loss of privacy in this context is a burden it seems reasonable for the insured to bear.

§ 7.8(g) LIMITATION OF ACTIONS

Courts have generally agreed that the limitation period applying to a cause of action for liability in excess of policy limits does not begin to run at the time of the company's wrongful failure to settle.[1] Because of a dearth of cases in which it would have made a difference, it is uncertain whether the limitation period begins to run at the time the tort judgment against the insured became final or instead at the time of some payment by the insured. Even if the time of payment is chosen as the standard, it seems unlikely that a payment other than to the claimant (for example, payment of a fee to an investigator or to an attorney employed by the insured to protect his interests after the company wrongfully refused to settle) would be held to start the running of the limitation period.

The choice of contract or tort theory as the explanation of the excess-liability claim may affect the limitation period. There is scant authority on this problem, and it includes support for the proposition that the action "sounds both in contract and tort" and the plaintiff may rely upon the contract theory to avoid a shorter statute of limitations applying to tort actions.[2]

1. *E.g.*, Attleboro Mfg. Co. v. Frankfort Marine, Acc. & Plate Glass Ins. Co., 240 F. 573 (1st Cir. 1917); American Mut. Liab. Ins. Co. v. Cooper, 61 F.2d 446 (5th Cir. 1932), *cert. denied*, 289 U.S. 736 (1933); Comunale v. Traders & Gen. Ins. Co., 50 Cal.2d 654, 328 P.2d 198 (1958), 68 A.L.R.2d 883 (1959); Linkenhoger v. American Fid. & Cas. Co., 152 Tex. 534, 260 S.W.2d 884 (1953). *But cf.* American Fid. & Cas. Co. v. All American Bus Lines, Inc., 190 F.2d 234 (10th Cir.), *cert.*

denied, 342 U.S. 851 (1951) (Oklahoma law) (assumption, perhaps only *arguendo*, that the cause of action was one for breach of contract and that the limitation period began to run when the wrongful rejection of a settlement offer occurred; however, the defense of limitation was rejected).

2. *E.g.*, Comunale v. Traders & Gen. Ins. Co., 50 Cal.2d 654, 328 P.2d 198 (1958), 68 A.L.R.2d 883 (1959).

§ 7.8(h) PROPOSALS FOR LEGISLATION OR REVISION OF POLICY FORMS

Legislative solutions of the excess-liability dilemma have been proposed. Most of them have been variations on the idea of an automatic increase or elimination of the limit of liability upon an insurer's refusal of an offer of settlement within the policy limit.[1] One important question on which relevant information is not available to the public is the difference in premium costs such a change would produce. One's judgment on this question might also be influenced by data on the costs of litigation over claims that the insurer's failure to settle amounted to bad faith or negligence. In the absence of such data, estimates of the relative costs of litigating these questions rather than applying an automatic increase or elimination of the limit upon refusal of the insurer to settle within the policy limit must be speculative at best.

SECTION 7.9 MULTIPLE CLAIMS UNDER A PER-ACCIDENT LIMIT OF COVERAGE; PREFERENTIAL SETTLEMENT

§ 7.9(a) CONFLICTING INTERESTS IN MULTIPLE-CLAIM CASES

Suppose a negligently driven car, the operation of which is covered by liability insurance having a per-accident coverage limit of $20,000, collides with a carefully driven car occupied by the driver and five passengers, all of whom are injured. Even if the negligent driver has some resources apart from the liability insurance, and the more so if he is otherwise financially irresponsible, the six victims have sharply conflicting interests in the liability insurance. For example, if the company is permitted to exhaust its per-accident limit by settling with two of the six victims, their interests are preferred over the interests of the other four.

The insured also has an interest that might be adversely affected by such settlements. His interest is best served by use of the limited coverage in such way as to minimize his risk of liability in excess of policy limits.

Apart from such duties as it may have to respect the various interests of the insured and the claimants, the insurance company might wish to use the $20,000 within the per-accident limit to settle such claims as would be likely to minimize its total payout, including all payments on judgments or by settlements and in defense costs as well.

Out of such conflicts of interest as these a number of distinctive problems arise.

1. See Keeton, *Liability Insurance and Responsibility for Settlement*, 67 Harv.L.Rev. 1136, 1183–1186 (1954).

§ 7.9(b) THE COMPANY'S DUTY TO THE INSURED

It is clear that a liability insurance company must give some weight to the distinctive interests of its insured as it decides its own course of conduct in multiple-claim cases. The duty to the insured regarding steps that might effect settlement of an individual claim within the per-person limit of coverage [2] extends to this multiple-claim situation as well,[3] though its application is affected by additional considerations. For example, even apart from the possibility that the company must also give reasonable weight to the interests of the claimants against preferential settlements with some among the entire group, it might best serve the insured's interest for the company to reject one offer of settlement, otherwise reasonable, in order to use the $20,000 within the per-accident limit for settlement of other claims that would expose the insured to greater risks of liability in excess of policy limits.

§ 7.9(c) PROTECTING CLAIMANTS AGAINST PREFERENTIAL SETTLEMENT

The question whether the company is free to disregard a claimant's interest against preferential settlement is debatable.

It has often happened that when a company has satisfied judgments or made settlements with one or more claimants, its liability to remaining claimants has been limited to the difference, if any, between its per-accident limit of coverage and the total already paid out in settlements.[1] This is plainly unfair because of the inequitable dis-

---

2. See § 7.8 *supra.*

3. *E.g.*, Liberty Mut. Ins. Co. v. Davis, 412 F.2d 475 (5th Cir. 1969) (Florida law; assignee of insured recovered on claim of bad faith refusal to settle arising from insurer's efforts to achieve a prorated, comprehensive settlement more for its own protection than for insured's); American Cas. Co. v. Glorfield, 216 F.2d 250 (9th Cir. 1954) (Washington law); Roberts v. American Fire & Cas. Co., 89 F.Supp. 827 (M.D.Tenn.1950), *aff'd per curiam,* 186 F.2d 921 (6th Cir. 1951) (Tennessee law). See generally Keeton, *Preferential Settlement of Liability Insurance Claims,* 70 Harv.L.Rev. 27, 28–36 (1956).

1. *E.g.*, Bartlett v. Travelers Ins. Co., 117 Conn. 147, 167 A. 180 (1933), 43 Yale L.J. 136; Williams' Adm'x v. Lloyds of London, 280 S.W.2d 527 (Ky.1955); Richard v. Southern Farm Bureau Cas. Ins. Co., 254 La. 429, 223 So.2d 858 (1969); Duprey v. Security Mut. Cas. Co., 22 App.Div.2d 544, 256

N.Y.S.2d 987 (3d Dep't 1965); Stolove v. Fidelity & Cas. Co., 157 Misc. 106, 282 N.Y.S. 263 (Sup.Ct.1935); Alford v. Textile Ins. Co., 248 N.C. 224, 103 S.E.2d 8 (1958), 70 A.L.R.2d 408 (1960). *Cf.* Lumbermens' Mut. Cas. Co. v. Yeroyan, 90 N.H. 145, 5 A.2d 726 (1939). *But cf.* Darrah v. Lion Bonding & Sur. Co., 200 S.W. 1101 (Tex.Civ.App.1918, no writ history). The court in *Darrah* indicated that in the absence of laches the claimant would have a right to participate in the insurance fund, enforceable in an action against the bonding company for the claimant's prorata share though the company had paid out the full amount of the bond in satisfaction of the judgments of other claimants. The bond, however, unlike the typical liability insurance policy provided that "suit may be brought and recovery had hereon by any person damaged, in his own name, against the principal and sureties hereon and hereof in the same action." Thus the claimant's interest in the insurance fund was more immediate than under a policy con-

tribution of the limited assets out of which the injured person could hope to recover compensation. The pattern is little, if any, less defensible in view of the special treatment sometimes accorded to claims that have been reduced to judgment. Some opinions have seemed to imply that even among such judgment creditors proration would be rejected in favor of the more rustic rule, "first come, first served." [2] The first-come-first-served rule is arguably supported by analogy to successive attachments or executions; in that context the prize ordinarily goes to the swift. But when a liability insurance company has tendered a sum into court in interpleader proceedings, proration has been ordered.[3] And proration in this context is supported by the analogy to surety-bond cases that apply it.[4] The right of proration among judgment creditors has been given explicit recognition in a New York statute.[5] However, the statute is subject to criticism because, as construed, it applies only when the insured is insolvent,[6] and because it applies only to injuries caused by certain

taining a typical "no action" clause. Under such a clause, the claimant's interest is customarily said to be "inchoate" before judgment against the insured on the tort claim.

See Le Van, *Distribution of a Limited Insurance Fund to Multiple Claimants*, 22 La.L.Rev. 214 (1961); Keeton, *Preferential Settlement of Liability Insurance Claims*, 70 Harv.L.Rev. 27, 37 (1956); Fisher, *Multiple Claims Under the Automobile Liability Policy*, 19 Ins.Counsel J. 419 (1952); Notes, 49 Harv.L.Rev. 658 (1936), 11 N.Y.U.L.Q.Rev. 447 (1934), 43 Yale L. J. 136 (1933).

2. *E.g.*, see Bruyette v. Sandini, 291 Mass. 373, 379, 197 N.E. 29, 32 (1935); Turk v. Goldberg, 91 N.J.Eq. 283, 287, 109 A. 732, 733 (Ch.1920); Pisciotta v. Preston, 170 Misc. 376, 377, 10 N.Y.S. 2d 44, 45 (Sup.Ct.1938); O'Donnell v. New Amsterdam Cas. Co., 50 R.I. 275, 276, 146 A. 770, 771 (1929).

3. *E.g.*, Century Indem. Co. v. Kofsky, 115 Conn. 193, 161 A. 101 (1932); Underwriters for Lloyds v. Jones, 261 S. W.2d 686 (Ky.1953). *Cf.* Fallon v. Pekarsky, 77 N.J.Super. 315, 186 A.2d 319 (1962) (money deposited with state by uninsured motorist held to be subject to pro rata distribution).

4. *E.g.*, Guffanti v. National Sur. Co., 196 N.Y. 452, 90 N.E. 174 (1909).

5. N.Y. Veh. & Traf. Law § 370 (McKinney 1970), applying only to bonds or policies required to be filed by certain vehicles carrying passengers for hire.

6. See Bleimeyer v. Public Serv. Mut. Cas. Ins. Corp., 250 N.Y. 264, 269, 165 N.E. 286, 288–289 (1929), distinguishing Long Island Coach Co. v. Hartford Acc. & Indem. Co., 233 App. Div. 331, 227 N.Y.S. 633 (1st Dep't), *aff'd mem.*, 248 N.Y. 629, 162 N.E. 552 (1928), as an action involving a solvent holder of a policy who had paid a claim for damages against himself and was seeking reimbursement. The latter case produced an astonishing result. The tortfeasor sued the insurance company to recover $600 the tortfeasor had paid on judgments obtained by claimants. The insurance company had settled with other claimants on 22 claims arising from one accident for a total of $3,298.50. In this suit it contended that under the statute the maximum due under its policy was to be apportioned ratably among judgment creditors, and that no liability could be enforced against it until all claims were reduced to judgment or were barred. The majority of a divided court awarded the insured a judgment for the $600, stating that the provision for ratable distribution of the insurance proceeds applied only in case of the insolvency of the insured. Thereafter another person injured in the same accident, and her husband, brought a proceeding on behalf of themselves and other judgment creditors of the insured tortfeasor, showing that the tortfeasor was insolvent and claiming the insurance proceeds. By the time this case was decided, the insurance company had paid out $3,383.50 in settlements and $618 to the insured under the judgment in the *Long Island* case. The court held that

vehicles carrying passengers for hire, by reason of which limited scope it is arguable that it may have done more to hinder than to promote general recognition of the principle of equitable proration.[7] Also, the statute fails to specify procedures for allocation, but one may defend this aspect of the statute on the ground that it is well to leave such matters of detail to courts.[8]

Recognition of a right of proration of limited insurance proceeds among judgment creditors serves well the aim of equitable distribution within this group. But the contribution to equity in this respect is matched and perhaps even outweighed by the negation of equity to other claimants that is implicit in applying the right of proration among judgment creditors only. That is, the victims whose tort claims have not been reduced to judgment are thus denied protection against an apportionment of the limited coverage that favors judgment creditors over other claimants. Thus the claimant who is lucky enough to get a quick trial and judgment collects his claim in full or with only such reduction as is necessary to give the same right to others who also have judgments at the time of the proceeding, whereas other claimants whose trials are delayed (often for reasons beyond their control) find that all the insurance coverage has been exhausted by the time their judgments can be obtained. The inequity seems too plain for dispute. This is, of course, a ground for criticism of both the New York statute and judicially developed rules of apportionment among judgment creditors.

It is argued that the risk of inequitable application of limited insurance coverage is an evil that must be accepted because measures taken to remedy it would interfere with the settlement process by which the vast majority of liability insurance claims are resolved.[9] But it is submitted that this counsel of pessimism is unwarranted.[10]

the insurance company was not entitled to credit against the policy limit for the amounts it had paid in settlements, and even more surprisingly held that the insurance company was entitled to credit for the $618 payment under judgment only to the extent that the two claimants' judgments it represented would participate ratably with other judgment creditors if the total judgments were in excess of the policy limit. Frank v. Hartford Acc. & Indem. Co., 136 Misc. 186, 239 N.Y.S. 397 (Sup.Ct.), aff'd mem., 231 App.Div. 707, 245 N.Y.S. 777 (1st Dep't 1930). The net consequence of this set of rules is both to deprive the insurance company of a fair opportunity for enforcement of its policy limit and to deter the insurer from settling.

7. For example, whether rightly so or not, it has in fact somewhat fortified arguments against rights of proration in cases involving types of vehicles to which it does not apply, the argument

being that the legislature deliberately refused to make proration applicable generally and that its action disabled the courts from taking the corrective action they might otherwise have taken. David v. Bauman, 24 Misc.2d 67, 196 N.Y.S.2d 746 (Sup.Ct.1960). However, the inference that the legislature meant to assume responsibility for the problem to the exclusion of further judicial innovation seems unwarranted. See Keeton, Venturing to Do Justice 78–82, 94–95 (1969).

8. See generally id at 83–92. Concerning procedures for enforcement of the New York statute, see Bleimeyer v. Public Serv. Mut. Cas. Ins. Corp., 250 N.Y. 264, 268, 165 N.E. 286, 288 (1929) (opinion by Cardozo, Ch. J.).

9. See, e.g., LeVan, Distribution of a Limited Insurance Fund to Multiple

10. See note 10 on page 525.

The simplest method of eliminating these problems of inequity would be a revision of policy forms eliminating the per-accident limit, which gives rise to this problem, or at least placing the per-accident limit ten or more times as high as the per-person limit.[11]

In the absence of a change in policy provisions increasing the per-accident limit in comparison with the per-person limit, perhaps the best avenue to solution of this problem is to recognize that the limited policy coverage per accident may be allocated equitably among the various claims.

Certainly if all the interested parties agree upon such an allocation it should be respected, and the company should be free to settle with a particular claimant for an amount within the limit allocated to him and be credited with the amount of that settlement toward exhaustion of its limit of liability.

It seems probable that, despite effectual technical objections of an earlier time, in most jurisdictions today there would be no *procedural* barrier to an insurer's instituting a proceeding in the nature of interpleader to obtain a court order allocating among various claims the limited fund within the per-accident limit of policy coverage,[12] if the substantive principle of equitable allocation were accepted. Insofar as procedural requirements are concerned, it seems appropriate to permit such a proceeding not only when the insurer tenders the fund into court but also when the insurer is contesting liability and is not prepared to make a tender but seeks an allocation of the per-accident limit among the individual claims.[13]

Claimants, 22 La.L.Rev. 214, 223–225 (1961); Fisher, *Multiple Claims Under the Automobile Liability Policy,* 19 Ins.Counsel J. 419, 424 (1952).

10. For further development of my position, see *Preferential Settlement of Liability Insurance Claims,* 70 Harv. L.Rev. 27 (1956).

11. For indications of the effect of raising the per-accident limit to ten times as much as the per-person limit, consider data for January—October, 1963, supplied by the New York Department of Motor Vehicles, Division of Research and Development, regarding the number of accidents in which various numbers of persons are reported as having been injured; these data disclose that among accidents producing personal injury or death the accidents involving more than ten persons numbered only 45 (6 involving one or more fatalities and 39 involving no fatalities). In contrast, the accidents involving more than nine persons numbered 95 (9 fatal and 86 non-

fatal), those involving more than five persons numbered 1,367 (75 fatal and 1,292 nonfatal) and those involving more than four persons numbered 2,888 (128 fatal and 2,760 nonfatal). Rating factors used in calculation of increased-limits liability insurance coverage indicate that the costs of this change to a per-accident limit ten times as high as the per-person limit would be modest.

12. *Cf.* State Farm Fire & Cas. Co. v. Tashire, 386 U.S. 523, 87 Sup.Ct. 1199, 18 L.Ed.2d 270 (1967). See generally Chafee, *The Federal Interpleader Act of 1936: II,* 45 Yale L.J. 1161 (1936); Chafee, *Federal Interpleader Since the Act of 1936,* 49 Yale L.J. 377 (1940); Keeton, *Preferential Settlement of Liability Insurance Claims,* 70 Harv.L.Rev. 27, 40–46 (1956).

13. For more detailed development of this point, see Keeton, *Preferential Settlement of Liability Insurance Claims,* 70 Harv.L.Rev. 27, 36–60 (1956).

The substantive issues, too, it would seem, should be resolved in favor of the principle of equitable allocation of limited proceeds and the right of each claimant to be protected against inequitable preference for other claims. The most feasible method of implementing this principle and this right is to permit proration of the per-accident limit of coverage among the various claims by agreement or by court order in the absence of agreement.

Once it is recognized not only that all interested parties may agree upon allocation of limited coverage but also that the company has a right to obtain a court order making such an allocation (thereby protecting itself against claims of violating either its duty to its insured [14] or its duty to other claimants), it then becomes feasible to recognize that the company has a duty to each person of whose potential claim it knows or should know, to give due weight to his interest against preferential settlement. Contrary to this position, however, is a substantial body of precedents favoring the insurer when a claim is made against it after it has paid out all or part of its policy limit to other claimants.[15] There have been decisions, also, denying a prayer for injunction against preferential settlement [16] or permitting collection of a judgment over objection of the insurer.[17] But it is submitted that these opinions do not present persuasive grounds for denying the equitable allocation of limited coverage that is proposed here, and the inference seems reasonable that in most instances the case for this kind of relief was not fully presented and considered.

If such a duty to respect the interests of claimants against preferential settlement is recognized, the question whether it should be enforceable by injunction remains a debatable issue. It may be argued that there will be adequate protection for claimants and less burden on the courts if a claimant's remedy is restricted to an action against the insurer for recovery of a money judgment up to the amount that should have been allocated to his claim under an equitable allocation, even if the company has already paid out amounts totaling as much as its per-accident limit of coverage. Under this rem-

---

14. In the absence of protection against liability on the theory of violation of its duty to the insured regarding settlement, it would seem inappropriate to allow an action by a claimant on the theory of preferential settlement. To do so would be to impose on the company conflicting obligations it could not satisfy. See Keeton, *Preferential Settlement of Liability Insurance Claims*, 70 Harv.L.Rev. 27, 49–50 (1956).

15. See n.1 *supra*.

16. *E.g.*, Liguori v. Allstate Ins. Co., 76 N.J.Super. 204, 184 A.2d 12 (1962) (attempt to enjoin settlement as preferential failed).

17. See, *e.g.*, Goad v. Fisher, 255 Md. 131, 257 A.2d 433 (1969) (Maryland Unsatisfied Claim and Judgment Law provides that no more than $30,000 may be recovered from the Fund on account of injury to or death of more than one person in any one accident and does not say whether judgments should be paid "first come, first serve" or instead by some system of proration; trial court ordered payment of a $3500 judgment in full from the Fund over objection of the Fund; Fund failed to show prejudice; held, affirmed; questions about what should be done under different facts reserved, and hope expressed that "the General Assembly will fill the void").

edy, the penalty against the company for making inequitably preferential settlements is that its credit toward exhaustion of its per-accident limit is restricted to the maximum sum that might reasonably have been allocated to the settled claims.[18]

SECTION 7.10   RECIPROCAL CLAIMS

§ 7.10(a)   THE EFFECT OF SETTLEMENT OF ONE CLAIM

Automobile accidents frequently give rise to reciprocal claims. If only the two drivers were involved, the problems arising from such claims would be relatively simple. But when collision insurance, liability insurance, or both apply to one or both cars, distinctive problems of conflicting interests are presented.

The most pervasive problem concerns the effect of settlement of one claim upon a reciprocal claim. For example, suppose that two persons, driving their respective cars, are in collision; that one of them has collision coverage under which he receives payment for the damage to his car less a deductible of $100; that his insurance company, acting pursuant to his liability insurance coverage, then pays the second person a small sum in settlement, taking a release of the tort claim of the second person against the first for both personal injury and property damage; that the first person, who was more severely injured, then asserts a tort claim against the second, in which the first person's insurance company joins as subrogee to the interest in the claim for damage to the first person's car; and that the second person's liability insurance company asserts that the previous settlement bars the reciprocal claim not only as to the subrogation interest of the first person's insurance company but also as to all interests of the first person himself.

---

18. Elsewhere I have argued that any interested party ought to be able to initiate proceedings for allocation of limited policy coverage. See *Preferential Settlement of Liability Insurance Claims*, 70 Harv.L.Rev. 27, 52–60 (1956). Perhaps the weightiest objections to allowing a claimant to initiate such proceedings are those concerned with the potential burden upon the courts from proceedings instituted from excessive zeal, or in spite, when there is no real need for an allocation. I am indebted to members of the New York Law Revision Commission for development of the idea (during consultation on this problem in 1962–1963) that limiting the right of initiation of such proceedings to the company might reduce the force of these objections without appreciably reducing the effectiveness of protection to the claimants. If the company is liable to partial disallowance of credit toward exhaustion of its policy limit per accident, it will be free to initiate such proceedings when there is real need for them, but would have little inducement to do so otherwise. Thus, it would seem acceptable to establish the companion rules that only the company may initiate such proceedings and that it is subject to disallowance of credit toward its policy limit if it fails to do so. Recognition of this set of rules would seem to be well within the province of a court exercising the blended powers of law and equity. As to the possibility of a statutory solution, compare Keeton & O'Connell, Basic Protection for the Traffic Victim 314–317, 425–428 (1965).

If there had been no insurance of any kind, a settlement in which the first person paid the second would have barred the reciprocal claim. This result can be supported on ordinary contract principles, since it is reasonable to infer that two parties with potential reciprocal claims intend, when one pays the other and takes a release, that no further claim be available to either of them. Perhaps it would be possible for them to enter into an agreement that preserved a reciprocal claim, but it is unlikely that they would wish to do so and not surprising that the rule applicable between two individuals is ordinarily stated without special provision for that contingency.[1]

Arguably this rule barring a reciprocal claim as between two parties holding all of the reciprocal rights and obligations may appropriately be applied against the first person's insurance company in the hypothetical case stated above.[2] The company settled with the second person, no special provision being made for preserving its reciprocal claim (as subrogee of the first person). But the inference that it was intended that there be no further claims is weaker if the second person has property damage liability insurance, since the reciprocal claim, though in form against the second person, will be paid, if at all, by his liability insurance company. Certainly if it is possible for the first person's insurance company and the second person to make a settlement that preserves the right of the company to proceed against the second person's insurance company, it is reasonable to suppose they might prefer to do so. Yet application of the rule that the reciprocal claim is barred may be justified on the ground that the second person has some interest, though not as much as his liability insurance company, in the claim against him, and ought not to be subjected to the reciprocal claim against himself and his company unless the first person's company required this reservation to be expressed as one of the terms of settlement.

Clearly distinguishable from the foregoing cases is the case in which the first person's collision insurance and liability insurance are written by different companies and the claimant knows this. Perhaps there is a good analogy to the foregoing cases if the two companies function as a group and the claimant is led to expect reasonably that no claim will be made against him to the extent of the subroga-

1. *Cf.* Lugena v. Hanna, 420 S.W.2d 335 (Mo.1967) (Lugena, having no liability insurance, obtained a release from Miss Hanna to meet the requirements of the Financial Responsibility Law for retaining his operator's license; thereafter he sued her for damages; summary judgment for defendant affirmed). *But cf.* Restifo v. McDonald, 426 Pa. 5, 230 A.2d 199 (1967), 34 A.L.R.3d 1365 (1970) (action by husband, wife, and minor children against estate of decedent; defendant joined coplaintiff wife as additional defendant on children's claims, also seeking contribution; wife pleaded general release given her by decedent; trial court sustained wife's motion for judgment on pleadings; held, reversed and remanded; defendant must show that a release of right to seek contribution was bargained for, and, when properly construed the release in instant litigation merely prevents recovery on action originating with releasor).

2. *Cf.* Wm. H. Heinemann Creameries, Inc. v. Milwaukee Auto. Ins. Co., 270 Wis. 443, 71 N.W.2d 395, 72 N.W.2d 102 (1955).

tion interest of the collision carrier. In the absence of such a basis for expectation that this reciprocal claim would not be asserted, the collision subrogation interest stands in a position more analogous to that of the claims of the first person himself, discussed immediately below.

Extending the rules discussed above so as to bar claims in which the first person holds the beneficial interest would be unwarranted. This point applies to any interest he may have in the property damage claim—because of the $100 deductible [3] or because of loss of use of his car while it was being repaired or replaced—and to any personal injury claim he may have as well. Since the first person did not participate in the settlement, to hold that it barred his reciprocal claims would be to give his insurance company (under the liability coverage) control over not only defense of the claim against him but also his reciprocal claim against the other driver. It would be most unjust to do this without holding his insurance company accountable, in exercising this power, for giving at least equal consideration to his interests in reciprocal claims.[4] Such a rule of accountability would be difficult to administer. It would seem both fairer and more efficient to treat the settlement between one person's insurance company and a second person as having no effect on the first person's interests.[5] The preferable rule, then, is that one's reciprocal claim is not barred by a settlement between his liability insurance company and the other party to an accident. This rule is supported by the great weight of authority.[6]

---

3. *E.g.*, Wm. H. Heinemann Creameries, Inc. v. Milwaukee Auto. Ins. Co., 270 Wis. 443, 71 N.W.2d 395, 72 N.W.2d 102 (1955). Rules against splitting what is usually regarded as a single cause of action for injury to one's person and property ought not to stand in the way of this solution, since the reasons for such rules are inapplicable in this context of distinctly conflicting interests between the insurers and their insureds. But some courts may apply the rule against splitting, declining to accept this purposive analysis of the issue. See, *e.g.*, Warner v. Hedrick, 147 W. Va. 262, 126 S.E.2d 371 (1962); Mills v. DeWees, 141 W.Va. 782, 93 S.E.2d 484 (1956), 62 A.L.R.2d 965 (1958). Concerning the impact of the rule against splitting in the context of subrogation, see § 3.10(c)(2) at nn.22, 23 *supra*.

4. Compare the duty of the insurer to give at least equal consideration to the interests of its insured in relation to a claim against him in excess of policy limits. See § 7.8(b) *supra*.

5. For more detailed development of the supporting arguments for this position, see Keeton, *Liability Insurance and Reciprocal Claims from a Single Accident*, 10 Sw.L.J. 1 (1956), reprinted 1957 Ins.L.J. 29.

6. *E.g.*, Fikes v. Johnson, 220 Ark. 448, 248 S.W.2d 362 (1952), 32 A.L.R.2d 934 (1953); Perry v. Faulkner, 98 N.H. 474, 102 A.2d 908 (1954); McGuire v. Commercial Union Ins. Co., 431 S.W. 2d 347 (Tex.1968); Eller v. Blackwelder, 204 Va. 292, 130 S.E.2d 426 (1963); Birkholz v. Cheese Makers Mut. Cas. Co., 274 Wis. 190, 79 N.W.2d 665 (1956). Ga.Laws 1963, p. 643, overturned a contrary decision in Aetna Cas. & Sur. Co. v. Brooks, 218 Ga. 593, 129 S.E.2d 798 (1963). *But cf.* Bradford v. Kelly, 260 N.C. 382, 132 S.E.2d 886 (1963) (insured must elect to ratify the insured's settlement by pleading it in bar, in which event plaintiff's own claim is barred, or repudiate it in which event claim against him is to be litigated, the amount paid by the insurer in settlement being credited against any judgment; insurer has no further responsibility, having been discharged by settlement).

Treating the reciprocal claims independently of each other in this way also avoids problems that would otherwise arise under the assistance and cooperation clause. Because of the independence of the claims in the sense this rule implies, plainly one does not violate the assistance and cooperation clause of his liability insurance coverage by the mere act of obtaining a settlement of his own reciprocal claim.[7] This does not mean, however, that he need have no concern at all about the effect what he says and does in pressing his own claim may have on the claim against him. For example, making a false assertion that not he but a friend was driving his car, in the hope of improving his own claim, could well constitute a violation of the assistance and cooperation clause of his liability insurance.[8]

§ 7.10(b) AGENCY AND FIDUCIARY CONCEPTS

It has sometimes been stated that the liability insurer acts as agent for the insured in defending or settling a claim against him on his behalf.[1] Typically, however, this characterization has not been essential to the decision; the same result might have been reached by recognizing that the insurer was a non-agent fiduciary holding a power to affect the interests of both the insurer and the insured.[2] Characterizing the relationship as one of agency may lead to the conclusion that a settlement made by the liability insurer has the same effect on the insured's reciprocal claim as if he had made it himself.[3] A basic fallacy in this position is the agency characterization. Unless there are special arrangements apart from the typical liability insurance policy, the insurer and its representatives are not agents of the insured even with respect to settlement of the claim against the insured or with respect to defense, much less with respect to settlement of the insured's reciprocal claim. The agency relationship involves not only a power in one person to affect another's interests but also a right in the other to direct and control its exercise.[4] The insured does not have this right in the typical liability insurance relationship. Thus, the agency characterization is erroneous, and as we have seen earlier in this section, factors apart from agency doctrine support the conclusion that the insurer and its representatives do not have the

---

7. *E.g.*, Utterback-Gleason Co. v. Standard Acc. Ins. Co., 179 N.Y.S. 836 (Sup.Ct.1920), *aff'd*, 193 App.Div. 646, 184 N.Y.S. 862 (3d Dep't 1920), *aff'd*, 233 N.Y. 549, 135 N.E. 913 (1922).

8. See generally § 7.5 *supra*.

1. For a collection of illustrative opinions referring to the liability insurer as agent of the insured, see Keeton, *Liability Insurance and Reciprocal Claims from a Single Accident*, 10 Sw.L.J. 1, 10 (1956), reprinted 1957 Ins.L.J. 29, 34.

2. *Cf.* Restatement (Second) of Agency §§ 138, 139 (1958), referring to this type of power as a power given as security. See also *id.*, §§ 12–14, 14H regarding distinctions between agents and other holders of a power to alter the legal relations between another and third persons.

3. See, *e.g.*, Aetna Cas. & Sur. Co. v. Brooks, 218 Ga. 593, 129 S.E.2d 798 (1963). This decision was promptly overturned by the Georgia legislature. Ga.Laws.1963, p. 643.

4. Restatement (Second) of Agency §§ 1, 14 (1958).

power to bar the insured's reciprocal claim by their settlement of the claim against the insured.

§ 7.10(c) EFFECTS OF JUDGMENTS

It might be argued that, because of the diverse interests involved and the practical complications encountered if trial of one claim on the merits is held to affect the reciprocal claim, the principle of treating reciprocal claims independently should be extended to trials on the merits as well as to settlements. But there are weighty countervailing interests in efficient and evenhanded administration of justice. Most of the disputed fact issues concerning fault that affect the separate claims will be identical. Probably less time will be expended in trials if one determination of those fact issues controls both cases (although the single trial will be somewhat longer than either of two separate trials would have been). Moreover, if two separate trials are allowed, they may produce conflicting resolutions of the fact issues, with adverse impact on both the appearance and the fact of evenhanded administration of justice. Considerations such as these underlie compulsory counterclaim rules applied in many states, and deviations for special treatment of reciprocal claims involving liability insurance seem difficult to justify at best.

On balance, then, it seems sound to extend to these cases of reciprocal claims the commonly applicable rules concerning estoppel by judgment.[1]

Also, it seems appropriate to hold a compulsory counterclaim rule applicable in the absence of any special provisions excluding these cases from its scope.[2] It does not follow, however, that final disposition of one claim after an action has been filed also disposes of the reciprocal claim. In the first place, when the parties to one of the claims wish to settle it, the court in which the claim and counterclaim are pending might appropriately order that they be severed and that the settlement of one not affect the other.[3] Second, if a defense attorney designated by the liability insurer has agreed to a disposition of the action against the insured without advising the insured regarding the compulsory counterclaim rule and without taking appropriate steps explicitly to preserve his reciprocal claim, a court may decline to enforce the bar of the compulsory counterclaim rule.[4]

---

1. *E.g.,* Sanderson v. Balfour, 109 N.H. 213, 247 A.2d 185 (1968); Ross v. Stricker, 153 Ohio St. 153, 91 N.E.2d 18 (1950). The result reached on the specific facts in *Ross* is debatable, even under the rule suggested in the text above. The case was settled while appeal was pending. Arguably the grounds of appeal were substantial and potentially meritorious, and in that event there was no final judgment on the merits. See generally Keeton, *Liability Insurance and Reciprocal Claims from a Single Accident,* 10 Sw.L.J. 1, 16–19, 26–27 (1956),

reprinted 1957 Ins.L.J. 29, 37–38, 41–42.

2. *Cf.* Wright, *Estoppel by Rule: The Compulsory Counterclaim under Modern Pleading,* 39 Iowa L.Rev. 255, 292–299 (1954), reprinted 38 Minn.L. Rev. 423, 458–465 (1954).

3. *E.g.,* McGuire v. Commercial Union Ins. Co., 431 S.W.2d 347 (Tex.1968).

4. *E.g.,* LaFollette v. Herron, 211 F. Supp. 919 (E.D.Tenn.1962) (insured had no contact with case except when

Also, compulsory counterclaim rules ordinarily allow a counterclaim to be asserted by amendment if the failure to plead it was due to oversight, inadvertence, or excusable neglect. If a liability insurance company and the attorney it employs to represent the insured fail to advise the insured of the existence and effect of a compulsory counterclaim rule, he should not lose the benefit of his claim on that account. Two possible avenues by which courts might achieve this result are apparent. One is to permit the insured to reopen the case even after judgment (by direct or collateral attack, as may be appropriate under the jurisdiction's procedure, and subject to the advantages and disadvantages of estoppel as to factfindings made if the case went to final judgment on the merits) for the purpose of filing and obtaining a judgment on his counterclaim. A second way a court might protect the insured is to hold that he has a cause of action against the company and the attorney for the loss of his counterclaim resulting from their failure to advise him properly. The first of these avenues of protection would seem to be the better rule, since it is more likely to allocate losses from the accident as they would have been allocated if the counterclaim had been filed in ordinary course.

A consent judgment against an insured indicating on its face that it was entered without a final adjudication on the merits and pursuant to a compromise between the third party claimant and the liability insurer, like a settlement between the same parties out of court, should not bar the insured's reciprocal claim. There is support for this view in precedents,[5] but also for the contrary view.[6]

Many decisions that might superficially appear to oppose the rule advanced here are better explained as instances of firm insistence that the insured take the proper procedural route of asserting that the insurer's settlement does not bar his reciprocal claim. Some of these cases involve, first, a record showing only a judgment on the

he was interviewed in hospital by claim agent and when he was served with papers; court "constrained to find" he did not have an opportunity to present his reciprocal claim before the settlement was made). There is some support for the more extreme step of holding that the compulsory counterclaim rule does not apply in this liability insurance setting. *E.g.*, Reynolds v. Hartford Acc. & Indem. Co., 278 F.Supp. 331 (S.D.N.Y.1967) (insured's action for judgment declaring that insurer-appointed attorney must assert insured's counterclaim dismissed on the ground that reciprocal claim need not be brought in the pending tort action since the compulsory counterclaim rule should be read as barring on an "estoppel" or "waiver" rather than a "merger" or "res judicata" basis). *But cf.* Kennedy v. Jones, 44 F.R.D. 52 (E.D.Va.1968) (claim against employer and employee

tried to judgment for defendant; employee had not been advised of compulsory counterclaim rule; his later action on his reciprocal claim was nevertheless dismissed as barred by compulsory counterclaim rule); Akers v. Simpson, 445 S.W.2d 957 (Tex.1969). See generally Barron & Holtzoff, Federal Practice & Procedure § 394.1 (Wright ed. 1960) [to be superseded by 6 Wright & Miller, Federal Practice & Procedure § 1417].

5. See, *e.g.*, Daniel v. Adorno, 107 A.2d 700 (Mun.Ct.App.D.C.1954); Perry v. Faulkner, 102 A.2d 908 (N.H.1954). See also Mass.Gen.Laws Ann. ch. 231, § 140A (1959).

6. *E.g.*, A.B.C. Truck Lines v. Kenemer, 247 Ala. 543, 25 So.2d 511 (1946). *Cf.* Ross v. Stricker, 153 Ohio St. 153, 91 N.E.2d 18 (1950), discussed in n.1 supra.

merits or a disposition with prejudice because of a compromise settlement and, second, a separate action on the reciprocal claim without any suitable proceeding, direct or collateral as may be required in the jurisdiction, to reform the first judgment to reflect the true nature of the disposition.[7] Other cases involve the insured's failing to file a counterclaim in the first proceeding even though he had ample opportunity to do so after being forewarned of the opponent's contention.[8] A judgment purporting to be an adjudication on the merits, or purporting to be entered pursuant to a compromise disposing of both the claim against the insured and his reciprocal claim, should be and probably is in most jurisdictions subject to reformation, by direct attack or by collateral attack as may be appropriate under the procedures of the jurisdiction, for the purpose of showing that it was in fact a consent judgment entered without the insured's agreeing that it should bar his reciprocal claim.[9] If such proof is established, the reformed judgment would then not bar the reciprocal claim.

It would seem also that a compulsory counterclaim rule should be held inapplicable to a "friendly suit" filed solely for the purpose of effecting a settlement between a claimant and a liability insurance company, and that a judgment purporting to be a final adjudication on the merits should be open to attack, direct or collateral, for the purpose of proving that it was in fact such a "friendly suit."

In light of the effect a judgment on the merits may have on a reciprocal claim because of a compulsory counterclaim rule and the doctrine of estoppel by judgment, the insured and his liability insurer have interests partly in conflict that may be affected by the adjudication of either the claim against the insured or the insured's reciprocal claim. With respect to the conduct of such litigation by either the insured or the company, it would seem that they should be held to

---

7. *E.g., compare* Akers v. Simpson, 445 S.W.2d 957 (Tex.1969) *with* McGuire v. Commercial Union Ins. Co., 431 S.W.2d 347 (Tex.1968).

8. *E.g.,* Datta v. Staab, 173 Cal.App.2d 613, 343 P.2d 977 (1st Dist. 1959).

9. Daniel v. Adorno, 107 A.2d 700 (Mun.Ct.App.D.C.1954); *semble* American Trust & Banking Co. v. Parsons, 21 Tenn.App. 202, 108 S.W.2d 187 (1937). *Cf.* Kelleher v. Lozzi, 7 N.J. 17, 80 A.2d 196 (1951); Smith v. Price, 253 N.C. 285, 116 S.E.2d 733 (1960) (friendly suit to approve settlement with infant plaintiff; one attorney represented defendants—two insurers and their several insureds including an infant defendant; the infant defendant's injuries were not called to court's attention; held, judgment irregular because of conflict of interest among defendants; infant defendant's motion to vacate judgment as to him allowed). The *Kelleher* opinion does not refer to the effect of insurance, but holds that extrinsic evidence may be received in a suit by A v. B to show that the suit of B v. A was in fact dismissed upon settlement and therefore not "without prejudice." Nevertheless, the effort to get a rehearing so plaintiff Kelleher might show that the settlement had been consummated by the company's attorney without her consent was unsuccessful. Docket No. 765 (Sup.Ct.N. J.1951). Direct attack on the consent judgment is required by the following decisions: Perry v. Faulkner, 98 N.H. 474, 102 A.2d 908 (1954); LaLonde v. Hubbard, 202 N.C. 771, 164 S.E. 359 (1932); Akers v. Simpson, 445 S.W.2d 957 (Tex.1969). See Comment, 32 N. C.L.Rev. 531 (1954). As to the requisites for direct and collateral attacks on judgments generally, see Restatement of Judgments §§ 11, 12 (1942).

have mutual obligations to give to their respective interests that degree of weight that would be given by an individual holding both interests.[10]

In light of the effect a consent judgment may have on a reciprocal claim, either as an absolute bar or because the insured must run a hazardous and potentially expensive obstacle course to get around it, the liability insurer and the insurer-appointed attorney should be held accountable to the insured for failure to use reasonable care to effectuate their settlement with the third party claimant in a way that not only takes account of the insurer's interest in an unassailable disposition of the tort claim against the insured but also gives at least equal weight to the insured's interest in being free to assert his reciprocal claim.[11] Ordinarily this principle would require that the insurer bear the expense of any direct or collateral attack on the consent judgment essential to reforming it so as to permit the assertion of the reciprocal claim. Also, if the attack failed without fault of the insured, this principle would require that the insurer compensate the insured for the value of his lost claim.

SECTION 7.11 DIRECT ACTIONS AND JOINDER OF THE INSURER

Liability insurance policies customarily provide that no action shall lie against the company until the amount of the insured's obligation to pay shall have been finally determined either by judgment against the insured after actual trial or by written agreement of the insured, the claimant, and the company.[1] The principal reason for inserting this "no action" clause in policy forms was to require an adjudication of the tort action against the insured without involving the insurer as a party and thereby incurring the disadvantage of jury prejudice against insurers. The practical effectiveness of the clause for this purpose has been gradually reduced over the years as liability insurance has become more prevalent and jurors increasingly have assumed the existence of such coverage regardless of the formality that the legal action is against the insured only. Courts also have tended to become less rigorous in their enforcement of doctrines designed to prevent the injection of insurance into the tort trial. Yet it is still the prevailing rule that the tort action must proceed to judgment against the insured before an action can be brought against the liability insurer on its promise to pay on behalf of the insured.[2] There are

10. Compare the liability insurer's duty to give at least equal weight to the insured's interest in relation to a claim against the insured in excess of policy limits, § 7.8(b) *supra*.

11. *Ibid.*

1. See Appendix H *infra*.

2. See, *e.g.*, Marchlik v. Coronet Ins. Co., 40 Ill.2d 327, 239 N.E.2d 799 (1968) (public policy of Illinois precludes use of Illinois courts for cases against automobile liability insurers under Wisconsin direct action statute). See generally Rudser, *Direct Actions Against Insurance Companies*, 45 N. D.L.Rev. 483 (1969); 8 Appleman, In-

a few jurisdictions, however, in which direct actions against the insurer are permitted, and in special circumstances many other jurisdictions as well may permit the insurer to be sued directly, either alone or in joinder with the insured, in an action in which both the tort liability of the insured and the contractual undertaking of the liability insurer are at issue.

By statutes a few states permit direct actions against liability insurers generally,[3] and other legislation either explicitly or as construed in the courts, has authorized direct actions in limited cases, commonly those involving insurers of public carriers.[4]

There is limited support for a judicially created doctrine allowing direct actions against liability insurers generally.[5]

There is also limited support for an *in rem* proceeding, nominally against the insured, but having in practical effect some of the consequences of a direct action against the insurer. Under this doctrine, the injured plaintiff files his tort action against the insured in a state where he cannot get personal jurisdiction over the insured, relying upon the liability insurer's obligations to the insured as an attachable "debt" to sustain *quasi in rem* jurisdiction and proceeding on the theory that this "debt" is attachable, if local law so permits, somewhere, and perhaps anywhere, the insurer can be found. Initiated by a divided court in *Seider v. Roth*,[6] and elaborated in a body of decisions, often too by divided courts,[7] this doctrine has been subjected to vigorous and cogent criticism.[8] Its future, in New York[9] and elsewhere as well,[10] is a matter of speculation.

Despite the several authorizations for direct actions against liability insurers, referred to above, it remains the prevailing rule that

surance Law §§ 4861–4866.25 (rev.ed. 1962).

3. *E.g.*, La.Rev.Stat.Ann. 22:655 (Supp. 1970); Puerto Rican Laws Ann. tit. 26, §§ 2001, 2003 (Supp.1968); Wis.Stat. §§ 204.30(4), 260.11(1) (Supp.1970); see also R.I.Gen.Laws Ann. § 27–7–2 (1968).

4. See 8 Appleman, Insurance Law § 4862 (rev.ed.1962).

5. *E.g.*, Beta Eta House Corp. v. Gregory, 237 So.2d 163 (Fla.1970) (rule that insurer may be joined as defendant applies to other forms of liability insurance as well as automobile; trial court may order separate trial on issue of coverage, before or after trial on merits); Shingleton v. Bussey, 223 So.2d 713 (Fla.1969) (opinion may be read as implying that joinder of the insured will be essential, and that action against insurer alone will not be permitted).

6. 17 N.Y.2d 111, 216 N.E.2d 312, 269 N.Y.S.2d 99 (1966).

7. *E.g.*, Minichiello v. Rosenberg, 410 F.2d 106 (2d Cir. 1969), *cert. denied*, 396 U.S. 844, 949 (1969); Simpson v. Loehmann, 21 N.Y.2d 305, 234 N.E.2d 669, 287 N.Y.S.2d 633 (1967), 33 A.L. R.3d 979 (1970) *reargument denied*, 21 N.Y.2d 990, 238 N.E.2d 319, 290 N.Y.S. 2d 914 (1968).

8. *E.g.*, Siegel, Supplementary Practice Commentary to CPLR 5201, N.Y.Civ. Prac.L.R. 18 (McKinney Supp.1969–70); Stein, *Jurisdiction by Attachment of Liability Insurance*, 43 N.Y. U.L.Rev. 1075 (1968).

9. See, *e.g.*, Siegel, op. cit. *supra* n.8 at 21–22.

10. See DeRentiis v. Lewis, 258 A.2d 464 (R.I.1969) (noting the controversial character of *Seider* and reserving judgment on its merits; ordering dismissal of attachment of liability insurance obligations as not supportable under Rhode Island statutes, distinguishable from those of New York).

the injured plaintiff is not permitted to sue the liability insurer directly, either alone or jointly with the insured, before establishing the tort liability of the insured. A court that adheres to this rule and rejects each of the doctrines discussed above may, however, find good reason for allowing the insurer to be joined as an additional defendant in the tort action against the insured in those exceptional cases involving such conflict of interest between the insurer and the insured that their respective interests in the defense of the tort action cannot be represented adequately by a single attorney.[11]

11.   See § 7.7(c) *supra*.

CHAPTER 8

INSURANCE INSTITUTIONS *

SECTION 8.1 ALLOCATION OF POWERS AMONG REGULATORY INSTITUTIONS

§ 8.1(a) THE UNEASY FEDERAL–STATE ACCOMMODATION

In the United States, administrative regulation of insurance has been and is primarily the responsibility of state rather than federal agencies. But there are elements of federal regulation as well. Proposals for shifting the major responsibility from state to federal agencies have long been disputed, and the arguments advanced by proponents and opponents of such a shift have changed with changing contexts.

On October 26, 1905, Louis D. Brandeis, later to become a distinguished Associate Justice of the Supreme Court of the United States but then an active member of the Boston Bar and a vigorous champion of the causes he supported, spoke before the Commercial Club of Boston as counsel for the Protective Committee of Policyholders in the Equitable Life Assurance Society. Then pending in the United States Senate was a bill, supported by some of the leading insurance executives of the day, to federalize insurance supervision. The Brandeis analysis of the bill was scathing:

"The sole effect of a Federal law would be . . . to free the companies from the careful scrutiny of the commissioners of some of the States. It seeks to rob the State even of the right to protect its own citizens from the legalized robbery to which present insurance measures subject the citizens, for by the terms of the bill a Federal license would secure the right to do business within the borders of the

---

* Insurance regulatory problems raise some of the fundamental questions of the administrative process and the federal system. This chapter is not intended to give adequate treatment to such problems, nor is it intended to deal with the many problems of enforcement encountered in making an insurance regulatory system effective. Rather, the purposes are, first, to consider the general characteristics of insurance regulation and governmental participation in insurance as they have developed in the United States and, second, to consider some principles that have affected and may continue to affect these developments in the future.

State, regardless of the State prohibitions, free from the State's protective regulation." [1]

By the time the *South-Eastern Underwriters* case [2] reached the Supreme Court, the political climate had changed. At that time, state agencies were less likely than federal agencies to be vigorous regulators, and the position of partisans was predictably reversed. Industry executives generally favored state regulation and opposed federal intrusions, and partisans of stricter controls favored federal assumption of increased responsibility for insurance regulation.

In *South-Eastern Underwriters* the Supreme Court determined that a group of insurance companies associating together for rate-making purposes were subject to the Sherman Anti-Trust Act. Reaction was prompt and strong. The forces preferring state regulation, though incapable of blocking the determination that Congress had ample power in the matter,[3] marshaled sufficient political support to curb the potential impact of the decision. The McCarran-Ferguson Act declared that the business of insurance should continue to be "subject to the laws of the several States which relate to the regulation or taxation of such business." [4] The Act also declared, however, that certain acts of Congress, after a temporary period for adjustment, would be "applicable to the business of insurance to the extent that such business is not regulated by State law."[5]

Promptly after the McCarran-Ferguson Act was passed, state insurance commissioners and industry representatives joined forces in a movement for state legislation to occupy the areas that were exempt from federal regulation to the extent of regulation by state law. Under the sponsorship of the National Association of Insurance Commissioners and with the active cooperation of an All-Industry Committee, model acts were prepared and recommended for adoption in the various states.[6] These acts were primarily concerned with rate regulation (together with standardization of policy forms) and fair trade practices. By 1950, rate regulatory legislation had been enacted in every state.[7]

State fair trade legislation had been scant before preparation of the N.A.I.C. Model Act, and the states did not respond as quickly to

1. Quoted in n.17 of the dissenting opinion of Justice Jackson, United States v. South-Eastern Underwriters Ass'n, 322 U.S. 533, 64 Sup.Ct. 1162, 88 L.Ed. 1440 (1944). True to Brandeis tradition, his argument was documented with data on stockholder dividends and insurance overhead.

2. United States v. South-Eastern Underwriters Ass'n, 322 U.S. 533, 64 Sup.Ct. 1162, 88 L.Ed. 1440 (1944).

3. Steps taken in an effort to forestall the decision included the filing of amicus curiae briefs by 35 states.

See n.18 in Justice Jackson's dissenting opinion.

4. 59 Stat. 33, 34 (1945), 15 U.S.C. § 1012 (1958).

5. *Ibid.*

6. See Donovan, *State Regulation of Insurance*, 1956 Ins.L.J. 11, 12; Donovan, *Regulation of Insurance Under the McCarran Act*, 15 Law & Contemp. Prob. 473, 483–488 (1950).

7. See 1 Richards, Insurance Law 216–220 (5th ed. Freedman 1952).

proposals for this kind of legislation as to those concerning rate regulation. The pace quickened, however, when the Federal Trade Commission initiated inquiries into promotional and advertising activities in the fields of accident and health insurance.[8] By the end of the year 1959, unfair trade practices acts had been adopted in all 50 states, the District of Columbia and Puerto Rico, most of the statutes being based on the N.A.I.C. Model Act.[9]

Another model act prepared by the All-Industry Committee and the National Association of Insurance Commissioners is the Unauthorized Insurers Service of Process Law.[10] This type of act provides for serving on the insurance commissioner process that is directed to an insurer not qualified to do business in the state under the state regulatory laws. Perhaps there would be a gap in state regulation, within the meaning of the conditional exemption from federal regulation in the McCarran-Ferguson Act, in the absence of such a law. Such regulation as is otherwise possible surely lacks something in effectiveness, though unauthorized insurers do not totally escape regulation by not being amenable to service in the state. Apparently concern about such a gap was an important factor behind the drafting of the Unauthorized Insurers Service of Process Law. And this concern may have been increased by the fact that effectuality of state control over the transactions of unauthorized insurers had been the focus of importation litigation.[11] However, even though the provision for jurisdiction of state courts over the nonadmitted insurer has thus been treated as a facet of insurance regulation, continuation of such state jurisdiction would seem consistent with even the most thoroughgoing Congressional occupation of the field of insurance regulation—a state of affairs that did not exist even during the interval between *South-Eastern Underwriters* and the enactment of the McCarran-Ferguson Act.

8. See Donovan, *State Regulation of Insurance*, 1956 Ins.L.J. 11, 13.

9. 1959 ABA Section Ins., Neg. & Comp.L.Proceedings 227.

10. See 1959 ABA Section Ins., Neg. & Comp.L.Proceedings 227, reporting adoption of statutes of this type in 49 states (excluding Alaska), the District of Columbia and Puerto Rico.

11. *E.g.*, McGee v. International Life Ins. Co., 355 U.S. 220, 78 Sup.Ct. 199, 2 L.Ed.2d 223 (1957) (respondent was not served with process in California but was served in accordance with a California statute, by registered mail at its principal place of business in Texas; Texas courts refused to enforce the California judgment in favor of a California resident on the respondent's contract of life insurance consummated by inter-state mail, respondent never having had any office or agent in California, and, so far as the record showed, never having solicited or done any insurance business in California apart from this policy, which was issued in substitution for the policy of an Arizona corporation whose obligations respondent assumed; held that the Texas courts erred in refusing to give the California judgment full faith and credit); Robertson v. California, 328 U.S. 440, 66 Sup.Ct. 1160, 90 L.Ed. 1366 (1946) (appellant was convicted in a state court of California of violating a provision of the California Insurance Code prohibiting a person from acting as agent for a nonadmitted insurer except under specified conditions; attack against the state action as inconsistent with the *South-Eastern Underwriters* decision rejected, and "explicitly without specific reliance upon" the McCarran-Ferguson Act).

The spate of state legislation following the McCarran-Ferguson Act did not still the controversy over the federal-state allocation of regulatory powers for long. Public complaints over automobile insurance rates led to congressional inquiries in the mid-1950's, but with no significant consequences. In the 1960's, the volume of public complaints rose again, and this time they focused not only on rates but also on insolvencies and harsh underwriting and cancellation practices. These renewed attacks against the industry and against ineffectual state regulation revived interest in proposals for a greater federal role in regulation and led to the initiation of a comprehensive study of automobile insurance in the Department of Transportation, commencing in 1968.[12]

Underlying this continuing controversy over Federal-state allocation of regulatory responsibility is a set of unanswered questions about the relative effectiveness of state and federal agencies.[13] The answers to these questions may differ from generation to generation, and they are likely to be debatable in every generation.

One's preference as between federal and state regulation is greatly influenced by his political philosophy in regard to the desirable balance between centralized and localized governmental power.[14] But there are also other issues of general policy.

One debatable issue concerns the risks of ineffectuality of administrative regulation. Most such risks are common to both state and federal regulation. The risk that the regulatory agency will become a "captive" of the regulated industry is an example. Is this risk substantially greater under one form of regulation than under the other? There is opportunity for the industry to concentrate all its power on influencing one agency, under a centralized system of regulation, but also greater likelihood of public awareness of such a concentration. Moreover, greater resources can be marshaled for counteraction.

A very important disadvantage of state regulation is the common lack of adequate funds and personnel in state insurance departments.

---

12. Among the reports on various aspects of the Department of Transportation study is one specifically concerned with regulation of insurance— Day, Economic Regulation of Insurance in the United States (U.S. Dep't Transp. Auto. Ins. & Comp. Study 1970).

13. See id. at 58–77. See also Denenberg, *Meeting the Insurance Crisis of Our Cities: An Industry in Revolution*, 1970 Ins.L.J. 205, 209–210; Kimball, *The Case for State Regulation of Insurance*, in Insurance, Government, and Social Policy 411 (Kimball & Denenberg eds. 1969).

14. For a succinct statement of the case for localized power, made how-

ever in discussing not the choice between federal and state regulation but rather the choice between governmental and privately written automobile insurance, see N.Y. Ins. Dep't, Report, Automobile Insurance . . .
For Whose Benefit? 77–78 (1970): "[D]ecentralized, variegated, responsive and smaller units of power are preferable to a monolithic and centralized monopoly of power. The reason is not efficiency; it is the desire to stimulate individual creativity, to encourage flexibility of response and healthy competition and to guard the public against the terrible consequences when centralized power goes wrong."

Cooperation among states is helpful, but is less efficient than centralized control. Although a centralized agency would not be entirely free of the impediments of inadequate funds and personnel, probably experience in other areas of regulation suggests that the problem would be less severe for the centralized agency, particularly in view of the economies possible in comparison with the duplication of effort by state agencies regulating an industry composed primarily of insurers operating nationally or regionally rather than locally.

Is a centralized system of regulation relatively at a disadvantage because of the fact that any single agency is likely to do well in some respects and poorly in others? Is it a significant advantage that, with multiple state agencies, there is a possibility that at least a few of them will focus on each major problem that needs attention, and that other states will benefit?

In addition to unresolved questions of general policy, there remain unresolved questions of more specialized and immediate concern.[15] To what extent, for example, does federal antitrust and Trade Commission legislation apply to insurance organizations and transactions? Since June 30, 1948, the guideline has been that such legislation is "applicable to the business of insurance to the extent that such business is not regulated by State law."[16] It has been held that prohibitory state legislation was enough to occupy the field of regulation of certain advertising practices challenged by the Federal Trade Commission, to which the Federal Trade Commission Act would otherwise have applied.[17] But the rationale of the opinion suggests the possibility that the mere enactment of some form of prohibitory statute is not conclusive of the question whether the business is "regulated by State law." It might be concluded, for example, that prohibitory legislation is alone enough to constitute preemptive regulation of the field of false advertising but that something more is required to preempt the more complex field of antitrust regulation. It may even be questioned whether state legislation will alone be enough to preclude application of the Federal Trade Commission Act in all circumstances.

Certainly it is open to the Supreme Court to conclude that, in determining whether the insurance business is to some extent "not regulated by State law," it may consider not only the statutes and the administrative structure established by statutory direction or authorization but also the practical effectiveness of the state regulatory scheme.[18] It is perhaps somewhat less likely that the Court will carry that practical assessment to the extent of taking into account such

15. See, *e.g.*, Atwell, *The McCarran-Ferguson Act—A Deceptive Panacea?* 5 Forum 339 (ABA Section Ins., Neg. & Comp.L.1970); Annot., 21 L.Ed.2d 938 (1969).

16. 15 U.S.C. § 1012(b) (1958).

17. Federal Trade Commission v. National Cas. Co., 357 U.S. 560, 78 Sup. Ct. 1260, 2 L.Ed.2d 1540 (1958).

18. *Cf.* Day, Economic Regulation of Insurance in the United States 42–44 (U.S. Dep't Transp. Auto. Ins. & Comp. Study 1970).

things as adequacy of the budget, and still less the qualifications of personnel in regulatory positions. Yet if the Court does not take a realistic view of the practical effectiveness of state regulation, the likelihood of further Congressional action is increased. It is an uneasy balance—a truce rather than a settled accommodation—that exists between proponents of regulation primarily by the states and proponents of increased federal participation in regulation of the insurance business.

§ 8.1(b) ALLOCATION OF POWERS AMONG LEGISLATURES, COURTS, AND ADMINISTRATIVE AGENCIES

Insurance transactions and institutions are subject to regulation, in a broad sense, not only at the hands of administrative agencies specially created for this purpose but also at the hands of legislatures and courts.

The insurance statutes of every state are a formidable body of enactments, if indeed they can be regarded as sufficiently unified either in form or in substantive content to be called a body. In an effort to achieve greater unity and coherence, a number of states have codified their insurance laws, or re-codified them in relatively recent time. An undertaking that is perhaps the most ambitious of all such efforts, with a staff of unparalleled excellence, was initiated in Wisconsin in 1965.[1]

In every state the legislature has in some respects directly effected regulation of insurance transactions and institutions, by statute. Statutory regulation of policy forms [2] is a prime example.

Each legislature has also initiated more comprehensive regulation by establishing provisions for continuing supervision of insurance transactions and institutions by a state agency under the direction of an officer usually called the commissioner of insurance. The staff and funds available to such an agency have varied widely. Some state agencies have been so understaffed and underfinanced that regulation has been largely illusory.[3] Others have suffered from severe fluctuations in administrative policy or in vigor of enforcement, or from manifested tendencies of constituent influence. Still

---

1. See Kimball & Denenberg, *Modern Insurance Code Revision: Reflections on the Art of Legislative Reform*, 21 C.L.U.J. No. 4, p. 34 (1967), reprinted with slight modification in Insurance, Government, and Social Policy 41 (Kimball & Denenberg eds. 1969). See also *Symposium: Insurance Regulation*, 1969 Wis.L.Rev. 1019.

2. See § 2.10 *supra*.

3. See Kimball & Hansen, *The Utah Insurance Commissioner: A Study of* *Administrative Regulation in Action*, 6 Utah L.Rev. 1, 19 (1958), reporting that the entire budget for the Insurance Department of Utah in 1956 was $33,274.51, over 10 per cent of which was charged to overhead costs of the parent Business Regulation Commission, leaving less than $30,000 for Insurance Department services to the insurance industry and the citizens of the state, even though the State collected more than three times that much from the industry in fees.

others, perhaps most notably New York, have been well staffed and generally effective.

Courts, too, have had a significant role in the regulation of insurance transactions and institutions. A very limited part of this role is concerned directly with judicial proceedings for enforcement of regulatory measures initiated by a commissioner of insurance within authorizations granted by statute. More significant is the continuing role of the courts in the regulation of insurance transactions through doctrinal developments. Notable among the doctrinal developments are those culminating in the recognition of rights at variance with policy provisions.[4]

SECTION 8.2 THE REACH OF INSURANCE REGULATORY MEASURES

§ 8.2(a) GENERALLY

Among the whole body of insurance regulatory measures—statutory, administrative, and decisional—some do and should have much greater reach than others. If properly attuned to needs, some will apply to all or nearly all types of insurance transactions and others to relatively few. One should be cautious, then, about relying upon a decision concerning the scope of one regulatory measure as precedent or even analogical support for giving the same scope to another measure. Yet the temptation to do this is strong, and especially so in relation to the basic issue of what constitutes an insurance transaction or doing an insurance business within the meaning of a statute or administrative rule, or a judicial doctrine that is designed explicitly as an insurance regulatory measure.

Many of the state statutes establishing systems of insurance regulation have failed to define insurance. Others have used definitions so broad and general as to be virtually useless as guides to determining applicability of the regulatory system in a disputed setting.[1] A

---

4. See generally Chapter 6 *supra*, and especially § 6.3 concerning the principle of honoring reasonable expectations even when inconsistent with a painstaking study of policy provisions.

1. The statutory definitions of insurance in California and Massachusetts are examples.

Calif.Ins.Code § 22 (West 1955): "Insurance is a contract whereby one undertakes to indemnify another against loss, damage, or liability arising from a contingent or unknown event."

Mass.Gen.Laws Ann. ch. 175, § 2 (1958): "A contract of insurance is an agreement by which one party for a consideration promises to pay money or its equivalent, or to do an act valuable

to the insured, upon the destruction, loss or injury of something in which the other party has an interest."

Arguably these statutes should be read not as stating that every transaction having the stated characteristics is insurance but only as saying that no transaction is insurance unless it has these characteristics. If so construed, there would seldom be any occasion to invoke them since it is not likely that a transaction lacking these characteristics would be alleged to be insurance even if there were no statutory definition of that term. Reading these statutes instead as stating that all transactions having these characteristics are insurance would be to give them a meaning plainly inconsistent with the

notable exception is the New York statute, to the drafting of which Patterson was a major contributor. It undertakes to specify, in both inclusory and exclusory terms, the reach of the regulatory statutes of the state.[2] In doing so, it defines both the term "insurance contract"[3] and the term "doing an insurance business."[4] This degree of differentiation in the scope of applicability of separate provisions in the total set of statutes seems a minimum; certainly a wisely designed regulatory system may well leave some types of occasional contracts unregulated even though regulation would be in order if the making of such contracts was a substantial part of the business of one of the contracting parties. And it may happen that this degree of differentiation is sufficient to deal with most of the problems of reach that a draftsman of a set of insurance laws faces. In any event such definitions of "insurance" and "doing an insurance business" should be viewed by the legislator (and within proper bounds by courts construing legislation) as the tools for expressing substantive decisions about the proper reach of regulatory measures, rather than

much narrower scope of regulation in practice. Many arrangements having these characteristics are never asserted to be insurance even by the most aggressive of regulatory officials.

2. See N.Y.Ins.Law § 41 (McKinney Supp.1970): *"Meaning of 'insurance contract' and 'doing an insurance business'*

"1. The term 'insurance contract,' as used in this chapter, shall, except as provided in subsection two, be deemed to include any agreement or other transaction whereby one party, herein called the insurer, is obligated to confer benefit of pecuniary value upon another party, herein called the insured or the beneficiary, dependent upon the happening of a fortuitous event in which the insured or beneficiary has, or is expected to have at the time of such happening, a material interest which will be adversely affected by the happening of such event. A fortuitous event is any occurrence or failure to occur which is, or is assumed by the parties to be, to a substantial extent beyond the control of either party.

"2. A contract of warranty, guaranty or suretyship is an insurance contract, within the meaning of this chapter, only if made by a warrantor, guarantor or surety who or which, as such, is doing an insurance business within the meaning of this chapter.

"3. Except as provided in subdivision four, any of the following acts in this state, effected by mail from outside this state or otherwise by any person,

firm, association, corporation or joint-stock company shall constitute doing an insurance business in this state . . .: (a) the making, as insurer, or proposing to make as insurer, of any insurance contract, . . .; (b) the making, as warrantor, guarantor or surety, or the proposing to make as warrantor, guarantor or surety, of any contract of warranty, guaranty or suretyship as a vocation and not as merely incidental to any other legitimate business or activity of the warrantor, guarantor or surety; (c) the collection of any premium, membership fee, assessment or other consideration for any policy or contract of insurance; (d) the doing of any kind of business, including a reinsurance business, specifically recognized as constituting the doing of an insurance business within the meaning of this chapter; (e) the doing or proposing to do any business in substance equivalent to any of the foregoing in a manner designed to evade the provisions of this chapter.

. . . .

"5. In the application of this chapter the fact that no profit is derived from the making of insurance contracts, agreements or transactions, or that no separate or direct consideration is received therefor, shall not be deemed conclusively to show that the making thereof does not constitute the doing of an insurance business."

3. *Id.*, paragraph 1.

4. *Id.*, paragraph 3.

rigid restraints against choosing a narrower or broader reach for a particular measure when on substantive grounds it seems appropriate to do so.

State statutes other than those of New York make little use of these tools of definition. Even those guidelines to definition of affected transactions that one can derive from judicial decisions are relatively insecure. There are advantages, however, to be weighed against the disadvantage of such uncertainty; one result is greater flexibility for both administrators and judges to make wise choices about the scope of different regulatory measures.[5] Moreover, the area of uncertainty is not as great as it might seem. Perhaps the best approach to a degree of certainty is through a classification of precedents according to the purposes of the particular regulatory measures and the types of transactions in which disputes over the applicability of such measures have come before the courts and administrative agencies.

Much of the regulation of insurance transactions on the initiative of courts, through judicial doctrine, concerns rights at variance with policy provisions.[6] There have been occasional instances when a court declined to extend these doctrines to particular contracts on the ground that they were not insurance transactions. For example, this theory has been used to save some party to a risk-transferring-and-distributing contract from the obligations courts impose upon an insurer in like circumstances.[7] One may be critical of such a definitional approach to problems. Certainly the perspectives from which regulatory precedents are appraised should include questioning whether the definition of insurance implicit in the scope of one insurance regulatory measure is a sound criterion for the scope of another particular doctrine under consideration. It may well be that the field of application of one doctrine of rights at variance with contract provisions should be either narrower or broader than that of another, or that such doctrines generally should have narrower or broader reach than that of the rather different kinds of regulatory measures ordinarily initiated by statute.

With respect to regulatory measures initiated by statute, as is noted elsewhere,[8] the principal objectives have been to avoid overreaching by insurers, to assure solidity and solvency of insurers, and to assure fair charges. The practical implementation of these objectives gives rise to a large number of distinct types of regulatory measures,[9] and it is reasonable that they too be varied in reach.[10]

---

5. Concerning the competing values of certainty and flexibility generally, see §§ 1.6, 2.7 *supra*.

6. See generally Chapter 6 *supra*.

7. See, *e.g.*, McIntosh v. Group Health Ass'n, 138 A.2d 496 (D.C.Mun.App. 1958). For further comments on this case, see § 8.2(b) at n.11 *infra*.

8. See § 8.3 *infra*.

9. *Ibid.*

10. For example, those to whom the power of decision is committed may well choose to leave a "consumer co-operative" health association free from the strictures of statutes aimed primarily at avoiding the conse-

§ 8.2(b) HEALTH PLANS

Most of the cases concerning various types of hospital and medical service plans for members of a group have held that a corporation organized for the purpose of providing such services is not subject to laws regulating insurance.[1] But there are cases holding that such groups are doing an insurance business. Most decisions of the latter type can be distinguished on the ground that details of the plans were materially different from those in cases deciding that no insurance was involved, but it is arguable that they represent a different point of view toward health plans generally.[2]

In *Jordan* v. *Group Health Ass'n*,[3] a leading case on the applicability of insurance regulatory statutes to group health plans, the opinion of Associate Justice Rutledge emphasized that the Association's undertaking was "not to supply the service, or see or guarantee that it is supplied, . . . but only to 'use its best efforts' to secure" service.[4] Nevertheless, the opinion suggested that the Association might be liable to suit by an individual member,[5] and subsequently that result was reached when a member sued after his claim had been denied on the theory that the treatment he needed was for a pre-existing condition.[6] Does this result indicate that the Association was in some respects a principal in the arrangement among itself, the physicians, and the Association members, and not merely an agent for the members or an agent for those supplying the medical services? And why was it not the case that an insurance business was being conducted either by the Association as principal, or by its principals if it was acting as an agent?

It would seem that if the Association was merely an agent for the physicians, its failure to use its best efforts to cause the physi-

quences of imprudent management of funded systems of risk distribution, while yet applying to the association's transactions a set of statutory and judicial doctrines aimed at disallowing unconscionable advantage and honoring reasonable expectations of individuals with whom the association contracts. See § 8.2(b) *infra*.

1. *E.g.*, Jordan v. Group Health Ass'n, 71 App.D.C. 38, 107 F.2d 239 (1939); California Physicians' Serv. v. Garrison, 28 Cal.2d 790, 172 P.2d 4 (1946), 167 A.L.R. 306 (1947); Commissioner of Banking and Ins. v. Community Health Serv., 129 N.J.L. 427, 30 A. 2d 44 (1943); State *ex rel.* Fishback v. Universal Serv. Agency, 87 Wash. 413, 151 P. 768 (1915); Annot., 167 A. L.R. 322 (1947).

2. *E.g.*, McCarty v. King County Medical Serv. Corp., 26 Wash.2d 660, 175 P.2d 653 (1947) (distinguishing *Jordan* and *Fishback*, n.1 *supra*, as each in-

volving (a) a non-profit corporation that was in nature a consumers' cooperative, rather than a private "charitable" corporation that was in nature an intermediary between beneficiaries and physicians; (b) less control in the association over determination of eligibility to receive medical services, the decisions by the association's medical director being concerned with medical questions only, rather than legal as well; and (c) relationships in which the association served as agent of those who provided the medical services, rather than as principal and moving spirit in control of the business contemplated by the contract).

3. 71 App.D.C. 38, 107 F.2d 239 (1939).

4. 71 App.D.C. at 45, 107 F.2d at 246.

5. *Ibid.*

6. Group Health Ass'n v. Shepherd, 37 A.2d 749 (D.C.Mun.App.1944).

cians to render services to a member would not have given rise to a cause of action in favor of the member *against the Association*, as distinguished from its principals. On the other hand, if the Association was merely an agent for the members, its failure to use its best efforts to obtain services would have been a breach of its obligations to one of its principals. This theory of liability is not a distinctive incident of agency law, however; rather, it is liability for breach of a contract, which happens to be an agency contract. Such liability of the agent is the liability of a party ("principal") to the contract establishing the agency relationship. The effect of such an agency contract is to transfer to the agent a part of the member's risk of medical expenses by causing the agent to assume a risk of legal responsibility for failure to be as effective as he should be in making arrangements transferring the risk of higher-than-average medical expenses from members to physicians. Also, the composite effect of a great number of such agency contracts is to establish a system of risk distribution through the agent as a conduit. The elements of assumption of risk by the agent and distribution of risk through the agent are minimized under an interpretation of the contract to mean that the agent assumes no greater obligation than to use its best efforts to obtain services, but nevertheless are still present since the extent to which it will be called upon to fulfill this promise will vary according to the state of health of members. Thus, irrespective of the theory of the Association's liability to a member (whether it be that the Association is a contractor, not an agent, or that the Association is a party to an agency contract with the member), there is an element of transference of risk from the member to the Association and use of the Association as a conduit for risk distribution.

If the Association is characterized as an agent for the physicians, the elements of participation in risk transference and distribution by its principals, the physicians, are even more striking.

Why, then, is the Association not engaged in the insurance business, either as itself an insurer or as agent for the insurer-physicians? In response to the suggestion that the Association's acting as insurance agent might not have been enough to make a case against the Association under the statutes involved, is it not a fair inference that this court would not have held that the alleged physician-principals were insurers, if that issue had been before the court? [7]

Although the arrangement challenged in *Jordan* was well conceived to minimize and subordinate the elements of risk transference and distribution through the Association, it is difficult to escape the conclusion that the decision was influenced by an appraisal of the arrangement as socially useful and as giving rise to less urgent need for public regulation than ordinary insurance arrangements. Note that

7. See Jordan v. Group Health Ass'n, 71 App.D.C. 38, 47, 107 F.2d 239, 248 (1939): "It is admitted that the identical plan and service rendered here would not be 'insurance' or 'indemnity' if offered by an organization owned, operated and controlled by physicians."

the opinion asserts that this arrangement is a consumer cooperative the primary purpose of which "is to reduce the cost rather than the risk of medical care." [8] Would different treatment be accorded an effort to establish a consumer cooperative to reduce the cost rather than the risk of funeral and burial expense? Note the comment that it is not the function of Group Health to accumulate capital for the needs of a distant day as distinguished from keeping a steady flow of current funds from patients to physicians, with little margin.[9] Thus the Group Health arrangement does not involve a great potential evil from inadequate provision of reserves.

It should be noted that the determination in *Jordan* that the Association's operations were not insurance for the purposes of applicability of the insurance regulatory laws there involved does not answer the question whether they should be classified as insurance in other contexts. For example, it should not be regarded as a precedent against the claim of a member to rights against the association at variance with the membership provisions, advanced on the theory that the membership contract has all the essential features of an insurance transaction in relation to insurance law rights at variance with policy provisions.[10] Yet a contrary view appears to have been taken. That is, the Municipal Court of Appeals, in denying the claim of a member against the Association, asserted on grounds that might be characterized as urging a right at variance with contract stipulations, noted that *Jordan* had determined that the Association was a cooperative concerned principally with getting service rendered to its members at low cost and remarked that "the principles governing in a member's suit are those of contract law and not . . . those rules of law peculiar to insurance cases." [11] But the arguably relevant "rules of law peculiar to insurance cases" are concerned with the construction and enforcement of contract provisions that may operate unfairly as between the insurer, represented by experts, and the layman with little bargaining power and poor understanding of the arrangement. The individual member of Group Health is in a position quite analogous to that of the untutored insured. The statutory definition of insurance (explicit or implicit) for the purpose of determining whether regulatory measures apply need not necessarily be identical with the definition of "insurance" to be inferred from the evolution of a judicial doctrine concerned with construction of agreements. Moreover, even if it be thought desirable to extend the statutory definition of insurance to general usage, it does not follow that the court should decline to apply the "rules of law peculiar to insurance cases" rather than extending them to closely analogous non-insurance cases. This criticism of the court's reasoning does not demonstrate that the result is not sound, however. Probably the same

---

8. 71 App.D.C. at 46, 107 F.2d at 247.

9. 71 App.D.C. at 50, 107 F.2d at 251.

10. Concerning such rights generally, see Chapter 6 *supra.*

11. McIntosh v. Group Health Ass'n, 138 A.2d 496, 498 (D.C.Mun.App.1958).

result should have been reached even if the case had been treated as one involving insurance.

Subrogation claims have presented another context in which it has been thought relevant to determine whether health plans or medical service contracts constituted insurance. For example, as one ground, albeit less emphasized than others, for holding that a hospital service association of the Blue Cross type was not subrogated to the subscriber's tort claim against a third party and could not obtain the benefit of a statute permitting "insurance companies" to join in actions against tortfeasors, a court observed that the association was not an insurance company and its contracts with subscribers were not insurance contracts.[12] Perhaps treating the statute on joinder as not applying to the association is defensible, but the conclusion that the contracts of the association with its subscribers were not insurance contracts, or contracts like insurance in a sense relevant to whether subrogation should be recognized, seems less defensible. In the first place, in most contexts and perhaps in all, arguments against classifying the arrangement as insurance are weaker as to Blue Cross and Blue Shield systems than as to a "consumer cooperative" such as that involved in *Jordan*. Secondly, arguments relevant to whether an association is subject to insurance regulatory statutes may have little relevance to whether it should be subrogated to tort claims for recovery of medical expenses it has reimbursed under one of its contracts. A sharp focus of policy arguments relevant to this latter question is likely to lead to the conclusion that subrogation should be allowed.[13] In a closely analogous context, one court, taking the position that it need not determine whether an association was an insurer or its contracts were insurance contracts, upheld the association's defense to a claim by a member who had settled with a third party tortfeasor, the defense being based on a provision declaring that the membership contract did not apply to any injury caused by negligence of another, except for benefits not available out of funds recoverable from the wrongdoer through reasonable efforts of the member.[14]

It is noteworthy, even in relation to the more limited context of questions concerning regulation of insurance transactions, that some state legislatures have enacted separate regulatory statutes for medical and health associations[15] rather than leaving courts to struggle with questions whether statutes applicable generally to insurers should be held to apply to associations of this type.

12. Michigan Hosp. Serv. v. Sharpe, 339 Mich. 357, 63 N.W.2d 638 (1954), 43 A.L.R.2d 1167 (1955).

13. See § 3.10 *supra*.

14. Barmeier v. Oregon Physicians' Serv., 194 Ore. 659, 243 P.2d 1053 (1952). Note that this is even more disadvantageous to the payee of benefits under the contract than is a subrogation provision. Under the latter, he is reimbursed promptly rather than having to wait for disposition of his tort claim.

15. *E.g.*, N.Y.Ins.Law §§ 250–260 (McKinney 1966 and McKinney Supp.1970).

§ 8.2(c) CONTRACTS FOR SERVICE OR FOR SALE OR RENTAL OF GOODS

Contracts for service or for the sale or rental of goods often involve both transference and distribution of risk. Assertions of jurisdiction over such transactions by insurance regulatory officials have sometimes been successful.

An automobile club operating with annual dues and with agreements declaring its members to be entitled to specified indemnities (including a $5,000 bail bond for manslaughter and traffic violation) and attorneys' services within a schedule of stipulated fees (the largest being $100) has been denied the authorization it sought, in declaratory proceedings, to continue its operations without complying with statutes applicable to those doing an insurance business in the state.[1]

Pre-need contracts for burial services have been subjected to regulation in a number of states.[2] Regulatory officials have sometimes resorted to the courts for enforcement orders; thus, a company has been enjoined from engaging in the business of making contracts under which, in consideration of weekly installments and an agreement to make specified purchases, it covenanted to allow a percentage discount from retail prices and to furnish embalming and hearse services at regular prices.[3]

A group of persons who contracted with each other for replacement of plate glass store windows regardless of the cause of breakage have been held to be carrying on an insurance business.[4]

A watchmaker who agreed to replace a watch if lost within a year has been held to be making a contract of insurance.[5]

A judgment of ouster from engaging in a line of business in violation of insurance regulatory laws has been entered against a company marketing its automobile tires with printed forms one of which guaranteed "against blowouts, cuts, bruises, rim-cuts, under-inflation, wheels out of alignment, faulty brakes or other road hazards that

---

1. Continental Auto Club, Inc. v. Navarre, 337 Mich. 434, 60 N.W.2d 180 (1953). *Cf.* Texas Ass'n of Qualified Drivers v. State, 361 S.W.2d 580 (Tex.Civ.App.1962, no writ history); National Auto. Serv. Corp. v. State, 55 S.W.2d 209 (Tex.Civ.App.1932, writ of error dismissed).

2. *E.g.*, State v. Memorial Gardens Dev. Corp., 143 W.Va. 182, 101 S.E.2d 425 (1957), 68 A.L.R.2d 1233 (1959). *But see* n.9 *infra.*

3. State *ex rel.* Att'y Gen. v. Smith Funeral Serv., Inc., 177 Tenn. 41, 145 S.W.2d 1021 (1940). The defendant unsuccessfully argued that the contracts were not insurance because the holder could call upon the defendant to furnish the casket and burial clothing at any time, rather than awaiting the contingency of death. The court, however, thought the effect of this right on the course of business would be negligible and that the business would, in reality, continue to be that of burial insurance. See also Long v. Mynatt, 207 Tenn. 319, 339 S.W.2d 26 (1960) (contract to furnish funeral services and merchandise at 50 per cent discount to purchaser or his successors held subject to regulation as life insurance).

4. *E.g.*, People v. Roschli, 275 N.Y. 26, 9 N.E.2d 763 (1937).

5. Ollendorff Watch Co. v. Pink, 279 N.Y. 32, 17 N.E.2d 676 (1938).

may render the tire unfit for further service (except fire and theft)" and another of which guaranteed the tire "to wear" for not less than a specified period, failing which the defendant agreed that it would "either repair it free or replace it with a new tire" subject to a proportionate charge for the period of use.[6]

In other types of factual settings, also, an assertion of regulatory jurisdiction has sometimes been sustained.[7]

In other instances, assertions of regulatory jurisdiction have failed.

A notable example involved proceedings initiated by a regulatory official against a company marketing its automobile tires with printed forms that guaranteed them for specified periods of time if used "under usual conditions"; a judgment of ouster was denied, the company also not being held accountable for alleged departures from the printed form by oral representations of salesmen that the guarantee would protect the purchaser "against such hazards as cuts, bruises, wheels out of alignment and blowouts." [8]

Other instances of denial of regulatory jurisdiction have involved rather different factual settings.[9]

Also, efforts of private litigants to invoke rights based on an alleged violation of insurance regulatory laws by an opposing party have sometimes failed on the ground that the regulatory statutes did not reach the transaction in question.[10]

It would be most difficult and perhaps impossible to formulate a definition of insurance that would reconcile all these cases—including within its scope all those transactions in which assertions of applicability of regulatory statutes have been successful while excluding all

---

6. State *ex rel.* Duffy v. Western Auto. Supply Co., 134 Ohio St. 163, 16 N.E. 2d 256 (1938), 119 A.L.R. 1236 (1939). *But cf.* State *ex rel.* Herbert v. Standard Oil Co., n.8 *infra*.

7. *E.g.*, 1964 Ops.Att'y Gen.Ohio No. 1304 (contract providing for automatic cancellation of debt at debtor's death substantially amounts to insurance, and national bank may not lawfully enter into such contracts without complying with insurance laws); 1958 Ops.Att'y Gen.Ohio No. 2897 (individual who guarantees that certain enumerated parts of an automobile are in good working condition and will not require repairs or replacement for a specified period of time, with normal usage, where there is no vendor-vendee relationship but rather a general scheme for distributing losses among subscribers, is engaging in the business of insurance within the meaning of Ohio Rev.Code Ann. § 3905.42 (Page 1954)).

8. State *ex rel.* Herbert v. Standard Oil Co., 138 Ohio St. 376, 35 N.E.2d 437 (1941). The court added: "In conclusion, it is not our intention to overrule the case of State ex rel. Duffy, . . . [n.6 supra], or abandon the principles there applied. We do think, however, the doctrine of that case should not be extended." 138 Ohio St. at 383, 35 N.E.2d at 441.

9. *E.g.*, 1954 Ops.Att'y Gen.Ohio No. 4610 (individual engaged in the business of executing bail bonds, recognizances and appeal bonds is not engaging in business of insurance nor is he entering into contracts "substantially amounting to insurance" within meaning of Ohio Rev.Code Ann. § 3905.42 (Page 1954); Memorial Gardens Assoc., Inc. v. Smith, 16 Ill.2d 116, 156 N.E.2d 587 (1959).

10. Transportation Gee. Co. v. Jellins, 29 Cal.2d 242, 174 P.2d 625 (1946).

in which such assertions have failed. But there is a more promising approach to harmonizing the cases—or at least as high a percentage of them as one should expect in light of the probability of differing judgments of different legislatures and courts about the proper scope of regulatory measures. To what extent, in each case, did the specific transactions or the general line of business at issue involve one or more of the evils at which the regulatory statutes were aimed? And were the elements of risk transference and risk distribution, characteristic of transactions at which the regulatory statutes were aimed, a central and relatively important element of the transactions or instead merely incidental to other elements that gave the transactions their distinctive character?

If one approaches from this point of view a set of transactions concerning services or involving sales or rental of goods, he is likely to conclude that insurance regulatory laws are not properly construed as aimed at an absolute prohibition against the inclusion of any risk-transfering-and-distributing provisions in contracts for services or for the sale or rental of goods. In short, the presence of a small element of insurance, if one wishes to call it that, closely associated with the predominant element of the transaction—the element that gives the transaction its distinctive character—does not conclusively demonstrate that the transaction is within the reach of insurance regulatory laws.

For example, it is one thing to classify the death benefits of a membership contract in the New York Stock Exchange as insurance for the purpose of calculating the federal tax on the estate of the deceased member,[11] and quite another to suggest that if the Exchange wishes to maintain such a provision in its membership agreements it must comply with all the requirements of state regulatory laws applicable to companies in an insurance business.

On similar grounds of permitting a marginal insurance-type element in a transaction that is in essence a truck maintenance contract, it may be held that a company agreeing to maintain trucks owned by the other party to a contract does not engage in an insurance business, subject to insurance regulatory laws, by including in its contracts an undertaking to make repairs, with no exception for repairs needed because of collision damage, or even an undertaking to cause the trucks to be insured.[12] And a similar view may be taken of like elements in contracts for rental of vehicles.[13] Even if one finds an element of what he regards as insurance in such transactions as these, he may yet find that, because it is relatively insubstantial and is closely tied in with and incidental to the main objective of the transaction, it does not bring the transaction within the scope of the insurance regulatory laws as properly construed. But when the insurance

---

11. See Commissioner of Internal Revenue v. Treganowan, 183 F.2d 288 (2d Cir. 1950), *cert. denied*, 340 U.S. 853 (1950).

12. Transportation Gee. Co. v. Jellins, 29 Cal.2d 242, 174 P.2d 625 (1946).

13. See the dictum, 29 Cal.2d at 253, 174 P.2d at 631–632.

element is as extraneous to a sale of goods as an agreement to replace the article if lost within a specified period (as in the watchmaker's case), there is less justification, if any at all, for permitting it as an adjunct to the sale transaction.

§ 8.2(d) VARIABLE ANNUITIES

Variable annuities plainly include an element of insurance.[1] But they also have some of the characteristics of securities, and the extent to which they are subject to regulation as insurance and are, as insurance, free of other regulation has been sharply disputed.[2]

The opinion of the Supreme Court in the first variable annuities case, delivered by Mr. Justice Douglas, includes these four assertions about the nature of insurance:

First: "[T]he concept of 'insurance' involves some investment risk-taking on the part of the company." Second: "In hard reality the issuer of a variable annuity that has no element of a fixed return assumes no true risk in the insurance sense." Third: "[I]n common understanding 'insurance' involves a guarantee that at least some fraction of the benefits will be payable in fixed amounts." Fourth: "There is no true underwriting of risks" in a variable annuity contract, except for such an ancillary feature as life insurance on a declining basis for a term of five years.[3]

All four of these propositions appear to be implications of the same premise—that in common understanding and as used by Congress in the relevant Acts, "insurance" involves an insurer's commitment to pay a fixed sum of money, not one dependent in any degree upon fluctuations in the value of investments purchased with the fund accumulated from premiums. Certainly that has been a characteristic of traditional life insurance policies. It is not so clearly true of other traditional types of insurance. For example, the exposure of a fire insurer under a five-year policy varies with market conditions in the sense that a given amount of physical damage, just enough to result in a $1,000 loss if occurring during the first year of coverage, may result in a much higher dollar loss if it occurs in a later year and there has been an intervening increase in market values and repair costs because of inflation. The concurring opinion of Justice Brennan and the dissenting opinion of Justice Harlan have in com-

1.　See § 1.3(i) *supra*.

2.　See generally 1 Loss, Securities Regulation 498–501 (1961), 4 *id.* 2511–2535 (1969); Martin, *The Status of the Variable Annuity as a Security: A Lesson in Legal Line Drawing*, 30 Ohio St.L.J. 736 (1969); Comment, *Commingled Trust Funds and Variable Annuities: Uniform Federal Regulation of Investment Funds Operated by Banks and Insurance Companies*, 82 Harv.L.Rev. 435 (1968); Kern, *Variable Annuities*, 54 A.B.A.J. 144 (1968); Galston, *The Regulation of Variable Annuities*, 1967 ABA Section Ins., Neg. & Comp.L.Proceedings 348; Bartlett, *Variable Annuities: Evaluation and Analysis*, 19 Stan.L.Rev. 150–166 (1966).

3.　Securities & Exchange Commission v. Variable Annuity Life Ins. Co. 359 U.S. 65, 71, 73, 79 Sup.Ct. 618, 622–623, 3 L.Ed.2d 640, 644, 645 (1959).

mon a point of view, preferable to that of the Douglas opinion it would seem, that the variable annuity plainly has elements characteristic of insurance and other elements characteristic of securities, making it necessary to decide the case on some basis other than the assertion that the arrangement is or is not insurance in common understanding or as used by Congress. The Brennan opinion argues that the securities aspects are predominant; the Harlan opinion, that the insurance aspects are at least so substantial that the history of Congressional restraint with respect to invasion of the field of insurance regulation points to inclusion of the variable annuity within the exemption of insurance from the operation of the securities acts.

Variable annuities are a socially desirable addition to the methods of providing for retirement.[4] Plainly, also, there are needs for public regulation of these contracts. The needs are in some respects like those for regulation of ordinary annuities and in other respects like those for regulation of securities transactions. For the present, at least, no single system of regulation has been developed; rather, industry operations in the variable annuities market are subject to regulation both under securities laws and under insurance laws.[5] There is risk, perhaps, that agencies primarily engaged in regulating securities transactions may seek to impose unduly restrictive measures on variable annuities in comparison with the somewhat competitive forms of open-end securities, and that agencies primarily engaged in regulating insurance transactions may seek to impose investment standards more appropriate to traditional life insurance payable in fixed sums than to variable annuities. In any event, the dispute over regulatory jurisdiction, spurred by competitive private interests as well as the differing interests and concerns of the various regulatory agencies involved, has had an adverse impact on the speed of development of variable annuities as a form of contract readily available to the public. And the present division of responsibility for regulation is surely less than a settled solution of the problem.

SECTION 8.3 AIMS AND AREAS OF INSURANCE REGULATION

Most measures of insurance regulation have been initiated to serve one or more of three main objectives: first, to avoid overreaching by insurers; second, to assure solidity and solvency of insurers; third, to assure that rating classifications and rates are reasonable and fair.[1]

4. See generally Greenough & King, Benefit Plans in American Colleges 43–99 (1969); Johnson & Grubbs, The Variable Annuity, ch. 1 (2d ed. 1970); Johnson, *Variable Annuities: What They Are and How They Can Be Used by Attorneys*, 48 Neb.L.Rev. 943 (1969).

5. See, *e.g.*, Securities & Exchange Commission v. National Securities,

Inc., 393 U.S. 453, 89 Sup.Ct. 564, 21 L.Ed.2d 668 (1969); Securities & Exchange Commission v. United Benefit Ins. Co., 387 U.S. 202, 87 Sup.Ct. 1557, 18 L.Ed.2d 673 (1967); 1 Loss, Securities Regulation 498–501 (1961), 4 *id.* 2511–2535 (1969).

1. Cf. Kimball, *The Regulation of Insurance*, in Insurance, Government and

Regulation to avoid overreaching is principally directed at marketing practices and arrangements and has been initiated both in statutes [2] and in judicially created doctrines.[3]

The aim of assuring solidity and solvency is served by regulation of insurance organizations and their funds to avoid the consequences of imprudent management,[4] and to lesser extent by an aspect of rate regulation concerned with adequacy as distinguished from reasonableness and equity.[5]

The aim of assuring that premium charges are reasonable and fair both in total amount and in proportionate allocation among policyholders is the chief objective of rate regulation generally.[6]

The areas of insurance regulation are numerous and varied. Some regulatory measures are focused on regulating insurance transactions; others, on regulating the institutions and the people engaged in such transactions as a business.

Insurance transactions are subject to regulatory doctrines developed in courts, affecting the terms of the various contracts offered to policyholders and the rights of policyholders and beneficiaries at variance with policy provisions.[7] Policy forms are, in addition, subject to statutory [8] and administrative regulation.[9]

Insurance transactions are also subject to much regulation in relation to the processing of claims. This is accomplished through regulation of forms,[10] through recognition of rights at variance with policy provisions,[11] through statutory penalties for delay in payment of claims,[12] through such devices as resident-agent statutes,[13] through

Social Policy 3, 5–10 (Kimball & Denenberg eds. 1969); Kimball, *The Purpose of Insurance Regulation: A Preliminary Inquiry in the Theory of Insurance Law*, 45 Minn.L.Rev. 471 (1961). Kimball also identifies "external objectives" that should be taken into account in thinking about insurance regulation, among which are the "libertarian objective" of freedom from governmental restraint, "local protectionism" that is in general opposed by the farsighted and nationally oriented but nevertheless has its impact, and the objective of wide dispersion of decision-making power, which he refers to as "federalism." *Id.* at 6–8. See also Stewart, *Ritual and Reality in Insurance Regulation*, in Insurance, Government and Social Policy 22, 24–32 (Kimball & Denenberg eds. 1969) ("A good, simple answer is that government is trying to help people get the most insurance for their money," and among the ideas this implies are assuring availability, quality and reliability, and reasonable pricing).

2. Consider, *e.g.*, legislation concerning the effect to be given to warranties in insurance law, § 6.5 *supra*.

3. Consider generally the judicially developed principles of denying unconscionable advantage and honoring reasonable expectations, §§ 6.2, 6.3 *supra*.

4. See generally Insurance, Government and Social Policy 63–190 (Kimball & Denenberg eds. 1969). See also § 8.5 *infra*.

5. See generally § 8.4 *infra*.

6. *Ibid.*

7. See generally Chapter 6 *supra*.

8. See § 2.10 *supra*.

9. *Ibid.*

10. *Ibid.*

11. See § 6.8 *supra*.

12. See § 7.4 *supra*.

13. *E.g.*, N.Y.Ins.Law § 59 (McKinney 1966).

administrative processes for responding to individual complaints,[14] and through provisions for administrative initiatives of more general scope.[15]

Rating practices are a matter of continuing concern and occasionally violent controversy.[16]

Marketing practices are subject to statutory, administrative, and judicial regulation. Judicial doctrines concerning rights at variance with policy provisions [17] are to a considerable extent responsive to abuses in marketing. In the period following enactment of the McCarran-Ferguson Act, legislation establishing sanctions against false advertising was adopted in the various states.[18] Other enactments, of longer standing, apply to rebating and discrimination.[19] In the 1960's increased legislative and administrative attention was given to complaints arising from cancellations and nonrenewals.[20]

Insurance institutions are subject to regulatory statutes, and administrative regulation thereunder, with respect to the forms of insurance organizations,[21] the maintenance of a secure financial status (the regulatory measures including controls over investments and reserves and requirements of deposits, reports, and audits),[22] processes of liquidation and rehabilitation,[23] and special provisions for protection of policyholders and others against the consequences of insurer insolvency.[24] Both insuring organizations and insurance agents and brokers are subject to licensing provisions.[25]

One of the troublesome areas in relation to qualification and licensing of agents for the marketing of insurance concerns tie-in transactions. For example, a legal entity engaged in consumer financing may itself seek to function as an agent for the sale of credit life insurance, or may participate in an arrangement in which persons associated with it do so as individuals but in a setting in which the tie-in is both commercially advantageous and subject to abuse. Similar arrangements may be established between sales of automobiles

---

14. For a summary of data concerning complaint records of the N.Y.Insurance Department in the years 1966–1968, see N.Y.Ins.Dep't, Report, Automobile Insurance . . . For Whose Benefit? 37 n.68 (1970).

15. The New York Insurance Department study of automobile insurance, cited in n.14 *supra* is a special instance of an initiative of broad scope. See generally § 8.1(b) *supra*.

16. See § 8.4 *infra*.

17. See generally Chapter 6 *supra*.

18. See § 8.1(a) *supra*.

19. *E.g.*, N.Y.Ins.Law §§ 188, 209 (McKinney Supp.1970).

20. See § 5.10(e) (3) *supra*.

21. See § 8.5 *infra*.

22. *E.g.*, N.Y.Ins.Law §§ 70–104 (McKinney Supp.1970).

23. *E.g.*, N.Y.Ins.Law §§ 510–546 (McKinney 1966).

24. *E.g.*, Wis.Stat.Ann. § 645.01–.10 (Supp.1970). See generally Insurance Accessibility for the Hard-to-Place Driver, Report of the Division of Industry Analysis, Bureau of Economics, Federal Trade Commission 73–77 (U. S.Dep't Transp.Auto.Ins. & Comp. Study 1970).

25. *E.g.*, N.Y.Ins.Law §§ 40, 110, 111 (McKinney 1966).

and automobile insurance, or between provision of funeral and burial services and the sale of funeral and burial insurance. Efforts to regulate such tie-in arrangements have sometimes succeeded [26] and sometimes failed.[27]

Federal as well as state antitrust laws are at least potentially applicable to insurance companies,[28] and the variable annuities cases [29] have demonstrated that there are other odds and ends of insurance regulation to be found outside the sources so labeled.

SECTION 8.4   INSURANCE RATING

§ 8.4(a) OBJECTIVES AND METHODS OF RATING AND REGULATION

Enlightened insurance rating is aimed at developing rates that are adequate and neither excessive nor unfairly discriminatory. This threefold set of objectives is more often stated, however, in twofold form—first, assuring that rates are adequate to provide funds for paying losses, costs of administration, and reasonable profits and, second, assuring that rates are neither excessive (with the result of unreasonable profits or costs) nor unfairly discriminatory (with the result of unreasonably high rates to some policyholders and unreasonably low rates to others).[1]

objectives of rating
adequate
not excessive
not unfairly discrimination

Relying to a large extent upon competition to produce rates that are neither excessive nor discriminatory has always been an underlying principle of insurance rating in the United States. Initially competition was virtually the sole mechanism relied upon. But the distinctive characteristics of the insurance business call for some degree of regulation to preserve and reinforce competition as an instrument for developing proper rates.

One factor of great significance is that the complexity of insurance transactions in the eyes of the ordinary consumer makes severe

---

26. *E.g.,* Daniel v. Family Security Life Ins. Co., 336 U.S. 220, 69 Sup.Ct. 550, 93 L.Ed. 632 (1949), 10 A.L.R.2d 945 (1950) (sustaining, against constitutional attack, a South Carolina statute prohibiting undertakers from serving as agents for life insurance companies).

27. *E.g.,* Department of Ins. v. Motors Ins. Corp., 236 Ind. 1, 138 N.E.2d 157 (1956) (overturning the Department's effort to prohibit automobile dealers from serving as agents for the sale of automobile insurance, holding such action to be an unconstitutional deprivation of the right to engage simultaneously in two lawful businesses; this conclusion of unconstitutionality seems strange in the modern setting).

28. See § 8.1(a) *supra.*

29. See § 8.2(d) *supra.*

1. See, *e.g.,* Williams, *Unfair Rate Discrimination in Property and Liability Insurance,* in Insurance, Government, and Social Policy 209 (Kimball & Denenberg eds. 1969); Kimball and Boyce, *The Adequacy of State Insurance Rate Regulation: The Mc-Carran-Ferguson Act in Historical Perspective,* 56 Mich.L.Rev. 545–546 (1958); Kulp, *The Rate-Making Process in Property and Casualty Insurance—Goals, Technics, and Limits,* 15 Law & Contemp.Prob. 493–494 (1950).

inroads upon the effectiveness of price competition. In the absence
of regulation of the package, if not the price, the proliferation of consumer products makes it a virtually hopeless task for the ordinary
consumer to compare the products and prices offered him from different sources.[2]

Unrestrained competition also endangers insurance companies
themselves, and in turn the members of the public they serve. For
example, it may lead to price competition that ends in the inability of
some companies to cover the losses against which they have contracted to insure. A rule of survival of the fittest may be defensible in relation to the interests of stockholder investors. But to permit the
less fit among insurance companies to go into insolvency without providing for the claims of their policyholders and others entitled to insurance benefits would be an intolerable injustice to persons who had
inadequate opportunity to judge the fitness of companies before taking insurance.

The perils to solvency of insurance companies arising from the
risk that rates might be set at unduly low levels, under the incentives
of unrestrained competition, is exacerbated by the danger of miscal-
culation of future losses. Actuarial prediction, in the pragmatic field
of insurance at least, is a process of developing a structure of precise
calculations all founded on guesses about the future. However precise the calculations may be, the conclusion is no more reliable than
the guesses on which the calculations are based. The element of
guesswork can be reduced in degree with relatively complete and reliable data about past experience, upon which predictions for the future are based, but in the end a degree of guesswork in setting rates
is inevitable. The best actuaries are persons shrewd in foresight and
skilled in analogical as well as logical reasoning.

On the other hand, an industry-wide practice of excessive caution about the unpredictable elements in future loss experience can
result in excessive rates—and this remains true whether it is the
product of concerted action or merely the cumulative effect of separate decisions by executives who prefer to express their competitive
urges in ways other than price reduction.

It happens also that competition cannot be expected to provide
adequate protection against discriminatory rates. Even if competition is functioning well, there will be collateral influences that make
some policyholders more or less attractive on grounds apart from

2. In the United States, there has been
relatively little regulation of life,
health, and accident insurance policy
forms and even less regulation of life,
health, and accident insurance rates.
One consequence is that it is extremely difficult for the ordinary purchaser
to make price comparisons. See, e.g.,
Young, A Study of Health Insurance
Policies Available in New York State
for the Purposes of Developing a Procedure for Their Evaluation and
Grading (1964), an excerpt from which
is quoted in Kimball & Pfennigstorf,
*Administrative Control of the Terms
of Insurance Contracts: A Comparative Study*, 40 Ind.L.J. 143, 214–215
(1965). Concerning life insurance
pricing generally, see Belth, *Life Insurance Price Measurement*, 57 Ky.L.
J. 687 (1969) [much of this article also
appears in 48 Neb.L.Rev. 897 (1969)].

pure assessment of the rated risk. Moreover, judgments must be made about the extent of multiplication of rating categories to reflect different degrees of risk. There comes a point at which the administrative costs of further refinements outweigh their utility. It is less than clear, to say the least, that unregulated competition will produce a wiser choice concerning the numbers of categories of rates, and their design, than can be produced under a somewhat regulated competition.

As surely as it is clear that unrestrained competition may be destructive rather than productive of rates that are adequate and neither excessive nor discriminatory, so too is it clear that unrestrained opportunities of cooperation among insurers would be contrary to the public interest. The risk that rates would be set at excessive levels is obvious, and though subtler perhaps, risks of discriminatory rating would surely exist under unrestrained cooperation. But this is not to say that all cooperation should be forbidden. Indeed, in a practical sense, any inroads upon free competition imply a degree of cooperation among insurers, even though under the scrutiny of a public official. Moreover, in some aspects of rating, cooperation is an affirmative good in itself rather than merely the converse of limiting competition. This is true, for example, of cooperation among insurers in accumulating and sharing data to produce a broader and more reliable base for predicting future losses.[3]

There is consensus, then, that some degree and form of regulation is needed to achieve an operable blend of competition and cooperation. But there is continuing controversy concerning just what that blend should be and how it should be effectuated.

In some contexts, regulation of rates has become in form absolute—that is, a governmental body has been given the power and responsibility of fixing rates.[4] A common usage in the industry refers to such an arrangement as one of governmental "rate-making" as distinguished from "regulation" of rates "made" by an individual insur-

[right margin handwritten note:] unrestrained also cooperation contrary to public interest

---

3. An interesting industry usage refers to the data, rather than merely the predictions based on the data, as more "credible" in these circumstances. Perhaps this is a reflection of a somewhat wishful view of the actuarial process that plays down the inevitable element of guesswork. But in any event the phrase "more credible data" can be viewed as useful shorthand for the more precise expression, "data that will support more credible predictions." Of course the data too may be more or less credible, depending on degrees of precision in gathering and recording information.

4. E.g., in relation to governmental rate setting for certain types of auto-

mobile insurance in two states, which are referred to in other contexts as the cradle of liberty and the bastion of individualism, see Mass.Gen.Laws Ann., ch. 175, § 113B (Supp.1970); Tex.Ins.Code Ann. art. 5.01 (1963). There are also other scattered instances of provisions for governmental rate-making. E.g., Tex.Ins.Code Ann. arts. 5.25–5.27 (fire rates), 5.55 (workmen's compensation rates), 5.69–5.71 (special rates for national defense contracts) (1963 and Supp.1970). See also La.Acts 1958 No. 125 (casualty rates), later amended to provide for approval rather than fixing of rates by the Casualty and Surety Division of the Rating Commission, La.Rev. Stat. § 22:1406 (Supp.1970).

er or by concerted action among insurers either on an ad hoc basis or through a regularly functioning rating bureau.

A more common arrangement for casualty insurance is one under which individual insurers or groups of insurers acting in concert set proposed rates that are subject to some form of regulation by some governmental agency. The forms of regulation have varied widely from systems of quite direct measures of rate regulation to systems depending on other types of regulations to achieve, with the aid of competition, the objectives of a sound rating system.

Rate *regulation* appears in practice to be less responsive to political pressures than *rate-making.* The experience with compulsory automobile insurance rates in Massachusetts is one of constant political pressure on the rate-*making* official to set the rates at levels that the insurers declare to be confiscatory. In contrast, rate *regulation* in most states has been neither vigorous nor effectual. There is greater risk under a rate-*making* system that in response to political pressures the rates will be set at a scale inadequate to produce sound protection of the insurance funds except by reliance upon profits from other lines of business that are free of the rate-making system (thus producing an unfair distribution of the costs of various types of insurance). And there is a greater risk under a system of rate *regulation* that the rates will be allowed to run too high because of the lack of vigor of the regulatory agency, or the lack of adequate funds and personnel to make an independent inquiry into the reasonableness of rates filed by the insurers.

In the history of changing patterns of insurance rate regulation, three distinctive periods can be identified—first, a period of very weak and exclusively state rather than federal regulation, ending in the aftermath of the 1944 decision in *South-Eastern Underwriters*; second, a predominantly state-prior-approval period extending until late in the 1960's; third, a period of re-consideration of the prior-approval practice and perhaps the federal-state accommodation as well.

Before 1944, insurance rating practices were generally understood to be subject to regulation in the various states and constitutionally protected from federal regulation. In that year the Supreme Court of the United States held insurance subject to federal regulation, and in particular to the federal antitrust legislation there invoked against the South-Eastern Underwriters Association, the members of which had long engaged in concerted action in setting rates.[5] In the face of severe doubts thus cast on existing rating practices and state regulation generally, Congress passed the McCarran-Ferguson Act, preserving in general the pre-1944 state competence and responsibility in insurance regulation, though with exceptions that are potentially very significant.[6]

---

5. United States v. South-Eastern Underwriters Ass'n, 322 U.S. 533, 64 Sup.Ct. 1162, 88 L.Ed. 1440 (1944).

6. See § 8.1(a) *supra.*

As a practical matter, however, the McCarran-Ferguson Act did not return matters to the pre-1944 status. In that earlier time, insurance regulation proceeded generally on the assumption that examination of reserves and investments would protect adequately against company failures, without specific examination of rates to assure their adequacy, and that generally competition, supplemented by antitrust and anti-discrimination legislation, would provide adequate protection against excessive and discriminatory rates. That view could no longer prevail after the *South-Eastern Underwriters* decision and the McCarran-Ferguson Act, for the latter protected the industry from the applications of federal antitrust legislation only to the extent that the insurance business is "regulated by State law." [7] There was immediate pressure from the insurance industry upon the states to occupy the field of insurance regulation more completely, and especially in relation to rating, to avoid the threat of federal regulation. An All-Industry Committee was formed and they quickly gained the sympathetic interest and cooperation of the National Association of Insurance Commissioners in developing and sponsoring state legislation.

In 1944, some kind of provision for rate regulation existed in two-thirds of the states, but insurance rate-making was on the whole under little effective supervision.[8] By 1951, many of the older statutes had been amended and rate regulatory legislation had been enacted in every state,[9] providing in most instances for specific concern with adequacy of rates as well as excessiveness and discrimination.[10] Many of these statutes are still in effect. And in many instances they apply only in the fields of fire, inland marine, and casualty insurance. The insurers' practice of acting in concert through rating organizations in these fields would run afoul of federal antitrust legisla-

---

7. 59 Stat. 33 (1945), 15 U.S.C. § 1012 (1958). Section 2(b) of the Act provides: "No Act of Congress shall be construed to invalidate, impair, or supercede any law enacted by any State for the purpose of regulating the business of insurance, or which imposes a fee or tax upon such business, unless such Act specifically relates to the business of insurance: *Provided*, That after January 1, 1948 . . . the Sherman Act, . . . the Clayton Act, and . . . the Federal Trade Commission Act, as amended, shall be applicable to the business of insurance to the extent that such business is not regulated by State law." The date January 1, 1948, was subsequently changed to June 30, 1948. 61 Stat. 448 (1947), 15 U.S.C. § 1012(b) (1958).

8. See Kimball and Boyce, *The Adequacy of State Insurance Rate Regulation: The McCarran-Ferguson Act in Historical Perspective*, 56 Mich.L.Rev.

545, 552 (1958). *Cf.* Day, Economic Regulation of Insurance in the United States 18–23 (U.S. Dep't Transp. Auto. Ins. & Comp. Study 1970).

9. See *id.* at 28. Concerning litigation incidental to the application of various rating statutes, see in general McCollough, *Insurance Rates in the Courts*, 1961 Ins.L.J. 381, 475.

10. "Under this model legislation the principle of concerted rate making under social control was established as nation-wide policy at the state level, in preference to the less sophisticated prohibition-of-concert principle of the Sherman Act." Kimball and Boyce, *The Adequacy of State Insurance Rate Regulation: The McCarran-Ferguson Act in Historical Perspective*, 56 Mich.L.Rev. 545, 556 (1958). *Cf.* Dirlam and Stelzer, *The Insurance Industry: A Case Study in the Workability of Regulated Competition*, 107 U.Pa.L.Rev. 199, 201–202 (1958).

tion if there were no state regulation. In the fields of life, health, and accident insurance, on the other hand, rates ordinarily have been made by each insurer separately rather than through a rating organization.[11]

Under these statutes enacted during the post-1944 period, the most common pattern for regulation of fire, inland marine, and casualty insurance rates is one in which rates must meet the prescribed standard that they not be excessive, inadequate, or unfairly discriminatory, rating manuals and rating plans must be filed with the State Insurance Commissioner for approval before use, companies may act in cooperation and concert through rating organizations licensed and supervised by the State, some rating deviations are provided for within the framework of the rating organizations, and there are provisions for administrative hearings and judicial review.[12]

The enactment, following the McCarran-Ferguson Act, of state legislation on regulation of rates for casualty insurance settled only temporarily, if at all, the controversy over methods of rating. The newly enacted state legislation was soon invoked in an effort to stifle competition by forcing insurance companies using the data-gathering facilities of a rating bureau to use the rates set by the bureau. In time this effort led to litigation over construction of some of the state statutes,[13] and to legislative amendments in some states for the purpose of making clear and explicit the rights of "partial subscribership" to a bureau, under which a company could get the benefits of bureau operations for a proper charge and yet be free, to some extent at least, to offer coverage at different rates from those the bureau set.

The rating systems operating under these statutes have posed serious practical obstacles to the use of rates other than the bureau

11. See Holz, *Administration of Insurance Law*, 1956 Ins.L.J. 24, 28.

12. Donovan, *State Regulation of Insurance*, 1956 Ins.L.J. 11, 13. For a more detailed treatment of the rating bills, see Gardner, *Insurance and the Anti-trust Laws—A Problem in Synthesis*, 61 Harv.L.Rev. 245, 259–265 (1948). Professor Gardner identifies five basic principles underlying the rating bills:

"First: All premiums shall be determined in accordance with written schedules, based on the analysis of past experience, and open to public inspection in a public office." *Id.* at 260.

"Second: The constitution of every rating organization shall be a matter of public record, and its services shall be available to every underwriting organization which desires to utilize such rating organization for the purpose of

determining its own rates." *Id.* at 261.

"Third: Every insuring organization may either file its own rates independently or adopt those of a licensed rating organization as it elects." *Id.* at 263.

"Fourth: The insured shall at all times have access, not only to the schedule by which his premium is determined, but to the statistics and computations on which it is based." *Id.* at 264.

"Fifth: The state insurance commissioner, or corresponding officer, may disapprove any premium schedule filed by anyone if, and only if, he finds that the rates are 'excessive, inadequate, or unfairly discriminatory.' " *Id.* at 265.

13. *E.g.*, Pacific Fire Rating Bureau v. Insurance Co. of N. Am., 83 Ariz. 369, 321 P.2d 1030 (1958); Fire Ins. Rating Bureau v. Rogan, 4 Wis.2d 558, 91 N. W.2d 372 (1958).

rates.[14] It has been stated that if you are a subscriber to a rating bureau "you must adhere to the rates so filed on your behalf unless you can comply with the deviation procedure provided by statute," which is a "cumbersome process that must be repeated each year." [15] Also, rating bureaus have argued that it is unfair for non-bureau companies to be allowed to use the data developed by the bureaus at considerable expense.[16]

Though partial subscribership adds some administrative problems that are not encountered under a system of full subscribership only, these are problems that can be met at a moderate cost. To one who opposes uniformity of rates, partial subscribership is desirable since otherwise the nonconformist insurers would be unable to take advantage of the cooperation among insurers in compilation of data relevant to rate-making. Surely the argument that it is unfair for non-bureau companies to use the bureau data can be met by charging non-bureau companies a fair proportion of the cost of accumulating the bureau data. It would be possible, for example, to require all insurers of the relevant class to report data to the bureau and to pay an assessment based on volume of business, leaving to each insurer the freedom to use the bureau rates or its own separate rates.

In general it would seem that this move toward increased freedom for competition was sound. The statutes on rate regulation enacted during the immediate aftermath of the McCarran-Ferguson Act wisely provided for cooperation in data gathering for rating purposes but went too far toward compelling cooperating companies to abide by bureau rates.

The near universal approval of cooperation among insurers in rating can be justified as a way of producing more widely based data, and at lower overall cost. Indeed there is hardly any dispute about the need for cooperation among insurers for this purpose.

Cooperation to achieve uniformity of rates is a different matter. It is true that arguments for uniformity may have contributed to approval of cooperation among insurers; one who favors uniformity of rates must also favor either cooperation among insurers (with or without public regulation) or else the maintenance of a public agency

---

14. See Dirlam and Stelzer, *The Insurance Industry: A Case Study in the Workability of Regulated Competition,* 107 U.Pa.L.Rev. 199 (1958).

15. Pacific Fire Ins. Bureau v. Insurance Co. of N. Am., 83 Ariz. 369, 375, 321 P.2d 1030, 1034 (1958).

16. "The pulling and tussling that is going on between the so-called bureau companies and those classed as independents would seem to call for another look at these laws. On the one hand the independent companies contend that some departments are using the laws to make rates by strict interpretations and by undue requirements for statistics, while on the other hand the bureau companies, particularly in the fire field, contend that the independents and those who may be partial subscribers at a bureau have no right to copy and use the bureau's surveys, rate books, tariffs, town classifications and other material in making their filings . . .." Stone, *Rate Regulation v. Rate-Making,* 1955 Ins.L.J. 107.

for rate-making. But the case for uniformity of rates seems much less persuasive than the case for cooperation in data gathering.[17]

A third distinctive period in the history of insurance rate regulation commenced late in the 1960's. Again, in this third period, significant changes in the patterns of rate regulation are occurring, but there is less consensus about the general direction and nature of the changes and there is greater diversity in the proposals and enactments. The new period of change was triggered by the worsening situation in automobile insurance. Mounting public dissatisfaction with various aspects of the automobile insurance system resulted in pressures against rate increases that insurers generally regarded as essential to their continued operations in this line of business. One pattern of response, developed by spokesmen for most segments of the industry [18] and state regulatory officials in some states,[19] has been a turn away from "prior approval" laws—the type most prevalent at the beginning of this new period of change—toward either "file and use" laws that, in theory at least, would open up somewhat greater competition, or "no-filing" laws (also referred to as "open competition" laws) that in theory would encourage far greater competition in rates by permitting a company to establish new rates freely and to place them in effect promptly. But just as this response was gaining momentum,[20] aided by the enactment of "open competition" legislation in Wisconsin [21] and New York [22] in 1969, proposals for exactly the reverse change were being advanced in states having "open competition" legislation.[23] These contradictory responses were symptomatic of difficulties of an even more fundamental character than the choice among methods of rate regulation. These difficulties, and the manifestations of public dissatisfaction they produced, were also commanding renewed interest in federal action affecting various aspects of the automobile reparations and insurance system.[24]

17. The case for uniformity of rates might be compared with the case for Fair Trade Acts bearing on *retail* price fixing by a *manufacturer*. In the insurance area, however, it is not contended that retail pricing by different agents of a single insurer should be competitive; rather the issue is whether prices of different insurers should be competitive.

18. See, *e.g.*, Williams, *Insurer Views on Property and Liability Insurance Rate Regulation*, 36 J. Risk & Ins. 217 (1969).

19. *E.g.*, N.Y. Ins. Dep't, Report, The Public Interest Now in Property and Liability Insurance Regulation 65–149 (1969). See generally Franson, *The Prior-Approval System of Property and Liability Insurance Rate Regulation: A Case Study*, 1969 Wis.L.Rev. 1104.

20. See Insurance Accessibility for the Hard-to-Place Driver, Report of the Division of Industry Analysis, Bureau of Economics, Federal Trade Commission 78–79 (U.S. Dep't Transp. Auto Ins. & Comp. Study 1970).

21. Wis. Laws of 1969, ch. 144, § 23; Wis.Stat.Ann. ch. 625 (Supp.1970).

22. N.Y.Ins.Law §§ 175–180 (McKinney 1966 and McKinney Supp.1970).

23. Competing views were expressed by speakers at the annual meeting of the American Insurance Association in May, 1970. See, *e.g.*, The Standard (New England's Insurance Weekly), May 22, 1970, pp. 1, 7–10. See also *id.*, April 10, 1970, pp. 1, 3, 20; March 27, 1970, p. 12.

24. See, *e.g.*, Insurance Accessibility for the Hard-to-Place Driver, Report

The new spirit of change revived also a long smoldering controversy over the consideration of investment income in casualty insurance rating.[25]

Rate regulation is in fact less pervasive and vigorous than the prevalence of state legislation might suggest. Most insurance consumers are unorganized, and their complaints about rates are seldom urged upon an insurance commission unless insurance rates become a political issue. In only a few states has the insurance commission the staff and financing required for a substantial inquiry beyond the data supplied from industry sources in support of their proposed rates. Thus, the interests of consumers, insofar as they are in conflict with those of insurers, are not effectively represented except when rates become a political issue, and in those circumstances there is danger that a politically-motivated resolution of the controversy will not give due weight to the public interest in adequacy of rates and want of discrimination.[26]

§ 8.4(b) EQUITY AND DISCRIMINATION

Rate regulatory standards customarily include a requirement that rates not be "unfairly discriminatory." [1]

The generality of this standard leaves wide leeway for evaluative determinations [2] regarding the number and nature of categories employed in a rating system. The difficulties of applying such a standard have figured in an assessment that no other objective of insurance regulation is as difficult to achieve as equitable rating.[3]

Administrative cost is a major factor in the choice concerning the degree to which a rating system is finely tailored to the magni-

of the Division of Industry Analysis, Bureau of Economics, Federal Trade Commission 73–85 (U.S. Dep't Transp. Auto. Ins. & Comp. Study 1970).

25. See, e.g., The Standard (New England's Insurance Weekly), Nov. 14, 1969, p. 1 (Mass. hearings), Nov. 21, 1969, p. 1 (N. H. Commission ruling). See generally, Birkinsha, *Investment Income and Underwriting Profit: "And Never the Twain Shall Meet"?* 13 Boston College Ind. & Com.L.Rev. 713 (1967); Comment, *Insurance Ratemaking Problems: Administrative Discretion, Investment Income, and Prepaid Expenses*, 16 Wayne L.Rev. 95 (1969).

26. *Cf.* Kimball and Boyce, *The Adequacy of State Insurance Regulation: The McCarran-Ferguson Act in Historical Perspective*, 56 Mich.L.Rev. 545, 556–565 (1958).

1. See § 8.4(a) n.1 *supra*.

2. Concerning the nature of evaluative issues generally, see § 1.6 *supra*.

3. See, *e.g.*, Kimball, *The Purpose of Insurance Regulation: A Preliminary Inquiry in the Theory of Insurance Law*, 45 Minn.L.Rev. 471, 495–498 (1961). The difficulties of determining whether rating classifications are "unfairly discriminatory" are enhanced by the political factors brought to bear. For example, it is common that some insurance purchasers are "subsidized" at the expense of others when, because of political pressures for allowing people to drive even when they are poor risks and without paying the full costs, rates for "assigned risk" insureds are not high enough to cover the cost to insurers of providing "assigned risk" coverages. *Cf.* Williams, *Unfair Rate Discrimination in Property and Liability Insurance*, in Insurance, Government and Social Policy 209, 222 (Kimball & Denenberg eds. 1969).

tude of risks assumed by the insurer in its contracts with various types of policyholders. In general there is an increase in administrative cost roughly proportionate to the degree of precision with which the classification system undertakes to measure the magnitude of risks. Obviously it is undesirable to use a system of classes tailored to different magnitudes of risk to the maximum extent that obtainable data will support. The cost of gathering the data and administering the resulting rating and marketing system would be so great that even the policyholders in the most favored rating classes would pay more than they would pay under a system with fewer and cruder classes. Even though there would be greater relative equity among policyholders, all policyholders, if reacting reasonably and apart from any motives of spite, would readily sacrifice such refined equity in favor of lower rates for everybody. Even those relatively less favorably treated by the cruder system of classification would nevertheless prefer it if persuaded that there was no way for them to achieve relatively more favorable treatment without also incurring higher costs for themselves as well as others. This principle of limiting refinements in categories by considerations of administrative cost explains the rejection in many contexts of arguments for more numerous and more finely graded rating classes.[4]

The impact of administrative cost on the rating system is well illustrated in the development of merit rating for automobile insurance. Merit rating systems have often been described as based on determinations of fault in the operation of motor vehicles. But even when formally designed to achieve that aim, in practical administration they have tended to be based on the more objective criterion of involvement rather than on genuine determinations of fault or even on objective criteria roughly identifying those at fault in particular motoring incidents.[5]

The first-party or third-party form of insurance contracts covering losses from bodily injury or property damage has influenced rating systems in a way that bears on equity. For example, first-party systems of insurance against loss from bodily injury tend to give little if any attention to a policyholder's characteristics bearing on the likelihood that he will impose costs on the insurance system by causing loss to others, and third-party systems tend to give little attention

4. See, *e.g.*, §§ 2.4(b) (inequities from insurer's liability for delay in acting on application); 2.8(a) at n.10 (group insurance); 2.11(b) and (d) (fringe additions to automobile and liability coverages); 4.2(c) (mortgagee-only insurance); 4.3(d) (vendor and purchaser); 5.5(c) (inequities from overlapping coverages); 5.10(b) (inequities arising from irregularities about anniversary date of policy) *supra* and § 8.6(c) n.13 (flood insurance) *infra*.

5. N.Y.Ins.Dep't, Report, Automobile Insurance . . . For Whose Benefit? 48 n.96 (1970): "Some insurance companies do indeed use 'merit rating' plans which are sometimes loosely thought of as varying one's premium rates according to the quality of one's driving. But even the merit rating plans do not depend upon fault law. Rather, premium surcharges and discounts are based on accident involvement. With a few exceptions for broad and objective categories, the merit rating plans do not significantly turn on legal fault or accident severity."

to a policyholder's characteristics (such as a high level of earned income and a long expectancy of working years) bearing on the likelihood that he will cost the system more than average whenever he is a victim. The debate over automobile insurance reform has served to focus attention on the fact, however, that it is feasible to adjust rates for either a first-party or a third-party system to take account of both these types of loss-causing potential.[6]

SECTION 8.5 / TYPES OF INSURERS

There are six major types of private, as distinguished from governmental,[1] insurers: natural persons; Lloyd's associations; stock companies; mutual companies; fraternal societies; and reciprocal associations (inter-insurance exchanges).[2]

Rather early in the development of public regulation of insurance transactions it became apparent that one of the important needs was for regulation of the juristic form of legal entities allowed to conduct an insurance business. State laws now commonly declare it a criminal offense for a person, association, or corporation to be engaged in what is commonly called "doing an insurance business" without having qualified as an insurer in conformity with the state laws and the administrative system established under them. The structure of the state laws for qualification to conduct an insurance business is thus a system regulating the forms of insuring organizations.

Even though the history of Lloyd's associations in England demonstrates that reasonable assurances of financial responsibility can be achieved in an insurance system relying largely upon such associations of individuals, American legislatures have generally disfavored the recognition of individuals and Lloyd's types of associations as qualified insurers. Even statutes authorizing so-called Lloyd's associations in some instances approve not associations of the type commonly indicated by that name—associations in which individuals may serve as the insurers—but rather legal entities very different in form from the Coffee House syndicates.[3] The trend away from recognition of individuals as insurers has extended also to the mutual insurers. State statutes provide for the incorporation of such insurers, and such incorporated entities are commonly referred to as mutual companies.

---

6. See Keeton, Compensation Systems —The Search for a Viable Alternative to Negligence Law 48–51 (1969), reprinted in Seavey, Keeton & Keeton, Cases and Materials on the Law of Torts 275–279 (1970 Supp.).

1. Concerning governmental organizations as insurers, see generally § 8.6 *infra*.

2. See generally § 1.4 *supra*.

3. See, *e.g.*, Tex.Ins.Code Ann. arts. 18.-01–18.24 (1963), sometimes referring to Lloyds' associations as "companies" (*id.* arts. 18.07, 18.11) and imposing requirements for maintaining assets and reserves equal to those required of a stock insurance company transacting the same kinds of business (*id.* arts. 18.05, 18.08).

Different sets of criteria for qualification have been developed for the various forms of organizations allowed to do an insurance business. Stock companies are generally subject to requirements regarding paid-in capital and surplus, to serve as a measure of assurance that the insurer will be able to perform its obligations. Since mutuals have no stock or stockholders, some other technique of accomplishing a comparable measure of assurance of performance must be used. Often a mutual is formed after a growing organization has developed as a stock company. In such circumstances, it is quite feasible to have the equivalent of paid-in capital and surplus, even if under some other designation. Another device in use is a form of insurance contract with each policyholder under which he is subject to assessments after losses. In practice, however, far more of the function of assuring financial responsibility, in relation to both stock and mutual insurers, is performed by statutory and administrative requirements for the maintenance of reserves bearing a reasonable relation to outstanding contractual obligations. Thus, mutuals are ordinarily permitted to issue non-assessable policies if adequate reserves are maintained.

Fraternal (mutual benefit) societies are commonly permitted to qualify as insurers under separate criteria. Initially these criteria were much less stringent, reflecting a public confidence and favoritism toward the fraternal associations. However, an unacceptable number of financial failures of such groups in time led to more stringent regulatory controls. Differences still exist, but they are less substantial than in earlier days.

The reciprocal exchange in pristine form was designed to make it as difficult as possible for effective legal proceedings to be brought against the exchange or its members. This arrangement tended to keep claims adjudication out of the hands of judges and juries, thus giving the management of the insurance organization a tighter control over claims practices. Often they could successfully resist the claims they thought fraudulent despite inability to prove the suspected fraud, since procedural obstacles could be used to block the assertion of the claims.

There were both advantages and disadvantages to membership in such a reciprocal exchange. As premium payer, one would be happy to become a member of an organization with a tight claims policy because of the potential saving in cost of insurance. The saving was potential, not certain, however, since a member of such an exchange was open to liability on assessments if losses of other members proved to be higher than anticipated. Also, the tight claims policy would be unattractive to a member as a potential claimant.

Under this type of organization, not only did a person face difficulties in proceeding against the exchange in case of a disputed claim, but also he was unprotected against part of the risk against which he might want insurance. A further disadvantage of the reciprocal exchange was the risk of inadequacy of the exchange's financial resources to meet claims. Thus, it was important for one considering membership in an exchange to have information about the reserves and financial stability of the organization. In many states at present, however, statutory and decisional developments have reduced to the point that they are no longer very troublesome both the risk of financial failure of the exchange and the difficulties of hailing the exchange into court.[4]

Through the combination of voluntary development in the market place and increasing statutory and administrative controls, the different types of insuring organizations have tended to become more alike both in formal structure and in practical performance. There may well be more difference, for example, between two stock companies and between two mutuals than between one of the stock and one of the mutual companies. Perhaps it is still the case, however, that differences of tendency and degree exist between the different groups.

One difference concerns identity of the persons to whom management is responsible. In stock companies, management is mainly responsible to the stockholders. Responsiveness to stockholder control in a corporation varies with factors such as the pattern of distribution of the stock. Usually however, there are one or more stockholders with substantial share holdings who exercise a significant voice in management. In a mutual, even if organized as a corporation with stockholders, management is expected to be responsible primarily to the policyholders. Ordinarily, however, no single policyholder has a relatively large interest in the company, and there is less tendency than in an ordinary stock company toward substantial shareholder influence on management decisions. Thus, the wide dispersion of ownership interests in mutuals, in contrast with a common situation of some concentration of share ownership in a stock company, creates a situation of greater independence of management of mutuals, in the absence of regulation.[5] While such independence may at times work to the advantage of the policyholders, it also creates a greater risk that mismanagement will go unchecked. Policyholders of a stock company need protection against management to serve stockholder interests in ways that may be detrimental to policyholders; in a mutual, this need is absent, but there is greater need than in a stock company for protection against management that is inefficient or is corruptly designed to further the interests of the officers themselves to the detriment of policyholders.

4. See, e.g., Long v. Sakleson, 328 Pa. 261, 195 A. 416 (1937) (attorney in fact of reciprocal exchange appeared specially to challenge jurisdiction over exchange based on service of the writ against the exchange by serving the Insurance Commissioner of Pennsylvania, arguing that neither the attorney in fact nor individual members of the exchange had been served and that the exchange was not a legal entity subject to jurisdiction; held, the court had jurisdiction); N.Y.Ins.Law §§ 410–424a (McKinney 1966). See also, e.g., Richardson v. Kelly, 144 Tex. 497, 191 S.W.2d 857 (1946), cert. denied, 329 U.S. 798 (1947) (class action against members of exchange).

5. See generally Hetherington, Fact v. Fiction: Who Owns Mutual Insurance Companies, 1969 Wis.L.Rev. 1068.

If management effectively represents the interests of the owners, the mutual form of organization is advantageous for policyholders, since they are the owners. Given equal efficiency of operations, the cost of insurance to the policyholder is less under the mutual form of organization, since all profits are in effect returned to policyholders. The participating stock company policies return some of the profit to policyholders, but presumably some is reserved for the stockholders. Arguably the stock company form of organization has prospects of greater efficiency, however, in view of the availability to it of the business acumen of its large-interest stockholders.

The financial responsibility of the insurer depends on the extent of holdings of assets in reserve to meet potential liabilities, but of course management decisions concerning reserves might be influenced by the form of organization.

The form of mutual organization in which obligations are met by assessments after loss has been unsatisfactory from the point of view of avoidance of insolvency, and regulatory statutes now commonly require the maintenance of substantial reserves. The need for maintenance of reserves by a stock company was more obvious from the outset, and requirements of such reserves were among the early forms of regulation.

The need for rate regulation and regulation aimed at avoidance of overreaching is less obvious and arguably less in degree as to mutuals than as to stock companies, since the policyholders are the owners of the mutuals. But the interests of the group of policyholders as owners are often in conflict with the interests of the individual policyholder. In relations between the management of the mutual and an individual policyholder the disparity of power creates substantially the same need for regulation as in the case of stock companies.

SECTION 8.6 GOVERNMENTAL SPONSORSHIP OF INSURANCE GENERALLY

§ 8.6(a) TECHNIQUES OF GOVERNMENTAL SPONSORSHIP

Governmental sponsorship of an insurance program may occur in one or more of the following ways:

First, through participation of a unit of government in the business of insuring, (i) as insurer, or (ii) as reinsurer, policies being issued to individual insureds by private insurers only.

Second, through governmental subsidy, by appropriations to a governmental unit that serves as insurer or reinsurer, or by grants to private insurers that meet specified standards.

Third, through coercion in aid of a program of private insurance, the coercive measures being aimed at inducing persons to apply for insurance through private channels and inducing insurers to accept applications.

Though governmental participation, subsidy, and coercion may all be used within a single program of government-sponsored insurance, somewhat different public policy considerations are applicable to these three techniques, and in general there has been more serious political opposition to participation than to either subsidy or coercion. The rejection of all three types of measures has sometimes been urged, even in the face of a concession that the government should in some manner take an interest in the accomplishment of an objective concerned with bearing fortuitous losses. Direct disaster relief, granted after losses have occurred, is an alternative to advance provision for future losses through insurance. During the debate over flood insurance in the mid-1950's, for example, it was urged that disaster relief, public and private, was preferable to government-sponsored insurance. The Federal Flood Insurance Act of 1956 [1] contained provisions for a form of disaster relief since, in addition to flood insurance and reinsurance, it provided for government-guaranteed loans for reconstruction of properties damaged by flood.

§ 8.6(b) AREAS OF GOVERNMENTAL SPONSORSHIP

In most insurance arrangements the coverage is provided by a private insurer (an individual, corporation, or unincorporated association) and governmental interest in the arrangement is limited to regulation and the provision of forums for resolution of disputes. Exceptional arrangements have been developed in considerable number, however; the following is an illustrative list, not exhaustive, of areas in which some unit of government in the United States, state or federal, participates in the business of insuring, either as insurer or as reinsurer: (1) social security benefits (including old-age, survivors, and disability insurance, and medicare); (2) unemployment insurance; (3) workmen's compensation; (4) unsatisfied judgment funds and similar arrangements regarding motor vehicle risks; (5) crop insurance; (6) bank deposit insurance; (7) bank guaranty funds; (8) public property insurance; (9) public official bonding funds; (10) animal-damage funds, financed by fines and used to pay damages even without proof of ownership of the malicious dogs or trespassing cattle causing the damage; (11) title insurance (the Torrens system); (12) housing mortgage insurance; (13) veterans' life insurance; (14) postal insurance; (15) war risk insurance; (16) atomic hazards insurance; (17) inner-city property insurance; and (18) flood insurance.

The possibility of governmental subsidy is inherent in every program of governmental participation in the business of insuring, whether as insurer or as reinsurer, since the program may prove not to be self-sustaining. It is doubtful that any program of governmental participation has ever operated without some degree of subsidy.

1. 70 Stat. 1078 (1956). These provisions were repealed with the enactment of the National Flood Insurance Act of 1968, 82 Stat. 572 (1968), 42 U.S.C.A. §§ 4001–4127 (Supp.1970).

The incidence of indirect subsidy has extended well beyond the areas of governmental participation in the business of insuring, since in many situations special tax treatment has been accorded to insurers and to insurance proceeds. Often the significance of such indirect subsidy, in relation to the overall economics of the type of insurance in question, is so small that it would be misleading to refer to the insurance as government-sponsored. The unqualified terms "subsidy" and "government-sponsored" through subsidy are reserved, in this discussion, for circumstances in which this element is a major factor in the operation of the insurance program.

In a few instances, governmental sponsorship of an insurance program has taken the form of coercive measures in aid of private insurance, without governmental participation in the business of insuring and without subsidy. The major part of the legislation so conceived consists of the motor vehicle financial responsibility acts, of both the compulsory and the safety-responsibility types.

§ 8.6(c) OBJECTIVES OF GOVERNMENTAL SPONSORSHIP

The variety of government-sponsored programs of insurance is itself suggestive of a variety of objectives. Moreover, it is a political fact that each such program is developed in response to multiple influences, some of the motivations for which are likely to be obscure. It is possible, nevertheless, to identify the most common objectives of governmental sponsorship of insurance. These objectives are not mutually exclusive.

(i) Implementation of legislation concerning economic security.

The motivation for governmental sponsorship is often independent of the requisites of a sound insurance plan. The aim in such cases is not the use of governmental measures to meet an insurance problem but rather the use of insurance, government-sponsored if need be, to meet a problem of economic security.

Two familiar examples of governmental sponsorship of an insurance program to meet social and economic problems of concern to the community as a whole are old-age and survivors' insurance, involving governmental participation in the business of insuring, and motor vehicle financial responsibility legislation, involving the use of coercive measures without governmental participation. Both involve participation of a very high percentage of the population as insureds. Other examples include programs of government-sponsored insurance available to relatively fewer members of the community. This was the nature of one of the oldest state insurance funds, the bank guaranty fund created in New York in 1829; certain banks were required to make annual payments into a safety fund that was used to pay debts of any contributing bank that later became insolvent.[1]

---

[1]. New York Laws 1829, ch. 94. Elder, *The Unsatisfied Judgment Fund and the Irresponsible Motorist*, in Current Trends in State Legislation, 1953–1954, 106–111 (Univ. of Mich.1955), calls attention to the following addi-

(ii) Compulsion or encouragement of potential insureds to participate.

The participation of only a small percentage of the total population ordinarily would provide the number and diversity of insureds essential to the sound operation of an insurance plan. The occasion for desiring *mass* participation is almost certainly not a distinctively insurance objective but a broader concern with arrangements for economic security of large numbers of persons in society who might otherwise be in need of public aid or private charity.[2] This fact does not rule out the possibility, however, that governmental sponsorship of a program of narrower scope might be urged on the ground that governmental sanctions would be needed to produce the number and diversity of insureds required for success of the program as one of insurance.

Probably old-age and survivors' insurance could have been provided on an actuarially sound basis through private insuring, but mass participation could not have been achieved through private initiative. Perhaps it would have been possible to provide the needed initiative by measures of governmental coercion, the insuring itself being left entirely in private hands; for example, proof that one carried such insurance could have been made a prerequisite to employment. Perhaps also the whole cost of the program could have been placed on employers, and private insurance alone could have been required, as is done in some states with respect to workmen's compensation for accidental injuries in the course of employment. Enforcement of measures aimed at mass participation in such types of programs, however, would have presented different and perhaps more difficult problems than those of the system now in effect. One of the factors relevant to the choice of governmental participation in the business of insuring was the greater ease of securing mass participation in this way.

In some circumstances, however, it is quite feasible to get very nearly universal participation among potential insureds without governmental participation in the business of insuring. Workmen's compensation insurance is provided in some states without reliance upon state participation, and compulsory motor vehicle liability insurance

tional examples of "the fund idea": (a) A motor vehicle liability security fund financed by contributions from insurers doing business in the state and used to pay automobile insurance claims against insolvent insurers. (b) Animal-damage funds, one type of which, existing in Massachusetts as early as 1794, was financed by fines against owners of trespassing cattle and was used to pay damages to lands, and another of which extended this principle to harm caused by malicious dogs. "[T]he frequent impossibility of determining ownership was a compelling incentive for this kind of

legislation." (c) The Torrens system of land registration, which includes an indemnity fund to compensate persons injured by operation of the system of certified titles. (d) Motor vehicle unsatisfied judgment funds, the first of which was created in the province of Manitoba in 1945.

2. Mass participation of potential insureds can seldom be achieved without governmental coercion. The wide distribution of homeowners insurance is perhaps the nearest approach to universal participation through private initiative.

has been provided in the same way in Massachusetts since 1927. Similarly safety-responsibility legislation, aimed at encouraging nearly universal motor vehicle liability insurance without resort to the extreme sanctions of a compulsory system, ordinarily does not include any provision for state participation in the business of insuring.

When sanctions or inducements are used to coerce or encourage applications and no state insurance fund is created, there is need for some provision for insuring those whom private insurers would prefer not to accept as insureds. With reference to automobile liability insurance, for example, the need has been met in some states by assigned-risk plans under which insurers who wish to write this kind of insurance in the state are required to participate in a pool, and the unwanted applicants for insurance are assigned, each insurer being required to take an appropriate number of them.[3] With anything less than universal participation by those who might be legally responsible for damages caused by motor vehicles, there are also needs for insurance to protect the victims of the financially irresponsible and the victims of hit-and-run accidents. These needs have been met in a few states by unsatisfied judgment funds or a similar arrangement under another designation.[4]

(iii) Provision of fringe benefits for government personnel.

Perhaps the most familiar example of governmental insurance as a fringe benefit is National Service Life Insurance for members of the armed services and veterans; within limits, service personnel are allowed insurance without premium charge and veterans are allowed insurance at costs to them substantially below self-sustaining rates. Other examples include retirement funds for public school teachers and other state employees. Once it has been determined that the state has an obligation to provide such fringe benefits, the arrangement is in the nature of state "self-insurance" insofar as the state makes contributions to the fund beyond those of the participants.[5]

(iv) Protection of the state or its political subdivisions.

Arrangements established for this purpose have included public deposits guaranty, public property insurance, and public official bonding funds. If the entire political structure of the state is considered as a unit, these arrangements, like those discussed in the preceding paragraph, are in the nature of "self-insurance" insofar as premiums are paid by the state or one of its political subdivisions.[6]

(v) Provisions for insurance as a motivation for economic development.

Governmental insurance of mortgage loans has been used as a device to encourage private lending on terms favorable to borrowers,

3. Concerning the assigned-risk problem generally, see § 8.6(f) *infra*.

4. See § 8.6(e) *infra*.

5. Cf. McCahan, State Insurance 272 (1929). Concerning "self-insuring" or

risk retention generally, see § 1.2(b) (6) *supra*.

6. Cf. McCahan, State Insurance 272 (1929). For a description of such funds, see *id.* at 222–239, 263–270.

and in turn to encourage new construction to meet housing shortages. A government-sponsored and subsidized program of atomic hazards insurance, supplementing a limited program of privately written insurance, has been used as a means of encouraging development of industrial uses of atomic energy. A government-sponsored and subsidized program of insurance and reinsurance of inner-city property has been used in an effort to revitalize urban centers and to redress inequities suffered by residents of those areas.[7] In other instances, influence on economic development may be an undesired by-product of a government-sponsored insurance program. One of the grounds of opposition to flood insurance has been that, if subsidized, it will tend to cause the uneconomic use of lowland areas that are subject to recurrent floods.

(vi) Provisions for use of insurance as an instrument of risk control.

Probably risk control has never been the primary objective of any government-sponsored insurance plan, but, as with private insurance, the effectiveness of a program of insurance is increased by risk-control measures that can be readily introduced as incidental aspects of the program. Thus, the National Flood Insurance Act of 1968 provides for measures designed to advance flood prevention and control and wise development of flood-exposed property.[8] And in Massachusetts under a system of governmental "rate-making" for compulsory automobile insurance, special instruction of young drivers has been encouraged by the allowance of a rate reduction for drivers under 25 who have completed an approved course of driver training.[9] In many states where governmental "rate regulation" rather than "rate-making" is applicable to automobile insurance, similar rate categories have been widely used, often along with merit rating that rewards those with records of safe driving. Experience rating has also been used extensively in workmen's compensation insurance. In general, it appears that more attention has been given to risk control in private than in government-sponsored insurance programs, but an increased emphasis on risk control might be achieved if it were a declared objective of governmental measures.

(vii) Experimental development of new types of insurance coverage.

If unavailability of a desired type of insurance appears to be caused by unwillingness of private insurers to enter an untested area,

7. See, e.g., Meeting the Insurance Crisis of Our Cities, Report by the President's National Advisory Panel on Insurance in Riot-Affected Areas (1968); Harris, Heilman, Stewart, & Wozencraft, *Revitalizing Our Cities: The Urban Core Insurance Crisis*, 24 Record, Assoc. of Bar of City of N.Y. 321 (1969); Bishop, *Federal Riot Reinsurance*, 1969 ABA Section Ins., Neg. & Comp.L.Proceedings 141; Denenberg, *Meeting the Insurance Crisis of Our Cities: An Industry in Revolution*, 1970 Ins.L.J. 205.

8. See 42 U.S.C. §§ 4101–4103.

9. See Hart & Sacks, The Legal Process 979 (temp. ed. 1958), discussing both this Massachusetts device and the possibility of flood insurance rating measures that would encourage flood prevention and control.

a program of governmental insurance may be created to break the ice. Another possibility is to provide encouragement to private insurers through governmental reinsurance; in this way private insurers are used as marketing agencies but are protected against the unusual risks of an untested type of coverage. Governmental participation in the business of insuring to foster development of new types of coverage is properly conceived as a temporary activity. Presumably private insurers will continue to offer the insurance without governmental aid if it proves to be self-sustaining. If the contrary is proved, the legislature will face the choice of abandoning the program or else continuing it for reasons other than experimentation.

(viii) Provisions for insurance that cannot be offered privately.

In some instances impediments to private development of new types of insurance coverage are permanent in character and cannot be overcome by an experimental program of governmental participation. For example, life insurance without limitations against coverage of war risks is disproportionately attractive to those persons who are subject to the greatest risks in wartime. Because of this problem of adverse selection [10] and the obvious difficulties of developing a graduated schedule of premiums that would meet it adequately, private insurers have commonly considered that it is not feasible to write new life insurance policies during wartime without provisions against full liability on account of death from a war risk. National Service Life Insurance fills this gap that otherwise would exist in the availability of insurance to members of the armed forces.

The potentially catastrophic nature of atomic hazards has caused private insurers to be unwilling to enter the field of insurance against atomic hazards except on a syndicate basis and with conservative limits upon the potential liability of each participating insurer. Provisions for governmental indemnity have been established as a supplement to the limited amount of private insurance that can be obtained.

During the debates over flood insurance in the mid-1950's, advocates of an experimental federal flood insurance program argued that the reluctance of private insurers to offer flood insurance on fixed properties in areas subject to flood risks could be overcome by the accumulation of data on losses and insurance costs during the period of a federally-sponsored experimental program. Opponents of such a program argued that there are impediments of a permanent nature: (a) Adverse selection [11] would occur because the insurance would be disproportionately attractive to the owners of the most exposed properties. (b) Because of such adverse selection, self-sustaining premium rates would be prohibitively high. (c) The potential loss from flood is catastrophic and it would not be possible to collect enough premiums to cover losses such as might occur.[12] These three arguments

---

10. Concerning adverse selection generally, see § 1.2(b) (7) *supra.*

11. *Ibid.*

12. See Overman, *The Flood Peril and the Federal Flood Insurance Act of 1956,* 309 Annals, Am.Academy of Pol. and Soc.Sci. 98, 99 (1957); Hart &

add up to the prediction that the risk of extraordinary losses in one flood or flood season would be too great and that, at self-sustaining premium rates, the number of persons willing to buy flood insurance would be too small for a practical program. This is a debatable estimate,[13] but if it is sound, then flood insurance cannot be maintained without permanent governmental subsidy, and the justification for such a program must be found in social and economic needs that are not adequately represented in a private insurance market. For example, one who recognizes a humanitarian obligation of the government to provide relief to flood victims might choose to establish a subsidized program of flood insurance on the theory that little if any more would be expended by the government on such a program than on direct relief, and that the net cost of relief measures, direct and indirect, would be reduced because the insurance fund accumulated from premiums paid by those exposed to the flood risk would pay part of the loss that is borne by the community generally in the absence of insurance; also, since the cost of subsidy would be at least partially offset by the reduction of revenue losses (because of flood damage deductions for income tax purposes as well as reduction of property taxes), one might conclude that the net cost of a subsidized flood insurance program would be quite moderate.[14]

Neither the objective of providing an experimental program nor the objective of providing insurance that cannot be offered privately is ever the sole or even primary motivation of governmental participation in the business of insuring, since each is concerned with unavailability of a type of insurance but not with need for it. National Service Life Insurance, for example, was intended to provide a fringe benefit for government personnel; atomic hazards insurance, to influence economic development; flood insurance, to meet a social and economic need by means other than direct disaster relief. In each instance, also, one or more of the other objectives discussed above had some influence.

Sacks, The Legal Process 970–980 (temp. ed. 1958).

13. The problem of potentially catastrophic losses in a short interval of time might arguably be met by a long-range program calculated to build a reserve in most years to offset heavy losses in an extraordinary year; the risk that extraordinarily heavy losses would occur in an early year of the program could be met by temporary governmental backing. The problem of obtaining an adequate number of insureds at self-sustaining premium rates might also be solved. Presumably the hypothetical economic man would not be deterred from buying flood insurance because of the fixing of rates at a self-sustaining level, provided they were also on a graduated scale adjusted with reasonable refinement to the varying degrees of flood risk to different properties. In the absence of such adjustment, the disproportionate attractiveness of the insurance to the owners of the most exposed properties in any rate class would be a serious obstacle. Two further questions should be considered. Might the response of real people be different from that of the economic man? Might prohibitive administrative costs be encountered in the attempt to adjust rates to the varying degrees of flood risk to different properties? Concerning this last question, see generally § 8.4(b) *supra*.

14. *Cf.* Hart & Sacks, The Legal Process 978 (temp. ed. 1958).

§ 8.6(d) COLLATERAL EFFECTS OF GOVERNMENTAL SPONSORSHIP

Any valid assessment of the desirability of a proposal for governmental sponsorship of some type of insurance must take account not only of the extent to which the proposed program will serve the intended objectives but also the extent to which it will produce other, unintended consequences.

A major cost of any such program is the resulting governmental intrusion into the business of insuring through private enterprise. Inevitably this cost will be in the forefront of any debate over a proposal for governmental sponsorship of insurance.[1]

More specialized consequences deserve consideration too. For example, one problem to be faced in designing a viable flood insurance program is to avoid encouraging the uneconomic use of floodlands for structures that cost more to maintain, in the face of flood risks, than they are worth.

There will also be less obvious costs and consequences, less certain to be fully considered. An example may be taken from the federal crop insurance program. The stated purpose of the 1947 Act is "to promote the national welfare by improving the economic stability of agriculture through a sound system of crop insurance and providing the means for the research and experience helpful in devising and establishing such insurance."[2] In most of the counties where federal crop insurance is available, the program is limited to the principal crop (e. g., wheat in one county and cotton in another).[3] This fact is relevant to the question whether the crop insurance program may have an unintended effect beyond the declared purpose and perhaps inconsistent with it. The limitation to a single crop tends to encourage concentration on the production of that crop in preference to diversification. That may be an unwanted agricultural and economic consequence of a choice (to limit the program in the county to one crop) made for other reasons (such as the need for large scale production of any crop within the program in order to provide a wide base for insurance).[4]

1. Compare the succinct statement of the case for a private enterprise solution of the automobile accident reparations problem in N.Y.Ins.Dep't, Report, Automobile Insurance . . . For Whose Benefit? 77–78 (1970), part of which is quoted in § 8.1(a) n.14 *supra*.

2. 61 Stat. 718 (1947), 7 U.S.C. § 1502 (1958). The declared purpose of the original act was "to promote the national welfare by alleviating the economic distress caused by wheatcrop failures due to drought and other causes, by maintaining the purchasing power of farmers, and by providing for stable supplies of wheat for domestic consumption and the orderly flow thereof in interstate commerce." 52 Stat. 72 (1938). An amendment in 1941 substituted "crop" for "wheatcrop" and "agricultural commodities" for "wheat." 55 Stat. 255 (1941). Concerning federal crop insurance generally, see Federal Disaster Insurance 272–299 (Staff Study, Com. on Banking and Currency, U.S. Senate, 84th Cong., 1st Sess., 1955).

3. See Graves, *Federal Crop Insurance: An Investment in Disappointment?* 7 Kan.L.Rev. 361, 362 (1959).

4. Compare the fifth objective of governmental sponsorship, discussed in § 8.6(c) *supra*.

§ 8.6(e) THE PROBLEM OF UNINSURED LOSSES

The undesirable social consequences of uninsured losses have given rise to proposals in varied contexts for governmental participation in some kind of insurance arrangement to meet this problem.

In relation to employee injuries, the problem of uninsured losses was initially staggering. The common law usually denied recovery against the employer, and the worker seldom had any form of voluntary insurance to cover his losses. These circumstances led to the enactment of workmen's compensation legislation, sometimes effectuated with government insurance and sometimes solely through privately written insurance. But there remained a problem of uninsured losses from work injuries primarily because of exceptions in the acts that left some employments outside their scope. The range of exclusions from workmen's compensation acts has been gradually reduced by amendments, but there remains an area of uninsured losses from work injuries—a situation that is hard to justify. It has also been suggested that the limitation of workmen's compensation to coverage of occupational as distinguished from nonoccupational injury has proved to be a shifting and debilitating restriction.[1]

The common law was substantially less adverse to compensation for traffic injuries than to compensation for work injuries. Moreover, practices of compromise settlement have sharply reduced the instances in which compensation for accidental loss is denied when liability insurance applies to the injury. As liability insurance became more prevalent and legislatures enacted financial responsibility laws to encourage its purchase, a more specialized problem emerged—the problem of the victim of an uninsured or hit-and-run driver. Measures taken in efforts to meet this problem of the uncompensated victim in motoring cases have included compulsory liability insurance laws,[2] unsatisfied judgment fund acts,[3] and a variety of other developments,[4] one of the most significant of which is uninsured motorist coverage.[5]

1. Henderson, *Should Workmen's Compensation Be Extended to Nonoccupational Injuries?* 48 Texas L.Rev. 117 (1969).

2. Mass.Gen.Laws Ann. ch. 90, §§ 1A, 3, 34A–34K (1969); N.Y.Veh. & Traf. Law §§ 310–321 (McKinney 1970 and McKinney Supp.1970); N.C.Gen. Stat. §§ 20–309 through 20–319 (1965 and Supp.1969). See also § 4.10 *supra* (nonfault insurance).

3. An act of this type was enacted in North Dakota in 1948, and later in New Jersey, Maryland, and Michigan. A variant on this general theme is the N.Y. Motor Vehicle Accident Indemnification Corporation (MVAIC) Law, N.Y.Ins.Law §§ 600–626 (McKinney 1966 and McKinney Supp.1970). Concerning unsatisfied judgment funds generally, see Elder, *The Unsatisfied Judgment Fund and the Irresponsible Motorist,* Current Trends in State Legislation, 1953–1954, 47 (Univ. of Mich.1955).

4. In Great Britain, with compulsory automobile liability insurance in effect, an agreement was made in 1946 between insurers and the Minister of Transport creating the Motor Insurers' Bureau for the purpose of providing compensation to motoring victims deprived of redress by the absence of effective insurance. The problem of the unidentified driver was not covered by this agreement, but it was

5. See Note 5 on page 580.

The primary objective of uninsured motorist coverage is to protect the policyholder and members of his family against the risk of being negligently injured by a financially irresponsible motorist. But policy draftsmen have incorporated into the forms a number of restrictive provisions somewhat inconsistent with the primary objective. In part they have done so to reduce incentives to fraud—an objective plainly serving public interest as well as insurers' interest. In part, too, policy draftsmen have sought—quite defensibly from their point of view but less so from the point of view of public interest—to reduce the uncertainties insurers face in offering the coverage. An example is a clause in the definition of the coverage declaring that it applies only if the injuries resulted from "physical contact" with the vehicle of the unidentified motorist. This requirement appears also in some of the statutes requiring that uninsured motorist coverage be included in each liability policy, either unconditionally or unless declined in writing by the policyholder.[6] If a statute requiring, conditionally or unconditionally, that uninsured motorist coverage be included in liability policies does not contain such a restrictive provision, its addition in a policy form may be challenged as an invalid attempt to diminish coverage to something less than that intended by the statute. But this contention is weak when the statute uses the phrase "hit-and-run" in describing the coverage because of the implication of physical contact in the word "hit".[7]

In the latter part of the 1960's, many uninsured motorist coverage forms were modified, in some instances by statutory compulsion, to apply to losses resulting from the insolvency of a liability insurer. Also, this problem of the victim with a claim against an insolvent insurer, in relation to either employee injuries or motoring injuries, has sometimes been met by the creation of a state security fund financed by periodic payments made by insurers doing the relevant type of business in the state.[8] Proposals for establishing a federal insolvency fund have also been advanced.[9]

soon stated that the Bureau would give consideration to making gratuitous payments of bona fide claims. See Shawcross & Lee, The Law of Motor Insurance 364, 377 (2d ed. 1949).

5. See generally § 4.9(e) *supra.* Concerning arbitration clauses in uninsured motorist coverage, see § 7.3(c) *supra.*

6. *E.g.,* N.Y.Ins.Law § 617 (McKinney 1966).

7. *Cf.* Prosk v. Allstate Ins. Co., 82 Ill. App.2d 457, 226 N.E.2d 498 (1st Dist. 1967), 25 A.L.R.3d 1294 (1969) (allegations that plaintiffs were forced to strike a parked vehicle because of the negligence of the driver of an unknown vehicle with which there was no contact; held, affirming judgment for insurer on pleadings, that the physical contact requirement of the policy did not conflict with the statute). See also Amidzich v. Charter Oak Fire Ins. Co., 44 Wis.2d 45, 170 N.W.2d 813 (1969); Widiss, A Guide to Uninsured Motorist Coverage § 2.41 (1969); Annot., 25 A.L.R.3d 1299 (1969).

8. *E.g.,* New Jersey Stat.Ann. §§ 39:6–92 through 39:6–104 (1961 and Supp. 1969) (motor vehicle insurance); N.Y. Ins.Law §§ 333, 334 (McKinney Supp. 1970); N.Y.Workmen's Comp.Law §§ 106–109j (McKinney 1965).

9. See, *e.g.,* Insurance Accessibility for the Hard-to-Place Driver, Report of the Division of Industry Analysis, Bureau of Economics, Federal Trade

§ 8.6(f) THE PROBLEM OF UNWANTED INSUREDS

The problem of the unwanted insured arises whenever the law requires insurance as a prerequisite to permission to engage in a specified activity. This occurs, for example, when insurance is declared to be a prerequisite to registration of a motor vehicle. Also, it occurs when insurance is required of all those who engage in a business within the scope of a workmen's compensation act. In each of these situations, if all insurers were free to refuse applicants, their refusal would effectively bar unwanted insureds from engaging in the specified activity. Yet a legislator might reasonably conclude that at least some of these unwanted insureds should not be barred. Moreover, provisions for insuring such persons strengthen the total arrangement against attack on constitutional grounds. This problem has been met in several ways. First, a few states have enacted a statute, in relation to workmen's compensation, requiring that insurers accept all qualified employers applying for insurance.[1] Second, in some states, either in combination with a statute of the foregoing type or separately, the legislature has created a competitive (non-exclusive) state fund [2] or a state-sponsored association [3] to write workmen's compensation insurance, and it "has sometimes been taken for granted that . . . . the fund or association should solve the undesirable-risk problem by acting as residual legatee of risks that private carriers do not want."[4] There is support, however, for the power of rejection of applications "in employments which involve hazards and risks of such a nature that it would, in all reasonable probability, result in the State Compensation Fund's becoming insolvent."[5] Third, in other states a monopolistic state fund has been created to write workmen's compensation insurance.[6] It has been suggested that the manager of such a fund might also have the power of rejection of risks that would probably result in insolvency of the fund, but the issue has not been squarely faced since in states having monopolistic

Commission 75–77 (U.S.Dept.Transp. Auto.Ins. & Comp.Study 1970).

1. See Larson, Workmen's Compensation Law, § 92.51 (1952). Also see n.3 *infra.*

2. *E.g.*, New York Workmen's Compensation Law, §§ 76–99.

3. *E.g.*, the Texas Employers' Insurance Association is an association of employers with statutory standing. Tex.Rev.Civ.Stat.Ann. art. 8308 (1967 and Supp.1970). In § 7 of this article it is stated that any employer who is subject to the Texas Workmen's Compensation Law or the Longshoremen's and Harbor Workers' Compensation Act of the United States "may become a subscriber to the Association." See the considered dicta in Texas Employ-

ers' Ins. Ass'n v. United States Torpedo Co., 26 S.W.2d 1057, 1059 (Tex. Comm'n App.1930), and Oil Well Drilling Co. v. Associated Indem. Corp., 153 Tex. 153, 157–158, 264 S.W.2d 697, 699 (1954), declaring that other insurers as well as the Texas Employers' Insurance Association are subject to the requirement of accepting any employer-applicant who is entitled to be covered by a policy of compensation insurance.

4. Larson, Workmen's Compensation Law 451–452 (1952).

5. Gene Autry Productions v. Industrial Commission, 67 Ariz. 290, 297, 195 P.2d 143, 147–148 (1948).

6. See Larson, Workmen's Compensation Law § 92.10 (1952).

funds it appears that all qualified employers are accepted as a matter of routine practice.[7] Fourth, many state statutes in the United States create assigned-risk plans for both workmen's compensation insurance [8] and automobile insurance,[9] distributing the unwanted insureds among the insurers through assignment by a public official or through a voluntary arrangement among insurers under administrative supervision. Fifth, in Canada the problem has been met by the "Canadian facility"—an arrangement among private insurers under which applications for insurance are generally accepted, even when the insurer regards the risk as undesirable, and the insurer is then free to reinsure with the facility up to a very high percentage of the risk.[10]

These ways of meeting the problem of unwanted insureds do not exhaust the possibilities, and continuing dissatisfaction with the functioning of automobile insurance may stimulate the development of other solutions.[11]

It is well settled that a state legislature may provide for the problem of the unwanted insured by compelling private insurers to meet it rather than providing for governmental participation in insuring, since this is the nature of assigned-risk plans.[12] It would

7. *Id.* § 92.52 (1952).

8. *E.g.*, Mass.Gen.Laws Ann. ch. 152, § 65A (1958). See Larson, Workmen's Compensation Law § 92.52 (1952).

9. *E.g.*, Mass.Gen.Laws, ch. 90, § 1A (1969), ch. 175, § 113H (Supp.1970).

10. For a brief description of the Canadian "Facility," see Insurance Accessibility for the Hard-to-Place Driver, Report of the Division of Industry Analysis, Bureau of Economics, Federal Trade Commission 81–82 (U.S.Dep't Transp. Auto. Ins. & Comp. Study 1970).

11. See Kozusko, *Reallocation Under Nonfault Automobile Insurance: Comments and Proposed Regulations*, 7 Harv.J.Legis. 423 (1970); Keeton, Compensation Systems—The Search for a Viable Alternative to Negligence Law 49–51 (1969), reprinted in Seavey, Keeton & Keeton, Cases and Materials on the Law of Torts 276–279 (Supp. 1970).

12. *E.g.*, California State Auto. Ass'n Inter-Ins. Bureau v. Maloney, 341 U.S. 105, 71 Sup.Ct. 601, 95 L.Ed. 788 (1951); Factory Mut. Liab. Ins. Co. v. Justices of the Superior Court, 300 Mass. 513, 16 N.E.2d 38 (1938). Birdwell v. Tri-State Ins. Co., 286 P.2d 736 (Okla.1955) is consistent with this conclusion though on cursory examination it might seem otherwise. In that case a person was denied insurance because he admittedly intended to drive his car, for a small part of the total use, in an illegal liquor traffic. The courts struck down an order of the Governing Committee of the Assigned Risk Plan, under which an insurance company would have been required to provide the insurance coverage applied for. Though the consequence is that some persons will be prevented from driving, this is not an unconstitutional legislative treatment of persons who are extremely bad risks from a point of view of concern not merely with insurance but also with social consequences generally.

See also Employers' Liab. Assur. Corp. v. Frost, 48 Ariz. 402, 62 P.2d 320 (1936), 107 A.L.R. 1413 (1937) (statute construed as requiring workmen's compensation insurer to insure every employer who applied to it for insurance; held to violate freedom of contract guaranteed by the Fourteenth Amendment). *Frost* might seem inconsistent with the theory that the legislature has power to meet the problem of the unwanted insured by requiring private insurers to accept applications from all except those whose operations are so excessively risky that the legislature wants to put them out of business. But it does not squarely face this question because it appears to pose

seem also to be within the competence of a legislature to provide for a system more like the "Canadian facility" than present assigned-risk plans. The range of additional possibilities includes other systems operated by private insurers as well as arrangements for government insurance.

Historically an interesting contrast has developed between, first, the use of *state* workmen's compensation funds in many states to cover the unwanted insureds and, second, the trend of rejection of *state* funds for automobile liability insurance in favor of assigned-risk plans. Probably the different choices are products of different political environments rather than relevant differences in characteristics of workmen's compensation and automobile liability insurance. State funds were started in the workmen's compensation field when compensation insurance, as distinguished from employer's liability insurance, was experimental. Private insurers were not so active and effective in trying to preserve that untested field of insurance for themselves as in trying in the 1950's [13] to keep the states out of the established field of automobile liability insurance.

the problem before the court as a choice between, on the one hand, holding that the company is free to reject any application and, on the other hand, holding that it must accept all applications without any exception for those whose operations are so excessively risky that it would be within the constitutional power of the legislature to prohibit their operations, either by a direct ban or by an indirect ban involving an insurance requirement. If the statute had been drafted to provide clearly for rejection of applications under such exceptional circumstances, but not otherwise, perhaps it would have been sustained by the Arizona court.

13. See, *e.g.*, California State Auto. Ass'n Inter-Ins. Bureau v. Maloney, 341 U.S. 105, 71 Sup.Ct. 601, 95 L.Ed. 788 (1951).

*

APPENDICES

Table of Appendices

APPENDIX A

Excerpts from New York Insurance Law
(McKinney 1966 and McKinney Supp. 1970)

Article III—Administrative and Procedural Provisions

§ 21. Regulations by superintendent

The superintendent shall have power to prescribe, in writing, official regulations, not inconsistent with the provisions of this chapter:

(a) governing the duties assigned to the members of the staff of the insurance department;

(b) effectuating any power, given to him under the provisions of this chapter, to prescribe forms or otherwise to make regulations;

(c) interpreting the provisions of this chapter;

(d) governing the procedure to be followed in the practice of the insurance department.

The superintendent may likewise, from time to time, withdraw, modify or amend any such regulation.

* * *

Article VII—The Insurance Contract

§ 141. Withdrawal of approval of policy forms

Whenever by the provisions of this chapter the superintendent is authorized to give his approval of any form of insurance policy, fraternal benefit certificate or annuity contract, he may, after notice and hearing given to the insurer which submitted such form for approval, withdraw an approval previously given, if the use of such form is contrary to the legal requirements applicable to such form at the time of such withdrawal, or in the case of any such policy form pertaining to accident or health insurance, or any application, rider or endorsement to be used in connection therewith (1) if the benefits provided therein are unreasonable in relation to the premium charged, or (2) if it contains provisions which encourage misrepresentation or are unjust, unfair, unequitable, misleading, deceptive, contrary to law or to the public policy of this state, or in the case of any such policy or certificate form pertaining to life insurance, or any application, rider or endorsement to be used in connection therewith, if in his judgment the use of such form would be prejudicial to the interests of its policyholders or members, or it contains provisions which are unjust, unfair or inequitable. Any such withdrawal shall be effective at the expiration of such period, not less than ninety days after the giving of notice of withdrawal, as the superintendent shall in such notice prescribe. The action of the superintendent in withdrawing approval of any such form shall be subject to judicial review.

§ 142. Policy to contain entire contract; statements of applicant to be representations and not warranties; alterations

1. Every policy of life, accident or health insurance, or contract of annuity, delivered or issued for delivery in this state shall contain the entire contract between the parties, and nothing shall be incorporated therein by reference to any constitution, by-laws, rules, application, or other writings, unless a copy thereof is endorsed upon or attached to the policy or contract when issued. No application for the issuance of any such policy or contract shall be admissible in evidence unless a true copy of such application was attached to such policy when issued.

2. Subsection one shall not apply to a table or schedule of rates, premiums or stipulated payments which is on file with the superintendent for use in connection with such policy or contract.

3. All statements made by, or by the authority of, the applicant for the issuance, reinstatement or renewal of a policy of life, accident or health insurance or annuity contract shall be deemed representations and not warranties, anything in such policy, contract or application to the contrary, notwithstanding.

4. No alteration of any written application for such insurance or annuity, by erasure or insertion or otherwise, shall be made by any person other than the applicant without his written consent, except that insertions may be made by the insurer for administrative purposes only in such manner as to indicate clearly that such insertions are not to be ascribed to the applicant.

5. If any policy of life, accident or health insurance delivered or issued for delivery in this state shall be reinstated or renewed, and the insured or the beneficiary or assignee of such policy shall make written request to the insurer for a copy of the application, if any, for such reinstatement or renewal, the insurer shall, within fifteen days after the receipt of such request at its home office or any branch office of the insurer, deliver or mail to the person making such request, a copy of such application. If such copy shall not be so delivered or mailed, the insurer shall be precluded from introducing such application as evidence in any action or proceeding based upon or involving such policy or its reinstatement or renewal.

6. Any waiver of the provisions of this section shall be void.

§ 143. Non-conforming contracts; law governing contracts

1. Except as otherwise specifically provided in this chapter any contract or policy of insurance or annuity contract delivered or issued for delivery in this state in violation of any of the provisions of this chapter shall be valid and binding upon the insurer making or issuing the same, but in all respects in which its provisions are in violation of the requirements or prohibitions of this chapter it shall be enforceable as if it conformed with such requirements or prohibitions. [Subsections 2 and 3 omitted.]

* * *

§ 146. Insurable interest in the person; consent required; exceptions

1. Any person of lawful age may on his own initiative procure or effect a contract of insurance upon his own person for the benefit of any person, firm, association or corporation, but no person shall procure or cause to be procured, directly or by assignment or otherwise any contract of insurance upon the person of another unless the benefits under such contract are payable to the person insured or his personal representatives, or to a person having, at the time when such contract is made, an insurable interest in the person insured. The term "contract of insurance upon the person", as used in this section, shall be deemed to include any contract of life insurance and any contract of accident or health insurance, and the term "person insured", as used in this section, shall be deemed to mean the natural person, or persons, whose life, health or bodily safety is thereby insured. If the beneficiary, assignee or other payee under any contract made in violation of this subsection shall receive from the insurer any benefits thereunder accruing upon the death, disablement or injury of the person insured, the person insured or his executor or administrator as the case may be, may maintain an action to recover such benefits from the person so receiving them.

2. The term, "insurable interest", as used in this section, shall mean: (a) In the case of persons related closely by blood or by law, a substantial interest engendered by love and affection; and (b) in the case of other persons, a lawful and substantial economic interest in having the life, health or bodily safety of the person insured continue, as distinguished from an interest which would arise only by, or would be enhanced in value by, the death, disablement or injury, as the case may be, of the person insured.

3. No contract of insurance upon the person, except a policy of group life insurance or of group or blanket accident or health insurance as defined in this chapter or family insurance, shall be made or effectuated unless at or before the making of such contract the person insured, being of lawful age or competent to contract therefor, applies therefor or consents in writing to the making thereof, except in the following cases:

(a) A wife or a husband may effectuate such insurance upon the person of the other.

(b) Any person having an insurable interest in the life of a minor under the age, as determined by nearest birthday, of fifteen years, or any person upon whom such minor is dependent for support and maintenance, may effectuate a contract of insurance upon the life of such minor, in an amount which shall not exceed the limits specified in section one hundred forty-seven which are applicable to such contract.

* * *

§ 148. Insurable interest in property

No contract or policy of insurance on property made or issued in this state, or made or issued upon any property in this state, shall be enforceable except for the benefit of some person having an insurable interest in the property insured. The term "insurable interest," as used in this section, shall be deemed to include any lawful and substantial economic interest in the safety or preservation of property from loss, destruction or pecuniary damage.

§ 149. Representations by the insured

1. A representation is a statement as to past or present fact, made to the insurer by or by the authority of the applicant for insurance or the prospective insured, at or before the making of the insurance contract as an inducement to the making thereof. A misrepresentation is a false representation, and the facts misrepresented are those facts which make the representation false.

2. No misrepresentation shall avoid any contract of insurance or defeat recovery thereunder unless such misrepresentation was material. No misrepresentation shall be deemed material unless knowledge by the insurer of the facts misrepresented would have led to a refusal by the insurer to make such contract.

3. In determining the question of materiality, evidence of the practice of the insurer which made such contract with respect to the acceptance or rejection of similar risks shall be admissible.

4. A misrepresentation that an applicant for life, accident or health insurance has not had previous medical treatment, consultation or observation, or has not had previous treatment or care in a hospital or other like institution, shall be deemed, for the purpose of determining its materiality, a misrepresentation that the applicant has not had the disease, ailment or other medical impairment for which such treatment or care was given or which was discovered by any licensed medical practitioner as a result of such consultation or observation. If in any action to rescind any such contract or to recover thereon, any such misrepresentation is proved by the insurer, and the insured or any other person having or claiming a right under such contract shall prevent full disclosure and proof of the nature of such medical impairment, such misrepresentation shall be presumed to have been material.

* * *

§ 150. Warranty defined; effect of breach

1. The term "warranty" as used in this section, means any provision of an insurance contract which has the effect of requiring, as a condition precedent of the taking effect of such contract or as a condition precedent of the insurer's liability thereunder, the existence of a fact which tends to diminish, or the non-existence of a fact which tends to increase, the risk of the occurrence of any loss, damage, or injury within the coverage of the contract. The term "occurrence of loss, damage, or injury" shall be deemed to include the occurrence of death, disability, injury, or any other

contingency insured against, and the term "risk" shall be deemed to include both physical and moral hazards.

2.   No breach of warranty shall avoid an insurance contract or defeat recovery thereunder unless such breach materially increased the risk of loss, damage or injury within the coverage of the contract.   If the insurance contract specified two or more distinct kinds of loss, damage or injury which are within its coverage, no breach of warranty shall avoid such contract or defeat recovery thereunder with respect to any kind or kinds of loss, damage or injury other than the kind or kinds to which such warranty relates and the risk of which is materially increased by the breach of such warranty.

3.   Nothing contained in this section shall affect the express or implied warranties under a contract of marine insurance in respect to, appertaining to or in connection with any and all risks or perils of navigation, transit, or transportation, including war risks, on, over or under any seas or inland waters, nor shall it affect any provision in an insurance contract requiring notice, proof or other conduct of the insured after the occurrence of loss, damage or injury.

*   *   *

§ 154.   Approval of life, accident, health and annuity contracts

1.   No policy of life insurance, industrial life insurance, group life insurance, accident or health insurance, group or blanket accident or health insurance or non-cancellable disability insurance, no fraternal benefit certificate or other evidence of any such insurance contract, and no annuity or pure endowment contract or group annuity contract shall be issued or delivered in this state unless a copy of the form thereof shall have been filed with the superintendent.   No application form shall be used with, and no rider and no endorsement, except as stated in subsection three, shall be attached to or printed or stamped upon such policy, certificate or contract unless the form of such application, rider or endorsement has been filed with the superintendent.   No individual certificate shall be used in connection with any such group or blanket insurance policy or group annuity contract unless the form thereof has been filed with the superintendent.   None of the aforementioned policies, contracts, certificates or other evidence of any such insurance contract shall be delivered or issued for delivery in this state and no applications, riders and endorsement shall be used in connection therewith unless approved by the superintendent as conforming to the requirements of this chapter and not inconsistent with law.   The superintendent may disapprove any such policy or certificate form pertaining to life insurance for delivery or issuance for delivery in this state, including any such issued by a cooperative life and accident insurance company or fraternal benefit society, and any application, rider or endorsement to be used in connection therewith, if in his judgment its issuance would be prejudicial to the interests of its policyholders or members or it contains provisions which are unjust, unfair or inequitable.   The superintendent may disapprove any such policy form, contract, certificate or other evidence of any such insurance contract pertaining to accident or health insurance for delivery or issuance for delivery in this state including any such issued by a cooperative life and accident insurance company or fraternal benefit society, and any application, rider or endorsement to be used in connection there-

with (1) if the benefits provided therein are unreasonable in relation to the premium charged, or (2) if any such form contains provisions which encourage misrepresentation or are unjust, unfair, inequitable, misleading, deceptive, contrary to law or to the public policy of this state. The superintendent shall, within a reasonable time after the filing of any form requiring approval, notify the insurer filing the same of his approval or his disapproval of such form. The action of the superintendent in disapproving such form shall be subject to judicial review.

* * *

3. The provisions of this section shall not apply to any special rider or endorsement on any such policy, certificate or contract, which relates only to the manner of distribution of benefits or to the reservation of rights and benefits under such policy, certificate or contract and which is used at the request of the individual policyholder, contract holder or certificate holder.

[Subsections 2 and 4–7 omitted.]

§ 155. Life insurance policies; standard provisions

[This section, several pages in length, states in considerable detail provisions that are required and others that are proscribed.]

* * *

§ 164. Individual accident and sickness policy provisions

[Comparable to § 155, but more lengthy and detailed; this section falls short of prescribing the whole policy form as is done for fire insurance by § 168, but does prescribe a very substantial part of the policy provisions].

* * *

§ 167. Liability insurance; standard provisions; right of injured person

1. No policy or contract insuring against liability for injury to person, except as stated in subsection three, or against liability for injury to, or destruction of, property shall be issued or delivered in this state, unless it contains in substance the following provisions or provisions which are equally or more favorable to the insured and to judgment creditors so far as such provisions relate to judgment creditors:

(a) A provision that the insolvency or bankruptcy of the person insured, or the insolvency of his estate, shall not release the insurer from the payment of damages for injury sustained or loss occasioned during the life of and within the coverage of such policy or contract.

(b) A provision that in case judgment against the insured or his personal representative in an action brought to recover damages for injury sustained or loss or damage occasioned during the life of the policy or contract, shall remain unsatisfied at the expiration of thirty days from the serving of notice of entry of judgment upon the attorney for the insured, or upon the insured, and upon the insurer, then an action may, except during a stay or limited stay of execution against the insured on such judgment, be maintained against the insurer under the terms of the policy or contract for the amount of such judgment not exceeding the amount of the applicable limit of coverage under such policy or contract.

(c) A provision that notice given by or on behalf of the insured, or written notice by or on behalf of the injured person or any other claimant, to any licensed agent of the insurer in this state, with particulars sufficient to identify the insured, shall be deemed notice to the insurer.

(d) A provision that failure to give any notice required to be given by such policy within the time prescribed therein shall not invalidate any claim made by the insured or by any other claimant thereunder if it shall be shown not to have been reasonably possible to give such notice within the prescribed time and that notice was given as soon as was reasonably possible.

2. No policy or contract of personal injury liability insurance or of property damage liability insurance, covering liability arising from the ownership, maintenance or operation of any motor vehicle or of any vehicle as defined in section three hundred eighty-eight of the vehicle and traffic law, or an aircraft, or any vessel as defined in section forty-eight of the navigation law, shall be issued or delivered in this state to the owner thereof, or shall be issued or delivered by any authorized insurer upon any such vehicle or aircraft or vessel then principally garaged or principally used in this state, unless it contains a provision insuring the named insured against liability for death or injury sustained, or loss or damage occasioned within the coverage of the policy or contract, as a result of negligence in the operation or use of such vehicle by any person operating or using the same with the permission, express or implied, of the named insured, or in the case of aircraft, as a result of the operation or use of the aircraft by any person operating or using the same with the permission, express or implied, of the named insured, or in the case of a vessel, as a result of the operation or use of the vessel by any person operating or using the same with the permission, express or implied, of the named insured.

2-a. No policy insuring against loss resulting from liability imposed by law for bodily injury or death suffered by any natural person arising out of the ownership, maintenance and use of a motor vehicle by the insured shall be issued or delivered by any authorized insurer upon any motor vehicle then principally garaged or principally used in this state unless it contains a provision whereby the insurer agrees that it will pay to the insured, as defined in such provision, subject to the terms and conditions set forth therein to be prescribed by the board of directors of the Motor Vehicle Indemnification Corporation and approved by the superintendent, all sums, not exceeding a maximum amount or limit of ten thousand dollars exclusive of interest and costs, on account of injury to, or death of, one person, in any one accident, and the maximum amount or limit, subject to such limit for any one person so injured or killed, of twenty thousand dollars, exclusive of interest or costs, on account of injury to, or death of, more than one person in any one accident, which the insured or his legal representative shall be entitled to recover as damages from an owner or operator of an uninsured motor vehicle, unidentified motor vehicle which leaves the scene of an accident, a motor vehicle registered in this state as to which at the time of the accident there was not in effect a policy of liability insurance, a stolen vehicle, a motor vehicle operated without permission of the owner, an insured motor vehicle where the insurer disclaims liability or denies coverage or an unregistered vehicle because of bodily injury, sickness or disease, including death resulting therefrom, sustained by the insured, caused by accident occurring in this state and arising out of the ownership, maintenance or use of such motor vehicle. Any such policy which does not contain the aforesaid provision shall be construed as if such condition were embodied therein.

3. No policy or contract shall be deemed to insure against any liability of an insured because of death of or injuries to his or her spouse or because of injury to, or destruction of property of his or her spouse unless express provision relating specifically thereto is included in the policy.

[Subsections 4–8 omitted.]

§ 168. Fire insurance contracts; standard policy provisions; permissible variations

1. The printed form of a policy of fire insurance, as set forth in subsection six [renumbered five by 1970 amendment], shall be known and designated as the "standard fire insurance policy of the state of New York."

2. No policy or contract of fire insurance shall be made, issued or delivered by any insurer or by any agent or representative thereof, on any property in this state, unless it shall conform as to all provisions, stipulations, agreements and conditions, with such form of policy. * * *

4. Appropriate forms of supplemental contract or contracts or extended coverage endorsements whereby the interest in the property described in such policy shall be insured against one or more of the perils which the insurer is empowered to assume, in addition to the perils covered by said standard fire insurance policy, may be approved by the superintendent, and their use in connection with a standard fire insurance policy may be authorized by him. The first page of the policy may in form approved by the superintendent be rearranged to provide space for the listing of amounts of insurance, rates and premiums for the basic coverages insured under the standard form of policy and for additional coverages or perils insured under endorsements attached, and such other data as may be conveniently included for duplication on daily reports for office records.

5. The form of the standard fire insurance policy of the state of New York (with permission to substitute for the word "company" a more accurate descriptive term for the type of insurer) shall be as follows: *

* Ed. note: In the portions of the statute reproduced on pp. 593–596 *infra*, pages 3 and 4 of the statutory policy form are omitted. Page 3 is blank except for the heading, "Third Page of Standard Fire Policy," and the instruction, "Attach Form Below This Line." The fourth page is headed "Back of Standard Fire Policy (Optional)" and contains the following in addition to spaces for identifying data: "It is important that the written portions of all policies covering the same property read exactly alike. If they do not, they should be made uniform at once."

FIRST PAGE OF STANDARD FIRE POLICY

No. ....

[Space for insertion of name of company or companies issuing the policy and other matter permitted to be stated at the head of the policy.]

[Space for listing amounts of insurance, rates and premiums for the basic coverages insured under the standard form of policy and for additional coverages or perils insured under endorsements attached.]

In Consideration of the Provisions and Stipulations herein or added hereto

and of ....Dollars Premium

this Company, for the term } from the .... day of ...., 19.... { at noon, Standard Time, at
of .... } to the .... day of ...., 19.... { location of property involved,

to an amount not exceeding .... Dollars,

does insure ....

and legal representatives, to the extent of the actual cash value of the property at the time of loss, but not exceeding the amount which it would cost to repair or replace the property with material of like kind and quality

[First page of Standard Fire Policy—Continued on page 594]

[A3422]

[Continued from page 595]

within a reasonable time after such loss, without allowance for any increased cost of repair or reconstruction by reason of any ordinance or law regulating construction or repair, and without compensation for loss resulting from interruption of business or manufacture, nor in any event for more than the interest of the insured, against all DIRECT LOSS BY FIRE, LIGHTNING AND BY REMOVAL FROM PREMISES ENDANGERED BY THE PERILS INSURED AGAINST IN THIS POLICY. EXCEPT AS HEREINAFTER PROVIDED, to the property described hereinafter while located or contained as described in this policy, or pro rata for five days at each proper place to which any of the property shall necessarily be removed for preservation from the perils insured against in this policy, but not elsewhere.

Assignment of this policy shall not be valid except with the written consent of this Company.

This policy is made and accepted subject to the foregoing provisions and stipulations and those hereinafter stated, which are hereby made a part of this policy, together with such other provisions, stipulations and agreements as may be added hereto, as provided in this policy.

In Witness Whereof, this Company has executed and attested these presents; but this policy shall not be valid unless countersigned by the duly authorized Agent of this Company at ....

....

.... Secretary.

.... President.

Countersigned this .... day of ...., 19....

.... AGENT.

[A3423]

SECOND PAGE OF STANDARD FIRE POLICY

[A3424]

Concealment, fraud. This entire policy shall be void if, whether before or after a loss, the insured has wilfully concealed or misrepresented any material fact or circumstance concerning this insurance or the subject thereof, or the interest of the insured therein, or in case of any fraud or false swearing by the insured relating thereto.

Uninsurable and excepted property. This policy shall not cover accounts, deeds, evidences of debt, money or securities; nor, unless specifically named hereon in writing, bullion or manuscripts.

Perils not included. This Company shall not be liable for loss by fire or other perils insured against in this policy caused, directly or indirectly, by: (a) enemy attack by armed forces, including action taken by military, naval or air forces in resisting an actual or an immediately impending enemy attack; (b) invasion; (c) insurrection; (d) rebellion; (e) revolution; (f) civil war; (g) usurped power; (h) order of any civil authority except acts of destruction at the time of and for the purpose of preventing the spread of fire, provided that such fire did not originate from any of the perils excluded by this policy; (i) neglect of the insured to use all reasonable means to save and preserve the property at and after a loss, or when the property is endangered by fire in neighboring premises; (j) nor shall this Company be liable for loss by theft.

Other insurance. Other insurance may be prohibited or the amount of insurance may be limited by endorsement attached hereto.

Conditions suspending or restricting insurance. Unless otherwise provided in writing added hereto this Company shall not be liable for loss occurring (a) while the hazard is increased by any means within the control or knowledge of the insured; or (b) while a described building, whether intended for occupancy by owner or tenant, is vacant or unoccupied beyond a period of sixty consecutive days; or (c) as a result of explosion or riot, unless fire ensue, and in that event for loss by fire only.

Other perils or subjects. Any other peril to be insured against or subject of insurance to be covered in this policy shall be by endorsement in writing hereon or added hereto.

relating to the interests and obligations of such mortgagee may be added hereto by agreement in writing.

Pro rata liability. This Company shall not be liable for a greater proportion of any loss than the amount hereby insured shall bear to the whole insurance covering the property against the peril involved, whether collectible or not.

Requirements in case loss occurs. The Insured shall give immediate written notice to this Company of any loss, protect the property from further damage, forthwith separate the damaged and undamaged personal property, put it in the best possible order, furnish a complete inventory of the destroyed, damaged and undamaged property, showing in detail quantities, costs, actual cash value and amount of loss claimed; and within sixty days after the loss, unless such time is extended in writing by this Company, the insured shall render to this Company a proof of loss, signed and sworn to by the insured, stating the knowledge and belief of the insured as to the following: the time and origin of the loss, the interest of the insured and of all others in the property, the actual cash value of each item thereof and the amount of loss thereto, all encumbrances thereon, all other contracts of insurance, whether valid or not, covering any of said property, any changes in the title, use, occupation, location, possession or exposures of said property since the issuing of this policy, by whom and for what purpose any building herein described and the several parts thereof were occupied at the time of loss and whether or not it then stood on leased ground, and shall furnish a copy of all the descriptions and schedules in all policies and, if required, verified plans and specifications of any building, fixtures or machinery destroyed or damaged. The insured, as often as may be reasonably required, shall exhibit to any person designated by this Company all that remains of any property herein described, and submit to examinations under oath by any person named by this Company, and subscribe the same; and, as often as may be reasonably required, shall produce for examination all books of account, bills, invoices and other vouchers, or certified copies thereof if originals be lost, at such reasonable time and place as may be designated by this Company or its representative, and shall permit extracts and copies thereof to be made.

Appraisal. In case the insured and this Company shall fail to agree as to the actual cash value or

[Second page of Standard Fire Policy—Continued on page 596]

[Continued from page 595]

42 **Added provisions.** The extent of the application of insurance
43 under this policy and of the contribution to
44 be made by this Company in case of loss, and any other pro-
45 vision or agreement not inconsistent with the provisions of this
46 policy, may be provided for in writing added hereto, but no pro-
47 vision may be waived except such as by the terms of this policy
48 is subject to change.
49 **Waiver** No permission affecting this insurance shall
50 **provisions.** exist, or waiver of any provision be valid,
51 unless granted herein or expressed in writing
52 added hereto. No provision, stipulation or forfeiture shall be
53 held to be waived by any requirement or proceeding on the part
54 of this Company relating to appraisal or to any examination
55 provided for herein.
56 **Cancellation** This policy shall be cancelled at any time
57 **of policy.** at the request of the insured, in which case
58 this Company shall, upon demand and sur-
59 render of this policy, refund the excess of paid premium above
60 the customary short rates for the expired time. This pol-
61 icy may be cancelled at any time by this Company by giving
62 to the insured a five days' written notice of cancellation with
63 or without tender of the excess of paid premium above the pro
64 rata premium for the expired time, which excess, if not ten-
65 dered, shall be refunded on demand. Notice of cancellation shall
66 state that said excess premium (if not tendered) will be re-
67 funded on demand.
68 **Mortgagee** If loss hereunder is made payable, in whole
69 **interests and** or in part, to a designated mortgagee not
70 **obligations.** named herein as the insured, such interest in
71 this policy may be cancelled by giving to such
72 mortgagee a ten days' written notice of can-
73 cellation.
74 If the insured fails to render proof of loss such mortgagee, upon
75 notice, shall render proof of loss in the form herein specified
76 within sixty (60) days thereafter and shall be subject to the pro-
77 visions hereof relating to appraisal and time of payment and of
78 bringing suit. If this Company shall claim that no liability ex-
79 isted as to the mortgagor or owner, it shall, to the extent of pay-
80 ment of loss to the mortgagee, be subrogated to all the mort-
81 gagee's rights of recovery, but without impairing mortgagee's
82 right to sue; or it may pay off the mortgage debt and require
83 an assignment thereof and of the mortgage. Other provisions

125 the amount of loss, then, on the written demand of either, each
126 shall select a competent and disinterested appraiser and notify
127 the other of the appraiser selected within twenty days of such
128 demand. The appraisers shall first select a competent and dis-
129 interested umpire; and failing for fifteen days to agree upon
130 such umpire, then, on request of the insured or this Company,
131 such umpire shall be selected by a judge of a court of record in
132 the state in which the property covered is located. The ap-
133 praisers shall then appraise the loss, stating separately actual
134 cash value and loss of each item; and, failing to agree, shall
135 submit their differences, only, to the umpire. An award in writ-
136 ing, so itemized, of any two when filed with this Company shall
137 determine the amount of actual cash value and loss. Each
138 appraiser shall be paid by the party selecting him and the ex-
139 penses of appraisal and umpire shall be paid by the parties
140 equally.
141 **Company's** It shall be optional with this Company to
142 **options.** take all, or any part, of the property at the
143 agreed or appraised value, and also to re-
144 pair, rebuild or replace the property destroyed or damaged with
145 other of like kind and quality within a reasonable time, on giv-
146 ing notice of its intention so to do within thirty days after the
147 receipt of the proof of loss herein required.
148 **Abandonment.** There can be no abandonment to this Com-
149 pany of any property.
150 **When loss** The amount of loss for which this Company
151 **payable.** may be liable shall be payable sixty days
152 after proof of loss, as herein provided, is
153 received by this Company and ascertainment of the loss is made
154 either by agreement between the insured and this Company ex-
155 pressed in writing or by the filing with this Company of an
156 award as herein provided.
157 **Suit.** No suit or action on this policy for the recov-
158 ery of any claim shall be sustainable in any
159 court of law or equity unless all the requirements of this policy
160 shall have been complied with, and unless commenced within
161 twelve months next after inception of the loss.
162 **Subrogation.** This Company may require from the insured
163 an assignment of all right of recovery against
164 any party for loss to the extent that payment therefor is made
165 by this Company.

[A3425]

* * *

[Subsection 6 of § 168 and § 168–a omitted.]

§ 169. Fire insurance and allied lines; power of superintendent to prescribe endorsements and supplemental contracts

1. The superintendent may, whenever he deems it necessary for the proper administration of any provision of law make or cause to be made, in accordance with article three, an examination of the books, records, policies, riders, endorsements, supplemental contracts and other documents of any insurer doing in this state the business of direct fire insurance or of any rating organization of which any such insurer is a member or subscriber.

2. If as a result of such examination or of any investigation of the forms of such riders, endorsements, supplemental contracts or other addenda, the superintendent determines that any rider, endorsement or other addendum for use in connection with a fire insurance contract should be uniform in this state or in any part thereof, he may, after reducing to writing such determination and his findings of fact relating thereto, prepare or cause to be prepared a standard form thereof, and thereupon give notice of such proposed form, together with his determination and findings of fact, to all insurers authorized in this state to do the business of direct fire insurance and to all rating organizations of which any such insurer is a member or subscriber and to all insurance brokers' associations incorporated in this state which shall have registered their names and addresses with the superintendent for this purpose. The superintendent may hold a public hearing thereon after notice to such insurers and rating organizations and such insurance brokers' associations. The superintendent may by official regulation prescribe the form or forms of any riders, endorsements or other addenda used in connection with any fire insurance contract covering any property located in this state, the extent to which the use of such form or forms shall be permitted and shall be exclusive of any other form or forms covering substantially the same agreement, the effect, if any, of the use of such form or forms upon rates, and the time when such regulation or regulations shall become effective, which shall be not less than thirty days after the giving of notice thereof to all such insurers and rating organizations and such insurance brokers' associations. Any insurer doing in this state the business of fire insurance which shall, in violation of any such regulation attach to, or otherwise make a part of, any contract of fire insurance covering any property located in this state, any rider, endorsement, clause, permit or other addendum which covers substantially the same agreement as such prescribed form and which is not in the precise language of such prescribed form, and any officer of such insurer who knowingly participates in such violation, shall be guilty of a misdemeanor.

[Subsections 3–5 omitted.]

§ 170. Executory contract not a change in interest, title or possession

The making of a contract to sell or to exchange real property shall not constitute a change in the interest, title or possession, within the meaning of the applicable provisions of any contract of fire insurance, including any contract supplemental thereto, hereafter made covering property located in this state.

* * *

APPENDIX B

Excerpt from New York Vehicle and Traffic Law
(McKinney 1970)

Article 6. Motor Vehicle Financial Security Act

§ 311. Definitions

As used in this article:

* * *

4. The term "owner's policy of liability insurance" shall mean a policy.[1]

(a) Affording coverage as defined in the minimum provisions prescribed in a regulation which shall be promulgated by the superintendent at least ninety days prior to effective date of this act. The superintendent before promulgating such regulations or any amendment thereof, shall consult with all insurers licensed to write automobile liability insurance in this state and shall not prescribe minimum provisions which fail to reflect the provisions of automobile liability insurance policies, other than motor vehicle liability policies as defined in section three hundred forty-five of this chapter, issued within this state at the date of such regulation or amendment thereof. Nothing contained in such regulation or in this article shall prohibit any insurer from affording coverage under an owner's policy of liability insurance more liberal than that required by said minimum provisions. Every such owner's policy of liability insurance shall provide insurance subject to said regulation against loss from the liability imposed by law for damages, including damages for care and loss of services, because of bodily injury to or death of any person and injury to or destruction of property arising out of the ownership, maintenance, use, or operation of a specific motor vehicle or motor vehicles within the state of New York, or elsewhere in the United States in North America or the Dominion of Canada, subject to a limit, exclusive of interest and costs, with respect to each such motor vehicle, of ten thousand dollars because of bodily injuries to or death of one person in any one accident and, subject to said limit for one person, to a limit of twenty thousand dollars because of bodily injury to or death of two or more persons in any one accident, and to a limit of five thousand dollars because of injury to or destruction of property of others in any one accident provided, however, that such policy need not be for a period coterminous with the registration period of the vehicle insured. Any insurer authorized to issue an owner's policy of liability insurance as provided for in this article may, pending the issue of such a policy, make an agreement, to be known as a binder, or may, in lieu of such a policy, issue a renewal endorsement or evidence of renewal of an existing policy; each of which shall be construed to provide indemnity or protection in like manner and to the same extent as such a policy. The provisions of this article shall apply to such binders, renewal endorsements or evidences of renewal; and

---

1. So in original. Period following
"policy" probably should be omitted.

(b) In the case of a vehicle registered in this state, a policy issued by an insurer duly authorized to transact business in this state; or

(c) In the case of a vehicle registered in another state, or in both this state and another state, in the name of a non-resident, either a policy issued by an authorized insurer, or a policy issued by an unauthorized insurer authorized to transact business in the state of his residence or in the state in which the vehicle is registered if such unauthorized insurer files with the commissioner in form to be approved by him a statement consenting to service of process and declaring its policies shall be deemed to be varied to comply with the requirements of this article; and

(d) The form of which has been approved by the superintendent. No such policy shall be issued or delivered in this state until a copy of the form of policy shall have been on file with the superintendent for at least thirty days, unless sooner approved in writing by the superintendent, nor if within said period of thirty days the superintendent shall have notified the carrier in writing that in his opinion, specifying the reasons therefor, the form of policy does not comply with the laws of this state.

* * *

APPENDIX C

Excerpts from British Marine Insurance Act, 1906, 6 Edw. 7, c. 41

MARINE INSURANCE.

1. A contract of marine insurance is a contract whereby the insurer undertakes to indemnify the assured, in manner and to the extent thereby agreed, against marine losses, that is to say, the losses incident to marine adventure. * * *

INSURABLE INTEREST.

4.—(1) Every contract of marine insurance by way of gaming or wagering is void.

(2) A contract of marine insurance is deemed to be a gaming or wagering contract—

    (a) Where the assured has not an insurable interest as defined by this Act, and the contract is entered into with no expectation of acquiring such an interest; or

    (b) Where the policy is made "interest or no interest," or "without further proof of interest than the policy itself," or "without benefit of salvage to the insurer," or subject to any other like term:

Provided that, where there is no possibility of salvage, a policy may be effected without benefit of salvage to the insurer.

5.—(1) Subject to the provisions of this Act, every person has an insurable interest who is interested in a marine adventure.

(2) In particular a person is interested in a marine adventure where he stands in any legal or equitable relation to the adventure or to any insurable property at risk therein, in consequence of which he may benefit by the safety or due arrival of insurable property, or may be prejudiced by its loss, or by damage thereto, or by the detention thereof, or may incur liability in respect thereof.

6.—(1) The assured must be interested in the subject-matter insured at the time of the loss though he need not be interested when the insurance is effected:

Provided that where the subject-matter is insured "lost or not lost," the assured may recover although he may not have acquired his interest until after the loss, unless at the time of effecting the contract of insurance the assured was aware of the loss, and the insurer was not.

(2) Where the assured has no interest at the time of the loss, he cannot acquire interest by any act or election after he is aware of the loss.

7.—(1) A defeasible interest is insurable, as also is a contingent interest.

(2) In particular, where the buyer of goods has insured them, he has an insurable interest, notwithstanding that he might, at his election, have rejected the goods, or have treated them as at the seller's risk, by reason of the latter's delay in making delivery or otherwise.

8. A partial interest of any nature is insurable.

9.—(1) The insurer under a contract of marine insurance has an insurable interest in his risk, and may re-insure in respect of it.

(2) Unless the policy otherwise provides, the orginal assured has no right or interest in respect of such re-insurance.

10. The lender of money on bottomry or respondentia has an insurable interest in respect of the loan.

11. The master or any member of the crew of a ship has an insurable interest in respect of his wages.

12. In the case of advance freight, the person advancing the freight has an insurable interest, in so far as such freight is not repayable in case of loss.

13. The assured has an insurable interest in the charges of any insurance which he may effect.

14.—(1) Where the subject-matter insured is mortgaged, the mortgagor has an insurable interest in the full value thereof, and the mortgagee has an insurable interest in respect of any sum due or to become due under the mortgage.

(2) A mortgagee, consignee, or other person having an interest in the subject-matter insured may insure on behalf and for the benefit of other persons interested as well as for his own benefit.

(3) The owner of insurable property has an insurable interest in respect of the full value thereof, notwithstanding that some third person may have agreed, or be liable, to indemnify him in case of loss.

15. Where the assured assigns or otherwise parts with his interest in the subject-matter insured, he does not thereby transfer to the assignee his rights under the contract of insurance, unless there be an express or implied agreement with the assignee to that effect.

But the provisions of this section do not affect a transmission of interest by operation of law.

INSURABLE VALUE.

16. Subject to any express provision or valuation in the policy, the insurable value of the subject-matter insured must be ascertained as follows:—

(1) In insurance on ship, the insurable value is the value, at the commencement of the risk, of the ship, including her outfit, provisions and stores for the officers and crew, money advanced for seamen's wages, and other disbursements (if any) incurred to make the ship fit for the voyage or adventure contemplated by the policy, plus the charges of insurance upon the whole:

The insurable value, in the case of a steamship, includes also the machinery, boilers, and coals and engine stores if owned by the assured, and, in the case of a ship engaged in a special trade, the ordinary fittings requisite for that trade:

(2) In insurance on freight, whether paid in advance or otherwise, the insurable value is the gross amount of the freight at the risk of the assured, plus the charges of insurance:

(3) In insurance on goods or merchandise, the insurable value is the prime cost of the property insured, plus the expenses of and incidental to shipping and the charges of insurance upon the whole:

(4) In insurance on any other subject-matter, the insurable value is the amount at the risk of the assured when the policy attaches, plus the charges of insurance.

DISCLOSURE AND REPRESENTATIONS.

17. A contract of marine insurance is a contract based upon the utmost good faith, and, if the utmost good faith be not observed by either party, the contract may be avoided by the other party.

18.—(1) Subject to the provisions of this section, the assured must disclose to the insurer, before the contract is concluded, every material circumstance which is known to the assured, and the assured is deemed to know every circumstance which, in the ordinary course of business, ought to be known by him. If the assured fails to make such disclosure, the insurer may avoid the contract.

(2) Every circumstance is material which would influence the judgment of a prudent insurer in fixing the premium, or determining whether he will take the risk.

(3) In the absence of inquiry the following circumstances need not be disclosed, namely:—

(a) Any circumstance which diminishes the risk;

(b) Any circumstance which is known or presumed to be known to the insurer. The insurer is presumed to know matters of common notoriety or knowledge, and matters which an insurer in the ordinary course of his business, as such, ought to know;

(c) Any circumstance as to which information is waived by the insurer;

(d) Any circumstance which it is superfluous to disclose by reason of any express or implied warranty.

(4) Whether any particular circumstance, which is not disclosed, be material or not is, in each case, a question of fact.

(5) The term "circumstance" includes any communication made to, or information received by, the assured.

19. Subject to the provisions of the preceding section as to circumstances which need not be disclosed, where an insurance is effected for the assured by an agent, the agent must disclose to the insurer—

(a) Every material circumstance which is known to himself, and an agent to insure is deemed to know every circumstance which in the ordinary course of business ought to be known by, or to have been communicated to, him; and

(b) Every material circumstance which the assured is bound to disclose, unless it come to his knowledge too late to communicate it to the agent.

20.—(1) Every material representation made by the assured or his agent to the insurer during the negotiations for the contract, and before the contract is concluded, must be true. If it be untrue the insurer may avoid the contract.

(2) A representation is material which would influence the judgment of a prudent insurer in fixing the premium, or determining whether he will take the risk.

(3) A representation may be either a representation as to a matter of fact, or as to a matter of expectation or belief.

(4) A representation as to a matter of fact is true, if it be substantially correct, that is to say, if the difference between what is represented and what is actually correct would not be considered material by a prudent insurer.

(5) A representation as to a matter of expectation or belief is true if it be made in good faith.

(6) A representation may be withdrawn or corrected before the contract is concluded.

(7) Whether a particular representation be material or not is, in each case, a question of fact.

* * *

THE POLICY.

22. Subject to the provisions of any statute, a contract of marine insurance is inadmissible in evidence unless it is embodied in a marine policy in accordance with this Act. The policy may be executed and issued either at the time when the contract is concluded, or afterwards.

* * *

27.—(1) A policy may be either valued or unvalued.

(2) A valued policy is a policy which specifies the agreed value of the subject-matter insured.

(3) Subject to the provisions of this Act, and in the absence of fraud, the value fixed by the policy is, as between the insurer and assured, conclusive of the insurable value of the subject intended to be insured, whether the loss be total or partial.

(4) Unless the policy otherwise provides, the value fixed by the policy is not conclusive for the purpose of determining whether there has been a constructive total loss.

28. An unvalued policy is a policy which does not specify the value of the subject-matter insured, but, subject to the limit of the sum insured, leaves the insurable value to be subsequently ascertained, in the manner herein-before specified.

* * *

30.—(1) A policy may be in the form in the First Schedule to this Act.

(2) Subject to the provisions of this Act, and unless the context of the policy otherwise requires, the terms and expressions mentioned in the First Schedule to this Act shall be construed as having the scope and meaning in that schedule assigned to them.

* * *

WARRANTIES, &c.

33.—(1) A warranty, in the following sections relating to warranties, means a promissory warranty, that is to say, a warranty by which the assured undertakes that some particular thing shall or shall not be done, or that some condition shall be fulfilled, or whereby he affirms or negatives the existence of a particular state of facts.

(2) A warranty may be express or implied.

(3) A warranty, as above defined, is a condition which must be exactly complied with, whether it be material to the risk or not. If it be not so complied with, then, subject to any express provision in the policy, the insurer is discharged from liability as from the date of the breach of warranty, but without prejudice to any liability incurred by him before that date.

34.—(1) Non-compliance with a warranty is excused when, by reason of a change of circumstances, the warranty ceases to be applicable to the circumstances of the contract, or when compliance with the warranty is rendered unlawful by any subsequent law.

(2) Where a warranty is broken, the assured cannot avail himself of the defence that the breach has been remedied, and the warranty complied with, before loss.

(3) A breach of warranty may be waived by the insurer.

35.—(1) An express warranty may be in any form of words from which the intention to warrant is to be inferred.

(2) An express warranty must be included in, or written upon, the policy, or must be contained in some document incorporated by reference into the policy.

(3) An express warranty does not exclude an implied warranty, unless it be inconsistent therewith.

* * *

39.—(1) In a voyage policy there is an implied warranty that at the commencement of the voyage the ship shall be seaworthy for the purpose of the particular adventure insured.

(2) Where the policy attaches while the ship is in port, there is also an implied warranty that she shall, at the commencement of the risk, be reasonably fit to encounter the ordinary perils of the port.

(3) Where the policy relates to a voyage which is performed in different stages, during which the ship requires different kinds of or further preparation or equipment, there is an implied warranty that at the commencement of each stage the ship is seaworthy in respect of such preparation or equipment for the purposes of that stage.

(4) A ship is deemed to be seaworthy when she is reasonably fit in all respects to encounter the ordinary perils of the seas of the adventure insured.

(5) In a time policy there is no implied warranty that the ship shall be seaworthy at any stage of the adventure, but where, with the privity of the assured, the ship is sent to sea in an unseaworthy state, the insurer is not liable for any loss attributable to unseaworthiness.

40.—(1) In a policy on goods or other moveables there is no implied warranty that the goods or moveables are seaworthy.

(2) In a voyage policy on goods or other moveables there is an implied warranty that at the commencement of the voyage the ship is not only seaworthy as a ship, but also that she is reasonably fit to carry the goods or other moveables to the destination contemplated by the policy.

41. There is an implied warranty that the adventure insured is a lawful one, and that, so far as the assured can control the matter, the adventure shall be carried out in a lawful manner.

* * *

ASSIGNMENT OF POLICY.

50.—(1) A marine policy is assignable unless it contains terms expressly prohibiting assignment. It may be assigned either before or after loss.

(2) Where a marine policy has been assigned so as to pass the beneficial interest in such policy, the assignee of the policy is entitled to sue thereon in his own name; and the defendant is entitled to make any defence arising out of the contract which he would have been entitled to make if the action had been brought in the name of the person by or on behalf of whom the policy was effected.

(3) A marine policy may be assigned by indorsement thereon or in other customary manner.

51. Where the assured has parted with or lost his interest in the subject-matter insured, and has not, before or at the time of so doing, expressly or impliedly agreed to assign the policy, any subsequent assignment of the policy is inoperative:

Provided that nothing in this section affects the assignment of a policy after loss.

* * *

LOSS AND ABANDONMENT.

55.—(1) Subject to the provisions of this Act, and unless the policy otherwise provides, the insurer is liable for any loss proximately caused by a peril insured against, but, subject as aforesaid, he is not liable for any loss which is not proximately caused by a peril insured against.

(2) In particular,—

(a) The insurer is not liable for any loss attributable to the wilful misconduct of the assured, but, unless the policy otherwise provides, he is liable for any loss proximately caused by a peril insured against, even though the loss would not have happened but for the misconduct or negligence of the master or crew;

(b) Unless the policy otherwise provides, the insurer on ship or goods is not liable for any loss proximately caused by delay, although the delay be caused by a peril insured against;

(c) Unless the policy otherwise provides, the insurer is not liable for ordinary wear and tear, ordinary leakage and breakage, inherent vice or nature of the subject-matter insured, or for any loss proximately caused by rats or vermin, or for any injury to machinery not proximately caused by maritime perils.

56.—(1) A loss may be either total or partial. Any loss other than a total loss, as hereinafter defined, is a partial loss.

(2) A total loss may be either an actual total loss, or a constructive total loss.

(3) Unless a different intention appears from the terms of the policy, an insurance against total loss includes a constructive, as well as an actual, total loss.

(4) Where the assured brings an action for a total loss and the evidence proves only a partial loss, he may, unless the policy otherwise provides, recover for a partial loss.

(5) Where goods reach their destination in specie, but by reason of obliteration of marks, or otherwise, they are incapable of identification, the loss, if any, is partial, and not total.

57.—(1) Where the subject-matter insured is destroyed, or so damaged as to cease to be a thing of the kind insured, or where the assured is irretrievably deprived thereof, there is an actual total loss.

(2) In the case of an actual total loss no notice of abandonment need be given.

58. Where the ship concerned in the adventure is missing, and after the lapse of a reasonable time no news of her has been received, an actual total loss may be presumed.

59. Where, by a peril insured against, the voyage is interrupted at an intermediate port or place, under such circumstances as, apart from any special stipulation in the contract of affreightment, to justify the master in landing and re-shipping the goods or other moveables, or in transhipping them, and sending them on to their destination, the liability of the insurer continues, notwithstanding the landing or transhipment.

60.—(1) Subject to any express provision in the policy, there is a constructive total loss where the subject-matter insured is reasonably abandoned on account of its actual total loss appearing to be unavoidable, or because it could not be preserved from actual total loss without an expenditure which would exceed its value when the expenditure had been incurred.

(2) In particular, there is a constructive total loss—

(i) Where the assured is deprived of the possession of his ship or goods by a peril insured against, and (*a*) it is unlikely that he can recover the ship or goods, as the case may be, or (*b*) the cost of recovering the ship or goods, as the case may be, would exceed their value when recovered; or

(ii) In the case of damage to a ship, where she is so damaged by a peril insured against that the cost of repairing the damage would exceed the value of the ship when repaired.

In estimating the cost of repairs, no deduction is to be made in respect of general average contributions to those repairs payable by other interests, but account is to be taken of the expense of future salvage operations and of any future general average contributions to which the ship would be liable if repaired; or

(iii) In the case of damage to goods, where the cost of repairing the damage and forwarding the goods to their destination would exceed their value on arrival.

61. Where there is a constructive total loss the assured may either treat the loss as a partial loss, or abandon the subject-matter insured to the insurer and treat the loss as if it were an actual total loss.

62.—(1) Subject to the provisions of this section, where the assured elects to abandon the subject-matter insured to the insurer, he must give notice of abandonment. If he fails to do so the loss can only be treated as a partial loss.

(2) Notice of abandonment may be given in writing, or by word of mouth, or partly in writing and partly by word of mouth, and may be given in any terms which indicate the intention of the assured to abandon his insured interest in the subject-matter insured unconditionally to the insurer.

(3) Notice of abandonment must be given with reasonable diligence after the receipt of reliable information of the loss, but where the information is of a doubtful character the assured is entitled to a reasonable time to make inquiry.

(4) Where notice of abandonment is properly given, the rights of the assured are not prejudiced by the fact that the insurer refuses to accept the abandonment.

(5) The acceptance of an abandonment may be either express or implied from the conduct of the insurer. The mere silence of the insurer after notice is not an acceptance.

(6) Where notice of abandonment is accepted the abandonment is irrevocable. The acceptance of the notice conclusively admits liability for the loss and the sufficiency of the notice.

(7) Notice of abandonment is unnecessary where, at the time when the assured receives information of the loss, there would be no possibility of benefit to the insurer if notice were given to him.

(8) Notice of abandonment may be waived by the insurer.

(9) Where an insurer has re-insured his risk, no notice of abandonment need be given by him.

63.—(1) Where there is a valid abandonment the insurer is entitled to take over the interest of the assured in whatever may remain of the subject-matter insured, and all proprietary rights incidental thereto.

(2) Upon the abandonment of a ship, the insurer thereof is entitled to any freight in course of being earned, and which is earned by her subsequent to the casualty causing the loss, less the expenses of earning it incurred after the casualty; and, where the ship is carrying the owner's goods, the insurer is entitled to a reasonable remuneration for the carriage of them subsequent to the casualty causing the loss.

PARTIAL LOSSES (INCLUDING SALVAGE AND GENERAL AVERAGE AND PARTICULAR CHARGES.)

64.—(1) A particular average loss is a particular loss of the subject-matter insured, caused by a peril insured against, and which is not a general average loss.

(2) Expenses incurred by or on behalf of the assured for the safety or preservation of the subject-matter insured, other than general average and salvage charges, are called particular charges. Particular charges are not included in particular average.

65.—(1) Subject to any express provision in the policy, salvage charges incurred in preventing a loss by perils insured against may be recovered as a loss by those perils.

(2) "Salvage charges" means the charges recoverable under maritime law by a salvor independently of contract. They do not include the expenses of services in the nature of salvage rendered by the assured or his agents, or any person employed for hire by them, for the purpose of averting a peril insured against. Such expenses, where properly incurred, may be recovered as particular charges or as a general average loss, according to the circumstances under which they were incurred.

66.—(1) A general average loss is a loss caused by or directly consequential on a general average act. It includes a general average expenditure as well as a general average sacrifice.

(2) There is a general average act where any extraordinary sacrifice or expenditure is voluntarily and reasonably made or incurred in time of peril for the purpose of preserving the property imperilled in the common adventure.

(3) Where there is a general average loss, the party on whom it falls is entitled, subject to the conditions imposed by maritime law, to a rateable contribution from the other parties interested, and such contribution is called a general average contribution.

(4) Subject to any express provision in the policy, where the assured has incurred a general average expenditure, he may recover from the insurer in respect of the proportion of the loss which falls upon him; and, in the case of a general average sacrifice, he may recover from the insurer in respect of the whole loss without having enforced his right of contribution from the other parties liable to contribute.

(5) Subject to any express provision in the policy, where the assured has paid, or is liable to pay, a general average contribution in respect of the subject insured, he may recover therefor from the insurer.

(6) In the absence of express stipulation, the insurer is not liable for any general average loss or contribution where the loss was not incurred for the purpose of avoiding, or in connexion with the avoidance of, a peril insured against.

(7) Where ship, freight, and cargo, or any two of those interests, are owned by the same assured, the liability of the insurer in respect of general average losses or contributions is to be determined as if those subjects were owned by different persons.

MEASURE OF INDEMNITY.

[§§ 67 and 69 are quoted in § 3.6(c) n. 7 *supra.*]

* * *

SCHEDULES.

FIRST SCHEDULE.

FORM OF POLICY.

BE IT KNOWN THAT   as well in

own name as for and in the name and names of all and every other person
or persons to whom the same doth, may, or shall appertain, in part or in
all doth make assurance and cause

and them, and every of them, to be insured lost or not lost, at and from

Upon any kind of goods and merchandises, and also upon the body, tackle,
apparel, ordnance, munition, artillery, boat, and other furniture, of and
in the good ship or vessel called the

whereof is master under God, for this present voyage,

or whosoever else shall go for master in the said ship, or by whatsoever
other name or names the said ship, or the master thereof, is or shall
be named or called; beginning the adventure upon the said goods and
merchandises from the loading thereof aboard the said ship,

upon the said ship, &c.

and so shall continue and endure, during her abode there, upon the said
ship, &c. And further, until the said ship, with all her ordnance, tackle,
apparel, &c., and goods and merchandises whatsoever shall be arrived at

upon the said ship, &c., until she hath moored at anchor twenty-four hours
in good safety; and upon the goods and merchandises, until the same be
there discharged and safely landed. And it shall be lawful for the said
ship, &c., in this voyage, to proceed and sail to and touch and stay at
any ports or places whatsoever

without prejudice to this insurance. The said ship, &c., goods and merchandises, &c., for so much as concerns the assured by agreement between
the assured and assurers in this policy, are and shall be valued at

Touching the adventures and perils which we the assurers are contented to bear and do take upon us in this voyage: they are of the seas,
men of war, fire, enemies, pirates, rovers, thieves, jettisons, letters of
mart and countermart, surprisals, takings at sea, arrests, restraints, and
detainments of all kings, princes, and people, of what nation, condition,
or quality soever, barratry of the master and mariners, and of all other
perils, losses, and misfortunes, that have or shall come to the hurt, detriment, or damage of the said goods and merchandises, and ship, &c., or
any part thereof. And in case of any loss or misfortune it shall be
lawful to the assured, their factors, servants and assigns, to sue, labour,
and travel for, in and about the defence, safeguards, and recovery of the
said goods and merchandises, and ship, &c., or any part thereof, without
prejudice to this insurance; to the charges whereof we, the assurers,
will contribute each one according to the rate and quantity of his sum
herein assured. And it is especially declared and agreed that no acts of
the insurer or insured in recovering, saving, or preserving the property in-

sured shall be considered as a waiver, or acceptance of abandonment. And it is agreed by us, the insurers, that this writing or policy of assurance shall be of as much force and effect as the surest writing or policy of assurance heretofore made in Lombard Street, or in the Royal Exchange, or elsewhere in London. And so we, the assurers, are contented, and do hereby promise and bind ourselves, each one for his own part, our heirs, executors, and goods to the assured, their executors, administrators, and assigns, for the true performance of the premises, confessing ourselves paid the consideration due unto us for this assurance by the assured, at and after the rate of

IN WITNESS whereof we, the assurers, have subscribed our names and sums assured in London.

N.B.—Corn, fish, salt, fruit, flour, and seed are warranted free from average, unless general, or the ship be stranded—sugar, tobacco, hemp, flax, hides and skins are warranted free from average, under five pounds per cent., and all other goods, also the ship and freight, are warranted free from average, under three pounds per cent. unless general, or the ship be stranded.

APPENDIX D

Mortality Tables

[Quoted, with permission, from Institute of Life Insurance, Life Insurance Fact Book, 1970, 118–119.]

Age	American Experience (1843–1858) Deaths Per 1000	Expectation of Life(Years)	Commissioners 1941 Standard Ordinary (1930–1940) Deaths Per 1000	Expectation of Life(Years)	Commissioners 1958 Standard Ordinary (1950–1954) Deaths Per 1000	Expectation of Life(Years)	Annuity Table for 1949—Male (1939–1949) Deaths Per 1000	Expectation of Life(Years)	United States Total Population (1959–1961) Deaths Per 1000	Expectation of Life(Years)
0	154.70	41.45	22.58	62.33	7.08	68.30	4.04	73.18	25.93	69.89
1	63.49	47.94	5.77	62.76	1.76	67.78	1.58	72.48	1.70	70.75
2	35.50	50.16	4.14	62.12	1.52	66.90	.89	71.59	1.04	69.87
3	23.91	50.98	3.38	61.37	1.46	66.00	.72	70.65	.80	68.94
4	17.70	51.22	2.99	60.58	1.40	65.10	.63	69.70	.67	67.99
5	13.60	51.13	2.76	59.76	1.35	64.19	.57	68.75	.59	67.04
6	11.37	50.83	2.61	58.92	1.30	63.27	.53	67.78	.52	66.08
7	9.75	50.41	2.47	58.08	1.26	62.35	.50	66.82	.47	65.11
8	8.63	49.90	2.31	57.22	1.23	61.43	.49	65.85	.43	64.14
9	7.90	49.33	2.12	56.35	1.21	60.51	.48	64.89	.39	63.17
10	7.49	48.72	1.97	55.47	1.21	59.58	.48	63.92	.37	62.19
11	7.52	48.08	1.91	54.58	1.23	58.65	.49	62.95	.37	61.22
12	7.54	47.45	1.92	53.68	1.26	57.72	.50	61.98	.40	60.24
13	7.57	46.80	1.98	52.78	1.32	56.80	.51	61.01	.48	59.26
14	7.60	46.16	2.07	51.89	1.39	55.87	.52	60.04	.59	58.29
15	7.63	45.50	2.15	50.99	1.46	54.95	.54	59.07	.71	57.33
16	7.66	44.85	2.19	50.10	1.54	54.03	.55	58.10	.82	56.37
17	7.69	44.19	2.25	49.21	1.62	53.11	.57	57.13	.93	55.41
18	7.73	43.53	2.30	48.32	1.69	52.19	.58	56.17	1.02	54.46
19	7.77	42.87	2.37	47.43	1.74	51.28	.60	55.20	1.08	53.52
20	7.80	42.20	2.43	46.54	1.79	50.37	.62	54.23	1.15	52.58
21	7.86	41.53	2.51	45.66	1.83	49.46	.65	53.27	1.22	51.64
22	7.91	40.85	2.59	44.77	1.86	48.55	.67	52.30	1.27	50.70
23	7.96	40.17	2.68	43.88	1.89	47.64	.70	51.33	1.28	49.76
24	8.01	39.49	2.77	43.00	1.91	46.73	.73	50.37	1.27	48.83
25	8.06	38.81	2.88	42.12	1.93	45.82	.77	49.41	1.26	47.89
26	8.13	38.12	2.99	41.24	1.96	44.90	.81	48.44	1.25	46.95
27	8.20	37.43	3.11	40.36	1.99	43.99	.85	47.48	1.26	46.00
28	8.26	36.73	3.25	39.49	2.03	43.08	.90	46.52	1.30	45.06
29	8.34	36.03	3.40	38.61	2.08	42.16	.95	45.56	1.36	44.12
30	8.43	35.33	3.56	37.74	2.13	41.25	1.00	44.61	1.43	43.18
31	8.51	34.63	3.73	36.88	2.19	40.34	1.07	43.65	1.51	42.24
32	8.61	33.92	3.92	36.01	2.25	39.43	1.14	42.70	1.60	41.30
33	8.72	33.21	4.12	35.15	2.32	38.51	1.21	41.75	1.70	40.37
34	8.83	32.50	4.35	34.29	2.40	37.60	1.30	40.80	1.81	39.44
35	8.95	31.78	4.59	33.44	2.51	36.69	1.39	39.85	1.94	38.51
36	9.09	31.07	4.86	32.59	2.64	35.78	1.49	38.90	2.09	37.58
37	9.23	30.35	5.15	31.75	2.80	34.88	1.61	37.96	2.28	36.66
38	9.41	29.62	5.46	30.91	3.01	33.97	1.73	37.02	2.49	35.74
39	9.59	28.90	5.81	30.08	3.25	33.07	1.87	36.08	2.73	34.83
40	9.79	28.18	6.18	29.25	3.53	32.18	2.03	35.15	3.00	33.92
41	10.01	27.45	6.59	28.43	3.84	31.29	2.22	34.22	3.30	33.02
42	10.25	26.72	7.03	27.62	4.17	30.41	2.48	33.30	3.62	32.13
43	10.52	26.00	7.51	26.81	4.53	29.54	2.80	32.38	3.97	31.25
44	10.83	25.27	8.04	26.01	4.92	28.67	3.19	31.47	4.35	30.37
45	11.16	24.54	8.61	25.21	5.35	27.81	3.63	30.57	4.76	29.50
46	11.56	23.81	9.23	24.43	5.83	26.95	4.12	29.68	5.21	28.64
47	12.00	23.08	9.91	23.65	6.36	26.11	4.66	28.80	5.73	27.79
48	12.51	22.36	10.64	22.88	6.95	25.27	5.25	27.93	6.33	26.94
49	13.11	21.63	11.45	22.12	7.60	24.45	5.88	27.07	7.00	26.11

Age	American Experience (1843–1858)		Commissioners 1941 Standard Ordinary (1930–1940)		Commissioners 1958 Standard Ordinary (1950–1954)		Annuity Table for 1949—Male (1939–1949)		United States Total Population (1959–1961)	
	Deaths Per 1000	Expectation of Life(Years)	Deaths Per 1000	Expectation of Life(Years)	Deaths Per 1000	Expectation of Life(Years)	Deaths Per 1000	Expectation of Life(Years)	Deaths Per 1000	Expectation of Life(Years)
50	13.78	20.91	12.32	21.37	8.32	23.63	6.56	26.23	7.74	25.29
51	14.54	20.20	13.27	20.64	9.11	22.82	7.28	25.40	8.52	24.49
52	15.39	19.49	14.30	19.91	9.96	22.03	8.04	24.58	9.29	23.69
53	16.33	18.79	15.43	19.19	10.89	21.25	8.84	23.78	10.05	22.91
54	17.40	18.09	16.65	18.48	11.90	20.47	9.68	22.99	10.82	22.14
55	18.57	17.40	17.98	17.78	13.00	19.71	10.56	22.20	11.61	21.37
56	19.89	16.72	19.43	17.10	14.21	18.97	11.49	21.44	12.49	20.62
57	21.34	16.05	21.00	16.43	15.54	18.23	12.46	20.68	13.52	19.87
58	22.94	15.39	22.71	15.77	17.00	17.51	13.48	19.93	14.73	19.14
59	24.72	14.74	24.57	15.13	18.59	16.81	14.54	19.20	16.11	18.42
60	26.69	14.10	26.59	14.50	20.34	16.12	15.66	18.48	17.61	17.71
61	28.88	13.47	28.78	13.88	22.24	15.44	16.87	17.76	19.17	17.02
62	31.29	12.86	31.18	13.27	24.31	14.78	18.20	17.06	20.82	16.34
63	33.94	12.26	33.76	12.69	26.57	14.14	19.67	16.37	22.52	15.68
64	36.87	11.67	36.58	12.11	29.04	13.51	21.28	15.68	24.31	15.03
65	40.13	11.10	39.64	11.55	31.75	12.90	23.07	15.01	26.22	14.39
66	43.71	10.54	42.96	11.01	34.74	12.31	25.03	14.36	28.28	13.76
67	47.65	10.00	46.56	10.48	38.04	11.73	27.19	13.71	30.53	13.15
68	52.00	9.47	50.46	9.97	41.68	11.17	29.58	13.08	33.01	12.55
69	56.76	8.97	54.70	9.47	45.61	10.64	32.20	12.46	35.73	11.96
70	61.99	8.48	59.30	8.99	49.79	10.12	35.09	11.86	38.66	11.38
71	67.67	8.00	64.27	8.52	54.15	9.63	38.27	11.28	41.82	10.82
72	73.73	7.55	69.66	8.08	58.65	9.15	41.77	10.71	45.30	10.27
73	80.18	7.11	75.50	7.64	63.26	8.69	45.62	10.15	49.15	9.74
74	87.03	6.68	81.81	7.23	68.12	8.24	49.85	9.61	53.42	9.21
75	94.37	6.27	88.64	6.82	73.37	7.81	54.50	9.09	57.99	8.71
76	102.31	5.88	96.02	6.44	79.18	7.39	59.61	8.58	62.96	8.21
77	111.06	5.49	103.99	6.07	85.70	6.98	65.22	8.10	68.67	7.73
78	120.83	5.11	112.59	5.72	93.06	6.59	71.37	7.63	75.35	7.26
79	131.73	4.74	121.86	5.38	101.19	6.21	78.11	7.17	83.02	6.81
80	144.47	4.39	131.85	5.06	109.98	5.85	85.50	6.74	92.08	6.39
81	158.60	4.05	142.60	4.75	119.35	5.51	93.59	6.32	102.19	5.98
82	174.30	3.71	154.16	4.46	129.17	5.19	102.44	5.92	112.44	5.61
83	191.56	3.39	166.57	4.18	139.38	4.89	112.11	5.54	121.95	5.25
84	211.36	3.08	179.88	3.91	150.01	4.60	122.67	5.18	130.67	4.91
85	235.55	2.77	194.13	3.66	161.14	4.32	134.18	4.84	143.80	4.58
86	265.68	2.47	209.37	3.42	172.82	4.06	146.71	4.51	158.16	4.26
87	303.02	2.18	225.63	3.19	185.13	3.80	160.33	4.20	173.55	3.97
88	346.69	1.91	243.00	2.98	198.25	3.55	175.12	3.90	190.32	3.70
89	395.86	1.66	261.44	2.77	212.46	3.31	191.15	3.62	208.35	3.45
90	454.55	1.42	280.99	2.58	228.14	3.06	208.49	3.36	227.09	3.22
91	532.47	1.19	301.73	2.39	245.77	2.82	227.19	3.12	245.98	3.02
92	634.26	.98	323.64	2.21	265.93	2.58	247.33	2.88	264.77	2.85
93	734.18	.80	346.66	2.03	289.30	2.33	268.96	2.67	282.84	2.69
94	857.14	.64	371.00	1.84	316.66	2.07	292.12	2.47	299.52	2.55
95	1,000.00	.50	396.21	1.63	351.24	1.80	316.83	2.28	314.16	2.43
96			447.19	1.37	400.56	1.51	343.12	2.10	329.15	2.32
97			548.26	1.08	488.42	1.18	370.97	1.94	344.50	2.21
98			724.67	.78	668.15	.83	400.35	1.79	360.18	2.10
99			1,000.00	.50	1,000.00	.50	431.20	1.65	376.16	2.01
100							463.41	1.52	392.42	1.91
101							496.87	1.40	408.91	1.83
102							531.39	1.29	425.62	1.75
103							566.76	1.20	442.50	1.67
104							602.71	1.10	459.51	1.60
105							638.96	1.02	476.62	1.53
106							675.14	.94	493.78	1.46
107							710.90	.86	510.95	1.40
108							745.82	.75	528.10	1.35
109							1,000.00	.50	545.19	1.29

APPENDIX E—Specimen Life Insurance Policy *

INSTITUTE LIFE

INSURANCE COMPANY, will pay the benefits provided in this policy, subject to its terms and conditions

NEW YORK, N. Y.

To the Student:

This policy is generally representative of contracts issued by life insurance companies in the United States. Since there are no "standard" life insurance policies, the contracts vary from company to company in wording and appearance. There are also some differences in policy provisions which under specific conditions may be quite significant.

| POLICY NUMBER | 00 000 000 | POLICY DATE MAY 1, 1969 | AGE 25 MALE |

ON LIFE OF JOHN DOE (THE INSURED)

OWNER THE INSURED

PLAN STRAIGHT LIFE WITH
ACCIDENTAL DEATH BENEFIT (ADB) AND
WAIVER OF PREMIUM BENEFIT (WP) AND
POLICY PURCHASE OPTION (PPO)

AMOUNT FACE AMOUNT $10,000.
ACCIDENTAL DEATH BENEFIT $10,000.
(ADB,WHEN PAYABLE,IS IN ADDITION
TO ANY OTHER DEATH BENEFIT)

BENEFICIARY FIRST —MARY DOE,WIFE OF INSURED
subject to change SECOND—CHILDREN BORN OF MARRIAGE OF INSURED TO
MARY DOE

PREMIUM SCHEDULE PREMIUMS PAYABLE AT ANNUAL INTERVALS,AS FOLLOWS

Beginning as of

Mo. Day Year	Premium	Specific amounts included in premium for stated supplementary benefits ADB	WP	PPO
5- 1-1967	$200.40	$7.80	$2.90	$16.00
5- 1-1982	$184.40	$7.80	$2.90	—
5- 1-2002	$181.50	$7.80	—	—
5- 1-2012	$173.70	—	—	—

SPECIMEN POLICY

The benefits, provisions and conditions on the following pages are part of this policy.

This policy is executed as of   MAY 1, 1969

which is its **DATE OF ISSUE**

Robert Jones
PRESIDENT

William A. Masters
SECRETARY

LIFE POLICY AS SHOWN UNDER PLAN.
PREMIUMS PAYABLE AS SHOWN IN PREMIUM SCHEDULE.
DIVIDEND CREDITS MAY BE USED TO SHORTEN PREMIUM PAYING PERIOD.
ANNUAL PARTICIPATION.

1
[A3426]

* Reproduced with permission of the Institute of Life Insurance.

INSURANCE BENEFIT

The death benefit proceeds under this policy will be paid to the beneficiary immediately upon receipt of due proof of the Insured's death. Such proceeds shall include the face amount of the policy together with any other benefit payable under the terms of the policy because of such death.

GENERAL PROVISIONS

1. The Contract

This policy and the application for it, a copy of which is attached to and made a part of the policy, constitute the entire contract. All statements made in the application will be deemed representations and not warranties. No statement will be used to invalidate the policy nor to defend against a claim under it unless contained in the application.

The contract is made in consideration of such application and the payment of premiums in accordance with the provisions of the policy.

Only the President, Executive Vice-President, Vice-President, Treasurer or Secretary of the Company at its Home Office can make or modify this contract or waive any of the Company's rights or requirements.

All payments by the Company under this policy are payable at the Company's Home Office in New York City.

2. Definitions

Every reference in this policy to:

"dividend credits" means outstanding dividends and dividend deposits and the reserve on outstanding dividend additions;

"indebtedness" means indebtedness to the Company against the policy;

"tabular cash value" means the cash value determined in accordance with the Table of Cash, Loan and Non-Forfeiture Values shown in the policy;

"age" means age nearest birthday. Any reference to a specified age in the Table of Cash, Loan and Non-Forfeiture Values or the Premium Schedule in the policy shall mean the policy anniversary on which the Insured's age, nearest birthday, is the specified age.

3. Effective Date of Policy

This policy is deemed to have taken effect as of the policy date shown on its first page. Policy years, months and anniversaries will be determined from the policy date.

4. Payment of Premiums

Premiums are payable during the Insured's lifetime in accordance with the Premium Schedule, in exchange for a receipt signed by the President or Secretary of the Company and duly countersigned. Any date in the Premium Schedule which was based on the assumption that the Insured would be a specified age on such date shall be corrected, if necessary, to agree with the Insured's true age, nearest birthday.

After payment of the first premium, failure to pay a premium on or before its due date, to the Company at its Home Office or to a duly authorized Office Manager of the Company, will constitute default in payment of premium.

Premiums may be made payable at annual, semi-annual, quarterly or monthly intervals at the Company's applicable premium rate for the mode of payment requested, subject to the Company's approval. Payment to and acceptance by the Company of a premium on a new mode of payment shall constitute a change in mode for subsequent premiums.

Grace Period. A grace period of thirty-one days will be allowed for payment of a premium in default, during which time this policy will continue in force. If a premium remains unpaid after expiration of the grace period, insurance will be in force only to the extent provided under the policy's Non-Forfeiture provisions.

5. Beneficiary

Unless otherwise provided in this policy or in a beneficiary designation in effect under the policy, the following provisions shall apply:

Beneficiary Classifications. The beneficiary for any death benefit proceeds under this policy will be classified as a first beneficiary, second beneficiary or third beneficiary. Such classification shall determine the interest of that beneficiary with respect to such death benefit proceeds. Surviving beneficiaries in the same beneficiary classification shall share equally in death benefit proceeds payable to the beneficiaries in that classification.

Payment to Beneficiaries. Death benefit proceeds payable to the beneficiaries under this policy will be paid:

to any first beneficiaries for such proceeds surviving at the time of the Insured's death; or

if no first beneficiary for such proceeds survives the Insured, to any second beneficiaries for such proceeds surviving at the time of the Insured's death; or

if no first or second beneficiary for such proceeds survives the Insured, to any third beneficiaries for such proceeds surviving at the time of the Insured's death.

Death of Beneficiary. If the last surviving beneficiary for any death benefit proceeds payable under this policy predeceases the Insured, the beneficial interest in such proceeds shall vest in the Owner. If any beneficiary dies simultaneously with the Insured or within fifteen days after the Insured but before due proof of the Insured's death has been received by the Company, the proceeds of the policy will be paid to the same payee or payees and in the same manner as though such beneficiary predeceased the Insured.

6. Change of Beneficiary

While the Insured is living, the beneficiary designation can be changed from time to time by written notice in form satisfactory to the Company. No such change will take effect unless recorded in the records of the Company at its Home Office. Upon being so recorded, the change will be effective as of the date the notice was signed, whether or not the Insured is living when the change is recorded, subject to any payment made or other action taken by the Company before such recording.

7. Ownership of Policy

All benefits, rights and privileges available under this policy during the Insured's lifetime are vested in the Owner and may be exercised without the consent of any beneficiary or Owner's Designee.

[A3427]

8. Arrangements for Transfer of Ownership

The Owner, by written request satisfactory to the Company accompanied by the policy for appropriate indorsement, can arrange for a transfer of his entire ownership

(a) to a new Owner, effective immediately, or

(b) to an Owner's Designee who, upon the death of the designating Owner before his rights of ownership terminate, will become the new Owner. Any designation of Owner's Designee can be terminated or changed from time to time in a similar manner.

Such new Owner shall succeed to the benefits, rights and privileges of the previous Owner, subject to the terms and conditions of the policy and the interest of any existing assignee. The new Owner is not an "assignee" and the transfer is not an "assignment" within the meaning of those words as used in this policy.

No arrangement for transfer of ownership will take effect unless it is indorsed on the policy, but upon being so indorsed will take effect as of the date such request was signed, subject to any payment made or other action taken by the Company before such indorsement.

Any interest as Owner's Designee shall automatically terminate if a transfer is made under (a) above or if such Owner's Designee does not survive the designating Owner. Transfer of ownership will not act to change the beneficiary nor to transfer the interest of the beneficiary.

9. Assignment

A duplicate copy of any assignment of this policy, or of any interest in it, must be filed with the Company. Any assignment shall be subject to any payment made or other action taken by the Company before the assignment is received and recorded at the Company's Home Office. The Company assumes no responsibility for the validity of any assignment.

The interest of any beneficiary or Owner's Designee under this policy shall be subordinate to the interest of any assignee and may be assigned by the Owner while the Insured is living.

An assignee cannot change the beneficiary nor exercise the rights set forth in the Arrangements for Transfer of Ownership provisions of this policy.

10. Dividends

This is a participating contract and its share of divisible surplus will be determined annually by the Company. On each anniversary of this policy, any share of divisible surplus apportioned to it will be payable as a dividend if this policy is then in force and all premiums due have been paid to such anniversary. The dividend, when payable, will be applied under one of the following options, as elected:

(a) *Cash* — Paid in cash.

(b) *Premium* — Applied toward payment of a premium due if the balance of such premium is paid.

(c) *Dividend Addition* — Applied at net single premium rates to provide a participating paid-up addition to the sum insured.

(d) *Dividend Deposit* — Left with the Company at interest, subject to withdrawal. On each succeeding policy anniversary, interest will be credited on outstanding dividend deposits at such rate (not less than 3% per annum) as the Company may declare.

If no option is elected, option (c) will apply.

It is not expected that a dividend will be payable on this policy before its second anniversary.

Any outstanding dividend addition can be surrendered at any time for an amount equal to the reserve on such addition as of the latest policy anniversary. Dividend additions and dividend deposits outstanding at the maturity of the policy by death will be payable as part of the policy proceeds.

Post-Mortem Dividend. If this policy matures by the death of the Insured, any post-mortem dividend apportioned to it will be paid as part of death benefit proceeds.

Fully Paid-up Policy Privilege. This policy will be made fully paid-up by application of dividend credits as of any premium due date on which its tabular cash value plus such dividend credits equals or exceeds the net single premium (calculated on the same basis as the premium for this policy) for such fully paid-up participating policy at the Insured's attained age, upon written request within thirty-one days of such premium due date.

Endowment Privilege. This policy will be matured as an endowment by application of dividend credits upon written request when its tabular cash value plus such dividend credits equals or exceeds the face amount of the policy.

11. Change Privilege

The following changes can be made in this policy:

(a) *Changes to Higher Premium Plans.* If no premium is in default, the plan of insurance will be changed to an endowment or limited payment life insurance plan for the same level face amount, but with a higher premium rate and a premium paying period which extends for at least five full years beyond the effective date of the change, without evidence of insurability and without any change in the classification of the risk, upon receipt by the Company at its Home Office of the Owner's written request for such change accompanied by the policy and a payment of:

(i) the difference in previously due premiums for the basic life or endowment insurance benefits under the two plans, where the change is to take effect on or before the second anniversary of this policy, or

(ii) 103% of the difference in the then current cash values for the two plans, where the change is to take effect after the second anniversary of this policy.

The new plan must be one which was available on the policy date of this policy. Subject to the same condition and such additional payment, if any, as may be required, provision for an Accidental Death Benefit may be included in the new plan if a corresponding provision is included in this policy. However, the inclusion in the new plan of a provision for any benefit other than such Accidental Death Benefit and the basic life or endowment insurance benefit on the life of the Insured shall be subject to the Company's approval and requirements.

(b) *Other Changes.* Any other change in this policy, including changes to a lesser amount of insurance or to a plan of insurance with a lower premium rate, shall be subject to the Company's approval and requirements.

12. Reinstatement

Within five years after default in payment of premium, this policy may be reinstated upon receipt by the Company of (a) evidence of insurability satisfactory to the Company, (b) payment of all overdue premiums with interest at 5% per annum from their respective due dates and (c) payment of any indebtedness outstanding at the end of the grace period, with compound interest at 5% per annum, plus any outstanding indebtedness incurred thereafter. However, if the Company receives the payments required under (b) and (c) within thirty-one days after expiration of the grace period for payment of the premium in default, the Company will not inquire into, nor require submission of, evidence of insurability but, in such case, reinstatement shall not take effect unless the Insured was living when such payments were received.

Upon the Owner's written request, all or part of the payment required to reinstate the policy can be charged against it as a loan under the Policy Loans provisions if the resulting indebtedness does not exceed the policy's loan value on the date of reinstatement.

13. Age and Sex

If the age or sex of the Insured has been misstated, any amount payable by the Company under this policy shall be such as the premium paid would have purchased on the basis of the correct age and sex.

GENERAL PROVISIONS (continued)

14. Suicide

Suicide of the Insured, while sane or insane, within two years from the date of issue, is a risk not assumed under this policy; in such event premiums paid for the policy, less any indebtedness, will be refunded.

15. Indebtedness

Any indebtedness will be deducted in determining the amount of proceeds payable in any settlement under this policy.

16. Settlement on Maturity or Surrender

This policy will be settled in accordance with its terms upon receipt of due proof of the Insured's death or upon its maturity as an endowment or its surrender for cash value. Surrender of the policy will be required when such settlement is made.

Death Benefit Premium Adjustment. Death benefit proceeds under this policy will be subject to adjustment, as follows:

(a) Such proceeds will be increased, if a premium was paid for the premium interval current at the time of the Insured's death, by such pro-rata part of that premium as is applicable to the period, if any, between the end of the policy month in which death occurs and the end of such premium interval;

(b) Such proceeds will be decreased, if the Insured dies during a grace period, by such pro-rata part of any overdue premium as would be applicable to the period ending with the last day of the policy month in which death occurs.

Interest on Single Sum Death Benefit. Interest at the rate (not less than 3% per annum) declared by the Company will be included in death benefit proceeds which are paid in a single sum. Such interest will be for the period from the date of the Insured's death to the date the proceeds are paid, but not for a period of more than two years.

17. Protection Against Creditors

To the extent allowed by law and subject to the terms and conditions of this policy, all benefits and money available or paid to any person and relating in any manner to this policy will be exempt and free from such person's debts, contracts and engagements, and from judicial process to levy upon or attach the same.

18. Incontestability

This policy shall be incontestable, except for non-payment of premium, after it has been in force during the lifetime of the Insured for two years from its date of issue. *See Waiver of Premium Benefit rider.*

LOAN PROVISIONS

1. Policy Loans

The Company will advance, on the sole security of the values provided under this policy, an amount up to its loan value at any time after the policy has a loan value, unless it is being continued as Extended Insurance. The loan value on a premium due date, or during the grace period, will be equal to the policy's cash value. The loan value at any other time will be the amount which, with interest, will equal the cash value on the next interest due date or next premium due date if earlier.

Such advance shall bear interest, at the rate of 5% per annum, due on each policy anniversary or on any other date approved by the Company. Interest not paid when due will be added to the principal and will bear interest at the same rate. Any such advance, together with interest as it accrues from day to day, will constitute an indebtedness.

The advance will be made upon receipt of such evidence of it as the Company may require. Any existing indebtedness will be deducted from such advance. The Company may defer making an advance, other than to pay any premium due the Company, for a period not exceeding six months from the date application for such advance is received by the Company.

Any indebtedness may be repaid, in whole or in part, at any time before this policy matures by the Insured's death or as an endowment, except that, if the policy is being continued under its Non-Forfeiture provisions, any indebtedness which was deducted in determining the non-forfeiture benefit may not be repaid unless the policy is reinstated.

Whenever the indebtedness exceeds the cash value, the policy shall be void thirty-one days after the Company has mailed notice to the last known address of the Owner and of the assignee of record, if any.

Term Insurance for Policy Loan. Before the policy anniversary on which the Insured's age is 65, the Owner may obtain term insurance, in accordance with the Company's rules with respect to such insurance, on the life of the Insured in the amount of any loan under this policy, subject to receipt of such evidence of insurability as the Company may require and payment of the appropriate premium according to the Company's premium rates for such insurance. If such insurance becomes payable, it will be applied against indebtedness.

2. Automatic Premium Loan Option

The automatic premium loan option will be in effect if requested in the application for this policy or in a written request received by the Company from the Owner before expiration of the grace period for payment of a premium in default. If this option is in effect, any premium in default will be automatically paid immediately before expiration of the grace period by making an advance, as under the Policy Loans provisions and subject to the terms and conditions of such provisions, sufficient to pay such premium unless (a) the resulting indebtedness would exceed the loan value of the policy, or (b) the two consecutive premiums immediately preceding such overdue premium were payable at other than monthly intervals and were paid by automatic premium loans, or (c) the six consecutive premiums immediately preceding such overdue premium were payable at monthly intervals and were paid by automatic premium loans.

Upon receipt by the Company of the Owner's written request for termination of this option, it will cease to be in effect with respect to any premium then due but unpaid and to subsequent premiums, but may be made effective again by the Owner's subsequent written request.

[A3429]

CASH AND NON-FORFEITURE BENEFITS

1. Cash Value

This policy can be surrendered for its cash value at any time after it first has such a value.

If no premium is in default, the cash value of this policy will be its tabular cash value plus any dividend credits. If the policy has become fully paid-up, its cash value will be the reserve on the paid-up insurance plus any dividend credits.

Within three months after the due date of a premium in default, the cash value of this policy will be the same as on that due date, reduced by any subsequent withdrawal of dividend credits.

After such three months, the cash value will be the reserve on any insurance provided under the policy's Non-Forfeiture provisions plus any dividend credits; however, if the policy is surrendered within thirty-one days after a policy anniversary, the reserve on such insurance will be taken as not less than on that anniversary.

The Company may defer payment of any cash value for a period not exceeding six months from the date of surrender. If payment is deferred for thirty days or more, such cash value, less any indebtedness, will bear interest at the rate of 3% per annum for the period of deferment.

2. Non-Forfeiture

The following non-forfeiture benefits will apply if this policy has a cash value and a premium in default remains unpaid:

(a) *Extended Insurance.* Upon expiration of the grace period, this policy will be automatically continued as non-participating term insurance commencing as from the due date of the premium in default. The amount of such insurance will be equal to the face amount of the policy plus any outstanding dividends, dividend deposits and dividend additions and less any indebtedness. The term period will be such as the cash value, less any indebtedness, would provide if applied as a net single premium at the Insured's attained age on the due date of the premium in default.

The election of Paid-up Insurance or the surrender of the policy for cash value within three months after the due date of such premium will revoke any Extended Insurance from such due date.

(b) *Paid-up Insurance.* Within three months after the due date of the premium in default, this policy will, upon written request, be continued as participating paid-up life insurance for such amount as the policy's cash value, less any indebtedness, would provide if applied as a net single premium at the Insured's attained age on such due date.

(c) *Cash Value.* The policy can be surrendered in accordance with the Cash Value provisions.

3. Basis of Computation

Tabular cash values and the corresponding non-forfeiture values are based on the assumptions that (a) this policy has been in force and all premiums due have been paid to the end of the number of policy years stated, (b) there are no dividend credits and (c) there is no indebtedness. Any value not shown in the table will be furnished by the Company upon request.

Tabular cash values are computed by the Standard Non-Forfeiture Value Method, using the applicable non-forfeiture factors set forth in the Table of Cash, Loan and Non-Forfeiture Values. Such values at any time during a policy year will be determined by the Company with due allowance for the time elapsed in that year and the date to which premiums that have become due have been paid. Tabular cash values are equal to the full net premium reserve from the policy anniversary specified in the table.

A detailed statement of the method of computation of cash and non-forfeiture values has been filed with the insurance supervisory official of the jurisdiction in which this policy is delivered. All values for this policy are equal to or greater than those required by statute in such jurisdiction.

Reserves, net single premiums, and cash and non-forfeiture values referred to in the Cash and Non-Forfeiture Benefits provisions, and reserves on, and net single premiums for, outstanding dividend additions wherever referred to in this policy, are based on the Commissioners 1958 Standard Ordinary Table of Mortality where the Insured is a male, or the Commissioners 1958 Standard Ordinary Female Table of Mortality where the Insured is a female, with continuous functions and interest at the rate of 3% compounded annually.

OPTIONAL METHODS OF SETTLEMENT

The death benefit, matured endowment or cash value proceeds of this policy, in whole or in part, can be settled under one of the following options instead of being paid in a single sum if every payee under the option is a natural person taking in his own right, subject to the terms and conditions of these Optional Methods of Settlement provisions.

Option 1. Withdrawable Deposit. Left on deposit, subject to withdrawal in sums of not less than $100. Interest will be credited annually at the rate (not less than 3%) declared by the Company each year under this option on the amount remaining with the Company on the interest credit date.

Option 2. Income for Specified Period. Equal monthly payments for the number of years elected, in accordance with the Option 2 Table.

Option 3. Annuity for Life:

With Certain Period. Equal monthly payments for five, ten, fifteen or twenty years (the certain period), as elected, and thereafter for the remaining lifetime of the payee; or

With Instalment Refund. Equal monthly payments until the sum of such payments equals the proceeds settled under this option (at which time the instalment refund period ends) and thereafter for the remaining lifetime of the payee.

The amount of each monthly payment will be in accordance with the Option 3 Table.

Option 4. Interest Payments. Left with the Company with interest payable at the rate declared by the Company each year under this option, until the death of the payee. The Company guarantees that such interest, per $1,000 remaining with the Company under this option on the interest due date, will not be less than the following, according to the frequency of payment elected:

Annual	Semi-annual	Quarterly	Monthly
$30.00	$14.89	$7.42	$2.47

Option 5. Income of Specified Amount. Equal monthly, quarterly, semi-annual or annual payments of specified amount, as elected, if the total amount payable each year is at least five percent of the proceeds settled under this option. Payments will be made until such proceeds, together with accrued interest at the rate (not less than 3%) declared by the Company each year under this option, have been paid.

Option 6. Annuity for Life — Two Persons. Equal monthly payments, in accordance with the Option 6 Table, for the joint lifetime of two payees and continuing for the remaining lifetime of the survivor. Such payments will be payable for ten years certain if both payees die sooner.

If one of the payees named in an election of Option 6 dies before becoming entitled to the first payment, settlement will be made instead under Option 3 (Ten Years Certain) with the surviving payee.

Deferred Settlement Option. Left with the Company at interest, as under Option 4, for not more than two years, subject to withdrawal in sums of not less than $100. At any time during such two year period the payee designated in the original election of this option may direct that any unpaid sum remaining with the Company, together with accrued interest thereon, be applied under any other optional method of settlement available under this policy. Any unpaid sum which has not been so applied at the end of such two year period will then be paid in a single sum.

Additional Interest Under Options 2, 3 and 6. The tables for Options 2, 3 and 6 are based on an interest rate of 3% per annum. The payment due on each anniversary of the due date of the first payment will be increased during the specified period of Option 2, or the certain period or instalment refund period of Option 3 or 6, by any additional interest as determined by the Company at the rate declared each year under the option, on the commuted value of the remaining payments for the applicable period.

Election of Options. Election of an optional method of settlement must be made by written notice in form satisfactory to the Company. While the policy is in force during the Insured's lifetime, a previous election can similarly be revoked or changed. Such election, revocation or change will, upon being recorded by the Company at its Home Office, take effect as of the date it was signed, whether or not the Insured is living when it is recorded, subject to any payment made or other action taken by the Company before such recording. An assignee cannot elect an optional method of settlement for unmatured death benefit proceeds nor revoke or change an election previously made.

An election for settlement of death benefit proceeds under these Optional Methods of Settlement provisions can be made by the person entitled to such proceeds if no previous election was in effect at the time of the Insured's death. Such election must be made before payment of the death benefit proceeds and within six months after the Insured's death. An election for settlement of matured endowment proceeds must be made within sixty days of maturity of this policy and an election for settlement of cash value proceeds must be made upon surrender of this policy.

Payee Not a Natural Person Taking in Own Right. Notwithstanding anything in these Optional Methods of Settlement provisions to the contrary, anyone, whether a natural person or not, who has the right to elect an optional method of settlement and who is acting for the benefit of the Insured, or the spouse, child or parent of the Insured, can elect to have death benefit, matured endowment or cash value proceeds settled under Option 2 or 5 or under Option 3 with amount and duration of payments based on the life of the person for whose benefit the election was made. In such case, either the person making the election or the person for whose benefit the election was made may be the payee, as elected.

In addition, any person, other than a natural person, who has the right to elect an optional method of settlement and who is taking in its own right, can elect to have death benefit, matured endowment or cash value proceeds settled under Option 2 or 5 or can elect to have matured endowment or cash value proceeds settled under Option 3 with amount and duration of payments based on the Insured's life. In any of these cases, either the person making such election or the Insured may be the payee, as elected.

Policy Assigned as Collateral. Any amount payable under this policy to a collateral assignee will be paid in a single sum but any remainder of the policy proceeds can be settled in accordance with these Optional Methods of Settlement provisions.

[A3431]

OPTIONAL METHODS OF SETTLEMENT (continued)

Purchase of Single Premium Life Annuity at Reduced Premium Rate. As a supplement to any settlement under these Optional Methods of Settlement provisions, the payee under the option, if a natural person taking in his own right, may purchase, on his own life, any single premium life annuity being issued by the Company on the date of such settlement by making appropriate written application to the Company within thirty-one days of such date accompanied by payment of the single premium for such annuity. The premium rate for such annuity will be 2% less than the Company's then published premium rate, and the amount of the single premium which can be paid for such annuity may not exceed the proceeds of this policy before deduction of any outstanding indebtedness.

Payments Other Than Monthly. In the election of an optional method of settlement, quarterly, semi-annual or annual payments may be requested. The amount of each such payment under Option 2, 3 or 6 will be determined by multiplying the amount of the monthly payment by the appropriate factor in the following table:

Option Elected	Frequency of Payment Elected		
	Quarterly	Semi-annual	Annual
Option 2	2.99	5.96	11.84
Option 3 or 6	2.99	5.94	11.74

Minimum Payment. If any monthly payment under an optional method of settlement would be less than $10, the frequency of payment will be automatically changed to quarterly. If any quarterly, semi-annual or annual payment would be less than $10, the Company may discharge its entire remaining obligation by payment of a single sum to the person who would be entitled to any amount then due.

Settlement Certificate. A settlement certificate setting forth the rights and benefits of the payee under any optional method of settlement elected will be issued when the proceeds of this policy become due. If the policy matures by the death of the Insured, the effective date of the settlement certificate will be the date of death; if the policy matures as an endowment or is surrendered for cash value, the effective date of the settlement certificate will be the date of maturity or surrender. The first payment under Option 2, 3, 5 or 6 will be payable as of the effective date of the settlement certificate except where such option is elected by the payee under a settlement certificate issued for a Deferred Settlement Option. Payments under Option 4 will be made at the end of each interest period according to the frequency of payment elected.

Miscellaneous Provisions. Any person making an election of an optional method of settlement can, at the time of such election, designate one or more contingent payees to receive any benefits which may be payable, after the death of the primary payee (the death of the survivor of the two primary payees under Option 6), under the provisions of a written settlement agreement. If no duly designated contingent payee is living at the time of such primary payee's death, such benefits, if any, will be settled by payment of a single sum to the executors or administrators of the deceased primary payee. The amount of any such single sum payment will be equal to:

Under Option 1, 4 or 5, any unpaid sum remaining with the Company together with any accrued interest to the date of death;

Under Option 2, 3 or 6, the commuted value as of the date of such death, on the basis of interest at the rate of 3% compounded annually, of any remaining payments (a) for the specified period of Option 2, (b) for the period certain of Option 6 or Option 3 (With Certain Period), or (c) as may be necessary to complete the payments which would equal in total the proceeds settled under Option 3 (With Instalment Refund).

If an optional method of settlement is elected by a person other than the payee and such person does not otherwise direct in writing, the benefits under such optional method of settlement will not be transferable nor subject to commutation, anticipation or encumbrance during the lifetime of the payee.

Evidence satisfactory to the Company may be required as to the age and continuing survival of any person on whose life Option 3 or 6 is based.

Special Agreements. Provision may be made for settlement of the proceeds of this policy in any other manner that may be agreed to by the Company.

TABLES OF MONTHLY PAYMENTS UNDER OPTIONAL METHODS OF SETTLEMENT
Per $1,000 of Proceeds Settled Under Option

Option 2. Income for Specified Period	Years	1	2	3	4	5	6	7	8	9	10	11	12	13	14	15
	Payment	$84.47	$42.86	$28.99	$22.06	$17.91	$15.14	$13.16	$11.68	$10.53	$9.61	$8.86	$8.24	$7.71	$7.26	$6.87
	Years	16	17	18	19	20	21	22	23	24	25	26	27	28	29	30
	Payment	$6.53	$6.23	$5.96	$5.73	$5.51	$5.32	$5.15	$4.99	$4.84	$4.71	$4.59	$4.47	$4.37	$4.27	$4.18

Option 3. Annuity for Life
(Based on payee's age on due date of first payment)

	Men					Women						Men					Women				
	Certain Period				Instal-ment Refund	Certain Period				Instal-ment Refund		Certain Period				Instal-ment Refund	Certain Period				Instal-ment Refund
Age	5 Years	10 Years	15 Years	20 Years		5 Years	10 Years	15 Years	20 Years		Age	5 Years	10 Years	15 Years	20 Years		5 Years	10 Years	15 Years	20 Years	
15*	$2.93	$2.92	$2.91	$2.90	$2.89	$2.86	$2.85	$2.84	$2.83	$2.82	50	$4.39	$4.35	$4.27	$4.17	$4.18	$3.97	$3.96	$3.93	$3.89	$3.87
16	2.95	2.94	2.93	2.92	2.91	2.88	2.87	2.86	2.85	2.84	51	4.48	4.43	4.35	4.24	4.25	4.04	4.02	3.99	3.95	3.94
17	2.97	2.96	2.95	2.94	2.93	2.89	2.88	2.87	2.86	2.85	52	4.58	4.52	4.43	4.30	4.32	4.12	4.10	4.06	4.01	4.00
18	2.98	2.97	2.96	2.95	2.94	2.90	2.89	2.88	2.87	2.86	53	4.68	4.62	4.51	4.37	4.40	4.20	4.18	4.14	4.08	4.07
19	3.00	2.99	2.98	2.97	2.96	2.92	2.91	2.90	2.89	2.88	54	4.79	4.72	4.60	4.44	4.49	4.28	4.26	4.21	4.15	4.14
20	3.02	3.01	3.00	2.99	2.98	2.94	2.93	2.92	2.91	2.90	55	4.90	4.82	4.69	4.51	4.58	4.37	4.34	4.29	4.21	4.22
21	3.04	3.03	3.02	3.01	3.00	2.95	2.94	2.93	2.92	2.91	56	5.02	4.93	4.78	4.58	4.67	4.47	4.44	4.38	4.28	4.29
22	3.06	3.05	3.04	3.03	3.02	2.97	2.96	2.95	2.94	2.93	57	5.15	5.04	4.87	4.64	4.77	4.57	4.53	4.46	4.35	4.38
23	3.08	3.07	3.06	3.05	3.04	2.99	2.98	2.97	2.96	2.95	58	5.28	5.16	4.97	4.71	4.87	4.68	4.64	4.55	4.43	4.47
24	3.11	3.10	3.09	3.08	3.07	3.00	2.99	2.98	2.97	2.96	59	5.42	5.29	5.07	4.78	4.97	4.80	4.75	4.65	4.50	4.56
25	3.13	3.12	3.11	3.10	3.09	3.02	3.01	3.00	2.99	2.98	60	5.57	5.42	5.17	4.85	5.09	4.92	4.86	4.75	4.58	4.66
26	3.16	3.15	3.14	3.13	3.12	3.04	3.03	3.02	3.01	3.00	61	5.73	5.55	5.27	4.91	5.21	5.05	4.98	4.85	4.65	4.76
27	3.18	3.17	3.16	3.15	3.14	3.06	3.05	3.04	3.03	3.02	62	5.90	5.70	5.38	4.98	5.33	5.20	5.11	4.96	4.73	4.87
28	3.21	3.20	3.19	3.18	3.17	3.09	3.08	3.07	3.06	3.05	63	6.08	5.85	5.48	5.04	5.46	5.35	5.25	5.07	4.80	4.98
29	3.24	3.23	3.22	3.21	3.20	3.11	3.10	3.09	3.08	3.07	64	6.28	6.00	5.59	5.09	5.60	5.51	5.39	5.18	4.87	5.11
30	3.27	3.26	3.25	3.24	3.22	3.13	3.12	3.11	3.10	3.09	65	6.48	6.17	5.70	5.15	5.75	5.68	5.54	5.29	4.94	5.23
31	3.30	3.29	3.28	3.27	3.26	3.16	3.15	3.14	3.13	3.12	66	6.70	6.34	5.80	5.20	5.90	5.87	5.70	5.41	5.01	5.37
32	3.33	3.32	3.31	3.30	3.29	3.18	3.17	3.16	3.15	3.14	67	6.93	6.51	5.90	5.24	6.06	6.06	5.86	5.52	5.07	5.51
33	3.37	3.36	3.35	3.34	3.32	3.21	3.20	3.19	3.18	3.17	68	7.18	6.69	6.00	5.28	6.23	6.28	6.04	5.64	5.13	5.66
34	3.41	3.40	3.39	3.37	3.35	3.24	3.23	3.22	3.21	3.20	69	7.44	6.87	6.09	5.32	6.41	6.50	6.22	5.75	5.19	5.82
35	3.45	3.44	3.43	3.41	3.39	3.27	3.26	3.25	3.24	3.23	70	7.72	7.05	6.18	5.35	6.60	6.74	6.40	5.86	5.24	5.99
36	3.49	3.48	3.47	3.45	3.43	3.30	3.29	3.28	3.27	3.26	71	8.01	7.23	6.27	5.38	6.80	7.00	6.59	5.97	5.29	6.17
37	3.53	3.52	3.51	3.49	3.47	3.33	3.32	3.31	3.30	3.29	72	8.32	7.42	6.35	5.41	7.01	7.27	6.78	6.07	5.33	6.36
38	3.58	3.57	3.56	3.53	3.51	3.37	3.36	3.35	3.34	3.32	73	8.64	7.60	6.42	5.43	7.23	7.57	6.98	6.17	5.37	6.56
39	3.63	3.62	3.60	3.58	3.55	3.40	3.39	3.38	3.37	3.36	74	8.98	7.78	6.49	5.45	7.46	7.87	7.18	6.27	5.40	6.77
40	3.68	3.67	3.65	3.62	3.60	3.44	3.43	3.42	3.41	3.40	75	9.33	7.95	6.55	5.46	7.71	8.20	7.38	6.36	5.42	6.99
41	3.74	3.73	3.70	3.67	3.64	3.48	3.47	3.46	3.45	3.43	76	9.70	8.12	6.60	5.48	7.96	8.54	7.58	6.44	5.45	7.23
42	3.80	3.78	3.76	3.72	3.69	3.52	3.51	3.50	3.49	3.47	77	10.07	8.28	6.65	5.49	8.24	8.90	7.77	6.51	5.46	7.48
43	3.86	3.84	3.81	3.77	3.74	3.57	3.56	3.55	3.53	3.52	78	10.45	8.44	6.69	5.49	8.52	9.28	7.97	6.58	5.48	7.74
44	3.92	3.90	3.87	3.82	3.80	3.62	3.61	3.60	3.58	3.56	79	10.84	8.58	6.73	5.50	8.82	9.67	8.15	6.63	5.49	8.02
45	3.99	3.97	3.93	3.88	3.85	3.67	3.66	3.64	3.62	3.61	80	11.24	8.72	6.76	5.50	9.14	10.07	8.33	6.68	5.50	8.32
46	4.06	4.04	4.00	3.93	3.91	3.72	3.71	3.70	3.67	3.65	81	11.64	8.84	6.79	5.50	9.46	10.49	8.50	6.73	5.50	8.63
47	4.14	4.11	4.06	3.99	3.97	3.78	3.77	3.75	3.72	3.71	82	12.04	8.96	6.81	5.50	9.81	10.92	8.65	6.76	5.50	8.97
48	4.22	4.19	4.13	4.05	4.04	3.84	3.83	3.81	3.78	3.76	83	12.45	9.06	6.82	5.50	10.18	11.36	8.80	6.79	5.50	9.33
49	4.30	4.26	4.20	4.11	4.10	3.90	3.89	3.87	3.83	3.81	84	12.86	9.15	6.84	5.50	10.57	11.81	8.94	6.81	5.50	9.70
	*and under		†and over								85†	13.27	9.24	6.85	5.50	10.97	12.28	9.06	6.83	5.50	10.11

Option 6. Annuity for Life — Ten Years Certain — Two Lives
(Based on payees' ages on due date of first payment)

Payees of Equal Age	One Man and One Woman	Two Men	Two Women	Payees of Equal Age	One Man and One Woman	Two Men	Two Women	Payees of Equal Age	One Man and One Woman	Two Men	Two Women	Payees of Equal Age	One Man and One Woman	Two Men	Two Women
25	$2.86	$2.88	$2.82	40	$3.19	$3.25	$3.13	55	$3.91	$4.07	$3.78	70	$5.69	$6.03	$5.43
26	2.87	2.90	2.84	41	3.23	3.29	3.16	56	4.00	4.17	3.86	71	5.89	6.23	5.63
27	2.89	2.92	2.85	42	3.27	3.33	3.19	57	4.08	4.26	3.93	72	6.09	6.44	5.82
28	2.91	2.94	2.87	43	3.30	3.37	3.22	58	4.17	4.36	4.01	73	6.29	6.64	6.01
29	2.93	2.96	2.89	44	3.34	3.41	3.26	59	4.25	4.45	4.09	74	6.49	6.84	6.21
30	2.95	2.97	2.90	45	3.37	3.45	3.29	60	4.33	4.54	4.16	75	6.69	7.05	6.40
31	2.97	3.00	2.92	46	3.42	3.51	3.33	61	4.45	4.67	4.27	76	6.91	7.25	6.63
32	2.99	3.02	2.94	47	3.47	3.56	3.37	62	4.56	4.80	4.38	77	7.13	7.46	6.86
33	3.01	3.05	2.96	48	3.51	3.61	3.42	63	4.68	4.93	4.48	78	7.35	7.66	7.08
34	3.03	3.07	2.98	49	3.56	3.67	3.46	64	4.79	5.06	4.59	79	7.57	7.87	7.31
35	3.05	3.10	3.00	50	3.61	3.72	3.50	65	4.91	5.19	4.69	80	7.79	8.08	7.54
36	3.08	3.13	3.03	51	3.67	3.79	3.56	66	5.07	5.35	4.84	81	7.98	8.25	7.75
37	3.11	3.16	3.05	52	3.73	3.86	3.61	67	5.22	5.52	4.99	82	8.18	8.41	7.97
38	3.14	3.19	3.08	53	3.79	3.93	3.67	68	5.38	5.69	5.14	83	8.37	8.58	8.18
39	3.17	3.22	3.10	54	3.85	4.00	3.72	69	5.54	5.86	5.28	84	8.57	8.75	8.40
												85 & over	8.76	8.92	8.61

The amount of the payment for any other combination of ages will be furnished by the Company on request.

8

[A3433]

ACCIDENTAL DEATH BENEFIT

These provisions are included in and made a part of the policy to which they are attached by the Company in consideration of the application for such provisions and payment of the amount that is included in the premium for such policy on account of the Accidental Death Benefit.

The amount of the Accidental Death Benefit and the amount included in the premium for the policy on account of such benefit are shown on the first page of this policy, and these Accidental Death Benefit provisions will be deemed to have taken effect as of the policy date of the policy, except where such provisions have been added to a policy which was already in force, in which case such amounts and such effective date shall be as specified in the provisions for Addition of Supplementary Benefits which make these Accidental Death Benefit provisions a part of this policy.

Subject to the terms and conditions of the policy and these Accidental Death Benefit provisions, the Company will pay the Accidental Death Benefit, as part of the policy's death benefit proceeds, upon receipt of due proof that the Insured's death resulted directly, and independently of all other causes, from accidental bodily injury and that such death occurred within 120 days after such injury and before the earliest of the following:

(1) expiration of the grace period following the due date of a premium in default;

(2) maturity of this policy as an endowment or its surrender for cash value;

(3) any other termination of coverage under these Accidental Death Benefit provisions.

However, the Accidental Death Benefit will not be payable if death occurs before the Insured's fifth birthday or results from (a) suicide, whether sane or insane, or (b) war (including any armed aggression resisted by the armed forces of any country or combination of countries), whether such war is declared or undeclared, or any act incident to any such war, or (c) travel or flight in any kind of aircraft (including falling or otherwise descending from or with such aircraft in flight) while the Insured is participating in aviation training in such aircraft, or is a pilot, officer or other member of the crew of such aircraft or has any duties aboard the aircraft while it is in flight if such duties relate in any way to the aircraft, its operation or equipment, or to any purpose of the flight; nor will such benefit be payable if death is caused or contributed to by infirmity of mind or body, or any illness or disease other than a bacterial infection occurring in consequence of an accidental injury on the exterior of the body.

The Company shall have the right and opportunity to examine the body and, unless prohibited by law, to make an autopsy.

These Accidental Death Benefit provisions will not affect tabular cash values under this policy.

Notwithstanding anything in this policy to the contrary, its Incontestability provision will not apply to these Accidental Death Benefit provisions where the Accidental Death Benefit provisions were added to the policy when it was already in force. Instead, in such case, these Accidental Death Benefit provisions shall be incontestable, except for nonpayment of premium, after the policy has been in force during the lifetime of the Insured for two years from the date of issue specified for these Accidental Death Benefit provisions in the applicable provisions for Addition of Supplementary Benefits.

Upon receipt by the Company within thirty-one days of any premium due date of the Owner's written request accompanied by this policy for appropriate indorsement, coverage under these Accidental Death Benefit provisions will terminate as of such premium due date. If not previously terminated, such coverage will terminate automatically on the policy anniversary when the Insured's age is 70.

Any premium due under this policy on or after termination of coverage under these Accidental Death Benefit provisions will be reduced by any amount included in such premium for the Accidental Death Benefit.

INSTITUTE LIFE INSURANCE COMPANY

BY ___*William G. Masters*___
Secretary

[A34

WAIVER OF PREMIUM BENEFIT

These provisions are included in and made a part of the policy to which they are attached by the Company in consideration of the application for such provisions and payment of the amount that is included in the premium for such policy on account of the Waiver of Premium Benefit.

The amount included in the premium for the policy on account of the Waiver of Premium Benefit is shown on the first page of this policy, and these Waiver of Premium Benefit provisions will be deemed to have taken effect as of the policy date of the policy, except where such provisions have been added to a policy which was already in force, in which case such amount and such effective date shall be as specified in the provisions for Addition of Supplementary Benefits which make these Waiver of Premium Benefit provisions a part of the policy.

If the Insured is totally disabled as defined below and has been continuously so disabled for at least six months, the Company will waive the payment of each premium falling due after such total disability began and during its uninterrupted continuance, subject to the terms and conditions of the policy and these Waiver of Premium Benefit provisions. Each premium waived will be the premium according to the mode of payment in effect when total disability began. No premium which fell due more than one year before written notice of claim is received by the Company at its Home Office will be waived unless it is shown that it was not reasonably possible to give such notice within one year after total disability began and that notice was given as soon as was reasonably possible.

Definition of Total Disability. Every reference in these Waiver of Premium Benefit provisions to "total disability" means a disability, resulting from bodily injury or disease, which prevents the Insured from engaging for remuneration or profit in any and every occupation or business for which he is reasonably suited by education, training or experience. The total and irrecoverable loss of the sight of both eyes, or of the use of both hands, both feet, or one hand and one foot will be regarded as total disability in any event.

If the Insured has not attained an age at which he is legally permitted to terminate his formal education, the reference to "engaging for remuneration or profit in any and every occupation or business for which he is reasonably suited by education, training or experience" shall mean "attending school".

Disabilities Not Covered. No benefit will be allowed under these Waiver of Premium Benefit provisions if the total disability began:

(a) before the Insured's fifth birthday, or

(b) while these provisions were not in force, or

(c) after expiration of the grace period following the due date of a premium in default, or

(d) after any other termination of coverage under these provisions; nor if such disability resulted:

(e) directly from injury wilfully and intentionally self-inflicted, or

(f) from war (including any armed aggression resisted by the armed forces of any country or combination of countries), whether such war is declared or undeclared, or any act incident to any such war, while the Insured is a member of any military, naval or air forces engaged in such war or is a member of an auxiliary or civilian noncombatant unit serving with such forces.

Notice of Claim and Proof of Total Disability. Before any premium is waived, written notice of claim and due proof of total disability must be given to the Company at its Home Office

(a) during the lifetime of the Insured and the continuance of such disability, and

(b) not later than one year after the due date of any premium in default, or maturity of this policy as an endowment or any other termination of the coverage under these Waiver of Premium Benefit provisions.

However, failure to give such notice and proof as required under (a) and (b) above will not invalidate nor diminish the claim if it is shown not to have been reasonably possible to give such notice or proof, and that each was given as soon as was reasonably possible.

The Company may require that due proof of the uninterrupted continuance of the total disability be furnished at reasonable intervals during the first two years of such disability, but thereafter such proof will not be required more often than once a year. If such proof is not furnished or if the Insured ceases to be totally disabled, premiums falling due thereafter under this policy will be payable in accordance with its terms. The Company may require, as part of due proof, that the Insured be examined by physicians satisfactory to it.

However, if any premium for this policy is payable after the policy anniversary when the Insured's age is 65 and if the Insured was totally disabled on that policy anniversary and such total disability had continued without interruption for five years or more, no further proof of the continuance of such disability will be required and the Company will continue to waive all premiums due after that anniversary, whether or not the Insured continues to be totally disabled.

Exception to Incontestability Provision.

Notwithstanding anything in this policy to the contrary, its Incontestability provision will not apply to these Waiver of Premium Benefit provisions. Instead, these Waiver of Premium Benefit provisions shall be incontestable, except for non-payment of premium, after the policy has been in force during the lifetime of the Insured for two years from the date of issue of these Waiver of Premium Benefit provisions unless the Insured becomes totally disabled within that year. The date of issue of these Waiver of Premium Benefit provisions will be the same as the date of issue of this policy except where they have been added to a policy which was already in force, in which case the date of issue of these provisions shall be as specified in the applicable provisions for Addition of Supplementary Benefits.

[A3435]

WAIVER OF PREMIUM BENEFIT (continued)

Miscellaneous Provisions. Any premium falling due before the Company approves a claim under these provisions will be payable in accordance with the terms of this policy. However, any premium paid to the Company and later waived will be refunded or, if such refund is not made before the Insured's death, will be payable as part of the death benefit proceeds.

If total disability begins during the grace period for a premium in default, failure to pay such premium shall not of itself invalidate any claim on account of such disability, but the overdue premium must be paid to the Company, with interest at 5% per annum, before any premium may be waived.

The amount payable in any settlement under this policy will not be reduced by premiums waived. Dividends and cash, loan and non-forfeiture benefits will be the same as if the waived premiums had been paid. These Waiver of Premium Benefit provisions will not affect tabular cash values under this policy.

Upon receipt by the Company within thirty-one days of any premium due date of the Owner's written request accompanied by this policy for appropriate indorsement, coverage under these Waiver of Premium Benefit provisions will terminate as of such premium due date. If not previously terminated, such coverage will terminate automatically on the policy anniversary when the Insured's age is 60 unless the premium paying period of this policy, determined in accordance with the Premium Schedule, extends beyond that anniversary but not beyond the policy anniversary when the Insured's age is 65, in which case such coverage will terminate automatically at the end of the premium paying period. However, any automatic termination of coverage shall not prejudice the Owner's right to any benefit provided under these Waiver of Premium Benefit provisions on account of total disability which began before such termination.

Any premium due under this policy on or after termination of coverage under these Waiver of Premium Benefit provisions will be reduced by any amount included in such premium for the Waiver of Premium Benefit.

INSTITUTE LIFE INSURANCE COMPANY

By _William G. Masters_
Secretary

PROVISIONS FOR APPLICATION OF DIVIDEND DEPOSITS TO PROVIDE ONE YEAR TERM INSURANCE

The Dividends provisions of this policy are hereby modified by the addition of these Provisions for Application of Dividend Deposits to Provide One Year Term Insurance.

These provisions will be deemed to have taken effect as of the policy date of the policy, except where they have been added to a policy which was already in force, in which case the effective date of these provisions shall be as specified in the provisions for Addition of Supplementary Benefits which make these Provisions for Application of Dividend Deposits to Provide One Year Term Insurance a part of this policy.

Provision for One Year Term Insurance

The Company, on each policy anniversary while these provisions are in effect, will withdraw from outstanding dividend deposits an amount sufficient to provide non-participating term insurance on the life of the Insured for a period of one year beginning on that policy anniversary. Such term insurance will be for an amount equal to this policy's tabular cash value on the next policy anniversary if outstanding dividend deposits are sufficient to provide that amount of term insurance. Otherwise, the amount of such term insurance will be the amount that can be provided by such application of all outstanding dividend deposits.

Outstanding dividend deposits will be applied to provide one year term insurance under these provisions at the Company's then current premium rate for such one year term insurance. The Company's premium rate for

such one year term insurance on standard risks will not exceed the net single premium therefor determined in accordance with the Commissioners 1958 Standard Ordinary Table of Mortality where the Insured is a male, or the Commissioners 1958 Standard Ordinary Female Table of Mortality where the Insured is a female, with continuous functions and interest at the rate of 3% compounded annually.

Conversion Privilege

While $2,000 or more of one year term insurance is in effect under these Provisions for Application of Dividend Deposits to Provide One Year Term Insurance, these provisions can be surrendered in exchange for a new policy on the life of the Insured as of any date before the policy anniversary on which the Insured's age is 60, if the Insured is living and is not totally disabled as defined in any Waiver of Premium Benefit of

PROVISIONS FOR APPLICATION OF DIVIDEND DEPOSITS TO PROVIDE ONE YEAR TERM INSURANCE *(continued)*

this policy and, where this policy provides endowment insurance, if at least five full years remain until the endowment date. Such exchange will be made upon receipt by the Company at its Home Office of a written request for it, accompanied by this policy for appropriate indorsement and by the first premium for the new policy, subject to the following conditions:

(a) The effective date of the new policy will be the date as of which the exchange is made;

(b) The amount of insurance under the new policy may not be greater than the amount of term insurance then in effect under these provisions nor less than $2,000;

(c) Subject to (d) below, the new policy may be on any life or endowment plan elected in the written request;

(d) The new policy shall be one which would be available on its effective date under the Company's rules as to amount, plan of insurance and age of the Insured. However, the inclusion in the new policy of any benefit other than the basic life or endowment insurance benefit shall be subject to the Company's approval and requirements, including evidence of insurability satisfactory to the Company.

The new policy will be of the same edition, with the same provisions and conditions, as policies being issued by the Company on the effective date of the new policy, and the premium for it will be based on the Company's then current rate for such policy at the Insured's attained age.

No change will be made in the classification of the risk and no evidence of insurability will be required in connection with any exchange effected under this Conversion Privilege except as may be required under (d) above.

The period of time specified in any provisions relating to Incontestability and Suicide in any new policy effected under this Conversion Privilege will run, not from the date of issue of the new policy, but from the date of issue of these Provisions for Application of Dividend Deposits to Provide One Year Term Insurance, except with respect to any benefit which required the Company's approval for inclusion in the new policy.

Incontestability and Suicide

Notwithstanding anything in this policy to the contrary, its Suicide and Incontestability provisions will not apply to these provisions where these Provisions for Application of Dividend Deposits to Provide One Year Term Insurance were added to this policy when it was already in force. Instead, in such case,

(a) suicide of the Insured, while sane or insane, within two years from the date of issue of these provisions is a risk not assumed under

these provisions and, in event of the Insured's suicide within that year, any amount withdrawn from outstanding dividend deposits to provide term insurance under these provisions will be refunded by crediting it to the policy as a dividend deposit; and

(b) these Provisions for Application of Dividend Deposits to Provide One Year Term Insurance shall be incontestable, after the policy has been in force during the lifetime of the Insured for two years from the date of issue of these provisions;

and the date of issue of these Provisions for Application of Dividend Deposits to Provide One Year Term Insurance shall be as specified in the applicable provisions for Addition of Supplementary Benefits.

Termination of Insurance

Any one year term insurance under these provisions will terminate on the date these provisions terminate. These provisions will automatically terminate:

(i) immediately before the policy anniversary next following receipt by the Company at its Home Office of the Owner's written request to terminate these provisions;

(ii) immediately before the policy anniversary on which a dividend option other than the Dividend Deposit option becomes effective;

(iii) upon termination of this policy by maturity, surrender or otherwise, or upon any non-forfeiture benefit becoming applicable;

(iv) upon exchange of this policy for a policy on another plan of insurance or a policy of lesser amount;

(v) upon exchange of these provisions for a new policy under the Conversion Privilege of these provisions;

(vi) upon issuance by the Company of a policy providing term insurance on the life of the Insured in accordance with the provisions for Term Insurance for Policy Loan under the Policy Loan Provisions of this policy;

(vii) immediately before any policy anniversary on which any indebtedness under this policy exceeds its loan value less the amount which would be withdrawn from outstanding dividend deposits on that anniversary to provide term insurance under these Provisions for Application of Dividend Deposits to Provide One Year Term Insurance.

If any one year term insurance provided under these provisions is terminated between policy anniversaries, its termination value will be equal to the pro rata part of the amount applied to provide such one year term insurance corresponding to the number of full policy months between the date such insurance is terminated and the end of the one year term period. Any such termination value will be credited to the policy as a dividend deposit.

INSTITUTE LIFE INSURANCE COMPANY

By *William G. Masters*
Secretary

[A3437]

POLICY PURCHASE OPTION

These provisions are included in and made a part of the policy to which they are attached by the Company in consideration of the application for such provisions and payment of the amount that is included in the premium for such policy on account of this Policy Purchase Option.

The amount included in the premium for the policy on account of the Policy Purchase Option is shown on the first page of this policy, and these provisions for a Policy Purchase Option will be deemed to have taken effect as of the policy date of the policy, except where such provisions have been added to a policy which was already in force, in which case such amount and such effective date shall be as specified in the provisions for Addition of Supplementary Benefits which make these provisions for a Policy Purchase Option a part of this policy.

While this policy is in force and these provisions for a Policy Purchase Option are in effect and applicable:

(a) the Owner of this policy may purchase a new policy on the life of the Insured as of each or any of the Option Dates or Alternative Option Dates specified in these provisions, without being required to furnish, in connection with such purchase, any evidence of insurability with respect to the condition of health, occupation, activities or residence of the Insured, such as is customarily required when new insurance is purchased; and

(b) the Company will automatically provide term insurance on the life of the Insured, beginning on the day of any marriage, birth or legal adoption which results in the establishment of an Alternative Option Date and expiring on the day preceding such Alternative Option Date;

all subject to the terms and conditions of this policy and these provisions for a Policy Purchase Option.

Purchase of New Policy

A new policy can be purchased under this Option upon submission of appropriate written application to the Company accompanied by the full first premium for the new policy, less that portion of the underwriting savings allowance which is credited, under the Company's rules, toward such premium, on or within sixty days before the date as of which such purchase is made, if premiums for this policy have been paid to, and the Insured is living on, the applicable Option Date or Alternative Option Date, subject to the following conditions:

(a) The new policy shall take effect on the Option Date or Alternative Option Date as of which it is purchased.

(b) The classification of the risk under the new policy will be the same as the classification of the risk under this policy.

(c) The new policy will provide a level amount of insurance which may not exceed the lesser of:

   (i) $20,000, or

   (ii) the face amount of the policy to which these provisions are attached (basic face amount on the life of the Insured where such policy provides insurance on more than one life, ultimate face amount where such policy is on the Insurance Builder Paid-up at Age 65 Plan).

However, in no event may the amount of insurance under the new policy be less than $5,000.

(d) The new policy:

   (i) will be of the same edition as similar policies that are being issued by the Company on the effective date of the new policy;

   (ii) will, subject to the other terms hereof, contain the same provisions and conditions, including any relating to war or aviation or any other limitation on the Company's liability, as the Company is then regularly including in newly purchased policies which provide coverage, under the same plan of insurance as the plan of such new policy, on a person of the same sex and attained age as the Insured;

   (iii) shall be a policy which would be available on its effective date under the Company's rules as to amount, plan of insurance and age of the Insured.

In addition, if this policy contains any provisions or conditions relating to war or aviation or any other limitation on the Company's liability under it, the new policy will contain corresponding provisions and conditions limiting the Company's liability in a similar manner; also any modifications made in the provisions of this policy because of the classification of the risk shall likewise be made in the corresponding provisions of the new policy.

(e) Subject to (c) and (d) above,

   (i) the new policy may be on any life or endowment plan except a plan which contains an option under which the face amount of insurance can be increased, or which provides insurance coverage on more than one person;

   (ii) provision for a Waiver of Premium Benefit may be included in the new policy if such a provision is included in the policy to which these provisions are attached, but, where the Insured has ever been totally disabled as defined in such provision of this policy, any new policy containing a Waiver of Premium Benefit provision must be on the Whole Life plan; and

   (iii) if the policy to which these provisions are attached includes a provision for an Accidental Death Benefit, the new policy may also include provision for an amount of Accidental Death Benefit equal to the amount of life or endowment insurance under the new policy.

However, the new policy may not include provisions for any benefit other than such Waiver of Premium Benefit, such Accidental Death Benefit and the basic life or endowment insurance benefit elected.

(f) The premium for the new policy will be based on the Company's premium rates current on its effective date for such a policy at the Insured's attained age on that date.

If the Owner does not have an insurable interest in the life of the Insured on any Option Date or Alternative Option Date and is, for that reason, prohibited by any applicable statute from purchasing the new policy under this Option, the Insured, instead of the Owner, may make such purchase in accordance with the provisions of this Option.

POLICY PURCHASE OPTION *(continued)*

Coverage Under New Policy. Insurance under any new policy purchased under this Option will take effect as of the new policy's effective date if the Insured is living on that date. If application is made for a new policy under this Option but the Insured dies before the new policy takes effect, a refund will be made, to the person who applied for such policy, of any payment made to the Company in connection with such application.

No insurance will be provided under the new policy before its effective date, and the new policy will not provide any benefits for death occurring, or disability beginning, before that date.

Option Dates. The Option Dates under this Option will be the seven policy anniversaries on which the Insured's age is 22, 25, 28, 31, 34, 37 and 40, excluding any such anniversaries which may have occurred on or before the date of issue of these provisions and any Option Date that has been eliminated by the exercise of this Option as of an Alternative Option Date.

Alternative Option Dates. The Alternative Option Dates under this Option will be the dates three months after

(i) the marriage of the Insured,

(ii) each birth of a living child to the Insured and his wife during the Insured's lifetime, and

(iii) legal adoption of each child adopted by the Insured,

if such marriage, birth or adoption occurs after the effective date of these provisions and before the policy anniversary on which the Insured's age is 40.

Each purchase of a new policy as of an Alternative Option Date will eliminate the first Option Date which occurs on or after such Alternative Option Date and which has not previously been so eliminated, and no purchase of a new policy can be made under this Option as of any Option Date which has been so eliminated. Where, because of a multiple birth or the simultaneous legal adoption of more than one child, more than one policy can be purchased on the same Alternative Option Date, but the Company permits such purchases to be combined in one purchase of a single policy, the number of Option Dates eliminated thereby will be determined on the same basis as if such purchases had not been combined. However, the elimination from these provisions of all future Option Dates shall not preclude the purchase of a new policy under this Option as of any subsequent Alternative Option Date.

Incontestability and Suicide under New Policy. The period of time specified in any provisions relating to Incontestability and Suicide in any new policy purchased under this Option will run, not from the date of issue of the new policy, but from the date of issue of these provisions for a Policy Purchase Option, and the new policy will so provide.

Interim Term Insurance Preceding Alternative Option Dates

The term insurance provided during the three months' period preceding an Alternative Option Date will be for an amount equal to the maximum amount of basic life or endowment insurance that could be purchased under a new policy on such Alternative Option Date. However, such term insurance will not be in effect if this Option is not in effect or if this policy is not in force or is being continued under its Non-Forfeiture provisions. Any term insurance payable under these provisions will be included as part of the death benefit proceeds under the policy to which such provisions are attached.

Underwriting Savings Allowance

An underwriting savings allowance will be made in connection with the purchase of each new policy under this Option. Such allowance is guaranteed to be not less than $5 plus an additional $1 for each full $1,000 by which the face amount of the new policy exceeds $5,000 and will be applied, in accordance with the Company's rules, as a credit against the premium or premiums for the first policy year for the new policy.

Incontestability of Provisions for Policy Purchase Option

Notwithstanding anything in this policy to the contrary, its Incontestability provisions will not apply to these provisions for a Policy Purchase Option where such Option was added to a policy when it was already in force. Instead, in such case, these provisions for a Policy Purchase Option shall be incontestable, except for non-payment of premium, after the policy has been in force during the lifetime of the Insured for one year from the date of issue specified for these provisions in the applicable provisions for Addition of Supplementary Benefits.

Miscellaneous Provisions

The provisions for this Option will not be applicable while this policy is being continued under any Non-Forfeiture provision nor will they affect tabular cash values under this policy.

The Company will require proof satisfactory to it of any marriage, birth or legal adoption which establishes an Alternative Option Date before any purchase of a new policy as of such Alternative Option Date can be effected, or payment is made of any term insurance benefit that is provided for the three months' period preceding such Alternative Option Date, under these provisions. The term "marriage", as used in the provisions for this Option, shall refer only to marriages where a marriage ceremony is performed by a person legally authorized to do so.

Upon receipt by the Company within thirty-one days of any premium due date of the Owner's written request accompanied by this policy for appropriate indorsement, the provisions for this Option will terminate as of such premium due date. If not previously terminated, these provisions will terminate automatically on the policy anniversary when the Insured's age is 40 or upon any earlier exchange of the policy to which these provisions are attached for a policy on another plan of insurance or a policy of lesser amount. However, any automatic termination of these provisions on the policy anniversary when the Insured's age is 40 will not prejudice the Owner's right to purchase a new policy, nor terminate any interim term insurance provided, under this Option because of a marriage, birth or legal adoption occurring less than three months before such anniversary.

Any premium due under this policy on or after any termination of these provisions will be reduced by any amount included in such premium for the Policy Purchase Option.

INSTITUTE LIFE INSURANCE COMPANY

BY *William G. Masters*
Secretary

[A3439]

PART 1 OF APPLICATION FOR INSURANCE

1. Full name of applicant USE BLACK INK ONLY
   JOHN DOE

2. A. Residence: Street
   City or Town **MONTCLAIR**
   County **ESSEX**   State **NEW JERSEY**

   B. Residence addresses (ST., CITY AND STATE) last three years
   35 HILLSIDE DR. MONTCLIRE N.J

   C. Do you contemplate a change in residence or foreign travel?
   IF SO, GIVE DETAILS

3. A. Occupation **ACCOUNTANT**

   B. Name of employer and business address
   BROWN + WHITE 300 BROAD STREET, NEWARK

   C. Previous occupations in last five years
   STUDENT + PRESENT POSTION

   D. Have you any other occupations? IF SO, GIVE DETAILS
   NONE

   E. Do you contemplate any change in occupation? IF SO, GIVE DETAILS
   NO

4. A. Have you ever piloted or have you any intention of piloting any type of aircraft? **NO**

   B. Have you taken any aerial flights in the last 12 months other than as a passenger? **NO**

   IF EITHER PART IS ANSWERED "YES" SUBMIT AVIATION SUPPLEMENT

5. Will insurance now being applied for replace insurance in this or any other company? IF SO, GIVE DETAILS **NO**

6. Are you insured in this Company? **NO**

7. A. Is your life insured in any other company or companies?
   IF SO, GIVE FULL DETAILS BELOW

NAMES OF COMPANIES	AMOUNTS	KINDS	DATES OF ISSUE	SPECIAL PROVISIONS WAIVER	DIS. INC.	A.D.B.
X LIFE INS. CO	$8,000	GROUP	1965			
X LIFE INS. CO	$2,000	STRAIGHT	1952			

   B. What would be the amount of your disability income, if disabled?
   EXCLUSIVE OF INSURANCE IN THIS COMPANY
   FROM 1. All life insurance policies $ per month
   FROM 2. All accident and health policies $ per month

8. Date of Birth   Month **APRIL**   Day **12**   Year **1942**   Age Last Birthday **25**

9. Birthplace CITY, STATE **DENVER COLORADO**

10. Are you CHECK   ☐ Single ☑ Married ☐ Widowed ☐ Divorced

11. During the past five years have you had advice, attendance, or treatment by a physician or any other person? If so, give nature of ailment, duration, approximate date and names and addresses of physicians or other persons consulted.

   LAST ANNUAL PHYSICAL EXAM JUNE 15, 1965

12. A. Plan of insurance
   STRAIGHT LIFE
   CHECK PROVISIONS DESIRED
   Waiver of   Policy   Accidental
   B. ☑ Premium Benefit C. ☑ Purchase Option D. ☑ Death Benefit

13. Amount of insurance $ **10,000**

14. Premiums payable in advance CHECK METHOD OF PAYMENT
   ☑ Annually ☐ Semiannually ☐ Quarterly ☐ Monthly

15. Beneficiary GIVEN NAME AND RELATIONSHIP
   MARY DOE, WIFE (IF LIVING) OTHERWISE CHILDREN BORN OF MARRIAGE OF INSURED TO MARY DOE
   (ENDOWMENTS ARE MADE PAYABLE TO THE INSURED AT MATURITY UNLESS OTHERWISE REQUESTED.)

16. Which of the following rights do you reserve as to a change of beneficiary, any change being subject to the consent of the Company?
   STRIKE OUT ONE
   A. The right to change and successively change to any beneficiary?
   B. No right to change except with the consent of all beneficiaries

17. Dividends to be: STRIKE OUT METHODS NOT DESIRED
   A. Paid in cash
   B. Applied in reduction of premium
   C. Used to purchase paid-up additions
   D. Dividend deposit
   E. Dividend deposits to provide one year term insurance

18. Is the Automatic Premium Loan Provision requested?   CHECK ☑ Yes ☐ No

19. Has the first premium on the insurance hereby applied for been paid? **YES**   If so, state amount paid $ **200.40**

I understand and agree that:
1. If the premium on the insurance herein applied for has been paid to the Company's agent, in exchange for the Company's signed advance premium receipt numbered the same as Part 1 hereof, the insurance as provided by the policy shall be effective from the date of Part 2 of this application PROVIDED the Company shall approve this application at its Home Office. If this application is not so approved, I will accept the return of the premium paid and surrender the advance premium receipt.

2. If the premium on the insurance herein applied for has not been paid, such insurance shall become effective on the date of issue stated in the policy PROVIDED the Company has approved this application at its Home Office, the premium has been paid, and the policy delivered to me while I am in good health.

I hereby declare that all the answers and statements herein contained are full, complete, and true, and have been correctly recorded.

Signed at **Montclair** CITY **New Jersy** STATE

and dated this **1** day of **May**, 19**69**

In My Presence **Oliver Wass**

General Agent submitting application

Applicant **John Doe**

Address all mail to **35 Hillside Drive Montclair N.J.**

Agent who actually solicited this application

INSTITUTE LIFE INSURANCE COMPANY, NEW YORK, NEW YORK

LIFE POLICY AS SHOWN UNDER PLAN.
PREMIUMS PAYABLE AS SHOWN IN PREMIUM SCHEDULE.
DIVIDEND CREDITS MAY BE USED TO SHORTEN PREMIUM PAYING PERIOD.
ANNUAL PARTICIPATION.

TABLE OF CASH, LOAN AND NON-FORFEITURE VALUES

PER $1,000 OF FACE AMOUNT

End of Policy Year	TABULAR CASH OR LOAN VALUE	PARTICIPATING PAID-UP INSURANCE	NON-PARTICIPATING EXTENDED INSURANCE (The period of years and days shown below is the same for policies of any amount.)		End of Policy Year
			YEARS	DAYS	
1	• • •	• • •	• •	• • •	1
2	$ 9	$ 31	4	244	2
3	23	76	11	162	3
4	38	122	16	175	4
5	53	166	19	318	5
6	64	195	21	155	6
7	76	226	22	274	7
8	88	255	23	266	8
9	100	282	24	160	9
10	113	311	25	28	10
11	126	338	25	189	11
12	139	364	25	297	12
13	153	390	26	32	13
14	167	415	26	88	14
15	181	439	26	110	15
16	195	462	26	101	16
17	210	485	26	96	17
18	225	507	26	64	18
19	240	528	26	11	19
20	255	548	25	303	20
AGE 60	500	780	20	334	AGE 60
AGE 65	582	832	18	288	AGE 65

NON-FORFEITURE FACTORS (applicable during premium paying period)
First   5   Policy Years $15.791
Thereafter $11.684   Tabular cash values equal full net premium reserve from   5TH   policy anniversary

[A3441]

APPENDIX F—Specimen Health and Accident
Insurance Policies *

THE HEALTH INSURANCE COMPANY

HOME OFFICE — NEW YORK

INSURED **Policy No.**

The benefits provided by this policy are indicated in the Policy Schedule.

POLICY SCHEDULE

Benefits marked "None" are not provided by this policy, and no premium charge is included therefor.

Policy
Date Premium $ for a term of months

Monthly Benefit for Total Disability $

Monthly Benefit for Partial Disability: Accident $ Sickness $

Elimination Period: Accident days; Sickness days

Maximum Benefit Period: Accident months; Sickness months
but not beyond the policy anniversary next following the Insured's 65th birthday except as provided herein.

Principal Sum — Death and Dismemberment and Loss of Sight $

Beneficiary: As designated in the application for this policy unless subsequently changed in accordance with the policy provisions. (Applicable only if Principal Sum provided herein.)

INSURING PROVISION

In consideration of the application herefor, a copy of which is attached hereto and made a part hereof, and the payment in advance of the premium specified in the Schedule, The Health Insurance Company does hereby insure the above-named Insured, subject to all the provisions, exceptions and reductions contained herein, attached hereto or endorsed hereon, against disability and loss, as indicated in the Schedule, resulting from:
  (a) Sickness or disease of the Insured which first manifests itself while this policy is in force, hereafter called "sickness," or
  (b) Accidental bodily injury occurring while this policy is in force, hereafter called "injury."
Coverage hereunder shall begin on the Policy Date.

NOTICE OF TEN DAY RIGHT TO EXAMINE POLICY

Within ten days after its delivery to the Insured, this policy may be surrendered by delivering or mailing it to the Home Office at New York, New York, or to any branch office or to the agent through whom it was purchased. Upon such surrender, the Company will return any premium paid and the policy shall be deemed void from the Policy Date.
The provisions written or printed by the Company on the following pages hereof are a part of this policy.
In Witness Whereof, The Health Insurance Company has caused this policy to be signed by its President and Secretary and countersigned by a Licensed Resident Agent on the Policy Date.

O. B. Risk
Secretary.

C. D. Carrier
President.

Examined by_____ Countersigned by_____
Licensed Resident Agent

NONCANCELLABLE AND GUARANTEED RENEWABLE TO AGE 65
DISABILITY INCOME POLICY

RENEWAL PROVISION

The first premium under this policy in the amount shown in the Schedule is payable on the Policy Date and will continue the policy for the term specified, subject to the Grace Period provided herein. The policy may be continued thereafter for like terms by the periodic payment of renewal premiums at the same rate until the policy anniversary next following the sixty-fifth birthday of the Insured when the coverage hereunder shall terminate with respect to any sickness contracted or injury occurring thereafter. However, except as provided in the "Misstatement of Age" provision, if the Company accepts a premium for a period of coverage beginning on or after the policy anniversary next following the sixty-fifth birthday of the Insured, coverage under this policy will continue until the end of the period for which such premium was accepted.

The only condition for the renewal of this policy is the timely payment of premiums as herein required. While this policy is maintained in force the Company cannot cancel the policy, increase the premium rate, reduce benefits because of change to a more hazardous occupation or place any restrictive rider hereon.

DEFINITIONS

Wherever used in this policy:

"total disability" means the complete inability of the Insured to perform any and every duty of his regular occupation, except that if benefits have been paid for sixty months of any continuous disability, and this policy provides benefits in excess thereof, then for the balance of the period of disability after said period of sixty months "total disability" shall mean complete inability of the Insured to engage in any gainful occupation for which he is reasonably fitted in consideration of his training, education, experience or prior average earnings. However, the total loss by the Insured of the use of both hands or both feet or one hand and one foot or the total loss of sight of both eyes shall be deemed to constitute "total disability" so long as such total loss of use or sight shall continue, irrespective of whether the Insured engages in his or any other gainful occupation;

"partial disability" means:

(a) a necessary and continuous loss of one-half or more of the time spent by the Insured in the usual daily performance of the duties of his occupation, or

(b) the inability of the Insured to perform one or more of the important daily duties of his occupation;

"elimination period" means the number of days at the beginning of the period of total disability, commencing with the first day thereof, for which no benefits are payable;

"physician" means a legally qualified physician or surgeon other than the Insured.

BENEFIT PROVISIONS

Total Disability Benefits — Accident. If, as the result of injury, the Insured suffers continuous total disability, and requires the attendance of a physician, the Company will pay periodically the Monthly Benefit for Total Disability specified in the Schedule, provided however, that no benefit will be payable for the Elimination

Period for Accident nor for any period of disability in excess of the Maximum Benefit Period for Accident as specified in said Schedule. It is further provided that:

(a) if Lifetime Accident Benefits are provided for disability by this policy the termination of this benefit on the anniversary next following the Insured's sixty-fifth birthday shall not apply, or

(b) that if fewer than twelve Monthly Benefit payments shall have been made for a continuous total disability of the Insured existing on the anniversary next following his sixty-fifth birthday, and Lifetime Accident Benefits are not provided for disability by this policy, the payment of Monthly Benefits will be continued during such a continuous disability until a total of twelve Monthly Benefit payments shall have been made.

Total Disability Benefits — Sickness. If, as the result of sickness, the Insured suffers continuous total disability commencing while this policy is in force, and requires the attendance of a physician, the Company will pay periodically the Monthly Benefit for Total Disability specified in the Schedule, provided however, that no benefit will be payable for the Elimination Period for Sickness nor for any period of disability in excess of the Maximum Benefit Period for Sickness as specified in said Schedule, except that if fewer than twelve Monthly Benefit payments shall have been made for a continuous total disability of the Insured existing on the anniversary next following his sixty-fifth birthday, the payment of Monthly Benefits will be continued during such a continuous disability until a total of twelve Monthly Benefit payments shall have been made.

Accidental Death, Dismemberment or Loss of Sight Benefits. If injury of the Insured shall, within ninety days of the accident, result in the loss of life, both hands, both feet or one hand and foot, or the sight of both eyes the Company will pay, in addition to any benefits payable for Accident Disability, the Principal Sum specified in the Schedule. It is further provided that said Principal Sum shall not be payable for more than one such loss as the result of any one accident and that loss of life resulting from suicide, while sane or insane, or from the voluntary inhalation of monoxide or any other gas or vapor shall not be covered.

Loss of hands or feet means complete severance at or above the wrist or ankle joints, and loss of sight must be entire and irrecoverable.

Partial Disability Benefits — Accident. If, as the result of injury, the Insured suffers partial disability, commencing on the date of said injury or following a period of compensable total disability, and requires the attendance of a physician, the Company will pay periodically the Monthly Benefit for Partial Disability specified in the Schedule for the period of such partial disability, but not to exceed six months during any one continuous disability, and provided that no benefit will be payable for the Elimination Period for Accident at the beginning of the period of disability, and that benefits for total and partial disability combined shall not be payable for any one continuous period in excess of the Maximum Benefit Period. It is further provided that:

(a) if Lifetime Accident Benefits are provided for disability by this policy the termination of this benefit on the anniversary

2

next following the Insured's sixty-fifth birthday shall not apply, or

(b) that if fewer than twelve Monthly Benefit payments shall have been made for a continuous total disability of the Insured existing on the anniversary next following his sixty-fifth birthday, and Lifetime Accident Benefits are not provided for disability by this policy, the payment of Monthly Benefits will be continued during such a continuous disability until a total of twelve Monthly Benefit payments shall have been made.

Partial Disability Benefits — Sickness. If, as the result of sickness, the Insured suffers partial disability following a period of compensable total disability, and requires the attendance of a physician, the Company will pay periodically the Monthly Benefit for Partial Disability specified in the Schedule for the period of such partial disability but not to exceed six months during any one continuous disability, and provided that benefits for total and partial disability combined shall not be payable for any one continuous period in excess of the Maximum Benefit Period, except that if fewer than twelve Monthly Benefit payments shall have been made for a continuous total disability of the Insured existing on the anniversary next following his sixty-fifth birthday, the payment of Monthly Benefits will be continued during such a continuous disability until a total of twelve Monthly Benefit payments shall have been made.

Recurrent Disability. If, following a period of disability due to sickness or injury, the Insured shall resume his regular occupation, or any occupation for which he is reasonably fitted, and shall perform all the important duties thereof for a continuous period of six months or more, any subsequent disability resulting from or contributed to be the same cause or causes shall be considered as a new period of disability and indemnified in accordance with the appropriate provisions of this policy, but if said period during which the Insured resumes such occupation shall be less than six months such subsequent disability shall be deemed a continuation of the same disability and the Company's liability for the entire period shall be subject to the limitations applicable in the part or parts of this policy under which the original period of disability was indemnified.

Waiver of Premium. After any total disability, for which total disability benefits are payable under this policy, has continued for ninety consecutive days, or for the elimination period if longer, the Company will refund any premiums due and paid during the continuance of such total disability and will waive all premiums coming due during such total disability; provided, however, that there shall be no waiver of any premium which falls due subsequent to the period for which total disability benefits are payable unless the Insured furnishes the Company proof of the continuance of such total disability within thirty-one days of such due date. Following such a period of disability during which the Company has waived premiums the insurance provided in this contract shall continue in full force and effect until the next premium due date, at which time the Insured shall have the right to resume payment of premiums as they become due.

EXCEPTIONS AND REDUCTIONS

This policy does not cover any loss caused by war or any act of war, whether declared or undeclared.

Any disability or loss resulting from inguinal, umbilical or post-operative hernia, ptomaines or bacterial infection shall be indemnified under the sickness provisions of this policy, except that pyogenic infections incurred through an accidental cut or wound shall be indemnified under the accident provisions.

The Insured shall not be entitled to concurrent benefits for disability contributed to or caused by both injury and sickness.

GENERAL PROVISIONS

Entire Contract: Changes. This policy, including the endorsements and the attached papers, if any, constitutes the entire contract of insurance. No change in this policy shall be valid until approved by an executive officer of the Company and unless such approval be endorsed hereon or attached hereto. No agent has authority to change this policy or to waive any of its provisions.

Incontestable. (a) After this policy has been in force for a period of two years during the lifetime of the Insured (excluding any period during which the Insured is disabled), it shall become incontestable as to the statements contained in the application

(b) No claim for loss incurred or disability (as defined in this policy) commencing after two years from the date of issue of this policy shall be reduced or denied on the ground that a disease or physical condition not excluded from coverage by name or specific description effective on the date of loss had existed prior to the effective date of coverage of this policy.

Grace Period. A grace period of thirty-one days will be granted for the payment of each premium falling due after the first premium, during which grace period this policy shall continue in force.

Reinstatement. If any renewal premium be not paid within the time granted the Insured for payment, a subsequent acceptance of premium by the Company or by any agent duly authorized by the Company to accept such premium, without requiring in connection therewith an application for reinstatement, shall reinstate this policy; provided, however, that if the Company or such agent requires an application for reinstatement and issues a conditional receipt for the premium tendered, this policy will be reinstated upon approval of such application by the Company or, lacking such approval, upon the forty-fifth day following the date of such conditional receipt unless the Company has previously notified the Insured in writing of its disapproval of such application. The reinstated policy shall cover only loss resulting from such accidental injury as may be sustained after the date of reinstatement and loss due to such sickness as may begin more than ten days after such date. In all other respects the Insured and the Company shall have the same rights thereunder as they had under this policy immediately before the due date of the defaulted premium, subject to any provisions endorsed hereon or attached hereto in connection with the reinstatement.

Notice of Claim. Written notice of claim must be given to the Company within twenty days after the occurrence or commencement of any loss covered by this policy, or as soon thereafter as is reasonably possible. Notice given by or on behalf of the Insured or the beneficiary (if designated in this policy) to the Company at its Home Office in New York, New York or to any authorized agent of the Company, with information sufficient to identify the Insured, shall be deemed notice to the Company.

Claim Forms: The Company, upon receipt of a notice of claim, will furnish to the claimant such forms as are usually furnished by it for filing proofs of loss. If such forms are not furnished within fifteen days after the giving of such notice the claimant shall be deemed to have complied with the requirements of this policy as to proof of loss upon submitting, within the time fixed in this policy for filing proofs of loss, written proof covering the occurrence, the character and the extent of the loss for which claim is made.

Proofs of Loss. Written proof of loss must be furnished to the Company at its said office in case of claim for loss for which this policy provides any periodic payment contingent upon continuing loss within ninety days after the termination of the period for which the Company is liable and in case of claim for any other loss within ninety days after the date of such loss. Failure to furnish such proof within the time required shall not invalidate nor reduce any claim if it was not reasonably possible to give proof within such time, provided such proof is furnished as soon as reasonably possible and in no event, except in the absence of legal capacity, later than one year from the time proof is otherwise required.

Time of Payment of Claims. Benefits payable under this policy for any loss other than loss for which this policy provides any periodic payment will be paid immediately upon receipt of due written proof of such loss. Subject to due written proof of loss, all accrued benefits for loss for which this policy provides periodic payment will be paid monthly and any balance remaining unpaid upon the termination of liability will be paid immediately upon receipt of due written proof.

Payment of Claims. The benefit for loss of life (if provided by this policy) will be payable in accordance with the beneficiary designation and the provisions respecting such payment which may be prescribed herein and effective at the time of payment. If no such designation or provision is then effective, such benefit shall be payable to the estate of the Insured. Any other accrued benefits unpaid at the Insured's death may, at the option of the Company, be paid either to such beneficiary or to such estate. All other benefits will be payable to the Insured.

If any benefit of this policy shall be payable to the estate of the Insured, or to an Insured or beneficiary (if designated in this policy) who is a minor or otherwise not competent to give a valid release, the Company may pay such benefit, up to an amount not exceeding $1,000, to any relative by blood or connection by marriage of the Insured or beneficiary who is deemed by the Company to be equitably entitled thereto. Any payment made by the Company in good faith pursuant to this provision shall fully discharge the Company to the extent of such payment.

Physical Examinations. The Company at its own expense shall have the right and opportunity to examine the person of the Insured when and as often as it may reasonably require during the pendency of a claim hereunder.

Legal Actions. No action at law or in equity shall be brought to recover on this policy prior to the expiration of sixty days after written proof of loss has been furnished in accordance with the requirements of this policy. No such action shall be brought after the expiration of three years after the time written proof of loss is required to be furnished.

Change of Beneficiary. The right to change beneficiary (if designated in this policy) is reserved to the Insured and the consent of the beneficiary or beneficiaries shall not be requisite to surrender or assignment of this policy or to any change of beneficiary or beneficiaries, or to any other changes in this policy.

Misstatement of Age. If the age of the Insured has been misstated, all amounts payable under this policy shall be such as the premium paid would have purchased at the correct age.

If, because of misstatement of the Insured's age, the Company shall accept any premium which falls due on a date when, according to the correct age, this policy would not have been issued or the coverage under this policy would have ceased, then the liability of the Company shall be limited to the refund, upon request, of all premiums paid for the period not covered by this policy.

Conformity with State Statutes. Any provision of this policy which, on its effective date, is in conflict with the statutes of the state in which the Insured resides on such date is hereby amended to conform to the minimum requirements of such statutes.

Payment of Premiums. All premiums are payable in advance, subject to the terms of the grace period provided herein, at the Home Office of the Company in New York, New York or to any authorized agent of the Company. Premiums may be paid annually, semi-annually or quarterly in advance in accordance with the Company's premium rates in force on the effective date of this policy, as elected in the application herefor and, except in any period during which the Insured is totally disabled, the mode of premium payment may be changed on any anniversary of the effective date of this policy upon request approved in writing by the Company at its Home Office. The payment of any premium shall not continue this policy in force beyond the date when the next premium is due and payable, except as may be otherwise provided by said grace period.

Premium Refund at Death. In the event of the death of the Insured while this policy is in force the Company will refund, on a pro-rata basis, any unearned premium paid by the Insured. Such refund may, at the option of the Company, be paid to beneficiary or to the estate of the Insured.

Form No. MW 5567
[A3445]

THE HEALTH INSURANCE COMPANY

HOME OFFICE — NEW YORK

Insured

Policy Number   SPECIMEN

First Premium

Date of Issue

SCHEDULE OF BENEFITS

BENEFIT	MAXIMUM AMOUNT	MAXIMUM PERIOD
Daily Hospital (Room and Board)	Per Day	90 Days
Hospital Services		—
Surgical Expense (Schedule Maximum)	$450.00	—

Maternity (Applicable only if both Insured and Insured's Spouse are covered family members) — benefit limited to those described in Maternity Benefit Provision

Deductible Amount — None   Not Applicable to Maternity Benefit

    The Health Insurance Company agrees to provide the benefits stated in this policy, subject to the provisions, conditions, exceptions and limitations set forth on this and the following pages, including the Policy Specifications above, all of which are a part of this contract. Among the exceptions from coverage are (1) charges incurred while confined in certain hospitals or other facilities provided by the government, (2) charges covered under government plans, and (3) any charges or disability which are due to any injury or sickness for which benefits are payable under any workmen's compensation or occupational disease law, all as set forth fully in the Exceptions provision of this policy.

    This policy is issued in consideration of the application, a copy of which is attached and made a part hereof. and of the payment of the first premium on or before the delivery of the policy and the payment of subsequent premiums as herein provided.

    Covered family members under this policy on its Date of Issue are the family members named in the application and accepted for insurance coverage. Commencement and termination of status as Insured or covered family member and addition of new covered family members are subject to General Provision 1.

GUARANTEED RENEWABLE TO AGE 65 — COMPANY CAN CHANGE TABLE OF PREMIUMS

    The Insured shall have the right to renew and continue this policy in force, in accordance with General Provision 2, until the latest of (a) the 65th birthday of the Insured; (b) the 65th birthday of the Insured's spouse, if a covered family member; and (c) the latest date of expiration of coverage of all dependent children who are covered family members, but coverage shall be continued on any renewal only for those covered family members whose coverage does not expire upon becoming entitled to "Medicare" coverage, or for any other reason, as set forth fully in General Provision 1(c). The Company reserves the right to change from time to time the table of rates applicable to renewal premiums but only on the basis indicated in General Provision 2.

Right of Policy Examination — If the Insured is not satisfied with this policy, it may be surrendered by delivering or mailing it within ten days after receipt by the Insured to the Company at New York, New York, or to the agent or agency office through which it was delivered. Immediately upon such delivering or mailing, the policy shall be deemed void from the beginning and any premium paid on it will be refunded.

    Signed for the Company at New York, New York.

O. B. Risk

Secretary

C. D. Carrier

President

HOSPITAL EXPENSE POLICY

Form No. MW 5767   Printed in U.S.A.   5
[A3446]

DEFINITIONS

Wherever used in this policy:

"Injury" means only accidental bodily injury sustained by any covered family member while such family member is covered under this policy.

"Sickness" means only sickness or disease of any covered family member, which is contracted and commences while such family member is covered under this policy, or which first manifests itself while such family member is covered under this policy.

"Hospital" means only an institution operated pursuant to law for the care and treatment of sick and injured persons, which institution provides 24 hour nursing care and has facilities both for diagnosis, and, except in the case of a hospital primarily concerned with the treatment of chronic diseases, for major surgery. The term "hospital" shall not be construed to include a hotel, rest home, nursing home, convalescent home, place for custodial care, home for the aged, or a place for the confinement or treatment of drug addicts or alcoholics.

"Inpatient" means only a person who is confined in a hospital as a resident patient and who is charged at least one day's room and board by the hospital.

"Surgical operation" means only a procedure listed in the Schedule of Surgical Operations and the following surgical procedures performed by a legally qualified physician: cutting, suturing, treatment of fracture, reduction of dislocation, electrocauterization, tapping (paracentesis), administration of artificial pneumothorax or pneumoperitoneum, removal of stone or foreign body by endoscopic means, or the injection treatment of hernia, hemorrhoids or varicose veins.

"Maximum Amount of the Daily Hospital Benefit," "Maximum Period of the Daily Hospital Benefit," "Maximum Amount of the Hospital Services Benefit," "Maximum Amount of the Surgical Expense Benefit" and "Deductible Amount" mean only the applicable amounts and period specified on pages 2 and 3 of policy.

DEDUCTIBLE AMOUNT PROVISION

(Applicable only if a Deductible Amount is shown on front page of this policy)

In determining the amount payable under any Benefit Provision of this policy to which this Deductible Amount Provision applies, the Deductible Amount shall be subtracted from the amount otherwise payable under said Benefit Provision; provided, however, that the Deductible Amount shall be subtracted only once from the sum of all benefits otherwise payable in the case of (a) recurrent hospital confinements which are considered as occurring during one

period of hospital confinement under the Hospital Expense Benefit, (b) successive surgical operations which are considered as due to the same or related causes or conditions under the Surgical Expense Benefit, (c) payment under more than one Benefit Provision during one period of hospital confinement, and (d) payment for all losses incurred by two or more covered family members as a result of the same accident.

BENEFIT PROVISIONS

Hospital Expense Benefit — If injury or sickness requires the confinement of a covered family member as an inpatient in a hospital and the confinement commences while such person is covered under this policy and while this policy is in force, the Company will pay, after applying the Deductible Amount Provision, the sum of the applicable benefits under Parts A and B:

Part A. Daily Hospital Benefit — An amount equal to the actual charges incurred each day of such confinement for room, board, and routine hospital services, but not exceeding the Maximum Amount of the Daily Hospital Benefit nor for longer than the Maximum Period of the Daily Hospital Benefit during any one period of hospital confinement.

Part B. Hospital Services Benefit — An amount equal to the actual charges incurred for services rendered and equipment and supplies used during such confinement only as follows: (a) anesthetics and the administration thereof, (b) ambulance service to and from the hospital, and (c) operating room, X-ray and fluoroscope, medicines, drugs, surgical dressings, oxygen and any other medical equipment or supplies for which a charge is made by the hospital, but no payment shall be made under this item (c) for room, board or routine hospital services or for services of physicians or nurses; provided, however, that the total amount payable under this Part B during any one period of hospital confinement shall not exceed the Maximum Amount of the Hospital Services Benefit.

If hospital charges are incurred on account of a covered family member (a) due to an injury and within 48 hours after the time of the accident causing such injury, or (b) on the day of and in connection with a surgical operation, such family member shall be deemed to be confined in a hospital as an inpatient for the purposes of this Part B and the Recurrent Hospital Confinements provision with respect to those charges otherwise payable under this Part B which are incurred within 48 hours after such accident or which are incurred on the day of and in connection with such operation.

Recurrent Hospital Confinements — If the confinement of a covered family member commences while such person is covered under this policy and while this policy is in force, and follows a prior confinement of such person with respect to which benefits were payable under this Hospital Expense Benefit, then such confinements shall be considered as occurring during one period of hospital confinement unless

(a) the cause of the subsequent confinement is entirely unrelated to the causes and conditions for which treatment was furnished during the prior confinement and such subsequent confinement is separated from the prior confinement by a resumption of full normal activities, or

(b) the successive periods of confinement are separated by an interval during which such family member resumes full normal activities for a continuous period of at least 6 months.

Form No. MW 5767
[A34471]

BENEFIT PROVISIONS — Continued

The Hospital Expense Benefit shall not cover any charge incurred due to pregnancy, including resulting childbirth, abortion or miscarriage.

Surgical Expense Benefit — If injury or sickness requires that a covered family member undergo a surgical operation while such family member is covered under this policy and while this policy is in force, or while the Daily Hospital Benefit is payable under the Hospital Expense Benefit with respect to such family member, the Company will pay, after applying the Deductible Amount Provision, an amount equal to the charges actually incurred for such operation but not exceeding the maximum payment provided therefor in accordance with the Schedule of Surgical Operations, except that:

(a) all surgical operations performed at the same operative session in the same operative field shall be considered as one surgical operation and the amount payable for such operation shall not exceed the maximum payment specified in the Schedule of Surgical Operations for the operation performed for which the Schedule of Surgical Operations provides the largest maximum payment;

(b) the amount payable for a bilateral surgical operation specified in the Schedule of Surgical Operations shall not exceed the maximum payment specified, and the amount payable for a bilateral surgical operation performed at one operative session and not specified in the Schedule of Surgical Operations shall not exceed one and one-half times the maximum payment specified in the Schedule of Surgical Operations for the surgical operation when not performed bilaterally; and

(c) the amount payable for all surgical operations performed at the same operative session in separate operative fields shall not exceed the total of (i) the maximum payment specified in the Schedule of Surgical Operations for the surgical operation performed for which the Schedule of Surgical Operations provides the largest maximum payment and (ii) one-half of the sum of the maximum payments specified in the Schedule of Surgical Operations for the other surgical operations performed during such operative session, provided, however, that determination of the maximum payments in (i) and (ii) shall be subject to paragraphs (a) and (b), and that the total amount payable under this paragraph (c) for all surgical operations performed at the same operative session shall not exceed one and one-half times the Maximum Amount of the Surgical Expense Benefit.

All surgical operations performed through the same incision or through the same natural body orifice shall be considered as being performed in the same operative field.

In no event shall the total amount payable under this Surgical Expense Benefit for all surgical operations performed on such family member due to any one accident or due to the same or related causes or conditions exceed one and one-half times the Maximum Amount of the Surgical Expense Benefit.

Successive Surgical Operations — If a surgical operation on a covered family member is performed while such person is covered under this policy and while this policy is in force, and following a prior surgical operation on such person with respect to which

benefits were payable under this Surgical Expense Benefit, then such operations shall be considered as due to the same or related causes or conditions unless

(a) the cause of the subsequent operation is entirely unrelated to the causes and conditions for which the prior operation was performed and such subsequent surgical operation is separated from the prior operation by a resumption of full normal activities, or

(b) the successive operations are separated by an interval during which such covered family member resumes full normal activities for a continuous period of at least 6 months.

The Surgical Expense Benefit shall not cover any charge incurred for dental procedures or due to pregnancy, including resulting childbirth, abortion or miscarriage.

Waiver of Premiums Benefit in Event of Total Disability

The Company will waive payment of the premium under this policy upon receipt at its Home Office of due proof that (1) an adult male covered family member, who is either the Insured or the Insured's spouse, is totally disabled on the premium due date as a result of injury or sickness, (2) such adult male was a covered family member both at the time the disability began and during the entire 6 months immediately preceding the date of the premium to be waived and that (3) such total disability has been continuous for the 6 months immediately preceding the date of the premium to be waived, and if such covered family member is over age 60 on the premium due date, such total disability commenced before such covered family member's 60th birthday and has been continuous since that date; and provided, however, that no premium payment shall be waived which is payable for any person who is not covered under this policy as of the date such covered family member becomes totally disabled. For the purpose of waiver of premiums only, such adult family member shall be deemed to be a covered family member although his status as a covered family member has otherwise terminated in accordance with General Provision 1(c)(i), 1(c)(ii) or 1(c)(v).

The phrase "total disability" means (a) such complete incapacity of such covered family member that he is able to perform none of the duties of any and every occupation, business or employment for remuneration or profit for which he is reasonably fitted by education, training or experience, except that total disability shall be deemed not to exist while such covered family member is engaged in any occupation, business or employment for remuneration or profit, or (b) the total loss by such covered family member of the use of both hands or both feet or one hand and one foot or the total and irrecoverable loss of the sight of both eyes.

No premiums shall be waived under this provision as of any premium due date on which such covered family member is not living or is not under the regular care and treatment of a legally qualified physician other than such covered member himself.

Waiver of premiums shall be in accordance with the interval of premium payment in effect when total disability commences.

If a premium becomes due and is not waived in accordance with this provision after one or more premiums have been so waived, the Insured shall have the right to pay such premium in accordance with and subject to the terms of this policy.

SCHEDULE OF SURGICAL OPERATIONS
(See Deductible Amount Provision)

This Schedule shows the maximum payments applicable to the respective surgical operations where the Maximum Amount of the Surgical Expense Benefit is $450.00. For any surgical operation neither specified nor expressly excluded, the Company will determine a maximum payment consistent with the payment for any listed operation of comparable difficulty and complexity, the maximum payment not to exceed the Maximum Amount of the Surgical Expense Benefit.

CARDIOVASCULAR SYSTEM

	Maximum Payment
Pericardiectomy	$300.00
Thromboendarterectomy of abdominal aorta	450.00
Valvulotomy or commissurotomy	
Aortic, pulmonic or tricuspid	450.00
Mitral	360.00
Varicose veins	
*Injection of sclerosing solution into vein(s) of leg	4.50
Cutting operation, with or without injection	
Ligation and division and complete stripping	
long or short saphenous veins, unilateral	90.00
long or short saphenous veins, bilateral	150.00
long and short saphenous veins, unilateral	120.00
long and short saphenous veins, bilateral	180.00
Ligation and division of short saphenous	
vein at saphenopopliteal junction	37.50

DIGESTIVE SYSTEM

	Maximum Payment
Adenoidectomy	30.00
*Anal papillectomy, one or more	15.00
Appendectomy	120.00
Appendicial abscess, transabdominal incision and drainage	90.00
*Aspiration biopsy of liver	15.00
Cholecystectomy	180.00
With open exploration of common duct	210.00
Cholecystotomy	150.00
Colectomy	
Partial resection of large intestine in two stages including first stage colostomy or cecostomy	300.00
Enterectomy	
Resection of small intestine with anastomosis or enterostomy	210.00
Esophagectomy	
Resection of esophagus trans pleural or extra pleural (upper two thirds)	360.00
Excision of submaxillary gland, tumor, or both	120.00
Fissurectomy with or without sphincterotomy	60.00
Fistulectomy or fistulotomy, subcutaneous	30.00
Fistulectomy or fistulotomy, submuscular	120.00
Gastrectomy with or without vagotomy	
Subtotal or hemi-gastrectomy	240.00
Total gastrectomy	300.00
Gastroduodenostomy or gastrojejunostomy	180.00
Gastroscopy or esophagoscopy	
Diagnostic, with or without biopsy	45.00
Gastrotomy or gastrorrhaphy	150.00
Hemorrhoids	
*Excision of external hemorrhoidal tabs	$ 15.00
External hemorrhoidectomy, complete	60.00

	Maximum Payment
External and internal, or internal hemorrhoidectomy	90.00
Hemorrhoidectomy and submuscular fistulotomy or fistulectomy	120.00
Hemorrhoidectomy and fissurectomy	90.00
*Incision of external thrombotic hemorrhoid	9.00
*Injection of sclerosing solution	6.00
Hernioplasty, herniorrhaphy, or herniotomy	
Epigastric, femoral, inguinal	105.00
Inguinal with orchidectomy or excision of hydrocele	120.00
Umbilical, under age 5 years	90.00
Umbilical, age 5 years or over	105.00
Incision and drainage of ischiorectal abscess	30.00
Laparotomy, exploratory	120.00
Marsupialization of cyst or abscess of liver	210.00
Pancreatectomy, total or subtotal	420.00
Proctectomy complete, combined abdominoperineal, one or two stages	300.00
Proctosigmoidoscopy	
Initial	9.00
Subsequent	6.00
With biopsy	15.00
With removal of polyp	21.00
With removal of polyps	27.00
Tonsillectomy, with or without adenoidectomy	
Under age 18 years	45.00
Age 18 years or over	60.00

EAR AND EYE

	Maximum Payment
Cataract	
Discission: needling of lens	
Initial	60.00
Subsequent	30.00
Extraction of lens, intracapsular, extracapsular, or linear	240.00
Enucleation of eyeball	120.00
Excision of pterygium	75.00
Fenestration of semicircular canal	300.00
Keratoplasty	
Corneal transplant, partial or complete, penetrating	330.00
Labyrinthectomy	300.00
Mastoidectomy, simple	150.00
*Myringotomy, tympanotomy, plicotomy	9.00
Reattachment of retina	
Electrocoagulation, scleral resection, buckling or partial tubing	300.00
Light coagulation of retinal breaks	120.00
*Removal of foreign body embedded in conjunctiva	$ 6.00
Stapedectomy, with reconstruction of ossicular chain, with or without vein graft	300.00
Stapes mobilization	210.00

*The Maximum Payment applicable shall be increased by $6.00 if the operation is performed while hospital confined as an inpatient.

Form No. MW 5767
[A3449]

SCHEDULE OF SURGICAL OPERATIONS — Continued

(See Deductible Amount Provision)

	Maximum Payment
ENDOCRINE, HEMIC, LYMPHATIC SYSTEMS	
Biopsy or excision of lymph node	
Anterior scalene	45.00
Other	15.00
Excision of cyst or adenoma of thyroid	120.00
Thyroidectomy	
For malignancy with radical neck dissection	300.00
Total or complete	210.00
Total thyroid lobectomy	150.00
FEMALE GENITAL SYSTEM	
Amputation of cervix	60.00
Biopsy of cervix or endometrium	9.00
Dilatation and curettage of uterus	
under general anesthesia	45.00
with conization	60.00
Excision of cautery destruction of Bartholin's	
gland or cyst	45.00
Hysterectomy	
Radical for cancer, including regional lymph nodes	300.00
Subtotal or supracervical	165.00
Total (corpus and cervix)	180.00
Repair of cystocele with or without urethrocele	105.00
Repair of cystocele, rectocele and perineoplasty,	
with or without repair of urethrocele	150.00
Repair of rectocele	90.00
Salpingectomy, oophorectomy or salpingo-oophorectomy, complete or partial, unilateral or bilateral	135.00
INTEGUMENTARY SYSTEM	
Breast	
Mastotomy with exploration of drainage of abscess, deep	30.00
Partial mastectomy, or excision of cyst or tumor	
Unilateral	45.00
Bilateral	75.00
Radical mastectomy, including breast, pectoral muscles and axillary lymph nodes	210.00
Simple mastectomy, complete	90.00
Excision of benign lesion of skin, subcutaneous tissue or mucous membrane, lesion diameter:	
¼ inch or less	12.00
over ¼ but not over ½ inch	15.00

Excision of malignant lesion of skin or mucous membrane of:	Lesion diameter: ¼ inch or less	over ¼ but not over ½ inch
Trunk, arms or legs	$18.00	$24.00
Face, scalp, ears, neck, hands, feet, genitalia	30.00	45.00
Eyelids, lips, mucous membrane	45.00	60.00

	Maximum Payment
*Incision ad drainage of sebaceous cysts, furuncle, carbuncle or any other subcutaneous abscess	6.00

	Maximum Payment
Suturing of wounds	
up to 2½ inches	
Arms, legs or trunk	$ 9.00
Axilla, cheeks, ear, neck, nose, hands or feet	12.00
Eyelids or lips	15.00
MALE GENITAL SYSTEM	
Circumcision, other than clamp or dorsal slit	30.00
Epididymectomy or excision of hydrocele or variocele	90.00
Orchidectomy, unilateral	60.00
Orchidectomy, bilateral	75.00
Prostatectomy (one or two stages, complete procedure)	240.00
MUSCULOSKELETAL SYSTEM	
Amputations, complete procedure	
Angle, with skin-plasty and resection of nerves	150.00
Arm through humerus or through radius and ulna	120.00
Digit, with or without split or Wolff graft, skin-plasty, tenodesis, or definitive resection volar digital nerves	
Finger or thumb	45.00
Toe	30.00
Disarticulation of hip	240.00
Disarticulation of knee	120.00
Disarticulation of shoulder	225.00
Foot, midtarsal or transmetatarsal	105.00
Hand, midcarpal or transmetacarpal	120.00
Leg through tibia and fibula	150.00
Thigh through femur, including supracondylar	180.00
Bones	
Excision of bone cyst or chondroma:	
Humerus, radius, ulna, pelvis, femur, tibia, or fibula	150.00
Carpal or tarsal bones	75.00
Fractures, treatment of chip or avulsion fractures	15.00
Fractures, closed reduction or treatment of other than chip or avulsion fractures:	
Ankle	
bimalleolar (including Pott's), simple	75.00
trimalleolar, simple	90.00
Astragalus or os calcis, simple	60.00
Carpal, one or more, simple	30.00
Clavicle, simple	45.00
Femur	
distal end, condyle(s), or both, simple	105.00
intertrochanteric, simple, with fixation or traction	135.00
neck, simple, with fixation or traction	150.00
shaft, including supracondylar, simple	120.00
Fibula	
distal end, malleolus, or both	45.00
shaft, simple	45.00
with tibia, shafts, simple	90.00
Humerus	
medial or lateral condyle	60.00
shaft, simple	75.00
surgical neck, simple	90.00
*Malar, simple or compound	15.00

*The Maximum Payment applicable shall be increased by $6.00 if the operation is performed while hospital confined as an inpatient.

SCHEDULE OF SURGICAL OPERATIONS — Continued

(See Deductible Amount Provision)

	Maximum Payment
Maxilla or mandible, simple or compound, with wiring of teeth	$ 90.00
Metacarpal, simple or compound	
one	30.00
more than one	37.50
Metatarsal, simple	30.00
*Nasal, simple or compound	15.00
Patella, simple	36.00
Pelvis, simple	30.00
Phalanx or phalanges, simple, one finger, thumb, or toe	15.00
Radius	
head or distal end, simple	45.00
shaft, with or without ulna, simple	60.00
Ribs, one or more, simple	19.50
Scapula or sternum, simple	36.00
Tarsal (other than astragalus or os calcis)	
one or more, simple	30.00
Tibia	
distal end, malleolus, simple	45.00
shaft, or proximal end, with or without condyle(s), or intercondylar spines, simple	75.00
with fibula, shafts, simple	90.00
Ulna, shaft, with or without radius, simple	60.00
Vertebral body (other than sacrum), one or more	90.00
Vertebral processes, one or more	24.00
Spinal fusion, two or more segments	300.00
Joints	
Arthrectomy	
Excision of intervertebral disc, with spinal fusion	360.00
Excision of semilunar cartilage, knee joint	150.00
Temporomandibular joint	225.00
Arthrotomy or capsulotomy with exploration, drainage, or removal of loose body	
Finger, thumb, or great toe	45.00
Hip	210.00
Shoulder, elbow, knee or ankle	150.00
Toe, other than great toe	30.00
Dislocations, closed reduction of	
Ankle or tarsal, simple	30.00
Clavicle, simple, with general anesthesia	30.00
*Wrist, elbow or shoulder (humerus), simple	15.00
*Finger, one or more joints, simple	9.00
Hip (femur) or knee (femoral-tibial joint), simple	60.00
*Metacarpal, one bone, simple	9.00
Metatarsal, one bone, simple	21.00
Patella, simple	9.00
*Temporomandibular, simple	15.00
*Thumb, simple	12.00
*Toe, one or more joints, simple	6.00
Vertebra, simple, using traction and general anesthesia	165.00
Suture or repair of joint capsule for recurrent shoulder dislocation	210.00

	Maximum Payment
Tendons, Tendon Sheaths and Fascia	
Excision	
Baker's cyst (synovial cyst of popliteal space)	$ 90.00
Lesion of tendon or fibrous sheath, or ganglion	
finger, thumb, or toe	30.00
in other locations	45.00
Repair or suture	
Extensor tendon, single	
forearm or leg	54.00
hand or foot, distal to wrist or ankle	36.00
Flexor tendon, single, finger, hand, or forearm	90.00
Transfer, transplant, or free graft of tendon, single	
Elbow to shoulder, knee to hip	150.00
Distal to elbow, distal to knee	120.00

NERVOUS SYSTEM

	Maximum Payment
Craniectomy, suboccipital, for brain tumor	450.00
Craniectomy, suboccipital, for section of cranial nerves	375.00
Craniotomy for drainage of brain abscess	225.00
Laminectomy for removal of intervertebral discs	270.00
Skull, burr holes, one or more, for ventriculography	60.00
Splanchnicectomy, unilateral	195.00
Splanchnicectomy, bilateral	240.00
Sympathectomy, cervical, unilateral	180.00
Sympathectomy, lumbar, unilateral	165.00
Sympathectomy, lumbar, bilateral	225.00

RESPIRATORY SYSTEM

	Maximum Payment
Antrotomy	
Intranasal, unilateral	45.00
Intranasal, bilateral	75.00
Radical (Caldwell-Luc), unilateral	150.00
Radical (Caldwell-Luc), bilateral	195.00
Bronchoscopy	
Initial	45.00
Subsequent	30.00
With biopsy	60.00
With removal of foreign body or tumor	75.00
Laryngectomy, with neck dissection	420.00
Nasal polypectomy	
*Single polyp	9.00
Multiple polyps, unilateral or bilateral, one or more stages	21.00
Pneumonectomy or lobectomy	300.00
Pulmonary resection with concomitant thoracoplasty	450.00
Tracheotomy	60.00

URINARY SYSTEM

	Maximum Payment
Cystolithotomy	150.00
Cystoscopy, while resident hospital inpatient	
Diagnostic	24.00
With ureteral catheterization	45.00
Cystoscopy with biopsy	30.00
Excision or fulguration of urethral caruncle	21.00
Pyelotomy, pyelolithotomy, pelviolithotomy	210.00
Removal of kidney	240.00

*The Maximum Payment applicable shall be increased by $6.00 if the operation is performed while hospital confined as an inpatient.

Form No. MW 5767
[A3451]

BENEFIT PROVISIONS — Continued

Conversion Privilege — In the event that coverage under this policy expires with respect to any dependent child in accordance with the terms of General Provision 1(c) (iii), or with respect to the Insured's spouse, if so provided by an amendment to this policy in the event of divorce, such person shall, subject to the conditions hereinafter stated, be entitled to have issued to him without evidence of insurability a policy of insurance (hereinafter referred to as the "converted policy") by making written application therefor together with payment of the first premium to the Company, within 31 days after such expiration of insurance, except that the Company shall not be required to issue a converted policy if its issuance would result in overinsurance or duplication of benefits according to the Company's standards. The premium for the converted policy shall be that applicable on such policy's effective date to the class of risk to which such person belongs, to the age of such person and to the form and amount of insurance provided. The effective date of the converted policy shall be the date of such expiration of insurance under this policy.

The converted policy shall be either (1) a primary policy providing (a) a Daily Hospital Benefit (for room and board) of $10.00 per day for a maximum period of 90 days, (b) a Maximum Surgical Expense Benefit according to a $450.00 Schedule and (c) a Hospital Services Benefit up to an amount not exceeding $100.00 or (2) at the option of the applicant for conversion, an alternate policy on the form then being offered by the Company for conversion which most closely resembles the coverage afforded by this policy. The primary policy may exclude any condition to the extent excluded expressly or by the operation of any maximum payment limit in this policy with respect to such person at the time of the expiration of his insurance hereunder and shall not exclude any other pre-existing conditions with respect to such person. However, any benefits otherwise payable under the primary policy may be reduced by the amount of any such benefits paid for the same loss under this policy with respect to such person after the expiration of coverage hereunder.

If a converted policy is issued, it shall be on a form authorized for issue on its effective date in the jurisdiction in which the applicant for conversion then resides.

Maternity Benefit (if both Insured and Insured's spouse are covered family members) — If, while this policy is in force and a Maternity Benefit is specified on page 3, the Insured's spouse (or the Insured, if a woman) becomes confined as an inpatient in a hospital due to pregnancy which commences (a) more than 30 days after both the Insured and the Insured's spouse become covered family members under this policy and (b) while both the Insured and the Insured's spouse are covered family members, the Company will pay an amount equal to the actual hospital charges incurred on account of such pregnancy but the total amount payable under this Benefit with respect to any one pregnancy shall not exceed the following, whichever is applicable:

(a) when hospital confinement commences within 2 years after the date coverage becomes effective on both the Insured and the Insured's spouse —

for normal delivery	8	Times Maximum Amount of the Daily Hospital Benefit
for a Caesarean section or operation for ectopic pregnancy	12	
for an abortion or miscarriage	4	

(b) when hospital confinement commences after 2 years from the date coverage becomes effective on both the Insured and the Insured's spouse —

for normal delivery	12	Times Maximum Amount of the Daily Hospital Benefit
for a Caesarean section or operation for ectopic pregnancy	16	
for an abortion or miscarriage	6	

The Deductible Amount Provision does not apply to this Benefit.

If the Insured's spouse (or the Insured, if a woman) becomes confined as an inpatient in a hospital due to complications of such pregnancy, the Insured may elect to have the pregnancy treated as a sickness for the purpose of receiving benefits solely under the Hospital Expense Benefit, subject to the Deductible Amount Provision, in lieu of any benefits under this Benefit which is not reduced by the Deductible Amount. Such an election may be changed by the Insured in order that payment may be elected under this Benefit or the Hospital Expense Benefit, whichever produces the greater benefit, provided, however, that in no event shall benefits be payable under both this Benefit and the Hospital Expense Benefit in connection with any one pregnancy. Complications due to pregnancy shall be deemed to include, but are not limited to, toxemia of pregnancy, postpartum hemorrhage and thrombophlebitis, but an abortion or miscarriage or a surgical operation performed in connection with an ectopic pregnancy or for the delivery of a child or children (including a Caesarean section) shall not be deemed as such a complication.

EXCEPTIONS

1. This policy does not cover any charge incurred with respect to any covered family member, and no premium shall be waived for total disability, which is due to:

   (a) (i) Any injury sustained by any covered family member prior to the date such family member becomes covered under this policy, (ii) any sickness contracted by any covered family member prior to the date such family member becomes covered under this policy unless such sickness had not manifested itself prior to such date or (iii) any sickness contracted by any covered family member resulting from a physical condition existent prior to the date such family member becomes covered under this policy unless such physical condition had not manifested itself prior to such date (this Exception 1(a) does not apply to any newborn child automatically covered in accordance with General Provision 1(d), and is subject to paragraph (b) of General Provision 7, entitled "Incontestability");

   (b) Any injury or sickness caused or contributed to by war, whether declared or undeclared, or by an act of war;

   (c) Any injury sustained or sickness contracted by such covered family member while on full-time active duty (other than active duty for training purposes only for not more than 2

Form No. MW 5767

EXCEPTIONS — Continued

consecutive months) in the armed forces of any country, international organization, or combination of countries (see General Provision 4, entitled "Refund of Unearned Premiums");

(d) Intentionally self-inflicted injury while sane, or self-inflicted injury while insane; or

(e) Any injury or sickness for which benefits are payable under any workmen's compensation or occupational disease law.

2. This policy does not cover any charge incurred for or on account of (a) any hospital confinement which has not been recommended and approved by a legally qualified physician or (b) any surgical operation performed by other than a legally qualified physician.

3. This policy does not cover any charge incurred with respect to any covered family member (other than a newborn child automatically covered in accordance with paragraph (d) of General Provision 1, entitled "Covered Family Members") for or on account of hospital confinement which commences or surgical operation which is performed within 6 months after such covered family member becomes covered under this policy if such confinement or operation is (a) for repair of abdomnial hernia,

(b) for removal or treatment of hemorrhoids, (c) for removal of tonsils, or adenoids, or both, (d) for removal of appendix concurrent with a surgical operation on the female generative organs performed through the same incision, or (e) for treatment of or operation on the female generative organs.

4. This policy does not cover any charge incurred with respect to any covered family member:

(a) While such covered family member is confined in any hospital owned, contracted for, or operated by a national or provincial government, for or on account of the treatment of members or ex-members of the armed forces;

(b) Due to pregnancy, including resulting childbirth, abortion, miscarriage or any complication due to pregnancy, except to the extent that coverage is expressly provided therefor under a Maternity Benefit Provision, if any, of this policy;

(c) Which neither the Insured nor any other covered family member is legally obligated to pay; or

(d) To the extent that any such charge is covered under any national, state or other government plan which is not limited to civilian governmental employees or their families. In the event benefits are reduced in accordance with this paragraph (d), an appropriate adjustment will be made in the premium, or dividend participation.

GENERAL PROVISIONS

1. Covered Family Members —

(a) Eligibility — After this policy has been issued, the Insured, the Insured's spouse or any dependent child whose age, nearest birthday, is less than 18 years, if not then a covered family member, shall be eligible for coverage, provided such person is insurable in accordance with the underwriting standards of the Company.

(b) Additions — Any such eligible member of the Insured's family shall be added from time to time as a covered family member upon the Company's approval of the Insured's application for the coverage and such premium payment as the Company may require.

(c) Expiration of Coverage — Status as a covered family member shall expire automatically on the earliest date applicable to such family member as follows (except for the purpose of continuance of waiver of premiums — see the Benefit Provision entitled "Waiver of Premiums Benefit in Event of Total Disability"):

    (i) the Insured, if a covered family member, at the end of the day before the 65th birthday of the Insured;

    (ii) the Insured's spouse, if a covered family member, at the end of the day before the 65th birthday of the said spouse;

    (iii) any dependent child, if a covered family member, at the end of the day before the policy anniversary next following the earlier of (a) the 23rd birthday of said child and (b) the cessation of dependency on the Insured;

    (iv) a covered family member, upon entry on full-time active duty (other than active duty for training purposes only for not more than 2 consecutive months) in the armed forces of any country, international organization, or combination of countries;

    (v) a covered family member, upon becoming entitled to "Medicare" coverage under Title XVIII of the Social Security Act, as amended.

(d) Automatic Coverage — Any child born to the Insured's spouse (or to the Insured, if a woman) while this policy is in force and while both the Insured and the Insured's spouse are covered family members shall, upon the attainment of the age of 14 days, automatically become a covered family member if this policy is then in force and, if the policy remains in force, coverage shall remain in effect on such child without additional charge until the next policy anniversary. The Company will waive the requirement that the Insured's spouse be a covered family member at time of birth if his status as a covered family member has terminated by operation of paragraph (c) above, or if such spouse is not living but was a covered family member under this policy at the time of death. Unless written notice of the child's birth is received by the Company on or before the next policy anniversary and unless the policy is renewed as of said next anniversary date by payment before the end of the grace period of the appropriate renewal premium, which premium shall include an additional charge for coverage of the child, the child shall cease to be a covered family member on the 31st day following the next anniversary date.

(e) Ownership — The Insured shall be the person so designated on page 3 of this policy, provided, however, that if the Insured dies, the spouse, if then a covered family member under this policy, shall automatically become the Insured under this policy, and all references in this policy to the Insured shall thereafter mean such spouse.

2. Guaranteed Renewable to Age 65 — Company Can Change Table of Premiums — The Insured shall have the right to renew

GENERAL PROVISIONS — Continued

and continue this policy in force until the latest of (a) the 65th birthday of the Insured; (b) the 65th birthday of the Insured's spouse, if a covered family member; and (c) the latest date of expiration of coverage of all dependent children who are covered family members, but coverage shall be continued on any renewal only for those covered family members whose coverage does not expire under the terms of the policy.

Any such renewal may be made only at the expiration of a period for a further period of the same duration as the expiring period and shall be subject to payment before the end of the grace period of the appropriate renewal premium, according to the Company's applicable table of premium rates in effect at the time of such renewal. The Company will not unilaterally reduce any benefits otherwise payable, shorten any Benefit Period, nor place any restrictive rider on this policy in connection with any such renewal. However, the Company reserves the right to change at any time and from time to time the table of rates applicable to renewal premiums thereafter payable under this policy, provided always that the Company's applicable table of rates shall be classified only by original age at entry and sex and shall apply to all policies theretofore or thereafter issued on this policy form. No change in the table of premium rates shall take effect for this policy until the policy anniversary following the date of such change.

3. Payment of Premiums — Payment of the first premium shall maintain this policy in force from the Date of Issue until the next succeeding premium due date, subject to General Provision 8, entitled "Grace Period." Policy years, policy months and policy anniversaries shall be determined from the Date of Issue.

Each premium after the first is due at the expiration of the period for which the preceding premium was paid. Premiums are payable at the Home Office of the Company or to a duly authorized agent. Receipts will be delivered in exchange for premium payments and will be valid only if signed by the President or the Secretary, and countersigned by the agent designated thereon. Payment of a premium shall not maintain this policy in force beyond the period for which such premium is paid except as may be otherwise provided herein. No further premium shall be required for coverage of the Insured, if a covered family member, beyond the end of the last full policy month next preceding the 65th birthday of the Insured, nor for coverage of the Insured's spouse, if a covered family member, beyond the end of the last full policy month next preceding the 65th birthday of the Insured's spouse.

When coverage expires on a covered family member, the renewal premium for this policy shall be reduced to the appropriate premium for coverage of the remaining covered family member or members.

If the Company fails to reduce a premium which should be reduced because of expiration of any family member's coverage, that family member shall continue to be covered under the policy, notwithstanding any provision for automatic expiration of covered family membership, until the end of the period for which such premium was accepted, subject to General Provision 17, entitled "Misstatement of Age."

4. Refund of Unearned Premiums — Upon receipt of notice that any covered family member has died or that his status as a covered family member has terminated by operation of General Provision 1(c), the Company will refund the premium paid, if any, for the inclusion of such covered family member for any period beyond the end of the policy month in which such death occurred or in which such status as a covered family member terminated.

5. Dividend Participation — This policy, while it is in force, will be entitled to the share, if any, of the divisible surplus as the Company shall annually determine and apportion to it. Any share will be distributed as a dividend payable in cash at the end of each policy year beginning with the third.

6. Entire Contract; Changes — This policy, including the endorsements and the attached papers, if any, constitutes the entire contract of insurance. No change in this policy shall be valid until approved by an executive officer of the Company and unless such approval is endorsed on or attached to the policy. No agent has authority to change this policy or to waive any of its provisions.

7. Incontestability — (a) This policy shall be incontestable as to the statements concerning any covered family member contained in the application for this policy, or in any subsequent application for coverage of a family member, after coverage on such family member has been in effect for 2 years during the lifetime of the Insured (excluding any period during which such family member is disabled).

(b) No claim for loss incurred or disability with respect to any covered family member after 2 years from the date coverage on such family member became effective shall be reduced or denied on the ground that a disease or physical condition had existed before such date unless, effective on the date of loss, such disease or physical condition was excluded from coverage by name or specific description.

8. Grace Period — A grace period of 31 days will be granted for the payment of each premium falling due after the first premium, during which grace period the policy shall continue in force.

9. Reinstatement — If any renewal premium is not paid within the time granted the Insured for payment, a subsequent acceptance of premium by the Company or by any agent duly authorized by the Company to accept such premium, without requiring in connection therewith an application for reinstatement, shall reinstate the policy. However, if the Company requires an application for reinstatement and issues a conditional receipt for the premium tendered, the policy shall be reinstated upon approval of such application by the Company or, lacking such approval, upon the 45th day following the date of such conditional receipt unless the Company has previously notified the Insured in writing of its disapproval of such application.

The reinstated policy shall cover only loss resulting from such accidental injury as may be sustained after the date of reinstatement and loss due to such sickness as may begin after such date. In all other respects the Insured and Company shall have the same rights under this policy as they had immediately before the due date of the defaulted premium, subject to any provisions endorsed on or attached to this policy in connection with the reinstatement.

10. Notice of Claim — Written notice of claim of any loss covered by this policy, other than a claim for waiver of premiums, must be given to the Company within 30 days after the occurrence or commencement of any such loss or as soon thereafter as reasonably possible. Written notice of any claim for waiver of premiums

GENERAL PROVISIONS — Continued

under the Benefit Provision entitled "Waiver of Premiums Benefit in Event of Total Disability" must be furnished to the Company within 30 days after the date as of which the first premium to be waived is due. Notice given by or on behalf of the Insured to the Company at its Home Office, New York, New York, or to any authorized agent of the Company, with information sufficient to identify the Insured, shall be deemed notice to the Company.

11. Claim Forms — The Company, upon receipt of a notice of claim, will furnish to the claimant such forms as are usually furnished by it for filing proofs of loss. If such forms are not furnished within 15 days after the giving of such notice the claimant shall be deemed to have complied with the requirements of this policy as to proof of loss upon submitting, within the time fixed in the policy for filing proofs of loss, written proof covering the occurrence, the character and the extent of the loss for which claim is made.

12. Proofs of Loss — Written proof of loss must be furnished to the Company at its Home Office within 90 days after the date of such loss, except that with respect to any claim for waiver of premiums under the Benefit Provision entitled "Waiver of Premiums Benefit in Event of Total Disability," proof of loss must be furnished within 90 days after the due date of the premium to be waived. Failure to furnish such proof within the time required shall not invalidate nor reduce any claim if it was not reasonably possible to give proof within such time, provided such proof is furnished as soon as reasonably possible and in no event, except in the absence of legal capacity, later than one year from the time proof is otherwise required.

13. Time of Payment of Claims — Benefits payable under this policy for any loss will be paid immediately upon receipt of due written proof of such loss.

14. Payment of Claims — Any benefit payable under this policy will be payable to the Insured, or at the Insured's death, to the estate of the Insured.

If any benefit under this policy is payable to the estate of the Insured, or to an Insured who is a minor or otherwise not competent to give a valid release, the Company may pay such benefit, up to an amount not exceeding $1,000, to any relative by blood or marriage of the Insured who is deemed by the Company to be equitably entitled to it. Any payment made by the Company in good faith in accordance with this provision shall fully discharge the Company to the extent of such payment.

15. Physical Examinations — The Company at its own expense shall have the right and opportunity to examine the person of any covered family member when and as often as it may reasonably require during the pendency of a claim under this policy.

16. Legal Actions — No action at law or in equity shall be brought to recover on this policy prior to the expiration of 60 days after written proof of loss has been furnished in accordance with the requirements of this policy. No such action shall be brought after the expiration of 3 years after the time written proof of loss is required to be furnished.

17. Misstatement of Age — If the age of any covered family member has been misstated, all amounts payable under this policy with respect to such person shall be such as the premium paid for the coverage of such person would have purchased at the correct age.

If, as a result of misstatement of the age of any covered family member, the Company accepts any premium or premiums for a period or periods beyond the date the coverage of any or all such persons would have ceased according to the correct ages, or if, according to the correct ages, the coverage provided by this policy for any or all such persons would not have become effective, then the liability of the Company with respect to such person or persons for the period during which their coverage would not have been effective shall be limited to the refund, upon request, of such amount, if any, by which the premium or premiums paid to the Company were increased on account of the coverage of such person or persons for such period.

18. Conformity with State Statutes — Any provision of this policy which, on its effective date, is in conflict with the statutes of the state in which the Insured resides on such date is hereby amended to conform to the minimum requirements of such statutes.

19. Assignment — The Company will not be on notice of any assignment unless it is in writing, nor until a duplicate of the original assignment has been filed at the Home Office of the Company. The Company assumes no responsibility for the validity or sufficiency of any assignment.

20. Termination of Policy — This policy will terminate on the earliest of (a) the first premium due date on which no person occupies the status of Insured, (b) the end of the grace period of 31 days after the due date of the first unpaid premium, and (c) the latest date of expiration of coverage of all covered family members.

Form No. MW 5767
[A3455]

ENDORSEMENTS

(To be made only by the Company at its Home Office in New York, New York.)

SPECIMEN

COPY OF APPLICATION

NOTE — This copy should be carefully examined and if any error or omission is found, full particulars, with the number of this policy, should be sent immediately to the Home Office of the Company, New York, New York.

Form No. MW 5767

THE HEALTH INSURANCE COMPANY

HOME OFFICE — NEW YORK

HOSPITAL EXPENSE POLICY

Countersigned (When required by law or regulation)

Date_____ _____
Resident Licensed Agent

In case of any question about this policy, write the Company at its Home Office, New York, New York, or any Agency of the Company.

SPECIMEN

THE HEALTH INSURANCE COMPANY

HOME OFFICE — NEW YORK

Insured

First Premium

Policy Number

Date of Issue

SCHEDULE OF BENEFITS

Maximum Benefit $10,000 for one injury or one sickness

Specific limits applicable to the following covered Medical Expenses:
Hospital Room and Board — $30 per day
Nursing Home Care — $15.00 per day (but for not more than 30 days)
Surgical Operations — $1,500 per operation (including related operations)

Percentages of Covered Medical Expenses Payable — subject to applicable limits:
None of First $750
75% of Next $10,000

Deductible Amount — $750

    The Health Insurance Company agrees to provide the benefits stated in this policy, subject to the provisions, conditions, exceptions and limitations set forth on this and the following pages, including the Policy Specifications above, all of which are a part of this contract. Among the exceptions from coverage are 1) charges incurred while confined in certain hospitals or other facilities provided by the government, (2) charges covered under government plans, and (3) any charges or disability which are due to any injury or sickness for which benefits are payable under any workmen's compensation or occupational disease law, all as set forth fully in the Exceptions provision of this policy.

    This policy is issued in consideration of the application, a copy of which is attached and made a part hereof, and of the payment of the first premium on or before the delivery of the policy and the payment of subsequent premiums as herein provided.

    Covered family members under this policy on its Date of Issue are the family members named in the application and accepted for insurance coverage. Commencement and termination of status as Insured or covered family member and addition of new covered family members are subject to General Provision 1.

GUARANTEED RENEWABLE TO AGE 65 — COMPANY CAN CHANGE TABLE OF PREMIUMS

    The Insured shall have the right to renew and continue this policy in force, in accordance with General Provision 2, until the latest of (a) the 65th birthday of the Insured; (b) the 65th birthday of the Insured's spouse, if a covered family member; and (c) the latest date of expiration of coverage of all dependent children who are covered family members, but coverage shall be continued on any renewal only for those covered family members whose coverage does not expire upon becoming entitled to "Medicare" coverage, or for any other reason, as set forth fully in General Provision 1(c). The Company reserves the right to change from time to time the table of rates applicable to renewal premiums but only on the basis indicated in General Provision 2.

Right of Policy Examination — If the Insured is not satisfied with this policy, it may be surrendered by delivering or mailing it within ten days after receipt by the Insured to the Company at New York, New York, or to the agent or agency office through which it was delivered. Immediately upon such delivering or mailing, the policy shall be deemed void from the beginning and any premium paid on it will be refunded.

    Signed for the Company at New York, New York.

A.B. Risk
Secretary

C.D. Carrier
President

MAJOR MEDICAL EXPENSE POLICY

DEFINITIONS

Wherever used in this policy:

"Injury" means only accidental bodily injury sustained by any covered family member while such family member is covered under this policy. "One injury" means every injury and all injuries resulting from one accident.

"Sickness" means only sickness or disease of any covered family member, which is contracted and commences while such family member is covered under this policy, or which first manifests itself while such family member is covered under this policy. "One sickness" means every sickness and all sicknesses (including recurrences) resulting from the same or related causes or conditions.

"Hospital" means only an institution operated pursuant to law for the care and treatment of sick and injured persons, which institution provides 24 hour nursing care and has facilities both for diagnosis, and, except in the case of a hospital primarily concerned with the treatment of chronic diseases, for major surgery. The term "hospital" shall not be construed to include a hotel, rest home, nursing home, convalescent home, place for custodial care, home for the aged, or a place for the confinement or treatment of drug addicts or alcoholics.

"Nursing home" means only an institution which (1) provides care for sick and injured persons, (2) complies with all licensing laws and regulations applicable to nursing homes, (3) has facilities for the care of 5 or more resident patients, (4) has available the services of a legally qualified physician, (5) provides continuous nursing care under the 24 hour a day supervision of a graduate registered nurse who is entitled to affix the initials "R.N." to her name and (6) is not primarily a hotel, rest home, place for custodial care, home for the aged, or a place for the confinement or treatment of drug addicts or alcoholics.

"Inpatient" means only a person who is confined in a hospital as a resident patient and who is charged at least one day's room and board by the hospital.

"Deductible Amount" means only the applicable amount so specified on page 3 of this policy which is subtracted from the sum of the Covered Medical Expenses incurred with respect to a covered family member during any Benefit Period under this policy.

"Maximum Benefit" and "Specific Limit" mean only the applicable amounts specified on page 3 of this policy.

BENEFIT PROVISIONS

Major Medical Benefit

. The Company will pay, subject to the Maximum Benefit provision, the applicable percentages (specified on page 3 of this policy) of the Covered Medical Expenses in excess of the Deductible Amount, which are incurred during a covered family member's Benefit Period and on account of the one injury or the one sickness of such covered family member, for which such Benefit Period was established. Covered Medical Expenses shall be deemed incurred when the applicable treatment, services or supplies are furnished, performed or received.

Covered Medical Expenses — Covered Medical Expenses are only the charges incurred for the following treatments, services and supplies provided for the medical and surgical care and treatment of an injury or sickness of a covered family member to the extent prescribed as necessary by the attending physician, except charges that are specifically excluded from coverage under the Exceptions provision of this policy, but in no event shall Covered Medical Expenses exceed the regular and customary charges for such treatments, services and supplies in the locality where provided:

1. Medical treatment (other than surgical operations including pre-operative and post-operative care) by a legally qualified physician;

2. Surgical operations (including pre-operative and post-operative care) by legally qualified physicians, but not exceeding for any one operation or series of related operations the Specific Limit for Surgical Operations;

3. Hospital room and board, including routine services and general nursing care, but not exceeding the Specific Limit for Hospital Room and Board;

4. Medical services and supplies provided by a hospital, other than room, board, routine services and general nursing care;

5. Nursing home care, including room and board, routine services and general nursing care, for not more than 30 days during any Benefit Period, provided the confinement in the nursing home commences within 7 days after a period of hospital confinement as an inpatient of at least 7 consecutive days, but in no event for an amount exceeding the Specific Limit for Nursing Home Care;

6. Drugs or medicines prescribed by a legally qualified physician;

7. Private duty nursing care:
   (a) in a hospital — full-time private duty special nursing services in a hospital by a licensed practical nurse or a graduate registered nurse who is entitled to affix the initials "R.N." to her name, but not including the services of a parent, spouse, brother, sister or child of any covered family member;
   (b) not in a hospital — three-fourths of the charges for full-time private duty special nursing services by a graduate registered nurse who is entitled to affix the initials "R.N." to her name, but not including the services of a parent, spouse, brother, sister or child of any covered family member or a nurse regularly employed by the nursing home where confined; and

8. Other treatments, services and supplies as follows:
   (a) local transportation by professional ambulance service to or from a local hospital;
   (b) artificial limbs or eyes;
   (c) casts, splints, trusses, braces or crutches;
   (d) oxygen and the rental of equipment for the administration thereof;
   (e) the rental of a wheel chair, of a hospital-type bed, of an iron lung or of other mechanical equipment required for the treatment of respiratory paralysis;
   (f) X-ray services;
   (g) laboratory tests;
   (h) the use of radium and radio-active isotopes;
   (i) physiotherapy;
   (j) anesthetics and the administration thereof; and
   (k) blood or blood plasma and the administration thereof.

Form No. MW 5667
[A3459]

BENEFIT PROVISIONS — Continued

Expense Requirement — To establish each Benefit Period for a covered family member, the respective covered family member must satisfy the Expense Requirement which shall be the requirement (a) that Covered Medical Expenses at least equal to the Deductible Amount be incurred with respect to such family member within a period of 180 consecutive days because of one injury or one sickness and (b) that such Covered Medical Expenses be incurred while this policy is in force and while coverage on such family member is in effect.

Benefit Period — A Benefit Period shall be the 3 year period beginning on the earliest date that the covered family member incurs any Covered Medical Expenses applied to satisfy the Expense Requirement establishing that Benefit Period.

If a Benefit Period has been established in connection with one injury or one sickness, Covered Medical Expenses incurred during such Benefit Period for treatment of the one injury or the one sickness cannot be used to satisfy the Expense Requirement again nor to establish a new Benefit Period.

After the expiration of any Benefit Period established in connection with one injury or one sickness, a new Benefit Period shall be established for the covered family member if Covered Medical Expenses for the treatment of the same one injury or the same one sickness are incurred thereafter so as to satisfy again the Expense Requirement, provided that the total amount payable for the prior and succeeding Benefit Periods shall be subject to the Maximum Benefit provision. The Deductible Amount shall be subtracted from the sum of Covered Medical Expenses incurred during such new Benefit Period.

Maximum Benefit — The total amount payable on account of one injury or one sickness of the covered family member shall not exceed the Maximum Benefit whether the Covered Medical Expenses are incurred during one Benefit Period or during several Benefit Periods. However, payment of the Maximum Benefit on account of any one injury or one sickness shall not preclude the payment of additional benefits because of an injury resulting from another accident or because of a sickness the cause of which is entirely unrelated to the one sickness for which the Maximum Benefit was paid.

Limited Benefit for Mental Sickness — The Company will pay the applicable percentages (specified on page 3 of this policy) of the Covered Medical Expenses in excess of the Deductible Amount, which are incurred on account of treatment of a mental sickness (including psychoneurosis and psychosis) of a covered family member while confined as an inpatient in a hospital, during such covered family member's Benefit Period established on account of such mental sickness, provided, however, that in no event shall the aggregate amount payable for all Covered Medical Expenses incurred on account of mental sicknesses of the covered family member exceed 25% of the Maximum Benefit.

Benefit for Complications Incident to Pregnancy — If charges are incurred with respect to the Insured's spouse (or to the Insured, if a woman) for treatment of complications incident to a pregnancy that begins while this policy is in force and while coverage on both the Insured and the Insured's spouse is in effect, the excess of (a) charges that are made in connection with such treatment and that, in all other respects, would be Covered Medical Expenses over (b)

the customary charges that would be incurred in connection with a normal pregnancy and childbirth shall be regarded as Covered Medical Expenses. A surgical procedure (including a caesarean section) for the delivery of a child or children shall not be considered a complication incident to pregnancy.

Benefit for Covered Family Members Involved in Same Accident or Contracting Same Contagious Disease — If Covered Medical Expenses are incurred with respect to two or more covered family members as a result of the same accident or as the result of contracting the same contagious disease within 30 days of each other, the Covered Medical Expenses shall be combined and considered as though they were incurred with respect to one covered family member. If the Expense Requirement is thereby satisfied, it shall be considered as satisfied for all such covered family members. The Benefit Periods for such covered family members shall thereupon commence simultaneously on the earliest date that any such Covered Medical Expenses are incurred. Only one Deductible Amount shall be subtracted from such combined Covered Medical Expenses in computing benefits payable. In other respects, the terms of the Major Medical Benefit provision shall apply to each covered family member separately.

Waiver of Premiums Benefit in Event of Total Disability

The Company will waive payment of the premium under this policy upon receipt at its Home Office of due proof that (1) an adult male covered family member, who is either the Insured or the Insured's spouse, is totally disabled on the premium due date as a result of injury or sickness, (2) such adult male was a covered family member both at the time the disability began and during the entire 6 months immediately preceding the date of the premium to be waived and that (3) such total disability has been continuous for the 6 months immediately preceding the date of the premium to be waived, and if such covered family member is over age 60 on the premium due date, such total disability commenced before such covered family member's 60th birthday and has been continuous since that date; and provided, however, that no premium payment shall be waived which is payable for any person who is not covered under this policy as of the date such covered family member becomes totally disabled. For the purpose of waiver of premiums only, such adult family member shall be deemed to be a covered family member although his status as a covered family member has otherwise terminated in accordance with General Provision 1(c)(i), 1(c)(ii) or 1(c)(v).

The phrase "total disability" means (a) such complete incapacity of such covered family member that he is able to perform none of the duties of any and every occupation, business or employment for remuneration or profit for which he is reasonably fitted by education, training or experience, except that total disability shall be deemed not to exist while such covered family member is engaged in any occupation, business or employment for remuneration or profit, or (b) the total loss by such covered family member of the use of both hands or both feet or one hand and one foot or the total and irrecoverable loss of the sight of both eyes.

No premiums shall be waived under this provision as of any premium due date on which such covered family member is not living or is not under the regular care and treatment of a legally qualified physician other than such covered member himself.

BENEFIT PROVISIONS — Continued

Waiver of premiums shall be in accordance with the interval of premium payment in effect when total disability commences.

If a premium becomes due and is not waived in accordance with this provision after one or more premiums have been so waived, the Insured shall have the right to pay such premium in accordance with and subject to the terms of this policy.

Conversion Privilege — In the event that coverage under this policy expires with respect to any dependent child in accordance with the terms of General Provision 1(c)(iii), or with respect to the Insured's spouse, if so provided by an amendment to this policy in the event of divorce, such person shall, subject to the conditions hereinafter stated, be entitled to have issued to him without evidence of insurability a policy of insurance (hereinafter referred to as the "converted policy") by making written application therefor together with payment of the first premium to the Company, within 31 days after such expiration of insurance, except that the Company shall not be required to issue a converted poilcy if its issuance would result in overinsurance or duplication of benefits according to the Company's standards. The premium for the converted policy shall be that applicable on such policy's effective date to the class of risk to which such person belongs, to the age of such person and to the form and amount of insurance provided. The effective date of

the converted policy shall be the date of such expiration of insurance under this policy.

The converted policy shall be either (1) a primary policy providing (a) a Daily Hospital Benefit (for room and board) of $10.00 per day for a maximum period of 90 days, (b) a Maximum Surgical Expense Benefit according to a $450.00 Schedule and (c) a Hospital Services Benefit up to an amount not exceeding $100.00 or (2) at the option of the applicant for conversion, an alternate policy on the form then being offered by the Company for conversion which most closely resembles the coverage afforded by this policy. The primary policy may exclude any condition to the extent excluded expressly or by the operation of any maximum payment limit in this policy with respect to such person at the time of the expiration of his insurance hereunder and shall not exclude any other pre-existing conditions with respect to such person. However, any benefits otherwise payable under the primary policy may be reduced by the amount of any such benefits paid for the same loss under this policy with respect to such person after the expiration of coverage hereunder.

If a converted policy is issued, it shall be on a form authorized for issue on its effective date in the jurisdiction in which the applicant for conversion then resides.

EXCEPTIONS

1. This policy does not cover any charge incurred with respect to any covered family member, and no premium shall be waived for total disability, which is due to:
   (a) (i) Any injury sustained by any covered family member prior to the date such family member becomes covered under this policy, (ii) any sickness contracted by any covered family member prior to the date such family member becomes covered under this policy unless such sickness had not manifested itself prior to such date or (iii) any sickness contracted by any covered family member resulting from a physical condition existent prior to the date such family member becomes covered under this policy unless such physical condition had not manifested itself prior to such date (this Exception 1(a) does not apply to any newborn child automatically covered in accordance with General Provision 1(d), and is subject to paragraph (b) of General Provision 7, entitled "Incontestability");
   (b) Any injury or sickness caused or contributed to by war, whether declared or undeclared, or by an act of war;
   (c) Any injury sustained or sickness contracted by such covered family member while on full-time active duty (other than active duty for training purposes only for not more than 2 consecutive months) in the armed forces of any country, international organization, or combination of countries (see General Provision 4, entitled "Refund of Unearned Premiums");
   (d) Intentionally self-inflicted injury while sane, or self-inflicted injury while insane;
   (e) Alcoholism or drug addiction; or
   (f) Any injury or sickness for which benefits are payable under any workmen's compensation or occupational disease law.

2. This policy does not cover any charge incurred due to:

   (a) Medical or surgical care or treatment of mental sickness (including psychoneuroses and psychoses), except as provided in the Benefit Provision entitled "Limited Benefit for Mental Sickness";
   (b) Dental work or dental X-rays, except where required because of injury to natural teeth;
   (c) Cosmetic surgery, except where performed to correct a condition resulting from injury or a congenital anomaly in a child automatically covered in accordance with General Provision 1(d); or
   (d) Hearing aids or eye glasses, or the fitting thereof, unless to correct a condition resulting from injury.

3. This policy does not cover any charge incurred with respect to any covered family member:
   (a) While such covered family member is confined in any hospital owned, contracted for, or operated by a national or provincial government, for or on account of the treatment of members or ex-members of the armed forces;
   (b) Due to pregnancy, including childbirth, abortion, miscarriage, or any complication due to pregnancy, except to the extent, if any, that coverage is provided under the Benefit Provision entitled "Benefit for Complications Incident to Pregnancy";
   (c) Which neither the Insured nor any other covered family member is legally obligated to pay; or
   (d) To the extent that the costs of the treatment, services or supplies for which the charge is incurred are covered under any national, state or other government plan which is not limited to civilian governmental employees or their families. In the event benefits are reduced in accordance with this paragraph (d), an appropriate adjustment will be made in the premium, or dividend participation.

20

Form No. MW 5667
[A3461]

GENERAL PROVISIONS

1. Covered Family Members —

(a) Eligibility — After this policy has been issued, the Insured, the Insured's spouse or any dependent child whose age, nearest birthday, is less than 18 years, if not then a covered family member, shall be eligible for coverage, provided such person is insurable in accordance with the underwriting standards of the Company.

(b) Additions — Any such eligible member of the Insured's family shall be added from time to time as a covered family member upon the Company's approval of the Insured's application for the coverage and such premium payment, if any, as the Company may require.

(c) Expiration of Coverage — Status as a covered famliy member shall expire automatically on the earliest date applicable to such family member as follows (except for the purpose of continuance of waiver of premiums — see the Benefit Provision entitled "Waiver of Premiums Benefit in Event of Total Disability"):

(i) the Insured, if a covered family member, at the end of the day before the 65th birthday of the Insured;

(ii) the Insured's spouse, if a covered family member, at the end of the day before the 65th birthday of the said spouse;

(iii) any dependent child, if a covered family member, at the end of the day before the policy anniversary next following the earlier of (a) the 23rd birthday of said child and (b) the cessation of dependency on the Insured;

(iv) a covered family member, upon entry on full-time active duty (other than active duty for training purposes only for not more than 2 consecutive months) in the armed forces of any country, international organization, or combination of countries;

(v) a covered family member upon becoming entitled to "Medicare" coverage under Title XVIII of the Social Security Act, as amended.

(d) Automatic Coverage — Any child born to the Insured's spouse (or to the Insured, if a woman) while this policy is in force and while both the Insured and the Insured's spouse are covered family members shall, at birth, automatically become a covered family member and, if the policy remains in force, coverage shall remain in effect on such child without additional charge until the next policy anniversary. The Company will waive the requirement that the Insured's spouse be a covered family member at time of birth if his status as a covered family member has terminated by operation of paragraph (c) above, or if such spouse is not living but was a covered family member under this policy at the time of death. Unless written notice of the child's birth is received by the Company on or before the next policy anniversary and unless the policy is renewed as of said next anniversary date by payment before the end of the grace period of the appropriate renewal premium, which premium shall include an additional charge for coverage of the child is required under General Provision 3, the child shall cease to be a covered family member on the 31st day following the next anniversary date.

(e) Ownership — The Insured shall be the person so designated on page 3 of this policy, provided, however, that if the Insured dies, the spouse, if then a covered family member under this policy, shall automatically become the Insured under this policy, and all references in this policy to the Insured shall thereafter mean such spouse.

2. Guaranteed Renewable to Age 65 — Company Can Change Table of Premiums — The Insured shall have the right to renew and continue this policy in force until the latest of (a) the 65th birthday of the Insured; (b) the 65th birthday of the Insured's spouse, if a covered family member; and (c) the latest date of expiration of coverage of all dependent children who are covered family members, but coverage shall be continued on any renewal only for those covered family members whose coverage does not expire under the terms of the policy.

Any such renewal may be made only at the expiration of a period for a further period of the same duration as the expiring period and shall be subject to payment before the end of the grace period of the appropriate renewal premium, according to the Company's applicable table of premium rates in effect at the time of such renewal. The Company will not unilaterally reduce any benefits otherwise payable, shorten any Benefit Period, nor place any restrictive rider on this policy in connection with any such renewal. However, the Company reserves the right to change at any time and from time to time the table of rates applicable to renewal premiums thereafter payable under this policy, provided always that the Company's applicable table of rates shall be classified only by original age at entry and sex and shall apply to all policies theretofore or thereafter issued on this policy form. No change in the table of premium rates shall take effect for this policy until the policy anniversary following the date of such change.

3. Payment of Premiums — Payment of the first premium shall maintain this policy in force from the Date of Issue until the next succeeding premium due date, subject to General Provision 8, entitled "Grace Period". Policy years, policy months and policy anniversaries shall be determined from the Date of Issue.

Each premium after the first is due at the expiration of the period for which the preceding premium was paid. Premiums are payable at the Home Office of the Company or to a duly authorized agent. Receipts will be delivered in exchange for premium payments and will be valid only if signed by the President or the Secretary, and countersigned by the agent designated thereon. Payment of a premium shall not maintain this policy in force beyond the period for which such premium is paid except as may be otherwise provided herein. No further premium shall be required for coverage of the Insured, if a covered family member, beyond the end of the last full policy month next preceding the 65th birthday of the Insured, nor for coverage of the Insured's spouse, if a covered family member, beyond the end of the last full policy month next preceding the 65th birthday of the Insured's spouse.

For any period during which one or more children (exclusive of any newborn child while automatically covered to the policy anniversary next following its birth under General Provision 1(d), are covered family members, a premium charge shall be made for the

GENERAL PROVISIONS — Continued

coverage of such child or children, which charge shall be the same whether one child or several children are covered family members. When coverage expires on a covered family member who is the Insured or the Insured's spouse, the renewal premium for this policy shall be reduced to the appropriate premium for coverage of the remaining covered family member or members. The premium charge made for the coverage of children shall not be reduced prior to the policy anniversary on which the last child ceased to be a covered family member under this policy.

If the Company fails to reduce a premium which should be reduced because of expiration of any family member's coverage, that family member shall continue to be covered under the policy, notwithstanding any provision for automatic expiration of covered family membership, until the end of the period for which such premium was accepted, subject to General Provision 17, entitled "Misstatement of Age".

4. Refund of Unearned Premiums — Upon receipt of notice that any covered family member has died or that his status as a covered family member has terminated by operation of General Provision 1(c), the Company will refund the premium paid, if any, for the inclusion of such covered family member for any period beyond the end of the policy month in which such death occurred or in which such status as a covered family member terminated.

5. Dividend Participation — This policy, while it is in force, will be entitled to the share, if any, of the divisible surplus as the Company shall annually determine and apportion to it. Any share will be distributed as a dividend payable in cash at the end of each policy year beginning with the third.

6. Entire Contract; Changes — This policy, including the endorsements and the attached papers, if any, constitutes the entire contract of insurance. No change in this policy shall be valid until approved by an executive officer of the Company and unless such approval is endorsed on or attached to the policy. No agent has authority to change this policy or to waive any of its provisions.

7. Incontestability — (a) This policy shall be incontestable as to the statements concerning any covered family member contained in the application for this policy, or in any subsequent application for coverage of a family member, after coverage on such family member has been in effect for 2 years during the lifetime of the Insured (excluding any period during which such family member is disabled).

(b) No claim for loss incurred or disability with respect to any covered family member after 2 years from the date coverage on such family member became effective shall be reduced or denied on the ground that a disease or physical condition had existed before such date unless, effective on the date of loss, such disease or physical condition was excluded from coverage by name or specific description.

8. Grace Period — A grace period of 31 days will be granted for the payment of each premium falling due after the first premium, during which grace period the policy shall continue in force.

9. Reinstatement — If any renewal premium is not paid within the time granted the Insured for payment, a subsequent acceptance of premium by the Company or by any agent duly authorized by the Company to accept such premium, without requiring in connection therewith an application for reinstatement, shall reinstate the policy. However, if the Company requires an application for reinstatement and issues a conditional receipt for the premium tendered, the policy shall be reinstated upon approval of such application by the Company or, lacking such approval, upon the 45th day following the date of such conditional receipt unless the Company has previously notified the Insured in writing of its disapproval of such application.

The reinstated policy shall cover only loss resulting from such accidental injury as may be sustained after the date of reinstatement and loss due to such sickness as may begin after such date. In all other respects the Insured and Company shall have the same rights under this policy as they had immediately before the due date of the defaulted premium, subject to any provisions endorsed on or attached to this policy in connection with the reinstatement.

10. Notice of Claim — Written notice of claim of any loss covered by this policy, other than a claim for waiver of premiums, must be given to the Company within 30 days after the occurrence or commencement of any such loss or as soon thereafter as reasonably possible. Written notice of any claim for waiver of premiums under the Benefit Provision entitled "Waiver of Premiums Benefit in Event of Total Disability" must be furnished to the Company within 30 days after the date as of which the first premium to be waived is due. Notice given by or on behalf of the Insured to the Company at its Home Office, New York, New York, or to any authorized agent of the Company, with information sufficient to identify the Insured, shall be deemed notice to the Company.

11. Claim Forms — The Company, upon receipt of a notice of claim, will furnish to the claimant such forms as are usually furnished by it for filing proofs of loss. If such forms are not furnished within 15 days after the giving of such notice the claimant shall be deemed to have complied with the requirements of this policy as to proof of loss upon submitting, within the time fixed in the policy for filing proofs of loss, written proof covering the occurrence, the character and the extent of the loss for which claim is made.

12. Proofs of Loss — Written proof of loss must be furnished to the Company at its Home Office within 90 days after the date of such loss, except that with respect to any claim for waiver of premiums under the Benefit Provision entitled "Waiver of Premiums Benefit in Event of Total Disability", proof of loss must be furnished within 90 days after the due date of the premium to be waived. Failure to furnish such proof within the time required shall not invalidate nor reduce any claim if it was not reasonably possible to give proof within such time, provided such proof is furnished as soon as reasonably possible and in no event, except in the absence of legal capacity, later than one year from the time proof is otherwise required.

Form No. MW 5667
[A3463]

GENERAL PROVISIONS — Continued

13. Time of Payment of Claims — Benefits payable under this policy for any loss will be paid immediately upon receipt of due written proof of such loss.

14. Payment of Claims — Any benefit payable under this policy will be payable to the Insured or, at the Insured's death, to the estate of the Insured.

If any benefit under this policy is payable to the estate of the Insured, or to an Insured who is a minor or otherwise not competent to give a valid release, the Company may pay such benefit, up to an amount not exceeding $1,000, to any relative by blood or marriage of the Insured who is deemed by the Company to be equitably entitled to it. Any payment made by the Company in good faith in accordance with this provision shall fully discharge the Company to the extent of such payment.

15. Physical Examinations — The Company at its own expense shall have the right and opportunity to examine the person of any covered family member when and as often as it may reasonably require during the pendency of a claim under this policy.

16. Legal Actions — No action at law or in equity shall be brought to recover on this policy prior to the expiration of 60 days after written proof of loss has been furnished in accordance with the requirements of this policy. No such action shall be brought after the expiration of 3 years after the time written proof of loss is required to be furnished.

17. Misstatement of Age — If the age of any covered family member has been misstated, all amounts payable under this policy with respect to such person shall be such as the premium paid for

the coverage of such person would have purchased at the correct age.

If, as a result of misstatement of the age of any covered family member, the Company accepts any premium or premiums for a period or periods beyond the date the coverage of any or all such persons would have ceased according to the correct ages, or if, according to the correct ages, the coverage provided by this policy for any or all such persons would not have become effective, then the liability of the Company with respect to such person or persons for the period during which their coverage would not have been effective shall be limited to the refund, upon request, of such amount, if any, by which the premium or premiums paid to the Company were increased on account of the coverage of such person or persons for such period.

18. Conformity with State Statutes — Any provision of this policy which, on its effective date, is in conflict with the statutes of the state in which the Insured resides on such date is hereby amended to conform to the minimum requirements of such statutes.

19. Assignment — The Company will not be on notice of any assignment unless it is in writing, nor until a duplicate of the original assignment has been filed at the Home Office of the Company. The Company assumes no responsibility for the validity or sufficiency of any assignment.

20. Termination of Policy — This policy will terminate on the earliest of (a) the first premium due date on which no person occupies the status of Insured, (b) the end of the grace period of 31 days after the due date of the first unpaid premium, and (c) the latest date of expiration of coverage of all covered family members.

ENDORSEMENTS

(To be made only by the Company at its Home Office in New York, New York.)

COPY OF APPLICATION

NOTE — This copy should be carefully examined and if any error or omission is found, full particulars, with the number of this policy, should be sent immediately to the Home Office of the Company, New York, New York.

THE HEALTH INSURANCE COMPANY

HOME OFFICE — NEW YORK

MAJOR MEDICAL EXPENSE POLICY

Countersigned (When required by law or regulation)

Date_____   _____

Resident Licensed Agent

150   Form No. MW 5667
[A3465]

APPENDIX G—General Liability—Automobile
Policy Form *

```
══════════════ GENERAL LIABILITY-AUTOMOBILE POLICY ══════════════

No. GLA                                          CAPITAL STOCK COMPANY
RENEWAL OF NUMBER


        SPACE FOR COMPANY NAME, INSIGNIA, AND LOCATION


DECLARATIONS
Item 1.  Named Insured and Address:   (No., Street, Town or City, County, State)
                                                    SPACE FOR
                                                PRODUCER'S NAME AND
                                                 MAILING ADDRESS

Item 2.  Policy Period:   (Mo. Day Yr.)
From                        to
        12:01 A.M., standard time at the address of the named insured as stated herein.
```

The **named insured** is:

☐ Individual   ☐ Partnership   ☐ Corporation   ☐ Joint Venture   ☐ Other: _____

Business of the **named insured** is: (ENTER BELOW)   Audit Period: Annual, unless otherwise stated. (ENTER BELOW)

Item 3. The insurance afforded is only with respect to the Coverage Part(s) indicated below by specific premium charge(s) and attached to and forming a part of this policy.

Advance Premiums	Coverage Part No(s).	Coverage Part(s)	Advance Premiums	Coverage Part No(s).	Coverage Part(s)
$		Automobile Medical Payments Insurance	$		Manufacturers' and Contractors' Liability Insurance
$		Automobile Physical Damage Insurance (Dealers)			
			$		Owner's and Contractor's Protective Liability Insurance
$		Automobile Physical Damage Insurance (Fleet Automatic)			
			$		Owners', Landlords' and Tenants' Liability Insurance
$		Automobile Physical Damage Insurance (Non-Fleet)			
			$		Personal Injury Liability Insurance
$		Completed Operations and Products Liability Insurance	$		Physicians', Surgeons' and Dentists' Professional Liability Insurance
$		Comprehensive Automobile Liability Insurance	$		Premises Medical Payments Insurance
$		Comprehensive General Liability Insurance	$		Protection Against Uninsured Motorists Insurance
$		Comprehensive Personal Insurance	$		Special Protective and Highway Liability Insurance New York Department of Transportation
$		Contractual Liability Insurance			
$		Druggists' Liability Insurance	$		Storekeeper's Insurance
$		Elevator Collision Insurance	$		
$		Farm Employers' Liability and Farm Employees' Medical Payments Insurance			
$		Farmer's Comprehensive Personal Insurance	$		
$		Farmer's Medical Payments Insurance			
$		Garage Insurance	$		
$		Hospital Professional Liability Insurance			
					Form numbers of endorsements, other than those entered on Coverage Part(s), attached at issue
$					
$		Total Advance Premium for this policy.			

* If the Policy Period is more than one year and the premium is to be paid in installments, premium is payable on:

Effective Date	1st Anniversary	2nd Anniversary
$	$	$

Item 4. During the past three years no insurer has cancelled insurance, issued to the **named insured**, similar to that afforded hereunder, unless otherwise stated herein:

Countersigned:

*Not applicable in Texas

OKP6300—1—E
(2-1-66)

By_____
Ptd. in U.S.A.   Authorized Representative

[A3466]

* Reproduced with permission of the Insurance Information Institute.

```
┌─────────────────────────────────────────────────────────────────┐
│            RESERVED FOR YOUR COMPANY'S NAME                       │
│        (A stock insurance company, herein called the company)     │
└─────────────────────────────────────────────────────────────────┘
```

In consideration of the payment of the premium, in reliance upon the statements in the declarations made a part hereof and subject to all of the terms of this policy, agrees with the **named insured** as follows:

DEFINITIONS

When used in this policy (including endorsements forming a part hereof):

"automobile" means a land motor vehicle, trailer or semi-trailer designed for travel on public roads (including any machinery or apparatus attached thereto), but does not include **mobile equipment**;

"bodily injury" means bodily injury, sickness or disease sustained by any person;

"collapse hazard" includes "structural property damage" as defined herein and **property damage** to any other property at any time resulting therefrom. "Structural property damage" means the collapse of or structural injury to any building or structure due to (1) grading of land, excavating, borrowing, filling, back-filling, tunnelling, pile driving, cofferdam work or caisson work or (2) moving, shoring, underpinning, raising or demolition of any building or structure or removal or rebuilding of any structural support thereof. The **collapse hazard** does not include **property damage** (1) arising out of operations performed for the named insured by independent contractors, or (2) included within the **completed operations hazard** or the **underground property damage hazard**, or (3) for which liability is assumed by the **insured** under an **incidental contract**;

"completed operations hazard" includes **bodily injury** and **property damage** arising out of operations or reliance upon a representation or warranty made at any time with respect thereto, but only if the **bodily injury** or **property damage** occurs after such operations have been completed or abandoned and occurs away from premises owned by or rented to the **named insured**. "Operations" include materials, parts or equipment furnished in connection therewith. Operations shall be deemed completed at the earliest of the following times:

(1) when all operations to be performed by or on behalf of the **named insured** under the contract have been completed,

(2) when all operations to be performed by or on behalf of the **named insured** at the site of the operations have been completed, or

(3) when the portion of the work out of which the injury or damage arises has been put to its intended use by any person or organization other than another contractor or subcontractor engaged in performing operations for a principal as a part of the same project.

Operations which may require further service or maintenance work, or correction, repair or replacement because of any defect or deficiency, but which are otherwise complete, shall be deemed completed.

The **completed operations hazard** does not include **bodily injury** or **property damage** arising out of

(a) operations in connection with the transportation of property, unless the **bodily injury** or **property damage** arises out of a condition in or on a vehicle created by the loading or unloading thereof,

(b) the existence of tools, uninstalled equipment or abandoned or unused materials, or

(c) operations for which the classification stated in the policy or in the company's manual specifies "including completed operations";

"damages" includes damages for death and for care and loss of services resulting from **bodily injury** and damages for loss of use of property resulting from **property damage**;

"elevator" means any hoisting or lowering device to connect floors or landings, whether or not in service, and all appliances thereof including any car, platform, shaft, hoistway, stairway, runway, power equipment and machinery; but does not include an **automobile** servicing hoist, or a hoist without a platform outside a building if without mechanical power or if not attached to building walls, or a hod or material hoist used in alteration, construction or demolition operations, or an inclined conveyor used exclusively for carrying property or a dumbwaiter used exclusively for carrying property and having a compartment height not exceeding four feet;

"explosion hazard" includes **property damage** arising out of blasting or explosion. The **explosion hazard** does not include **property damage** (1) arising out of the explosion of air or steam vessels, piping under pressure, prime movers, machinery or power transmitting equipment, or (2) arising out of operations performed for the **named insured** by independent contractors, or (3) included within the **completed operations hazard** or the **underground property damage hazard**, or (4) for which liability is assumed by the **insured** under an **incidental contract**;

"incidental contract" means any written (1) lease of premises, (2) easement agreement, except in connection with construction or demolition operations on or adjacent to a railroad, (3) undertaking to indemnify a municipality required by municipal ordinance, except in connection with work for the municipality, (4) sidetrack agreement, or (5) **elevator** maintenance agreement;

"insured" means any person or organization qualifying as an insured in the "Persons Insured" provision of the applicable insurance coverage. The insurance afforded applies separately to each **insured** against whom claim is made or suit is brought, except with respect to the limits of the company's liability;

"mobile equipment" means a land vehicle (including any machinery or apparatus attached thereto), whether or not self-propelled, (1) not subject to motor vehicle registration, or (2) maintained for use exclusively on premises owned by or rented to the **named insured**, including the ways immediately adjoining, or (3) designed for use principally off public roads, or (4) designed or maintained for the sole purpose of affording mobility to equipment of the following types forming an integral part of or permanently attached to such vehicle: power cranes, shovels, loaders, diggers and drills; concrete mixers (other than the mix-in-transit type); graders, scrapers, rollers and other road construction or repair equipment; air-compressors, pumps and generators, including spraying, welding and building cleaning equipment; and geophysical exploration and well servicing equipment;

"named insured" means the person or organization named in Item 1. of the declarations of this policy;

"named insured's products" means goods or products manufactured, sold, handled or distributed by the **named insured** or by others trading under his name, including any container thereof (other than a vehicle), but **"named insured's products"** shall not include a vending machine or any property other than such container, rented to or located for use of others but not sold;

"occurrence" means an accident, including injurious exposure to conditions, which results, during the policy period, in **bodily injury** or **property damage** neither expected nor intended from the standpoint of the **insured**;

"policy territory" means:

(1) the United States of America, its territories or possessions, or Canada, or

(2) international waters or air space, provided the **bodily injury** or **property damage** does not occur in the course of travel or transportation to or from any other country, state or nation, or

(3) anywhere in the world with respect to **damages** because of **bodily injury** or **property damage** arising out of a product which was sold for use or consumption within the territory described in paragraph (1) above, provided the original suit for such damages is brought within such territory;

"products hazard" includes **bodily injury** and **property damage** arising out of the **named insured's products** or reliance upon a representation or warranty made at any time with respect thereto, but only if the **bodily injury** or **property damage** occurs away from premises owned by or rented to the **named insured** and after physical possession of such products has been relinquished to others;

"property damage" means injury to or destruction of tangible property;

"underground property damage hazard" includes underground property damage as defined herein and **property damage** to any other property at any time resulting therefrom. "Underground property damage" means **property damage** to wires, conduits, pipes, mains, sewers, tanks, tunnels, any similar property, and any apparatus in connection therewith, beneath the surface of the ground or water, caused by and occurring during the use of mechanical equipment for the purpose of grading land, paving, excavating, drilling, borrowing, filling, back-filling or pile driving. The **underground property damage hazard** does not include **property damage** (1) arising out of operations performed for the named insured by independent contractors, or (2) included within the **completed operations hazard**, or (3) for which liability is assumed by the **insured** under an **incidental contract**.

SUPPLEMENTARY PAYMENTS

The company will pay, in addition to the applicable limit of liability:

(a) all expenses incurred by the company, all costs taxed against the **insured** in any suit defended by the company and all interest on the entire amount of any judgment therein which accrues after entry of the judgment and before the company has paid or tendered or deposited in court that part of the judgment which does not exceed the limit of the company's liability thereon;

(b) premiums on appeal bonds required in any such suit, premiums on bonds to release attachments in any such suit for an amount not in excess of the applicable limit of liability of this policy, and the cost of bail bonds required of the **insured** because of accident or traffic law violation arising out of the use of any vehicle to which this policy applies, not to exceed $250 per bail bond, but the company shall have no obligation to apply for or furnish any such bonds;

(c) expenses incurred by the **insured** for first aid to others at the time of an accident, for **bodily injury** to which this policy applies;

(d) reasonable expenses incurred by the **insured** at the company's request, including actual loss of wages or salary (but not loss of other income) not to exceed $25 per day because of his attendance at hearings or trials at such request.

[A3467]

Attach Coverage Part(s) and Endorsement(s) (If Any) Here

CONDITIONS

1. Premium: All premiums for this policy shall be computed in accordance with the company's rules, rates, rating plans, premiums and minimum premiums applicable to the insurance afforded herein.

Premium designated in this policy as "advance premium" is a deposit premium only which shall be credited to the amount of the earned premium due at the end of the policy period. At the close of each period (or part thereof terminating with the end of the policy period) designated in the declarations as the audit period the earned premium shall be computed for such period and, upon notice thereof to the **named insured**, shall become due and payable. If the total earned premium for the policy period is less than the premium previously paid, the company shall return to the **named insured** the unearned portion paid by the **named insured.**

The **named insured** shall maintain records of such information as is necessary for premium computation, and shall send copies of such records to the company at the end of the policy period and at such times during the policy period as the company may direct.

2. Inspection and Audit: The company shall be permitted but not obligated to inspect the **named insured's** property and operations at any time. Neither the company's right to make inspections nor the making thereof nor any report thereon shall constitute an undertaking, on behalf of or for the benefit of the **named insured** or others, to determine or warrant that such property or operations are safe.

The company may examine and audit the **named insured's** books and records at any time during the policy period and extensions thereof and within three years after the final termination of this policy, as far as they relate to the subject matter of this insurance.

3. Financial Responsibility Laws: When this policy is certified as proof of financial responsibility for the future under the provisions of any motor vehicle financial responsibility law, such insurance as is afforded by this policy for **bodily injury** liability or for **property damage** liability shall comply with the provisions of such law to the extent of the coverage and limits of liability required by such law. The **insured** agrees to reimburse the company for any payment made by the company which it would not have been obligated to make under the terms of this policy except for the agreement contained in this paragraph.

4. Insured's Duties in the Event of Occurrence, Claim or Suit:

(a) In the event of an **occurrence,** written notice containing particulars sufficient to identify the **insured** and also reasonably obtainable information with respect to the time, place and circumstances thereof, and the names and addresses of the injured and of available witnesses, shall be given by or for the **insured** to the company or any of its authorized agents as soon as practicable. The **named insured** shall promptly take at his expense all reasonable steps to prevent other **bodily injury** or **property damage** from arising out of the same or similar conditions, but such expense shall not be recoverable under this policy.

(b) If claim is made or suit is brought against the **insured,** the **insured** shall immediately forward to the company every demand, notice, summons or other process received by him or his representative.

(c) The **insured** shall cooperate with the company and, upon the company's request, assist in making settlements, in the conduct of suits and in enforcing any right of contribution or indemnity against any person or organization who may be liable to the **insured** because of **bodily injury** or **property damage** with respect to which insurance is afforded under this policy; and the **insured** shall attend hearings and trials and assist in securing and giving evidence and obtaining the attendance of witnesses. The **insured** shall not, except at his own cost, voluntarily make any payment, assume any obligation or incur any expense other than for first aid to others at the time of accident.

5. Action Against Company: No action shall lie against the company unless, as a condition precedent thereto, there shall have been full compliance with all of the terms of this policy, nor until the amount of the **insured's** obligation to pay shall have been finally determined either by judgment against the **insured** after actual trial or by written agreement of the **insured,** the claimant and the company.

Any person or organization or the legal representative thereof who has secured such judgment or written agreement shall thereafter be entitled to recover under this policy to the extent of the insurance afforded by this policy. No person or organization shall have any right under this policy to join the company as a party to any action against the **insured** to determine the **insured's** liability, nor shall the company be impleaded by the **insured** or his legal representative. Bankruptcy or insolvency of the **insured** or of the **insured's** estate shall not relieve the company of any of its obligations hereunder.

6. Other Insurance: The insurance afforded by this policy is primary insurance, except when stated to apply in excess of or contingent upon the absence of other insurance. When this insurance is primary and the **insured** has other insurance which is stated to be applicable to the loss on an excess or contingent basis, the amount of the company's liability under this policy shall not be reduced by the existence of such other insurance.

When both this insurance and other insurance apply to the loss on the same basis, whether primary, excess or contingent, the company shall not be liable under this policy for a greater proportion of the loss than that stated in the applicable contribution provision below:

(a) **Contribution by Equal Shares.** If all of such other valid and collectible insurance provides for contribution by equal shares, the company shall not be liable for a greater proportion of such loss than would be payable if each insurer contributes an equal share until the share of each insurer equals the lowest applicable limit of liability under any one policy or the full amount of the loss is paid, and with respect to any amount of loss not so paid the remaining insurers then continue to contribute equal shares of the remaining amount of the loss until each such insurer has paid its limit in full or the full amount of the loss is paid.

(b) **Contribution by Limits.** If any of such other insurance does not provide for contribution by equal shares, the company shall not be liable for a greater proportion of such loss than the applicable limit of liability under this policy for such loss bears to the total applicable limit of liability of all valid and collectible insurance against such loss.

7. Subrogation: In the event of any payment under this policy, the company shall be subrogated to all the **insured's** rights of recovery therefor against any person or organization and the **insured** shall execute and deliver instruments and papers and do whatever else is necessary to secure such rights. The **insured** shall do nothing after loss to prejudice such rights.

8. Changes: Notice to any agent or knowledge possessed by any agent or by any other person shall not effect a waiver or a change in any part of this policy or estop the company from asserting any right under the terms of this policy; nor shall the terms of this policy be waived or changed, except by endorsement issued to form a part of this policy.

9. Assignment: Assignment of interest under this policy shall not bind the company until its consent is endorsed hereon; if, however, the **named insured** shall die, such insurance as is afforded by this policy shall apply (1) to the **named insured's** legal representative, as the **named insured,** but only while acting within the scope of his duties as such, and (2) with respect to the property of the **named insured,** to the person having proper temporary custody thereof, as **insured,** but only until the appointment and qualification of the legal representative.

10. Three Year Policy: If this policy is issued for a period of three years, the limits of the company's liability shall apply separately to each consecutive annual period thereof.

11. Cancellation: This policy may be cancelled by the **named insured** by surrender thereof to the company or any of its authorized agents or by mailing to the company written notice stating when thereafter the cancellation shall be effective. This policy may be cancelled by the company by mailing to the **named insured** at the address shown in this policy, written notice stating when not less than ten days thereafter such cancellation shall be effective. The mailing of notice as aforesaid shall be sufficient proof of notice. The time of surrender or the effective date and hour of cancellation stated in the notice shall become the end of the policy period. Delivery of such written notice either by the **named insured** or by the company shall be equivalent to mailing.

If the **named insured** cancels, earned premium shall be computed in accordance with the customary short rate table and procedure. If the company cancels, earned premium shall be computed pro rata. Premium adjustment may be made either at the time cancellation is effected or as soon as practicable after cancellation becomes effective, but payment or tender of unearned premium is not a condition of cancellation.

12. Declarations: By acceptance of this policy, the **named insured** agrees that the statements in the declarations are his agreements and representations, that this policy is issued in reliance upon the truth of such representations and that this policy embodies all agreements existing between himself and the company or any of its agents relating to this insurance.

°**In Witness Whereof,** the company has caused this policy to be executed and attested, but this policy shall not be valid unless countersigned by a duly authorized representative of the company.

°Company's language may be substituted as desired.

INSERT SIGNATURES AND
TITLES OF PROPER OFFICERS

[A3468]

NUCLEAR ENERGY LIABILITY EXCLUSION ENDORSEMENT
(BROAD FORM)

This endorsement modifies the provisions of this policy relating to **ALL AUTOMOBILE LIABILITY, GENERAL LIABILITY AND MEDICAL PAYMENTS INSURANCE OTHER THAN FAMILY AUTOMOBILE, SPECIAL PACKAGE AUTOMOBILE, COMPREHENSIVE PERSONAL AND FARMER'S COMPREHENSIVE PERSONAL INSURANCE.**

It is agreed that:

I. This policy does not apply:

A. Under any Liability Coverage, to **bodily injury** or **property damage**

(1) with respect to which an **insured** under this policy is also an insured under a nuclear energy liability policy issued by Nuclear Energy Liability Insurance Association, Mutual Atomic Energy Liability Underwriters or Nuclear Insurance Association of Canada, or would be an insured under any such policy but for its termination upon exhaustion of its limit of liability; or

(2) resulting from the **hazardous properties** of **nuclear material** and with respect to which (a) any person or organization is required to maintain financial protection pursuant to the Atomic Energy Act of 1954, or any law amendatory thereof, or (b) the **insured** is, or had this policy not been issued would be, entitled to indemnity from the United States of America, or any agency thereof, under any agreement entered into by the United States of America, or any agency thereof, with any person or organization.

B. Under any Medical Payments Coverage, or under any Supplementary Payments provision relating to first aid, to expenses incurred with respect to **bodily injury** resulting from the **hazardous properties** of **nuclear material** and arising out of the operation of a **nuclear facility** by any person or organization.

C. Under any Liability Coverage, to **bodily injury** or **property damage** resulting from the **hazardous properties** of **nuclear material**, if

(1) the **nuclear material** (a) is at any **nuclear facility** owned by, or operated by or on behalf of, an **insured** or (b) has been discharged or dispersed therefrom;

(2) the **nuclear material** is contained in **spent fuel** or **waste** at any time possessed, handled, used, processed, stored, transported or disposed of by or on behalf of an **insured**; or

(3) the **bodily injury** or **property damage** arises out of the furnishing by an **insured** of services, materials, parts or equipment in connection with the planning, construction, maintenance, operation or use of any **nuclear facility**, but if such facility is located within the United States of America, its territories or possessions or Canada, this exclusion (3) applies only to **property damage** to such **nuclear facility** and any property thereat.

II. As used in this endorsement:

"**hazardous properties**" include radioactive, toxic or explosive properties;

"**nuclear material**" means **source material, special nuclear material** or **byproduct material**;

"**source material**", "**special nuclear material**", and "**byproduct material**" have the meanings given them in the Atomic Energy Act of 1954 or in any law amendatory thereof;

"**spent fuel**" means any fuel element or fuel component, solid or liquid, which has been used or exposed to radiation in a **nuclear reactor**;

"**waste**" means any waste material (1) containing **byproduct material** and (2) resulting from the operation by any person or organization of any **nuclear facility** included within the definition of **nuclear facility** under paragraph (a) or (b) thereof;

"**nuclear facility**" means

(a) any **nuclear reactor**,

(b) any equipment or device designed or used for (1) separating the isotopes of uranium or plutonium, (2) processing or utilizing **spent fuel**, or (3) handling, processing or packaging **waste**,

(c) any equipment or device used for the processing, fabricating or alloying of **special nuclear material** if at any time the total amount of such material in the custody of the **insured** at the premises where such equipment or device is located consists of or contains more than 25 grams of plutonium or uranium 233 or any combination thereof, or more than 250 grams of uranium 235,

(d) any structure, basin, excavation, premises or place prepared or used for the storage or disposal of **waste**,

and includes the site on which any of the foregoing is located, all operations conducted on such site and all premises used for such operations;

"**nuclear reactor**" means any apparatus designed or used to sustain nuclear fission in a self-supporting chain reaction or to contain a critical mass of fissionable material;

"**property damage**" includes all forms of radioactive contamination of property.

[A3469]

COVERAGE PART

L 6102
(Ed. 2-66)

COMPREHENSIVE GENERAL LIABILITY INSURANCE

For attachment to Policy No._____, to complete said policy.

ADDITIONAL DECLARATIONS

Location of all premises owned by, rented to or controlled by the **named insured** (ENTER ''SAME'' IF SAME LOCATION AS ADDRESS SHOWN IN ITEM 1 OF DECLARATIONS)

Interest of **named insured** in such premises (CHECK BELOW)

☐ Owner   ☐ General Lessee   ☐ Tenant   ☐ Other _____

Part occupied by **named insured** (ENTER BELOW)

The following discloses all hazards insured hereunder known to exist at the effective date of this policy, unless otherwise stated herein.

SCHEDULE

The insurance afforded is only with respect to such of the following Coverages as are indicated by specific premium charge or charges. The limit of the company's liability against each such Coverage shall be as stated herein, subject to all the terms of this policy having reference thereto.

Limits of Liability			Coverages		
each person	each occurrence	aggregate			
$	$	$	A—Bodily Injury Liability		
	$	$	B—Property Damage Liability		

Advance Premiums		Rates		Premium Bases	Code No.	Description of Hazards
Bodily Injury	Property Damage	B.I.	P.D.			
						Premises - Operations
		(a) Per 100 Sq. Ft. of Area (b) Per Linear Foot (c) Per $100 of Remuneration (d) Per $100 of Receipts (e) Per Unit		(a) Area (Sq. Ft.) (b) Frontage (c) Remuneration (d) Receipts (e) Units		
		Per Elevator		Number Insured		**Elevators (Number at Premises)**
		Per $100 of Cost		Cost		**Independent Contractors**
		(a) Per $1,000 of Receipts		(a) Receipts		**Completed Operations**
		(b) Per $1,000 of Sales		(b) Sales		**Products**
$	$	Total Advance B.I. and P.D. Premiums				Form numbers of endorsements attached at issue
$						
$	Total Advance Premium					

When used as a premium basis:

1. **"admissions"** means the total number of persons, other than employees of the **named insured**, admitted to the event insured or to events conducted on the **premises** whether on paid admission tickets, complimentary tickets or passes;

2. **"cost"** means the total cost to the **named insured** with respect to operations performed for the **named insured** during the policy period by independent contractors of all work let or sub-let in connection with each specific project, including the cost of all labor, materials and equipment furnished, used or delivered for use in the execution of such work, whether furnished by the owner, contractor or subcontractor, including all fees, allowances, bonuses or commissions made, paid or due;

3. **"receipts"** means the gross amount of money charged by the **named insured** for such operations by the **named insured** or by others during the policy period as are rated on a receipts basis other than receipts from telecasting, broadcasting or motion pictures, and includes taxes, other than taxes which the **named insured** collects as a separate item and remits directly to a governmental division;

4. **"remuneration"** means the entire remuneration earned during the policy period by proprietors and by all employees of the **named insured**, other than chauffeurs (except operators of mobile equipment) and aircraft pilots and co-pilots, subject to any overtime earnings or limitation of remuneration rule applicable in accordance with the manuals in use by the company;

5. **"sales"** means the gross amount of money charged by the **named insured** or by others trading under his name for all goods and products sold or distributed during the policy period and charged during the policy period for installation, servicing or repair, and includes taxes, other than taxes which the **named insured** and such others collect as a separate item and remit directly to a governmental division.

(over)

[A3470]

I. COVERAGE A—BODILY INJURY LIABILITY
COVERAGE B—PROPERTY DAMAGE LIABILITY

The company will pay on behalf of the **insured** all sums which the **insured** shall become legally obligated to pay as **damages** because of

A. **bodily injury** or
B. **property damage**

to which this insurance applies, caused by an **occurrence**, and the company shall have the right and duty to defend any suit against the **insured** seeking **damages** on account of such **bodily injury** or **property damage**, even if any of the allegations of the suit are groundless, false or fraudulent, and may make such investigation and settlement of any claim or suit as it deems expedient, but the company shall not be obligated to pay any claim or judgment or to defend any suit after the applicable limit of the company's liability has been exhausted by payment of judgments or settlements.

Exclusions

This insurance does not apply:

(a) to liability assumed by the **insured** under any contract or agreement except an **incidental contract**; but this exclusion does not apply to a warranty of fitness or quality of the **named insured's products** or a warranty that work performed by or on behalf of the **named insured** will be done in a workmanlike manner;

(b) to **bodily injury** or **property damage** arising out of the ownership, maintenance, operation, use, loading or unloading of

(1) any **automobile** or aircraft owned or operated by or rented or loaned to the **named insured**, or

(2) any other **automobile** or aircraft operated by any person in the course of his employment by the **named insured**;

but this exclusion does not apply to the parking of an **automobile** on premises owned by, rented to or controlled by the **named insured** or the ways immediately adjoining, if such **automobile** is not owned by or rented or loaned to the **named insured**;

(c) to **bodily injury** or **property damage** arising out of and in the course of the transportation of **mobile equipment** by an **automobile** owned or operated by or rented or loaned to the **named insured**;

(d) to **bodily injury** or **property damage** arising out of the ownership, maintenance, operation, use, loading or unloading of any watercraft, if the **bodily injury** or **property damage** occurs away from premises owned by, rented to or controlled by the **named insured**; but this exclusion does not apply to **bodily injury** or **property damage** included within the **products hazard** or the **completed operations hazard** or resulting from operations performed for the **named insured** by independent contractors or to liability assumed by the **insured** under an **incidental contract**;

(e) to **bodily injury** or **property damage** due to war, whether or not declared, civil war, insurrection, rebellion or revolution or to any act or condition incident to any of the foregoing, with respect to

(1) liability assumed by the **insured** under an **incidental contract**, or

(2) expenses for first aid under the Supplementary Payments provision;

(f) to **bodily injury** or **property damage** for which the **insured** or his indemnitee may be held liable, as a person or organization engaged in the business of manufacturing, distributing, selling or serving alcoholic beverages or as an owner or lessor of premises used for such purposes, by reason of the selling, serving or giving of any alcoholic beverage

(1) in violation of any statute, ordinance or regulation,

(2) to a minor,

(3) to a person under the influence of alcohol, or

(4) which causes or contributes to the intoxication of any person;

(g) to any obligation for which the **insured** or any carrier as his insurer may be held liable under any workmen's compensation, unemployment compensation or disability benefits law, or under any similar law;

(h) to **bodily injury** to any employee of the **insured** arising out of and in the course of his employment by the **insured**; but this exclusion does not apply to liability assumed by the **insured** under an **incidental contract**;

(i) to **property damage** to

(1) property owned or occupied by or rented to the **insured**,

(2) property used by the **insured**, or

(3) property in the care, custody or control of the **insured** or as to which the **insured** is for any purpose exercising physical control;

but parts (2) and (3) of this exclusion do not apply with respect to liability under a written sidetrack agreement and part (3) of this exclusion does not apply with respect to **property damage** (other than to **elevators**) arising out of the use of an **elevator** at premises owned by, rented to or controlled by the **named insured**;

(j) to **property damage** to premises alienated by the **named insured** arising out of such premises or any part thereof;

(k) to **bodily injury** or **property damage** resulting from the failure of the **named insured's products** or work completed by or for the **named insured** to perform the function or serve the purpose intended by the **named insured**, if such failure is due to a mistake or deficiency in any design, formula, plan, specifications, advertising material or printed instructions prepared or developed by any **insured**; but this exclusion does not apply to **bodily injury** or **property damage** resulting from the active malfunctioning of such products or work;

(l) to **property damage** to the **named insured's products** arising out of such products or any part of such products;

(m) to **property damage** to work performed by or on behalf of the **named insured** arising out of the work or any portion thereof, or out of materials, parts or equipment furnished in connection therewith;

(n) to **damages** claimed for the withdrawal, inspection, repair, replacement, or loss of use of the **named insured's products** or work completed by or for the **named insured** or of any property of which such products or work form a part, if such products, work or property are withdrawn from the market or from use because of any known or suspected defect or deficiency therein;

(o) to **property damage** included within:

(1) the **explosion hazard** in connection with operations identified in this policy by a classification code number which includes the symbol "x",

(2) the **collapse hazard** in connection with operations identified in this policy by a classification code number which includes the symbol "c",

(3) the **underground property damage hazard** in connection with operations identified in this policy by a classification code number which includes the symbol "u".

II. PERSONS INSURED

Each of the following is an **insured** under this insurance to the extent set forth below:

(a) if the **named insured** is designated in the declarations as an individual, the person so designated but only with respect to the conduct of a business of which he is the sole proprietor;

(b) if the **named insured** is designated in the declarations as a partnership or joint venture, the partnership or joint venture so designated and any partner or member thereof but only with respect to his liability as such;

(c) if the **named insured** is designated in the declarations as other than an individual, partnership or joint venture, the organization so designated and any executive officer, director or stockholder thereof while acting within the scope of his duties as such;

(d) any person (other than an employee of the **named insured**) or organization while acting as real estate manager for the **named insured**; and

(e) with respect to the operation, for the purpose of locomotion upon a public highway, of **mobile equipment** registered under any motor vehicle registration law,

(i) an employee of the **named insured** while operating any such equipment in the course of his employment, and

(ii) any other person while operating with the permission of the **named insured** any such equipment registered in the name of the **named insured** and any person or organization legally responsible for such operation, but only if there is no other valid and collectible insurance available, either on a primary or excess basis, to such person or organization;

provided that no person or organization shall be an **insured** under this paragraph (e) with respect to:

(1) **bodily injury** to any fellow employee of such person injured in the course of his employment, or

(2) **property damage** to property owned by, rented to, in charge of or occupied by the **named insured** or the employer of any person described in subparagraph (ii).

This insurance does not apply to **bodily injury** or **property damage** arising out of the conduct of any partnership or joint venture of which the **insured** is a partner or member and which is not designated in this policy as a **named insured**.

III. LIMITS OF LIABILITY

Regardless of the number of (1) **insureds** under this policy, (2) persons or organizations who sustain **bodily injury** or **property damage**, or (3) claims made or suits brought on account of **bodily injury** or **property damage**, the company's liability is limited as follows:

Coverage A—The limit of **bodily injury** liability stated in the schedule as applicable to "each person" is the limit of the company's liability for all **damages** because of **bodily injury** sustained by one person as the result of any one **occurrence**; but subject to the above provision respecting "each person", the total liability of the company for all **damages** because of **bodily injury** sustained by two or more persons as the result of any one **occurrence** shall not exceed the limit of **bodily injury** liability stated in the schedule as applicable to "each **occurrence**".

Subject to the above provisions respecting "each person" and "each **occurrence**", the total liability of the company for all **damages** because of (1) all **bodily injury** included within the **completed operations hazard** and (2) all **bodily injury** included within the **products hazard** shall not exceed the limit of **bodily injury** liability stated in the schedule as "aggregate".

Coverage B—The total liability of the company for all **damages** because of all **property damage** sustained by one or more persons or organizations as the result of any one **occurrence** shall not exceed the limit of **property damage** liability stated in the schedule as applicable to "each **occurrence**".

Subject to the above provision respecting "each **occurrence**", the total liability of the company for all **damages** because of all **property damage** to which this coverage applies and described in any of the numbered subparagraphs below shall not exceed the limit of **property damage** liability stated in the schedule as "aggregate":

(1) all **property damage** arising out of premises or operations rated on a remuneration basis or contractor's equipment rated on a receipts basis, including **property damage** for which liability is assumed under any **incidental contract** relating to such premises or operations, but excluding **property damage** included in subparagraph (2) below;

(2) all **property damage** arising out of and occurring in the course of operations performed for the **named insured** by independent contractors and general supervision thereof by the **named insured**, including any such **property damage** for which liability is assumed under any **incidental contract** relating to such operations, but this subparagraph (2) does not include **property damage** arising out of maintenance or repairs at premises owned by or rented to the **named insured** or structural alterations at such premises which do not involve changing the size of or moving buildings or other structures;

(3) all **property damage** included within the **products hazard** and all **property damage** included within the **completed operations hazard**.

Such aggregate limit shall apply separately to the **property damage** described in subparagraphs (1), (2) and (3) above, and under subparagraphs (1) and (2), separately with respect to each project away from premises owned by or rented to the **named insured**.

Coverages A and B—For the purpose of determining the limit of the company's liability, all **bodily injury** and **property damage** arising out of continuous or repeated exposure to substantially the same general conditions shall be considered as arising out of one **occurrence**.

IV. POLICY PERIOD; TERRITORY

This insurance applies only to **bodily injury** or **property damage** which occurs during the policy period within the **policy territory**.

[A3471]

COVERAGE PART

COMPREHENSIVE AUTOMOBILE LIABILITY INSURANCE

AL 6114
(Ed. 5-66)

For attachment to Policy No._____, to complete said policy.

SCHEDULE

The insurance afforded is only with respect to such of the following Coverages as are indicated by specific premium charge or charges. The limit of the company's liability against each such Coverage shall be as stated herein, subject to all the terms of this policy having reference thereto.

Limits of Liability	Coverages
thousand dollars each person thousand dollars each occurrence	C—Bodily Injury Liability
thousand dollars each occurrence	D—Property Damage Liability

Advance Premiums		Description of Hazards					
BI	PD	**1. Owned Automobiles — Premium Basis — Per Automobile**					
		Town or City and State In Which the Automobile Will Be Principally Garaged	Year of Model	Trade Name	Body Type and Model; Truck Size; Tank Gallonage Capacity; or Bus Seating Capacity	Identification Number Serial Number Motor Number	Purposes of Use

2. Hired Automobiles — Premium Basis — Cost of Hire

Types Hired	Locations Where Automobiles Will Be Principally Used	Purposes of Use	Estimated Cost of Hire	Rates Per $100 Cost of Hire	
				BI	PD

3. Non-Owned Automobiles — Premium Basis — Class 1 Persons and Class 2 Employees

Class 1 Persons—Name of Each	Location of Headquarters of Persons Named Herein	

Class 2 Employees—Estimated Average Number	Location of Headquarters of Class 2 Employees	Rates Per Employee	
		BI	PD

$	$	**Total Advance B.I. and P.D. Premiums**	**Form numbers of endorsements attached at issue**
$			
$	**Total Advance Premium**		

When used as a premium basis:

A. **"cost of hire"** means the amount incurred for (a) the hire of **automobiles**, including the entire remuneration of each employee of the **named insured** engaged in the operation of such **automobiles** subject to an average weekly maximum remuneration of $100, and for (b) pick-up, transportation or delivery service of property or passengers, other than such services performed by motor carriers which are subject to the security requirements of any motor carrier law or ordinance. The rates for each $100 of "cost of hire" shall be 5% of the applicable **hired automobile** rates, provided the owner of such **hired automobile** has purchased **automobile Bodily Injury** Liability and **Property Damage** Liability insurance covering the interest of the **named insured** on a direct primary basis as respects such **automobile** and submits evidence of such insurance to the **named insured**;

B. **"Class 1 persons"** means the following persons, provided their usual duties in the business of the **named insured** include the use of **non-owned automobiles**: (a) all employees, including officers, of the **named insured** compensated for the use of such **automobiles** by salary, commission, terms of employment, or specific operating allowance of any sort; (b) all direct agents and representatives of the **named insured**;

C. **"Class 2 employees"** means all employees, including officers, of the **named insured**, not included in Class 1 persons.

(over)

[A3472]

I. COVERAGE C—BODILY INJURY LIABILITY

COVERAGE D—PROPERTY DAMAGE LIABILITY

The company will pay on behalf of the **insured** all sums which the **insured** shall become legally obligated to pay as **damages** because of

C. **bodily injury** or

D. **property damage**

to which this insurance applies, caused by an **occurrence** and arising out of the ownership, maintenance or use, including loading and unloading, of any **automobile**, and the company shall have the right and duty to defend any suit against the **insured** seeking **damages** on account of such **bodily injury** or **property damage**, even if any of the allegations of the suit are groundless, false or fraudulent, and may make such investigation and settlement of any claim or suit as it deems expedient, but the company shall not be obligated to pay any claim or judgment or to defend any suit after the applicable limit of the company's liability has been exhausted by payment of judgments or settlements.

Exclusions

This insurance does not apply:

(a) to liability assumed by the **insured** under any contract or agreement;

(b) to any obligation for which the **insured** or any carrier as his insurer may be held liable under any workmen's compensation, unemployment compensation or disability benefits law, or under any similar law;

(c) to **bodily injury** to any employee of the **insured** arising out of and in the course of his employment by the **insured**, but this exclusion does not apply to any such injury arising out of and in the course of domestic employment by the **insured** unless benefits therefor are in whole or in part either payable or required to be provided under any workmen's compensation law;

(d) to **property damage** to

(1) property owned or being transported by the **insured**, or

(2) property rented to or in the care, custody or control of the **insured**, or as to which the **insured** is for any purpose exercising physical control, other than **property damage** to a residence or private garage by a **private passenger automobile** covered by this insurance;

(e) to **bodily injury** due to war, whether or not declared, civil war, insurrection, rebellion or revolution or to any act or condition incident to any of the foregoing, with respect to expenses for first aid under the Supplementary Payments provision.

II. PERSONS INSURED

Each of the following is an **insured** under this insurance to the extent set forth below:

(a) the **named insured**;

(b) any partner or executive officer thereof, but with respect to a **non-owned automobile** only while such **automobile** is being used in the business of the **named insured**;

(c) any other person while using an **owned automobile** or a **hired automobile** with the permission of the **named insured**, provided his actual operation or (if he is not operating) his other actual use thereof is within the scope of such permission, but with respect to **bodily injury** or **property damage** arising out of the loading or unloading thereof, such other person shall be an **insured** only if he is:

(1) a lessee or borrower of the **automobile**, or

(2) an employee of the **named insured** or of such lessee or borrower;

(d) any other person or organization but only with respect to his or its liability because of acts or omissions of an **insured** under (a), (b) or (c) above.

None of the following is an **insured**:

(i) any person while engaged in the business of his employer with respect to **bodily injury** to any fellow employee of such person injured in the course of his employment;

(ii) the owner or lessee (of whom the **named insured** is a sub-lessee) of a **hired automobile** or the owner of a **non-owned automobile**, or any agent or employee of any such owner or lessee;

(iii) an executive officer with respect to an **automobile** owned by him or by a member of his household;

(iv) any person or organization, other than the **named insured**, with respect to:

(1) a motor vehicle while used with any **trailer** owned or hired by such person or organization and not covered by like insurance in the company (except a **trailer** designed for use with a **private passenger automobile** and not being used for business purposes with another type motor vehicle), or

(2) a **trailer** while used with any motor vehicle owned or hired by such person or organization and not covered by like insurance in the company;

(v) any person while employed in or otherwise engaged in duties in connection with an **automobile business**, other than an **automobile business** operated by the **named insured**.

This insurance does not apply to **bodily injury** or **property damage** arising out of (1) a **non-owned automobile** used in the conduct of any partnership or joint venture of which the **insured** is a partner or member and which is not designated in this policy as a **named insured**, or (2) if the **named insured** is a partnership, an **automobile** owned by or registered in the name of a partner thereof.

III. LIMITS OF LIABILITY

Regardless of the number of (1) **insureds** under this policy, (2) persons or organizations who sustain **bodily injury** or **property damage**, (3) claims made or suits brought on account of **bodily injury** or **property damage** or (4) **automobiles** to which this policy applies, the company's liability is limited as follows:

Coverage C—The limit of **bodily injury** liability stated in the schedule as applicable to "each person" is the limit of the company's liability for all **damages** because of **bodily injury** sustained by one person as the result of any one **occurrence**; but subject to the above provision respecting "each person", the total liability of the company for all **damages** because of **bodily injury** sustained by two or more persons as the result of any one **occurrence** shall not exceed the limit of **bodily injury** liability stated in the schedule as applicable to "each **occurrence**".

Coverage D—The total liability of the company for all **damages** because of all **property damage** sustained by one or more persons or organizations as the result of any one **occurrence** shall not exceed the limit of **property damage** liability stated in the schedule as applicable to "each **occurrence**".

Coverages C and D—For the purpose of determining the limit of the company's liability, all **bodily injury** and **property damage** arising out of continuous or repeated exposure to substantially the same general conditions shall be considered as arising out of one **occurrence**.

IV. POLICY PERIOD; TERRITORY

This insurance applies only to **bodily injury** or **property damage** which occurs during the policy period within the territory described in paragraph (1) or (2) of the definition of **policy territory**.

V. ADDITIONAL DEFINITIONS

When used in reference to this insurance (including endorsements forming a part of the policy):

"automobile business" means the business or occupation of selling, repairing, servicing, storing or parking **automobiles**;

"hired automobile" means an **automobile** not owned by the **named insured** which is used under contract in behalf of, or loaned to, the **named insured**, provided such **automobile** is not owned by or registered in the name of (a) a partner or executive officer of the **named insured** or (b) an employee or agent of the **named insured** who is granted an operating allowance of any sort for the use of such **automobile**;

"non-owned automobile" means an **automobile** which is neither an **owned automobile** nor a **hired automobile**;

"owned automobile" means an **automobile** owned by the named insured;

"private passenger automobile" means a four wheel private passenger or station wagon type **automobile**;

"trailer" includes semi-trailer but does not include **mobile equipment**.

VI. ADDITIONAL CONDITION

Excess Insurance—Hired and Non-Owned Automobiles

With respect to a **hired automobile** or a **non-owned automobile**, this insurance shall be excess insurance over any other valid and collectible insurance available to the **insured**.

[A3473]

APPENDIX H—Family Combination Automobile
Policy Form *

════════════════════════════ FAMILY COMBINATION AUTOMOBILE POLICY ════════════════════════════

No. ACF | | CAPITAL STOCK COMPANY

RENEWAL OF NUMBER

SPACE FOR COMPANY NAME, INSIGNIA, AND LOCATION

DECLARATIONS

Item 1. Named Insured and Address: (No., Street, Town or City, County, State)

SPACE FOR
PRODUCER'S NAME AND
MAILING ADDRESS

Item 2. Policy Period: (Mo. Day Yr.)   (Months)

From   to
12:01 A.M., standard time at the address of the named insured as stated herein.

Occupation of the named insured is IF MARRIED WOMAN, GIVE HUSBAND'S OCCUPATION OR BUSINESS (ENTER BELOW)

Item 3.   The insurance afforded is only with respect to such of the following coverages as are indicated by specific premium charge or charges. The limit of the company's liability against each such coverage shall be as stated herein, subject to all the terms of this policy having reference thereto.

CAR 1	PREMIUMS	CAR 2	LIMITS OF LIABILITY		COVERAGES	
$		$	thousand dollars each person thousand dollars each occurrence	A	Bodily Injury Liability	
$		$	thousand dollars each occurrence	B	Property Damage Liability	
$		$	dollars each person	C	Medical Payments	
			$ Actual Cash Value*	D	(1) Comprehensive (excluding Collision)	
$		$	$ 100		(2) Personal Effects	
			Actual Cash Value less	E	Collision	
$		$	$ deductible			
$		$	$	F	Fire, Lightning and Transportation	
$		$	$	G	Theft	
$		$	$	H	Combined Additional Coverage	
$		$	$ 25 per disablement	I	Towing and Labor Costs	
$		$	thousand dollars each person thousand dollars each accident	J	Uninsured Motorists	
					Form numbers of endorsements attached to policy at issue	
$						
$		$	Total Car 1 - Car 2			
$	**Total Premium**					

* STRIKE OUT "ACTUAL CASH VALUE" AND INSERT AMOUNT IF POLICY IS WRITTEN ON STATED AMOUNT BASIS.

Item 4.   Description of owned automobile or trailer

Year of Model	Trade Name	Body Type; Model	Identification Number (I) Serial Number (S) Motor Number (M)	F.O.B. List Price or Delivered Price at Factory	Purct-sed Month, Year New or Used	Class & Rating Symbol	Sub-Class (if any)
Car 1							
Car 2							

Item 5.   Loss Payee: Any loss under Part III is payable as interest may appear to the named insured and (NAME AND ADDRESS—ENTER BELOW)

Item 6.   The owned automobile will be principally garaged in the town or city designated in Item 1 above, unless otherwise stated herein: (ENTER BELOW)

Item 7.   During the past three years no insurer has canceled insurance, issued to the named insured, similar to that afforded hereunder, unless otherwise stated herein:

Countersigned:

By_____
                                    Authorized Representative

[A3474]

OKP 6013-0-G
(Rev. 1-1-63)

* Reproduced with permission of the Insurance Information Institute.

RESERVED FOR YOUR COMPANY'S NAME

(A stock insurance company, herein called the company)

Agrees with the insured, named in the declarations made a part hereof, in consideration of the payment of the premium and in reliance upon the statements in the declarations and subject to all of the terms of this policy:

PART I — LIABILITY

Coverage A—Bodily Injury Liability; Coverage B—Property Damage Liability: To pay on behalf of the insured all sums which the insured shall become legally obligated to pay as damages because of:

A. bodily injury, sickness or disease, including death resulting therefrom, hereinafter called "bodily injury," sustained by any person;

B. injury to or destruction of property, including loss of use thereof, hereinafter called "property damage";

arising out of the ownership, maintenance or use of the owned automobile or any non-owned automobile, and the company shall defend any suit alleging such bodily injury or property damage and seeking damages which are payable under the terms of this policy, even if any of the allegations of the suit are groundless, false or fraudulent; but the company may make such investigation and settlement of any claim or suit as it deems expedient.

Supplementary Payments: To pay, in addition to the applicable limits of liability:

(a) all expenses incurred by the company, all costs taxed against the insured in any such suit and all interest on the entire amount of any judgment therein which accrues after entry of the judgment and before the company has paid or tendered or deposited in court that part of the judgment which does not exceed the limit of the company's liability thereon;

(b) premiums on appeal bonds required in any such suit, premiums on bonds to release attachments for an amount not in excess of the applicable limit of liability of this policy, and the cost of bail bonds required of the insured because of accident or traffic law violation arising out of the use of an automobile insured hereunder, not to exceed $100 per bail bond, but without any obligation to apply for or furnish any such bonds;

(c) expenses incurred by the insured for such immediate medical and surgical relief to others as shall be imperative at the time of an accident involving an automobile insured hereunder and not due to war;

(d) all reasonable expenses, other than loss of earnings, incurred by the insured at the company's request.

Persons Insured: The following are insureds under Part I:

(a) with respect to the owned automobile,

(1) the named insured and any resident of the same household,

(2) any other person using such automobile with the permission of the named insured, provided his actual operation or (if he is not operating) his other actual use thereof is within the scope of such permission, and

(3) any other person or organization but only with respect to his or its liability because of acts or omissions of an insured under (a) (1) or (2) above;

(b) with respect to a non-owned automobile,

(1) the named insured,

(2) any relative, but only with respect to a private passenger automobile or trailer,

provided his actual operation or (if he is not operating) the other actual use thereof is with the permission, or reasonably believed to be with the permission, of the owner and is within the scope of such permission, and

(3) any other person or organization not owning or hiring the automobile, but only with respect to his or its liability because of acts or omissions of an insured under (b) (1) or (2) above.

The insurance afforded under Part I applies separately to each insured against whom claim is made or suit is brought, but the inclusion herein of more than one insured shall not operate to increase the limits of the company's liability.

Definitions: Under Part I:

"named insured" means the individual named in Item 1 of the declarations and also includes his spouse, if a resident of the same household;

"insured" means a person or organization described under "Persons Insured";

"relative" means a relative of the named insured who is a resident of the same household;

"owned automobile" means

(a) a private passenger, farm or utility automobile described in this policy for which a specific premium charge indicates that coverage is afforded,

(b) a trailer owned by the named insured,

(c) a private passenger, farm or utility automobile ownership of which is acquired by the named insured during the policy period, provided

(1) it replaces an owned automobile as defined in (a) above, or

(2) the company insures all private passenger, farm and utility automobiles owned by the named insured on the date of such acquisition and the named insured notifies the company during the policy period or within 30 days after the date of such acquisition of his election to make this and no other policy issued by the company applicable to such automobile, or

(d) a temporary substitute automobile;

"temporary substitute automobile" means any automobile or trailer, not owned by the named insured, while temporarily used with the permission of the owner as a substitute for the owned automobile or trailer when withdrawn from normal use because of its breakdown, repair, servicing, loss or destruction;

"non-owned automobile" means an automobile or trailer not owned by or furnished for the regular use of either the named insured or any relative, other than a temporary substitute automobile;

"private passenger automobile" means a four wheel private passenger, station wagon or jeep type automobile;

"farm automobile" means an automobile of the truck type with a load capacity of fifteen hundred pounds or less not used for business or commercial purposes other than farming;

"utility automobile" means an automobile, other than a farm automobile, with a load capacity of fifteen hundred pounds or less of the pick-up body, sedan delivery or panel truck type not used for business or commercial purposes;

"trailer" means a trailer designed for use with a private passenger automobile, if not being used for business or commercial purposes with other than a private passenger, farm or utility automobile, or a farm wagon or farm implement while used with a farm automobile;

"automobile business" means the business or occupation of selling, repairing, servicing, storing or parking automobiles;

"use" of an automobile includes the loading and unloading thereof;

"war" means war, whether or not declared, civil war, insurrection, rebellion or revolution, or any act or condition incident to any of the foregoing.

Exclusions: This policy does not apply under Part I:

(a) to any automobile while used as a public or livery conveyance, but this exclusion does not apply to the named insured with respect to bodily injury or property damage which results from the named insured's occupancy of a non-owned automobile other than as the operator thereof;

(b) to bodily injury or property damage caused intentionally by or at the direction of the insured;

(c) to bodily injury or property damage with respect to which an insured under this policy is also an insured under a nuclear energy liability policy issued by Nuclear Energy Liability Insurance Association, Mutual Atomic Energy Liability Underwriters or Nuclear Insurance Association of Canada, or would be an insured under any such policy but for its termination upon exhaustion of its limit of liability;

(d) to bodily injury or property damage arising out of the operation of farm machinery;

(e) to bodily injury to any employee of the insured arising out of and in the course of (1) domestic employment by the insured, if benefits therefor are in whole or in part either payable or required to be provided under any workmen's compensation law, or (2) other employment by the insured;

(f) to bodily injury to any fellow employee of the insured injured in the course of his employment if such injury arises out of the use of an automobile in the business of his employer, but this exclusion does not apply to the named insured with respect to injury sustained by any such fellow employee;

(g) to an owned automobile while used by any person while such person is employed or otherwise engaged in the automobile business, but this exclusion does not apply to the named insured, a resident of the same household as the named insured, a partnership in which the named insured or such resident is a partner, or any partner, agent or employee of the named insured, such resident or partnership;

(h) to a non-owned automobile while maintained or used by any person while such person is employed or otherwise engaged in

(1) the automobile business of the insured or of any other person or organization,

(2) any other business or occupation of the insured, but this exclusion (h) (2) does not apply to a private passenger automobile operated or occupied by the named insured or by his private chauffeur or domestic servant or a trailer used therewith or with an owned automobile;

(i) to injury to or destruction of (1) property owned or transported by the insured or (2) property rented to or in charge of the insured other than a residence or private garage;

(j) to the ownership, maintenance, operation, use, loading or unloading of an automobile ownership of which is acquired by the named insured during the policy period or any temporary substitute automobile therefor, if the named insured has purchased other automobile liability insurance applicable to such automobile for which a specific premium charge has been made.

Financial Responsibility Laws: When this policy is certified as proof of financial responsibility for the future under the provisions of any motor vehicle financial responsibility law, such insurance as is afforded by this policy for bodily injury liability or for property damage liability shall comply with the provisions of such law to the extent of the coverage and limits of liability required by such law, but in no event in excess of the limits of liability stated in this policy. The insured agrees to reimburse the company for any payment made by the company which it would not have been obligated to make under the terms of this policy except for the agreement contained in this paragraph.

Limits of Liability: The limit of bodily injury liability stated in the declarations as applicable to "each person" is the limit of the company's liability for all damages, including damages for care and loss of services, arising out of bodily injury sustained by one person as the result of any one occurrence; the limit of such liability stated in the declarations as applicable to "each occurrence" is, subject to the above provision respecting each person, the total limit of the company's liability for all such damages arising out of bodily injury sustained by two or more persons as the result of any one occurrence.

The limit of property damage liability stated in the declarations as applicable to "each occurrence" is the total limit of the company's liability for all damages arising out of injury to or destruction of all property of one or more persons or organizations, including the loss of use thereof, as the result of any one occurrence.

Other Insurance: If the insured has other insurance against a loss covered by Part I of this policy the company shall not be liable under this policy for a greater proportion of such loss than the applicable limit of liability stated in the declarations bears to the total applicable limit of liability of all valid and collectible insurance against such loss; provided, however, the insurance with respect to a temporary substitute automobile or non-owned automobile shall be excess insurance over any other valid and collectible insurance.

PART II — EXPENSES FOR MEDICAL SERVICES

Coverage C—Medical Payments: To pay all reasonable expenses incurred within one year from the date of accident for necessary medical, surgical, X-ray and dental services, including prosthetic devices, and necessary ambulance, hospital, professional nursing and funeral services:

Division 1. To or for the named insured and each relative who sustains bodily injury, sickness or disease, including death resulting therefrom, hereinafter called "bodily injury", caused by accident,

(a) while occupying the owned automobile,

(b) while occupying a non-owned automobile, but only if such person has, or reasonably believes he has, the permission of the owner to use the automobile and the use is within the scope of such permission, or

(c) through being struck by an automobile or by a trailer of any type;

Division 2. To or for any other person who sustains bodily injury, caused by accident, while occupying

(a) the owned automobile, while being used by the named insured, by any resident of the same household or by any other person with the permission of the named insured; or

(b) a non-owned automobile, if the bodily injury results from

(1) its operation or occupancy by the named insured or its operation on his behalf by his private chauffeur or domestic servant, or

[A3475]

(Attach Endorsements Here)

(2) its operation or occupancy by a relative, provided it is a private passenger automobile or trailer,

but only if such operator or occupant has, or reasonably believes he has, the permission of the owner to use the automobile and the use is within the scope of such permission.

Definitions: The definitions under Part I apply to Part II, and under Part II:

"**occupying**" means in or upon or entering into or alighting from.

Exclusions: This policy does not apply under Part II to bodily injury:

(a) sustained while occupying (1) an owned automobile while used as a public or livery conveyance, or (2) any vehicle while located for use as a residence or premises;

(b) sustained by the named insured or a relative while occupying or through being struck by
(1) a farm type tractor or other equipment designed for use principally off public roads, while not upon public roads, or (2) a vehicle operated on rails or crawler-treads;

(c) sustained by any person other than the named insured or a relative,
(1) while such person is occupying a non-owned automobile while used as a public or livery conveyance, or
(2) resulting from the maintenance or use of a non-owned automobile by such person while employed or otherwise engaged in the automobile business, or
(3) resulting from the maintenance or use of a non-owned automobile by such person while

Coverage D (1)—Comprehensive (excluding Collision); (2)—Personal Effects:

(1) To pay for loss caused other than by collision to the owned automobile or to a non-owned automobile. For the purpose of this coverage, breakage of glass and loss caused by missiles, falling objects, fire, theft or larceny, explosion, earthquake, windstorm, hail, water, flood, malicious mischief or vandalism, riot or civil commotion, or colliding with a bird or animal, shall not be deemed to be loss caused by collision.

(2) To pay for loss caused by fire or lightning to robes, wearing apparel and other personal effects which are the property of the named insured or a relative, while such effects are in or upon the owned automobile.

Coverage E—Collision: To pay for loss caused by collision to the owned automobile or to a non-owned automobile but only for the amount of each such loss in excess of the deductible amount stated in the declarations as applicable hereto. The deductible amount shall not apply to loss caused by a collision with another automobile insured by the company.

Coverage F—Fire, Lightning and Transportation: To pay for loss to the owned automobile or a non-owned automobile, caused (a) by fire or lightning, (b) by smoke or smudge due to a sudden, unusual and faulty operation of any fixed heating equipment serving the premises in which the automobile is located, or (c) by the stranding, sinking, burning, collision or derailment of any conveyance in or upon which the automobile is being transported.

Coverage G—Theft: To pay for loss to the owned automobile or to a non-owned automobile caused by theft or larceny.

Coverage H—Combined Additional Coverage: To pay for loss to the owned automobile or a non-owned automobile caused by windstorm, hail, earthquake, explosion, riot or civil commotion, or the forced landing or falling of any aircraft or its parts or equipment, flood or rising waters, malicious mischief or vandalism, external discharge or leakage of water except loss resulting from rain, snow or sleet whether or not wind-driven; provided, with respect to each automobile $25 shall be deducted from each loss caused by malicious mischief or vandalism.

Coverage I—Towing and Labor Costs: To pay for towing and labor costs necessitated by the disablement of the owned automobile or of any non-owned automobile, provided the labor is performed at the place of disablement.

Supplementary Payments: In addition to the applicable limit of liability:

(a) to reimburse the insured for transportation expenses incurred during the period commencing 48 hours after a theft covered by this policy of the entire automobile has been reported to the company and the police, and terminating when the automobile is returned to use or the company pays for the loss; provided that the company shall not be obligated to pay aggregate expenses in excess of $10 per day or totaling more than $300.

(b) to pay general average and salvage charges for which the insured becomes legally liable, as to the automobile being transported.

Definitions: The definitions of "named insured", "relative", "temporary substitute automobile", "private passenger automobile", "farm automobile", "utility automobile", "automobile business", "war", and "owned automobile" in Part I apply to Part III, but "owned automobile" does not include, under Part III, (1) a trailer owned by the named insured on the effective date of this policy and not described herein, or (2) a trailer ownership of which is acquired during the policy period unless the company insures all private passenger, farm and utility automobiles and trailers owned by the named insured on the date of such acquisition and the named insured notifies the company during the policy period or within 30 days after the date of such acquisition of his election to make this and no other policy issued by the company applicable to such trailer.

"**insured**" means

(a) with respect to an owned automobile,

employed or otherwise engaged in any other business or occupation, unless the bodily injury results from the operation or occupancy of a private passenger automobile by the named insured or by his private chauffeur or domestic servant, or of a trailer used therewith or with an owned automobile;

(d) sustained by any person who is employed in the automobile business, if the accident arises out of the operation thereof and if benefits therefor are in whole or in part either payable or required to be provided under any workmen's compensation law;

(e) due to war.

Limit of Liability: The limit of liability for medical payments stated in the declarations as applicable to "each person" is the limit of the company's liability for all expenses incurred by or on behalf of each person who sustains bodily injury as the result of any one accident.

Other Insurance: If there is other automobile medical payments insurance against a loss covered by Part II of this policy the company shall not be liable under this policy for a greater proportion of such loss than the applicable limit of liability stated in the declarations bears to the total applicable limit of liability of all valid and collectible automobile medical payments insurance; provided, however, the insurance with respect to a temporary substitute automobile or non-owned automobile shall be excess insurance over any other valid and collectible automobile medical payments insurance.

PART III — PHYSICAL DAMAGE

(1) the named insured, and

(2) any person or organization (other than a person or organization employed or otherwise engaged in the automobile business or as a carrier or other bailee for hire) maintaining, using or having custody of said automobile with the permission of the named insured and within the scope of such permission;

(b) with respect to a non-owned automobile, the named insured and any relative while using such automobile, provided his actual operation or (if he is not operating) the other actual use thereof is with the permission, or reasonably believed to be with the permission, of the owner and is within the scope of such permission;

"**non-owned automobile**" means a private passenger automobile or trailer not owned by or furnished for the regular use of either the named insured or any relative, other than a temporary substitute automobile, while said automobile or trailer is in the possession or custody of the insured or is being operated by him;

"**loss**" means direct and accidental loss of or damage to (a) the automobile, including its equipment, or (b) other insured property;

"**collision**" means collision of an automobile covered by this policy with another object or with a vehicle to which it is attached or by upset of such automobile;

"**trailer**" means a trailer designed for use with a private passenger automobile, if not being used for business or commercial purposes with other than a private passenger, farm or utility automobile, and if not a home, office, store, display or passenger trailer.

Exclusions: This policy does not apply under Part III:

(a) to any automobile while used as a public or livery conveyance;

(b) to loss due to war;

(c) to loss to a non-owned automobile arising out of its use by the insured while he is employed or otherwise engaged in the automobile business;

(d) to loss to a private passenger, farm or utility automobile or trailer owned by the named insured and not described in this policy or to any temporary substitute automobile therefor, if the insured has other valid and collectible insurance against such loss;

(e) to damage which is due and confined to wear and tear, freezing, mechanical or electrical breakdown or failure, unless such damage results from a theft covered by this policy;

(f) to tires, unless damaged by fire, malicious mischief or vandalism, or stolen or unless the loss be coincident with and from the same cause as other loss covered by this policy;

(g) to loss due to radioactive contamination;

(h) under coverage E, to breakage of glass if insurance with respect to such breakage is otherwise afforded.

Limit of Liability: The limit of the company's liability for loss shall not exceed the actual cash value of the property, or if the loss is of a part thereof the actual cash value of such part, at time of loss, nor what it would then cost to repair or replace the property or such part thereof with other of like kind and quality, nor, with respect to an owned automobile described in this policy, the applicable limit of liability stated in the declarations; provided, however, the limit of the company's liability (a) for loss to personal effects arising out of any one occurrence is $100, and (b) for loss to any trailer not owned by the named insured is $500.

Other Insurance: If the insured has other insurance against a loss covered by Part III of this policy, the company shall not be liable under this policy for a greater proportion of such loss than the applicable limit of liability of this policy bears to the total applicable limit of liability of all valid and collectible insurance against such loss; provided, however, the insurance with respect to a temporary substitute automobile or non-owned automobile shall be excess insurance over any other valid and collectible insurance.

[A3476]

PART IV — PROTECTION AGAINST UNINSURED MOTORISTS

Coverage J—Uninsured Motorists (Damages for Bodily Injury): To pay all sums which the insured or his legal representative shall be legally entitled to recover as damages from the owner or operator of an uninsured automobile because of bodily injury, sickness or disease, including death resulting therefrom, hereinafter called "bodily injury," sustained by the insured, caused by accident and arising out of the ownership, maintenance or use of such uninsured automobile; provided, for the purposes of this coverage, determination as to whether the insured or such representative is legally entitled to recover such damages, and if so the amount thereof, shall be made by agreement between the insured or such representative and the company or, if they fail to agree, by arbitration.

No judgment against any person or organization alleged to be legally responsible for the bodily injury shall be conclusive, as between the insured and the company, of the issues of liability of such person or organization or of the amount of damages to which the insured is legally entitled unless such judgment is entered pursuant to an action prosecuted by the insured with the written consent of the company.

Definitions: The definitions under Part I, except the definition of "insured," apply to Part IV, and under Part IV:

"insured" means:
(a) the named insured and any relative;
(b) any other person while occupying an insured automobile; and
(c) any person, with respect to damages he is entitled to recover because of bodily injury to which this Part applies sustained by an insured under (a) or (b) above.
The insurance afforded under Part IV applies separately to each insured, but the inclusion herein of more than one insured shall not operate to increase the limits of the company's liability.

"insured automobile" means:
(a) an automobile described in the policy for which a specific premium charge indicates that coverage is afforded,
(b) a private passenger, farm or utility automobile, ownership of which is acquired by the named insured during the policy period, provided
 (1) it replaces an insured automobile as defined in (a) above, or
 (2) the company insures under this Coverage all private passenger, farm and utility automobiles owned by the named insured on the date of such acquisition and the named insured notifies the company during the policy period or within 30 days after the date of such acquisition of his election to make the Liability and Uninsured Motorist Coverages under this and no other policy issued by the company applicable to such automobile,
(c) a temporary substitute automobile for an insured automobile as defined in (a) or (b) above, and
(d) a non-owned automobile while being operated by the named insured; and the term "insured automobile" includes a trailer while being used with an automobile described in (a), (b), (c) or (d) above, but shall not include:
 (1) any automobile or trailer owned by a resident of the same household as the named insured,
 (2) any automobile while used as a public or livery conveyance, or
 (3) any automobile while being used without the permission of the owner.

"uninsured automobile" includes a trailer of any type and means:
(a) an automobile or trailer with respect to the ownership, maintenance or use of which there is, in at least the amounts specified by the financial responsibility law of the state in which the insured automobile is principally garaged, no bodily injury liability bond or insurance policy applicable at the time of the accident with respect to any person or organization legally responsible for the use of such automobile, or with respect to which there is a bodily injury liability bond or insurance policy applicable at the time of the accident but the company writing the same denies coverage thereunder or
(b) a hit-and-run automobile;
but the term "uninsured automobile" shall not include:
 (1) an insured automobile or an automobile furnished for the regular use of the named insured or a relative,
 (2) an automobile or trailer owned or operated by a self-insurer within the meaning of any motor vehicle financial responsibility law, motor carrier law or any similar law,
 (3) an automobile or trailer owned by the United States of America, Canada, a state, a political subdivision of any such government or an agency of any of the foregoing,
 (4) a land motor vehicle or trailer if operated on rails or crawler-treads or while located for use as a residence or premises and not as a vehicle, or
 (5) a farm type tractor or equipment designed for use principally off public roads, except while actually upon public roads.

"hit-and-run automobile" means an automobile which causes bodily injury to an insured arising out of physical contact of such automobile with the insured or with an automobile which the insured is occupying at the time of the accident, provided: (a) there cannot be ascertained the identity of either the operator or the owner of such "hit-and-run automobile"; (b) the insured or someone on his behalf shall have reported the accident within 24 hours to a police, peace or judicial officer or to the Commissioner of Motor Vehicles, and shall have filed with the company within 30 days thereafter a statement under oath that the insured or his legal representative has a cause or causes of action arising out of such accident for damages against a person or persons whose identity is unascertainable, and setting forth the facts in support thereof; and (c) at the company's request, the insured or his legal representative makes available for inspection the automobile which the insured was occupying at the time of the accident.

"occupying" means in or upon or entering into or alighting from.

"state" includes the District of Columbia, a territory or possession of the United States, and a province of Canada.

Exclusions: This policy does not apply under Part IV:
(a) to bodily injury to an insured while occupying an automobile (other than an insured automobile) owned by the named insured or a relative, or through being struck by such an automobile;
(b) to bodily injury to an insured with respect to which such insured, his legal representative or any person entitled to payment under this coverage shall, without written consent of the company, make any settlement with any person or organization who may be legally liable therefor;
(c) so as to inure directly or indirectly to the benefit of any workmen's compensation or disability benefits carrier or any person or organization qualifying as a self-insurer under any workmen's compensation or disability benefits law or any similar law.

Limits of Liability:
(a) The limit of liability for uninsured motorists coverage stated in the declarations as applicable to "each person" is the limit of the company's liability for all damages, including damages for care or loss of services, because of bodily injury sustained by one person as the result of any one accident and, subject to the above provision respecting each person, the limit of liability stated in the declarations as applicable to "each accident" is the total limit of the company's liability for all damages, including damages for care or loss of services, because of bodily injury sustained by two or more persons as the result of any one accident.
(b) Any amount payable under the terms of this Part because of bodily injury sustained in an accident by a person who is an insured under this Part shall be reduced by
 (1) all sums paid on account of such bodily injury by or on behalf of (i) the owner or operator of the uninsured automobile and (ii) any other person or organization jointly or severally liable together with such owner or operator for such bodily injury including all sums paid under Coverage A, and
 (2) the amount paid and the present value of all amounts payable on account of such bodily injury under any workmen's compensation law, disability benefits law or any similar law.
(c) Any payment made under this Part to or for any insured shall be applied in reduction of the amount of damages which he may be entitled to recover from any person insured under Coverage A.
(d) The company shall not be obligated to pay under this Coverage that part of the damages which the insured may be entitled to recover from the owner or operator of an uninsured automobile which represents expenses for medical services paid or payable under Part II.

Other Insurance: With respect to bodily injury to an insured while occupying an automobile not owned by the named insured, the insurance under Part IV shall apply only as excess insurance over any other similar insurance available to such insured and applicable to such automobile as primary insurance, and this insurance shall then apply only in the amount by which the limit of liability for this coverage exceeds the applicable limit of liability of such other insurance.

Except as provided in the foregoing paragraph, if the insured has other similar insurance available to him and applicable to the accident, the damages shall be deemed not to exceed the higher of the applicable limits of liability of this insurance and such other insurance, and the company shall not be liable for a greater proportion of any loss to which this Coverage applies than the limit of liability hereunder bears to the sum of the applicable limits of liability of this insurance and such other insurance.

Arbitration: If any person making claim hereunder and the company do not agree that such person is legally entitled to recover damages from the owner or operator of an uninsured automobile because of bodily injury to the insured, or do not agree as to the amount of payment which may be owing under this Part, then, upon written demand of either, the matter or matters upon which such person and the company do not agree shall be settled by arbitration in accordance with the rules of the American Arbitration Association, and judgment upon the award rendered by the arbitrators may be entered in any court having jurisdiction thereof. Such person and the company each agree to consider itself bound and to be bound by any award made by the arbitrators pursuant to this Part.

Trust Agreement: In the event of payment to any person under this Part:
(a) the company shall be entitled to the extent of such payment to the proceeds of any settlement or judgment that may result from the exercise of any rights of recovery of such person against any person or organization legally responsible for the bodily injury because of which such payment is made;
(b) such person shall hold in trust for the benefit of the company all rights of recovery which he shall have against such other person or organization because of the damages which are the subject of claim made under this Part;
(c) such person shall do whatever is proper to secure and shall do nothing after loss to prejudice such rights;
(d) if requested in writing by the company, such person shall take, through any representative designated by the company, such action as may be necessary or appropriate to recover such payment as damages from such other person or organization, such action to be taken in the name of such person; in the event of a recovery, the company shall be reimbursed out of such recovery for expenses, costs and attorneys' fees incurred by it in connection therewith;
(e) such person shall execute and deliver to the company such instruments and papers as may be appropriate to secure the rights and obligations of such person and the company established by this provision.

CONDITIONS

Conditions 1, 2, 3, 6, 14, 15, 16 and 18 apply to all Parts. Conditions 4 and 5, 7 through 13, and 17 apply only to the Parts noted thereunder.

1. Policy Period, Territory: This policy applies only to accidents, occurrences and loss during the policy period while the automobile is within the United States of America, its territories or possessions, or Canada, or is being transported between ports thereof.

2. Premium: If the named insured disposes of, acquires ownership of, or replaces a private passenger, farm or utility automobile or, with respect to Part III, a trailer, any premium adjustment necessary shall be made as of the date of such change in accordance with the manuals in use by the company. The named insured shall, upon request, furnish reasonable proof of the number of such automobiles or trailers and a description thereof.

3. Notice: In the event of an accident, occurrence or loss, written notice containing particulars sufficient to identify the insured and also reasonably obtainable information with respect to the time, place and circumstances thereof, and the names and addresses of the injured and of available witnesses, shall be given by or for the insured to the company or any of its authorized agents as soon as practicable. In the event of theft the insured shall also promptly notify the police. If claim is made or suit is brought against the insured, he shall immediately forward to the company every demand, notice, summons or other process received by him or his representative.

If, before the company makes payment of loss under Part IV, the insured or his legal representative shall institute any legal action for bodily injury against any person or organization legally responsible for the use of an automobile involved in the accident, a copy of the summons and complaint or other process served in connection with such legal action shall be forwarded immediately to the company by the insured or his legal representative.

4. Two or More Automobiles—Parts I, II and III: When two or more automobiles are insured hereunder, the terms of this policy shall apply separately to each, but an automobile and a trailer attached thereto shall be held to be one automobile as respects limits of liability under Part I of this policy, and separate automobiles under Part III of this policy, including any deductible provisions applicable thereto.

5. Assistance and Cooperation of the Insured—Parts I and III: The insured shall cooperate with the company and, upon the company's request, assist in making settlements, in the conduct of suits and in enforcing any right of contribution or indemnity against any person or organization who may be liable to the insured because of bodily injury, property damage or loss with respect to which insurance is afforded under this policy; and the insured shall attend hearings and trials and assist in securing and giving evidence and obtaining the attendance of witnesses. The insured shall not, except at his own cost, voluntarily make any payment, assume any obligation or incur any expense other than for such immediate medical and surgical relief to others as shall be imperative at the time of accident.

Part IV: After notice of claim under Part IV, the company may require the insured to take such action as may be necessary or appropriate to preserve his right to recover damages from any person or organization alleged to be legally responsible for the bodily injury; and in any action against the company, the company may require the insured to join such person or organization as a party defendant.

6. Action Against Company—Part I: No action shall lie against the company unless, as a condition precedent thereto, the insured shall have fully complied with all the terms of this policy, nor until the amount of the insured's obligation to pay shall have been finally determined either by judgment against the insured after actual trial or by written agreement of the insured, the claimant and the company.

Any person or organization or the legal representative thereof who has secured such judgment or written agreement shall thereafter be entitled to recover under this policy to the extent of the insurance afforded by this policy. No person or organization shall have any right under this policy to join the company as a party to any action against the insured to determine the insured's liability, nor shall the company be impleaded by the insured or his legal representative. Bankruptcy or insolvency of the insured or of the insured's estate shall not relieve the company of any of its obligations hereunder.

Parts II, III and IV: No action shall lie against the company unless, as a condition precedent thereto, there shall have been full compliance with all the terms of this policy nor, under Part III, until thirty days after proof of loss is filed and the amount of loss is determined as provided in this policy.

7. Medical Reports; Proof and Payment of Claim—Part II: As soon as practicable the injured person or someone on his behalf shall give to the company written proof of claim, under oath if required, and shall, after each request from the company, execute authorization to enable the company to obtain medical reports and copies of records. The injured person shall submit to physical examination by physicians selected by the company when and as often as the company may reasonably require.

The company may pay the injured person or any person or organization rendering the services and such payment shall reduce the amount payable hereunder for such injury. Payment hereunder shall not constitute an admission of liability of any person or, except hereunder, of the company.

8. Insured's Duties in Event of Loss—Part III: In the event of loss the insured shall:
(a) protect the automobile, whether or not the loss is covered by this policy, and any further loss due to the insured's failure to protect shall not be recoverable under this policy; reasonable expenses incurred in affording such protection shall be deemed incurred at the company's request;
(b) file with the company, within 91 days after loss, his sworn proof of loss in such form and including such information as the company may reasonably require and shall, upon the company's request, exhibit the damaged property and submit to examination under oath.

9. Proof of Claim; Medical Reports—Part IV: As soon as practicable, the insured or other person making claim shall give to the company written proof of claim, under oath if required, including full particulars of the nature and extent of the injuries, treatment, and other details entering into the determination of the amount payable. The insured and every other person making claim shall submit to examinations under oath by any person named by the company and subscribe the same, as often as may reasonably be required. Proof of claim shall be made upon forms furnished by the company unless the company shall have failed to furnish such forms within 15 days after receiving notice of claim.

The injured person shall submit to physical examinations by physicians selected by the company when and as often as the company may reasonably require and he, or in the event of his incapacity his legal representative, or in the event of his death his legal representative or the person or persons entitled to sue therefor, shall upon each request from the company execute authorization to enable the company to obtain medical reports and copies of records.

10. Appraisal—Part III: If the insured and the company fail to agree as to the amount of loss, either may, within 60 days after proof of loss is filed, demand an appraisal of the loss. In such event the insured and the company shall each select a competent appraiser, and the appraisers shall select a competent and disinterested umpire. The appraisers shall state separately the actual cash value and the amount of loss and failing to agree shall submit their differences to the umpire. An award in writing of any two shall determine the amount of loss. The insured and the company shall each pay his chosen appraiser and shall bear equally the other expenses of the appraisal and umpire.

The company shall not be held to have waived any of its rights by any act relating to appraisal.

11. Payment of Loss—Part III: The company may pay for the loss in money; or may repair or replace the damaged or stolen property; or may, at any time before the loss is paid or the property is so replaced, at its expense return any stolen property to the named insured, or at its option to the address shown in the declarations, with payment for any resultant damage thereto; or may take all or such part of the property at the agreed or appraised value but there shall be no abandonment to the company. The company may settle any claim for loss either with the insured or the owner of the property.

Part IV: Any amount due is payable (a) to the insured, or (b) if the insured be a minor to his parent or guardian, or (c) if the insured be deceased to his surviving spouse, otherwise (d) to a person authorized by law to receive such payment or to a person legally entitled to recover the damages which the payment represents; provided, the company may at its option pay any amount due in accordance with division (d) hereof.

12. No Benefit to Bailee—Part III: The insurance afforded by this policy shall not inure directly or indirectly to the benefit of any carrier or other bailee for hire liable for loss to the automobile.

13. Subrogation—Parts I and III: In the event of any payment under this policy, the company shall be subrogated to all the insured's rights of recovery therefor against any person or organization and the insured shall execute and deliver instruments and papers and do whatever else is necessary to secure such rights. The insured shall do nothing after loss to prejudice such rights.

14. Changes: Notice to any agent or knowledge possessed by any agent or by any other person shall not effect a waiver or a change in any part of this policy or estop the company from asserting any right under the terms of this policy; nor shall the terms of this policy be waived or changed, except by endorsement issued to form a part of this policy.

15. Assignment: Assignment of interest under this policy shall not bind the company until its consent is endorsed hereon; if, however, the insured named in Item 1 of the declarations, or his spouse if a resident of the same household, shall die, this policy shall cover (1) the survivor as named insured, (2) his legal representative as named insured but only while acting within the scope of his duties as such (3) any person having proper temporary custody of an owned automobile, as an insured, until the appointment and qualification of such legal representative, and (4) under division 1 of Part II any person who was a relative at the time of such death.

16. Cancelation: This policy may be canceled by the insured named in Item 1 of the declarations by surrender thereof to the company or any of its authorized agents or by mailing to the company written notice stating when thereafter the cancelation shall be effective. This policy may be canceled by the company by mailing to the insured named in Item 1 of the declarations at the address shown in this policy written notice stating when not less than ten days thereafter such cancelation shall be effective. The mailing of notice as aforesaid shall be sufficient proof of notice. The time of the surrender or the effective date and hour of cancelation stated in the notice shall become the end of the policy period. Delivery of such written notice either by such insured or by the company shall be equivalent to mailing.

If such insured cancels, earned premium shall be computed in accordance with the customary short rate table and procedure. If the company cancels, earned premium shall be computed pro rata. Premium adjustment may be made either at the time cancelation is effected or as soon as practicable after cancelation becomes effective, but payment or tender of unearned premium is not a condition of cancelation.

17. Cancelation by Company Limited—Part I: After this policy has been in effect for sixty days or, if the policy is a renewal, effective immediately, the company shall not exercise its right to cancel the insurance afforded under Part I unless:
1. the named insured fails to discharge when due any of his obligations in connection with the payment of premium for this policy or any installment thereof whether payable directly or under any premium finance plan; or
2. the insurance was obtained through fraudulent misrepresentation; or
3. the insured violates any of the terms and conditions of the policy; or
4. the named insured or any other operator, either resident in the same household, or who customarily operates an automobile insured under the policy,
   (a) has had his driver's license suspended or revoked during the policy period, or
   (b) is or becomes subject to epilepsy or heart attacks, and such individual cannot produce a certificate from a physician testifying to his unqualified ability to operate a motor vehicle, or
   (c) is or has been convicted of or forfeits bail, during the 36 months immediately preceding the effective date of the policy or during the policy period, for:
      (1) any felony, or
      (2) criminal negligence resulting in death, homicide or assault, arising out of the operation of a motor vehicle, or
      (3) operating a motor vehicle while in an intoxicated condition or while under the influence of drugs, or
      (4) leaving the scene of an accident without stopping to report, or
      (5) theft of a motor vehicle, or
      (6) making false statements in an application for a driver's license, or
      (7) a third violation, committed within a period of 18 months, of (i) any ordinance or regulation limiting the speed of motor vehicles or (ii) any of the provisions in the motor vehicle laws of any state, the violation of which constitutes a misdemeanor, whether or not the violations were repetitions of the same offense or were different offenses.

18. Declarations: By acceptance of this policy, the insured named in Item 1 of the declarations agrees that the statements in the declarations are his agreements and representations, that this policy is issued in reliance upon the truth of such representations and that this policy embodies all agreements existing between himself and the company or any of its agents relating to this insurance.

---

*In Witness Whereof, the company has caused this policy to be executed and attested, but this policy shall not be valid unless countersigned by a duly authorized representative of the company.

°Company's language may be substituted as desired.

INSERT SIGNATURES AND
TITLES OF PROPER OFFICERS

[A3478]

APPENDIX I—Personal Property Floater Form *

INLAND MARINE

PPF 1335

IM 2149
(Ed. 8-66)

PERSONAL PROPERTY FLOATER

Attached to and forming part of policy No.

or supplemental

endorsement (form) No.

attached to policy No.

issued to

by

at its Agency

located

Date

CITY AND STATE

(When this endorsement forms a part of a supplemental endorsement (form) the word "policy" wherever appearing in the following provisions is to be construed to mean "supplemental endorsement (form)".)

PROPERTY COVERED

1. Personal property owned, used or worn by the person in whose name this policy is issued and members of the Insured's family of the same household, while in all situations, except as hereinafter provided.

PERILS INSURED

2. All risks of loss of or damage to property covered except as hereinafter provided.

AMOUNTS OF INSURANCE

3. Insurance attaches only with respect to those items in this paragraph for which an amount is shown and only for such amount.

ITEM		AMOUNT	
(a)	$		On unscheduled personal property, except as hereinafter provided.
(b)	$		On personal jewelry, watches, furs, fine arts and other property as per schedules attached hereto. Each item considered separately insured.
(c)	$		On unscheduled personal jewelry, watches and furs, in addition to the amount of $250.00 provided in Paragraph 5 (b), against fire and lightning only.

TOTAL $

(See other side for Paragraphs 4, 5 and 6)

DECLARATIONS OF THE INSURED

7. The following are the approximate values of the unscheduled personal property, other than jewelry, watches and furs, as estimated by the Insured, at the time of issuance of this policy:

	Wherever Located	(Of which the following amounts involve personal property ordinarily situated throughout the year at residences other than principal residence.)
(a) Silverware and pewter	$	($)
(b) Linens (including dining room and bedroom)	$	($)
(c) Clothing (men's, women's, children's)	$	($)
(d) Rugs (including floor coverings) and draperies	$	($)
(e) Books	$	($)
(f) Musical instruments (including pianos)	$	($)
(g) Television sets, radios, record players and records	$	($)
(h) Paintings, etchings, pictures and other objects of art	$	($)
(i) China and glassware (including bric-a-brac)	$	($)
(j) Cameras and photographic equipment	$	($)
(k) Golf, hunting, fishing and other sports and hobby equipment	$	($)
(l) Refrigerators, washing machines, stoves, electrical appliances and other kitchen equipment	$	($)
(m) Bedding (including blankets, comforters, covers, pillows, mattresses, and springs)	$	($)
(n) Furniture (including tables, chairs, sofas, desks, beds, chests, lamps, mirrors, clocks)	$	($)
(o) All other personal property (including wines, liquors, foodstuff, garden and lawn tools and equipment, trunks, traveling bags, children's playthings, miscellaneous articles in basement and attic) and professional equipment, if any, covered under Paragraph 6 (b)	$	($)
TOTAL	$	($)

NOTE: If the total value ordinarily situated throughout the year at residences other than the principal residence exceeds ten per cent of the amount of the insurance granted under Item (a) Paragraph 3, such excess value is not insured hereunder unless specifically endorsed hereon.

THE PROVISIONS PRINTED ON THE BACK OF THIS FORM ARE HEREBY REFERRED TO AND MADE A PART HEREOF.

Agent

[A3479]

* Reproduced with permission of the Insurance Information Institute.

EXTENSIONS

4. (a) Subject otherwise to all of the conditions of this policy, Item (a) Paragraph 3, includes, at the sole option of the Insured, personal property of others while on the premises of the residences of the Insured, and personal property of servants while they are actually engaged in the service of the Insured and while in the physical custody of such servants outside such residences;

(b) The Company will also pay:

(1) The actual loss of or damage (except by fire) to property of the Insured not specifically excluded by this policy caused by theft or attempt thereat; or by vandalism or malicious mischief to the interior of the residences of the Insured;

(2) Actual loss of or damage to improvements, alterations or additions made by the Insured to buildings occupied as residences by but not owned by the Insured, or to premises occupied by the Insured in condominiums, caused by fire, lightning, windstorm, cyclone, tornado, hail, explosion, riot, riot attending a strike, smoke, damage by vehicles or aircraft but as respects such loss or damage, the liability of the Company is limited to 10% of the amount of insurance under Item (a) Paragraph 3;

(c) **Automatic Reinstatement of Losses—Unscheduled Property.** Any loss payment hereunder shall not reduce the amount of insurance under Items (a) and (c) of Paragraph 3;

but in no event shall the Company's combined liability for loss or damage covered under this Paragraph 4 and for insurance attaching under Item (a) Paragraph 3, exceed the amount of insurance shown in Item (a) Paragraph 3.

LIMITATIONS

5. (a) As respects unscheduled personal property ordinarily situated throughout the year at residences other than the principal residence of the Insured, the Company shall not be liable in excess of ten per cent of the amount of insurance set forth in Item (a) Paragraph 3.

(b) As respects any one loss of unscheduled jewelry, watches and furs, the Company shall not be liable for more than $250.00 unless the loss is covered under Item (c) Paragraph 3, in which event the Company's liability for such loss is limited to the amount stated therein.

(c) As respects any one loss of money including numismatic property, the Company shall not be liable for more than $100.00. As respects any one loss of notes, securities, stamps including philatelic property, accounts, bills, deeds, evidences of debt, letters of credit, passports, documents and railroad and other tickets, the Company shall not be liable for more than $500.00.

EXCLUSIONS

6. This policy does not insure

(a) animals; automobiles, motorcycles, aircraft, boats or other conveyances (except bicycles, tricycles, baby carriages, invalid chairs and similar conveniences), or their equipment or furnishings except when removed therefrom and actually on the premises of residences of the Insured; property of any government or subdivision thereof;

(b) unscheduled property pertaining to a business, profession or occupation of the persons whose property is insured hereunder, excepting professional books, instruments and other professional equipment owned by the Insured while actually within the residences of the Insured;

(c) against breakage of eye glasses, glassware, statuary, marbles, bric-a-brac, porcelains and similar fragile articles (jewelry, watches, bronzes, cameras and photographic lenses excepted), unless occasioned by theft or attempt thereat, vandalism or malicious mischief, or by fire, lightning, windstorm, earthquake, explosion, falling aircraft, rioters, strikers, collapse of building, accident to conveyance or other similar casualty, nor unless likewise occasioned, against marring or scratching of any property not specifically scheduled herein;

(d) against mechanical breakdown; against loss or damage to electrical apparatus caused by electricity other than lightning unless fire ensues and then only for loss or damage by such ensuing fire;

(e) against wear and tear; against loss or damage caused by dampness of atmosphere or extremes of temperature unless directly caused by rain, snow, sleet, hail, bursting of pipes or apparatus and provided further that such loss or damage is not specifically excluded under subsection (h) hereof; against deterioration, insect, vermin and inherent vice; against damage to property (watches, jewelry and furs excepted) occasioned by or actually resulting from any work thereon in the course of any refinishing, renovating or repairing process;

(f) property on exhibition at fairgrounds or on the premises of any national or international exposition unless such premises are specifically herein described;

(g) against loss or damage caused by or resulting from: (1) hostile or warlike action in time of peace or war, including action in hindering, combating or defending against an actual, impending or expected attack, (a) by any government or sovereign power (de jure or de facto), or by any authority maintaining or using military, naval or air forces; or (b) by military, naval or air forces; or (c) by an agent of any such government, power, authority or forces; (2) any weapon of war employing atomic fission or radioactive force whether in time of peace or war; (3) insurrection, rebellion, revolution, civil war, usurped power, or action taken by governmental authority in hindering, combating or defending against such an occurrence, seizure or destruction under quarantine or customs regulations, confiscation by order of any government or public authority, or risks of contraband or illegal transportation or trade;

(h) unscheduled property at premises owned, rented, occupied or controlled by the Insured or any other party whose property is insured hereunder, against loss caused by, resulting from, contributed to or aggravated by any of the following:

(1) flood, surface water, waves, tidal water or tidal wave, overflow of streams or other bodies of water, or spray from any of the foregoing, all whether driven by wind or not;

(2) water which backs up through sewers or drains;

(3) water below the surface of the ground including that which exerts pressure on or flows, seeps or leaks through sidewalks, driveways, foundations, walls, basement or other floors, or through doors, windows or other openings in such sidewalks, driveways, foundations, walls or floors;

unless loss by fire or explosion ensues and the Company shall then be liable only for such ensuing loss;
But this exclusion (h) shall not apply to loss arising from theft;

(i) against loss or damage caused by animals or birds owned or kept by an insured or by a residence employee of an insured unless loss by fire, explosion or smoke ensues and the Company shall then be liable only for such ensuing loss;

(j) against loss by nuclear reaction or nuclear radiation or radioactive contamination, all whether controlled or uncontrolled, and whether such loss be direct or indirect, proximate or remote, or be in whole or in part caused by, contributed to, or aggravated by the peril(s) insured against in this policy; however, subject to the foregoing and all provisions of this policy, direct loss by fire resulting from nuclear reaction or nuclear radiation or radioactive contamination is insured against by this policy.

7. DECLARATIONS OF THE INSURED (See Face)

8. Unless otherwise endorsed hereon, no other insurance against the risks hereby insured is permitted on the property covered hereunder except as to property described under Paragraphs 4(a) and (b), 5(b) and (c), 6(a) and (b). If at the time of loss or damage, there is any other valid and collectible insurance which would attach on the property described in Paragraphs 4(a) and (b), 5(b) and (c), 6(a) and (b) had this policy not been effected, then this insurance shall apply only as excess insurance over all such other insurance and in no event as contributing insurance.   [A3480]

TABLE OF CASES

References are to Pages

*

INDEX

References are to Pages